TEACHER'S EDITION

PRENTICE HALL
LITERATURE

Timeless Voices, Timeless Themes

THE AMERICAN EXPERIENCE

VOLUME II

Upper Saddle River, New Jersey

Needham, Massachusetts

ISBN 0-13-180444-8

3 4 5 6 7 8 9 10   08 07 06 05 04

PRENTICE HALL
LITERATURE

Timeless Voices, Timeless Themes

THE AMERICAN EXPERIENCE

PEARSON

Prentice Hall

Upper Saddle River, New Jersey
Needham, Massachusetts

ISBN 0-13-180436-7

2 3 4 5 6 7 8 9 10   08 07 06 05 04

Cover: *Travel by Ox-Drawn Covered Wagons,* Artist unknown, Courtesy of the Bancroft Library, University of California, Berkeley

ACKNOWLEDGMENTS

Grateful acknowledgment is made to the following for copyrighted material:

Amistad Research Center, administered by Thompson and Thompson "From the Dark Tower" by Countee Cullen published in *Copper Sun,* Harper & Bros., © 1927, renewed 1954 by Ida Cullen. Copyrights held by the Amistad Research Center, administered by Thompson and Thompson, New York, NY. Used by permission.

Arte Público Press "To Walt Whitman" by Angela de Hoyos from *In Other Words: Literature by Latinas of the United States* (Houston: Arte Público Press, University of Houston, 1994).

The James Baldwin Estate "The Rockpile" is collected in *Going to Meet the Man,* (c) 1965 by James Baldwin. Copyright renewed. Published by Vintage Books. Used by arrangement with the James Baldwin Estate.

Peter Basch, Literary Agent "When Grizzlies Walked Upright" (Modoc) from *American Indian Myths and Legends,* selected and edited by Richard Erdoes and Alfonso Ortiz, published by Pantheon Books. Copyright © 1984 by Richard Erdoes and Alfonso Ortiz.

Susan Bergholz Literary Services "Antojos" by Julia Alvarez, copyright © 1991 by Julia Alvarez. Later published in slightly different form in *How the Garcia Girls Lost Their Accents,* copyright © 1991 by Julia Alvarez. Published by Plume, an imprint of Dutton Signet, a division of Penguin USA, Inc., and originally in hardcover by Algonquin Books of Chapel Hill. "Straw into Gold" by Sandra Cisneros. Copyright © 1987 by Sandra Cisneros. First published in *The Texas Observer,* September 1987. Reprinted by permission of Susan Bergholz Literary Services, New York. All rights reserved.

(Acknowledgments continue on page R58, which constitutes an extension of this copyright page.)

PRENTICE HALL
LITERATURE

Timeless Voices, Timeless Themes

COPPER

BRONZE

SILVER

GOLD

PLATINUM

THE AMERICAN EXPERIENCE

THE BRITISH TRADITION

CONTRIBUTING AUTHORS

The contributing authors guided the direction and philosophy of *Prentice Hall Literature: Timeless Voices, Timeless Themes*. Working with the development team, they helped to build the pedagogical integrity of the program and to ensure its relevance for today's teachers and students.

Kate Kinsella

Kate Kinsella, Ed.D., is a faculty member in the Department of Secondary Education at San Francisco State University. A specialist in second-language acquisition and adolescent reading and writing, she teaches coursework addressing language and literacy development across the secondary curricula. She has taught high-school ESL and directed SFSU's *Intensive English Program* for first-generation bilingual college students. She maintains secondary classroom involvement by teaching an academic literacy class for second-language learners through the University's *Step to College* partnership program. A former Fulbright lecturer and perennial institute leader for TESOL, the California Reading Association, and the California League of Middle Schools, Dr. Kinsella provides professional development nationally on topics ranging from learning-style enhancement to second-language reading. Her scholarship has been published in journals such as the *TESOL Journal,* the *CATESOL Journal,* and the *Social Studies Review.* Dr. Kinsella earned her M.A. in TESOL from San Francisco State University and her Ed.D. in Second Language Acquisition from the University of San Francisco.

Kevin Feldman

Kevin Feldman, Ed.D., is the Director of Reading and Early Intervention with the Sonoma County Office of Education (SCOE). His career in education spans thirty-one years. As the Director of Reading and Early Intervention for SCOE, he develops, organizes, and monitors programs related to K–12 literacy and prevention of reading difficulties. He also serves as a Leadership Team Consultant to the California Reading and Literature Project and assists in the development and implementation of K–12 programs throughout California. Dr. Feldman earned his undergraduate degree in Psychology from Washington State University and has a Master's degree in Special Education, Learning Disabilities, and Instructional Design from U.C. Riverside. He earned his Ed.D. in Curriculum and Instruction from the University of San Francisco.

Colleen Shea Stump

Colleen Shea Stump, Ph.D., is a Special Education Supervisor in the area of Resource and Inclusion for Seattle Public Schools. She has served as a professor and chairperson for the Department of Special Education at San Francisco State University. She continues as a lead consultant in the area of collaboration for the California State Improvement Grant and travels the state of California providing professional development training in the areas of collaboration, content literacy instruction, and inclusive instruction. Dr. Stump earned her doctorate at the University of Washington, her M.A. in Special Education from the University of New Mexico, and her B.S. in Elementary Education from the University of Wisconsin–Eau Claire.

Joyce Armstrong Carroll

In her forty-year career, Joyce Armstrong Carroll, Ed. D., has taught on every grade level from primary to graduate school. In the past twenty years, she has trained teachers in the teaching of writing. A nationally known consultant, she has served as president of TCTE and on NCTE's Commission on Composition. More than fifty of her articles have appeared in journals such as *Curriculum Review, English Journal, Media & Methods, Southwest Philosophical Studies, English in Texas,* and the *Florida English Journal.* With Edward E. Wilson, Dr. Carroll co-authored *Acts of Teaching: How to Teach Writing* and co-edited *Poetry After Lunch: Poetry to Read Aloud.* She co-directs the New Jersey Writing Project in Texas.

Edward E. Wilson

A former editor of *English in Texas,* Edward E. Wilson has served as a high-school English teacher and a writing consultant in school districts nationwide. Wilson has served on both the Texas Teacher Professional Practices Commission and NCTE's Commission on Composition. Wilson's poetry appears in Paul Janeczko's anthology *The Music of What Happens.* With Dr. Carroll, he co-wrote *Acts of Teaching: How to Teach Writing* and co-edited *Poetry After Lunch: Poetry to Read Aloud.* Wilson co-directs the New Jersey Writing Project in Texas.

PROGRAM ADVISORS

The program advisors provided ongoing input throughout the development of *Prentice Hall Literature: Timeless Voices, Timeless Themes*. Their valuable insights ensure that the perspectives of the teachers throughout the country are represented within this literature series.

Diane Cappillo
English Department Chair
Barbara Goleman Senior High School
Miami, Florida

Anita Clay
Language Arts Instructor
Gateway Institute of Technology
St. Louis, Missouri

Ellen Eberly
Language Arts Instructor
Catholic Memorial High School
West Roxbury, Massachusetts

Nancy Fahner
L.A.M.P. Lansing Area Manufacturing
   Partnership
Ingham Intermediate School District
Mason, Michigan

Terri Fields
Instructor of Language Arts,
   Communication Arts, and Author
Sunnyslope High School
Phoenix, Arizona

Susan Goldberg
Language Arts Instructor
Westlake Middle School
Thornwood, New York

Margo L. Graf
English Department Chair, Speech,
   Yearbook, Journalism
Lane Middle School
Fort Wayne, Indiana

Christopher E. Guarraia
Language Arts Instructor
Lakewood High School
Saint Petersburg, Florida

V. Pauline Hodges
Teacher, Educational Consultant
Forgan High School
Forgan, Oklahoma

Karen Hurley
Language Arts Instructor
Perry Meridian Middle School
Indianapolis, Indiana

Lenore D. Hynes
Language Arts Coordinator
Sunman-Dearborn Community
   Schools
Sunman, Indiana

Linda Kramer
Language Arts Instructor
Norman High School North
Norman, Oklahoma

Thomas S. Lindsay
Assistant Superintendent of Schools
Manheim District 83
Franklin Park, Illinois

Agathaniki (Niki) Locklear
English Department Chair
Simon Kenton High School
Independence, Kentucky

Ashley MacDonald
Language Arts Instructor
South Forsyth High School
Cumming, Georgia

Mary Ellen Mastej
Language Arts Instructor
Scott Middle School
Hammond, Indiana

Nancy L. Monroe
English, Speed Reading Teacher
Bolton High School
Alexandria, Louisiana

Jim Moody
Language Arts Instructor
Northside High School
Fort Smith, Arkansas

David Morris
Teacher of English, Writing,
   Publications, Yearbook
Washington High School
South Bend, Indiana

Rosemary A. Naab
English Department Chair
Ryan High School
Archdiocese of Philadelphia
Philadelphia, Pennsylvania

Ann Okamura
English Teacher
Laguna Creek High School
Elk Grove, California

Tucky Roger
Coordinator of Languages
Tulsa Public Schools
Tulsa, Oklahoma

Jonathan L. Schatz
English Teacher/Team Leader
Tappan Zee High School
Orangeburg, New York

John Scott
Assistant Principal
Middlesex High School
Saluda, Virginia

Ken Spurlock
Assistant Principal, Retired
Boone County High School
Florence, Kentucky

Dr. Jennifer Watson
Secondary Language Arts
   Coordinator
Putnam City Schools
Oklahoma City, Oklahoma

Joan West
Assistant Principal
Oliver Middle School
Broken Arrow, Oklahoma

UNIT 1 *Beginnings–1750*

Introduction 2

Richard Lederer **The Development of American English: Our Native American Heritage** 12

PART 1 Meeting of Cultures

Comparing Literary Works

Onondaga **The Earth on Turtle's Back** .... Myth 16
Modoc **When Grizzlies Walked Upright** .... Myth 19
Navajo *from* **The Navajo Origin Legend** .... Legend 22
Iroquois *from* **The Iroquois Constitution** .... Nonfiction 24

Comparing Literary Works

Alvar Núñez Cabeza de Vaca **A Journey Through Texas** .... Nonfiction 32

García López de Cárdenas **Boulders Taller Than the Great Tower of Seville** .... Nonfiction 37

Olaudah Equiano *from* **The Interesting Narrative of the Life of Olaudah Equiano** .... Nonfiction 44

Connections: Literature Past and Present

Darryl Babe Wilson **Diamond Island: Alcatraz** .... Nonfiction 52

PART 2 Focus on Literary Forms: Narrative Accounts

Christopher Columbus *from* **Journal of the First Voyage to America** .... Nonfiction 62

A Closer Look
Captivity Narratives: Colonial Pulp Fiction 68

Comparing Literary Works

John Smith *from* **The General History of Virginia** .... Nonfiction 72
William Bradford *from* **Of Plymouth Plantation** .... Nonfiction 78

Reading Informational Materials: *Web Sites*
Plimoth–on–Web .... Web site 88

Connections: Literature Past and Present

Tom Wolfe *from* **The Right Stuff** .... Nonfiction 92

PART 3   The Puritan Influence

Comparing Literary Works

Edward Taylor	**Huswifery**...Poem	100
Anne Bradstreet	**To My Dear and Loving Husband**...............................Poem	102
Jonathan Edwards	*from* **Sinners in the Hands of an Angry God** ....Speech	108

SKILLS WORKSHOPS

Writing About Literature: Analyze Literary Periods 116

Writing Workshop: Narration: Autobiographical Narrative 118

Listening and Speaking Workshop: Delivering a Speech.................................. 122

Assessment Workshop: Summaries of Written Texts...................................... 123

 This selection is featured in
the *Reader's Companion* series.

UNIT 2

A Nation Is Born (1750–1800)

INTRODUCTION 124

Richard Lederer   **The Development of American English:
Noah Webster and the American Language** 136

PART 1   Voices for Freedom

RC   Benjamin Franklin

Comparing Literary Works
from **The Autobiography** .... Nonfiction 140
from **Poor Richard's Almanack** .... Nonfiction 146

A Closer Look
All the News That's Fit to Print: Colonial Newspapers..... *152*

RC   Thomas Jefferson

Thomas Paine

Comparing Literary Works
The Declaration of Independence .... Nonfiction 156
from **The Crisis, Number 1** .... Nonfiction 160

RC
RC   USA Today

Robert N. Weiner

Reading Informational Materials: *Newspaper Editorials*
Lawyers Leave Poor Behind .... Editorials 167
Pro Bono Work Still Valued .... Editorials 168

Phillis Wheatley

Comparing Literary Works
An Hymn to the Evening .... Poem 172
To His Excellency, General Washington .... Poem 174

Dr. Martin Luther King, Jr.

Connections: Literature Past and Present
from **Letter From Birmingham City Jail**.............. Nonfiction 180

PART 2   Focus on Literary Forms: Speeches

RC   Patrick Henry

Benjamin Franklin

Comparing Literary Works
Speech in the Virginia Convention.......................... Speech 186
Speech in the Convention... Speech 191

John F. Kennedy

Connections: Literature Past and Present
Inaugural Address .... Speech 196

PART 3   Defining an American

          ⌐Comparing Literary Works

Abigail Adams   **Letter to Her Daughter from the New**
White House.. Letter   204   **RC**

Michel-Guillaume Jean
de Crèvecoeur   *from* **Letters from an American Farmer**........ Letter/epistle   208   **RC**

         Connections: Literature Past and Present

Alex Haley   *from* **Roots**... Nonfiction   214

SKILLS WORKSHOPS

Writing About Literature: Evaluate Literary Themes 218

Writing Workshop: Problem-and-Solution Essay... 220

Listening and Speaking Workshop: Analyze Persuasive Techniques 224

Assessment Workshop: Cause-and-Effect Relationships 225

RC This selection is featured in
the *Reader's Companion* series.

UNIT 3

A Growing Nation (1800–1870)

| INTRODUCTION | | | 228 |

Richard Lederer **The Development of American English: The Truth About O.K.** 238

PART 1   Fireside and Campfire

Washington Irving **The Devil and Tom Walker**................................. Short Story 242

┌ Comparing Literary Works

Henry Wadsworth Longfellow **A Psalm of Life** .... Poem 258

The Tide Rises, The Tide Falls.................................. Poem 260

┌ Comparing Literary Works

William Cullen Bryant **Thanatopsis** .... Poem 267

Oliver Wendell Holmes **Old Ironsides** .... Poem 270

James Russell Lowell **The First Snowfall** .... Poem 272

John Greenleaf Whittier *from* **Snowbound** .... Poem 274

┌ Comparing Literary Works

Meriwether Lewis **Crossing the Great Divide** .... Nonfiction 286

John Wesley Powell **The Most Sublime Spectacle on Earth**.............. Nonfiction 289

Reading Informational Materials: *Memorandums*

Thomas Jefferson **Commission of Meriwether Lewis**............................... Historic Memorandum 296

Connections: Literature Past and Present

Annie Dillard *from* **Pilgrim at Tinker Creek, Seeing** .... Nonfiction 300

PART 2   Shadows of the Imagination

┌ Comparing Literary Works

Edgar Allan Poe **The Fall of the House of Usher**...........................Short Story 308

The Raven...Poem 326

Nathaniel Hawthorne **The Minister's Black Veil** .... Short Story 336

Herman Melville *from* **Moby-Dick**... Fiction 354

Connections: Literature Past and Present

Joyce Carol Oates **Where** *Is* **Here?**.. Short Story 374

PART 3   The Human Spirit and the Natural World

A Closer Look
Transcendentalism: The Seekers... *384*

Ralph Waldo Emerson

⌐Comparing Literary Works
from **Nature**... Nonfiction 388
from **Self-Reliance** .... Nonfiction 391
Concord Hymn... Poem 393
The Snowstorm .... Poem 394

Henry David Thoreau

⌐Comparing Literary Works
from **Walden**.. Nonfiction 402
from **Civil Disobedience**.. Nonfiction 412

PART 4   Focus on Literary Forms: Poetry

Emily Dickinson

⌐Comparing Literary Works
Because I could not stop for Death—........................ Poem 420
I heard a Fly buzz—when I died—........................... Poem 422
There's a certain Slant of light,................................ Poem 424
My life closed twice before its close— .... Poem 424
The Soul selects her own Society—.......................... Poem 425
The Brain—is wider than the Sky— .... Poem 426
There is a solitude of space .... Poem 427
Water, is taught by thirst.. Poem 428

Walt Whitman

⌐Comparing Literary Works
from **Preface to the 1855 Edition of Leaves
of Grass**.. Nonfiction 434
from **Song of Myself**... Poem 436
When I Heard the Learn'd Astronomer.................... Poem 440
By the Bivouac's Fitful Flame.................................... Poem 441
I Hear America Singing .... Poem 442
A Noiseless Patient Spider ....Poem 444

Connections: Literature Past and Present

Langston Hughes   **I, Too** ....Poem 448

Angela de Hoyos   **To Walt Whitman**.......................................Poem 450

SKILLS WORKSHOPS

Writing About Literature: Compare and Contrast Literary Trends........................ 452
Writing Workshop: Narration: Reflective Essay 454
Listening and Speaking Workshop: Analyzing Media 458
Assessment Workshop: Inferences and Generalizations.................................. 459

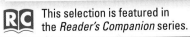
This selection is featured in
the *Reader's Companion* series.

Division, Reconciliation, and Expansion (1850–1914)

INTRODUCTION 460

Richard Lederer   **The Development of American English:
Mark Twain and the American Language** 472

PART 1   A Nation Divided

RC

Comparing Literary Works

Stephen Crane   **An Episode of War** .... Short Story   476

Stephen Foster,
George Cooper   **Willie Has Gone to the War** .... Song   481

Comparing Literary Works

Spiritual   **Swing Low, Sweet Chariot** .... Song   488
Go Down, Moses .... Song   490

RC

Frederick Douglass   *from* **My Bondage and My Freedom** .... Nonfiction   496

Ambrose Bierce   **An Occurrence at Owl Creek Bridge** .... Short Story   508

Comparing Literary Works

Abraham Lincoln   **The Gettysburg Address** .... Speech   522
Second Inaugural Address .... Speech   523

Robert E. Lee   **Letter to His Son** .... Letter   525

Reading Informational Materials: *Public Documents*

RC

Abraham Lincoln   **Emancipation Proclamation** .... Public Document   530

PART 2   Focus on Literary Forms: Diaries, Journals, and Letters

Comparing Literary Works

Mary Chesnut   *from* **Mary Chesnut's Civil War** .... Nonfiction   536

Warren Lee Goss   **Recollections of a Private** .... Nonfiction   540

Randolph McKim   **A Confederate Account of the Battle
of Gettysburg** .... Nonfiction   542

Stonewall Jackson   **An Account of the Battle of Bull Run** .... Nonfiction   544

Rev. Henry M. Turner   **Reaction to the Emancipation Proclamation** .... Nonfiction   545

Sojourner Truth   **An Account of an Experience With
Discrimination** .... Nonfiction   547

Connections: Literature Past and Present

Molly Moore   **Gulf War Journal** *from* **A Woman at War** .... Nonfiction   552

PART 3   Forging New Frontiers

A Closer Look
Mark Twain: The American Bard... *560*

Mark Twain
    Comparing Literary Works
    from **Life on the Mississippi** .... Nonfiction 564
    **The Notorious Jumping Frog of
    Calaveras County** .... Short Story 569 **RC**

Bret Harte
    The Outcasts of Poker Flat................................ Short Story 580

Miriam Davis Colt
    Comparing Literary Works
    Heading West .... Nonfiction 596

Chief Joseph
    I Will Fight No More Forever.................................. Speech 602

Jack London
    To Build a Fire.. Short Story 608

    Connections: Literature Past and Present

Larry McMurtry
    from **Lonesome Dove** .... Fiction 626

PART 4   Living in a Changing World

Kate Chopin
    The Story of an Hour .... Short Story 634 **RC**

Edith Wharton
    April Showers... Short Story 644

Paul Laurence Dunbar
    Comparing Literary Works
    Douglass .... Poem 658
    We Wear the Mask .... Poem 660

Edwin Arlington Robinson
    Comparing Literary Works
    Luke Havergal... Poem 666
    Richard Cory .... Poem 668

Edgar Lee Masters
    Lucinda Matlock ....Poem 669
    Richard Bone .... Poem 670

Willa Cather
    A Wagner Matinée...................................... Short Story 676

    Connections: Literature Past and Present

Anna Quindlen
    Cats.. Fiction 688

SKILLS WORKSHOPS

Writing About Literature: Compare and Contrast Literary Themes............................ 692
Writing Workshop: Research: Research Paper 694
Listening and Speaking Workshop: Critique Persuasive Arguments............................ 700
Assessment Workshop: Context Clues.. 701

RC This selection is featured in
the *Reader's Companion* series.

UNIT 5

Disillusion, Defiance, and Discontent (1914–1946)

| INTRODUCTION | | | 704 |
| Richard Lederer | The Development of American English: Slang as It Is Slung | | 714 |

PART 1 Facing Troubled Times

| T. S. Eliot | The Love Song of J. Alfred Prufrock | Poem | 718 |

Comparing Literary Works

Ezra Pound	A Few Don'ts by an Imagiste	Nonfiction	729
	The River-Merchant's Wife: A Letter	Poem	732
	In a Station of the Metro	Poem	734
William Carlos Williams	The Red Wheelbarrow	Poem	735
	The Great Figure	Poem	735
	This Is Just to Say	Poem	736
H. D.	Pear Tree	Poem	737
	Heat	Poem	738

| **RC** F. Scott Fitzgerald | Winter Dreams | Short Story | 744 |
| John Steinbeck | The Turtle *from* The Grapes of Wrath | Fiction | 768 |

Comparing Literary Works

E. E. Cummings	old age sticks	Poem	776
	anyone lived in a pretty how town	Poem	777
W. H. Auden	The Unknown Citizen	Poem	779

| **RC** Thomas Wolfe | The Far and the Near | Short Story | 786 |

Comparing Literary Works

Wallace Stevens	Of Modern Poetry	Poem	796
	Anecdote of the Jar	Poem	797
Archibald MacLeish	Ars Poetica	Poem	798
Marianne Moore	Poetry	Poem	800

PART 2 Focus on Literary Forms: The Short Story

Comparing Literary Works

RC Ernest Hemingway	In Another Country	Short Story	809
Sherwood Anderson	The Corn Planting	Short Story	815
RC Eudora Welty	A Worn Path	Short Story	820

Connections: Literature Past and Present

| Grace Paley | Anxiety | Short Story | 832 |

PART 3   From Every Corner of the Land

Carl Sandburg
Comparing Literary Works
Chicago .... Poem 838
Grass .... Poem 840

Katherine Anne Porter
The Jilting of Granny Weatherall .... Short Story 846

William Faulkner
Comparing Literary Works
Race at Morning .... Short Story 860
Nobel Prize Acceptance Speech .... Speech 875

Robert Frost
Comparing Literary Works
Birches .... Poem 882
Stopping by Woods on a Snowy Evening .... Poem 885
Mending Wall .... Poem 886
"Out, Out—" .... Poem 888
The Gift Outright .... Poem 890
Acquainted With the Night .... Poem 892

James Thurber
E. B. White
Comparing Literary Works
The Night the Ghost Got In .... Nonfiction 898
from **Here Is New York** .... Nonfiction 903

A Closer Look
The Harlem Renaissance: A Cultural Revolution 910

Zora Neale Hurston
from **Dust Tracks on a Road** .... Nonfiction 914

Langston Hughes
Comparing Literary Works
The Negro Speaks of Rivers .... Poem 926
Ardella .... Poem 927
Dream Variations .... Poem 928
Refugee in America .... Poem 929

Claude McKay
The Tropics in New York .... Poem 930

(continued)

This selection is featured in the *Reader's Companion* series.

┌ Comparing Literary Works

Countee Cullen | **From the Dark Tower** .... Poem 936
Arna Bontemps | **A Black Man Talks of Reaping** .... Poem 937
Jean Toomer | **Storm Ending**.. Poem 938

Reading Informational Materials: *Public Relations Documents*
Museum of Afro American History........ Mission Statement
....Calendar of Events 942

Connections: *Literature Past and Present*
Ricardo Sánchez | **i yearn** .... Poem 946

SKILLS WORKSHOPS

Writing About Literature: Evaluate Literary Trends 948
Writing Workshop: Research: Multimedia Presentation 950
Listening and Speaking Workshop: Evaluating Communication Methods................... 954
Assessment Workshop: Sentence-Completion Questions............................... 955

UNIT 6

Prosperity and Protest (1946–Present)

INTRODUCTION 958

Richard Lederer   **The Development of American English:
Brave New Words** 968

PART 1   Literature Confronts the Everyday

Flannery O'Connor	**The Life You Save May Be Your Own**	Short Story	972
Bernard Malamud	**The First Seven Years**	Short Story	988
John Updike	**The Brown Chest**	Short Story	1002

Comparing Literary Works

Robert Lowell	**Hawthorne**	Poem	1014
Robert Penn Warren	**Gold Glade**	Poem	1017
William Stafford	**Traveling Through the Dark**	Poem	1019
Theodore Roethke	**The Light Comes Brighter**	Poem	1021
	The Adamant	Poem	1022

Anne Tyler	**Average Waves in Unprotected Waters**	Short Story	1028

Comparing Literary Works

N. Scott Momaday	*from* **The Names**	Nonfiction	1042
Naomi Shihab Nye	**Mint Snowball**	Nonfiction	1047
Joy Harjo	**Suspended**	Nonfiction	1049

Alice Walker	**Everyday Use**	Short Story	1056
Maxine Hong Kingston	*from* **The Woman Warrior**	Nonfiction	1070
Julia Alvarez	**Antojos**	Short Story	1082

Comparing Literary Works

Lorna Dee Cervantes	**Freeway 280**	Poem	1098
Martín Espada	**Who Burns for the Perfection of Paper**	Poem	1100
Diana Chang	**Most Satisfied by Snow**	Poem	1101
Simon Ortiz	**Hunger in New York City**	Poem	1102
Garret Hongo	**What For**	Poem	1103

(continued)

 This selection is featured in
the *Reader's Companion* series.

Contents ◆ *xvii*

xvii

UNIT 6

Prosperity and Protest (1946–Present) (continued)

PART 2   Focus on Literary Forms: Essay

Comparing Literary Works

Carson McCullers	*from* **The Mortgaged Heart**	Nonfiction	1112
William Safire	**Onomatopoeia**	Nonfiction	1115
Ian Frazier	**Coyote v. Acme**	Nonfiction	1118

Comparing Literary Works

Sandra Cisneros	**Straw Into Gold: The Metamorphosis of the Everyday**	Nonfiction	1128
Rita Dove	**For the Love of Books**	Nonfiction	1133
Amy Tan	**Mother Tongue**	Nonfiction	1136

PART 3   Social Protest

James Baldwin	**The Rockpile**	Short Story	1148

Comparing Literary Works

John Hersey	*from* **Hiroshima**	Nonfiction	1162
Randall Jarrell	**Losses**	Poem	1173
	The Death of the Ball Turret Gunner	Poem	1174

Comparing Literary Works

Sylvia Plath	**Mirror**	Poem	1180
Adrienne Rich	**In a Classroom**	Poem	1181
Gwendolyn Brooks	**The Explorer**	Poem	1182
Robert Hayden	**Frederick Douglass**	Poem	1183
	Runagate Runagate	Poem	1184

Comparing Literary Works

Colleen McElroy	**For My Children**	Poem	1192
Louise Erdrich	**Bidwell Ghost**	Poem	1195

E. L. Doctorow	**The Writer in the Family**	Short Story	1202

Comparing Literary Works

Yusef Komunyakaa	**Camouflaging the Chimera**	Poem	1220
Tim O'Brien	**Ambush** *from* **The Things They Carried**	Short Story	1222

A Closer Look
Twentieth Century Drama: America On Stage 1228

Comparing Literary Works

Arthur Miller **The Crucible**.. Drama

Act I.. 1233

Act II... 1267

Act III.. 1291

Act IV 1319

Reading Informational Materials: *Critical Commentaries*

Arthur Miller *from* **On Social Plays**........................... Critical Commentary 1338 **RC**

Skills Workshops

Writing About Literature: Analyze Literary Trends 1342

Writing Workshop: Workplace Writing: Job Portfolio 1344

Listening and Speaking Workshop: Analyze the Impact of the Media...................... 1348

Assessment Workshop: Punctuation, Usage, and Sentence Structure...................... 1349

Resources

Suggestions for Sustained Reading................................... R1

Glossary R7

Tips for Improving Reading Fluency.................................... R10

Literary Terms Handbook R12

Grammar and Mechanics Handbook R22

Internet Research Handbook R29

Citing Sources R31

Rubric Handbook R33

Preparing for College Entrance and AP^{TM} Exams........... R37

Handbook of Academic Writing... R40

   College Application Essays R40

   Writing About Literature R41

Formatting Business Letters R46

Commonly Misspelled Words R47

Index of Authors and Titles... R48

Index of Skills R50

Index of Features... R57

Acknowledgments (continued) R58

Art Credits R61

 **RC** This selection is featured in the *Reader's Companion* series.

Comparing Literary Works

Comparing Works in the Oral Tradition
The Earth on Turtle's Back 16
Onondaga
When Grizzlies Walked Upright 19
Modoc
from The Navajo Origin Legend 22
Navajo
from The Iroquois Constitution 24
Iroquois

Comparing Authors' Styles
A Journey Through Texas 32
Alvar Núñez Cabeza de Vaca
Boulders Taller Than the Great Tower of Seville 37
García López de Cárdenas

Comparing Historical Accounts
from The General History of Virginia 72
John Smith
from Of Plymouth Plantation 78
William Bradford

Comparing Apostrophe and Direct Address
Huswifery 100
Edward Taylor
To My Dear and Loving Husband 102
Anne Bradstreet

Comparing Theme of Self Improvement
from The Autobiography •
from Poor Richard's Almanack 140
Benjamin Franklin

Comparing Audience
The Declaration of Independence 156
Thomas Jefferson
from The Crisis, Number 1 160
Thomas Paine

Comparing Poems of Praise
Phillis Wheatley's Poetry 172

Comparing Diction
Speech in the Virginia Convention 186
Patrick Henry
Speech in the Convention 191
Benjamin Franklin

Comparing Primary Source Documents
Letter to Her Daughter From the
New White House 204
Abigail Adams
from Letters From an American Farmer 208
Michel-Guillaume Jean de Crèvecoeur

Comparing Mood
Henry Wadsworth Longfellow's Poetry 258

Comparing Mood
Thanatopsis 267
William Cullen Bryant
Old Ironsides 270
Oliver Wendell Holmes
The First Snowfall 272
James Russell Lowell
from Snowbound 274
John Greenleaf Whittier

Comparing Writer's Style
Crossing the Great Divide 286
Meriwether Lewis
The Most Sublime Spectacle on Earth 289
John Wesley Powell

Comparing Gothic Style
The Fall of the House of Usher 308
The Raven 326
Edgar Allan Poe

Comparing Relationships
Ralph Waldo Emerson's Writings 388

Comparing Metaphor
Henry David Thoreau's Writings 402

Comparing Theme
Emily Dickinson's Poetry 420

Comparing Diction
Walt Whitman's Poetry 434

Comparing Depictions of War
An Episode of War 476
Stephen Crane
Willie Has Gone to the War 481
Stephen Foster, George Cooper

Comparing Mood
Spirituals 488

Comparing Insights Into History
The Gettysburg Address 522
Second Inaugural Address 523
Abraham Lincoln
Letter to His Son 525
Robert E. Lee

Comparing Historical Perspectives
Civil War Writings 536

Comparing Humor

from Life on the Mississippi 564

The Notorious Jumping Frog
of Calaveras County 569

Mark Twain

Comparing Mood

Heading West 596

Miriam Davis Colt

I Will Fight No More Forever 602

Chief Joseph

Comparing Depictions of African American Experience

Douglass • We Wear the Mask 658

Paul Lawrence Dunbar

Comparing Views of Life and Death

Edwin Arlington Robinson's Poetry 666

Edgar Lee Masters's Poetry 669

Comparing Poems to Philosophy

A Few Don'ts by an Imagiste •
The River-Merchant's Wife: A Letter 729

Ezra Pound

The Red Wheelbarrow • The Great Figure •
This Is Just to Say 735

William Carlos Williams

Pear Tree • Heat 737

H. D.

Comparing Satiric Tone

old age sticks 776

anyone lived in a pretty how town 777

E. E. Cummings

The Unknown Citizen 779

W. H. Auden

Comparing Imagery

Of Modern Poetry • Anecdote of the Jar 796

Wallace Stevens

Ars Poetica 798

Archibald MacLeish

Poetry 800

Marianne Moore

Comparing Narrative Points of View

In Another Country 809

Ernest Hemingway

The Corn Planting 815

Sherwood Anderson

A Worn Path 820

Eudora Welty

Comparing Personification

Carl Sandburg's Poetry 838

Comparing Story to Philosophy

William Faulkner's Writing 860

Comparing Depictions of Rural Life

Robert Frost's Poetry 882

Comparing Humor

The Night the Ghost Got In 898

James Thurber

from Here Is New York 903

E. B. White

Comparing Images of Homeland

The Negro Speaks of Rivers • Ardella •
Dream Variations • Refugee in America 926

Langston Hughes

The Tropics in New York 930

Claude McKay

Comparing Imagery

From the Dark Tower 936

Countee Cullen

A Black Man Talks of Reaping 937

Arna Bontemps

Storm Ending 938

Jean Toomer

Comparing Subject Matter

Hawthorne 1014

Robert Lowell

Gold Glade 1017

Robert Penn Warren

Traveling Through the Dark 1019

William Stafford

The Light Comes Brighter •
The Adamant 1021

Theodore Roethke

Comparing Rites of Passage

from The Names 1042

N. Scott Momaday

Mint Snowball 1047

Naomi Shihab Nye

Suspended 1049

Joy Harjo

Comparing Theme of Alienation

Freeway 280 1098

Lorna Dee Cervantes

Who Burns for the Perfection of Paper 1100

Martín Espada

Most Satisfied by Snow 1101

Diana Chang

Hunger in New York City 1102

Simon Ortiz

What For 1103

Garret Hongo

Comparing Tone
from The Mortgaged Heart 1112
Carson McCullers
Onomatopoeia 1115
William Safire
Coyote v. Acme 1118
Ian Frazier

Comparing Identity
**Straw Into Gold: The Metamorphosis
of the Everyday** 1128
Sandra Cisneros
For the Love of Books 1133
Rita Dove
Mother Tongue 1136
Amy Tan

Comparing Objectivity and Subjectivity
from Hiroshima 1162
John Hersey
**Losses • The Death of the
Ball Turret Gunner** 1173
Randall Jarrell

Comparing Social Criticism
Mirror 1180
Sylvia Plath
In a Classroom 1181
Adrienne Rich
The Explorer 1182
Gwendolyn Brooks
**Frederick Douglass •
Runagate Runagate** 1183
Robert Hayden

Comparing Portrayals of Time
For My Children 1192
Colleen McElroy
Bidwell Ghost 1195
Louise Erdrich

Comparing Form
Camouflaging the Chimera 1220
Yusef Komunyakaa
Ambush from The Things They Carried 1222
Tim O'Brien

READING INFORMATIONAL MATERIALS

	Plimoth-on-Web .... Web Site	88
USA Today	**Lawyers Leave Poor Behind** .... Editorial	167
Robert N. Weiner	**Pro Bono Work Still Valued** .... Editorial	168
Thomas Jefferson	**Commission of Meriwether Lewis** .... Historic Memorandum	296
Abraham Lincoln	**Emancipation Proclamation** .... Public Document	530
	Museum of Afro-American History ...... Mission Statement	943
	.... Calendar of Events	944
Arthur Miller	*from* **On Social Plays** .... Critical Commentary	1338

CONNECTIONS: LITERATURE PAST AND PRESENT

Darryl Babe Wilson	**Diamond Island: Alcatraz** .... Nonfiction	52
Tom Wolfe	*from* **The Right Stuff** .... Nonfiction	92
Martin Luther King Jr.	*from* **Letter From Birmingham City Jail** .... Nonfiction	180
John F. Kennedy	**Inaugural Address** .... Speech	196
Alex Haley	*from* **Roots** .... Nonfiction	214
Annie Dillard	*from* **Pilgrim at Tinker Creek, Seeing** .... Nonfiction	300
Joyce Carol Oates	**Where *Is* Here?** .... Short Story	374
Langston Hughes	**I, Too** .... Poem	448

Angela de Hoyos	**To Walt Whitman**	Poem	450
Molly Moore	**Gulf War Journal** *from* **A Woman at War**	Nonfiction	552
Larry McMurtry	*from* **Lonesome Dove**	Fiction	626
Anna Quindlen	**Cats**	Nonfiction	688
Grace Paley	**Anxiety**	Short Story	832
Ricardo Sánchez	**i yearn**	Poem	946

WRITING WORKSHOPS

Analyze Literary Periods 116

Narration: Autobiographical Narrative 118

Evaluate Literary Themes 218

Problem-and-Solution Essay 220

Compare and Contrast Literary Trends 452

Narration: Reflective Essay 454

Compare and Contrast Literary Themes 692

Research: Research Paper 694

Evaluate Literary Trends 948

Research: Multimedia Presentation 950

Analyze Literary Trends 1342

Workplace Writing: Job Portfolio 1344

LISTENING AND SPEAKING WORKSHOPS

Delivering a Speech 122

Analyze Persuasive Techniques 224

Analyze Media 458

Critique Persuasive Arguments 700

Evaluate Communication Methods 954

Analyze the Impact of the Media 1348

ASSESSMENT WORKSHOPS

Summaries of Written Texts 123

Cause-and-Effect Relationships 225

Inferences and Generalizations 459

Context Clues 701

Sentence-Completion Questions 955

Punctuation, Usage, and Sentence Structure 1349

Unit Objectives

1. To read American literature selections written between 1914 and 1946

2. To apply strategies for reading poetry that are appropriate for these selections

3. To analyze literary elements

4. To use a variety of strategies to read unfamiliar words and to build vocabulary

5. To learn elements of grammar, usage, and style.

6. To use recursive writing processes to write in a variety of forms

7. To develop listening and speaking skills

8. To express and support responses to various types of texts

9. To prepare, organize, and present literary interpretations

Meeting the Objectives

With each selection, you will find instructional materials through which students can meet these objectives. Further, you will find additional practice pages for reading strategies, literary analysis, vocabulary, and grammar in the **Selection Support: Skills Development Workbook** in your **Teaching Resources.**

Background

Art

Nighthawks, by Edward Hopper

Edward Hopper (1882–1967) worked for twenty years as a commercial illustrator; only after he was forty was he able to begin to focus entirely on art. Hopper specialized in two types of subject matter: New England rural life and New York City urban scenes.

1. What mood does the painting create, and how?
   Possible response: Most students will respond that the painting's nighttime setting and the apparent isolation of the figures create a mood of loneliness.

2. Make up a story about one of the people in the coffee shop.
   Possible response: Students' stories should indicate why the person is there and how he or she feels in the moment.

UNIT 5 Disillusion, Defiance, and Discontent (1914–1946)

Nighthawks, 1942, Edward Hopper, The Art Institute of Chicago

UNIT FEATURES

Connections	Reading Informational Material
Every unit contains a feature that connects literature to a related topic, such as art, science, or history. In this unit: Part 2: **Grace Paley: Anxiety** on p. 832; Part 3: **Ricardo Sanchez: i yearn** on p. 946. Use the information and questions on the Connections pages to help students enrich their understanding of the selections presented within the unit.	These selections will help students learn to analyze and evaluate informational texts, such as workplace documents, technical directions, and consumer materials. They will expose students to the organization and features unique to nonnarrative texts. In this unit, the focus is on Policy Statements. The **NCAA Policy Statement** is on p. 942.

" *We asked the cyclone*
to go around our barn
but it didn't hear us. "

— Carl Sandburg
from *The People, Yes*

ASSESSMENT RESOURCES

- **Selection Support:** Skills Development Workbook
- **Formal Assessment**
- **Open Book Tests**
- **Performance Assessment and Portfolio Management**
- **Extension Activities**

Assessing Student Progress

Listed below are the tools that are available to measure the degree to which students meet the unit objectives.

Informal Assessment

The questions in the Review and Assess sections are a first level of response to the concepts and skills presented within the selections. Students' responses are a brief, informal measure of their grasp of the material. These responses can indicate where further instruction and practice are needed. Then follow up with the practice pages in the **Selection Support: Skills Development Workbook.**

Formal Assessment

The **Formal Assessment** booklet contains Selection Tests and Unit Tests.

- Selection Tests measure comprehension and skills acquisition for each selection or group of selections.
- Each Unit Test provides students with thirty multiple-choice questions and five essay questions designed to assess students' knowledge of the literature and skills taught in the unit.

The **Open-Book Tests** ask students to demonstrate their ability to synthesize and communicate information from selections or groups of selections.

To assess student writing, you will find rubrics and scoring models in the **Performance Assessment and Portfolio Management** booklet. In this booklet you will also find scoring rubrics for listening and speaking activities.

Alternative Assessment

The **Extension Activities** booklet contains writing activities, listening and speaking activities, and research and technology activities that are appropriate for students with different ability levels. You may also use these activities as an alternative measurement of students' growth.

Using the Timeline

The Timeline can serve a number of instructional purposes, as follows:

Getting an Overview

Use the Timeline to help students get a quick overview of themes and events of the period. This approach will benefit all students but may be especially helpful for Visual/Spatial Learners, English Learners, and Less Proficient Readers. (For strategies in using the Timeline as an overview, see the bottom of this page.)

Thinking Critically

Questions are provided on the facing page. Use these questions to have students review the events, discuss their significance, and examine the *so what* behind the *what happened.*

Connecting to Selections

Have students refer back to the Timeline when they begin to read individual selections. By consulting the Timeline regularly, they will gain a better sense of the period's chronology. In addition, they will appreciate what was occurring in the world that gave rise to these works of literature.

Projects

Students can use the Timeline as a launching pad for projects like these:

- **Focused Timeline** Have students research the events leading up to an item on the timeline and create a smaller, more focused timeline to record them. For example, students can use the biography of T.S. Eliot on p. 716, as well as other sources, to show the events leading up to the publication of *The Waste Land* in 1922.

- **News Presentation** Have students scan a section of the Timeline, assimilate the information on it, and summarize the important events of this period in a brief oral presentation for their classmates. They can model their presentations on television or radio news reports.

Timeline 1914–1946

1915   **1920**   **1925**

American Events

- **1915** Olympic track and field champion Jim Thorpe begins his professional football career. ◀
- **1916** *Chicago Poems* by Carl Sandburg appears.
- **1917** United States enters World War I.
- **1918** President Wilson announces his 14 Points in peace plan.
- **1919** Prohibition becomes law; repealed in 1933.
- **1919** Sherwood Anderson publishes *Winesburg, Ohio.*

- **1920** Nineteenth Amendment to Constitution gives U.S. women the right to vote. ▲
- **1922** T. S. Eliot publishes *The Waste Land.*
- **1923** Wallace Stevens publishes *Harmonium.*

- **1925** F. Scott Fitzgerald publishes *The Great Gatsby.*
- **1926** Langston Hughes publishes *The Weary Blues.*
- **1926** Ernest Hemingway publishes *The Sun Also Rises.*
- **1927** Charles Lindbergh flies solo and nonstop from New York to Paris.
- **1929** Stock market crashes in October, followed by Great Depression of the 1930s. ▶

World Events

- **1915** England: Because of the war in Europe, travelers are cautioned against transatlantic voyages. The *Lusitania* would be sunk despite these warnings.
- **1917** Russia: Bolsheviks seize control of Russia in October Revolution.
- **1918** Worldwide influenza epidemic kills as many as 20 million people.
- **1919** France: Treaty of Versailles ends World War I. ▶

- **1921** England: D. H. Lawrence publishes *Women in Love.*
- **1922** Ireland: James Joyce publishes *Ulysses.*
- **1924** Germany: Thomas Mann publishes *The Magic Mountain.*

- **1925** England: Virginia Woolf publishes *Mrs. Dalloway.*
- **1925** France: French sign Pact of Locarno with Germany, committing both parties to avoid using force to change the boundary line between them.
- **1928** China: Chiang Kai-shek becomes head of Nationalist government.
- **1928** Germany: Kurt Weill and Bertolt Brecht write and produce *The Threepenny Opera.*
- **1929** Japan: Collapse of American silk market hurts workers and farmers.

704 ◆ *Disillusion, Defiance, and Discontent (1914–1946)*

American and World Events

- **1933** President Roosevelt closes banks; Congress passes New Deal laws.
- **1939** John Steinbeck publishes *The Grapes of Wrath.*
- **1939** *The Wizard of Oz* and *Gone With the Wind* appear in movie theaters. ▼

...we here highly resolve that these dead shall not have died in vain...

REMEMBER DEC. 7th!

- **1940** Richard Wright publishes *Native Son.*
- **1940** Civil Aeronautics Board is created to regulate U.S. commercial air traffic.
- **1941** Japanese bomb American naval base at Pearl Harbor, bringing U.S. into World War II. ▲
- **1944** Roosevelt is reelected president for an unprecedented fourth term.

- **1945** Atom bombs dropped on Hiroshima and Nagasaki.
- **1945** Truman declares September 2 V-J Day, or Victory Over Japan Day. World War II ends. ▼

- **1930** India: Mahatma Gandhi leads famous march to the sea to protest British tax on salt.
- **1931** Spain: Salvador Dali paints *Persistence of Memory.* ▶
- **1933** Germany: Adolf Hitler becomes German chancellor.
- **1936** Spain: Spanish Civil War begins.
- **1939** Poland: German blitzkrieg invasion of Poland sets off World War II.

- **1940** France: French government signs armistice with Germany.
- **1942** France: Albert Camus completes *The Stranger.*

- **1945** Germany: Dresden is hit by Allied firebombing raid. Firestorm virtually destroys city.
- **1945** United Nations Charter signed at end of World War II.

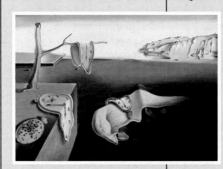

Analyzing the Timeline

1. (a) When did the United States enter World War I? **(b)** What does this date of entry suggest about feelings in the United States toward the war?
Answer: (a) The Untied States entered World War I in 1917. **(b)** The lateness of this date—the war had been going on for several years—suggests that the United States was reluctant to become involved in a European conflict.

2. (a) Name a feat of flying that occurred in the period 1925–1930. **(b)** What does this event indicate about the development of technology?
Answer: (a) In 1927, Charles Lindbergh flew solo and nonstop from New York to Paris. **(b)** It indicates better methods of transportation were shrinking the globe.

3. (a) What is the time span between the end of World War I and the beginning of World War II? **(b)** Judging by this Timeline, how would you characterize the ten years leading up to World War II?
Answer: (a) The time span is a period of twenty years, from 1919 to 1939. **(b)** In 1929, the stock market crashed, leading to the Great Depression of the 1930s. This item suggests that the 1930s were a time of economic hardship.

4. (a) When did World War II break out in Europe? When did the United States enter the war? **(b)** What connection can you make between the date the United States entered World War II and its behavior in World War I?
Answer: (a) World War II broke out in Europe in 1939; the United States entered the war in 1941. **(b)** In World War I, the United States also seemed reluctant to join in the fighting.

5. (a) For how many terms was President Roosevelt elected? **(b)** Judging by events on this Timeline, what might account for this success?
Answer: (a) In 1944, he won an unprecedented fourth term. **(b)** In 1933, he seems to have dealt decisively with the Depression. Also, people may have wanted to keep a trusted leader during a time of crisis such as World War II.
continued

Continued from right column

▶**Critical Viewing**

1. What does the illustration for the stock market crash of 1929 suggest about the state of the nation? **[Infer]**
Possible response: It suggests that people who had become very wealthy suddenly became poor; it also suggests that the wealthiest Americans were resented by many.

2. Compare and contrast the photograph of Dorothy, the scarecrow, and the tin man (1939) with that of the sailor kissing a nurse on V-J day. **[Compare and Contrast]**

Possible response: Dorothy is in a world of innocent fantasy; the sailor and the nurse, while joyous, are at the end of a long transformative experience.

3. What mood does Salvador Dali's painting (1931) convey? **[Analyze]**
Possible response: With its limp watches, apparently dead horse, and stretch of open ground, the painting conveys a mood of fear and uncertainty.

- Amid the optimism of pre-World War I America, T.S. Eliot was hearing a more melancholy strain and helping to create a new kind of verse. Students can appreciate his achievement by reading "The Love Song of J. Alfred Prufrock," p. 716.

- In Ernest Hemingway's short story "In Another Country," p. 806, students will experience the sense of disillusionment that resulted from World War I.

- As they read F. Scott Fitzgerald's story "Winter Dreams," p. 742, students will come to understand the dreams that tantalized Americans during the 1920s.

▶ **Critical Viewing**

Possible response: Some students may respond that the poster is corny. Others may feel that its inspirational, patriotic message—with a heroic-looking sailor beckoning toward the flag and liberty hovering at the top—would have been effective.

Disillusion, Defiance, and Discontent
(1914–1946)

The America that entered the twentieth century was a nation achieving world dominance while simultaneously losing some of its youthful innocence and brash confidence. Two world wars, a dizzying decade of prosperity, and a devastating worldwide depression marked this era. With these events came a new age in American literature. The upheavals of the early twentieth century ushered in a period of artistic experimentation and lasting literary achievement.

Historical Background

The years immediately preceding World War I were characterized by an overwhelming sense of optimism. Numerous technological advances occurred, dramatically affecting people's lives and creating a sense of promise for the future. While a number of serious social problems still existed, politicians began to initiate reforms aimed at solving those problems. When World War I broke out in 1914, however, President Woodrow Wilson was forced to turn his attention away from the troubles at home and focus on the events in Europe.

War in Europe World War I was one of the bloodiest and most tragic conflicts ever to occur. It involved a struggle between the Allies (Britain, France, Belgium, Italy, Serbia, Montenegro, Japan, and Russia; later, Russia would drop out of the conflict and the United States would join) and the Central Powers (Germany, Austria-Hungary, and Turkey). When the initial advances of the German forces were halted, the conflict in Europe was transformed into a trench war. The introduction of the machine gun made it virtually impossible for one side to launch a successful attack on its opponents' trenches, however, and the war dragged on for several years, claiming almost an entire generation of European men.

President Wilson wanted the United States to remain neutral in the war, but that proved impossible. In 1915, a German submarine sank the *Lusitania*, pride of the British merchant fleet. More than 1,200 people on board lost their lives, including 128 Americans. After the sinking, American public opinion favored the Allies. When Germany resumed unrestricted submarine warfare two years later, the United States joined the Allied cause.

At first, the reality of war did not sink in. Americans were confident and carefree as the troops set off overseas. That cheerful mood soon passed. A number of famous American writers saw the war firsthand and learned of its horror. E. E. Cummings, Ernest Hemingway, and John Dos Passos served as

THE NAVY NEEDS YOU! DON'T READ AMERICAN HISTORY— MAKE IT!

U·S·NAVY RECRUITING STATION

▲ **Critical Viewing**
Recruiting posters like this one urged Americans to help the war effort during World War I. Why do you think this poster would or would not have been effective in persuading people to enlist? **[Evaluate an Advertisement]**

✳ ENRICHMENT: Social Studies Connection

Ethnic Groups in the U.S. Army

People from every ethnic group enlisted to fight in World War I. About 20,000 Puerto Ricans served in the armed forces. Many Filipinos also served. Scores of soldiers were immigrant who had recently arrived in the United States.

At first, the armed forces did not allow African Americans in combat. When the government changed the rules, more than two million African Americans registered for the draft. Nearly 400,000 were accepted

for duty. They were forced into segregated "black-only" units commanded mostly by white officers.

Ask students what the willingness to serve in the army, despite barriers, indicates about the loyalty of ethnic groups.
Possible response: It suggests that ethnic Americans felt a strong commitment to the country and its cause.

ambulance drivers. Hemingway later served in the Italian infantry and was seriously wounded. Other, less famous writers fought and died in France. Among them were the poets Joyce Kilmer, who wrote "Trees," and Alan Seeger, who wrote "I Have a Rendezvous with Death."

Prosperity and Depression The era following the end of the Great War in November 1918 was not a peaceful one for America: President Wilson's dream of seeing the United States join the League of Nations failed, and in the big cities of America, from 1920 to 1933, Prohibition made the sale of liquor illegal, leading to bootlegging, speakeasies, widespread law breaking, and sporadic warfare among competing gangs.

Throughout the 1920s, the nation seemed to be on a binge. After a brief recession in 1920 and 1921, the economy boomed. New buildings rose everywhere, creating new downtown sections in many cities—Omaha, Des Moines, and Minneapolis among them. Radio arrived, and so did jazz. Movies became big business, and spectacular movie palaces sprang up across the country. Fads

Close-up on History

Women Get the Vote

One of the most important events of the immediate postwar period was the passage of the Nineteenth Amendment to the Constitution, giving women the right to vote.

The struggle to grant women the vote, or suffrage, went back many years, but it gathered significant momentum in the early 1900s. Carrie Chapman Catt, a former school principal and reporter, spoke out forcefully for women's suffrage. Catt was also a brilliant organizer, and she devised a state-by-state campaign to win the vote for women. Her campaign succeeded as year by year more states in the West and Midwest gave women the vote, although in most cases, they could exercise this right only in state elections. Gradually, more women called for an amendment to the Constitution to give them a voice in national elections, too.

The suffragist leader Alice Paul and others met with President Wilson soon after he took office in 1913. Although Wilson was not opposed to women's suffrage, he did not support a constitutional amendment. Suffragists became disillusioned after numerous meetings with Wilson and, in January 1917, began to picket at the White House. After several months, police began arresting the protesters. Paul and other arrested women went on a hunger strike, but prison officials force-fed them. Upon their release from prison, Paul and the other women resumed their picketing. They were a determined group.

By early 1918, not long before the end of World War I, the tide began to turn in favor of the suffrage cause. The tireless work of Catt, Paul, and others began to pay off. President Wilson agreed to support the suffrage amendment.

Finally, in 1919, Congress passed the Nineteenth Amendment, and by August 1920, three fourths of the states had ratified it. The amendment doubled the number of eligible voters in the United States and eliminated a long-standing injustice.

Background

Automobiles

The auto industry was the engine of the American economy in the 1920s. Car sales grew rapidly during the decade. The auto boom spurred growth in related fields, such as steel and rubber.

One reason for the auto boom was a drop in prices. By 1924, the cost of a Model T had decreased from $850 to $290. As a result, ordinary Americans—not just the rich—could afford to buy a car. Car prices fell because factories became more efficient. Henry Ford had introduced the assembly line in his factory in 1913. The goal, he said, was to make the cars identical. Before the assembly line, it took 14 hours to put together a Model T. In Ford's new factory, workers could assemble a Model T in 93 minutes!

The assembly line was a key idea in the expansion of manufacturing. It could apply to many industries, ensuring rapid manufacture of less expensive goods. Other companies copied Ford's methods. In 1927, General Motors passed Ford as the top auto maker. General Motors sold cars in a variety of models and colors.

CUSTOMIZE INSTRUCTION FOR UNIVERSAL ACCESS

For Less Proficient Readers	For English Learners	For Advanced Readers
Help these students approach and understand the Historical Background and Literature of the Period by instructing them to focus on the two world wars. What historical causes and effects are associated with the wars? What connections does the essay make between the wars and literature?	These students may find the literary concepts associated with Modernism to be particularly challenging. First, explain that World War I was a key influence on these literary movements. Then, have them read through Literature of the Period slowly, pausing to identify words that might reflect that influence.	As these students read, encourage them to take notes on how World War I influenced the literature of the period. Then, have them discuss the cultural impact of World War I and speculate on the cultural impact that World War II—which ends this historical period—might have on the era to come.

Background

Greenwich Village

During the 1920s, artists and writers flocked to Greenwich Village in New York City. Older buildings in the area, including barns, stables, and houses, were converted to studios, nightclubs, theaters, and shops. In 1923, playwright Eugene O'Neill founded the Greenwich Village Theatre, where experimental dramas were performed.

▶ **Critical Viewing**

Possible response: They probably flourish because people have money to spend and more leisure time in which to enjoy themselves.

Historical Background

Comprehension Check

1. What was the prevailing mood in the years preceding World War I?
   Answer: There was a mood of optimism.

2. What tragic event during World War I turned opinion in America toward the Allies?
   Answer: The event was the sinking of the *Lusitania*, which resulted in 128 American deaths.

3. After World War I, what law caused an outbreak of criminal activity in American cities?
   Answer: In 1919, Prohibition made the sale of liquor illegal, a measure that caused widespread crime as liquor was smuggled into America and sold illegally.

4. How healthy was the economy during most of the 1920s?
   Answer: During most of the 1920s, the economy boomed.

5. Name the event that, in 1929, started the economic downturn known as the Depression.
   Answer: That event was the stock market crash.

6. What caused the United States to enter World War II?
   Answer: The Japanese attack on Pearl Harbor on December 7, 1941, caused the United States to enter the war.

Critical Thinking

1. In what way could you support the assertion that, between 1914 and 1939, the mood of Americans alternated between optimism and pessimism? **[Support]**

continued

---

abounded: raccoon coats, flagpole sitting, and a dance called the Charleston. The great literary interpreter of the Roaring Twenties was F. Scott Fitzgerald. In *This Side of Paradise* and *The Great Gatsby*, Fitzgerald vividly captured the essence of life during this frenzied decade.

Writers flocked to Greenwich Village, in New York City. In 1923, playwright Eugene O'Neill founded the Greenwich Village Theatre, where experimental dramas were performed. Thomas Wolfe taught English at New York University in the Village while writing his novel *Look Homeward Angel*.

In late October 1929, the stock market crashed, marking the beginning of the Great Depression. By mid-1932, about 12 million people—one quarter of the work force—were out of work. Even as bread lines formed and the numbers of unemployed grew, most business leaders remained optimistic. However, the situation continued to worsen. In the presidential election of 1932, New York's governor Franklin D. Roosevelt defeated incumbent president Herbert Hoover. Roosevelt initiated the New Deal, a package of major economic reforms, to strengthen the economy. Roosevelt's policies helped bring an end to the Depression, and these policies, together with his leadership in World War II, earned him reelection in 1936, 1940, and again in 1944.

World War II Only twenty years after the Treaty of Versailles had ended World War I, the German invasion of Poland touched off World War II. As in the earlier war, most Americans wanted to remain neutral. Even after the fall of France in 1940, the dominant mood in the United States was one of isolationism. However, when the Japanese attacked Pearl Harbor, Hawaii, on December 7, 1941, America could stay neutral no longer. The United States declared war on the Axis powers—Japan, Germany, and Italy.

After years of bitter fighting on two fronts, the Allies—the United States, Great Britain, the Soviet Union, and France—defeated Nazi Germany. Japan surrendered three months later, after the United States had dropped atomic bombs on two Japanese cities. Peace, and the atomic age, had arrived.

Literature of the Period

The Birth of Modernism The devastation of World War I brought about an end to the sense of optimism that had characterized the years immediately preceding the war. Many people were left with a feeling of uncertainty and disillusionment. No longer trusting the ideas and values of the world out of which the war had developed, people sought to find new ideas that better suited twentieth-century life. The quest for new ideas occurred in the world of literature as well, and a major literary movement known as Modernism was born.

Modernists experimented with a wide variety of new approaches and techniques, producing a remarkably diverse body of literature. Yet the Modernists shared a common purpose: They sought to capture the essence of modern life

708 ◆ *Disillusion, Defiance, and Discontent (1914–1946)*

▲ **Critical Viewing**
The Charleston was a popular dance during the Roaring Twenties. Why do nightclubs featuring music and dance flourish during periods of prosperity? **[Make an Inference]**

Historical Background continued

Possible response: Before World War I, Americans were optimistic. The war brought Americans face to face with bitter realities. However, the 1920s produced a new optimism as the economy boomed. Then spirits declined as the Depression set in.

2. Judging by what you know about the 1920s, what do you think F. Scott Fitzgerald's stories and novels are like? **[Infer]** Possible response: Students may respond that they capture the dazzle,

dreams—and perhaps the disillusion—of a fast-moving, showy era.

3. Do the historical events suggest that 1914–1946 would be a time of experimentation in literature? Why or why not? **[Draw Conclusions]** Possible response: The rapid changes, dramatic world events, and fluctuations in mood might inspire writers to experiment with new forms and new approaches to language.

in both the form and content of their work. To reflect the fragmentation of the modern world, the Modernists constructed their works out of fragments, omitting the expositions, transitions, resolutions, and explanations used in traditional literature. In poetry, they abandoned traditional forms and meters in favor of free verse, whose rhythms they improvised to suit individual poems. The themes of their works were usually implied, rather than directly stated, creating a sense of uncertainty and forcing readers to draw their own conclusions. In general, Modernist works demanded more from readers than the works of earlier American writers. At the same time, the Modernists helped to earn American literature a place in the world's esteem.

Imagism The Modernist movement was ushered in by a poetic movement known as Imagism. This movement, which lasted from 1909 to 1917, attracted followers in both the United States and England. The Imagists rebelled against the sentimentality of nineteenth-century poetry. They demanded

Point/Counterpoint

Women, Followers—or Cofounders—of Modernism?

Were the female writers and editors who worked alongside men like Pound and Eliot useful followers and helpers of these men, or were they fully contributing cofounders of Modernism? Two scholars disagree about where the credit for founding Imagism should be given.

Women, Followers of Modernism "With energy and dispatch, Pound began collecting poetry. . . . He then asked Hilda Doolittle to show him some poems in the tearoom of the British Museum, in the 'rather prissy milieu of some infernal bun shop full of English spinsters,' as Aldington put it. Pound read Hilda's new poems with admiration. According to Aldington, Pound popped his pince-nez, an affectation he had learned from Yeats, when he read her 'Hermes of the Ways,' a poem he immediately cut and changed to make its pristine clarity even more penetrating, and signed the poem 'H.D., Imagiste.' In the space of a few moments Pound had created a literary movement and its first acolytes."
—John Tytell,
Ezra Pound: The Solitary Volcano

Women, Cofounders of Modernism "It is also apparent that a number of women's achievements have been credited to Pound in whole or in part. H.D. made the first real critical comments about the poetry of Marianne Moore, and Moore credited H.D. with suggesting that Moore write prose for the *Dial*—both activities that have been attributed to Pound. Cyrena Pondrom has demonstrated that H.D. also created the poetic style that became known as Imagism. . . . H.D., and especially Amy Lowell, played central roles in disseminating Imagism. . . . Literary histories, however, often give Pound full credit for the development and promotion of Imagism."
—Jayne E. Marek,
Women Editing Modernism

→← *POINT/COUNTERPOINT*
Underscore that Ezra Pound frequently interacted with other writers and poets, discussing their work and his own. Scholars still debate the degree to which Pound influenced these writers—and possibly deserves credit for the movements they began. Then, ask the following questions:

1. What do these two viewpoints have in common?
   Possible response: Both imply that the Modernist period was a time of great literary innovation, and that Pound and H.D. were at the heart of Imagism.

2. In what ways do these viewpoints differ?
   Possible response: They differ on the question of Pound's influence. Tytell believes Pound created Imagism through his influence on H.D., while Marek believes Pound has been credited for other writers' accomplishments.

3. Can you think of contemporary examples of similar debates over who gets credit for a certain development—literary, artistic, or otherwise? Explain.
   Possible response: Students may be able to refer to any number of new forms in the arts or entertainment, such as film genres or formats for television shows. Be sure students are able to identify and explain the debate over credit for any developments they list.

✳ ENRICHMENT: Humanities Connection

The Movies

Leisure gained a new meaning in the 1920s. Rising wages and labor-saving appliances gave families more time and money, and they looked for new ways to have fun.

In the 1920s, the movie industry came of age and provided Americans with the fun they were seeking. Southern California's warm and sunny climate allowed filming all year round. Soon, Hollywood became the movie capital of the world.

Over the course of the decade, millions of Americans went to the movies. They thrilled to westerns, romances, adventures, and comedies. In small towns, theaters were bare rooms with hard chairs. In cities, they were huge palaces with red velvet seats.

The first movies had no sound. Audiences followed the plot by reading "title cards" that appeared on the screen. A pianist in the theater played music that went with the action.

Critical Thinking

Possible response: Students may respond that the photograph reveals something of the economic hardship of the period, and that the expression of the woman in the photograph conveys the fear and uncertainty many Americans experienced.

instead hard, clear expression, concrete images, and the language of everyday speech. Their models came from Greek and Roman classics, Chinese and Japanese poetry, and the free verse of the French poets of their day. Among the writers associated with the earliest phase of Imagism were H.D. (Hilda Doolittle) and Ezra Pound. When Pound moved on from Imagism, other leaders took over, among them H.D. Amy Lowell, a Massachusetts poet, led the Imagist movement in the United States in its final years.

The Expatriates Postwar disenchantment led a number of American writers to become expatriates, or exiles. Many of these writers settled in Paris, where they were influenced by Gertrude Stein, the writer who coined the phrase "lost generation" to describe those who were disillusioned by World War I. Stein lived in Paris from 1902 until her death in 1946, and her home attracted many major authors, including Sherwood Anderson, F. Scott Fitzgerald, and Ernest Hemingway.

Fitzgerald and Hemingway are the best known of the expatriates, but they are by no means the only ones. Ezra Pound spent most of his adult life in England, France, and Italy. T. S. Eliot, born in St. Louis, went to Europe in 1914, soon settled in England, and lived there until his death in 1965. Some critics have called Eliot's long, despairing poem *The Waste Land* the most important poem of the century.

Most of the "lost generation" saw very little in their civilization to praise or even accept. Archibald MacLeish, an expatriate from 1923 to 1928, wrote several volumes of verse expressing the chaos and hopelessness of those years. MacLeish eventually broke with the expatriates, however. He returned to the United States in the 1930s and became increasingly concerned about the rise of dictatorships. A supporter of President Roosevelt's New Deal, he served as Librarian of Congress during World War II.

New Approaches During the years between the two world wars, writers in both the United States and Europe explored new literary territories. Influenced by developments in modern psychology, writers began using the stream-of-consciousness technique, attempting to re-create the natural flow of a character's thoughts. Drawing its name from the work of psychologist William James, this technique involves the presentation of a series of thoughts, memories, and insights, connected only by a character's natural associations.

The landmark stream-of-consciousness novel is *Ulysses*, published in 1922 by the Irish writer James Joyce. A number of American novelists soon adopted the technique, most notably William Faulkner in

▼ **Critical Viewing**
Dorothea Lange took this photograph, which has become a symbol of the Great Depression. What does it "say" about this period?
[Draw a Conclusion]

710 ◆ *Disillusion, Defiance, and Discontent (1914–1946)*

The Sound and the Fury. Katherine Anne Porter's short stories and the three novels in John Dos Passos's *U.S.A.* also use stream-of-consciousness narration. The trilogy by Dos Passos includes other devices unusual in a fictional work, such as brief biographies of well-known Americans and quotations from newspapers and magazines.

Poets also sought to stretch the old boundaries. E. E. Cummings's poems attracted special attention because of their wordplay, unique typography, and special punctuation. These devices are more than mere oddities in Cummings's poetry. They are vital to its intent and its meaning.

William Carlos Williams, a New Jersey physician and poet, began by writing poetry like that of John Keats, radically changed his style under the influence of Imagism, and turned an attentive eye on his local world. Unlike the writers who traveled to Europe, Williams sought meaning in American sights and sounds and used informal, conversational speech. His epic poem, *Paterson*, is named for a New Jersey city. He had a great influence on two important poets of the next generation, Allen Ginsberg and A.R. Ammons.

Wallace Stevens, an insurance executive, wrote a more intellectual and self-consciously elegant poetry than that of Williams. Throughout his work, Stevens explored the shifting relationship between reality and the fictions that the imagination creates. His poetry was inspirational for such later poets as James Merrill and John Ashbery.

Marianne Moore is famous for her lines measured by syllable counts, her use of quotations from such real-world texts as "business documents and school books," and her quirky, unforgettable images—in "Poetry," she compares an "immovable critic twitching his skin" to "a horse."

Writers of International Renown The Modernists dramatically altered the complexion of American literature. At the same time, many of these writers earned international acclaim that equaled that of their European literary contemporaries.

Proof of this acclaim is the number of Americans who won the Nobel Prize for Literature. This international award was established in 1901 with funds bequeathed by Alfred Nobel, the Swedish inventor of dynamite. The first American to win the Nobel Prize for Literature was Sinclair Lewis. A native of Sauk Center, Minnesota, Lewis fictionalized his hometown as Gopher Prairie in his first important novel, *Main Street*. Lewis, one of the great satirists of the era, wrote two more classics within the next few years. *Babbitt* was about an American businessman, while *Arrowsmith* dealt with the medical profession.

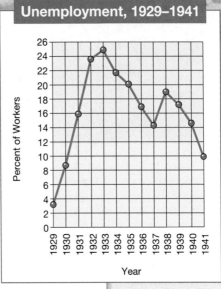

Unemployment, 1929–1941

Percent of Workers / *Year*

▲ **Critical Viewing** During the Depression, millions of Americans were out of work. According to the graph, what happened to unemployment between 1936 and 1941? **[Interpret a Pattern]**

Background

John Dos Passos

John Dos Passos is still remembered as a radical social critic. After graduating from Harvard University, Dos Passos drove ambulances during World War I and traveled extensively in Europe as a newspaper correspondent. When Italian immigrant Nicola Sacco and Bartolomeo Vanzetti were executed after what many critics declared to be a false conviction, Dos Passos developed the conviction that there were, in fact, two Americas—one for the wealthy and a second for the powerless. The idea of "two nations" within the United States inspired the trilogy *U.S.A.*, in which the author used radical stylistic experimentation to address burning social issues of the day. It is because of *U.S.A.* that Dos Passos is remembered as a critic of American life. Yet the author became disillusioned with the social beliefs behind his great trilogy, and by the end of his life his writing clearly reflected a growing conservativism.

▶ **Critical Viewing**

Answer: According to the graph, the percentage of unemployed workers fell from 1936 to 1937 (from about 17% to about 14%), rose again from 1937 to 1938 (from 14% to about 19%), and then declined from 1938 to 1941 (from about 19% to 10%).

▶ **Critical Viewing**

Possible response: In a single panorama, it dramatizes a sequence of events in the history of African Americans. Figures are shown in silhouette, gesturing dramatically, while a rising sun symbolizes hope for the future.

Background

William Faulkner

William Faulkner's Nobel Prize arrived as the writer's career was undergoing a revival. Faulkner's most famous work had been written and published years before, but his reputation in America began to grow with the publication of an anthology, *The Portable Faulkner*, in 1946. The 1949 Nobel Prize, actually presented in 1950, finally solidified Faulkner's place as one of the great American writers. His acceptance speech, which students can read on p. 875, was justly famous. In it, he proclaimed his faith in the human race, even as the world entered the atomic age.

Lewis's Nobel Prize in 1930 was the first of many for American writers. In 1936, the prize went to Eugene O'Neill, ranked by most critics as America's greatest playwright. Among his best-known plays are *Desire Under the Elms*, *The Iceman Cometh*, and *Long Day's Journey Into Night*. O'Neill's plays are sometimes autobiographical, generally tragic, and often experimental. His *Strange Interlude*, produced in 1928, uses stream-of-consciousness asides to reveal the inner feelings of characters. These feelings often contrast with their actual spoken words.

Then, in 1938, the Nobel Prize for Literature went to Pearl S. Buck, an American who spent her early years in China. Buck wrote about that country with understanding and compassion. *The Good Earth* is considered her finest work.

After T. S. Eliot, who had become a British subject, won the award in 1948, William Faulkner won it the following year. Most of Faulkner's novels and short stories are set in mythical Yoknapatawpha County, Mississippi, which closely resembled the region of Mississippi where Faulkner lived. In addition to *The Sound and the Fury*, Faulkner wrote such enduring works as *Light in August* and *The Hamlet*.

Later, Ernest Hemingway and John Steinbeck also won Nobel Prizes for Literature. Hemingway's simple, direct, journalistic style of writing, evident in such novels as *The Sun Also Rises* and *A Farewell to Arms*, influenced a generation of young writers. Much of his best writing focuses on World War I and its aftermath. Many of Steinbeck's works depict the Depression, especially as it affected migrant workers and dust-bowl farmers. Two of Steinbeck's most memorable novels are *Of Mice and Men* and *The Grapes of Wrath*.

The Harlem Renaissance A new literary age was dawning, not only in Greenwich Village and among expatriates in Paris, but also in northern Manhattan, in Harlem. African American writers, mostly newcomers from the South, were creating their own renaissance there. It began in 1921 with the publication of Countee Cullen's "I Have a Rendezvous With Life (with apologies to Alan Seeger)." Another poem by a promising young African American writer—"The Negro Speaks of Rivers," by Langston Hughes—followed six months later.

What occurred thereafter was a burst of creative activity by African American writers, few of whom, other than Cullen, had been born in New York City. Most of them moved to Harlem during the renaissance. Claude

▲ **Critical Viewing** Aaron Douglas, an African American artist, lived and painted during the Harlem Renaissance. How does his painting "From Slavery Through Reconstruction" communicate the experience of African Americans? **[Analyze Art]**

☀ **ENRICHMENT: Music Connection**

Jazz

The early part of the twentieth century was an era of experimentation and innovation in music and art, as well as literature. Drawing upon the complex rhythms of traditional West African folk music and the harmonies of black folk music of the nineteenth century, African Americans created a vibrant new type of music known as jazz. By the 1920s, listening and dancing to jazz had become a national craze. Due to the success of performers like Duke Ellington (1899–1974) and Fats Waller (1904–1943), Harlem became the nation's jazz center.

If possible, find and play for students a recording of Ellington's "Take the A Train." Ask these questions:

1. Describe this piece of music for someone who has never heard it. **Possible response:** Students may say that the music is free-flowing but focused.

2. How does the music reflect the modern age? **Possible response:** It is quick and innovative, and it has a nervous energy.

McKay, for example, was from Jamaica. His most famous book was *Harlem Shadows,* a collection of poems published in 1922. A year later came Jean Toomer's *Cane,* a collection of stories, verses, and a play.

The Harlem Renaissance was publicly recognized in March 1924, when young African American writers met the literary editors of the city. Carl Van Doren, editor of the *Century,* noted that black writers, long "oppressed and handicapped . . . have gathered stores of emotion and are ready to burst forth with a new eloquence."

The Harlem phenomenon continued throughout the 1920s and into the 1930s. Arna Bontemps, born in Louisiana, published his first novel, *God Sends Sunday,* in 1931. The writers of this renaissance belonged to no single school of literature, but they did form a coherent group. They saw themselves as part of a new and exciting movement. In addition to producing their own exceptional works, they opened the door for the African American writers who would follow them.

A Continuing Tradition World War II did not end the literary revival that had begun after World War I. Many of the older writers continued to produce novels, short stories, plays, and poems. Meanwhile, a new generation of writers arose after World War II to keep American literature at the leading edge of the world's artistic achievement.

A Writer's Voice

Anne Spencer, Poet of the Harlem Renaissance
Women who participated in the Harlem Renaissance tend to get less attention than the men. That is why it is worth mentioning Anne Spencer (1882–1975), a poet whose work compares favorably with that of her more famous contemporaries: James Weldon Johnson, Langston Hughes, Jean Toomer, and Claude McKay.

Spencer grew up and was educated in Virginia. Her poetry became well known when Johnson selected some of her work to appear in *The Book of American Negro Poetry* (1922). During the Harlem Renaissance, she received visits from such distinguished writers as Johnson, McKay, and W.E.B. Du Bois, author of *The Souls of Black Folk* (1903).

In the following brief poem, Spencer writes in the voice of Paul Laurence Dunbar (1872–1906), an African American poet of the previous generation. Dunbar had written powerful poems like "Douglass" and "We Wear the Mask" (see pages 658 and 660). Here, Spencer indicates the value of his work by having him rank himself with three famous British Romantic poets, all of whom, like Dunbar himself, died young.

Dunbar (1920)
Ah, how poets sing and die!
Make one song and Heaven takes it;
Have one heart and Beauty breaks it;
Chatterton, Shelley, Keats, and I—
Ah, how poets sing and die!

Literature of the Period
Comprehension Check

1. What purpose was shared by Modernist writers?
Answer: They sought to capture the essence of modern life in the form and content of their work.

2. Name three qualities favored by Imagist poets.
Answer: They wanted clear expression, concrete images, and the language of everyday speech.

3. (a) What prompted writers to leave the United States and become expatriates in Europe? **(b)** Which two writers are the best known of the expatriates?
Answer: **(a)** Disenchantment stemming from World War I prompted writers to move to Europe. **(b)** Hemingway and Fitzgerald are the best-known expatriate writers.

4. What is the stream-of-consciousness technique pioneered by writers in this era?
Answer: It involves the presentation of a series of thoughts, memories, and insights, linked only by a character's natural associations.

5. Name at least two American writers who won the Nobel Prize for Literature during this era.
Possible response: Sinclair Lewis (1930), Eugene O'Neill (1936), and Pearl Buck (1938) all won the Nobel Prize for Literature. In later years, Eliot, Faulkner, Hemingway, and Steinbeck also won the prize.

6. What was the Harlem Renaissance?
Answer: It was a flowering of creative activity in the 1920s and 1930s by black writers and artists associated with the New York City community of Harlem.

Critical Thinking

1. What qualities of the modern world are reflected in the literary movement known as Modernism? **[Connect]** Possible response: Modernism reflects the nervous energy, quick and baffling transitions, and fragmentary qualities of the modern world.

continued

Literature of the Period continued

2. What do you think the expatriates were looking for in Europe that they could not find in America? **[Speculate]** Possible response: Reasonable answers include: They may have been looking for a chance to cut free from traditional ties and develop their own viewpoints. They may have seen Europe as a place where moral standards were not so rigid.

3. What factors might have brought about the Harlem Renaissance? **[Analyze Causes and Effects]** Possible response: Young African Americans from more rural areas may have been inspired by the freedom of the big city and by the loose, free-flowing rhythms of jazz, a form of music newly invented by African Americans.

Critical Thinking

1. Why do you think people use slang? **[Speculate]**

Possible response: Certain types of slang qualify the user as part of an "in" crowd. Slang may also have an appeal because it is fresh and new.

2. How much slang do you use? **[Relate]**

Possible response: Give students some methods by which they can evaluate the slang quotient of their own speech, to see whether slang makes up more or less than a fifth of the words they use. For example, they could tape record a brief conversation with a friend and then analyze its slang content.

Activity

Encourage students to gather slang words and phrases for their glossaries by keeping small notepads and pencils handy as they go through their school day, and to write down any slang they hear. If they encounter words or expressions with which they are not familiar, they should try to ask about their meanings. Encourage students to develop consistent formats for their glossaries. They may want to include pronunciations as well as definitions. Student glossaries should be as comprehensive as possible.

THE DEVELOPMENT OF AMERICAN ENGLISH
Slang As It Is Slung

BY RICHARD LEDERER

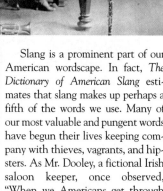

Slang is hot and slang is cool. Slang is nifty and slang is wicked. Slang is the bee's knees and the cat's whiskers. Slang is far out, groovy, and outa sight. Slang is fresh, fly, and phat. Slang is bodacious and fantabulous. Slang is ace, awesome, copacetic, the max, and totally tubular.

Those are many ways of saying that, if variety is the spice of life, slang is the spice of language. Slang adds gusto to the feast of words, as long as speakers and writers remember that too much spice can kill the feast of any dish.

Slang has added spice to the feast of American literature as American writers have increasingly written in an American voice, with the words and rhythms of everyday American discourse. Listen to the Harlem Renaissance poet Langston Hughes:

Good morning, daddy!
Ain't you heard
The boogie-woogie rumble
Of a dream deferred?

DEFINING THE "LINGO"

What is slang? In the preface to their *Dictionary of American Slang*, Harold Wentworth and Stuart Berg Flexner define slang as "the body of words and expressions frequently used by or intelligible to a rather large portion of the general American public, but not accepted as good, formal usage by the majority." Slang, then, is seen as a kind of vagabond language that prowls the outskirts of respectable speech, yet few of us can get along without it. Even our statespersons have a hard time getting by without such colloquial or slang expressions as "hit the nail on the head," "team effort," or "pass the buck."

WHAT'S IN THIS NAME?

Nobody is quite sure where the word *slang* comes from. According to H. L. Mencken, the word slang developed in the eighteenth century (it was first recorded in 1756) either from an erroneous past tense of *sling* (*sling-slang-slung*) or from language itself, as in *(thieve)s'lang(uage)* and *(beggar)s'lang(uage)*. The second theory makes the point that jargon and slang originate and are used by a particular trade or class group, but slang words come to be slung around to some extent by a whole population.

Slang is a prominent part of our American wordscape. In fact, *The Dictionary of American Slang* estimates that slang makes up perhaps a fifth of the words we use. Many of our most valuable and pungent words have begun their lives keeping company with thieves, vagrants, and hipsters. As Mr. Dooley, a fictional Irish saloon keeper, once observed, "When we Americans get through with the English language, it will look as if it has been run over by a musical comedy."

ACTIVITY

Student slang is a rich vein of metaphor and word formation. With your classmates, compile a dictionary of the slang used in your school. Provide a sentence or two illustrating the use of each slang term you define.

✳ ENRICHMENT: Social Studies Connection

More on Slang

Point out to students that slang can contribute to the growth of the language. Often, words that we take for granted today were once regarded as outrageous and unacceptable examples of slang.

The following are several slang terms that have gradually become acceptable to most speakers:

joke   slump   row   crank   boom   fad

Have students list slang terms that they use. Ask them to predict which of their slang terms will have staying power and which will fall away. If possible have them explain their choices.

Possible response: One factor predictive of a word's lasting value may be its ability to describe something better than a more standard word does; another is its ability to describe something for which there is no standard word.

Facing Troubled Times

No Place to Go, 1935, Maynard Dixon. The Herald Clark Memorial Collection, Courtesy of Brigham Young University Museum of Fine Arts

Selection Planning Guide

The selections in this section reflect the pain and disillusionment Americans felt during the years between the two world wars—a time when many Americans questioned an increasingly complex and impersonal society. "The Love Song of J. Alfred Prufrock" provides students with a glimpse of a troubled individual trapped in conventions. Pound's "In a Station of the Metro" reflects the transient nature of relationships and of society. Similarly, Fitzgerald's short story "Winter Dreams" shows the tentative nature of love in a status-conscious world. "The Unknown Citizen" raises questions about the nature of conformity. This section ends with the Billy Joel song "Allentown," a 1980s lament over a dying steel town.

Background

Art

No Place to Go, by Maynard Dixon

Point out that this painting dates from the Great Depression; elicit students' knowledge about that time in American history. Encourage students to contrast this painting with the painting on page 226 that shows a man taking in the wonders of Niagara Falls. Both paintings show a traveler in a natural setting. However, they are very different in content and mood. Encourage students to relate these differences to historical and social developments.

Have students link the painting to the focus of this part (Facing Troubled Times) by answering the following questions:

• Considering the painting's title, who might the man in it be, and what reasons might he have for traveling on foot in the American West?
Possible response: He may be a factory worker who has lost his job and is looking for another one. He may be a farmer whose farm has been repossessed and whose quest for an agricultural job has been fruitless.

TOMIZE INSTRUCTION FOR UNIVERSAL ACCESS

n assigning the selections in this part, keep in mind these factors:

Love Song of J. Alfred Prufrock"

engthy poem may present difficulty for some.

Is Just to Say"

n Imagist poem with appealing sensory imagery

ge sticks"; "anyone lived . . ."

Cummings's poetry may delight some students while presenting challenges to others; you may eed to clarify unconventional punctuation.

"The Unknown Citizen"

• An accessible poem about the dangers of uniformity in society

"Of Modern Poetry"; "Ars Poetica"; "Poetry"

• Three poems demonstrate their subject—the techniques and subject matter of poetry.

The Love Song of J. Alfred Prufrock

Lesson Objectives

1. **To analyze and respond to literary elements**
   - Literary Analysis: Dramatic Monologue
   - Connecting Literary Elements: Allusion

2. **To read, comprehend, analyze, and critique a poem**
   - Reading Strategy: Listening
   - Reading Check questions
   - Review and Assess questions
   - Assessment Practice (ATE)

3. **To develop word analysis skills, fluency, and systematic vocabulary**
   - Vocabulary Development Lesson: Greek Prefix: *di-*

4. **To understand and apply written and oral language conventions**
   - Spelling Strategy
   - Grammar and Style Lesson: Adjectival Modifiers

5. **To understand and apply appropriate writing and research strategies**
   - Writing Lesson: Character Analysis
   - Extension Activity: Report

6. **To understand and apply listening and speaking strategies**
   - Extension Activity: Role-Play

STEP-BY-STEP TEACHING GUIDE	PACING GUIDE
PRETEACH	
Motivate Students and Provide Background	
Use the Motivation activity (ATE p. 716)	5 min.
Read and discuss author and background features (SE/ATE pp. 716, 718) A	5 min.
Introduce the Concepts	
Introduce the Literary Analysis and Reading Strategy (SE/ATE p. 717) A	15 min.
Pronounce the vocabulary words and read their definitions (SE p. 717)	5 min.
TEACH	
Monitor Comprehension	
Informally monitor comprehension by circulating while students read independently or in groups A	25 min.
Monitor students' comprehension with the Reading Check notes (SE/ATE pp. 719, 721)	as students read
Develop vocabulary with Vocabulary notes (SE pp. 718, 720, 721; ATE p. 720)	as students read
Develop Understanding	
Develop students' understanding of dramatic monologue with the Literary Analysis annotations (SE pp. 719, 720; ATE pp. 719, 720) A	5 min.
Develop students' ability to paraphrase insights about the selection with the Reading Strategy annotations (SE pp. 718, 721; ATE pp. 718, 721)	5 min.
ASSESS	
Assess Mastery	
Assess students' mastery of the Reading Strategy and Literary Analysis by having them answer the Review and Assess questions (SE/ATE p. 723)	15 min.
Use one or more of the print and media Assessment Resources (ATE p. 725) A	up to 45 min.
EXTEND	
Apply Understanding	
Have students complete the Vocabulary Development Lesson and the Grammar and Style Lesson (SE p. 724) A	20 min.
Apply students' ability to revise for accuracy by using the Writing Lesson (SE/ATE p. 725) A	45 min.
Apply students' understanding using one or more of the Extension Activities (SE p. 725)	20–90 min.

 ACCELERATED INSTRUCTION:
Use the strategies and activities identified with an A.

UNIVERSAL ACCESS
- ● = Below Level Students
- ▲ = On-Level Students
- ■ = Above Level Students

Time and Resource Manager

RESOURCES		
PRINT 📖	**TRANSPARENCIES** 🗒	**TECHNOLOGY** 💿 🎧 📼
• **Beyond Literature,** Cross-Curricular Connection: Art, p. 39 ▲ ■		• **Interest Grabber Video,** Tape 5 ● ▲ ■
• **Selection Support Workbook:** ● ▲ ■ Literary Analysis, p. 177 Reading Strategy, p. 176 Build Vocabulary, p. 174	• **Literary Analysis and Reading Transparencies,** pp. 77 and 78 ● ▲ ■	
• **Literatura en español** ● ▲ • **Literary Analysis for Enrichment** ■		
• **Formal Assessment:** Selection Test, pp. 185–187 ● ▲ ■ • **Open Book Test,** pp. 115–117 ● ▲ ■ • **Performance Assessment and Portfolio Management,** p. 23 ● ▲ ■ **PRENTICE HALL ASSESSMENT SYSTEM** ● ▲ ■	**PRENTICE HALL ASSESSMENT SYSTEM** ● ▲ ■ Skills Practice Answers and Explanations on Transparencies	• **Test Bank Software** ● ▲ ■ • **Got It! Assessment Videotapes,** Tape 4 ● ▲
• **Selection Support Workbook:** ● ▲ ■ Grammar and Style, p. 175 • **Writing and Grammar,** Ruby Level ● ▲ ■ • **Extension Activities,** p. 39 ● ▲ ■	• **Daily Language Practice Transparencies** ● ▲ • **Writing Models and Graphic Organizers on Transparencies,** p. 67 ● ▲ ■	• **Writing and Grammar iText CD-ROM** ● ▲ ■ 🖥 *Take It to the Net* www.phschool.com

▨ **BLOCK SCHEDULING:** Use one 90-minute class period to preteach the selection and have students read it. Use a second 90-minute class period to assess students' mastery of skills and have them complete one of the Extension Activities.

Motivation

This dramatic monologue about a critical turning point in the speaker's life surrounds a theme students will find universal—the challenge of seizing an opportunity for emotional connection and the anguish that results when that opportunity goes unrealized. To get students involved in the theme, ask them to imagine you have invited a much-admired celebrity to visit the class. Ask students to record their feelings about such a visit in a journal. How would they express their admiration? What apprehensions might they have about the visitor's reactions? How might their feelings for the visitor affect their ability to communicate during the visit? Invite volunteers to share their entries.

Interest Grabber Video

As an alternative, you may wish to play "T.S. Eliot" on Tape 5 to engage student interest.

❶ Background

More About the Author

In some works, including "Prufrock," Eliot and other Modernists used a technique known as stream of consciousness, in which they tried to reproduce the natural tendency of the human mind to jump from association to association. Rather than providing answers, the Modernists most often left it up to readers to draw their own conclusions about the meaning of a work.

Prepare to Read

❶ The Love Song of J. Alfred Prufrock

T. S. Eliot (1888–1965)

Always well-spoken and somberly attired, Thomas Stearns Eliot was outwardly the model of convention. His work, in contrast, was revolutionary in both form and content.

Beginnings Born into a wealthy family in St. Louis, Missouri, Eliot grew up in an environment that promoted his intellectual development. He attended Harvard University, where he published a number of poems in *The Harvard Advocate*, the school's literary magazine. In 1910, the year Eliot received his master's degree in philosophy, he completed "The Love Song of J. Alfred Prufrock."

A Literary Sensation Just before the outbreak of World War I, Eliot moved to England. In 1915, he married Vivien Haigh-Wood, a deeply troubled young woman with whom he had a tumultuous relationship. During this period, he also became acquainted with Ezra Pound, another young American poet. Pound urged Harriet Monroe, the editor of *Poetry* magazine, to publish "Prufrock," thus making Eliot's work available to the public for the first time. Shortly thereafter, Eliot published a collection titled *Prufrock and Other Observations* (1917), which caused a sensation in the literary world. Eliot had used techniques, such as an intentionally fragmented structure, that were utterly new. Focusing on the frustration and despair of modern urban life, the poems in Eliot's first book also set the tone for the other poems he would write during the early stages of his career. These early poems alone earned Eliot a lasting place among the finest writers of the twentieth century.

Facing a New World Eliot made his literary mark against the backdrop of a rapidly changing society. Telephones, radios, automobiles—all were transforming life at an unprecedented pace in the early decades of the twentieth century. Uncertain and disillusioned with the values and ideologies that had produced the devastation of World War I, many people were searching for new ideas and values. Eliot was among a group of such writers and visual artists who called themselves Modernists. Modernist poets sought a break with the literary traditions of the past. They believed that poetry had to reflect the genuine, fractured experience of life in the twentieth century, not a romanticized idea of what life was once like. Eliot's exploration of the uncertainty of modern life struck a chord among readers, who were stunned by his revolutionary poetic imagery.

In 1922, Eliot published *The Waste Land*, his most celebrated work. Although Eliot himself once dismissed *The Waste Land* as "a piece of rhythmical grumbling," most readers saw it as a profound critique of the spiritual barrenness of the modern world. The poem is filled with allusions to classical and world literature and to Eastern culture and religion. It was widely read and had an enormous impact on writers and critics. *The Waste Land* is still considered one of the finest works ever written.

A Return to Tradition In his search for something beyond the "waste land" of modern society, Eliot became a member of the Church of England in 1927. He began to explore religious themes in poems such as "Ash Wednesday" (1930) and *Four Quartets* (1943)—works that suggest that he believed religion could heal the wounds inflicted by society. In later years, he wrote several plays, including *Murder in the Cathedral* (1935) and *The Cocktail Party* (1949), as well as a sizable body of literary criticism. In 1948, Eliot received the Nobel Prize for Literature.

TEACHING RESOURCES

The following resources can be used to enrich or extend the instruction for pp. 716–717.

Motivation

■ **Interest Grabber Video**, Tape 5 ■

Background

📖 **Beyond Literature**, p. 39

 Take It to the Net

Visit www.phschool.com for Background and hotlinks for "The Love Song of J. Alfred Prufrock."

Literary Analysis

📖 **Literary Analysis and Reading Transparencies,** Dramatic Monologue, p. 78 ■

Reading

📖 **Literary Analysis and Reading Transparencies,** Listening, p. 77

📖 **Selection Support:** Reading Strategy, p. 176; Building Vocabulary, p.174

■ **BLOCK SCHEDULING:** Resources marked with this symbol provide varied instruction during 90-minute blocks.

Preview

Connecting to the Literature

You may be able to remember occasions when you have wished you had a different personality. Maybe you would have preferred to be more outgoing or more assertive—the type of person who makes things happen. The character of J. Alfred Prufrock speaks to this feeling in all of us.

❷ Literary Analysis

Dramatic Monologue

A troubled J. Alfred Prufrock invites an unidentified companion—perhaps a part of his own personality—to walk with him as he reflects aloud about his bitter realization that life and love are passing him by. Prufrock's so-called love song is a **dramatic monologue**—a poem or speech in which a character addresses a silent listener. As you read this dramatic monologue, use a chart like the one shown to record Prufrock's observations about life, details of his personality, and internal conflicts.

Connecting Literary Elements

Just as you might refer to a movie you once saw or a book you once read, Prufrock refers to people and historical or literary events that hold meaning for him. For example, in this passage, he alludes to Shakespeare:

No! I am not Prince Hamlet, nor was meant to be;
Am an attendant lord, one that will do
To swell a progress, start a scene or two . . .

These references, or **allusions,** form a literary shorthand that paints a picture of Prufrock and his culture. As you read, use footnotes and guided reading questions to help you understand these allusions.

> **Prufrock's Observations**
>
> **Personality Traits**
>
> **Internal Conflicts**

❸ Reading Strategy

Listening

This poem contains some of the most famous and haunting passages in literature. One of the reasons the poem affects readers so intensely is its musicality—the sweep and fall of the lines, the repetition and rhyme, and the sounds of the words. To fully appreciate the poem, you must **listen** to it. Try reading the poem aloud, paying attention to the rhythms and repetitions. Consider how the musicality of the poem contributes to its mood and meaning.

Vocabulary Development

insidious (in sid′ ē əs) *adj.* secretly treacherous (p. 718)

digress (dī gres′) *v.* depart temporarily from the main subject (p. 720)

malingers (mə liŋ′ gerz) *v.* pretends to be ill (p. 720)

meticulous (mə tik′ yōō ləs) *adj.* extremely careful about details (p. 721)

obtuse (äb tōōs′) *adj.* slow to understand or perceive (p. 721)

The Love Song of J. Alfred Prufrock ◆ 717

---

❷ Literary Analysis

Dramatic Monologue

- Tell students that as they read "The Love Song of J. Alfred Prufrock," they will focus on understanding dramatic monologue, a literary genre in which one character addresses a silent listener.

- Have a volunteer read aloud the first sentence of the Literary Analysis instruction. Call attention to the suggestion that the person that Prufrock addresses may be part of his own personality. Encourage students to keep this possibility in mind as they read.

- Use the instruction for **Connecting Literary Elements** to point out that students can use Prufrock's allusions to build understanding of his character.

- Review the chart shown and then encourage students to complete a similar one as they read the poem.

❸ Reading Strategy

Listening

- Tell students that this poem contains a conversation—or at least one half of a conversation. As such it should be read aloud. The reading skill of listening can help students access the poem more fully.

- To listen critically, students must focus on many aspects of the poem's sound. Review those discussed in the Reading Strategy instruction and confirm students' understanding of each.

- Remind students to read the poem aloud in order to practice listening.

Vocabulary Development

Pronounce each vocabulary word for students and read the definitions as a class. Have students identify any words with which they are already familiar.

 E-Teach

Visit E-Teach at www.phschool.com for teachers' essays on how to teach, with questions and answers.

CUSTOMIZE INSTRUCTION FOR UNIVERSAL ACCESS

For Less Proficient Readers	For English Learners	For Advanced Readers
Have students listen as you read the poem aloud. This will enable them to hear the poem read fluidly. Then, encourage students to read the poem aloud themselves to hear its sounds spoken in their own voices.	Emphasize to students that they can appreciate the musicality of this poem even at places where they find it difficult to understand. Encourage students to trust their reactions to the poem's sounds and rhythms. These will suggest moods, which can in turn help students decipher the poet's meaning.	Point out to students that Eliot uses many questions in his poem. These questions are posed rhetorically, in other words, they are left unanswered by any other voice in the poem. Ask students to consider as they read, the impact on readers of the questions. How does this structure engage readers' attention.

717

CUSTOMIZE INSTRUCTION
For Bodily/Kinesthetic Learners

Encourage students to consider choreographing a mime or dance performance based on "The Love Song of J. Alfred Prufrock" to be performed outside of class. Students might divide the events in the poem into Act I in the narrow streets mentioned by the speaker, Act II at the party, and Act III on a beach. Encourage students to choose appropriate music to accompany each passage.

❶ About the Selection

This poem invites readers into the mind of its speaker J. Alfred Prufrock, as he agonizes, in a dramatic monologue, over whether and how to declare his love to a woman. Prufrock reviews his superficial personal life, and recognizes his sense of alienation and failure, all the while visualizing a scene of amorous declaration that may take place if he summons the courage. By accompanying Prufrock on his internal journey, the reader recognizes how someone might vacillate over which path to take at a fork in life's road, and how that decision-making process can reveal important facets of character.

❷ Reading Strategy

Listening

• Have a volunteer read aloud lines 1–12. Invite students to point out the repetitions in these lines. Then, have students discuss the rhythm of these lines.

• Ask students the Reading Strategy question on p. 718: In what ways do the rhythms and repetitions of this opening stanza invite readers into the poem? **Answer:** Students may note that the words "Let us go" invite readers to join Prufrock on his journey. In addition, the rhythm of the stanza sounds like footsteps, with a repetition of stressed and unstressed words.

---

❶ *The Love Song of*
J. Alfred Prufrock
T. S. Eliot

Background

In this poem, surely one of the strangest "love songs" ever written, J. Alfred Prufrock, a stuffy and inhibited man who is pained by his own passivity, invites the reader, or some unnamed visitor, to join him in a journey. Where Prufrock is and where he is going—to a party, a museum, a tea party, or some other gathering—is open to debate. The most important part of this journey, however, takes place within the inner landscape of Prufrock's emotions, memory, and intellect as he meditates on his life.

S'io credessi che mia risposta fosse
a persona che mai tornasse al mondo,
questa fiamma staria senza più scosse.
Ma per ciò che giammai di questo fondo
non tornò vivo alcun, s'i'odo il vero,
senza tema d'infamia ti rispondo.[1]

Let us go then, you and I,
When the evening is spread out against the sky
Like a patient etherized[2] upon a table;
Let us go, through certain half-deserted streets,
5 The muttering retreats
❷ Of restless nights in one-night cheap hotels
And sawdust restaurants with oyster-shells:
Streets that follow like a tedious argument
Of <u>insidious</u> intent
10 To lead you to an overwhelming question . . .
Oh, do not ask, "What is it?"
Let us go and make our visit.

Reading Strategy
Listening In what ways do the rhythms and repetitions of this opening stanza invite readers into the poem?

insidious (in sid′ ē əs) *adj.* secretly treacherous

---

1. ***S'io credessi . . . ti rispondo*** The epigraph is a passage from Dante's *Inferno,* in which one of the damned, upon being requested to tell his story, says: "If I believed my answer were being given to someone who could ever return to the world, this flame (his voice) would shake no more. But since no one has ever returned alive from this depth, if what I hear is true, I will answer you without fear of disgrace."
2. **etherized** (ē′ thə rīzd) *v.* anesthetized with ether.

TEACHING RESOURCES

The following resources can be used to enrich or extend the instruction for pp. 718–722.

Literary Analysis

📖 **Writing Models and Graphic Organizers on Literary Analysis and Reading Transparencies,** p. 67

📖 **Selection Support:** Literary Analysis, p. 177

Reading

📖 **Selection Support:** Reading Strategy, p. 176; Build Vocabulary, p. 174

BLOCK SCHEDULING: Resources marked with this symbol provide varied instruction during 90-minute blocks.

In the room the women come and go
Talking of Michelangelo.[3]

15 The yellow fog that rubs its back upon the window-panes,
The yellow smoke that rubs its muzzle on the window-panes,
Licked its tongue into the corners of the evening,
Lingered upon the pools that stand in drains,
Let fall upon its back the soot that falls from chimneys,
20 Slipped by the terrace, made a sudden leap,
And seeing that it was a soft October night,
Curled once about the house, and fell asleep.

And indeed there will be time[4]
For the yellow smoke that slides along the street
25 Rubbing its back upon the window-panes;
There will be time, there will be time
To prepare a face to meet the faces that you meet;
There will be time to murder and create,
And time for all the works and days[5] of hands
30 That lift and drop a question on your plate;
Time for you and time for me,
And time yet for a hundred indecisions,
And for a hundred visions and revisions.
Before the taking of a toast and tea.

35 In the room the women come and go
Talking of Michelangelo.
And indeed there will be time
To wonder, "Do I dare?" and, "Do I dare?"
Time to turn back and descend the stair,
40 With a bald spot in the middle of my hair—
(They will say: "How his hair is growing thin!")
My morning coat, my collar mounting firmly to the chin,
My necktie rich and modest, but asserted by a simple pin–
(They will say: "But how his arms and legs are thin!")
45 Do I dare
Disturb the universe?
In a minute there is time
For decisions and revisions which a minute will reverse.

For I have known them all already, known them all—
50 Have known the evenings, mornings, afternoons,
I have measured out my life with coffee spoons;
I know the voices dying with a dying fall

---

3. **Michelangelo** (mī´ kel an´ je lō) a famous Italian artist and sculptor (1475–1564).
4. **there will be time** These words echo the narrator's plea in English poet Andrew Marvell's "To His Coy Mistress": "Had we but world enough and time . . . "
5. **works and days** Ancient Greek poet Hesiod wrote a poem about farming called "Works and Days."

Literary Analysis
Dramatic Monologue and Allusion What might Prufrock's allusion to Michelangelo suggest about the women at the party?

Literary Analysis
Dramatic Monologue What emotions does the speaker express in the description of his physical appearance?

5 ✔**Reading Check**
At what time of day is the poem set?

---

❸ Literary Analysis

Dramatic Monologue and Allusion

- Remind students of the definition of an allusion, using the Connecting Literary Elements instruction on p. 717 if necessary.
- Discuss with students what conclusions might be drawn about people who stroll about "talking of Michelangelo."
- Then, ask students the Literary Analysis question on p. 719: What might Prufrock's allusion to Michelangelo suggest about the women at the party?
  Possible response: It could suggest that they are educated and that perhaps they intimidate Prufrock.

❹ Literary Analysis

Dramatic Monologue

- Have students close their eyes as you read aloud the bracketed passage. Ask them to list the details related to Prufrock's appearance. Then, encourage them to visualize Prufrock using these details.
  Answer: He is thin and balding, wearing a buttoned up coat with a simple but expensive necktie.
- Ask students the second Literary Analysis question on p. 719: What emotions does the speaker express in the description of his physical appearance?
  Answer: He seems to express some insecurity, focusing largely on negatives in his appearance and on the negative reaction he expects from others about it.

❺ ✔Reading Check

Answer: The poem is set in the early evening, at teatime.

CUSTOMIZE INSTRUCTION FOR UNIVERSAL ACCESS

For Less Proficient Readers	For English Learners	For Advanced Readers
Students may find Eliot's many cultural references and historical allusions confusing. Encourage students to make full use of the numbered footnotes, many of which explain Eliot's allusions. Invite students' questions about the footnotes and offer clarification as necessary.	Spanish- or Italian-speaking students may be able to help their classmates understand Eliot's reference to Dante's Inferno. Invite any students who are able to read the epigraph aloud in Italian. Then have a native English speaker read footnote 1. After students fiinish the poem, discuss the meaning of the epigraph as a class.	Point out that Eliot's language is filled with cultural references and historical allusions. Have students select a list of these references to share and explain to the class. You might suggest that they use a library or the Internet to find literary criticism that explores Eliot's references.

❻ Vocabulary Development

The Greek Prefix di-

- Call students' attention to the word *digress* and its definition. Tell students that the Greek prefix *di–* (or *dis–*) means "apart" or "away."

- Have students suggest words that contain this prefix, and write them on the chalkboard. Possibilities include: divide, differ, diffuse, diverge

- Have students locate the etymologies of these words in a dictionary. Ensure that they can distinguish between the prefixes *di-* or *dis-* meaning "apart" or "away" and the prefix *di-* or *dia-*, which means "through," as in " diagonal" or "diameter."

❼ Literary Analysis

Dramatic Monologue

- Direct students to consider the surrounding context of Prufrock's remark.

- Ask the Literary Analysis question on p. 720: When he says "I have seen the moment of my greatness flicker," what observation does Prufrock make about himself?
  Answer: He acknowledges that he isn't going to express his feelings to the woman he loves. He observes that he lacks the greatness, or courage, to do it.

▶ Monitor Progress Direct students' attention to the chart they began on p. 717. Help them complete it with the evidence of the bracketed text. Charts should look similar to the following.

Prufrock's Observations
"I am no prophet—and here's no great matter."

Personality Traits
Highly educated, ironic, uncertain of himself

Internal Conflicts
Desire for love conflicts with fear

Beneath the music from a farther room.
   So how should I presume?

55 And I have known the eyes already, known them all—
The eyes that fix you in a formulated phrase,
And when I am formulated, sprawling on a pin,
When I am pinned and wriggling on the wall,
Then how should I begin
60 To spit out all the butt-ends of my days and ways?
   And how should I presume?

And I have known the arms already, known them all—
Arms that are braceleted and white and bare
(But in the lamplight, downed with light brown hair!)
65 Is it perfume from a dress
That makes me so <u>digress</u>?
Arms that lie along a table, or wrap about a shawl.
   And should I then presume?
   And how should I begin?
   . . . .

70 Shall I say, I have gone at dusk through narrow streets
And watched the smoke that rises from the pipes
Of lonely men in shirt-sleeves, leaning out of windows? . . .

I should have been a pair of ragged claws
Scuttling across the floors of silent seas.[6]

   . . . .

75 And the afternoon, the evening, sleeps so peacefully!
Smoothed by long fingers,
Asleep . . . tired . . . or it <u>malingers,</u>
Stretched on the floor, here beside you and me.
Should I, after tea and cakes and ices,
80 Have the strength to force the moment to its crisis?
But though I have wept and fasted, wept and prayed,
Though I have seen my head (grown slightly bald) brought in
   upon a platter,[7]
I am no prophet—and here's no great matter;
I have seen the moment of my greatness flicker,
85 And I have seen the eternal Footman[8] hold my coat, and snicker.
And in short, I was afraid.

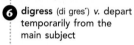

---

6. **I should . . . seas** In Shakespeare's *Hamlet,* the hero, Hamlet, mocks the aging Lord Chamberlain, Polonius, saying, "You yourself, sir, should be old as I am, if like a crab you could go backward" (II.ii. 205–206).
7. **head . . . platter** a reference to the prophet John the Baptist, whose head was delivered on a platter to Salome as a reward for her dancing (Matthew 14:1–11).
8. **eternal Footman** death.

720 ◆ *Disillusion, Defiance, Discontent (1914–1946)*

❻ digress (di gres′) *v.* depart temporarily from the main subject

malingers (mə lin′ gərz) *v.* pretends to be ill

Literary Analysis
Dramatic Monologue
When he says "I have seen the moment of my greatness flicker," what observation does Prufrock make about himself?

✷ ENRICHMENT: Cultural Connection

The Importance of Tea

Eliot's poem revolves around his observations during of an afternoon tea party. In the late nineteenth century and early twentieth centuries, afternoon tea parties were social events; people dressed up for the occasion and tables were elegantly set. Small sandwiches and pastries were served in addition to tea. The tea party provided an opportunity for well-born people to "see and be seen." Tea parties were quiet, well-mannered affairs, often, as here, embellished with music and cultural discussions.

Have students compare and contrast Prufrock's party with their own social gatherings. Points of comparison might include:

(1) reasons for the gathering,

(2) social behavior at the gathering,

(3) appropriate dress,

(4) topics of conversation.

And would it have been worth it, after all,
After the cups, the marmalade, the tea,
Among the porcelain, among some talk of you and me,
90 Would it have been worth while,
To have bitten off the matter with a smile,
To have squeezed the universe into a ball
To roll it towards some overwhelming question.
To say: "I am Lazarus,[9] come from the dead,
95 Come back to tell you all. I shall tell you all"—
If one, settling a pillow by her head,
        Should say: "That is not what I meant at all.
        That is not it, at all."

And would it have been worth it, after all,
100 Would it have been worth while,
After the sunsets and the dooryards and the sprinkled streets,
After the novels, after the teacups, after the skirts that trail
        along the floor—
And this, and so much more?—
It is impossible to say just what I mean!
105 But as if a magic lantern[10] threw the nerves in patterns on a
        screen:
Would it have been worth while
If one, settling a pillow or throwing off a shawl,
And turning toward the window, should say:
        "That is not it at all,
110   That is not what I meant, at all."

                . . . .

No! I am not Prince Hamlet, nor was meant to be;
Am an attendant lord, one that will do
To swell a progress,[11] start a scene or two,
Advise the prince; no doubt, an easy tool,
115 Deferential, glad to be of use,
Politic, cautious, and meticulous;
Full of high sentence,[12] but a bit obtuse;
At times, indeed, almost ridiculous—
Almost, at times, the Fool.

120 I grow old . . . I grow old . . .
I shall wear the bottoms of my trousers rolled.

Shall I part my hair behind? Do I dare to eat a peach?
I shall wear white flannel trousers, and walk upon the beach.
I have heard the mermaids singing, each to each.

---

9. **Lazarus** (laz´ ə rəs) Lazarus is resurrected from the dead by Jesus in John 11:1–44.
10. **magic lantern** an early device used to project images on a screen.
11. **To swell a progress** to add to the number of people in a parade or scene from a play.
12. **Full of high sentence** speaking in a very ornate manner, often offering advice.

The Love Song of J. Alfred Prufrock ◆ 721

Reading Strategy

Listening How does the use of rhyme contribute to the effect of this stanza?

meticulous (mə tik´ yo͞o ləs) *adj.* extremely careful about details

obtuse (äb to͞os´) *adj.* slow to understand or perceive

❾ ✔**Reading Check**
What question does Prufrock repeatedly ask himself?

❽ **Reading Strategy**

Listening

• Invite students to listen as you read aloud the bracketed passage. Then have students read it aloud themselves. Together, identify the rhymes in lines 102–103, 104–105, and 107–110.

• Ask students to describe the tone of this stanza and to characterize the poem's speaker based on what they have learned thus far. Then, have students evaluate the relationship between the rhythm of the stanza and its content. What effect does this rhythm have on the content?

▶ **Monitor Progress** Ask students the Reading Strategy question on p. 721: How does the use of rhyme contribute to the effect of this stanza?

Answer: The rhyme gives the stanza a sing-song quality, almost like a nursery rhyme. Some students may observe that this lends a satirical, ironic tone to Prufrock's observations.

❾ ✔**Reading Check**

Answer: Prufrock asks himself, "would it have been worth it, after all?"

CUSTOMIZE INSTRUCTION FOR UNIVERSAL ACCESS

For Less Proficient Readers	For Special Needs Students
Remind students that a dramatic monologue consists of a single individual's speech, either to another person or to him- or herself. Ask students what the purpose of a dramatic monologue might be. Help students understand that it allows the speaker to give voice freely to his or her innermost thoughts and emotions. This is what Prufrock does, saying things that he does not dare speak aloud to others.	Relate the monologue format to students' own experiences talking or thinking aloud to themselves. Emphasize that the monologue reveals feelings Prufrock cannot share with others. Encourage students to use the graphic organizer introduced on p. 717 to build a profile of Prufrock from his dramatic monologue. Model how to complete the organizer with Prufrock's views on life and then help students gather information about his personality traits and internal conflicts from the text of the poem.

Answers for p. 722

Review and Assess

1. **(a)** and **(b)** Students' responses should indicate a clear understanding of the poem.

2. **(a)** He says that because he is damned, he may speak freely because no one ever returns from the dead to share these secrets. **(b)** It suggests that Eliot intends the reader to see Prufrock as a man living in his own private hell, speaking the truth even if only to himself.

3. **(a)** He says he has a bald spot and thinning hair, has thin arms and legs, and is dressed elegantly and conservatively. **(b)** He is likely on the verge of middle age.

4. **(a)** He describes lower-class neighborhoods, where men as lonely as he lean out of windows, smoking their pipes. **(b)** They are the streets of the poor, of a crowded urban neighborhood rather than the wider, more spacious streets of Prufrock's cultured society.

5. **(a)** He uses the image of coffee spoons. **(b)** He has lived a careful life, with little risk, and he has lived a life filled with trivial, but well-mannered social occasions.

6. **(a)** Her reaction is to deny whatever interest in him Prufrock may have dared to read into her conversation. **(b)** He doesn't think they will sing to him. **(c)** He expects them to reject him.

7. **(a)** Prufrock sees "the eternal Footman hold my coat, and snicker." **(b)** Prufrock is afraid both of death and of other people's derision.

8. **(a)** In the opening stanza, Prufrock prepares to go to a party, which will present the opportunity for him to make a declaration of love. In the closing stanza, he compares the women he admires to mermaids, and his own self-knowledge to death by drowning. **(b)** The first is hopeful, the second is not.

9. **(a)** and **(b)** Students should be able to support their views with specific examples of contemporary behavior.

125 I do not think that they will sing to me.

I have seen them riding seaward on the waves
Combing the white hair of the waves blown back
When the wind blows the water white and black.

We have lingered in the chambers of the sea
130 By sea-girls wreathed with seaweed red and brown
Till human voices wake us, and we drown.

Review and Assess

Thinking About the Selection

1. **(a) Respond:** What is your primary feeling for Prufrock—pity or irritation? Why? **(b) Respond:** What advice would you give him if he were your friend?

2. **(a) Recall:** What does the speaker say in the opening quotation from Dante's *Inferno*? **(b) Interpret:** What does this quotation suggest about the content of the poem that follows?

3. **(a) Recall:** What details does Prufrock use in lines 36–45 to describe his appearance? **(b) Infer:** At what stage of life is Prufrock?

4. **(a) Recall:** In lines 69–71, what kind of streets does Prufrock describe? **(b) Interpret:** In what ways do these streets differ from those that Prufrock would more customarily visit?

5. **(a) Recall:** In lines 48–53, what image does Prufrock use to describe how he has "measured out" his life? **(b) Analyze:** Judging from this metaphor, how has Prufrock lived?

6. **(a) Recall:** In lines 96–97, what is the woman's reaction to Prufrock? **(b) Recall:** In line 124, how does Prufrock describe the mermaids' reaction to him? **(c) Connect:** How does Prufrock seem to feel about women's interest in him?

7. **(a) Recall:** In line 85, who or what does Prufrock see? **(b) Make a Judgment:** Do you think Prufrock is simply afraid of death, or are his fears more complicated? Explain.

8. **(a) Interpret:** Describe the scenes outlined in the poem's opening and closing stanzas. **(b) Compare and Contrast:** How do the moods of these scenes differ?

9. **(a) Generalize:** Do you think that Prufrock accurately represents many people today? **(b) Relate:** Do we live in a time when it is difficult, even impossible, to be the heroes of our own lives? Explain.

ASSESSMENT PRACTICE: Reading Comprehension

Anticipate Missing Words **(For more practice, see Test Preparation Workbook, p. 41.)**

Many tests ask students to correctly answer sentence-completion questions. Use the following examples to show students how to use context and their prior knowledge to choose the word that would best complete the following passage.

Always somberly attired and well-spoken, Thomas Stearns Eliot was outwardly the model of _____. His work, in contrast, was revolutionary in both form and content.

A rebellion   **C** illiteracy
B convention   **D** fashion

The context clues "somberly attired" and "well-spoken" provide the key to completing the sentence. In addition, "in contrast" indicates that the word must be the opposite of *revolutionary*. *B* is the most logical choice.

Review and Assess

Literary Analysis

Dramatic Monologue

1. What do his descriptions of the sky and the city in lines 1–12 suggest about Prufrock's outlook on life?
2. (a) How can the first line of this **dramatic monologue** be interpreted to suggest that Prufrock sees himself as divided, both seeking and fearing action? (b) At what other points does he express a deeply conflicted sense of self?

Connecting Literary Elements

3. Some of Prufrock's **allusions** paint imaginary portraits that reveal his sense of self. Use a chart like the one shown to examine these allusions and what they suggest about Prufrock's self-image.

Allusion		Prufrock's Meaning	His Self-Image
No! I am not Prime Hamlet . . .	....▶		

4. (a) What is suggested by the repeated reference to Michelangelo? (b) In what ways would the portrayal of Prufrock's world be quite different if that reference were to something less refined?

Reading Strategy

Listening

5. In the lines referring to Michelangelo, what is the impact of the use of rhyme?
6. What is the effect of the repetition of "there will be time" in lines 23–34 and again in lines 37–48?
7. What effect do the ellipsis points (three dots used to indicate an elongated pause or an omission) have on the way you hear lines 120–121?

Extend Understanding

8. **Humanities Connection:** Prufrock says there will be time "To prepare a face to meet the faces that you meet." Does this statement accurately describe how people relate to each other? All the time? Sometimes? Explain.

The Love Song of J. Alfred Prufrock ◆ 723

Quick Review

In a **dramatic monologue,** the speaker addresses a silent listener.

Allusions are references to well-known people, historical events, and literary works.

Listen to the music of a poem by reading it aloud and noting sound devices such as rhythm, and rhyme.

 Take It to the Net
www.phschool.com
Take the interactive self-test online to check your understanding of the selection.

Answers for p. 723

Review and Assess

1. The gloomy images, such as that of an etherized patient and of cheap hotels, imply a pessimistic outlook on life.

2. **(a)** Prufrock refers to himself as "you and I." **(b)** He refers to himself as divided in line 30 when he says "Time for you and time for me." Also, his vacillation between the desire to speak and his inability to do so suggests deep internal conflict.

3. Possible response: Allusion: "No! I am not Prince Hamlet . . ."; Prufrock's Meaning: He is not a heroic figure; His Self-Image: He sees himself as inadequate.

4. **(a)** Possible response: Prufrock suggests that the women are highly cultured and refined. **(b)** It might make the women seem less intimidating and more accessible.

5. It gives the lines a sing-song quality that make the women seem a bit ridiculous.

6. This repetition heightens the tension as readers wonder whether Prufrock will actually get the job done while there is still time. Also, the repetition conveys Prufrock's anxiety about the task ahead.

7. They make these lines sound wearied and slow, which emphasizes their meaning about growing old.

8. Possible response: This line accurately suggests the way people often compose their outward demeanor for the world.

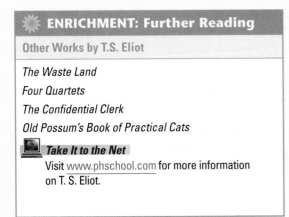

✳ ENRICHMENT: Further Reading

Other Works by T.S. Eliot

The Waste Land

Four Quartets

The Confidential Clerk

Old Possum's Book of Practical Cats

Take It to the Net
Visit www.phschool.com for more information on T. S. Eliot.

❶ Vocabulary Development

Word Analysis

1. true
2. false
3. false

Spelling Strategy

1. insidious
2. perfidious
3. invidious

Concept Development: Synonyms

1. c
2. a
3. a
4. c
5. b

❷ Grammar and Style

Practice

1. modifier: of tea; modifies: cups
2. modifier: talking in the next room; modifies: guests
3. modifier: who secretly disliked each other; modifies: People
4. modifier: to serve tea; modifies: time
5. modifier: crowded with indifferent faces; modifies: drawing room

Writing Application

Paragraphs should describe Prufrock and include at least two correctly used adjectival modifiers.

Integrate Language Skills

❶ Vocabulary Development Lesson

Word Analysis: Greek Prefix *di-*

The Greek prefix *di-* (or *dis-*) means "apart" or "away." The word digress means "to move away from a subject." Each of the following sentences includes a word containing the prefix *di-*. Indicate whether each sentence is true or false.

1. A path *diverges* if it branches off.
2. If you are *diverted*, your focus is sharp.
3. A *diverse* menu features many similar foods.

Spelling Strategy

When you form adjectives by adding the *-ious* suffix to stems ending in *d*, use the spelling *-ious*, as in *studious*. An exception to this rule is the word *hideous*. Add the correctly spelled *-ious* suffix to each stem below.

1. insid_____   2. perfid_____   3. invid_____

Concept Development: Synonyms

Review the words from the vocabulary list on page 717. Then, choose the letter of the word that is the best synonym, or word with a similar meaning, for the first word.

1. insidious: (a) innocent, (b) wealthy, (c) dangerous, (d) certified
2. digress: (a) wander, (b) contain, (c) hesitate, (d) elaborate
3. malingers: (a) fakes, (b) studies, (c) boasts, (d) anticipates
4. meticulous: (a) messy, (b) absurd, (c) careful, (d) tart
5. obtuse: (a) intense, (b) stupid, (c) friendly, (d) prompt

❷ Grammar and Style Lesson

Adjectival Modifiers

Adjectival modifiers, phrases or clauses which modify nouns or pronouns, can have many different grammatical structures. In the examples below, the adjectival modifiers are italicized.

> **Prepositional Phrase:** sawdust restaurants *with oyster shells* (modifies *restaurants*)
>
> **Participial Phrase:** a patient *etherized upon a table* (modifies *patient*)
>
> **Adjective Clause:** Streets *that follow like a tedious argument* (modifies *streets*)
>
> **Infinitive Phrase:** prepare a face *to meet the faces . . .* (modifies *face*)

Practice Copy these sentences. Underline the adjectival modifier, and then circle the noun it modifies in each of the sentences below.

1. The cups of tea sat on the tray.
2. The guests talking in the next room were gossiping about J. Alfred Prufrock.
3. People who secretly disliked each other chatted politely.
4. The hostess said it was time to serve tea.
5. Prufrock entered a drawing room crowded with indifferent faces.

Writing Application Write a brief paragraph describing J. Alfred Prufrock. Include at least two adjectival modifiers in your description.

𝒲𝒢 *Prentice Hall Writing and Grammar Connection: Chapter 19, Sections 1–3*

724 ◆ *Disillusion, Defiance, and Discontent (1914–1946)*

TEACHING RESOURCES

The following resources can be used to enrich or extend the instruction for pp. 724–725.

Vocabulary

📖 **Selection Support,** Build Vocabulary, p. 174

📖 **Vocabulary and Spelling Practice Book** (Use this booklet for skills enrichment.)

Grammar

📖 **Selection Support,** Grammar and Style, p. 175

𝒲𝒢 **Writing and Grammar,** Ruby Level, p. 434

▨ **Daily Language Practice Transparencies** ▨

Writing

𝒲𝒢 **Writing and Grammar,** Ruby Level, p. 304 ▨

⊚ **Writing and Grammar iText CD-ROM**

▨ **Writing Models and Graphic Organizers on Transparencies,** p. 67

▨ **BLOCK SCHEDULING:** Resources marked with this symbol provide varied instruction during 90-minute blocks.

❸ Writing Lesson

Character Analysis

Ever since Eliot's "Love Song" was published in 1915, J. Alfred Prufrock has fascinated readers. For some, Prufrock is merely a man who fails to achieve his dreams. For others, Prufrock embodies larger failings of the modern age—an absence of heroism, or a general weariness. Write an essay analyzing Prufrock's character, and make your own judgment about this famous literary creation.

Prewriting   Reread the poem, taking notes about Prufrock's character. Pay attention to details that suggest reasons for Prufrock's passivity and fears, and cite passages to use as support for your point of view.

Drafting   Begin by noting the title and author of the work, and stating what you believe about Prufrock's character. Use quotes from the poem and precise language to develop your ideas in each body paragraph.

Revising   Review your essay. Highlight any words that seem vague or inappropriate, and replace them with better, more specific word choices.

Model: Revising for Accuracy

         sweeping   *pines for*

Prufrock's lament is ~~big~~. He ~~talks about~~ all that he has lost

or that he never had—youth and love. He is keenly aware

        even tormented by

of, ~~and really upset about~~ the passage of time.

> Replacing vague words with specific ones makes a piece of writing more accurate and powerful.

Prentice Hall Writing and Grammar Connection: Chapter 14, Section 2

❹ Extension Activities

Listening and Speaking With a classmate, **role-play** a talk-show host's interview with Prufrock. Explore the reasons for Prufrock's poor self-esteem, and try to build his self-image. Consider the following tips as you plan:

- Create a list of appropriate interview questions that require in-depth responses.
- Develop Prufrock's responses within the context of his character.

Present your role play. **[Group Activity]**

Research and Technology Modernism has had a lasting effect on art, literature, and popular culture. Use printed and online sources to research the movement and its impact. If possible, download some appropriate examples of Modernist literature or artwork to illustrate your conclusions. Present your findings in a **report.**

 **Take It to the Net**   www.phschool.com

Go online for an additional research activity using the Internet.

The Love Song of J. Alfred Prufrock ◆ 725

---

❸ Writing Lesson

- Review with students the basic elements of a character analysis: vivid description of the character's appearance, attitudes, and behaviors, along with discussion of reasons for these elements.

- To aid prewriting, have students use the Branching Organizer in **Writing Models and Graphic Organizers on Transparencies,** p. 67 to gather details about Prufrock's character. Model how to label each branch with headings such as "motivations" and "fears."

- Read through the Writing Lesson steps with students and clarify any confusion.

- Use the Response to Literature rubric in **Performance Assessment and Portfolio Management,** p. 23 to evaluate students' character analyses.

❹ Listening and Speaking

- Before students team up, lead a class discussion about typical features of poor self-esteem. Invite students' comments about this fairly common teenage experience.

- Encourage partners to read both questions and answers aloud before finalizing them. Stress that conversation should sound natural, rather than scripted.

- Provide time for rehearsal so that partners will be prepared to present their role-play without scripts.

CUSTOMIZE INSTRUCTION
For Universal Access

To address different learning styles, use the activities suggested in the Extension Activities booklet, p. 39.

For Interpersonal and Verbal/Linguistic Learners, use Activity 5.

For Visual/Spatial Learners, use Activity 6.

For Bodily/Kinesthetic, Musical/Rhythmic, and Interpersonal Learners, use Activity 7.

ASSESSMENT RESOURCES

The following resources can be used to assess students' knowledge and skills.

Selection Assessment

- 📖 **Formal Assessment,** pp. 185–187
- 📖 **Open Book Test,** pp. 115–117
- 📼 **Got It! Assessment Videotapes,** Tape 4
- 💿 **Test Bank Software**
- 🖥 *Take It to the Net*
  Visit www.phschool.com for self-tests and additional questions on "The Love Song of J. Alfred Prufrock."

Writing Rubric

- 📖 **Performance Assessment and Portfolio Management,** p. 23

PRENTICE HALL
ASSESSMENT SYSTEM

- 📖 **Workbook**
- 📖 **Skill Book**
- 🖥 **Transparencies**
- 💿 **CD-ROM**

The Imagist Poets

Lesson Objectives

1. **To analyze and respond to literary elements**
   - Literary Analysis: Imagist Poetry
   - Comparing Literary Works

2. **To read, comprehend, analyze, and critique nonfiction and poetry**
   - Reading Strategy: Engaging Your Senses
   - Reading Check questions
   - Review and Assess questions
   - Assessment Practice (ATE)

3. **To develop word analysis skills, fluency, and systematic vocabulary**
   - Vocabulary Development Lesson: Forms of *appear*

4. **To understand and apply written and oral language conventions**
   - Spelling Strategy
   - Grammar and Style Lesson: Concrete and Abstract Nouns

5. **To understand and apply appropriate writing and research strategies**
   - Writing Lesson: An Editor's Review of Manuscript
   - Extension Activity: Poetry Illustration

6. **To understand and apply listening and speaking strategies**
   - Extension Activity: Informal Debate

STEP-BY-STEP TEACHING GUIDE	PACING GUIDE
PRETEACH	
Motivate Students and Provide Background	
Use the Motivation activity (ATE p. 726)	5 min.
Read and discuss author and background features (SE/ATE pp. 726–727, 729) A	5 min.
Introduce the Concepts	
Introduce the Literary Analysis and Reading Strategy (SE/ATE p. 728) A	15 min.
Pronounce the vocabulary words and read their definitions (SE p. 728)	5 min.
TEACH	
Monitor Comprehension	
Informally monitor comprehension by circulating while students read independently or in groups A	30 min.
Monitor students' comprehension with the Reading Check notes (SE/ATE pp. 729, 731, 733, 737)	as students read
Develop vocabulary with Vocabulary notes (SE pp. 729, 734; ATE p. 734)	as students read
Develop Understanding	
Develop students' understanding of imagist poetry with the Literary Analysis annotations (SE pp. 730, 732, 733; ATE pp. 730, 732, 733) A	5 min.
Develop students' ability to engage their senses while reading by using the Reading Strategy annotations (SE pp. 731, 737; ATE pp. 731, 736, 737)	5 min.
ASSESS	
Assess Mastery	
Assess students' mastery of the Reading Strategy and Literary Analysis by having them answer the Review and Assess questions (SE/ATE p. 739)	15 min.
Use one or more of the print and media Assessment Resources (ATE p. 741) A	up to 45 min.
EXTEND	
Apply Understanding	
Have students complete the Vocabulary Development Lesson and the Grammar and Style (SE p. 740) A	20 min.
Apply students' ability to write briefly and clearly by using the Writing Lesson (SE/ATE p. 741) A	45 min.
Apply students' understanding using one or more of the Extension Activities (SE p. 741)	20–90 min.

 ACCELERATED INSTRUCTION:
Use the strategies and activities identified with an A.

UNIVERSAL ACCESS
- ● = Below Level Students
- ▲ = On-Level Students
- ■ = Above Level Students

Time and Resource Manager

RESOURCES		
PRINT 📖	**TRANSPARENCIES**	**TECHNOLOGY** 💿 🎧 📼
• **Beyond Literature,** Cross-Curricular Connection: Music, p. 40 ▲ ■		• **Interest Grabber Video,** Tape 5 ● ▲ ■
• **Selection Support Workbook:** ● ▲ ■ Literary Analysis, p. 181 Reading Strategy, p. 180 Build Vocabulary, p. 178	• **Literary Analysis and Reading Transparencies,** pp. 79 and 80 ● ▲ ■	
		• **Listening to Literature** ● ▲ ■ Audiocassettes, Sides 24, 25 Audio CDs, CD 14
• **Literatura en español** ● ▲ • **Literary Analysis for Enrichment** ■		
• **Formal Assessment:** Selection Test, pp. 188–190 ● ▲ ■ • **Open Book Test,** pp. 118–120 ● ▲ ■ • **Performance Assessment and Portfolio Management,** p. 23 ● ▲ ■ • **PRENTICE HALL ASSESSMENT SYSTEM** ● ▲ ■	• **PRENTICE HALL ASSESSMENT SYSTEM** ● ▲ ■ Skills Practice Answers and Explanations on Transparencies	• **Test Bank Software** ● ▲ ■ • **Got It! Assessment Videotapes,** Tape 4 ● ▲
• **Selection Support Workbook:** ● ▲ ■ Grammar and Style, p. 179 • **Writing and Grammar,** Ruby Level ● ▲ ■ • **Extension Activities,** p. 40 ● ▲ ■	• **Daily Language Practice Transparencies** ● ▲	• **Writing and Grammar iText CD-ROM** ● ▲ ■ 🖥️ *Take It to the Net* www.phschool.com

BLOCK SCHEDULING: Use one 90-minute class period to preteach the selection and have students read it. Use a second 90-minute class period to assess students' mastery of skills and have them complete one of the Extension Activities.

PRETEACH

Step-by-Step Teaching Guide for pp. 726–728

Motivation

When students read Pound's essay and these vivid poems, their senses will stand at attention. To jump-start students' interest in the selections, arrange a variety of sensory stimuli in the classroom: several dramatic photographs; a strongly scented item of food or greenery; textural examples such as carpet or a bowl of dried beans; musical objects or audiotaped sounds. Invite students to tour and interact with the stimuli. Then urge them to free write for a few moments about the images generated by the stimuli. What do they expect to encounter in poetry created under the banner: "It is better to present one Image in a lifetime than to produce voluminous work"?

▭ Interest Grabber Video

As an alternative, you may wish to play "Reading and Student Response" on Tape 5 to engage student interest.

❶ Background

More About the Authors

Ezra Pound spent most of his life in Europe, where he became a vital part of the Modernist movement. After 1920, Pound focused his efforts on writing *The Cantos*, a long poetic sequence in which he expresses his beliefs, reflects upon history and politics, and alludes to a variety of foreign languages and literatures. In all he produced 116 cantos of varying quality.

Prepare to Read

❶ The Imagist Poets

Ezra Pound (1885–1972)

As both an editor and a poet, Ezra Pound inspired the dramatic changes in American poetry that characterized the Modern Age. Pound's insistence that writers "make it new" led many poets to discard the forms, techniques, and ideas of the past and to experiment with new approaches to poetry.

Pound influenced the work of the Irish poet William Butler Yeats, as well as that of T. S. Eliot, William Carlos Williams, H. D., Marianne Moore, and Ernest Hemingway—a "who's who" of the literary voices of the age. He is best remembered, however, for his role in the development of Imagism.

Despite his preoccupation with originality and inventiveness, Pound's work often drew upon the poetry of ancient cultures. Many of his poems are filled with literary and historical allusions, which can make the poems difficult to interpret without having the appropriate background information.

Fall From Grace In 1925, Pound settled in Italy. Motivated by the mistaken belief that a country governed by a powerful dictator was the most conducive environment for the creation of art, Pound became an outspoken supporter of Italian dictator Benito Mussolini during World War II. In 1943, the American government indicted Pound for treason; in 1945, he was arrested by American troops and imprisoned. After being flown back to the United States in 1945, he was judged psychologically unfit to stand trial and was confined to a hospital for the criminally insane. There he remained until 1958, when he was released due largely to the efforts of the literary community he had so doggedly supported over the years. He returned to Italy, where he lived until his death.

William Carlos Williams (1883–1963)

Unlike his fellow Imagists, William Carlos Williams spent most of his life in the United States, where he pursued a double career as a poet and a pediatrician in New Jersey. He felt that his experiences as a doctor helped provide him with inspiration as a poet, crediting medicine for his ability to "gain entrance to . . . the secret gardens of the self."

The child of immigrants, Williams grew up speaking Spanish, French, and British English. Nevertheless, he was enamored of American language and life. He rejected the views of his college friend, Ezra Pound, who believed in using allusions to history, religion, and ancient literature. Williams focused instead on capturing the essence of modern American life by depicting ordinary people, objects, and experiences using current, everyday language.

The Poetry of Daily Life In volumes such as *Spring and All* (1923) and *In the American Grain* (1925), Williams captured the essence of American life and landscape. He avoided offering explanations, remarking that a poet should deal in "No ideas but in things"—concrete images that speak for themselves, evoking emotions and ideas.

In his later work, Williams departed from pure Imagism in order to write more expansively. His five-volume poem *Paterson* (1946–58) explores the idea of a city as a symbol for a man. The poem is based on the real city of Paterson, New Jersey.

Williams continued to write even after his failing health forced him to give up his medical practice. In 1963, he received a Pulitzer Prize for *Pictures from Breughel and Other Poems*, his final volume of poetry.

726 ◆ *Disillusion, Defiance, and Discontent (1914–1946)*

TEACHING RESOURCES

The following resources can be used to enrich or extend the instruction for pp. 726–728.

Motivation
▭ **Interest Grabber Video**, Tape 5 ▭

Background
▯ **Beyond Literature**, p. 40

▭ *Take It to the Net*
Visit www.phschool.com for Background and hotlinks for the selections.

Literary Analysis
▭ **Literary Analysis and Reading Transparencies**, Imagist Poetry, p. 80 ▭

▯ **Selection Support:** Literary Analysis, p. 181

Reading
▭ **Literary Analysis and Reading Transparencies**, Engaging Your Senses, p. 79

 BLOCK SCHEDULING: Resources marked with this symbol provide varied instruction during 90-minute blocks.

H. D. (Hilda Doolittle) (1886–1961)

In 1913, when Ezra Pound reshaped three of Hilda Doolittle's poems and submitted them to *Poetry* magazine under the name "H. D., Imagiste," the Imagist movement was born.

The publication of the poems also served to launch the successful career of the young poet, who continued to publish under the name H. D. throughout her life.

Born in Pennsylvania, Doolittle was only fifteen when she first met Ezra Pound, who was studying at the University of Pennsylvania. In 1911, Doolittle moved to London and renewed her acquaintance with Pound. She married a close friend of his, the English poet Richard Aldington, but the marriage struggled and failed during World War I when Aldington left to fight in France. Doolittle remained a short while in London, where she became a leader of the Imagist group. She returned to the United States and settled in California, where she remained for a year before going back to England. In 1921, she moved to Switzerland, and lived there until her death.

Classically Inspired Like the Greek lyrics that she so greatly admired, H. D.'s early poems were brief, precise, and direct. Often emphasizing light, color, and physical textures, she created vivid, emotive images. Like other Imagist poets, H. D. used everyday speech, carefully and sparingly chosen to evoke an emotional response, to freeze a single moment in time. She also abandoned traditional rhythmical patterns, instead creating innovative musical lines in her poetry. With these unusual techniques, H. D. focused much of her poetry and prose on the issues of her day—World Wars I and II, the growing interest in the human psyche created by Sigmund Freud's work, and the blossoming film medium.

In 1925, almost all of H. D.'s early poems were gathered in *Collected Poems*, a volume that also contained her translations from the *Odyssey* and from the Greek poet Sappho. She also wrote a play—*Hippolytus Temporizes*, which appeared in 1927—and two prose works—*Palimpsest* (1926) and *Hedylus* (1928). During the later stages of her career, she focused on writing longer works, including an epic poem. H. D. is best remembered, however, for her early Imagist poetry.

Background on Imagism

Imagism was a literary movement established in the early 1900s by Ezra Pound and other poets. As the name suggests, the Imagists concentrated on the direct presentation of images, or word pictures. An Imagist poem expressed the essence of an object, person, or incident, without providing explanations. Through the spare, clean presentation of an image, the Imagists hoped to freeze a single moment in time and to capture the emotions of that moment. To accomplish this purpose, the Imagists used the language of everyday speech, carefully choosing each word. They also shied away from traditional poetic patterns, focusing instead on creating new, musical rhythms.

The Imagists were strongly influenced by traditional Chinese and Japanese poetry. Many Imagist poems bear a close resemblance to the Japanese verse forms of haiku and tanka, which generally evoke an emotional response through the presentation of a single image or a pair of contrasting images.

The Imagist movement was short-lived, lasting only until about 1918. However, for many years that followed, the poems of Pound, Williams, H.D. and other Imagists continued to influence the work of other poets, including Wallace Stevens, T.S. Eliot, and Hart Crane.

In his later work, William Carlos Williams departed from pure Imagism in order to write more expansively. His five-volume poem *Paterson* (1946–58) explores the idea of a city as a symbol for a man. The poem is based on the real city of Paterson, New Jersey.

H. D.'s reflections on Sigmund Freud's controversial work of the 1930s grew out of personal experience—she herself underwent psychoanalysis with Freud. Both her reflections on this, *Tribute to Freud* (1956), and the later work, *Bid Me Live* (1960), had autobiographical elements. H. D. spent the World War II years in London, recording those experiences in three long poems: *The Walls Do Not Fall* (1944), *Tribute to the Angels* (1945), and *The Flowering of the Rod* (1946).

CUSTOMIZE INSTRUCTION FOR UNIVERSAL ACCESS

For Less Proficient Readers	For English Learners	For Advanced Readers
Direct students' attention to the Reading Strategy instruction on p. 728. Explain that engaging the senses is particularly useful in reading free verse poetry, which can be confusing. Urge students to begin by reading the poetry for a sensory and emotional response rather than for literal meaning.	Free verse may be confusing to English language learners. Remind them that the Imagists sought to make sensory impressions more than convey their ideas. Encourage students to focus on engaging their senses. They can do this by reading the poems aloud to find the natural pauses to find the sensory images.	Draw students' attention to the vivid and sensory language of Imagist poetry. Then challenge students to write brief descriptive paragraphs about the scenes each poem describes. Ask students to respond analytically to the following question: How do the sensory images of these poems convey so much with so few words?

❷ Literary Analysis
Imagist Poetry

- Tell students that as they read the Imagist Poets, they will focus on how the poems reflect the Imagist literary movement and its primary characteristics.

- Discuss the example given in the Literary Analysis instruction. Explain that the words of "In a Station of the Metro" were chosen with extreme precision in order to paint a vivid picture. The poem demands that the reader consider the meaning of each word.

- Use the Imagist Poetry transparency in **Literary Analysis and Reading Transparencies,** p. 80 to identify and discuss characteristics of Imagist poetry.

❸ Reading Strategy
Engaging Your Senses

- Tell students that engaging their senses can help them appreciate the vivid images of these poems.

- Invite students to give their own examples of sensory language, perhaps drawing on those they explored in the Motivation activity.

- Discuss the example on the student page, leading students to feel the images H.D.'s language evokes. Point out that H.D. produces her effect on the reader's senses by treating heat as a solid object, capable of being cut, plowed, and turned, like earth.

- Model how to use the chart on the student page to record sensory images. Direct students to complete similar charts as they read the poetry.

Vocabulary Development

Pronounce each vocabulary word for students, and read the definitions as a class. Have students identify any words with which they are already familiar.

 E-Teach

Visit E-Teach at www.phschool.com for teachers' essays on how to teach, with questions and answers.

Preview
Connecting to the Literature

You may know what it is like to have a song stick in your mind, but have you ever had an image lodge there? The poems you are about to read capture in words some of the striking images that lodged in the minds and emotions of the Imagists.

❷ Literary Analysis
Imagist Poetry

Imagist poems focus on evoking emotion and sparking the imagination through the vivid presentation of a limited number of images. "In a Station of the Metro," for example, presents just two images and consists of only two lines and fourteen well-chosen words. Few poems have been written that convey so much meaning with such brevity.

Comparing Literary Works

In his essay "A Few Don'ts by an Imagiste," Ezra Pound describes the image as something more than a simple word-picture. Instead, he says it is "that which presents an intellectual and emotional complex in an instant of time."

For Pound, the image brings the reader a new way of seeing—on the physical level through the senses, and on higher levels through the emotions and intellect. As you read these poems, think about which ones best achieve the effect of "that sense of sudden growth" that Pound believed was the highest achievement of art.

❸ Reading Strategy
Engaging Your Senses

These poems are filled with vivid imagery—words or phrases that appeal to the senses. As you encounter each image, **engage your senses** by re-creating in your mind the sights, sounds, smells, tastes, and physical sensations associated with the image. Also note that some images appeal to more than one sense. For example, you can almost see and feel the thickness in the air as H. D. calls on the wind in "Heat":

> Cut the heat— / plow through it, / Turning it on either side

Use a chart like the one shown to record the ways in which you engage your senses as you read these poems.

Vocabulary Development

voluminous (və lōom′ ə nəs) *adj.* of enough material to fill volumes (p. 729)

dogma (dôg′ mə) *n.* authoritative doctrines or beliefs (p. 729)

apparition (ap′ ə rish′ ən) *n.* act of appearing or becoming visible (p. 734)

728 ◆ *Disillusion, Defiance, and Discontent (1914–1946)*

TEACHING RESOURCES

The following resources can be used to enrich or extend the instruction for pp. 729–738.

Literary Analysis

Literary Analysis and Reading Transparencies, p. 84

Reading

Selection Support: Reading Strategy, p. 193; Build Vocabulary, p. 191

Listening to Literature Audiocassettes, Sides 24, 25

Listening to Literature Audio CDs, CD 14

BLOCK SCHEDULING: Resources marked with this symbol provide varied instruction during 90-minute blocks.

❶ A Few Don'ts by an
IMAGISTE[1]

Ezra Pound

Background

Ezra Pound was one of the leading figures in the Imagist movement. As the name suggests, Imagists concentrated on the focused presentation of images, or word-pictures. For example, Pound's original draft of "In a Station of the Metro" consisted of 30 lines. Pound whittled away at the poem until he arrived at a work of only 14 words of great precision and power. In this essay, Pound discusses his beliefs about what poetry should and should not be.

An "Image" is that which presents an intellectual and emotional complex in an instant of time. I use the term "complex" rather in the technical sense employed by the newer psychologists, such as Hart, though we might not agree absolutely in our application.

It is the presentation of such a "complex" instantaneously which gives that sense of sudden liberation; that sense of freedom from time limits and space limits; that sense of sudden growth, which we experience in the presence of the greatest works of art.

It is better to present one Image in a lifetime than to produce voluminous works.

All this, however, some may consider open to debate. The immediate necessity is to tabulate A LIST OF DON'TS for those beginning to write verses. But I can not put all of them into Mosaic negative.[2]

To begin with, consider the three rules recorded by Mr. Flint,[3] . . . not as dogma—never consider anything as dogma—but as the result of long contemplation, which, even if it is some one else's contemplation, may be worth consideration. . . .

LANGUAGE

Use no superfluous word, no adjective, which does not reveal something.

voluminous (və lm′ ə nəs) *adj.* of enough material to fill volumes

dogma (dôg′ mə) *n.* authoritative doctrines or beliefs

❷ **Reading Check**
According to Pound, what is an image?

---

1. **Imagiste** French for *Imagist.*
2. **Mosaic negative** refers to the ten commandments presented by Moses to the Israelites in the Old Testament of the Bible. Many of the commandments are in the negative and begin with the words "Thou shalt not . . ."
3. **the three rules recorded by Mr. Flint** English Imagist poet Frank Stuart Flint noted that Imagist poets adhered to the following three rules or guidelines.
   1. Direct treatment of the "thing," whether subjective or objective.
   2. To use absolutely no word that did not contribute to the presentation.
   3. As regarding rhythm to compose in sequence of the musical phrase, not in sequence of a metronome.

A Few Don'ts by an Imagiste ◆ 729

TEACH

Step-by-Step Teaching Guide for pp. 729–738

CUSTOMIZE INSTRUCTION
For Visual/Spatial Learners

Point out that Imagist poetry is highly visual. Have students preview the illustrations that accompany the poems. What images and moods do these illustrations evoke?

❶ About the Selection

As one of the founders of Imagism, Ezra Pound helped define its philosophy. In his essay warning Imagist poets against writing pitfalls, Pound quickly establishes his essential idea: less is more.

❷ ✓ Reading Check

Answer: "An image is that which presents an intellectual and emotional complex in an instant of time." In other words, an image presents an evocative description that speaks to both mind and heart.

CUSTOMIZE INSTRUCTION FOR UNIVERSAL ACCESS

For Special Needs Students	For Less Proficient Readers	For Gifted/Talented Students
To help students understand Pound's central ideas, have them read each paragraph several times. Ask students what they think Pound means in each sentence, working together to build meaning. Then encourage students to recall these basic meanings as they read the Imagist poetry.	Direct students to read the essay carefully in preparation for reading the Imagist poetry that follows. In particular, draw their attention to the footnoted material beneath the essay. Discuss and explain this material as you and your students progress through the essay's pages.	Provide, or have students locate, the complete text of Pound's essay. Challenge them to summarize this essay, which is also known as "The Imagist Manifesto." Urge students to share summaries with the class in preparation for reading the Imagist poems that follow.

❸ Literary Analysis

Imagist Poetry

- Have students paraphrase the bracketed passage. Make sure students clarify the meaning of "Go in fear of abstractions."

- Then, ask students the Literary Analysis question on p. 730: Why is this rule of avoiding abstractions consistent with the goals of Imagist poetry?

Possible response: Imagist poets sought to evoke specific and vivid images for readers. Abstract ideas do not lend themselves to such specificity.

❹ Background

Art

Ezra Pound by Wyndham Lewis

This painting is a portrait of the poet, Ezra Pound, perhaps resting or silently contemplating his work. Use these questions for discussion:

1. How does the painting's style mirror Pound's preference for the "concrete"?

Answer: The pictured scene is rendered simply and with great clarity.

2. According to Pound, a painter can best describe a landscape. What elements does Lewis incorporate to capture the landscape of his subject?

Answer: These elements include black clothing, the poet's contemplative and somewhat serious expression, the newspaper, the importance of the figure in the composition. Like a landscape, the portrait includes a wide area around the subject rather than focusing on a face.

❺ ▶ Critical Viewing

Possible response: An Imagist poem might emphasize details such as the objects on the table and the expression on the figure's face.

730

Don't use such an expression as "dim lands *of peace*." It dulls the image. It mixes an abstraction with the concrete. It comes from the writer's not realizing that the natural object is always the *adequate* symbol.

❸ Go in fear of abstractions. Don't retell in mediocre verse what has already been done in good prose. Don't think any intelligent person is going to be deceived when you try to shirk all the difficulties of the unspeakably difficult art of good prose by chopping your composition into line lengths. . . .

Don't imagine that the art of poetry is any simpler than the art of music, or that you can please the expert before you have spent at least as much effort on the art of verse as the average piano teacher spends on the art of music. . . .

RHYTHM AND RHYME

. . . Don't imagine that a thing will "go" in verse just because it's too dull to go in prose.

Don't be "viewy"—leave that to the writers of pretty little philosophic essays. Don't be descriptive; remember that the painter can describe a landscape much better than you can, and that he has to know a deal more about it.

Literary Analysis
Imagist Poetry Why is this rule of avoiding abstractions consistent with the goals of Imagist poetry?

❹

❺ ▲ **Critical Viewing** What key details might be emphasized in an Imagist poem about this portrait of Ezra Pound? **[Synthesize]**

When Shakespeare talks of the "Dawn in russet mantle clad" he presents something which the painter does not present. There is in this line of his nothing that one can call description; he presents. . . .

Don't chop your stuff into separate *iambs*.[4] Don't make each line stop dead at the end, and then begin every next line with a heave. Let the beginning of the next line catch the rise of the rhythm wave, unless you want a definite longish pause.

In short, behave as a musician, a good musician, when dealing with that phase of your art which has exact parallels in music. The same laws govern, and you are bound by no others. . . .

A rhyme must have in it some slight element of surprise if it is to give pleasure; it need not be bizarre or curious, but it must be well used if used at all. . . .

Don't mess up the perception of one sense by trying to define it in terms of another. This is usually only the result of being too lazy to find the exact word. To this clause there are possibly exceptions.

The first three simple proscriptions[5] will throw out nine-tenths of all the bad poetry now accepted as standard and classic; and will prevent you from many a crime of production. . . .

---

4. **iambs** (ī′ ambz′) *n.* metrical feet consisting of two syllables, the first unaccented, the other accented.
5. **The first three simple proscriptions** reference to Flint's three rules outlined in footnote #3.

Review and Assess

Thinking About the Selection

1. **Respond:** What is your reaction to Pound's ideas about poetry?

2. **(a) Recall:** What three rules does Pound invite readers to consider? **(b) Define:** What is the difference between dogma and the results of "long contemplation"?
   (c) Speculate: Why did Pound prefer a list of "don'ts" to a list of "do's"?

3. **(a) Recall:** What does Pound consider preferable to abstractions? **(b) Analyze:** Why would the use of abstractions be offensive to an Imagist poet?

4. **(a) Recall:** Does Pound consider Shakespeare's image an example of description or presentation? **(b) Distinguish:** How does presentation differ from description?

5. **(a) Recall:** What rule does Pound suggest should govern the rhythm of a poem? **(b) Interpret:** What does a good musician do that a poet should emulate?

6. **Evaluate:** Do you think following Pound's "don'ts" would make it easier or more difficult to write poetry?

A Few Don'ts by an Imagiste ◆ 731

❻ Reading Strategy
Engaging Your Senses

- Read aloud the bracketed text, using hand gestures to convey the physical aspects of the description.

- Encourage students to clarify the meaning of this passage. What exactly is Pound advocating?

- Then, ask students the Reading Strategy question on p. 731: What physical sensations are suggested by the rhythmic wave Pound advocates?
  Possible response: Students may mention a lifting feeling that propels them forward like ocean waves.

Answers for p. 731

Review and Assess

1. Possible response: Students' opinions should be supported by citations from the text.

2. **(a)** The three rules are direct treatment of the topic, use no extra words, use a natural musical rhythm. **(b)** The results of "long contemplation" have been carefully thought out, whereas dogma is mindlessly followed. **(c)** A list of "do's" might be infinitely long, while a list of key "don'ts" is manageable.

3. **(a)** Pound considers the concrete better than the abstract. **(b)** Imagists seek to capture emotion in spare, concrete images. This doesn't work with abstractions.

4. **(a)** Pound considers it presentation. **(b)** Presentation puts forth only the concrete object. Description puts the characteristics of the concrete object at a greater remove from the reader.

5. **(a)** Pound suggests using the same rules used in composing music. **(b)** A good musician allows the rhythm to rise and fall naturally.

6. Students may say that Pound's rules make it more difficult.

CUSTOMIZE INSTRUCTION FOR UNIVERSAL ACCESS

For Less Proficient Readers	For Advanced Readers
Pound wrote his essay for readers whom he presumed were highly educated and well read. Less proficient readers may struggle, therefore, with Pound's elaborate sentences. To help students to better understand the writer's position, have them paraphrase Pound's directives in the form of a list.	Remind students about Pound's extraordinary influence during the twentieth century. This brief essay was one of Pound's best efforts to convey to a broader audience what he had imparted to fellow poets. One strategy for developing an understanding of this selection is to find or create examples of all the "negatives" he warns against. For example, when students read Pound's caution against using superfluous words in a poem, they should find superfluous words in another poem or examine their own work for superfluity.

Ezra Pound's poetry exemplifies the credo he espouses in his essay. In "The River-Merchant's Wife: A Letter," the speaker, who was married as a young girl by the arrangement of her parents, comes gradually to love her husband. By vividly describing her emotions and experiences during his absence, she demonstrates the simple power of human emotion. "In a Station of the Metro" evokes the crowd of a train station in just fourteen words.

8 Literary Analysis

Imagist Poetry

- Read aloud the Literary Analysis question on p. 732: What details in this stanza are most effective in conveying an image?

- Have volunteers take turns reading aloud the bracketed lines. Invite students to suggest details they find especially effective. Then, have students answer the question.

Possible answers: Effective images include "hair was still cut straight across my forehead," "on bamboo stilts, playing horse," "playing with blue plums."

▶ Monitor Progress Remind students of Imagism's commitment to precision and brevity. Have students evaluate this stanza based on these criteria. Do students find any superfluous words in the stanza?

The 7 River-Merchant's Wife: *A Letter*

Ezra Pound

8
> While my hair was still cut straight across my forehead
> I played about the front gate, pulling flowers.
> You came by on bamboo stilts, playing horse,
> You walked about my seat, playing with blue plums.
> 5   And we went on living in the village of Chokan:[1]
> Two small people, without dislike or suspicion.
>
> At fourteen I married My Lord you.
> I never laughed, being bashful.
> Lowering my head, I looked at the wall.
> 10   Called to, a thousand times, I never looked back.
>
> At fifteen I stopped scowling,
> I desired my dust to be mingled with yours
> Forever and forever and forever.
> Why should I climb the lookout?
>
> 15   At sixteen you departed,
> You went into far Ku-to-yen,[2] by the river of swirling eddies,
> And you have been gone five months.
> The monkeys make sorrowful noise overhead.

**Literary Analysis
Imagist Poetry** What details in this stanza are most effective in conveying an image?

---

1. **Chokan** (chō´ kän´) a suburb of Nanking, a city in the People's Republic of China.
2. **Ku-to-yen** (kōō´ tō´ yen´) an island in the Yangtze (yaŋk´ sē) River.

✳ ENRICHMENT: Cultural Connection

Customs

Pound's poem was adapted from a Chinese poem by Li T'ai Po. At the time that Li T'ai Po was writing, marriages in China were commonly arranged by family leaders rather than by the bride and groom. Love was expected to grow after the marriage. Point out that Pound's poem suggests the system worked, as strong love does grow between the young speaker and her husband.

Acknowledge to students that arranged marriages, while common in Li T'ai Po's time, are more unusual now. Customs such as this one are often unique to a time and culture. Invite students to brainstorm for customs of your community—annual festivals, young people's gathering places, decorated doorways on special holidays. Then urge students to interview longtime residents of the community to learn how these customs originated and changed over time.

You dragged your feet when you went out.
20 By the gate now, the moss is grown, the different mosses,
Too deep to clear them away!
The leaves fall early this autumn, in wind.
The paired butterflies are already yellow with August
Over the grass in the West garden;
25 They hurt me. I grow older.
If you are coming down through the narrows of the river Kiang,

Please let me know beforehand,
And I will come out to meet you
      As far as Cho-fu-Sa.[3]

By Rihaku

Literary Analysis
Imagist Poetry What details make this stanza appeal to both the senses and the emotions?

✓ **Reading Check**
Who is the speaker in this poem? Whom does she address?

---

3. **Cho-fu-Sa** (chŏ′ foo′ sä′) a beach along the Yangtze River, several hundred miles from Nanking.

Landscape Album in Various Styles, Ch'a Shih-piao, The Cleveland Museum of Art

▲ **Critical Viewing** In what ways does the mood of this drawing mirror the mood of "The River-Merchant's Wife: A Letter"? **[Analyze]**

A River-Merchant's Wife: A Letter ◆ 733

---

❾ Literary Analysis

Imagist Poetry

- Have students read lines 19–26 several times independently. Discuss the difference between senses and emotions.

- Have students list all the details in this poem that appeal to the senses and the emotions. Encourage them to list these details in two separate columns.

- Then, ask them the Literary Analysis question on p. 733: What details make this stanza appeal to both the senses and the emotions?
  Possible response: Details such as "dragged your feet," "They hurt me. I grow older" appeal to both senses by creating strong visual images and emotions by suggesting the speaker's sadness.

❿ Background

Art

Landscape Album in Various Styles by Ch'a Shih-piao

This piece of art depicts a landscape similar to the one described by the river-merchant's wife. Its artist was well-known for somber and melancholy landscapes such as this one. Use this question for discussion:

How would the setting depicted here make it difficult for the poem's speaker to learn of her husband's progress home?
Answer: The setting is isolated, making long-distance communication difficult.

⓫ ▶Critical Viewing

Answer: The mood is somewhat desolate, created by bare trees, an isolated house, and a stark landscape, suggesting the speaker's loneliness for her husband.

⓬ ✓Reading Check

Answer: The speaker is a young bride. She addresses her husband.

CUSTOMIZE INSTRUCTION FOR UNIVERSAL ACCESS

For Less Proficient Readers	For Special Needs Students	For Gifted/Talented Students
To help these students understand the concept of imagery, review the Reading Strategy instruction on p. 728. Model the use of the chart to identify sensory images and monitor students as they complete the chart with images from "The River-Merchant's Wife: A Letter."	To help these students experience the vivid images of Pound's poem, focus discussion on a few specific images. For example, you might point out the falling leaves, wind, and colorful butterflies as images that can be felt and heard as well as seen. Help students identify the emotions the images are intended to evoke.	Challenge students to create their own Imagist poetry. Direct them to try to capture the essence of an object, person, or incident in a brief Imagist poem. Tell them to use language that is precise and suggestive, and that appeals to the senses with its images.

733

Forms of *appear*

- Draw students' attention to the word *apparition* on page 734, and to its definition.

- Let students know that several common English words are forms of the word *appear*, which means "to come into sight or into being" or "to become understood."

- Invite students to volunteer other forms of the word that they may know.
  Possibilities include: apparent, appearance

Answers for p. 734

Review and Assess

1. Encourage students to share their responses.

2. **(a)** She marries her husband at the age of fourteen. **(b)** When she first marries, she does not love her husband, but at fifteen she does love him.

3. **(a)** Her husband goes away. **(b)** She is unhappy about it.

4. **(a)** He compares the people's faces with the "petals on a wet, black bough." **(b)** It creates an intensely vivid image of the train station crowd. **(c)** One doesn't usually see rain-covered tree branches in a train station.

5. Students should support their opinions with examples from the poetry.

⓻ In a Station of the Metro[1]

Ezra Pound

⓭ | The <u>apparition</u> of these faces in the crowd;
Petals on a wet, black bough.

apparition (ap′ ə rish′ ən)
n. act of appearing or becoming visible

---

1. **Metro** the Paris subway.

Review and Assess

Thinking About the Selections

1. **Respond:** Of all the images contained in the two poems by Ezra Pound, which did you find the most striking? Why?

2. **(a) Recall:** In "The River-Merchant's Wife," how old is the speaker when she marries? **(b) Compare and Contrast:** In what ways are her feelings for her husband at age fifteen different from those when she first marries?

3. **(a) Recall:** What happens when the river-merchant's wife is sixteen? **(b) Analyze:** How does she feel about this change?

4. **(a) Recall:** In "In a Station of the Metro," what two things does Pound compare? **(b) Interpret:** In what ways does this poem capture the essence of a single moment?
   (c) Analyze: Given the poem's setting, why is the image of "Petals on a wet, black bough" surprising?

5. **Take a Position:** What do you like about Pound's poetry? What do you dislike? Explain.

✵ ENRICHMENT: Social Studies Connection

Rail Transportation

"In a Station of the Metro" captures a brief moment inside the Paris Metro, or subway. Subways are rail systems designed to move people around in an urban area. Many are largely underground, though some systems include street level or elevated stations. London built the first subway, known still as the "underground," in 1863. Stations occur at frequent intervals, perhaps as little as a few blocks distance, so that passengers can arrive close to their exact destination. Riders reach underground subway stations by descending stairs to underground platforms. At busy times such as the morning and evening rush hours, crowds of passengers such as Pound describes, cluster on the platform to await trains. Together with commuter trains, subways form the largest part of passenger rail travel in the U.S. today.

The Red Wheelbarrow

William Carlos Williams

so much depends
upon

a red wheel
barrow

5   glazed with rain
water

beside the white
chickens.

The Great Figure

William Carlos Williams

Among the rain
and lights
I saw the figure 5
in gold
5   on a red
fire truck
moving
tense
unheeded
10   to gong clangs
siren howls
and wheels rumbling
through the dark city.

The Figure 5 in Gold, Charles Demuth, Metropolitan Museum of Art

16 ▶ Critical Viewing Artist Charles Demuth created this work of art to accompany his friend Williams's poem. What elements of his illustration convey the energy and clamor of the poem? [Connect]

14 ▶ About the Selections

These three poems by William Carlos Williams illustrate the power of strong sensory images to evoke emotions and responses from readers. Whether capturing an everyday farm scene of animals and equipment, freezing in time the tension of a speeding fire engine, or interpreting a letter of apology, the poems use straightforward language to create images that demand attention.

15 ▶ Background

Art

The Figure 5 in Gold, by Charles Demuth

This painting evokes many of the images in "The Great Figure" as well as the character of the poet Williams. Point out the artist's inclusion of the nickname Bill at the top of the image, alluding to William Carlos Williams even more deliberately. *The Figure 5 in Gold* captures, as does Williams's poem, the modern world's growing awareness of machines and technology.

Use this question for discussion:

How does the painting respond to the poem?
Answer: It distills the poem's topic to its visual core.

16 ▶ Critical Viewing

Answer: The expanding and repeated "5," which seems to shout at viewers, the fragmented bands of lights that explode from the center of the image, and the bright colors against a dark background all create a mood of urgency and clamor.

- Ask students the following question: What senses are stimulated by the bracketed lines? Direct students to cite specific words from the poem in answering.

- Have students use a sensory details chart to record their responses. Charts should look similar to the following.

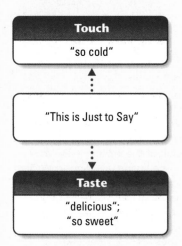

Touch
"so cold"

"This is Just to Say"

Taste
"delicious";
"so sweet"

Answers for p. 736

Review and Assess

1. Students' responses should include citations from the poems.

2. **(a)** It appeals most to the sense of sight. **(b)** The poem focuses on finite, focused images rather than on the speaker's reactions to them.

3. **(a)** He divides the words *wheelbarrow* and *rainwater*. **(b)** It forces readers to slow down and take notice.

4. **(a)** The detail is the figure 5. **(b)** He may be saying that beauty can be found in unlikely places and that modern life is so hectic and impersonal that people do not notice what is going on around them.

5. **(a)** The speaker intends to apologize. **(b)** Details such as "delicious," "sweet," and "cold" suggest that the speaker truly enjoyed the plums and doesn't really regret eating them.

6. Simple everyday moments or images, the subject matter of these poems, suggest the poet's interest and pleasure in everyday life.

---

⑭ # THIS IS JUST TO SAY

William Carlos Williams

I have eaten
the plums
that were in
the icebox
5 and which
you were probably
saving
for breakfast

Forgive me
⑰ 10 they were delicious
so sweet
and so cold

Review and Assess

Thinking About the Selections

1. **Respond:** Which of the three poems by Williams evokes the strongest emotional response in you? Why?

2. **(a) Classify:** In "The Red Wheelbarrow," to what sense does the image appeal most? **(b) Analyze:** In what way does this poem reflect the Imagist emphasis on the concrete?

3. **(a) Recall:** Which words has Williams divided to run on two separate lines? **(b) Analyze:** What is the effect of this arrangement of words?

4. **(a) Recall:** In "The Great Figure," what detail is the focus of the speaker's experience of the fire truck? **(b) Interpret:** In focusing on this detail, what might Williams be saying about beauty and modern life?

5. **(a) Recall:** What is the intention of the speaker in "This Is Just to Say"? **(b) Connect:** Which details in the second stanza challenge the speaker's sincerity?

6. **Evaluate:** Which elements of these poems reflect Williams's interest in portraying—and celebrating—everyday American life?

✷ ENRICHMENT: Art Connection

Landscape Painting

H.D.'s poem "Pear Tree" works like a landscape painting to capture the essential image of a fruit tree in full bloom. Describing nature in words or pictures is a long-standing artistic tradition. Many art historians assert that landscape painting in America reached its peak during the nineteenth century when artists of the Hudson River School were active. Characterized by contrast between wilderness and a smaller human element, these landscapes highlighted the magnificence of the American landscape and the relative transience of human occupancy.

Have students view examples of American landscape painting in books or online museum exhibits. Discuss how these images capture the same sense of responsive wonder as does the poem "Pear Tree."

PEAR TREE H.D.

Silver dust
lifted from the earth,
higher than my arms reach,
you have mounted,
5   O silver,
higher than my arms reach
you front us with great mass;

no flower ever opened
so staunch a white leaf,
10 no flower ever parted silver
from such rare silver;

O white pear,
your flower-tufts
thick on the branch
15 bring summer and ripe fruits
in their purple hearts.

▼ Critical Viewing

Which phrases from the poem best describe this image of a pear tree in full flower? **[Evaluate]**

☑ Reading Check

What image does the poet use to describe the pear tree flowers?

About the Selections

These Imagist poems illustrate nature with words so evocative they hardly need accompanying illustrations. In both poems, the poet describes and responds to nature. "Pear Tree" presents H.D.'s rapturous emotional response to a pear tree in bloom while "Heat" brings the physical experience of a sweltering day into sharp focus for readers. One poem adores nature while the other complains to it, but together they demonstrate the emotional and sensory impact of carefully chosen words.

Reading Strategy

Engaging Your Senses

• Have a volunteer read aloud the bracketed stanza. Invite students to close their eyes as they listen, paying attention to the sensory details.

• Ask students this question: What sensory experience does the line "higher than my arms reach" create?
Answer: It creates the experience of stretching up toward the sky.

► Critical Viewing

Answer: Effective descriptive phrases include "Silver dust/lifted from the earth" and "your flower-tufts/thick on the branch."

☑ Reading Check

Answer: She uses the image of silver dust.

CUSTOMIZE INSTRUCTION FOR UNIVERSAL ACCESS

For Less Proficient Readers

Remind students of the admonition that Ezra Pound includes in his essay on Imagist poetry: "Go in fear of abstractions." The opposite of an abstraction is the concrete image, which impresses itself on the senses upon reading.

All the poems included in this grouping should have this effect. Use "Pear Tree" as an example, and ask students for sensory descriptions from it. Ask: what senses are affected by the poem? After students complete the organizer, help them find other poems from the grouping that contains images that appeal to those senses missing from "Pear Tree."

22 ▶ Critical Viewing

Answer: Some students will say the image is effective for its depiction of the thick and hanging air. Others will say it is not, citing the painting's scene as less oppressive than the feelings of the poem.

Answers for p. 738

Review and Assess

1. Encourage students to share their responses. Have them support their answers with specific images and phrases from the poems.

2. **(a)** The silver dust refers to the leaves and flowers of the pear tree. **(b)** The pear tree grows upward.

3. **(a)** It waits for summer and fruit. **(b)** It is spring.

4. **(a)** It cannot fall through the thick, hot air. **(b)** The speaker seems to describe the heat of the sun on a torrid summer day.

5. **(a)** The speaker uses the words *rend, cut, plow,* and *turn.* **(b)** They create the impression that the heat is almost a solid substance.

6. The poet feels deeply involved with nature and is also impressed by its power.

18 HEAT
H. D.

O wind, rend open the heat,
cut apart the heat,
rend it to tatters.

5 Fruit cannot drop
through this thick air—
fruit cannot fall into heat
that presses up and blunts
the points of pears
and rounds the grapes.

10 Cut the heat—
plow through it,
turning it on either side
of your path.

Overhanging Cloud in July, (1947/1959), Charles Burchfield, Watercolor on paper, 39 1/2" x 35 1/2", Collection of Whitney Museum of American Art, Purchase, with funds from the Friends of the Whitney Museum of American Art

22 ▲ Critical Viewing
Does this painting capture the oppressive heat of a humid summer day as effectively as the poem does? Explain. **[Evaluate]**

Review and Assess

Thinking About the Selections

1. **Respond:** How do these two poems by H. D. make you feel?
2. **(a) Recall:** What is the "silver dust" referred to in the first stanza of "Pear Tree"? **(b) Interpret:** In what sense is the silver dust "lifted from the earth"?
3. **(a) Recall:** What does the pear tree's blossom anticipate? **(b) Infer:** What time of year is the speaker describing?
4. **(a) Recall:** In "Heat," what is the reaction of the fruit to the air? **(b) Interpret:** What specific type of heat is the speaker describing?
5. **(a) Recall:** Which verbs does the speaker use to describe lessening the heat? **(b) Analyze:** What impression of the heat do these verbs create?
6. **Generalize:** Based on these two poems, how would you define the poet's relationship to nature?

ASSESSMENT PRACTICE: Reading Comprehension

Anticipate Missing Words   (For more practice, see Test Preparation Workbook, p. 42)

Many tests ask students to correctly answer sentence-completion questions. Use the following example to show students how to use context and prior knowledge to choose the word that best completes the following passage.

The Imagist poets strove for a spare, clean presentation of an image. To accomplish this purpose, the Imagists carefully avoided using _____ words.

A easy   **C** simple
B everyday   **D** unnecessary

The context clues *spare* and *clean* provide the key to completing the sentence. The correct answer will describe words that would prevent something from being spare and clean. *D* is the most logical choice.

Review and Assess

Literary Analysis

Imagist Poetry

1. Does "The River-Merchant's Wife: A Letter" qualify as a purely **Imagist poem**? Why or why not?
2. What effect does Pound's choice of the word *apparition*—commonly used to describe a ghostly figure—to mean "appearance" contribute to "In a Station of the Metro"?

Comparing Literary Works

3. In what ways is Pound's advice to (a) avoid abstractions and (b) avoid superfluous words evident in all of these poems?
4. (a) Use a chart like the one shown to compare and contrast the use of color in the poems by H. D. and Williams. (b) What emotions do these uses of color evoke?

Poem	Color(s)	Emotional Effect

5. Although Pound wrote "the painter can describe a landscape much better than you can," in what ways are these poems like paintings?
6. Which of these poems best exemplifies Pound's idea of the image as "that which presents an intellectual and emotional complex in an instant of time"? Explain your choice.

Reading Strategy

Engaging Your Senses

7. What other **senses**, besides sight, can you engage to re-create the images of "Petals on a wet, black bough"? Explain.
8. Identify two examples of passages in "The River-Merchant's Wife" in which you were able to engage the sense of smell.

Extend Understanding

9. **Literature Connection:** "The River-Merchant's Wife: A Letter" is an adaptation of a poem by the Chinese poet Li T'ai Po. What challenges and opportunities face a poet in translating a work of literature from one language and culture to another?

Quick Review

Imagist poetry focuses on evoking emotion and vivid mental associations through the presentation of concise, unadorned images.

By **engaging your senses,** you can fully experience the images in poetry.

 Take It to the Net
www.phschool.com
Take the interactive self-test online to check your understanding of these selections.

The Imagist Poets ◆ 739

Answers for p. 739

Review and Assess

1. **Possible responses:** Some students may say that the poem is not a purely Imagist poem because it includes descriptive lines and abstract words. Others may observe that the speaker's descriptions are spare evocations of scenes and images that only suggest, rather than explore, her feelings.

2. The word *apparition* enhances the feeling of isolation and anonymity within the crowd.

3. **(a)** In general, the poems focus on very specific, concrete topics and images. **(b)** The poems are short and succinct.

4. **(a) Possible responses:** "The Great Figure": Colors: gold, red; Effect: These colors suggest a vibrant, demanding image; "Pear Tree": Colors: silver, white; Effect: These colors suggest a clean, spare, and brilliant image. **(b)** Williams's colors suggest emotions of tension or excitement, while H.D.'s colors suggest emotions of peace, awe, or wonder.

5. They are extremely visual in nature, using imagery to help readers "see" the poems.

6. Students should support their choices with specific examples from the poem.

7. The sense of touch can be engaged to feel the petals and the wet bough. The sense of smell can be engaged to smell the wet bough and the petals.

8. Passages include "I played about the front gate, pulling flowers," and "The paired butterflies are already yellow with August/Over the grass in the West garden."

9. The challenge is to maintain the poem's essential ideas, mood, and cultural context. The opportunity is to evoke an entirely different world for readers, to transport them to another time or place.

739

❶ Vocabulary Development

Word Analysis

1. appearance
2. apparent
3. apparition

Concept Development: Synonyms

1. a
2. c
3. b

Spelling Strategy

1. aggressor
2. assign
3. approve

❷ Grammar and Style

Practice

1. abstract; abstract
2. concrete; concrete
3. concrete; concrete
4. concrete
5. concrete; concrete

Looking at Style

The Imagists believed in evoking concrete images rather than abstract ideas.

Integrate Language Skills

❶ Vocabulary Development Lesson

Word Analysis: Forms of *appear*

Several common English words are forms of the verb *appear*, meaning "to come into sight or into being" or "to become understood."

apparent   appearance   apparition

Complete each of the following sentences with the correct word from the list above.

1. He made a brief ___?___ at the awards dinner—just long enough to pick up his trophy and say a few words.
2. When midnight found the toddlers still running around the house, it became ___?___ that the babysitter was no longer in control.
3. The ___?___ of a face at the window nearly stopped her heart with fear.

❷ Grammar and Style Lesson

Concrete and Abstract Nouns

Nouns can be classified according to the item they name. A **concrete noun** names something that can be perceived with one or more of the five senses. Concrete nouns have a physical, tangible reality. An **abstract noun** names something that cannot be seen, heard, smelled, tasted, or touched. These may be qualities, characteristics, emotions, or ideas that are not perceived mainly through the senses.

> **Concrete:** *I* played about the front *gate*, pulling *flowers*.
>
> **Abstract:** Two small people, without *dislike* or *suspicion*.

_WG_ *Prentice Hall Writing and Grammar Connection: Chapter 17, Section 1*

740 ◆ *Disillusion, Defiance, and Discontent (1914–1946)*

Concept Development: Synonyms

Select the letter of the best synonym, or word of similar meaning, for the numbered word.

1. dogma: (a) doctrine, (b) legality, (c) statement
2. voluminous: (a) loud, (b) arrogant, (c) comprehensive
3. apparition: (a) suspicious, (b) vision, (c) face

Spelling Strategy

You may need to drop the *d* when adding the prefix *ad-* to a word or word stem beginning with the consonants *p*, *g*, *s*, or *c*. If so, you must also double the consonant, as in *appear*. Use this principle to correctly spell the words below.

1. *ad-* + gressor   2. *ad-* + sign   3. *ad-* + prove

Practice Label the italicized nouns in these sentences as either *concrete* or *abstract*.

1. Don't use such an *expression* as "dim lands of *peace*."
2. The *leaves* fell early this autumn, in *wind*.
3. I saw the figure 5 in gold on a red firetruck moving tense unheeded to gong *clangs* siren howls and wheels rumbling through the dark *city*.
4. Cut the *heat*—plow through it . . .
5. I have eaten the *plums* that were in the icebox and which you were probably saving for *breakfast*.

Looking at Style Explain why you would expect to find mainly concrete nouns in an Imagist poem.

TEACHING RESOURCES

The following resources can be used to enrich or extend the instruction for pp. 740–741.

Vocabulary

📖 **Selection Support:** Build Vocabulary, p. 178

📖 **Vocabulary and Spelling Practice Book** (Use this booklet for skills enrichment.) ■

Grammar

📖 **Selection Support:** Grammar and Style, p. 179

_WG_ **Writing and Grammar,** Ruby Level, p. 364

📄 **Daily Language Practice Transparencies** ■

Writing

_WG_ **Writing and Grammar,** Ruby Level, p. 346

💿 **Writing and Grammar iText CD-ROM**

■ **BLOCK SCHEDULING:** Resources marked with this symbol provide varied instruction during 90-minute blocks.

❸ Writing Lesson

An Editor's Review of Manuscript

Imagine that you are a magazine editor who has just received a manuscript from an Imagist poet. Write a letter to the poet explaining why you will or will not publish his or her poems. Be simple, honest, and kind, and include constructive criticism.

Prewriting   Choose a poet and reread the poems. Take notes on the strengths and weaknesses of each poem, citing relevant passages.

Drafting   Write a letter that explains why you will or will not publish the poems. Discuss strengths, and identify flaws. Select specific words that best convey your meaning.

Revising   Review your draft, highlighting any words that are inaccurate or vague. Then, replace those words with better, more specific choices.

Model: Revising for Brevity and Clarity

deceptively simple

Your poems are small and ~~not complex~~, but are rich in imagery

wry

and ideas. I especially enjoyed the ~~incredible~~ tone of "This Is

Just to Say."

> Replacing vague words with specific words helps to express ideas exactly.

*W*G *Prentice Hall Writing and Grammar Connection: Chapter 16, Section 1*

❹ Extension Activities

Listening and Speaking Of "The Red Wheelbarrow," Roy Harvey Pearce writes: "At its worst this is togetherness in a chickenyard. At its best it is an exercise in the creation of the poetic out of the anti-poetic." Which view do you hold? Defend your view in an **informal debate** with classmates. To prepare, keep these tips in mind:

- Find examples to support both positions, and then decide which you will argue.
- Use examples for the opposing side to develop arguments against that position.

As you debate, be as clear and as eloquent as possible. **[Group Activity]**

Research and Technology Select one of the Imagist poems and **illustrate** it, either with artworks of your own or with clippings or printouts from magazines, the Internet, and other sources. If possible, create your illustration using graphic arts software and integrate them in a file with the text of the poem. Then, post your work in the classroom with a brief explanation of its imagery, and use it as the basis for an oral interpretation or reading of the poem.

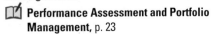 **Take It to the Net**   www.phschool.com

Go online for an additional research activity using the Internet.

The Imagist Poets ◆ 741

Lesson Support for p. 741

❸ Writing Lesson

- Encourage students to reread Pound's essay for ideas on how to construct critical analysis about writing. Remind them, however, that they need not adopt Pound's viewpoints.
- After discussing the steps in the Writing Lesson, emphasize the importance of clearly identifying strengths and weaknesses in the poem. Suggest that students use a two-column chart headed "Strengths" and "Weaknesses" as they prewrite.
- Stress that critical writing should remain professional in tone. Students should develop constructive criticism, especially when rejecting a poem for publication.
- Use the rubric for Response to Literature in **Performance Assessment and Portfolio Management**, p. 23, to evaluate students' reviews.

❹ Research and Technology

- Help students become familiar with graphic arts software available in your school or local library. You might also lead them in downloading such software from appropriate Internet sources.
- Allow students the alternative of illustrating in a manual medium.
- Encourage students looking for ideas to review the illustrations and photographs that accompany the Imagist poems in the grouping.

CUSTOMIZE INSTRUCTION
For Universal Access

To address different learning styles, use the activities suggested in the Extension Activities booklet, p. 40.

For Intrapersonal and Verbal/Linguistic Learners, use Activity 5.

For Visual/Spatial Learners, use Activity 6.

For Musical/Rhythmic and Interpersonal Learners, use Activity 7.

ASSESSMENT RESOURCES

The following resources can be used to assess students' knowledge and skills.

Selection Assessment

📖 **Formal Assessment**, pp. 188–190

📖 **Open Book Test**, pp. 118–120

📼 **Got It! Assessment Videotapes**, Tape 3

💿 **Test Bank Software**

 **Take It to the Net**

Visit www.phschool.com for self-tests and additional questions on the selections.

Writing Rubric

📖 **Performance Assessment and Portfolio Management**, p. 23

 PRENTICE HALL **ASSESSMENT SYSTEM**

📖 **Workbook**   📄 **Transparencies**

📖 **Skill Book**   💿 **CD-ROM**

Winter Dreams

Lesson Objectives

1. **To analyze and respond to literary elements**
   - Literary Analysis: Characterization
   - Connecting Literary Elements: Motivation of Character

2. **To read, comprehend, analyze, and critique a short story**
   - Reading Strategy: Drawing Conclusions About Characters
   - Reading Check Questions
   - Review and Assess Questions
   - Assessment Practice (ATE)

3. **To develop word analysis skills, fluency, and systematic vocabulary**
   - Vocabulary Development Lesson: Word Analysis: Latin Root: -somn-

4. **To understand and apply written and oral language conventions**
   - Spelling Strategy
   - Grammar Lesson: Dashes

5. **To understand and apply appropriate writing and research strategies**
   - Writing Lesson: Character Analysis
   - Extension Activity: Report

6. **To understand and apply listening and speaking strategies**
   - Extension Activity: Musical Presentation

STEP-BY-STEP TEACHING GUIDE	PACING GUIDE
PRETEACH	
Motivate Students and Provide Background	
Use the Motivation activity (ATE p. 742)	5 min.
Read and discuss author and background features (SE/ATE p. 742)	10 min.
Introduce the Concepts	
Introduce the Literary Analysis and Reading Strategy (SE/ATE p. 742) A	15 min.
Pronounce the vocabulary words and read their definitions (SE p. 743)	5 min.
TEACH	
Monitor Comprehension	
Informally monitor comprehension by circulating while students read independently or in groups A	60 min.
Monitor students' comprehension with the Reading Check notes (SE/ATE pp. 745, 747, 749, 751, 753, 755, 757, 759, 761,)	as students read as students read
Develop vocabulary with Vocabulary notes (SE p. 759 ATE p. 759)	
Develop Understanding	
Develop students' understanding of characterization with the Literary Analysis annotations (SE/ATE pp. 746, 747, 750–753, 755, 756, 759, 761) A	5 min.
Develop students' ability to draw conclusions about characters by using the Reading Strategy annotations (SE/ATE pp. 745, 749, 757, 758)	5 min.
ASSESS	
Assess Mastery	
Assess students' mastery of the Reading Strategy and Literary Analysis by having them answer the Review and Assess questions (SE/ATE p. 763)	15 min.
Use one or more of the print and media Assessment Resources (ATE p. 765) A	up to 45 min.
EXTEND	
Apply Understanding	
Have students complete the Vocabulary Development Lesson and the Grammar Lesson (SE p. 764) A	20 min.
Apply students' ability to elaborate informatively by using the Writing Lesson (SE/ATE p. 765) A	45 min.
Apply students' understanding using one or more of the Extension Activities (SE p. 765)	20–90 min.

A **ACCELERATED INSTRUCTION:** Use the strategies and activities identified with an **A**.

UNIVERSAL ACCESS
● = Below Level Students
▲ = On-Level Students
■ = Above Level Students

RESOURCES		
PRINT 📖	**TRANSPARENCIES**	**TECHNOLOGY** 💿 🎧
• **Beyond Literature,** Media Connection: Music, p. 41 ▲ ■		• **Interest Grabber Video,** Tape 5 ● ▲ ■
• **Selection Support Workbook:** ● ▲ ■ Literary Analysis, p. 185 Reading Strategy, p. 184 Build Vocabulary, p. 182	• **Literary Analysis and Reading Transparencies,** pp. 81 and 82 ● ▲ ■	
		• **Listening to Literature** ● ▲ ■ Audiocassettes, Side 25–26 Audio CDs, CD 14–15
• **Literatura en español** ● ▲ • **Literary Analysis for Enrichment** ■		
• **Formal Assessment:** Selection Test, p. 191 ● ▲ ■ • **Open-Book Test,** p. 121 ● ▲ ■ • **Performance Assessment and Portfolio Management,** p. 30 ● ▲ ■ • PRENTICE HALL **ASSESSMENT** *SYSTEM* ● ▲ ■	• PRENTICE HALL **ASSESSMENT** *SYSTEM* ● ▲ ■ Skills Practice Answers and Explanations on Transparencies	• **Test Bank Software** ● ▲ ■ • **Got It! Assessment Videotapes,** Tape 4 ● ▲
• **Selection Support Workbook:** ● ▲ ■ Build Grammar Skills, p. 183 • **Writing and Grammar,** Ruby Level ● ▲ ■ • **Extension Activities,** p. 41 ● ▲ ■	• **Daily Language Practice Transparencies** ● ▲ • **Writing Models and Graphic Organizers on Transparencies,** p. 67 ● ▲ ■	• **Writing and Grammar iText CD-ROM** ● ▲ ■ 💻 *Take It to the Net* www.phschool.com

BLOCK SCHEDULING: Use one 90-minute class period to preteach the selection and have students read it. Use a second 90-minute class period to assess students' mastery of skills and have them complete one of the Extension Activities.

Step-by-Step Teaching Guide for pp. 742–743

Motivation

Students may discover that this sad story of obsessive love is reminiscent of many films, books, and real-life experiences. The power of any love story evolves from its characters. Introduce students to Fitzgerald's vividly drawn and alluring centerpiece character—Judy Jones—by reading aloud the following:

> She drew down the corners of her mouth, smiled, glanced furtively around, her eyes in transit falling for an instant on Dexter . . . The smile again—radiant, blatantly artful—convincing."

Have students discuss what this description reveals about Judy. Then, have them predict what might happen when another character falls desperately in love with her. After students have read the story, invite them to discuss their predictions and compare them against the actual plot.

▄▄▄ Interest Grabber Video

As an alternative, you may wish to play "The Roaring Twenties" on Tape 5 to engage student interest.

❶ Background

More About the Author

People had aspired to wealth long before Fitzgerald's time, but during the 1920s—the decade in which Fritzgerald's fame was at its peak—wealth and status became more accessible than ever. The restricted world of America's wealthy established families had begun to open its doors. Making money—rather than inheriting it—became honorable and admired. Thus, F. Scott Fitzgerald's own desire for wealth became realistic, an achievable goal. Unfortunately, Fitzgerald's wealth and fame were not simple gifts. He struggled with alcoholism, financial and marital problems, and saw the star of his literary success fall into eclipse.

Prepare to Read

❶ Winter Dreams

F. Scott Fitzgerald (1896–1940)

When you open the pages of one of F. Scott Fitzgerald's books, you are transported back in time to the Roaring Twenties, a decade unlike any other in American history. Many Americans lived with reckless abandon, attending wild parties, wearing glamorous clothing, and striving for fulfillment through material wealth. Yet, this quest for pleasure was often accompanied by a sense of inner despair. Fitzgerald was able to successfully capture the paradox of this glittering, materialistic, and often self-destructive lifestyle because he actually lived it. Like many of his characters, he led a fast-paced life and longed to attain the wealth and social status of the upper class. He also experienced the emptiness conveyed in his stories.

A Quick Rise to Fame Francis Scott Key Fitzgerald was born in St. Paul, Minnesota, into a family with high social aspirations but little wealth. The family had a small claim on history: One of their distant relatives was Francis Scott Key, the writer of "The Star Spangled Banner," after whom Fitzgerald was named. As a young man, Fitzgerald was eager to improve his social standing. He entered Princeton University in 1913, where he pursued the type of high-profile social life for which he would later become famous. Fitzgerald failed to graduate, perhaps as a result of his self-indulgent lifestyle, and soon enlisted in the army.

His first novel, *This Side of Paradise* (1920), published shortly after his discharge from the service, was an instant success. With the fame and wealth the novel brought him, Fitzgerald was able to court Zelda Sayre, a southern belle with whom he had fallen in love while in the army. They married in 1920. Together, they blazed an extravagant trail across the societies of both New York and Europe, mingling with rich and famous artists and aristocrats and spending money recklessly.

An American Masterpiece Despite the couple's pleasure-seeking lifestyle, Fitzgerald remained a productive writer, publishing dozens of short stories. In 1925, he published his most successful novel, *The Great Gatsby*, the story of a self-made man whose dreams of love and social acceptance lead to scandal and corruption and ultimately end in tragedy. The novel displayed Fitzgerald's fascination with—and growing distrust of—the wealthy society he had embraced. The book is widely considered to be Fitzgerald's masterpiece, one of the greatest novels in American literature.

Fortunes Turn After the 1929 stock market crash, Fitzgerald's world began to crumble. His wife suffered a series of nervous breakdowns, his reputation as a writer declined, and financial setbacks forced him to seek work as a Hollywood screenwriter. Despite these setbacks, however, he managed to produce many more short stories and a fine second novel, *Tender Is the Night* (1934). Though well-regarded by critics, the book was not a financial success. In the last year of his life, Fitzgerald, who had once been the highest-paid author in the country, earned just $13.13 from his writing.

Fitzgerald was in the midst of writing *The Last Tycoon*, a novel about a Hollywood film mogul, when he died of a heart attack in 1940. His editor approached the novelist John O'Hara about finishing the book, but O'Hara declined. In a letter O'Hara wrote to author John Steinbeck, he explained his refusal, saying that "Fitzgerald was a better just plain writer than all of us put together. Just words writing."

742 ◆ Disillusion, Defiance, and Discontent (1914–1946)

TEACHING RESOURCES

The following resources can be used to enrich or extend the instruction for pp. 742–743.

Motivation
▄▄▄ **Interest Grabber Video**, Tape 5 ▄

Background
📖 **Beyond Literature**, p. 41

🖥 *Take It to the Net*
Visit www.phschool.com for Background and hotlinks for "Winter Dreams." ▄

Literary Analysis
📖 **Literary Analysis and Reading Transparencies**, Characterization, p. 82

Reading
📖 **Literary Analysis and Reading Transparencies**, Drawing Conclusions About Characters, p. 81

📖 **Selection Support**: Reading Strategy, p. 184; Build Vocabulary, p. 182

 **BLOCK SCHEDULING:** Resources marked with this symbol provide varied instruction during 90-minute blocks.

Preview

Connecting to the Literature

Even when you know, deep down, that someone is not right for you, you may continue to long for that person. Such a struggle between reason and emotion forms the heart of this story.

❷ Literary Analysis

Characterization

Fitzgerald creates intimate portraits of Dexter and Judy through **characterization**—the revelation of characters' personalities.

- In **direct characterization,** the writer tells the reader what the character is like.
- In **indirect characterization,** characters' traits are revealed through their thoughts, actions, and words, and by what other characters say to or about them.

Fitzgerald brings characters into sharp focus through both methods.

Connecting Literary Elements

Characters' motivations—their reasons for acting as they do—may come from internal sources, such as feelings of loneliness, or external sources, such as danger. As you read, identify characters' motivations for their actions.

❸ Reading Strategy

Drawing Conclusions About Characters

Fitzgerald often leaves it up to the reader to draw conclusions about his characters. To **draw conclusions,** combine information from the story with your own experience. Consider this example:

> Dexter stood perfectly still . . . if he moved forward a step his stare would be in her line of vision—if he moved backward he would lose his full view of her face.

If you have ever wanted to hide your interest in someone but could not stop looking, you can conclude that Dexter is enthralled by Judy. Use a chart like the one shown to draw conclusions.

Vocabulary Development

fallowness (fal′ ō nis) *n.* inactivity (p. 745)

preposterous (prē päs′ tər əs) *adj.* ridiculous (p. 746)

fortuitous (fôr tōō′ ə təs) *adj.* fortunate (p. 747)

sinuous (sin′ yōō əs) *adj.* moving in and out; wavy (p. 751)

mundane (mun′ dān′) *adj.* commonplace; ordinary (p. 752)

poignant (poin′ yənt) *adj.* sharply painful to the feelings (p. 756)

pugilistic (pyōō′ jəl is′ tik) *adj.* looking for a fight (p. 758)

somnolent (säm′ nə lənt) *adj.* sleepy; drowsy (p. 759)

Winter Dreams ◆ 743

❷ Literary Analysis

Characterization

- Tell students that as they read "Winter Dreams," they will focus on characterization, the technique authors use to create and develop characters.
- Read the instruction about characterization aloud. Point out the two distinct methods of characterization— direct and indirect— and use these passages to highlight the difference:
  Direct: Whatever Judy wanted, she went after.
  Indirect: She swung her mashie impatiently and without interest. Invite students to notice how the second example conveys information by describing a character's behavior, while the first simply states what the character is like.
- Use the **Connecting Literary Elements** instruction to emphasize that identifying characters' motivations will help students better understand Fitzgerald's characters.

❸ Reading Strategy

Drawing Conclusions About Characters

- Remind students that drawing conclusions can help them fully appreciate Fitzgerald's vivid characters.
- To draw conclusions about characters, readers must look carefully at characters' motivations, pay attention to the author's characterization, and consider their own knowledge of human behavior.
- Direct students to the chart on the student page. Urge them to record text and life clues that lead them to draw specific conclusions about Dexter and Judy.

Vocabulary Development

- Pronounce each vocabulary word for students, and read the definitions as a class. Have students identify any words with which they are already familiar.

 E-Teach

Visit E-Teach at www.phschool.com for teachers' essays on how to teach, with questions and answers.

CUSTOMIZE INSTRUCTION FOR UNIVERSAL ACCESS

For Less Proficient Readers	For English Learners	For Advanced Readers
Prepare students to draw conclusions about characters by presenting the Drawing Conclusions About Characters transparency in **Literary Analysis and Reading Transparencies,** p. 81. Invite a volunteer to read each numbered passage aloud. Discuss the text clues in each that lead to the conclusions noted.	Discuss the idea that human behavior may be influenced by cultural attitudes, but human emotions remain the same in people everywhere. Encourage students to trust their own knowledge of human behavior to draw conclusions about characters even if the cultural setting of the story is unfamiliar.	Drawing conclusions about characters can help more advanced students appreciate Fitzgerald's power-packed portrayal of even minor characters. Have students locate details from the text to support conclusions about one or more minor characters.

Step-by-Step Teaching Guide for pp. 744–762

CUSTOMIZE INSTRUCTION
For Musical/Rhythmic Learners

Give students the opportunity to share in Dexter's sensory experiences. Play a recording of the songs noted in the story (p. 750)—available on Jazz Age song collections. Have students identify other sounds in the referenced scene. As they listen to the recording, urge students to imagine all the sounds Dexter hears. Lead students to appreciate how these various sounds might affect Dexter's mood.

❶ About the Selection

This story illustrates the powerful magnetism of love and suggests the extremes to which a person might go in pursuit of it. Dexter Green, an up-and-coming young man, becomes passionately obsessed with capturing Judy Jones and gaining entrance into her wealthy society. No matter how badly she behaves, Dexter remains steadfast in his passion, finding Judy and the glittering life around her both captivating and desirable. As Dexter repeatedly returns to Judy's side to hungrily grasp at her erratic goodwill, he demonstrates with poignant force the glory and despair of loving a fantasy—a romantic ideal for which sacrificing all seems worthwhile.

WINTER DREAMS

F. Scott Fitzgerald

Background

Written in 1922, this story unfolds against the background of the Jazz Age. Focusing on Dexter Green's obsession with Judy Jones, a beautiful young woman from a prominent wealthy family, Fitzgerald explores the connections between love, money, and social status. Through Dexter, he shows what life was like in the 1920s for an ambitious young man driven by the desire for "glittering things."

I

Some of the caddies were poor as sin and lived in one-room houses with a neurasthenic[1] cow in the front yard, but Dexter Green's father owned the second best grocery store in Black Bear—the best one was "The Hub," patronized by the wealthy people from Sherry Island—and Dexter caddied only for pocket money.

---

1. **neurasthenic** (noor′ əs then′ ik) *adj.* here, weak, tired.

744 ◆ *Disillusion, Defiance, and Discontent (1914–1946)*

TEACHING RESOURCES

The following resources can be used to enrich or extend the instruction for pp. 744–762.

Literary Analysis
- Writing Models and Graphic Organizers on Transparency, pp. 82
- Selection Support: Literary Analysis, p. 185

Literary Analysis
- ◯ Listening to Literature Audiocassettes, Sides 25–26 ▪
- ◉ Listening to Literature Audio CDs, CDs 14–15 ▪

■ **BLOCK SCHEDULING:** Resources marked with this symbol provide varied instruction during 90-minute blocks.

In the fall when the days became crisp and gray, and the long Minnesota winter shut down like the white lid of a box, Dexter's skis moved over the snow that hid the fairways of the golf course. At these times the country gave him a feeling of profound melancholy—it offended him that the links should lie in enforced <u>fallowness</u>, haunted by ragged sparrows for the long season. It was dreary, too, that on the tees where the gay colors fluttered in summer there were now only the desolate sandboxes knee deep in crusted ice. When he crossed the hills the wind blew cold as misery, and if the sun was out he tramped with his eyes squinted up against the hard dimensionless glare.

In April the winter ceased abruptly. The snow ran down into Black Bear Lake scarcely tarrying for the early golfers to brave the season with red and black balls. Without elation, without an interval of moist glory, the cold was gone. Dexter knew that there was something dismal about this Northern spring, just as he knew there was something gorgeous about the fall. Fall made him clinch his hands and tremble and repeat idiotic sentences to himself, and make brisk abrupt gestures of command to imaginary audiences and armies. October filled him with hope which November raised to a sort of ecstatic triumph, and in this mood the fleeting brilliant impressions of the summer at Sherry Island were ready grist to his mill. He became a golf champion and defeated Mr. T. A. Hedrick in a marvelous match played a hundred times over the fairways of his imagination, a match each detail of which he changed about untiringly—sometimes he won with almost laughable ease, sometimes he came up magnificently from behind. Again, stepping from a Pierce-Arrow automobile, like Mr. Mortimer Jones, he strolled frigidly into the lounge of the Sherry Island Golf Club—or perhaps, surrounded by an admiring crowd, he gave an exhibition of fancy diving from the springboard of the club raft. . . . Among those who watched him in open-mouthed wonder was Mr. Mortimer Jones.

And one day it came to pass that Mr. Jones—himself and not his ghost—came up to Dexter with tears in his eyes and said that Dexter was the——best caddy in the club, and wouldn't he decide not to quit if Mr. Jones made it worth his while, because every other——caddy in the club lost one ball a hole for him—regularly——

"No, sir," said Dexter decisively, "I don't want to caddy any more." Then, after a pause: "I'm too old."

"You're not more than fourteen. Why the devil did you decide just this morning that you wanted to quit? You promised that next week you'd go over to the state tournament with me."

"I decided I was too old."

Dexter handed in his "A Class" badge, collected what money was due him from the caddy master, and walked home to Black Bear Village.

"The best——caddy I ever saw," shouted Mr. Mortimer Jones over a drink that afternoon. "Never lost a ball! Willing! Intelligent! Quiet! Honest! Grateful!"

fallowness (fal´ ō nis) *n.* inactivity

Reading Strategy
Drawing Conclusions About Characters What conclusions do you draw about Dexter's circumstances and desires based on this description of his "winter dreams"?

 Reading Check
What does Dexter do for pocket money?

❷ **Reading Strategy**
Drawing Conclusions About Characters

- Read the bracketed passage aloud to students. Ask them to paraphrase it.

  Possible response: Dexter fantasizes about becoming wealthy and then using his golf and diving talents to gain status and show off at the golf club.

- Then, ask students the Reading Strategy question on p. 745: What conclusions do you draw about Dexter's circumstances and desires based on this description of his "winter dreams"?
  Answer: Dexter lacks wealth or status but would like to attain both.

❸ ✔ **Reading Check**
Answer: He caddies at the golf club.

CUSTOMIZE INSTRUCTION FOR UNIVERSAL ACCESS

For Special Needs Students	For English Learners
Tell students that there are two groups of people portrayed in this story—the wealthy members of the golf club, and the workers, people like Dexter Green who serve the wealthy. Help students set up a two-column chart to record information about these two groups as they read.	Walk students through the many names—of places, people, cars, and months—included on pp. 744–745. Make sure students know what each name identifies and demonstrate how its correct pronunciation. Then, ask students to name the months of April, October, and November in their home language. Point out these months on a calendar to help students make appropriate seasonal associations with them.

- Direct students to read the bracketed passage. Remind them to consider elements of both direct and indirect characterization as they answer the Literary Analysis question.

- Ask students the Literary Analysis question on p. 746: What methods of characterization does Fitzgerald use in this passage about Judy Jones?

  Answer: He uses indirect characterization, describing Judy through Dexter's perception of her, and direct characterization, describing Judy's physical beauty.

▶ Monitor Progress On the chalkboard, draw a two-column chart like the one shown. Lead students in completing the chart with details from the passage.

Direct	Indirect

❹ The little girl who had done this was eleven—beautifully ugly as little girls are apt to be who are destined after a few years to be inexpressibly lovely and bring no end of misery to a great number of men. The spark, however, was perceptible. There was a general ungodliness in the way her lips twisted down at the corners when she smiled, and in the—Heaven help us!—in the almost passionate quality of her eyes. Vitality is born early in such women. It was utterly in evidence now, shining through her thin frame in a sort of glow.

She had come eagerly out on to the course at nine o'clock with a white linen nurse and five small new golf clubs in a white canvas bag which the nurse was carrying. When Dexter first saw her she was standing by the caddy house, rather ill at ease and trying to conceal the fact by engaging her nurse in an obviously unnatural conversation graced by startling and irrelevant grimaces from herself.

"Well, it's certainly a nice day, Hilda," Dexter heard her say. She drew down the corners of her mouth, smiled, and glanced furtively around, her eyes in transit falling for an instant on Dexter.

Then to the nurse:

"Well, I guess there aren't very many people out here this morning, are there?"

The smile again—radiant, blatantly artificial—convincing.

"I don't know what we're supposed to do now," said the nurse looking nowhere in particular.

"Oh, that's all right. I'll fix it up."

Dexter stood perfectly still, his mouth slightly ajar. He knew that if he moved forward a step his stare would be in her line of vision—if he moved backward he would lose his full view of her face. For a moment he had not realized how young she was. Now he remembered having seen her several times the year before—in bloomers.

Suddenly, involuntarily, he laughed, a short abrupt laugh—then, startled by himself, he turned and began to walk quickly away.

"Boy!"

Dexter stopped.

"Boy——"

Beyond question he was addressed. Not only that, but he was treated to that absurd smile, that preposterous smile—the memory of which at least a dozen men were to carry into middle age.

"Boy, do you know where the golf teacher is?"

"He's giving a lesson."

"Well, do you know where the caddy master is?"

"He isn't here yet this morning."

"Oh." For a moment this baffled her. She stood alternately on her right and left foot.

"We'd like to get a caddy," said the nurse. "Mrs. Mortimer Jones sent us out to play golf, and we don't know how without we get a caddy."

Here she was stopped by an ominous glance from Miss Jones, followed immediately by the smile.

Literary Analysis
Characterization
What methods of characterization does Fitzgerald use in this passage about Judy Jones?

preposterous (prē päs′ tər əs) *adj.* ridiculous

✳ ENRICHMENT: Cultural Connection

The Rising Popularity of Golf

Though golf was once a game played mostly in private clubs reserved for the wealthy and closed to most non-whites, in recent years the game has become more widely accessible and popular in America. As a result, top golfers can now be found among many American cultures and ethnic groups. In 1997, for example, Tiger Woods—whose mother is Southeast Asian and whose father is African American, Native American, and Chinese—won golf's most prestigious prize, the Masters Tournament. At just 21 years of age, Tiger became the youngest Masters champion in history. In the seasons of 2000–2001, Tiger topped this achievement by winning the Masters a second time and becoming the simultaneous titleholder of such major golf tournaments as the U.S. Open, British Open, PGA Championship, and The Players Championship.

In 2001, the world of professional golf saw another significant change in the form of a Supreme Court ruling granting golfer Casey Martin, who has a disability, the right to use a golf cart during competition. Although there are vocal opponents of the Supreme Court's decision, for most observers Martin's case means that athletes with disabilities who are able to complete at an elite level will now be allowed to do so.

"There aren't any caddies here except me," said Dexter to the nurse, "and I got to stay here in charge until the caddy master gets here."

"Oh."

Miss Jones and her retinue now withdrew, and at a proper distance from Dexter became involved in a heated conversation, which was concluded by Miss Jones taking one of the clubs and hitting it on the ground with violence. For further emphasis she raised it again and was about to bring it down smartly upon the nurse's bosom, when the nurse seized the club and twisted it from her hands.

"You little mean old *thing*!" cried Miss Jones wildly.

Another argument ensued. Realizing that the elements of the comedy were implied in the scene, Dexter several times began to laugh, but each time restrained the laugh before it reached audibility. He could not resist the monstrous conviction that the little girl was justified in beating the nurse.

The situation was resolved by the <u>fortuitous</u> appearance of the caddy master, who was appealed to immediately by the nurse.

"Miss Jones is to have a little caddy, and this one says he can't go."

"Mr. McKenna said I was to wait here till you came," said Dexter quickly.

"Well, he's here now." Miss Jones smiled cheerfully at the caddy master. Then she dropped her bag and set off at a haughty mince toward the first tee.

"Well?" The caddy master turned to Dexter.

"What you standing there like a dummy for? Go pick up the young lady's clubs."

"I don't think I'll go out today," said Dexter.

"You don't——"

"I think I'll quit."

The enormity of his decision frightened him. He was a favorite caddy, and the thirty dollars a month he earned through the summer were not to be made elsewhere around the lake. But he had received a strong emotional shock, and his perturbation required a violent and immediate outlet.

It is not so simple as that, either. As so frequently would be the case in the future, Dexter was unconsciously dictated to by his winter dreams.

II

Now, of course, the quality and the seasonability of these winter dreams varied, but the stuff of them remained. They persuaded Dexter several years later to pass up a business course at the State university—his father, prospering now, would have paid his way—for the precarious advantage of attending an older and more famous university in the East, where he was bothered by his scanty funds. But do not get the impression, because his winter dreams happened to be concerned at first with musings on the rich, that there was anything

Literary Analysis
Characterization and Character's Motivation
What motivates Judy Jones's behavior in fighting with her nurse?

fortuitous (fôr tōō′ ə təs) *adj.* fortunate

6 ✓**Reading Check**
What does Dexter do when told to go out and caddy for Miss Jones?

⑤ Literary Analysis
Characterization and Character's Motivation

- Have three students act out the scene described in the bracketed passage in which Dexter observes Judy with her nurse.
- Then, ask students the Literary Analysis question on p. 747: What motivates Judy Jones's behavior in fighting with her nurse?
  Answer: She wants to get her own way and to remind the nurse that she is the boss, despite her youth.

⑥ ✓Reading Check
Answer: He quits his job as a caddy.

CUSTOMIZE INSTRUCTION FOR UNIVERSAL ACCESS		
For Less Proficient Readers	**For English Language Learners**	**For Advanced Students**
Students may find the link between Dexter's "winter dreams" and his behavior on meeting Judy Jones unclear. Review the paraphrases generated in response to the Reading Strategy question on p. 745. Then, help students summarize Dexter's meeting with Judy. Explain that Dexter doesn't want Judy to view him as a servant.	Point out the link between Dexter's "winter dreams" (described on p. 745) and his covetous perception of Judy. Note the adjectives, for example "brilliant" and "glow," that Fitzgerald uses to describe both. Explain that these words share similar connotations. Have students look for additional examples of this connection as they read.	Challenge students to draw on their knowledge of F. Scott Fitzgerald's life to link his hopes and dreams with those of Dexter Green. Fitzgerald, too, came from a modest background but aspired to wealth and glamour. Given this similarity, how do students think Fitzgerald wanted readers to feel about Dexter?

Art

Golf Course–California 1917, by George Wesley Bellows

This picture is a lithograph—an image printed from an inked stone or metal plate. It depicts a golf course much like the one where Dexter and Judy meet in the story. George Wesley Bellows was known for both lithography and painting, especially of sports and action scenes. A serious amateur athlete, Bellows had intimate knowledge of these activities. This image, like a photograph, captures the energy and motion of a golf game in mid-play.

Use these questions for discussion:

1. What do the people depicted here suggest about the manners and expectations of Fitzgerald's characters?
   Answer: They are dressed in almost uniformlike clothing, suggesting a "club" that only some can enter. They appear to be moving slowly and gently, as if they have few cares.
2. How does the golf club and its members depicted here compare with your image of Dexter and Judy at their golf club?
   Answer: Students may say that they envisioned the course as more densely covered in trees making the people less visible to one another.

8 ▶ Critical Viewing

Answer: Students may note that in this private and privileged setting, Dexter would see Judy as somewhat unattainable and more attractive.

7

merely snobbish in the boy. He wanted not association with glittering things and glittering people—he wanted the glittering things themselves. Often he reached out for the best without knowing why he wanted it—and sometimes he ran up against the mysterious denials and prohibitions in which life indulges. It is with one of those denials and not with his career as a whole that this story deals.

He made money. It was rather amazing. After college he went to the city from which Black Bear Lake draws its wealthy patrons. When he was only twenty-three and had been there not quite two years, there were already people who liked to say: "Now *there's* a boy—" All about him rich men's sons were peddling bonds precariously, or investing patrimonies precariously, or plodding through the two dozen volumes of the "George Washington Commercial Course," but Dexter borrowed a thousand dollars on his college degree and his confident mouth, and bought a partnership in a laundry.

It was a small laundry when he went into it, but Dexter made a specialty of learning how the English washed fine woolen golf stockings without shrinking them, and within a year he was catering to the trade that wore knickerbockers. Men were insisting that their Shetland hose and sweaters go to his laundry, just as they had insisted on a caddy who could find golf balls. A little later he was doing their wives' lingerie as well—and running five branches in different parts of the city. Before he was twenty-seven he owned the largest string of laundries in his section of the country. It was then that he sold out and went to New York. But the part of his story that concerns us goes back to the days when he was making his first big success.

When he was twenty-three Mr. Hart—one of the gray-haired men who like to say "Now there's a boy"—gave him a guest card to the Sherry Island Golf Club for a weekend. So he signed his name one day on the register, and that afternoon played golf in a foursome with Mr. Hart and Mr. Sandwood and Mr. T. A. Hedrick. He did not consider it necessary to remark that he had once carried Mr. Hart's bag over this same links, and that he knew every trap and gully with his eyes shut—but he found himself glancing at the four caddies who trailed them, trying to catch a gleam or gesture that would remind him of himself, that would lessen the gap which lay between his present and his past.

It was a curious day, slashed abruptly with fleeting, familiar impressions. One minute he had the sense of being a trespasser—in the next he was impressed by the tremendous superiority he felt toward Mr. T. A. Hedrick, who was a bore and not even a good golfer any more.

8 ▲ Critical Viewing
Golf was once a game reserved for the wealthy. It is on a golf course like the one in this painting that Dexter meets Judy for the first time. How might this setting have affected Dexter's perception of Judy? **[Analyze]**

✷ ENRICHMENT: Career Connections

Job Search	Costume Design
Review with students the characteristics associated with Judy—vital, beautiful, athletic, superficial, flirtatious, charming, greedy, self-centered. Encourage students to brainstorm for ways that her character and physical qualities could serve Judy in the workplace. For what jobs might she be suited and why? Have students examine the employment ads in a local newspaper or online source to see if they can find a match.	Dexter believes that by donning the costume of the privileged class, he will be able to join it. Film and theatrical costume designers develop clothing that enables an actor to enter the life and cultural setting of a character. Have interested students read about costume design. Then, invite students to apply costume-design methods to create costumes appropriate to several subgroups in contemporary American culture.

Golf Course–California, 1917, George Wesley Bellows, Cincinnati Art Museum

Then, because of a ball Mr. Hart lost near the fifteenth green, an enormous thing happened. While they were searching the stiff grasses of the rough there was a clear call of "Fore!" from behind a hill in their rear. And as they all turned abruptly from their search a bright new ball sliced abruptly over the hill and caught Mr. T. A. Hedrick in the abdomen.

"By Gad!" cried Mr. T. A. Hedrick, "they ought to put some of these crazy women off the course. It's getting to be outrageous."

A head and a voice came up together over the hill:

"Do you mind if we go through?"

"You hit me in the stomach!" declared Mr. Hedrick wildly.

"Did I?" The girl approached the group of men. "I'm sorry. I yelled 'Fore!' "

Her glance fell casually on each of the men—then scanned the fairway for her ball.

"Did I bounce into the rough?"

It was impossible to determine whether this question was ingenuous or malicious. In a moment, however, she left no doubt, for as her partner came up over the hill she called cheerfully:

"Here I am! I'd have gone on the green except that I hit something."

As she took her stance for a short mashie shot, Dexter looked at her closely. She wore a blue gingham dress, rimmed at throat and shoulders with a white edging that accentuated her tan. The quality of exaggeration, of thinness, which had made her passionate eyes and down-turning mouth absurd at eleven, was gone now. She was arrestingly beautiful. The color in her cheeks was centered like the color in a picture—it was not a "high" color, but a sort of fluctuating and feverish warmth, so shaded that it seemed at any moment it would recede and disappear. This color and the mobility of her mouth gave a continual impression of flux, of intense life, of passionate vitality—balanced only partially by the sad luxury of her eyes.

She swung her mashie impatiently and without interest, pitching the ball into a sand pit on the other side of the green. With a quick, insincere smile and a careless "Thank you!" she went on after it.

"That Judy Jones!" remarked Mr. Hedrick on the next tee, as they waited—some moments—for her to play on ahead. "All she needs is to be turned up and spanked for six months and then to be married off to an old-fashioned cavalry captain."

"My God, she's good looking!" said Mr. Sandwood, who was just over thirty.

9

Reading Strategy
Drawing Conclusions About Characters What does Judy's behavior toward the men on the golf course suggest about her character?

10 ☑ **Reading Check**

What "enormous thing" happens near the fifteenth green?

Winter Dreams ◆ 749

---

9 Reading Strategy
Drawing Conclusions About Characters

- Call on a volunteer to read the bracketed passage aloud. Then, help students hear the call ons and careless tone in Judy's voice when she speaks.

▶ **Monitor Progress** Ask students the Reading Strategy question on p. 749: What does Judy's behavior toward the men on the golf course suggest about her character? Answer: It suggests that she is selfish and self-centered, oblivious to other people's concerns. Judy apparently sees herself as entitled to this selfish attitude.

10 ☑ **Reading Check**

Answer: Judy hits another golfer with a ball, but she appears not to care. For Dexter, the "enormous thing" is his seeing Judy Jones again.

CUSTOMIZE INSTRUCTION FOR UNIVERSAL ACCESS

For Less Proficient Readers

Review the Build Grammar Skills lesson on Dashes in **Selection Support**, p. 183 with students. Then, work with them to clarify sentences on pp. 748–749, in which Fitzgerald uses dashes to insert asides or draw attention. For example, you might note the sentence: "Her glance fell casually on each of the men—then scanned the fairway for her ball." Discuss Fitzgerald's use of the dash to emphasize an aspect of Judy's character. By creating a dramatic pause, the dash indicates Judy's perusal of each man as a possible audience for her charms. When she finds each lacking, she moves on.

For English Learners

Fitzgerald's creative sentence structure, especially his use of dashes, will likely challenge students. Urge students to read the story in manageable chunks, rephrasing difficult sentences for clarification. You may want to break the story into the numbered sections the author has already provided.

- Discuss with students what each man says about Judy in the bracketed passage.

- Ask students the Literary Analysis questions on p. 750: What information about Judy Jones does Fitzgerald provide in this discussion among the golfers? **Answer:** She's good looking, she's immature, she's a pretty good golfer but she doesn't work at it, she has a nice figure, she's a flirt.

▶ Monitor Progress Ask students to identify whether these details about Judy's character are examples of direct or indirect characterization.
Answer: This information is conveyed through the use of dialogue. Therefore, it represents examples of indirect Characterization.

"Good looking!" cried Mr. Hedrick contemptuously, "she always looks as if she wanted to be kissed! Turning those big coweyes on every calf in town!"

⑪ It was doubtful if Mr. Hedrick intended a reference to the maternal instinct.

"She'd play pretty good golf if she'd try," said Mr. Sandwood.

"She has no form," said Mr. Hedrick solemnly.

"She has a nice figure," said Mr. Sandwood.

"Better thank the Lord she doesn't drive a swifter ball," said Mr. Hart, winking at Dexter.

Later in the afternoon the sun went down with a riotous swirl of gold and varying blues and scarlets, and left the dry, rustling night of Western summer. Dexter watched from the veranda of the golf club, watched the even overlap of the waters in the little wind, silver molasses under the harvest moon. Then the moon held a finger to her lips and the lake became a clear pool, pale and quiet. Dexter put on his bathing suit and swam out to the farthest raft, where he stretched dripping on the wet canvas of the springboard.

There was a fish jumping and a star shining and the lights around the lake were gleaming. Over on a dark peninsula a piano was playing the songs of last summer and of summers before that—songs from *Chin-Chin* and *The Count of Luxemburg* and *The Chocolate Soldier*[2]— and because the sound of a piano over a stretch of water had always seemed beautiful to Dexter he lay perfectly quiet and listened.

The tune the piano was playing at that moment had been gay and new five years before when Dexter was a sophomore at college. They had played it at a prom once when he could not afford the luxury of proms, and he had stood outside the gymnasium and listened. The sound of the tune precipitated in him a sort of ecstasy and it was with that ecstasy he viewed what happened to him now. It was a mood of intense appreciation, a sense that, for once, he was magnificently attuned to life and that everything about him was radiating a brightness and a glamor he might never know again.

A low, pale oblong detached itself suddenly from the darkness of the Island, spitting forth the reverberate sound of a racing motorboat. Two white streamers of cleft water rolled themselves out behind it and almost immediately the boat was beside him, drowning out the hot tinkle of the piano in the drone of its spray. Dexter raising himself on his arms was aware of a figure standing at the wheel, of two dark eyes regarding him over the lengthening space of water—then the boat had gone by and was sweeping in an immense and purposeless circle of spray round and round in the middle of the lake. With equal eccentricity one of the circles flattened out and headed back toward the raft.

"Who's that?" she called, shutting off her motor. She was so near now that Dexter could see her bathing suit, which consisted apparently of pink rompers.

---

2. ***Chin-Chin . . . The Chocolate Soldier*** popular operettas of the time.

☀ ENRICHMENT: Community Connection

Sports Venues

Point out to students that the golf course featured in Dexter's story is a significant physical element in the community. A typical golf course has 18 holes that require walking 7,000 yards (70 football fields) to complete. Most courses are carefully landscaped and may even incorporate natural features such as ponds, streams, or woods. Because they require intensive chemical upkeep to maintain, golf courses sometimes generate ecological problems for the water supplies or wetland areas of surrounding communities. This can cause conflict between golf course owners and residents. Ask students to identify some sports venues—either indoor or outdoor—in your community. How do these facilities affect the community? Have these venues generate any conflicts or controversies? Urge students to consider issues of business activity, traffic flow and parking, visitor density, and the ecological and visual impact of the venues.

The nose of the boat bumped the raft, and as the latter tilted rakishly he was precipitated toward her. With different degrees of interest they recognized each other.

"Aren't you one of those men we played through this afternoon?" she demanded.

He was.

"Well, do you know how to drive a motorboat? Because if you do I wish you'd drive this one so I can ride on the surfboard behind. My name is Judy Jones"—she favored him with an absurd smirk—rather, what tried to be a smirk, for, twist her mouth as she might, it was not grotesque, it was merely beautiful—"and I live in a house over there on the Island, and in that house there is a man waiting for me. When he drove up at the door I drove out of the dock because he says I'm his ideal."

There was a fish jumping and a star shining and the lights around the lake were gleaming. Dexter sat beside Judy Jones and she explained how her boat was driven. Then she was in the water, swimming to the floating surfboard with a <u>sinuous</u> crawl. Watching her was without effort to the eye, watching a branch waving or a sea gull flying. Her arms, burned to butternut, moved sinuously among the dull platinum ripples, elbow appearing first, casting the forearm back with a cadence of falling water, then reaching out and down, stabbing a path ahead.

They moved out into the lake; turning, Dexter saw that she was kneeling on the low rear of the now uptilted surfboard.

"Go faster," she called, "fast as it'll go."

Obediently he jammed the lever forward and the white spray mounted at the bow. When he looked around again the girl was standing up on the rushing board, her arms spread wide, her eyes lifted toward the moon.

"It's awful cold," she shouted. "What's your name?"

He told her.

"Well, why don't you come to dinner tomorrow night?"

His heart turned over like the flywheel of the boat, and, for the second time, her casual whim gave a new direction to his life.

III

Next evening while he waited for her to come downstairs, Dexter peopled the soft deep summer room and the sun porch that opened from it with the men who had already loved Judy Jones. He knew the sort of men they were—the men who when he first went to college had entered from the great prep schools with graceful clothes and the deep tan of healthy summers. He had seen that, in one sense, he was better than these men. He was newer and stronger. Yet in acknowledging to himself that he wished his children to be like them he was admitting that he was but the rough, strong stuff from which they eternally sprang.

Literary Analysis
Characterization and Characters' Motivations
What motivates Judy Jones to get in her boat and approach Dexter?

sinuous (sin′ yōō əs) *adj.* moving in and out; wavy

⓭ ✔**Reading Check**
Where is Dexter when he meets Judy Jones for the third time?

⓬ **Literary Analysis**

Characterization and Characters' Motivations

- After students read the bracketed passage, direct their attention to the description of Judy's smirk. Discuss what such an expression might suggest about Judy's attitude.

  Answer: It suggests a dismissiveness, almost a contempt, on her part.

- Then, ask students the Literary Analysis question on p. 751: What motivates Judy Jones to get in her boat and approach Dexter? Urge students to carefully read the last sentence of the bracketed text before answering.

  Answer: She wants to get away from a man at her house. He has complimented her too much and made himself seem too easy, too accessible.

⓭ ✔**Reading Check**

Answer: He is relaxing on a raft in the lake next to the golf club.

CUSTOMIZE INSTRUCTION FOR UNIVERSAL ACCESS

For Special Needs Students	For Less Proficient Readers	For English Learners
A story of this length may challenge the capacity of students to sustain interest over its course. One way to help students meet this challenge is to have them note the importance of the section breaks inserted by the author. Tell students that each break provides a place to pause and reflect on what has passed so far in the story.	Less proficient readers may find the abrupt time shifts in this long story quite confusing. Suggest that they use a timeline to chart the story's events in the sequence in which they occur. If they wish, students can divide their timeline into sections according to those inserted by the author.	Draw students' attention to the time shift that occurs in Part II. Point out that the events described here take place many years after Dexter's caddying job. Have students note the time shifts on a timeline or sequential record.

- Read the bracketed passage aloud to students. Ask them to summarize the information they learn.

- Then, ask students what the information about Dexter's mother's name and her speaking broken English means.
  Answer: Explain that Dexter's reference to his mother's name acknowledges his family's origins in Eastern Europe. His mother spoke broken English because it was not her first language.

15 Literary Analysis

Characterization

- Have students read the bracketed passage, taking brief notes about Judy's behavior and apparent feelings. Then, ask them how Dexter reacts to Judy.
  Possible response: Judy speaks petulantly, sulks moodily, smiles in a forced manner. She seems unhappy. Dexter reacts with concern and anxiety, but he is also fascinated by her.

- Ask students the Literary Analysis question on p. 752 What does this description reveal about Dexter's and Judy's relationship?
  Possible response: It reveals a one-sided relationship in which Judy's emotional state sets the tone and Dexter is constantly worried that he will not measure up.

14 When the time had come for him to wear good clothes, he had known who were the best tailors in America, and the best tailors in America had made him the suit he wore this evening. He had acquired that particular reserve peculiar to his university, that set it off from other universities. He recognized the value to him of such a mannerism and he had adopted it; he knew that to be careless in dress and manner required more confidence than to be careful. But carelessness was for his children. His mother's name had been Krimelich. She was a Bohemian of the peasant class and she had talked broken English to the end of her days. Her son must keep to the set patterns.

At a little after seven Judy Jones came downstairs. She wore a blue silk afternoon dress, and he was disappointed at first that she had not put on something more elaborate. This feeling was accentuated when, after a brief greeting, she went to the door of a butler's pantry and pushing it open called: "You can serve dinner, Martha." He had rather expected that a butler would announce dinner, that there would be a cocktail. Then he put these thoughts behind him as they sat down side by side on a lounge and looked at each other.

"Father and mother won't be here," she said thoughtfully.

He remembered the last time he had seen her father, and he was glad the parents were not to be here tonight—they might wonder who he was. He had been born in Keeble, a Minnesota village fifty miles farther north, and he always gave Keeble as his home instead of Black Bear Village. Country towns were well enough to come from if they weren't inconveniently in sight and used as footstools by fashionable lakes.

They talked of his university, which she had visited frequently during the past two years, and of the nearby city which supplied Sherry Island with its patrons, and whither Dexter would return next day to his prospering laundries.

15 During dinner she slipped into a moody depression which gave Dexter a feeling of uneasiness. Whatever petulance she uttered in her throaty voice worried him. Whatever she smiled at—at him, at a chicken liver, at nothing—it disturbed him that her smile could have no root in mirth, or even in amusement. When the scarlet corners of her lips curved down, it was less a smile than an invitation to a kiss.

Then, after dinner, she led him out on the dark sun porch and deliberately changed the atmosphere.

"Do you mind if I weep a little?" she said.

"I'm afraid I'm boring you," he responded quickly.

"You're not. I like you. But I've just had a terrible afternoon. There was a man I cared about, and this afternoon he told me out of a clear sky that he was poor as a church mouse. He'd never even hinted it before. Does this sound horribly <u>mundane</u>?"

"Perhaps he was afraid to tell you."

"Suppose he was," she answered. "He didn't start right. You see, if I'd thought of him as poor—well, I've been mad about loads of poor men, and fully intended to marry them all. But in this case, I hadn't thought of him that way, and my interest in him wasn't strong

752 ◆ *Disillusion, Defiance, and Discontent (1914–1946)*

Literary Analysis
Characterization What does this description reveal about Dexter's and Judy's relationship?

mundane (mun dān´) *adj.* commonplace; ordinary

⚙ **ENRICHMENT: Science Connection**

The Anatomy of Emotion

As Dexter reacts to Judy Jones's vacillating interest and personal charms, his emotions control his body. Emotions, while they arise from the brain, are associated with the heart. In fact, the heart and other physical elements change in response to emotion. Feelings of love, for example, may result in a faster heart rate, sweaty palms, weak knees, and loss of concentration.

Tell students that as the story progresses and Dexter begins to question his attachment to Judy, his reason battles with his emotions. Reason and

decision making are governed by the cerebrum, the largest part of the human brain. The cerebrum has two parts known as the left brain and the right brain, each of which controls the opposite side of the body. Scientists now believe there are important contrasts between the right and left brains of men and women, which contribute to differences in behavior.

Have students use this information to analyze Dexter's reactions to and decisions about Judy.

enough to survive the shock. As if a girl calmly informed her fiancè that she was a widow. He might not object to widows, but——

"Let's start right," she interrupted herself suddenly. "Who are you, anyhow?"

For a moment Dexter hesitated. Then:

"I'm nobody," he announced. "My career is largely a matter of futures."

"Are you poor?"

"No," he said frankly, "I'm probably making more money than any man my age in the Northwest. I know that's an obnoxious remark, but you advised me to start right."

There was a pause. Then she smiled and the corners of her mouth drooped and an almost imperceptible sway brought her closer to him, looking up into his eyes. A lump rose in Dexter's throat, and he waited breathless for the experiment, facing the unpredictable compound that would form mysteriously from the elements of their lips. Then he saw—she communicated her excitement to him, lavishly, deeply, with kisses that were not a promise but a fulfillment. They aroused in him not hunger demanding renewal but surfeit that would demand more surfeit . . . kisses that were like charity, creating want by holding back nothing at all.

It did not take him many hours to decide that he had wanted Judy Jones ever since he was a proud, desirous little boy.

IV

It began like that—and continued, with varying shades of intensity, on such a note right up to the denouement. Dexter surrendered a part of himself to the most direct and unprincipled personality with which he had ever come in contact. Whatever Judy wanted, she went after with the full pressure of her charm. There was no divergence of method, no jockeying for position or premeditation of effects—there was a very little mental side to any of her affairs. She simply made men conscious to the highest degree of her physical loveliness. Dexter had no desire to change her. Her deficiencies were knit up with a passionate energy that transcended and justified them.

When, as Judy's head lay against his shoulder that first night, she whispered, "I don't know what's the matter with me. Last night I thought I was in love with a man and tonight I think I'm in love with you——" it seemed to him a beautiful and romantic thing to say. It was the exquisite excitability that for the moment he controlled and owned. But a week later he was compelled to view this same quality in a different light. She took him in her roadster to a picnic supper, and after supper she disappeared, likewise in her roadster, with another man. Dexter became enormously upset and was scarcely able to be decently civil to the other people present. When she assured him that she had not kissed the other man, he knew she was lying— yet he was glad that she had taken the trouble to lie to him.

Literary Analysis
Characterization What does this conversation reveal about the characters of Dexter and Judy?

Literary Analysis
Characterization and Character's Motivation Why is Dexter so willing to accept Judy's lies?

Reading Check
Where do Dexter and Judy have dinner?

16 Literary Analysis

Characterization

- Invite two students to read aloud the conversation between Dexter and Judy, with you speaking the narrator's text. Ask students to explain their reactions to the characters as Fitzgerald portrays them here.

  Possible response: Students will likely react with sympathy for Dexter, and with criticism for Judy's callowness.

- Ask students the Literary Analysis question on p. 753 What does this conversation reveal about the characters of Dexter and Judy?

  Answer: Dexter is basically honest, sympathetic, and eager to be accepted. Judy is superficial, petty, and coy, but also frank and direct.

17 Literary Analysis

Characterization and Character's Motivation

- Ask students if they have ever wished someone would lie to them, perhaps to avoid facing an unpleasant truth.

- Invite a volunteer to read the bracketed text aloud. Have students think about why Dexter might be glad that Judy "had taken the trouble to lie to him."

- Then, ask the Literary Analysis question on p. 753 Why is Dexter so willing to accept Judy's lies?

  Answer: He wants to believe that Judy cares about him enough to protect his feelings.

18 Reading Check

Answer: They have dinner at Judy's house.

CUSTOMIZE INSTRUCTION FOR UNIVERSAL ACCESS

For Special Needs Students	For English Learners	For Advanced Readers
To help students create a word picture of Judy Jones, work with them to pare Dexter's descriptions of her appearance and behavior down to a few essential words. Model this process with the description that begins Section IV. Using these word lists, lead students to see that Judy is inconsistent, indifferent, and insensitive.	Explain that *denouement* p. 753 is a French word that literally means "untying" but used to refer to the final outcome or resolution of a situation. The word has been absorbed into English with its original French spelling intact. Invite any French speakers in the class to pronounce the word and use it in a French sentence.	Have students look up the word *mundane*, which Judy uses to describe her reaction to a suitor's poverty. Discuss the word's connotations with students. Then, ask students to speculate about what effect Fitzgerald was trying to achieve by having Judy use this word. What image of herself is she trying to convey to Dexter?

⓳ Background

Art

The Morning Sun 1920, by Pauline Palmer

This painting shows a young woman much like Judy Jones contemplating herself in the mirror. The artist, Pauline Palmer, was a first-generation American born to German and French parents. She studied in Chicago and Paris, where she became interested in the soft brush-work of Impressionism. Although Palmer is relatively unknown today, in her time she was hugely popular with both critics and collectors.

The Morning Sun is typical of Plamer's work, capturing mood and emotion through the use of light and color.

Use these questions for discussion:

1. If this portrait were of Judy Jones, what might the young woman be thinking at this moment?
Answer: Judy would likely be thinking about a dress or a man—her thoughts would not be analytical or introspective.

2. How does this painting reflect the privileged world in which Judy Jones lives?
Answer: The room is furnished with delicate fabrics and decorative objects. The woman wears impractical clothing, as if for a day of lounging and leisure.

⓴ ▶Critical Viewing

Answer: The painting would show the woman's full face and more movement. It might also depict her interacting with others.

He was, as he found before the summer ended, one of a varying dozen who circulated about her. Each of them had at one time been favored above all others—about half of them still basked in the solace of occasional sentimental revivals. Whenever one showed signs of dropping out through long neglect, she granted him a brief honeyed hour, which encouraged him to tag along for a year or so longer. Judy made these forays upon the helpless and defeated without malice, indeed half unconscious that there was anything mischievous in what she did.

When a new man came to town everyone dropped out—dates were automatically canceled.

The helpless part of trying to do anything about it was that she did it all herself. She was not a girl who could be "won" in the kinetic sense—she was proof against cleverness, she was proof against charm; if any of these assailed her too strongly she would immediately resolve the affair to a physical basis, and under the magic of her physical splendor the strong as well as the brilliant played her game and not their own. She was entertained only by the gratification of her desires and by the direct exercise of her own charm. Perhaps from so much youthful love, so many youthful lovers, she had come, in self-defense, to nourish herself wholly from within.

Succeeding Dexter's first exhilaration came restlessness and dissatisfaction. The helpless ecstasy of losing himself in her was opiate rather than tonic. It was fortunate for his work during the winter that those moments of ecstasy came infrequently. Early in their acquaintance it had seemed for a while that there was a deep and spontaneous mutual attraction—that first August, for example—three days of long evenings on her dusky veranda, of strange wan kisses through the late afternoon, in shadowy alcoves or behind the protecting trellises of the garden arbors, of mornings when she was fresh as a dream and almost shy at meeting him in the clarity of the rising day. There was all the ecstasy of an engagement about it, sharpened by his realization that there was no engagement. It was during those three days that, for the first time, he had asked her to marry him. She said "maybe some day," she said "kiss me," she said, "I'd like to marry you," she said "I love you"—she said—nothing.

The three days were interrupted by the arrival of a New York man who visited at her house for half September. To Dexter's agony, rumor engaged them. The man was the son of the president of a great trust company. But at

⓴ ▼Critical Viewing
The mood of this painting is serene. How might this portrait be different if the artist were striving to communicate Judy Jones's energy and magnetic beauty? **[Modify]**

The Morning Sun, © 1920, Pauline Palmer, Rockford Art Museum

754 ◆ *Disillusion, Defiance, and Discontent (1914–1946)*

✹ ENRICHMENT: Communications Connection

The Grapevine

Because Judy's suitors are obsessed by her, they continually "report" her actions to each other. Even if the information is true, remind students that this method of communication may be considered gossip and could have potentially dangerous results.

Ask students to consider how news and information travel through communities large and small. Beyond the formal channels of television, radio, and print journalism, community leaders such as school principals, police personnel, and the clergy can also distribute news. Point out that students get only a small percentage of their information through such official sources. Students may get their news in the halls between classes or in the other free time they spend with friends.

Link the discussion to the story by asking how Dexter feels about hearing that Judy dates several men. Would he have felt differently if he had *seen* newspaper photos of Judy with the many other men in her life?

754

the end of a month it was reported that Judy was yawning. At a dance one night she sat all evening in a motorboat with a local beau, while the New Yorker searched the club for her frantically. She told the local beau that she was bored with her visitor, and two days later he left. She was seen with him at the station, and it was reported that he looked very mournful indeed.

On this note the summer ended. Dexter was twenty-four, and he found himself increasingly in a position to do as he wished. He joined two clubs in the city and lived at one of them. Though he was by no means an integral part of the stag lines at these clubs, he managed to be on hand at dances where Judy Jones was likely to appear. He could have gone out socially as much as he liked—he was an eligible young man, now, and popular with downtown fathers. His confessed devotion to Judy Jones had rather solidified his position. But he had no social aspirations and rather despised the dancing men who were always on tap for the Thursday or Saturday parties and who filled in at dinners with the younger married set. Already he was playing with the idea of going East to New York. He wanted to take Judy Jones with him. No disillusion as to the world in which she had grown up could cure his illusion as to her desirability.

Remember that—for only in the light of it can what he did for her be understood.

Eighteen months after he first met Judy Jones he became engaged to another girl. Her name was Irene Scheerer, and her father was one of the men who had always believed in Dexter. Irene was light-haired and sweet and honorable, and a little stout, and she had two suitors whom she pleasantly relinquished when Dexter formally asked her to marry him.

Summer, fall, winter, spring, another summer, another fall—so much he had given of his active life to the incorrigible lips of Judy Jones. She had treated him with interest, with encouragement, with malice, with indifference, with contempt. She had inflicted on him the innumerable little slights and indignities possible in such a case—as if in revenge for having ever cared for him at all. She had beckoned him and yawned at him and beckoned him again and he had responded often with bitterness and narrowed eyes. She had brought him ecstatic happiness and intolerable agony of spirit. She had caused him untold inconvenience and not a little trouble. She had insulted him, and she had ridden over him, and she had played his interest in her against his interest in his work—for fun. She had done everything to him except to criticize him—this she had not done—it seemed to him only because it might have sullied the utter indifference she manifested and sincerely felt toward him.

When autumn had come and gone again it occurred to him that he could not have Judy Jones. He had to beat this into his mind but he convinced himself at last. He lay awake at night for a while and argued it over. He told himself the trouble and the pain she had caused him, he enumerated her glaring deficiencies as a wife. Then he said to himself that he loved her, and after a while he fell asleep. For a week,

Literary Analysis
Characterization What do Judy Jones's varying responses to Dexter's marriage proposals reveal about her feelings for him?

22 Reading Check
Does Judy have more than one suitor? Explain.

---

21 Literary Analysis
Characterization

- Have students read the bracketed text aloud. Then, ask them to list the several responses Judy makes to Dexter's proposals. Point out the quotation marks that indicate Judy's words.
  Answer: She says "maybe some day," "kiss me," "I'd like to marry you," and "I love you."

▶ **Monitor Progress** Ask students the Literary Analysis question on p. 755: What do Judy Jones's varying responses to Dexter's marriage proposals reveal about her feelings for him?
Possible response: They reveal that her feelings change continually, probably as a result of how much control she's feeling over him at that moment. Her responses may also reveal that she's intentionally manipulating him or that she's flighty and doesn't know her own feelings.

22 ✔Reading Check
Answer: Yes, she has several suitors. Dexter is merely one of them.

CUSTOMIZE INSTRUCTION FOR UNIVERSAL ACCESS

For Less Proficient Readers	For English Learners	For Gifted/Talented Students
Have students create a chronology of Dexter's and Judy's relationship. Lead students in constructing the following order: Dexter and Judy meet while he is a caddy (ages 14 and 11); they meet again on the golf course (ages 23 and 20); they date for 18 months; Dexter becomes engaged to Irene Scheerer (age 25).	Review with students English words related to the passage of time. For example, clarify the difference between days, months, and seasons. Encourage students to keep careful track of when various events take place for Dexter and Judy, perhaps adding to the time line they began earlier.	Help these students to appreciate the depth of Dexter's tumult. Despite having renounced Judy in favor of sturdy Irene Scheerer, Dexter remains painfully entranced by Judy. Challenge students to look back and read forward to find other examples of Dexter's doomed struggle to stop wanting Judy Jones.

lest he imagined her husky voice over the telephone or her eyes opposite him at lunch, he worked hard and late, and at night he went to his office and plotted out his years.

At the end of a week he went to a dance and cut in on her once. For almost the first time since they had met he did not ask her to sit out with him or tell her that she was lovely. It hurt him that she did not miss these things—that was all. He was not jealous when he saw that there was a new man tonight. He had been hardened against jealousy long before.

24 He stayed late at the dance. He sat for an hour with Irene Scheerer and talked about books and about music. He knew very little about either. But he was beginning to be master of his own time now, and he had a rather priggish[3] notion that he—the young and already fabulously successful Dexter Green—should know more about such things.

That was in October, when he was twenty-five. In January, Dexter and Irene became engaged. It was to be announced in June, and they were to be married three months later.

The Minnesota winter prolonged itself interminably, and it was almost May when the winds came soft and the snow ran down into Black Bear Lake at last. For the first time in over a year Dexter was enjoying a certain tranquility of spirit. Judy Jones had been in Florida, and afterward in Hot Springs, and somewhere she had been engaged, and somewhere she had broken it off. At first, when Dexter had definitely given her up, it had made him sad that people still linked them together and asked for news of her, but when he began to be placed at dinner next to Irene Scheerer people didn't ask him about her any more—they told him about her. He ceased to be an authority on her.

May at last. Dexter walked the streets at night when the darkness was damp as rain, wondering that so soon, with so little done, so much of ecstasy had gone from him. May one year back had been marked by Judy's poignant, unforgivable, yet forgiven turbulence—it had been one of those rare times when he fancied she had grown to care for him. That old penny's worth of happiness he had spent for this bushel of content. He knew that Irene would be no more than a curtain spread behind him, a hand moving among gleaming teacups, a voice calling to children . . . fire and loveliness were gone, the magic of nights and the wonder of the varying hours and seasons . . . slender lips, down-turning, dropping to his lips and bearing him up into a heaven of eyes . . . The thing was deep in him. He was too strong and alive for it to die lightly.

In the middle of May when the weather balanced for a few days on the thin bridge that led to deep summer he turned in one night

---

3. **priggish** (prig´ gish) *adj.* excessively proper and smug.

at Irene's house. Their engagement was to be announced in a week now—no one would be surprised at it. And tonight they would sit together on the lounge at the University Club and look on for an hour at the dancers. It gave him a sense of solidity to go with her—she was so sturdily popular, so intensely "great."

He mounted the steps of the brownstone house and stepped inside. "Irene," he called.

Mrs. Scheerer came out of the living room to meet him.

"Dexter," she said, "Irene's gone upstairs with a splitting headache. She wanted to go with you but I made her go to bed."

"Nothing serious, I——"

"Oh, no. She's going to play golf with you in the morning. You can spare her for just one night, can't you, Dexter?"

Her smile was kind. She and Dexter liked each other. In the living room he talked for a moment before he said good night.

Returning to the University Club, where he had rooms, he stood in the doorway for a moment and watched the dancers. He leaned against the doorpost, nodded at a man or two—yawned.

"Hello, darling."

The familiar voice at his elbow startled him. Judy Jones had left a man and crossed the room to him—Judy Jones, a slender enameled doll in cloth of gold: gold in a band at her head, gold in two slipper points at her dress's hem. The fragile glow of her face seemed to blossom as she smiled at him. A breeze of warmth and light blew through the room. His hands in the pockets of his dinner jacket tightened spasmodically. He was filled with a sudden excitement.

"When did you get back?" he asked casually.

"Come here and I'll tell you about it."

She turned and he followed her. She had been away—he could have wept at the wonder of her return. She had passed through enchanted streets, doing things that were like provocative music. All mysterious happenings, all fresh and quickening hopes, had gone away with her, come back with her now.

She turned in the doorway.

"Have you a car here? If you haven't, I have."

"I have a coupé."

In then, with a rustle of golden cloth. He slammed the door. Into so many cars she had stepped—like this—like that—her back against the leather, so—her elbow resting on the door—waiting. She would have been soiled long since had there been anything to soil her—except herself—but this was her own self outpouring.

With an effort he forced himself to start the car and back into the street. This was nothing, he must remember. She had done this before, and he had put her behind him, as he would have crossed a bad account from his books.

He drove slowly downtown and, affecting abstraction, traversed the deserted streets of the business section, peopled here and there where a movie was giving out its crowd or where consumptive or

Reading Strategy
Drawing Conclusions About Characters What conclusions about Dexter's feelings for Irene do you draw from this description of "a sense of solidity"?

Reading Check
What is Dexter's relationship to Irene Scheerer?

Reading Strategy
Drawing Conclusions About Characters

- Read the bracketed text aloud to students, striving to infuse it with Dexter's longing and sadness. Ask students to list the things Dexter describes losing.
  Answer: He describes losing fire, loveliness, magic, wonder, slender lips, a heaven of eyes.

- Ask students the Reading Strategy question on p. 757: What conclusions about Dexter's feelings for Irene do you draw from this description of a "sense of solidity"?
  Answer: His feelings for Irene are not romantic. He sees her as a practical choice for a wife—reliable and trustworthy, but not exciting.

Reading Check

Answer: Dexter and Irene are going to announce their engagement in a week.

CUSTOMIZE INSTRUCTION FOR UNIVERSAL ACCESS

For English Learners

Point out to students the sentence "That old penny's worth of happiness he had spent for this bushel of content." Help students identify the meaning of unfamiliar words. For example, confirm their understanding that a penny is a minute monetary unit. Explain too that a bushel is a measure of weight usually reserved for measuring fruit or vegetables. It is a fairly large quantity when compared to what a penny would buy. With this explanation, help students understand that Dexter has traded a tiny moment of real happiness—with Judy—for a much larger quantity of contentment—with Irene. To emphasize the comparison, help students rank the degree of meaning in "happiness" and "content." Lead them to see that happiness is a much stronger emotion or state than is contentment. Make sure students understand that Dexter feels he has settled for a practical life rather than a passionate one.

- Have students describe Judy as she appears in the passage.
  Answer: She seems pensive, sad, and vulnerable.

- Ask students the Reading Strategy question on p. 758: Given the information Fitzgerald provides in this conversation, what can you conclude about Judy's experiences during her absence?
  Answer: You can conclude that she didn't have a very good time and that her ego was bruised in some way.

pugilistic youth lounged in front of pool halls. The clink of glasses and the slap of hands on the bars issued from saloons, cloisters of glazed glass and dirty yellow light.

She was watching him closely and the silence was embarrassing, yet in this crisis he could find no casual word with which to profane the hour. At a convenient turning he began to zigzag back toward the University Club.

"Have you missed me?" she asked suddenly.

"Everybody missed you."

He wondered if she knew of Irene Scheerer. She had been back only a day—her absence had been almost contemporaneous with his engagement.

"What a remark!" Judy laughed sadly—without sadness. She looked at him searchingly. He became absorbed in the dashboard.

"You're handsomer than you used to be," she said thoughtfully. "Dexter, you have the most rememberable eyes."

He could have laughed at this, but he did not laugh. It was the sort of thing that was said to sophomores. Yet it stabbed at him.

"I'm awfully tired of everything, darling." She called everyone darling, endowing the endearment with careless, individual camaraderie.[4] "I wish you'd marry me."

27 The directness of this confused him. He should have told her now that he was going to marry another girl, but he could not tell her. He could as easily have sworn that he had never loved her.

"I think we'd get along," she continued, on the same note, "unless probably you've forgotten me and fallen in love with another girl."

Her confidence was obviously enormous. She had said, in effect, that she found such a thing impossible to believe, that if it were true he had merely committed a childish indiscretion—and probably to show off. She would forgive him, because it was not a matter of any moment but rather something to be brushed aside lightly.

"Of course you could never love anybody but me," she continued, "I like the way you love me. Oh, Dexter, have you forgotten last year?"

"No, I haven't forgotten."

"Neither have I!"

Was she sincerely moved—or was she carried along by the wave of her own acting?

"I wish we could be like that again," she said, and he forced himself to answer:

"I don't think we can."

"I suppose not. . . . I hear you're giving Irene Scheerer a violent rush."

There was not the faintest emphasis on the name, yet Dexter was suddenly ashamed.

"Oh, take me home," cried Judy suddenly; "I don't want to go back to that idiotic dance—with those children."

---

4. **camaraderie** (käm´ ə räd´ ə rē) *n.* warm, friendly feelings.

pugilistic (pyoo´ jə lis´ tik) *adj.* looking for a fight

Reading Strategy
Drawing Conclusions About Characters Given the information Fitzgerald provides in this conversation, what can you conclude about Judy's experiences during her absence?

✻ ENRICHMENT: Cultural Connection

Marriage Customs

In other times and cultures Dexter would have had little to say about whether he married Judy or Irene. The choice of marriage partner is sometimes severely restricted by cultural and religious beliefs. For example, in cultures such as apartheid South Africa with very distinct ethnic and social groups, intermarriage amongst groups was strongly discouraged. In other cultures—Islam or Orthodox Judaism, for example—marriages might be arranged by parents of the couple. Even in the largely open cul-

ture of America, the idea of marrying for love without parental guidance is a fairly recent trend. Marriages have often been influenced by economic reasons, as families seek to expand holdings or shore up finances.

Ask students to contribute information about marriage customs in cultures with which they are familiar. Then, discuss with students which methods they feel are most likely to produce successful marriages.

Then, as he turned up the street that led to the residence district, Judy began to cry quietly to herself. He had never seen her cry before.

The dark street lightened, the dwellings of the rich loomed up around them, he stopped his coupé in front of the great white bulk of the Mortimer Joneses' house, <u>somnolent</u>, gorgeous, drenched with the splendor of the damp moonlight. Its solidity startled him. The strong walls, the steel of the girders, the breadth and beam and pomp of it were there only to bring out the contrast with the young beauty beside him. It was sturdy to accentuate her slightness—as if to show what a breeze could be generated by a butterfly's wing.

He sat perfectly quiet, his nerves in wild clamor, afraid that if he moved he would find her irresistibly in his arms. Two tears had rolled down her wet face and trembled on her upper lip.

29 "I'm more beautiful than anybody else," she said brokenly, "why can't I be happy?" Her moist eyes tore at his stability—her mouth turned slowly downward with an exquisite sadness: "I'd like to marry you if you'll have me, Dexter. I suppose you think I'm not worth having, but I'll be so beautiful for you, Dexter."

A million phrases of anger, pride, passion, hatred, tenderness fought on his lips. Then a perfect wave of emotion washed over him, carrying off with it a sediment of wisdom, of convention, of doubt, of honor. This was his girl who was speaking, his own, his beautiful, his pride.

"Won't you come in?" He heard her draw in her breath sharply. Waiting.

"All right," his voice was trembling, "I'll come in."

V

It was strange that neither when it was over nor a long time afterward did he regret that night. Looking at it from the perspective of ten years, the fact that Judy's flare for him endured just one month seemed of little importance. Nor did it matter that by his yielding he subjected himself to a deeper agony in the end and gave serious hurt to Irene Scheerer and to Irene's parents, who had befriended him. There was nothing sufficiently pictorial about Irene's grief to stamp itself on his mind.

Dexter was at bottom hard-minded. The attitude of the city on his action was of no importance to him, not because he was going to leave the city, but because any outside attitude on the situation seemed superficial. He was completely indifferent to popular opinion. Nor, when he had seen that it was no use, that he did not possess in himself the power to move fundamentally or to hold Judy Jones, did he bear any malice toward her. He loved her, and he would love her until the day he was too old for loving—but he could not have her. So he tasted the deep pain that is reserved only for the strong, just as he had tasted for a little while the deep happiness.

Even the ultimate falsity of the grounds upon which Judy terminated the engagement that she did not want to "take him away" from

28 somnolent (säm′ nə lənt) *adj.* sleepy; drowsy

Literary Analysis
Characterization
What does this wistful remark about her lack of happiness add to Fitzgerald's portrait of Judy's character?

30 ☑ **Reading Check**
How long does Dexter's romance with Judy Jones last?

Winter Dreams ◆ 759

---

28 **Vocabulary Development**

- Draw students' attention to Fitzgerald's use of the word *somnolent*, and read its definition. Then, tell students that the word derives from the Latin root *-somn-*, which means "sleep."

- Read aloud Fitzgerald's sentence containing the word *somnolent*. Invite students to describe the Mortimer Joneses' house in their own words.

- Then, ask this question: How does understanding the root of *somnolent* enhance your image of the house?
  Answer: Responses should recognize the house's grandeur and sense of solidity or immobility, and they should reflect students' understanding of the word *somnolent*.

29 **Literary Analysis**

Characterization

- Refer students to the line near the top of p. 759: " . . . Judy began to cry quietly to herself. He had never seen her cry before." Ask students what they think Judy's crying reveals about her.
  Answer: It suggests that she has had a difficult time, but also that she wants to win Dexter's sympathy.

- Have students read the bracketed text, keeping in mind that Dexter has never seen Judy cry before. Then, ask the Literary Analysis question on p. 759: What does this wistful remark about her lack of happiness add to Fitzgerald's portrait of Judy's character?
  Answer: It adds a dimension of frailty and poignancy to Judy's character, although readers never know for sure whether Judy's unhappiness is genuine or posed.

30 ☑ **Reading Check**

Answer: It lasts one month.

CUSTOMIZE INSTRUCTION FOR UNIVERSAL ACCESS

For Less Proficient Readers	For Gifted/Talented Students	For Advanced Readers
To help students follow the story to its conclusion, have them jot down notes while listening to the story in audio format, either on **Listening to Literature Audiotapes**, Sides 25–26 or **Audio CDs**, CDs 14–15. Encourage students to listen for Dexter's and Judy's emotions in the different stages of their relationship. Point out how little these really change.	Invite students to explore Fitzgerald's descriptive language by rewriting the scene between Dexter and Judy that takes place in the car (pp. 758–759) as a scene from a play. Have students tranform Fitzgerald's descriptions into stage directions indicating the physical environment, as well as the actors' body language and vocal inflections.	Invite students to read back in the story and explore questions about a change in human relationships: In what ways, if any, has the relationship between Dexter and Judy changed? Do the two of them truly know each other? With these questions in mind, how do students anticipate the ending of the story?

The Jazz Age was a time of parties and the pursuit of fun. Young men and women became increasingly rebellious, breaking long-held rules about relationships and engaging in casual love affairs without serious commitment. The eager pursuit of wealth and glamour and an increasingly flexible sense of social advancement added to the energy of the decade. When the stock markets crash of 1929 ended the economic boom, social mores resumed a more sober tone. It would not be until the 1960s that a strong economy and a powerful youth culture would again challenge the traditional rules of courtship and decorum.

Irene—Judy who had wanted nothing else—did not revolt him. He was beyond any revulsion or any amusement.

He went East in February with the intention of selling out his laundries and settling in New York—but the war came to America in March and changed his plans. He returned to the West, handed over the management of the business to his partner, and went into the first officers' training camp in late April. He was one of those young thousands who greeted the war with a certain amount of relief, welcoming the liberation from webs of tangled emotion.

VI

This story is not his biography, remember, although things creep into it which have nothing to do with those dreams he had when he was young. We are almost done with them and with him now. There is only one more incident to be related here, and it happens seven years farther on.

It took place in New York, where he had done well—so well that there were no barriers too high for him. He was thirty-two years old, and, except for one flying trip immediately after the war, he had not been West in seven years. A man named Devlin from Detroit came into his office to see him in a business way, and then and there this incident occurred, and closed out, so to speak, this particular side of his life.

"So you're from the Middle West," said the man Devlin with careless curiosity. "That's funny—I thought men like you were probably born and raised on Wall Street. You know—wife of one of my best friends in Detroit came from your city. I was an usher at the wedding."

Dexter waited with no apprehension of what was coming.

"Judy Simms," said Devlin with no particular interest; "Judy Jones she was once."

"Yes, I knew her." A dull impatience spread over him. He had heard, of course, that she was married—perhaps deliberately he had heard no more.

"Awfully nice girl," brooded Devlin meaninglessly, "I'm sort of sorry for her."

"Why?" Something in Dexter was alert, receptive, at once.

"Oh, Lud Simms has gone to pieces in a way. I don't mean he ill-uses her, but he drinks and runs around——"

"Doesn't she run around?"

"No. Stays at home with her kids."

"Oh."

"She's a little too old for him," said Devlin.

"Too old!" cried Dexter. "Why, man, she's only twenty-seven."

When World War I ended in 1918, Americans were desperate for a good time. They roared into the 1920s at breakneck speed, overthrowing rules about clothing, decorum, and personal style. The flapper, with her short dresses, bobbed hair, and complicated social life became a symbol of the times. She rode in sporty automobiles and danced until dawn to the sounds of jazz, a new kind of music critics blamed for a loosening moral code.

F. Scott Fitzgerald's work and life reflected the gaiety of this time, as well as the emptiness many felt when their pleasure seeking did not prove satisfying. Fitzgerald was not only part of the age, he helped to shape it, naming it the Jazz Age. Through both his life and his fiction, he created some of the decade's most enduring images.

He was possessed with a wild notion of rushing out into the streets and taking a train to Detroit. He rose to his feet spasmodically.

"I guess you're busy," Devlin apologized quickly. "I didn't realize——"

"No, I'm not busy," said Dexter, steadying his voice. "I'm not busy at all. Not busy at all. Did you say she was—twenty-seven? No, I said she was twenty-seven."

"Yes, you did," agreed Devlin dryly.

"Go on, then. Go on."

"What do you mean?"

"About Judy Jones."

Devlin looked at him helplessly.

"Well, that's—I told you all there is to it. He treats her like the devil. Oh, they're not going to get divorced or anything. When he's particularly outrageous she forgives him. In fact, I'm inclined to think she loves him. She was a pretty girl when she first came to Detroit."

A pretty girl! The phrase struck Dexter as ludicrous.

"Isn't she—a pretty girl, anymore?"

"Oh, she's all right."

"Look here," said Dexter, sitting down suddenly. "I don't understand. You say she was a 'pretty girl' and now you say she's 'all right.' I don't understand what you mean—Judy Jones wasn't a pretty girl, at all. She was a great beauty. Why, I knew her. I knew her. She was ——"

Devlin laughed pleasantly.

"I'm not trying to start a row," he said. "I think Judy's a nice girl and I like her. I can't understand how a man like Lud Simms could fall madly in love with her, but he did." Then he added: "Most of the women like her."

Dexter looked closely at Devlin, thinking wildly that there must be a reason for this, some insensitivity in the man or some private malice.

"Lots of women fade just like *that*," Devlin snapped his fingers. "You must have seen it happen. Perhaps I've forgotten how pretty she was at her wedding. I've seen her so much since then, you see. She has nice eyes."

A sort of dullness settled down upon Dexter. For the first time in his life he felt like getting very drunk. He knew that he was laughing loudly at something Devlin had said, but he did not know what it was or why it was funny. When, in a few minutes, Devlin went he lay down on his lounge and looked out the window at the New York skyline into which the sun was sinking in dull lovely shades of pink and gold.

He had thought that having nothing else to lose he was invulnerable at last—but he knew that he had just lost something more, as surely as if he had married Judy Jones and seen her fade away before his eyes.

The dream was gone. Something had been taken from him. In a sort of panic he pushed the palms of his hands into his eyes and tried to bring up a picture of the waters lapping on Sherry Island and the moonlit veranda, and gingham on the golf links and the dry sun and the gold color of her neck's soft down. And her mouth damp to his kisses and her eyes plaintive with melancholy and her freshness

Literary Analysis
Characterization and Character's Motivation
Why do you think Dexter is "obsessed by a wild notion"? What need drives his behavior?

32 **Literary Analysis**

Characterization and Character's Motivation

- Have two volunteers act out the entire conversation between Dexter and Devlin. Discuss how students think Dexter feels during the conversation.
  Answer: He feels agitated.

- Ask students the Literary Analysis questions on p. 761: Why do you think Dexter is "obsessed by a wild notion"? What need drives his behavior?
  Answer: He is so agitated by the thought of Judy Jones's beauty and spark having been diminished that he wants to go to Detroit and prove Devlin wrong. He needs to believe that Judy Jones, as he recalls her, still exists in the world.

33 ☑ **Reading Check**

Answer: She's become ordinary. She is no longer beautiful and no longer captures men's attention everywhere. Women now like her, whereas before they found her threatening.

33 ☑ **Reading Check**
According to Devlin, in what ways has Judy changed since Dexter last saw her?

Winter Dreams ◆ 761

CUSTOMIZE INSTRUCTION FOR UNIVERSAL ACCESS

For Less Proficient Readers

Tell students that one of the qualities that made Fitzgerald a great writer was his capacity to develop characters with psychological depth and realism. His characters can surprise readers, just as real people may do.

Draw a graphic organizer like the one shown to help students draw

conclusions about Judy Jones's character: Was she a selfish person in the end? Upon what actions do students base their conclusions? Have students suggest actions to fill out both sides of the organizer. If students have trouble finding unselfish actions, remind them about the final scene of the story.

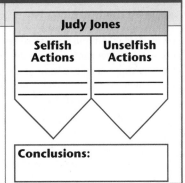

Answers for p. 762

Review and Assess

1. Students should support their answers with clear reasons.

2. **(a)** In the fall and winter, he feels melancholy but filled with hopeful fantasies. In spring, he feels dismal. **(b)** Dexter fantasizes about the summer and sees himself achieveing success and glamour. **(c)** Dexter's memories of summer are idealized.

3. **(a)** He wants the glittering things of wealth. **(b)** She cares only for pleasure, for the glitter in life. Like wealth and luxury, she is tantalizing but unobtainable.

4. **(a)** After their first meeting, he quits his job as a caddy. After their second meeting, she becomes his new pursuit, his reason for striving. **(b)** She causes him to quit his caddying job, and later leads him to break off an engagement.

5. **(a)** Irene is sweet and honorable, pleasant-looking, and a little stout. **(b)** It symbolizes his abandoning his pursuit of Judy Jones and settling for a more stable life.

6. **(a)** He responds by dropping whatever he's doing in order to see her. **(b)** He is obsessed with her and the ideal that she represents to him.

7. Students may answer that many people in today's world are also obsessed with money and status.

---

like new fine linen in the morning. Why, these things were no longer in the world! They had existed and they existed no longer.

For the first time in years the tears were streaming down his face. But they were for himself now. He did not care about mouth and eyes and moving hands. He wanted to care, and he could not care. For he had gone away and he could never go back any more. The gates were closed, the sun was gone down, and there was no beauty but the gray beauty of steel that withstands all time. Even the grief he could have borne was left behind in the country of illusion, of youth, of the richness of life, where his winter dreams had flourished.

"Long ago," he said, "long ago, there was something in me, but now that thing is gone. Now that thing is gone, that thing is gone. I cannot cry. I cannot care. That thing will come back no more."

Review and Assess

Thinking About the Selection

1. **Respond:** Do you feel sorry for Judy? For Dexter? Explain.

2. **(a) Recall:** What emotions does Dexter feel during the different seasons of the year? **(b) Interpret:** During the winter, how does Dexter reflect upon his summer activities? **(c) Make a Judgment:** Would you say Dexter's memories of the summer are accurate or idealized? Explain.

3. **(a) Recall:** At the beginning of Section II, what does the narrator say Dexter wants? **(b) Interpret:** In what ways does Judy embody Dexter's ambitions?

4. **(a) Recall:** What actions does Dexter take as a result of his first two meetings with Judy? **(b) Connect:** Find two examples in the story that demonstrate the effects of Judy's casual decisions or behavior on Dexter's life.

5. **(a) Interpret:** What is Irene like? Briefly describe her. **(b) Draw Conclusions:** What does the decision to become engaged to Irene symbolize for Dexter?

6. **(a) Interpret:** What is Dexter's response to Judy whenever she reappears in his life? **(b) Analyze:** Why do Dexter's feelings for Judy remain unchanged even after he finally loses her?

7. **Evaluate:** Are Dexter's values and ideals influenced by the times in which he lived, or would his feelings for Judy Jones have been the same in any era? Explain.

762 ◆ Disillusion, Defiance, and Discontent (1914–1946)

✒ ASSESSMENT PRACTICE: Reading Comprehension

Analyze Sentence Meaning

On many standardized tests, students are asked to correctly answer sentence-completion questions. Use the following example to show students how to use the meaning of a sentence to choose the word that best completes the passage.

    F. Scott Fitzgerald was able to successfully capture the glittering and _____ lifestyle of the Roaring Twenties. Like many of his characters, he longed to attain the wealth and social status of

the upper class.

Select the word that best completes the sentence:

  A repressed   **C** simplistic
  B materialistic **D** frugal

The meaning of the second sentence supports answer *B*, *materialistic*, as the most logical answer. Answer choices *C* and *D* contradict the second sentence, and choice *A*, *repressed*, does not fit with the meaning of *glittering*.

Review and Assess

Literary Analysis

Characterization

1. (a) Use a chart like the one shown to analyze Fitzgerald's use of **characterization** to portray Judy and Dexter. (b) What do you learn about the characters in each example?

2. Note ways in which both types of characterization work together to create consistent portraits.
3. (a) What traits do Dexter and Judy share? (b) In what ways are they different? (c) Which details of characterization lead you to your answers?

Connecting Literary Elements

4. What details in the story reveal Dexter's **motivation** to be successful?
5. (a) What need drives Judy? (b) For what does she yearn?
6. Judy tells Dexter that she cannot be happy. In what ways does her behavior throughout the story contribute to her unhappiness?

Reading Strategy

Drawing Conclusions About Characters

7. Demonstrate what you have learned about the characters of Dexter and Judy by writing an account of their last meeting. What did they say and how did they act as their relationship ended?
8. In what ways do the characters of Dexter and Judy reflect Fitzgerald's complex views of material wealth and social status?

Extend Understanding

9. **Social Studies Connection:** (a) How do you think Fitzgerald defines the American Dream? (b) Do you agree with critics who have said that Fitzgerald's vision of that dream is conflicted, or divided? Explain.

Quick Review

Writers use both **direct** and **indirect** methods of **characterization** to reveal the personalities of their characters.

A **character's motivations** are the needs and desires that drive his or her behavior, thoughts, feelings, and speech.

To **draw conclusions about characters**, connect clues from the text with your own life experiences.

 Take It to the Net
www.phschool.com
Take the interactive self-test online to check your understanding of the selection.

Answers for p. 763

Review and Assess

1. **(a)** and **(b)** Judy: Direct: Judy Jones was "not a girl who could be 'won' in the kinetic sense . . . "; Indirect: Judy Jones's treatment of Dexter at the beginning of the story; What I Learn: Judy is beautiful, unapproachable, self-centered, and insensitive; Dexter: Direct: Dexter wanted the "glittering things themselves"; Indirect: Dexter's reaction to Judy Jones at the beginning of the story reveals his pride; What I Learn: Dexter is ambitious and proud.

2. Direct characterization allows the author to emphasize particular characteristics or motivations. Indirect characterization makes the characters come alive through their interactions with others.

3. **(a)** Both are materialistic. **(b)** Judy comes from a wealthy background, while Dexter does not. **(c)** Students should use evidence from the text to support their responses.

4. He works as a caddy for extra money and is known as the best caddy at the club, a tribute to his talents and work ethic. He chooses a college for the social advancement it may provide. He works hard at his laundry.

5. **(a)** Judy appears to need a great deal of male attention. **(b)** In a brief moment of vulnerability, she appears to yearn for happiness.

6. She continually steps on other people's feelings or needs in order to get her own way and to remain carefree and unattached.

7. Students should be able to create likely scenarios.

8. Judy and Dexter symbolize the forever divided "have's" and "have-not's" that Fitzgerald saw in the world around him. Judy reflects a lifetime of privilege and entitlement. Dexter reflects a lifetime spent striving to enter the inner circle of privilege.

9. **(a)** Possible answer: Fitzgerald saw the American Dream as the achievement of wealth and status. **(b)** It was conflicted. Fitzgerald saw how people's efforts to realize the American Dream often resulted in the destruction of their happiness and even their lives.

763

❶ Vocabulary Development

Word Analysis

Check to see that students have used each word correctly.

Spelling Strategy

1. antagonistic
2. futuristic
3. angelic

Students should use each word correctly in a meaningful sentence.

Concept Development: Antonyms

1. a
2. a
3. b
4. a
5. b
6. a
7. b
8. a

❷ Grammar and Style

1. Mr. Hart—one of those golfers who liked to yell *Fore!* at the top of their lungs—gave him a guest card to a prestigious local golf club.

2. He was glad her parents were not there—they might wonder who he was.

3. Whatever she smiled at—at him, at a chicken liver, at nothing—it disturbed him. . . .

4. He had the notion that she—and this was the strange part—actually had feelings for him.

5. "I'd like to marry you," she said "I love you"—she said—nothing.

Writing Application

Check to see that students do not overuse dashes in their descriptions.

Integrate Language Skills

❶ Vocabulary Development Lesson

Word Analysis: Latin Root -somn-

The word *somnolent* meaning "sleepy," is built on the Latin root -somn-, which means "sleep." Using each of the words defined below, write a brief paragraph about a student who keeps nodding off in class.

1. insomnia: *n.* inability to sleep
2. somnolent: *adj.* sleepy; drowsy
3. somniloquist: *n.* one who talks while asleep

Spelling Strategy

Usually, when forming adjectives by adding the suffix -ic, do not change the spelling of the base word: *pugilist* becomes *pugilistic*. Add -ic to the words below. Then, use each adjective in a sentence.

1. antagonist   2. futurist   3. angel

Concept Development: Antonyms

Review the vocabulary list on page 743. Then, choose the letter of the word that is the better antonym, or word of opposite meaning, for each numbered word.

1. fallowness   (a) activity, (b) emptiness
2. preposterous   (a) serious, (b) sarcastic
3. fortuitous   (a) wealthy, (b) cursed
4. sinuous   (a) straight, (b) slippery
5. mundane   (a) legal, (b) amazing
6. poignant   (a) dull, (b) moving
7. pugilistic   (a) tough, (b) peace-loving
8. somnolent   (a) alert, (b) hard

❷ Grammar and Style Lesson

Dashes

Dashes (—) are a form of punctuation which create a longer, more emphatic pause than commas. They signal information that interrupts the flow of text. Dashes can indicate an abrupt change of thought, a dramatic interrupting idea, or a summary statement.

In Fitzgerald's story, dashes draw readers' attention to the information they set off. Look at this example:

Example: When he was twenty-three, Mr. Hart—one of the gray-haired men who liked to say "Now *there's* a boy"—gave him a guest card to the Sherry Island Golf Club for a weekend.

Practice Insert dashes where necessary in the following sentences.

1. Mr. Hart one of those golfers who like to yell *Fore!* at the top of their lungs gave him a guest card to a prestigious local golf club.
2. He was glad her parents were not there they might wonder who he was.
3. Whatever she smiled at him, at a chicken liver, at nothing it disturbed him . . .
4. He had the notion that she and this was the strange part actually had feelings for him.
5. "I'd like to marry you," she said "I love you" she said nothing.

Writing Application Write a brief description of someone you admire. Use dashes to set off a few pieces of information you want readers to notice.

W̶G Prentice Hall *Writing and Grammar Connection: Chapter 27, Section 5*

764 ◆ *Disillusion, Defiance, and Discontent (1914–1946)*

BLOCK SCHEDULING: Resources marked with this symbol provide varied instruction during 90-minute blocks.

❸ Writing Lesson

Character Analysis

Fitzgerald portrays Dexter Green as a fully rounded character with believable thoughts, feelings, strengths, and weaknesses. Explore Dexter's behavior and motivations in a character analysis. Support your ideas with examples from the story.

Prewriting   Scan the story for examples of Dexter's appearance, words, actions, and motivations. Note how he changes during the story, and then decide whether Dexter's actions are heroic or simply foolish.

Drafting   In your introduction, name the author, title, and featured character, and then state your most important idea. Describe Dexter's behavior with specific examples, and quote from the text to support your judgment.

Model: Elaborating for Information

Dexter was an outsider looking in on an elegant world. He was so close to it, he could almost touch it, and that combination of proximity and distance drove him. As Fitzgerald tells us, "He wanted not association with glittering things and glittering people—he wanted the glittering things themselves."

> Direct quotations from the text provide support for the analysis.

Revising   Make sure your essay clearly communicates your opinion. Where needed, add quotations or other details to support your points.

W͏G Prentice Hall Writing and Grammar Connection: Chapter 14, Section 3

❹ Extension Activities

Listening and Speaking Select a song that might remind Dexter of Judy. Play the song for the class and give a **presentation** about why it is appropriate. Use these tips to guide your work:

- Consider both current music and music from the Jazz Age.
- Alternate between discussion and musical passages, using the song to emphasize your points.

Conclude by addressing the relationship between music and emotions, and speculate about why songs are so powerful.

Research and Technology Using a variety of sources, research the lives of F. Scott and Zelda Fitzgerald. Then, write a **report** on their relationship and lifestyle. Incorporate various critical views of the connections between F. Scott's relationship with Zelda and his fiction and take a position to explain which one seems most accurate to you.

 **Take It to the Net**   www.phschool.com

Go online for an additional research activity using the Internet.

Lesson Support for p. 761

❸ Writing Lesson

- Review the Literary Analysis, Connecting Literary Elements, and Reading Strategy instruction to refresh students' understanding of the elements of literary characters.
- To aid prewriting, have students use the Branching Organizer in **Writing Models and Graphic Organizers on Transparencies,** p. 67, to gather details about Dexter's character.
- Read through the Writing Lesson steps with students, and clarify any confusion.
- Urge students to focus on developing a central idea about Dexter's character. They can then focus on details that support their main idea.

❹ Listening and Speaking

- Provide, or direct students to sources of Jazz Age music. Point out, however, that students may wish to use contemporary music or music from another time period. Suggest online or local music libraries where students can hear many options.
- Encourage students to play the song in its entirety before they begin speaking and then to play it again in portions as they discuss it.
- Have students use the Peer Assessment form for Delivering a Speech rubric, p. 30 in **Performance Assessment and Portfolio Management.**

CUSTOMIZE INSTRUCTION
For Universal Access

To address different learning styles, use the activities suggested in the Extension Activities booklet, p. 43.

For Visual/Spatial Learners, use Activity 5.

For Intrapersonal Learners, use Activity 6.

For Interpersonal Learners, use Activity 7.

ASSESSMENT RESOURCES

The following resources can be used to assess students' knowledge and skills.

Selection Assessment

- 📖 **Formal Assessment,** pp. 191
- 📖 **Open-Book Test,** pp. 121
- 📼 **Got It! Videotapes,** Tape 4
- 💿 **Test Bank Software**
- 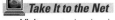 **Take It to the Net**
   Visit www.phschool.com for self-tests and additional questions on "Winter Dreams."

Listening and Speaking Rubric

- 📖 **Performance Assessment and Portfolio Management,** p. 30

PRENTICE HALL
ASSESSMENT SYSTEM

- 📖 **Workbook**
- 📖 **Skills Book**
- 📗 **Transparencies**
- 💿 **CD-ROM**

The Turtle from The Grapes of Wrath

Lesson Objectives

1. **To analyze and respond to literary elements**
   - Literary Analysis: Theme
   - Connecting Literary Elements: Symbol

2. **To read, comprehend, analyze, and critique a short story**
   - Reading Strategy: Finding Clues to Theme
   - Reading Check Questions
   - Review and Assess Questions
   - Assessment Practice (ATE)

3. **To develop word analysis skills, fluency, and systematic vocabulary**
   - Vocabulary Development Lesson: Latin Prefix: *pro-*

4. **To understand and apply written and oral language conventions**
   - Spelling Strategy
   - Grammar and Style Lesson: Parallel Structure

5. **To understand and apply appropriate writing and research strategies**
   - Writing Lesson: Essay About Historical Context
   - Extension Activity: Cartoon

6. **To understand and apply listening and speaking strategies**
   - Extension Activity: Interview

STEP-BY-STEP TEACHING GUIDE	PACING GUIDE
PRETEACH	
Motivate Students and Provide Background	
Use the Motivation activity (ATE p. 766)	5 min.
Read and discuss author and background features (SE/ATE p. 766) **A**	5 min.
Introduce the Concepts	
Introduce the Literary Analysis and Reading Strategy (SE/ATE p. 767) **A**	15 min.
Pronounce the vocabulary words and read their definitions (SE p. 767)	5 min.
TEACH	
Monitor Comprehension	
Informally monitor comprehension by circulating while students read independently or in groups **A**	15 min.
Monitor students' comprehension with the Reading Check note (SE/ATE p. 769)	as students read
Develop vocabulary with Vocabulary note (SE p. 769; ATE p. 769)	as students read
Develop Understanding	
Develop students' understanding of theme with the Literary Analysis annotation (SE p. 770; ATE p. 770) **A**	5 min.
Develop students' ability to find clues to the theme in their reading by using the Reading Strategy annotation (SE p. 769; ATE p. 769)	5 min.
ASSESS	
Assess Mastery	
Assess students' mastery of the Reading Strategy and Literary Analysis by having them answer the Review and Assess questions (SE/ATE p. 771)	15 min.
Use one or more of the print and media Assessment Resources (ATE p. 773) **A**	up to 45 min.
EXTEND	
Apply Understanding	
Have students complete the Vocabulary Development Lesson and the Grammar and Style Lesson (SE p. 772) **A**	20 min.
Apply students' ability to provide internal documentation in writing by using the Writing Lesson (SE/ATE p. 773) **A**	45 min.
Apply students' understanding using one or more of the Extension Activities (SE p. 773)	20–90 min.

 ACCELERATED INSTRUCTION:
Use the strategies and activities identified with an **A**.

UNIVERSAL ACCESS
● = Below Level Students
▲ = On-Level Students
■ = Above Level Students

Time and Resource Manager

RESOURCES		
PRINT 📖	**TRANSPARENCIES**	**TECHNOLOGY**
• **Beyond Literature,** Workplace Skills: Survival, p. 42 ▲ ■		• **Interest Grabber Video,** Tape 5 ● ▲ ■
• **Selection Support Workbook:** ● ▲ ■ Literary Analysis, p. 189 Reading Strategy, p. 188 Build Vocabulary, p. 186	• **Literary Analysis and Reading Transparencies,** pp. 83 and 84 ● ▲ ■	
• **Adapted Reader's Companion** ● • **Reader's Companion** ●		• **Listening to Literature** ● ▲ ■ Audiocassettes, Side 26 Audio CDs, CD 15
• **English Learner's Companion** ● ▲ • **Literatura en español** ● ▲ • **Literary Analysis for Enrichment** ■		
• **Formal Assessment:** Selection Test, p. 194 ● ▲ ■ • **Open Book Test,** p. 124 ● ▲ ■ • **Performance Assessment and Portfolio Management,** p. 21 ● ▲ ■ • **PRENTICE HALL ASSESSMENT SYSTEM** ● ▲ ■	• **PRENTICE HALL ASSESSMENT SYSTEM** ● ▲ ■ Skills Practice Answers and Explanations on Transparencies	• **Test Bank Software** ● ▲ ■ • **Got It! Assessment Videotapes,** Tape 4 ● ▲
• **Selection Support Workbook:** ● ▲ ■ Grammar and Style, p. 187 • **Writing and Grammar,** Ruby Level ● ▲ ■ • **Extension Activities,** p. 42 ● ▲ ■	• **Daily Language Practice Transparencies** ● ▲ • **Writing Models and Graphic Organizers on Transparencies,** p. 95 ● ▲ ■	• **Writing and Grammar iText CD-ROM** ● ▲ ■ 💻 *Take It to the Net* www.phschool.com

BLOCK SCHEDULING: Use one 90-minute class period to preteach the selection and have students read it. Use a second 90-minute class period to assess students' mastery of skills and have them complete one of the Extension Activities.

Step-by-Step Teaching Guide for pp. 766–767

Motivation

Students can appreciate this "Little Engine That Could" story on two levels: as a highly detailed and literal account of a turtle's efforts to cross the road and as a thematic statement about the human struggles of the Great Depression. You might engage students' interest in the story by focusing on the first level. Read aloud the following passages:

"As the embankment grew steeper and steeper, the more frantic were the efforts of the land turtle."

"Pushing hind legs strained and slipped. . . ."

"Little by little the shell slid up the embankment . . ."

Ask students whether they think the turtle will succeed in climbing the embankment. Invite students to empathize with the turtle as they read the story.

■ Interest Grabber Video

As an alternative, play "The Dust Bowl" on Tape 5 to engage student interest.

❶ Background

More About the Author

Steinbeck wrote in many genres. For example, in addition to the novels and short stories for which he is famous, Steinbeck wrote screenplays. His novel *The Grapes of Wrath* was made into a hugely successful film and led to several screenwriting assignments for the author. In particular, Steinbeck received critical praise for his *Viva Zapata!* screenplay. He also developed screenplays for the film adaptations of his stories "The Pearl" and "The Red Pony." In addition, Steinbeck wrote travel sketches, served as a war correspondent in World War II, and wrote nonfiction social commentaries that often formed the basis for his fiction.

Prepare to Read

❶ The Turtle *from* The Grapes of Wrath

John Steinbeck (1902–1968)

No writer captures more vividly than John Steinbeck what it was like to live through the Great Depression of the 1930s.

His stories and novels, many of which are set in the agricultural region of northern California where he grew up, capture the poverty, desperation, and social injustice experienced by many working-class Americans during this bleak period in our nation's history. As in the works of Naturalist writers like Stephen Crane and Jack London, Steinbeck's characters struggle desperately against forces beyond their understanding or control. Many of those characters suffer tragic fates, yet they almost always manage to exhibit bravery and retain a sense of dignity throughout their struggles. Steinbeck's ability to combine harsh critiques of the political and social systems of his times with genuine artistry in his characterization, plot, and language is unique in American literature.

Modest Beginnings Steinbeck was born in Salinas, California, the son of a county official and a schoolteacher. By his late teens, he was already supporting himself by working as a laborer. After graduating from high school, he enrolled at Stanford University. He left before graduating, however, and spent the next five years drifting across the country, working in a variety of odd jobs, including that of fish hatcher, fruit picker, laboratory assistant, surveyor, apprentice painter, and journalist. Through these experiences, Steinbeck discovered firsthand what it means to survive by manual labor. He also gathered material that he would later use in his books to create authentic portraits of working-class life.

First Success Steinbeck's first three books received little—or negative—attention from critics. However, this changed in 1935 when he published *Tortilla Flat*, his fourth book. The book received the California Commonwealth Club's Gold Medal for best novel by a California author. Two years later, the author earned even greater recognition and acclaim with *Of Mice and Men* (1937). This novel, which portrays two migrant workers whose dream of owning a farm ends in tragedy, became a bestseller and was made into a Broadway play and a movie.

The Great American Novel Steinbeck went on to write what is generally regarded as his finest novel. *The Grapes of Wrath* (1939) is the historically authentic story of the Joad family, Oklahoma farmers dispossessed of their land and forced to become migrant farmers in California. "The Turtle" is an excerpt from the opening pages of this novel, which won the National Book Award and the Pulitzer Prize. The book aroused public sympathy for the plight of migratory farm workers and established Steinbeck as one of the most highly regarded writers of his day.

Steinbeck produced several more successful works during his later years, including *Cannery Row* (1945), *The Pearl* (1947), *East of Eden* (1952), and *The Winter of Our Discontent* (1961). In 1962, he received the Nobel Prize for Literature. In accepting that award, Steinbeck noted his belief that literature can sustain people through hard times. He added that it is the writer's responsibility to celebrate the human "capacity for greatness of heart and spirit—for gallantry in defeat, for courage, compassion and love. In the endless war against weakness and despair, these are the bright rally flags of hope and of emulation." Steinbeck's belief in social justice, and in the human ability to learn from and rise above suffering, infused all his work.

TEACHING RESOURCES

The following resources can be used to enrich or extend the instruction for pp. 766–767.

Motivation

■ **Interest Grabber Video**, Tape 5 ■

Background

📖 **Beyond Literature**, p. 42

Take It to the Net
Visit www.phschool.com for Background and hotlinks for "The Turtle."

Literary Analysis

📄 **Literary Analysis and Reading Transparencies**, Theme, p. 84 ■

📖 **Selection Support**: Literary Analysis, p. 189

Reading

📄 **Literary Analysis and Reading Transparencies**, Finding Clues to Theme, p. 83

■ **BLOCK SCHEDULING:** Resources marked with this symbol provide varied instruction during 90-minute blocks.

Preview

Connecting to the Literature

Sometimes, a single event can seem to mirror all of life. For example, one long and complicated journey with many detours and wrong turns might be seen as representing the experience of growing up. As you read this selection, think about how the small events it describes could represent something much bigger.

❷ Literary Analysis

Theme

John Steinbeck's narrative about a brief episode in a turtle's life conveys an important **theme,** or insight into life. An author's theme is rarely directly stated. Instead, it is revealed indirectly through these means:

- Characters' comments and actions
- Events in the plot
- The use of literary devices, such as symbols

Sometimes, even small details can serve an important role in conveying a theme, and deserve attention as you read.

Connecting Literary Elements

At first glance, this is just a simple story about a turtle. However, when looked at symbolically, the story grows in power and meaning. Steinbeck's use of **symbols**—people, places, or things that represent something larger than their literal meanings—helps to communicate his theme. To understand the story's symbolism, think about the qualities Steinbeck attributes to each person, place, animal, or object, and how each one might represent some aspect of life.

❸ Reading Strategy

Finding Clues to Theme

To interpret the theme of a story, become a literary detective. Look carefully for **clues to the theme** in the writer's use of symbols, his choice of details, and the ways characters react to one another. For example, Steinbeck includes only slight descriptions of how two motorists react when they spot the turtle. As brief as they are, these descriptions provide important clues to the theme. When you encounter such clues, consider the broader or underlying meanings they suggest. Gather clues in a chart like the one shown.

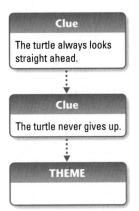

Vocabulary Development

embankment (em baŋk′ mənt) *n.* mound of earth or stone built to hold back water or support a roadway (p. 769)

protruded (prō trood′ id) *v.* pushed or thrust outward (p. 769)

The Turtle from *The Grapes of Wrath* ◆ 767

❷ Literary Analysis

Theme

- Tell students that as they read "The Turtle," they will focus on theme, an important insight into life that is usually conveyed indirectly in a literary work.

- Read aloud the instruction on theme. Draw students' attention to the ways in which theme can be implied through various story elements. To emphasize this point, discuss how all the passages students heard in the Motivation activity suggest a theme of struggle.

- Use the instruction for **Connecting Literary Elements** to help students recognize symbols that may suggest theme. Invite students' ideas about what the turtle might symbolize.

- Display the Theme transparency in **Literary Analysis and Reading Transparencies,** p. 84 and explain to students how each element in the story contributes to the theme. Encourage students to watch for these elements as they read.

❸ Reading Strategy

Finding Clues to Theme

- Tell students that because writers do not state themes directly, readers must make inferences from clues in the text. Remind students of previous instruction on making inferences and stress that finding clues to theme follows a similar process.

- To find clues to theme, readers must approach each portion of text on multiple levels: literal, figurative, and thematic. Tell students to read the story several times, on each occasion seeking a different level of understanding.

- Direct students to the chart on the student page. Urge them to record thematic clues as they read "The Turtle."

Vocabulary Development

- Pronounce each vocabulary word for students, and read the definitions as a class. Have students identify any words with which they are already familiar.

 E-Teach

Visit E-Teach at www.phschool.com for teachers' essays on how to teach, with questions and answers.

CUSTOMIZE INSTRUCTION FOR UNIVERSAL ACCESS

For Special Needs Students	For Less Proficient Readers	For English Learners
Have students read the adapted version of "The Turtle" in the **Adapted Reader's Companion.** This version provides basic-level instruction in an interactive format with questions and write-on lines. Completing the adapted version will prepare students to read the selection in the Student Edition.	Have students read "The Turtle" in the **Reader's Companion.** This version provides basic-level instruction in an interactive format with questions and write-on lines. After students finish the selection in **Reader's Companion,** have them complete the questions and activities in the Student Edition.	Have students read the adapted version of "The Turtle" in the **English Learner's Companion.** This version provides basic-level instruction in an interactive format with questions and write-on lines. Completing the adapted version will prepare students to read the selection in the Student Edition.

CUSTOMIZE INSTRUCTION
Verbal/Linguistic Learners
This story is highly visual. To help students grasp the movement in the story, pair them with visual/spatial learners to create a map of the turtle's progress.

❶ About the Selection

This story proclaims the virtues of persistence, illustrating how an individual can achieve a difficult goal through steady effort. Readers may initially doubt the turtle's ability to achieve its goal—to climb the embankment of a highway—but will increasingly admire its dogged efforts. When the turtle is rebuffed, first by the landscape and then by speeding cars, its ability to renew its commitment and continue on symbolizes the underlying stamina and resilience of both nature and human beings.

❷ ▶ Critical Viewing

Answer: Students may respond that the turtle has short, strong legs well suited to demanding terrain, and a tough shell to protect it from harsh sunlight, or physical accidents.

The Turtle
from **The Grapes of Wrath**
John Steinbeck

❷ ▲ Critical Viewing
What elements of this turtle's anatomy make it especially suited for the landscape Steinbeck describes? **[Connect]**

Background

The Great Depression of the 1930s was a time of unequaled economic distress. In 1932, a quarter of Americans—at least 12 million—were out of work. One of many factors contributing to the Depression was a widespread drought in Oklahoma. The drought was so severe that farmland literally blew away in massive dust storms. Hoping to find relief and work, many farmers fled to the city. This is the situation faced by the Joad family, whose story is told by Steinbeck in his novel *The Grapes of Wrath*. This tale of the turtle serves as the introduction to that epic book, and provides a point of reference for the story of human struggle that follows.

768 ◆ *Disillusion, Defiance, and Discontent (1914–1946)*

TEACHING RESOURCES

The following resources can be used to enrich or extend the instruction for pp. 768–770.

Literary Analysis
📖 **Writing Models and Graphic Organizers on Transparencies,** p. 95
📖 **Literary Analysis and Reading Transparencies,** p. 84

Reading
📖 **Selection Support:** Reading Strategy, p. 188; Build Vocabulary, p. 186

📖 **Reader's Companion,**
📖 **English Learner's Companion,**
🎧 **Listening to Literature Audiocassettes,** Side 26 ▦
💿 **Listening to Literature Audio CDs,** CD 15 ▦

▦ **BLOCK SCHEDULING:** Resources marked with this symbol provide varied instruction during 90-minute blocks.

The concrete highway was edged with a mat of tangled, broken, dry grass, and the grass heads were heavy with oat beards to catch on a dog's coat, and foxtails to tangle in a horse's fetlocks, and clover burrs to fasten in sheep's wool; sleeping life waiting to be spread and dispersed, every seed armed with an appliance of dispersal, twisting darts and parachutes for the wind, little spears and balls of tiny thorns, and all waiting for animals and for the wind, for a man's trouser cuff or the hem of a woman's skirt, all passive but armed with appliances of activity, still, but each possessed of the anlage[1] of movement.

The sun lay on the grass and warmed it, and in the shade under the grass the insects moved, ants and ant lions to set traps for them, grasshoppers to jump into the air and flick their yellow wings for a second, sow bugs like little armadillos, plodding restlessly on many tender feet. And over the grass at the roadside a land turtle crawled, turning aside for nothing, dragging his high-domed shell over the grass. His hard legs and yellow-nailed feet threshed slowly through the grass, not really walking, but boosting and dragging his shell along. The barley beards slid off his shell, and the clover burrs fell on him and rolled to the ground. His horny beak was partly opened, and his fierce, humorous eyes, under brows like fingernails, stared straight ahead. He came over the grass leaving a beaten trail behind him, and the hill, which was the highway <u>embankment</u>, reared up ahead of him. For a moment he stopped, his head held high. He blinked and looked up and down. At last he started to climb the embankment. Front clawed feet reached forward but did not touch. The hind feet kicked his shell along, and it scraped on the grass, and on the gravel. As the embankment grew steeper and steeper, the more frantic were the efforts of the land turtle. Pushing hind legs strained and slipped, boosting the shell along, and the horny head <u>protruded</u> as far as the neck could stretch. Little by little the shell slid up the embankment until at last a parapet[2] cut straight across its line of march, the shoulder of the road, a concrete wall four inches high. As though they worked independently the hind legs pushed the shell against the wall. The head upraised and peered over the wall to the broad smooth plain of cement. Now the hands, braced on top of the wall, strained and lifted, and the shell came slowly up and rested its front end on the wall. For a moment the turtle rested. A red ant ran into the shell, into the soft skin inside the shell, and suddenly head and legs snapped in, and the armored tail clamped in sideways. The red ant was crushed between body and legs. And one head of wild oats was clamped into the shell by a front leg. For a long moment the turtle lay still, and then the neck crept out and the old humorous frowning eyes looked about and the legs and tail came out. The back legs went to work, straining like elephant legs, and the shell tipped

---

1. **anlage** (än′ lä′ gə) *n.* foundation; basis; the initial cell structure from which an embryonic part develops.
2. **parapet** (par′ ə pet′) *n.* a low wall or edge of a roof, balcony, or similar structure.

The Turtle from *The Grapes of Wrath* ◆ 769

❼ Literary Analysis

Theme and Symbol

- Direct students to reread the bracketed passage and to paraphrase the events it describes.
  Answer: The turtle is hit by a truck, rights itself, and continues on.

- Have students offer a definition of *symbol*. Ask students if they think the turtle's actions are symbolic.

▶ Monitor Progress Ask students the Literary Analysis question on p. 770: What symbolic meaning might be given to the turtle's actions after it is hit by the truck?
Answer: Even the most difficult of challenges—including the threat of injury or death—can be overcome through patience and persistence.

Answers for p. 770

Review and Assess

1. Students may report that they felt anxious about the turtle's success.

2. (a) The turtle encounters the highway embankment, parapet, the hot surface of the road, and two vehicles. (b) The vehicles are the most dangerous.

3. (a) In the first encounter, the turtle is unharmed though startled into its shell. In the second encounter, the turtle is struck and knocked off the highway. (b) The first driver is careful and kind, swerving to avoid the turtle. The second driver is angry and cruel, and intentionally strikes the turtle.

4. (a) It is crushed by the turtle's shell. (b) The turtle can defend itself well against dangers of certain kinds.

5. (a) The seed is planted. (b) Possible answer: He is suggesting that different forms of life interact, even helping each other overcome obstacles.

6. Possible answer: Yes, the turtle makes a good symbol because he encounters many obstacles yet perseveres and finally succeeds.

to an angle so that the front legs could not reach the level cement plain. But higher and higher the hind legs boosted it, until at last the center of balance was reached, the front tipped down, the front legs scratched at the pavement, and it was up. But the head of wild oats was held by its stem around the front legs.

Now the going was easy, and all the legs worked, and the shell boosted along, waggling from side to side. A sedan driven by a forty-year-old woman approached. She saw the turtle and swung to the right, off the highway, the wheels screamed and a cloud of dust boiled up. Two wheels lifted for a moment and then settled. The car skidded back onto the road, and went on, but more slowly. The turtle had jerked into its shell, but now it hurried on, for the highway was burning hot.

And now a light truck approached, and as it came near, the driver saw the turtle and swerved to hit it. His front wheel struck the edge of the shell, flipped the turtle like a tiddly-wink, spun it like a coin, and rolled it off the highway. The truck went back to its course along the right side. Lying on its back, the turtle was tight in its shell for a long time. But at last its legs waved in the air, reaching for something to pull it over. Its front foot caught a piece of quartz and little by little the shell pulled over and flopped upright. The wild oat head fell out and three of the spearhead seeds stuck in the ground. And as the turtle crawled on down the embankment, its shell dragged dirt over the seeds. The turtle entered a dust road and jerked itself along, drawing a wavy shallow trench in the dust with its shell. The old humorous eyes looked ahead, and the horny beak opened a little. His yellow toe nails slipped a fraction in the dust.

Review and Assess

Thinking About the Selection

1. **Respond:** How did you feel as you watched the turtle proceed?
2. (a) **Recall:** What obstacles does the turtle encounter? (b) **Make a Judgment:** Which of these is most dangerous?
3. (a) **Recall:** What happens to the turtle in his encounter with the two drivers? (b) **Compare and Contrast:** Based on their actions, what kinds of people do the two drivers seem to be?
4. (a) **Recall:** What happens to the red ant that slips inside the turtle's shell? (b) **Distinguish:** What does this event suggest about the turtle's capacity to defend itself?
5. (a) **Recall:** What happens to the wild oat head at the end of the story? (b) **Analyze:** What is the author suggesting about the relationships between different forms of life?
6. **Evaluate:** Do you think the turtle makes an effective symbol of the struggles of ordinary people? Explain.

Literary Analysis
Theme and Symbol
What symbolic meaning might be given to turtle's actions after it is hit by the truck?

ASSESSMENT PRACTICE: Reading Comprehension

Analyze Sentence Meaning (For more practice, see Test Preparation Workbook, p. 44.)

Many tests require students to correctly answer sentence-completion questions. Often, more than one choice can complete a sentence. Use the following sample item to show students how to analyze sentence meaning, decide whether it is positive or negative, and eliminate choices that have the opposite sense.

John Steinbeck captured the poverty and desperation experienced by many Americans during the Great Depression, a(n) _____ period in our nation's history.

A comfortable **C** bleak
B inconvenient **D** prosperous

The context of the sentence indicates that the correct answer will have a negative connotation, so A and D are eliminated. Answer choice B is too mild to compare to the words *poverty* and *desperation*. C is the best choice.

Review and Assess

Literary Analysis

Theme

1. What parallels do you see between the experiences of the turtle and human experiences?
2. In what way are the wild oat seeds related to the story's **theme**?
3. What connection do the images from the beginning of the story of "sleeping life waiting to be spread" have to the story's theme?
4. Using your answers to questions 1–3, state the story's theme.

Connecting Literary Elements

5. Knowing that this story served as the introduction to *The Grapes of Wrath*, a novel about a displaced Depression-era farming family seeking a better life, what do you think the turtle symbolizes?
6. (a) Use a chart like the one shown to examine the turtle's actions at each stage of its journey. (b) What does the turtle's journey symbolize?

	Obstacles	Turtle's Reactions	Symbolic Meaning
Climbs Embankment			
Crosses Road			

Reading Strategy

Finding Clues to Theme

7. Steinbeck uses the words *dragging*, *turning aside for nothing*, and *thrashed slowly* to describe the turtle. (a) What effect do these words have on your perception of the turtle? (b) How do you think Steinbeck wants readers to respond to the turtle?
8. (a) Which characters can be seen as representing nature—or the simple life—and which represent the modern world? Explain. (b) Which does Steinbeck likely feel is more important? Explain.

Extend Understanding

9. **Career Connection:** Which of the turtle's personal qualities would be advantageous or disadvantageous in today's business world? Explain.

The Turtle from The Grapes of Wrath ◆ 771

Quick Review

A story's **theme** is its central message.

Symbols are people, places, or things that represent ideas or qualities larger than their literal meanings.

To **find clues to theme**, consider the details a writer provides and identify their underlying meaning.

 Take It to the Net
www.phschool.com

Take the interactive self-test online to check your understanding of the selection.

Answers for p. 771

Review and Assess

1. The turtle faces obstacles that seem almost insurmountable. Life presents people with challenges that are equally daunting.

2. The wild oat seed represents potential life which is surprisingly adaptable and resilient. The turtle's struggle allows the seed to be planted and therefore succeed. This symbolizes the larger theme of success through struggle.

3. These images suggest the latent power and abundance of all forms of life, even those that seem fragile.

4. Possible answer: Life is difficult, but obstacles— including those presented by the modern world—can be overcome.

5. Possible answer: The turtle symbolizes those who were poor and struggling during the Great Depression.

6. (a) Climbs Embankment: Obstacles: steep sides, the parapet; Turtle's Reactions: stubborn persistence and sheer determination; Symbolic Meaning: determination people summon when facing "uphill" battles; Crosses Road: Obstacles: traffic; Reactions: retreats into shell, then regroups and goes on; Symbolic Meaning: Even when it seems impossible, keep trying (b) The turtle's journey symbolizes the struggles of people facing terrible obstacles during the Great Depression.

7. (a) These words personify the turtle and make readers perceive it as a fighter. (b) He wants them to be sympathetic toward it.

8. (a) The turtle and the woman who swerves to avoid it can be seen as representing nature and the simple life. The truck driver may represent the modern world. (b) Steinbeck probably feels nature is more important.

9. The turtle's persistence would be advantageous in today's complex business world. His slow speed might be seen as a disadvantage.

❶ Vocabulary Development

Word Analysis

1. *Project* means to plan or look ahead; We *project* high sales next quarter.

2. *Proceed* means to continue forward; *Proceed* to the next corner and turn left.

3. *Progress* means to move forward; The turtle's steady *progress* is amazing.

4. *Prohibit* means to forbid or keep from moving forward; Because of the danger they present, we *prohibit* trucks on this road.

5. *Produce* means to generate; The turtle's persistence will *produce* success in the end.

6. *Propose* means to suggest a plan; I *propose* using the turtle's experience as a motivational tool.

Fluency: True or False?

1. False
2. True

Spelling Strategy

1. no
2. no
3. yes

❷ Grammar and Style

1. ...all waiting <u>for animals</u> and <u>for the wind</u>, <u>for a man's trouser cuff</u>...

2. ...a land turtle crawled, <u>turning aside for nothing</u>, <u>dragging his high domed shell over the grass</u>.

3. His front wheel <u>struck the edge</u> of the shell, <u>flipped the turtle</u> like a tiddly-wink, <u>spun it like a coin</u>, and <u>rolled it</u> off the highway.

4. ...ants and ant lions to <u>set traps for them</u>, grasshoppers to <u>jump into the air</u>...

5. A red ant ran <u>into the shell</u>, <u>into the soft skin</u>...

Writing Application

Paragraphs should contain at least three examples of parallel structure. Students should be able to identify these examples in discussion.

Integrate Language Skills

❶ Vocabulary Development Lesson

Word Analysis: Latin Prefix *pro-*

In this story, John Steinbeck uses the word *protruded*, which begins with the Latin prefix *pro-*, meaning "forward." Knowing this meaning helps you to define the whole word *protruded*, which means "thrust forward," and other words beginning with the prefix *pro-*.

Add the prefix *pro-* to the word roots below. Then, write a brief definition of each word and use it in a sentence.

1. *-ject*
2. *-ceed*
3. *-gress*
4. *-hibit*
5. *-duce*
6. *-pose*

Fluency: True or False?

Use your knowledge of the words from the vocabulary list on page 767 to decide whether these statements are true or false.

1. An *embankment* is at the bottom of a lake.
2. When the cat's paw *protruded*, it stuck out.

Spelling Strategy

In some words, the prefix or suffix is embedded, and removing the prefix or suffix leaves only a word part. For each of the following words, note whether or not the underlined prefix or suffix can be removed to make a base word.

1. terri<u>fy</u>
2. <u>ag</u>gress<u>or</u>
3. <u>im</u>possible

❷ Grammar and Style Lesson

Parallel Structure

Parallel structure is the expression of similar ideas using similar grammatical form. Parallel structures can involve the use of adjectives, verbs, phrases, or entire sentences.

The use of parallel structures helps to emphasize key ideas and link similar concepts. In "The Turtle," John Steinbeck uses numerous parallel structures to add sophistication to his writing and to indicate the connection between actions and ideas. Look at these examples.

> **Adjectives:** The concrete highway was edged with a mat of *tangled, broken, dry* grass . . .
>
> **Infinitive Phrases:** . . . the grass heads were heavy with oat beards *to catch* on a dog's coat, and foxtails *to tangle* in a horse's fetlocks, and clover burrs *to fasten* in sheep's wool . . .

Practice Identify the parallel grammatical elements in each sentence.

1. . . . all waiting for animals and for the wind, for a man's trouser cuff . . .

2. . . . a land turtle crawled, turning aside for nothing, dragging his high-domed shell over the grass.

3. His front wheel struck the edge of the shell, flipped the turtle like a tiddly-wink, spun it like a coin, and rolled it off the highway.

4. . . . ants and ant lions to set traps for them, grasshoppers to jump into the air . . .

5. A red ant ran into the shell, into the soft skin . . .

Writing Application Write a short description of a natural event, like a storm or a flight of geese. Use parallel structure to call attention to the key details in your description.

*W*G *Prentice Hall Writing and Grammar Connection: Chapter 20, Section 6*

772 ◆ Disillusion, Defiance, and Discontent (1914–1946)

TEACHING RESOURCES

The following resources can be used to enrich or extend the instruction for pp. 772–773.

Vocabulary

📖 **Selection Support:** Build Vocabulary, p. 186

📖 **Vocabulary and Spelling Practice Book** (Use this booklet for skills enrichment.) ▪

Grammar

📖 **Selection Support:** Grammar and Style, p. 187

*W*G **Writing and Grammar,** Ruby Level, p. 504

▪ **Daily Language Practice Transparencies** ▪

Writing

*W*G **Writing and Grammar,** Ruby Level, p. 257

💿 **Writing and Grammar iText CD-ROM**

▪ **Writing Models and Graphic Organizers on Transparencies,** p. 95

▪ **BLOCK SCHEDULING:** Resources marked with this symbol provide varied instruction during 90-minute blocks.

❸ Writing Lesson

Essay About Historical Context

John Steinbeck wrote "The Turtle" as a prelude for his novel *The Grapes of Wrath*, which portrays the struggles of a Depression-era farm family. Steinbeck intended that readers draw parallels between the prelude and the novel. Write an essay connecting the events described in "The Turtle" to the lives of ordinary people during the Great Depression.

Prewriting   Research the Great Depression to learn how people reacted to adverse economic circumstances. Then, review "The Turtle" and draw parallels.

Drafting   First, provide information about the Depression. In your body paragraphs, note facts and data and explain parallels you found to "The Turtle." Cite the sources of these facts as you draft.

Model: Providing Internal Documentation

The Great Depression of the 1930s was a time of economic disaster. Stock prices fell 40 percent, 9,000 banks failed, and 9 million savings accounts were wiped out. (*http://www.britannica.com*, Great Depression)

> When citing sources without providing a full reference list at the end of the essay, include all source information parenthetically.

Revising   Review your essay. Make sure that you have provided enough historical context to support your observations. Add information as needed, and provide correct citations about where you found the material.

Prentice Hall Writing and Grammar Connection: Chapter 12, Section 5

❹ Extension Activities

Listening and Speaking   After preparing a list of questions, conduct an **interview** with someone who lived through the Great Depression. Share your findings with the class. Use the following tips:

- Come to the interview with a tape recorder and writing materials.
- Request your subject's permission to record the conversation.

Frame your post-interview presentation with an engaging introduction and conclusion.

Research and Technology   With a partner, pare "The Turtle" down to its essential thematic message. Write and illustrate a **cartoon strip** conveying that message. If possible, use graphic arts software to lay out and generate your cartoon. **[Group Activity]**

 Take It to the Net   www.phschool.com

Go online for an additional research activity using the Internet.

The Turtle from *The Grapes of Wrath* ◆ 773

---

❸ Writing Lesson

- Review possible research sources with students, including the use of search engines for online research.
- To aid prewriting, have students use the Outline Transparency in **Writing Models and Graphic Organizers on Transparencies**, p. 95, to plan their subtopics and supporting ideas.
- Read through the Writing Lesson steps with students and clarify any questions.
- Urge students to use descriptive details to convey information about the Great Depression in a vivid manner.
- Adapt the Research: Documented Essay rubric in **Performance Assessment and Portfolio Management**, p. 21, to evaluate students' essays.

❹ Research and Technology

- Refer students to the Literary Analysis and Reading Strategy instruction for help in identifying the essential thematic message of the story.
- Emphasize that drawing ability will not be evaluated and that students may draw manually or electronically.
- Suggest that students use slideshow software to animate their cartoons.

CUSTOMIZE INSTRUCTION
For Universal Access

To address different learning styles, use the activities suggested in the **Extension Activities** booklet, p. 42.

For Interpersonal and Visual/Spatial Learners, use Activity 5.

For Verbal/Linguistic Learners, use Activity 6.

For Intrapersonal Learners, use Activity 7.

ASSESSMENT RESOURCES

The following resources can be used to assess students' knowledge and skills.

Selection Assessment

- 📖 **Formal Assessment**, pp. 194–196
- 📖 **Open Book Test**, pp. 124–126
- 📼 **Got It! Assessment Videotapes**, Tape 4
- 💿 **Test Bank Software**
- 💻 **Take It to the Net**
  Visit www.phschool.com for self-tests and additional questions on "The Turtle."

Writing Rubric

- 📖 **Performance Assess. and Portfolio Mgmt.**, p. 21

PRENTICE HALL *ASSESSMENT SYSTEM*

- 📖 **Workbook**
- 📖 **Skill Book**
- 📺 **Transparencies**
- 💿 **CD-ROM**

old age sticks ✦ anyone lived in a pretty how town ✦ The Unknown Citizen

Lesson Objectives

1. **To analyze and respond to literary elements**
   - Literary Analysis: Satire
   - Comparing Literary Works
2. **To read, comprehend, analyze, and critique poetry**
   - Reading Strategy: Relating Structure to Meaning
   - Reading Check questions
   - Review and Assess questions
   - Assessment Practice (ATE)
3. **To develop word analysis skills, fluency, and systematic vocabulary**
   - Vocabulary Development Lesson: Greek Root: -psych-
4. **To understand and apply written and oral language conventions**
   - Spelling Strategy
   - Grammar and Style Lesson: Parentheses
5. **To understand and apply appropriate writing and research strategies**
   - Writing Lesson: Introduction to a Poetry Reading
   - Extension Activity: Written Report
6. **To understand and apply listening and speaking strategies**
   - Extension Activity: Group Discussion

STEP-BY-STEP TEACHING GUIDE	PACING GUIDE
PRETEACH	
Motivate Students and Provide Background	
Use the Motivation activity (ATE p. 774)	5 min.
Read and discuss author and background features (SE/ATE pp. 774, 777) [A]	5 min.
Introduce the Concepts	
Introduce the Literary Analysis and Reading Strategy (SE/ATE p. 775) [A]	15 min.
Pronounce the vocabulary words and read their definitions (SE p. 775)	5 min.
TEACH	
Monitor Comprehension	
Informally monitor comprehension by circulating while students read independently or in groups [A]	10 min.
Monitor students' comprehension with the Reading Check notes (SE/ATE pp. 777, 779)	as students read
Develop vocabulary with Vocabulary notes (SE pp. 779, 780)	as students read
Develop Understanding	
Develop students' understanding of satire with the Literary Analysis annotations (ATE p. 775) [A]	5 min.
Develop students' ability to relate structure to meaning by using the Reading Strategy annotations (SE pp. 778, 780; ATE pp. 775, 778, 780)	5 min.
ASSESS	
Assess Mastery	
Assess students' mastery of the Reading Strategy and Literary Analysis by having them answer the Review and Assess questions (SE/ATE p. 781)	15 min.
Use one or more of the print and media Assessment Resources (ATE p. 783) [A]	up to 45 min.
EXTEND	
Apply Understanding	
Have students complete the Vocabulary Development Lesson and the Grammar and Style Lesson (SE p. 782) [A]	20 min.
Apply students' ability to use details to support meaning by using the Writing Lesson (SE/ATE p. 783) [A]	45 min.
Apply students' understanding using one or more of the Extension Activities (SE p. 783)	20–90 min.

[A] **ACCELERATED INSTRUCTION:**
Use the strategies and activities identified with an [A].

UNIVERSAL ACCESS
- ● = Below Level Students
- ▲ = On-Level Students
- ■ = Above Level Students

Time and Resource Manager

Reading Level: Challenging, Challenging, Average
Average Number of Instructional Days: 3

RESOURCES		
PRINT 📖	**TRANSPARENCIES** 🎞	**TECHNOLOGY** 💿 🎧 📼
• **Beyond Literature,** Humanities Connection: Art, p. 43 ▲ ■		• **Interest Grabber Video,** Tape 5 ● ▲ ■
• **Selection Support Workbook:** ● ▲ ■ Literary Analysis, p. 193 Reading Strategy, p. 192 Build Vocabulary, p. 190	• **Literary Analysis and Reading Transparencies,** pp. 85 and 86 ● ▲ ■	
		• **Listening to Literature** ● ▲ ■ Audiocassettes, Sides 26, 27 Audio CDs, CD 15
• **Literatura en español** ● ▲ • **Literary Analysis for Enrichment** ■		
• **Formal Assessment:** Selection Test, pp. 197–199 ● ▲ ■ • **Open Book Test,** pp. 127–129 ● ▲ ■ • **Performance Assessment and Portfolio Management,** p. 19 ● ▲ ■ • PRENTICE HALL ASSESSMENT *SYSTEM* ● ▲ ■	• PRENTICE HALL ASSESSMENT *SYSTEM* ● ▲ ■ Skills Practice Answers and Explanations on Transparencies	• **Test Bank Software** ● ▲ ■ • **Got It! Assessment Videotapes,** Tape 4 ● ▲
• **Selection Support Workbook:** ● ▲ ■ Grammar and Style, p. 191 • **Writing and Grammar,** Ruby Level ● ▲ ■ • **Extension Activities,** p. 43 ● ▲ ■	• **Daily Language Practice Transparencies** ● ▲ • **Writing Models and Graphic Organizers on Transparencies,** p. 87 ● ▲ ■	• **Writing and Grammar iText CD-ROM** ● ▲ ■ *Take It to the Net* www.phschool.com

BLOCK SCHEDULING: Use one 90-minute class period to preteach the selection and have students read it. Use a second 90-minute class period to assess students' mastery of skills and have them complete one of the Extension Activities.

Step-by-Step Teaching Guide for pp. 774–775

Motivation

Read an excerpt from Jerry Seinfeld's book *Seinlanguage* or a column by Dave Barry, or share a video of the stand-up comedy of Jay Leno or David Letterman to show that no subject is off limits to columnists and comedians who challenge and satirize society and its rituals. Ask students whether they enjoyed the contemporary satire. How do they view the role of writers and artists in analyzing society? Tell them that they're about to encounter a group of poems that comment on society.

■ Interest Grabber Video

As an alternative, play "Reading and Student Response" on Tape 5 to engage student interest.

❶ Background

More About the Authors

The poems of E.E. Cummings are often instantly recognizable because of their style. In addition, Cummings wrote *concrete poetry*—poetry in which the shape of the poem reinforces its meaning. For example, his poem about a grasshopper, "r-p-o-p-h-e-s-s-a-g-r," forms the shape of a grasshopper hopping and reforming itself.

After leaving Oxford, Auden taught school from 1930 to 1935 and later worked for a government film unit. Auden was the most active of the group of young English poets who, in the late 1920s and early 1930s, saw themselves bringing new techniques and attitudes to English poetry.

Prepare to Read

❶ old age sticks ♦ anyone lived in a pretty how town ♦ The Unknown Citizen

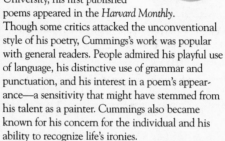

E. E. Cummings (1894–1962)

After working in the French ambulance corps and spending three months behind bars as a political prisoner during World War I, Edward Estlin Cummings studied painting in Paris and subsequently began writing poetry in New York City. A graduate of Harvard University, his first published poems appeared in the *Harvard Monthly*. Though some critics attacked the unconventional style of his poetry, Cummings's work was popular with general readers. People admired his playful use of language, his distinctive use of grammar and punctuation, and his interest in a poem's appearance—a sensitivity that might have stemmed from his talent as a painter. Cummings also became known for his concern for the individual and his ability to recognize life's ironies.

Form vs. Content Although Cummings's poems tend to be unconventional in form and style, they generally express traditional ideas. In his finest poems, Cummings explores the customary poetic terrain of love and nature but makes innovative use of grammar and punctuation to reinforce meaning. Many of his poems also contain comic touches as Cummings addresses the confusing aspects of modern life. Cummings was also a skillful satirist who used his poems to challenge accepted notions and fixed beliefs.

Cummings received a number of awards for his work, including the Boston Fine Arts Poetry Festival Award and the Bollingen Prize in Poetry. In 1968, six years after his death, a volume of his poetry, *The Complete Poems, 1913–1968*, was published. At the time of his death, he was the second most widely read poet in the United States, after Robert Frost.

W. H. Auden (1907–1973)

Although he was influenced by the Modernist poets, Wystan Hugh Auden adopted only those aspects of Modernism with which he felt comfortable. At the same time, he maintained many elements of traditional poetry. Throughout his career, he wrote with insight about people struggling to preserve their individuality in an increasingly conformist society.

Auden was born in England and attended Oxford University. At age twenty-three, he both published his first volume of poetry and developed a passionate interest in politics. He spoke out against poverty in England and the rise of Nazism in Germany.

A New Country In 1939, just before World War II, Auden moved from England to the United States. That move was coincident with his rediscovery of his Christian beliefs. His works *The Double Man* (1941) and *For the Time Being* (1944) depict religion as a way of coping with a disjointed modern society. Despite the comfort he found in religion, Auden became disillusioned with modern life in his later years. He used his poetry to explore the responsibilities of the artist in what he saw as a faithless modern age.

Auden earned the Pulitzer Prize in 1948 for his long narrative poem *The Age of Anxiety* (1947), which explores the confusion associated with post-World War II life. He later produced several more volumes of poetry and a large body of literary criticism. He also anthologized others' works and coauthored at least one musical composition—a libretto for the opera *The Rake's Progress*. From 1954 to 1973, Auden served as Chancellor of the Academy of American Poets.

774 ♦ Disillusion, Defiance, and Discontent (1914–1946)

TEACHING RESOURCES

The following resources can be used to enrich or extend the instruction for pp. 774–775.

Motivation
- ■ Interest Grabber Video, Tape 3 ■

Background
- 📖 Beyond Literature, p. 43
- 💻 *Take It to the Net*
  Visit www.phschool.com for Background and hotlinks for the selections.

Literary Analysis
- 📄 Literary Analysis and Reading Transparencies, Satire, p. 86

Reading
- 📖 Selection Support: Reading Strategy, p. 192; Build Vocabulary, p. 190 ■
- 📄 Literary Analysis and Reading Transparencies, Relate Structure to Meaning, p. 85

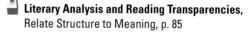

■ **BLOCK SCHEDULING:** Resources marked with this symbol provide varied instruction during 90-minute blocks.

Preview

Connecting to the Literature

Do you ever wonder how you can express your individuality and distinguish yourself from the rest of humanity—or even from your immediate circle of friends? The following poems address this human desire.

❷ Literary Analysis

Satire

Satire is writing in which an author uses humor to ridicule or criticize certain individuals, institutions, types of behavior, or even humanity in general. The purpose of satire is to promote changes in society or in the world. By poking fun at problems, satirists use the force of laughter to persuade readers to accept their point of view. As you read, think about the serious point each poet makes through satire.

Comparing Literary Works

Satirical writings vary in **tone**—a quality that reveals a writer's attitude toward his or her subject, characters, or audience. The tone of a satirical work may be tolerant, humorous, bitter, or biting, and is revealed through the writer's choices of words and details. For example, in naming his characters "anyone" and "noone," Cummings suggests the lack of distinction that comes with excessive conformity. His satire is biting, though it is softened by other elements of the poem:

> one day anyone died i guess
> (and noone stooped to kiss his face)

As you read these poems, compare each poet's tone, and identify the varying kinds of satire that result.

❸ Reading Strategy

Relating Structure to Meaning

You can often connect the ideas of poetry with the form the words take:

- **Structure** is the way a poem is put together in words, lines, and stanzas.
- **Meaning** is the central idea the poet wants to convey.

In his poems, Cummings plays typographical games and breaks rules of grammar and syntax. His structure suits his theme: individual challenges to convention. Use a chart like the one shown to link structure to meaning.

Vocabulary Development

statistics (stə tis′ tiks) *n.* science of collecting and arranging facts about a particular subject in the form of numbers (p. 779)

psychology (sī käl′ ə jē) *n.* science dealing with the mind and with mental and emotional processes (p. 780)

"anyone lived in a pretty how town"

Structure	Meaning
Nine stanzas of four lines apiece	The regularity of the stanzas emphasizes the routine of town life.

old age sticks / anyone lived in a pretty how town / The Unknown Citizen ◆ 775

- Explain to students that in *satire*, an author uses humor for a specific purpose: to ridicule a problem in the world and promote change. Satire can take aim at people, institutions, or societies.

- Use the instruction on p. 775 to explain to students the role of *tone* in satire. Have students discuss the tone of the lines quoted in Comparing Literary Works. What is Cummings satirizing?

- As students read the selection, have them consider the following questions: What is being ridiculed? What is the tone? What kind of change might the poet be promoting?

- Use the Satire transparency in **Literary Analysis and Reading Transparencies**, p. 86, to demonstrate how to recognize and analyze satire.

❸ Reading Strategy

Relating Structure to Meaning

- Read aloud the definitions of *structure* and *meaning* listed in the Reading Strategy instruction on p. 775. Emphasize to students the difference between the two concepts.

- Explain to students that a poem's structure helps to communicate its meaning. Use the graphic organizer on p. 775 to show a relationship between stanza structure and meaning.

- Encourage students to use such a chart to relate the structures of poems to their meanings. Review the strategy using the Relate Structure to Meaning transparency in **Literary Analysis and Reading Transparencies**, p. 85.

Vocabulary Development

- Pronounce each vocabulary word for students, and read the definitions as a class. Have students identify any words with which they are already familiar.

 E-Teach

Visit E-Teach at www.phschool.com for teachers' essays on how to teach, with questions and answers.

CUSTOMIZE INSTRUCTION FOR UNIVERSAL ACCESS

For Less Proficient Readers	For English Learners	For Advanced Readers
Students might find the syntax in this selection extremely challenging. Point out that Cummings often plays with word order; urge students to reorganize words to gain understanding. Suggest that they use the line breaks in Auden's poem to divide his long sentences into manageable phrases.	Warn these students that E.E. Cummings breaks many rules of syntax and punctuation. To help these students negotiate Cummings's work, pair them with more advanced students to read aloud and analyze the poems.	Challenge more advanced students to analyze Cummings's syntax by punctuating a stanza or two from either poem. What do the punctuated versions highlight about Cummings's syntax? These students can also assist less proficient readers and English learners in decoding these poems.

CUSTOMIZE INSTRUCTION
For Logical/Mathematical Learners

Explain to these students that some elements of a poem's structure can be measured very precisely. The pattern of stressed and unstressed syllables in a poem is called *meter*, and it is a part of a poem's structure that can contribute to its meaning. Use the Relating Structure to Meaning transparency in **Literary Analysis and Reading Transparencies** to teach students to study structure closely.

❶ About the Selections

Cummings challenges the way people live in both of these poems. In "old age sticks," Cummings illustrates the cyclical nature of human experience. Youth's liveliness is contrasted with old age's conservatism, but gradually youth becomes old age. "anyone lived in a pretty how town" paints a picture for readers of an anonymous town in which people live routine and unremarkable lives. The seasons pass with regular predictability as the main characters, "anyone" and his wife "noone," do nothing special and are basically unnoticed by the town's other occupants. With their unusual syntax and satirical views, these poems explore the relationship between the individual and society's structure.

❶.old age sticks

E. E. Cummings

    old age sticks
    up Keep
    Off
    signs)&

5   youth yanks them
    down(old
    age
    cries No

    Tres)&(pas)
10 youth laughs
    (sing
    old age

    scolds Forbid
    den Stop
15 Must
    n't Don't

    &)youth goes
    right on
    gr
20 owing old

Remember Now the Days of Thy Youth, 1950, Paul Starrett Sample, Hood Museum of Art, Dartmouth College, Hanover, NH

❸ ▲ **Critical Viewing** Do you think that the elderly men in this painting could belong to the group that Cummings describes, or are they a different sort? On what details did you base your conclusion? **[Speculate]**

TEACHING RESOURCES

The following resources can be used to enrich or extend the instruction for pp. 776–780.

Literary Analysis
📖 **Selection Support:** Literary Analysis, p. 193

Reading
🎧 **Listening to Literature Audiocassettes,** Sides 26, 27 ▪

💿 **Listening to Literature Audio CDs,** CD 15 ▪

▪ **BLOCK SCHEDULING:** Resources marked with this symbol provide varied instruction during 90-minute blocks.

●1 anyone lived in a pretty how town

E. E. Cummings

Background

E. E. Cummings's style is among the most distinctive of any American poet. He molded his poems into unconventional shapes by varying line lengths and inserting unusual spaces between letters and lines. Many of his poems contain little punctuation; the few marks that do appear often highlight important ideas. In addition, Cummings rarely uses capital letters, except for emphasis. Another distinguishing mark of his style is his use of the lower-case *i* when his speakers refer to themselves. This small *i* is meant to convey the idea of a self as a small part of mass society and Cummings's belief in the need for modesty.

anyone lived in a pretty how town
(with up so floating many bells down)
spring summer autumn winter
he sang his didn't he danced his did.

5 Women and men(both little and small)
cared for anyone not at all
they sowed their isn't they reaped their same
sun moon stars rain

children guessed(but only a few
10 and down they forgot as up they grew
autumn winter spring summer)
that noone loved him more by more

when by now and tree by leaf
she laughed his joy she cried his grief
15 bird by snow and stir by still
anyone's any was all to her

●4 ✔ **Reading Check**
Which words are repeated in these stanzas?

anyone lived in a pretty how town ◆ 777

●2 **Background**

Art

Remember Now the Days of Thy Youth, by Paul Starrett Sample

American painter Paul Starrett Sample discovered art while convalescing from tuberculosis. While living in Los Angeles and later in New England, Sample painted scenes of American life that made him immensely popular. His work was included in exhibitions such as the 1939 New York World's Fair. Many critics today consider Sample one of America's most important but under-recognized painters. *Remember Now the Days of Thy Youth,* much like Sample's famous *Maple Sugaring in Vermont,* captures an everyday moment in the lives of ordinary people. Ask:

1. How do the figures in the painting represent the contrasting groups in the poem "old age sticks"?
   Answer: The old men on the porch represent "old age"; the mother and baby and the young couple represent "youth."

2. In the world of the poem, how would you expect the young couple depicted here to behave toward "old age" on the porch?
   Possible response: They would either ignore or overrule "old age," perhaps blocking their view.

●3 ▶ **Critical Viewing**

Possible response: Students may say that the men are of the "sticks up Keep Off signs" group because they are old, and because they are watching instead of participating. Others may say the men are not interfering with youth as it heads on its way.

●4 ✔ **Reading Check**

Answer: The word "anyone" is repeated, as are the names of the seasons: "spring," "summer," "autumn," and "winter."

- Call students' attention to the poem's *stanzas*—its groups of lines. Ask students to identify what characteristics the stanzas all share.
  Answer: Each stanza has four lines. Students may also notice internal rhymes and repetition.

- Point out that the common features make stanzas regular. Then, ask them the Reading Strategy question on p. 778: How do the regular stanzas reinforce the ideas of the poem? Possible response: The regularity of the stanzas emphasizes the monotonous routine of town life.

Answers for p. 778

Review and Assess

1. Possible response: Students may feel that they are scolded by their elders as "youth" is by "old age"; they may also feel that their lives are as routine as those of "anyone" and "noone."

2. **(a)** Old age "sticks up Keep Off signs," "cries," and "scolds." Youth yanks the signs down and "laughs." **(b)** Possible response: Youth is carefree and lively; old age is conservative and authoritarian.

3. **(a)** Youth is "growing old." **(b)** Possible response: Youth shows no care for old age, yet youth is growing old.

4. **(a)** He names the male character "anyone" and the female character "noone." **(b)** Possible response: He might view them as unimportant because no one around them notices or cares about them.

5. **(a)** They "laughed their cryings" and "slept their dreams." **(b)** Possible response: "Laughed their cryings" implies that they hid their feelings. "Slept their dreams" means they lived unimaginative, unfulfilled lives.

6. Possible response: Students may respond that the poem criticizes society for stifling and ignoring the individual. Some students may see the love anyone and noone share as an escape from their cold and anonymous world.

---

someones married their everyones
laughed their cryings and did their dance
(sleep wake hope and then)they
20 said their nevers they slept their dream

stars rain sun moon
(and only the snow can begin to explain
how children are apt to forget to remember
with up so floating many bells down)

❺
25 one day anyone died i guess
(and noone stooped to kiss his face)
busy folk buried them side by side
little by little and was by was

all by all and deep by deep
30 and more by more they dream their sleep
noone and anyone earth by april
wish by spirit and if by yes.

Women and men(both dong and ding)
summer autumn winter spring
35 reaped their sowing and went their came
sun moon stars rain

Review and Assess

Thinking About the Selections

1. **Respond:** What parts of your life do you see in these poems? Explain.

2. **(a) Recall:** In "old age sticks," what actions do old age and youth take? **(b) Compare and Contrast:** Explain the differences Cummings points out between youth and old age.

3. **(a) Recall:** In the final stanza of "old age sticks," what does the poem say is happening to youth? **(b) Interpret:** Explain the irony in this final stanza.

4. **(a) Recall:** What does Cummings name the main male and female characters in "anyone lived in a pretty how town"? **(b) Speculate:** What is the poet suggesting in this choice?

5. **(a) Recall:** What does Cummings say the people do with their cryings and their dreams? **(b) Interpret:** What message is the poet conveying about the ideas of individuality and conformity?

6. **Evaluate:** Which poem presents a more positive view of life? Explain.

✳ ENRICHMENT: Math Connection

The Census

In "The Unknown Citizen," W.H. Auden pokes fun at the amount of data collected on people in the United States. One basic means of collecting such data is the census. A population census—a count of the number of people—is taken in the United States every ten years. The first United States Census was a population count that began in 1790. It took about eighteen months and revealed that fewer than four million people lived in the country. Since then, the population—and the way it is counted—has grown.

The census is now conducted by the Bureau of the Census, part of the Department of Commerce. In 1990, the U.S. population was over 280 million. Data collected in that census included information such as population, age, sex, ethnicity, marital status, and more.

Why is the information collected by the census useful to the American people? Encourage students to look for the positive side of the fascination with data that Auden satirizes in this poem.

The Unknown Citizen

W. H. Auden

(To JS/07/M/378 This Marble Monument Is Erected by the State)

Turret Lathe Operator, Grant Wood, Cedar Rapids Museum of Art, Cedar Rapids, Iowa. Courtesy Associated American Artists, © Estate of Grant Wood/Licensed by VAGA, New York, NY

▲ **Critical Viewing** In what ways does the man in this painting appear to fit Auden's description of "the unknown citizen"? **[Analyze]**

He was found by the Bureau of <u>Statistics</u> to be
One against whom there was no official complaint,
And all the reports on his conduct agree
That, in the modern sense of an old-fashioned word, he was a saint,
5   For in everything he did he served the Greater Community.
Except for the War till the day he retired
He worked in a factory and never got fired,
But satisfied his employers, Fudge Motors Inc.
Yet he wasn't a scab or odd in his views,
10   For his Union reports that he paid his dues,
(Our report on his Union shows it was sound)

statistics (stə tis′ tiks) *n.* science of collecting and arranging facts about a particular subject in the form of numbers

✓ Reading Check
What makes the subject of the poem "a saint"?

The Unknown Citizen ◆ 779

---

❻ **About the Selection**

This poem highlights how society can become so concerned with recording data that it obliterates individuals and their emotions or beliefs. The poem's central character, the unknown citizen, is documented, analyzed, and studied, yet no one knows anything about his true personal experience of the world.

❼ **Background**

Art

Turret Lathe Operator, by Grant Wood

Grant Wood was born and lived much of his life in or near Anamosa, Iowa. There he painted, taught art, and promoted regional art, especially that capturing the unique Midwestern experience. *Turret Lathe Operator* is part of a series commissioned by a dairy equipment manufacturer to show quality craftsmanship in its factory. Ask:

> Why might the unknown citizen in the painting or poem not communicate his unhappiness to the world?
> Possible response: He might assume the world is not interested in his opinions.

❽ ▶ **Critical Viewing**

Possible response: Students may say he looks like an ordinary man who would not challenge or surprise anyone. In the factory, as long as his machine keeps going, no one will notice him.

❾ **✓ Reading Check**

Answer: He is "a saint" because he appears to have "served the Greater Community" rather than himself.

CUSTOMIZE INSTRUCTION FOR UNIVERSAL ACCESS

For English Learners	For Gifted/Talented Students
Stress that Auden's poem is not meant to be read literally. Help them locate examples of exaggeration, such as lines 14, 15, 19, 24, and 26, and discuss the *tone* these examples convey. Reading along with **Listening to Literature** Audiocassette Sides 26 and 27 or Audio CD 15 can help students recognize tone.	If these students are interested by the parallels between the poems in this selection and the paintings on pp. 776–777 and 779, encourage them to learn more about the artists, Paul Starrett Sample and Grant Wood. Students can deliver presentations on the artists, including reproductions of their paintings.

⓾ Reading Strategy
Relating Structure to Meaning

- Call students' attention to line 18. Be sure that they recognize the capitalization of "Producers Research" and "High-Grade Living." Ask students what these terms describe.
  Answer: They are bureaucratic groups in the Unknown Citizens' society.

- Ask the Reading Strategy question on p. 780: Why do you think Auden capitalizes words in line 18?
  Possible response: Auden implies that these groups are falsely elevating their own status.

▶ Monitor Progress Encourage students to discuss the meaning of other examples of unusual capitalization in the poem.

Answers for p. 780

Review and Assess

1. Possible response: Students who have had interaction with bureaucracies—from government offices to standardized tests—may have experienced this feeling.

2. (a) The state identifies him as JS/07/M/378. (b) Possible response: They suggest the impersonal nature of the society; they suggest that he has no true identity.

3. (a) He worked in a factory for most of his life; he paid union dues; he was married and had children. (b) Possible response: The state knows nothing about his feelings or concerns. (c) Possible response: These are not data that can be easily monitored.

4. (a) The speaker calls the questions "Was he free?" and "Was he happy?" absurd. (b) Possible response: Students will probably say that these questions are very important. (c) The final lines are strongly satiric. The speaker cares little and knows less about the citizen's reality. The poet is poking fun at the bureaucratic structure of society.

5. Possible response: Our government has a large, bureaucratic system in place like the one described in the poem. However, the poem exaggerates the idea of bureaucratic control over the individual.

6. Possible response: Information about the man's inner life—about his loves, fears, hopes, and dreams—is missing from the poem.

And our Social <u>Psychology</u> workers found
That he was popular with his mates and liked a drink.
The Press are convinced that he bought a paper every day
15 And that his reactions to advertisements were normal in every way.
Policies taken out in his name prove that he was fully insured,
And his Health-card shows he was once in hospital but left it cured.
⓾ Both Producers Research and High-Grade Living declare
He was fully sensible to the advantages of the Installment Plan
20 And had everything necessary to the Modern Man,
A phonograph, a radio, a car and a frigidaire.
Our researchers into Public Opinion are content
That he held the proper opinions for the time of year;
When there was peace, he was for peace; when there was war,
    he went.
25 He was married and added five children to the population.
Which our Eugenist[1] says was the right number for a parent of
    his generation,
And our teachers report that he never interfered with their
    education.
Was he free? Was he happy? The question is absurd:
Had anything been wrong, we should certainly have heard.

---

1. **Eugenist** (yōō jen´ ist) *n.* a specialist in eugenics, the movement devoted to improving the human species through genetic control.

psychology (sī käl´ ə jē) *n.* science dealing with the mind and with mental and emotional processes

Reading Strategy
Relating Structure to Meaning Why do you think Auden capitalizes words in line 18?

Review and Assess

Thinking About the Selection

1. **Respond:** Have you ever felt as though you have been reduced to a number? Explain your answer.

2. **(a) Recall:** How does the state identify the unknown citizen in the poem's subtitle? **(b) Interpret:** What do these numbers and letters suggest?

3. **(a) Recall:** Identify at least three facts the state knows about the citizen's life. **(b) Interpret:** In what ways is the citizen "unknown" to the state? **(c) Deduce:** Why might the state have heard nothing about these aspects of the citizen's life?

4. **(a) Recall:** What questions does the speaker refer to as "absurd"? **(b) Make a Judgment:** Are these questions actually absurd? Explain. **(c) Analyze:** In what ways do the final two lines clarify the poet's attitude or beliefs?

5. **Apply:** Which aspects of the society in the poem are like contemporary America? Which are different? Explain.

6. **Evaluate:** What types of information about the man do you feel are missing from the poem? Explain.

780 ◆ *Disillusion, Defiance, and Discontent (1914–1946)*

 ASSESSMENT PRACTICE: Reading Comprehension

Try Words in a Sentence   (For more practice, see Test Preparation Workbook, p. 45.)

Many tests require students to correctly answer sentence-completion questions. Use the following sample item to show students that they can often eliminate choices because they are illogical, the wrong part of speech, or inconsistent with the sentence meaning.

Thomas Wolfe's first novel, *Look Homeward, Angel*, was a critical and _____ success and earned Wolfe widespread _____.

A moral; abuse

B financial; recognition

C personal; apathy

D profit; applause

The first word in answer choice *D* is the wrong part of speech. The context of the sentence indicates that the second word will have a positive meaning, eliminating choices *A* and *C*. Answer *B* is the best choice.

Review and Assess

Literary Analysis

Satire

1. What changes might E.E. Cummings like to see in the world of "old age sticks"?

2. Based on "anyone lived in a pretty how town," what small-town qualities and behaviors does Cummings **satirize**?

3. (a) Using a chart like the one shown here, name four groups that report on the unknown citizen's activities. (b) What do the concerns of the state and these groups reveal about society as a whole?

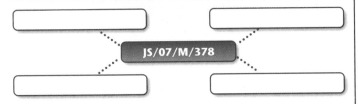

JS/07/M/378

4. (a) Based on "The Unknown Citizen," what values do you think Auden holds dear? (b) What type of society do you think he supports?

Comparing Literary Works

5. In what way does each of the poems explore the conflict between individuality and conformity to a group?

6. (a) Identify the tone, or attitude, of each poem. (b) Note two details from each poem that reveal the tone. (c) Which tone do you find most effective for the purpose of satire? Explain.

Reading Strategy

Relating Structure to Meaning

7. How does the **structure** of "old age sticks" relate to the idea of rules and rule-breaking as it is presented in the poem?

8. Discuss how Auden's style of capitalization affects the meaning and tone of his poem.

Extend Understanding

9. **Cultural Connection:** In what way have bureaucracies such as government agencies or corporations affected our sense of individuality and identity? Explain.

old age sticks / anyone lived in a pretty how town / The Unknown Citizen ◆ 781

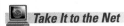

Answers for p. 781

Review and Assess

1. Possible response: He might like to see "old age" become more tolerant of "youth" and "youth" become more attentive toward "old age."

2. Possible response: He satirizes the conformity of small towns that stifles creativity and individualism, as well as the anonymity and coldness with which people treat each other.

3. (a) Possible response: his Union; High-Grade Living; Public Opinion researchers; the Eugenist (b) Possible response: It is a society in which people have little freedom and are controlled by the state.

4. (a) Auden probably values freedom, individuality, and empathy. (b) Possible response: He probably supports a society that places greater emphasis on individuality and freedom.

5. Possible response: "old age sticks" suggests that young people have more individuality than "old age"; "anyone lived in a pretty how town" suggests that individuals can lose their identities in society; and "The Unknown Citizen" argues that some societies can deny identity to individuals.

6. (a) Possible response: The tone in "old age sticks" is resigned to the conflict between youth and age; the tone in "anyone lived in a pretty how town" is disdainful of the way most people lead lives that lack imagination, creativity, or a sense of meaning; and the tone in "The Unknown Citizen" is full of contempt for an oppressive society. (b) Details in "old age sticks" include the description of old age endlessly putting up signs and youth tearing them down, which suggest a cycle that won't change. Details in "anyone lived in a pretty how town" include "cared for anyone not at all" and "children are apt to forget to remember." Details in "The Unknown Citizen" include "The question is absurd" and the last line. (c) Possible response: Students may find that Auden's tone is most effective because it

continued

Answers continued

contrasts with the detached nature of the poet's speaker.

7. Possible response: The regular length of the lines corresponds to old age's tendency toward rules. The other structural elements are nontraditional, in keeping with rule-breaking youth. Also, references to old age and its rules are in parentheses, suggesting unimportance.

8. Possible response: Students should recognize that Auden capitalizes state and societal institutions, reinforcing their formality and officiality.

9. Possible response: American citizens are depersonalized by large corporations and bureaucracies. For example, the emergence of "superstores" has obliterated neighborhood businesses and made main streets more conformist.

❶ Vocabulary Development

Word Analysis

1. *psychiatry*: the branch of medicine concerned with the study, treatment, and prevention of disorders of the mind. Possible response: He specialized in *psychiatry* in medical school.

2. *psychosomatic*: a physical disorder of the body originating in or aggravated by the psychic or emotional process. Possible response: The doctor labeled his patient's symptoms as *psychosomatic* when he could find no physical cause for them.

3. *psychotic*: of, or having the nature of, a psychosis. Possible response: The serial killer was a confirmed *psychotic*.

4. *psychiatrist*: a doctor of medicine specializing in disorders of the mind. Possible response: The *psychiatrist* diagnosed the patient with schizophrenia.

Spelling Strategy

1. *psychopath*; Possible response: She ranted as if she was a *psychopath*.

2. *psychic*; Possible response: He asked the *psychic* what his future would hold.

3. *psoriasis*; Possible response: His skin showed signs of *psoriasis*.

Fluency: Context

1. psychology
2. statistics
3. psychology
4. statistics
5. psychology

❷ Grammar and Style

1. (at least no sensible person)
2. (except for the love poems)
3. (especially when read by an actor)
4. (I'd guess)
5. (except for their different punctuation styles)

Writing Application

Paragraphs should use parentheses to set off related or interruptive material at least twice.

782

Integrate Language Skills

❶ Vocabulary Development Lesson

Word Analysis: Greek Root *-psych-*

The name Psyche—a heroine in a Greek myth—comes from a Greek word meaning "breath" or "soul." The Greek root *-psych-* means "soul" or "mind," and it forms the basis for a number of English words, including *psychology*. Write definitions for the following *-psych-* words. Then, write a sentence using each word.

1. psychiatry
2. psychosomatic
3. psychotic
4. psychiatrist

Spelling Strategy

Some words begin with the *s* sound but are actually spelled *ps*: *psychology*, *psalm*. These words derive from the Greek letter *psi*, pronounced *si*. Complete the spelling of the words below. Then, write a sentence for each.

1. __ychopath
2. __ychic
3. __oriasis

❷ Grammar and Style Lesson

Parentheses

Parentheses are used to enclose extra information that is interruptive or loosely related to the rest of the sentence but that does not deserve special attention. Use parentheses instead of dashes and commas to set off such information.

Example: My father's new truck (the one he bought last month) has a lot of power.

Practice Rewrite each of the following sentences, adding parentheses to improve the clarity.

1. No person at least no sensible person could accuse Cummings of being a conformist.

Fluency: Context

The word *psychology* refers to the science dealing with mental and emotional processes. The word *statistics* refers to the science of tabulation or counting. Decide whether each of the following situations relates more closely to psychology or statistics.

1. Teacher assigns class lesson on grieving process.
2. Teacher keeps records of completed assignments.
3. You explain your dream to a friend.
4. Scientist publishes paper on blood diseases in New York State.
5. A star athlete's endorsement boosts product sales in the first two weeks following an advertisement's release.

2. Cummings's unconventional poetry except for the love poems can be silly, serious, and witty.
3. Auden's poetry especially when read by an actor always affects listeners.
4. Auden's political viewpoints I'd guess were formed over time.
5. The works of two poets except for their different punctuation styles have much in common.

Writing Application Write a paragraph about one of your hobbies, using parentheses at least twice to set off information.

WG *Prentice Hall Writing and Grammar Connection: Chapter 27, Section 5*

TEACHING RESOURCES

The following resources can be used to enrich or extend the instruction for pp. 782–783.

Vocabulary

📖 **Selection Support:** Build Vocabulary, p. 190

📖 **Vocabulary and Spelling Practice Book** (Use this booklet for skills enrichment.) ■

Grammar

📖 **Selection Support:** Grammar and Style, p. 191

WG **Writing and Grammar,** Ruby Level, p. 746 ■

📖 **Daily Language Practice Transparencies**

Writing

WG **Writing and Grammar,** Ruby Level, p. 304 ■

⊙ **Writing and Grammar iText CD-ROM**

📖 **Writing Models and Graphic Organizers on Transparencies,** p. 87

 **BLOCK SCHEDULING:** Resources marked with this symbol provide varied instruction during 90-minute blocks.

❸ Writing Lesson

Introduction to a Poetry Reading

Poetry readings—in coffee shops, bookstores, libraries, or community centers—often feature the work of more than one writer. Imagine that you have been asked to organize a reading of Auden's and Cummings's poetry. Write an introduction that welcomes your audience, provides some background information on the poets, and briefly compares their work.

Prewriting Reread the poems. Develop a central idea about similarities and differences in the work of Cummings and Auden. Jot down details or examples from the poems that support this main idea.

> ### Model: Gathering Details of Support
>
> **Theme:** Cummings uses a highly ordered stanza structure in "anyone lived in a pretty how town."
>
> **Structure:** In "The Unknown Citizen," Auden explores the effect of a highly organized society on individuals.
>
> > Specific references to poetry will strengthen an introduction to the works.

Drafting Keep your remarks brief but informative and well supported with details. Use a conversational writing style suitable to oral delivery.

Revising Make sure you provide enough information to prepare the audience for the poetry they will hear. Revise to ensure that your details are relevant and support your main points.

W̶G Prentice Hall Writing and Grammar Connection: Chapter 14, Section 2

❹ Extension Activities

Listening and Speaking The poem "anyone lived in a pretty how town" is set in the country. How might the poem be different if it were set in a city? In a **group discussion,** brainstorm the topic. Consider the following:

- What kinds of lives would people live?
- How would the setting change the activities?
- In what ways might it affect relationships?

After discussing the differences, write a revision based on an urban setting, and share it with the class. [Group Activity]

Research and Technology Auden speaks out against totalitarianism—a system in which the government takes control of civil life. Use the Internet to investigate totalitarian governments in Europe after World War I. Compile your findings in a **written report.** Incorporate spreadsheets on the topic in your word-processor document.

 **Take It to the Net** www.phschool.com

Go online for an additional research activity using the Internet.

old age sticks / anyone lived in a pretty how town / The Unknown Citizen ◆ 783

---

❸ Writing Lesson

- Explain to students that their introductions should provide background information about each poet. Review the background information provided on p. 774.

- To begin prewriting, lead a discussion of the poems in this selection. What do all three share? Encourage students to use the Comparison-and-Contrast transparency on p. 87 of **Writing Models and Graphic Organizers on Transparencies** to organize their notes.

- As students begin drafting, remind them that their introductions are meant to be read aloud. Students should write in a conversational tone.

- Use the Comparison-and-Contrast Essay rubric on p. 19 of **Performance Assessment and Portfolio Management** to assess students' work.

❹ Listening and Speaking

- Put students in groups to re-read "anyone lived in a pretty how town." Have groups consider the bulleted questions on p. 783. Encourage students to take notes on their discussions.

- Before students begin to write their poems, remind them to keep Cummings's themes and tone as they change the poem's setting.

- Have students practice reading their poems in groups before presenting them to the class.

CUSTOMIZE INSTRUCTION
For Universal Access

To address different learning styles, use the following activities suggested in the **Extension Activities** booklet, p. 43.

For Bodily/Kinesthetic and Interpersonal Learners, use Activity 5.

For Spatial/Visual Learners, use Activity 6.

For Verbal/Linguistic Learners, use Activity 7.

ASSESSMENT RESOURCES

The following resources can be used to assess students' knowledge and skills.

Selection Assessment

- **Formal Assessment,** pp. 197–199
- **Open Book Test,** pp. 127–129
- **Got It! Assessment Videotapes,** Tape 4
- **Test Bank Software**

Take It to the Net
Visit www.phschool.com for self-tests and additional questions on the selections.

Writing Rubric

- **Performance Assess. and Portfolio Mgmt.,** p. 19

PRENTICE HALL ASSESSMENT SYSTEM

- **Workbook**
- **Skill Book**
- **Transparencies**
- **CD-ROM**

The Far and the Near

Lesson Objectives

1. **To analyze and respond to literary elements**
   - Literary Analysis: Climax and Anticlimax
   - Connecting Literary Elements: Rising Action

2. **To read, comprehend, analyze, and critique a short story**
   - Reading Strategy: Predicting
   - Reading Check Questions
   - Review and Assess Questions
   - Assessment Practice (ATE)

3. **To develop word analysis skills, fluency, and systematic vocabulary**
   - Vocabulary Development Lesson: Latin Root -temp-

4. **To understand and apply written and oral language conventions**
   - Spelling Strategy
   - Grammar and Style Lesson: Restrictive and Nonrestrictive Participial Clauses

5. **To understand and apply appropriate writing and research strategies**
   - Writing Lesson: Compare and Contrast Essay
   - Extension Activity: Written Report

6. **To understand and apply listening and speaking strategies**
   - Extension Activity: Interview

STEP-BY-STEP TEACHING GUIDE	PACING GUIDE
PRETEACH	
Motivate Students and Provide Background	
Use the Motivation activity (ATE p. 784)	5 min.
Read and discuss Author and Background information (SE/ATE p. 784) **A**	5 min.
Introduce the Concepts	
Introduce the Literary Analysis and Reading Strategy (SE/ATE p. 785) **A**	15 min.
Pronounce the vocabulary words and read their definitions (SE p. 785)	5 min.
TEACH	
Monitor Comprehension	
Informally monitor comprehension by circulating while students read independently or in groups **A**	20 min.
Monitor students' comprehension with the Reading Check notes (SE/ATE pp. 787, 789)	as students read
Develop vocabulary with Vocabulary notes (SE pp. 788, 790; ATE p. 788)	as students read
Develop Understanding	
Develop students' understanding of climax and anticlimax with the Literary Analysis annotations (SE pp. 787, 788, 789; ATE pp. 787, 789) **A**	5 min.
ASSESS	
Assess Mastery	
Assess students' mastery of the Reading Strategy and Literary Analysis by having them answer the Review and Assess questions (SE/ATE p. 791)	15 min.
Use one or more of the print and media Assessment Resources (ATE p. 793) **A**	up to 45 min.
EXTEND	
Apply Understanding	
Have students complete the Vocabulary Development Lesson and the Grammar Lesson (SE p. 792) **A**	20 min.
Apply students' ability to build contrast in writing by using the Writing Lesson (SE/ATE p. 793) **A**	45 min.
Apply students' understanding using one or more of the Extension Activities (SE p. 793)	20–90 min.

 ACCELERATED INSTRUCTION:
Use the strategies and activities identified with an **A**.

UNIVERSAL ACCESS
● = Below Level Students
▲ = On-Level Students
■ = Above Level Students

Time and Resource Manager

RESOURCES		
PRINT 📖	**TRANSPARENCIES** 🎴	**TECHNOLOGY** 💿 🎧 📼
• **Beyond Literature,** p. 44 ▲ ■		• **Interest Grabber Video,** Tape 5 ● ▲ ■
• **Selection Support Workbook:** ● ▲ ■ Literary Analysis, p. 197 Reading Strategy, p. 196 Build Vocabulary, p. 194	• **Literary Analysis and Reading Transparencies,** pp. 87 and 88 ● ▲ ■	
• **Adapted Reader's Companion** ● • **Reader's Companion** ●		• **Listening to Literature** ● ▲ ■ Audiocassettes, Side 27 Audio CDs, CD 15
• **English Learner's Companion** ● ▲ • **Literatura en español** ● ▲ • **Literary Analysis for Enrichment** ■	• **Fine Art Transparencies,** Volume 1, Transparency 10	
• **Formal Assessment:** Selection Test, p. 200–202 ● ▲ ■ • **Open Book Test,** p. 130–132 ● ▲ ■ • **Performance Assessment and Portfolio Management,** p. 19 ● ▲ ■ • PRENTICE HALL **ASSESSMENT** *SYSTEM* ● ▲ ■	• PRENTICE HALL **ASSESSMENT** *SYSTEM* ● ▲ ■ Skills Practice Answers and Explanations on Transparencies	• **Test Bank Software** ● ▲ ■ • **Got It! Assessment Videotapes,** Tape 4 ● ▲
• **Selection Support Workbook:** ● ▲ ■ Grammar and Style, p. 195 • **Writing and Grammar,** Ruby Level ● ▲ ■ • **Extension Activities,** p. 44 ● ▲ ■	• **Daily Language Practice Transparencies** ● ▲ • **Writing Models and Graphic Organizers on Transparencies,** pp. 41, 87 ● ▲ ■	• **Writing and Grammar iText CD-ROM** ● ▲ ■ 🖥️ *Take It to the Net* www.phschool.com

BLOCK SCHEDULING: Use one 90-minute class period to preteach the selection and have students read it. Use a second 90-minute class period to assess students' mastery of skills and have them complete one of the Extension Activities.

Step-by-Step Teaching Guide
for pp. 784–785

Motivation

Thomas Wolfe's story juxtaposes two perspectives on life—the far and the near views. As students read, they will discover the sharp contrast between these two perspectives. Engage students' interest in the story by involving them in the following demonstration. Have students describe a distant part of the school, such as the gymnasium or library. Then, visit the identified location as a class. Again, invite students to describe it. How do the two descriptions differ? Challenge students to explain the contrast.

❶ Background

More About the Author

Thomas Wolfe's autobiographical novel *Look Homeward Angel* has become a classic of American literature. Since its publication in 1929, it has never gone out of print. The book describes Wolfe's boyhood in Asheville, North Carolina with such frankness and realism that the town would not permit it to be purchased for the public libraries for over seven years. Today, however, Wolfe is regarded as one of Asheville's most illustrious citizens, and his boyhood home —the house he called "Dixieland" in the novel—has become a site attracting thousands of literary tourists each year.

Prepare to Read

❶ The Far and the Near

Thomas Wolfe
(1900–1938)

A man of tremendous energy, appetites, and size, Thomas Wolfe poured out thousands of pages of fiction during his brief career. Driven by the desire to experience all life had to offer, he pursued variety. He lived in the city and in the country, in America and in Europe, in the North and in the South. He reflected this passion for life in his work—in its sheer volume, in the expanses of time and territory it covers, and in his characters who were symbols of greater humanity.

An Instant Success Born in Asheville, North Carolina, Wolfe grew up in a large, eccentric family whose members later served as models for his fiction. His mother speculated in real estate. His father made tombstones. Shortly before the age of sixteen, Wolfe entered the University of North Carolina. There, he became interested in playwriting, a focus he pursued during and after his postgraduate studies at Harvard. Wolfe eventually moved to New York City, where he taught composition at New York University and wrote plays in his spare time.

Unable to find success as a playwright, Wolfe turned to writing fiction. With the assistance of Maxwell Perkins, the leading editor of the time, Wolfe published his first novel in 1929, the loosely autobiographical *Look Homeward, Angel*. The novel was a critical and financial success and earned Wolfe widespread recognition. In 1930, Wolfe was awarded a Guggenheim fellowship that allowed him to travel extensively in Europe.

A New Direction Inspired by the success of his first novel, Wolfe began working on a sequel. Once again, Perkins helped him shorten and shape the novel, which was published in 1935 as *Of Time and the River*. The novel sold well, yet Wolfe was criticized for basing his work too closely on his own life and for his reliance on Perkins.

A New Direction Stung by the criticism, Wolfe switched publishers and struck out on a new course. He became obsessed with the idea that his duty as a writer was to act as a social historian, to interpret his time and place. Unfortunately, he died of a brain infection before he could finish another novel.

Wolfe did, however, leave several thousand pages of manuscript in the hands of another editor, Edward Aswell. Aswell shaped Wolfe's drafts into two more books, *The Web and the Rock* (1939) and *You Can't Go Home Again* (1940).

Sharp Contrasts The contrasts between Wolfe's early, highly personal writings and his later, more socially focused work can perhaps be traced to the differences between his brooding, ambitious mother and his outgoing but self-indulgent father. Certainly, contrast plays a key role in much of Wolfe's writing.

As if to nurture To develop these differences in his work, Wolfe pursued life with an enormous appetite. He said, "I will go everywhere and see everything. I will meet all the people I can. I will think all the thoughts, feel all the emotions I am able, and I will write, write, write."

Final Assessment Had he not died so young, there is little doubt that Wolfe's literary output would have been great. Despite the criticism that he lacked discipline, his talent was profound. In his novels and short stories he displayed a strong sense of time and place, an ability to create vivid and realistic descriptions, and a deep understanding of the human condition. All of these abilities find expression in Wolfe's story "The Far and the Near," which explores the often painful disparity between imagination and real life.

784 ◆ *Disillusion, Defiance, and Discontent (1914–1946)*

TEACHING RESOURCES

The following resources can be used to enrich or extend the instruction for pp. 784–785.

Motivation

📼 **Interest Grabber Video**, Tape 5

Background

📖 **Beyond Literature**, p. 44

Take It to the Net

Visit www.phschool.com for Background and hotlinks for the author.

Literary Analysis

📖 **Literary Analysis and Reading Transparencies,** Climax and Anticlimax, p. 88

Reading

📖 **Selection Support:** Reading Strategy, p. 196; Build Vocabulary, p. 194

📖 **Literary Analysis and Reading Transparencies,** Predicting, p. 87

Preview
Connecting to the Literature
At some time in your life, you have probably looked forward to an experience, only to find that it was not what you had dreamed of. In this story, a man learns the difference between hopes, dreams, and sober reality.

❷ Literary Analysis
Climax and Anticlimax
The **climax** in a story is the high point of interest, the moment at which the conflict is resolved. When that resolution is unexpectedly disappointing, ridiculous, or trivial, it is called an **anticlimax.** Like a climax, an anticlimax is the biggest moment in the story, but it is more a low point than a high point in the action. The reader, who has been led to expect that something important or serious is about to occur, is suddenly confronted with the letdown of a seemingly inappropriate resolution. When used effectively, anticlimax can create a variety of effects, from pathos—sorrow or sympathy—to humor.

Connecting Literary Elements
To keep readers engaged, writers must grab their interest early. Once a story's central conflict is introduced, the events leading up to the climax help build readers' anticipation. These events constitute a story's **rising action.** As you read, identify the elements of the rising action to see how they add to your expectations of the climax.

❸ Reading Strategy
Predicting
This story about a train engineer's life is a bit like a real train ride: Signposts guide the way to the final destination. These clues enable you to **predict** upcoming events and outcomes. Watch for signals in the story's details that can help you predict where the action is headed. Consider this passage from the story:

> Every day, a few minutes after two o'clock in the afternoon, the limited express . . . passed this spot.

Because the writer tells you the place is important, you might predict that the story will involve "this spot" in some way. As you read, predict what is to come. Record the information in a chart like the one shown here.

Clues

+

Prior Knowledge, Experience, or Expectations

=

Prediction

Vocabulary Development
tempo (tem′ pō) *n.* rate of activity of a sound or motion; pace (p. 788)

sallow (sal′ ō) *adj.* sickly; pale yellow (p. 789)

sullen (sul′ ən) *adj.* sulky; glum (p. 790)

timorous (tim′ ər əs) *adj.* full of fear (p. 790)

visage (viz′ ij) *n.* appearance (p. 790)

The Far and the Near ◆ 785

❷ Literary Analysis
Climax and Anticlimax
- Read the instruction on Climax and Anticlimax aloud.
- Invite a volunteer to describe the concepts of climax and anticlimax in their own words.
- Then, ask one or two students to relate the plot line of a favorite film or TV show. As each student speaks, tell the class to identify the climax—the moment of highest tension or suspense.
- Invite students to suggest examples from movies or television shows of anticlimax —when the viewer's expectations are disappointed in some way, and the story resolves in a trivial or meaningless outcome.
- Urge students as they read this story to pay attention to the ways in which the author builds and then foils their expectations.

❸ Reading Strategy
Predicting
- Have a volunteer read the instruction about Predicting aloud.
- Draw students' attention to the ideas of signposts or clues provided by the author. Tell students that an author deliberately includes such clues to build readers' expectations.
- Conduct a discussion about the variety of clues given in the passage from the story on p. 785. What can readers predict about "the limited express" or "the spot" noted in the passage?
Answer: The story will involve the train and the place in some important way.

Vocabulary Development
- Pronounce each vocabulary word for students, and read the definitions as a class. Have students identify any words with which they are already familiar.

 E-Teach

Visit E-Teach at www.phschool.com for teachers' essays on how to teach, with questions and answers.

CUSTOMIZE INSTRUCTION FOR UNIVERSAL ACCESS

For Special Needs Students	For Less Proficient Readers	For English Learners
Have students read the adapted version of "The Far and the Near" in the **Adapted Reader's Companion**. This version provides basic-level instruction in an interactive format with questions and write-on lines. Completing the adapted version will prepare students to read the selection in the Student Edition.	Have students read "The Far and the Near" in the **Reader's Companion**. This version provides basic-level instruction in an interactive format with questions and write-on lines. After students finish the selection in **Reader's Companion**, have them complete the questions and activities in the Student Edition.	Have students read the adapted version of Wolfe's story in the **English Learner's Companion**. This version provides basic-level instruction in an interactive format with questions and write-on lines. Completing the adapted version will prepare students to read the selection in the Student Edition.

Step-by-step Teaching Guide for pp. 786–790

CUSTOMIZE INSTRUCTION
For Bodily/Kinesthetic Learners

Students will appreciate the changing perspective best by experiencing it physically. Select an object that is both definite in form and highly detailed. Show students the object from a distance. Invite their observations. Then, show them the object close up. Again, invite their observations. Discuss how the changing proximity affects their responses.

❶ About the Selection

The central character, a train engineer, passes by a house every day for twenty years. A woman and her daughter appear each time and wave. Through the difficulties the engineer endures in his career, the image of the women remains constant. When he retires, he visits them, only to discover that the women are unattractive and unfriendly—nothing like what he had expected. The story underscores the idea that distance and anticipation are often more pleasant than reality.

❷ Background

Art

Stone City, Iowa, by Grant Wood

Grant Wood, an American painter, was a lifelong resident of Iowa. He studied painting in Europe before returning to Iowa to embrace the inspiration he found in its familiar people and places.

Stone City, Iowa is a perfect example of Wood's interest in everyday objects and scenes. Although the painting depicts realistic elements, the almost geometric forms give the picture a surrealistic air. Use this question for discussion:

What elements in the painting underscore the importance of perspective addressed in Wolfe's story? Possible answer: The picture's rising foreground and diminishing background frame the town, making it a focal point. In addition, the perspective omits any unpleasant details, making the town seem idyllic. Similarly, in the story, the engineer's distance from the women makes them a focal point for his imagination, and erases the possibilities of their flaws or failings.

786

❶ The Far and the Near

Thomas Wolfe

Stone City, Iowa, Grant Wood, Joslyn Art Museum, Omaha, Nebraska, © Estate of Grant Wood/Licensed by VAGA, New York, NY

Background

With the driving of the "golden spike" on May 10, 1869, at Promontory, Utah, the first transcontinental rail link was completed. Finishing the western half had taken more than six years, the work of thousands, and the lives of many. With its completion, America's love affair with the railways had officially begun. Now, people could travel the width of the young nation in relative comfort; they could strike out for the inexpensive land available to homesteaders; they could return East to visit relatives. In many ways, the nation grew more united. Cities grew at railroad hubs such as Chicago and St. Louis. As the railroad crisscrossed the nation, untamed land and lifestyles, like those of cowboys, disappeared. America became a nation of towns like the one the engineer in "The Far and the Near" observes from his perch in the train engine.

O n the outskirts of a little town upon a rise of land that swept back from the railway there was a tidy little cottage of white boards, trimmed vividly with green blinds. To one side of the house there was a garden neatly patterned with plots of growing vegetables, and an arbor for the grapes which ripened late in August. Before the house there were three mighty oaks which sheltered it in their clean and massive shade in summer, and to the other side there was a border of gay flowers. The whole place had an air of tidiness, thrift, and modest comfort.

Every day, a few minutes after two o'clock ❸ in the afternoon, the limited express between two cities passed this spot. At that moment the great train, having halted for a breathing

❹ ◀ **Critical Viewing** In what ways might this painting reflect the engineer's perspective on the farms and villages he sees along his train route? **[Analyze]**

Literary Analysis
Climax, Anticlimax, and Rising Action What effect does the routine of "every day" have on your expectations of the story?

❺ ✔ **Reading Check**

What happens everyday a few minutes after two o'clock?

The Far and the Near ◆ 787

❸ **Literary Analysis**
Climax, Anticlimax, and Rising Action

- Remind students that readers' expectations build as the action of a story progresses.

- Have students read the bracketed passage silently. Then, ask them to describe the scene described in the first paragraph and to note what happens "every day"?
  Answer: Every day, the train passes by a tidy cottage on the outskirts of a small town.

- Ask students the Literary Analysis question on p. 787: What effect does the routine of "every day" have on your expectations of the story?
  Possible answer: It suggests that the story will involve the cottage, and perhaps some alteration to the daily routine.

❹ ▶ **Critical Viewing**

Possible answer: Students may note that the painting depicts the town from afar and above in a way that mirrors the engineer's perspective.

❺ ✔ **Reading Check**

Answer: A train traveling between two unnamed cities passes a small cottage.

CUSTOMIZE INSTRUCTION FOR UNIVERSAL ACCESS

For Less Proficient Readers	For English Learners	For Advanced Readers
Although Wolfe's story is very brief, it covers a time period of twenty years. To ensure that students gain a clear understanding of when events are taking place, urge them to note words and phrases related to time. For example, on p. 787, draw their attention to the words "Every day."	Some of Wolfe's sophisticated sentences may challenge students. Help students to rephrase difficult sentences using a simple subject-verb-object construction.	This story depicts experiences that fail to live up to a character's expectations. Encourage students to extend their exploration of the story by comparing and contrasting it with other pieces of literature or movies that deal with a similar theme. In what ways do various characters respond to their disappointments?

❻ Vocabulary Development

Latin Word Root -temp-

• Draw students' attention to Wolfe's use of the word *tempo*, and read its definition. Then, tell students that the Latin root -*temp*- means "time."

• Have students suggest other words that contain this root, and list them on the chalkboard. Possible answers: temporary, extemporaneous, temporal, contemporary

• Have students look up the meanings of these words in a dictionary.

• Finally, have them write sentences using these words correctly.

❼ Literary Analysis

Climax, Anticlimax, and Rising Action

• Invite a volunteer to read the bracketed passage aloud.

• As students listen, instruct them to pay close attention to the description of the engineer's experiences during his working years. Why do they think Wolfe elaborates on the circumstances that caused him grief, but provides no details about the joys? Possible answer: Wolfe wants the reader to understand that the man has experienced tragedies, even if he witnessed them largely from the distant perspective of the passing train.

• Then, ask students the Literary Analysis question on p. 788: In what ways does this detailed description of the old man's experiences with "grief and joy" add to your expectations of the story? Possible answer: The description increases our understanding that the engineer's fantasy of the two women is deeply important to him. It adds to the expectation that the resolution of his conflict will be a moment of high drama.

---

space at the town nearby, was beginning to lengthen evenly into its stroke, but it had not yet reached the full drive of its terrific speed. It swung into view deliberately, swept past with a powerful swaying motion of the engine, a low smooth rumble of its heavy cars upon pressed steel, and then it vanished in the cut. For a moment the progress of the engine could be marked by heavy bellowing puffs of ❻ smoke that burst at spaced intervals above the edges of the meadow grass, and finally nothing could be heard but the solid clacking <u>tempo</u> of the wheels receding into the drowsy stillness of the afternoon.

Every day for more than twenty years, as the train had approached this house, the engineer had blown on the whistle, and every day, as soon as she heard this signal, a woman had appeared on the back porch of the little house and waved to him. At first she had a small child clinging to her skirts, and now this child had grown to full womanhood, and every day she, too, came with her mother to the porch and waved.

The engineer had grown old and gray in service. He had driven his great train, loaded with its weight of lives, across the land ten thousand times. His own children had grown up and married, and four times he had seen before him on the tracks the ghastly dot of tragedy converging like a cannon ball to its eclipse of horror at the boiler head[1]—a light spring wagon filled with children, with its clustered row of small stunned faces; a cheap automobile stalled upon the tracks, set with the wooden figures of people paralyzed with fear; a battered hobo walking by the rail, too deaf and old to hear the whistle's warning; and a form flung past his window with a scream—all this the man had seen and known. He had known all the grief, the joy, the peril and the labor such a man could know; he had grown seamed and weathered in his loyal service, and now, schooled by the qualities of faith and courage and humbleness that attended his labor, he had grown old, and had the grandeur and the wisdom these men have.

But no matter what peril or tragedy he had known, the vision of the little house and the women waving to him with a brave free motion of the arm had become fixed in the mind of the engineer as something beautiful and enduring, something beyond all change and ruin, and something that would always be the same, no matter what mishap, grief or error might break the iron schedule of his days.

The sight of the little house and of these two women gave him the most extraordinary happiness he had ever known. He had seen them in a thousand lights, a hundred weathers. He had seen them through the harsh bare light of wintry gray across the brown and frosted stubble of the earth, and he had seen them again in the green luring sorcery of April.

❼ He felt for them and for the little house in which they lived such tenderness as a man might feel for his own children, and at length the picture of their lives was carved so sharply in his heart that he

---

1. **boiler head** the front section of a steam locomotive.

tempo (tem´ pō) *n.* rate of activity of a sound or motion; pace

**Literary Analysis
Climax, Anticlimax, and Rising Action** In what ways does this detailed description of the old man's experiences with "grief and joy" add to your expectations of the story?

felt that he knew their lives completely, to every hour and moment of the day, and he resolved that one day, when his years of service should be ended, he would go and find these people and speak at last with them whose lives had been so wrought into his own.

That day came. At last the engineer stepped from a train onto the station platform of the town where these two women lived. His years upon the rail had ended. He was a pensioned servant of his company, with no more work to do. The engineer walked slowly through the station and out into the streets of the town. Everything was as strange to him as if he had never seen this town before. As he walked on, his sense of bewilderment and confusion grew. Could this be the town he had passed ten thousand times? Were these the same houses he had seen so often from the high windows of his cab? It was all as unfamiliar, as disquieting as a city in a dream, and the perplexity of his spirit increased as he went on.

Presently the houses thinned into the straggling outposts of the town, and the street faded into a country road—the one on which the women lived. And the man plodded on slowly in the heat and dust. At length he stood before the house he sought. He knew at once that he had found the proper place. He saw the lordly oaks before the house, the flower beds, the garden and the arbor, and farther off, the glint of rails.

Yes, this was the house he sought, the place he had passed so many times, the destination he had longed for with such happiness. But now that he had found it, now that he was here, why did his hand falter on the gate; why had the town, the road, the earth, the very entrance to this place he loved turned unfamiliar as the landscape of some ugly dream? Why did he now feel this sense of confusion, doubt and hopelessness?

At length he entered by the gate, walked slowly up the path and in a moment more had mounted three short steps that led up to the porch, and was knocking at the door. Presently he heard steps in the hall, the door was opened, and a woman stood facing him.

And instantly, with a sense of bitter loss and grief, he was sorry he had come. He knew at once that the woman who stood there looking at him with a mistrustful eye was the same woman who had waved to him so many thousand times. But her face was harsh and pinched and meager; the flesh sagged wearily in <u>sallow</u> folds, and the small eyes peered at him with timid suspicion and uneasy doubt. All the brave freedom, the warmth and the affection that he had read into her gesture, vanished in the moment that he saw her and heard her unfriendly tongue.

And now his own voice sounded unreal and ghastly to him as he tried to explain his presence, to tell her who he was and the reason he had come. But he faltered on, fighting stubbornly against the

8
The American Experience

The American Railroad

The first railroad in America was built in 1826; it ran three miles—from Quincy, Massachusetts, to the Neponset River. Fourteen years later, the first steam locomotive was built in New York, running seventeen miles from Albany to Schenectady. By the late 1800s, a complete network of rail lines linked the entire nation, opening every corner of the country to settlement and growth. Businesses and towns developed where rail lines crossed. As the railroads expanded, the economy of the country also grew. Freight cars carried coal and other products while passenger rails made it easy for people to resettle or visit relatives in other parts of the country. Thousands of new jobs were created, and the United States soon became the greatest industrial nation in the world. Thus began America's love for the railroad.

Literary Analysis
Climax and Anticlimax
Explain why the woman's appearance is anticlimactic.

sallow (sal' ō) *adj.* sickly; pale yellow

10 ✓ **Reading Check**
What does the engineer do after retiring from the railroad?

The Far and the Near ◆ 789

---

8 ● **Background**
The American Railroad

The railroad affected the development of the United States in countless ways. Not only did the railroad spur the growth of American industry, it gave farmers and ranchers in the nation's west access to the markets of the densely populated east. This was, in part, how the nation grew more united, as the note on p. 789 suggests. The railroad also influenced popular culture. Songs and literature about the emerging railroad abounded, including folksongs like "I've Been Working on the Railroad."

9 ● Literary Analysis
Climax and Anticlimax

• Before they read the bracketed passage, have students briefly review the story so far. Guide them to recognize the rising action. Use the Climax and Anticlimax transparency in **Literary Analysis and Reading Transparencies,** p. 88 to clarify any confusion.

• Have students read the bracketed passage. Point out that the engineer is "sorry he had come." Ask students if this moment represents a climax or an anticlimax.
Answer: The moment is an anticlimax.

• Then, ask the Literary Analysis question on p. 789: Explain why the woman's appearance is anticlimactic.
Answer: The engineer expects her to be "beautiful and enduring" (p. 788). Now he sees that she is ordinary and unattractive. This moment, which the engineer thought would be so momentous, is disappointing—an anticlimax.

▶ Monitor Progress Ask students for their reactions to this anticlimactic moment. Encourage them to discuss how they would have reacted if Wolfe had fulfilled the engineer's hopes in a climax instead.

10 ● ✓ Reading Check
Answer: He goes to visit the mother and daughter whose house he had passed every day for twenty years.

Answers for p. 790

Review and Assess

1. Possible answer: Most students will hope that he will find the "something beautiful and enduring" which he is seeking. Students should offer reasons for their responses.

2. **(a)** While riding his train, the engineer passes a cottage on the outskirts of a small town and a woman and her daughter wave at him. **(b)** Possible answer: It suggests his life is unchanging, monotonous.

3. **(a)** He idealizes them. **(b)** Possible answer: It represents companionship, the comforts of a tidy home, a simple way of life.

4. **(a)** He retires from his career. **(b)** The town is not as he imagined it; it is ordinary, somewhat squalid. He finds it bewildering. **(c)** Possible response: He realizes it as soon as he steps off the train.

5. **(a)** He realizes that his magical vision is gone forever. **(b)** Possible response: In his imagination, the women had come to represent warmth and beauty. As it turns out, they are unfriendly and unattractive.

6. Possible response: He is suggesting that human longing is extremely powerful.

7. Possible response: Some students may feel that hope and reality are inherently contradictory. Others may be more optimistic. Encourage students to discuss their opinions.

---

horror of regret, confusion, disbelief that surged up in his spirit, drowning all his former joy and making his act of hope and tenderness seem shameful to him.

At length the woman invited him almost unwillingly into the house, and called her daughter in a harsh shrill voice. Then, for a brief agony of time, the man sat in an ugly little parlor, and he tried to talk while the two women stared at him with a dull, bewildered hostility, a <u>sullen</u>, <u>timorous</u> restraint.

And finally, stammering a crude farewell, he departed. He walked away down the path and then along the road toward town, and suddenly he knew that he was an old man. His heart, which had been brave and confident when it looked along the familiar vista of the rails, was now sick with doubt and horror as it saw the strange and unsuspected <u>visage</u> of an earth which had always been within a stone's throw of him, and which he had never seen or known. And he knew that all the magic of that bright lost way, the vista of that shining line, the imagined corner of that small good universe of hope's desire, was gone forever, could never be got back again.

sullen (sul′ ən) *adj.* sulky; glum

timorous (tim′ ər əs) *adj.* full of fear

visage (viz′ ij) *n.* appearance

Review and Assess

Thinking About the Selection

1. **Respond:** As you read about the engineer's approaching visit to the little town, what did you hope he would find?

2. **(a) Recall:** What has been the engineer's daily experience for the last twenty years? **(b) Interpret:** What does this tell you about the engineer's life?

3. **(a) Recall:** How does the engineer feel about the little house and the two women? **(b) Infer:** What do the house and the women represent to him?

4. **(a) Recall:** What event makes the engineer's visit to the town possible? **(b) Recall:** What is the engineer's first impression of the town when he comes to visit? **(c) Connect:** When does he first sense that his experience is unlikely to match his expectations?

5. **(a) Recall:** What realization does the engineer come to at the end of the story? **(b) Contrast:** In what ways do the engineer's observations in the final scene contrast with his expectations?

6. **Analyze:** Considering the title of the story, what do you think Wolfe is saying about human longing?

7. **Apply:** The engineer is crushed when he discovers his optimism was not based on reality. Is it possible to confront reality and remain hopeful about life at the same time? Explain.

ASSESSMENT PRACTICE: Reading Comprehension

Try Words in a Sentence   **(For more practice, see Test Preparation Workbook, p. 46.)**

Many tests require students to correctly answer sentence-completion questions. Use the following sample item to show students that they can often eliminate choices because they are illogical, the wrong part of speech, or inconsistent with the sentence meaning.

Have you ever felt a conflict between asserting your _____ and maintaining your _____ toward society?

  A duty; obligation

  B uniqueness; separateness

  C independence; indifference

  D individuality; responsibility

Because the sentence uses the word *conflict*, the correct pair will have somewhat opposite meanings, eliminating *A* and *B. C* is illogical. Answer *D* is the best choice.

Review and Assess

Literary Analysis
Climax and Anticlimax

1. (a) What is the story's **anticlimax**? Support your answer. (b) In what way does the anticlimax resolve the story's central conflict?
2. What effect does the anticlimax have on both the engineer and the reader?
3. Why do you suppose Wolfe chose to give this story an anticlimax rather than a **climax**? Explain.
4. If you were to rewrite this story with a climax rather than an anticlimax: (a) What details would change? (b) How would such a revised story end?

Connecting Literary Elements

5. (a) When in the story does the rising action begin? (b) Using a chart like the one shown, list three events in the rising action that led to the moment of greatest tension.

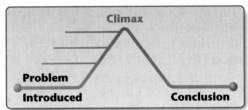

6. How does the repetition of the engineer's attachment to the woman and her house contribute to the tension created in the story's **rising action**?

Reading Strategy
Predicting

7. When you read about the engineer's decision to visit the two women after retiring, what did you **predict** would happen?
8. Based on your own experience, did you predict that the engineer's view of the world would change when he stepped down from the "high windows of his cab"? Explain.

Extend Understanding

9. **Cultural Connection:** In what way does the romantic notion of train travel add to the distortion between the engineer's view of the world from far away and his view up close?

❶ Vocabulary Development

Word Analysis

1. *temporary:* fleeting, not lasting

2. *contemporary:* of the moment, modern

3. *extemporaneous:* spontaneous, unplanned

4. *tempo:* the rhythm or beat of a musical work

Spelling Strategy

1. edge

2. generous

3. reject

Fluency: Words in Context

Possible answers:

1. After being bedridden for weeks, the man's complexion had become *sallow.*

2. The child's *timorous* voice revealed her fear about going to the dentist.

3. Grinning with nervousness as he made his feeble excuses, the student's *visage* nearly gave him away.

4. The *sullen* girl disliked her school, her job, and even her friends.

5. As everyone struggles to meet the deadlines, the *tempo* of work in an office becomes very fast.

❷ Grammar and Style

Practice

1. *nonrestrictive participial phrase:* schooled by the humbleness that attended . . . *Comma use:* and now, schooled by the humbleness that attended his labor, he had grown old

2. *restrictive participial phrase:* converging like a cannon ball to its eclipse . . . ; no commas needed)

3. *restrictive participial phrase:* loaded with its weight of lives . . . ; (no commas needed)

4. *restrictive participial phrase:* receding into the drowsy stillness . . . ; (no commas needed)

5. *nonrestrictive participial phrase:* trimmed with green blinds. *Comma use:* On the outskirts of a little town was a tidy little cottage, trimmed with green blinds.

Integrate Language Skills

❶ Vocabulary Development Lesson

Word Analysis: Latin Root *-temp-*

Built on the Latin root *-temp-*, meaning "time," *tempo* means "pace" or "the rate of activity of a sound or motion." Using this knowledge define the following words:

1. temporary
2. contemporary
3. extemporaneous
4. tempo

Spelling Strategy

The *j* sound can be spelled in a few ways, including *ge* as in *visage*, or *j* as in *juice*. In your notebook, complete each of the following words using either *j* or *g*.

1. ed__e   2. __enerous   3. re__ect

❷ Grammar and Style Lesson

Restrictive and Nonrestrictive Participial Phrases

A **participial phrase** consists of a participle (a form of a verb that acts as an adjective) and its modifiers or complements. The entire phrase acts as an adjective. If the phrase is essential to the sentence's meaning, it is **restrictive** and not set off by commas. If it is not essential, it is **nonrestrictive** and should be set off by commas.

> **Restrictive:** . . . a light spring wagon *filled with children.* (essential)
>
> **Nonrestrictive:** And finally, *stammering a crude farewell*, he departed. (not essential)

Practice Copy these passages, identifying participial phrases and adding commas as necessary.

1. . . . and now schooled by the humbleness that attended his labor he had grown old . . .

W̶G Prentice Hall Writing and Grammar Connection: Chapter 19, Section 2

792 ◆ *Disillusion, Defiance, and Discontent (1914–1946)*

Fluency: Words in Context

For each item, follow the directions by writing a sentence using a word from the vocabulary list on page 785.

1. Describe a man who has been ill for many weeks.

2. Describe how a child might feel before visiting the dentist.

3. Describe a student giving an outrageous excuse for failing a test.

4. Write the first sentence of a story about a girl who is unhappy and angry about her life.

5. Describe an activity in a busy office.

2. . . . four times he had seen before him on the tracks a ghastly dot of tragedy converging like a cannon ball to its eclipse of horror at the boiler head . . .

3. . . . He had driven his great train loaded with its weight of lives across the land ten thousand times.

4. . . . nothing could be heard but the solid clacking tempo of the wheels receding into the drowsy stillness of the afternoon.

5. On the outskirts of a little town was a tidy little cottage trimmed with green blinds.

Looking at Style Explain how each of the participial phrases in the Practice enables Wolfe to insert action into a description.

Writing Application Describe a let down you have experienced, using two participial phrases.

❸ Writing Lesson

Comparison-and-Contrast Essay

Write an essay in which you compare the two viewpoints suggested by the title "The Far and the Near." Explain how the engineer's view of things depends on distance from or proximity to them. Consider what the story suggests about the dreams we dream from afar.

Prewriting Reread the story and note passages that reflect the engineer's thoughts and feelings about the world from a distance.

Drafting Address each of the passages you have selected, comparing the engineer's thoughts and reflections while riding the train to the realities he later experiences.

Revising Reread your essay to make sure you have drawn a strong comparison between the engineer's experiences of life from both vantage points. Strengthen your word choices to emphasize contrasts.

Model: Revising to Build Contrast

green and lush

From a distance, the backyards appear ~~pretty~~ and the

tidy little cottages

~~houses~~ look like havens of hospitality and warmth. Up close,

overgrown weeds,   *peeling clapboard*

however, the ~~grass~~, scattered trash, and ~~siding~~ tell another story

cold and neglected

of a community.

> The additional descriptive details make a contrast more striking.

 Prentice Hall Writing and Grammar Connection: Chapter 9, Section 2

❹ Extension Activities

Speaking and Listening Some people feel that train travel is truly magical. Conduct an **interview** with someone who has traveled by rail. Start by asking questions like these:

- How did the landscape appear from the train?
- What was romantic or exciting about the journey?
- In what way is rail travel different from auto trips?

Share your findings with the class.

Research and Technology In a group, research the evolution of the railroad and the nation's love affair with it. Devise a research outline. Then, contribute sections to a **written report** explaining the history of the railroad and the changes that have taken place in recent decades. **[Group Activity]**

Take It to the Net www.phschool.com

Go online for an additional research activity using the Internet.

The Far and the Near ◆ 793

ASSESSMENT RESOURCES

The following resources can be used to assess students' knowledge and skills.

Selection Assessment

- **Formal Assessment,** pp. 200–202
- **Open Book Test,** pp. 130–132
- **Got It! Assessment Videotapes,** Tape 5
- **Test Bank Software**

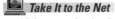 **Take It to the Net**

Visit www.phschool.com for self-tests and additional questions on the selections.

Writing Rubric

- **Performance Assess. and Portfolio Mgmt.,** p. 19

PRENTICE HALL ASSESSMENT SYSTEM

- **Workbook**
- **Skill Book**
- **Transparencies**
- **CD-ROM**

---

❸ Writing Lesson

- Remind students that their comparison-and-contrast essays should clearly explain--and use supporting details to show--the differences between the engineer's changing perspectives.

- Have students reread the story, marking passages to use in their essays.

- Use the Comparison and Contrast transparency in **Writing Models and Graphic Organizers on Transparencies**, p. 87, to help students organize their analysis.

- Draw students' attention to the model on p. 793 to help them strengthen their contrasts with concrete detail.

- Use the Comparison and Contrast essay rubric in **Performance Assessment and Portfolio Management**, p. 19, to assess students' work.

❹ Research and Technology

- Remind students that their written reports should explain both the history of the railroad and the ways in which it changed American culture.

- Suggest that students assign specific research tasks, such as the building of the railroad, the completion of the transcontinental rails, and so on. Once they have gathered enough material, students can then meet to focus their ideas.

- Use the Research Report model in **Writing Models and Graphic Organizers on Transparencies,** p. 41, to assist students in completing their reports.

CUSTOMIZE INSTRUCTION
For Universal Access

To address different learning styles, use the activities suggested in the **Extension Activities** booklet, p. 44.

For Visual/Spatial learners, use Activity 5.

For Musical/Rhythmic learners, use Activity 6.

For Interpersonal Learners, use Activity 7.

Lesson Objectives

1. **To analyze and respond to literary elements**
   - Literary Analysis: Simile
   - Comparing Literary Works
2. **To read, comprehend, analyze, and critique poetry**
   - Reading Strategy: Paraphrasing
   - Review and Assess questions
   - Assessment Practice (ATE)
3. **To develop word analysis skills, fluency, and systematic vocabulary**
   - Vocabulary Development Lesson: Latin Root: *-satis-*
4. **To understand and apply written and oral language conventions**
   - Spelling Strategy
   - Grammar and Style Lesson: Subject Complements
5. **To understand and apply appropriate writing and research strategies**
   - Writing Lesson: Definition
   - Extension Activity: Poetry Collection
6. **To understand and apply listening and speaking strategies**
   - Extension Activity: Round-table Discussion

STEP-BY-STEP TEACHING GUIDE	PACING GUIDE
PRETEACH	
Motivate Students and Provide Background	
Use the Motivation activity (ATE p. 794)	5 min.
Read and discuss author and background features (SE/ATE p. 794) **A**	5 min.
Introduce the Concepts	
Introduce the Literary Analysis and Reading Strategy (SE/ATE p. 795) **A**	15 min.
Pronounce the vocabulary words and read their definitions (SE p. 795)	5 min.
TEACH	
Monitor Comprehension	
Informally monitor comprehension by circulating while students read independently or in groups **A**	25 min.
Develop vocabulary with Vocabulary notes (SE pp. 796, 797, 798, 800, 801; ATE p. 796)	as students read
Develop Understanding	5 min.
Develop students' understanding of simile with the Literary Analysis annotations (SE pp. 798, 800; ATE pp. 798, 800) **A**	5 min.
Develop students' ability to recognize and understand the use of paraphrasing by using the Reading Strategy annotations (SE p. 796; ATE p. 797)	
ASSESS	
Assess Mastery	15 min.
Assess students' mastery of the Reading Strategy and Literary Analysis by having them answer the Review and Assess questions (SE/ATE p. 802)	up to 45 min.
Use one or more of the print and media Assessment Resources (ATE p. 804) **A**	
EXTEND	
Apply Understanding	20 min.
Have students complete the Vocabulary Development Lesson and the Grammar and Style Lesson (SE p. 803) **A**	45 min.
Apply students' ability to provide necessary background information in writing a definition by using the Writing Lesson (SE/ATE p. 804) **A**	20–90 min.
Apply students' understanding using one or more of the Extension Activities (SE p. 804)	

 ACCELERATED INSTRUCTION:
Use the strategies and activities identified with an **A**.

UNIVERSAL ACCESS
- ● = Below Level Students
- ▲ = On-Level Students
- ■ = Above Level Students

Time and Resource Manager

Reading Level: Challenging, Challenging, Challenging, Challenging
Average Number of Instructional Days: 4

RESOURCES		
PRINT 📖	**TRANSPARENCIES** 🎞	**TECHNOLOGY** 💿 🎧 📼
• **Beyond Literature,** Humanities Connection: Photography, p. 45 ▲ ■		• **Interest Grabber Video,** Tape 5 ● ▲ ■
• **Selection Support Workbook:** ● ▲ ■ Literary Analysis, p. 201 Reading Strategy, p. 200 Build Vocabulary, p. 198	• **Literary Analysis and Reading Transparencies,** pp. 89 and 90 ● ▲ ■	
		• **Listening to Literature** ● ▲ ■ Audiocassettes, Side 27 Audio CDs, CD 15
• **Literatura en español** ● ▲ • **Literary Analysis for Enrichment** ■		
• **Formal Assessment:** Selection Test, p. 203 ● ▲ ■ • **Open Book Test,** p. 133 ● ▲ ■ • **Performance Assessment and Portfolio Management,** p. 55 ● ▲ ■ • **PRENTICE HALL ASSESSMENT SYSTEM** ● ▲ ■	• **PRENTICE HALL ASSESSMENT SYSTEM** ● ▲ ■ Skills Practice Answers and Explanations on Transparencies	• **Test Bank Software** ● ▲ ■ • **Got It! Assessment Videotapes,** Tape 4 ● ▲
• **Selection Support Workbook:** ● ▲ ■ Grammar and Style, p. 199 • **Writing and Grammar,** Ruby Level ● ▲ ■ • **Extension Activities,** p. 45 ● ▲ ■	• **Daily Language Practice Transparencies** ● ▲ • **Writing Models and Graphic Organizers on Transparencies,** p. 87 ● ▲ ■	• **Writing and Grammar iText CD-ROM** ● ▲ ■ 💻 *Take It to the Net* www.phschool.com

BLOCK SCHEDULING: Use one 90-minute class period to preteach the selection and have students read it. Use a second 90-minute class period to assess students' mastery of skills and have them complete one of the Extension Activities.

Step-by-Step Teaching Guide for pp. 794–795

Prepare to Read

❶ **Of Modern Poetry** ◆ **Anecdote of the Jar** ◆
Ars Poetica ◆ **Poetry**

Motivation

Use students' interest in music as a hook to motivate them to read these poems. Start with a class activity in which students share the ways in which their favorite music affects them. Write the responses on the chalkboard. Then, have students discuss the role that song lyrics play in eliciting the types of responses they've noted. Using the ideas that have been generated, work as a class to come up with a short definition of what song lyrics are and how they affect people. Then, point out that poetry shares many of the same qualities as song lyrics. Explain to students that they are about to read three poets' definitions of poetry and its importance within a culture. Focus students' reading by having them compare the poets' definitions of poetry with their own definitions of song lyrics.

▣ Interest Grabber Video

As an alternative, play "Phillip Fried on Modern Poetry" on Tape 5 to engage student interest.

❶ Background

More About the Authors

The three poets represented in this grouping began to publish their poetry in the same period—the decade of the 1920s, when such writers as T.S. Eliot and Ezra Pound dominated modern verse. MacLeish and Moore became active figures in American cultural life, Moore as the editor of *The Dial* and MacLeish as the Librarian of Congress and later as a professor at Harvard University. Stevens, however, continued in his career as an insurance company executive. He was recognized with a Pulitzer Prize in the last years of his life and has since been hailed as one of the most significant poets in American literature.

Wallace Stevens (1879–1955)

Wallace Stevens believed that the goal of poetry was to capture the interaction between fantasy and reality. He spent his career writing poems that delve into the imagination and the ways in which it shapes our perception of the physical world. He uses elaborate imagery and precise words to express his philosophical themes. Stevens depended largely on the natural world for his inspiration because nature, he said, is the only certainty.

Insurance Executive by Day Stevens was born and raised in Reading, Pennsylvania. After completing his education at Harvard University, he took a job at the Hartford Accident and Indemnity Company, an insurance company in Hartford, Connecticut, and eventually became the company's vice president. He did not publish his first collection of poetry, *Harmonium* (1923), until he was forty-three years old. In *Harmonium* and much of his other work, Stevens uses dazzling imagery to capture the beauty of the physical world while expressing the dependence of that beauty on the perceptions of the observer. Although the book received little public attention, it was praised by critics and launched Stevens's literary career.

Stevens published many volumes of poetry, including *Ideas of Order* (1935), *Parts of a World* (1942), *Transport to Summer* (1947), and *The Auroras of Autumn* (1950). His *Collected Poems* earned him the Pulitzer Prize in 1955. Despite his success as a poet, however, Stevens continued his career in insurance until the end of his life. "It gives a man character as a poet to have this daily contact with a job," he once said. A brilliant and unusual figure, he is now regarded as one of the most important poets of the twentieth century.

Archibald MacLeish (1892–1982)

Archibald MacLeish was born in Glencoe, Illinois. MacLeish was trained as a lawyer but, unlike Stevens, he turned his back on his first career to devote himself completely to poetry. His early poems, such as "Ars Poetica," are experimental in form, reflecting the influence of the Modernists. By contrast, his later poems are more traditional and accessible. As unrest spread throughout the world in the 1930s, MacLeish used poetry to explore political and social issues. Over the course of his career, MacLeish produced more than thirty books and won three Pulitzer Prizes.

Marianne Moore (1887–1972)

Born in Kirkwood, Missouri, Marianne Moore first gained a footing in the literary world as the editor of *The Dial*, a highly regarded literary journal. In that role, she encouraged many new writers by publishing their work. However, she was hesitant to publish her own work, although it had been admired by many noted poets. In fact, her first book, *Poems* (1921), was published without her knowledge.

As a Modernist, Moore wrote poems that were unconventional, precise, inventive, and witty. Unlike most other Modernists, however, she chose not to write about the state of modern civilization. Instead, she explored subjects such as animals and nature. "Poetry," one of her best-known poems, delves into the subject of poetry itself.

TEACHING RESOURCES

The following resources can be used to enrich or extend the instruction for pp. 794–795.

Motivation

▣ **Interest Grabber Video**, Tape 5 ▣

Background

▣ **Beyond Literature**, p. 45

▣ *Take It to the Net*
Visit www.phschool.com for Background and hotlinks for the selections.

Literary Analysis

▣ **Literary Analysis and Reading Transparencies,** Similes, p. 90

Reading

▣ **Selection Support:** Reading Strategy, p. 200; Build Vocabulary, p. 198 ▣

▣ **Literary Analysis and Reading Transparencies,** Paraphrasing, p. 89

 BLOCK SCHEDULING: Resources marked with this symbol provide varied instruction during 90-minute blocks.

Preview

Connecting to the Literature

You probably have your own special way of looking at the subjects you care about most deeply. In these selections, three major poets present their views on a subject about which they are deeply passionate: poetry.

❷ Literary Analysis

Simile

A **simile** is a comparison between two seemingly different things. Signal words such as *like* or *as* indicate the comparison. For example, the word *like* signals the comparison in the following simile:

> The sound of the explosion echoed through the air like thunder.

By comparing the sound of an explosion to thunder, the simile stresses its loud, jarring power. Like poetry itself, similes show us the world in startling new ways. As you read, compare the similes used by each poet.

Comparing Literary Works

The poets whose works appear in these selections devote their attention to the genre of poetry itself. Although the art of writing poetry defies definition, each writer attempts an explanation. The poets use imagery to give body to their ideas. Like similes, **imagery** creates word pictures for readers. Most often, imagery works by appealing to the five senses—sight, smell, touch, sound, or taste. Compare the types of images each poet presents and determine the ways in which these images advance each poet's explanation of poetry.

❸ Reading Strategy

Paraphrasing

Because poetry is written in verse and is likely to contain unexpected words and images, it can be difficult to understand. One way to make sure that you grasp what you are reading is to **paraphrase**—to identify key ideas and restate them in your own words. Paraphrasing can remove barriers that make some poems seem too difficult to understand. In a chart like the one shown, list the difficult passages and paraphrase them.

Difficult Passage
"I, too, dislike it: there are things that are more important beyond/all this fiddle."

Paraphrased
I also dislike poetry. It's nonsense, and a lot of other things are more important.

Vocabulary Development

suffice (sə fīs´) *v.* be adequate; meet the needs of (p. 796)

insatiable (in sā´ shə bəl) *adj.* constantly wanting more (p. 796)

slovenly (sluv´ ən lē) *adj.* untidy (p. 797)

dominion (də min´ yən) *n.* power to rule (p. 797)

palpable (pal´ pə bəl) *adj.* able to be touched, felt, or handled (p. 798)

derivative (də riv´ ə tiv) *adj.* not original; based on something else (p. 800)

literalists (lit´ ər əl ists) *n.* those who take words at their exact meaning (p. 801)

Of Modern Poetry / Anecdote of the Jar / Ars Poetica / Poetry ◆ 795

CUSTOMIZE INSTRUCTION FOR UNIVERSAL ACCESS

For Less Proficient Readers	For English Learners	For Advanced Readers
The reading skill for this selection, paraphrasing, may be especially helpful for students. Use the Reading Strategy page in the **Selection Support Workbook**, p. 200, to reinforce the skill. Encourage students to use a dictionary to help define unfamiliar words as they work their way through each poem.	Students may find the reading skill for this selection, paraphrasing, to be challenging. Help them by previewing the poems, noting and defining unfamiliar or difficult words and phrases. Encourage students to create their own glossary of terms to which they can refer as they read.	To make the reading skill for this selection, paraphrasing, more challenging for students, instruct them to create paraphrase charts in which they explain the significance of passages in addition to paraphrasing them.

---

❷ Literary Analysis

Simile

- Explain to students that in a *simile*, an author compares two unlike things using the words "like" or "as." Note that some similes are highly imaginative, while others, like the example on p. 795, are more ordinary.

- Using the Simile transparency in **Literary Analysis and Reading Transparencies,** p. 90, guide students through an analysis of two other similes from the selections.

- Have students complete the final example on the **Simile** transparency.
  Answer: Two unlike things: "A poem," "a globed fruit"; connecting word: "As"

- Encourage students to identify and diagram other similes they find in the poems in this grouping.

❸ Reading Strategy

Paraphrasing

- Explain to students that poetry can be especially challenging for readers because it is often dense with meaning.

- Use the difficult passage included in the model Paraphrasing chart on p. 795 to illustrate the challenge of reading poetry. Encourage students to discuss the meaning of the passage.

- Direct student attention to the paraphrased text in the model chart. Point out that the paraphrase uses more accessible language and makes the passage's meaning easier to understand.

- Encourage students to use paraphrasing to decode difficult passages in the poems.

Vocabulary Development

- Pronounce each vocabulary word for students, and read the definitions as a class. Have students identify any words with which they are already familiar.

 E-Teach

Visit E-Teach at www.phschool.com for teachers'' essays on how to teach, with questions and answers.

795

Step-by-Step Teaching Guide for pp. 796–801

CUSTOMIZE INSTRUCTION
For Verbal/Linguistic Learners

Pair students with visual/spatial learners to expand their experience of the poem's imagery. Have students read the poem aloud as their visual/spatial partners illustrate its images with original or found visuals.

❶ About the Selections

The poems by Stevens explore the creative process as he defined it. They break down that process into the intimate moments of imagination, inspiration, and painstaking perfectionism that together work to create poetry.

❷ Vocabulary Development

The Latin Root -satis-

- Call students' attention to the word *insatiable* and its definition. Tell students that the Latin word root -satis- means "enough."

- Have students suggest words and phrases that contain this root, and list them on the chalkboard. Possible answers: *satisfy, satisfactory, satiate,* and *satiety.*

- Next, have students look up the meanings of these words in a dictionary.

- Finally, direct students to reread the poem, looking for places where they can replace an existing word or phrase with a word containing the Latin root -satis-. Call on volunteers to read their new sentences aloud.

Of Modern Poetry ❶

Wallace Stevens

Background

Wallace Stevens's poetry reflects the influence of the Symbolist literary movement. Originating in the last half of the nineteenth century, Symbolist poets believed that ideas and emotions are difficult to communicate because people perceive the world in such personal ways. These poets tried to convey meaning through symbols—people, places, and objects that represent ideas beyond their concrete meaning. As a result, the work of Symbolist poets like Stevens can often be interpreted in many different ways.

The poem of the mind in the act of finding
What will <u>suffice</u>. It has not always had
To find: the scene was set; it repeated what
Was in the script.
     Then the theatre was changed
5 To something else. Its past was a souvenir.

It has to be living, to learn the speech of the place.
It has to face the men of the time and to meet
The women of the time. It has to think about war
And it has to find what will suffice. It has
10 To construct a new stage. It has to be on that stage
❷ And, like an <u>insatiable</u> actor, slowly and
With meditation, speak words that in the ear,
In the delicatest ear of the mind, repeat,
Exactly, that which it wants to hear, at the sound
15 Of which, an invisible audience listens,
Not to the play, but to itself, expressed
In an emotion as of two people, as of two
Emotions becoming one. The actor is
❸ A metaphysician[1] in the dark, twanging
20 An instrument, twanging a wiry string that gives
Sounds passing through sudden rightnesses, wholly
Containing the mind, below which it cannot descend,
Beyond which it has no will to rise.
       It must
Be the finding of a satisfaction, and may
25 Be of a man skating, a woman dancing, a woman
Combing. The poem of the act of the mind.

suffice (sə fīs´) *v.* be adequate; meet the needs of

insatiable (in sā´ shə bəl) *adj.* constantly wanting more

Reading Strategy
Paraphrasing Restate the sentence in lines 18–24 in your own words.

1. **metaphysician** (met´ ə fə zish´ ən) *n.* a person versed in philosophy, especially those branches that seek to explain the nature of being or of the universe.

TEACHING RESOURCES

The following resources can be used to enrich or extend the instruction for pp. 796–801.

Literary Analysis

📖 **Selection Support:** Literary Analysis, p. 201

📠 **Literary Analysis and Reading Transparencies,** p. 90

Reading

📠 **Literary Analysis and Reading Transparencies,** p. 89

🎧 **Listening to Literature Audiocassettes,** Side 27 ■

💿 **Listening to Literature Audio CDs,** CD 15 ■

BLOCK SCHEDULING: Resources marked with this symbol provide varied instruction during 90-minute blocks.

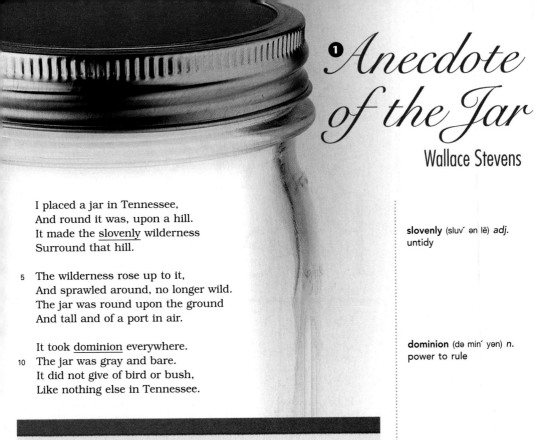

Anecdote of the Jar

Wallace Stevens

I placed a jar in Tennessee,
And round it was, upon a hill.
It made the <u>slovenly</u> wilderness
Surround that hill.

5   The wilderness rose up to it,
And sprawled around, no longer wild.
The jar was round upon the ground
And tall and of a port in air.

It took <u>dominion</u> everywhere.
10 The jar was gray and bare.
It did not give of bird or bush,
Like nothing else in Tennessee.

slovenly (sluv´ ən lē) *adj.*
untidy

dominion (də min´ yən) *n.*
power to rule

Review and Assess

Thinking About the Selections

1. **(a) Recall:** In the first stanza of "Of Modern Poetry," what does the poet say happened to the theater?
   (b) Interpret: What does "the theatre" represent?

2. **(a) Recall:** What does the poem suggest about the relationship poetry must have with the people of its time?
   (b) Analyze: Does the poet believe the work of poetry to be difficult? Explain.

3. **(a) Recall:** In "Anecdote of the Jar," how does the wilderness receive the jar? **(b) Analyze:** How does the jar affect the wilderness?

4. **(a) Recall:** What words describe the jar in the first and third stanzas? **(b) Compare and Contrast:** How does the image of the jar in the third stanza differ from its depiction in the first?

5. **Evaluate:** Does the jar effectively symbolize the human imagination? Support your answer.

Paraphrasing

- Point out that paraphrasing—restating a passage in your own words—can make poetry easier to understand.

- Use the Paraphrasing transparency in **Literary Analysis and Reading Transparencies,** p. 89, to model a paraphrase chart for students.

- Present the Reading Strategy task on p. 796 to students: Restate the sentence in lines 18–24 in your own words. Ask students to use a paraphrase chart to develop their responses.
  Possible response: The poet must listen carefully to inspiration, experimenting with different forms and testing each word against an inner, trusted instinct.

▶ Monitor Progress Encourage students to discuss how paraphrasing helps to clarify the poem's meaning.

Answers for p. 797

Review and Assess

1. **(a)** It "was changed/To something else." **(b)** Possible response: It represents society, which changed dramatically as the modern age began.

2. **(a)** It has to "face the men of the time" and "meet the women of the time." **(b)** Possible response: The poet does believe it is difficult work; poetry must "learn the speech" of the modern world and "construct a new stage" for itself.

3. **(a)** The wilderness rises up to the jar and "sprawl[s] around," tamed. **(b)** Possible response: The jar gives order to the wilderness.

4. **(a)** The words "round," "gray," and "bare" describe the jar. **(b)** Possible response: In the first stanza, the jar is simply part of the landscape. In the third stanza, the jar has taken "dominion everywhere."

5. Possible response: Students may respond that it does because it gives order to the wilderness.

CUSTOMIZE INSTRUCTION FOR UNIVERSAL ACCESS

For Less Proficient Readers	For English Learners	For Advanced Readers
The difficult vocabulary and abstract nature of these poems will challenge students. Explain that Stevens sought to define a subject that cannot be grasped easily via the senses, but is "an act of the mind." Preview difficult vocabulary and have students paraphrase after every few lines to aid comprehension.	Students may find the images and similes in these poems challenging. Encourage students to discuss the meaning of the literary devices, beginning with the significance of concrete images that are relatively easy to comprehend.	More advanced readers can analyze the symbolism in these poems through critical reading and paraphrasing. Organize students into small groups or teams and have them both identify and explain symbolic elements in their own words.

This poem catalogs in vivid sensory images and figurative language the myriad ways in which poetry can touch the human spirit. MacLeish portrays poetry as a living force, rendering it as the outlet for human emotion expressed through concrete and accessible images.

❺ **Literary Analysis**

Simile

- Remind students that in a *simile*, a writer compares two unlike things using the words "like" or "as."

- Use the Simile transparency in **Literary Analysis and Reading Transparencies,** p. 90 to model similes for the class.

- Have students read the bracketed passage. Then, ask the Literary Analysis question on p. 798: Identify the simile in line 5 and explain what two things MacLeish compares.
  Answer: The entire stanza is a simile; MacLeish compares poetry with a smooth and mossy stone.

▶ Monitor Progress Ask students to explain the effect of this simile. What does the simile communicate to the reader?
Possible response: The comparison stresses that poetry should communicate through its sensory images, not through rhetoric.

❻ ▶**Critical Viewing**

Possible response: Students should identify the images in lines 9–14: the moon climbing, bare trees against a moonlit night, and the moon behind the winter leaves.

⁴.Ars Poetica¹
Archibald MacLeish

A poem should be <u>palpable</u> and mute
As a globed fruit.

Dumb
As old medallions to the thumb,

5   Silent as the sleeve-worn stone
Of casement ledges where the moss has grown—

A poem should be wordless
As the flight of birds.

A poem should be motionless in time
10   As the moon climbs,

palpable (pal′ pə bəl) *adj.* able to be touched, felt, or handled

Literary Analysis
Simile Identify the simile in line 5 and explain what two things MacLeish compares.

---

1. **Ars Poetica** The title is an allusion to Horace's "Ars Poetica," or "The Art of Poetry," which was composed about 20 B.C.

❻ ◀**Critical Viewing** Which of the poem's images can be found in this photograph? **[Interpret]**

✳ **ENRICHMENT: Science Connection**

The Moon's Orbit

The moon's climb is not really motionless, of course, just slow enough that the movement is difficult to see. It takes 27 days, 7 hours, and 43 minutes for the moon to complete an orbit around the Earth. Each night the moon appears to rise in the sky, both because it is orbiting around the Earth and because the Earth itself is turning. The moon's light—a reflection of the Sun's light—takes different shapes, or phases, as the lit portion of the moon's surface rotates through our path of vision.

Have students work in groups to calculate the moon's rate of movement through the night sky and create an accurate, movable model of the moon and Earth.

Leaving, as the moon releases
Twig by twig the night-entangled trees,

Leaving, as the moon behind the winter leaves.
Memory by memory the mind—

15 A poem should be motionless in time
As the moon climbs.

A poem should be equal to:
Not true.

For all the history of grief
20 An empty doorway and a maple leaf.

For love
The leaning grasses and two lights above the sea—

A poem should not mean
But be.

Review and Assess
Thinking About the Selection

1. **Respond:** Do you like the way poetry is described in this poem? Why or why not?

2. **(a) Recall:** Identify at least three items the speaker compares to poetry. **(b) Analyze:** What do you think the speaker means by saying that a poem should be "palpable and mute," "wordless," and "motionless in time"?

3. **(a) Recall:** With what images can a poem show the history of grief, as the speaker states? **(b) Recall:** With what images should it show love? **(c) Speculate:** Why do you think MacLeish chose to focus on these emotions?

4. **(a) Interpret:** What contradiction do you see in lines 7–8? **(b) Analyze:** What do you think this contradiction suggests about the subject, poetry?

5. **(a) Interpret:** What contrast does the poet make in the final two lines? **(b) Define:** How would you define the difference between *meaning* and *being*?

6. **Extend:** In what ways do you think poetry can touch the human spirit? Explain.

Ars Poetica ◆ 799

CUSTOMIZE INSTRUCTION FOR UNIVERSAL ACCESS

For Special Needs Students	For Gifted/Talented Students	For Advanced Readers
Encourage students to first read instinctively for an overall impression of each poem, rather than trying to analyze literal meaning. Then, have them reread each poem. Students may read along with the recordings on **Listening to Literature: Audiocassettes,** Side 17; **Audio CDs,** CD 15.	The poems in this grouping are about the art of poetry and the nature of creative expression. Ask students to choose an idea expressed in one of the poems and use it as the starting point for a collage or other visual expression. Challenge them to incorporate phrases from the poem into this visual format.	Provide students with the following passage from Horace's "Ars Poetica," to which MacLeish alludes in his title: "It is not enough that poems have beauty of form; they must have charm. . . ." Then, ask students to explain the passage and tell whether they think MacLeish would agree with it or not.

---

❼ **Critical Thinking**

Interpret

- Read the bracketed passage aloud. Ask students to explain what the poet is saying in the final stanza. Possible response: Most students will respond that poetry should not simply convey ideas but should reach the reader directly through the emotions and senses.

- Invite students to describe their personal responses to the final stanza. What does it mean to them? Possible response: Students may mention times of grief or love when poetry moved them.

Answers for p. 799

Review and Assess

1. Possible response: Students may respond that they like the description of poetry as a concrete living entity. Students should provide a clear explanation of their reactions.

2. **(a)** The speaker compares a poem to a "globed fruit," "old medallions," "sleeve-worn stone of casement ledges," and "the flight of birds." **(b)** Possible response: Poetry appeals to the sense of touch, expresses meaning through concrete images, and is timeless.

3. **(a)** A poem shows the history of grief in "an empty doorway and a maple leaf." **(b)** It shows love in "leaning grasses and two lights above the sea." **(c)** Possible response: They are two of the strongest emotions.

4. **(a)** Poetry, which is composed of words, cannot be literally "wordless." **(b)** Possible response: It suggests that poetry should rely on images appealing to the senses and emotions rather than the intellect.

5. **(a)** The poet distinguishes between a poem's *meaning* something and its *being* something. **(b)** *Meaning* suggests that a poem refers to a subject; it implies distance from an experience. *Being* suggests that the poem is an experience in its own right.

6. Possible response: Students may respond that poetry expresses the deepest human emotions.

799

❽Poetry

Marianne
Moore

Untitled, 1984, Alexander Calder, Solomon R. Guggenheim Museum, New York

I, too, dislike it: there are things that are important beyond all this
    fiddle.
  Reading it, however, with a perfect contempt for it, one discovers in
it after all, a place for the genuine.
    Hands that can grasp, eyes
5   that can dilate, hair that can rise
      if it must, these things are important not because a

high-sounding interpretation can be put upon them but because they
    are
useful. When they become so <u>derivative</u> as to become unintelligible,
the same thing may be said for all of us, that we
    do not admire what
10   we cannot understand: the bat
      holding on upside down or in quest of something to

eat, elephants pushing, a wild horse taking a roll, a tireless wolf under
  a tree, the immovable critic twitching his skin like a horse that feels
    a flea, the base-
ball fan, the statistician—
15   nor is it valid
      to discriminate against "business documents and

❿ ▲ Critical Viewing
Write a sentence describing this painting "with a perfect contempt for it." Explain what the result shows you about Moore's point in lines 2–3. **[Connect]**

derivative (də riv′ ə tiv) *adj.* not original; based on something else

Literary Analysis
Simile What does the simile comparing a critic to a horse suggest about the speaker's attitude toward critics?

❾

school-books"; all these phenomena are important. One must make a
   distinction
however: when dragged into prominence by half poets, the result is
   not poetry,
nor till the poets among us can be
20   "literalists of
   the imagination"—above
      insolence and triviality and can present

for inspection, "imaginary gardens with real toads in them," shall we
   have
it. In the meantime, if you demand on the one hand,
25   the raw material of poetry in
      all its rawness and
      that which is on the other hand
         genuine, you are interested in poetry.

literalists (lit´ ər əl ists)
n. those who take
words at their exact
meaning

Review and Assess

Thinking About the Selection

1. **Respond:** In your opinion, which word or phrase best describes Moore's poem—"fiddle," "derivative," or "genuine"? Explain.
2. **(a) Recall:** What does the speaker say a person discovers when reading poetry "with a perfect contempt for it"?
   (b) Interpret: What type of poetry does the speaker dislike?
3. **(a) Recall:** What does the speaker say happens when poems become derivative? **(b) Synthesize:** What qualities does the speaker believe good poetry should possess?
4. **(a) Interpret:** What apparent contradiction exists in the phrase "literalists of the imagination"? **(b) Analyze:** In what way is the meaning of this phrase furthered by Moore's image of "imaginary gardens with real toads"? **(c) Generalize:** From where is Moore suggesting good poetry derives its power?
5. **Extend:** Do you think that the lyrics of today's popular music meet Moores' criteria for good poetry? Why or why not?

Poetry ◆ 801

ASSESS

Answers for p. 801

Review and Assess

1. Possible response: Students may feel that Moore's poem deserves her own highest praise—"genuine." Students should provide a clear explanation for their responses.
2. **(a)** Some of it is good and worthwhile; there is a place in it for the "genuine."
   (b) Possible response: The speaker dislikes poetry that is pretentious or obscure, requiring "high-sounding interpretations."
3. **(a)** They become "unintelligible" and cannot be admired.
   (b) Possible response: She believes that poems should be accessible and concrete.
4. **(a)** Literalism suggests a dedication to fact, while imagination suggests the possibility of fancy.
   (b) Flights of fancy are implied by the idea of "imaginary gardens," but "real toads" suggests a reliance on things ordinary, concrete, and even ugly—the literal. **(c)** Moore suggests that good poetry derives its power from the concrete objects and experiences of everyday life.
5. Possible answers: Students may respond that if song lyrics rely on concrete images and evoke clear emotions Moore might consider them to be poetry.

✎ ASSESSMENT PRACTICE: Reading Comprehension

Analyze Sentence Meaning   (For more practice, see Test Preparation Workbook, p. 47.)

Many tests require students to correctly answer sentence-completion questions. Often, more than one choice can complete a sentence. Use the following sample item to show students how to analyze sentence meaning to eliminate incorrect choices.

The Symbolist poets believed that the Modern Age was a time of uncertainty, and that people's ideas and emotions were _____ to communicate.

A easy   **C** difficult
B fair   **D** enjoyable

The context of the sentence indicates that the correct answer will have a negative connotation, so *A* and *D* are eliminated. Answer choice *B* does not make sense in the sentence. *C* is the best choice.

Review and Assess

1. Possible response: It should approach some ideal, rounded form.

2. Possible responses: *Items compared*: a poem and a flight of birds; The simile uses the word *as*. *Interpretation*: Poetry should convey movement rather than words about movement.

3. Possible response: All of the similes combine to create a sense of a poem as an organic, living thing one can experience directly.

4. Possible response: Poetry must both absorb and reflect the realities of the modern world.

5. **(a)** The image is of the moon climbing above the trees in the winter. **(b)** Possible response: The image suggests that poetry must transcend the specific moment that produced it in order to be timeless.

6. **(a)** They appeal to the sense of sight, but also to touch and physical sensation. **(b)** Possible response: The images allow Moore to suggest the raw, physical energy she believes poetry can—and should—contain.

7. Possible responses: **(a)** Stevens: "It has to be. . . like an insatiable actor"; MacLeish: "A poem should be. . . silent as the sleeve-worn stone"; Moore: "imaginary gardens with real toads in them" **(b)** All three want poetry to touch people's souls through their senses and to be relevant to people's lives. **(c)** Steven's ideas are more intellectual and abstract. MacLeish's ideas emphasize the emotional and sensory aspects of poetry. Moore's ideas emphasize the clarity and directness she prizes in poetry.

8. Possible responses: **(a)** The wilderness enveloped the jar and both the landscape and the jar were improved. **(b)** These things are important because they are practical, not lofty or intellectual.

9. Possible response: Students may identify music or theater, and argue for various criteria by which to judge quality work.

Review and Assess

Literary Analysis

Simile

1. In "Ars Poetica," what does the word "globed" suggest about a poem?

2. Find four **similes** in "Ars Poetica" and interpret their meaning. Analyze them in a chart like the one shown.

Items Compared · · · · ▶ ☐ **like** / ☐ **as** · · · · ▶ **Interpretation**

3. How do all the similes work together in this poem to create a vision of poetry as something that "should not mean / But be"?

Comparing Literary Works

4. Based on "Of Modern Poetry," how would you summarize Steven's definition of poetry?

5. **(a)** Identify the **image** in lines 9–14 in "Ars Poetica." **(b)** How does this image help you understand MacLeish's definition of poetry?

6. **(a)** To what senses do Marianne Moore's images of animal behavior appeal? **(b)** What unites the images in defining poetry for Moore?

7. **(a)** Select one key image from each poem that captures the poet's beliefs about poetry. Explain your choice. **(b)** How do the poets' ideas about poetry compare? **(c)** How do they contrast?

Reading Strategy

Paraphrasing

8. Paraphrase the following passages from the poems, giving them straightforward and direct meanings:
(a) from "Anecdote of the Jar," lines 5–8
(b) from "Poetry," lines 6–8 ("these things . . . useful.")

Extend Understanding

9. **Career Connection:** These poems express distinct ideas about the characteristics good poems possess. Select another field of artistic endeavor and identify various elements that make for quality work.

802 ◆ Disillusion, Defiance, and Discontent (1914–1946)

Quick Review

A **simile** is a comparison between two seemingly dissimilar things and is indicated by a connecting word such as *like* or *as*.

Imagery is descriptive language used to create word pictures for the readers and to appeal to the senses.

To **paraphrase,** identify key passages and restate them in your own words.

 **Take It to the Net**
www.phschool.com
Take the interactive self-test online to check your understanding of these selections.

★ ENRICHMENT: Further Reading

Other Works by the Poets

Works by Wallace Stevens

Harmonium
The Man With the Blue Guitar

Works by Archibald MacLeish

J.B.: A Play in Verse
Poetry and Experience

Works by Marianne Moore

Complete Poems of Marianne Moore

Integrate Language Skills

❶ Vocabulary Development Lesson

Word Analysis: Latin Root -satis-

The word *insatiable* contains the Latin root *-satis-*, which means "enough." Combined with the prefix *in-*, meaning "not," you can determine that *insatiable* will suggest "not enough." Use your knowledge of *-satis-* to define each word below.

1. satisfy
2. satisfactory
3. satiate
4. satiety

Spelling Strategy

When choosing between the suffixes *-able* and *-ible* to form adjectives, opt for *-able* if you are unsure of the spelling. Like *insatiable*, many more adjectives are formed with *-able* than with *-ible*. Add *-able* or *-ible* to each word part below. Then, check your choice in a dictionary.

1. avail__
2. reli__
3. palp__
4. illeg__
5. fall__
6. pli__

Fluency: Context

Follow the instructions below to write a sentence for each item, using a word from the vocabulary list on page 795. Use each word once.

1. Describe someone who never exercises imagination.
2. Define the territory governed by a king.
3. Describe the quality of a peach in a beautiful painting.
4. Explain why a friend's room is always such a terrible mess.
5. Criticize a musician whose work lacks originality.
6. Explain why a minimum amount of nutritional food is not enough to maintain one's health.
7. Criticize a sibling who always wants more possessions.

❷ Grammar and Style Lesson

Subject Complements

Subject complements are nouns, pronouns, and adjectives that follow linking verbs (often forms of the word "to be") and identify or describe the subjects.

Sentences containing subject complements are effective when defining something.

> Noun: The actor is a *metaphysican* . . .
> (S) (LV) (SC)
>
> Pronoun: The poet is *she* who is a literalist of the imagination.
> (S) (LV) (SC)
>
> Adjective: A poem should be *wordless* . . .
> (S) (LV) (SC)

Practice Copy each of the following sentences. Underline the subject complement in each one and label it a noun, a pronoun, or an adjective.

1. The winner of this year's poetry prize is you!
2. The subject of the poem was a waterfall.
3. Good poetry should be thrilling.
4. Poets are deep thinkers.
5. The oldest book in the library is a volume of poetry.

Writing Application Write a brief descriptive poem about a familiar person or object. Begin each line with the name of the person or object. Follow it with a linking verb and a subject complement.

𝒲𝒢 *Prentice Hall Writing and Grammar Connection: Chapter 18, Section 3*

EXTEND

Answers for p. 803

❶ Vocabulary Development

Word Analysis

1. to fulfill the needs of
2. good enough to fulfill a need
3. to provide with more than enough
4. the state of having had more than enough

Spelling Strategy

1. available
2. reliable
3. palpable
4. illegible
5. fallible
6. pliable

Fluency: Context

1. Possible response: Someone who never uses his or her imagination is a *literalist*.
2. Possible response: The territory governed by a king is his *dominion*.
3. Possible response: In a beautiful painting, the peach looks *palpable* and ripe.
4. Possible response: My friend has *slovenly* habits.
5. Possible response: The musician's work is very *derivative*.
6. Possible response: That amount of nutrition will not *suffice* to maintain your health.
7. Possible response: My sibling has an *insatiable* appetite for possessions.

❷ Grammar and Style

Practice

1. you; pronoun
2. waterfall; noun
3. thrilling; adjective
4. thinkers; noun
5. volume; noun

Writing Application

Students' poems should maintain an appropriate descriptive focus on one person or object; each line should contain a subject complement.

❸ Writing Lesson

- Remind students that their essays should clearly explain each poem's main idea, as well as compare and contrast those ideas.

- Guide students in rereading the poems. You may paraphrase the ideas in all four poems as a class.

- Show students how to organize their ideas for drafting using the Comparison and Contrast transparency in **Writing Models and Graphic Organizers on Transparencies,** p. 87.

- As students draft, be sure that they include necessary background information on each poet's beliefs, as the instruction on p. 804 urges.

❹ Listening and Speaking

- Have students create and discuss their own definitions of poetry. Remind them that poetry analysis is highly subjective; they should develop ideas they can support.

- Divide the class into two groups. They should begin by analyzing each poet's views before moving on to the round-table discussion.

- Remind students to remain consistent to the poets' ideas and to adopt appropriate behavior for a discussion, listening and speaking respectfully.

- Adapt the Persuasive Speech rubric in **Performance Assessment and Portfolio Management,** p. 55, to assess students' participation in the discussion.

CUSTOMIZE INSTRUCTION
For Universal Access

To address different learning styles, use the activities in the **Extension Activities** booklet, p. 45.

For Visual/Spatial and Musical/Rhythmic Learners, use Activity 5.

For Visual/Spatial Learners, use Activity 6.

For Interpersonal Learners, use Activity 7.

---

❸ Writing Lesson

Definition

Stevens, Moore, and MacLeish were not only three of the most important American poets of the twentieth century, they were three of the deepest thinkers about the art of poetry. Write an essay in which you compare and contrast the ideas expressed in two of these poems about poetry. Note the distinct ways in which each poet explains, above all, why poetry is important.

Prewriting Reread each poem and paraphrase the ideas it presents. Compare and contrast the ideas and determine an organizing principle or main idea to develop in your essay.

Drafting Begin by introducing each poet and providing a general statement about his or her beliefs about poetry. Then, write a brief statement of your main point. Develop your ideas, with quotes from the poems in the body paragraphs.

Model: Providing Necessary Background

Wallace Stevens believed that human beings perceive the world in an entirely subjective way. For Stevens, reality itself was an expression of the imagination. These views come through in his ideas about poetry.

> The inclusion of general information about a subject's point of view clarifies the ideas that will follow.

Revising Review your draft, making sure that you have supported your ideas with appropriate quotations from the poem. Replace any less effective quotations with better choices.

W̶G̶ Prentice Hall Writing and Grammar Connection: Chapter 9, Section 3

❹ Extension Activities

Speaking and Listening In a small group, analyze different poets' views of poetry. Then, stage a **round-table discussion** on the issue "What Is Poetry?" Each group member should take a poet's position. Use the following tips as a guide:

- Develop a central argument of your view.
- Include logical appeals based on examples.
- Incorporate emotional appeals, such as a poem's impact on you or others.

Share the results of your discussion.
[Group Activity]

Research and Technology Create a **collection of poems** on another topic, such as sports or nature, that focus on a guiding question. Use print and online poetry reference sources to locate appropriate poems. Include an introduction that explains how the poems relate to one another.

 **Take It to the Net**   www.phschool.com

Go online for an additional research activity using the Internet.

ASSESSMENT RESOURCES

The following resources can be used to assess students' knowledge and skills.

Selection Assessment
- 📖 **Formal Assessment,** p. 203
- 📖 **Open Book Test,** p. 133
- 📼 **Got It! Assessment Videotapes,** Tape 4
- 💿 **Test Bank Software**
- 💻 *Take It to the Net*
  Visit www.phschool.com for self-tests and additional questions on the selections.

Listening and Speaking Rubric
- 📖 **Performance Assess. and Portfolio Mgmt.,** p. 55

PRENTICE HALL
ASSESSMENT SYSTEM

- 📖 **Workbook**   📗 **Transparencies**
- 📖 **Skill Book**   💿 **CD-ROM**

Focus on Literary Forms: The Short Story

Do It Yourself Landscape, Andy Warhol, Museum Ludwig, Cologne, photo courtesy of Rheinisches Bildarchiv Köln

...ort story has been a part of American literature since ...r Allan Poe defined the genre in the 1800s. Every ...n of writers brings a new energy to the form, ...g it by reflecting the changing values, attitudes, ...s of the times. The Modern Age was a critical ...the growth of the American short story, as ...ch as Hemingway and Fitzgerald carried the ...ew heights.

...TRUCTION FOR UNIVERSAL ACCESS

...elections in this part, keep in mind these factors:

reveals much about life's trials

...story dealing
...n emotions
...tion on

...story that

- Less proficient readers may need to read the story in sections

"A Worn Path"

- Less proficient readers may need help distinguishing between actual events and the main character's lapses into reverie

- English language learners may need help with story dialect

"Anxiety"

- Students may need help following dialogue written without quotation marks
- Accessible message about fear of nuclear annihilation

Selection Planning Guide

The selections in this section deal with the anxiety and fear felt by many during the modern era, that is, from the period of World War I to the present. "In Another Country" is told through the eyes of a wounded American World-War-I volunteer recuperating in a hospital in Italy. A soldier's fear of death, the fragility of life, the disillusionment with modern technology, and the futility of careful planning are poignantly brought out in this Hemingway story. In "The Corn Planting," an American farm couple, isolated from fast-paced society, cope with the unexpected death of their son by communing with nature through the planting of corn. "A Worn Path" presents an elderly woman with a mission. In spite of her anxiety over making an arduous journey, and over becoming confused at times, a grandmother walks many miles into town to pick up medicine for her injured grandson. She has made this ritualistic journey many times since the young boy swallowed lye long ago. Part 2 ends with a story appropriately titled "Anxiety." This short story examines a particular fear of contemporary society, that of annihilation from nuclear war.

Background
Art

Do It Yourself Landscape, Andy Warhol

Andy Warhol (1930–1987) led the Pop Art movement during the 1960s, making artworks out of commonplace elements of popular culture. In this artwork, Warhol cleverly imitates the look of a partially finished paint-by-number painting, popular during the 1950s and early 1960s. Explain that such a painting would start out like the outlined white spaces on this work, the numbers indicating which color to use within each space.

Ask the following question:

- What seems peculiarly American and twentieth-century about the idea of do-it-yourself art?
  Possible response: Such art is democratic—no one needs to be specially skilled or inspired. It also reflects the techniques of modern mass-production.

805

In Another Country ✦ The Corn Planting ✦ A Worn Path

Lesson Objectives

1. **To analyze and respond to literary elements**
   - Literary Analysis: Point of View
   - Comparing Literary Works
2. **To read, comprehend, analyze, and critique short fiction**
   - Reading Strategy: Identifying With Characters
   - Reading Check Questions
   - Review and Assess Questions
   - Assessment Practice (ATE)
3. **To develop word analysis skills, fluency, and systematic vocabulary**
   - Vocabulary Development Lesson: Latin Root -val-
4. **To understand and apply written and oral language conventions**
   - Spelling Strategy
   - Grammar and Style Lesson: Punctuating Dialogue
5. **To understand and apply appropriate writing and research strategies**
   - Writing Lesson: Memorial Speech
   - Extension Activity: Research Report
6. **To understand and apply listening and speaking strategies**
   - Extension Activity: Sequel

STEP-BY-STEP TEACHING GUIDE	PACING GUIDE
PRETEACH	
Motivate Students and Provide Background	
Use the Motivation activity (ATE p. 806)	5 min.
Read and discuss author and background features (SE/ATE p. 806) **A**	15 min.
Introduce the Concepts	
Introduce the Literary Analysis and Reading Strategy (SE/ATE p. 807) **A**	15 min.
Pronounce the vocabulary words and read their definitions (SE p. 807)	5 min.
TEACH	
Monitor Comprehension	
Informally monitor comprehension by circulating while students read independently or in groups **A**	90 min.
Monitor students' comprehension with the Reading Check notes (SE/ATE pp. 811–817, 821–827)	as students read as students read
Develop vocabulary with Vocabulary notes (SE pp. 814, 821, 827; ATE p. 814)	
Develop Understanding	
Develop students' understanding point of view with the Literary Analysis annotations (SE pp. 810, 815, 817, 822, 823, 825–827; ATE pp. 810, 815, 816, 823, 825–827) **A**	15 min.
Develop students' ability to identify with characters by using the Reading Strategy annotations (SE pp. 812, 818, 822; ATE pp. 812, 818, 822, 825, 827)	15 min.
ASSESS	
Assess Mastery	
Assess students' mastery of the Reading Strategy and Literary Analysis by having them answer the Review and Assess questions (SE/ATE p. 829)	20 min.
Use one or more of the print and media Assessment Resources (ATE p. 831) **A**	up to 45 min.
EXTEND	
Apply Understanding	
Have students complete the Vocabulary Development Lesson and the Grammar Lesson (SE p. 830) **A**	20 min.
Apply students' ability to elaborate to add emotional appeal to writing by using the Writing Lesson (SE/ATE p. 831) **A**	45 min.
Apply students' understanding using one or more of the Extension Activities (SE p. 831)	20–90 min.

 ACCELERATED INSTRUCTION:
Use the strategies and activities identified with an **A**.

UNIVERSAL ACCESS
● = Below Level Students
▲ = On-Level Students
■ = Above Level Students

Time and Resource Manager

Reading Level: Average, Easy, Challenging
Average Number of Instructional Days: 6

RESOURCES		
PRINT	**TRANSPARENCIES**	**TECHNOLOGY**
• **Beyond Literature,** Cross-Curricular Connection: Health, p. 46 ▲ ■		• **Interest Grabber Video,** Tape 5 ● ▲ ■
• **Selection Support Workbook:** ● ▲ ■ Literary Analysis, p. 205 Reading Strategy, p. 204 Build Vocabulary, p. 202	• **Literary Analysis and Reading Transparencies,** pp. 91 and 92 ● ▲ ■	
• **Adapted Reader's Companion** ● • **Reader's Companion** ●		• **Listening to Literature** ● ▲ ■ Audiocassettes, Side 27–28 Audio CDs, CD 15–16
• **English Learner's Companion** ● ▲ • **Literatura en español** ● ▲ • **Literary Analysis for Enrichment** ■	• **Fine Art Transparencies,** Volume 1, Transparency 10	
• **Formal Assessment:** Selection Test, p. 210 ● ▲ ■ • **Open Book Test,** p. 136 ● ▲ ■ • **Performance Assessment and Portfolio Management,** p. 22 ● ▲ ■ PRENTICE HALL ASSESSMENT SYSTEM ● ▲ ■	PRENTICE HALL ASSESSMENT SYSTEM ● ▲ ■ Skills Practice Answers and Explanations on Transparencies	• **Test Bank Software** ● ▲ ■ • **Got It! Assessment Videotapes,** Tape 4 ● ▲
• **Selection Support Workbook:** ● ▲ ■ Grammar and Style, p. 203 • **Writing and Grammar,** Ruby Level ● ▲ ■ • **Extension Activities,** p. 46 ● ▲ ■	• **Daily Language Practice Transparencies** ● ▲ • **Writing Models and Graphic Organizers on Transparencies,** p. 95 ● ▲ ■	• **Writing and Grammar iText CD-ROM** ● ▲ ■ **Take It to the Net** www.phschool.com

BLOCK SCHEDULING: Use one 90-minute class period to preteach the selection and have students read it. Use a second 90-minute class period to assess students' mastery of skills and have them complete one of the Extension Activities.

Step-by-Step Teaching Guide for pp. 806–808

Motivation

Tell students that it is likely that at some time in their lives they will find themselves in the unenviable position of being the bearer of bad news. Then, divide students into groups. Hand each group an index card with news of an injury, accident, incarceration, dire financial reversal, and so on. Tell them that it is their job to pass on that news to someone who will probably find it very upsetting. Give a different piece of bad news to each group.

Groups can discuss and role-play ways in which to break the news to the people most affected by it. Should they be direct? Should they try to soften the blow? Should they be comforting? Should they deliver the news and then disappear? Have students talk or write about how they think it would feel to give bad news. Students who actually have had that responsibility can volunteer to describe their experiences. Explain to students that each of the stories they're about to read focuses on how people handle difficult situations such as the ones they dealt with in the activity.

▐▐▐ Interest Grabber Video

As an alternative, you may wish to play "World War I" on Tape 5 to engage student interest.

Prepare to Read

❶ In Another Country ◆ The Corn Planting ◆ A Worn Path

Ernest Hemingway (1899–1961)

Ernest Hemingway's fiction expressed the sentiments of many members of the post-World War I generation. He wrote about people's struggles to maintain a sense of dignity while living in a sometimes hostile world.

The Red Cross Hemingway, the son of a physician, was born and raised in Oak Park, Illinois, a suburb of Chicago. In high school, he played football and wrote newspaper columns. Eager to serve in World War I, he tried to join the army but was repeatedly turned away due to an eye defect. He joined the Red Cross ambulance corps instead and, in 1918, was sent to the Italian front. Just before his nineteenth birthday, he was severely wounded and spent several months recovering in a hospital in Milan, Italy. His experiences during the war helped shape his view of the world and provide material for his writing.

Expatriates After the war, Hemingway had a difficult time readjusting to life in the United States. To establish himself as a writer, he went to Paris as a foreign correspondent for the *Toronto Star*. In Paris, he befriended Ezra Pound, Gertrude Stein, F. Scott Fitzgerald, and other American writers and artists living overseas. The literary advice of these friends and his work as a journalist helped him develop his concise, concrete, and highly charged writing style.

In 1925, Hemingway published his first major work, *In Our Time*, a series of loosely connected short stories. A year later he published *The Sun Also Rises*, a novel about a group of British and American expatriates trying to overcome the pain and disillusionment of life in the modern world.

Hemingway became as famous for his lifestyle as he was for his writing. Constantly pursuing adventure, he hunted big game in Africa, attended bullfights in Spain, held records for deep-sea fishing in the Caribbean, and participated in amateur boxing.

The full body of Hemingway's work—including *A Farewell to Arms* (1929), *For Whom the Bell Tolls* (1940), and *The Old Man and the Sea* (1952)—earned him the Nobel Prize for Literature in 1954.

Sherwood Anderson (1876–1941)

Sherwood Anderson was one of the most influential American writers of the first half of the twentieth century. The third of seven children, Anderson was raised in a small town in Ohio. His father was a harness maker and house painter who was not always able to earn enough money to support the family. At fourteen, Anderson dropped out of high school to work, taking a variety of unskilled jobs. He eventually joined the army to serve in the Spanish-American War, which ended just before he arrived in Cuba. At the age of twenty-three, after a year of military service, Anderson returned to his hometown and finished high school.

His Best-known Work After, completing high-school, Anderson moved to Chicago to pursue a writing career. He worked as an advertising copywriter and met poets Carl Sandburg and Edgar Lee Masters and novelist Theodore Dreiser. After witnessing the success of Masters's *Spoon River Anthology*, Anderson began his own fictional explorations of life in rural America. Using his boyhood observations and experiences as material, he created his best-known work, *Winesburg, Ohio* (1919), a unified collection of short stories. In this work, Anderson presents small-town life in a strikingly different manner from earlier works of literature. He looks beneath the surface of the characters' lives to construct psychological portraits. He also uses

---

TEACHING RESOURCES

The following resources can be used to enrich or extend the instruction for pp. 806–808

Motivation

▐▐▐ **Interest Grabber Video,** Tape 5 ▪

Background

📖 **Beyond Literature,** p. 46

Take It to the Net
Visit www.phschool.com for Background and hotlinks for the authors.

Literary Analysis

📖 **Selection Support:** Literary Analysis, p. 205 ▪

📄 **Literary Analysis and Reading Transparencies,** Point of View, p. 92

Reading

📄 **Literary Analysis and Reading Transparencies,** Identifying with Characters, p. 91

▐ **BLOCK SCHEDULING:** Resources marked with this symbol provide varied instruction during 90-minute blocks.

everyday speech to capture the essence of characters, a technique he borrowed from Mark Twain.

In addition to writing, Anderson became a successful businessman heading the Anderson Manufacturing Company, which made paint and roof-pitch. He did not enjoy business, and in his mid-thirties, he abandoned the company to devote himself to writing. Although Anderson's literary reputation rests mainly on *Winesburg, Ohio*, he also published other successful books, including *Windy McPherson's Son* (1916), *The Triumph of the Egg* (1921), *Horses and Men* (1923), and *Death in the Woods and Other Stories* (1933).

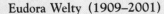

Eudora Welty (1909–2001)

Eudora Welty's stories and novels capture life in the deep South, creating images of the landscape and conveying the shared attitudes and values of the people. She often confronts the hardships of life in poor rural areas. Despite her awareness of people's suffering, her writing remains optimistic. Welty was born in Jackson, Mississippi, where she spent most of her life. She attended Mississippi State College for Women before transferring to the University of Wisconsin, from which she graduated in 1929. Hoping to pursue a career in advertising, she moved to New York and enrolled at Columbia University School of Business. However, because of the worsening economic depression, she was unable to find steady employment and returned to Jackson in 1931.

Writing Fiction After accepting a job as a publicist for a government agency, Welty spent several years traveling throughout Mississippi, taking photographs and interviewing people. Her experiences and observations inspired her to write, and in 1936 her first short story, "Death of a Traveling Salesman," was published.

In her fiction, Welty displays an acute sense of detail and a deep sense of compassion toward her characters. For example, in "A Worn Path," she paints a sympathetic portrait of an old woman whose feelings of love and sense of duty motivate her to make a long, painful journey through the woods.

One of the leading American writers of the twentieth century, Welty published numerous collections of short stories and novels. In 1973, her novel *The Optimist's Daughter* won the Pulitzer Prize.

Background

World War I was the first truly global war, involving nations on every continent but Antarctica. The Great War, as it was also called, began in Europe in 1914, sparked by nationalist pride and systems of alliances among nations. The Central Powers (Germany, Austria, Turkey) fought the Allies (England, France, Russia) with other nations joining one side or the other. Italy, where Hemingway's "In Another Country" takes place, was not strategically important, but it helped the Allies by drawing Central Power troops away from other battle areas.

The war lasted four brutal years. Throughout most of the conflict, a stalemate existed. Both sides were dug into trenches, and took turns rushing one another. Each rush was greeted by a barrage of machine-gun fire, with thousands falling dead. Other soldiers fell to new weapons of killing—inventions such as airplanes, long-range artillery, and poison gas—that many people had hoped would deter aggressors and prevent war. Many of the wounded were saved, however, by advances in medical treatment, such as surgical disinfectants and rehabilitative techniques to strengthen injured limbs.

In his time, Sherwood Anderson was enormously influential in the world of American literature. *Winesburg, Ohio* appeared just after World War I and can be seen as heralding an important literary moment in the United States. Anderson's experimental use of everyday language directly influenced Ernest Hemingway's style. Anderson's influence worked on other levels, as well. Hemingway owed his first book publication to the older author.

Hemingway became famous with his first novel, *The Sun Also Rises*, and his literary star quickly outshone Anderson's. In 1926, Hemingway published *Torrents of Spring*, a mean-spirited satire of Anderson's work. As Anderson's importance seemed to fade, Hemingway emerged as perhaps the most famous and influential American author of the twentieth century. Tragically, he took his own life in 1961, but he remains a giant literary figure whose influence continues to this day.

Eudora Welty matured as a writer in a literary landscape permanently changed by such authors as Anderson and Hemingway. While her style and immediate subject matter—the people of small-town Mississippi—seem very different from the two older writers, her explorations of human relationships travel ground broken by the generation of writers that immediately preceded her generation, American fiction has continued to evolve.

CUSTOMIZE INSTRUCTION FOR UNIVERSAL ACCESS

For Special Needs Students	For Less Proficient Readers	For English Learners
Have students read the adapted version of the selections in the **Adapted Reader's Companion.** This version provides basic-level instruction in an interactive format with questions and write-on lines. Completing the adapted version will prepare students to read the selection in the Student Edition.	Have students read the selections in the **Reader's Companion.** This version provides basic-level instruction in an interactive format with questions and write-on lines. After students finish the selection in **Reader's Companion**, have them complete the questions and activities in the Student Edition.	Have students read the adapted version of the selections in the **English Learner's Companion.** This version provides basic-level instruction in an interactive format with questions and write-on lines. Completing the adapted version will prepare students to read the selection in the Student Edition.

❷ Literary Analysis

Point of View

- Explain that a narrator who is a character and speaks to the reader using the words "I" or "we" is a *first-person narrator.* One who is not a character and describes the actions using "he," "she," and "they" is a *limited third-person narrator.*

- Be sure students understand that different kinds of narrators have different *points of view* on the action in a story.

- Provide examples of different kinds of narrators and points of view using the Point of View transparency in **Literary Analysis and Reading Transparencies,** p. 92.

- Direct students' attention to the Point of View chart on p. 808. Have students create similar charts for each of the stories to better understand point of view.

❸ Reading Strategy

Identifying With Characters

- Explain to students that by identifying with characters they can appreciate and understand stories more fully.

- As an example, point out that the narrator of the first story is an injured soldier being consoled by a doctor. Readers who have also been injured may know how the narrator feels. Those who have not been physically injured may nonetheless understand the emotional turmoil the soldier experiences.

- Model for students the chart on the Identifying With Characters transparency in **Literary Analysis and Reading Transparencies,** p. 91.

- Encourage students to use similar charts to identify with the characters in these selections.

Vocabulary Development

- Pronounce each vocabulary word for students, and read the definitions as a class. Have students identify any words with which they are already familiar.

 E-Teach

Visit E-Teach at www.phschool.com for teachers' essays on how to teach, with questions and answers.

808

Preview
Connecting to the Literature

In each of these stories, characters undertake journeys that dramatically affect their lives. As you read, notice the ways in which their journeys compare to ones that you have made.

❷ Literary Analysis
Point of View

The **point of view** of a story is the perspective from which it is told.

- In stories told from the **first-person point of view,** the person telling the story participates in the action, uses the pronoun *I,* and shares his or her own thoughts and feeling about events.

- Stories told from a **limited third-person point of view** are told by an anonymous speaker who stands outside the action and does not use the pronoun *I.* The speaker both relates the events of the story and conveys the thoughts of one of the characters.

As you read, use a chart like the one shown to analyze the type of narration each story demonstrates.

Comparing Literary Works

Each of these stories is told from a different point of view. In each case, the **narrator,** or person telling the story, controls information and directly influences the reader's perceptions. Examine the effects of different points of view by comparing the information each narrator shares. Notice the biases each displays and the level of sympathy or interest each generates. Finally, determine the reasons you think each author chose the narrative point of view he or she did and how that choice gives a specific shape to the story.

❸ Reading Strategy
Identifying With Characters

Even if your journeys differ from the ones taken by these characters, you might feel as though you know them. When you **identify with characters,** you relate to their thoughts and feelings and connect them with your own experiences. As you read, identify with characters by comparing your life experiences with theirs.

Vocabulary Development

invalided (in′ və lid′ id) *v.* released because of illness or disability (p. 814)

grave (grāv) *adj.* serious; solemn (p. 821)

limber (lim′ bər) *adj.* flexible (p. 821)

obstinate (äb′ stə nit) *adj.* stubborn (p. 827)

Story

| Notes About Narrator |

Type of Narrator

TEACHING RESOURCES

The following resources can be used to enrich or extend the instruction for pp. 809–828.

Literary Analysis
- **Literary Analysis and Reading Transparencies,** p. 92

Reading
- **Selection Support:** Reading Strategy, p. 204; Build Vocabulary, p. 202

- **Adapted Reader's Companion**
- **English Learner's Companion**
- **Reader's Companion**
- **Literary Analysis and Reading Transparencies,** p. 91

Extension
- **Fine Art Transparencies,** Volume 1, Art Transparency 10

❶ IN ANOTHER COUNTRY

ERNEST HEMINGWAY

I n the fall the war[1] was always there, but we did not go to it any more. It was cold in the fall in Milan[2] and the dark came very early. Then the electric lights came on, and it was pleasant along the streets looking in the windows. There was much game hanging outside the shops, and the snow powdered in the fur of the foxes and the wind blew their tails. The deer hung stiff and heavy and empty, and small birds blew in the wind and the wind turned their feathers. It was a cold fall and the wind came down from the mountains.

---

1. **the war** World War I (1914–1918).
2. **Milan** (mi lan´) a city in northern Italy.

❷ ▲ **Critical Viewing** What mood is conveyed in this image of a hospital serving soldiers during World War I? Which details contribute to the mood? **[Interpret]**

In Another Country ◆ 809

CUSTOMIZE INSTRUCTION
For Bodily/Kinesthetic Learners

Invite students to develop an exercise program for someone like the major or the narrator in the first story in the selection, "In Another Country." Their goal is to strengthen or increase the use of a particular injured limb. Students should assume that the complex scientific equipment that exists today is not available. Students can also consider how their program will be presented to the patients.

❶ About the Selection

True to Hemingway's style, this story of a soldier in a World War I military hospital describes a time, but does not create and then resolve a single conflict. The narrator, an American serving as an officer in the Italian army during World War I, convalesces after a serious injury to his leg. He befriends other wounded soldiers, but once they decide his medals were awarded because he is an American while theirs were won for acts of valor and self-sacrifice, he feels isolated from them. The narrator is "in another country," both physically and emotionally. It is a place where he feels no connection to anyone else.

❷ ▶Critical Viewing

The image conveys a mood of calm, but with trouble and pain close by. Details that add to this mood include the white sheets and the placid expression on the nurse's face combined with the haunted or pained look of the American soldier.

CUSTOMIZE INSTRUCTION FOR UNIVERSAL ACCESS

For Less Proficient Readers	For English Learners	For Advanced Readers
Some of the situations and ideas in these stories may be confusing. You may find it useful to stop and clarify things periodically, asking *Who? Where? Why? What? How?* and *When?* questions to make sure students are on track.	Guide students to use context clues or a dictionary to discover the meanings of words not highlighted and defined on the page. *Pavilions, lurched,* and *jostle* are examples from the first story. *Gnarled, loitered,* and *harrowing* are examples from the second. In the last story, students may not know the meanings of *meditative, ravine,* and *lolling*.	Each of these stories includes references that add levels of meaning and complexity. Have students analyze examples in the stories of irony, symbolism, imagery, and foreshadowing. Encourage them to keep notes on their observations.

809

- Remind students that *point of view* refers to the narrator's perspective. In first-person point of view, the narrator is a character in the story who speaks to the reader using the words "I" and "we."

- Instruct students to create Point of View charts for "In Another Country" based on the model on p. 808.

- Before they fill in the boxes on their charts, ask students what type of narrator tells this story. Answer: The story has a first-person narrator.

- Ask the Literary Analysis question on p. 810: How can you tell right from the start that the story is told from a first-person point of view? Possible response: The narrator uses the words "we" and "I". The narrator is a character in the story.

We were all at the hospital every afternoon, and there were different ways of walking across the town through the dusk to the hospital. Two of the ways were alongside canals, but they were long. Always, though, you crossed a bridge across a canal to enter the hospital. There was a choice of three bridges. On one of them a woman sold roasted chestnuts. It was warm, standing in front of her charcoal fire, and the chestnuts were warm afterward in your pocket. The hospital was very old and very beautiful, and you entered through a gate and walked across a courtyard and out a gate on the other side. There were usually funerals starting from the courtyard. Beyond the old hospital were the new brick pavilions, and there we met every afternoon and were all very polite and interested in what was the matter, and sat in the machines that were to make so much difference.

The doctor came up to the machine where I was sitting and said: "What did you like best to do before the war? Did you practice a sport?"

I said: "Yes, football."

"Good," he said. "You will be able to play football again better than ever."

My knee did not bend and the leg dropped straight from the knee to the ankle without a calf, and the machine was to bend the knee and make it move as in riding a tricycle. But it did not bend yet, and instead the machine lurched when it came to the bending part. The doctor said: "That will all pass. You are a fortunate young man. You will play football again like a champion."

In the next machine was a major who had a little hand like a baby's. He winked at me when the doctor examined his hand, which was between two leather straps that bounced up and down and flapped the stiff fingers, and said: "And will I too play football, captain-doctor?" He had been a very great fencer, and before the war the greatest fencer in Italy.

The doctor went to his office in a back room and brought a photograph which showed a hand that had been withered almost as small as the major's, before it had taken a machine course, and after was a little larger. The major held the photograph with his good hand and looked at it very carefully. "A wound?" he asked.

"An industrial accident," the doctor said.

"Very interesting, very interesting," the major said, and handed it back to the doctor.

"You have confidence?"

"No," said the major.

There were three boys who came each day who were about the same age I was. They were all three from Milan, and one of them was to be a lawyer, and one was to be a painter, and one had intended to be a soldier, and after we were finished with the machines, sometimes we walked back together to the Café Cova, which was next door to the Scala.[3] We walked the short way through the communist quarter

---

3. **the Scala** (ska´ la) an opera house in Milan.

✳ ENRICHMENT: Career Connection

Physical Therapy and Therapists

Physical therapy is the treatment of injury or illness by physical means. Physical therapists work with a wide range of patients, from those who have severe injuries and are in need of intensive therapy, to the throngs of Americans suffering from lower back pain. The tools of the physical therapist are exercise, massage, infrared or ultraviolet light, electrotherapy, and heat.

Interested students can research to find out more about the daily activities of physical therapists. Students can learn about how a physical therapist's approach to healing differs from that of chiropractors, psychiatrists, orthopedists, acupuncturists, and other practitioners. Also, students can research the nature of the education and training physical therapists undergo, as well as the necessary licensing requirements.

because we were four together. The people hated us because we were officers, and from a wine-shop someone called out, "A basso gli ufficiali!"[4] as we passed. Another boy who walked with us sometimes and made us five wore a black silk handkerchief across his face because he had no nose then and his face was to be rebuilt. He had gone out to the front from the military academy and been wounded within an hour after he had gone into the front line for the first time. They rebuilt his face, but he came from a very old family and they could never get the nose exactly right. He went to South America and worked in a bank. But this was a long time ago, and then we did not any of us know how it was going to be afterward. We only knew then that there was always the war, but that we were not going to it any more.

We all had the same medals, except the boy with the black silk bandage across his face, and he had not been at the front long enough to get any medals. The tall boy with a very pale face who was to be a lawyer had been a lieutenant of Arditi[5] and had three medals of the sort we each had only one of. He had lived a very long time with death and was a little detached. We were all a little detached, and there was nothing that held us together except that we met every afternoon at the hospital. Although, as we walked to the Cova through the tough part of town, walking in the dark, with light and singing coming out of the wine-shops, and sometimes having to walk into the street when the men and women would crowd together on the sidewalk so that we would have had to jostle them to get by, we felt held together by there being something that had happened that they, the people who disliked us, did not understand.

We ourselves all understood the Cova, where it was rich and warm and not too brightly lighted, and noisy and smoky at certain hours, and there were always girls at the tables and the illustrated papers on a rack on the wall. The girls at the Cova were very patriotic, and I found that the most patriotic people in Italy were the café girls— and I believe they are still patriotic.

The boys at first were very polite about my medals and asked me what I had done to get them. I showed them the papers, which were written in very beautiful language and full of *fratellanza* and *abnegazione*,[6] but which really said, with the adjectives removed,

---

4. **"A basso gli ufficiali!"** (a ba´ so lye oo fe cha´ le) "Down with officers!" (Italian).
5. **Arditi** (är dē´ tē) a select group of soldiers chosen specifically for dangerous campaigns.
6. *fratellanza* (frä täl än´ tsä) and *abnegazione* (äb´ nä gä tzyō´ nä) "brotherhood" and "self-denial" (Italian).

❺ "The War to End All Wars"
In this story, the characters struggle courageously against their disillusionment with war and technology. World War I resulted in astonishing destruction and massive death as a result of new technologies such as airplanes, poison gas, and long-range artillery. Many who enlisted did so expecting a swift victory, but the war lasted four grueling years. Up to ten million soldiers died, as well as many civilians. Some people believed that the widespread destruction and loss of life would make World War I "The War to End All Wars," but subsequent conflicts have proved them wrong.

❻ ✓ Reading Check
What do the narrator and the "three boys" have in common?

In Another Country ◆ 811

❹ Critical Thinking
Infer

• Read the bracketed passage out loud with the class. Discuss with students their impressions of the narrator and the three "boys."

• Ask students: How old do you think the narrator and the other "boys" are? Why?
Possible response: Students may say that the young soldiers are perhaps 18–20 years old because none of them had careers before the war; their plans are for what they are "to be."

• Remind students that wars, for the most part, are fought by soldiers who are their age and just a little older.

❺ Background
"The War to End All Wars"

World War I was a nineteenth-century war fought with twentieth-century weapons; the military tactics lagged behind the capabilities of the weaponry. As a result, casualties were staggering and the wounds extraordinary and appalling. Although some soldiers came home with psychological wounds and others with illnesses, some were simply ripped apart. It has been estimated that more than 12 percent of all injured soldiers suffered from facial wounds. Perhaps a third of these unfortunate men were permanently disfigured. Polite society sometimes shunned them. Much of the support the hundreds of decorated veterans received was from their fellow victims. Attempting to dignify their experience, they bonded together to form mutual-aid societies.

❻ ✓ Reading Check
Answer: They are about the same age, serve in the Italian military, earned similar medals, and have been wounded.

CUSTOMIZE INSTRUCTION FOR UNIVERSAL ACCESS

For Special Needs Students	For Gifted/Talented Students	For Advanced Readers
If students are confused by the story's setting and do not seem to understand what is happening, preview the story with students and explain its central events.	After reading about the wounded men walking to the Cova, have these students discuss what it means to feel detached. Ask them to explain why these men are "a little detached" and to offer reasons why people come to feel aloof and indifferent. Then, ask each student to write a short poem about the feeling of detachment.	Call students' attention to the sentence, "We only knew then that there was always the war, but that we were not going to it anymore." Point out that here the narrator rephrases the opening sentence of the story. Have students discuss the effect of this repetition.

Identifying With Characters

❽ **Background**

Hemingway

that I had been given the medals because I was an American. After that their manner changed a little toward me, although I was their friend against outsiders. I was a friend, but I was never really one of them after they had read the citations, because it had been different with them and they had done very different things to get their medals. I had been wounded, it was true; but we all knew that being wounded, after all, was really an accident. I was never ashamed of the ribbons, though, and sometimes, after the cocktail hour, I would imagine myself having done all the things they had done to get their medals; but walking home at night through the empty streets with the cold wind and all the shops closed, trying to keep near the street lights, I knew that I would never have done such things, and I was very much afraid to die, and often lay in bed at night by myself, afraid to die and wondering how I would be when I went back to the front again.

The three with the medals were like hunting-hawks; and I was not a hawk, although I might seem a hawk to those who had never hunted; they, the three, knew better and so we drifted apart. But I stayed good friends with the boy who had been wounded his first day at the front, because he would never know now how he would have turned out; so he could never be accepted either, and I liked him because I thought perhaps he would not have turned out to be a hawk either.

The major, who had been the great fencer, did not believe in bravery, and spent much time while we sat in the machines correcting my grammar. He had complimented me on how I spoke Italian, and we talked together very easily. One day I had said that Italian seemed such an easy language to me that I could not take a great interest in it; everything was so easy to say. "Ah yes," the major said. "Why, then, do you not take up the use of grammar?" So we took up the use of grammar, and soon Italian was such a difficult language that I was afraid to talk to him until I had the grammar straight in my mind.

The major came very regularly to the hospital. I do not think he ever missed a day, although I am sure he did not believe in the machines. There was a time when none of us believed in the machines, and one day the major said it was all nonsense. The machines were new then and it was we who were to prove them. It was an idiotic idea, he said, "a theory, like another." I had not learned my grammar, and he said I was a stupid impossible disgrace, and he was a

fool to have bothered with me. He was a small man and he sat straight up in his chair with his right hand thrust into the machine and looked straight ahead at the wall while the straps thumped up and down with his fingers in them.

"What will you do when the war is over if it is over?" he asked me. "Speak grammatically!"

"I will go to the States."

"Are you married?"

"No, but I hope to be."

"The more of a fool you are," he said. He seemed very angry. "A man must not marry."

"Why, Signor Maggiore?"[7]

"Don't call me 'Signor Maggiore.'"

"Why must not a man marry?"

"He cannot marry. He cannot marry," he said angrily. "If he is to lose everything, he should not place himself in a position to lose that. He should not place himself in a position to lose. He should find things he cannot lose."

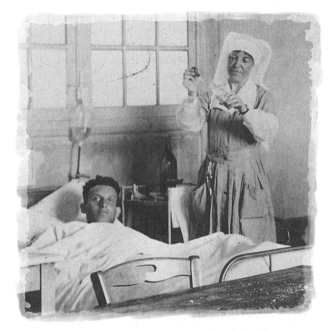

He spoke very angrily and bitterly, and looked straight ahead while he talked.

"But why should he necessarily lose it?"

"He'll lose it," the major said. He was looking at the wall. Then he looked down at the machine and jerked his little hand out from between the straps and slapped it hard against his thigh. "He'll lose it," he almost shouted. "Don't argue with me!" Then he called to the attendant who ran the machines. "Come and turn this damned thing off."

He went back into the other room for the light treatment and the massage. Then I heard him ask the doctor if he might use his telephone and he shut the door. When he came back into the room, I was sitting in another machine. He was wearing his cape and had his cap on, and he came directly toward my machine and put his arm on my shoulder.

"I am so sorry," he said, and patted me on the shoulder with his good hand. "I would not be rude. My wife has just died. You must forgive me."

"Oh—" I said, feeling sick for him. "I am so sorry."

He stood there biting his lower lip. "It is very difficult," he said. "I cannot resign myself."

---

7. **Signor Maggiore** (sēn yōr′ mäj jō′ rā) "Mr. Major" (Italian); a respectful way of addressing an officer.

11 ▲ Critical Viewing
Does this World War I military hospital compare with the hospital Hemingway describes? Explain. [Compare and Contrast]

12 ✔ Reading Check
Why does the mayor believe "a man must not marry"?

In Another Country ◆ 813

9 ▶ Critical Viewing

Interpret

The cold metallic appearance of the room would probably have been frightening.

10 Critical Thinking

Interpret

• Have students read the bracketed passage. Encourage students to discuss their reactions to the information the major reveals. Did it surprise them?

• Ask students to reread the exchange between the narrator and the major on p. 813 regarding marriage. Guide them to recognize that the major's anger is a response to his wife's death.

• Then, ask students: Why did the major respond to learning of his loss by being angry?
Possible response: Some students might say that anger is a common reaction to tragedy. Others might say that the major has not yet accepted the loss.

11 ▶ Critical Viewing

Possible response: Students may say that the place Hemingway has described seems to be a clinic housed in an impressive building. It appears to be full of machines, not crowded with beds filled with badly wounded men.

12 Reading Check

Answer: A man must not marry because "[h]e should not place himself in a position to lose" something as important as a spouse.

CUSTOMIZE INSTRUCTION FOR UNIVERSAL ACCESS

For Less Proficient Readers	For English Learners
Students may find the narrator's conversation with the major on p. 813 to be challenging. Have them read the passage once through for a general impression. Then, have them reread the passage as they listen to it read aloud on **Listening to Literature: Audiocassettes,** Sides 27–28; Audio CDs, CDs 15–16. Guide students to understand that the major becomes highly emotional on the subject of marriage. Encourage them to speculate on what might be the cause of the major's anger.	You may wish to use the major's thoughts on grammar for discussion. Students can understand that speaking Italian was easy for the narrator when he was unaware of correct grammar. Then, as soon as he tried to speak correctly, Italian became difficult. Ask students learning English if they face the same problem. Discuss whether there is an everyday English that is easy to speak and a "classroom" grammar that is difficult to learn.

⓭ Vocabulary Development

The Latin Root -val-

- Call students' attention to the word *invalided* and read its definition. Tell students that the Latin root -val- means "strength" or "value."

- Have students suggest words and phrases that contain this root, and list them on the chalkboard. Possible answers: *equivalent, valor, prevail.*

- Then, have students look up the meanings of these words in a dictionary and write sentences in which they use each word correctly.

Answers for p. 814

Review and Assess

1. Possible response: Students may say that the story aroused pity for all the injured men.

2. **(a)** The narrator was wounded in the leg and is receiving physical therapy to restore muscle activity. **(b)** Possible response: The Italian boys are proud of their accomplishments—and their wounds—because they have fought for their country.

3. **(a)** He says that they "were to make so much difference," that they are new, and that these men are the first to use them. **(b)** Possible response: His leg does not bend despite the machines.

4. **(a)** The people hate them just because they are officers. **(b)** Possible response: The abuse creates a stronger bond between the wounded men.

5. **(a)** The major's wife dies. **(b)** He reacts with anger. **(c)** Possible answer: It is ironic because the major escaped death in the war, but his wife, protected from such dangers, died after a short illness.

6. Possible response: Grammar follows rules; it can be understood and mastered. By contrast, the war is confusing and seems to have no rules.

7. Possible response: Advancements in modern technology have brought weapons of destruction that have maimed countless thousands of men like

continued

814

He looked straight past me and out through the window. Then he began to cry. "I am utterly unable to resign myself," he said and choked. And then crying, his head up looking at nothing, carrying himself straight and soldierly, with tears on both his cheeks and biting his lips, he walked past the machines and out the door.

⓭ The doctor told me that the major's wife, who was very young and whom he had not married until he was definitely <u>invalided</u> out of the war, had died of pneumonia. She had been sick only a few days. No one expected her to die. The major did not come to the hospital for three days. Then he came at the usual hour, wearing a black band on the sleeve of his uniform. When he came back, there were large framed photographs around the wall of all sorts of wounds before and after they had been cured by the machines. In front of the machine the major used were three photographs of hands like his that were completely restored. I do not know where the doctor got them. I always understood we were the first to use the machines. The photographs did not make much difference to the major because he only looked out of the window.

invalided (in´ və lid id) v. released because of illness or disability

Review and Assess

Thinking About the Selection

1. **Respond:** What emotion did this story arouse most strongly in you? Explain.

2. **(a) Recall:** Why does the narrator go to the hospital every day? **(b) Infer:** What type of attitudes would you say he encounters from other patients at the hospital in the same situation? Explain.

3. **(a) Recall:** What does the narrator say about the machines at the hospital? **(b) Interpret:** Why do you think he has developed this attitude toward the machines?

4. **(a) Recall:** How do the people in the communist quarter of the city react to the officers? **(b) Relate:** How do you think these reactions make the officers feel?

5. **(a) Recall:** What happens to the major's wife? **(b) Recall:** How does the major react? **(c) Analyze:** Do you find what happened ironic or surprising? Explain.

6. **Interpret:** Given the setting of the story, a hospital during wartime, what might be the significance of the major's interest in grammar?

7. **Apply:** Do you think this story reflects the sense of disillusionment that arose among writers and artists during World War I? Explain.

---

continued from left column

those in the story; constructive uses of technology, represented by the rehabilitation machines, seem far less effective than their destructive counterparts. The story seems to be saying that the advance of civilization has created more, not less, suffering, and thus expresses a strong sense of disillusionment.

The Corn PLANTING

SHERWOOD ANDERSON

The farmers who come to our town to trade are a part of the town life. Saturday is the big day. Often the children come to the high school in town.

It is so with Hatch Hutchenson. Although his farm, some three miles from town, is small, it is known to be one of the best-kept and best-worked places in all our section. Hatch is a little gnarled old figure of a man. His place is on the Scratch Gravel Road and there are plenty of poorly kept places out that way.

Hatch's place stands out. The little frame house is always kept painted, the trees in his orchard are whitened with lime halfway up the trunks, and the barn and sheds are in repair, and his fields are always clean-looking.

Hatch is nearly seventy. He got a rather late start in life. His father, who owned the same farm, was a Civil War man and came home badly wounded, so that, although he lived a long time after the war, he couldn't work much. Hatch was the only son and stayed at home, working the place until his father died. Then, when he was nearing fifty, he married a schoolteacher of forty, and they had a son. The schoolteacher was a small one like Hatch. After they married, they both stuck close to the land. They seemed to fit into their farm life as certain people fit into the clothes they wear. I have noticed something about people who make a go of marriage. They grow more and more alike. Then even grow to look alike.

Their one son, Will Hutchenson, was a small but remarkably strong boy. He came to our high school in town and pitched on our town baseball team. He was a fellow always cheerful, bright and alert, and a great favorite with all of us.

For one thing, he began as a young boy to make amusing little drawings. It was a talent. He made drawings of fish and pigs and cows, and they looked like people you knew. I never did know, before, that people could look so much like cows and horses and pigs and fish.

Literary Analysis
Point of View From whose point of view is this story being told? Support your answer.

 **Reading Check**

What is the overall condition of the Hutchenson farm?

The Corn Planting ◆ 815

About the Selection

Told from the point of view of a friend of the family, this story describes the alienation of a son from his parents. The narrator describes the Hutchensons as people who "fit into their farm life." When their son, Will, leaves to study art in Chicago, his parents live for news of his life; he frequently sends letters that they treasure. The Hutchensons claim that they can never visit Chicago because of the demands of the farm. When a friend of the narrator receives a telegraph about Will's death, he and the narrator both go out to the farm to inform his parents. In an eerily silent reaction to the news, the Hutchensons grieve in the only way they know how: they go out into the night to plant corn.

Literary Analysis

Point of View

- Remind students that a narrator who speaks to the reader using "I" tells a story from a *first-person point of view*.

- Have students read the bracketed passage. Ask them to look for indications as to who is telling the story.

- Ask students the Literary Analysis question on p. 815: From whose point of view is this story being told? Support your answer.
  Answer: The story is told by a first-person narrator who lives in the place he is describing and knows the inhabitants. This point of view is indicated by the narrator's use of "I" and detailed descriptions.

▶ **Monitor Progress** Encourage students to create Point of View charts for this story, based on the model on p. 808.

✔ Reading Check

Answer: The farm is so neat and well-maintained that it stands out from its surroundings.

When he had finished in the town high school, Will went to Chicago, where his mother had a cousin living, and he became a student in the Art Institute out there. Another young fellow from our town was also in Chicago. He really went two years before Will did. His name was Hal Weyman, and he was a student at the University of Chicago. After he graduated, he came home and got a job as principal of our high school.

Hal and Will Hutchenson hadn't been close friends before, Hal being several years older than Will, but in Chicago they got together, went together to see plays, and, as Hal later told me, they had a good many long talks.

I got it from Hal that, in Chicago, as at home here when he was a young boy, Will was immediately popular. He was good-looking, so the girls in the art school liked him, and he had a straightforwardness that made him popular with all the young fellows.

Hal told me that Will was out to some party nearly every night, and right away he began to sell some of his amusing little drawings and to make money. The drawings were used in advertisements, and he was well paid.

He even began to send some money home. You see, after Hal came back

816 ◁ Disillusion, Defiance, and Discontent (1914–1946)

✵ ENRICHMENT: History Connection

Chicago

Chicago was a major city in the Midwest when Will Hutchenson went there to study at the Art Institute. In 1837, when it was incorporated, Chicago had a population of about 4,200. By the time of its Great Fire in 1871, the population had soared to 300,000. By 1893, the city had sufficiently recovered to host the World Columbian Exposition commemorating the 400th anniversary of the European discovery of America. With unlimited opportunities to rebuild after the Great Fire, Chicago provided America's finest architects with an unprecedented boost; the city filled up with decorative and monumental buildings. The Art Institute is one such structure which today houses an impressive collection of artwork. Tell students that Ernest Hemingway grew up in Chicago.

here, he used to go quite often out to the Hutchenson place to see Will's father and mother. He would walk or drive out there in the afternoon or on summer evenings and sit with them. The talk was always of Will.

Hal said it was touching how much the father and mother depended on their one son, how much they talked about him and dreamed of his future. They had never been people who went about much with the town folks or even with their neighbors. They were of the sort who work all the time, from early morning till late in the evenings, and on moonlight nights, Hal said, and after the little old wife had got the supper, they often went out into the fields and worked again.

You see, by this time old Hatch was nearing seventy and his wife would have been ten years younger. Hal said that whenever he went out to the farm they quit work and came to sit with him. They might be in one of the fields, working together, but when they saw him in the road, they came running. They had got a letter from Will. He wrote every week.

The little old mother would come running following the father. "We got another letter, Mr. Weyman," Hatch would cry, and then his wife, quite breathless, would say the same thing, "Mr. Weyman, we got a letter."

The letter would be brought out at once and read aloud. Hal said the letters were always delicious. Will larded them with little sketches. There were humorous drawings of people he had seen or been with, rivers of automobiles on Michigan Avenue in Chicago, a policeman at a street crossing, young stenographers hurrying into office buildings. Neither of the old people had ever been to the city and they were curious and eager. They wanted the drawings explained, and Hal said they were like two children wanting to know every little detail Hal could remember about their son's life in the big city. He was always at them to come there on a visit and they would spend hours talking of that.

"Of course," Hatch said, "we couldn't go."

"How could we?" he said. He had been on that one little farm since he was a boy. When he was a young fellow, his father was an invalid and so Hatch had to run things. A farm, if you run it right, is very exacting. You have to fight weeds all the time. There are the farm animals to take care of. "Who would milk our cows?" Hatch said. The idea of anyone but him or his wife touching one of the Hutchenson cows seemed to hurt him. While he was alive, he didn't want anyone else plowing one of his fields, tending his corn, looking after things about the barn. He felt that way about his farm. It was a thing you couldn't explain, Hal said. He seemed to understand the two old people.

It was a spring night, past midnight, when Hal came to my house and told me the news. In our town we have a night telegraph operator at the railroad station and Hal got a wire. It was really addressed to Hatch Hutchenson, but the operator brought it to Hal. Will Hutchenson was dead, had been killed. It turned out later that he

18

19

20 ☑ **Reading Check**
How does the narrator describe Hal's relationship to Will?

Literary Analysis
Point of View and Narrator How does the narrator interact with other characters?

---

18 Literary Analysis
Point of View and Narrator

- Remind students that with *first-person point of view*, we learn about the actions of the story through one character, the narrator.

- Have students read the bracketed passage. Be sure they recognize that this information about the Hutchensons was given to the narrator by Hal.

- Ask students the Literary Analysis question on p. 816: How does the narrator interact with other characters?
Possible response: The narrator appears to be in regular communication with Hal, who tells him what the Hutchensons do and say. Students should recognize that he does not interact directly with the Hutchensons at all.

19 Vocabulary Development
The Latin Root -val-

- Call students' attention to the word "invalid" in this passage. Remind them that the Latin root -val- means "strength" or "value."

- Ask students to use this fact along with their knowledge of the root -in-, which means "not," to construct a definition of "invalid."
Answer: As it is used here, "invalid" means "a disabled person."

20 ☑ Reading Check

Answer: Hal, who is older than Will, knew Will at home but they were not close. They became good friends in Chicago.

CUSTOMIZE INSTRUCTION FOR UNIVERSAL ACCESS

For Less Proficient Readers	For English Learners	For Advanced Readers
Students may wonder why, if they love their son so much and are so curious about his life, the Hutchensons do not visit him in Chicago. Introduce these two possibilities: that their reluctance stems from a powerful sense of responsibility and connection to their land; that it comes from a fear of and disconnection from modern life.	Point out to students that it is unconventional to present what two different speakers say in one paragraph. Explain that Anderson puts Hatch and his wife's dialogue in one paragraph because the narrator is relating this information second-hand and Hatch and his wife are essentially saying the same thing.	Have students contrast Will's life in Chicago with the farm life his parents knew. Explain that Will and his parents are separated by a period of enormous change. Hal bridges the two generations and serves as a link between Will and his parents. Encourage students to research the differences between Will's generation and his parents'.

Speculate

- Instruct students to pause before reading the bracketed passage. Ask them to describe their responses to the Hutchensons' reaction to Hal's news.
  Possible response: Most students will find the Hutchensons' reaction believable, although some will observe that they have not yet fully absorbed the news.

- Have students read the bracketed passage. Then, ask them to predict what the Hutchensons are going to do once they emerge from the house.
  Possible response: Students' predictions will vary but may include ideas such as: they will kill themselves; they will begin digging a grave; they will sit somewhere in the field and pray or meditate; they will bury his letters; and so on.

❷② Reading Strategy

Identifying With Characters

- Remind students that identifying with characters can make it easier to understand them. Model the strategy using the Identifying With Characters transparency in **Literary Analysis and Reading Transparencies**, p. 91.

- Have students read the bracketed passage. Encourage them to consider carefully the emotions it describes.

- Ask the Reading Skills question on p. 817: Putting yourself in Hal's place, how do you think he felt telling the Hutchensons about Will's death?
  Possible response: Hal knows how much the Hutchensons loved their son, and dreads having to tell them of his death.

▶ **Monitor Progress** Encourage students to discuss how their responses help them to understand Hal's character.

was at a party with some other young fellows and there might have been some drinking. Anyway, the car was wrecked, and Will Hutchenson was killed. The operator wanted Hal to go out and take the message to Hatch and his wife, and Hal wanted me to go along.

I offered to take my car, but Hal said no, "Let's walk out," he said. He wanted to put off the moment, I could see that. So we did walk. It was early spring, and I remember every moment of the silent walk we took, the little leaves just coming on the trees, the little streams we crossed, how the moonlight made the water seem alive. We loitered and loitered, not talking, hating to go on.

Then we got out there, and Hal went to the front door of the farmhouse while I stayed in the road. I heard a dog bark, away off somewhere. I heard a child crying in some distant house. I think that Hal, after he got to the front door of the house, must have stood there for ten minutes, hating to knock.

Then he did knock, and the sound his fist made on the door seemed terrible. It seemed like guns going off. Old Hatch came to the door, and I heard Hal tell him. I know what happened. Hal had been trying, all the way out from town, to think up words to tell the old couple in some gentle way, but when it came to the scratch, he couldn't. He blurted everything right out, right into old Hatch's face.

That was all. Old Hatch didn't say a word. The door was opened, he stood there in the moonlight, wearing a funny long white night-gown, Hal told him, and the door went shut again with a bang, and Hal was left standing there.

He stood for a time, and then came back out into the road to me. "Well," he said, and "Well," I said. We stood in the road looking and listening. There wasn't a sound from the house.

And then—it might have been ten minutes or it might have been a half-hour—we stood silently, listening and watching, not knowing what to do—we couldn't go away——"I guess they are trying to get so they can believe it," Hal whispered to me. I got his notion all right. The two old people must have thought of their son Will always only in terms of life, never of death.

We stood watching and listening, and then, suddenly, after a long time, Hal touched me on the arm. "Look," he whispered. There were two white-clad figures going from the house to the barn. It turned out, you see, that old Hatch had been plowing that day. He had finished plowing and harrowing a field near the barn.

The two figures went into the barn and presently came out. They went into the field, and Hal and I crept across the farmyard to the barn and got to where we could see what was going on without being seen.

It was an incredible thing. The old man had got a hand corn-planter out of the barn and his wife had got a bag of seed corn, and there, in the moonlight, that night, after they got that news, they were planting corn.

It was a thing to curl your hair—it was so ghostly. They were both in their nightgowns. They would do a row across the field, coming

818 ◆ *Disillusion, Defiance, and Discontent (1914–1946)*

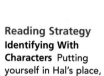

Reading Strategy Identifying With Characters Putting yourself in Hal's place, how do you think he felt telling the Hutchensons about Will's death?

Corn

Corn, a member of the grass family, was first cultivated in Central America. In the history of the domestication of plants, corn is actually a latecomer, trailing by a thousand years the cultivation of beans and squash. The original wild corn is small. The much larger size and shape of the modern corncob is a result of centuries of selective breeding.

Corn has long been a staple of Native American societies throughout North America, and different groups have celebrated its cultivation in one way or another. For example, the Pueblo people have traditionally honored their Corn Mothers by providing all newborn children with corn fetishes. Mississippian groups like the Muskogee, Chickasaw, Choctaw, and Cherokee have held Green Corn Dances after each summer's harvest. Invite students to learn more about the specifics of the Green Corn Dance or other Native American ceremonies that honor this key crop. They can share their findings with the class.

quite close to us as we stood in the shadow of the barn, and then, at the end of each row, they would kneel side by side by the fence and stay silent for a time. The whole thing went on in silence. It was the first time in my life I ever understood something, and I am far from sure now that I can put down what I understood and felt that night— I mean something about the connection between certain people and the earth—a kind of silent cry, down into the earth, of these two old people, putting corn down into the earth. It was as though they were putting death down into the ground that life might grow again— something like that.

They must have been asking something of the earth, too. But what's the use? What they were up to in connection with the life in their field and the lost life in their son is something you can't very well make clear in words. All I know is that Hal and I stood the sight as long as we could, and then we crept away and went back to town, but Hatch Hutchenson and his wife must have got what they were after that night, because Hal told me that when he went out in the morning to see them and to make the arrangements for bringing their dead son home, they were both curiously quiet and Hal thought in command of themselves. Hal said he thought they had got something. "They have their farm and they have still got Will's letters to read," Hal said.

Review and Assess

Thinking About the Selection

1. **Respond:** With which character did you identify the most in this story? Why?
2. **(a) Recall:** Why does Hatch Hutchenson choose not to go off to make his own way in the world? **(b) Interpret:** What does the narrator mean by the statement that Hatch "got a rather late start in life"?
3. **(a) Recall:** What did the Hutchensons always do when Hal came to visit? **(b) Analyze:** Why do you think they did this? **(c) Infer:** Why do you think the Hutchensons spend so much time working in their fields?
4. **(a) Recall:** Why is Hal given the task of taking the bad news to the Hutchensons? **(b) Evaluate:** Do you think Hal does a good job of telling them about Will's death? Why or why not?
5. **(a) Recall:** What do the Hutchensons do after learning their son has died? **(b) Interpret:** How does the narrator explain their reaction? **(c) Evaluate:** Do you agree with his assessment? Explain.
6. **Apply:** What message about life do you think this story conveys? Support your answer.

CUSTOMIZE INSTRUCTION FOR UNIVERSAL ACCESS

For Special Needs Students	For Less Proficient Readers	For Advanced Readers
Students may be confused by the story's conclusion. After they complete the story, ask students to explain what the Hutchensons did in response to their son's death. If they are unsure, have them read pp. 818–819 again. You can also use the **Adapted Reader's Companion** to facilitate comprehension.	If students are challenged by the Hutchensons' response to their son's death, ask them for interpretations of why the elderly couple would grieve in this way. Guide students to recognize that after their son, their farm and their land were the most important things in the Hutchensons' lives.	Ask students to consider the Hutchensons' response to their son's death. Point out that Hal says, "They must have been asking something of the earth." What were they asking? Did they find it, as Hal believes? Encourage students to write paragraphs interpreting the story's conclusion.

Answers for p. 819

Review and Assess

1. **Possible response:** Students may identify with the narrator, who witnesses powerful emotions without really being a part of them. Student explanations should include details from the story.
2. **(a)** Hatch has to care for his injured father. **(b)** Possible response: He did not begin an independent life of his own until he was almost fifty, when he finally married.
3. **(a)** The Hutchensons talked with Hal about their son, Will. **(b)** Possible response: They depend on Will, their only son, to provide them with hope for the future. **(c)** Possible response: They love the farm and the land more than anything except their son. They feel more comfortable working the land than doing anything else.
4. **(a)** Hal is quite close to the Hutchensons and has always acted as a conduit for information about Will. **(b)** Possible response: Some students will say Hal did a poor job because he blurted the news out without any preamble. Others will say it is a difficult enough task and that his willingness to do it at all makes it a good job.
5. **(a)** They plant row after row of corn under the moonlight. **(b)** He describes their behavior as a way of planting death so that life might grow again. **(c)** Possible response: Yes. They seem to turn to the other love in their lives, the land—to gain control of their experience, and to find comfort.
6. Possible response: The story conveys the message that life in unpredictable and that tragedy can strike anyone at any time. Student responses should be supported with references to the story.

819

Art

Miz Emily, by Joseph Holston

This piece of art shows an African American woman pausing to look out into the distance. The dramatic juxtaposition of light and shadow as well as the facial expression and posture of the woman help to bring out her character. Use these questions for discussion:

1. What can you infer about this woman and her life based on her facial expression, her stance, and her clothing?

   Possible response: Students may say that she looks like she is used to hard work; she wears an apron and a head wrap, which indicate she is some kind of laborer. Her loose sweater indicates that she is old and sensitive to the cold. She grasps a walking stick, suggesting that she is taking a walk. She may be pausing for rest or to take stock of her work for the day.

2. Notice how the light streams in on the woman's face. What might the artist mean by this?

   Possible response: Students may say that the light represents a higher calling, or a gleam of hope in the distance to contrast with the hard life she seems to lead. The light could signify sunrise or sunset, suggesting a change: either a new dawn or an ending.

Miz Emily, Joseph Holston, Holston Reproductions

820 ◆ *Disillusion, Defiance, and Discontent (1914–1946)*

㉔A Worn Path

Eudora Welty

It was December—a bright frozen day in the early morning. Far out in the country there was an old Negro woman with her head tied in a red rag, coming along a path through the pinewoods. Her name was Phoenix Jackson. She was very old and small and she walked slowly in the dark pine shadows, moving a little from side to side in her steps, with the balanced heaviness and lightness of a pendulum in a grandfather clock. She carried a thin, small cane made from an umbrella, and with this she kept tapping the frozen earth in front of her. This made a <u>grave</u> and persistent noise in the still air, that seemed meditative like the chirping of a solitary little bird.

grave (grāv) *adj.* serious; solemn

She wore a dark striped dress reaching down to her shoe tops, and an equally long apron of bleached sugar sacks, with a full pocket all neat and tidy, but every time she took a step she might have fallen over her shoelaces, which dragged from her unlaced shoes. She looked straight ahead. Her eyes were blue with age. Her skin had a pattern all its own of numberless branching wrinkles and as though a whole little tree stood in the middle of her forehead, but a golden color ran underneath, and the two knobs of her cheeks were illumined by a yellow burning under the dark. Under the red rag her hair came down on her neck in the frailest of ringlets, still black, and with an odor like copper.

Now and then there was a quivering in the thicket. Old Phoenix said, "Out of my way, all you foxes, owls, beetles, jack rabbits, coons and wild animals! . . . Keep out from under these feet, little bobwhites[1]. . . . Keep the big wild hogs out of my path. Don't let none of those come running my direction. I got a long way." Under her small black-freckled hand her cane, <u>limber</u> as a buggy whip, would switch at the brush as if to rouse up any hiding things.

limber (lim´ bər) *adj.* flexible

On she went. The woods were deep and still. The sun made the pine needles almost too bright to look at, up where the wind rocked. The cones dropped as light as feathers. Down in the hollow was the mourning dove—it was not too late for him.

The path ran up a hill. "Seem like there is chains about my feet, time I get this far," she said, in the voice of argument old people keep to use with themselves. "Something always take a hold of me on this hill—pleads I should stay."

---

1. **bobwhites** *n.* partridges.

㉕ ◀ **Critical Viewing** What details in this image suggest Phoenix's strong character? **[Connect]**

㉖ ☑**Reading Check**
What are some of Phoenix Jackson's distinguishing features?

CUSTOMIZE INSTRUCTION FOR UNIVERSAL ACCESS

For English Learners	For Advanced Readers
You can help students to understand the meaning of the dialectical grammar Phoenix uses by supplying missing verbs and helping verbs, pronouns, and inflected endings. If necessary, use the **English Learner's Companion** to preview the story's plot.	Explain to students that birds play a key symbolic role in this story. Point out, for example, that the name *Phoenix* refers to the mythological Egyptian bird that rose from the ashes of its own funeral pyre. Suggest that students make note of and interpret this and other references to birds in the story.

27 Reading Strategy

Identifying With Characters

- Ask students to pause when they reach the bracketed passage. Guide them to recognize Phoenix's familiarity with the path she is walking.

- Have students read the bracketed passage. Point out Phoenix's running commentary, emphasizing that she uses figurative language to describe the difficult parts of her journey.

- Ask students the Reading Strategy question on p. 822: Why do you suppose Phoenix is talking her way through the woods?
Possible response: Students may say that the sound of her voice soothes her. By identifying the obstacles she faces, she may eliminate her fear that the woods present an unknown challenge.

▶ Monitor Progress Encourage students to discuss what they might have in common with Phoenix's feelings about the woods.

28 Literary Analysis

Point of View and Narrator

- Have a volunteer read the bracketed passage aloud. As they listen, tell students to note any information that a passerby would not be able to perceive.

- Then, ask the literary analysis question on p. 822: What private information does the narrator share in the paragraph beginning "But she sat down to rest." What is the effect?
Answer: Phoenix's hallucination of a boy offering her cake is entirely private. It allows the reader to understand that Phoenix's grasp of reality is not always firm.

After she got to the top she turned and gave a full, severe look behind her where she had come. "Up through pines," she said at length. "Now down through oaks."

Her eyes opened their widest, and she started down gently. But **27** before she got to the bottom of the hill a bush caught her dress.

Her fingers were busy and intent, but her skirts were full and long, so that before she could pull them free in one place they were caught in another. It was not possible to allow the dress to tear. "I in the thorny bush," she said. "Thorns, you doing your appointed work. Never want to let folks pass, no sir. Old eyes thought you was a pretty little *green* bush."

Finally, trembling all over, she stood free, and after a moment dared to stoop for her cane.

"Sun so high!" she cried, leaning back and looking, while the thick tears went over her eyes. "The time getting all gone here."

At the foot of this hill was a place where a log was laid across the creek.

"Now comes the trial," said Phoenix.

Putting her right foot out, she mounted the log and shut her eyes. Lifting her skirt, leveling her cane fiercely before her, like a festival figure in some parade, she began to march across. Then she opened her eyes and she was safe on the other side.

"I wasn't as old as I thought," she said.

But she sat down to rest. She spread her skirts on the bank **28** around her and folded her hands over her knees. Up above her was a tree in a pearly cloud of mistletoe. She did not dare to close her eyes, and when a little boy brought her a plate with a slice of marble cake on it she spoke to him. "That would be acceptable," she said. But when she went to take it there was just her own hand in the air.

So she left that tree, and had to go through a barbed-wire fence. There she had to creep and crawl, spreading her knees and stretching her fingers like a baby trying to climb the steps. But she talked loudly to herself: she could not let her dress be torn now, so late in the day, and she could not pay for having her arm or her leg sawed off if she got caught fast where she was.

At last she was safe through the fence and risen up out in the clearing. Big dead trees, like black men with one arm, were standing in the purple stalks of the withered cotton field. There sat a buzzard.

"Who you watching?"

In the furrow she made her way along.

"Glad this not the season for bulls," she said, looking sideways, "and the good Lord made his snakes to curl up and sleep in the winter. A pleasure I don't see no two-headed snake coming around that tree, where it come once. It took a while to get by him, back in the summer."

She passed through the old cotton and went into a field of dead corn. It whispered and shook and was taller than her head. "Through the maze now," she said, for there was no path.

Then there was something tall, black, and skinny there, moving before her.

822 ◆ *Disillusion, Defiance, and Discontent (1914–1946)*

Reading Strategy
Identifying With Characters Why do you suppose Phoenix is talking her way through the woods?

Literary Analysis
Point of View and Narrator What private information does the narrator share in the paragraph beginning "But she sat down to rest." What is the effect?

✳ ENRICHMENT: Cultural Connection

The Journey and Egyptian Myths

The journey, with its obstacles and travails, has been a common element in literature for thousands of years. Phoenix Jackson's story parallels Egyptian myths relating the journey of the dead through the twelve gates of Osiris's underworld. The bull and the two-headed snake are two of the many mythical creatures who guard the underworld. That journey ended when the travelers faced the god, who pronounced judgment on them. The dead person's heart was weighed on a balancing scale overseen by

Truth. If the person failed the test, he or she was destroyed by a ferocious beast called the Devourer of Souls. If the person passed and was judged worthy of the afterlife, he or she entered eternity, free to pursue the same pleasures enjoyed on earth.

Invite interested students to investigate journey or quest myths of other cultures. For example, they might look into the Buddhist story of Siddhartha, or the Nibelung saga of ancient Teutonic mythology.

822

At first she took it for a man. It could have been a man dancing in the field. But she stood still and listened, and it did not make a sound. It was as silent as a ghost.

"Ghost," she said sharply, "who be you the ghost of? For I have heard of nary death close by."

But there was no answer—only the ragged dancing in the wind.

She shut her eyes, reached out her hand, and touched a sleeve. She found a coat and inside that an emptiness, cold as ice.

"You scarecrow," she said. Her face lighted. "I ought to be shut up for good," she said with laughter. "My senses is gone. I too old. I the oldest people I ever know. Dance, old scarecrow," she said, "while I dancing with you."

She kicked her foot over the furrow, and with mouth drawn down, shook her head once or twice in a little strutting way. Some husks blew down and whirled in streamers about her skirts.

Then she went on, parting her way from side to side with the cane, through the whispering field. At last she came to the end, to a wagon track where the silver grass blew between the red ruts. The quail were walking around like pullets, seeming all dainty and unseen.

"Walk pretty," she said. "This the easy place. This the easy going."

She followed the track, swaying through the quiet bare fields, through the little strings of trees silver in their dead leaves, past cabins silver from weather, with the doors and windows boarded shut, all like old women under a spell sitting there. "I walking in their sleep," she said, nodding her head vigorously.

In a ravine she went where a spring was silently flowing through a hollow log. Old Phoenix bent and drank. "Sweet gum[2] makes the water sweet," she said, and drank more. "Nobody know who made this well, for it was here when I was born."

The track crossed a swampy part where the moss hung as white as lace from every limb. "Sleep on, alligators, and blow your bubbles." Then the track went into the road.

Deep, deep the road went down between the high green-colored banks. Overhead the live-oaks met, and it was as dark as a cave.

A black dog with a lolling tongue came up out of the weeds by the ditch. She was meditating, and not ready, and when he came at her she only hit him a little with her cane. Over she went in the ditch, like a little puff of milkweed.[3]

Down there, her senses drifted away. A dream visited her, and she reached her hand up, but nothing reached down and gave her a pull. So she lay there and presently went to talking. "Old woman," she said to herself, "that black dog come up out of the weeds to stall you off, and now there he sitting on his fine tail, smiling at you."

A white man finally came along and found her—a hunter, a young man, with his dog on a chain.

---

2. **sweet gum** _n._ a tree that produces a fragrant juice.
3. **milkweed** _n._ a plant with pods that, when ripe, release feathery seeds.

Literary Analysis
Point of View From what point of view is the story being told? How do you know?

 Reading Check
What is Phoenix Jackson's attitude as she walks?

29 Literary Analysis
Point of View

- Remind students that they can determine a story's *point of view* by looking closely at the way the narrator speaks to readers and the information the narrator presents about characters.

- Have students read the bracketed passage.

- Then, ask students the Literary Analysis question on p. 823: From what point of view is the story being told? How do you know? Answer: The story is told through the limited third-person point of view, in which events are viewed from the perspective of Phoenix Jackson. Students should note that the story includes both real and imagined events that could only be known by the main character.

30 ☑ Reading Check
Answer: She is determined, even as she struggles with obstacles and her own confusion.

CUSTOMIZE INSTRUCTION FOR UNIVERSAL ACCESS

For Special Needs Students	For Less Proficient Readers	For Advanced Readers
Be sure that students understand that the story describes a journey taken on foot by an old African American woman in the South. If students are confused, have them read along with **Listening to Literature: Audiocassettes,** Sides 27–28; Audio CDs, CDs 15–16.	Guide students to distinguish between the story's concrete details that describe Jackson's journey and the imagined details that reveal the daydreams her mind creates. Encourage students to construct charts listing both concrete and imagined details.	Ghosts are only one of the many images of death in this story. Ask students to identify other words and images the author uses to create a grim atmosphere. Students may mention, in addition to the bull and two-headed snake, "dark pine shadows," "frozen earth," "mourning dove," "big dead trees," and "buzzard."

Art

Georgia Red Clay, by Nell Choate Jones

This oil painting offers a surreal representation of a dirt road winding through the Georgia countryside. Use these questions for discussion:

1. How would you describe the mood of this painting?
   Possible response: Students may describe it as dark, foreboding, eerie, or dreamlike.

2. This painting depicts a rural scene in Georgia. What elements of this work relate to Welty's story, which is set in Mississippi?
   Possible response: Students may say that the painting depicts a hilly, winding country path, such as the one described in the story. The gnarled trees are foreboding, suggesting Phoenix's frame of mind during parts of her walk. The odd light suggests the haze through which she views events.

③ ▶ **Critical Viewing**

Possible response: Some students may say that the surrealistic nature of the painting mirrors the dreamlike state in which Phoenix seems to exist. Others may say that Phoenix's path lay through dense pine woods, neither passing farmhouses nor hardwood trees, as depicted in the painting.

"Well, Granny!" he laughed. "What are you doing there?"

"Lying on my back like a June bug waiting to be turned over, mister," she said, reaching up her hand.

He lifted her up, gave her a swing in the air, and set her down. "Anything broken, Granny?"

"No sir, them old dead weeds is springy enough," said Phoenix, when she had got her breath. "I thank you for your trouble."

③ ▼ **Critical Viewing**
Does this image accurately represent the path Phoenix travels? Why or why not? **[Evaluate]**

"Where do you live, Granny?" he asked, while the two dogs were growling at each other.

"Away back yonder, sir, behind the ridge. You can't even see it from here."

"On your way home?"

"No sir, I going to town."

"Why, that's too far! That's as far as I walk when I come out myself, and I get something for my trouble." He patted the stuffed bag he carried, and there hung down a little closed claw. It was one of the bobwhites, with its beak hooked bitterly to show it was dead. "Now you go on home, Granny!"

"I bound to go to town, mister," said Phoenix. "The time come around."

He gave another laugh, filling the whole landscape. "I know you old colored people! Wouldn't miss going to town to see Santa Claus!"

But something held old Phoenix very still. The deep lines in her face went into a fierce and different radiation. Without warning, she had seen with her own eyes a flashing nickel fall out of the man's pocket onto the ground.

"How old are you, Granny?" he was saying.

"There is no telling, mister," she said, "no telling."

Then she gave a little cry and clapped her hands and said, "Git on away from here, dog! Look! Look at that dog!" She laughed as if in admiration. "He ain't scared of nobody. He a big black dog." She whispered, "Sic him!"

"Watch me get rid of that cur," said the man. "Sic him, Pete! Sic him!"

Phoenix heard the dogs fighting, and heard the man running and throwing sticks. She even heard a gunshot. But she was slowly bending forward by that time, further and further forward, the lids stretched down over her eyes, as if she were doing this in her sleep. Her chin was lowered almost to her knees. The yellow palm of her hand came out from the fold of her apron. Her fingers slid down and along the ground under the piece of money with the grace and care they would have in lifting an egg from under a setting hen. Then she slowly straightened up, she stood erect, and the nickel was in her apron pocket. A bird flew by. Her lips moved. "God watching me the whole time. I come to stealing."

The man came back, and his own dog panted about them. "Well, I scared him off that time," he said, and then he laughed and lifted his gun and pointed it at Phoenix.

She stood straight and faced him.

"Doesn't the gun scare you?" he said, still pointing it.

"No, sir, I seen plenty go off closer by, in my day, and for less than what I done," she said, holding utterly still.

He smiled, and shouldered the gun. "Well, Granny," he said, "you must be a hundred years old, and scared of nothing. I'd

Georgia Red Clay, 1946, Nell Choate Jones, Morris Museum of Art, Augusta, Georgia

Literary Analysis
Point of View What detail in this paragraph reveals the point of view from which the story is told? Explain.

Reading Check
Whom and what does Phoenix encounter on her journey?

A Worn Path ◆ 825

Literary Analysis
Point of View
- Before students read the bracketed passage, ask them to pause and consider point of view.
- Guide students to recognize that if the story were told from the hunter's viewpoint, they would learn in a more direct way that he considers Phoenix to be inferior. As it is written, the reader infers the hunter's feelings based on his language and behavior.
- Have students read the bracketed passage. Then, ask the Literary Analysis question on p. 825: What detail in this paragraph reveals the point of view from which the story is told? Explain.
  Answer: The nickel that falls from the man's pocket reveals that the story is told from Phoenix's point of view, because she is the only one who sees it.
- Be sure students understand that Phoenix lives in dire poverty at a time when 5 cents was not an insignificant sum; a nickel could mean the difference between eating a meal or going hungry.

Reading Strategy
Identifying With Characters
- Have students read the bracketed passage. Ask them to pause and consider Phoenix's actions.
- Point out that Phoenix's act of taking the nickel that fell and her awareness that she is stealing show both her poverty and her sense of honor.
- Ask students: What does it say about Phoenix that she is used to having a gun pointed at her or near to her? Possible response: Students may say that it indicates that she was once a slave and had experienced the bullying of armed overseers or perhaps that she was a poor sharecropper accustomed to harsh treatment by callous landowners.

Reading Check
Answer: Phoenix is knocked down by a stray dog and then encounters a hunter with his own dog.

CUSTOMIZE INSTRUCTION FOR UNIVERSAL ACCESS

For Special Needs Students	For Advanced Readers
Have students read the conversation between Phoenix and the hunter once on their own to form a general impression. Then, ask them to describe the encounter. If they are confused about what is happening—Phoenix has fallen over when the white man spots her and helps her up; she tells him she is going to town; she sees he has dropped a nickel, distracts him, and picks it up; he frightens away a stray dog with his gun—use the **Adapted Reader's Companion** to aid comprehension.	Explain to students that when this story was first published in 1941, the term *colored people* was commonly used to refer to African Americans. The term is no longer considered acceptable. Encourage students to identify and research other aspects of relations between black and white characters in this story that are no longer accepted today, such as the openly patronizing attitude the hunter displays towards Phoenix.

825

Speculate

- Read the bracketed passage out loud for students. Review with them the actions and details the passage describes: Phoenix enters a large building, goes up many stairs, and enters a door marked by a framed document with a gold seal.

- Ask students: Why does Welty not identify the building with the gold seal?

  Possible response: Students may suggest that the narrator is describing the building as Phoenix herself sees it.

- Encourage students to keep the narrator's point of view in mind as they read on.

37 Literary Analysis

Point of View

- Remind the class that this story is told from a limited third-person point of view. A third-person narrator describes events from Phoenix's perspective—including events in her mind.

- Have students read the bracketed passage. Guide them to recognize that the attendant's comment reveals her assumptions about Phoenix.

- Ask students the Literary Analysis question on p. 826: What response does this dialogue describing the way others see Phoenix evoke in you? Why?

  Possible response: Students are likely to be empathetic toward Phoenix, who has just made a formidable journey on her grandson's behalf, and who is now being treated with coldness and condescension.

 Monitor Progress Be sure that students understand that point of view can influence readers' sympathies toward characters.

---

give you a dime if I had any money with me. But you take my advice and stay home, and nothing will happen to you."

"I bound to go on my way, mister," said Phoenix. She inclined her head in the red rag. Then they went in different directions, but she could hear the gun shooting again and again over the hill.

She walked on. The shadows hung from the oak trees to the road like curtains. Then she smelled woodsmoke, and smelled the river, and she saw a steeple and the cabins on their steep steps. Dozens of little black children whirled around her. There ahead was Natchez[4] shining. Bells were ringing. She walked on.

In the paved city it was Christmas time. There were red and green electric lights strung and criss-crossed everywhere, and all turned on in the daytime. Old Phoenix would have been lost if she had not distrusted her eyesight and depended on her feet to know where to take her.

She paused quietly on the sidewalk where people were passing by. A lady came along in the crowd, carrying an armful of red-, green- and silver-wrapped presents; she gave off perfume like the red roses in hot summer, and Phoenix stopped her.

"Please, missy, will you lace up my shoe?" She held up her foot.

"What do you want, Grandma?"

"See my shoe," said Phoenix. "Do all right for out in the country, but wouldn't look right to go in a big building."

"Stand still then, Grandma," said the lady. She put her packages down on the sidewalk beside her and laced and tied both shoes tightly.

"Can't lace em with a cane," said Phoenix. "Thank you, missy. I doesn't mind asking a nice lady to tie up my shoe, when I gets out on the street."

36 Moving slowly and from side to side, she went into the big building, and into a tower of steps, where she walked up and around and around until her feet knew to stop.

She entered a door, and there she saw nailed up on the wall the document that had been stamped with the gold seal and framed in the gold frame, which matched the dream that was hung up in her head.

"Here I be," she said. There was a fixed and ceremonial stiffness over her body.

"A charity case, I suppose," said an attendant who sat at the desk before her.

But Phoenix only looked above her head. There was sweat on her face, the wrinkles in her skin shone like a bright net.

"Speak up, Grandma," the woman said. "What's your name?
37 We must have your history, you know. Have you been here before? What seems to be the trouble with you?"

Old Phoenix only gave a twitch to her face as if a fly were bothering her.

"Are you deaf?" cried the attendant.

But then the nurse came in.

---

4. **Natchez** (nach′ iz) a town in southern Mississippi.

Literary Analysis
Point of View What response does this dialogue describing the way others see Phoenix evoke in you? Why?

"Oh, that's just old Aunt Phoenix," she said. "She doesn't come for herself—she has a little grandson. She makes these trips just as regular as clockwork. She lives away back off the Old Natchez Trace." She bent down. "Well, Aunt Phoenix, why don't you just take a seat? We won't keep you standing after your long trip." She pointed.

The old woman sat down, bolt upright in the chair.

"Now, how is the boy?" asked the nurse.

Old Phoenix did not speak.

"I said, how is the boy?"

But Phoenix only waited and stared straight ahead, her face very solemn and withdrawn into rigidity.

"Is his throat any better?" asked the nurse. "Aunt Phoenix, don't you hear me? Is your grandson's throat any better since the last time you came for the medicine?"

With her hands on her knees, the old woman waited, silent, erect and motionless, just as if she were in armor.

"You mustn't take up our time this way, Aunt Phoenix," the nurse said. "Tell us quickly about your grandson, and get it over. He isn't dead, is he?"

At last there came a flicker and then a flame of comprehension across her face, and she spoke.

"My grandson. It was my memory had left me. There I sat and forgot why I made my long trip."

"Forgot?" The nurse frowned. "After you came so far?"

Then Phoenix was like an old woman begging a dignified forgiveness for waking up frightened in the night. "I never did go to school. I was too old at the Surrender,"[5] she said in a soft voice. "I'm an old woman without an education. It was my memory fail me. My little grandson, he is just the same, and I forgot it in the coming."

"Throat never heals, does it?" said the nurse, speaking in a loud, sure voice to old Phoenix. By now she had a card with something written on it, a little list. "Yes. Swallowed lye. When was it?— January—two-three years ago—"

Phoenix spoke unasked now. "No, missy, he not dead, he just the same. Every little while his throat begin to close up again, and he not able to swallow. He not get his breath. He not able to help himself. So the time come around, and I go on another trip for the soothing medicine."

"All right. The doctor said as long as you came to get it, you could have it," said the nurse. "But it's an obstinate case."

"My little grandson, he sit up there in the house all wrapped up, waiting by himself," Phoenix went on. "We is the only two left in the world. He suffer and it don't seem to put him back at all. He got a sweet look. He going to last. He wear a little patch quilt and peep out holding his mouth open like a little bird. I remembers so plain now. I not going to forget him again, no, the whole enduring time. I could tell him from all the others in creation."

---

5. **the Surrender** the surrender of the Confederate army, which ended the Civil War.

Literary Analysis
Point of View and Narrator Here, the narrator does not share Phoenix's thoughts. How does this affect you as a reader? Explain.

obstinate (äb′ stə nət) *adj.* stubborn

40 ✔ Reading Check
Why is Phoenix at the doctor's office?

A Worn Path ◆ 827

---

38 Literary Analysis
Point of View and Narrator
- Remind students that the point of view of a story is shaped by its narrator, and not simply by whether the narrator is first- or third-person; the narrator's perspective also affects point of view.
- Have students read the bracketed passage. Guide them to recognize that while the narrator has previously shared Phoenix's thoughts, here they are not revealed.
- Ask students the Literary Analysis question on p. 827: Here, the narrator does not share Phoenix's thoughts. How does this affect you as a reader? Explain.
  Possible response: Students may note that since Phoenix arrived at the doctor's office, her thoughts have not been revealed; instead, the narrator shows us how she appears from the attendant and nurse's perspective. The change in perspective may make students angry at the attendant and nurse for their patronizing, dismissive attitude.

39 Reading Strategy
Identify With Characters
- Have students read the bracketed passage. Encourage them to consider the emotions that Phoenix reveals here.
- Ask students: Can you identify with Phoenix Jackson's feelings in this situation? Explain.
  Possible response: Most students will sympathize with Phoenix, inferring that she has had a hard life and asks little of the attendants at the clinic. Many, however, will say that they have not experienced such a situation and cannot truly identify with her.

40 ✔ Reading Check
Answer: She is there to get medicine for her grandson, who suffers the lingering effects of swallowing Lye.

Review and Assess

1. Possible response: Students may say that Welty's use of language suits her story because it not only communicates the action, but conveys the subtleties of Phoenix's feelings and thoughts.

2. **(a)** It takes place in December, near Christmas. **(b)** Possible response: The behavior of the other characters towards Phoenix contrasts with the true Christmas spirit.

3. **(a)** Obstacles include the distance she must travel on foot, a thorny bush, a log bridge across a creek, barbed-wire fencing, a pathless field, a scarecrow, a dog, a hunter, and a desk attendant. **(b)** Possible response: She deals with the obstacles with steady determination. Although some are more difficult for her than others, no obstacle stops her.

4. **(a)** Phoenix goes to Natchez to pick up her grandson's medicine. **(b)** Possible response: Phoenix's journey expresses her profound love for her grandson.

5. **(a)** At first, she fails to respond, saying she momentarily forgot why she came. **(b)** Possible response: The attendant and the nurse regard Phoenix with a mixture of helpfulness, irritation, and wondrous disbelief. **(c)** Possible response: Students may say that Phoenix sees herself as more physically fit and mentally sharp than others see her.

6. Possible response: Students may respond that she is named Phoenix because she rises from every obstacle, including her own collapses, and completes her journey.

7. Possible response: Phoenix shows perseverance during her long journey as well as optimism when difficulties occur. Life in troubled times has made Phoenix a strong person.

"All right." The nurse was trying to hush her now. She brought her a bottle of medicine. "Charity," she said, making a check mark in a book.

Old Phoenix held the bottle close to her eyes, and then carefully put it into her pocket.

"I thank you," she said.

"It's Christmas time, Grandma," said the attendant. "Could I give you a few pennies out of my purse?"

"Five pennies is a nickel," said Phoenix stiffly.

"Here's a nickel," said the attendant.

Phoenix rose carefully and held out her hand. She received the nickel and then fished the other nickel out of her pocket and laid it beside the new one. She stared at her palm closely, with her head on one side.

Then she gave a tap with her cane on the floor.

"This is what come to me to do," she said. "I going to the store and buy my child a little windmill they sells, made out of paper. He going to find it hard to believe there such a thing in the world. I'll march myself back where he is waiting, holding it straight up in this hand."

She lifted her free hand, gave a little nod, turned around, and walked out of the doctor's office. Then her slow step began on the stairs, going down.

Review and Assess

Thinking About the Selection

1. **Respond:** Do you think Welty's use of language suits her story, or would you have used language differently? Explain.

2. **(a) Recall:** At what time of year does the story take place? **(b) Interpret:** What is significant about the story taking place at this time?

3. **(a) Recall:** What obstacles does Phoenix encounter on her journey? **(b) Analyze:** How does she deal with each of those obstacles?

4. **(a) Recall:** For what reason does Phoenix make her journey? **(b) Interpret:** What emotions does her journey express?

5. **(a) Recall:** In what way does Phoenix initially respond to the questions asked by the attendant and the nurse? **(b) Infer:** What does their reaction reveal about their attitudes toward her? **(c) Assess:** Do you think Phoenix sees herself as others see her?

6. **Synthesize:** In mythology, the Phoenix is a bird that rises from the ashes. Why do you think the author named the main character of this story Phoenix?

7. **Assess:** In what specific ways do you think Phoenix Jackson's character has been shaped by hardship? Explain.

✏ ASSESSMENT PRACTICE: Reading Comprehension

Analyze Sentence Meaning	(For more practice, see Test Preparation Workbook, p. 48.)

Many tests require students to correctly answer sentence-completion questions. Often, more than one choice can complete a sentence. Use the following sample item to show students how to analyze sentence meaning, decide whether it is positive or negative, and eliminate choices that have the opposite sense.

Ironically, despite the devastation of World War I, modern medicine _____ during the period.

A advanced   **C** regressed
B declined   **D** changed

The signal words *Ironically* and *despite* indicate the correct answer will have a positive connotation. *B* and *C* can be eliminated. *D* is too mild an answer. *A* is the best choice.

Review and Assess

Literary Analysis

Point of View

1. (a) Identify three details that show Hemingway's story was written using a **first-person point of view**. (b) How would the story be different if Hemingway had used a **third-person point of view**?

2. (a) What point of view does Anderson use in "The Corn Planting"? (b) Is the narrator of "The Corn Planting" the best character to tell the story? Why or why not?

3. How would "A Worn Path" be different if Welty had told the story from Phoenix Jackson's first-person point of view?

4. Using a different point of view from the original, rewrite a paragraph from one of the stories. Then, compare the two versions. (a) What is gained in your version? (b) What is lost?

Comparing Literary Works

5. (a) For each selection, identify the type of **narrator** being used. (b) Note specific ways in which each narrator allows some information to be revealed and some to be hidden.

6. (a) Compare the emotions the narrator evokes in you in each story. (b) In what way does the author's choice of a narrator create a different level of emotional involvement in each story?

Reading Strategy

Identifying With Characters

7. Among the three stories, choose the characters with whom you **identify** most and least. Provide reasons for your choices.

8. Did you find yourself sympathizing with Phoenix Jackson? Why or why not?

9. Using a diagram like the one shown, list one personality trait, interest, or value you might share with a character in each story.

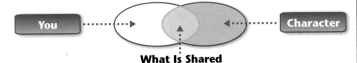

What Is Shared

Extend Understanding

10. **Social Studies Connection:** What does Hemingway's story tell you about war that a history textbook might not?

In Another Country / The Corn Planting / A Worn Path ◆ 829

Quick Review

Point of view is the perspective from which a story is told. The **first-person point of view** features a narrator who participates in the action. In a story using **limited third-person point of view**, the story is told by a narrator who stands outside the action and conveys the thoughts and feelings of a single character.

The **narrator** is the speaker who tells the story.

To **identify with characters,** connect their thoughts and feelings with your own experiences.

 Take It to the Net
www.phschool.com

Take the interactive self-test online to check your understanding of these selections.

Answers for p. 829

Review and Assess

1. (a) Details include the narrator's use of "I" and "we," presence as the story's central character, and description of his own thoughts and feelings. (b) Possible response: The thoughts and feelings of all the characters might have been presented.

2. (a) Anderson uses a first-person point of view, but his narrator is not a part of the main action of the story. (b) The narrator is ideally suited to tell the story; his distance from the events and his close understanding of the people and community allow him to present the story clearly and with great empathy.

3. Possible response: It might have focused in greater detail on Phoenix's emotions.

4. Paragraphs must demonstrate an understanding of point of view.

5. (a) "In Another Country": first-person; "A Corn Planting": first-person; "A Worn Path": third-person. (b) Both first-person points of view limit the narrator to his own perceptions. The third-person point of view could convey the perceptions of all characters.

6. Possible answers: (a) and (b) Students' responses should be supported by details from the story.

7. Possible response: Students may say they identified most with the narrator of "In Another Country," because he is close to their age, and least with the Hutchensons, people from a different generation.

8. Possible response: Students may say they sympathize with Phoenix because she undertakes an arduous journey in order to help her grandson.

9. Possible response for "In Another Country": **You:** Wants to be brave; never served in war **Narrator:** Living in Italy; injured in war **What Is Shared:** Young and uncertain.

10. Possible answers: Wounded soldiers felt camaraderie; certain kinds of rehabilitative machines were first used during the war.

 Take It to the Net

Visit www.phschool.com for self-tests and additional questions on on the authors.

✵ ENRICHMENT: Further Reading

Other Works by the Authors

Works by Ernest Hemingway

The Sun Also Rises

A Farewell to Arms

For Whom the Bell Tolls

The Old Man and the Sea

Works by Sherwood Anderson

Winesburg, Ohio

Windy McPherson's Sons

Triumph of the Egg

Horses and Men

Works by Eudora Welty

The Optimist's Daughter

Delta Wedding

The Ponder Heart

Losing Battles

We suggest that you preview these works.

❶ Vocabulary Development

Word Analysis

1. Having legal force or power, correct. **Possible response:** Something that is *valid* has the <u>strength</u> of accuracy behind it.

2. Equal in value, amount, or force. **Possible response:** Things which are *equivalent* are of equal <u>value</u> or <u>strength</u>.

3. Strength of mind or spirit, especially in the face of danger. **Possible response:** It takes great <u>strength</u> to have *valor*.

4. To gain the advantage; to be victorious or triumphant. **Possible response:** One must be <u>strong</u> to *prevail*.

Spelling Strategy

1. gnu   **3.** knit
2. knife   **4.** gnat

Fluency: Clarify Word Meaning

1. No. Someone who is invalided has been removed from service to recover from an injury.
2. No. Grave news is serious or solemn; therefore, the bearer of the news would be in a similar mood.
3. Yes. Athletes, especially gymnasts, need to make their limbs limber before attempting difficult movements.
4. No. An obstinate person would be unlikely to compromise as is needed in a successful collaborative effort.

❷ Grammar and Style

1. "No," said the major.
2. "Well," he said, and "Well," I said.
3. "Don't argue with me!"
4. I offered to take my car, but Hal said "No, let's walk out."
5. "How old are you, Granny?" he was asking.

Looking at Style

Possible response: The lack of dialogue forces readers to see the actions of Hal and the Hutchensons only as the narrator hears about and sees them. The reader understands the characters only as much as the narrator does.

Integrate Language Skills

❶ Vocabulary Development Lesson

Word Analysis: Latin Root *-val-*

The Latin root *-val-* means "strength" or "value." Use a dictionary to define each of the words below. Then, write a sentence explaining how each word's definition might relate to the meaning of *-val-*.

1. valid   **3.** valor
2. equivalent   **4.** prevail

Spelling Strategy

When words begin with the letters *gn* or *kn*, as in *gnarled, gnaw, knee,* and *knock,* the *g* or *k* is silent. In your notebook, complete the spelling of the following words.

1. __nu   **3.** __nit
2. __nife   **4.** __nat

❷ Grammar and Style Lesson

Punctuating Dialogue

Dialogue is one of the most effective tools in a writer's toolkit. Dialogue brings characters to life by letting readers "hear" the characters' own words. Because each writer carefully punctuates the dialogue, you can easily tell who is speaking each line.

To correctly punctuate dialogue, always put quotation marks around the speaker's exact words. Place periods and commas inside the quotation marks.

> **Example:** "Ghost," she said sharply, "who be you the ghost of? For I have heard of nary death close by."

Fluency: Clarify Word Meaning

Review the words from the vocabulary list on page 808 and notice the way each word is used in the selections. Then, answer yes or no to each question. Explain each of your answers.

1. If a soldier is *invalided*, has he or she been transferred to combat duty?

2. Would someone bringing *grave* news be smiling?

3. Would a gymnast need to be *limber* before performing?

4. Would you want to pair up for a project with someone described as *obstinate*?

Practice The punctuation marks in the following pieces of dialogue have been misplaced or omitted. Rewrite each item, using correct punctuation.

1. "No" said the major.
2. "Well, he said, and "Well," I said.
3. "Don't argue with me"!
4. I offered to take my car, but Hal said No, Let's walk out.
5. "How old are you, Granny"? he was asking.

Looking at Style When you compare the amount of dialogue in these three stories, you'll notice that "The Corn Planting" has the least. How does this difference affect the way you relate to the characters? Explain.

WG   *Prentice Hall Writing and Grammar Connection: Chapter 5, Section 4*

TEACHING RESOURCES

The following resources can be used to enrich or extend the instruction for pp. 830–831

Vocabulary

📖 **Selection Support:** Build Vocabulary, p. 202

📖 **Vocabulary and Spelling Practice Book** (Use this booklet for skills enrichment.)

Grammar

📖 **Selection Support:** Grammar and Style, p. 203

WG **Writing and Grammar,** Ruby Level, p. 724

▨ **Daily Language Practice Transparencies** ▨

WG **Writing and Grammar,** Ruby Level, p. 788 ▨

💿 **Writing and Grammar iText CD-ROM** ▨

📄 **Writing Models and Graphic Organizers on Transparencies,** p. 95

▨ **BLOCK SCHEDULING:** Resources marked with this symbol provide varied instruction during 90-minute blocks.

❸ Writing Lesson

Memorial Speech

As Hal Weyman in "The Corn Planting," write the speech you might give at Will's memorial service. In your remarks, acknowledge both Will's family and his dreams. Also include personal traits revealed from the story.

Prewriting   Reread the story and note personal details about Will. Look for Hal's opinions about Will's strength, talents, and personality.

Drafting   To begin, identify Will Hutchenson, and explain the sad occasion for the speech. Organize your main points in order of importance, noting the memories of greatest significance. Retell anecdotes in a style reflecting Hal's character.

Revising   Reread your speech to make sure it reveals Will's personality and expresses his dreams. Highlight and revise vague words and add details that evoke emotion.

Model: Revising to Add Emotional Appeal

person whom I'll never forget because
he had endless enthusiasm for life.

Will Hutchenson was a ~~great guy.~~ An only child, he was the source of pride for his parents. ~~He was talented.~~ He dreamed of becoming a successful artist, and he had talent that was too young to die.

> Phrases such as *endless enthusiasm for life* and *a talent that was too young to die* add emotional appeal.

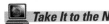 *Prentice Hall Writing and Grammar Connection: Chapter 28, Section 1*

❹ Extension Activities

Speaking and Listening   Write and narrate **a sequel** to Welty's "A Worn Path" that describes what happens when Phoenix Jackson gets home. Use these questions to help you plan:

- Is Phoenix's grandson alive?
- Is anyone else present?
- What does Phoenix feel and do?
- How will your story end?

In an oral presentation, share your story with your class.

Research and Technology   Hemingway's story drew upon his service in the Italian army. Conduct research on the Internet and in the library to find information on the role Italy played in World War I, as well as on Hemingway's participation. Prepare a **research report** on your findings, including maps and charts as visual aids.

 **Take It to the Net**   www.phschool.com

Go online for an additional research activity using the Internet.

In Another Country / The Corn Planting / A Worn Path ◆ 831

---

❸ Writing Lesson

- Remind students that their speeches should capture Will's personality, hopes, and ambitions, as well as the strength of the bond in Will's family.

- As students reread, remind them that their speech is from Hal's point of view. They should note Hal's knowledge of Will and feelings for his family.

- Remind students that they should organize their ideas either in order of importance or in chronological order. Use the Outline transparency in **Writing Models and Graphic Organizers on Transparencies,** p. 95 as a model.

- When students begin to revise, encourage them to include at least one emotional detail in each paragraph.

❹ Research and Technology

- Remind students to collect information for creating maps and other visuals. Have them use varied resources, including textbooks, encyclopedias, atlases, databases, and the Internet.

- If students have difficulty finding information, tell them to search under "Italian Front in World War I" and "Hemingway."

- After they gather their research materials, have students determine if they have appropriate information to use for maps, charts, and diagrams.

- Adapt the Research Paper rubric in **Performance Assessment and Portfolio Management,** p. 22, to assess students' reports.

CUSTOMIZE INSTRUCTION
For Universal Access

To address different learning styles, use the activities suggested in the **Extension Activities** booklet, p. 46.

For Bodily/Kinesthetic Learners, use Activity 5.

For Interpersonal Learners, use Activity 6.

For Verbal/Linguistic Learners, use Activity 7.

Lesson Objectives

1. To understand the connection between the anxiety expressed by a late-twentieth century writer such as Grace Paley and that expressed by the Modernist writers in Part 2

2. To understand the common characteristics of twentieth century short stories, and the differences between short stories written at the start and end of that century

Connections

The American twentieth century was a time of fragmentation, uncertainty and anxiety. For the Modernist authors in Part 2, much of the anxiety stemmed from World War I; Grace Paley faced the anxiety of the nuclear age. Have students reread the selections in Part 2 after completing "Anxiety." What common themes do these short stories explore? How do they differ from Paley's story?

Facing Troubled Times

- Remind students that when the Modernist authors from Part 2 were writing—the years following World War I—many people were deeply uncertain about the values and meanings of life.

- Explain to students that at the turn of the twentieth century—a time of rapid technological, economic, and social change— anxieties that echo those of the Modernist period abound.

- Suggest to students that the short story is a literary form ideally suited to exploring such themes as fragmentation, uncertainty, and anxiety. The brief narratives and small number of characters and settings in short stories match the anxious lives they depict.

- Encourage students to look for the themes "Anxiety" shares with the short stories in Part 2, and also for the differences in the ways the stories treat these themes.

CONNECTIONS
Literature Past and Present
Facing Troubled Times

The Modernist writers had a deep sense of uncertainty. The war that had cost the world so much seemed to have accomplished little. Searching for values suited to a new era, Modernists focused on themes of confusion and the apparent meaninglessness of life. For contemporary Americans today, the world is even more fragmented. Grace Paley's story "Anxiety," with its implied theme of world doom, reflects the uncertainty brought about by changes in technology and politics.

Twentieth Century Short Stories The stories by Ernest Hemingway, Sherwood Anderson, Eudora Welty, and Paley were all written during the twentieth century, and share themes of uncertainty, ambiguity, and disillusionment. Paley's contemporary short story reflects the pace of our increasingly urban culture. Her story also raises new issues of concern—nuclear warfare, for example—and, consisting almost entirely of unpunctuated dialogue, blurs structural form more than do the other stories.

ANXIETY
Grace Paley

The young fathers are waiting outside the school. What curly heads! Such graceful brown mustaches. They're sitting on their haunches eating pizza and exchanging information. They're waiting for the 3 P.M. bell. It's springtime, the season of first looking out the window. I have a window box of greenhouse marigolds. The young fathers can be seen through the ferny leaves.

The bell rings. The children fall out of school, tumbling through the open door. One of the fathers sees his child. A small child. Is she Chinese? A little. Up u-u-p, he says and hoists her to his shoulders. U-u-p, says the second father, and hoists his little boy. The little boy sits on top of his father's head for a couple of seconds before sliding to his shoulders. Very funny, says the father.

They start off down the street, right under and past my window. The two children are still laughing. They try to whisper a secret. The fathers haven't finished their conversation. The frailer father is uncomfortable; his little girl wiggles too much.

Stop it this minute, he says.

Oink oink, says the little girl.

832 ◆ Disillusion, Defiance, and Discontent (1914–1946)

What'd you say?

Oink oink, she says.

The young father says What! three times. Then he seizes the child, raises her high above his head, and sets her hard on her feet.

What'd I do so bad, she says, rubbing her ankle. Just hold my hand, screams the frail and angry father.

I lean far out the window. Stop! Stop! I cry.

The young father turns, shading his eyes, but sees. What? he says. His friend says, Hey? Who's that? He probably thinks I'm a family friend, a teacher maybe.

Who're you? he says.

I move the pots of marigold aside. Then I'm able to lean my elbow way out into unshadowed visibility. Once, not too long ago, the tenements were speckled with women like me in every third window up to the fifth story, calling the children from play to receive orders and instruction. This memory enables me to say strictly, Young man, I am an older person who feels free because of that to ask questions and give advice.

Oh? he says, laughs with a little embarrassment, says to his friend, Shoot if you will that old gray head.[1] But he's joking, I know, because he has established himself, legs apart, hands behind his back, his neck arched to see and hear me out.

How old are you? I call. About thirty or so?

Thirty-three.

First I want to say you're about a generation ahead of your father in your attitude and behavior toward your child.

Really? Well? Anything else, ma'am.

Son, I said, leaning another two, three dangerous inches toward him. Son, I must tell you that madmen intend to destroy this beautifully made planet. That the murder of our children by these men has got to become a terror and a sorrow to you, and starting now, it had better interfere with any daily pleasure.

Speech, speech, he called.

I waited a minute, but he continued to look up. So, I said, I can tell by your general appearance and loping walk that you agree with me.

I do, he said, winking at his friend; but turning a serious face to mine, he said again, Yes, yes, I do.

Well then, why do you become so angry at that little girl whose future is like a film which suddenly cuts to white. Why did you nearly slam this little doomed person to the ground in your uncontrollable anger.

Let's not go too far, said the young father. She *was* jumping around on my poor back and hollering oink oink.

---

1. **Shoot . . . head** a reference to John Greenleaf Whittier's 1864 Civil War poem, "Barbara Frietchie," which contains the line, "'Shoot, if you must, this old gray head, / But spare your country's flag,' she said."

✔**Reading Check**

Answer: The fathers sit, eat pizza and talk, "exchanging information."

✔**Reading Check**

What do the young fathers do while they wait outside the school?

Connections: Anxiety ◆ 833

CUSTOMIZE INSTRUCTION FOR UNIVERSAL ACCESS

For Less Proficient Readers	For English Learners	For Advanced Readers
These students may be confused by the lack of standard quotation punctuation in this short story. Suggest that they read the story aloud in groups, round-robin style, to "hear" the dialogue and determine who is speaking to whom.	These students may find the lack of standard quotation punctuation to be challenging. Place these students in pairs, mixing English skill levels if possible. Have each pair read the story together, inserting standard punctuation for clarification.	Point out to these students that the story does not use standard quotation punctuation. As they read, encourage them to make note of the effects of Paley's decision. Afterwards, have them discuss these effects. What does the lack of quotation marks reveal about the story's narrator and point of view?

Connecting Literature Past and Present

1. Possible response: The soldiers in "In Another Country" are anxious about physical recovery and death. In "The Corn Planting," the Hutchensons are anxious about the world's complexity and the meaning of their son's death. Welty's Phoenix Jackson is anxious about being able to complete her long journey.

2. Possible response: Some students may say that the nuclear age is more troubling because a nuclear war could destroy the planet. Others might say that the post-World War I period is more troubling because they do not find living in the contemporary world particularly unsettling.

When were you angriest—when she wiggled and jumped or when she said oink?

He scratched his wonderful head of dark well-cut hair. I guess when she said oink.

Have you ever said oink oink? Think carefully. Years ago, perhaps? No. Well maybe. Maybe.

Whom did you refer to in this way?

He laughed. He called to his friend, Hey Ken, this old person's got something. The cops. In a demonstration. Oink oink, he said, remembering, laughing.

The little girl smiled and said, Oink oink.

Shut up, he said.

What do you deduce from this?

That I was angry at Rosie because she was dealing with me as though I was a figure of authority, and it's not my thing, never has been, never will be.

I could see his happiness, his nice grin, as he remembered this.

So, I continued, since those children are such lovely examples of what may well be the last generation of humankind, why don't you start all over again, right from the school door, as though none of this had ever happened.

Thank you, said the young father. Thank you. It would be nice to be a horse, he said, grabbing little Rosie's hand. Come on Rosie, let's go. I don't have all day.

U-up, says the first father. U-up, says the second.

Giddap, shout the children, and the fathers yell neigh neigh, as horses do. The children kick their fathers' horsechests, screaming giddap giddap, and they gallop wildly westward.

I lean way out to cry once more, Be careful! Stop! But they've gone too far. Oh, anyone would love to be a fierce fast horse carrying a beloved beautiful rider, but they are galloping toward one of the most dangerous street corners in the world. And they live beyond that trisection across other dangerous avenues.

So I must shut the window after patting the April-cooled marigolds with their rusty smell of summer. Then I sit in the nice light and wonder how to make sure that they gallop safely home through the airy scary dreams of scientists and the bulky dreams of automakers. I wish I could see just how they sit down at their kitchen tables for a healthy snack (orange juice or milk and cookies) before going out into the new spring afternoon to play.

Connecting Literature Past and Present

1. Explain how the title "Anxiety" might fit the stories by Hemingway, Anderson and Welty.

2. Which time period do you find more uncertain—post World War I or Grace Paley's nuclear age? Explain.

Grace Paley

(b. 1922)

Grace Paley, a native New Yorker, has a strong concern for urban community life. This concern, along with her interest in social issues, is reflected in her highly praised short story collections, such as *Enormous Changes at the Last Minute* (1974) and *Later the Same Day* (1985). Sometimes referred to as a writer's writer, Paley's work is often studied in writing workshops. Her style is crisp and deceptively simple. Nonetheless, "Anxiety" embodies an implicit theme of moral concern worth consideration in our age.

From Every Corner of the Land

The Tower, Charles Demuth, Columbus Museum of Art, Ohio

The works in this section reflect the breadth of American literature in the early-to-mid- twentieth century. This literary look at the regional diversity of the United States takes students from Carl Sandburg's rough and ready "Chicago" and E.B. White's dynamic urban portrait in *Here Is New York* to the Southern bayous of Faulkner's Mississippi in "Race at Morning." Katherine Anne Porter uses a stream-of-consciousness style to tell the tale of a rural woman's life in "The Jilting of Granny Weatherall," a story that is likely to both challenge and intrigue students. Frost's poetry, set against a vividly painted New England backdrop, has a depth and power that belie its simple language. The engaging excerpt from Zora Neale Hurston's *Dust Tracks on a Road* introduces a sampling of poetry by the leading writers of the Harlem Renaissance. These easy-to-read poems are rich with images and metaphors that express what it meant to be an African American at a time when memories of both slavery and the Civil War were still fresh in the American consciousness.

Background

Art

The Tower 1920, by Charles Demuth

Sir Christopher Wren (1632–1723), to whom this painting pays tribute, was England's most famous architect. After the Great Fire of London in 1666, he redesigned at least portions of more than half of the churches that had been burnt. His church spires, in particular, are admired for their grace and variety.

Use these questions for discussion:

1. Why is this painting called *The Tower?* Possible response: Most students will see the connection with the old-fashioned spire in the center of the painting, but point out the other towers in the image, including the faceted blue futuristic structure in the background.

2. What various facets of America do you see reflected in this painting? Possible response: This painting reflects America's New England roots, its combination of past and future, its social variety.

MIZE INSTRUCTION FOR UNIVERSAL ACCESS

igning the selections in this part, keep in mind these factors:

"Grass"
essible poems.
will enjoy the bold imagery and rhythms of
"
of Granny Weatherall"
y written in stream-of-consciousness style.
may need help clarifying the sequence of

orning"
ry filled with regional dialect that may
e students.

The Poetry of Robert Frost
- Most students will enjoy the rhythm and imagery of these poems.

"Dust Tracks on a Road"
- Most students will enjoy the light-hearted tone of this autobiographical selection.

Poetry of the Harlem Renaissance
- These brief, easy-to-read poems have many layers of meaning.

"I Yearn"
- Many students will relate to this contemporary poem about longing for home.

Chicago ✦ Grass

Lesson Objectives

1. **To analyze and respond to literary elements**
   - Literary Analysis: Apostrophe
   - Comparing Literary Works
2. **To read, comprehend, analyze, and critique poetry**
   - Reading Strategy: Responding
   - Reading Check questions
   - Review and Assess questions
   - Assessment Practice (ATE)
3. **To develop word analysis skills, fluency, and systematic vocabulary**
   - Vocabulary Development Lesson: Related Words: *brutal*
4. **To understand and apply written and oral language conventions**
   - Spelling Strategy
   - Grammar and Style Lesson: Sentence Types
5. **To understand and apply appropriate writing and research strategies**
   - Writing Lesson: Essay Analyzing the Use of Repetition
   - Extension Activity: Report
6. **To understand and apply listening and speaking strategies**
   - Extension Activity: Stand-up Comedy Routine

STEP-BY-STEP TEACHING GUIDE	PACING GUIDE
PRETEACH	
Motivate Students and Provide Background	
Use the Motivation activity (ATE p. 836)	5 min.
Read and discuss author and background features (SE/ATE pp. 836, 839)	5 min.
Introduce the Concepts	
Introduce the Literary Analysis and Reading Strategy (SE/ATE p. 837) A	15 min.
Pronounce the vocabulary words and read their definitions (SE p. 837)	5 min.
TEACH	
Monitor Comprehension	
Informally monitor comprehension by circulating while students read independently or in groups A	20 min.
Monitor students' comprehension with the Reading Check notes (SE/ATE p. 839)	as students read
Develop vocabulary with Vocabulary notes (SE p. 839; ATE p. 839)	as students read
Develop Understanding	
Develop students' understanding of apostrophe with the Literary Analysis annotations (ATE pp. 837, 839) A	5 min.
Develop students' ability to respond to reading with the Reading Strategy annotations (ATE p. 837)	5 min.
ASSESS	
Assess Mastery	
Assess students' mastery of the Reading Strategy and Literary Analysis by having them answer the Review and Assess questions (SE/ATE p. 841)	15 min.
Use one or more of the print and media Assessment Resources (ATE p. 843) A	up to 45 min.
EXTEND	
Apply Understanding	
Have students complete the Vocabulary Development Lesson and the Grammar and Style Lesson (SE p. 842) A	20 min.
Apply students' ability to connect contradictory information using the Writing Lesson (SE/ATE p. 843) A	45 min.
Apply students' understanding using one or more of the Extension Activities (SE p. 843)	20–90 min.

A **ACCELERATED INSTRUCTION:**
Use the strategies and activities identified with an A.

UNIVERSAL ACCESS
● = Below Level Students
▲ = On-Level Students
■ = Above Level Students

Time and Resource Manager

Reading Level: Easy, Average
Average Number of Instructional Days: 3

PRINT	TRANSPARENCIES	TECHNOLOGY
RESOURCES		
• **Beyond Literature,** Career Connection: Marketing, p. 47 ▲ ■		• **Interest Grabber Video,** Tape 5 ● ▲ ■
• **Selection Support Workbook:** ● ▲ ■ Literary Analysis, p. 211 Reading Strategy, p. 210 Build Vocabulary, p. 208	• **Literary Analysis and Reading Transparencies,** pp. 93 and 94 ● ▲ ■	
		• **Listening to Literature** ● ▲ ■ Audiocassettes, Side 29 Audio CDs, CD 16
• **Literatura en español** ● ▲ • **Literary Analysis for Enrichment** ■		
• **Formal Assessment:** Selection Test, pp. 218–220 ● ▲ ■ • **Open Book Test,** pp. 139–141 ● ▲ ■ • **PRENTICE HALL ASSESSMENT** *SYSTEM* ● ▲ ■	• **PRENTICE HALL ASSESSMENT** *SYSTEM* ● ▲ ■ Skills Practice Answers and Explanations on Transparencies	• **Test Bank Software** ● ▲ ■ • **Got It! Assessment Videotapes,** Tape 4 ● ▲
• **Selection Support Workbook:** ● ▲ ■ Grammar and Style, p. 209 • **Writing and Grammar,** Ruby Level ● ▲ ■ • **Extension Activities,** p. 47 ● ▲ ■	• **Daily Language Practice Transparencies** ● ▲ • **Writing Models and Graphic Organizers on Transparencies,** p. 25 ● ▲ ■	• **Writing and Grammar iText CD-ROM** ● ▲ ■ *Take It to the Net* www.phschool.com

BLOCK SCHEDULING: Use one 90-minute class period to preteach the selection and have students read it. Use a second 90-minute class period to assess students' mastery of skills and have them complete one of the Extension Activities.

836b

Step-by-Step Teaching Guide
for pp. 836–837

Motivation

Obtain the video of the John Hughes 1986 film *Ferris Bueller's Day Off*, which offers viewers a whirlwind tour of the "City of the Big Shoulders" as it looks in modern times. Play portions of the movie to show scenes in which the teen and his high school friends are in the Loop, at the Board of Trade, at a Cubs game at Wrigley Field, at a parade down Michigan Avenue, and at a posh French restaurant. Ask students to give their impressions of the city. Then, tell students that they are going to read a famous poem about Chicago, written nearly a century ago. Have them keep modern Chicago in mind as they read. Invite them to compare the images from the film with the images Sandburg presents.

Interest Grabber Video

As an alternative, play "Chicago Stockyards" on Tape 5 to engage student interest.

❶ Background

More About the Author

Quoting Rudyard Kipling to describe himself, Carl Sandburg once said, "I will be the word of the people. Mine will be the bleeding mouth from which the gag is snatched. I will say everything." Both poems collected here offer profound images of the people or comments on their behalf. In particular, "Grass" speaks out against the human waste of war.

Sandburg was part of a group of writers known as the Chicago School. These men—Sherwood Anderson and Theodore Dreiser, among others—lived and wrote in Chicago in the early 20th century. Sandburg also wrote for children, in his humorous stories *Rootabaga Stories* (1922), *Rootabaga Pigeons* (1923), and *Potato Face* (1930).

Prepare to Read

❶ Chicago ◆ Grass

Carl Sandburg (1878–1967)

You may enjoy the work of a contemporary poet or songwriter who seems to speak right to you. The poetry of Carl Sandburg seemed to speak directly to many of the people of his time. It celebrated the lives and the vitality of ordinary Americans, and made Sandburg one of the most popular poets of his day.

No writer better captured the spirit of industrial America than did Carl Sandburg, whose poems paint vivid portraits of the working class, capturing its energy and enthusiasm. In his poems about mills and factories, meatpacking houses, and railroads, he paid tribute to the struggles and hopes of the poor.

Modest Beginnings The son of Swedish immigrants, Sandburg was born and raised in Galesburg, Illinois. He was forced to leave school after eighth grade in order to help support his family. As an adolescent, he worked as a laborer, and when he was nineteen, he set out to see the country. He did so by hitching rides on freight trains. In 1898, after spending six years working at a variety of odd jobs, Sandburg enlisted in the army. Though the Spanish-American War was being fought at the time, Sandburg did not see combat. After the war, he attended Lombard College, but dropped out before graduating. He then spent several years traveling around the country, again working at a variety of jobs.

The Bard of Chicago In 1912, Sandburg settled in Chicago, one of the nation's great industrial cities. He made his living as a newspaper reporter and began to publish poetry in *Poetry* magazine, a highly regarded literary journal based in Chicago. His first book, *Chicago Poems*, published in 1916, sold well and was praised for its passion and vigor. Sandburg soon earned widespread recognition and helped establish Chicago as one of the nation's leading literary centers. During the next ten years, he published three more successful collections of poetry: *Cornhuskers* (1918), *Smoke and Steel* (1920), and *Slabs of the Sunburnt West* (1922).

Writing Lincoln's Life While continuing to write poetry, Sandburg began touring the country, delivering lectures on Walt Whitman and Abraham Lincoln—two men whom he greatly admired—and starting a career as a folk singer. He also spent a great deal of time collecting material for a biography of Lincoln, and he prepared an anthology of American folk songs he had heard during his travels. He collected these songs from cowboys, lumberjacks, factory workers, and hobos. *The American Songbag* appeared in 1927. In 1940, Carl Sandburg received a Pulitzer Prize for his multi-volume biography of Lincoln, and in 1951 he received a second Pulitzer Prize for his *Complete Poems*. Sandburg was also awarded the United States Presidential Medal in 1964, and he was asked to address a joint session of Congress on the 150th anniversary of Lincoln's birth.

Power of Positive Thinking Sandburg was an optimist who believed in the power of ordinary Americans to fulfill their dreams. He was not interested in experimenting with complicated syntax or images, as were some other poets of his generation. Instead, he reached out to his readers with poems that were concrete and direct. Sandburg offered a variety of definitions of poetry, among them these two: "Poetry is a search for syllables to shoot at the barriers of the unknown and the unknowable," and "Poetry is the opening and closing of a door, leaving those who look through to guess about what is seen during a moment."

836 ◆ *Disillusion, Defiance, and Discontent (1914–1946)*

TEACHING RESOURCES

The following resources can be used to enrich or extend the instruction for pp. 836-837.

Motivation

Interest Grabber Video, Tape 5

Background

Beyond Literature, p. 47

Take It to the Net
Visit www.phschool.com for Background and hotlinks for the selections.

Literary Analysis

Literary Analysis and Reading Transparencies, Apostrophe, p. 94

Reading

Literary Analysis and Reading Transparencies, Responding, p. 93

Selection Support: Reading Strategy, p. 210

BLOCK SCHEDULING: Resources marked with this symbol provide varied instruction during 90-minute blocks.

Preview

Connecting to the Literature

If you have ever celebrated the comeback of someone who seemed to have been defeated, then you understand the spirit in which Carl Sandburg wrote. In reading these poems, you will see that Sandburg recognized people's and cities' failures, but he cheered the invincibility of their souls.

❷ Literary Analysis

Apostrophe

Apostrophe is a literary device in which the speaker or narrator directly addresses a person or thing. For example, in "Chicago," Sandburg addresses the city as if it were a person:

> They tell me you are wicked and I believe them . . .

> And they tell me you are crooked and I answer: Yes . . .

As you read "Chicago," think about the effect of this technique, and identify the reasons that Sandburg chose to speak directly to the city of Chicago.

Comparing Literary Works

These poems concern two very different subjects and evoke distinct emotions. "Chicago" is a celebration of life in an industrial city, while "Grass" is a lament for loss of life in war. In "Chicago," the speaker addresses the city directly; in "Grass," it is the grass itself that speaks. Despite these differences, the poet uses similar techniques to achieve his aims. For example, both poems use **personification,** figurative language in which a non-human subject is given human qualities. As you read, use a chart like the one shown to examine the ways in which Sandburg uses personification, but to different effect in each poem.

❸ Reading Strategy

Responding

When you **respond** to a poem, you think about the message that the poet has conveyed and reflect on how you feel personally about the topic. You take the time to consider how the poet's message relates to your own life and to the world in which you live, and to think about how you can use or apply what you have learned from the poem. As you read these poems, connect your own experiences to the images and ideas Sandburg presents.

Vocabulary Development

brutal (brōōt′ əl) *adj.* cruel and without feeling; savage; violent (p. 839)

wanton (wän′ tən) *adj.* senseless; unjustified (p. 839)

cunning (kun′ iŋ) *adj.* skillful in deception; crafty; sly (p. 839)

Detail expressing human trait

⬆
⋮

"Chicago"

"Grass"

⋮
⬇

Detail expressing human trait

---

❷ Literary Analysis

Apostrophe

- Tell students that as they read Carl Sandburg's poems, they will focus on *apostrophe*, a literary device in which the poet addresses a person or thing directly.

- Have a volunteer read aloud the excerpts in the Literary Analysis instruction. Point out the specific word ("you") that makes these lines examples of apostrophe.

- Discuss the instruction under Comparing Literary Works, and use it to help students understand how personification and apostrophe work together.

- Model the use of the chart on this page, and direct students to complete a similar chart as they read the poems.

❸ Reading Strategy

Responding

- Explain to students that responding includes thoughts, feelings, associations, and any other reactions evoked by a reading.

- Remind students that responding to poetry is at the core of their reading experience. Encourage them to trust their reactions, even when they don't "understand" the poem.

Vocabulary Development

- Pronounce each vocabulary word for students, and read the definitions as a class. Have students identify any words with which they are already familiar.

CUSTOMIZE INSTRUCTION FOR UNIVERSAL ACCESS

For Less Proficient Readers	For English Learners	For Advanced Readers
Display the Responding Transparency, p. 97 of **Literary Analysis and Reading Transparencies**. Read aloud some of the questions from the transparency. Then, walk students through the questions to help them understand the many ways to respond to a poem.	Tell students that reading in a second language can make it more difficult to respond to the content or messages of a poem. However, readers can focus on their emotional responses—to sounds, rhythms, and images. Encourage students to focus on the responses evoked by the familiar words.	Have students contrast the general feelings and emotions behind the two poems as they read them. How are the messages similar and different? Then, ask students to contrast their responses to the poems. In what ways are these similar or different?

 E-Teach

Visit E-Teach at www.phschool.com for teachers' essays on how to teach, with questions and answers.

CUSTOMIZE INSTRUCTION
For Visual/Spatial Learners

Provide photos of the Chicago Sandburg portrays as well as "before and after" photos of Gettysburg and the World War I battlefields. Ask students to think about whether the tone of the poems matches the visual images in these pictures.

❶ About the Selections

Using spirited but simple words and phrases, Sandburg expresses his love and admiration for what he sees as a vital, brawny, sweating giant of a city.

In "Grass," Carl Sandburg observes that today there is only grass where once monumental battles between great armies took place. The serenity of nature obscures the horror and futility of war.

❷ ▶ Critical Viewing

Answer: It shows the mosaic of people and activities, the bustle of business and the marketplace, and the vitality and struggle of people to survive.

❶ Chicago

Carl Sandburg

838 ◆ *Disillusion, Defiance, and Discontent (1914–1946)*

TEACHING RESOURCES

The following resources can be used to enrich or extend the instruction for pp. 838–840.

Literary Analysis

📖 **Writing Models and Graphic Organizers on Transparencies,** p. 25

📖 **Selection Support:** Literary Analysis, p. 211 ▪

Reading

🎧 **Listening to Literature Audiocassettes,** Side 29

💿 **Listening to Literature Audio CDs,** CD 16

▪ **BLOCK SCHEDULING:** Resources marked with this symbol provide varied instruction during 90-minute blocks.

Background

The 1920s was a time of excitement in America. The economy was booming, and jazz was the rage. Sandburg's poems of industrial America celebrate the energy of the times.

Hog Butcher for the World,
Tool Maker, Stacker of Wheat,
Player with Railroads and the Nation's Freight Handler;
Stormy, husky, brawling,
5   City of the Big Shoulders:

They tell me you are wicked and I believe them, for I have seen
    your painted women under the gas lamps luring the farm
    boys.
And they tell me you are crooked and I answer: Yes, it is true I
    have seen the gunman kill and go free to kill again.
And they tell me you are <u>brutal</u> and my reply is: On the faces of
    women and children I have seen the marks of <u>wanton</u> hunger.
And having answered so I turn once more to those who sneer at
    this my city, and I give them back the sneer and say to them:
10 Come and show me another city with lifted head singing so proud
    to be alive and coarse and strong and <u>cunning</u>.
Flinging magnetic curses amid the toil of piling job on job, here is
    a tall bold slugger set vivid against the little soft cities;
Fierce as a dog with tongue lapping for action, cunning as a
    savage pitted against the wilderness,
        Bareheaded,
        Shoveling,
15   Wrecking,
        Planning,
        Building, breaking, rebuilding,
Under the smoke, dust all over his mouth, laughing with
    white teeth,
Under the terrible burden of destiny laughing as a young man
    laughs,
20 Laughing even as an ignorant fighter laughs who has never lost
    a battle,
Bragging and laughing that under his wrist is the pulse, and
    under his ribs the heart of the people,
        Laughing!
Laughing the stormy, husky, brawling laughter of Youth, half-
    naked, sweating, proud to be a Hog Butcher, Tool Maker,
    Stacker of Wheat, Player with Railroads and Freight Handler
    to the Nation.

② ◄ Critical Viewing In what ways does this bustling street scene of Chicago reflect Sandburg's poem **[Connect]**

brutal (broot´ əl) *adj.* cruel and without feeling; savage; violent

wanton (wän´ tən) *adj.* senseless; unjustified

cunning (kun´ iŋ) *adj.* skillful in deception; crafty; sly

⑤ ✔Reading Check
Who is the "you" the speaker addresses?

Chicago ◆ 839

❸ Vocabulary Development

Related Words: *brutal*

- Call students' attention to the word *brutal* and its definition. Tell students that there are several words related to *brutal*.
- List the words presented in the Vocabulary Development Lesson on p. 842: *brute, brutality, brutalize,* and *brutish.* Have students look up these words in a dictionary.
- Have students create sentences using these words based on the two Sandburg poems presented here.

❹ Literary Analysis

Apostrophe and Personification

- Read aloud lines 10–11 to students. Have students identify the type of figurative language that Sandburg uses in these lines. Lead students to see that Sandburg personifies the city.
- Ask students to describe the effect of this personification. What qualities of the city are expressed in these lines?
  Answer: The use of personification makes the city seem a vibrant, loud, and bustling place.

❺ ✔Reading Check

Answer: The speaker addresses the city of Chicago as "you."

CUSTOMIZE INSTRUCTION FOR UNIVERSAL ACCESS

For Less Proficient Readers	For Special Needs Students	For Gifted/Talented Students
Guide students to understand that with the rough, robust, and coarse images at the beginning of the poem, Sandburg is celebrating the essence of Chicago, not complaining about the city. Help them to appreciate that to him these images are rich and heroic. Read the poem aloud to convey its gusto.	Have students listen to you read the poem aloud. Help them define any words or phrases they do not understand. Then, ask them how the poem makes them feel. Guide them to see the vital personality Sandburg gives his city. Emphasize that this is the most important message of the poem.	After reading the poem aloud, invite students to render Sandburg's personified "City of the Big Shoulders" in another medium. Regardless of the medium they choose, they should try to capture the vitality and energy of Sandburg's portrayal.

1. Students should be prepared to explain their responses.

2. **(a)** He uses the names "Hog Butcher for the World, Tool Maker, Stacker of Wheat, Player with Railroads, the Nation's Freight Handler, and City of the Big Shoulders." **(b)** They tell you that the city is full of industry and business, that it is a transportation center, and that it is a busy, vibrant place.

3. **(a)** The city is wicked, crooked, and brutal. **(b)** The speaker thinks the city is wonderful despite its faults. If anything, he thinks these faults contribute to the city's vitality.

4. **(a)** It claims to cover the evidence of war. **(b)** He is saying that the death and destruction of war are futile, for they will be covered up and forgotten by nature.

5. **(a)** Responses should show an awareness of regional variations. **(b)** It is highly varied and unique, yet also similar to Chicago in its vitality.

Grass Carl Sandburg

Pile the bodies high at Austerlitz and Waterloo.[1]
Shovel them under and let me work—
    I am the grass; I cover all.

And pile them high at Gettysburg
5   And pile them high at Ypres and Verdun.[2]
Shovel them under and let me work.
Two years, ten years, and passengers ask the conductor:
    What place is this?
    Where are we now?

10   I am grass.
    Let me work.

---

1. **Austerlitz** (ôs′ tər lits′) **and Waterloo** sites of battles of the Napoleonic Wars.
2. **Ypres** (ē′ pr) **and Verdun** (ver dun′) sites of battles of World War I.

Review and Assess

Thinking About the Selections

1. **Respond:** Unlike some poets, Sandburg tells you what to feel and think. How do you react to his directness? Why?

2. **(a) Recall:** In "Chicago," what names does the speaker use to address the city in the first stanza? **(b) Interpret:** What do these names tell you about the city's economy and atmosphere?

3. **(a) Recall:** What three specific faults concerning his city does the speaker acknowledge? **(b) Interpret:** In what ways do these faults affect the speaker's attitude toward the city?

4. **(a) Recall:** In the first stanza of "Grass," what does the grass claim to be able to do? **(b) Draw Conclusions:** Is Sandburg suggesting that the death and destruction of war can be covered over and easily forgotten? Support your answer.

5. **(a) Distinguish:** In what ways is the city described in "Chicago" similar to and different from other cities with which you are familiar? **(b) Apply:** What do the differences among American cities reveal about the nation's character?

ASSESSMENT PRACTICE: Reading Comprehension

Analyze Sentence Meaning   (For more practice, see Test Preparation Workbook, p. 50.)

Many tests require students to correctly answer sentence-completion questions. Often, more than one choice can complete a sentence. Use the following sample item to show students how to analyze sentence meaning, decide whether it is positive or negative, and eliminate choices that have the opposite sense.

Carl Sandburg's poems focus on the lives of the working classes. By writing about mills and factories, he honored the _____ and hopes of the poor.

A cowardice   **C** struggles
B avarice   **D** idleness

The context indicates that the missing word will have a positive connotation. *A, B,* and *D* are all negative in this context. *C* is the best choice.

Review and Assess

Literary Analysis

Apostrophe

1. (a) In which lines of "Chicago" does Sandburg address the city directly? (b) What effect does this use of **apostrophe** create?
2. (a) Using a chart like the one shown, contrast the lines in the poem that directly address the city with those that address others. (b) Which section contains more positive images?

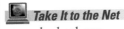

Imagery	Chicago	Others	Imagery

Comparing Literary Works

3. (a) Compare and contrast the use of specific details in "Chicago" and "Grass." (b) In what ways does the choice and amount of detail suit each poem's subject? (c) What distinct moods do these details evoke?
4. (a) Identify at least one feeling Sandburg has for Chicago that he might feel toward a friend. Support your answer with examples. (b) In "Grass," with what two words does the poet **personify** the grass?
5. In what ways do the uses of personification serve the distinct goals of each of these poems? Explain

Reading Strategy

Responding

6. Which words or images in "Chicago" were most striking to you? Explain.
7. (a) In what tone of voice do you imagine the grass speaks? (b) What is your **response** to the grass's message?

Extend Understanding

8. **Literature Connection:** Some critics have said that Sandburg opened poetry to new subjects by writing about industry and laborers. Other poets of his day, like T.S. Eliot, wrote about more intellectual subjects. What benefits or harm do you see—for poetry or popular culture—in Sandburg's appeal to the common person?

Quick Review

Apostrophe is a literary device in which a speaker directly addresses a person or thing.

Personification is a type of figurative language in which a nonhuman subject is given human traits.

To **respond** to a literary work, think about what it says, consider how it makes you feel, and notice the thoughts it triggers in your mind.

 Take It to the Net
www.phschool.com

Take the interactive self-test online to check your understanding of these selections.

Chicago / Grass ◆ 841

---

❶ Vocabulary Development

Related Words

1. brute
2. brutality
3. brutish
4. brutalize

Concept Development: Synonyms

1. b
2. c
3. c

Spelling Strategy

1. barest
2. piling
3. smokily
4. caring

❷ Grammar and Style

1. Shovel me under and let me work. (Imperative)
2. I have seen hunger on children's faces. (Declarative)
3. Where are we now? (Interrogative)
4. Show me another city. (Imperative)
5. I am overjoyed by this response! (Exclamatory)

Writing Application

Check to see that students have included and properly punctuated all four types of sentences.

Integrate Language Skills

❶ Vocabulary Development Lesson

Related Words: *brutal*

The word *brutal* means "cruel, crude, or harsh." Use this information and your knowledge about parts of speech to complete each sentence using a related word from the list below.

brute   brutality   brutalize   brutish

1. Sam was so rough with my brother that I told him he was behaving like a ___?___ and asked him to leave.

2. Many who participated in World War I were stunned by the ___?___ on the front lines.

3. Use your knife and fork, and stop that ___?___ behavior at once!

4. Those who ___?___ innocent animals should receive the harshest punishment.

Concept Development: Synonyms

Select the letter of the word that is closest in meaning to each of the numbered vocabulary words.

1. brutal: (a) unwise, (b) violent, (c) heavy
2. cunning: (a) suspicious, (b) diligent, (c) crafty
3. wanton: (a) rapid, (b) kind, (c) rash

Spelling Strategy

In the word *brute*, the final *e* marks the long sound of the vowel that precedes it. When a suffix beginning with a vowel is added to such a word, the final *e* is usually dropped: *brute* becomes *brutish*. For each of the following words, create a new word containing the given suffix.

1. bare (add -*est*)   3. smoke (add -*ily*)
2. pile (add -*ing*)   4. care (add -*ing*)

❷ Grammar and Style Lesson

Sentence Types

There are four sentence types. A **declarative** sentence makes a statement and ends with a period. An **interrogative** sentence asks a question and ends with a question mark. An **imperative** sentence is a statement and gives a command or makes a request; it ends with a period. An **exclamatory** sentence expresses a strong emotion and ends with an exclamation point.

> **Declarative:** I am grass.
>
> **Interrogative:** What place is this?
>
> **Imperative:** Pile the bodies high.
>
> **Exclamatory:** Look at that man!

Practice Add the correct end punctuation, and label the sentence type for each of the following examples.

1. Shovel me under and let me work
2. I have seen hunger on children's faces
3. Where are we now
4. Show me another city
5. I am overjoyed by this response

Writing Application Write a paragraph in which you praise and/or criticize your city or town. Use all four types of sentences in your essay.

W_G *Prentice Hall Writing and Grammar Connection: Chapter 20, Section 1*

TEACHING RESOURCES

The following resources can be used to enrich or extend the instruction for pp. 842–843.

Vocabulary

📖 **Selection Support:** Build Vocabulary, p. 208

📖 **Vocabulary and Spelling Practice Book**
(Use this booklet for skills enrichment.)

Grammar

📖 **Selection Support:** Grammar and Style, p. 209

W_G **Writing and Grammar,** Ruby Level, p. 476 ▪

Daily Language Practice Transparencies

Writing

W_G **Writing and Grammar,** Ruby Level, p. 311

💿 **Writing and Grammar iText CD-ROM** ▪

Writing Models and Graphic Organizers on Transparencies, p. 25

▪ **BLOCK SCHEDULING:** Resources marked with this symbol provide varied instruction during 90-minute blocks.

❸ Writing Lesson

Essay Analyzing the Use of Repetition

Using either "Chicago," or "Grass," write an essay analyzing Sandburg's use of repetition. Explain the ways in which the poet's use of repetition emphasizes particular ideas and heightens specific emotions.

Prewriting	Select a poem to analyze, and examine it for examples of repetition. Note which elements—words, phrases, sentence structures, or grammatical forms—are repeated, and consider their effect.
Drafting	In your introduction, briefly summarize the poem, and state your main point about its use of repetition. Develop your ideas, with quotes from the poem, in the body paragraphs.
Revising	Review your draft, and make sure that you have explained your ideas in a consistent way. Use contrasting colors to underline any contradictory information. If you cannot connect the contradictions to your main idea, delete them.

Model: Revising to Connect Contradictory Information

Reading "Chicago" is like riding the rapids on a river; you are

swept along in a stream of words, and <u>do not stop to examine the</u>

However,

validity of the ideas. The ideas in a Sandburg poem are important.

Transitional words, such as "however" connect contradictory information to a main idea.

Prentice Hall Writing and Grammar Connection: Chapter 8, Section 2

❹ Extension Activities

Listening and Speaking Acting as the city of Chicago, deliver a **stand-up comedy routine.** First, research Chicago's history for events you can turn into anecdotes. Then, use these tips to prepare:

- Decide what your attitude will be—tough or sensitive.
- Find body language to fit your attitude.

When presenting your routine, appeal to your audience's experiences, and create a bond that will result in laughter.

Research and Technology Using the Internet and other sources, research the population of Chicago. Collect statistics related to that population, including totals of men, women, and children, and so on. Create a **report** that demonstrates how the population of Chicago today reflects its history.

 **Take It to the Net** www.phschool.com

Go online for an additional research activity using the Internet.

Chicago / Grass ◆ 843

Lesson Support for p. 843

❸ Writing Lesson

- Reread the poems with students, identifying examples of repetition.
- Refer students to Writing Process Model 5: Written Evaluation, p. 25 in **Writing Models and Graphic Organizers on Transparencies** for ideas on how to construct a literary analysis.
- Review the Writing Lesson to guide students in developing their essay.

❹ Research and Technology

- If you wish, divide the class into groups to research different time periods in Chicago history.
- Discuss the types of research sources students might use. Suggest almanacs and Web sites such as those created by the City of Chicago.
- Encourage students to include some kind of graphic organizer, such as a chart or graph, in their report.

CUSTOMIZE INSTRUCTION
For Universal Access

To address different learning styles, use the activities suggested in the **Extension Activities** booklet, p. 47.

For Intrapersonal Learners, use Activity 5.

For Visual/Spatial Learners, use Activity 6.

For Verbal/Linguistic Learners, use Activity 7.

ASSESSMENT RESOURCES

The following resources can be used to assess students' knowledge and skills.

Selection Assessment

- **Formal Assessment,** pp. 218–220
- **Open Book Test,** pp. 139–141
- **Got It! Assessment Videotapes,** Tape 4
- **Test Bank Software**

 **Take It to the Net**
Visit www.phschool.com for self-tests and additional questions on the selections.

PRENTICE HALL ASSESSMENT SYSTEM

- **Workbook**
- **Skill Book**
- **Transparencies**
- **CD-ROM**

The Jilting of Granny Weatherall

Lesson Objectives

1. **To analyze and respond to literary elements**
   - Literary Analysis: Stream of Consciousness
   - Connecting Literary Elements: Flashback

2. **To read, comprehend, analyze, and critique a short story**
   - Reading Strategy: Clarifying Sequence of Events
   - Reading Check Questions
   - Review and Assess Questions
   - Assessment Practice (ATE)

3. **To develop word analysis skills, fluency, and systematic vocabulary**
   - Vocabulary Development Lesson: Greek Prefix: *dys-*

4. **To understand and apply written and oral language conventions**
   - Spelling Strategy
   - Grammar and Style Lesson: Imperative Sentences

5. **To understand and apply appropriate writing and research strategies**
   - Writing Lesson: Stream -of- Consciousness Monologue
   - Extension Activity: Report on Hospice Care

6. **To understand and apply listening and speaking strategies**
   - Extension Activity: Conversation

STEP-BY-STEP TEACHING GUIDE	PACING GUIDE
PRETEACH	
Motivate Students and Provide Background	
Use the Motivation activity (ATE p. 844)	5 min.
Read and discuss author and background features (SE/ATE p. 844)	5 min.
Introduce the Concepts	
Introduce the Literary Analysis and Reading Strategy (SE/ATE p. 845) A	15 min.
Pronounce the vocabulary words and read their definitions (SE p. 845)	5 min.
TEACH	
Monitor Comprehension	
Informally monitor comprehension by circulating while students read independently or in groups A	35 min.
Monitor students' comprehension with the Reading Check notes (SE/ATE pp. 852, 853, 854)	as students read
Develop vocabulary with Vocabulary notes (SE pp. 852, 853, 854; ATE p. 853)	as students read
Develop Understanding	
Develop students' understanding of stream of consciousness with the Literary Analysis annotations (SE pp. 846, 849, 850, 851, 852, 853; ATE pp. 846, 849, 850, 851, 852, 853	5 min.
Develop students' ability to clarify the sequence of events by using the Reading Strategy annotations (ATE p. 848)	5 min.
ASSESS	
Assess Mastery	
Assess students' mastery of the Reading Strategy and Literary Analysis by having them answer the Review and Assess questions (SE/ATE p. 855)	15 min.
Use one or more of the print and media Assessment Resources (ATE p. 857) A	up to 45 min.
EXTEND	
Apply Understanding	
Have students complete the Vocabulary Development Lesson and the Grammar and Style Lesson (SE p. 856) A	20 min.
Apply students' ability to create a vivid character by using the Writing Lesson (SE/ATE p. 857) A	45 min.
Apply students' understanding using one or more of the Extension Activities (SE p. 857)	20–90 min.

A **ACCELERATED INSTRUCTION:**
Use the strategies and activities identified with an A.

UNIVERSAL ACCESS
- ● = Below Level Students
- ▲ = On-Level Students
- ■ = Above Level Students

Time and Resource Manager

RESOURCES		
PRINT 📖	**TRANSPARENCIES**	**TECHNOLOGY** 💿 🎧 📼
• **Beyond Literature,** Media Connection: Film Biography, p. 48 ▲ ■		• **Interest Grabber Video,** Tape 5 ● ▲ ■
• **Selection Support Workbook:** ● ▲ ■ Literary Analysis, p. 215 Reading Strategy, p. 214 Build Vocabulary, p. 212	• **Literary Analysis and Reading Transparencies,** pp. 95 and 96 ● ▲ ■	
		• **Listening to Literature** ● ▲ ■ Audiocassettes, Side 30 Audio CDs, CD 17
• **Literatura en español** ● ▲ • **Literary Analysis for Enrichment** ■		
• **Formal Assessment:** Selection Test, p. 221 ● ▲ ■ • **Open Book Test,** p. 142 ● ▲ ■ • **Performance Assessment and Portfolio Management,** p. 15 ● ▲ ■ • **PRENTICE HALL ASSESSMENT** *SYSTEM* ● ▲ ■	• **PRENTICE HALL ASSESSMENT** *SYSTEM* ● ▲ ■ Skills Practice Answers and Explanations on Transparencies	• **Test Bank Software** ● ▲ ■ • **Got It! Assessment Videotapes,** Tape 4 ● ▲
• **Selection Support Workbook:** ● ▲ ■ Grammar and Style, p. 213 • **Writing and Grammar,** Ruby Level ● ▲ ■ • **Extension Activities,** p. 48 ● ▲ ■	• **Daily Language Practice Transparencies** ● ▲ • **Writing Models and Graphic Organizers on Transparencies,** p. 67 ● ▲ ■	• **Writing and Grammar iText CD-ROM** ● ▲ ■ 🖥 *Take It to the Net* www.phschool.com

BLOCK SCHEDULING: Use one 90-minute class period to preteach the selection and have students read it. Use a second 90-minute class period to assess students' mastery of skills and have them complete one of the Extension Activities.

Step-by-Step Teaching Guide for pp. 844–845

Motivation

Write the word "granny" on the chalkboard. Ask students to begin with that word and then freewrite their thoughts and associations as they occur. Encourage them to write quickly for about five minutes, without stopping to organize or order their impressions. Have small groups of students share their freewriting, and discuss the associations that led them from one thought to the next. Do they notice any common threads? Tell students that they have just created a piece of stream-of-consciousness writing—the same style used in the short story they are about to read.

 Interest Grabber Video

As an alternative, play "Through Different Eyes" on Tape 5 to engage student interest.

❶ Background

More About the Author

Katherine Anne Porter sometimes described her life with a certain measure of creative license. According to some historians, at one time Porter described her childhood as refined and her schooling as in-depth (though this was far from true). She also borrowed from her own life to create her fiction. For example, she based the novel *Ship of Fools* in part on her own 1931 journey from Mexico to Europe.

Prepare to Read

❶ The Jilting of Granny Weatherall

Katherine Anne Porter (1890–1980)

Katherine Anne Porter's life spanned World War I, the Great Depression, World War II, and the rise of the nuclear age, making her deeply aware of what she called "the heavy threat of world catastrophe." For Porter, her exceptionally well-crafted fiction was an "effort to grasp the meaning of those threats, to trace them to their sources, and to understand the logic of this majestic and terrible failure of the life of man in the Western world." Her stories were often set in the South and featured characters at pivotal moments in their lives, faced with dramatic change, the constricting bonds of family, and the weight of the past.

A descendant of legendary pioneer Daniel Boone, Porter was born in Indian Creek, Texas. She was raised in poverty and haphazardly educated in convent schools. Commenting on her schooling, Porter said that she received a "fragmentary, but strangely useless and ornamental education." Instead, she added, her true education came by reading five writers—American authors Henry James, T.S. Eliot, and Ezra Pound, Irish writer James Joyce, and Irish poet W.B. Yeats.

Beginnings as a Writer Porter began writing at an early age, though she did not publish her first book until she was forty years old. As a young adult, she worked as a journalist. Her work took her to many places, including Mexico City, where she lived for eight years. She became deeply involved in Mexican politics and culture, even writing a study of Mexican crafts. While in Mexico, Porter also developed an interest in writing fiction, and in 1922 she published her first story, "María Concepción," in *Century*, a highly regarded literary magazine. Eight years later, she published her first book, *Flowering Judas* (1930). The book, a collection of six short stories, was praised by critics and earned Porter widespread recognition. *Flowering Judas and Other Stories*, an expanded edition of the book containing ten stories, was published in 1935.

Literary Achievements Katherine Anne Porter went on to produce several other major works, including *Noon Wine* (1937); *Pale Horse, Pale Rider* (1939); *The Leaning Tower and Other Stories* (1944); and *Ship of Fools* (1962)—Porter's only novel. Her last major work, *The Never-Ending Wrong*, a nonfiction account of the trial of Sacco and Vanzetti during the 1920s, was published in 1977. Although her body of work was relatively small in comparison to those of other major writers of her time, her work consistently received high praise from critics and earned her a place among the finest writers of the twentieth century. Her *Collected Stories* (1965) was awarded the Pulitzer Prize and the National Book Award. In addition, her novel, *Ship of Fools*, was made into a popular film.

A First-Rate Artist In his review of *The Leaning Tower and Other Stories*, critic Edmund Wilson tried to account for the "elusive" quality that made Porter an "absolutely first-rate artist." He said, "These stories are not illustrations of anything that is reducible to a moral law or a political or social analysis or even a principle of human behavior. What they show us are human relationships in their constantly shifting phases and in the moments of which their existence is made. There is no place for general reflections; you are to live through the experiences as the characters do." You will discover that Wilson's observations can be applied to "The Jilting of Granny Weatherall," which takes readers on a journey through the various phases of an elderly woman's life in the moments leading up to her death.

TEACHING RESOURCES

The following resources can be used to enrich or extend the instruction for pp. 844–845.

Motivation

 Interest Grabber Video, Tape 5 ▪

Background

📖 **Beyond Literature**, p. 48

💻 *Take It to the Net*

Visit www.phschool.com for background and hotlinks for "The Jilting of Granny Weatherall." ▪

Literary Analysis

📄 **Literary Analysis and Reading Transparencies,** Stream of Consciousness, p. 96

📖 **Selection Support:** Literary Analysis, p. 215

Reading

📄 **Literary Analysis and Reading Transparencies,** Clarifying Sequence of Events, p. 95

BLOCK SCHEDULING: Resources marked with this symbol provide varied instruction during 90-minute blocks.

Preview

Connecting to the Literature

Think about the drifting thoughts and images that greet you as you fall asleep. If you can remember these semi-conscious thoughts of yours, you may be able to understand Granny Weatherall a little better. The old woman in this story is visited by a host of such images from her past. As you read, try to uncover the meaning of her memories.

Literary Analysis

Stream of Consciousness

People's thoughts do not flow in neat patterns; they proceed in streams of insight, memory, and reflection. During the early 1900s, some writers began using a literary device called **stream of consciousness**, in which they tried to capture the natural flow of thought. These narratives usually

- present sequences of thought as if they were issuing directly from a character's mind.
- omit transitional words and phrases found in ordinary prose.
- connect details only through a character's associations.

Note the way Granny Weatherall's thoughts wander among memories, dream-like images, and accurate perceptions of the present moment.

Connecting Literary Elements

Stream-of-consciousness narratives often involve the use of **flashback**, or interruptions in which an earlier event is described. A flashback may take the form of a character's memory, a story told by a character, a dream or daydream, or a switch by the narrator to a time in the past.

As you read, pay attention to the details that trigger Granny's flashbacks, determine the form of the flashback, and decide how each relates to events in the present. Use a chart like the one shown to link past to present in the story.

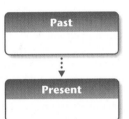

Reading Strategy

Clarifying Sequence of Events

This story evokes an array of different moments spanning eighty years as Granny Weatherall drifts in and out of reality. To stay oriented, **clarify the sequence of events**. Watch for jumps in Granny's thinking, often signaled by a shift from present-moment dialogue to Granny's inner thoughts.

Build Vocabulary

piety (pī′ ə tē) *n.* devotion to religious duties (p. 852)

frippery (frip′ ər ē) *n.* showy display of elegance (p. 853)

dyspepsia (dis pep′ shə) *n.* indigestion (p. 854)

---

❷ Literary Analysis

Stream of Consciousness

- Tell students that as they read Porter's story, they will focus on stream of consciousness, a writing style in which the flow of text mirrors the natural streams of human thoughts.
- Read the instruction about stream of consciousness aloud, focusing on the bulleted text.
- Remind students of the Motivation activity from p. 844. Clarify the idea that stream-of-consciousness writing follows similar connecting bridges of associations.
- Use the Connecting Literary Elements instruction to note how stream of consciousness can jump about in time. Urge students to use this instruction to navigate the story's events.

❸ Reading Strategy

Clarifying Sequence of Events

- Tell students that clarifying the sequence of events will enable them to keep track of the story as it jumps about in time.
- To clarify the sequence of events, readers must look for signals that suggest sequence. Mentions of Granny's age or contextual details, for example, can suggest sequence.
- Have students list key moments in Granny's life and then number them in sequence.
- Encourage students, to use a chart like the one shown to record key moments in the narrative.

Vocabulary Development

- Pronounce each vocabulary word for students, and read the definitions as a class. Have students identify any words with which they are already familiar.

 E-Teach

Visit E-Teach at www.phschool.com for teachers' essays on how to teach, with questions and answers.

CUSTOMIZE INSTRUCTION FOR UNIVERSAL ACCESS

For Less Proficient Readers	For English Learners	For Advanced Readers
Suggest that students read this difficult story at least twice in order to better grasp the meaning of Granny Weatherall's stream-of-consciousness narration. As they read, encourage students to use the chart shown on this page to help them clarify their understanding of the sequence of events.	Tell students that Granny's thoughts jump from one topic to another, often across connecting bridges that may be unfamiliar to English language learners. To aid their comprehension, make sure students understand who is talking at any given point in the story.	Have students compare and contrast the stream-of-consciousness technique used by Porter in "The Jilting of Granny Weatherall" with that used by T. S. Eliot in "The Love Song of J. Alfred Prufrock."

CUSTOMIZE INSTRUCTION
For Interpersonal Learners

As the story progresses Granny passes in and out of lucidity. When she is lucid, she feels proud and doesn't want her daughter humoring or babying her. Help students recognize that Granny is in Cornelia's home, under her care, and that Cornelia believes that her mother is neither thinking clearly nor capable of caring for herself.

❶ About the Selection

On her deathbed, between visits from her daughter, her doctor, and her priest, old Ellen Weatherall, who is referred to as "Granny," thinks back on her life as she slips in and out of consciousness. She recalls George, who left her standing at the alter on their wedding day, and John, who became her husband but died when their children were still young. She reflects with pleasure and pride on her raising of the children, but remains deeply troubled by the recollection of having been jilted sixty years earlier. Unable to come to terms with the pain of that experience and haunted by the death of her daughter, Hapsy, Ellen suddenly realizes that death has come to claim her. As she is about to die, she suffers one last jilting—her loss of faith—when God fails to provide a sign that would indicate that He is waiting for her with open arms.

❷ Literary Analysis

Stream of Consciousness

- Have students read the bracketed passage. Discuss the doctor's actions as clues to the actual events occurring in the story.

- Ask students the Literary Analysis question on p. 846: While Granny is engaged in a dialogue with the doctor, what is really happening in the room?
Answer: The doctor examines her and then departs.

---

❶ The Jilting of Granny Weatherall

Katherine Anne Porter

Background

Katherine Anne Porter's view of life and the literature she created were shaped by the universal sense of disillusionment resulting from World War I, the despair of the Great Depression, and the World War II horrors of Nazism and nuclear warfare. Sometimes, as in the novel *Ship of Fools*, Porter focused on social and political issues such as Nazism. In contrast, works like "The Jilting of Granny Weatherall" pinpointed the dissolving families and communities of the modern age.

She flicked her wrist neatly out of Doctor Harry's pudgy careful fingers and pulled the sheet up to her chin. The brat ought to be in knee breeches. Doctoring around the country with spectacles on his nose! "Get along now, take your schoolbooks and go. There's nothing wrong with me."

Doctor Harry spread a warm paw like a cushion on her forehead where the forked green vein danced and made her eyelids twitch. "Now, now, be a good girl, and we'll have you up in no time."

"That's no way to speak to a woman nearly eighty years old just because she's down. I'd have you respect your elders, young man."

"Well, Missy, excuse me," Doctor Harry patted her cheek. "But I've got to warn you, haven't I? You're a marvel, but you must be careful or you're going to be good and sorry."

"Don't tell me what I'm going to be. I'm on my feet now, morally speaking. It's Cornelia. I had to go to bed to get rid of her."

Her bones felt loose, and floated around in her skin, and Doctor Harry floated like a balloon around the foot of the bed. He floated and pulled down his waistcoat and swung his glasses on a cord. "Well, stay where you are, it certainly can't hurt you."

❷ "Get along and doctor your sick," said Granny Weatherall. "Leave a well woman alone. I'll call for you when I want you. . . . Where were you forty years ago when I pulled through milk leg[1] and double pneumonia? You weren't even born. Don't let Cornelia lead you on,"

---

1. **milk leg** painful swelling of the leg.

846 ◆ Disillusion, Defiance, and Discontent (1914–1946)

Literary Analysis
Stream of Consciousness
While Granny is engaged in a dialogue with the doctor, what is really happening in the room?

TEACHING RESOURCES

The following resources can be used to enrich or extend the instruction for pp. 846–854.

Reading

📖 **Selection Support:** Reading Strategy, p. 214;
Build Vocabulary, p. 212

🎧 **Listening to Literature Audiocassettes,**
Side 30 ■

💿 **Listening to Literature Audio CDs,** CD 17 ■.

■ **BLOCK SCHEDULING:** Resources marked with this symbol provide varied instruction during 90-minute blocks.

❸

Garden of Memories, Charles Burchfield, The Museum of Modern Art

❹ ▲ **Critical Viewing** What elements of this surreal illustration of an old woman in her "garden of memories" might represent Granny Weatherall? **[Connect]**

she shouted, because Doctor Harry appeared to float up to the ceiling and out. "I pay my own bills, and I don't throw my money away on nonsense!"

She meant to wave good-bye, but it was too much trouble. Her eyes closed of themselves, it was like a dark curtain drawn around the bed. The pillow rose and floated under her, pleasant as a hammock in a light wind. She listened to the leaves rustling outside the window.

❺

☑ **Reading Check**

Where is Granny Weatherall as she speaks to the doctor?

The Jilting of Granny Weatherall ◆ 847

❸ Background

Art

Garden of Memories by Charles Burchfield

This picture shows an old woman sitting in a nearly immobile posture. She and the buildings and landscape around her reflect the drooping apathy of extreme old age and the haunting sense of memory and emotion. The artist created this "drooping" effect with his individualistic combination of crayon and watercolor.

Use this question for discussion:

• How would you describe the mood of this piece of art? How does the mood mirror the mood of the story?
Answer: The painting is sinister and filled with strange apparitions and melancholy. Granny also feels strange, sees "apparitions" as she revisits memories, and experiences melancholy.

❹ ▶**Critical Viewing**

Answer: The old woman sunk in a chair and surrouded by apparitions might represent Granny. Also, the drooping, somewhat distorted landscape and buildings could represent Granny's experience of the world around her.

❺ ☑**Reading Check**

Answer: Granny Weatherall is in her bed.

House Calls

Prior to the 1930s, babies were almost exclusively born at home, people were treated at home, and they almost always died at home rather than in the hospital. In the course of a typical day, a general practitioner might make as many as 15 to 20 house calls, in addition to seeing patients in his or her office.

❼ Reading Strategy

Clarifying Sequence of Events

- Read aloud the bracketed passage to students, pausing slightly at "The box in the attic. . ." to suggest a possible mental bridge.

- Ask the following question: Are the images of household items memories of the past or pictures of the present? Direct students to reread the bracketed passage again before answering the question. Point out the word *afterwards* in the passage as a clue to sequence.

Answer: The images that begin the passage are memories of the past. The discussion of the boxes of letters could be past, present, or both as Granny experiences a passing moment of lucidity in which she realizes that she is dying.

No, somebody was swishing newspapers: no, Cornelia and Doctor Harry were whispering together. She leaped broad awake, thinking they whispered in her ear.

"She was never like this, never like this!" "Well, what can we expect?" "Yes, eighty years old. . . ."

Well, and what if she was? She still had ears. It was like Cornelia to whisper around doors. She always kept things secret in such a public way. She was always being tactful and kind. Cornelia was dutiful; that was the trouble with her. Dutiful and good: "So good and dutiful," said Granny, "that I'd like to spank her." She saw herself spanking Cornelia and making a fine job of it.

"What'd you say, Mother?"

Granny felt her face tying up in hard knots.

"Can't a body think, I'd like to know?"

"I thought you might want something."

"I do. I want a lot of things. First off, go away and don't whisper."

She lay and drowsed, hoping in her sleep that the children would keep out and let her rest a minute. It had been a long day. Not that she was tired. It was always pleasant to snatch a minute now and then. There was always so much to be done, let me see: tomorrow.

Tomorrow was far away and there was nothing to trouble about. Things were finished somehow when the time came; thank God there was always a little margin over for peace: then a person could spread out the plan of life and tuck in the edges orderly. It was good to have everything clean and folded away, with the hair brushes and tonic bottles sitting straight on the white embroidered linen: the day started without fuss and the pantry shelves laid out with rows of jelly glasses and brown jugs and white stone-china jars with blue whirligigs and words painted on them: coffee, tea, sugar, ginger, cinnamon, allspice: **❼** and the bronze clock with the lion on top nicely dusted off. The dust that lion could collect in twenty-four hours! The box in the attic with all those letters tied up, well, she'd have to go through that tomorrow. All those letters—George's letters and John's letters and her letters to them both—lying around for the children to find afterwards made her uneasy. Yes, that would be tomorrow's business. No use to let them know how silly she had been once.

While she was rummaging around she found death in her mind and it felt clammy and unfamiliar. She had spent so much time preparing for death there was no need for bringing it up again. Let it take care of itself now. When she was sixty she had felt very old, finished, and went around making farewell trips to see her children and grandchildren, with a secret in her mind: This is the very last of your mother, children! Then she made her will and came down with

❻ *Literature* in context History Connection

House Calls

In this story, eighty-year-old Ellen Weatherall dies at home, having been attended by the family doctor. Up until the 1930s, it was a common practice for doctors to deliver most of their services in the home. At that time, medical technology was simple enough that home treatment was as good as—or better than—treatment given in the hospital. However, after World War II, the field of medicine changed dramatically. New techniques for diagnosing and treating illness required special facilities. For example, doctors making house calls could not use X-rays or blood tests to diagnose patients, nor could they perform surgery. People went to the hospital where the resources were available, and the doctor's house call faded into memory.

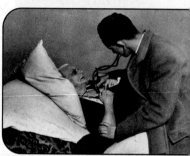

✳ ENRICHMENT: Career Connection

Gerontology

As people today live longer and longer, the care and treatment of older people and issues involving the elderly have grown in prominence. Those interested in the problems facing America's elderly population will find many career opportunities. From jobs in geriatric medicine, dentistry, psychology, social work, and physical and occupational therapy, to work in estate planning and elder law, there are many jobs geared to planning for old age and improving the circumstances of the elderly.

Invite interested students to explore career opportunities in one or more of the aforementioned fields. Ask them to do research to track the changes the field has undergone in recent years and to predict the direction in which it is going. Students can gather their information from the library, by contacting associations like the AARP, and by interviewing people working in the field.

a long fever. That was all just a notion like a lot of other things, but it was lucky too, for she had once for all got over the idea of dying for a long time. Now she couldn't be worried. She hoped she had better sense now. Her father had lived to be one hundred and two years old and had drunk a noggin of strong hot toddy on his last birthday. He told the reporters it was his daily habit, and he owed his long life to that. He had made quite a scandal and was very pleased about it. She believed she'd just plague Cornelia a little.

"Cornelia! Cornelia!" No footsteps, but a sudden hand on her cheek. "Bless you, where have you been?"

"Here, mother."

"Well, Cornelia, I want a noggin of hot toddy."

"Are you cold, darling?"

"I'm chilly, Cornelia. Lying in bed stops the circulation. I must have told you that a thousand times."

Well, she could just hear Cornelia telling her husband that Mother was getting a little childish and they'd have to humor her. The thing that most annoyed her was that Cornelia thought she was deaf, dumb, and blind. Little hasty glances and tiny gestures tossed around her and over her head saying, "Don't cross her, let her have her way, she's eighty years old," and she sitting there as if she lived in a thin glass cage. Sometimes Granny almost made up her mind to pack up and move back to her own house where nobody could remind her every minute that she was old. Wait, wait, Cornelia, till your own children whisper behind your back!

In her day she had kept a better house and had got more work done. She wasn't too old yet for Lydia to be driving eighty miles for advice when one of the children jumped the track, and Jimmy still dropped in and talked things over: "Now, Mammy, you've a good business head, I want to know what you think of this?. . . " Old. Cornelia couldn't change the furniture around without asking. Little things, little things! They had been so sweet when they were little. Granny wished the old days were back again with the children young and everything to be done over. It had been a hard pull, but not too much for her. When she thought of all the food she had cooked, and all the clothes she had cut and sewed, and all the gardens she had made—well, the children showed it. There they were, made out of her, and they couldn't get away from that. Sometimes she wanted to see John again and point to them and say, Well, I didn't do so badly, did I? But that would have to wait. That was for tomorrow. She used to think of him as a man, but now all the children were older than their father, and he would be a child beside her if she saw him now. It seemed strange and there was something wrong in the idea. Why, he couldn't possibly recognize her. She had fenced in a hundred acres once, digging the post holes herself and clamping the wires with just a negro boy to help. That changed a woman. John would be looking for a young woman with the peaked Spanish comb in her hair and the painted fan. Digging post holes changed a woman. Riding country roads in the winter when women had

Literary Analysis
Stream of Consciousness
Notice the path of Granny's thoughts. What are some topics she touches on, and how are they linked in her mind?

Reading Check
What journey did Granny Weatherall take when she was sixty years old? Why?

❽ Literary Analysis
Stream of Consciousness

- Have a volunteer read aloud the bracketed text, striving for a natural flow of thoughts.

- Ask students the Literary Analysis question on p. 849: Notice the path of Granny's thoughts. What are some topics she touches on, and how are they linked in her mind?
  Answer: Granny's thoughts run back to a time twenty years earlier when she had originally faced her mortality. Then, she thinks of her long-lived father, a hot toddy, and the annoyance of having to live with her daughter.

 Have students begin an organizer like the one shown on p. 845. As you reread the bracketed text, invite students to complete the organizer showing Granny's thoughts and the mental connecting bridges she moves across.

❾ ✔Reading Check

Answer: She thought she was dying and made farewell trips to each of her children.

CUSTOMIZE INSTRUCTION FOR UNIVERSAL ACCESS

For Less Proficient Readers	For English Learners	For Advanced Readers
Direct students to the passage at the bottom of p. 848, in which Granny recalls making a trip at age sixty. Help students understand Granny's attitude toward death. Guide them to see that she is resigned to it now, unafraid, having had the experience twenty years earlier of facing it.	Read aloud the passage at the bottom of p. 848, in which Granny recalls a trip she made at age sixty. Confirm that students understand the age "sixty." Then, clarify the meanings of the word *will*. Explain that the word *will* can refer to a document describing a person's wishes concerning the disposal of personal property after death.	Challenge students to learn about the concept of a living will, in which a person creates a will describing his or her wishes when ill or infirm. Discuss the kind of living will Granny might have created after her brush with death at age sixty. What might she instruct her children to do should she become terminally ill?

- Invite students to read the bracketed passage at least twice. Encourage them to visualize the scene Granny recalls and to share their visualizations.

- Ask students the Literary Analysis question on p. 850: What do you learn about Granny from this flashback to a time when her children were small?
  Answer: You learn that she was deeply religious, that her children trusted her, and that they lived in simple surroundings without electricity.

⑪ **Literary Analysis**

Stream of Consciousness

- Ask volunteers to read the bracketed passage.

- Discuss the Literary Analysis question on p. 850: What memory does Granny try to keep from surfacing? Why?
  Answer: She doesn't want to remember being jilted at the altar. The experience was deeply painful to her.

---

their babies was another thing: sitting up nights with sick horses and sick children and hardly ever losing one. John, I hardly ever lost one of them! John would see that in a minute, that would be something he could understand, she wouldn't have to explain anything!

It made her feel like rolling up her sleeves and putting the whole place to rights again. No matter if Cornelia was determined to be everywhere at once, there were a great many things left undone on this place. She would start tomorrow and do them. It was good to be strong enough for everything, even if all you made melted and changed and slipped under your hands, so that by the time you finished you almost forgot what you were working for. What was it I set out to do? she asked herself intently, but she could not remember. A fog rose over the valley, she saw it marching across the creek swallowing the trees and moving up the hill like an army of ghosts. Soon it would be at the near edge of the orchard, and then it was time to go in and light the lamps. Come in, children, don't stay out in the night air.

⑩ Lighting the lamps had been beautiful. The children huddled up to her and breathed like little calves waiting at the bars in the twilight. Their eyes followed the match and watched the flame rise and settle in a blue curve, then they moved away from her. The lamp was lit, they didn't have to be scared and hang on to mother any more. Never, never, never more. God, for all my life I thank Thee. Without Thee, my God, I could never have done it. Hail Mary, full of grace.

I want you to pick all the fruit this year and see that nothing is wasted. There's always someone who can use it. Don't let good things rot for want of using. You waste life when you waste good food. Don't let things get lost. It's bitter to lose things. Now, don't let me get to thinking, not when I am tired and taking a little nap before supper. . . .

The pillow rose about her shoulders and pressed against her heart and the memory was being squeezed out of it: oh, push down the pillow, somebody: it would smother her if she tried to hold it. Such a fresh breeze blowing and such a green day with no threats in it. But he had not come, just the same. What does a woman do when she has put on the white veil and set out the white cake for a man and he doesn't come? She tried to remember. No, I swear he never harmed me but in that. He never harmed me but in that . . . and what if he did? There was the day, the day, but a whirl of dark smoke rose and covered it,

⑪ crept up and over into the bright field where everything was planted so carefully in orderly rows. That was hell, she knew hell when she saw it. For sixty years she had prayed against remembering him and against losing her soul in the deep pit of hell, and now the two things were mingled in one and the thought of him was a smoky cloud from hell that moved and crept in her head when she had just got rid of Doctor Harry and was trying to rest a minute. Wounded vanity, Ellen, said a sharp voice in the top of her mind. Don't let your wounded vanity get the upper hand of you. Plenty of girls get jilted. You were jilted, weren't you? Then stand up to it. Her eyelids wavered and let in streamers of

Literary Analysis
Stream of Consciousness and Flashback What do you learn about Granny from this flashback to a time when her children were small?

Literary Analysis
Stream of Consciousness What memory does Granny try to keep from surfacing? Why?

✳ ENRICHMENT: History Connection

Rural Women

Rural women, living far from hospitals and medical doctors, often depended on the services of neighbors and midwives in delivering their babies. Students may be surprised at Granny's elation in recalling that she "hardly ever lost one" of the sick children or animals she nursed. Inform them that at that time, infant mortality rates were far higher than they are today; it was not uncommon for children to die of illnesses or diseases that are easily treated with modern medicine.

For example, once-common childhood diseases such as measles, mumps, diphtheria, and whooping cough could be deadly. Today, nearly all American children are vaccinated against these and other diseases. As a result, the incidence of some diseases—for example, polio—has been reduced to almost zero. Such advances in medical care would have made Granny Weatherall's life as a rural woman much, much easier.

blue-gray light like tissue paper over her eyes. She must get up and pull the shades down or she'd never sleep. She was in bed again and the shades were not down. How could that happen? Better turn over, hide from the light, sleeping in the light gave you nightmares. "Mother, how do you feel now?" and a stinging wetness on her forehead. But I don't like having my face washed in cold water!

Hapsy? George? Lydia? Jimmy? No, Cornelia, and her features were swollen and full of little puddles. "They're coming, darling, they'll all be here soon." Go wash your face, child, you look funny.

Instead of obeying, Cornelia knelt down and put her head on the pillow. She seemed to be talking but there was no sound. "Well, are you tongue-tied? Whose birthday is it? Are you going to give a party?"

Cornelia's mouth moved urgently in strange shapes. "Don't do that, you bother me, daughter."

"Oh, no, Mother. Oh, no. . . ."

Nonsense. It was strange about children. They disputed your every word. "No what, Cornelia?"

"Here's Doctor Harry."

"I won't see that boy again. He just left five minutes ago."

"That was this morning, Mother. It's night now. Here's the nurse."

"This is Doctor Harry, Mrs. Weatherall. I never saw you look so young and happy!"

"Ah, I'll never be young again—but I'd be happy if they'd let me lie in peace and get rested."

She thought she spoke up loudly, but no one answered. A warm weight on her forehead, a warm bracelet on her wrist, and a breeze went on whispering, trying to tell her something. A shuffle of leaves in the everlasting hand of God, He blew on them and they danced and rattled. "Mother, don't mind, we're going to give you a little hypodermic." "Look here, daughter, how do ants get in this bed? I saw sugar ants yesterday." Did you send for Hapsy too?

It was Hapsy she really wanted. She had to go a long way back through a great many rooms to find Hapsy standing with a baby on her arm. She seemed to herself to be Hapsy also, and the baby on Hapsy's arm was Hapsy and himself and herself, all at once, and there was no surprise in the meeting. Then Hapsy melted from within and turned flimsy as gray gauze and the baby was a gauzy shadow, and Hapsy came up close and said, "I thought you'd never come," and looked at her very searchingly and said, "You haven't changed a bit!" They leaned forward to kiss, when Cornelia began whispering from a long way off, "Oh, is there anything you want to tell me? Is there anything I can do for you?"

Yes, she had changed her mind after sixty years and she would like to see George. I want you to find George. Find him and be sure to tell him I forgot him. I want him to know I had my husband just the same and my children and my house like any other woman. A good house too and a good husband that I loved and fine children out of him. Better than I hoped for even. Tell him I was given back everything he took

The Jilting of Granny Weatherall ◆ 851

Literary Analysis
Stream of Consciousness
What actual events are taking place in the room, and in what ways do they affect Granny's thoughts?

13 ✓**Reading Check**
What happened to Granny sixty years ago?

---

⑫ Literary Analysis
Stream of Consciousness

- Call on a volunteer to read aloud the bracketed passage. Review where Granny is during this sequence of dialogue and description, clarifying if necessary that she is in her bed under the care of her daughter Cornelia.

- Ask students the Literary Analysis question on p. 851: What actual events are taking place in the room, and in what ways do they affect Granny's thoughts?
  Answer: Granny's daughter Cornelia is weeping and talking to her mother. Doctor Harry also returns and examines Granny. Granny's thoughts reflect the physical environment but in distorted ways.

⑬ **Reading Check**

Answer: She was jilted at the altar by George.

CUSTOMIZE INSTRUCTION FOR UNIVERSAL ACCESS

For Less Proficient Readers	For English Learners	For Advanced Readers
Make sure students recognize that Granny is drifting in and out of consciousness. Elicit from students that Granny, at the moment, is thinking way back into her past and imagining that Hapsy, her deceased daughter, is there with her now. She barely hears or recognizes Cornelia, who is caring for her.	Explain to students that when Granny recalls the time she "put on the white veil and set out the white cake" and the man didn't come, she is remembering having been jilted, or left standing at the altar, by the man she was supposed to marry.	Ask students whether they believe Granny has fully recovered from her jilting. Ask them to support their response with evidence from Granny's memories of the event sixty years past. Discuss Granny's prayers to forget that moment and her link to a hellish image of fiery smoke.

Stream of Consciousness and Flashback

- Direct students' attention to the opening phrase "Since the day the wedding cake was not cut, but thrown out and wasted." Discuss with students what this phrase refers to.

- Ask students the Literary Analysis question on p. 852: What event central to Granny's life do you learn more about in this flashback? **Answer:** Readers learn more detail about the day Granny was jilted at the altar.

---

away and more. Oh, no, oh, God, no, there was something else besides the house and the man and the children. Oh, surely they were not all? What was it? Something not given back. . . . Her breath crowded down under her ribs and grew into a monstrous frightening shape with cutting edges; it bored up into her head, and the agony was unbelievable: Yes, John, get the Doctor now, no more talk, my time has come.

When this one was born it should be the last. The last. It should have been born first, for it was the one she had truly wanted. Everything came in good time. Nothing left out, left over. She was strong, in three days she would be as well as ever. Better. A woman needed milk in her to have her full health.

"Mother, do you hear me?"

"I've been telling you—"

"Mother, Father Connolly's here."

"I went to Holy Communion only last week. Tell him I'm not so sinful as all that."

"Father just wants to speak to you."

He could speak as much as he pleased. It was like him to drop in and inquire about her soul as if it were a teething baby, and then stay on for a cup of tea and a round of cards and gossip. He always had a funny story of some sort, usually about an Irishman who made his little mistakes and confessed them, and the point lay in some absurd thing he would blurt out in the confessional showing his struggles between native <u>piety</u> and original sin. Granny felt easy about her soul. Cornelia, where are your manners? Give Father Connolly a chair. She had her secret comfortable understanding with a few favorite saints who cleared a straight road to God for her. All as surely signed and sealed as the papers for the new Forty Acres. Forever . . . heirs and assigns[2] forever. Since the day the wedding cake was not cut, but thrown out and wasted. The whole bottom dropped out of the world, and there she was blind and sweating with nothing under her feet and the walls falling away. His hand had caught her under the breast, she had not fallen, there was the freshly polished floor with the green rug on it, just as before. He had cursed like a sailor's parrot and said, "I'll kill him for you." Don't lay a hand on him, for my sake leave something to God. "Now, Ellen, you must believe what I tell you. . . ."

So there was nothing, nothing to worry about any more, except sometimes in the night one of the children screamed in a nightmare, and they both hustled out shaking and hunting for the matches and calling, "There, wait a minute, here we are!" John, get the doctor now, Hapsy's time has come. But there was Hapsy standing by the bed in a white cap. "Cornelia, tell Hapsy to take off her cap. I can't see her plain."

Her eyes opened very wide and the room stood out like a picture she had seen somewhere. Dark colors with the shadows rising towards the ceiling in long angles. The tall black dresser gleamed with nothing

---

2. **assigns** persons to whom property is transferred.

piety (pī´ ə tē) *n.* devotion to religious duties

Literary Analysis
Stream of Consciousness and Flashback What event central to Granny's life do you learn more about in this flashback?

CUSTOMIZE FOR UNIVERSAL ACCESS

For Less Proficient Readers

To reteach sequence of events, have students create timelines. Instruct them to write the events of the story on note cards or paper cut into strips. Each event should be stated in a few words. When all the events are noted, students should put the cards or paper strips in chronological order and number them. Then, organize the numbered events into a timeline.

on it but John's picture, enlarged from a little one, with John's eyes very black when they should have been blue. You never saw him, so how do you know how he looked? But the man insisted the copy was perfect, it was very rich and handsome. For a picture, yes, but it's not my husband. The table by the bed had a linen cover and a candle and a crucifix. The light was blue from Cornelia's silk lampshades. No sort of light at all, just <u>frippery</u>. You had to live forty years with kerosene lamps to appreciate honest electricity. She felt very strong and she saw Doctor Harry with a rosy nimbus around him.

"You look like a saint, Doctor Harry, and I vow that's as near as you'll ever come to it."

"She's saying something."

"I heard you, Cornelia. What's all this carrying on?"

"Father Connolly's saying—"

Cornelia's voice staggered and bumped like a cart in a bad road. It rounded corners and turned back again and arrived nowhere. Granny stepped up in the cart very lightly and reached for the reins, but a man sat beside her and she knew him by his hands, driving the cart. She did not look in his face, for she knew without seeing, but looked instead down the road where the trees leaned over and bowed to each other and a thousand birds were singing a Mass. She felt like singing too, but she put her hand in the bosom of her dress and pulled out a rosary, and Father Connolly murmured Latin in a very solemn voice and tickled her feet.[3] My God, will you stop that nonsense? I'm a married woman. What if he did run away and leave me to face the priest by myself? I found another a whole world better. I wouldn't have exchanged my husband for anybody except St. Michael[4] himself, and you may tell him that for me with a thank you in the bargain.

Light flashed on her closed eyelids, and a deep roaring shook her. Cornelia, is that lightning? I hear thunder. There's going to be a storm. Close all the windows. Call the children in. . . . "Mother, here we are, all of us." "Is that you, Hapsy?" "Oh, no, I'm Lydia. We drove as fast as we could." Their faces drifted above her, drifted away. The rosary fell out of her hands and Lydia put it back. Jimmy tried to help, their hands fumbled together, and Granny closed two fingers around Jimmy's thumb. Beads wouldn't do, it must be something alive. She was so amazed her thoughts ran round and round. So, my dear Lord, this is my death and I wasn't even thinking about it. My children have come to see me die. But I can't, it's not time. Oh, I always hated surprises. I wanted to give Cornelia the amethyst set—Cornelia, you're to have the amethyst set, but Hapsy's to wear it when she wants, and, Doctor Harry, do shut up. Nobody sent for you. Oh, my dear Lord, do wait a minute. I meant to do something about the Forty Acres, Jimmy doesn't need it and Lydia will later on, with that worthless husband of hers. I meant to finish the altar cloth and send six bottles of wine to

---

3. **murmured . . . feet** administered the last rites of the Catholic Church.
4. **St. Michael** one of the archangels.

frippery (frip´ ər ē) *n.* showy display of elegance

Literary Analysis
Stream of Consciousness
What is the connecting link between Granny's thoughts about her amethyst set, the Forty acres, and the altar cloth?

 Reading Check

What does Granny finally realize is happening to her?

The Jilting of Granny Weatherall ◆ 853

⓱ Vocabulary Development

Word Analysis: Greek Prefix *dys-*

- Draw students' attention to the word *dyspepsia* and invite a volunteer to read aloud its definition.

- Explain that the word includes the Greek prefix *dys-*, meaning "difficult" or "bad." Ask the class to brainstorm for other words beginning with this prefix. If necessary, prompt students with ideas from the dictionary. Possible answers: dysfunctional; dyslexia.

Answers for p. 854

Review and Assess

1. Students might tell Granny that her life has been a success: she married a good man and raised children of whom she is proud.

2. **(a)** Her daughter Cornelia sits with her. **(b)** Granny is largely annoyed with Cornelia.

3. **(a)** Her children are named Hapsy, Lydia, Jimmy, and Cornelia. **(b)** She longs to see Hapsy. **(c)** Hapsy is dead.

4. **(a)** Granny wants to avoid the memory of being jilted at the altar by George, but the memory eventually surfaces. **(b)** She tries to tell herself that he never meant to harm her, that jilting happens to many girls.

5. **(a)** Granny's memories of caring for her children and farm, of helping neighbors with sick children and animals, and of enduring both the jilting and her husband's early death suggest her strengths. **(b)** Granny has weathered many difficult situations during her life.

6. **(a)** She doesn't feel ready to go because she is waiting for a sign of how to face death. **(b)** As she faces death, she sees no sign from God of any welcome to the afterlife. She feels jilted by her faith as she once felt jilted by George.

7. Students should offer explanations for their answers.

⓱ Sister Borgia for her <u>dyspepsia</u>. I want to send six bottles of wine to Sister Borgia, Father Connolly, now don't let me forget.

Cornelia's voice made short turns and tilted over and crashed. "Oh, Mother, oh, Mother, oh Mother. . . ."

"I'm not going, Cornelia. I'm taken by surprise. I can't go."

You'll see Hapsy again. What about her? "I thought you'd never come." Granny made a long journey outward, looking for Hapsy. What if I don't find her? What then? Her heart sank down and down, there was no bottom to death, she couldn't come to the end of it. The blue light from Cornelia's lampshade drew into a tiny point in the center of her brain, it flickered and winked like an eye, quietly it fluttered and dwindled. Granny lay curled down within herself, amazed and watchful, staring at the point of light that was herself; her body was now only a deeper mass of shadow in an endless darkness and this darkness would curl around the light and swallow it up. God, give a sign!

For the second time there was no sign. Again no bridegroom and the priest in the house. She could not remember any other sorrow because this grief wiped them all away. Oh, no, there's nothing more cruel than this—I'll never forgive it. She stretched herself with a deep breath and blew out the light.

dyspepsia (dis pep′ she) *n.* indigestion

Review and Assess

Thinking About the Selection

1. **Respond:** If you were at Granny Weatherall's deathbed, what would you say to help comfort her?

2. **(a) Recall:** Who sits with Granny during her final hours? **(b) Analyze:** What is Granny's attitude toward this person?

3. **(a) Recall:** What are the names of Granny's children? **(b) Interpret:** Which of her children does Granny long to see? **(c) Deduce:** Why is she unable to see this child?

4. **(a) Recall:** As she drifts in and out of consciousness, what memory is "squeezed out" of Granny's heart? **(b) Interpret:** How does Granny try to talk herself out of the pain of this memory?

5. **(a) Interpret:** What memories and details suggest Granny's physical and emotional strength? **(b) Analyze:** Why might the author have chosen "Weatherall" as an appropriate surname for Granny?

6. **(a) Infer:** As she nears death, why does Granny say she "can't go"? **(b) Connect:** What is the connection between her experience of having been jilted sixty years ago and her experiences in the final paragraph?

7. **Speculate:** In what ways might this story have been different if Granny had confronted George after he jilted her?

ASSESSMENT PRACTICE: Reading Comprehension

Analyze Sentence Meaning   (For more paractice, see Test Preparation Workbook, p. 5.)

Many tests ask students to correctly answer sentence-completion questions. Often, more than one choice can complete a sentence. Use the following sample item to show students how to analyze sentence meaning, decide whether it is positive or negative, and eliminate choices that have the opposite sense.

Katherine Anne Porter's work reflects the disillusionment of the postwar era. Many of her works examine the drifting and _____ families and communities of the modern age.

    A growing   **C** reflective
    B uniting   **D** dissolving

The context clues *disillusionment* and *drifting* indicate the correct answer will have a negative connotation. *D* is the best choice.

Review and Assess

Literary Analysis

Stream of Consciousness

1. What effect does the use of **stream of consciousness** have on the reader's perceptions of Granny's children and of Doctor Harry?

2. (a) Find two points at which Granny's thoughts drift from one subject to another that is seemingly unrelated. (b) What natural associations connect her thoughts in each of these examples?

3. In what ways does the stream-of-consciousness technique allow for ambiguity—the presence of different and even conflicting meanings—for specific events or for the story as a whole?

4. Is stream of consciousness an effective technique for this story? Explain.

Connecting Literary Elements

5. (a) What details trigger Granny's **flashback** to lighting the lamps when her children were young? (b) What is the connection between this flashback and her experiences in the present?

6. Use a chart like the one shown to analyze three flashbacks in the story. Identify the form each flashback takes (dream, memory, and so on) and note what you learn about Granny's life from each one.

Form	Trigger		What we learn
		...▶	

Reading Strategy

Clarifying Sequence of Events

7. **Clarify the sequence of events** presented in this story by rearranging them in chronological order.

8. Does the jumbled sequence of events as they appear in the story create a complete picture of Granny's life? Explain.

Extend Understanding

9. **Psychology Connection:** This story was written around 1930. Do you think a young person's experience of being left at the altar would have a less profound impact on his or her life if it happened today? Explain your answer.

Quick Review

Stream of consciousness is a literary device used in a story to capture the natural flow of people's thoughts.

Flashback is an interruption in a narrative that describes an event from the past.

To **clarify the sequence of events,** reorganize events in the order in which they occurred.

 Take It to the Net
www.phschool.com
Take the interactive self-test online to check your understanding of the selection.

The Jilting of Granny Weatherall ◆ 855

✷ ENRICHMENT: Further Reading

Other Works by Katherine Anne Porter

Flowering Judas

Pale Horse, Pale Rider

The Leaning Tower

Collected Short Stories

Ship of Fools

Noon Wine

 Take It to the Net
Visit www.phschool.com for self-tests and additional questions on Katherine Anne Porter.

Answers for p. 855

Review and Assess

1. The reader learns snippets of often unrelated information about Granny's children and Doctor Harry. This information is both limited and subjective.

2. **(a and b)** Possible answer: Granny thinks of tasks to be done, and her thoughts drift to possessions, then to fears of her children reading her love letters. When the priest arrives, Granny's thoughts drift from thoughts about his personality to his need for a chair, to religious reflections. His religious affiliation spurs her thoughts about God.

3. By keeping readers' grasp of events somewhat loose, the stream-of-consciousness format invites readers to bring their own interpretations to Granny's experiences, memories and thoughts.

4. Porter's use of stream of consciousness powerfully conveys a sense of the fractured, complex, and emotional experience of death.

5. **(a)** She recalls darkness falling around the farm. **(b)** The room seems to be growing darker as Granny slips toward death.

6. Flashback: Fainting in church when George doesn't show up. Trigger: Father Connolly reminds her of being in church. Form: memory; What you learn: That Granny was deeply upset by the experience of being jilted.

7. Possible response: As a young woman, Granny is jilted by George. She later marries John and has children, one of who dies. After John dies, Granny continues to raise her children and run the household alone. At age sixty, she prepares for death and visits her children. She eventually moves into Cornelia's home, and, at age eighty, Granny dies.

8. No, it presents a picture of those moments Granny finds important as she faces death.

9. Possible response: In today's world, with marriage one of many options, jilting might be less of a social embarrassment.

Answer for p. 856

❶ Vocabulary Development

Word Analysis

Possible responses:

1. dysentery: a disturbance or disease of the intestines
2. dysfunctional: not working properly
3. dyslexia: a difficulty with words and reading
4. dyspepsia: a difficulty with digestion
5. dystopia: a place filled with difficulties

Fluency: Sentence Completion

1. piety
2. dyspepsia
3. frippery

Spelling Strategy

1. anxiety
2. illegality
3. creativity

❷ Grammar and Style

Practice

1. b
2. b
3. b
4. a
5. a

Writing Application

1. Leave a well woman alone.
2. Don't let Cornelia lead you on.
3. Let a body think.

Integrate Language Skills

❶ Vocabulary Development Lesson

Word Analysis: Greek Prefix *dys-*

The Greek prefix *dys-*, which means "difficult" or "bad," can help you unlock the meanings of many challenging words.

Write a definition of each word below by combining the meaning of the prefix *dys-* with the clues in parentheses. After you have finished, check your definitions in a dictionary and revise if necessary.

1. dysentery (*entery* = intestine)
2. dysfunctional (*functional* = working properly)
3. dyslexia (*lexis* = word or speech)
4. dyspepsia (*pepsis* = digestion)
5. dystopia (*topos* = place)

Fluency: Sentence Completions

Select the word from the vocabulary list on p. 845 that best completes each sentence.

1. Kelly showed her ___?___ by attending religious services daily.
2. "Pizza aggravates my ___?___," said Mr. Otis.
3. The skaters strutted by, displaying their ___?___ for all to admire.

Spelling Strategy

The suffixes *-ety* and *-ity* change an adjective into a noun. The suffix may be accompanied by other spelling changes as well. For example, *pious* becomes *piety*. For each word below, create a new word using the suffix *-ety* or *-ity*.

1. anxious   2. illegal   3. creative

❷ Grammar and Style Lesson

Imperative Sentences

An **imperative sentence** states a request or gives an order. The subject, *you*, is implied and thus is usually not stated. In this example, notice that the sentence contains three verbs and an implied subject:

> **Example:** "Get along now, take your schoolbooks and go." (*The subject* you *is implied.*)

Practice Review each of the following pairs of sentences. In each pair, identify which example is imperative.

1. (a) Will you get along and doctor your sick?
   (b) Get along and doctor your sick.
2. (a) I want you to stay where you are.
   (b) Stay where you are.
3. (a) They shouldn't be whispering.
   (b) Go away and don't whisper.
4. (a) Be a good girl, and you'll get well.
   (b) If you are good, you'll get well.
5. (a) Don't worry about it.
   (b) You need not worry about it.

Writing Application Rewrite these sentences to make them imperative:

1. Won't you please leave a well woman alone?
2. You shouldn't let Cornelia lead you on.
3. Can't a body think?

𝒲𝒢 *Prentice Hall Writing and Grammar Connection: Chapter 20, Section 1*

TEACHING RESOURCES

The following resources can be used to enrich or extend the instruction for pp. 856–857.

Vocabulary

📖 **Selection Support:** Build Vocabulary, p. 212

📖 **Vocabulary and Spelling Practice Book** (Use this booklet for skills enrichment.) ▪

Grammar

📖 **Selection Support:** Grammar and Style, p. 213

𝒲𝒢 **Writing and Grammar,** Ruby Level, p. 476

📖 **Daily Language Practice Transparencies** ▪

Writing

𝒲𝒢 **Writing and Grammar,** Ruby Level, p. 82

💿 **Writing and Grammar iText CD-ROM**

📖 **Writing Models and Graphic Organizers on Transparencies,** p. 67

▪ **BLOCK SCHEDULING:** Resources marked with this symbol provide varied instruction during 90-minute blocks.

Writing Lesson

Stream-of-Consciousness Monologue

A monologue is a dramatic form in which only a single character speaks. Create a character, and write a monologue. Like Katherine Anne Porter, incorporate the character's thoughts and memories in a stream-of-consciousness presentation.

Prewriting   List descriptive words and phrases you associate with your character. Group these under the headings "Actions," "Feelings," "Comments," and "Attitudes."

Drafting   Select several memories around which to organize the monologue. To heighten the stream-of-consciousness effect, write without transitions.

Model: Using Details to Create a Vivid Character

Here's the jetway, a chute, really, can't go back. *Tickets out, please!* Flying alone that night—was I nine, eleven?—daring myself to peer at the tiny lights outside the scratched plastic oval, and the awesome blackness of the lake beyond.

> The use of specific images emphasizes the character's feelings.

Revising   Read your monologue aloud to hear whether or not it sounds like a genuine and private voice. Add clues to help your audience follow the thought stream and clarify the purpose of the monologue.

 *Prentice Hall Writing and Grammar Connection: Chapter 5, Section 4*

Extension Activities

Listening and Speaking Suppose that Ellen Weatherall (Granny) and George meet ten years after the jilting. With a partner, role-play the **conversation** they have. To prepare, keep these tips in mind:

- Note details about Ellen's life and how it has changed since the jilting.
- Create a story to explain George's behavior and his life since the jilting.

As you role-play, use language to express the characters' feelings and thoughts and to reflect the time and place in which they live. **[Group Activity]**

Research and Technology Hospice care—benevolent care of terminally ill people—is a growing area of medical specialization. Using a variety of sources, including the Internet and community resources, research the growing hospice field. Use your findings to prepare an **oral report** detailing how Granny might have been cared for in a modern hospice.

 *Take It to the Net*   www.phschool.com

Go online for an additional research activity using the Internet.

The Jilting of Granny Weatherall ◆ 857

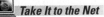
---

❸ Writing Lesson

- Review the Literary Analysis and Connecting Literary Elements instruction to help students clarify the features of stream-of-consciousness writing.

- To aid prewriting, have students use the Branching Organizier in **Writing Models and Graphic Organizers on Transparencies,** p. 67, to organize key personality traits and descriptive words and phrases for their monologues. Model how to add additional branches to the organizer if students wish.

- Read through the Writing Lesson steps with students and clarify any confusion.

- Guide students to think about whether their character might be dominated by a particular emotion. If so, urge students to choose memories that explain that emotion.

- Adapt the Short Story rubric in **Performance Assessment and Portfolio Management,** p.15 to evaluate students' monologues.

❹ Listening and Speaking

- Invite students to recap events from the story that pertain to Granny and George's relationship. Note these events on the chalkboard for all to see.

- Encourage students to determine the two characters' attitudes toward each other.

- Have students try out their explanatory stories on another team before developing the final script for their role-play.

CUSTOMIZE INSTRUCTION
For Universal Access

To address different learning styles, use the activities suggested in the **Extension Activities** booklet, p. 48.

For Verbal/Linguistic and Interpersonal Learners, use Activity 5.

For Visual/Spatial Learners, use Activity 6.

For Musical/Rhythmic and Bodily/Kinesthetic Learners, use Activity 7.

Race at Morning

Lesson Objectives

1. **To analyze and respond to literary elements**
   - Literary Analysis: Dialect
   - Connecting Literary Elements: Regionalism

   OR: Comparing Literary Works

2. **To read, comprehend, analyze, and critique a short story and a speech**
   - Reading Strategy: Break Down Long Sentences
   - Reading Check questions
   - Review and Assess questions
   - Assessment Practice (ATE)

3. **To develop word analysis skills, fluency, and systematic vocabulary**
   - Vocabulary Development Lesson: Latin Suffixes: *-ery*

4. **To understand and apply written and oral language conventions**
   - Spelling Strategy
   - Grammar and Style Lesson: Correct Use of Irregular Verb Forms

5. **To understand and apply appropriate writing and research strategies**
   - Writing Lesson: Critical Review
   - Extension Activity: Musical Research

6. **To understand and apply listening and speaking strategies**
   - Extension Activity: Broadcast

STEP-BY-STEP TEACHING GUIDE	PACING GUIDE
PRETEACH	
Motivate Students and Provide Background	
Use the Motivation activity (ATE p. 858)	5 min.
Read and discuss author and background features (SE/ATE p. 858) [A]	10 min.
Introduce the Concepts	
Introduce the Literary Analysis and Reading Strategy (SE/ATE p. 859) [A]	20 min.
Pronounce the vocabulary words and read their definitions (SE p. 859)	10 min.
TEACH	
Monitor Comprehension	
Informally monitor comprehension by circulating while students read independently or in groups [A]	70 min.
Monitor students' comprehension with the Reading Check notes (SE/ATE pp. 861–873)	as students read
Develop vocabulary with Vocabulary notes (SE pp. 861, 862, 868; ATE p. 861)	as students read
Develop Understanding	
Develop students' understanding of dialect with the Literary Analysis annotations (SE pp. 861, 863, 865, 867; ATE pp. 861, 863, 865, 867) [A]	15 min.
Develop students' ability to break down long sentences by using the Reading Strategy annotations (SE pp. 862, 868, 870; ATE pp. 862, 868, 870)	10 min.
ASSESS	
Assess Mastery	
Assess students' mastery of the Reading Strategy and Literary Analysis by having them answer the Review and Assess questions (SE/ATE p. 877)	20 min.
Use one or more of the print and media Assessment Resources (ATE p. 879) [A]	up to 45 min.
EXTEND	
Apply Understanding	
Have students complete the Vocabulary Development Lesson and the Grammar and Style Lesson (SE p. 878) [A]	20 min.
Apply students' ability to elaborate to support an argument by using the Writing Lesson (SE/ATE p. 879) [A]	45 min.
Apply students' understanding using one or more of the Extension Activities (SE p. 879)	20–90 min.

[A] ACCELERATED INSTRUCTION:
Use the strategies and activities identified with an [A].

UNIVERSAL ACCESS
- ● = Below Level Students
- ▲ = On-Level Students
- ■ = Above Level Students

Time and Resource Manager

Reading Level: Average, Easy
Average Number of Instructional Days: 6

PRINT	TRANSPARENCIES	TECHNOLOGY
• **Beyond Literature,** Workplace Skills: Finding a Balance, p. 49 ▲ ■		• **Interest Grabber Video,** Tape 5 ● ▲ ■
• **Selection Support Workbook:** ● ▲ ■ Literary Analysis, p. 219 Reading Strategy, p. 218 Build Vocabulary, p. 216	• **Literary Analysis and Reading Transparencies,** pp. 97 and 98 ● ▲ ■	
• **Adapted Reader's Companion** ● • **Reader's Companion** ●		• **Listening to Literature** ● ▲ ■ Audiocassettes, Side 31 Audio CDs, CD 17
• **English Learner's Companion** ● ▲ • **Literatura en español** ● ▲ • **Literary Analysis for Enrichment** ■		
• **Formal Assessment:** Selection Test, pp. 224–226 ● ▲ ■ • **Open Book Test,** pp. 151–153 ● ▲ ■ • **Performance Assessment and Portfolio Management,** p. 23 ● ▲ ■ **PRENTICE HALL ASSESSMENT SYSTEM** ● ▲ ■	**PRENTICE HALL ASSESSMENT SYSTEM** ● ▲ ■ Skills Practice Answers and Explanations on Transparencies	• **Test Bank Software** ● ▲ ■ • **Got It! Assessment Videotapes,** Tape 4 ● ▲
• **Selection Support Workbook:** ● ▲ ■ Build Grammar Skills, p. 217 • **Writing and Grammar,** Ruby Level ● ▲ ■ • **Extension Activities,** p. 49 ● ▲ ■	• **Daily Language Practice Transparencies** ● ▲ • **Writing Models and Graphic Organizers on Transparencies** ● ▲ ■	• **Writing and Grammar iText CD-ROM** ● ▲ ■ *Take It to the Net* www.phschool.com

BLOCK SCHEDULING: Use one 90-minute class period to preteach the selection and have students read it. Use a second 90-minute class period to assess students' mastery of skills and have them complete one of the Extension Activities.

858b

Step-by-Step Teaching Guide
for pp. 858–859

Motivation

On one side of the classroom, post a sign that says "Hunting is a worthwhile activity that serves a purpose." On the other side, post a sign that says "Hunting is wrong. Place more restrictions on it." Invite students to take one side or the other and, with their group, develop a list of points that make their case. Record their points on the chalkboard. Then, tell students that the story they are about to read focuses on a hunting trip through the bayous of Mississippi. Explain, however, that hunting is not the true focus of the story; prompt them to respond to the symbolic significance of the story as they read.

Interest Grabber Video

As an alternative, play "Rites of Passage" on Tape 5 to engage student interest.

❶ Background
More About the Author

As he notes in his Nobel Prize acceptance speech, William Faulkner felt it was his task as a writer to highlight what he called the "eternal verities." These values—love, honor, pity, pride, compassion, and sacrifice—often appeared in Faulkner's works only in contrast to dark and violent elements in society. Though he was often criticized for the violence and abnormality in his stories, Faulkner felt the contrast helped him accomplish his goal.

Prepare to Read

❶ Race at Morning ◆ Nobel Prize Acceptance Speech

William Faulkner
(1897–1962)

For some writers, the place of their roots is a wellspring of story material. Oxford, Mississippi, was such a place for William Faulkner. It became the basis for the imaginary world of Yoknapatawpha County—the setting of many of his novels and stories.

A Writer's Roots Although Faulkner never finished high school, he read a great deal and developed an interest in writing from an early age. In 1918, he enlisted in the British Royal Flying Corps and was sent to Canada for training. However, World War I ended before he had a chance to see combat, and he returned to Mississippi. A few years later, longing for a change of scene, Faulkner moved to New Orleans. There, he became friends with author Sherwood Anderson, who offered encouragement and helped get Faulkner's first novel, *Soldier's Pay*, published. In 1926, Faulkner returned home to Oxford, Mississippi, to devote himself to his writing.

A Gold Mine of Inspiration In what he called his "own little postage stamp of native soil," Faulkner uncovered a "gold mine" of inspiration. So compelling and complex was this source of inspiration that Faulkner decided to create a "cosmos of my own"—the fictional county of Yoknapatawpha. From Oxford, Faulkner wrote a series of novels about the decay of traditional values as small communities became swept up in the changes of the modern age. He saw immense dramas acted out in his small, rural town, and he used jumbled time sequences, stream-of-consciousness narration, dialect, page-long sentences, and other difficult techniques to show what he called "the human heart in conflict with itself."

A Slow Spread of Recognition For many years, Faulkner was dismissed as an eccentric—an unimportant regional writer. Gradually, however, critics began to take him seriously. Today, Faulkner is generally considered the most innovative American writer of his time.

Experimenting With Narration The novel that first earned him critical acclaim was *The Sound and the Fury* (1929), a complex book exploring the downfall of an old southern family as seen through the eyes of three brothers, one of whom suffers from severe mental retardation. A year later, Faulkner published *As I Lay Dying*, the story of a poor family's six-day journey to bury their mother. Told from fifteen different points of view and exploring people's varying perspectives of death, the novel was a masterpiece of narrative experimentation. Other innovative works followed, including *Absalom, Absalom!* (1936), which is told by four speakers offering different interpretations of events.

Hollywood Years To earn money during the 1930s and 1940s, Faulkner wrote screenplays in Hollywood. Many of the films he worked on—including *Gunga Din* (1939), *To Have and Have Not* (1945), and *The Big Sleep* (1946)—have become classics of the American cinema.

In some of Faulkner's later works, such as *The Unvanquished* (1938) and *The Hamlet* (1940), he returned to a more traditional style. Yet in these novels, Faulkner continued developing the history of Yoknapatawpha County and its people.

Despite the critical success of his fiction, Faulkner did not earn widespread public recognition until 1946, when *The Portable Faulkner* was published. Four years later, he was awarded the Nobel Prize following the publication of *Intruder in the Dust* (1948), a novel in which he confronted the issue of racism. The narrative techniques he pioneered continue to challenge and inspire writers today.

TEACHING RESOURCES

The following resources can be used to enrich or extend the instruction for pp. 858–859.

Motivation

▣ **Interest Grabber Video**, Tape 5 ▣

Background

📖 **Beyond Literature**, p. 49

💻 **Take It to the Net**
Visit www.phschool.com for Background and hotlinks for the selections.

Literary Analysis

📄 **Literary Analysis and Reading Transparencies**, Dialect, p. 98 ▣

Reading

📄 **Literary Analysis and Reading Transparencies**, Breaking Down Long Sentences, p. 97

📖 **Selection Support:** Reading Strategy, p. 218; Build Vocabulary, p. 216

■ **BLOCK SCHEDULING:** Resources marked with this symbol provide varied instruction during 90-minute blocks.

Preview

Connecting to the Literature

You may have experienced moments when you felt a bond with another person, even though few words passed between you. In this story, a boy confirms his bond to a father figure, not in words, but in an activity the two share—a hunting expedition in the bayous of rural Mississippi.

❷ Literary Analysis

Dialect

Faulkner is a master of **dialect,** a manner of speaking that is common to a particular region or group. Dialect affects pronunciation, word choice, and grammatical structure. Look at the italicized words in this example:

> It was *jest dust-dark*; I had *jest* fed the horses and *clumb* back down . . .

Jest is the way the narrator pronounces *just*. *Dust-dark* is his word for *dusk*, and *clumb* is the way he forms the past participle of *climb*. Faulkner's brilliant use of dialect helps to paint portraits of the characters and lets the reader know more about the fictional world he explores.

Comparing Literary Works

In his famous Nobel Prize acceptance speech, Faulkner voiced some of his beliefs about the importance of literature. He noted that the urgency of a story—its reason for existing—must reflect "the old universal truths . . . —love and honor and pity and pride and compassion and sacrifice." As you read "Race at Morning," think about how it mirrors the beliefs about literature Faulkner expresses in his speech.

❸ Reading Strategy

Breaking Down Long Sentences

Faulkner is famous for writing in long sentences. To meet the challenge, **break down each long sentence** into smaller units of meaning. Using the punctuation as a guide, divide the sentence into sections. Determine the meaning of each section. Then, look for transitions that show how the sections fit together. Use a chart like the one shown to help you.

Vocabulary Development

bayou (bī′ o͞o′) *n.* marshy inlet (p. 860)

distillery (di stil′ ər ē) *n.* place where alcoholic liquors are distilled (p. 861)

buck (buk) *n.* male animal, especially a male deer (p. 862)

moiling (moi′ liŋ) *v.* churning; swirling (p. 862)

switch (swich) *n.* slender, flexible twig or whip (p. 862)

scrabbling (skrab′ liŋ) *v.* scrambling (p. 866)

swag (swag) *n.* suspended cluster of branches (p. 868)

glade (glād) *n.* open space surrounded by woods (p. 868)

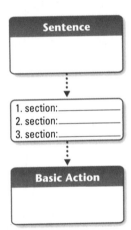

❷ Literary Analysis

Dialect

- Tell students that as they read Faulkner's story, they will focus on dialect, a manner of speaking typical of a particular region or group.

- Have a volunteer read aloud the example, using the spelling to develop pronunciation.

- After students read the instruction under Comparing Literary Works, invite their opinion on the importance of Faulkner's universal truths.

- Encourage students to work at hearing the characters' dialect as they read.

❸ Reading Strategy

Breaking Down Long Sentences

- Remind students that breaking down long sentences will help them access the meaning of Faulkner's complex writing.

- Tell students that it may be helpful to break extremely long sentences into a series of several shorter sentences.

- Draw students' attention to the graphic organizer on p. 859. Post the organizer on the board and model its use for students.

Vocabulary Development

Pronounce each vocabulary word for students, and read the definitions as a class. Have students identify any words with which they are already familiar.

CUSTOMIZE INSTRUCTION FOR UNIVERSAL ACCESS

For Less Proficient Readers	For English Learners	For Advanced Readers
Students will be challenged by Faulkner's use of dialect. Point out, however, that the dialect can help them differentiate the characters. Help students develop a list of key characters that they can refer to as they read. Encourage them to write examples of each character's dialect on the list. This will help them "hear" each character as unique.	Students learning English will find Faulkner's long sentences full of regional dialect difficult to follow. Encourage students to use context clues to figure out the meanings of expressions heavy in dialect. They may also find it helpful to read passages aloud; the pronunciation of some dialect words can provide clues to their meaning.	Once students find the rhythm of Faulkner's dialects, challenge them to develop additional dialogue for the various characters. Invite students to present their dialogue orally. Discuss the differences in dialect between the characters and ask students to suggest reasons for those variations, for example, differences in education.

 E-Teach

Visit E-Teach at www.phschool.com for teachers' essays on how to teach, with questions and answers.

CUSTOMIZE INSTRUCTION
For Visual/Spatial Learners

The story takes place in the bayou, a sluggish swampy region with which few students will be familiar. Obtain and show a geography video or sets of photos of bayou country to acquaint them with this unique environment and its inhabitants.

❶ About the Selection

Every year, Mister Ernest and his men spend two-weeks in the bayou hunting a large, elusive buck. In his distinctive Southern dialect, the narrator, a twelve-year-old boy, relates the events of the final day of hunting season, when he and Mister Ernest embark on a battle of wits with the legendary buck. When given the opportunity, Mister Ernest intentionally fails to shoot the deer, thus teaching the boy about the importance of respecting nature and valuing the possibilities of life.

❷ Background

Art

Buck and Doe Alerted
by Arthur Fitzwilliam Tait

This realistic landscape painting depicts a scene common to North American wildlife. A pair of deer have stopped in their tracks, alerted perhaps by the sound of hunters in the distance. The sense of danger is also suggested by the receding line of geese in flight. Use these questions for discussion:

1. How does the artist express his attitude toward nature in this picture?
Answer: His respect for nature is evident from the way he positions the deer in the center of the canvas and depicts them as beautiful, powerful, and vulnerable.

2. How does this attitude compare with Faulkner's attitude in the story?
Answer: Students should realize that both the artist and the author share a great respect for nature.

❶ •Race at Morning
William Faulkner

❷

Buck and Doe Alerted, Arthur Fitzwilliam Tait, Superstock

I was in the boat when I seen him. It was jest dust-dark; I had jest fed the horses and clumb back down the bank to the boat and shoved off to cross back to camp when I seen him, about half a quarter up the river, swimming; just his head above the water, and it no more than a dot in that light. But I could see that rocking chair he toted on it and I knowed it was him, going right back to that canebrake[1] in the fork of the <u>bayou</u> where he lived all year until the day before the season opened, like the game wardens had give him a calendar, when he would clear out and disappear, nobody knowed where, until the day after the season closed. But here he was, coming

1. **canebrake** *n.* area overgrown with the tall, woody reeds of cane plants.

860 ◆ *Disillusion, Defiance, and Discontent (1914–1946)*

❸ ▲ **Critical Viewing**
Compare the mood of this painting with the narrator's description of the bayou on page 862. **[Compare]**

bayou (bī′ ōō′) *n.* marshy inlet

TEACHING RESOURCES

The following resources can be used to enrich or extend the instruction for pp. 860–876.

Literary Analysis

📖 **Selection Support:** Literary Analysis, p. 219

Reading

🎧 **Listening to Literature Audiocassettes,** Side 31 ▪

💿 **Listening to Literature Audio CDs,** CD 17 ▪

▪ **BLOCK SCHEDULING:** Resources marked with this symbol provide varied instruction during 90-minute blocks.

back a day ahead of time, like maybe he had got mixed up and was using last year's calendar by mistake. Which was jest too bad for him, because me and Mister Ernest would be setting on the horse right over him when the sun rose tomorrow morning.

So I told Mister Ernest and we et supper and fed the dogs, and then I holp Mister Ernest in the poker game, standing behind his chair until about ten o'clock, when Roth Edmonds said, "Why don't you go to bed, boy?"

"Or if you're going to set up," Willy Legate said, "why don't you take a spelling book to set up over? He knows every cuss word in the dictionary, every poker hand in the deck and every whisky label in the distillery, but he can't even write his name. Can you?" he says to me.

"I don't need to write my name down," I said. "I can remember in my mind who I am."

"You're twelve years old," Walter Ewell said. "Man to man now, how many days in your life did you ever spend in school?"

"He ain't got time to go to school," Willy Legate said. "What's the use in going to school from September to middle of November, when he'll have to quit then to come in here and do Ernest's hearing for him? And what's the use in going back to school in January, when in jest eleven months it will be November fifteenth again and he'll have to start all over telling Ernest which way the dogs went?"

"Well, stop looking into my hand, anyway," Roth Edmonds said.

"What's that? What's that?" Mister Ernest said. He wore his listening button in his ear all the time, but he never brought the battery to camp with him because the cord would bound to get snagged ever time we run through a thicket.

"Willy says for me to go to bed!" I hollered.

"Don't you never call nobody 'mister'?" Willy said.

"I call Mister Ernest 'mister.'" I said.

"All right," Mister Ernest said. "Go to bed then. I don't need you."

"That ain't no lie," Willy said. "Deaf or no deaf, he can hear a fifty-dollar raise if you don't even move your lips."

So I went to bed, and after a while Mister Ernest come in and I wanted to tell him again how big them horns looked even half a quarter away in the river. Only I would 'a' had to holler, and the only time Mister Ernest agreed he couldn't hear was when we would be setting on Dan, waiting for me to point which way the dogs was going. So we jest laid down, and it wasn't no time Simon was beating the bottom of the dishpan with the spoon, hollering, "Raise up and get your four o'clock coffee!" and I crossed the river in the dark this time, with the lantern, and fed Dan and Roth Edmondziz horse. It was going to be a fine day, cold and bright; even in the dark I could see the white frost on the leaves and bushes—jest exactly the kind of day that big old son of a gun laying up there in that brake would like to run.

Then we et, and set the stand-holder across for Uncle Ike McCaslin to put them on the stands where he thought they ought to be, because he was the oldest one in camp. He had been hunting deer in these

Race at Morning ◆ 861

Literary Analysis
Dialect What can you infer are the meanings of *jest* and *setting on*?

distillery (di stil´ ə rē) *n.* place where alcoholic liquors are distilled

6 ☑ **Reading Check**
Whom or what does the narrator see from the boat?

---

3 ▶ **Critical Viewing**
Answer: Students may say that both the painting and the description convey the uneasiness and excitement that would precede a hunt.

4 **Literary Analysis**
Dialect
- Have a volunteer read the bracketed sentence aloud. Correct pronunciation if necessary until the class hears the dialect as written.
- Ask students the Literary Analysis question on p. 861: What can you infer are the meanings of *jest* and *setting on*?
  Answer: *Jest* means "just" and *setting on* meaning "sitting on."

▶ Monitor Progress Have students paraphrase the sentence in their own words.
  Answer: It was too bad for the buck that he was still in view, because the speaker and Mister Ernest will be hunting for him the next day.

5 **Vocabulary Development**
The Latin Suffix -ery
- Have students read the bracketed sentence. Point out the word *distillery*.
- Invite a volunteer to read aloud the definition of *distillery*. Explain that the Latin suffix *-ery* means "a place of" in this context. It can also mean "a state of." Discuss what *distill* means and help students build a definition from the two word parts.
- Cite additional examples such as *bravery* and *hatchery*. Ask students to use their understanding of *-ery* to define these words as well.

6 ☑ **Reading Check**
Answer: He sees the buck that everyone wants to hunt down.

CUSTOMIZE INSTRUCTION FOR UNIVERSAL ACCESS

For Special Needs Students	For Less Proficient Readers	For English Learners
Help students clarify who is who in the story. Ask them to identify the men in the group on p. 861. Explain that Mister Ernest is the leader of the group, and that the boy is in his charge. Help students infer that the others—Willy, Walter, and Roth—are men who know or may work for Mister Ernest.	To help readers keep track of who's who in the story, review and discuss the character list they began earlier. Guide students to understand, for example, that Dan is a horse. Point out that later they will meet Eagle, who is a dog. Encourage students to reread passages as needed to digest this dense story.	Explain that some of Faulker's characters remain unnamed. For example, guide students to see that the *him* that the boy refers to in the opening paragraph is the buck the hunters are after. What the boy refers to as "the rocking chair he toted" is the buck's impressive rack of antlers.

- Read aloud the bracketed sentence to students very slowly, working to create meaningful sections with your pacing.

- Then, recreate the organizer from p. 859 on the chalkboard and work with the class to respond to the Reading Strategy prompt on p. 863: Break down the long sentence beginning "Because me and Mister Ernest," into sections to clarify the action.

  Answer: Students should suggest breaks that reflect the punctuation. The sentence action describes the deer hiding on an island to wait for other prey to draw the dogs away from him. Here is a suggested breakdown:

1. Because me and Mister Ernest knowed exactly where he would be—

2. a little canebrake island in the middle of the bayou where he could lay up until whatever doe or little deer the dogs had happened to jump could go up or down the bayou in either direction and take the dogs on away

3. so he could steal out and creep back down the bayou to the river and swim it

4. and leave the country like he always done the day the season opened.

---

woods for about a hundred years, I reckon, and if anybody would know where a <u>buck</u> would pass, it would be him. Maybe with a big old buck like this one, that had been running the woods for what would amount to a hundred years in a deer's life, too, him and Uncle Ike would sholy manage to be at the same place at the same time this morning—provided, of course, he managed to git away from me and Mister Ernest on the jump. Because me and Mister Ernest was going to git him.

Then me and Mister Ernest and Roth Edmonds sent the dogs over, with Simon holding Eagle and the other old dogs on leash because the young ones, the puppies, wasn't going nowhere until Eagle let him, nohow. Then me and Mister Ernest and Roth saddled up, and Mr. Ernest got up and I handed him up his pump gun and let Dan's bridle[2] go for him to git rid of the spell of bucking he had to git shut of ever morning until Mister Ernest hit him between the ears with a gun barrel. Then Mister Ernest loaded the gun and give me the stirrup,[3] and I got up behind him and we taken the fire road up toward the bayou, the four big dogs dragging Simon along in front with his single-barrel britch-loader slung on a piece of plow line across his back, and the puppies <u>moiling</u> along in ever'body's way. It was light now and it was going to be jest fine; the east already yellow for the sun and our breaths smoking in the cold still bright air until the sun would come up and warm it, and a little skim of ice in the ruts, and ever leaf and twig and <u>switch</u> and even the frozen clods frosted over, waiting to sparkle like a rainbow when the sun finally come up and hit them. Until all my insides felt light and strong as a balloon, full of that light cold strong air, so that it seemed to me like I couldn't even feel the horse's back I was straddle of—jest the hot strong muscles moving under the hot strong skin, setting up there without no wait atall, so that when old Eagle struck and jumped, me and Dan and Mister Ernest would go jest like a bird, not even touching the ground. It was jest fine. When that big old buck got killed today, I knowed that even if he had put it off another ten years, he couldn't 'a' picked a better one.

And sho enough, as soon as we come to the bayou we seen his foot in the mud where he had come up out of the river last night, spread in the soft mud like a cow's foot, big as a cow's, big as a mule's, with Eagle and the other dogs laying into the leash rope now until Mister Ernest told me to jump down and help Simon hold them. Because me and Mister Ernest knowed exactly where he would be—a little canebrake island in the middle of the bayou, where he could lay up until whatever doe or little deer the dogs had happened to jump could go up or down the bayou in either direction and take the dogs on away, so he could steal out and creep back down the bayou to the river and swim it, and leave the country like he always done the day the season opened.

Which is jest what we never aimed for him to do this time. So we left Roth on his horse to cut him off and turn him over Uncle Ike's

---

2. bridle *n.* headgear with which a horse is guided.

3. stirrup *n.* rings or other devices attached to the saddle of a horse and used to support the rider's feet.

buck (buk) *n.* male animal, especially a male deer

moiling (moil´ in) *v.* churning; swirling

switch (swich) *n.* slender, flexible twig or whip

Reading Strategy
Breaking Down Long Sentences Break down the long sentence beginning "Because me and Mister Ernest," into sections to clarify the action.

✹ ENRICHMENT: Cultural Connection

Deer as Symbols

Many Native American peoples use the deer as a symbolic figure in their dance rituals and ceremonies. To gain power over the deer before a hunt, the Yaqui perform a deer dance at fiestas. The footwork, postures, and gestures of the dance are meant to represent the deer's behavior during the hunt. While this ceremony is performed as a solo dance, the deer dance in San Juan, Puerto Rico, is performed by eighteen men, fourteen of whom run away at the end of the dance, leaving four to be symbolically hunted and killed. For many nations, such as the Hopi, the deer dance is performed to help bring rain and to promote abundant harvests.

Among the Zuni, the deer dance is performed to help cure sickness. During the performance, dancers use actual parts or symbolic representations of parts of a deer, such as antlers, hoofs, and hide.

standers if he tried to slip back down the bayou, and me and Simon, with the leashed dogs, walked on up the bayou until Mister Ernest on the horse said it was fur enough; then turned up into the woods about half a quarter above the brake because the wind was going to be south this morning when it riz, and turned down toward the brake, and Mister Ernest give the word to cast them,[4] and we slipped the leash and Mr. Ernest give me the stirrup again and I got up.

Old Eagle had done already took off because he knowed where that old son of a gun would be laying as good as we did, not making no racket atall yet, but jest boring on through the buck vines with the other dogs trailing along behind him, and even Dan seemed to know about that buck, too, beginning to souple up and jump a little through the vines, so that I taken my holt in Mister Ernest's belt already before the time had come for Mister Ernest to touch him. Because when we got strung out, going fast behind a deer, I wasn't on Dan's back much of the time nohow, but mostly jest strung out from my holt on Mister Ernest's belt, so that Willy Legate said that when we was going through the woods fast, it looked like Mister Ernest had a boy-size pair of empty overalls blowing out of his hind pocket.

So it wasn't even a strike, it was a jump. Eagle must 'a' walked right up behind him or maybe even stepped on him while he was laying there still thinking it was day after tomorrow. Eagle jest threw his head back and up and said, "There he goes," and we even heard the buck crashing through the first of the cane. Then all the other dogs was hollering behind him, and Dan give a squat to jump, but it was against the curb[5] this time, not jest the snaffle,[6] and Mister Ernest let him down into the bayou and swung him around the brake and up the other bank. Only he never had to say, "Which way?" because I was already pointing past his shoulder, freshening my holt on the belt jest as Mister Ernest touched Dan with that big old rusty spur on his nigh heel, because when Dan felt it he would go off jest like a stick of dynamite, straight through whatever he could bust and over and under what he couldn't, over it like a bird or under it crawling on his knees like a mole or a big coon, with Mister Ernest still on him because he had the saddle to hold on to, and me still there because I had Mister Ernest to hold on to; me and Mister Ernest not riding him, but jest going along with him, provided we held on. Because when the jump come, Dan never cared who else was there neither; I believe to my soul he could 'a' cast and run them dogs by hisself, without me or Mister Ernest or Simon or nobody.

That's what he done. He had to; the dogs was already almost out of hearing. Eagle must 'a' been looking right up that big son of a gun's

---

4. **cast them** send them ranging overland in search of a trail.
5. **curb** *n.* chain or strap used to restrain a horse.
6. **snaffle** *n.* the part of a bridle that is inserted into the mouth of a horse.

Literary Analysis
Dialect In the phrase "beginning to souple up," which word shows the speaker is using dialect? What does the word mean in Standard English?

9 ✓**Reading Check**
What do the hunters notice in the mud of the bayou?

❽ Literary Analysis
Dialect
- Have students read the bracketed passage. Ask them to identify any unfamiliar words. *(souple)*
- Direct students to answer the Literary Analysis question on p. 863: In the phrase "beginning to souple up," which word shows the speaker is using dialect? What does the word mean in Standard English?
  Answer: The word *souple* indicates dialect. It means "to get excited" or "revved up."
▶ Monitor Progress Have students restate the phrase in their own words. Urge them to use surrounding context clues to aid their inference.
  Answer: Students should grasp the essential meaning that Dan is excited.

❾ ✓**Reading Check**
Answer: They see a footprint left by the buck they are hunting.

CUSTOMIZE INSTRUCTION FOR UNIVERSAL ACCESS

For Special Needs Students	For English Learners	For Advanced Readers
It may help students understand the story's events if they picture them visually. Explain, for example, that as Dan, the horse, starts to gallop, the boy, who sits behind Mister Ernest, is hanging on to the man's belt for dear life. He is practically lifted off the horse's back. Students may enjoy sketching their vision of this image.	Tell students that in dialect, familiar words may be used in unfamiliar ways. For example, you might point out that in the boy's hunting community, the word *standers* refers to members of the hunting party who do not participate in the chase. Instead, they wait in readiness for game to be driven within shooting range.	Guide students to note that the ride through the bayou is filled with references that reflect the Mississippi bayou setting: the mud, the canebreak island, the deer's escape route from bayou to river. As students read, have them consider how the "race" might have been different had it taken place in another part of the country.

⑩ Background

Art

Winter in Southern Louisiana
by Ellsworth Woodward

This colorful landscape depicts a serene, still, bayou scene. The long shadows and silhouetted trees in the background suggest that it is either early morning or late afternoon. The painting shows the bayou to consist of water, low-lying land, and towering trees that provide little shade. It is early winter, judging by the shades of red, yellow, brown, and orange in the foliage. Use these questions for discussion:

1. How does this painting illustrate some of the difficulties deer hunters might face in the bayou?
   Answer: The painting shows dense, high brush; mucky, watery areas; straggling branches; and limited visibility.

2. How would you describe the mood created by such a setting? Is this mood reflected in the story?
   Answer: The bayou has an eerie, mystical, or even forbidding feel to it. The story shares some of that mood, but the boy is so comfortable in the bayou that it seems less forbidding than in the picture.

⑪ ▶ Critical Viewing

Answer: Students may respond that the bayou is more dense, watery, and impenetrable than they had imagined. The painting can also help students appreciate the eerie beauty of such a setting.

---

⑩ tail until he finally decided he better git on out of there. And now they must 'a' been getting pretty close to Uncle Ike's standers, and Mister Ernest reined Dan back and held him, squatting and bouncing and trembling like a mule having his tail roached,[7] while we listened for the shots. But never none come, and I hollered to Mister Ernest we better go on while I could still hear the dogs, and he let Dan off, but still there wasn't no shots, and now we knowed the race had done already passed the standers, like that old son of a gun actually was a hant,[8] like Simon and the other field hands said he was, and we busted out of a thicket, and sho enough there was Uncle Ike and Willy standing beside his foot in a soft patch.

"He got through us all," Uncle Ike said. "I don't know how he done it. I just had a glimpse of him. He looked big as a elephant, with a rack on his head you could cradle a yellin' calf in. He went right on down the ridge. You better get on, too; that Hog Bayou camp might not miss him."

So I freshened my holt and Mister Ernest touched Dan again. The ridge run due south; it was clear of vines and bushes so we could go fast, into the wind, too, because it had riz now, and now the sun was up, too; though I hadn't had time to notice it, bright and strong and level through the woods, shining and sparkling like a rainbow on the frosted leaves. So we would hear the dogs again any time now as the wind got up; we could make time now, but still holding Dan back to a canter,[9] because it was either going to be quick, when he got down to the standers from that Hog Bayou camp eight

Winter in Southern Louisiana, Ellsworth Woodward, Mississippi Museum of Art

⑪ ▲ Critical Viewing
In what ways does this painting add to your appreciation of the story's bayou setting? [Connect]

---

7. **roached** *v.* cut so that the remainder stands upright, as with an animal's mane.
8. **hant** *n.* ghost.
9. **canter** *n.* three-beat gait resembling, but smoother and slower than, a gallop.

CUSTOMIZE INSTRUCTION FOR UNIVERSAL ACCESS

For Advanced Readers

The critic Irving Howe commented on William Faulkner's work: " . . . At a time when men in mass society often believe that their possibilities are shrinking, Faulkner insists upon the largeness of human possibility. He returned to traditional dramatic gestures; he reasserted the claims of uncompromising tragedy, extreme melodrama, wild comedy. The force of human desire breaks through in his novels with a grandeur and terror that are almost unequaled in our time. Indeed, it is this readiness for confronting the largest ranges of experience which helps explain the hold Faulkner has won upon modern readers . . . "

Read aloud Howe's critique and ask students to paraphrase it. Then, have students discuss these questions:

1. How does Faulkner express the force of human desire in *Race at Morning*?

2. Do you agree that the experience described in this story will hold interest for modern readers? Why or why not?

miles below ourn, or a long time, in case he got by them, too. And sho enough, after a while we heard the dogs; we was walking Dan now to let him blow a while, and we heard them, the sound coming faint up the wind, not running now, but trailing because the big son of a gun had decided a good piece back, probably, to put a end to this foolishness, and picked hisself up and soupled out and put about a mile between hisself and the dogs—until he run up on them other standers from that camp below. I could almost see him stopped behind a bush, peeping out and saying, "What's this? What's this? Is this whole durn country full of folks this morning?" Then looking back over his shoulder at where old Eagle and others was hollering along after him while he decided how much time he had to decide what to do next.

Except he almost shaved it too fine. We heard the shots; it sounded like a war. Old Eagle must 'a' been looking right up his tail again and he had to bust on through the best way he could. "Pow, pow, pow, pow" and then "Pow, pow, pow, pow," like it must 'a' been three or four ganged right up on him before he had time even to swerve, and me hollering, "No! No! No! No!" because he was ourn. It was our beans and oats he et and our brake he laid in; we had been watching him every year, and it was like we had raised him, to be killed at last on our jump, in front of our dogs, by some strangers that would probably try to beat the dogs off and drag him away before we could even git a piece of the meat.

"Shut up and listen," Mister Ernest said. So I done it and we could hear the dogs; not just the others, but Eagle, too, not trailing no scent now and not baying[10] no downed meat neither, but running hot on sight long after the shooting was over. I jest had time to freshen my holt. Yes, sir, they was running on sight. Like Willy Legate would say, if Eagle jest had a drink of whisky he would ketch that deer; going on, done already gone when we broke out of the thicket and seen the fellers that had done the shooting, five or six of them, squatting and crawling around, looking at the ground and the bushes, like maybe if they looked hard enough, spots of blood would bloom out on the stalks and leaves like frogstools or hawberries, with old Eagle still in hearing and still telling them that what blood they found wasn't coming out of nothing in front of him.

"Have any luck, boys?" Mister Ernest said.

"I think I hit him," one of them said. "I know I did. We're hunting blood now."

"Well, when you find him, blow your horn and I'll come back and tote him in to camp for you," Mister Ernest said.

So we went on, going fast now because the race was almost out of hearing again, going fast, too, like not jest the buck, but the dogs, too, had took a new leash on life from all the excitement and shooting.

---

10. **baying** *v.* barking with long, deep tones.

Literary Analysis
Dialect What elements of dialect do you find in this description of the hunt?

Reading Check
What are the second group of hunters searching for "on the stalks and leaves"?

Literary Analysis

Dialect

- Read aloud the bracketed passage to students, lending as much authenticity to the dialect as possible. Have students identify words that are not Standard English. Encourage them to consider these words when answering the Literary Analysis question that follows.
  Possible answers: "sho enough," "was walking," "faint up the wind," "good piece back," "hisself," "soupled out," "durn."

- Ask students the Literary Analysis question on p. 865: What elements of dialect do you find in this description of the hunt?
  Answer: Students may cite any of the words listed above, but may also comment on phrases such as "let him blow awhile," which while not strictly dialect are particular to riding communities.

Reading Check

Answer: They are looking for spots of blood that would suggest the deer had been hit.

CUSTOMIZE INSTRUCTION FOR UNIVERSAL ACCESS

For Less Proficient Readers	For English Learners	For Gifted/Talented Students
Guide students to understand that another group of hunters has spotted the buck and is firing at it. The boy is outraged because he believes that the prize belongs to his group alone.	To help students follow the plot, suggest that they work in pairs to summarize and discuss any questions. Encourage them to describe the events to date. Explain to students that discussing their summaries will help them clarify information, answer questions, and focus on the main ideas.	Invite students to explore the dramatic tension of the scene in which the second group of hunters arrives. To help them structure their exploration, have students begin the Listening and Speaking Activity on p. 879. Ask students to share their broadcast of this scene. Urge them to include the boy's reactions, perhaps through an interview.

⓮ Background

A Guide to Yoknapatawpha County

Perhaps one reason Faulkner could make his fictional county so detailed and rich is that its real-life model also had many layers and facets. Oxford, Mississippi, in Lafayette County, housed the state's university along with the county's government. Residents could also watch important trials in the federal district court located there. In addition, Faulkner's own family had a colorful history. For example, his great grand father— considered by some critics to be the model for Faulkner's character John Sartoris—was twice accused of murder.

We was in strange country now because we never had to run this fur before, we had always killed before now; now we had come to Hog Bayou that runs into the river a good fifteen miles below our camp. It had water in it, not to mention a mess of down trees and logs and such, and Mister Ernest checked Dan again, saying, "Which way?" I could just barely hear them, off to the east a little, like the old son of a gun had give up the idea of Vicksburg or New Orleans, like he first seemed to have, and had decided to have a look at Alabama, maybe, since he was already up and moving; so I pointed and we turned up the bayou hunting for a crossing, and maybe we could 'a' found one, except that I reckon Mister Ernest decided we never had time to wait.

We come to a place where the bayou had narrowed down to about twelve or fifteen feet, and Mister Ernest said, "Look out, I'm going to touch him," and done it; I didn't even have time to freshen my holt when we was already in the air, and then I seen the vine—it was a loop of grapevine nigh as big as my wrist, looping down right across the middle of the bayou—and I thought he seen it, too, and was jest waiting to grab it and fling it over our heads to go under it, and I know Dan seen it because he even ducked his head to jump under it. But Mister Ernest never seen it atall until it skun back along Dan's neck and hooked under the head of the saddle horn,[11] us flying on through the air, the loop of the vine gitting tighter and tighter until something somewhere was going to have to give. It was the saddle girth. It broke, and Dan going on and <u>scrabbling</u> up the other bank bare nekkid except for the bridle, and me and Mister Ernest and the saddle, Mister Ernest still setting in the saddle holding the gun, and me still holding onto Mister Ernest's belt, hanging in the air over the bayou in the tightened loop of that vine like in the drawed-back loop of a big rubber-banded slingshot, until it snapped back and shot across the bayou and flang us clear, me still holding onto Mister Ernest's belt and on the bottom now, so that when we lit I would 'a' had Mister Ernest and the saddle both on top of me if I hadn't clumb fast around the saddle and up Mister Ernest's side, so that when we landed, it was the saddle first, then Mister Ernest, and me on top, until I jumped up, and Mister Ernest still laying there with jest the white rim of his eyes showing.

"Mister Ernest!" I hollered, and then clumb down to the bayou and scooped my cap full of water and clumb back and throwed it in his face, and he opened his eyes and laid there on the saddle cussing me.

"God dawg it," he said, "why didn't you stay behind where you started out?"

---

11. **saddle horn** *n.* knob at the front and top of a saddle.

866 ◆ *Disillusion, Defiance, and Discontent (1914–1946)*

𝓛iterature in context Literature Connection

⓮ *A Guide to Yoknapatawpha County*

This story, like most of William Faulkner's work, is set in or near the fictional county of Yoknapatawpha (Yok´ nuh puh TAW´ fuh). Using his real home of Lafayette County as a pattern, Faulkner created an amazingly detailed world—one that was as precise in its geography, history, characters, and language as any real place. In his 1936 novel *Absalom, Absalom!*, Faulkner included a map of Yoknapatawpha county (detail shown below) that he had drawn and annotated. In the map's key, he included information about the county's geographical size (2,400 square miles) and its population (Total: 15,611; Whites, 6298; Negroes, 9313). He also signed the map "William Faulkner, Sole Owner & Proprietor." According to Faulkner, the name Yoknapatawpha is derived from two Chickasaw words, yocona and petopha, and means "water flowing slow through the flatland."

scrabbling (skrab´ lin) *v.* scrambling

✷ ENRICHMENT: Culture Connection

Hunting

Faulkner's story focuses on hunting—an activity that is part of the heritage of all cultures. While farming has been practiced for about one percent of human history, hunting was humankind's occupation for more than half a million years. Anthropologists believe that hunting may have encouraged the development of many traits common to human beings in modern society, including cooperation, organization, and aggression.

There are few hunting and gathering societies left in the world. The only people who still exist solely by hunting are the Mbuti Pygmies of the Central African rain forest and the disappearing Bushmen of the Kalahari in Southern Africa. Societies that combine hunting with other means of sustenance include the Eskimos, the Pacific Northwest Indians, some Plains Indians, the Siriono Indians of Bolivia, and the Aborigines of Australia.

"You was the biggest!" I said. "You would 'a' mashed me flat!"

"What do you think you done to me?" Mister Ernest said. "Next time, if you can't stay where you start out, jump clear. Don't climb on top of me no more. You hear?"

"Yes, sir," I said.

So he got up then, still cussing and holding his back, and clumb down to the water and dipped some in his hand onto his face and neck and dipped some more up and drunk it, and I drunk some, too, and clumb back and got the saddle and the gun, and we crossed the bayou on the down logs. If we could jest ketch Dan; not that he would have went them fifteen miles back to camp, because, if anything, he would have went on by hisself to try to help Eagle ketch that buck. But he was about fifty yards away, eating buck vines, so I brought him back, and we taken Mister Ernest's galluses[12] and my belt and tied the saddle back on Dan. It didn't look like much, but maybe it would hold.

"Provided you don't let me jump him through no more grapevines without hollering first," Mister Ernest said.

"Yes, sir," I said. "I'll holler first next time—provided you'll holler a little quicker when you touch him next time, too." But it was all right; we jest had to be a little easy getting up. "Now which-a-way?" I said. Because we couldn't hear nothing now, after wasting all this time. And this was new country, sho enough. It had been cut over and growed up in thickets we couldn't 'a' seen over even standing up on Dan.

But Mister Ernest never even answered. He jest turned Dan along the bank of the bayou where it was a little more open and we could move faster again, soon as Dan and us got used to that homemade cinch strop[13] and got a little confidence in it. Which jest happened to be east, or so I thought then, because I never paid no particular attention to east then because the sun—I don't know where the morning had went, but it was gone, the morning and the frost, too—was up high now, even if my insides had told me it was past dinnertime.

And then we heard him. No, that's wrong; what we heard was shots. And that was when we realized how fur he had come, because the only camp we knowed about in that direction was the Hollyknowe camp, and Hollyknowe was exactly twenty-eight miles from Van Dorn, where me and Mister Ernest lived—jest the shots, no dogs nor nothing. If old Eagle was still behind him and the buck was still alive, he was too wore out now to even say, "Here he comes."

"Don't touch him!" I hollered. But Mister Ernest remembered that cinch strop, too, and he jest let Dan off the snaffle. And Dan heard them shots, too; picking his way through the thickets, hopping the vines and logs when he could and going under them when he couldn't. And sho enough, it was jest like before—two or three men squatting

---

12. **galluses** *n.* suspenders.
13. **cinch strop** *n.* strap that encircles the body of an animal and is used to fasten something on its back.

Literary Analysis
Dialect How would you restate the passage beginning "If we could jest ketch Dan" in Standard English?

 Reading Check
What happens to Mister Ernest when Dan hits the grapevine?

Race at Morning ◆ 867

15 **Literary Analysis**

Dialect

- Ask a volunteer to read aloud the bracketed passage. Invite students to make note of unfamiliar words.

- Have students suggest words from the passage that they think are examples of dialect. Write these on the chalkboard.
  Answer: Students may note "jest ketch," "hisself," and "galluses."

- Ask students the Literary Analysis question on p. 867: How would you restate the passage beginning "If we could jest ketch Dan" in Standard English?
  Possible response: We need to catch Dan, though he's probably nearby. He would try to help Eagle instead of going all the way back to camp. He was about fifty yards away, eating buck vines. We brought him back and used Mister Ernest's suspenders and my belt to tie the saddle onto Dan. It was makeshift, but maybe it would work.

16 ✔ **Reading Check**

Answer: He gets thrown from the horse and knocked unconscious by the fall.

CUSTOMIZE INSTRUCTION FOR UNIVERSAL ACCESS

For Less Proficient Readers	For English Learners	For Gifted/Talented Students
Play Audiocassette 31 or Audio CD 17 on **Listening to Literature** for students. Tell students that listening to the story on tape may enhance their comprehension or help them appreciate the vitality, richness, and humor of Faulkner's prose.	Obtain images of a typical saddle and bridle combination. As students listen to the grapevine scene read aloud on **Listening to Literature,** Audiocassette 31 or Audio CD 17, use the images to clarify the series of mishaps that occurs.	After students listen to text on pp. 866–867 on **Listening to Literature,** Audiocassette 31 or Audio CD 17, offer the following challenge. Ask students to write what happened in this part of the story from the buck's point of view. Suggest that they write about what he saw, what he would say to Mister Ernest and the boy, and how he feels about thus far escaping death.

867

- To help students' comprehension, slowly read aloud the bracketed passage. Emphasize the punctuation to help students hear the many separate thoughts.

- Discuss with students the action in the story up to this point and how the participants, both human and animal, might feel. **Possible answer:** Both men and animals might feel tired but exhilarated.

- Ask students the Reading Strategy question on p. 868: Why do you think Faulkner chose to combine all of this information into one long sentence beginning "There wasn't no sound"? **Possible answer:** The long sentence suggests the length of the trek home. It also shows how all the participants belong together, even though they have been at odds during the hunt.

and creeping among the bushes, looking for blood that Eagle had done already told them wasn't there. But we never stopped this time, jest trotting on by with Dan hopping and dodging among the brush and vines dainty as a dancer. Then Mister Ernest swung Dan until we was going due north.

"Wait!" I hollered. "Not this way."

But Mister Ernest jest turned his face back over his shoulder. It looked tired, too, and there was a smear of mud on it where that ere grapevine had snatched him off the horse.

"Don't you know where he's heading?" he said. "He's done done his part, give everybody a fair open shot at him, and now he's going home, back to that brake in our bayou. He ought to make it exactly at dark."

And that's what he was doing. We went on. It didn't matter to hurry now. There wasn't no sound nowhere; it was that time in the early afternoon in November when don't nothing move or cry, not even birds, the peckerwoods and yellowhammers and jays, and it seemed to me like I could see all three of us—me and Mister Ernest and Dan—and Eagle, and the other dogs, and that big old buck, moving through the quiet woods in the same direction, headed for the same place, not running now but walking, that had all run the fine race the best we knowed how, and all three of us now turned like on a agreement to walk back home, not together in a bunch because we didn't want to worry or tempt one another, because what we had all three spent this ⓱ morning doing was no playacting jest for fun, but was serious, and all three of us was still what we was—that old buck that had to run, not because he was skeered, but because running was what he done the best and was proudest at; and Eagle and the dogs that chased him, not because they hated or feared him, but because that was the thing they done the best and was proudest at; and me and Mister Ernest and Dan, that run him not because we wanted his meat, which would be too tough to eat anyhow, or his head to hang on a wall, but because now we could go back and work hard for eleven months making a crop, so we would have the right to come back here next November—all three of us going back home now, peaceful and separate, but still side by side, until next year, next time.

Then we seen him for the first time. We was out of the cut-over now; we could even 'a' cantered, except that all three of us was long past that, and now you could tell where west was because the sun was already half-way down it. So we was walking, too, when we come on the dogs—the puppies and one of the old ones—played out, laying in a little wet <u>swag</u>, panting, jest looking up at us when we passed, but not moving when we went on. Then we come to a long open <u>glade</u>, you could see about half a quarter, and we seen the three other old dogs and about a hundred yards ahead of them Eagle, all walking, not making no sound; and then suddenly, at the fur end of the glade, the buck hisself getting up from where he had been resting for the dogs to come up, getting up without no hurry, big, big as a mule, tall as a

Reading Strategy
Breaking Down Long Sentences Why do you think Faulkner chose to combine all of this information into one long sentence beginning "There wasn't no sound"?

swag (swag) *n.* suspended cluster of branches

glade (glād) *n.* open space surrounded by woods

⚙ ENRICHMENT: Community Connection

Hunting Season

The characters in this story wait all year for the opening day of deer-hunting season. Explain to students that states carefully regulate when, where, and for how long particular animals can be hunted or fish caught. Have them imagine what it would be like for casual hikers and campers if hunting was permitted year round! Point out that regulations also require most people to obtain licenses before they may hunt or fish. Hunters sometimes also wear special clothing to make sure other hunters can see them.

Have students discuss the reasons for allowing the shooting of certain animals and for limiting hunting and fishing seasons. Invite interested students to contact your state's fish and game office to learn about hunting regulations in your area, including what precautionary measures hunters need to take. Have them find out about the procedures and requirements for obtaining a hunting or fishing license.

Old Man and the Boy, John Head, Russell A. Fink Gallery

Art

Old Man and the Boy by John Head

This painting depicts an old man and a young boy, presumably out for a walk by a secluded lake or stream. Our eyes are drawn to the boy in his red hat, the only splash of bold color in the landscape. He and the dog have spotted or heard something in the distance, perhaps a deer, a turkey, or a waterfowl. Use this question for discussion:

In what ways do the people and animal in the painting seem similar to or different from those in the story?
Answer: The people and animal in the picture include a boy, older man, and dog just as in the story. However, the people and animal in the picture aren't hunting. They have no gun, bow, or other hunting gear, nor are they dressed like hunters.

19 ▶**Critical Viewing**

Answer: Students may say that the painting is effective because it depicts people and animals similar to those in the story. However, the painting clearly doesn't depict a hunting scene nor does the environment it shows closely resemble that of the bayou.

20 ✓**Reading Check**

Answer: Mister Ernest removes the ammunition from his gun.

mule, and turned without no hurry still, and the white underside of his tail for a second or two more before the thicket taken him.

It might 'a' been a signal, a good-bye, a farewell. Still walking, we passed the other three old dogs in the middle of the glade, laying down, too, now jest where they was when the buck vanished, and not trying to get up neither when we passed; and still that hundred yards ahead of them, Eagle, too, not laying down, because he was still on his feet, but his legs was spraddled and his head was down; maybe jest waiting until we was out of sight of his shame, his eyes saying plain as talk when we passed, "I'm sorry, boys, but this here is all."

Mister Ernest stopped Dan. "Jump down and look at his feet," he said.

"Ain't nothing wrong with his feet," I said. "It's his wind has done give out."

"Jump down and look at his feet," Mister Ernest said.

So I done it, and while I was stooping over Eagle I could hear the pump gun go, "Snick-cluck, Snick-cluck. Snick-cluck" three times, except that I never thought nothing then. Maybe he was jest running the shells through to be sho it would work when we seen him again or maybe to make sho they was all buckshot.[14] Then I got up again, and

---

14. **buckshot** *n.* large lead shot used for shooting deer and other big game.

19 ▲**Critical Viewing** Do you think this painting effectively illustrates the story? Explain. **[Evaluate]**

20 ✓**Reading Check**

What does Mister Ernest do with the pump gun as the boy checks Dan's feet?

CUSTOMIZE INSTRUCTION FOR UNIVERSAL ACCESS

For Special Needs Students	For Less Proficient Readers	For Advanced Readers
Students may miss the underlying essence of the boy's interaction with Eagle. Guide them in drawing an inference about the scene. Mister Ernest is using the pretence of checking on Eagle's condition to divert the boy's attention from his own actions with the gun. Tell students that they will learn the reason for this diversion as they read.	Point out that Faulkner uses his animal characters in many different ways. For example, in the bracketed passage on p. 868, he describes how everyone, including the dogs, is spent and weary. With this description, Faulkner invites even readers to slow down.	Point out to students that when the speaker puts words into Eagle's mouth, it is just one of many times that animals communicate messages to people in the story. Ask students to identify examples of this communication as they read or reread the story.

㉑ Reading Strategy

Breaking Down Long Sentences

- Read aloud the bracketed passage slowly and clearly, pausing at meaningful breaks.

- Ask students the Reading Strategy question on p. 870: What information is conveyed in the long sentence beginning "He crashed just once"? Why do you think Faulkner chose to provide this information in such a long sentence?

Possible answer: The sentence describes four main elements—the grandeur and beauty of the buck, Mister Ernest's "Shooting" of the buck, the buck's departure, and Mister Ernest's reaction. Faulkner's use of the long sentence effectively conveys the breathless excitement with which the boy observes these events.

we went on, still walking; a little west of north now, because when we seen his white flag that second or two before the thicket hid it, it was on a beeline for that notch in the bayou. And it was evening, too, now. The wind had done dropped and there was a edge to the air and the sun jest touched the tops of the trees now, except jest now and then, when it found a hole to come almost level through onto the ground. And he was taking the easiest way, too, now, going straight as he could. When we seen his foot in the soft places he was running for a while at first after his rest. But soon he was walking, too, like he knowed, too, where Eagle and the dogs was.

And then we seen him again. It was the last time—a thicket, with the sun coming through a hole onto it like a searchlight. He crashed jest once; then he was standing there broadside to us, not twenty yards away, big as a statue and red as gold in the sun, and the sun sparking on the tips of his horns—they was twelve of them—so that he looked like he had twelve lighted candles branched around his head, standing there looking at us while Mister Ernest raised the gun and aimed at his neck, and the gun went, "Click. Snick-cluck. Click, Snick-cluck. Click. Snick-cluck" three times, and Mister Ernest still holding the gun aimed while the buck turned and give one long bound, the white underside of his tail like a blaze of fire, too, until the thicket and the shadows put it out; and Mister Ernest laid the gun slow and gentle back across the saddle in front of him, saying quiet and peaceful, and not much louder than jest breathing, "God dawg. God dawg."

Then he jogged me with his elbow and we got down, easy and careful because of that ere cinch strop and he reached into his vest and taken out one of the cigars. It was busted where I had fell on it, I reckon, when we hit the ground. He throwed it away and taken out the other one. It was busted, too, so he bit off a hunk of it to chew and throwed the rest away. And now the sun was gone even from the tops of the trees and there wasn't nothing left but a big red glare in the west.

"Don't worry," I said. "I ain't going to tell them you forgot to load your gun. For that matter, they don't need to know we ever seed him."

"Much oblige," Mister Ernest said. There wasn't going to be no moon tonight neither, so he taken the compass off the whang leather loop in his buttonhole and handed me the gun and set the compass on a stump and stepped back and looked at it. "Just about the way we're headed now," he said, and taken the gun from me and opened it and put one shell in the britch and taken up the compass, and I taken Dan's reins and we started, with him in front with the compass in his hand.

And after a while it was full dark; Mister Ernest would have to strike a match ever now and then to read the compass, until the stars come out good and we could pick out one to follow, because I said, "How fur do you reckon it is?" A little more than one box of matches." So we used a star when we could, only we couldn't see it

Reading Strategy
Breaking Down Long Sentences What information is conveyed in the long sentence beginning "He crashed just once"? Why do you think Faulkner chose to provide this information in such a long sentence?

CUSTOMIZE INSTRUCTION FOR UNIVERSAL ACCESS

For Less Proficient Readers

Suggest that students break a long sentence into shorter segments using punctuation as a guide. Have students write a sentence from this page on the left side of a piece of paper. Then, have them put a box around each thought within the longer sentence. Finally, have students restate the text in their own words on the right side. An example is shown.

Text:

"And that was when we realized how fur he had come, because the only camp we knowed about in that direction was the Hollyknowe camp, and Hollyknowe was exactly twenty-eight miles from Van Dorn, where me and Mister Ernest lived—jest the shot, no dogs or nothing."

In My Own Words:

We realized how far he had come.
The only camp we knew about in that direction was the Hollyknowe camp.
Hollyknowe was twenty-eight miles from Van Dorn.
We heard shots and no dogs.

all the time because the woods was too dense and we would git a little off until he would have to spend another match. And now it was good and late, and he stopped and said, "Get on the horse."

"I ain't tired," I said.

"Get on the horse," he said. "We don't want to spoil him."

Because he had been a good feller ever since I had knowed him, which was even before that day two years ago when maw went off with the Vicksburg roadhouse feller and the next day pap didn't come home neither, and on the third one Mister Ernest rid Dan up to the door of the cabin on the river he let us live in, so pap could work his piece of land and run his fish line, too, and said, "Put that gun down and come on here and climb up behind."

So I got in the saddle even if I couldn't reach the stirrups, and Mister Ernest taken the reins and I must 'a' went to sleep, because the next thing I knowed a button hole of my lumberjack was tied to the saddle horn with that ere whang cord off the compass, and it was good and late now and we wasn't fur, because Dan was already smelling water, the river. Or maybe it was the feed lot itself he smelled, because we struck the fire road not a quarter below it, and soon I could see the river, too, with the white mist laying on it soft and still as cotton. Then the lot, home; and up yonder in the dark, not no piece akchully, close enough to hear us unsaddling and shucking corn prob'ly, and sholy close enough to hear Mister Ernest blowing his horn at the dark camp for Simon to come in the boat and git us, that old buck in his brake in the bayou; home, too, resting, too, after the hard run, waking hisself now and then, dreaming of dogs behind him or maybe it was the racket we was making would wake him, but not neither of them for more than jest a little while before sleeping again.

Then Mister Ernest stood on the bank blowing until Simon's lantern went bobbing down into the mist; then we clumb down to the landing and Mister Ernest blowed again now and then to guide Simon, until we seen the lantern in the mist, and then Simon and the boat; only it looked like ever time I set down and got still, I went back to sleep, because Mister Ernest was shaking me again to git out and climb the bank into the dark camp, until I felt a bed against my knees and tumbled into it.

Then it was morning, tomorrow; it was all over now until next November, next year, and we could come back. Uncle Ike and Willy and Walter and Roth and the rest of them had come in yestiddy, soon as Eagle taken the buck out of hearing and they knowed that deer was gone, to pack up and be ready to leave this morning for Yoknapatawpha, where they lived, until it would be November again and they could come back again.

So, as soon as we et breakfast, Simon run them back up the river in the big boat to where they left their cars and pickups, and now it wasn't nobody but jest me and Mister Ernest setting on the back against the kitchen wall in the sun; Mister Ernest smoking a cigar—a whole one this time that Dan hadn't had no chance to jump

22 ✓ Reading Check

What does Mister Ernest do when he sees the buck for the last time?

Race at Morning ◆ 871

22 ✓ Reading Check

Answer: He fires an empty gun at it so as not to hurt it.

CUSTOMIZE INSTRUCTION FOR UNIVERSAL ACCESS

For Less Proficient Readers	For English Learners	For Advanced Readers
Use the Dialect and Breaking Down Long Sentences transparencies, pp. 97–98 in **Literary Analysis and Reading Transparencies** as support tools for students. Invite them to highlight passages that they find confusing. Work with students to complete the organizers shown on the appropriate transparency.	To support students in their reading of dialect, present the Grammar and Style instruction on p. 878. Discuss with students how English verbs are formed and conjugated. Then, have students complete the Dialect transparency organizer, p. 97 in **Literary Analysis and Reading Transparencies.**	Challenge students to use the Dialect transparency, p. 101, in **Literary Analysis and Reading Transparencies,** as a guide in writing their own paragraph of dialect. Provide a passage written in Standard English for students to "translate" into dialect. Invite students to read their completed paragraphs aloud.

Analyze

- Read the bracketed passage to students. Ask them to identify the word that the speaker repeats a number of times in this paragraph. Lead students to see that he repeats the word *home*.

- Ask students what might make the idea of home especially meaningful to the speaker.
  Answer: The home he shares with Mister Ernest is probably the first real home he's ever known. It is his place of refuge and the only place where anyone has ever truly cared for him.

24 Background

Two Influential Writers

Just as Faulkner had his home country in Mississippi, Ernest Hemingway had a special place growing up—Walloon Lake, Michigan, where his family spent summers. Despite an apparently happy childhood, Hemingway struggled throughout his larger-than-life adulthood to find peace. Depressed and ill, Hemingway took his own life in 1961.

through a grapevine and bust. He hadn't washed his face neither where that vine had throwed him into the mud. But that was all right, too; his face usually did have a smudge of mud or tractor grease or beard stubble on it, because he wasn't jest a planter; he was a farmer, he worked as hard as ara one of his hands and tenants—which is why I knowed from the very first that we would git along, that I wouldn't have no trouble with him and he wouldn't have no trouble with me, from that very first day when I woke up and maw had done gone off with that Vicksburg roadhouse feller without even waiting to cook breakfast, and the next morning pap was gone, too, and it was almost night the next day when I heard a horse coming up and I taken the gun that I had already throwed a shell into the britch when pap never came home last night, and stood in the door while Mister Ernest rid up and said, "Come on. Your paw ain't coming back neither."

"You mean he give me to you?" I said.

"Who cares?" He said. "Come on. I brought a lock for the door. We'll send the pickup back tomorrow for whatever you want."

So I come home with him and it was all right, it was jest fine—his wife had died about three years ago—without no women to worry us or take off in the middle of the night with a durn Vicksburg roadhouse jake without even wanting to cook breakfast. And we would go home this afternoon, too, but not jest yet; we always stayed one more day after the others left because Uncle Ike always left what grub they hadn't et, and the rest of the homemade corn whisky he drunk and that town whisky of Roth Edmondziz he called Scotch that smelled like it come out of a old bucket of roof paint; setting in the sun for one more day before we went back home to get ready to put in next year's crop of cotton and oats and beans and hay; and across the river yonder, behind the wall of trees where the big woods started, that old buck laying up today in the sun, too—resting today, too, without nobody to bother him until next November.

So at least one of us was glad it would be eleven months and two weeks before he would have to run that fur that fast again. So he was glad of the very same thing we was sorry of, and so all of a sudden I thought about how maybe planting and working and then harvesting oats and cotton and beans and hay wasn't jest something me and Mister Ernest done three hundred and fifty-one days to fill in the time until we could come back hunting again, but it was something we had to do, and do honest and good during the three hundred and fifty-one days, to have the right to come back into the big woods and hunt for the other fourteen; and the fourteen days that old buck run in front of dogs wasn't jest something to fill his time until the three hundred and fifty-one when he didn't have to, but the running and the risking in front of guns and dogs was

The American Experience

24 *Two Influential Writers*

William Faulkner and Ernest Hemingway were probably the most influential American writers of the twentieth century, even though they were near-opposites in almost all aspects of their lives and work.

Although Faulkner longed for adventure as a young man, he settled in a tiny corner of rural Mississippi from where he churned out masterpieces. His prose was dense and complex, and featured enormously long sentences.

Hemingway, on the other hand, lived a personal life of epic adventure, traveling the world and hunting big game. He became a celebrity due to both the grandeur of his personality and the brilliance of his prose. That prose—precise and unadorned—introduced a new way of writing to American literature.

Both men won the Nobel Prize—Faulkner in 1950 and Hemingway in 1954—and they shared a grudging respect. However, they also waged famous wars of words. Hemingway said that Faulkner "wrote like an old grandmother," and Faulkner replied that the famously terse Hemingway was "afraid to use a word of more than five letters."

☀ **ENRICHMENT: Social Studies Connection**

Social Welfare Programs

Although Mister Ernest probably felt no real connection to or affection for the boy, he knew he could not just leave him alone in the cabin. He does the right thing by taking the boy into his care, with no questions asked, no legalities considered.

As small towns gave way to large cities, American communities had to find new ways to care for abandoned or dependent children. Beginning in the early 20th century, the U.S. government instituted programs to support dependent children, especially those living with single female parents. Those programs expanded throughout the 20th century as more and more women faced raising children alone (18% by the end of the 20th century). Today, the U.S. offers a network of social welfare programs designed to support children.

something he had to do for fourteen days to have the right not to be bothered for the other three hundred and fifty-one. And so the hunting and the farming wasn't two different things atall—they was jest the other side of each other.

"Yes," I said. "All we got to do now is put in that next year's crop. Then November won't be no time away at all."

"You ain't going to put in the crop next year," Mister Ernest said. "You're going to school."

So at first I didn't even believe I had heard him. "What?" I said. "Me? Go to school?"

"Yes," Mister Ernest said. "You must make something out of yourself."

"I am," I said. "I'm doing it now. I'm going to be a hunter and a farmer like you."

"No," Mister Ernest said. "That ain't enough any more. Time was when all a man had to do was just farm eleven and a half months, and hunt the other half. But not now. Now just to belong to the farming business and the hunting business ain't enough. You got to belong to the business of mankind."

"Mankind?" I said.

"Yes," Mister Ernest said. "So you're going to school. Because you got to know why. You can belong to the farming and hunting business and you can learn the difference between what's right and what's wrong, and do right. And that used to be enough—just to do right. But not now. You got to know why it's right and why it's wrong, and be able to tell the folks that never had no chance to learn it; teach them how to do what's right, not just because they know it's right, but because they know now why it's right because you just showed them, told them, taught them why. So you're going to school."

"It's because you been listening to that durn Will Legate and Walter Ewell!" I said.

"No," Mister Ernest said.

"Yes!" I said. "No wonder you missed that buck yestiddy, taking ideas from the very fellers that let him get away, after me and you had run Dan and the dogs durn nigh clean to death! Because you never even missed him! You never forgot to load that gun! You had done already unloaded it a purpose! I heard you!"

"All right, all right," Mister Ernest said. "Which would you rather have? His bloody head and hide on the kitchen floor yonder and half his meat in a pickup truck on the way to Yoknapatawpha County,

25 ✔**Reading Check**

What is the reason the boy will not plant the crop next year?

Race at Morning ◆ 873

CUSTOMIZE INSTRUCTION FOR UNIVERSAL ACCESS

For Less Proficient Readers	For English Learners	For Gifted/Talented Students
Help students understand the boy's description of dividing the year into two parts. The first of these parts is the 11½ months he spends farming and the deer spends safe from hunting. The second is the two weeks of hunting season. Explain that although the times are not equal, the boy feels these two parts of his life are of equal value.	Review the time language in the boy's description of the year's division into hunting and farm activities. Make sure students understand the quantities "three hundred and fifty-one" and "fourteen." You might use numerals or even manipulatives to demonstrate these quantities.	Invite students to create a visual representation of the concept the boy devises about his divided year. Students might create a poster, coin, or painting that conveys the idea of a life split into two parts, unequal in size but not in value.

Answers for p. 874

Review and Assess

1. Students should be prepared to explain their responses.

2. **(a)** He doesn't go to school. **(b)** It foreshadows the ending, when the boy learns he will be attending school.

3. **(a)** They abandoned him. **(b)** Mister Ernest adopts the speaker when the boy's parents, who are Mister Ernest's tenants, disappear. **(c)** Examples might include the boy's trust in holding onto Mister Ernest atop a galloping horse, and the way he speaks his mind to Mister Ernest.

4. **(a)** Mister Ernest has secretly unloaded the gun. **(b)** There is more pleasure in possibility than in certainty.

5. **(a)** The boy will be sent to school. **(b)** He hopes the boy will learn about important human values and why things are right or wrong, so that he can teach others.

6. Possible response: Faulkner successfully connects the two events by making the point that the boy needs an education in order to understand the reasoning—and emotions— behind Mister Ernest's decision not to shoot the buck.

7. **(a)** Possible answer: Mister Ernest lives by a code that requires treating others decently and taking responsibility. For example, he takes in the boy even though he doesn't have to. **(b)** Possible answer: Most people would say that they hold some responsibility for a neighbor in need, though this value may be held more dearly in a small town environment.

874

---

or him with his head and hide and meat still together over yonder in that brake, waiting for next November for us to run him again?"

"And git him, too," I said. "We won't even fool with no Willy Legate and Walter Ewell next time."

"Maybe," Mister Ernest said.

"Yes," I said.

"Maybe," Mister Ernest said. "The best word in our language, the best of all. That's what mankind keeps going on: Maybe. The best days of his life ain't the ones when he said 'Yes' beforehand: they're the ones when all he knew to say was 'Maybe.' He can't say 'Yes' until afterward because he not only don't know it until then, he don't want to know 'Yes' until then . . . Step in the kitchen and make me a toddy. Then we'll see about dinner."

"All right," I said. I got up. "You want some of Uncle Ike's corn or that town whisky of Roth Edmondziz?"

"Can't you say Mister Roth or Mister Edmonds?" Mister Ernest said.

"Yes, sir," I said. "Well, which do you want? Uncle Ike's corn or that ere stuff of Roth Edmondziz?"

Review and Assess

Thinking About the Selection

1. **Respond:** If you had the opportunity, would you join the hunters on their yearly trip to the bayou? Explain.

2. **(a) Recall:** During the card game, what do the men reveal about the narrator's school career? **(b) Speculate:** Why might Faulkner include a discussion about school early in the story?

3. **(a) Recall:** What happened to the boy's parents? **(b) Recall:** Under what circumstances did the boy go to live with Mister Ernest? **(c) Support:** Find two examples from the story that support the conclusion that the boy trusts and feels relaxed with Mister Ernest.

4. **(a) Infer:** When Mister Ernest fires at the deer, it does not die. Why not? **(b) Analyze:** According to Mister Ernest, why is it better to have let the deer live than to have killed it?

5. **(a) Recall:** Why does Mister Ernest say the boy will not be planting next year's crop? **(b) Interpret:** What are Mr. Ernest's hopes for the boy?

6. **Evaluate:** Evaluate Faulkner's success in connecting the significance of the hunt to the significance of Mister Ernest's plans for the boy.

7. **(a) Generalize:** What values or moral code do you think Mister Ernest lives by? **(b) Take a Position:** Are Mister Ernest's values universal, or are they particular to a time and place? Explain.

874 ◆ Disillusion, Defiance, and Discontent (1914–1946)

✳ ENRICHMENT: Culture Connection

The Nobel Prize

The Nobel Prize for Literature, given each year by the Swedish Academy in Stockholm, is awarded without regard to national origin. It is usually based on an author's entire body of work, rather than on any single book. Tell students that recent award winners in literature include Seamus Heaney (Ireland), Kenzaburo Oe (Japan), Toni Morrison (United States), Derek Walcott (West Indies), Nadine Gordimer (South Africa), and Octavio Paz (Mexico).

The fund for the Nobel Prize Awards was established in the will of Alfred Nobel (1833–1896). The prize's financial benefits are significant; the prize now brings a reward of about $1 million. Nobel specified that the annual awards should go to those people who, during the preceding year, conferred the greatest benefit on humankind. William Faulkner received his award in 1950 for his contributions in 1949.

Nobel Prize Acceptance Speech

26

WILLIAM FAULKNER

Background

The Swedish chemist Alfred Nobel earned fame as the inventor of dynamite. Nobel had intended dynamite to be used safely in mining and construction, but disasters often occurred, and his name became associated with tragedy. Nobel eventually succeeded in making dynamite safer. Later, he sought to make the world a better place by establishing a foundation to encourage achievement and diplomacy. The Nobel Prizes, given for achievement in the fields of physics, chemistry, medicine, literature, and world peace, are the result of his efforts. They are the world's most prestigious awards. When William Faulkner received the Nobel Prize for literature in 1950, he gave an acceptance speech that is among the simplest and most moving examples of oratory in our literature.

Stockholm, Sweden
December 10, 1950

I feel that this award was not made to me as a man, but to my work—a life's work in the agony and sweat of the human spirit, not for glory and least of all for profit, but to create out of the materials of the human spirit something which did not exist before. So this award is only mine in trust. It will not be difficult to find a dedication for the money part of it commensurate with the purpose and significance of its origin. But I would like to do the same with the acclaim too, by using this moment as a pinnacle from which I might be listened to by the young men and women already dedicated to the same anguish and travail, among whom is already that one who will some day stand here where I am standing.

Our tragedy today is a general and universal physical fear so long sustained by now that we can even bear it. There are no longer problems of the spirit. There is only the question: When will I be blown up? Because of this, the young man or woman writing today has forgotten the problems of the human heart in conflict with itself which alone can make good writing because only that is worth writing about, worth the agony and the sweat.

He must learn them again. He must teach himself that the basest of all things is to be afraid; and, teaching himself that, forget it forever, leaving no room in his workshop for anything but the old verities and

27 ✓ **Reading Check**

What does Faulkner believe is the only subject that can yield good writing?

26 **About the Selecti[on]**

In his gracious acceptance sp[eech] Faulkner expresses his concer[n that] the question of physical surviva[l has] diverted young writers from deal[ing] with what truly matters in life and literature: love, honor, compassion, and sacrifice. He states his belief that humanity will not only endure, but prevail, because man alone possesses an immortal soul and compassionate spirit. The writer is both obliged and privileged to remind humanity of its nobler capabilities and, thus, can help ensure the success of the human race.

27 ✓ **Reading Check**

Answer: The only subject that can yield good writing is one focused on the problems of the human heart in conflict.

CUSTOMIZE INSTRUCTION FOR UNIVERSAL ACCESS

For Less Proficient Readers	For Advanced Readers
Increase students' access to Faulkner's speech by providing the following information: In 1950 the United States was involved in a Cold War with the Soviet Union. The relationship between the two nations was strained, and the buildup of nuclear weapons in both countries produced a tremendous amount of distrust and fear.	Encourage students to explore works of Nobel Prize winners from countries other than the United States. Students can read with the purpose of learning how literature reflects the values and culture of its country of origin. You may wish to have each student select a different Nobel Prize-winning author to research. Students can then share their findings in a series of oral reports. As a whole class, discuss which themes or concerns the authors share in common, despite their different cultural backgrounds. Do students think the works discussed meet Faulkner's criteria for good literature?

on

ech, that has g

76

ess

... responses should ...ct an understanding of Faulkner's criteria for good literature.

2. (a) People are too worried about being killed. **(b)** It is the fear of nuclear destruction.

3. (a) Acccording to Faulkner, the problems of the human heart in conflict are the sole subject of good writing.
(b) He sees modern literature as being concerned with trivial or passing emotions and problems rather than with "old universal truths."

4. **(a)** Humanity will prevail. **(b)** Enduring is merely continuing to exist, while prevailing expresses the ability to lift the human spirit.

5. **(a)** It is a writer's duty to write about compassion, courage, honor, hope, pride, pity, and sacrifice. **(b)** The poet's voice can be a prop or pillar to help people prevail.

6. **(a)** The use of atom bombs in World War II and Russia's testing of an atom bomb soon afterward led to widespread fear that nuclear war was about to destroy the human race. **(b)** Responses will vary. Students should be able to support their responses.

truths of the heart, the old universal truths lacking which any story is ephemeral and doomed—love and honor and pity and pride and compassion and sacrifice. Until he does so, he labors under a curse. He writes not of love but of lust, of defeats in which nobody loses anything of value, of victories without hope and, worst of all, without pity or compassion. His griefs grieve on no universal bones, leaving no scars. He writes not of the heart but of the glands.

Until he relearns these things, he will write as though he stood among and watched the end of man. I decline to accept the end of man. It is easy enough to say that man is immortal simply because he will endure: that when the last ding-dong of doom has clanged and faded from the last worthless rock hanging tideless in the last red and dying evening, that even then there will still be one more sound: that of his puny inexhaustible voice, still talking. I refuse to accept this. I believe that man will not merely endure: he will prevail. He is immortal, not because he alone among creatures has an inexhaustible voice, but because he has a soul, a spirit capable of compassion and sacrifice and endurance. The poet's, the writer's, duty is to write about these things. It is his privilege to help man endure by lifting his heart, by reminding him of the courage and honor and hope and pride and compassion and pity and sacrifice which have been the glory of his past. The poet's voice need not merely be the record of man, it can be one of the props, the pillars to help him endure and prevail.

Review and Assess

Thinking About the Selection

1. **Respond:** Do you agree with Faulkner's definition of good literature? If not, how would you revise it?
2. **(a) Recall:** According to Faulkner, why are there no longer problems of the spirit? **(b) Deduce:** What is the physical fear to which he refers?
3. **(a) Recall:** According to Faulkner, what alone is the subject matter of good writing? **(b) Interpret:** Why does he view most modern literature as ephemeral?
4. **(a) Recall:** According to Faulkner, will humanity endure or prevail? **(b) Define:** In what way does Faulkner define the difference between enduring and prevailing?
5. **(a) Recall:** According to Faulkner, what is a writer's "duty"? **(b) Interpret:** What distinction does he draw about "the poet's voice" in his explanation of how humanity can prevail?
6. **(a) Extend:** What events not long before 1950 gave rise to the fear of which Faulkner speaks? **(b) Hypothesize:** If he were alive today, would he say we have lost or retained that fear? Explain.

ASSESSMENT PRACTICE: Reading Comprehension

Anticipate Missing Words **(For more practice, see Test Preparation Workbook, p. 52.)**

Many tests ask students to correctly answer sentence-completion questions. Use the following example to show students how to use context and their own knowledge to guess a word that would complete the following passage.

Because he wrote about his home in Oxford, Mississippi, William Faulkner was for many years dismissed as an unimportant _________ writer.

A experimental
B regional
C eccentric
D untalented

After reading the passage, students might think that the word *local* completes the sentence. *B, regional,* is the best choice.

Review and Assess

Literary Analysis

Dialect

1. Use a chart like the one shown to analyze the following passage of **dialect** in "Race at Morning."

   > So I come home with him and it was all right, it was jest fine—his wife had died about three years ago—without no women to worry us or take off in the middle of the night with a durn Vicksburg roadhouse jake . . .

   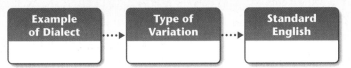

Example of Dialect	Type of Variation	Standard English

2. If you were to rewrite "Race at Morning" in Standard English, (a) What would be lost? (b) What would be gained?

Comparing Literary Works

3. (a) In what ways does Mister Ernest's insistence on the boy's attending to the "business of mankind" reflect the message of Faulkner's speech? (b) What is the "business of mankind"?

4. (a) According to Mister Ernest, why is "maybe" the best word in the language? (b) In what ways does Mr. Ernest's explanation relate to the message of human potential in Faulkner's speech?

Reading Strategy

Breaking Down Long Sentences

5. Select a long sentence from "Race at Morning." (a) Using the punctuation as a guide, divide the sentence into sections. (b) Identify the section of the sentence that contains its subject. (c) Rewrite each section as a separate sentence, connected by transitions.

6. In **breaking down** his **long sentences,** what insights do you gain into Faulkner's style?

Extend Understanding

7. **Media Connection:** Identify several popular films you have seen. Then, decide whether Faulkner would have approved of each one. Explain your responses.

Race at Morning / Nobel Prize Acceptance Speech ◆ 877

Quick Review

Dialect is a manner of speaking that is common to a particular region or group. Dialect affects pronunciation, word choice, and grammatical structure.

Break down long sentences into smaller units of meaning in order to better understand them.

 Take It to the Net
www.phschool.com

Take the interactive self-test online to check your understanding of these selections.

Answers for p. 877

Review and Assess

1. Possible responses: come, grammatical structure, came; jest, pronunciation, just; without no, grammatical structure; without any; durn, pronunciation, darn; jake, pronunciation/word choice, jerk

2. (a) The story's authentic ring and strong sense of place would be lost by removing dialect. (b) Readers might gain easier access to the story without the dialect.

3. (a) Mister Ernest wants the boy to be a teacher of men, one who helps mankind find its way, just as Faulkner says writers must do. (b) It is to behave with honor and compassion, to teach right from wrong and to stand by one another.

4. (a) It offers possibility and hope. (b) Faulkner also suggests that people must have hope and optimism about the future in order to realize their potential.

5. (a) Sample answer (from p. 862): Then Mister Ernest loaded the gun . . . the stirrup,/ and I got up . . . toward the bayou,/ the four big dogs . . . across his back,/ and the puppies moiling along in ever'body's way. (b) The first section contains the subject *Mister Ernest*; the second contains the subjects *I* and *we*. (c) Students' responses should demonstrate correct punctuation and use of transitions.

6. Faulkner seems to prefer the long, winding sentences as a way of expressing the boy's excitement and rapid-fire observations.

7. Students should be able to support their responses.

Answers for p. 878

❶ Vocabulary Development

Word Analysis

1. A *creamery* is a place where dairy products—things made from cream—are produced.

2. *Finery* is showy or elaborate decoration, clothing, or jewels.

3. *Snobbery* is snobbish behavior.

Spelling Strategy

1. trickery
2. dietary
3. dictionary

Concept Development: Definitions

1. No
2. No
3. Yes
4. No
5. Yes
6. Yes
7. Yes
8. Yes

❷ Grammar and Style

1. *ate*; We ate by the campfire.
2. *rose*; I rose with the sun.
3. *went*; We went east when we heard the dogs barking.
4. *gave*; We gave the chase all our effort.
5. *threw*; The tension of the vine threw the saddle through the air.

Writing Application

Sentences from the story should contain incorrectly used irregular verbs. Rewritten sentences should reflect Standard English usage for these verbs, and also should be free of grammatical or mechanical errors.

Integrate Language Skills

❶ Vocabulary Development Lesson

Word Analysis: Latin Suffix -ery

The Latin suffix *-ery* (or *-ry*), meaning "state or quality of," "place of," or "a kind of behavior," is used to form nouns from verbs or other nouns. For example, the verb *distill* means "to refine" or "to extract." The noun *distillery* means a place where something is distilled. Use this information to define each of the following words.

1. creamery   2. finery   3. snobbery

Spelling Strategy

Nouns meaning "state or quality of" or "place of" often end in *-ery*, as in the words *slavery* and *refinery*. The ending *-ary* is usually reserved for nouns designating a person or thing related to or connected with something (such as *functionary*) or for adjectives meaning "related to" or "connected with" (such as *budgetary*). Create new nouns for the words below using one of these two suffixes.

1. trick   2. diet   3. diction

❷ Grammar and Style Lesson

Correct Use of Irregular Verb Forms

The narrator of "Race at Morning" often mistakenly conjugates **irregular verbs**—verbs whose past tenses and past participles are not formed by adding *-ed* or *-d* to the present form—as regular verbs. While the boy's speech captures his dialect, helping Faulkner place the story in a specific setting, these kinds of conjugations are considered incorrect in Standard English.

> **Incorrect:** I *knowed* it was him.
>
> **Correct:** I *knew* it was him.

W̶G *Prentice Hall Writing and Grammar Connection: Chapter 21, Section 1*

878 ◆ *Disillusion, Defiance, and Discontent (1914–1946)*

Concept Development: Definitions

Review the vocabulary list on p. 859. Then, answer each of the following questions, basing your answers on the meaning of the italicized words.

1. Can you plow a *bayou*?

2. Are the typical products of a *distillery* suitable for children to consume?

3. Is a *buck* a male animal?

4. Would a *moiling* puppy be standing still?

5. Might you find a *switch* in the woods?

6. Is *scrabbling* a quick movement?

7. Is a *swag* something you would find in the forest?

8. If you wanted to get some sun, would you head for a *glade*?

Practice Rewrite each incorrect verb that follows in its correct irregular form. Then, write a sentence that uses each verb correctly.

1. eated   4. gived
2. rised   5. throwed
3. goed

Writing Application Select three sentences from "Race at Morning" in which the characters conjugate irregular verbs incorrectly. Then, rewrite the sentences using Standard English. Consult a grammar book, if necessary.

TEACHING RESOURCES

The following resources can be used to enrich or extend the instruction for pp. 878–879.

Vocabulary

📖 **Selection Support:** Build Vocabulary, p. 216

📖 **Vocabulary and Spelling Practice Book** (Use this booklet for skills enrichment.) ▪

Grammar

📖 **Selection Support:** Grammar and Style, p. 217

W̶G **Writing and Grammar,** Ruby Level, p. 520

📄 **Daily Language Practice Transparencies** ▪

Writing

W̶G **Writing and Grammar,** Ruby Level, p. 309

💿 **Writing and Grammar iText CD-ROM**

📄 **Writing Models and Graphic Organizers on Transparencies,** p. 75

📄 **BLOCK SCHEDULING:** Resources marked with this symbol provide varied instruction during 90-minute blocks.

❸ Writing Lesson

Critical Review

In his Nobel Prize acceptance speech, Faulkner notes that the writer's duty is to help people "endure by lifting their hearts, by reminding them of the courage and honor and hope and pride and compassion and pity and sacrifice which have been the glory of their past." Choose a short story and evaluate it in terms of how well the author fulfills Faulkner's ideal.

Prewriting   Choose a story for analysis, and read it closely. Make notes about whether the author has succeeded or failed, according to Faulkner's standards.

Drafting   Start your review with a statement of your position. Then, elaborate by providing details and passages from the story.

Model: Drafting to Elaborate on an Idea

In "The Story of an Hour," Kate Chopin fulfills Faulkner's criteria for writing about "truths of the heart." The core of the tale rests in Mrs. Mallard's thoughts and feelings as she greets the prospect of personal freedom: "Free! Body and soul free!" she exults.

> Including specific information elaborates on a basic idea.

Revising   Reread your review to confirm you have provided solid supporting evidence for your ideas.

W̶G *Prentice Hall Writing and Grammar Connection: Chapter 14, Section 3*

❹ Extension Activities

Listening and Speaking As a radio announcer, create a **broadcast** of the hunt in "Race at Morning." Prepare your broadcast by reviewing the story closely and making an outline of events. To the basic outline, add details about

- the weather.
- the activities.
- the apparent feelings of the men, horses, dogs, and deer.

Allow your voice to reveal tension or excitement as your reading of the hunt progresses. Close with an insight into the story's events.

Research and Technology With a classmate, stage a **debate** about the pros and cons of hunting. Prepare for the debate by gathering information, opinions, and facts that represent the wide range of opinions on this subject. Then, argue the subject from the point of view of farmers, animals rights supporters, hunting enthusiasts, and others. **[Group Activity]**

 **Take It to the Net**   www.phschool.com

Go online for an additional research activity using the Internet.

---

❸ Writing Lesson

- Have student groups brainstorm for possible short stories, discussing those each group member has recently found interesting.
- Provide students with the Argument Transparency, p. 75 in **Writing Models and Graphic Organizers on Transparencies** as a tool to organize details to support their arguments.
- Read through the Writing Lesson steps with students and clarify any confusion.
- Use the Response to Literature rubric in **Performance Assessment and Portfolio Management,** p. 23, to assess student's critical review.

❹ Listening and Speaking

- Play audio recordings or have students listen to live radio broadcasts of sporting events. Discuss with students the techniques announcers use to heighten tension and engage audience interest.
- Have students work in pairs to develop ideas about the weather, activities, and emotions implied by the story.
- Stage a radio broadcast hour, with students presenting their broadcasts in turn. Position presenters so that they can be heard, but not seen, by listening students.

CUSTOMIZE INSTRUCTION
For Universal Access

To address different learning styles, use the activities suggested in the Extension Activities booklet, p. 49.

For Interpersonal and Verbal/Linguistic Learners, use Activity 5.

For Verbal/Linguistic Learners, use Activity 6.

For Visual/Spatial Learners, use Activity 7.

The Poetry of Robert Frost

Lesson Objectives

1. **To analyze and respond to literary elements**
   - Literary Analysis: Blank Verse
   - Connecting Literary Elements: Pastorals

2. **To read, comprehend, analyze, and critique poetry**
   - Reading Strategy: Reading Blank Verse
   - Reading Check questions
   - Review and Assess questions
   - Assessment Practice (ATE)

3. **To develop word analysis skills, fluency, and systematic vocabulary**
   - Vocabulary Development Lesson: Latin Root: *-lum-*

4. **To understand and apply written and oral language conventions**
   - Spelling Strategy
   - Grammar and Style Lesson: Uses of Infinitives

5. **To understand and apply appropriate writing and research strategies**
   - Writing Lesson: Introduction to an Anthology
   - Extension Activity: Interpretive Presentation

6. **To understand and apply listening and speaking strategies**
   - Extension Activity: Eulogy

STEP-BY-STEP TEACHING GUIDE	PACING GUIDE
PRETEACH	
Motivate Students and Provide Background	
Use the Motivation activity (ATE p. 880)	5 min.
Read and discuss author and background features (SE/ATE pp. 880, 882, 890) 🅰	5 min.
Introduce the Concepts	
Introduce the Literary Analysis and Reading Strategy (SE/ATE p. 881) 🅰	15 min.
Pronounce the vocabulary words and read their definitions (SE p. 881)	5 min.
TEACH	
Monitor Comprehension	
Informally monitor comprehension by circulating while students read independently or in groups 🅰	60 min.
Monitor students' comprehension with the Reading Check notes (SE/ATE pp. 883, 885)	as students read
Develop vocabulary with Vocabulary notes (SE pp. 883, 889, 892; ATE p. 892)	as students read
Develop Understanding	
Develop students' understanding of blank verse with the Literary Analysis annotations (SE pp. 883, 885, 886, 888, 889, 892; ATE pp. 883, 885, 886, 888, 889, 892) 🅰	5 min.
Develop students' ability to read blank verse by using the Reading Strategy annotations (SE pp. 884, 887, 891; ATE pp. 884, 887, 891)	15 min.
ASSESS	
Assess Mastery	
Assess students' mastery of the Reading Strategy and Literary Analysis by having them answer the Review and Assess questions (SE/ATE p. 893)	15 min.
Use one or more of the print and media Assessment Resources (ATE p. 895) 🅰	up to 45 min.
EXTEND	
Apply Understanding	
Have students complete the Vocabulary Development Lesson and the Grammar and Style Lesson (SE p. 894) 🅰	20 min.
Apply students' ability to use transitions to show examples by using the Writing Lesson (SE/ATE p. 895) 🅰	45 min.
Apply students' understanding using one or more of the Extension Activities (SE p. 895)	20–90 min.

 ACCELERATED INSTRUCTION:
Use the strategies and activities identified with an 🅰.

UNIVERSAL ACCESS
● = Below Level Students
▲ = On-Level Students
■ = Above Level Students

Time and Resource Manager

Reading Level: Average, Average, Average, Easy, Average, Challenging
Average Number of Instructional Days: 5

RESOURCES		
PRINT 📖	**TRANSPARENCIES**	**TECHNOLOGY** 💿 🎧 📼
• **Beyond Literature,** Humanities Connection: Photography, p. 50 ▲ ■		• **Interest Grabber Video,** Tape 5 ● ▲ ■
• **Selection Support Workbook:** ● ▲ ■ Literary Analysis, p. 223 Reading Strategy, p. 222 Build Vocabulary, p. 220	• **Literary Analysis and Reading Transparencies,** pp. 99 and 100 ● ▲ ■	
• **Authors In Depth,** The American Experience, p. 140 ■		• **Listening to Literature** ● ▲ ■ Audiocassettes, Sides 31, 32 Audio CDs, CDs 17, 18
• **Literatura en español** ● ▲ • **Literary Analysis for Enrichment** ■		
• **Formal Assessment:** Selection Test, pp. 227–229 ● ▲ ■ • **Open Book Test,** pp. 148–150 ● ▲ ■ • **Performance Assessment and Portfolio Management,** p. 30 ● ▲ ■ • **ASSESSMENT SYSTEM** ● ▲ ■	• **ASSESSMENT SYSTEM** ● ▲ ■ Skills Practice Answers and Explanations on Transparencies	• **Test Bank Software** ● ▲ ■ • **Got It! Assessment Videotapes,** Tape 4 ● ▲
• **Selection Support Workbook:** ● ▲ ■ Grammar and Style, p. 221 • **Writing and Grammar,** Ruby Level ● ▲ ■ • **Extension Activities,** p. 50 ● ▲ ■	• **Daily Language Practice Transparencies** ● ▲ • **Writing Models and Graphic Organizers on Transparencies,** pp. 83–85, 95–97 ● ▲ ■	• **Writing and Grammar iText CD-ROM** ● ▲ ■ 💻 **Take It to the Net** www.phschool.com

BLOCK SCHEDULING: Use one 90-minute class period to preteach the selection and have students read it. Use a second 90-minute class period to assess students' mastery of skills and have them complete one of the Extension Activities.

Motivation

Before class, set up a low wall down the center of the room, out of boxes, desks, chairs, or masking tape. On either side of the "wall" post a sign that says, "Good fences make good neighbors." As students enter, have them sit on either side of the wall so that about half the class is on each side. Ask students to tell how it feels to be separated from each other. Draw attention to the quotation and ask them to respond to it. Then tell students that they will be reading poems by Robert Frost, one of which explores a response to the line they have discussed.

 Interest Grabber Video

As an alternative, play "Reading and Students Response" on Tape 5 to engage student interest.

❶ Background

More About the Author

Despite the apparent insularity of Frost's New England experience, the poetry that resulted from his residence there has been overwhelmingly influential. The scholar Earl J. Wilcox declares that, "between 1915 and 1980 more than three hundred articles focusing on Frost and his poetry appeared in popular journals such as *Reader's Digest* and *The Saturday Evening Post* . . . It has become commonplace during the three decades since his death to see almost daily lines quoted or paraphrased from the poet's most accessible poems in advertisements for computer companies ('Take the road less traveled,' reads one blurb), for sporting goods, for musical events, and an array of other business and cultural events. It seems obvious that Frost remains in the American consciousness in a deep and potent dimension."

Prepare to Read

❶ Robert Frost's Poetry

Robert Frost
(1874–1963)

In becoming one of America's most loved and respected poets, Robert Frost displayed the same rugged persistence and determination exhibited by the rural New Englanders he depicted in his poems. Although he eventually received four Pulitzer Prizes and read at a presidential inauguration, Frost's success as a poet did not come overnight or easily. Only after years of rejection by book and magazine publishers did he finally achieve the acceptance for which he had worked so hard.

Early Struggles Frost was born in San Francisco, California. His father died when Frost was eleven, and his mother moved the family to the textile city of Lawrence, Massachusetts. After graduating from high school, Frost briefly attended Dartmouth College. Disliking college life, he left school and spent time working as a farmer, mill hand, journalist, and schoolteacher. During his spare time, he wrote poetry and dreamed of someday being able to support himself solely by writing.

The English Years Frost married and spent ten years farming in New Hampshire. In 1912, unable to get his poems published, he sold the farm and moved his family to England. Once there, he hoped to establish himself as a poet. While living in England, Frost befriended a number of well-known poets, including Ezra Pound, and succeeded in publishing two collections of poetry, *A Boy's Will* (1913) and *North of Boston* (1914). When Frost returned to the United States in 1915, he discovered that his success in England had spread across the Atlantic, and he was on the road to fame.

Critical Acclaim Frost went on to publish several more volumes of poetry, for which he received many awards. He also taught at Amherst College, the University of Michigan, Harvard University, and Dartmouth College and lectured and read at dozens of other schools. Recognition of his poetry did not stop him from farming in Vermont and New Hampshire. In 1960, at John F. Kennedy's invitation, Frost became the first poet to read his work at a presidential inauguration.

New England Life Frost's poetry was popular not only with critics and intellectuals, but also among the general public. He used traditional verse forms and conversational language to paint vivid portraits of the New England landscape and lifestyle. Despite their apparent simplicity, however, his poems are filled with profound meanings, compelling readers to delve beneath the surface to fully appreciate his work.

"Ice on a hot stove" Frost was emphatic about his belief that a poem should reveal its meaning in a continuous process. He wrote: "Like a piece of ice on a hot stove the poem must ride on its own melting. A poem may be worked over since it is in being, but may not be worried into being. Its most precious quality will remain its having run itself and carried away the poet with it. Read it a hundred times: it will forever keep its freshness as a petal keeps its fragrance. It can never lose its sense of a meaning that once unfolded by surprise as it went."

Like his poetry, Frost's personality also had multiple levels. In his public appearances, Frost presented himself as a jovial, folksy farmer who just happened to write poetry. In reality, however, Frost was a deep thinker whose darker, complicated personality sometimes mystified those who knew him.

880 ◆ *Disillusion, Defiance, and Discontent (1914–1946)*

TEACHING RESOURCES

The following resources can be used to enrich or extend the instruction for pp. 880–881.

Motivation

 Interest Grabber Video, Tape 5

Background

📖 **Beyond Literature**, p.50

 *Take It to the Net*
Visit www.phschool.com for Background and hotlinks for the selections.

Literary Analysis

📄 **Literary Analysis and Reading Transparencies**, Blank Verse, p. 100

📖 **Selection Support**: Literary Analysis, p. 223

Reading

📄 **Literary Analysis and Reading Transparencies**, Reading Blank Verse, p. 99

 **BLOCK SCHEDULING:** Resources marked with this symbol provide varied instruction during 90-minute blocks.

Preview

Connecting to the Literature

Popular psychology holds that we are, at least in part, products of our environments, suggesting that the way we feel and act on a busy city street will be different from our emotions and behavior when surrounded by nature. In these poems, the setting plays an integral role in creating mood and meaning.

❷ Literary Analysis

Blank Verse

Many of Frost's poems do not contain rhyme, but their lines have a regular pattern of stressed and unstressed syllables, or *meter*.

- The basic unit of meter is a *foot*—usually one stressed syllable and one or more unstressed syllables.
- The most common foot is the *iamb*—one unstressed syllable followed by a stressed syllable.
- A line containing five iambs is written in *iambic pentameter*.
- Verse consisting of unrhymed lines of iambic pentameter is called **blank verse.**

As you read Frost's poems, use a chart like the one shown to identify those that have been written in blank verse and those that are in rhyming iambic pentameter.

Comparing Literary Works

Five of these poems by Frost can be categorized as **pastorals**—poems that deal with rural settings. Traditionally, pastoral poems have presented idealized views of rural life. In Frost's hands, however, rural life is sometimes fraught with ethical lapses, accidents, and even violence. As you read these poems, look closely at how the poet portrays rural life, and examine the differing ways in which the setting contributes to each poem's larger meaning.

❸ Reading Strategy

Reading Blank Verse

One way to appreciate **blank verse** is to read it aloud in sentences rather than in poetic lines. Avoid pausing at the end of each line. Instead, follow the punctuation as if you were reading prose: pause briefly after commas, and pause longer after periods. Notice how the flow of blank verse recreates the natural cadences of speech.

Vocabulary Development

poise (poiz) *n.* balance; stability (p. 883)

rueful (rōō´ fəl) *adj.* feeling or showing someone sorrow or pity (p. 889)

luminary (lōō´ mə ner´ ē) *adj.* giving off light (p. 892)

Sample Lines

When Í see bírches bénd tŏ léft and right

Ăcróss thĕ línes ŏf stráightĕr dárker trees,

↓

Five Beats per line:
Yes ____
No ____

↓

Rhyme:
Yes ____
No ✓

↓

Blank verse:
Yes ____
No ____

Robert Frost's Poetry ◆ 881

❷ Literary Analysis

Blank Verse

- Tell students that as they read Robert Frost's poems, they will focus on blank verse—unrhymed iambic pentameter.

- Have volunteers read aloud the bulleted items under Literary Analysis. Post the Blank Verse transparency, p. 104, **Literary Analysis and Reading Transparencies.** Refer to it as you define blank verse and other elements of meter.

- Point out the chart on the student page and model its use, urging students to complete a similar chart as they read.

- Discuss the instruction under **Comparing Literary Works.** Urge students to explore why Robert Frost chose to use blank verse in some of his pastoral poems.

❸ Reading Strategy

Reading Blank Verse

- Explain that blank verse should be read as sentences, rather than in poetic rhythm.

- Have a volunteer read aloud the Reading Strategy instruction. Model how to read blank verse, using the lines on the Reading Blank Verse transparency, p. 103 in **Literary Analysis and Reading Transparencies.**

- Briefly review the pauses indicated by various levels of punctuation, noting for example that colons indicate longer pauses than do commas.

Vocabulary Development

- Pronounce each vocabulary word for students, and read the definitions as a class. Have students identify any words with which they are already familiar.

E-Teach

Visit E-Teach at www.phschool.com for teachers' essays on how to teach, with questions and answers.

CUSTOMIZE INSTRUCTION
For Intrapersonal Learners

Although Frost's poetry invokes natural outdoor settings, it also mines the inner landscape of human values and beliefs. Encourage students to compare their own reactions to Frost's ideas. For example, ask students to consider their own views on walls or to respond to "Stopping by Woods on a Snowy Evening."

❶ About the Selection

The speaker, an older man, remembers the childhood pleasure of swinging from birches. He muses about how exploring his environment prepared him for life's greater challenges. Yet, despite preparation, adulthood sometimes feels so burdensome that it helps to recall carefree times as a boy swinging from birches, when his whole life was still ahead of him.

❷ ▶ Critical Viewing

Answer: Students should be able to explain their responses with specific details from the photograph.

Birches

Robert Frost

Background

Robert Frost spent most of his life in New Hampshire, Vermont, and Massachusetts. Much of his poetry reflects not only the New England landscape, but also its distinctive personalities. Despite Frost's city roots, he was able to gain the acceptance of his country neighbors and to enter their world—a place that was usually closed to outsiders. In so doing, Frost gathered a wealth of material for his poetry.

When I see birches bend to left and right
Across the lines of straighter darker trees,
I like to think some boy's been swinging them.
But swinging doesn't bend them down to stay
5   As ice storms do. Often you must have seen them
Loaded with ice a sunny winter morning
After a rain. They click upon themselves
As the breeze rises, and turn many-colored
As the stir cracks and crazes their enamel.
10   Soon the sun's warmth makes them shed crystal shells
Shattering and avalanching on the snow crust—
Such heaps of broken glass to sweep away
You'd think the inner dome of heaven had fallen.
They are dragged to the withered bracken by the load,
15   And they seem not to break; though once they are bowed

❷ ▲ Critical Viewing
Frost's poem is based on his reaction to birch trees. What response does this photograph of birches evoke in you? [Connect]

882 ◆ *Disillusion, Defiance, and Discontent (1914–1946)*

TEACHING RESOURCES

The following resources can be used to enrich or extend the instruction for pp. 882–892.

Literary Analysis

📖 **Writing Models and Graphic Organizers on Transparencies,** pp. 83–85, 95–97

Reading

📖 **Selection Support:** Reading Strategy, p. 222; Build Vocabulary, p. 220

🎧 **Listening to Literature Audiocassettes,** Sides 31, 32 ▪

💿 **Listening to Literature Audio CDs,** CDs 17, 18 ▪

Extension

📖 **Authors In Depth:** Ruby Level (The collection includes eleven additional selections by Robert Frost for extended reading.) ▪

▪ **BLOCK SCHEDULING:** Resources marked with this symbol provide varied instruction during 90-minute blocks.

❸ Literary Analysis

Blank Verse and Pastorals

- Read aloud the bracketed lines for students, emphasizing the blank verse rhythm of the poetry. Invite students to close their eyes and visualize the boy's activities as they listen.

- Ask students the Literary Analysis question on p. 883: What picture of rural life is conveyed in this description of the boy's summer activities?
  Possible answer: The picture is one of a carefree, if perhaps an isolated summer.

❹ ✓ **Reading Check**

Answer: He thinks of times he swung from birches as a boy.

So low for long, they never right themselves:
You may see their trunks arching in the woods
Years afterwards, trailing their leaves on the ground
Like girls on hands and knees that throw their hair
20 Before them over their heads to dry in the sun.
But I was going to say when Truth broke in
With all her matter of fact about the ice storm,
I should prefer to have some boy bend them
As he went out and in to fetch the cows—
25 Some boy too far from town to learn baseball,
Whose only play was what he found himself,
Summer or winter, and could play alone.
One by one he subdued his father's trees
By riding them down over and over again
30 Until he took the stiffness out of them,
And not one but hung limp, not one was left
For him to conquer. He learned all there was
To learn about not launching out too soon
And so not carrying the tree away
35 Clear to the ground. He always kept his poise
To the top branches, climbing carefully

Literary Analysis
Blank Verse and Pastorals
What picture of rural life is conveyed in this description of the boy's summer activities?

poise (poiz) *n.* balance; stability

❹ ✓ **Reading Check**
What does the speaker think of when he sees birches bend to left and right?

Birches ◆ 883

Reading Blank Verse

- Invite a volunteer to read aloud lines 43–47 several times until he or she achieves a sentence rhythm. Discuss what students think the lines mean.
  Answer: Adult life is sometimes confusing and hard to navigate.

- Ask students the Reading Strategy question on p. 884: Does reading lines 43–47 as a sentence help to clarify their meaning?
  Answer: Most students will answer yes.

Answers for p. 884

Review and Assess

1. Many students will admit to the occasional need to escape.

2. (a) The ice storm makes the trees bend over. (b) He hopes they are bent because a boy has been playing on them, not because of violent storms. (c) He prefers his version of the facts.

3. (a) The boy is an image of the speaker as a youth. (b) It symbolizes freedom and the experience of learning.

4. (a) He'd like to begin his life over again. (b) He sees the violence in nature and the burdens of daily life, yet still loves Earth and life.

5. Possible response: The speaker may be troubled by relationships, responsibilities, or frustrations.

With the same pains you use to fill a cup
Up to the brim, and even above the brim.
Then he flung outward, feet first, with a swish,
40   Kicking his way down through the air to the ground.
So was I once myself a swinger of birches.
And so I dream of going back to be.
It's when I'm weary of considerations,
And life is too much like a pathless wood
45   Where your face burns and tickles with the cobwebs
Broken across it, and one eye is weeping
From a twig's having lashed across it open.
I'd like to get away from earth awhile
And then come back to it and begin over.
50   May no fate willfully misunderstand me
And half grant what I wish and snatch me away
Not to return. Earth's the right place for love:
I don't know where it's likely to go better.
I'd like to go by climbing a birch tree,
55   And climb black branches up a snow-white trunk
Toward heaven, till the tree could bear no more,
But dipped its top and set me down again.
That would be good both going and coming back.
One could do worse than be a swinger of birches.

Review and Assess

Thinking About the Selection

1. **Respond:** Do you ever yearn to escape from reality for a while? Why or why not?

2. **(a) Recall:** What is the connection between the ice storm and the bent birches? **(b) Recall:** What does the speaker prefer to think when he sees birches "bend to left and right"? **(c) Interpret:** What does the speaker feel about the facts concerning the real causes of the bowed trees?

3. **(a) Recall:** What is the connection between the "swinger of birches" and the speaker? **(b) Interpret:** What does the activity of swinging on birches come to symbolize for the speaker in the poem?

4. **(a) Interpret:** What does the speaker say he'd like to "begin over"? **(b) Analyze:** What aspects of this poem reflect the speaker's conflicting attitudes about life?

5. **Speculate:** What kinds of events, experiences, and feelings in his life might have caused the speaker to make the admission contained in lines 48–49?

884 ◆ Disillusion, Defiance, and Discontent (1914–1946)

Reading Strategy
Reading Blank Verse
Does reading lines 43–47 as a sentence help to clarify its meaning? Explain.

 ENRICHMENT: Cultural Connection

Trees as Symbols

Certain trees have come to symbolize a culture or nation. The cedars of Lebanon are included in the nation's flag and have been associated with that country since Biblical times. Unfortunately, few giant cedars remain in Lebanon today; most were cut down in previous centuries to provide wood for building ships and temples. The graceful weeping willow tree, native to China, appears frequently in Chinese art. The American elm has long been part of our nation's heritage. Elms lined many streets in early American villages; to this day most towns and cities still have an Elm Street.

Discuss with students some characteristics that make trees meaningful and enduring symbols. Point out that trees are a visual reference to the cycles of the seasons and therefore to life and death. Note the fact that trees withstand harsh weather and storms and live for many years.

Stopping by Woods on a Snowy Evening

⑥

Robert Frost

Whose woods these are I think I know.
His house is in the village though;
He will not see me stopping here
To watch his woods fill up with snow.

5 My little horse must think it queer
To stop without a farmhouse near
Between the woods and frozen lake
The darkest evening of the year.

He gives his harness bells a shake
10 To ask if there is some mistake.
The only other sound's the sweep
Of easy wind and downy flake.

The woods are lovely, dark and deep,
But I have promises to keep,
15 And miles to go before I sleep,
And miles to go before I sleep.

⑦ ▲ Critical Viewing
What elements of this scene differ from the scene the speaker describes? What do the two scenes have in common? **[Compare and Contrast]**

⑧ Literary Analysis
Blank Verse Is this poem an example of blank verse? Explain.

⑨ ☑ Reading Check
At what exact time of year is this poem set?

Stopping by Woods on a Snowy Evening ◆ 885

---

⑥ About the Selection
The speaker of this poem, on a nighttime journey through a wintry forest, stops to observe the beauty of the scene and to temporarily escape the demands of his life. Although he would like to rest and take in the beauty of the scene, he thinks of the many tasks he must complete. This decision suggests he forestalls death to keep the promises of his life. The poem mines the meaning of life and the things people value most.

⑦ ▶ Critical Viewing
Answer: Students should note that the wooded area in the photo is brightly moonlit, open, and still, rather than dark, windy, and filled with falling snow. Both scenes are peaceful nighttime depictions of snow-covered woods.

⑧ Literary Analysis
Blank Verse
- Direct students to read the poem silently. Have them count the number of feet in the first two lines and determine the pattern of unstressed and stressed syllables.
- Then, ask them the Literary Analysis question on p. 885: Is this poem an example of blank verse? Explain.
- Students should note that this poem cannot be an example of blank verse, because it is rhymed.
- Explain to students that poetry using this pattern is an example of iambic tetrameter, as each line has four iambs. Distinguish tetrameter from pentameter, in which each line has five iambs.
- Ask students for possible reasons why Frost chose rhymed iambic tetrameter for this poem. Possible answer: The quicker rhythm might have suggested the sound of a horse's hooves, evoking the ride through the snowy woods.

⑨ ☑ Reading Check
Answer: It is set "during the darkest evening of the year," the winter solstice.

❿ **About the Selection**

The speaker and his neighbor make an annual walk along the fieldstone wall that separates their property to repair the breaks they find. The speaker sees this as an unnecessary act, but the neighbor holds that "Good fences make good neighbors." The speaker suggests that because walls create unnatural separations, natural forces will always work to break them down.

⓫ **Literary Analysis**

Blank Verse and Pastorals

- Call on a volunteer to read aloud the lines 5–9, stopping after "yelping dogs." Help students paraphrase the lines.
  Answer: The speaker has repaired the breaks in the wall created by hunters trying to oust a hiding rabbit.

- Ask students the Literary Analysis question on p. 886: What activities do lines 5–9 suggest are part of rural life?
  Answer: They suggest that rural life includes hunting for rabbits with dogs, and repairing walls.

⓬ ▶ **Critical Viewing**

Answer: Students may respond that weeds have grown right up through the rock wall as if it offered no resistance. Also, some rocks have fallen, due perhaps to frost heaves or animals or people climbing on them.

Mending Wall

⓾

Robert Frost

Something there is that doesn't love a wall,
That sends the frozen-ground-swell under it
And spills the upper boulders in the sun,
And makes gaps even two can pass abreast.
5   The work of hunters is another thing:
I have come after them and made repair
Where they have left not one stone on a stone,
But they would have the rabbit out of hiding,
To please the yelping dogs. The gaps I mean,
10 No one has seen them made or heard them made,
But at spring mending-time we find them there.
I let my neighbor know beyond the hill;
And on a day we meet to walk the line
And set the wall between us once again.
15 We keep the wall between us as we go.
To each the boulders that have fallen to each.
And some are loaves and some so nearly balls
We have to use a spell to make them balance:
"Stay where you are until our backs are turned!"
20 We wear our fingers rough with handling them.
Oh, just another kind of outdoor game,
One on a side. It comes to little more:
There where it is we do not need the wall:

⓫

Literary Analysis
Blank Verse and Pastorals
What activities do lines 5–9 suggest are part of rural life?

⓬ ▼ **Critical Viewing**
What elements of this picture suggest that walls do not belong in the natural world? **[Analyze]**

886 ◆ *Disillusion, Defiance, and Discontent (1914–1946)*

He is all pine and I am apple orchard.
25 My apple trees will never get across
And eat the cones under his pines, I tell him.
He only says, "Good fences make good neighbors."
Spring is the mischief in me, and I wonder
If I could put a notion in his head:
30 "*Why* do they make good neighbors? Isn't it
Where there are cows? But here there are no cows.
Before I built a wall I'd ask to know
What I was walling in or walling out,
And to whom I was like to give offense.
35 Something there is that doesn't love a wall,
That wants it down." I could say "Elves" to him,
But it's not elves exactly, and I'd rather
He said it for himself. I see him there,
Bringing a stone grasped firmly by the top
40 In each hand, like an old-stone savage armed.
He moves in darkness as it seems to me,
Not of woods only and the shade of trees.
He will not go behind his father's saying,
And he likes having thought of it so well
45 He says again, "Good fences make good neighbors."

Reading Strategy
Reading Blank Verse
Read lines 28–31 as sentences. In what ways are their meanings clarified?

Review and Assess

Thinking About the Selections

1. **Respond:** Which of the poems on pages 885–887 made the strongest impression on you? Explain.

2. **(a) Recall:** In the first stanza of "Stopping by Woods on a Snowy Evening," what two actions does the speaker engage in? **(b) Infer:** What internal conflict do the actions create?

3. **(a) Recall:** What phrase is repeated in the poem's last two lines? **(b) Analyze:** How does this repetition reinforce the theme?

4. **(a) Recall:** In "Mending Wall," what two causes of gaps in walls does the speaker identify? **(b) Speculate:** In what ways are these two causes expressions of a general force the speaker struggles to name? **(c) Interpret:** Why does this force not love a wall?

5. **(a) Recall:** What saying does the neighbor repeat? **(b) Interpret:** What does this saying mean?

6. **(a) Recall:** What image does the speaker use to characterize his neighbor as he repairs the wall? **(b) Interpret:** What is the meaning of the "darkness" in which the man walks?

7. **Make a Judgment:** Are both the neighbor's and the speaker's ideas about the value of walls valid? Explain.

CUSTOMIZE FOR UNIVERSAL ACCESS

For Less Proficient Readers	For English Learners	For Advanced Readers
Brainstorm with the class for reasons not to love a wall, as well as for valid reasons to support putting up walls. You may use the Motivation activity on p. 880 to help students visualize the concept. Encourage students to think metaphorically as well as concretely.	To help these students recognize the poem's meanings about walls, write the saying "Good fences make good neighbors" on the chalkboard. Explain that the phrase is figurative. The fences create the opportunity for good relationships between neighbors, they don't literally make the good neighbors.	Challenge students to restate the logic the speaker puts forth in lines 28–34 to argue against his neighbor's viewpoint about walls. Invite other students to refute this argument in a debate setting.

⓭ Reading Strategy

Reading Blank Verse

• Invite volunteers to take turns reading aloud lines 28–31 so that the class hears the lines several times. Make sure students read the lines as sentences.

• Ask students the Reading Strategy question on p. 887: Read lines 28–31 as sentences. In what ways are their meanings clarified? Answer: Reading the lines as sentences can help students recognize the speaker's reasoning about walls: he believes there should be reasons for their existence.

Answers for p. 887

Review and Assess

1. Students should be able to support their responses.

2. **(a)** He stops in the woods; he watches the snow fall. **(b)** He is torn between the desire to enjoy nature's beauty and the awareness that he has commitments to fulfill.

3. **(a)** The speaker repeats "And miles to go before I sleep." **(b)** The repetition creates finality and reinforces the conflict between life's demands and the sleep of death.

4. **(a)** The speaker names the freezing and thawing of the earth and the work of hunters as culprits. **(b)** Both causes reflect natural forces, first of the seasons and second of the human thirst for control. **(c)** Nature doesn't love a wall because it marks territories and claims false ownership.

5. **(a)** He repeats "Good fences make good neighbors." **(b)** It means that walls clearly define the boundaries and thus leave less possibility for conflict.

6. **(a)** He uses the image of a stone-age "savage." **(b)** The darkness may be a lack of imagination or thought.

7. Possible response: Each view is valid. While walls may be unnecessary in certain circumstances, they may keep the peace between enemies.

This shocking, understated poem presents a horrific story of death. Late one ordinary day, a young boy using a power saw to cut wood momentarily loses his concentration and severely cuts his hand. Unfortunately, not only does the boy lose his hand, he loses his life. However, the harsh reality of rural life demands that family members go about their chores because farm life must go on even after a senseless death.

⓯ Literary Analysis

Blank Verse

- Direct students to read lines 10–12. Then, have a volunteer read aloud the lines, and ask students to describe the meter of the lines.

- Then, ask students the Literary Analysis question on p. 888: Which words or phrases in lines 10–12 capture the rhythms of everyday speech?
  Answer: The phrase "call it a day" sounds in particular like everyday speech, though the entire sentence captures an everyday cadence as well.

▶ Monitor Progress Have students complete the organizer from p. 881 with information about the lines. Students should respond that there is no rhyme scheme and that the poem is written in blank verse.

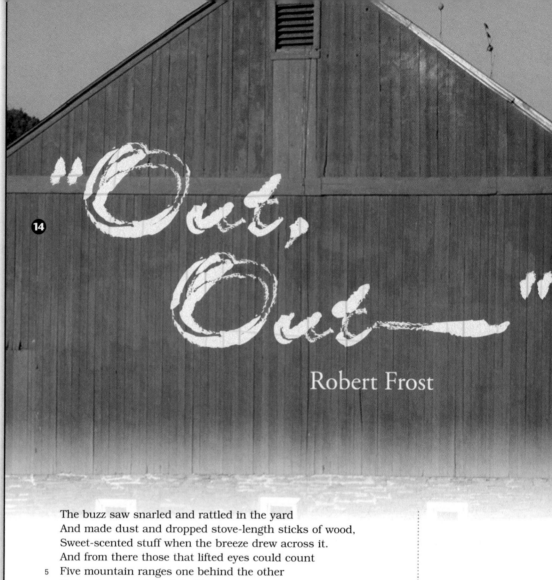

⓮

"Out, Out—"

Robert Frost

The buzz saw snarled and rattled in the yard
And made dust and dropped stove-length sticks of wood,
Sweet-scented stuff when the breeze drew across it.
And from there those that lifted eyes could count
5 Five mountain ranges one behind the other
Under the sunset far into Vermont.
And the saw snarled and rattled, snarled and rattled,
As it ran light, or had to bear a load.
And nothing happened: day was all but done.
10 Call it a day, I wish they might have said
To please the boy by giving him the half hour
That a boy counts so much when saved from work.
His sister stood beside them in her apron
To tell them "Supper." At the word, the saw,
15 As if to prove saws knew what supper meant,

Literary Analysis
Blank Verse Which words or phrases in lines 10–12 capture the rhythms of everyday speech?

☀ ENRICHMENT: Health/Safety Connection

Job Safety

Statistics for fatalities from plane crashes, natural disasters, or epidemic illnesses are widely publicized. However, we rarely hear about the significant number of casualties that occur each year on farms. Nearly one-third of all reported farm accidents involve contact with equipment or machinery.

Brainstorm with the class for different types of farm equipment or machinery that could cause injury, and then for measures workers could take to protect themselves. Have interested students contact the U.S. Labor Department to gather recent statistics on farm-related injuries. Students can present their findings in a chart or graph, and provide a list of safety measures.

Leaped out at the boy's hand, or seemed to leap—
He must have given the hand. However it was,
Neither refused the meeting. But the hand!
The boy's first outcry was a <u>rueful</u> laugh,
20 As he swung toward them holding up the hand,
Half in appeal, but half as if to keep
The life from spilling. Then the boy saw all—
Since he was old enough to know, big boy
Doing a man's work, though a child at heart—
25 He saw all spoiled. "Don't let him cut my hand off—
The doctor, when he comes. Don't let him, sister!"
So. But the hand was gone already.
The doctor put him in the dark of ether.[1]
He lay and puffed his lips out with his breath.
30 And then—the watcher at his pulse took fright.
No one believed. They listened at his heart.
Little—less—nothing!—and that ended it.
No more to build on there. And they, since they
Were not the one dead, turned to their affairs.

---

1. **ether** (ē′ ther) *n.* chemical compound used as an anesthetic.

rueful (rōō′ fəl) *adj.* feeling or showing someone sorrow or pity

Literary Analysis
Blank Verse and Pastorals
In what ways do lines 19–34 portray a harsh view of rural life?

Review and Assess

Thinking About the Selection

1. **Respond:** What do you find more disturbing—the boy's death or the onlookers' reaction to it? Explain.

2. **(a) Recall:** Where is the poem set? **(b) Connect:** In what ways does the description of the setting contrast with the events of the poem?

3. **(a) Recall:** At what time of day does the accident occur? **(b) Support:** What is ironic about the fact that the boy is cut at precisely that moment?

4. **(a) Recall:** What are the boy's first and second responses to the accident? **(b) Interpret:** What does the speaker mean by the expression "the boy saw all" in line 22?

5. **(a) Recall:** In the last line, what is the family's response to the boy's death? **(b) Speculate:** How do you explain this response?

6. **Connect:** The poem's title comes from a scene in William Shakespeare's *Macbeth* in which Macbeth laments the death of his wife with these words: "Out, out, brief candle! / Life's but a walking shadow, a poor player, / That struts and frets his hour upon the stage, / And then is heard no more." What does this quotation reveal about the poem's theme?

"Out, Out—" ◆ 889

🔟 Literary Analysis
Blank Verse and Pastorals

- After students have read the lines 19–34, ask them to describe what has happened.
  Answer: The boy cuts himself badly. The doctor comes to help him, but he dies anyway. His family returns to work.

- Then, ask students the Literary Analysis question on p. 889: In what ways do lines 19–34 portray a harsh view of rural life?
  Answer: They show how easily injury and even death can occur on a farm. They also suggest that the family cannot even take time from the ongoing chores in order to grieve.

Answers for p. 889

Review and Assess

1. Students should support their responses.

2. **(a)** It is set on a Vermont farm in the summer. **(b)** The setting is very peaceful, while the events are quite violent.

3. **(a)** The accident occurs just before supper. **(b)** The boy was finished with work for the day and—theoretically—out of danger.

4. **(a)** First he laughs ruefully, then he asks his sister not to let the doctor amputate his hand. **(b)** Possible response: The boy understood the severity of his injury.

5. **(a)** They go on with their affairs. **(b)** Possible response: They were in shock and unable to process the reality of the death.

6. It conveys the fact that life is short and fragile in nature.

CUSTOMIZE INSTRUCTION FOR UNIVERSAL ACCESS

For Less Proficient Readers	For English Learners	For Advanced Readers
Guide students to recognize the impact Frost creates in lines 14–18 by personifying the saw. Help them understand that Frost describes the saw as though it had a mind and could understand that it was time to be fed, as though the saw "eats" the boy's hand.	To help students visualize the tool that plays such a key role in this poem, display pictures of buzz saws or buzz saw blades. Students who have used a buzz saw or have heard one in operation can describe its loud whining sound.	Ask students to identify words in the opening lines that personify the saw. Discuss how these words, along with those linking dust to death, create an uneasy sense of foreboding. Challenge students to look for other clues in the poem that hint at the tragedy ahead.

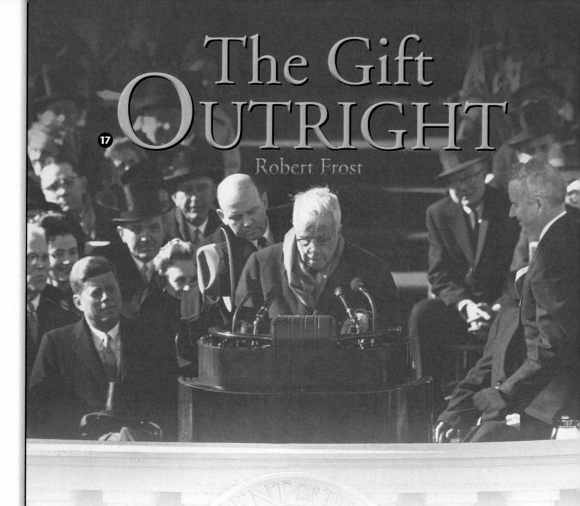

The Gift OUTRIGHT

17 Robert Frost

17 About the Selections

This poem celebrates the birth of a nation and reminds readers of the human connection to the hope and potential of the landscape. The speaker examines the American colonists' struggle to understand their future on the strange continent. He suggests that— spurred on by a love of the land and high hopes for a future that was as yet unformed—colonists broke free from English rule to form an independent nation.

Drawing on darkness as a time of isolation and loneliness, "Acquainted With the Night" is the city partner of "Stopping by Woods on a Snowy Evening." Here, Frost's speaker views his life as having had times of isolation, loneliness, and despair, but he accepts this as his lot.

Background

During the planning stages of John F. Kennedy's presidential inauguration, his staff approached Robert Frost with a request: Would the poet write and recite a poem for the inauguration? Frost declined to write something new but agreed to recite "The Gift Outright." President Kennedy had a second request: Would Frost change the word "would" to "will" in the last line of the poem? The poet agreed. Shortly before the inauguration date, Frost was struck by inspiration and, despite his earlier refusal, drafted a forty-two-line poem, "Dedication," especially for the ceremony. The weather on inauguration day was windy, clear, and sunny. As Frost stood at the podium reading his new poem, the glare of the sun and the whipping wind made it almost impossible for him to see the words on the page. After struggling through the first half of "Dedication," he gave up the effort, and recited "The Gift Outright" from memory.

890 ◆ *Disillusion, Defiance, and Discontent*

CUSTOMIZE INSTRUCTION FOR UNIVERSAL ACCESS

For Advanced Readers

Suggest that students read additional works by Robert Frost. Provide students with the titles listed in the Enrichment box, ATE p. 893. You may also wish to use **Authors In Depth,** The American Experience, which contains the following selections:

- "The Death of the Hired Man" (poem, p. 143)
- "The Sound of Trees" (poem, p. 148)
- "A Brook in the City" (poem, p. 149)
- "Nothing Gold Can Stay" (poem, p. 150)

- "The Tuft of Flowers" (poem, p. 151)
- "Take Something Like a Star" (poem, p. 152)
- "On 'Choose Something Like a Star' "(nonfiction, p. 153)
- "Fragmentary Blue" (poem, p. 154)
- "Misgiving" (poem, p. 155)
- "For Once, Then, Something" (poem, p. 156)
- from "*Paris Review* Interview with Richard Poirier" (nonfiction, p. 157)

The land was ours before we were the land's.
She was our land more than a hundred years
Before we were her people. She was ours
In Massachusetts, in Virginia,
5   But we were England's, still colonials,
Possessing what we still were unpossessed by,
Possessed by what we now no more possessed.
Something we were withholding made us weak
Until we found out that it was ourselves
10 We were withholding from our land of living,
And forthwith found salvation in surrender.
Such as we were we gave ourselves outright
(The deed of gift was many deeds of war)
To the land vaguely realizing westward,
15 But still unstoried, artless, unenhanced,
Such as she was, such as she would become.

Reading Strategy
Reading Blank Verse In what ways does reading this poem aloud as sentences help clarify the poet's meaning?

Review and Assess

Thinking About the Selection

1. **Respond:** What does this poem make you feel about America's past and future? Explain.

2. **(a) Recall:** According to the speaker, what was the relationship between the land and the people in colonial America? **(b) Interpret:** What do you think the poet means by the phrase "the land was ours"?

3. **(a) Recall:** According to the speaker, where did the national allegiance of most Americans in colonial America lie? **(b) Interpret:** To where does the speaker say this sense of allegiance shifted?

4. **(a) Recall:** According to the speaker, what were we "withholding" in early America? **(b) Infer:** To what does the speaker suggest earlier generations surrendered in order to become true Americans? **(c) Synthesize:** What does this poem suggest about the meaning of citizenship?

5. **(a) Recall:** In what action did the early Americans find salvation? **(b) Connect:** What is the meaning of the poem's title?

6. **(a) Interpret:** Does the poet suggest there was a price to pay for the "gift outright"? **(b) Analyze:** According to the poet, what was that price, and who paid it?

7. **Generalize:** What picture of American history does this poem create? **(b) Evaluate:** Do you think this poem suggests that American history is a story of continuous progress? Explain.

⑱ Reading Strategy

Reading Blank Verse

- Have volunteers read lines 5–16 twice, first in poetic fashion and then as sentences. Encourage students to listen carefully for the difference.

- Then, ask students the Reading Strategy question on p. 891: In what ways does reading this poem aloud as sentences help clarify the poet's meaning?
  Answer: It helps listeners organize the long sentences into meaningful ideas.

Answers for p. 891

Review and Assess

1. Students should support their responses.

2. **(a)** The people took America while still feeling allegiance to England. **(b)** The speaker means that the colonials lived on it, but did not yet truly possess it.

3. **(a)** It lay in England. **(b)** It shifted to the land.

4. **(a)** We were withholding ourselves. **(b)** They surrendered to the need to fight and sacrifice for freedom. **(c)** It suggests that citizenship means a willingness to fight for your country.

5. **(a)** They found salvation in surrender. **(b)** It means that Americans should give themselves without reservation.

6. **(a)** Yes, he does. **(b)** The deeds of war were the price paid by those who fought for freedom.

7. **(a)** It creates a picture of heroic sacrifice. **(b)** Yes, it suggests that the nation had yet to write its history and develop its potential.

CUSTOMIZE INSTRUCTION FOR UNIVERSAL ACCESS

For Less Proficient Readers

To help students get meaning from reading blank verse, suggest that they not stop or pause at the end of a line unless there is punctuation. Explain that stopping at the end of each line will produce a choppy effect and will distract from the meaning.

Have students work in groups of two or three to read one of Frost's poems aloud. Ask one person to read aloud, stopping at the end of each complete thought, which usually ends in punctuation. Instruct the others

to listen. Then, listeners should briefly state the idea in the lines that were read aloud. Students may exchange roles of reader and listener.

To help students get the rhythm when reading the lines aloud, they can emphasize the stresses in each line as shown here.

Súch as wé were
gáve oursélves óutright

⑲ Literary Analysis

Blank Verse

- Direct students to read the entire poem silently. Then read it aloud together as a class.

- Ask students the Literary Analysis question on p. 892: How do you know that this poem is not an example of blank verse?
  Answer: It contains rhyme.

⑳ Vocabulary Development

The Latin Word Root -lum-

- Draw students' attention to the word *luminary* and its definition. Tell students that the word root -lum- derives from the Latin word *lumen*, which means "light."

- Have students suggest words that contain this word root, and list them on the chalkboard. Possibilities include: *illuminate, luminous, luminescent*

- Have students confirm the meanings of these words in a dictionary.

- Then, ask students to look through the poems, and find places where they might replace an existing word with a word containing the Latin root -lum-.

Answers for p. 892

Review and Assess

1. Students should support their responses.

2. **(a)** He avoids making eye contact. **(b)** Possible responses: He is unwilling to explain his presence.

3. **(a)** He hears an interrupted cry. **(b)** He wishes someone would interact with him.

4. **(a)** The time is neither wrong nor right. **(b)** A state of lonely acceptance is proclaimed by the final stanza.

5. **(a)** It might symbolize a feeling of being apart from the human mainstream. **(b)** The use of repetition draws readers back to the poem's beginning, referring perhaps to the speaker's continual sense of being apart.

6. It uses an everyday setting, a city street, to explore themes such as isolation and loneliness.

⑰ ACQUAINTED WITH THE NIGHT

Robert Frost

I have been one acquainted with the night.
I have walked out in rain—and back in rain.
I have outwalked the furthest city light.

I have looked down the saddest city lane.
5   I have passed by the watchman on his beat
And dropped my eyes, unwilling to explain.

⑲   I have stood still and stopped the sound of feet
When far away an interrupted cry
Came over houses from another street,

10   But not to call me back or say good-by;
And further still at an unearthly height
One <u>luminary</u> clock against the sky

Proclaimed the time was neither wrong nor right.
I have been one acquainted with the night.

Literary Analysis
Blank Verse How do you know that this poem is not an example of blank verse?

⑳ **luminary** (lo͞o′ mə ner′ ē)
adj. giving off light

Review and Assess

Thinking About the Selection

1. **Respond:** How did this poem make you feel? Explain.

2. **(a) Recall:** What is the speaker's reaction when he sees the night watchman? **(b) Interpret:** What is the speaker "unwilling to explain"?

3. **(a) Recall:** What does the speaker hear in the third stanza? **(b) Infer:** From line 10, what does it seem the speaker hoped for?

4. **(a) Recall:** What is proclaimed in the final stanza? **(b) Analyze:** What emotional state is suggested by this proclamation?

5. **(a) Generalize:** What does night symbolize in this poem? **(b) Analyze:** In what ways does Frost's use of repetition heighten the symbolism of the poem?

6. **Evaluate:** How does this poem demonstrate Frost's ability to write poems that seem simple but present deeper meaning?

892 ◆ *Disillusion, Defiance, and Discontent (1914–1946)*

✎ ASSESSMENT PRACTICE: Reading Comprehension

Try Words in a Sentence   (For more practice, see Test Preparation Workbook, p. 53.)

Use the following item to show students that they can often eliminate choices because they are illogical, the wrong part of speech, or inconsistent with meaning.

Robert Frost moved to England in 1912 hoping to have his poetry accepted, and his strategy worked. He found that his _____ abroad had spread and that he was on the road to _____.

A failure; ruin   **C** reputation; despair
B success; fame   **D** defeat; glory

From the context, students can tell that the correct words should be positive and should have similar meanings. *B* is the best choice.

Review and Assess

Literary Analysis

Blank Verse

1. (a) Find two instances in "Out, Out—" where Frost deviates from **blank verse.** (b) In what ways do these metrical variations emphasize a specific idea or image?

2. (a) Identify the two poems presented here that are not written in blank verse. (b) What poetic device distinguishes them from the other poems? (c) How is the sound of these poems different from those that are written in blank verse?

Comparing Literary Works

3. (a) What details of "Out, Out—" and "Mending Wall" present a dark view of rural life? (b) What human failings do these poems depict?

4. What ideas about land ownership and boundaries do "Stopping by Woods on a Snowy Evening" and "Mending Wall" express?

5. In "Birches," the speaker expresses ambivalence about life, though he adds "Earth's the right place for love." (a) Use a chart like the one shown to determine the nature of his ambivalence. (b) Do Frost's other poems express similar ambivalence? Explain.

Reading Strategy

Reading Blank Verse

6. (a) Rewrite "The Gift Outright" as five sentences. (b) What is the effect of this approach?

7. Read "Out, Out—", pausing at the end of each of the poetic lines. Then, read the poem as a series of sentences. How does each reading affect your understanding of the poem?

Extend Understanding

8. **Psychology Connection:** Pausing to observe nature provides the speaker with a temporary escape from reality in "Stopping by Woods on a Snowy Evening." Why do you think people sometimes need to find this type of temporary escape?

Robert Frost's Poetry ◆ 893

Quick Review

Blank verse is poetry written in unrhymed iambic pentameter.

A **pastoral** is a poem that features people in rural settings.

Reading blank verse as sentences (rather than as poetic lines) helps you appreciate how blank verse captures the rhythms of everyday speech.

 Take It to the Net
www.phschool.com

Take the interactive self-test online to check your understanding of these selections.

ENRICHMENT: Further Reading

Other Works by Robert Frost

North of Boston

A Boy's Will

In the Clearing

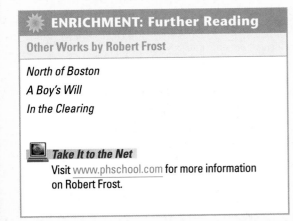

Take It to the Net
Visit www.phschool.com for more information on Robert Frost.

Answers for p. 893

Review and Assess

1. **(a)** While blank verse is frequently not exact, Frost makes clear breaks in lines 27 and 32. **(b)** The breaks in lines 27 and 32 emphasize the severity of the injury.

2. **(a)** Neither "Stopping by Woods on a Snowy Evening" nor "Acquainted with the Night" is written in blank verse. **(b)** The use of rhyme and repetition distinguishes them from the other poems. **(c)** They have a more regular rhythm than that of the blank verse poems.

3. **(a)** In "Out, Out" the boy's injury and his family's stoicism in the face of tragedy show a dark side of rural life. In "Mending Wall" the image of hunters and yelping dogs, as well as the closed mind of the neighbor shows a dark side to rural life. **(b)** "Out, Out" shows indifference; "Mending Wall" shows aggression and self-satisfaction.

4. Both suggest a vision in which land ownership and boundaries are irrelevant.

5. **(a)** Negative ideas and images: heaps of broken glass; withered bracken, bowed [branches], pathless wood; cobwebs broken across it; Positive ideas and images: kicking his way through the air, toward heaven, subdued his father's trees, swinger of birches **(b)** Frost's poems contain hopeful images of people in everyday moments, but also show violent and gloomy moments in life.

6. **(a)** Students should write five sentences ending with the periods shown in the poem. **(b)** Content becomes more accessible.

7. Students may find that reading the poem and pausing at line breaks produces choppiness that interferes with comprehension. Reading blank verse as a series of sentences is a more effective method for retaining meaning.

8. Possible response: People find the demands of modern life exhausting. Nature soothes with beauty and the promise of continuity.

❶ Vocabulary Development

Word Analysis

1. b
2. a
3. c

Concept Development: Analogies

1. luminary
2. poise
3. rueful

Spelling Strategy

1. blissful
2. mournful

❷ Grammar and Style

Practice

1. to fetch the cows: adv.
2. to walk the line: adv.
3. to keep, to go: adj.
4. to conquer: adverb
5. to sweep away: adj.

Writing Application

Students' paragraphs should be free of mechanical errors and make proper use of at least three infinitives or infinitive phrases.

Integrate Language Skills

❶ Vocabulary Development Lesson

Word Analysis: Latin Root -lum-

Along with several related English words, including *luminous* and *illuminate*, the word *luminary* (which means "giving off light") is based on the Latin root *-lum-*, meaning "light."

Complete these sentences using the appropriate word from the list below.

    a. luminous   **b.** illuminate   **c.** illumination

1. Is that single bulb enough to ___?___ the entire room?

2. The leaves of the linden tree were bathed in ___?___ sunlight.

3. The students found ___?___ in the wise words of the philosopher.

❷ Grammar and Style Lesson

Uses of Infinitives

An **infinitive** is a verb form consisting of the base form of a verb, usually with the word *to*. An **infinitive phrase** consists of an infinitive plus any modifiers or complements, all acting together as a single part of speech. Infinitives and infinitive phrases can be used as adjectives, adverbs, or nouns.

Adverb: But swinging doesn't bend them down *to stay*. (The infinitive acts as an adverb that modifies *bend*.)

Noun: Before I built a wall I'd ask *to know* . . . (The infinitive acts as a noun serving as the direct object of the verb *ask*.)

Concept Development: Analogies

Complete the following analogies using the words from the vocabulary list on page 881.

1. *Scorching* is to *fire* as ___?___ is to *moon*.
2. *Swiftness* is to *runner* as ___?___ is to *dancer*.
3. *Joyful* is to *celebrant* as ___?___ is to *mourner*.

Spelling Strategy

The one-syllable word *full* is spelled with two *l*'s. However, in words of more than one syllable, such as *rueful* and *stressful*, the suffix *-ful* is spelled with only one *l*. Turn each of the following phrases into a word using a form of the key word and the suffix *-ful*.

    1. full of bliss   **2.** full of mourning

Practice For each of the following items, identify the infinitive or infinitive phrase and determine whether it functions as a noun, an adjective, or an adverb.

1. As he went out . . . to fetch the cows— . . .
2. And on a day we meet to walk the line . . .
3. But I have promises to keep, / And miles to go before I sleep . . .
4. Not one was left . . . to conquer.
5. Such heaps of broken glass to sweep away . . .

Writing Application Using at least three infinitives or infinitive phrases, describe an outdoor activity in which you recently participated.

W̶G   *Prentice Hall Writing and Grammar Connection: Chapter 19, Section 2*

894 ◆ *Disillusion, Defiance, and Discontent (1914–1946)*

TEACHING RESOURCES

The following resources can be used to enrich or extend the instruction for pp. 894–895.

Vocabulary

📖 **Selection Support:** Build Vocabulary, p. 220
📖 **Vocabulary and Spelling Practice Book** (Use this booklet for skills enrichment.) 📘

Grammar

📖 **Selection Support:** Grammar and Style, p. 221
W̶G **Writing and Grammar,** Ruby Level, p. 442
📄 **Daily Language Practice Transparencies** 📘

Writing

W̶G **Writing and Grammar,** Ruby Level, p. 37
💿 **Writing and Grammar iText CD-ROM**
📄 **Writing Models and Graphic Organizers on Transparencies,** pp. 83–85, 95–97

📄 **BLOCK SCHEDULING:** Resources marked with this symbol provide varied instruction during 90-minute blocks.

❸ Writing Lesson

Introduction to an Anthology

An anthology is a collection of literature often focused on a specific theme or time period. Anthologies frequently include an introduction that provides an overview of the content and comments on the works. Write an introduction to an anthology that includes poems by Robert Frost.

Prewriting   Reread Frost's poems, and make notes about his style and themes. Select the characteristics you will address, and identify poems to cite. Then, sketch out a table of contents.

Drafting   Start with a general statement about the poems you chose. Follow by touching on a few key points related to this statement. Focus each paragraph on one key point, supported with passages from the poems.

Revising   As you review your work, make sure that you have clearly linked your ideas. Add transitions to introduce examples where necessary.

Model: Revising to Smooth Transitions

For example,

Frost's appreciation of beauty is never simple. In "Stopping

by Woods on a Snowy Evening," he reminds us that

someone else owns the lovely scene.

> Phrases like *for example* provide transitions that improve clarity.

W̶G̶ Prentice Hall Writing and Grammar Connection: Chapter 3, Section 2

❹ Extension Activities

Listening and Speaking   Present a **eulogy** for the boy whose death is described in "Out, Out—." Use these tips to prepare:

- Use clues in the poem to create a sense of the boy's personality.
- Pay tribute to the boy "who did a man's work."
- Address the boy's family in an appropriate manner.

Deliver the eulogy at a "memorial service" in the classroom. **[Group Activity]**

Research and Technology   Using a variety of sources, locate recordings of Frost reciting his poems. Select two poems that appeal to you and play the recordings for the class as part of an **interpretive presentation.** Deliver a brief analysis of each poem in which you consider the impressions created by Frost's delivery.

 **Take It to the Net**   www.phschool.com

Go online for an additional research activity using the Internet.

Lesson Support for p. 895

❸ Writing Lesson

- Organize students in groups to discuss characteristics shared by various Frost poems and to brainstorm logical groupings.
- Suggest that students use the Analysis Map or Outline transparencies in **Writings Models and Graphic Organizers on Transparencies,** pp. 83–85 and pp. 95–97 to plan their introductions.
- Work with students to develop a list of possible transition words.

❹ Listening and Speaking

- Suggest that students read some eulogies or share knowledge of eulogies they may have heard. Discuss the key elements of a eulogy.
- Urge students to use their imaginations to extend Frost's description and paint a vivid picture of the boy.
- Encourage students to include appropriate quotes from other works of literature to reflect the boy's circumstances.
- Have students use the Peer Assessment form for Delivering a Speech, p. 30, in **Performance Assessment and Portfolio Management.**

**CUSTOMIZE INSTRUCTION
For Universal Access**

To address different learning styles, use the activities suggested in the **Extension Activities** booklet, p. 50.

For Verbal/Linguistic and Interpersonal Learners, use Activity 5.

For Visual/Spatial Learners, use Activity 6.

For Musical/Rhythmic and Bodily/Kinesthetic Learners, use Activity 7.

ASSESSMENT RESOURCES

The following resources can be used to assess students' knowledge and skills.

Selection Assessment

- 📖 **Formal Assessment,** pp. 227–229
- 📖 **Open Book Test,** pp. 148–150
- 📼 **Got It! Assessment Videotapes,** Tape 5
- 💿 **Test Bank Software**

 **Take It to the Net**

Visit www.phschool.com for self-tests and additional questions on the selections.

Listening and Speaking Rubric

- 📖 **Performance Assess. and Portfolio Mgmt.,** p. 30

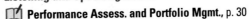 **PRENTICE HALL ASSESSMENT SYSTEM**

- 📖 **Workbook**
- 📖 **Skill Book**
- 🗄 **Transparencies**
- 💿 **CD-ROM**

The Night the Ghost Got In ✦ *from* Here Is New York

Lesson Objectives

1. **To analyze and respond to literary elements**
   - Literary Analysis: Informal Essay
   - Comparing Literary Works
2. **To read, comprehend, analyze, and critique nonfiction**
   - Reading Strategy: Recognizing Hyperbole
   - Reading Check Questions
   - Review and Assess Questions
   - Assessment Practice (ATE)
3. **To develop word analysis skills, fluency, and systematic vocabulary**
   - Vocabulary Development Lesson: Latin Word Root: *-terr-*
4. **To understand and apply written and oral language conventions**
   - Spelling Strategy
   - Grammar and Style Lesson: Commas in Series
5. **To understand and apply appropriate writing and research strategies**
   - Writing Lesson: Critical Response
   - Extension Activity: Written Report
6. **To understand and apply listening and speaking strategies**
   - Extension Activity: Role-play

STEP-BY-STEP TEACHING GUIDE	PACING GUIDE
PRETEACH	
Motivate Students and Provide Background	
Use the Motivation activity (ATE p. 896)	5 min.
Read and discuss author and background features (SE/ATE p. 896)	10 min.
Introduce the Concepts	
Introduce the Literary Analysis and Reading Strategy (SE/ATE p. 897) A	15 min.
Pronounce the vocabulary words and read their definitions (SE p. 897)	5 min.
TEACH	
Monitor Comprehension	
Informally monitor comprehension by circulating while students read independently or in groups A	
Monitor students' comprehension with the Reading Check notes (SE/ATE pp. 899, 901, 905)	as students read
Develop vocabulary with Vocabulary notes (SE pp. 899, 902, 904; ATE p. 904)	as students read
Develop Understanding	
Develop students' understanding of the informal essay with the Literary Analysis annotations (SE pp. 898, 899, 901, 905; ATE pp. 898, 899, 901, 903, 905) A	5 min.
Develop students' ability to recognize hyperbole by using the Reading Strategy annotations (SE p. 904; ATE pp. 900, 904)	5 min.
ASSESS	
Assess Mastery	
Assess students' mastery of the Reading Strategy and Literary Analysis by having them answer the Review and Assess questions (SE/ATE p. 907)	15 min.
Use one or more of the print and media Assessment Resources (ATE p. 909) A	up to 45 min.
EXTEND	
Apply Understanding	
Have students complete the Vocabulary Development Lesson and the Grammar and Style Lesson (SE p. 908) A	20 min.
Apply students' ability to incorporate quotations by using the Writing Lesson (SE/ATE p. 909) A	45 min.
Apply students' understanding using one or more of the Extension Activities (SE p. 909)	20–90 min.

A **ACCELERATED INSTRUCTION:**
Use the strategies and activities identified with an **A**.

UNIVERSAL ACCESS
● = Below Level Students
▲ = On-Level Students
■ = Above Level Students

Time and Resource Manager

Reading Level: Average, Easy
Average Number of Instructional Days: 4

RESOURCES

PRINT 📖	TRANSPARENCIES	TECHNOLOGY 💿 🎧 📼
• **Beyond Literature,** Community Connection: The Police, p. 51 ▲ ■		• **Interest Grabber Video,** Tape 5 ● ▲ ■
• **Selection Support Workbook:** ● ▲ ■ Literary Analysis, p. 227 Reading Strategy, p. 226 Build Vocabulary, p. 224	• **Literary Analysis and Reading Transparencies,** pp. 101 and 102 ● ▲ ■	
		• **Listening to Literature** ● ▲ ■ Audiocassettes, Side 32 Audio CDs, CD 18
• **Literatura en español** ● ▲ • **Literary Analysis for Enrichment** ■	• **Fine Art Transparencies, Volume 1,** Art Transparency 14 ● ▲ ■	
• **Formal Assessment:** Selection Test, p. 230 ● ▲ ■ • **Open Book Test,** p. 151 ● ▲ ■ • **Performance Assessment and Portfolio Management,** p. 23 ● ▲ ■ • PRENTICE HALL ASSESSMENT *SYSTEM* ● ▲ ■	• PRENTICE HALL ASSESSMENT *SYSTEM* ● ▲ ■ Skills Practice Answers and Explanations on Transparencies	• **Test Bank Software** ● ▲ ■ • **Got It! Assessment Videotapes,** Tape 4 ● ▲
• **Selection Support Workbook:** ● ▲ ■ Grammar and Style, p. 225 • **Writing and Grammar,** Ruby Level ● ▲ ■ • **Extension Activities,** p. 51 ● ▲ ■	• **Daily Language Practice Transparencies** ● ▲ • **Writing Models and Graphic Organizers on Transparencies,** p. 37 ● ▲ ■	• **Writing and Grammar iText CD-ROM** ● ▲ ■ 🖥 *Take It to the Net* www.phschool.com

BLOCK SCHEDULING: Use one 90-minute class period to preteach the selection and have students read it. Use a second 90-minute class period to assess students' mastery of skills and have them complete one of the Extension Activities.

Step-by-Step Teaching Guide for pp. 896–897

Motivation

Bring in a few sample copies of *The New Yorker*—issues from the 1930s and 40s, if these are available from the library—and give students a chance to leaf through them. Explain that both Thurber and White wrote for *The New Yorker* for many years. Thurber also contributed many cartoons to the magazine. Point out *The New Yorker's* distinctive features: its cover illustrations, cartoons and drawings, typeface, and poems. Have students read a paragraph here or a story there to absorb something of the magazine's unique sense of humor. Tell them that they are about to read two essays by writers who helped define the magazine's style.

▣ Interest Grabber Video

As an alternative, play "The Big Apple" on Tape 5 to engage students' interest.

❶ Background

More About the Authors

Thurber and White met for the first time in 1927. White introduced Thurber to the magazine's editor, Harold Ross, and was thus responsible for Thurber's joining the staff. Thurber's office quickly became conspicuous for the cartoons he drew all over the walls. White urged Thurber to show his drawings to the magazine's art department; when Thurber hesitated, White retrieved some of his friend's cartoons from the trashcan and submitted them for consideration.

Comparing Literary Works

Prepare to Read

❶ The Night the Ghost Got In ◆ *from* Here Is New York

James Thurber (1894–1961)

James Thurber's essays, plays, sketches, cartoons, and short stories, such as the well-known "The Secret Life of Walter Mitty," generally evolved from his own experiences. In his humorous autobiographical sketches, Thurber embellishes facts and describes events in an amusing manner. In his short stories, Thurber's characters typically struggle against the unpleasant realities of modern life, often with comical consequences. In his cartoons, Thurber portrays men, women, and a profusion of animals—especially dogs—facing the trials of everyday life.

The New Yorker Thurber was born in Columbus, Ohio. After attending Ohio State University, he joined *The New Yorker* magazine staff in 1927 as managing editor. From there, or so he claimed, he quickly worked his way down to writer. Until the end of his life, Thurber regularly contributed stories, essays, and cartoons to the magazine's pages. He also worked closely with the celebrated writer E. B. White.

Thurber is one of the few humorists whose work is part of the American literary canon. About his comic genius, Thurber was quite modest: "I write humor the way a surgeon operates, because it is a livelihood, because I have a great urge to do it, because many interesting challenges are set up, and because I have the hope it may do some good."

In much of his work, Thurber's humor reveals an edge of unhappiness, especially in his later years when his failing vision caused him much pain and bitterness. Yet he continued to write and draw as well as he could.

Thurber's many published works include *The Owl in the Attic and Other Perplexities* (1931), *The Seal in the Bedroom and Other Predicaments* (1932), *Fables for Our Time* (1940), and the bestselling *My World and Welcome to It* (1942).

E. B. White (1899–1985)

Capturing the interest of adults as well as children, E(lwyn) B(rooks) White established himself as one of the best-loved writers of the twentieth century. His precisely worded essays set a standard against which today's essays can still be judged.

White grew up in Mount Vernon, New York, and studied literature at Cornell University. As an undergraduate, White served as the editor of the *Cornell Daily Sun*. Later, he began a long association with *The New Yorker* magazine. His humorous, topical essays helped to establish *The New Yorker* as one of the nation's most successful general-interest magazines. White produced essays for *The New Yorker* on a weekly basis until 1938. In these essays, many of which are collected in his books *Every Day Is Saturday* (1934) and *Quo Vadimus?* (1939), White used his talents as a humorist to explore numerous social and political themes.

Transcendentalist Influence Influenced by the writings and philosophies of Henry David Thoreau, White believed in simplicity and individualism. These values emerge in nearly everything he wrote. A brilliant observer, he often satirized the complexities of modern life. In fact, in an effort to simplify his own life, White bought a farmhouse in Brooklin, Maine, in 1939; thereafter, he and his family spent most of their time there. White said that the animals in the barn gave him ideas. Some of these ideas took shape in White's work for children.

Two of his children's books—*Stuart Little* (1945) and *Charlotte's Web* (1952)—are among the most beloved children's books of all time. In addition, White's revision of William Strunk, Jr.'s classic style manual, *The Elements of Style*, has become a classic in its own right.

896 ◆ *Disillusion, Defiance, and Discontent (1914–1946)*

TEACHING RESOURCES

The following resources can be used to enrich or extend the instruction for pp. 896–897.

Motivation

▣ **Interest Grabber Video,** Tape 5 ▣

Background

▤ **Beyond Literature,** p. 51

 Take It to the Net
Visit www.phschool.com for Background and hotlinks for "The Night the Ghost Got In" and "Here Is New York"

Literary Analysis

▨ **Literary Analysis and Reading Transparencies,** Informal Essay, p. 102 ▣

Reading

▤ **Selection Support:** Reading Strategy, p. 226; Build Vocabulary, p. 224

▨ **Literary Analysis and Reading Transparencies,** Recognizing Hyperbole, p. 101

 **BLOCK SCHEDULING:** Resources marked with this symbol provide varied instruction during 90-minute blocks.

Preview

Connecting to the Literature

Different people are amused by different things. You can discover something about yourself by noting which parts of these essays make you laugh.

❷ Literary Analysis

Informal Essay

"The Night the Ghost Got In" and "Here Is New York" are both **informal essays,** brief nonfiction pieces characterized by a relaxed, conversational style and structure. Informal essays usually address a narrow subject, are loosely organized, and include digressions from the main point. Consider this example from "The Night the Ghost Got In":

> Glass tinkled into the bedroom occupied by a retired engraver named Bodwell and his wife. Bodwell had been for some years in rather a bad way and was subject to mild "attacks."

Informal essays give you a glimpse into a writer's personality. As you read these selections, consider what each suggests about its author. Record your findings in a chart like the one shown.

Comparing Literary Works

Although the topics are entirely different, both of these selections are humorous and intended to provoke laughter. Thurber's **humor** revolves around an exaggerated account of a childhood experience, while White's humor satirizes—pokes fun at—New York City. Humor writers must have the ability to perceive the ridiculous, comical, or ludicrous aspects of a personality or situation. Humorists often exaggerate details and embellish facts for comic effect. As you read, compare the elements that make these essays humorous.

❸ Reading Strategy

Recognizing Hyperbole

These informal essays draw humor from **hyperbole,** or exaggerations and outrageous overstatements. Examples include bizarre events in Thurber's essay and White's litany of probable disasters. To recognize hyperbole, look for details that seem too absurd to be true.

Vocabulary Development

intuitively (in tōō´ i tiv lē) *adv.* instinctively (p. 899)

blaspheming (blas fēm´ iŋ) *v.* cursing (p. 902)

aspiration (as´ pə rā´ shən) *n.* strong ambition (p. 904)

subterranean (sub´ tə rā´ nē ən) *adj.* underground (p. 904)

claustrophobia (klôs´ trə fō´ bē ə) *n.* fear of being in a confined space (p. 904)

cosmopolitan (käz´ mə päl´ ə tən) *adj.* at ease in all countries or places (p. 904)

Writer's Style

⬇

Writer's Purpose

⬇

Writer's Personality

The Night the Ghost Got In / from *Here Is New York* ◆ 897

---

❷ Literary Analysis

Informal Essay

- Tell students that *essay* is from the French verb *essayer* (es • say • YAY), meaning "to try or attempt." An essay is an attempt to share something with the reader—a story, an emotion, or a belief.

- Essayists write for a variety of purposes. An essay can persuade, inform, narrate, or entertain—or it can do some or all of these things at once. As students read these two essays, have them identify each author's purpose in writing.

❸ Reading Strategy

Recognizing Hyperbole

- Explain that the word *hyperbole* derives from two Greek words literally meaning "to overthrow." In Greek as in English, the compound word *hyperbole* means "excess" or "exaggeration." Compare a verbal exaggeration to an overthrown foul shot in basketball—a shot that goes too far or too high to catch the hoop.

- Ask students why a writer would want to use hyperbole. Write the following quotation from "The Notorious Jumping Frog of Calaveras County" (Unit 4) on the chalkboard: *Thish-yere Smiley had a mare—the boys called her the fifteen-minute nag, but that was only in fun, you know, because of course she was faster than that.*

  Point out that "the boys" exaggerate the mare's slowness "for fun." Answer: The usual purpose of hyperbole is to add humor to a text.

- As students read the two essays, have them look for examples of hyperbole and think about what this element contributes to each essay.

Vocabulary Development

- Pronounce each vocabulary word for students, and then read the definitions as a class. Have students identify any words with which they are already familiar.

 E-Teach

Visit E-Teach at www.phschool.com for teachers' essays on how to teach, with questions and answers.

CUSTOMIZE INSTRUCTION
For Musical/Rhythmic Learners

Point out to students that "The Night the Ghost Got In" relies heavily on sound—the footsteps in the dining-room, the smash of the neighbor's window, the New York accents of the policemen, and so on. Have students pay close attention to Thurber's uses of sound and discuss what they contribute to the essay and how they help to draw readers into the story. As an extension, students can apply the same approach to White's essay.

❶ About the Selection

One night, the narrator steps out of the bathtub and is startled to hear footsteps in the dining-room below. He awakens his brother, who also hears the sounds. In turn, the brothers awaken their mother, who breaks a window in the house next door to attract attention and get help. When the police come, they make matters worse by damaging the front doors and arousing the wrath of the narrator's crazy grandfather.

❷ ▶ Critical Viewing

Answer: Students may find the facial expressions—the friendly-looking ghost, and the frightened person—comical.

❸ Literary Analysis

Informal Essay

- Have students read the first two paragraphs of the essay. Ask them: Why did Thurber write this essay? Which details in the first paragraph lead you to your response?
  Answer: He wants to tell a story; the details include highlights of the plot and a quick preview of the characters. Thurber wants to entertain: the details are funny.

- Then, ask the Literary Analysis question on page 898: What characteristics of the informal essay does this passage include?
  Answer: The tone is conversational and friendly, like someone sharing a funny story at the dinner table.

❶ The Night the Ghost Got In

James Thurber

The ghost that got into our house on the night of November 17, 1915, raised such a hullabaloo of misunderstandings that I am sorry I didn't just let it keep on walking, and go to bed. Its advent caused my mother to throw a shoe through a window of the house next door and ended up with my grandfather shooting a patrolman. I am sorry, therefore, as I have said, that I ever paid any attention to the footsteps.

They began about a quarter past one o'clock in the morning, a rhythmic, quick-cadenced walking around the dining-room table. My mother was asleep in one room upstairs, my brother Herman in another; grandfather was in the attic, in the old walnut bed which, as you will remember, once fell on my father. I had just stepped out of the bathtub and was busily rubbing myself with a towel when I heard the steps. They were the steps of a man walking rapidly around the dining-room table downstairs. The light from the bathroom shone down the back steps, which dropped directly into the dining-room; I could see the faint shine of plates on the plate-rail; I couldn't see the table. The steps kept going round and round the table; at regular intervals a board creaked, when it was trod upon. I supposed at first that it was my father or my brother Roy, who had gone to Indianapolis but were expected home at any time. I suspected next that it was a burglar. It did not enter my mind until later that it was a ghost.

After the walking had gone on for perhaps three minutes, I tiptoed to Herman's room. "Psst!" I hissed, in the dark, shaking him. "Awp," he said, in the low, hopeless tone of a despondent beagle—he always half suspected that something would "get him" in the night. I told him who I was. "There's something downstairs!" I said. He got up and followed me to the head of the back staircase. We listened together. There was no sound. The steps had ceased. Herman looked at me in some alarm: I had only the bath towel around my waist. He wanted to go back to bed, but I gripped his arm. "There's something down

898 ◆ Disillusion, Defiance, and Discontent (1914–1946)

❷ ▲ Critical Viewing
The humor in Thurber's drawing echoes the humor in his story. What makes this sketch funny? **[Analyze]**

Literary Analysis
Informal Essay What characteristics of the informal essay does this passage include?

TEACHING RESOURCES

The following resources can be used to enrich or extend the instruction for pp. 898–906.

Literary Analysis
📖 **Selection Support:** Literary Analysis, p. 227

Reading
🎧 **Listening to Literature Audiocassettes,** Side 32 ■

💿 **Listening to Literature Audio CDs,** CD 18 ■

Extension
📄 **Fine Art Transparencies,** Volume 1, Art Transparency 14

■ **BLOCK SCHEDULING:** Resources marked with this symbol provide varied instruction during 90-minute blocks.

there!" I said. Instantly the steps began again, circled the dining-room table like a man running, and started up the stairs toward us, heavily, two at a time. The light still shone palely down the stairs; we saw nothing coming; we only heard the steps. Herman rushed to his room and slammed the door. I slammed shut the door at the stairs top and held my knee against it. After a long minute, I slowly opened it again. There was nothing there. There was no sound. None of us ever heard the ghost again.

The slamming of the doors had aroused mother: she peered out of her room. "What on earth are you boys doing?" she demanded. Herman ventured out of his room. "Nothing," he said, gruffly, but he was, in color, a light green. "What was all that running around downstairs?" said mother. So she had heard the steps, too! We just looked at her. "Burglars!" she shouted intuitively. I tried to quiet her by starting lightly downstairs.

"Come on, Herman," I said.

"I'll stay with Mother," he said. "She's all excited."

I stepped back onto the landing.

"Don't either of you go a step," said mother. "We'll call the police." Since the phone was downstairs, I didn't see how we were going to call the police—nor did I want the police—but mother made one of her quick, incomparable decisions. She flung up a window of her bedroom which faced the bedroom windows of the house of a neighbor, picked up a shoe, and whammed it through a pane of glass across the narrow space that separated the two houses. Glass tinkled into the bedroom occupied by a retired engraver named Bodwell and his wife. Bodwell had been for some years in rather a bad way and was subject to mild "attacks." Most everybody we knew or lived near had *some* kind of attacks.

It was now about two o'clock of a moonless night; clouds hung black and low. Bodwell was at the window in a minute, shouting, frothing a little, shaking his fist. "We'll sell the house and go back to Peoria," we could hear Mrs. Bodwell saying. It was some time before mother "got through" to Bodwell. "Burglars!" she shouted. "Burglars in the house!" Herman and I hadn't dared to tell her that it was not burglars but ghosts, for she was even more afraid of ghosts than of burglars. Bodwell at first thought that she meant there were burglars in his house, but finally he quieted down and called the police for us over an extension phone by his bed. After he had disappeared from the window, mother suddenly made as if to throw another shoe, not because there was further need of it, but, as she later explained, because the thrill of heaving a shoe through a window glass had enormously taken her fancy. I prevented her.

The police were on hand in a commendably short time: a Ford sedan full of them, two on motorcycles, and a patrol wagon with about eight in it and a few reporters. They began banging at our front door. Flashlights shot streaks of gleam up and down the walls, across the yard, down the walk between our house and Bodwell's. "Open up!"

intuitively (in tōō´ i tiv lē) *adv.* instinctively

Literary Analysis
Informal Essay and Humor What does the humorous digression about the thrill of heaving a shoe reveal about the mother?

⑤ ✓ Reading Check
Who does Mother think the intruders are?

The Night the Ghost Got In ◆ 899

Art

James Thurber was a cartoonist and illustrator as well as a writer. His pen-and-ink cartoons and drawings frequently appeared in *The New Yorker* as well as in his books.

By the time he was in his mid-50s, Thurber was almost totally blind. He continued drawing, using special tools such as a magnifier, an illuminated board, and a mechanized pencil that produced a glowing neon line. His deteriorating eyesight may explain the lack of detail in his simple drawings. Use these questions for discussion:

1. Which character from the essay appears in the cartoon on p. 900? How do you know?
   Answer: The cartoon depicts the scene described on the previous page in which the mother throws a shoe at the house next door.

2. In what ways is the cartoon of the policemen on p. 901 an example of hyperbole?
   Answer: Their puzzlement is exaggerated. There are too many of them looking for clues in a small space.

❼ ▶ Critical Viewing

Answer: The picture shows just how incongruous and hilarious the mother's actions are.

❽ Reading Strategy

Recognizing Hyperbole

- Ask students whether they recognize the hyperbole in the bracketed passage. Have them explain their answers.
  Answer: Students should realize that the narrator exaggerates the policemen's behavior. Since they are looking for a burglar, the police do not need to ransack the house.

- Then, have students discuss the effect of the hyperbole.
  Answer: The hyperbole adds to the story's humor. It creates a mood like that of a slapstick comedy and creates sympathy for the family.

▶ Monitor Progress Ask students to consider how the policemen's speech is an example of hyperbole.
Answer: The policemen's speech exaggerates a certain street-smart, rough-and-tumble accent.

cried a hoarse voice. "We're men from Headquarters!" I wanted to go down and let them in, since there they were, but mother wouldn't hear of it. "You haven't a stitch on," she pointed out. "You'd catch your death." I wound the towel around me again. Finally the cops put their shoulders to our big heavy front door with its thick beveled glass and broke it in: I could hear a rending of wood and a splash of glass on the floor of the hall. Their lights played all over the living-room and crisscrossed nervously in the dining-room, stabbed into hallways, shot up the front stairs and finally up the back. They caught me standing in my towel at the top. A heavy policeman bounded up the steps. "Who are you?" he demanded. "I live here," I said. "Well, whattsa matta, ya hot?" he asked. I was, as a matter of fact, cold; I went to my room and pulled on some trousers. On my way out, a cop stuck a gun into my ribs. "Whatta you doin' here?" he demanded. "I live here," I said.

❽ The officer in charge reported to mother. "No sign of nobody, lady," he said. "Musta got away—whatt'd he look like?" "There were two or three of them," mother said, "whooping and carrying on and slamming doors." "Funny," said the cop. "All ya windows and doors was locked on the inside tight as a tick."

Downstairs, we could hear the tromping of the other police. Police were all over the place; doors were yanked open, drawers were yanked open, windows were shot up and pulled down, furniture fell with dull thumps. A half-dozen policemen emerged out of the darkness of the front hallway upstairs. They began to ransack the floor: pulled beds away from walls, tore clothes off hooks in the closets, pulled suitcases and boxes off shelves. One of them found an old zither[1] that Roy had won in a pool tournament. "Looky here, Joe," he said, strumming it with a big paw. The cop named Joe took it and turned it over. "What is it?" he asked me. "It's an old zither our guinea pig used to sleep on," I said. It was true that a pet guinea pig we once had would never sleep anywhere except on the zither, but I should never have said so. Joe and the other cop looked at me a long time. They put the zither back on a shelf.

"No sign o' nuthin'," said the cop who had first spoken to mother. "This guy," he explained to the others, jerking a thumb at me, "was nekked. The lady seems historical." They all nodded, but said nothing;

The Night the Ghost Got In, Copyright 1933, 1961, James Thurber, From *My Life and*

❼ ▲ Critical Viewing Thurber created this cartoon to accompany "The Night the Ghost Got In." Describe the way in which the illustration adds to the humorous effect of the essay. [Assess]

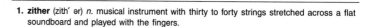

---

1. **zither** (zith′ ər) *n.* musical instrument with thirty to forty strings stretched across a flat soundboard and played with the fingers.

900 ◆ *Disillusion, Defiance, and Discontent (1914–1946)*

CUSTOMIZE INSTRUCTION FOR UNIVERSAL ACCESS

For Gifted/Talented Students

Thurber's cartoons inspired Professor Peter Schickele, better known as P.D.Q. Bach, to compose a piece of music entitled *Thurber's Dogs.* Invite students to locate a collection of Thurber's dog cartoons and a recording of the Schickele composition. Students can then browse through the cartoons, listen to the music, and discuss their opinions of Schickele's response to the drawings.

just looked at me. In the small silence we all heard a creaking in the attic. Grandfather was turning over in bed. "What's 'at?" snapped Joe. Five or six cops sprang for the attic door before I could intervene or explain. I realized that it would be bad if they burst in on grandfather unannounced, or even announced. He was going through a phase in which he believed that General Meade's men, under steady hammering by Stonewall Jackson, were beginning to retreat and even desert.

When I got to the attic, things were pretty confused. Grandfather had evidently jumped to the conclusion that the police were deserters from Meade's army, trying to hide away in his attic. He bounded out of bed wearing a long flannel nightgown over long woolen underwear, a nightcap, and a leather jacket around his chest. The cops must have realized at once that the indignant white-haired old man belonged in the house, but they had no chance to say so. "Back, ye cowardly dogs!" roared grandfather. "Back t' the lines, ye yellow, lily-livered cattle!" With that, he fetched the officer who found the zither a flat-handed smack alongside his head that sent him sprawling. The others beat a retreat, but not fast enough; grandfather grabbed Zither's gun from its holster and let fly. The report seemed to crack the rafters; smoke filled the attic. A cop cursed and shot his hand to his shoulder. Somehow, we all finally got downstairs again and locked the door against the old gentleman. He fired once or twice more in the darkness and then went back to bed. "That was grandfather," I explained to Joe, out of breath. "He thinks you're deserters." "I'll say he does," said Joe.

Literary Analysis
Informal Essay Which words in this paragraph reflect a relaxed, conversational style?

10 ✔Reading Check
What does grandfather think is happening?

The Night the Ghost Got In, Copyright 1933, 1961, James Thurber, From *My Life and Hard Times,* published by Harper & Row.

11 ◀Critical Viewing
Compare this illustration with Thurber's description of the police investigation. What makes each funny?
[Evaluate]

The Night the Ghost Got In ◆ 901

Review and Assess

1. Students should support their responses with details from the text.

2. **(a)** The narrator hears footsteps in the dining-room. **(b)** The narrator wants to uncover the cause of the noise. Herman wants to hide. The mother wants to call the police. **(c)** He seems to be the only calm, sane person in the house.

3. **(a)** The mother breaks the neighbor's window and asks him to call the police. **(b)** The neighbor's misunderstanding—first thinking that the mother broke their window for fun (which is true, in part), then thinking that they have burglars in their house—is another step in a series of miscommunications and missteps that combine to create humor.

4. **(a)** He attacks them, grabs one of their guns, and shoots. **(b)** He thinks the policmen are deserters from the Union army.

5. They might have been more frightened.

6. Yes; nothing in the essay suggests that it takes place at a particular time in history or that the situational comedy offers less than a universal appeal.

The cops were reluctant to leave without getting their hands on somebody besides grandfather; the night had been distinctly a defeat for them. Furthermore, they obviously didn't like the "layout"; something looked—and I can see their viewpoint—phony. They began to poke into things again. A reporter, a thin-faced, wispy man, came up to me. I had put on one of mother's blouses, not being able to find anything else. The reporter looked at me with mingled suspicion and interest. "Just what the heck is the real lowdown here, Bud?" he asked. I decided to be frank with him. "We had ghosts," I said. He gazed at me a long time as if I were a slot machine into which he had, without results, dropped a nickel. Then he walked away. The cops followed him, the one grandfather shot holding his now-bandaged arm, cursing and <u>blaspheming</u>. "I'm gonna get my gun back from that old bird," said the zither-cop. "Yeh," said Joe. "You—and who else?" I told them I would bring it to the station house the next day.

"What was the matter with that one policeman?" mother asked, after they had gone. "Grandfather shot him," I said. "What for?" she demanded. I told her he was a deserter. "Of all things!" said mother. "He was such a nice-looking young man."

Grandfather was fresh as a daisy and full of jokes at breakfast next morning. We thought at first he had forgotten all about what had happened, but he hadn't. Over his third cup of coffee, he glared at Herman and me. "What was the idee of all them cops tarry-hootin' round the house last night?" he demanded. He had us there.

blaspheming (blas fēm′ iŋ)
v. cursing

Review and Assess

Thinking About the Selection

1. **Respond:** What do you consider the most humorous point in the essay? Why?

2. **(a) Recall:** What event sets off the family's reactions?
   (b) Classify: Describe how each member of the family reacts.
   (c) Distinguish: In what way does Thurber's portrayal of himself in the situation differ from his portrayal of the other characters?

3. **(a) Recall:** Why are the police summoned?
   (b) Support: How does this lack of communication contribute to the humor of the essay?

4. **(a) Recall:** What does grandfather do when the police burst into his room? **(b) Infer:** Why do you think he does this?

5. **Speculate:** In what way might the narrator's family and the police have reacted if they thought it was a ghost in the house?

6. **Take a Position:** This essay describes an event that took place in 1915. Do you think modern readers can still enjoy it? Why or why not?

from HERE IS NEW YORK

E. B. White

Background

America has a strong tradition of humor writing. Much of that humor builds on self-ridicule, with people poking fun at their own missteps and failures. Americans seem especially willing to laugh at themselves when they fail to achieve all that they attempt. Although he loves New York City and its energy and excitement, E. B. White still finds plenty to satirize in "Here Is New York."

New York is nothing like Paris; it is nothing like London; and it is not Spokane multiplied by sixty, or Detroit multiplied by four. It is by all odds the loftiest of cities. It even managed to reach the highest point in the sky at the lowest moment of the Depression. The Empire State Building shot 1250 feet into the air when it was madness to put out as much as six inches of new growth. (The building has a mooring mast that no dirigible[1] has ever tied to; it employs a man to flush toilets in slack times; it has been hit by an airplane in a fog, struck countless times by lightning, and been jumped off of by so many unhappy people that pedestrians instinctively quicken step when passing Fifth Avenue and Thirty-fourth Street.)

Manhattan has been compelled to expand skyward because of the absence of any other direction in which to grow. This,

---

1. **dirigible** (dirʹə jə bəl) *n.* large, long airship.

▶ **Critical Viewing**
What objects in this photograph confirm White's attitude about New York? Explain. **[Connect]**

from *Here Is New York* ◆ 903

---

⑫ About the Selection

E.B. White describes the city of New York, with its soaring buildings, its huge crowds, and its unique inconveniences. He notes that though the city can seem inhospitable and unmanageable to tourists, it is really a huge collection of tiny neighborhoods just like those they left behind.

⑬ Literary Analysis

Informal Essay

• As students begin to read, ask them why they think White wrote this essay. Have students identify details in the opening paragraph to support their answers.
Answer: White wanted to describe New York. Each detail in the opening paragraph advances his view of the city as a place of extremes. He wants to share his feelings about the city with readers.

• Ask: Which aspects of this paragraph suggest that this is an informal essay?
Answer: Casual language like "shot up into the air," mention of a man employed to flush toilets, and a humorous reference to pedestrians quickening their step when they pass the Empire State Building add to the essay's sense of informality.

⑭ ▶ Critical Viewing

Answer: White describes New York as the "loftiest" of cities. All the buildings in the photographs, including the Empire State Building shown at far left, are tall.

15 ▶ Critical Thinking

Analyzing

- Ask students: How does White create a sense of the city as a living, breathing personality, like a character in a story?
  Answer: White anthropomorphizes the city. He describes the challenges it has weathered and uses vivid verbs that suggest the city is responsible for its own success.

- Then, have students list words that describe the character of New York City as White depicts it.
  Possible answers: Students might describe the city as brave, enduring, or strong.

16 Vocabulary Development

- Draw students' attention to White's use of the word *subterranean*, and read its definition. Tell them that the word combines the Latin prefix *sub-*, meaning "under," with the root *-terr-*, which means "ground."

- Invite students to brainstorm for other words that share the root *-terr-*. Write students' suggestions on the chalkboard. Possible responses: terrestrial, terrain, terra-cotta

- Then, have students use each of these *-terr-* words in a sentence describing a city.

17 Reading Strategy

Recognizing Hyperbole

- Have a volunteer read aloud the bracketed paragraph. Then, ask students how White creates humor in this passage.
  Answer: White uses vivid verbs that help the reader "see" what might have happened to the city. Because the reader knows that the city was not destroyed, he or she enjoys the exaggerated depictions of its demise.

- Then, ask the Reading Strategy question on page 904: Which details in the passage beginning "Long ago" are examples of hyperbole?
  Answer: White exaggerates the damage that any one of a list of evils might have done to New York.

---

more than any other thing, is responsible for its physical majesty. It is to the nation what the white church spire is to the village—the visible symbol of aspiration and faith, the white plume saying that the way is up. The summer traveler swings in over Hell Gate Bridge and from the window of his sleeping car as it glides above the pigeon lofts and back yards of Queens looks southwest to where the morning light first strikes the steel peaks of midtown, and he sees its upward thrust unmistakable: the great walls and towers rising, the smoke rising, the heat not yet rising, the hopes and ferments of so many awakening millions rising—this vigorous spear that presses heaven hard.

It is a miracle that New York works at all. The whole thing is implausible. Every time the residents brush their teeth, millions of gallons of water must be drawn from the Catskills and the hills of Westchester. When a young man in Manhattan writes a letter to his girl in Brooklyn, the love message gets blown to her through a pneumatic[2] tube—*pfft*—just like that. The subterranean system of telephone cables, power lines, steam pipes, gas mains, and sewer pipes is reason enough to abandon the island to the gods and the weevils. Every time an incision is made in the pavement, the noisy surgeons expose ganglia[3] that are tangled beyond belief. By rights New York should have destroyed itself long ago, from panic or fire or rioting or failure of some vital supply line in its circulatory system or from some deep labyrinthine short circuit. Long ago the city should have experienced an insoluble traffic snarl at some impossible bottleneck. It should have perished of hunger when food lines filed for a few days. It should have been wiped out by a plague starting in its slums or carried in by ships' rats. It should have been overwhelmed by the sea that licks at it on every side. The workers in its myriad cells should have succumbed to nerves, from the fearful pall of smoke-fog that drifts over every few days from Jersey, blotting out all light at noon and leaving the high offices suspended, men groping and depressed, and the sense of world's end. It should have been touched in the head by the August heat and gone off its rocker.

Mass hysteria is a terrible force, yet New Yorkers seem always to escape it by some tiny margin: they sit in stalled subways without claustrophobia, they extricate themselves from panic situations by some lucky wisecrack, they meet confusion and congestion with patience and grit—a sort of perpetual muddling through. Every facility is inadequate—the hospitals and schools and the playgrounds are overcrowded, the express highways are feverish, the unimproved highways and bridges are bottlenecks, there is not enough air and not enough light, and there is usually either too much heat or too little. But the city makes up for its hazards and its deficiencies by supplying its citizens with massive doses of a supplementary vitamin: the sense of belonging to something unique, cosmopolitan, mighty, and unparalleled.

---

2. **pneumatic** (noo mat′ ik) *adj.* filled with compressed air.
3. **ganglia** (gaŋ′ glē ə) *n.* mass of nerve cells serving as center of force, energy, activity.

aspiration (as′ pə rā′ shən) *n.* strong ambition

subterranean (sub′ tə rā′ nē ən) *adj.* underground

Reading Strategy
Recognizing Hyperbole
Which details in the passage beginning "Long ago" are examples of hyperbole?

claustrophobia (klôs′ trə fō′ bē ə) *n.* fear of being in a confined space

cosmopolitan (käz′ mə päl′ ə tən) *adj.* at ease in all countries or places

---

✷ ENRICHMENT

New York, New York

In 1626, the Dutch West India Company established the tiny settlement of New Amsterdam on the southern shore of what was then known as Manna-hata Island. In May of that year, Peter Minuit bought the land from a band of Native Americans, who probably did not own it, for the now infamous price of $24. The tiny village expanded northward, eventually encompassing the entire island. Today, New York City consists of five boroughs—Manhattan Island, Brooklyn, Queens, the Bronx, and Staten Island.

Most of Manhattan is laid out on a grid pattern. Wide north-south avenues are numbered from east to west—First Avenue, Second Avenue, and so on—and narrower east-west cross-streets are numbered from south to north—Fourteenth Street, Fifteenth Street, and so on. Broadway, a former Indian trail and the city's longest and oldest street, runs the full length of Manhattan Island. Its diagonal direction was not altered when the grid plan was instituted.

To an outlander a stay in New York can be and often is a series of small embarrassments and discomforts and disappointments: not understanding the waiter, not being able to distinguish between a sucker joint and a friendly saloon, riding the wrong subway, being slapped down by a bus driver for asking an innocent question, enduring sleepless nights when the street noises fill the bedroom. Tourists make for New York, particularly in summertime—they swarm all over the Statue of Liberty (where many a resident of the town has never set foot), they invade the Automat,[4] visit radio studios, St. Patrick's Cathedral, and they window shop. Mostly they have a pretty good time. But sometimes in New York you run across the disillusioned—a young couple who are obviously visitors, newlyweds perhaps, for whom the bright dream has vanished. The place has been too much for them; they sit languishing in a cheap restaurant over a speechless meal.

The oft-quoted thumbnail sketch of New York is, of course: "It's a wonderful place, but I'd hate to live there." I have an idea that people from villages and small towns, people accustomed to the convenience and the friendliness of neighborhood over-the-fence living, are unaware that life in New York follows the neighborhood pattern. The city is literally a composite of tens of thousands of tiny neighborhood units. There are, of course, the big districts and big units: Chelsea and Murray Hill and Gramercy (which are residential units), . . . Greenwich Village (a unit dedicated to the arts and other matters), and there is Radio City (a commercial development), Peter Cooper Village (a housing unit), the Medical Center (a sickness unit) and many other sections each of which has some distinguishing characteristic. But the curious thing about New York is that each large geographical unit is composed of countless small neighborhoods. Each neighborhood is virtually self-sufficient. Usually it is no more than two or three blocks long and a couple of blocks wide. Each area is a city within a city within a city. Thus, no matter where you live in New York, you will find within a block or two a grocery store, a barbershop, a newsstand and shoeshine shack, an ice-coal-and-wood cellar (where you write your order on a pad outside as you walk by), a dry cleaner, a laundry, a delicatessen (beer and sandwiches delivered at any hour to your door), a flower shop, an undertaker's parlor, a movie house, a radio-repair shop, a stationer, a haberdasher,[5] a tailor, a drugstore, a garage, a tearoom, a saloon, a hardware store, a liquor store, a shoe-repair shop. Every block or two, in most residential sections of New York, is a little main street. A man starts for work in the morning and before he has gone two hundred yards he has completed half a dozen missions: bought a paper, left a pair of shoes to be soled, picked up a pack of cigarettes, . . . written a message to the unseen forces of the wood cellar, and notified the dry cleaner that a pair of trousers awaits call. Homeward-bound

---

4. **Automat** *n.* restaurant in which patrons get food from small compartments with doors opened by putting coins into slots.
5. **haberdasher** *n.* person whose work is selling men's clothing, such as hats, shirts, neckties, and gloves.

Literary Analysis
Informal Essay What does the relaxed, conversational style of this passage reveal about White's attitude toward New York?

20 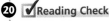 **Reading Check**
According to the writer, what difficulties might a visitor to New York encounter?

from *Here Is New York* ◆ 905

⓲ Literary Analysis
Informal Essay

- Ask students to identify White's purpose in this passage.
  Answer: White explains an outsider's perspective of New York as an overwhelming, noisy, unfriendly place.

- Ask students the Literary Analysis question on page 905: What does the relaxed, conversational style of this passage reveal about White's attitude toward New York?
  Answer: White regards New York with affection. He understands why some people find it bewildering and why others would never live anywhere else.

⓳ ▶ Critical Thinking
Compare and Contrast

- Have students compare this long descriptive paragraph to the paragraph that precedes it. What is the main idea of each paragraph?
  Answer: Shorter paragraph: New York can be intimidating to tourists. Longer paragraph: New York is not so overwhelming; it is simply a big collection of small neighborhoods.

- Then, have students consider why White might make these somewhat contradictory points in sequence.
  Answer: White sets up the tourists' point of view only to show that there is far more to the story.

⓴ ✓ Reading Check
Answer: Tourists to New York might encounter unintelligible waiters, "sucker joints," confusing subway maps, rudeness, and noise.

905

Answers for p. 906

Review and Assess

1. Possible answers: No, because he stresses the city's unfriendliness to visitors; yes, because he makes it sound exciting and alive.

2. **(a)** They make jokes, they don't suffer from claustrophobia, and they exercise patience and grit. **(b)** It gives them a sense of community and variety.

3. **(a)** It can be confusing and unwelcoming. **(b)** Such a person might say that people planning to visit New York should read about the city, get advice from friends who live there, and remain open to adventure instead of being intimidated. They might add that New York is full of beauty and vitality and can offer visitors a wonderful experience.

4. **(a)** He says that they are tiny villages. **(b)** They are just like small towns. Just like many small-town dwellers who never move away from home, many New Yorkers never leave their own neighborhoods.

5. **(a)** It has endurance and strength. **(b)** It is a marvelous and unique place and those who live there are lucky.

6. A politician might disagree that the city is challenging for for visitors, but would agree that it is a great place to live.

---

eight hours later, he buys a bunch of pussy willows, a Mazda bulb, a drink, a shine—all between the corner where he steps off the bus and his apartment. So complete is each neighborhood, and so strong the sense of neighborhood, that many a New Yorker spends a lifetime within the confines of an area smaller than a country village. Let him walk two blocks from his corner and he is in a strange land and will feel uneasy till he gets back.

Storekeepers are particularly conscious of neighborhood boundary lines. A woman friend of mine moved recently from one apartment to another, a distance of three blocks. When she turned up, the day after the move, at the same grocer's that she had patronized for years, the proprietor was in ecstasy—almost in tears—at seeing her. "I was afraid," he said, "now that you've moved away I wouldn't be seeing you anymore." To him, *away* was three blocks, or about 750 feet.

I am, at the moment of writing this, living not as a neighborhood man in New York but as a transient, or vagrant, in from the country for a few days. Summertime is a good time to reexamine New York and to receive again the gift of privacy, the jewel of loneliness. In summer the city contains (except for tourists) only die-hards and authentic characters. No casual, spotty dwellers are around, only the real article. And the town has a somewhat relaxed air, and one can lie in a loincloth, gasping and remembering things.

Review and Assess

Thinking About the Selection

1. **Respond:** Would you like to visit the New York City of E. B. White's description? Why or why not?

2. **(a) Recall:** According to this essay, what are three ways in which New Yorkers escape mass hysteria? **(b) Connect:** What does New York City offer its citizens in return to help them cope with the city's deficiencies?

3. **(a) Recall:** According to White, what is New York City like for tourists? **(b) Hypothesize:** Describe the way in which someone working in New York City's tourist industry might respond to E. B. White's representation of the city for "outlanders"?

4. **(a) Recall:** What terms does White use to describe New York's neighborhoods? **(b) Compare and Contrast:** In what ways do these neighborhoods compare to small towns?

5. **(a) Draw Conclusions:** What qualities of New York City enable it to function against all odds? **(b) Summarize:** What general conclusions does White's essay reach about the city?

6. **Extend:** How might the city's mayor or a New York State Senator respond to White's description?

✍ ASSESSMENT PRACTICE: Reading Comprehension

Fill In Missing Words	(For more practice, see Test Preparation Workbook, p. 54.)

Many tests require students to complete sentences by choosing from a list of possible words. Use the following sample test item to give students practice at this skill.

Magazines have been important in nurturing American humor. For years *The New Yorker* has _____ the work of cartoonists and humorous writers.

Which word best fills the blank?

A concealed   **C** showcased
B reserved   **D** hidden

The second sentence of the passage is intended to illustrate the point made in the first sentence. *The New Yorker* could not nurture artists and writers by concealing, reserving, or hiding their work. Choice *C* is correct.

Review and Assess

Literary Analysis

Informal Essay

1. Cite an especially strong example of language that reflects the conversational style of Thurber's **informal essay.** Explain your choice.
2. What does "Here Is New York" suggest about White's attitude toward New York and the modern world it symbolizes? Support your answer.
3. What does their calm detachment in the midst of describing chaotic events reveal about the writers' views of the world around them?

Comparing Literary Works

4. (a) How would you describe the dominant type of **humor** Thurber uses in his informal essay? (b) In what ways does it compare to the humor used by E.B. White?
5. Although White uses humor to make fun of New York, his writing actually reveals some of the city's unique qualities. Using a chart like the one shown, cite three examples of hidden praise.

Humorous Passage	What It Reveals

6. (a) What does each author's use of humor add to his exploration of social or political issues? (b) Does the presence of humor allow the writer to convey ideas that would otherwise be difficult for readers to accept? Explain.

Reading Strategy

Recognizing Hyperbole

7. Cite an example of **hyperbole** from each essay and explain in what ways it represents an exaggeration.
8. For what purpose does Thurber exaggerate the behavior of his grandfather in his essay?
9. How is White's use of hyperbole appropriate for his subject?

Extend Understanding

10. **Career Connection:** Name three careers in today's world that might provide work for humorists. Explain how humor is used in each case.

The Night the Ghost Got In / from Here Is New York ◆ 907

Answers continued

10. Possible answers: A political cartoonist uses humor to expose serious evils in government. A stand-up comic uses humor to expose problems in society. A teacher can use humor to impart lessons.

Answers for p. 907

Review and Assess

1. Sample answer: The opening sentence is a blend of the calm and hysteria that make the whole essay so funny.
2. White admires the city as a great achievement of the modern age. He describes it as the modern equivalent of the village church steeple; a symbol of human aspiration.
3. They are amused by the world around them. They observe it even as they participate in it.
4. (a) Thurber's humor rests in the contrast between the narrator's calm behavior and the zaniness with which he is surrounded. (b) Like Thurber's, part of White's humor comes from the author's sense of detached observation. Both write humor that is gentle, not biting.
5. Possible answers: The city is exuberant and energetic. The city offers immense variety in foods and consumer goods. The city has spectacular tourist attractions. For its residents, New York is as homey as any small town.
6. (a) White uses humor to highlight a cultural divide between residents of New York City and nonresidents. Thurber's use of humor allows him to portray a rather extreme police search in a nonthreatening way. (b) White's use of humor allows him to criticize New York City and to poke fun at tourists without causing offense. Thurber's use of humor allows him to portay family members in a less than flattering light.
7. Possible response: Thurber: the number of policemen who come to the house is exaggerated. White: the grocer nearly crying when his customer who had moved down the street returned is an exaggerated description. Most grocers would not cry in such circumstances.
8. Thurber wants to make the reader laugh.
9. New York itself is an example of hyperbole: the buildings are taller, the crowds larger, and the streets noisier than anywhere else.

continued

907

❶ Vocabulary Development

Word Analysis

1. b
2. c

Spelling Strategy

1. photograph
2. symphony

Fluency: Words in Context

1. No; an aspiration is a goal or dream.
2. Yes; subterranean pipes are those below ground.
3. Yes; blaspheming means cursing.
4. Yes; a cosmopolitan person would feel comfortable anywhere.
5. Yes; a loud bang would startle most people.
6. No; an elevator is a small, enclosed space.

❷ Grammar and Style

Practice

1. . . . telephone cables, power lines, steam pipes, gas mains, and . . .
2. . . .began again, circled the dining room table like a man running, and . . .
3. . . . dining-room, stabbed into hallways, shot up the front stairs, and . . .
4. . . . a grocery store, a barbershop, a newsstand, and . . .
5. . . . open, drawers were yanked open, windows were shot up and pulled down, furniture . . .

Writing Application

Have students check one another's paragraphs to make sure they have used two sets of commas in series.

Integrate Language Skills

❶ Vocabulary Development Lesson

Word Analysis: Latin Root -terr-

The prefix *sub-* means "under" and the Latin root *-terr-* means "earth" or "land." Therefore, the word *subterranean* means "under Earth's surface." Use the meaning of *-terr-* and context clues to choose the best word for each sentence.

a. terrain   b. extraterrestrial   c. terrarium

1. The ___?___ visited from another planet.
2. Put some earth in a glass jar and plant some seeds to make a ___?___.

Spelling Strategy

Words such as *blaspheme* and *telephone* spell the *f* sound with *ph*. These words derive from Greek and are spelled with the Greek letter *phi* (fi). Write a *ph* word that fits each definition.

1. a portrait taken with a camera
2. a piece of music for an orchestra

❷ Grammar and Style Lesson

Commas in Series

Commas in series are placed between three or more parallel items to link them. Sometimes, coordinating conjunctions such as "and," "or," or "but" precede the final item. Separate the items in a list with commas.

> **Example:** Bodwell was at the window in a minute, shouting, frothing a little, shaking his fist.

Practice Rewrite these sentences, inserting commas in their appropriate places.

1. The subterranean system of telephone cables power lines steam pipes gas mains and sewer pipes is the reason to . . .

W̶G *Prentice Hall Writing and Grammar Connection: Chapter 27, Section 2*

908 ◆ *Disillusion, Defiance, and Discontent (1914–1946)*

Fluency: Words in Context

Review the vocabulary list on page 897. Then, answer *yes* or *no* to each question below. Explain your responses.

1. If Susan has an *aspiration* to sail around the world, does she have a vague notion?
2. Must you dig to reach *subterranean* pipes in a city?
3. Would you get in trouble for *blaspheming* in class?
4. Would a *cosmopolitan* person enjoy the streets of Paris?
5. If you heard a very loud bang, would you *intuitively* wince?
6. Would a person suffering from *claustrophobia* enjoy riding in an elevator?

2. Instantly the steps began again circled the dining room table like a man running and started up the stairs toward us . . .
3. Their lights . . . crisscrossed nervously in the dining-room stabbed into hallways shot up the front stairs and finally up the back.
4. You will find within a block or two a grocery store a barbershop a newsstand and shoeshine rack . . .
5. Doors were yanked open drawers were yanked open windows were shot up and pulled down furniture fell with dull thumps.

Writing Application Write a paragraph, using two sets of commas in series.

TEACHING RESOURCES

The following resources can be used to enrich or extend the instruction for pp. 908–909.

Vocabulary

📖 **Selection Support:** Build Vocabulary, p. 224
📖 **Vocabulary and Spelling Practice Book**
(Use this booklet for skills enrichment.) ▪

Grammar

📖 **Selection Support:** Grammar and Style, p. 225
W̶G **Writing and Grammar,** Ruby Level, p. 696
▪ **Daily Language Practice Transparencies** ▪

Writing

▪ **Writing Models and Graphic Organizers on Transparencies,** p. 37
W̶G **Writing and Grammar,** Ruby Level, p. 309 ▪
💿 **Writing and Grammar iText CD-ROM**

▪ **BLOCK SCHEDULING:** Resources marked with this symbol provide varied instruction during 90-minute blocks.

❸ Writing Lesson

Critical Response

E. B. White once said, "The most widely appreciated humorists are those who create characters and tell tales . . ." Write an essay responding to this statement. Cite passages from these humorous essays for support.

Prewriting	Review the selections and identify the most humorous characters. Jot down notes about what makes each of them funny. Select the ones you will write about to support your opinions.
Drafting	Begin by presenting your response to White's statement. Then, use the examples of humorous characters and passages from the selections to support your position.
Revising	Strengthen your essay by incorporating direct quotations that clearly support your opinions.

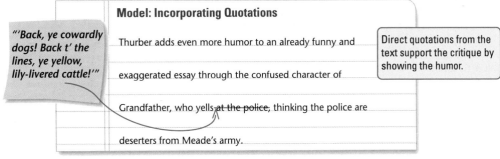

Model: Incorporating Quotations

"'Back, ye cowardly dogs! Back t' the lines, ye yellow, lily-livered cattle!'"

Thurber adds even more humor to an already funny and

exaggerated essay through the confused character of

Grandfather, who yells at the police, thinking the police are

deserters from Meade's army.

Direct quotations from the text support the critique by showing the humor.

 *Prentice Hall Writing and Grammar Connection: Chapter 14, Section 3*

❹ Extension Activities

Listening and Speaking With a partner, conduct a **role play** of Thurber and White discussing their essays in the offices of *The New Yorker*. Constructively criticize each other's work, considering the following:

• What makes the essays funny?
• In what ways are they similar?
• In what ways do they differ?
• What would you add or change?

Present your role play to the class.

Research and Technology Thurber and White both worked for *The New Yorker*. Using the Internet and other sources, research "The Algonquin Roundtable," a group of wits associated with *The New Yorker* who met on a regular basis. With classmates, deliver your findings in a **written report. [Group Activity]**

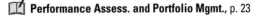 **Take It to the Net** www.phschool.com

Go online for an additional research activity using the Internet.

The Night the Ghost Got In / from Here Is New York ◆ 909

---

❸ Writing Lesson

• Have students choose one of the two essays for this assignment; they need not write about both.

• Remind students to cite specific examples of humor from the text. Since Thurber's illustrations were created specifically for his essay, students may also take those into account in their reviews.

• Remind students that the assignment allows them to criticize the chosen essay for not being funny. If students believe that either White or Thurber has failed to "create characters and tell tales," they are free to defend that point of view.

• Have students use writing Model 7 in **Writing Models and Graphic Organizers on Transparencies,** p. 33, for help in drafting their essays.

• Use the Response to Literature rubric in **Performance Assessment and Portfolio Management,** p. 23, to evaluate students' letters.

❹ Research and Technology

• Tell students that this group of writers is known as the Algonquin Round Table because they met for lunch or cocktails at the large round table in the lounge of the Algonquin Hotel, located on 44th Street near the offices of *The New Yorker*.

• Members of the Algonquin Round Table included short-story writer and poet Dorothy Parker, *The New Yorker* editor Harold Ross, playwright George S. Kaufman, and sportswriter Ring Lardner.

CUSTOMIZE INSTRUCTION
for Universal Access

To address different learning styles, use the following activities suggested in the **Extension Activities** booklet, p. 51.

For Spatial/Visual Learners, use Activities 5 and 6.

For Verbal/Linguistic Learners, use Activities 6 and 7.

Background

African American writers made enormous contributions to prose as well as poetry. Nella Larsen, Arna Bontemps, and Zora Neale Hurston are only a few of the numerous Harlem Renaissance novelists. Larsen wrote two critically acclaimed novels, *Quicksand* (1928) and *Passing* (1929). Her career came to an unfortunate halt soon after her rise when she was accused of plagiarizing a short story by a well-known writer. Although Larsen was fully acquitted, her career was over. She never published again. Her two novels, however, document life in 1920s Harlem and, on a broader scale, life in 1920s America for a black woman.

▶ **Critical Viewing**

Answer: The picture is busy; there is something to look at in every corner. The picture is full of movement and action. The instruments have prominent positions in the picture, helping the viewer "hear" the music.

A Closer Look

The Harlem Renaissance: A Cultural Revolution

In the 1920s, the New York City neighborhood of Harlem became the artistic home of black America.

Harlem in the 1920s: For some it conjures images of wild times, of jazz sessions at hot spots like the Cotton Club, of seedy speakeasies with names like the Clam Bake and the Hot Feet.

For others, it brings to mind the artistic genius of writers like Langston Hughes and Zora Neale Hurston, and painters like Aaron Douglas. Harlem in the 1920s was home to an event that America had never seen before—a flowering of African American talent that left an astonishing cultural legacy.

A Celebration of African American Life Known as the Harlem Renaissance, this remarkable period in America's cultural life marked the first time that African American artists were taken seriously by the culture at large. The artists of the Harlem Renaissance celebrated their culture and exalted their heritage. "Negro life is seizing its first chances for group expression and self determination," wrote sociologist Alain Locke in 1926. Harlem became what Locke termed "the center of a spiritual coming of age."

The artists and writers of the Renaissance did not share a style. Langston Hughes's realistic poems of downtrodden but determined people bear little resemblance to Countee Cullen's elegant sonnets. Instead, these artists shared the urgent need to document the experiences of their people.

The Center of the World Life for African Americans after World War I was filled with grave disappointment. Although many had served side-by-side with white soldiers in Europe, they returned home to find continued racism barring their paths to the American Dream. In the early 1900s, hundreds of thousands of African Americans embarked on what has come to be called the Great Migration, moving from the rural South to the industrial cities of the North. As more and more African Americans settled in Harlem, the neighborhood became a meeting ground for writers, musicians, performers, and thinkers.

The work they produced was unique. Before the Renaissance, many African American writers sought to emulate whites. By contrast, the

▼ **Critical Viewing** In this image of jazz great Duke Ellington leading his band, how do the positioning of the musicians and the use of light and shadow echo the rhythms and energy of jazz music? **[Analyze]**

910 ◆ *Disillusion, Defiance, and Discontent (1914–1946)*

 ENRICHMENT: Music Connection

Plenty o' Nothin'

One of the best-known works to come out the the Harlem Renaissance is *Porgy and Bess*, George Gershwin's jazz opera of DuBose and Dorothy Heyward's novel and play *Porgy* (1925). *Porgy* was a bestselling novel of a Gullah African American community in a Charleston neighborhood called Catfish Row. Porgy, who has lost the use of his legs and wheels himself about on a small platform, falls in love with the beautiful Bess, who is also pursued by the flashy drug dealer Sportin' Life. Gershwin and

Heyward's opera premiered on Broadway and toured 29 countries; tragically, the Metropolitan Opera company did not produce the work that is considered the greatest American opera until the 1980s. The score's combination of jazz, spirituals, popular song, and music from the European classical tradition have ensured its enduring popularity.

Renaissance writers celebrated their racial identity. The goal was to create, as Hughes put it, "an expression of our individual dark-skinned selves."

An Outpouring of Expression Their output was impressive. From the 1920s through the mid-1930s, sixteen African American writers published more than fifty volumes of poetry and fiction—an astounding amount of work at the time. Other African American artists made their marks in painting, music, and theater. Blues singer Bessie Smith performed to packed houses. Musicians Jelly Roll Morton, Louis Armstrong, and Duke Ellington laid the foundations of jazz, a form of music scholars argue is the only truly American art form. In the visual arts, Aaron Douglas incorporated African images into his paintings and illustrations.

Although he was one of the youngest in the movement, Langston Hughes may have been its most influential advocate. His poems combined the rhythms of jazz and blues with stories of Harlem life and captured the struggles of "workers, roustabouts, and singers and job hunters."

Other writers, such as Countee Cullen and Claude McKay, a Jamaican immigrant, wrote in more classical forms. Novelist Zora Neale Hurston combined African folklore with realistic narratives. Today, her novel *Their Eyes Were Watching God* is considered a major work.

A Powerful Legacy In the decades since it ended, the impact of the Harlem Renaissance has been a subject of debate. Most scholars agree that it opened doors for the acceptance of art and writing by African Americans. However, some say that the Renaissance artists were too interested in seeking the approval of the white establishment. Even Langston Hughes admitted that few African Americans had read his work.

Still, the Harlem Renaissance gave Americans a language with which to begin to discuss the problems of racism. It also broke ground for writers who came later. Mid-century writers such as Richard Wright, Ralph Ellison, and James Baldwin stand in a direct line of descent from the writers of the Renaissance.

Today, Nobel Prize–winner Toni Morrison, novelist and poet Alice Walker, popular mystery writer Walter Mosley, and hundreds of other writers, painters, and musicians owe a debt to the artists of the Harlem Renaissance. In its own time, it raised America's consciousness about racism. For thousands of aspiring writers and artists, the Harlem Renaissance was proof that art excludes no one. On the contrary, music, art, and literature provide all human beings the tools with which we can express and celebrate ourselves.

Zora and Langston, Phoebe Beasley

▲ **Critical Viewing** What elements of the lives and works of Langston Hughes and Zora Neale Hurston are expressed in this image of the two writers? **[Interpret]**

The Harlem Renaissance: A Cultural Revolution ◆ 911

Critical Thinking

1. Why was it important for the writers and artists of the Harlem Renaissance to live and work together in one community? **Answer:** They depended on one another for inspiration and support. In the 1920s, black people were still not considered first-class citizens. These artists all shared a common ancestry and a common culture, and their work flourished in the supportive environment of a creative community.

from Dust Tracks on a Road

Lesson Objectives

1. **To analyze and respond to literary elements**
   - Literary Analysis: Social Context in Autobiography
   - Connecting Literary Elements: Dialogue

2. **To read, comprehend, analyze, and critique nonfiction**
   - Reading Strategy: Analyzing How a Writer Achieves Purpose
   - Reading Check Questions
   - Review and Assess Questions
   - Assessment Practice (ATE)

3. **To develop word analysis skills, fluency, and systematic vocabulary**
   - Vocabulary Development Lesson: Greek Root: *-graph-*

4. **To understand and apply written and oral language conventions**
   - Spelling Strategy
   - Grammar and Style Lesson: Parellelism in Coordinate Elements

5. **To understand and apply appropriate writing and research strategies**
   - Writing Lesson: Moment of Inspiration
   - Extension Activity: Folk-Tale Collection

6. **To understand and apply listening and speaking strategies**
   - Extension Activity: Campaign Speech

STEP-BY-STEP TEACHING GUIDE	PACING GUIDE
PRETEACH	
Motivate Students and Provide Background	
Use the Motivation activity (ATE p. 912)	5 min.
Read and discuss author and background features (SE/ATE p. 912) [A]	5 min.
Introduce the Concepts	
Introduce the Literary Analysis and Reading Strategy (SE/ATE p. 913) [A]	15 min.
Pronounce the vocabulary words and read their definitions (SE p. 913)	5 min.
TEACH	
Monitor Comprehension	
Informally monitor comprehension by circulating while students read independently or in groups [A]	40 min.
Monitor students' comprehension with the Reading Check notes (SE/ATE pp. 915, 917, 919)	as students read
Develop vocabulary with Vocabulary notes (SE pp. 915, 916, 917, 918; ATE p. 917)	as students read
Develop Understanding	
Develop students' understanding of social context in autobiography with the Literary Analysis annotations (SE pp. 915, 916; ATE pp. 915, 916) [A]	5 min.
Develop students' ability to analyze how a writer achieves purpose by using the Reading Strategy annotations (SE pp. 917, 918; ATE pp. 917, 918)	5 min.
ASSESS	
Assess Mastery	
Assess students' mastery of the Reading Strategy and Literary Analysis by having them answer the Review and Assess questions (SE/ATE p. 921)	15 min.
Use one or more of the print and media Assessment Resources (ATE p. 923) [A]	up to 45 min.
EXTEND	
Apply Understanding	
Have students complete the Vocabulary Development Lesson and the Grammar and Style Lesson (SE p. 922) [A]	20 min.
Apply students' ability to analyze cause and effect in their writing by using the Writing Lesson (SE/ATE p. 923) [A]	45 min.
Apply students' understanding using one or more of the Extension Activities (SE p. 923)	20–90 min.

 ACCELERATED INSTRUCTION:
Use the strategies and activities identified with an [A].

UNIVERSAL ACCESS
- ● = Below Level Students
- ▲ = On-Level Students
- ■ = Above Level Students

Time and Resource Manager

RESOURCES		
PRINT 📖	**TRANSPARENCIES**	**TECHNOLOGY** 💿 🎧 📼
• **Beyond Literature,** Community Connection: Community and Personal Identity, p. 52 ▲ ■		• **Interest Grabber Video,** Tape 5 ● ▲ ■
• **Selection Support Workbook:** ● ▲ ■ Literary Analysis, p. 231 Reading Strategy, p. 230 Build Vocabulary, p. 228	• **Literary Analysis and Reading Transparencies,** pp. 103 and 104 ● ▲ ■	
		• **Listening to Literature** ● ▲ ■ Audiocassettes, Side 32 Audio CDs, CD 18
• **Literatura en español** ● ▲ • **Literary Analysis for Enrichment** ■		
• **Formal Assessment:** Selection Test, p. 233 ● ▲ ■ • **Open Book Test,** p. 54 ● ▲ ■ • **Performance Assessment and Portfolio Management,** p. 20 ● ▲ ■ • PRENTICE HALL **ASSESSMENT** *SYSTEM* ● ▲ ■	• PRENTICE HALL **ASSESSMENT** *SYSTEM* ● ▲ ■ Skills Practice Answers and Explanations on Transparencies+	• **Test Bank Software** ● ▲ ■ • **Got It! Assessment Videotapes,** Tape 4 ● ▲
• **Selection Support Workbook:** ● ▲ ■ Grammar and Style, p. 229 • **Writing and Grammar,** Ruby Level ● ▲ ■ • **Extension Activities,** p. 52 ● ▲ ■	• **Daily Language Practice Transparencies** ● ▲ • **Writing Models and Graphic Organizers on Transparencies,** p. 91 ● ▲ ■	• **Writing and Grammar iText CD-ROM** ● ▲ ■ 💻 *Take It to the Net* www.phschool.com

BLOCK SCHEDULING: Use one 90-minute class period to preteach the selection and have students read it. Use a second 90-minute class period to assess students' mastery of skills and have them complete one of the Extension Activities.

Step-by-Step Teaching Guide for pp. 912–913

Motivation

Ask students which books were their favorites when they were in fifth or sixth grade. List titles on the board and ask students to bring some of their old books to pass around in class. Have students explain why they liked these books and how the books influenced them. Tell students that they are about to read an autobiographical story of a girl whose love of reading would shape her whole life.

▣ Interest Grabber Video

As an alternative, play "Harlem Renaissance" on Tape 5 to engage students' interest.

❶ More About the Author

Zora Neale Hurston was born in a small hamlet near Tuskegee, Alabama. When she was a child, her family resettled in Eatonville, Florida, the first incorporated African American community in America. Her father served three terms as mayor there. Hurston's Eatonville childhood deeply affected her life. Unlike many—or most—African Americans of her day, Hurston grew up without experiencing the sting of racism. Instead, her community openly expressed pride in African culture, and celebrated its heritage. This environment led the future folkorist to develop a profound self-confidence, as well as a deep appreciation for folklore and literature.

Prepare to Read

❶ *from* Dust Tracks on a Road

Zora Neale Hurston (1891–1960)

Throughout her career as a writer, Zora Neale Hurston was recognized as an influential author and a pioneering force in the documentation of African American culture. Still, she died penniless and was buried in an unmarked grave in a segregated cemetery in Fort Pierce, Florida. Hurston was almost entirely forgotten until author Alice Walker set out on a mission to locate and mark her grave, recording the experience in a 1975 *Ms.* magazine article. Walker's effort restored Hurston to her rightful place in American literature as "the dominant black woman writer" of her time.

Early Influences Hurston was one of the first American writers to recognize that a cultural heritage was valuable in its own right. Her unshakable self-confidence and strong sense of personal worth were fostered by a childhood in Eatonville, Florida, America's first fully incorporated African American township. One of eight children, Hurston was, by her own account, a spirited, curious child who "always wanted to go." Her mother explained this urge to wander by claiming that travel dust had been sprinkled at the door the day Zora was born.

Hurston's childhood abruptly ended when her mother died. Hurston went to live with a series of friends and relatives. By age fourteen, she was supporting herself.

Two Careers Hurston developed an interest in writing while studying at Howard University. In 1925, she moved to New York City, where her gift for storytelling and her outgoing personality helped her to make friends quickly. She soon published a story and a play, firmly establishing herself as one of the bright new talents of the Harlem Renaissance, the blossoming of literature and painting among African Americans in the 1920s, centered in New York. She began attending Barnard College, where her work came to the attention of prominent anthropologist Franz Boas, who convinced Hurston to begin graduate studies in anthropology at Columbia University. With an academic grant, she began a second career as a folklorist.

Preserving a Culture During the Great Migration, when African Americans from the South migrated by the hundreds of thousands to the north—where jobs awaited them in industrial cities like Detroit and Chicago—Hurston moved against the tide. She returned to the South for six years to document the art of "the Negro farthest down." She collected African American folk tales and, in 1935, published *Mules and Men*, the first volume of black American folklore compiled by an African American. Hurston's work helped to document the roots of African American tales in the stories, songs, and myths of Africa. Her second folklore collection, *Tell My Horse* (1938), also provided descriptions of African American cultural beliefs and ritual practices transported from Africa.

The Road to Obscurity Hurston achieved strong critical and popular success during the 1930s and 1940s after publishing the novels *Jonah's Gourd Vine* (1934), *Their Eyes Were Watching God* (1937), and *Moses, Man of the Mountain* (1939). She also wrote numerous short stories, plays, and her prize-winning autobiography, *Dust Tracks on a Road* (1942), which was the most commercially successful of her works.

Unfortunately, controversy and personal scandal led Hurston's career into obscurity. At the time of her death, none of her books were in print. It was not until the 1970s that, with the assistance of Alice Walker, there was a resurgence of interest in Hurston's work. Rescued from the shadows of literary history, she is now generally regarded as one of the important literary figures of the twentieth century.

912 ◆ *Disillusion, Defiance, and Discontent (1914–1946)*

TEACHING RESOURCES

The following resources can be used to enrich or extend the instruction for pp. 912–913.

Motivation

▣ **Interest Grabber Video**, Tape 5

Background

📖 **Beyond Literature**, p. 52

💻 *Take It to the Net*

Visit www.phschool.com for background and hotlinks for "Dust Tracks on a Road."

Literary Analysis

▤ **Literary Analysis and Reading Transparencies,** Social Context in Autobiography, p. 104

Reading

📖 **Selection Support:** Reading Strategy, p. 230; Build Vocabulary, p. 228

▤ **Literary Analysis and Reading Transparencies,** Analyzing How a Writer Achieves Purpose, p. 103

 **BLOCK SCHEDULING:** Resources marked with this symbol provide varied instruction during 90-minute blocks.

Preview

Connecting to the Literature

As a child, Zora Neale Hurston was passionate about literature, and that passion led to her success as a writer. As you read, think about an interest of your own that may not only shape your character but also change your life.

Literary Analysis

Social Context in Autobiography

Autobiography is a nonfiction account of a writer's life told in his or her own words. Autobiographical writing documents the writer's feelings about key events and experiences. In addition to personal insights, autobiographies also reveal **social context**—the attitudes and customs of the culture in which the writer lived. The excerpt from Hurston's autobiography recalls an event from her childhood and provides a glimpse of life in her African American community in the South.

Connecting Literary Elements

In this selection, Hurston helps the scenery and settings of her memories come to life through the use of **dialogue**. The words the people speak reflect their culture and reveal their personalities. By showcasing human interaction, dialogue makes literature more conversational, readable, and enjoyable. As you read, notice the ways in which the dialogue adds nuance and color to your understanding of Hurston's experience.

Reading Strategy

Analyzing How a Writer Achieves Purpose

Hurston's **purpose**—to share her personal experience and show the vitality of the African American community—determines her choice of words, details, characters, and events. By linking her choices to her goals, you can analyze her success in achieving her purpose.

As you read, note key words, details, characters, and events in a chart like the one shown. Then review your notes to evaluate how Hurston achieves her purpose.

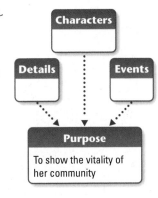

Vocabulary Development

foreknowledge (fôr′ näl ij) *n.* awareness of something before it happens or exists (p. 915)

brazenness (brā′ zən nis) *n.* shamelessness; boldness; impudence (p. 915)

caper (kā′ pər) *n.* prank (p. 915)

exalted (eg zôlt′ id) *adj.* filled with joy or pride; elated (p. 916)

geography (jē äg′ rə fē) *n.* study of Earth's surface (p. 917)

avarice (av′ ə ris) *n.* extreme desire for wealth; greed (p. 918)

from *Dust Tracks on a Road* ◆ 913

913

CUSTOMIZE INSTRUCTION
For Intrapersonal Learners

Point out that Zora's most obvious personality trait is her independence of judgment. Ask students if they identify with this characteristic. As they read the selection, have them think about how her confidence and self-reliance affect Zora's relation-ships with family members, teachers, other children, and the two women visitors, and how it is likely to affect her life beyond the period described in this excerpt.

❶ About the Selection

Hurston recalls how forward and assured she was as a child, alarming her parents and grandmother by "looking white folks right in the face." She recalls two white women who hear her read aloud in school one day and invite her to visit their hotel. They give Hurston a roll of new pennies and later send her boxes of clothing and books. Hurston recalls the fascination that folk tales, Norse mythology, and Old Testament stories held for her.

❷ ▶ Critical Viewing

Answer: Although the classroom appears orderly and the children work diligently at their studies, their bare feet and the battered furniture suggest poverty.

❶ *from*
Dust Tracks on a Road
Zora Neale Hurston

© Hulton Getty/Archive Photos

❷ ▲ **Critical Viewing** What elements of this photograph document the economic realities many of these children probably faced? **[Analyze]**

914 ◆ *Disillusion, Defiance, and Discontent (1914–1946)*

TEACHING RESOURCES

The following resources can be used to enrich or extend the instruction for pp. 914–920.

Literary Analysis
📖 **Selection Support:** Literary Analysis, p. 231

Reading
🎧 **Listening to Literature Audiocassettes,** Side 32 ▪
💿 **Listening to Literature Audio CDs,** CD 18 ▪

▪ **BLOCK SCHEDULING:** Resources marked with this symbol provide varied instruction during 90-minute blocks.

Background

In this excerpt from Zora Neale Hurston's autobiography, the young Zora experiences an event that opens her eyes to the world of literature and sets the stage for her career as a writer. Hurston would go on to compile African American folklore—traditional stories—and to write her own critically acclaimed fiction.

I used to take a seat on top of the gatepost and watch the world go by. One way to Orlando[1] ran past my house, so the carriages and cars would pass before me. The movement made me glad to see it. Often the white travelers would hail me, but more often I hailed them, and asked, "Don't you want me to go a piece of the way with you?"

They always did. I know now that I must have caused a great deal of amusement among them, but my self-assurance must have carried the point, for I was always invited to come along. I'd ride up the road for perhaps a half-mile, then walk back. I did not do this with the permission of my parents, nor with their foreknowledge. When they found out about it later, I usually got a whipping. My grandmother worried about my forward ways a great deal. She had known slavery and to her my brazenness was unthinkable.

"Git down offa dat gate-post! You li'l sow, you! Git down! Setting up dere looking dem white folks right in de face! They's gowine[2] to lynch you, yet. And don't stand in dat doorway gazing out at 'em neither. Youse too brazen to live long."[3]

Nevertheless, I kept right on gazing at them, and "going a piece of the way" whenever I could make it. The village seemed dull to me most of the time. If the village was singing a chorus, I must have missed the tune.

Perhaps a year before the old man[4] died, I came to know two other white people for myself. They were women.

It came about this way. The whites who came down from the North were often brought by their friends to visit the village school. A Negro school was something strange to them, and while they were always sympathetic and kind, curiosity must have been present, also. They came and went, came and went. Always, the room was hurriedly put in order, and we were threatened with a prompt and bloody death if we cut one caper while the visitors were present. We always sang a spiritual, led by Mr. Calhoun himself. Mrs. Calhoun always stood

---

1. **Orlando** (ôr lan´ dō) city in central Florida, about five miles from Eatonville, Hurston's hometown.
2. **gowine** "going."
3. **"Git down . . . live long"** Hurston's grandmother's fears reflect the belief of many people at the time that it was inappropriate for African Americans to be assertive toward whites.
4. **the old man** white farmer who had developed a friendship with Hurston.

from *Dust Tracks on a Road* ◆ 915

Literary Analysis
Social Context in Autobiography What do you learn about the social context from Zora's parents' stern warning about talking with white folk?

foreknowledge (fôr´ näl´ ij) *n.* awareness of something before it happens or exists

brazenness (brā´ zən nis) *n.* shamelessness; boldness; impudence

caper (kā´ pər) *n.* prank

⑤ ✓ Reading Check
Why does her grandmother worry about Zora's sitting on the gatepost and accepting rides from strangers?

---

❸ Literary Analysis
Social Context in Autobiography

- Read the first four paragraphs of the excerpt aloud.

- Then, ask students the Literary Analysis question on page 915: What do you learn about the social context from Zora's parents' stern warning about talking with white folk?
Answer: Zora clearly lives in a society in which blacks and whites experience little interaction, and blacks do not expect whites to treat them well.

- Ask students: What does the white travelers' treatment of Zora suggest about the parents' and grandmother's fears?
Answer: The travelers are amused by Zora, but are friendly and kind to her. This suggests that the family's fears are less justified than one might assume, given the time and place of the story.

▶ **Monitor Progress** Ask students whether they think Zora's fearlessness affects the ways in which the white people respond to her. Have them explain their answers.
Answer: Students may say that Zora's bold assumption of welcome and kindness makes the white people respond well to her.

❹ Critical Thinking
Infer

- Ask students what they can infer about Zora's character from her actions.
Answer: She is fearless and adventurous. She wants to see what lies beyond the village.

- Then, ask: Do you think Zora's family worries about her because of her personality or because they are distrustful of white people? Explain.
Answer: They are afraid for her because she lacks caution. At the same time, Zora's grandmother had "known slavery" and so her distrust of white people is well justified.

❺ ✓ Reading Check
Answer: The grandmother is afraid for Zora's safety.

915

Social Context in Autobiography

- Remind students that social context—the culture in which the writer lives—plays an important role in autobiography.

- Ask students: What does Mrs. Calhoun's palmetto switch reveal about the society in which Zora grew up?
  Answer: Teachers are permitted to maintain discipline by whipping student.

- Then, ask the Literary Analysis question on page 916: What social context is revealed in this passage about preparation for visitors?
  Answer: The people who run the school want to be sure that they present their students and themselves in the best possible light.

▶ Monitor Progress Have students consider what the warning to wear shoes on the day visitors are expected tells them about the social context.
  Answer: If not given the warning, children would go to school barefoot. This suggests that their families can't often afford shoes for them. In order to keep shoes from wearing out too fast they are probably reserved for church and special occasions.

❼ Background

Art

School Bell Time, by Romare Bearden

Romare Bearden (1914–1988) grew up in Harlem. During the Depression, he became a member of the Harlem Artists' Guild, along with Jacob Lawrence, Aaron Douglas, and others. After World War II, Bearden studied at the Sorbonne in Paris. He was greatly influenced by Cubist painters such as Pablo Picasso. The scraps of fabric and paper cutouts pasted to the canvas make this painting a collage. Use the following questions for discussion:

1. How would you describe the composition of this painting?
   Answer: Students may say that it combines abstract and representational elements in a collage-like design with human figures and geometrical patterns.

916

---

in the back, with a palmetto switch[5] in her hand as a squelcher. We were all little angels for the duration, because we'd better be. She would cut her eyes and give us a glare that meant trouble, then turn her face towards the visitors and beam as much as to say it was a great privilege and pleasure to teach lovely children like us. They couldn't see that palmetto hickory in her hand behind all those benches, but we knew where our angelic behavior was coming from.

❻ Usually, the visitors gave warning a day ahead and we would be cautioned to put on shoes, comb our heads, and see to ears and fingernails. There was a close inspection of every one of us before we marched in that morning. Knotty heads, dirty ears and fingernails got hauled out of line, strapped and sent home to lick the calf over again.

This particular afternoon, the two young ladies just popped in. Mr. Calhoun was flustered, but he put on the best show he could. He dismissed the class that he was teaching up at the front of the room, then called the fifth grade in reading. That was my class.

So we took our readers and went up front. We stood up in the usual line, and opened to the lesson. It was the story of Pluto and Persephone. It was new and hard to the class in general, and Mr. Calhoun was very uncomfortable as the readers stumbled along, spelling out words with their lips, and in mumbling undertones before they exposed them experimentally to the teacher's ears.

Then it came to me. I was fifth or sixth down the line. The story was not new to me, because I had read my reader through from lid to lid, the first week that Papa had bought it for me.

That is how it was that my eyes were not in the book, working out the paragraph which I knew would be mine by counting the children ahead of me. I was observing our visitors, who held a book between them, following the lesson. They had shiny hair, mostly brownish. One had a looping gold chain around her neck. The other one was dressed all over in black and white with a pretty finger ring on her left hand. But the thing that held my eyes were their fingers. They were long and thin, and very white, except up near the tips. There they were baby pink. I had never seen such hands. It was a fascinating discovery for me. I wondered how they felt. I would have given those hands more attention, but the child before me was almost through. My turn next, so I got on my mark, bringing my eyes back to the book and made sure of my place. Some of the stories I had reread several times, and this Greco-Roman myth was one of my favorites. I was <u>exalted</u> by it, and that is the way I read my paragraph.

"Yes, Jupiter had seen her (Persephone). He had seen the maiden picking flowers in the field. He had seen the chariot of the dark monarch pause by the maiden's side. He had seen him when he seized Persephone. He had seen the black horses leap down Mount Aetna's fiery throat. Persephone was now in Pluto's dark realm and he had made her his wife."

---

5. **palmetto** (pal met′ ō) **switch** whip made from the fan-shaped leaves of the palmetto, a type of palm tree.

exalted (eg zôlt′ id) *adj.* filled with joy or pride; elated

---

2. Which figures in the painting are suggestive of characters in Hurston's autobiography?
   Answer: The woman ringing the school bell in the lower right corner may remind students of Mrs. Calhoun, while they may identify the man in the schoolyard as Mr. Calhoun.

The two women looked at each other and then back to me. Mr. Calhoun broke out with a proud smile beneath his bristly moustache, and instead of the next child taking up where I had ended, he nodded to me to go on. So I read the story to the end, where flying Mercury, the messenger of the Gods, brought Persephone back to the sunlit earth and restored her to the arms of Dame Ceres, her mother, that the world might have springtime and summer flowers, autumn and harvest. But because she had bitten the pomegranate[6] while in Pluto's kingdom, she must return to him for three months of each year, and be his queen. Then the world had winter, until she returned to earth.

The class was dismissed, and the visitors smiled us away and went into a low-voiced conversation with Mr. Calhoun for a few minutes. They glanced my way once or twice and I began to worry. Not only was I barefooted, but my feet and legs were dusty. My hair was more uncombed than usual, and my nails were not shiny clean. Oh, I'm going to catch it now. Those ladies saw me, too. Mr. Calhoun is promising to 'tend to me. So I thought.

Then Mr. Calhoun called me. I went up thinking how awful it was to get a whipping before company. Furthermore, I heard a snicker run over the room. Hennie Clark and Stell Brazzle did it out loud, so I would be sure to hear them. The smart-aleck was going to get it. I slipped one hand behind me and switched my dress tail at them, indicating scorn.

"Come here, Zora Neale," Mr. Calhoun cooed as I reached the desk. He put his hand on my shoulder and gave me little pats. The ladies smiled and held out those flower-looking fingers towards me. I seized the opportunity for a good look.

"Shake hands with the ladies, Zora Neale," Mr. Calhoun prompted and they took my hand one after the other and smiled. They asked if I loved school, and I lied that I did. There was *some* truth in it, because I liked geography and reading, and I liked to play at recess time. Who ever it was invented writing and arithmetic got no thanks from me. Neither did I like the arrangement where the teacher could sit up there with a palmetto stem and lick me whenever he saw fit. I hated things I couldn't do anything about. But I knew better than to bring that up right there, so I said yes, I *loved* school.

---

6. **pomegranate** (päm′ gran′ it) *n.* round, red-skinned fruit with many seeds.

School Bell Time, 1978 From the Profile/Part 1: The Twenties series (Mecklenburg County), Romare Bearden, Collection: Kingsborough Community College, The City University of New York; © Romare Bearden Foundation/Licensed by VAGA, New York, NY

❽ ▲ Critical Viewing
How does the mood of this image compare or contrast with the mood of Hurston's writing? Explain. **[Compare and Contrast]**

Reading Strategy
Analyzing How a Writer Achieves Purpose Why do you think Hurston includes this description of her response to taunting classmates? How does it help you to understand young Zora's experience?

geography (jē äg′ rə fē) *n.* study of Earth's surface

❿ ✓Reading Check
Why is Zora afraid to approach her teacher after reading so well?

❽ ▶Critical Viewing
Answer: The faces seem solemn and the face of the figure at far left seems almost desperate. Such joylessness is not characteristic of Hurston's ebullient personality or her writing. However, the bright colors of the image more closely echo Hurston's work.

❾ Reading Strategy
Analyzing How a Writer Achieves Purpose
• Read aloud the bracketed passage to students.
• Ask the Reading Strategy question on page 917: Why do you think Hurston includes this description of her response to taunting classmates? How does it help you to understand young Zora's experience?
Answer: Zora's reaction to her classmates shows her fearlessness and also her difference. She is taunted, at least in part, for being smart.

❿ Vocabulary Development
Greek Root -graph-
• Draw students' attention to Hurston's use of the word *geography*, and read its definition.
• Tell students that the word combines the prefix *geo-*, meaning "earth," with the root *-graph-*, meaning "to write."
• Write the following prefixes and their meanings on the board: *auto-* = "self"; *topo-* = "place," *biblio-* = "book," *bio-* = "life."
• Have students combine these prefixes with the root *-graph-* to create new words. Ask students to define each of the new words they create. **Answers:** An autograph is a signature. Topography is the contour of the land; the terrain. A bibliography is a list of books. A biography is a life story.

⓫ ✓Reading Check
Answer: Zora looks dirty and untidy. She expects to be punished.

Analyzing How a Writer Achieves Purpose

- Ask students: Why does Hurston mention the "strange things" the ladies offer her to eat?

  Answer: She wants to stress how foreign and exotic the women seemed to her.

- Then, have students explain why Hurston describes the gift of the pennies in detail.

  Answer: She was overwhelmed by the gift and still remembers it years later. She wants readers to understand what a miracle it was for a black child in the Depression to have a hundred shiny pennies.

- Then, ask the Reading Strategy question on page 918: Why do you think Hurston includes this incident in which her mother prepares her for meeting the women at the hotel?

  Answer: Hurston wants to show how important this visit was to her family. She wants to emphasize that her invitation was a special, unusual event.

"I can tell you do," Brown Taffeta gleamed. She patted my head, and was lucky enough not to get sandspurs in her hand. Children who roll and tumble in the grass in Florida are apt to get sandspurs in their hair. They shook hands with me again and I went back to my seat.

When school let out at three o'clock, Mr. Calhoun told me to wait. When everybody had gone, he told me I was to go to the Park House, that was the hotel in Maitland,[7] the next afternoon to call upon Mrs. Johnstone and Miss Hurd. I must tell Mama to see that I was clean and brushed from head to feet, and I must wear shoes and stockings. The ladies liked me, he said, and I must be on my best behavior.

The next day I was let out of school an hour early, and went home to be stood up in a tub full of suds and be scrubbed and have my ears dug into. My sandy hair sported a red ribbon to match my red and white checked gingham dress, starched until it could stand alone. Mama saw to it that my shoes were on the right feet, since I was careless about left and right. Last thing, I was given a handkerchief to carry, warned again about my behavior, and sent off, with my big brother John to go as far as the hotel gate with me.

First thing, the ladies gave me strange things, like stuffed dates and preserved ginger, and encouraged me to eat all that I wanted. Then they showed me their Japanese dolls and just talked. I was then handed a copy of *Scribner's Magazine*,[8] and asked to read a place that was pointed out to me. After a paragraph or two, I was told with smiles, that that would do.

I was led out on the grounds and they took my picture under a palm tree. They handed me what was to me then a heavy cylinder done up in fancy paper, tied with a ribbon, and they told me goodbye, asking me not to open it until I got home.

My brother was waiting for me down by the lake, and we hurried home, eager to see what was in the thing. It was too heavy to be candy or anything like that. John insisted on toting it for me.

My mother made John give it back to me and let me open it. Perhaps, I shall never experience such joy again. The nearest thing to that moment was the telegram accepting my first book. One hundred goldy-new pennies rolled out of the cylinder. Their gleam lit up the world. It was not <u>avarice</u> that moved me. It was the beauty of the thing. I stood on the mountain. Mama let me play with my pennies for a while, then put them away for me to keep.

That was only the beginning. The next day I received an Episcopal hymn-book bound in white leather with a golden cross stamped into the front cover, a copy of *The Swiss Family Robinson*, and a book of fairy tales.

I set about to commit the song words to memory. There was no music written there, just the words. But there was to my consciousness music in between them just the same. "When I Survey the Wondrous Cross"

---

7. **Maitland** (māt′ lənd) city in Florida, close to Eatonville.
8. *Scribner's Magazine* literary magazine no longer published.

Reading Strategy
Analyzing How a Writer Achieves Purpose Why do you think Hurston includes this incident in which her mother prepares her for her meeting with the women at the hotel?

avarice (av′ ər is) *n.* extreme desire for wealth; greed

✳ ENRICHMENT: Literature Connection

The Boxes of Books

Jonathan Swift's satire *Gulliver's Travels* (1727) recounts the amazing lands discovered by his fictional hero Lemuel Gulliver. The Lilliputians are miniature people, the Brobdingnagians are giants, and the Houyhnhnms are civilized horses whose servants are human savages.

Odin, Thor, and other Norse gods have counterparts in Greek and Roman mythology. Odin, like Zeus, is the unhappily-married chief of all the gods. Like Zeus' wife

Hera, Odin's wife Fricka is the goddess of marriage and fidelity. Brunnhilde, Odin's favorite daughter, is a warrior maiden like Athena.

Robert Louis Stevenson (page 920) is best known for his adventure stories—*Treasure Island, Kidnapped,* and *The Black Arrow*. Rudyard Kipling's *Just So Stories* is a collection of original Anglo-Indian legends explaining, among other things, how the camel got its hump and how the alphabet was invented.

seemed the most beautiful to me, so I committed that to memory first of all. Some of them seemed dull and without life, and I pretended they were not there. If white people liked trashy singing like that, there must be something funny about them that I had not noticed before. I stuck to the pretty ones where the words marched to a throb I could feel.

A month or so after the young ladies returned to Minnesota, they sent me a huge box packed with clothes and books. The red coat with a wide circular collar and the red tam[9] pleased me more than any of the other things. My chums pretended not to like anything that I had, but even then I knew that they were jealous. Old Smarty had gotten by them again. The clothes were not new, but they were very good. I shone like the morning sun.

But the books gave me more pleasure than the clothes. I had never been too keen on dressing up. It called for hard scrubbings with Octagon soap suds getting in my eyes, and none too gentle fingers scrubbing my neck and gouging in my ears.

In that box were *Gulliver's Travels, Grimm's Fairy Tales, Dick Whittington, Greek and Roman Myths,* and best of all, *Norse Tales.* Why did the Norse tales strike so deeply into my soul? I do not know, but they did. I seemed to remember seeing Thor swing his mighty short-handled hammer as he sped across the sky in rumbling thunder, lightning flashing from the tread of his steeds and the wheels of his chariot. The great and good Odin, who went down to the well of knowledge to drink, and was told that the price of a drink from that fountain was an eye. Odin drank deeply, then plucked out one eye without a murmur and handed it to the grizzly keeper, and walked away. That held majesty for me.

Of the Greeks, Hercules moved me most. I followed him eagerly on his tasks. The story of the choice of Hercules as a boy when he met Pleasure and Duty, and put his hand in that of Duty and followed her steep way to the blue hills of fame and glory, which she pointed out at the end, moved me profoundly. I resolved to be like him. The tricks and turns of the other Gods and Goddesses left me cold. There were other thin books about this and that sweet and gentle little girl who gave up her heart to Christ and good works. Almost always they died from it, preaching as they passed. I was utterly indifferent to their deaths. In the first place I could not conceive of death, and in the next place they never had any funerals that amounted to a hill of beans, so I didn't care how soon they rolled up their big, soulful, blue eyes and kicked the bucket. They had no meat on their bones.

But I also met Hans Andersen and Robert Louis Stevenson. They seemed to know what I wanted to hear and said it in a way that

---

9. **tam** (tam) *n.* cap with a wide, round, flat top and sometimes a center pompom.

The American Experience

⓭ *Zora Neale Hurston Rediscovered*

Although she died in a welfare home in 1960 penniless and unknown, the rediscovery of Zora Neale Hurston in the 1970s is among the most dramatic events in American literary history. Hurston became a subject of author Alice Walker's 1983 essay, "In Search of Our Mother's Gardens." Ten years earlier, Walker's article "Looking for Zora" described her 1973 search to find and mark Hurston's unknown grave.

In both of her writings, Walker speaks of the importance of recovering and remembering Hurston as one of the greatest African American folklorists of all time and a major American writer. Walker championed the cause to resurrect Hurston's literary reputation and, once again, give her a prominent place in our literary heritage.

⓯ ✓**Reading Check**
Of all the gifts she receives, what gives Zora the most pleasure? Explain.

from Dust Tracks on a Road ◆ 919

⓭ Background
Alice Walker

Alice Walker's best-known novel is *The Color Purple*, published in 1982. This controversial book was a huge bestseller and won both a Pulitzer Prize and a National Book Award. It tells the story of Celie, a young black woman who is separated from her sister, forced into marriage to an uncaring and unfaithful husband, but who eventually triumphs over all her difficulties.

⓮ Critical Thinking
Compare and Contrast

- Based on Hurston's descriptions of her favorite stories, ask students to compare and contrast Thor, Odin, and Hercules.
  Answer: Thor and Hercules are strong heroes. Odin and Hercules both make sacrifices for what they want (knowledge and glory).

- How is Zora like her heroes? How is she different?
  Answer: Like her heroes, Zora takes risks to get what she wants. She is brave. Her heroes have adventures and she, too, seeks adventure.

- Then, ask students to contrast Zora's personality with that of the "sweet and gentle little girl" she describes in the last paragraph on this page. Why do these stories bore her?
  Answer: Zora is the opposite of "sweet and gentle"; she is smart-alecky, disobedient, and high-spirited. She likes stories about bold spirits and is bored by tales of the lifeless and obedient.

⓯ ✓Reading Check

Answer: Zora likes the books best because they tell exciting tales of bold characters whom she admires.

1. Students who like fantasy and adventure should share Zora's taste in stories.

2. **(a)** She calls to them and offers to accompany them up the road. **(b)** She is outgoing and assertive, likes talking to new people, and isn't afraid of strangers.

3. **(a)** Mrs. Johnstone and Miss Hurd are from Minnesota. Their interest in the school and their gifts to Zora suggest that they are involved in charity work. **(b)** Everything about them, from their hands to their clothing to the food they offer her, fascinates Zora. Their gift of the new roll of pennies resulted in one of the shining moments of Zora's life.

4. **(a)** Zora finds nearly everything about them fascinating, but is most taken with their hands. **(b)** She hasn't met many people outside her own community. Most of the people she knows are just like her and her family.

5. **(a)** She is happy with the clothes and thrilled by the pennies. It is the books that have the most enduring impact on her. **(b)** She loves to read, and likes things that appeal to her intelligence and imagination.

6. Students should say yes. People respond best to those who believe in and respect themselves.

---

tingled me. Just a little below these friends was Rudyard Kipling in his *Jungle Books.* I loved his talking snakes as much as I did the hero.

I came to start reading the Bible through my mother. She gave me a licking one afternoon for repeating something I had overheard a neighbor telling her. She locked me in her room after the whipping, and the Bible was the only thing in there for me to read. I happened to open to the place where David[10] was doing some mighty smiting, and I got interested. David went here and he went there, and no matter where he went, he smote 'em hip and thigh. Then he sung songs to his harp awhile, and went out and smote some more. Not one time did David stop and preach about sins and other things. All David wanted to know from God was who to kill and when. He took care of the other details himself. Never a quiet moment. I liked him a lot. So I read a great deal more in the Bible, hunting for some more active people like David. Except for the beautiful language of Luke and Paul,[11] the New Testament still plays a poor second to the Old Testament for me. The Jews had a God who laid about Him when they needed Him. I could see no use waiting until Judgment Day to see a man who was just crying for a good killing, to be told to go and roast. My idea was to give him a good killing first, and then if he got roasted later on, so much the better.

---

10. **David** in the Bible, the second king of Israel, the land of the Hebrews.
11. **Luke and Paul** two Christian Apostles who wrote parts of the New Testament.

Review and Assess

Thinking About the Selection

1. **Respond:** What do you think about young Zora's preferences in reading? Which of the stories would you like to read?

2. **(a) Recall:** What does Zora do when white travelers pass by her house? **(b) Infer:** What does this activity tell you about her?

3. **(a) Recall:** Who are the two white women Zora meets, and why are they at her school? **(b) Support:** How can you tell that these two women made an impression on Hurston?

4. **(a) Recall:** What does Zora find fascinating about the two visitors? **(b) Infer:** What does her fascination suggest about her life experiences so far?

5. **(a) Recall:** Describe Zora's response to the gifts she receives. **(b) Infer:** What does her preference reveal about her?

6. **Evaluate:** Do you think it is important to have self-confidence, as Zora did, in order to succeed in life? Why or why not?

920 ◆ *Disillusion, Defiance, and Discontent (1914–1946)*

✎ ASSESSMENT PRACTICE: Reading Comprehension

Sentence Completion	(For more practice, see Test Preparation Workbook, p. 55.)

Many tests ask students to choose the best word to complete a sentence. Use the following sample test item to give students practice at this skill.

> For African Americans, folklore and oral history served as an important means of preserving their cultural heritage. Thanks to anthropologists and writers such as Hurston, this folk tradition is now _____ preserved in writing.

Which word best completes this passage?

A permanently   **C** emphatically
B temporarily   **D** tentatively

Students should know that short of deliberate destruction, written records last forever. The correct answer is *A.*

Review and Assess

Literary Analysis

Social Context in Autobiography

1. (a) Why might Zora's grandmother be worried about her granddaughter's brazenness? (b) What can you infer about the **social context** and cultural attitudes, based on her grandmother's statements?

2. What do you learn about the social context through the following details of Hurston's **autobiography:** (a) the schoolroom being cleaned for visitors, (b) students reading mythology, and (c) Zora going to school barefoot?

3. Find three more details that reveal the attitudes of Hurston's culture. Record them in a chart like the one shown.

Detail of Social Context	⋯▶	Attitude It Reveals

Connecting Literary Elements

4. What important information about Hurston is revealed in the opening **dialogue** she has with her grandmother?

5. Identify an example of dialogue that reveals a distinct trait of Hurston's personality. Explain how it does so.

6. What general impression do you get of the school and of education in the community based on the dialogue between Hurston, her teacher, and the two visitors?

Reading Strategy

Analyzing How a Writer Achieves Purpose

7. Why does Hurston include the actual words of her grandmother in dialect?

8. What small incidents and details does Hurston use to reveal her reputation as a smart-aleck in school?

9. For what purpose do you think Hurston included her meeting with the Minnesotans in her autobiography?

Extend Understanding

10. **Cultural Connection:** In what ways can relationships with mentors such as Hurston's improve a young person's life?

Quick Review

In **autobiography,** a writer tells his or her own life story.

Autobiographies often reveal **social context**— the attitudes or customs of a culture or specific time period.

The use of **dialogue,** or conversation between characters, makes a scene come alive and helps to define such things as the characters' personalities, social class, and education.

To **analyze how a writer achieves purpose,** consider the way details and events that are described work toward a specific goal.

 Take It to the Net
www.phschool.com
Take the interactive self-test online to check your understanding of the selection.

from Dust Tracks on a Road ◆ 921

✿ ENRICHMENT: Further Reading

Other Works by Zora Neale Hurston

Their Eyes Were Watching God

Jonah's Gourd Vine

Mules and Men

 Take It to the Net
Visit www.phschool.com for more information on Zora Neale Hurston.

Review and Assess

1. **(a)** She's afraid that Zora will get herself into trouble. **(b)** Experience tells the grandmother that many white people want black people to behave in a subservient manner, not to display the bold confidence that Zora shows.

2. **(a)** The teachers want to make a good impression on visitors; this suggests that they depend on the visitors in some way. **(b)** Students are exposed to classical literature. **(c)** The community is poor. The children's parents probably want to reserve shoes for special occasions.

3. Possible answers: Zora's classmates stumble through their reading; the culture is not highly literate. The ladies' gifts to Zora; some white people seek to redress the wrongs done to blacks. Zora's fascination with the ladies' slender white hands; she is used to seeing work-worn hands on women.

4. She risks punishment to do what she wants.

5. "Don't you want me to go a piece of the way with you?" shows that Hurston is gregarious and wants adventure.

6. The teachers seem to deal with the students as a group, not as individuals. They use force to disciple the children. An intelligent, curious child like Zora probably finds limited stimulation.

7. She wants to portray her grandmother realistically. She wants to remind readers of the heritage of slavery—fear and ignorance.

8. She reads aloud much better than the other students. Even when she thinks she is about to be punished, she makes a scornful gesture to the students who snicker at her.

9. Their gifts of books marked a turning point in her life. It gave her access in print to new places, stories, and people.

10. Mentors can share their life experiences, listen to confidences, give advice, and provide a model of success.

❶ Vocabulary Development

Word Analysis

1. to write one's signature
2. to send a message over wires
3. the story of someone's life
4. written or drawn

Spelling Strategy

1. judge
2. fudge
3. budge

Concept Development: Analogies

1. foreknowledge
2. caper
3. brazenness
4. exalted
5. geography
6. avarice

❷ Grammar and Style

1. circles
2. capture
3. come
4. flash
5. describes

Writing Application

1. I kept right on gazing at them, and "going a piece of the way..."; conjunction: and
2. with the permission of my parents, nor with their foreknowledge; conjunction: nor
3. David sung songs and went out and smote; conjunction: and (twice)
4. I must tell Mama... and I must wear shoes and stockings; conjunction: and
5. I was given...warned... and sent off; conjunction: and

Writing Application

Have students exchange papers and check for the required grammatical elements. Students may review Writing and Grammar, Ruby Level, to settle any disagreements.

Integrate Language Skills

❶ Vocabulary Development Lesson

Word Analysis: Greek Root -graph-

The Greek root -graph- means "write." For example, *geography* means "the study of, or writing about, Earth." Define the following words, incorporating the meaning of -graph- into your definitions.

1. autograph
2. telegraph
3. biography
4. graphic

Spelling Strategy

In many words, the *j* sound is spelled -dg-, as in *knowledge* or *pudgy*. Complete each sentence with a word in which the *j* sound is spelled -dg-.

1. A ____?____ rules in a court.
2. I ordered a hot ____?____ sundae.
3. The heavy table would not ____?____ .

Concept Development: Analogies

Review the vocabulary list on page 913 and note how each word is used in the context of the selection. Then, select the correct word to complete each of the following analogies.

1. *Hindsight* is to *past* as ____?____ is to *future*.
2. *Trick* is to *magician* as ____?____ is to *prankster*.
3. *Indifference* is to *concern* as ____?____ is to *shyness*.
4. *Dejected* is to *loser* as ____?____ is to *winner*.
5. *Zoology* is to *animals* as ____?____ is to *Earth's surface*.
6. *Cruelty* is to *kindness* as ____?____ is to *selflessness*.

❷ Grammar and Style Lesson

Parallelism in Coordinate Elements

Parallel coordinate elements—those linked by coordinating conjunctions such as *and, but, or, nor,* or *so*—may be nouns, adjectives, adverbs, clauses, or phrases. To make elements that are linked with coordinating conjunctions parallel, put them in the same grammatical form.

> **Example:** She *cut* her eyes <u>and</u> *gave* us a glare that meant trouble. (past tense verb)

Practice Copy the following sentences. Circle the coordinating conjunction(s) and underline the parallel coordinate elements.

1. Nevertheless, I kept right on gazing at them, and "going a piece of the way" . . .

2. I did not do this with the permission of my parents, nor with their foreknowledge.
3. Then [David] sung songs to his harp awhile, and went out and smote some more.
4. I must tell Mama to see that I was clean and brushed from head to feet, and I must wear shoes and stockings.
5. I was given a handkerchief to carry, warned again about my behavior, and sent off . . .

Writing Application Write a paragraph about the importance of self-confidence. Include at least two parallel coordinate elements linked by coordinating conjunctions.

W̶G Prentice Hall Writing and Grammar Connection: Chapter 20, Section 6

TEACHING RESOURCES

The following resources can be used to enrich or extend the instruction for pp. 922–923.

Vocabulary

📖 **Selection Support:** Build Vocabulary, p. 228

📖 **Vocabulary and Spelling Practice Book** (Use this booklet for skills enrichment). ▪

Grammar

📖 **Selection Support:** Grammar and Style, p. 229

W̶G **Writing and Grammar**, Ruby Level, p. 504

▪ **Daily Language Practice Transparencies** ▪

Writing

W̶G **Writing and Grammar**, Ruby Level, p. 52 ▪

⊙ **Writing and Grammar iText CD-ROM**

▪ **Writing Models and Graphic Organizers on Transparencies,** p. 91.

▪ **BLOCK SCHEDULING:** Resources marked with this symbol provide varied instruction during 90-minute blocks.

❸ Writing Lesson

Moment of Inspiration

Hurston's encounter with the Minnesotans was a turning point in her life, leading to a greater love of reading and learning. Write a personal narrative about a moment in your life that inspired you to act or think differently.

Prewriting   Jot down some of your interests, such as sports, hobbies, movies, or travel, and consider their origins. Think of incidents that were "moments of inspiration." Select one as the focus of your narrative, and explore its impact in a cause-and-effect diagram like the one shown.

Model: Analyzing Cause and Effect

Cause	Effects
My ninth-grade teacher introduced me to writing poetry in a creative way.	As a result, I feel confident in my ability and want to pursue a career as a poet.

Drafting   Start your essay by showing the effects of your moment of inspiration and then flashing back to reconstruct the moment itself. Use the details in your cause-and-effect diagram to help you.

Revising   Reread your narrative to make sure the connection between inspiration and reaction is clear. Make sure you have demonstrated, rather than explained, its impact on your life.

W̶G *Prentice Hall Writing and Grammar Connection: Chapter 4, Section 2*

❹ Extension Activities

Listening and Speaking Develop and deliver a **campaign speech** in which young Zora hopes to persuade her classmates to elect her class president. Include details that reveal Zora's self-image and portray her character. The following tips will help you:

- Review the selection to identify Zora's qualities.
- Outline her accomplishments.
- Discuss goals that will benefit the class.

Practice the speech with a partner before presenting it to your class.

Research and Technology With a group, select three folk tales from Hurston's *Mules and Men* or from another book of folk tales collected in the United States. Compile them in a booklet, creating a **folk tale collection**. In the booklet, write an introduction, prepare a table of contents, choose art or illustrations and include brief reviews of each tale. **[Group Activity]**

 **Take It to the Net**   www.phschool.com

Go online for an additional research activity using the Internet.

from Dust Tracks on a Road ◆ 923

Lesson Support for p. 923

❸ Writing Lesson

- Students may find it helpful to begin by identifying a person who has strongly influenced their lives.
- Review the cause-and-effect chart. Explain to students that the impact of their chosen incident will be the effect.
- As an alternative, have students use the Cause-and-Effect organizer in **Writing Models and Graphic Organizers on Transparencies,** p. 91.
- Tell students that the effect they define will be the main idea of their personal narratives. All the ideas and details they include in their narratives should all contribute to this main idea.
- Adapt the Cause-and-Effect rubric in **Performance Assessment and Portfolio Management,** p. 20, to evaluate students' essays.

❹ Research and Technology

- Encourage students to choose folk tales from a variety of cultures.
- Challenge students to write their own versions of old stories they heard while growing up.
- Students may want to collaborate on this project, with some students writing stories, others drawing illustrations, others working on the introductions, and others organizing the elements to create the actual books.

CUSTOMIZE INSTRUCTION for Universal Access

To address different learning styles, use the following activities suggested in the **Extension Activities** booklet, p. 52.

For Visual/Spatial Learners, use Activity 5.

For Bodily/Kinesthetic Learners, use Activity 6.

For Verbal/Linguistic Learners, use Activities 6 and 7.

ASSESSMENT RESOURCES

The following resources can be used to assess students' knowledge and skills.

Selection Assessment
- **Formal Assessment,** p. 233
- **Open Book Test,** p. 154
- **Got It! Assessment Videotapes,** Tape 4
- **Test Bank Software**
- **Take It to the Net**
  Visit www.phschool.com for self-tests and additional questions on "Dust Tracks on a Road."

Writing Rubric
- **Performance Assess. and Portfolio Mgmt.,** p.20

PRENTICE HALL
ASSESSMENT SYSTEM
- **Workbook**
- **Skill Book**
- **Transparencies**
- **CD-ROM**

The Negro Speaks of Rivers ✦ Ardella ✦ Dream Variations ✦ Refugee in America ✦ The Tropics in New York

Lesson Objectives

1. **To analyze and respond to literary elements**
   - Literary Analysis: Speaker
   - Comparing Literary Works
2. **To read, comprehend, analyze, and critique poetry**
   - Reading Strategy: Drawing Inferences
   - Reading Check Questions
   - Review and Assess Questions
   - Assessment Practice (ATE)
3. **To develop word analysis skills, fluency, and systematic vocabulary**
   - Vocabulary Development Lesson: Latin Word Root: -lib-
4. **To understand and apply written and oral language conventions**
   - Spelling Strategy
   - Grammar and Style Lesson: Verb Tenses: Past and Present Perfect
5. **To understand and apply appropriate writing and research strategies**
   - Writing Lesson: Poetry Comparison
   - Extension Activity: Poster
6. **To understand and apply listening and speaking strategies**
   - Extension Activity: Presentation

STEP-BY-STEP TEACHING GUIDE	PACING GUIDE
PRETEACH	
Motivate Students and Provide Background	
Use the Motivation activity (ATE p. 924)	5 min.
Read and discuss author and background features (SE/ATE p. 924) [A]	10 min.
Introduce the Concepts	
Introduce the Literary Analysis and Reading Strategy (SE/ATE p. 925) [A]	15 min.
Pronounce the vocabulary words and read their definitions (SE p. 925)	5 min.
TEACH	
Monitor Comprehension	
Informally monitor comprehension by circulating while students read independently or in groups [A]	25 min.
Develop vocabulary with Vocabulary notes (SE pp. 926, 929; ATE p. 929)	as students read
Develop Understanding	
Develop students' ability to draw inferences by using the Reading Strategy annotations (SE p. 928; ATE pp. 926, 928, 929)	5 min.
	5 min.
ASSESS	
Assess Mastery	
Assess students' mastery of the Reading Strategy and Literary Analysis by having them answer the Review and Assess questions (SE/ATE p. 931)	15 min.
Use one or more of the print and media Assessment Resources (ATE p. 933) [A]	up to 45 min.
EXTEND	
Apply Understanding	
Have students complete the Vocabulary Development Lesson and the Grammar and Style Lesson (SE p. 932) [A]	20 min.
Apply students' ability to use quotations to connect themes by using the Writing Lesson (SE/ATE p. 933) [A]	45 min.
Apply students' understanding using one or more of the Extension Activities (SE p. 933)	20–90 min.

 ACCELERATED INSTRUCTION:
Use the strategies and activities identified with an [A].

UNIVERSAL ACCESS
- ● = Below Level Students
- ▲ = On-Level Students
- ■ = Above Level Students

Time and Resource Manager

Reading Level: Challenging, Average, Challenging, Average, Challenging
Average Number of Instructional Days: 3

RESOURCES		
PRINT 📖	**TRANSPARENCIES**	**TECHNOLOGY** 💿 🎧 📼
• **Beyond Literature,** Cross-Curricular Connection: Science, p. 53 ▲ ■		• **Interest Grabber Video,** Tape 5 ● ▲ ■
• **Selection Support Workbook:** ● ▲ ■ Literary Analysis, p. 235 Reading Strategy, p. 234 Build Vocabulary, p. 232	• **Literary Analysis and Reading Transparencies,** pp. 105 and 106 ● ▲ ■	
• **Authors In Depth,** The American Experience, p. 165 ■		• **Listening to Literature** ● ▲ ■ Audiocassettes, Side 33 Audio CDs, CD 19
• **Literatura en español** ● ▲ • **Literary Analysis for Enrichment** ■	• **Fine Art Transparencies, Volume 1,** Art Transparency 17 ● ▲ ■	
• **Formal Assessment:** Selection Test, p. 236 ● ▲ ■ • **Open Book Test,** p. 157 ● ▲ ■ • **Performance Assessment and Portfolio Management,** p. 23 ● ▲ ■ • (ASSESSMENT SYSTEM) ● ▲ ■	• (PRENTICE HALL ASSESSMENT SYSTEM) ● ▲ ■ Skills Practice Answers and Explanations on Transparencies	• **Test Bank Software** ● ▲ ■ • **Got It! Assessment Videotapes,** Tape 4 ● ▲
• **Selection Support Workbook:** ● ▲ ■ Grammar and Style, p. 233 • **Writing and Grammar,** Ruby Level ● ▲ ■ • **Extension Activities,** p. 53 ● ▲ ■	• **Daily Language Practice Transparencies** ● ▲ • **Writing Models and Graphic Organizers on Transparencies,** p. 37, 103 ● ▲ ■	• **Writing and Grammar iText CD-ROM** ● ▲ ■ *Take It to the Net* www.phschool.com

BLOCK SCHEDULING: Use one 90-minute class period to preteach the selection and have students read it. Use a second 90-minute class period to assess students' mastery of skills and have them complete one of the Extension Activities.

Step-by-Step Teaching Guide for pp. 924–925

Motivation

Play for the class the famous jazz song "Take the A Train" (composed by Billy Strayhorn, and arranged by Duke Ellington). Explain that during the 1920s, New York City's Harlem was a thriving center for literature, music, and the arts. This group of poems includes work by two important writers of the Harlem Renaissance: Langston Hughes and Claude McKay.

Interest Grabber Video

As an alternative, you may wish to play "Harlem Today" on Tape 5 to engage students' interest.

❶ Background

More About the Authors

In much of his work, which included lyrics, plays, and short stories as well as the poetry for which he is most famous, Langston Hughes sought to express the energy, immediacy, and improvisational feel of jazz and the blues. Although some critics took issue with these efforts, Hughes's insistence on the seriousness and integrity of these musical forms is one of his great artistic achievements. Hughes's interest in music was also evident in his work as a writer of librettos, including the one he wrote for the Kurt Weill/ Elmer Rice opera *Street Scene* (1947), that critics have praised as a groundbreaking work of the American musical theater.

For many critics, Claude McKay's poems of social protest, which he wrote fairly early in his career, remain his best and most influential work. Traditional in form but full of highly charged content, these poems influenced many of the younger writers of the Harlem Renaissance, including Langston Hughes. McKay wrote one of these poems of protest, the sonnet "If We Must Die," in response to a period of racial violence against blacks known as the Red Summer of 1919. The poem is an anthem of resistance to oppression and was later quoted by Winston Churchill during World War II.

924

Prepare to Read

❶ The Negro Speaks of Rivers ◆ Ardella ◆ Dream Variations ◆ Refugee in America ◆ The Tropics in New York

Langston Hughes (1902–1967)

Langston Hughes emerged from the Harlem Renaissance, a cultural movement of the 1920s, as the most prolific and successful African American writer in the country. In his poetry, he expressed pride in his heritage and voiced displeasure with the oppression he witnessed. Although Hughes is best known for his powerful poetry, he also wrote plays, fiction, autobiographical sketches, and screenplays.

Born in Missouri and raised in Kansas, Illinois, and Ohio, Hughes attended high school in Cleveland, where he contributed poetry to the school literary magazine. In 1921, he moved to New York City to attend Columbia University, but a year later he left school to travel to Europe and to Africa as a merchant seaman.

First Success On his return to New York, Hughes published his first volume of poetry, *The Weary Blues* (1926). The book attracted attention and earned him wide recognition. Hughes published several other volumes of poetry, including *The Dream Keeper* (1932), *Fields of Wonder* (1947), and *Montage of a Dream Deferred* (1951). He experimented with a variety of forms and techniques in his poetry and often tried to re-create the rhythms of contemporary jazz.

Like many of the Harlem Renaissance writers, Hughes was not born in Harlem and lived a large part of his life elsewhere. Nevertheless, he identified Harlem as a source of inspiration for black artists. Harlem was where he felt most welcome and nourished. Today, Hughes is recognized as one of the most popular and enduring African American writers of the twentieth century.

Claude McKay (1890–1948)

In much of his work, Claude McKay—poet, novelist, journalist, and activist—evokes the colors and rhythms of life on his native island of Jamaica. While McKay retained a lifelong attachment to Jamaica, he regarded Harlem as a spiritual home. Although he frequently lived elsewhere in the United States and overseas, including England, Russia, France, Germany, and Morocco, it was to Harlem that he would return in both his life and his work. Writing from abroad in 1930 to fellow Harlem Renaissance poet Langston Hughes, McKay said, "I write of America as home [although] I am really a poet without a country."

Jamaican Roots The son of farm workers, Festus Claudius McKay received his early education from his brother, Uriah Theophilus, who was a schoolteacher. When he was fourteen, McKay moved to Kingston, Jamaica's capital. While living in Kingston, McKay met a British folklorist who encouraged him to begin writing poetry that reflected Jamaica's indigenous culture. When his collection *Songs of Jamaica* (1912) won an award from the Institute of Arts and Letters, McKay was able to emigrate to the United States. He claimed he was coming to America to study agriculture, but he really came to advance his literary career.

After spending time at Tuskegee Institute and Kansas State College, McKay moved to Harlem in 1914. There, he held down various jobs and opened a restaurant with a friend. McKay's poem "The Tropics in New York" is marked by nostalgia for his homeland—a feeling echoed in the title of his autobiography, *A Long Way From Home* (1937).

924 ◆ Disillusion, Defiance, and Discontent (1914–1946)

TEACHING RESOURCES

The following resources can be used to enrich or extend the instruction for pp. 924–925.

Motivation

▪ **Interest Grabber Video**, Tape 5

Background

📖 **Beyond Literature**, p. 53 ▪

💻 *Take It to the Net*
Visit www.phschool.com for Background and hotlinks for the selections.

Literary Analysis

📄 **Literary Analysis and Reading Transparencies**, Speaker, p. 106 ▪

Reading

📖 **Selection Support:** Reading Strategy, p. 234; Build Vocabulary, p. 232

📄 **Literary Analysis and Reading Transparencies**, Drawing Inferences About the Speaker, p. 105

 BLOCK SCHEDULING: Resources marked with this symbol provide varied instruction during 90-minute blocks.

Preview

Connecting to the Literature

Many factors shape our identities—the places we come from, the people who nurture us or cause us pain, and the experiences that touch our lives. In these poems, two eloquent writers examine the factors that helped to shape their identities.

❷ Literary Analysis

Speaker

The **speaker** is the voice of a poem. Often, the speaker is the poet. However, a speaker may also be an imaginary person, a group of people, an animal, or an inanimate object. In "The Tropics in New York," Claude McKay's speaker is a homesick adult who is probably the poet himself:

> A wave of longing through my body swept,
> And, hungry for the old, familiar ways
> I turned aside and bowed my head and wept.

As you read these poems, look for clues that reveal the identity of the speaker. Use a chart like the one shown to record your observations.

Comparing Literary Works

Through imagery and vivid memories, each of these poems expresses a sense of African American culture, identity, or homeland. For example, both "The Negro Speaks of Rivers" and "The Tropics in New York" describe homelands through references to ancient rivers, to the Mississippi, and to the tropics. As you read these poems, compare the images of African American culture and identity the poets describe.

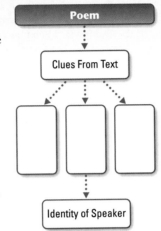

❸ Reading Strategy

Drawing Inferences About the Speaker

Most often, a poem's speaker is not revealed directly. Instead, the reader must **draw inferences,** or come to conclusions, based on the speaker's choice of words and the details included in the poem. Once you have determined the speaker's identity, you can draw inferences about the speaker's attitudes, feelings, and experiences.

As you read these poems, look for clues about the speakers, and draw inferences about both their personal qualities and the attitude toward life each expresses.

Vocabulary Development

lulled (luld) *v.* calmed or soothed by a gentle sound or motion (p. 926)

dusky (dus′ kē) *adj.* dim; shadowy (p. 926)

liberty (lib′ ər tē) *n.* condition of being free from control by others (p. 929)

The Negro Speaks of Rivers / Ardella / Dream Variations / Refugee in America / The Tropics in New York ◆ 925

CUSTOMIZE INSTRUCTION FOR UNIVERSAL ACCESS

For Less Proficient Readers	For English Learners	For Advanced Readers
Have students create a word web for each poem. In the center of each web, have students write the word *speaker*. Then, on the web's rays, invite them to list all the characteristics they have inferred about each speaker. They should also indicate the lines in each poem that support each inference.	Have students clarify the language and meaning of the poems by reading each one aloud with a partner. Remind students to read the poems as sentences, pausing where punctuation marks indicate. As they finish their oral readings, ask students to discuss their impressions of the speaker.	Invite students to read the author biographies on p. 924 and to conduct additional research into the lives and work of both Hughes and McKay. After students have read all the poems in the grouping, ask them to discuss whether or not they feel the speakers of each poem are the poets themselves.

---

❷ Literary Analysis

Speaker

- Explain that a speaker is to a poem what a narrator is to a work of prose. The poem presents the speaker's point of view, just as a story shares the narrator's point of view.

- List the following poems from previous units on the chalkboard and ask students to identify the speakers: "The Love Song of J. Alfred Prufrock" (a fictional character named Prufrock); excerpt from "Song of Myself" (Walt Whitman); "I heard a Fly buzz—when I died—" (speaker may or may not be the poet).

- Use this exercise to remind students that a speaker is simply a narrator, not necessarily the poet. In some cases, the speaker and the poet may be one and the same, but they are often completely different.

- Challenge students to try to characterize the speaker of each poem in this grouping.

❸ Reading Strategy

Drawing Inferences About the Speaker

- Critical Thinking annotations throughout this teacher's edition give students practice at drawing inferences. Briefly review this skill. An inference is a conclusion made from hints and implications in a text.

- Because the poems in this grouping are brief, students must infer almost all the information about the speakers—gender, appearance, age, and so on.

- Invite students to list the characteristics of each speaker and identify clues in the text that support each of their choices.

Vocabulary Development

- Pronounce each vocabulary word for students and read the definitions as a class. Have students identify any words with which they are already familiar.

 E-Teach

Visit E-Teach at www.phschool.com for teachers' essays on how to teach, with questions and answers.

Step-by-Step Teaching Guide for pp. 926–930

CUSTOMIZE INSTRUCTION
For Visual Learners

Invite students to choose any two poems and write brief essays comparing and contrasting the ways in which each poet uses words to create visual images. Do the poets create similar images? Do they use similar techniques to create vastly different images? How would students illustrate these poems if they had the opportunity?

❶ About the Selections

Four poems by Langston Hughes explore themes of ancestry, love, aspiration, and the longing for freedom and justice. Coming face to face with a window display of tropical fruit, the speaker of a Claude McKay poem is overcome with longing for home.

❷ Reading Strategy

Drawing Inferences About the Speaker

• Ask students what they can infer about the speaker of this poem. Have them explain their answers.
Answer: The speaker describes memories of three African rivers, so he or she is probably of African descent. The speaker's reference to Lincoln and the Mississippi suggest that he or she has lived in the United States. The references to rivers suggest that they play an important role in the speaker's daily life.

▶ **Monitor Progress** Have students use a graphic organizer like the one shown to determine who the speaker is in this poem. Help students to see that the final lines of the poem underscore the collective identity of the speaker.

clues
I've known rivers I bathed in the Euphrates I looked upon the Nile …when Abe Lincoln…

⋮

Inference

926

---

❶The Negro Speaks of Rivers

LANGSTON HUGHES

Background

"The Negro Speaks of Rivers" was Langston Hughes's first great poem. Hughes is said to have written it when he was a senior in high school, although it was published several years later. Hughes's poetry was influenced by Carl Sandburg and by Walt Whitman, whom he considered to be the greatest American poets. Like Whitman's "Song of Myself," "The Negro Speaks of Rivers" uses the first-person point of view to express the experience and identity of an entire community.

I've known rivers:
I've known rivers ancient as the world and older than the flow
    of human blood in human veins.

My soul has grown deep like the rivers.

I bathed in the Euphrates when dawns were young.
5   I built my hut near the Congo and it <u>lulled</u> me to sleep.
I looked upon the Nile and raised the pyramids above it.
I heard the singing of the Mississippi when Abe Lincoln went
    down to New Orleans, and I've seen its muddy bosom turn
    all golden in the sunset.

I've known rivers:
Ancient, <u>dusky</u> rivers.

10   My soul has grown deep like the rivers.

lulled (luld) *v.* calmed or soothed by a gentle sound or motion

dusky (dus′ kē) *adj.* dim; shadowy

926 ◆ *Disillusion, Defiance, and Discontent (1914–1946)*

TEACHING RESOURCES

The following resources can be used to enrich or extend the instruction for pp. 926–930.

Literary Analysis

📖 **Writing Models and Graphic Organizers on Transparencies,** Context Chart, p. 103 ■

📘 **Selection Support:** Literary Analysis, p. 235

Reading

🎧 **Listening to Literature Audiocassettes,** Side 33 ■

💿 **Listening to Literature Audio CDs,** CD 19 ■

Extension

📖 **Fine Art Transparencies,** Volume 1, Art Transparency 17

Ardella

LANGSTON HUGHES

3

I would liken you
To a night without stars
Were it not for your eyes.
I would liken you
5   To a sleep without dreams
Were it not for your songs.

Review and Assess

Thinking About the Selections

1. **(a) Respond:** What do you associate with the places Hughes describes in "The Negro Speaks of Rivers"? **(b) Respond:** What places do you associate with your culture or your ancestry?

2. **(a) Recall:** In "The Negro Speaks of Rivers," what has happened to the speaker's soul? **(b) Interpret:** Based on lines 3 and 10, what do you think is the theme of this poem?

3. **(a) Recall:** Identify four rivers the speaker names in "The Negro Speaks of Rivers." **(b) Interpret:** What does the age of rivers imply about people of African ancestry?

4. **Apply:** In what respects can the human race as a whole be compared with rivers?

5. **(a) Recall:** To what two images does the speaker compare Ardella? **(b) Interpret:** What is unusual about these comparisons? **(c) Infer:** What is the speaker's feeling toward Ardella?

6. **Evaluate:** Is Hughes's comparison in "Ardella" effective? Why or why not?

7. **(a) Speculate:** Why do love poems often compare people to nature? **(b) Evaluate:** What is the effect of such comparisons?

Ardella ◆ 927

---

❸ Critical Thinking

Infer

- Have students read the entire poem. Then, ask them how they would describe Ardella.
  Possible answers: She is solemn and quiet except for her bright eyes and her dreamy songs. Her personality seems dark and somewhat mysterious.

- Ask: What do you think the speaker's relationship with Ardella is like? Why do you think so?
  Possible answers: The poem suggests that their relationship is romantic or that the speaker would like it to be. The speaker's stress on the darkness of Ardella's personality suggests that their relationship is not happy.

Answers for p. 927

Review and Assess

1. **(a)** and **(b)** Students' responses will vary.

2. **(a)** It has "grown deep like the rivers." **(b)** The theme is the endurance of the African American people.

3. **(a)** The speaker names the Euphrates, Congo, Nile, Mississippi Rivers. **(b)** It implies that African Americans have roots that extend back to the earliest civilizations.

4. Both have endured for many centuries.

5. **(a)** The speaker compares Ardella to a night without stars and a sleep without dreams. **(b)** The images dwell on darkness or on absence. **(c)** Students may suggest that the speaker is in love with Ardella or that he or she feels compassion for Ardella's dark melancholy.

6. **Possible answer:** Yes, because readers can easily visualize a dark night or a dreamless sleep.

7. **(a) Possible answer:** People often find the natural world full of beauty and mystery—traits that one often attributes to a loved one. **(b)** Make sure students support their responses with details from this or other poems.

Art

Girls Skipping, 1949, by Hale Woodruff

Hale Woodruff (1900–1980) was a painter, printmaker, muralist, and teacher. Born in Cairo, Illinois, he studied at the John Heron Art Institute and the Fogg Art Museum. He also studied with the great Mexican muralist Diego Rivera.

Use this question for discussion:

> How does the artist create a sense of motion?
> Answer: The swirls of color suggest motion. The girls' skirts and hair seem to blow in the breeze made by their movement. Looking from the bottom right corner, each figure leans or gestures toward the next, creating a circle of figures that ends at the top right.

❺ ▶Critical Viewing

Answer: The poem is full of action verbs like *fling*, *whirl*, and *dance*. The figures enact these verbs.

❻ Reading Strategy

Drawing Inferences About the Speaker

- Explain to students that the poem describes experiences for which the speaker longs. What do students think the speaker's daily life is like?
  Answer: This poem works on at least two levels. On one level, the speaker dreams of playing in the sunshine and resting at night. The reader infers that he or she probably can't do these things. At the same time, the speaker is also expressing longing for a world in which darkness—like the skin of an African American person—is accepted. There is a strong suggestion that the speaker's daily life is full of struggle.

- Ask the Reading Strategy question on page 928: Based on lines 10–12, describe the speaker's personality.
  Answer: The speaker is burdened, but hopeful and optimistic.

Dream Variations

LANGSTON HUGHES

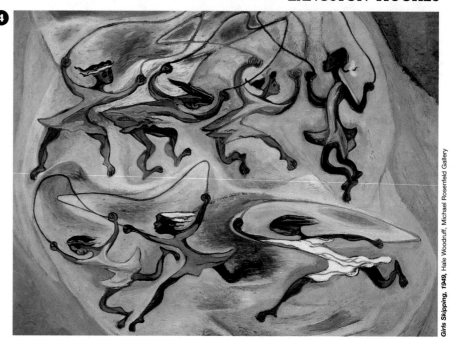

Girls Skipping, 1949, Hale Woodruff, Michael Rosenfeld Gallery

To fling my arms wide
In some place of the sun,
To whirl and to dance
Till the white day is done.
5   Then rest at cool evening
Beneath a tall tree
While night comes on gently,
    Dark like me—
That is my dream!

10   To fling my arms wide
In the face of the sun,
Dance! Whirl! Whirl!
Till the quick day is done.
Rest at pale evening . . .
15   A tall, slim tree . . .
Night coming tenderly
    Black like me.

928 ◆ *Disillusion, Defiance, and Discontent (1914–1946)*

❺ ▲ Critical Viewing
How does the motion of the figures in this drawing reflect the mood of the poem? **[Connect]**

Reading Strategy
Drawing Inferences About the Speaker
Based on lines 10–12, describe the speaker's personality.

CUSTOMIZE INSTRUCTION FOR UNIVERSAL ACCESS

For Advanced Readers

Invite students to analyze the form and style of the five poems in this grouping. Each is written in a different verse form; each uses rhyme differently; each has a different rhythm. Have students analyze the effect of each poem's form on its meaning and overall effect.

Students can consider how changes in form and style might have altered each poem's message. How do the poet's choices of form reveal their purposes in writing?

For example, "The Tropics in New York" echoes the sonnet form but is two lines short of a complete sonnet. Why might McKay have written only twelve lines instead of the usual fourteen? In traditional fourteen-line sonnets, what function does that final couplet often serve? By omitting it, in what ways does McKay reinforce the poem's meaning, and emphasize the speaker's feelings of loss and displacement?

Refugee in America

LANGSTON HUGHES

There are words like *Freedom*
Sweet and wonderful to say.
On my heart-strings freedom sings
All day everyday.

❼

⁵ There are words like *Liberty*
That almost make me cry.
If you had known what I knew
You would know why.

❽

liberty (lib´ ər tē) *n.* condition of being free from control by others

---

Review and Assess

Thinking About the Selections

1. **Respond:** What mood or emotions did you feel in reading "Dream Variations"? Explain.

2. **(a) Recall:** In "Dream Variations," what does the speaker want to do till the "white" day is done? **(b) Analyze:** What double meaning can you identify in the phrase "white day"?

3. **(a) Recall:** What words does Hughes use to describe color or images of darkness? **(b) Analyze:** In what ways are color and images of darkness used to express meaning?

4. **(a) Recall:** In "Refugee in America," what is the speaker's reaction to words like "freedom" and "liberty"? **(b) Interpret:** In what way does the title of the poem connect these words to the poem itself?

5. **(a) Recall:** What words of emotion are expressed in "Refugee in America"? **(b) Evaluate:** In what way do these emotions contribute to the mood conveyed by the poem? Explain.

6. **Apply:** What common goal do the speakers in these poems share? Explain.

Refugee in America ◆ 929

Answers continued

and *cry* **(b)** They show that the speaker's emotions are heightened and intensify the poem's power.

6. Both speakers long for freedom and an end to struggle.

❶ The Tropics in New York
Claude McKay

Bananas ripe and green, and ginger-root,
   Cocoa in pods and alligator pears,
And tangerines and mangoes and grape fruit,
   Fit for the highest prize at parish fairs,

5 Set in the window, bringing memories
   Of fruit-trees laden by low-singing rills,
And dewy dawns, and mystical blue skies
   In benediction over nun-like hills.

My eyes grew dim, and I could no more gaze;
10   A wave of longing through my body swept,
And, hungry for the old, familiar ways
   I turned aside and bowed my head and wept.

Review and Assess
Thinking About the Selection

1. **Respond:** The fruit in the window evokes memories of the speaker's birthplace. What objects could evoke memories of your own past?

2. **(a) Recall:** What fruits are set in the window? **(b) Assess:** In what regions are such fruits generally grown?

3. **(a) Recall:** What specific memories does the fruit stir in the speaker? **(b) Infer:** Why do you think the speaker weeps?

4. **(a) Interpret:** How does the title "The Tropics in New York" contribute to the poem's meaning? **(b) Interpret:** What is ironic about the title and the actual meaning of the poem?

5. **Analyze:** What impressions of his homeland does the speaker convey in this poem?

6. **Take a Position:** Do you think people can find happiness after they have made drastic changes? Why or why not?

930 ◆ *Disillusion, Defiance, and Discontent (1914–1946)*

✎ ASSESSMENT PRACTICE: Reading Comprehension

Sentence Completion   **(For more practice see the Test Preparation Workbook, p. 56.)**

Many tests require students to choose the best word to complete a sentence. Use the following sample test item to give students practice at this skill.

  In the 1920s, many writers identified Harlem as a source of _____ for African American artists, a supportive place where they felt a sense of _____.

Which pair of words best completes this sentence?

  A embarrassment, loss

  B inspiration, community

  C comfort, bewilderment

  D pride, abandonment

  Only choices *A* and *B* contain pairs of words that work together. The word *supportive* in the sentence shows that Harlem was a good place for writers and artists. The correct answer is *B*.

Review and Assess

Literary Analysis

Speaker

1. (a) Who is the **speaker** of "The Negro Speaks of Rivers"? (b) What effect does the title have on your ability to identify the speaker? Explain.
2. What can you infer about the identity and circumstances of the speaker in "Ardella"?
3. Describe the speaker of "Refugee in America."
4. What might the effect of "Tropics in New York" be if it were delivered by an adolescent son or daughter of the speaker?

Comparing Literary Works

5. (a) Compare the references to homeland in "The Negro Speaks of Rivers" and "The Tropics in New York." (b) Which derive from personal experience? (c) Which are almost mythic? Explain.
6. Compare the messages about freedom in "Refugee in America" and "Dream Variations," citing specific lines.
7. Explain the importance of place to the speakers in each poem.
8. What do these poems reveal about the shared experiences of African Americans with different backgrounds?

Reading Strategy

Drawing Inferences About the Speaker

9. In the third stanza of "The Negro Speaks of Rivers," what can you infer about the identity of a speaker who has raised the ancient pyramids and was also in New Orleans thousands of years later?
10. In each poem, find one line that reveals a characteristic of the speaker. Record your findings in a chart like the one shown.

Passage	What It Reveals About Speaker

Extend Understanding

11. **Cultural Connection:** What kinds of community and commercial services would you suggest to help immigrants stay in touch with their culture?

To **draw inferences about the speaker,** look closely at the speaker's choice of words and details included in a work.

 Take It to the Net

www.phschool.com

Take the interactive self-test online to check your understanding of these selections.

The Negro Speaks of Rivers / Ardella / Dream Variations / Refugee in America / The Tropics in New York ◆ 931

Answers for p. 931

Review and Assess

1. **(a)** The speaker symbolizes all African Americans. **(b)** The title suggests that the speaker is not a single individual.
2. The speaker is probably a man who is in love with Ardella.
3. The speaker is a refugee in the United States from another country. He seeks escape from oppression.
4. One would presume that an adolescent had not made the personal choice to live in the United States; therefore, the poem might have an additional poignancy.
5. **(a)** The speaker in "Rivers" does not seem to long for the past. The rivers and other references are symbolic. The speaker in "Tropics" longs for specific, tangible elements of home. **(b)** McKay's poem seems to be based on personal experience. **(c)** Hughes's poem presents a sweeping, almost mythic perspective that covers many centuries of history.
6. **(a)** "Variations": lines 1–4 and lines 10–13. "Refugee": lines 1, 3, and 5. **(b)** The first speaker longs for freedom; the second has found it.
7. Their identities are shaped by the places in which they have lived.
8. The poems suggest that all African Americans have longed for, and sometimes found, freedom.
9. The speaker symbolizes a race of people whose history spans both places and times.
10. Possible answers: "Rivers" line 10: speaker is enduring. "Ardella" lines 1–3: speaker is unhappily in love with Ardella. "Variations" line 17: speaker is African American. "Refugee" lines 7–8: speaker has suffered oppression. "Tropics" line 12: speaker is homesick.
11. Students may suggest programs offered by churches or community centers.

✵ ENRICHMENT: Further Reading

Other Works by the Authors

Other Works by Langston Hughes

The Weary Blues

Not Without Laughter

Mulebone (with Zora Neale Hurston)

Other Works by Claude McKay

Home to Harlem

Spring in New Hampshire

Banana Bottom

 Take It to the Net

Visit www.phschool.com for more information on the authors.

❶ Vocabulary Development

Word Analysis

1. c
2. a
3. d
4. b

Fluency: Completing Sentences

1. dusky
2. lulled
3. liberty

Spelling Strategy

1. dull
2. steal
3. spell
4. extol

❷ Grammar and Style

1. has grown; present perfect
2. turned, bowed, wept; past
3. have known; present perfect
4. had known, past perfect; knew, past
5. bathed, were; past

Writing Application

Have students exchange papers with partners and check one another's work. Partners can review papers together and resolve any disagreements by referring to Writing and Grammar; Ruby Level.

Integrate Language Skills

❶ Vocabulary Development Lesson

Word Analysis: Latin Root -lib-

The root -lib- derives from liber, the Latin word for "free." Match the following words with their definitions.

1.	liberty	a.	improvise
2.	ad-lib	b.	generous
3.	liberate	c.	freedom
4.	liberal	d.	release from slavery

Fluency: Completing Sentences

Use words from the vocabulary list on page 925 to complete the following sentence.

The fading light, ___?___ and soft, ___?___ the prisoner to sleep, and soon he was dreaming again of his lost ___?___ .

Spelling Strategy

One-syllable words, such as lull and roll, end in double l because the words have only one vowel. By contrast, one-syllable words such as seal and peal end with only one l because the words have two vowels. Considering this rule, choose a word that ends with a single or double l for each definition.

1. not shiny or bright (d____)
2. to take something that does not belong to you (st____)
3. to write the letters of a word correctly (sp____)
4. to praise someone (ext____)

❷ Grammar and Style Lesson

Verb Tenses: Past and Present Perfect

The tenses of verbs allow you to express time within one of three main catergories; the present, the past, and the future. The **past tense** shows an action or condition that began and ended at a given time in the past. By contrast, the **present perfect tense** shows an action or condition that occurred at an indefinite time in the past—or one that begins in the past and continues into the present. This tense is formed with the helping verb have or has used before the past participle of the main verb.

> **Past:** I built my hut near the Congo and it lulled me to sleep. (action ended)
>
> **Present Perfect:** I've known rivers . . . (action continues into present)

Practice Copy these sentences in your notebook. Circle the verbs in each sentence, and label each verb as past tense or present perfect tense.

1. My soul has grown deep like the rivers.
2. I turned aside and bowed my head and wept.
3. I've known rivers ancient as the world and older than the flow of human blood in human veins.
4. If you had known what I knew . . .
5. I bathed in the Euphrates when dawns were young.

Writing Application Write a paragraph about a memory you have of your past. Include verbs in both the past tense and the present perfect tense.

W̶G *Prentice Hall Writing and Grammar Connection: Chapter 21, Section 2*

TEACHING RESOURCES

The following resources can be used to enrich or extend the instruction for pp. 932–933.

Vocabulary

📖 **Selection Support:** Build Vocabulary, p. 232

📖 **Vocabulary and Spelling Practice Book** (Use this booklet for skills enrichment.) ■

Grammar

📖 **Selection Support:** Grammar and Style, p. 233

W̶G **Writing and Grammar,** Ruby Level, p. 532

📄 **Daily Language Practice Transparencies**

W̶G **Writing and Grammar,** Ruby Level, p. 172 ■

💿 **Writing and Grammar iText CD-ROM**

Writing

📄 **Writing Models and Graphic Organizers on Transparencies,** p. 37

■ **BLOCK SCHEDULING:** Resources marked with this symbol provide varied instruction during 90-minute blocks.

● Writing Lesson

Poetry Comparison

Langston Hughes committed himself to writing about the African American experience. His poetry focuses on themes of racial identity, pride, and perseverance. To add to your knowledge of Hughes's work, read "I, Too" on page 449. Write an essay addressing the themes you find in the Hughes poems you have read.

Prewriting   As you read the poems, list the images and messages you find in each one. Compare your notes and identify common themes that you can address.

Drafting   Begin your draft by introducing the common themes. In the body of your essay, include direct quotations to support your ideas. End with a conclusion that ties your ideas together.

> **Model: Using Quotations to Connect Themes**
>
> In "Refugee in America," Hughes refers to past suffering, saying, "If you had known what I knew." This message of perseverance parallels Hughes's message in "I, Too," in which he says, "But I laugh,/And eat well,/And grow strong."
>
> Using quotations from the poems helps to make clear connections to the themes.

Revising   Reread your essay to make sure you have made strong connections between the poems. Review your introduction and conclusion to be sure they support your main points and provide insight to readers.

W̶G̶ Prentice Hall Writing and Grammar Connection: Chapter 9, Section 2

● Extension Activities

Listening and Speaking Examine pictures, library books, and historic records of Jamaican life, and list the characteristics you find most intriguing. Consider the following in your research:

- What are the unique aspects of Jamaican culture?
- Compare these ideas, beliefs, or customs with their parallels in American culture.

Give a **presentation** to classmates comparing American and Jamaican cultures.

Research and Technology Using text and graphics, design a series of **posters** that depict the variety of cultural contributions made by African Americans during the 1920s. Include a range of mediums, such as literature, art, and drama. Display the work for your classmates.

 Take It to the Net   www.phschool.com

Go online for an additional research activity using the Internet.

The Negro Speaks of Rivers / Ardella / Dream Variations / Refugee in America / The Tropics in New York ◆ 933

❸ Writing Lesson

- Students may want to read additional poems by Hughes and take them into account in their essays.
- Remind students that they should look for both similarities and differences among the poems.
- Have students use the Interpreting a Work of Literature Model in **Writing Models and Graphic Organizers on Transparencies,** p. 37 to help draft their essays.
- Use the Response to Literature Rubric, p. 23, in **Performance Assessment and Portfolio Management** to assess students' essays.

❹ Research and Technology

- The Harlem Renaissance influenced all areas of cultural activity, including literature, the visual arts, music, theater, philosophy, and social reform. Encourage students to focus their research on no more than three of these areas, but make sure that the full breadth of Renaissance activity is covered by the class as a whole.
- Encourage students to use a variety of research sources, including the Internet.
- Because students are creating posters, encourage them to find the most interesting images possible. Suggest a variety of ways in which to incorporate informational text, such as headlines, captions, quotes, and brief passages.
- Remind students that a poster should capture a central idea—theme or distinguishing trait—of its subject.
- Display students' finished posters in the classroom.

CUSTOMIZE INSTRUCTION for Universal Access

To address different learning styles, use the following activities suggested in the **Extension Activities** booklet, p. 53.

For Intrapersonal Learners, use Activity 5.

For Musical/Rhythmic Learners, use Activity 6.

For Interpersonal Learners, use Activity 7.

From the Dark Tower ✦ A Black Man Talks of Reaping ✦ Storm Ending

Lesson Objectives

1. **To analyze and respond to literary elements**
   - Literary Analysis: Metaphor
   - Comparing Literary Works
2. **To read, comprehend, analyze, and critique poetry**
   - Reading Strategy: Connecting to Historical Context
   - Reading Check Questions
   - Review and Assess Questions
   - Assessment Practice (ATE)
3. **To develop word analysis skills, fluency, and systematic vocabulary**
   - Vocabulary Development Lesson: Latin Word Root: -cree-
4. **To understand and apply written and oral language conventions**
   - Spelling Strategy
   - Grammar and Style Lesson: Placement of Adjectives
5. **To understand and apply appropriate writing and research strategies**
   - Writing Lesson: Comparison-and-Contrast Essay
   - Extension Activity: Research Report
6. **To understand and apply listening and speaking strategies**
   - Extension Activity: Dramatic Reading

STEP-BY-STEP TEACHING GUIDE	PACING GUIDE
PRETEACH	
Motivate Students and Provide Background	
Use the Motivation activity (ATE p. 934)	5 min.
Read and discuss author and background features (SE/ATE p. 934) [A]	10 min.
Introduce the Concepts	
Introduce the Literary Analysis and Reading Strategy (SE/ATE p. 935) [A]	15 min.
Pronounce the vocabulary words and read their definitions (SE p. 935)	5 min.
TEACH	
Monitor Comprehension	
Informally monitor comprehension by circulating while students read independently or in groups [A]	20 min.
Monitor students' comprehension with the Reading Check note (SE/ATE p. 934)	as students read
Develop vocabulary with Vocabulary notes (SE pp. 936, 937; ATE p. 936)	as students read
Develop Understanding	
Develop students' ability to connect to the historical context by using the Reading Strategy annotations (SE p. 938; ATE p. 937)	5 min.
	5 min.
ASSESS	
Assess Mastery	
Assess students' mastery of the Reading Strategy and Literary Analysis by having them answer the Review and Assess questions (SE/ATE p. 939)	15 min.
Use one or more of the print and media Assessment Resources (ATE p. 941) [A]	up to 45 min.
EXTEND	
Apply Understanding	
Have students complete the Vocabulary Development Lesson and the Grammar and Style Lesson (SE p. 940) [A]	20 min.
Apply students' ability to identify points of comparison by using the Writing Lesson (SE/ATE p. 941) [A]	45 min.
Apply students' understanding using one or more of the Extension Activities (SE p. 941)	20–90 min.

 ACCELERATED INSTRUCTION:
Use the strategies and activities identified with an [A].

UNIVERSAL ACCESS
- ● = Below Level Students
- ▲ = On-Level Students
- ■ = Above Level Students

Time and Resource Manager

RESOURCES		
PRINT 📖	**TRANSPARENCIES**	**TECHNOLOGY** 💿 🎧
• **Beyond Literature,** Cross-Curricular Connection: Social Studies, p. 54 ▲ ■		• **Interest Grabber Video,** Tape 5 ● ▲ ■
• **Selection Support Workbook:** ● ▲ ■ Literary Analysis, p. 239 Reading Strategy, p. 238 Build Vocabulary, p. 236	• **Literary Analysis and Reading Transparencies,** pp. 107 and 108 ● ▲ ■	
		• **Listening to Literature** ● ▲ ■ Audiocassettes, Side 33 Audio CDs, CD 19
• **Literatura en español** ● ▲ • **Literary Analysis for Enrichment** ■	• **Fine Art Transparencies, Volume 1,** Transparencies 7, 18 ● ▲ ■	
• **Formal Assessment:** Selection Test, p. 239 ● ▲ ■ • **Open Book Test,** p. 160 ● ▲ ■ • **Performance Assessment and Portfolio Management,** p. 23 ● ▲ ■ • ⬤ PRENTICE HALL **ASSESSMENT** *SYSTEM* ● ▲ ■	• ⬤ PRENTICE HALL **ASSESSMENT** *SYSTEM* ● ▲ ■ Skills Practice Answers and Explanations on Transparencies	• **Test Bank Software** ● ▲ ■ • **Got It! Assessment Videotapes,** Tape 4 ● ▲
• **Selection Support Workbook:** ● ▲ ■ Grammar and Style, p. 237 • **Writing and Grammar,** Ruby Level ● ▲ ■ • **Extension Activities,** p. 54 ● ▲ ■	• **Daily Language Practice Transparencies** ● ▲ • **Writing Models and Graphic Organizers on Transparencies.** ● ▲ ■	• **Writing and Grammar iText CD-ROM** ● ▲ ■ 💻 *Take It to the Net* www.phschool.com

BLOCK SCHEDULING: Use one 90-minute class period to preteach the selection and have students read it. Use a second 90-minute class period to assess students' mastery of skills and have them complete one of the Extension Activities.

Step-by-Step Teaching Guide for pp. 934–935

Motivation

Obtain and display works by Harlem Renaissance artists such as Aaron Douglas, Hale Woodruff, or Palmer Hayden. Encourage volunteers to share their responses to the art. Tell students that both the art and the poems were created by some of the leading lights of the Harlem Renaissance. As they read, have students look for images or ideas in the poems that reflect those in the art.

Interest Grabber Video

As an alternative, play "Reading and Student Response" on Tape 5 to engage students' interest.

❶ Background

More About the Authors

God Sends Sunday, Arna Bontemps's first novel, tells the story of Little Augie, the most successful black jockey in St. Louis. In 1939, Bontemps and Countee Cullen collaborated on a musical play based on this novel. Titled *St. Louis Woman*, the play combined songs with folk beliefs to tell the story of Little Augie's romances as well as his life on the track. *St. Louis Woman* had a successful run on Broadway in 1946.

Prepare to Read

❶ From the Dark Tower ◆ A Black Man Talks of Reaping ◆ Storm Ending

Countee Cullen (1903–1946)

Unlike most other poets of his day, Countee Cullen used traditional forms and methods. Yet, no other poet expressed the sentiments of African Americans during the early 1900s more eloquently than did Cullen.

A Literary Life Cullen was born in Louisville, Kentucky, and raised by foster parents in New York. An outstanding student, Cullen worked on his high-school newspaper and literary magazine and began to write poetry seriously. He graduated from New York University and later earned a master's degree in English and French from Harvard University. His first collection of poetry, *Color*, was published in 1925. This was followed by *Copper Sun* (1927), *The Ballad of the Brown Girl* (1927), and *The Black Christ* (1929). In 1932, Cullen published *One Way to Heaven*, a satirical novel. In his later years, he published two children's books, *The Lost Zoo* (1940) and *My Lives and How I Lost Them* (1942).

Arna Bontemps (1902–1973)

Arna Bontemps was one of the most scholarly figures of the Harlem Renaissance. Throughout his career as an editor, a novelist, a dramatist, and a poet, his work for social justice made him "the conscience of an era."

Born in Louisiana and raised in California, Bontemps came to New York during the height of the Harlem Renaissance. After teaching at several religious academies, he wrote *Black Thunder* (1936), a highly acclaimed novel about a Virginia slave revolt. In subsequent years, he published poems, biographies, dramas, and books for young readers. He also ran the library at Fisk University in Nashville, making it a major center for African American studies. In 1967, after the death of his friend Langston Hughes, Bontemps compiled *Hold Fast to Dreams* (1969), a poetry anthology. The bulk of the extensive correspondence between Hughes and Bontemps was donated to Yale University, where scholars can study this vivid chronicle of African American literary life.

Jean Toomer (1894–1967)

Like other Harlem Renaissance writers, Jean Toomer was interested in the cultural roots of his people. In his work, he expressed the cultural belief that black heritage and pride were vital to the happiness and freedom of African Americans.

A Major Work Born in Washington, D.C., Nathan Pinchback Toomer attended New York University. He then taught for a few years in Georgia. In 1920, Toomer changed his first name to Jean, to honor the hero of a novel that inspired him. Following the appearance of *Cane* (1923), an unusual book of prose sketches, poems, stories, and a one-act play, Toomer was widely viewed as one of the most talented writers of the Harlem Renaissance. When Toomer's publishing output dwindled, *Cane* fell into obscurity. In recent years, however, *Cane* has been recognized and celebrated as a significant work of the Harlem Renaissance.

TEACHING RESOURCES

The following resources can be used to enrich or extend the instruction for pp. 934–935.

Motivation

📼 **Interest Grabber Video**, Tape 5

Background

📓 **Beyond Literature**, p. 54 ▪

🖥️ *Take It to the Net*

Visit www.phschool.com for background and hotlinks for "From the Dark Tower," "A Black Man Talks," and "Storm Ending."

Literary Analysis

📖 **Literary Analysis and Reading Transparencies**, Metaphor, p. 108 ▪

Reading

📓 **Selection Support**: Reading Strategy, p. 238; Build Vocabulary, p. 236

📖 **Literary Analysis and Reading Transparencies**, Connecting to Historical Context, p. 107 ▪

▪ **BLOCK SCHEDULING**: Resources marked with this symbol provide varied instruction during 90-minute blocks.

Preview

Connecting to the Literature

If you see trouble ahead, you might say that a storm is brewing. In the same way, these poems capture the experiences of the African American people through striking images of nature or familiar activities and events.

Literary Analysis

Metaphor

A **metaphor** is an implied comparison between two seemingly dissimilar things used to make writing more vivid, and meaningful. In these lines, Countee Cullen compares African American life to the toil of planting.

> We shall not always plant while others reap
> The golden increment of bursting fruit . . .

Although metaphors are usually brief, they may also be elaborate, lengthy comparisons. An **extended metaphor** is a comparison that is developed throughout the course of a poem. As you read "Storm Ending," look for the extended metaphor Toomer develops.

Comparing Literary Works

Metaphors are often conveyed through the use of **imagery**—descriptive language that appeals to the senses. These three poets use imagery to express their feelings about the African American experience. Two of these poems offer images of planting, while the third presents images of a huge storm. Usually, readers associate agricultural imagery with growth, and storm imagery with destruction. However, these poems challenge readers' expectations. As you read, use a chart like the one shown to analyze each poem's imagery, and to assess the emotions and attitudes it conveys.

Reading Strategy

Connecting to Historical Context

Many works of literature bear a direct relation to the time and place in which they were written. A reader must **connect** such works to their **historical contexts** in order to understand and appreciate them. To fully grasp the following poems—born in the cultural movement known as the Harlem Renaissance in the 1920s—review the information on page 910.

Vocabulary Development

increment (in´krə mənt) *n.* increase, as in a series (p. 936)

countenance (koun´ tə nəns) *v.* approve; tolerate (p. 936)

beguile (bē gīl´) *v.* charm or delight (p. 936)

stark (stärk) *adj.* severe (p. 937)

reaping (rēp´ iŋ) *v.* cutting or harvesting grain from a field (p. 937)

glean (glēn) *v.* collect the remaining grain after reaping (p. 937)

Metaphor

African Americans compared to farm workers.

↓

Image

silently working hard in fields of gold, weeping

↓

Emotion / Ideas

sorrow, anger

From the Dark Tower / A Black Man Talks of Reaping / Storm Ending ◆ 935

Metaphor

- Remind students of the difference between metaphor and simile. A simile is a comparison that states "A is like B." A metaphor is a more direct comparison stating that "A is B."

- List the following comparisons on the chalkboard and challenge students to identify similes and metaphors.

    "A poem should be palpable and mute"/As a globed fruit. (simile) ("Ars Poetica" by Archibald MacLeish)

    "The actor is a metaphysician in the dark. . . . "(metaphor) ("Of Modern Poetry" by Wallace Stevens)

    "And indeed there will be time for the yellow smoke that slides along the street/Rubbing its back upon the window-panes. . . . "(metaphor) ("The Love Song of J. Alfred Prufrock" by T.S. Eliot)

❸ Reading Strategy

Connecting to Historical Context

- Review the Literary Analysis instruction Social Context in Autobiography (page 913) with students. Explain that all writers are products of the time and place in which they live. Readers can best appreciate literature if they have some understanding of the writer's social and historical circumstances.

- Have students read the author biographies on page 934. In addition, you might encourage them to do a little further reading about these poets, or you may give the class a talk on both these poets and the Harlem Renaissance as a whole. Urge students to keep this information about the historical context in mind as they read.

Vocabulary Development

- Pronounce each vocabulary word for students, and read the definitions as a class. Have students identify any words with which they are already familiar.

 E-Teach

Visit E-Teach at www.phschool.com for teachers' essays on how to teach, with questions and answers.

CUSTOMIZE INSTRUCTION FOR UNIVERSAL ACCESS

For Less Proficient Readers	For English Learners	For Advanced Readers
Remind students that the end of a line of poetry is often not the end of the sentence or complete thought. Urge students to pay attention to punctuation, not to where the lines end, so that they will gain a better sense of the poems as they read.	Have students try reading the poems aloud with partners. They can take alternating stanzas or choose other stopping places. In order to better understand the poems, remind them to pause at periods, commas, and other punctuation marks, not at the ends of lines.	Have students choose partners with whom to read each poem aloud and then discuss it. Partners can consider the effects of such literary elements as alliteration, assonance, rhythm, and rhyme on the poem's overall power and meaning.

Step-by-Step Teaching Guide for pp. 936–938

CUSTOMIZE INSTRUCTION
For Visual Learners

Have students consider the visual effects of each poem's language. Students can choose any two poems and write brief essays comparing and contrasting how each poet uses words to create visual images. Do the poets create similar images? Do they use similar techniques to create widely different images? How would students illustrate these poems if they had the opportunity?

❶ About the Selections

Three poems use extended metaphors—two of planting and one of a thunderstorm—to comment on social and historical issues.

❷ Vocabulary Development

The Latin Root -cre-

- Call attention to the word *increment*, and have a volunteer read its definition.

- Tell students that increment shares the root -cre- with the words *create* and *increase*.

- Ask students this question: Based on these words what do you think the root -cre- means?
  Answer: The root -cre- means to "grow".

Answers for p. 936

Review and Assess

1. Most students will empathize with the feeling of doing the work and watching others take the profits.

2. **(a)** "not" **(b)** The repetition gives the poem the quality of a protest.

3. **(a)** contrast between the dark night and the white stars **(b)** Darkness is not inherently ugly.

4. **(a)** "We" can symbolize any oppressed people; Cullen probably had African Americans in mind.
   (b) "We" do the work while "others" take the profits.

5. Possible Answer: Waiting is appropriate because while the speakers wait, they build up strength.

---

❶ From The Dark Tower
Countee Cullen (To Charles S. Johnson)

Background

Countee Cullen dedicated this poem to Charles S. Johnson, an African American sociologist, editor, and author of a landmark study of race relations in the 1920s. Johnson was the editor of the publication *Opportunity: Journal of Negro Life* and helped to nurture the writers and artists of the Harlem Renaissance. Cullen served as assistant editor of the publication.

> We shall not always plant while others reap
> ❷ The golden <u>increment</u> of bursting fruit,
> Not always <u>countenance</u>, abject and mute,
> That lesser men should hold their brothers cheap;
> 5 Not everlastingly while others sleep
> Shall we <u>beguile</u> their limbs with mellow flute,
> Not always bend to some more subtle brute;
> We were not made eternally to weep.
>
> The night whose sable breast relieves the stark,
> 10 White stars is no less lovely being dark,
> And there are buds that cannot bloom at all
> In light, but crumple, piteous, and fall;
> So in the dark we hide the heart that bleeds,
> And wait, and tend our agonizing seeds.

increment (in´ krə mənt) *n.* increase, as in a series

countenance (koun´ tə nəns) *v.* approve; tolerate

beguile (bē gīl´) *v.* charm or delight

Review and Assess

Thinking About the Selection

1. **Respond:** Can you identify or empathize with the speaker of this poem? Why or why not?

2. **(a) Recall:** Which word is repeated five times in the first stanza? **(b) Analyze:** What is the effect of this repetition?

3. **(a) Recall:** What contrast or opposition does the speaker set up in lines 9–10? **(b) Interpret:** What does Cullen mean by "no less lovely being dark"?

4. **(a) Infer:** Who is the "we" in the poem? **(b) Interpret:** What distinction does the speaker draw between the circumstances of "we" and those of "others"?

5. **Evaluate:** Do you think that waiting is an appropriate response to the conflicts described in the poem? Explain.

TEACHING RESOURCES

The following resources can be used to enrich or extend the instruction for pp. 936–938.

Literary Analysis
📖 **Selection Support:** Literary Analysis, p. 239

Reading
🎧 **Listening to Literature Audiocassettes,** Side 33

💿 **Listening to Literature Audio CDs,** CD 19

Extension
🖼 **Fine Art Transparencies,** Volume 1, Art Transparencies 7, 18

■ **BLOCK SCHEDULING:** Resources marked with this symbol provide varied instruction during 90-minute blocks.

Hoeing, Robert Gwathmey, Carnegie Institute Museum of Art, Pittsburgh, Pennsylvania, © Estate of Robert Gwathmey/Licensed by VAGA, New York, NY

❸

◄ Critical Viewing
What emotion does this image convey? In what way does it compare with the mood of the poem? [Compare and Contrast]

❸ ► Critical Viewing
Answer: The workers are all either toiling or pausing in exhaustion. The landscape is barren. Like the poem, the painting suggests that workers do not profit from their own labor.

❹ Reading Strategy
Connecting to Historical Context

• Ask students to consider the poem's title. How does it affect their reading of the poem's meaning?
Answer: The title suggests that the poem is about race relations, not about sowing and reaping.

▶ Monitor Progress Then, ask students to explain what Bontemps is saying about race relations.
Answer: Bontemps suggests that black people work and others reap the fruits of their labor.

❺ ✓Reading Check

The speaker gains only "what the hand can hold." The speaker does not profit from his work.

A Black Man Talks of Reaping ❹
Arna Bontemps

I have sown beside all waters in my day.
I planted deep, within my heart the fear
that wind or fowl would take the grain away.
I planted safe against this <u>stark</u>, lean year.

5   I scattered seed enough to plant the land
in rows from Canada to Mexico
but for my <u>reaping</u> only what the hand
can hold at once is all that I can show.

Yet what I sowed and what the orchard yields
10   my brother's sons are gathering stalk and root;
small wonder then my children <u>glean</u> in fields
they have not sown, and feed on bitter fruit.

stark (stärk) *adj.* severe

reaping (rēp´ iŋ) *v.* cutting or harvesting grain from a field

glean (glēn) *v.* collect the remaining grain after reaping

✓Reading Check **❺**

What does the speaker have to show for all his labor?

A Black Man Talks of Reaping ◆ 937

CUSTOMIZE INSTRUCTION FOR UNIVERSAL ACCESS

For Special Needs Students	For Gifted/Talented Students
Organize students into small groups to answer the questions on pages 936 and 938. Each group can then report on its answers to entire class. If there is significant disagreement, have students identify words, phrases, and lines from the poems that support their interpretations.	Have each student choose one of the three poems and write a detailed analysis and interpretation of its meaning. Students can try paraphrasing lines and stanzas in their search for what the poems mean. Encourage them to do some background reading about Cullen, Bontemps, and Toomer, and to examine other works by the poets as they work on their interpretations.

6 Reading Strategy

Connecting to Historical Context

- Have students freewrite about the idea of storms and thunder.

- Invite them to share some of the associations they discover through their freewriting. Possible responses: Students may respond that storms and thunder can be symbols of nature's or even God's wrath.

- Then, ask students the Reading Strategy question on p. 938: How might the imagery of thunder relate to the ending of slavery? Answer: The images of thunder suggest a powerful onslaught, as though nature itself is angry. These images, likened to flowers and honey, imply that the thunder is positive and nurturing, marking the end of a terrible evil, such as slavery.

Answers for p. 938

Review and Assess

1. Possible response: I saw farmers toiling in fields, dark places with people hiding; I heard thunder and rain.

2. (a) The speaker is afraid that shallowly planted seeds would be stolen. (b) It might be a time in which people suffer from hunger or, symbolically, from a lack of freedom.

3. (a) He scatters an enormous amount of seed. (b) He can only harvest a handful. (c) His brother's sons reap what he has sown.

4. (a) a thunderstorm (b) The speaker is awed, impressed, and excited. (c) The words "gorgeously," "great," "full-lipped," and "golden" suggest the grandeur and beauty of the thunder.

5. (a) They have received only "the bitter fruit." (b) It suggests that this statement is not true in situations where people are denied their basic rights and freedoms.

Storm Ending

Jean Toomer

Thunder blossoms gorgeously above our heads,
Great, hollow, bell-like flowers,
Rumbling in the wind,
Stretching clappers to strike our ears . . .
5   Full-lipped flowers
Bitten by the sun
Bleeding rain
Dripping rain like golden honey—
And the sweet earth flying from the thunder.

6

Reading Strategy
Connecting to Historical Context How might imagery of thunder relate to the ending of slavery?

Review and Assess

Thinking About the Selections

1. **Respond:** What did you see as you read these poems? What did you hear?

2. **(a) Recall:** In "A Black Man Talks of Reaping," why does the speaker plant "deep"? **(b) Draw Conclusions:** What do you think is meant by the "stark, lean year"?

3. **(a) Recall:** In "A Black Man Talks of Reaping," how much seed does the speaker scatter? **(b) Recall:** How much grain is he allowed to harvest? **(c) Infer:** Who reaps what the speaker has sown?

4. **(a) Recall:** In "Storm Ending," what natural event does the poem describe? **(b) Analyze:** What is the speaker's attitude toward the event described? **(c) Support:** Which words best convey this attitude?

5. **(a) Infer:** What does Bontemps suggest about what African Americans have received in exchange for their hard work? **(b) Apply:** In what way does Bontemps's poem comment on the idea that "Whatsoever a man soweth, that shall he also reap"?

✎ ASSESSMENT PRACTICE: Reading Comprehension

Sentence Completion   (For more practice, see Test Preperation Workbook, p. 57.)

Many tests require students to choose the best word to complete a sentence. Use the following sample test item to give students practice at this skill.

Although the forms and techniques used by Harlem Renaissance writers varied widely, the poets and novelists had ____ purposes for creating their art.

Which word best completes this sentence?

    A complex   **C** similar
    B unusual   **D** different

The word *although* in the sentence suggests that the blank space must be filled by an antonym for *varied widely*. The correct answer is *C*.

Review and Assess

Literary Analysis

Metaphor

1. (a) Identify the **metaphors** Countee Cullen uses in "From the Dark Tower." (b) What details does he use to extend them?
2. (a) What metaphor appears in Bontemps's poem? (b) How does he express and develop the metaphor in each stanza?
3. (a) What two things are compared in the extended metaphor presented in "Storm Ending"? (b) Describe the way in which Toomer establishes this comparison in the first four lines. (c) Describe how he develops it in the lines that follow.

Comparing Literary Works

4. Using a chart like the one shown, identify and analyze the dominant **image** conveyed by each poem.

Poem	Image	Interpretation	Emotion

5. (a) What theme or central message do these poems share? (b) In what ways do their uses of imagery serve to convey those messages?
6. Rank the three poems from most optimistic to most pessimistic. Explain your decisions.

Reading Strategy

Connecting to Historical Context

7. How can you deepen your appreciation of "From the Dark Tower" by reflecting on the northern migration of nearly one million African Americans in the late 1800s and early 1900s?
8. Identify a fact of **historical context** that enriches your reading of "A Black Man Talks of Reaping." Explain.
9. Does your interpretation of "Storm Ending" change when you connect to historical context? Explain.

Extend Understanding

10. **Historical Connection:** What historical factors may have contributed to the decline of the Harlem Renaissance around 1935?

From the Dark Tower / A Black Man Talks of Reaping / Storm Ending ◆ 939

ENRICHMENT: Further Reading

Other Works by the Authors

Works by Countee Cullen
Color, Copper Sun, The Ballad of the Brown Girl

Works by Arna Bontemps
God Sends Sunday, Black Thunder, Drums at Dusk

Works by Jean Toomer
Cane, Essentials, The Blue Meridian

 Take It to the Net
Visit www.phschool.com for self-tests and additional questions on the authors.

939

❶ Vocabulary Development

Word Analysis

1. A crescendo is a steady increase in sound.

2. A creation is something that is made.

3. An increment is a measure of growth.

Spelling Strategy

1. first g is hard, second g is soft

2. first g is hard, second g is soft

3. first g is soft, second g is hard

Concept Development: Synonyms

1. a

2. b

3. a

4. c

5. c

❷ Grammar and Style

1. The wind, cold and merciless, chilled us.

2. We saw the vast, cobalt ocean.

3. The refugees, penniless but determined, came to America to start anew.

4. The cold, hungry bird pecked the ground for worms.

5. We tired workers fell to exhaustion.

Writing Application

Have students exchange papers with partners and check one another's work. Partners can go over papers together and resolve any disagreements by referring to the Writing and Grammar book.

Integrate Language Skills

❶ Vocabulary Development Lesson

Word Analysis: Latin Root -cre-

Like *increase*, and *create*, the word *increment* contains the Latin root *-cre-*, which means "to grow." Use your knowledge of the root *-cre-* to define these words:

1. crescendo
2. creation
3. increment

Spelling Strategy

The letter *g* usually makes a "hard" sound when it is followed by *a*, *h*, *o*, or *u*, as in *gather*, *ghost*, and *beguile*. For a "soft" sound, *g* is usually followed by *e*, *i*, or *y*. Indicate whether the *g* sounds in these words are hard or soft.

1. gorgeously   2. garbage   3. gyromagnetic

Concept Development: Synonyms

Review the vobcaulary list on page 935. Then, write the letter of the best synonym for each numbered word.

1. reap: (a) harvest, (b) sow, (c) plow

2. countenance: (a) cheer, (b) tolerate, (c) disregard

3. increment: (a) increase, (b) stability, (c) decrease

4. stark: (a) gentle, (b) steep, (c) severe

5. glean: (a) distribute, (b) weigh, (c) collect

❷ Grammar and Style Lesson

Placement of Adjectives

An **adjective** is a word used to describe a noun or a pronoun. Adjectives can be placed *before* or *after* the nouns or pronouns they modify.

> **Before:** this *stark, lean* <u>year</u> (modifies *year*)
>
> **After:** I've scattered <u>seed</u> *enough* to plant the land (modifies *seed*)

When adjectives follow the noun they modify, they may have more emphasis in a sentence.

In poetry, a literary form characterized by precise word choice and deliberately sculpted lines and stanzas, adjectives can effectively add meaning and build imagery. While poets choose adjectives with care, they also select nouns and verbs to achieve poetic effects.

Practice Rewrite the following sentences, altering the position of the italicized adjectives. Be sure that the adjectives modify the same noun in your sentence as in the original. Make any necessary changes in wording and punctuation.

1. The *cold, merciless* wind chilled us.

2. We saw the ocean, *vast and cobalt*.

3. The *penniless but determined* refugees came to America to start anew.

4. The bird, *cold and hungry*, pecked the ground for worms.

5. *Tired*, we workers fell to exhaustion.

Writing Application Write a paragraph about a poem in this grouping. Include three adjectives and vary the placement of these modifiers.

WG Prentice Hall Writing and Grammar Connection: Chapter 27, Section 2

TEACHING RESOURCES

The following resources can be used to enrich or extend the instructions for pp. 940–941.

Vocabulary

📖 **Selection Support:** Build Vocabulary, p. 236

📖 **Vocabulary and Spelling Practice Book** (Use this booklet for skills enrichment.) ■

Grammer

📖 **Selection Support:** Grammar and Style, p. 237

WG **Writing and Grammar,** Ruby Level, p. 696

Daily Language Practice Transparencies ■

Writing

📖 **Writing Models and Graphic Organizers on Transparencies,** p. 87

WG **Writing and Grammar,** Ruby Level, p. 172 ■

💿 **Writing and Grammar iText CD-ROM**

■ **BLOCK SCHEDULING:** Resources marked with this symbol provide varied instruction during 90-minute blocks.

Writing Lesson

Comparison-and-Contrast Essay

Although Countee Cullen and Jean Toomer were associated with the same literary movement, each had a distinct style. In an essay, compare and contrast the qualities of Cullen's structured sonnet and Toomer's open lyric.

Prewriting In a chart, identify the points of comparison between the two poets, such as their uses of metaphors and imagery. Then, consider each poem's message and its sound—the musical quality, which may be lilting and gentle or harsh and driving.

Model: Identifying Points of Comparison

Drafting In your introduction, briefly describe the poems. Then, using your chart, draft a point-by-point comparison, addressing each element of comparison with examples from the poems.

Revising Reread your essay to be sure you have addressed both similarities and differences between the two poems. Add vivid and descriptive language to strengthen comparisons, quoting sufficiently from the poems to support them.

W̶G Prentice Hall Writing and Grammar Connection: Chapter 9, Section 2

Extension Activities

Listening and Speaking Select and compare two other poems by Countee Cullen, and give a **dramatic reading** to the class. As you practice, consider these tips:

- Select the poems based on connections between theme and image.
- As you read, enhance meaning by emphasizing key words.

After reading the poems, invite questions and comments from the class.

Research and Technology With a group, choose an artist or musician from the Harlem Renaissance period and research his or her life and accomplishments. Present your findings to your class in an organized **research report.** [Group Activity]

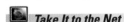 **Take It to the Net** www.phschool.com

Go online for an additional research activity using the Internet.

Lesson Support for p. 941

❸ Writing Lesson

- Suggest that students try reading the poems aloud to compare their sound effects. Students may prefer to listen to the poems read on the audiocassettes or CDs.

- In addition to the instruction and comparison chart given in the Writing Lesson, use the Comparison-and-Contrast organizer in **Writing Models and Graphic Organizers on Transparencies,** p. 87. to help students analyze the poems.

- Have students consider form as well as content in their essays.

- Use the Response to Literature Rubric in **Performance Assessment and Portfolio Management,** p. 23, to assess students' essays.

❹ Research and Technology

- Have students clear their choices with you before they begin working. Students may want to work with partners or in small groups.

- This activity lends itself to a variety of class presentations. Encourage students to incorporate, recordings, works of art, dramatic readings, or other elements into their presentations.

CUSTOMIZE INSTRUCTION for Universal Access

To address different learning styles, use the following activities suggested in the **Extension Activities** booklet, p. 54.

For Intrapersonal Learners, use Activity 5.

For Verbal/Linguistic Learners, use Activity 6.

For Interpersonal Learners, use Activity 7.

ASSESSMENT RESOURCES

The following resources can be used to assess students' knowledge and skills.

Selection Assessment
- 📖 **Formal Assessment,** p. 239
- 📖 **Open Book Test,** p. 160
- 📼 **Got It! Assessment Videotapes,** Tape 4
- 💿 **Test Bank Software**

📖 **Take It to the Net**
Visit www.phschool.com for self-tests and additional questions on the selections.

Writing Rubric
- 📖 **Performance Assess. and Portfolio Mgmt.,** p. 31

PRENTICE HALL ASSESSMENT SYSTEM
- 📖 **Workbook**
- 📄 **Transparencies**
- 📖 **Skill Book**
- 💿 **CD-ROM**

Lesson Objectives

1. To learn to make inferences
2. To learn to identify various kinds of public relations documents
3. To understand the elements of effective public relations documents

About Public Relations Documents

- Have students read "About Public Relations Documents." Review the bulleted points to focus students' attention on the distinguishing features of one of the most important types of public relations documents—the mission statement.

- Ask students to identify a variety of ways in which a non-profit organization might use its mission statement.

  Answer: Mission statements communicate to donors, prospective donors, and the general public the reasons that the organization exists, the goals it hopes to accomplish, and the ways in which it will use donated funds. Mission statements might be printed on direct mail pieces, on pamphlets, or on programs to be handed out at performances.

- Add that many for-profit organizations publish mission statements as well.

Reading Strategy

Making Inferences

- Have students read the Reading Strategy section.

- Explain to students that they make inferences all the time, including in casual conversation or when watching movies. For example, at the end of a film, two characters that have spent the movie insulting each other, grin and walk off. The audience infers that the two characters have come to like each other.

- Draw students' attention to the chart describing the process by which readers make inferences.

- Ask students to suggest other examples, from either their daily lives, casual reading, or school work, of inferences they have made.

Public Relations Documents

About Public Relations Documents

Businesses and organizations create many documents to convey messages to the public. These documents include brochures, advertisements, and flyers. They also include press releases and public service announcements. All of these documents are important; however, the heart of an organization lies in its mission, or purpose. For that reason, an organization's mission statement is one of its most important documents. Most mission statements contain three kinds of information:

- **Who We Are**—This is a set of basic facts about the business or organization that has issued the statement.
- **What We Do**—These details show what the business or organization offers.
- **Why We Do It**—This information expresses the philosophy and goals of the business or organization.

The mission statement at right outlines the *Who, What,* and *Why* for a museum in Boston, Massachusetts. As you read it, think about the information that it provides, why this information is offered, who is the intended audience, and why such a document would be useful.

Reading Strategy

Making Inferences

As you read, you gather information. Some information is stated in the text itself. Other information may take the form of assumptions that are based on what you know. Such assumptions, which combine a reading of the text with your own experience, are called inferences.

Making an inference requires you to combine two kinds of knowledge and then to determine whether unstated information is likely to be supported by that knowledge.

Look for Details		Relate Your Experience		Make and Check an Inference
In an article about a fire, notice details about the intensity of the blaze.	+	Recall fires that you have seen.	=	Both skill and courage played a part in putting out the fire. Check against firefighters' actions. Verify.

942 ◆ *Disillusion, Defiance and Discontent (1914–1946)*

Mission Statement

Most businesses and organizations create informational documents that communicate to potential partners, customers, or contributors their overall purpose and the scope of their activities. The examples shown here include a mission statement on this page that briefly expresses the organization's purpose and a calendar of events on page 944 that shows how that purpose is carried out and invites people to come and participate.

MUSEUM OF AFRO-AMERICAN HISTORY

Boston and Nantucket

Mission Statement

A Foundation for the Future

The mission of the Museum of Afro-American History is to preserve, conserve and interpret the contributions of people of African descent and those who have found common cause with them in the struggle for liberty, dignity, and justice for all Americans. Therefore, we:

- collect and exhibit artifacts of distinction in this field and acquire and maintain physical structures and sites through the end of the 19th century;

- educate the public about the importance of the Afro-American historical legacy in general, its Boston and New England heritages, in particular;

- celebrate the enduring vitality of African American culture;

- and advance on our own and in collaboration with others an appreciation of the past for the benefit of the custodians of the future.

> In one well-crafted sentence, the museum says, "This is *who we are.*" More details follow, but this is the single most important statement about the museum.

> As part of a list of museum features, this explains *what we do* information. Similar information appears at the end of the statement, but its purpose is more general.

> Here is *why we do it* information—an expression of the museum's philosophy and goals.

Mission Statement

- Tell students that the mission statement of the Museum of Afro-American History is typical of such documents.

- Have students read the mission statement and the notes that identify its key elements.

- Call students' attention to the first paragraph, which concisely expresses the museum's overarching reason for existing. Ask students what kinds of programs and activities they think such an organization would undertake to fulfill its mission.

- Then, draw students' attention to the bulleted items that follow the first paragraph. Ask students if this list of bulleted items satisfies their expectations of what such an organization might do. Are these bulleted items highly specific? In what types of documents might students find more detailed information about the organization's activities?
  Answer: The bulleted items do not provide exact program names or dates. One might expect to find more detailed information about specific programs in a calendar, flyer, brochure, or pamphlet.

CUSTOMIZE INSTRUCTION FOR UNIVERSAL ACCESS

For Less Proficient Readers	For English Learners
The museum uses the words *preserve* and *conserve* to describe two elements of its primary mission. Help students understand the subtle differences between these words. While both words mean to "protect from harm," in this context the word *preserve* refers to protecting ideas—things of the intellect and spirit—while the word *conserve* refers to protection of physical objects and places.	Some of the language the Museum of Afro-American History uses in its mission statement may be challenging for students. Review with them the words *artifacts, vitality, legacy,* and *collaboration.* Also note for students that here, the word *custodians*—which they may believe is synonymous with *janitor*—refers to caretakers in a more embracing way.

943

Calendars of Events

- Tell students that in order to fulfill their missions, many organizations provide programs that are offered for varying costs, and aimed at a variety of audiences.

- Have students read the Museum of Afro-American History's calendar of events.

- Then, ask students to organize the museum's public programs into the following categories: cost, target audience, and type of event (educational workshop, youth program, cultural event, or partnerships with another organization).

- Ask students to compare the general goals described in the mission statement with the programs offered on the calendar. Do students feel that these programs fulfill the museum's mission?

Answer: These programs and events, which are offered for free or for nominal fees, promote the museum's interest in educating the public about Afro-American history.

A calender of events provides basic information, such as where and when activities take place.

MUSEUM OF AFRO-AMERICAN HISTORY BOSTON

Calendar of Events

Events take place at 8 Smith Court, Beacon Hill, unless otherwise noted.

SATURDAY, FEB. 3, 7:30 P.M.

READING AND BOOK SIGNING

On Her Own Ground: The Life and Times of Madam C.J. Walker

A'Lelia Bundles, former deputy bureau chief of ABC News in Washington and great-great granddaughter of Madam C.J. Walker, will discuss the writing of *On Her Own Ground*, the first historically accurate account of this legendary entrepreneur and social activist.

Sponsored by the Collection of African American Literature, a partnership between the Museum of Afro-American History, Suffolk University, and Boston African American Historic Site.

REFRESHMENTS AND BOOK SALES FOLLOWING. FREE

Information about sponsoring organizations is usually included.

TUESDAYS, 10:30-11:30 A.M.

Stories from African American Literature and Lore

Vibrant stories and activities presenting history for preschool aged children and parents. FREE

FRIDAY, FEB. 16, 6 P.M.-9 A.M.

Museum Overnight: Underground Railroad

Descriptions of events are brief but inviting.

Spend the night at the Museum exploring the Underground Railroad through the escape routes on Beacon Hill. Design and build your own safe house. Includes dinner, storytelling, activities, breakfast and a special "bundle" to take home.

GRADE 5-6. $30 NON-MEMBER $25 MEMBERS.

SUNDAY, MARCH 18, 3 P.M.

Marian Anderson/Roland Hayes Concert Series: A New Beginning

Makanda Ken McIntyre Jazz Quartet. Original jazz selections and standard favorites from this world-class composer and improviser. McIntyre, a Boston native and NY resident, is a master of the alto sax, bass clarinet, oboe, flute, and bassoon. Reception immediately following.

Sponsored in part by the Office of Community Collaborations and Program Development at the New England Conservatory.

Any fees must be indicated.

$10 NON-MEMBER; FREE MEMBER; GROUP RATES AVAILABLE.

Check Your Comprehension

1. Summarize the museum's mission, and name two goals that result from that mission.
2. Review the calendar of events to determine (a) in what ways the museum collaborates with others and (b) in what ways the museum educates the public.

Applying the Reading Strategy

Making Inferences

3. Copy and complete this chart of inferences about the Museum of Afro-American History. Verify each inference by noting a supporting detail from the mission statement or calendar of events.

Inference	Verification
Some African American artists found a creative outlet in New England.	
The museum founders thought that African American history had been misrepresented.	
The museum has little information about the civil rights movement of the 1960s.	

Activity

Writing a Mission Statement

Write a mission statement for one of the following organizations:

- a museum devoted to a scientific or artistic topic
- a magazine devoted to a sport or hobby
- a Web site devoted to a historical person

Before you write, think about the philosophy—a system of values—that you believe merits public attention. Then, identify the goals related to your topic that would arise from that philosophy.

Comparing Informational Materials

Comparative Mission Statements

Prepare a list of questions that you could use to evaluate the effectiveness of mission statements. Then, using either print sources or the Internet, find mission statements from two similar businesses or organizations. You might compare restaurants, hospitals, libraries, or charities. Apply your questions. Then, prepare a presentation in which you explain which mission statement you find more effective.

Answers continued

Comparing Informational Materials

Students' lists of questions and comparisons should reflect their understanding of the purposes of mission statements.

Answers for p. 945

Check Your Comprehension

1. The museum seeks to educate the public about and preserve artifacts that represent the cultural contributions of African Americans. Two goals that express this mission include their intention to collect and exhibit artifacts for public viewing and to provide educational programs for the public.

2. **(a)** The museum presents two programs—the talk about Madame C.J. Walker and the Marian Anderson/Roland Hayes concert—in collaboration with other organizations. **(b)** All of the programs listed on the calendar provide some form of public education. The Museum Overnight program for children is particularly educational.

Applying the Reading Strategy

3. Inference 1: The museum exhibits artifacts, which one infers includes artworks, created by African American artists in Boston and New England. Inference 2: In its mission statement, the museum emphasizes the importance of accurately interpreting the contributions of people of African descent. Inference 3: The museum's work focuses on African American history through the end of the nineteenth century but does not extend into the twentieth century.

Activity

Emphasize that before they begin to write their mission statements, students should first identify a solution to a problem or a set of values that they believe their organization should address. That solution or set of values must underlie all elements of their mission statement. In addition, make sure that students understand that a successful mission statement is extremely brief and concise, although it can contain lyrical and even impassioned language. Most mission statements include a general, all-purpose paragraph, followed by bulleted items or shorter paragraphs that provide additional details.

continued

Lesson Objectives

1. To understand the connection between the diverse perspectives of the writers in Part 3 and the multiculturalism expressed by Ricardo Sánchez

2. To understand how American literature that celebrates diversity has changed from the period covered in Unit 5 to the present

Connections

Just as American authors from 1914–1946 began to write about their far-ranging backgrounds, authors of diverse ethnicities have been gaining wide audiences today by writing about their own cultures—about how their cultures both mesh and conflict with mainstream American attitudes and values. Ask students to consider what the works in Part 3 and Sánchez's "i yearn" reveal about their authors' struggles to belong to two worlds.

From Every Corner of the Land

• Remind students that during the first half of the twentieth century, American writers celebrated the nation's diversity by focusing on the regions and ethnic and racial backgrounds from which they came.

• Point to the writers represented in Part 3—especially those of the Harlem Renaissance: Zora Neale Hurston, Langston Hughes, Claude McKay, Countee Cullen, Arna Bontemps, and Jean Toomer—as examples.

• Explain that the United States is even more diverse and multicultural today. Point out that some experts predict that by the middle of the 21st century, over one-fifth of the U.S. population will be of Spanish-speaking origin.

• Instruct students to look for themes relating to multiculturalism in "i yearn," and encourage them to compare Sánchez's treatment of these themes to that in the other works in Part 3.

CONNECTIONS
Literature Past and Present
From Every Corner of the Land

In the past, historians described the United States as a "melting pot" to suggest that people of different ethnic backgrounds came to the country and blended into a single American culture. Today, many Americans argue that the "melting pot" metaphor is not accurate. They say that the United States is a multicultural society in which many distinct cultures exist side by side, retaining their individual identities. New phrases that describe the country's diversity call the United States a quilt, a rainbow, a salad bowl, or a mosaic.

In today's United States, ethnic communities nurture their own cultures and traditions while they still hold many distinctly American beliefs such as freedom and equality. Just a few examples of such communities are the Chinatowns in New York and San Francisco, Arab communities in Michigan, and Scandinavian communities in the Midwest.

Writers Celebrate Differences Today's writers explore the many ways of being an American. Hispanic Americans are growing in number and becoming increasingly vocal. Hispanic novelists, playwrights, and poets such as Ricardo Sánchez reflect on the ways in which their Hispanic roots intersect with American culture to create new influences and identities.

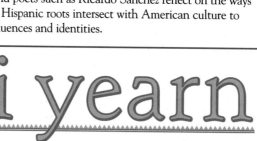

Ricardo Sánchez

i yearn this morning
what i've yearned
since i left

almost a year ago . . .

5   it is hollow
this
being away
from everyday life

946 ◆ *Disillusion, Defiance, and Discontent (1914–1946)*

 ENRICHMENT: Art Connection

Folk Art

Identify the embroidered object that occupies part of the background for this poem as a *huipil* (blouse) from the Tarascan people of Michoacan. Michoacan is a state in Mexico that borders on the Pacific Ocean, about two-thirds of the way to Guatemala; the Tarascans are Native Americans who live there.

Invite students to find out more about the folk arts associated with a culture of their choice. For example, they might investigate and describe the characteristic pottery of the Acoma people of New Mexico, the beautiful hand-woven *dhurrie* rugs of India, the dramatic batik work of Indonesia, or the delicate lacework of the people of Saba, in the Caribbean. Students can find representative examples of the folk art, and research how particular techniques or styles developed—and how they are preserved and continued today.

in the barrios[1]
10   of my homeland . . .
all those cities
like el paso, los angeles,
albuquerque,
denver, san antonio
15   (off into chicano
      infinitum![2]);

i yearn
to hear spanish
spoken in caló[3]—
20   that special way
chicanos[4] roll their
   tongues
to form
words
25   which dart or glide;

i yearn
for foods
that have character
and strength—the kind
30   that assail yet caress
you with the zest of life;

more than anything,
i yearn, my people,
for the warmth of you
35   greeting me with "¿qué tal,
hermano?"[5]
and the knowing that you
   mean it
when you tell me that you love
40   the fact that we exist . . .

---

1. **barrios** (bär´ ē ōs) *n.* Spanish-speaking neighborhood.
2. **infinitum** (in´ fə nīt´ əm) *n.* Latin for "that which is endless."
3. **caló** (kä lō´) *n.* slang.
4. **chicanos** (chē kä´ nōs) *n.* Mexican Americans, usually capitalized.
5. **¿qué tal, hermano?** (kā täl´ er mä´ nō) Spanish for "How are things, brother?"

Connecting Literature Past and Present

1. Compare Ricardo Sánchez's homesickness in "i yearn" to that of Claude McKay in "The Tropics in New York."
2. (a) According to this poem, what are the difficulties of a multicultural society? (b) What are the benefits?

Ricardo Sanchez

(1941–1995)

Born in El Paso, Texas, and raised in a Hispanic neighborhood, Ricardo Sánchez believed that his mission was to bring Mexican culture and traditions into the lives of his fellow Mexican Americans. He often wrote about the challenge faced by those who try to create a coherent identity from a mix of two cultures: Mexican and American. Sánchez was an activist as well as a writer and an academic. As a lecturer, consultant, developer of television programs, and poet, Sánchez worked to educate all Americans about Mexican American culture.

Background

Chicano Culture

The speaker of this poem reveals how much he misses being with fellow Chicanos: hearing the slang they speak, eating the zesty foods they enjoy, and most of all, being relaxed and easy with people who share common bonds.

Answers

Connecting Literature Past and Present

1. **Possible response:** Both poets focus on the foods of their own homes and cultures, yearning for their bright colors and strong flavors. While Sánchez yearns for the food of his memories along with other aspects of his home, McKay is drawn into intense homesickness by the sight of imported tropical fruits.

2. **Possible responses: (a)** The difficulties include how the mainstream culture can separate individuals from their heritages, leaving them homesick and yearning. **(b)** The benefits include the chance for anyone to experience the languages, foods, and warmth of which Sánchez and McKay write.

CUSTOMIZE INSTRUCTION FOR UNIVERSAL ACCESS

For Less Proficient Readers	For English Learners	For Advanced Learners
These students might be challenged by Sánchez's use of Spanish words and punctuation, as well as his nonstandard capitalization. Help them read the poem, and guide them to recognize that these artistic decisions give readers a vision of the culture for which the poet yearns.	This poem may speak directly to many of these students' experiences. Encourage these students to discuss Sánchez's use of Spanish words and punctuation. How do these inclusions enhance the poem's expression of its themes?	Have these students pay close attention to Sánchez's use of Spanish words and conventions in this poem. Then, ask them to find similar uses of language and cultural materials in the poems of the Harlem Renaissance in Part 3. What does a comparison of this technique reveal about the poems' themes?

Prewriting

- Instruct students to reread Pound's essay "A Few Don'ts by an Imagiste," on pp. 729–731. Ask students to carefully take notes identifying Pound's major ideas.

- Tell students to turn Pound's ideas into criteria for imagist poetry by paraphrasing them, or rewriting the ideas in students' own words. As an example, ask them to paraphrase the following: "Use no superfluous word, no adjective, which does not reveal something." *Possible response:* An imagist poem should have no purely descriptive adjectives.

- Students should select poems to evaluate from Unit 5. Encourage students to photocopy the poems they choose, possibly blowing them up to make note taking easier.

- Call students' attention to the Analyzing According to Criteria model scorecard. Explain that by using a scorecard such as this, they can determine whether a poem meets or fails to meet the criteria. They can also identify why a poem succeeds or fails by these standards.

Writing About Literature
Evaluate Literary Trends

The Imagist poets wrote with clear ideas about poetry and provided specific criteria with which to judge the success or failure of a poem. Ezra Pound expressed these ideas in his essay "A Few Don'ts by an Imagiste." To a great extent, poems by such Imagists as Pound, William Carlos Williams, and H.D. can be measured according to the criteria Pound defined.

Using the assignment outlined in the yellow box, write an essay evaluating this literary trend.

Prewriting

Summarize Pound's main points. Reread Pound's essay, and take careful notes about each of his main points. Avoid using Pound's own language in your notes. Instead, paraphrase—or restate in your own words—his ideas. Translating his advice into your own words will allow you to be sure you understand his often complex concepts. It will also help you to determine which of his ideas will require additional explanation or definition for your readers.

Evaluate line by line. In all works of literature, every word plays an important part within the whole. In Imagist poetry, which, by its very nature, is compressed and focused, a single word carries even greater weight than in most other genres. Judge the success of each poem you have selected by weighing each word according to Pound's criteria. You may want to make a photocopy of the poems and write notes directly on the pages.

Create a scorecard. Use your notes to create an Imagist scorecard, like the one shown below. In the first column, list the criteria you will use to judge each poem. Across the top, list the titles of the poems you have chosen to analyze. In each box, place a *P* (for *Pass*) for each criterion that a given poem fulfills. Place an *F* (for *Fail*) for each criterion that a poem fails to meet.

Model: Analyzing According to Criteria

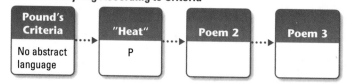

For each of the poems you are discussing, use the results of your scorecard to write a one-sentence statement about whether or not it fulfills Pound's criteria. These statements will serve as the foundation for the concepts you will develop more completely as you draft. Your statement should note the most prominent ways in which the poem succeeds or fails.

Assignment: Following the Rules

Write an analytical essay that evaluates the success with which at least three Imagist poems fulfill the goals set out in Pound's essay "A Few Don'ts by an Imagiste."

Criteria:

- Clearly restate Pound's main ideas.
- Evaluate the effectiveness of specific words, lines, and images in at least three poems according to Pound's ideas.
- Approximate length: 1,500 words.

Read to Write

As you read each poem, ask yourself whether it meets Pound's criteria. The point is not whether or not you like the poem, but whether it fulfills specific artistic objectives.

TEACHING RESOURCES

The following resources can be used to enrich or extend the instruction for pp. 948–949

Writing and Grammar, Ruby Level, Chapter 14, pp. 298–317

Performance Assessment and Portfolio Management, p. 13

Writing and Grammar iText

Students can use the following tools as they complete their evaluation of literary trends:

- Chart Organizer
- Transition Word Bin
- Vague Adjectives Revising Tool

Drafting

Transform your notes into sentences. Notes written in preparation for writing an essay are abbreviated ideas—kernels of the points you will develop more completely in a draft. Using the notes you made as part of your prewriting activities, construct one or more complete sentences that fully express the idea each note represents.

Combine sentences into paragraphs. Write at least one paragraph on Pound's essay and at least one on each poem you have analyzed. In each paragraph about a poem, evaluate the author's success in meeting Pound's criteria. Refer to your scorecard for details. Make sure each sentence supports or explains your "grade."

Revising and Editing

Review content: Check the soundness of your thinking. Check your evaluation of each poem to make sure it is based on the criteria you have compiled from Pound's essay. Remember: The point is not whether you personally like a poem but whether it fulfills the stated requirements.

> ### Model: Revising to Focus on Criteria
>
> "In a Station of the Metro" almost perfectly obeys Pound's dictate that a poem should "go in fear of abstractions." This brief description of faces in a crowd is intensely visual and concrete. ~~I love this poem because I know exactly what he means.~~ *One possible weakness is the word* apparition. *Because the word refers to something that is not really there, it can be interpreted as an abstraction.*

Review style: Vary sentence length and word choice. Poets select and arrange words not only for their meanings but also for their sounds and rhythms. Learn from their example. When revising your essay, work to avoid using the same words repeatedly, and make changes to avoid using sentences of the same length and structure.

Publishing and Presenting

Give an oral presentation. Share your ideas with the class. If possible, use an overhead projector or a slideshow program to project the poems you are discussing. Alternatively, you can simply copy the poems on the board. Then, as you read your essay aloud for the class, use a pointer to indicate words or phrases that are especially relevant to your discussion. Invite questions and comments from the class.

WG Prentice Hall Writing and Grammar Connection: Chapter 14

✏ Write to Learn
As you work on your essay, you may discover new ideas about the poems. Allow for this, and incorporate your discoveries into your work.

✏ Write to Explain
The foundation of your essay is your examination of Pound's essay. Make sure that your explanation of Pound's ideas is simple and clear.

Drafting

- Explain to students that their notes are the beginning of sentences for their essays. Refer to the model scorecard on p. 948 and ask students to draw an essay sentence from it.
  Possible response: H.D.'s poem "Heat" lives up to Pound's requirement that poems use no abstract language.

- Suggest that students plan their essays with one paragraph to explain Pound's criteria and then one paragraph for each poem evaluated. Point out that this plan can easily be turned into an outline.

- Explain to students that their Analyze According to Criteria scorecards can provide the main points and evidence for each of their evaluation paragraphs.

Revising and Editing

- Be sure students understand that they are evaluating poems by *Pound's* standards—not by their own. Call their attention to the model on p. 949. Guide them to see the difference between the deleted passage and the revision.

- Encourage students to use the Transition Word Bin at **Writing and Grammar Interactive** to help them revise for varied word choice.

Publishing and Presenting

- Point out that in their presentations, students can project Pound's criteria as well as their poems.

- As students prepare their oral presentations, suggest that they include specific examples from the poems in their notes. Then, during presentations, students can point to specific words or phrases from the poems and explain why they meet or fail to meet Pound's criteria.

- You may wish to use the assessment rubric for Multimedia Presentation in **Performance Assessment and Portfolio Management**, p. 13, to assess students' presentations.

CUSTOMIZE INSTRUCTION FOR UNIVERSAL ACCESS

For Less Proficient Writers	For English Learners	For Advanced Writers
These students may need help revising for variety. If they have drawn on their notes in drafting, their sentences and paragraphs may be highly repetitive. Have them vary their paragraphs by organizing their support for each evaluation differently. The Word Bins at **Writing and Grammar iText** may also be helpful.	These students may find revising for variety in word choice challenging. Encourage them to build vocabulary and vary word choice by using a thesaurus to find synonyms for repeated words. Then, have them look up the definitions of the new words in a dictionary. Be sure that they understand the difference between a synonym and a definition.	As these students revise, encourage them to pay close attention to varying sentence structure. You might require students to incorporate two each of specific types of sentences—compound sentences, complex sentences, sentences using subordinate clauses, and so on—throughout their essays.

Research: Multimedia Presentation

Model From Literature

The vivid language of William Faulkner's "Nobel Prize Acceptance Speech" (p. 875) might work well with visual media. Encourage students to imagine how a multimedia presentation could enhance Faulkner's message.

Prewriting

- Explain to students that their topics must be subjects about which they have something to say, as well as subjects about which there will be multimedia material—music, video material, art or photographs, recorded interviews, and so on—available.

- Call student attention to the media checklist. Instruct students to use this list as they research their topics. Encourage them to try to find material in each medium.

- Ask students to evaluate the model checklist. Will this presentation be an interesting one? Explain. Possible response: Students should notice that of the six media categories, the students have found material in all but "computer presentation"—so the presentation is likely to be interesting.

- As they research, remind students that their multimedia presentations should *involve* the audience's interest. They should find material that are both informative and involving.

- Before students draft their essays, have them review the Rubric for Self-Assessment (p. 953), so they know what is expected.

A **multimedia presentation** is a technique for sharing information with an audience by enhancing narration and explanation with media, including video images, slides, audiotape recordings, music, and fine art. In this workshop, you will plan, draft, and revise a multimedia presentation.

Assignment Criteria Your multimedia presentation should have the following characteristics:

- Integrated audio and visual components
- Reinforcement of each element by the appropriate medium
- A clear and logical organization
- Innovative use of media to convey concepts

To preview the criteria on which your multimedia presentation may be assessed, see the Rubric on page 953.

Prewriting

Choose a topic. Select a subject for which multimedia material will be readily available. To narrow the field of possible topics, **list** musicians or artists whose work you enjoy, films you know well, or professional sports teams you watch regularly. Make sure you can imagine the audio or visual material that would support your ideas. Then, choose a topic.

Create a media checklist. In a chart, list the various kinds of media that would be available for the topic you have chosen. Use the right-hand column of the chart to note specific media that would be most useful for your topic.

Media Checklist	
☑ Music	*Mysterious music*
☑ Videos	*Historic roller coaster*
☑ Art	*Sketches of design*
☑ Photographs	*Dragon memorabilia*
☐ Computer Presentation	
☑ Interviews	*People waiting in line*

Research your topic. As you gather materials, note creative ways to involve viewers. Consult your library for audio or video clips of interviews, documentaries, music, and art resources. Search the Internet for a wide range of resources. Remember: almost any medium can be used with your presentation, provided it helps to explain your topic.

Identify a thesis. Review your notes and the materials you have gathered. Develop a main idea—one clear statement that will express the focus of your multimedia presentation. You may include this statement in whatever portion of your presentation will best convey the idea, whether audiotape, videotape, art, or text.

950 ◆ Disillusion, Defiance, and Discontent (1914–1946)

TEACHING RESOURCES

The following resources can be used to enrich or extend the instruction for pp. 950–953

WG **Writing and Grammar,** Ruby Level, Chapter 16, pp. 344–354

📖 **Performance Assessment and Portfolio Management,** p. 13

Writing Models and Graphic Organizers on Transparencies, p. 96

🔍 **Writing and Grammar iText**

Students can use the following tools as they complete their evaluation of literary trends:

- Research Topic Bank
- Cluster Diagram Organizer
- Sensory Word Bin
- Language Variety Revising Tool

Student Model

Before you begin writing, read this student model and review the characteristics of effective multimedia presentations.

Afton Kapala
Ventura, California

The Dragon's Lair

Text

(cue video and audio) For thousands of years, dragons have played a major role in the human imagination. They represent the awesome power of nature, and the extremes of human emotion.

Today, Bombshell Roller Coasters harnesses the power of dragon lore in our latest roller coaster design. (pause for emphasis; cue video) . . . the Dragon's Lair. (pause as video plays)

(cue slide) Our design represents the latest and best in roller coaster technology. (use pointer to highlight features) The coaster will begin with a 95-meter peak, followed by a drop, followed by a 76-meter peak and drop. The rest of the ride includes banked turns, loops, and a smaller hill.

(cue audio and first slide) After they buy tickets, customers will enter our air-conditioned concourse, (cue second slide) where they can buy snacks and dragon memorabilia. (cue third slide) Our Ground Dragons—customer service agents in costume—will provide customers with great photo opportunities.

(cue slide) Why would Magic Mountain want to buy this ride? For nearly two centuries roller coasters have been a huge public attraction. (cue video)

All of those great coasters represent the past, but the Dragon's Lair is the future. It will keep crowds coming, generating great revenues for years to come.

Video and Audio

Video: dragons from ancient China, Babylonia, Rome, to Wales, and Anglo-Saxon England, to today (film and TV shows)
Audio: music from ancient past to today

Video: computer animation of Dragon's Lair in motion with zooms in and out to show detail

Slide: coaster route schematic design

Slide: dragon memorabilia (hats, flashlights, stuffed animals, etc.)
Slide: costumed ground dragon

Slide: question mark
Video with voiceover: historic roller coasters—Russian Mountains (1800s), the Cyclone (1900s), the Fireball (1920s), and the Skyliner (1960s)
Video morphs to: computer-animated image of the Dragon's Lair

> Afton's subject is rich and well-suited to a multimedia format.

> Afton does not attempt to be flashy if it is not appropriate. This slide of a schematic design is appropriate for the text.

> The text, audio, and visual elements convey an increasing level of detail in a clear, logical way.

> This use of video transforming into computer animation is an innovative and effective use of media.

Student Model

- Explain that the Student Model is a sample, and that presentations might be longer.
- Call students' attention to Afton's subject—the power of dragons in the imagination. Ask students to evaluate this topic. Will it grab the audience's attention? Explain. Possible response: Students will likely agree that dragons are a very interesting subject, especially for a multimedia presentation that might have exciting visuals.
- After they have read the second note, be sure students understand that multimedia material should not overwhelm the topic of a presentation. Therefore, the slide is more appropriate here than an exciting videotape.
- Emphasize that, like an essay, a multimedia project must be organized properly. Here, the presentation moves from general to more specific information about the roller coaster.
- Call students' attention to the final note and encourage them to be innovative in their presentations, as well.

Real-World Connection

Tell students that in many businesses, multimedia presentations can be an important tool for selling services and products, communicating goals and agendas, or simply informing audiences. Multimedia material can grab an audience's attention and direct it to a presentation's key points, making it ideally suited to the business world—but also to the classroom! Have any of your teachers presented multimedia lessons?

If so, did the presentations generate interest and excitement in the class?

CUSTOMIZE INSTRUCTION FOR UNIVERSAL ACCESS

For Less Proficient Writers	For English Learners	For Advanced Writers
These students may find the research process challenging. Help them to choose topics for which they will be able to find multimedia materials. Then, encourage them to write descriptions of each multimedia source. Students can use their notes to select appropriate materials for the presentation.	Conducting multimedia research may be challenging for these students, especially if they encounter audio and video materials using unfamiliar vocabulary. Have these students research in small, mixed-skill level groups. Encourage group members to help one another determine the meanings of unfamiliar words and phrases.	Encourage these students to find multimedia sources that express different positions on their topics. Using these sources, students should address a controversy over their topics as part of their presentations. Be sure students take a clear position and support it effectively.

Drafting

- Remind students that like an essay, a multimedia presentation needs to be well organized. Then, review the Organize Your Presentation chart on p. 952 with the class. Explain that this chart is a good starting point for an outline.
- After they have organized the introduction, body, and conclusion of their essays, instruct students to organize the multimedia elements. Refer to the Student Model on p. 951 as an example. Ask students what struck them most about its use of multimedia material. Possible response: Students may say they were impressed by ways Afton used multimedia elements to communicate information and emphasize his points.
- Tell students not to overload their presentations with audio and visual materials. Be sure they understand that they must balance these elements with their narrative.
- Remind students to include stage directions for themselves, indicating how they will deliver the presentation.
- Students may wish to use the Outline Blackline Master, p. 96 in **Writing Models and Graphic Organizers on Transparencies**, to help them draft their presentations.

Revising

- Explain to students that the best way to revise their presentations is to practice delivering them. Without practicing, they will not be able to know what aspects need to be reconsidered.
- Point out that presentations need to flow smoothly—and this flow can be interrupted when students stop to change media. Use the model on p. 952 as an example of revising to smooth transitions between different media.

(continued on page 953)

952

Writing WORKSHOP *continued*

Drafting

Sketch an outline. Before you begin to draft actual text, create a working outline to shape your sequence of ideas. The chart shown here details an effective sequence for a presentation.

Organize your presentation. Once you have gathered sufficient information, elaborate on your outline sketch by planning the media elements to include under each main heading. Jot down any additional ideas for incorporating other media to convey your ideas.

Plan your delivery. Draft a script based on the outline sketch. Use stage direction format to indicate posture, body language, and voice inflection during your presentation. Note points at which you may wish to use a pointer or other tool.

Strike a balance. As you draft, strive to strike a balance between the narrative, audio, and visual elements you will use. As in all research writing, weave your ideas into those of others using transitions and appropriate recognition of sources.

Revising

Revise to clarify sequence. A seamless presentation is the goal of any multimedia demonstration. Because your presentation may involve apparatus that requires time for setup, hold a test-run with a partner.

1. Run through your presentation, incorporating all audiovisual elements.
2. Ask your partner to comment on parts that lacked clarity or seemed unpolished.

If necessary, revise the sequence to clarify connections between ideas or eliminate awkward transitions.

Organize Your Presentation

Introduction: Address the topic and introduce the thesis statement in an innovative, attention-getting way.

Body: Offer in-depth coverage of the topic and provide at least two examples—at least one of which should be conveyed in a medium other than text—to reinforce the thesis.

Conclusion: Sum up research and restate the thesis.

Model: Revising to Smooth Transitions

(cue slide)

~~(cue video)~~ Our design represents the latest and best in roller coaster technology. ~~(cue slide and audio)~~ (pointer to highlight features) The coaster will begin with a 95-meter peak, followed by a drop, followed by a 76-meter peak and drop. The rest of the ride includes banked turns, loops, and a smaller hill.

~~Video: computer animation of Dragon's Lair~~
Slide: coaster route schematic design
~~Audio: People screaming~~

Afton deleted the video and audio elements of this section because the transitions were too complicated to handle smoothly.

952 ◆ *Disillusion, Defiance, and Discontent (1914–1946)*

USING TECHNOLOGY IN WRITING

As students will likely be aware, there are many technology resources that can be very useful in preparing and delivering multimedia presentations. If you have access to audiocassette players, videocassette players and monitors, and slide projectors for your class, encourage your students to make full use of them. A Power Point display can also be a very effective part of a multimedia presentation. If students are not familiar with any equipment, arrange for Audio/Visual staff members to give a tutorial. Students can also use the organizing tools and revision checkers on **Writing and Grammar iText**.

Revise to vary media. Review your script for overuse of one form of media. By using a variety of media to enhance your narration, you can spice up your presentation, and hold your viewers' interest.

Without Variety: Play audio interview of quarterback
Play audio interview of ballerina

With Variety: Show video footage of quarterback
Voiceover interview of ballerina

The plans below show the multimedia element of a presentation. Compare the model and the nonmodel. Why is the model more effective than the nonmodel?

Nonmodel	Model
Slide: computer schematic	**Video:** computer animation of Dragon's Lair
Slide: station schematics	**Slide:** station schematics
Slide: train schematics	**Hand-outs:** circulate design specifications
Slide: people standing on line	**Video:** interviews with customers waiting on line

Publishing and Presenting

Consider this activity to share your writing with a wider audience.

Deliver an oral presentation. Deliver your multimedia presentation for your classmates. Invite questions. Afterwards, write a brief analysis of your experience.

- Get to know your material so you can speak without a script, and familiarize yourself with the equipment you will be using.
- Give a practice performance to friends or family members.
- Give equipment a final check for problems before delivering your presentation.

W̶G Prentice Hall Writing and Grammar Connection: Chapter 13

Rubric for Self-Assessment

Evaluate your multimedia presentation using the following criteria and rating scale:

Criteria	Rating Scale				
	Not very				Very
How well does the presentation integrate audio and visual components?	1	2	3	4	5
How effectively is each element reinforced by the appropriate medium?	1	2	3	4	5
Is the presentation clear and logically organized?	1	2	3	4	5
How innovatively does the presentation make use of media to convey concepts?	1	2	3	4	5

Revising (continued)

- Call students' attention to the "Without Variety/With Variety" example on p. 953. Then, ask them the question below: Compare the model and the nonmodel. Why is the model more effective than the nonmodel? Answer: The only medium the nonmodel uses is slides. The model is more interesting because it uses a variety of media—videos, a slide, and a handout.

Publishing and Presenting

- Remind students to think about the audience they had in mind when they prepared their presentations.
- Suggest that students rehearse their presentations once again after they have completed revising.
- Instruct students to write short essays analyzing what was most effective in their own presentations, as well as what aspects might need work.

Assessment

- Review the assessment criteria with the class.
- Suggest that students use the rubric as they rehearse their presentations. The criteria can be used to assess the presentations and guide the revision process.
- The rubric on this page can be found on p. 13 of **Performance Assessment and Portfolio Management.**

TEST-TAKING TIP

Explain to students that, while few tests will require them to make attention-grabbing multimedia presentations, many tests will include prompts that require them to be equally focused on keeping an audience's attention. Point out that multimedia presentations such as the Student Model on p. 951 are a form of persuasive writing, a type of writing required by many tests. When responding to such prompts, students should consider their audiences. When selecting evidence to use, students should ask themselves: Can I make this information as involving as an exciting presentation would be?

Evaluating Communication Methods

Many of the communication methods we are most affected by, such as television broadcasts or films, appear in a visual medium. Listening skills can be useful in analyzing such materials and identifying the techniques used to present information and opinions. The strategies described below will help you interpret arguments and understand information presented through such media. Use the form on this page to record your responses.

Evaluate Presentations

Evaluate Presentations

• Call students' attention to the chart on p. 954. Explain that they will use this chart to evaluate audiovisual media communication methods.

• Tell students to begin their evaluations by determining the purpose of the media format. Ask: What do you think the purpose of a television newsmagazine program is?
Possible response: Some students may say that their purpose is to inform; others will note that such programs also entertain.

• Explain to students that the structure of media communication—the length of news stories, for example, or the balance between audio and video—affects the way in which the message is conveyed.

• Be sure that students understand the difference between objective and subjective communication. Point out that the difference is not always obvious; for example, they may need to analyze a news program to determine its position.

Evaluate Communication Techniques

• Encourage students to pay close attention to the music used with such audiovisual communication as a television news program. Does the music affect the viewer emotionally?

• Instruct students to be on the lookout for sounds and images that appeal to the emotions without conveying relevant information.

Use the following strategies to evaluate presentations.

• **Recognize purpose.** Distinct forms of media have specific goals. Some seek to entertain, some seek to persuade, and others seek to inform. Some seek to do all three.

• **Analyze structure.** Note the ways in which each form of media structures information. For example, the evening news might build on short oral summaries supported by photographs or film footage. An advertisement might present a short persuasive message accompanied by a series of quick images. Learn to notice the ways in which the structure affects your perception.

• **Weigh objectivity and subjectivity.** News reports, for example, are meant to present current events in an objective manner, without bias or opinion. Often, such shows also include editorials that convey subjective opinions. Consider how the objectivity or subjectivity of a presentation affects your understanding of events.

Evaluate Communication Techniques

Media makers use various techniques to communicate information. Look for the following in evaluating audiovisual media:

• **Music or slogans:** Audiovisual media makers may use music to set a mood or emphasize visual imagery. Slogans, which you will often hear repeated, grab your attention and stick in your mind.

• **Charged sounds and images:** Powerful images, such as videos of gurgling babies or of starving children, evoke strong emotional reactions. Used responsibly, they give substance to reported facts.

Activity:
Listen, View, and Evaluate Watch the television news, a film documentary, or a news magazine/interview program. Use the evaluation form shown here to interpret media techniques.

954 ◆ *Disillusion, Defiance, and Discontent (1914–1946)*

Feedback Form for Audiovisual Media

Presentation
Topic: entertainment _____ information _____
Structure: length _____
    balance between visual and audio _____
Point of view: objective _____ subjective _____

Techniques
Note your responses to media makers' use of the techniques listed below. Use this ranking system:
+ = effective, ✔ = acceptable, – = inappropriate.
Music/slogans: _____
Loaded sounds/images: _____

Your Evaluation
Do you feel the events addressed by this medium were presented objectively and thoroughly?

How did the techniques you identified affect your response to the media? Explain.

CUSTOMIZE INSTRUCTION FOR UNIVERSAL ACCESS

For Special Needs Students	For Less Proficient Readers	For English Learners
Students may need to practice with videotapes of television news reports. Show students a news report, asking them to focus on and write down the facts of the story. Then, show the report again, this time having them evaluate presentation. Have them watch a third time for communication techniques.	Students may find weighing objectivity and subjectivity challenging. Be sure that they understand that while a media format such as a news report may seem to be objective, it may have a subjective bias. Instruct them to search even seemingly objective media formats for signs of subjectivity.	These students may find the vocabulary of audiovisual media difficult, but they may be especially adept at recognizing the impact of music and charged sounds and images. Suggest that these students watch a news report, paying attention only to these techniques. What messages do they find?

Assessment WORKSHOP

Sentence-Completion Questions

The reading sections of some tests require you to correctly answer sentence-completion questions. Use the following strategies to help you understand and answer these types of questions.

- Use the context and your own knowledge to predict which word would best complete the sentence.
- If the word you anticipated is not among the answers presented, look for a synonym of the word or other related words.
- Analyze the sentence meaning, deciding if it is positive or negative, and eliminate choices that have the opposite sense.

Test-Taking Strategy

Try each word choice in the sentence to see whether it makes sense. Often, you can eliminate some of the choices because they are illogical, the wrong part of speech, or inconsistent with the sentence's meaning.

Sample Test Item

Directions: Read the following sentences and select the answers that best complete their meanings.

1. When Julie skipped three classes and two band practices after months of perfect attendance, her friends wondered about her _____?_____ behavior.

   A erratic

   B reasonable

   C slow

   D arrogant

2. Olivia's mastery of formal etiquette was just one example of her _____?_____ behavior.

   A crude

   B suspicious

   C refined

   D temporary

Answer and Explanation

1. The correct answer is *A,* because it is closest to the meaning of the sentence. Julie's behavior is erratic, or inconsistent. The other choices are not supported by the information in the paragraph.

2. The correct answer is *C.* Formal etiquette suggests refined behavior.

Practice

Directions: Read the following sentences and select the answer that best completes each sentence.

1. Those who believe it is barbaric and cruel to keep large animals in captivity think that to visit a zoo is _____?_____.

   A unfortunate

   B advisable

   C immoral

   D courageous

2. Although my good friend had _____?_____ the movie, I was _____?_____ by the weak plot.

   A recommended; disappointed

   B enjoyed; impressed

   C criticized; convinced

   D proposed; frightened

3. Surprisingly, Umberto loved peanuts but found peanut butter _____?_____.

   A creamy

   B exquisite

   C old-fashioned

   D repugnant

Assessment Workshop ◆ 955

Lesson Objectives

To correctly answer sentence completion items in a standardized test situation

Applying Reading Strategies

Explain to students that engaging their senses as they did when reading Imagist poems can help them answer sentence-completion questions. Instead of trying to visualize images, however, they should try to imagine situations in order to anticipate the missing words.

Test-Taking Skills

- Have students read sample test item one. Then, ask them to visualize and describe the situation. Possible response: Students should recognize that Julie's behavior seems alarming and unusual, especially because her friends "wondered" about it.

- Next, have students read the choice of answers. Guide them to recognize that only **A**, *erratic*, matches the situation they have visualized.

Answers

1. The correct answer is **C**. The passage indicates that the people who think this also believe zoos are "barbaric and cruel." Only C, *immoral*, matches this sentiment. *B* and *D* are opposed to the negative sentiment, and *A*, while negative, is not strong enough to match "barbaric and cruel."

2. The correct answer is **A**. The passage indicates that the two words should reflect opposite reactions to the movie; the word "weak" indicates that the second word should be negative. The two words in answer *B* are not opposed, and the second word in answer *C* is positive. Answer *D* makes no sense, leaving only answer *A*.

3. The correct answer is **D**. The sentence makes clear that Umberto's response to peanut butter was contrary to his fondness for peanuts. Answer *D* is the only choice that makes this clear.

TEACHING RESOURCES

The following resources can be used to enrich or extend the instruction for pp. 954–955.

PRENTICE HALL ASSESSMENT SYSTEM

- 📖 **Workbook**
- 📖 **Skill Book**
- 📄 **Transparencies**
- 💿 **CD-ROM**

Prosperity and Protest (1946–Present)

Unit Objectives

1. To read selections from American literature written during the period of 1946 to the present
2. To apply a variety of reading strategies, particularly strategies for reading fiction, appropriate for reading these selections
3. To analyze literary elements
4. To use a variety of strategies to read unfamiliar words and to build vocabulary
5. To learn elements of grammar, usage, and style
6. To use recursive writing processes to write in a variety of forms
7. To develop listening and speaking skills
8. To express and support responses to various types of texts
9. To prepare, organize, and present literary interpretations

Meeting the Objectives

With each selection, you will find instructional materials through which students can meet these objectives. Further, you will find additional practice pages for reading strategies, literary analysis, vocabulary, and grammar in the **Selection Support: Skills Development Workbook** in your **Teaching Resources.**

Background

Art

Telephones (detail), by Colleen Browning

In this painting, the artist has painted on plywood, which gives the image a rough, grainy quality. Have students link the painting to the focus of Unit 6, Prosperity and Protest, by answering the following questions:

1. Does the painting emphasize a sense of community or a sense of isolation? Explain.
   Possible response: The painting emphasizes isolation by showing people in separate phone booths, none relating to the others.

Continued

Telephones (detail), 1954, Colleen Browning, Butler Institute of American Art

Continued from left column

2. How does the painting relate to the unit's theme, prosperity and protest?
   Possible response: Students may say that the painting's picture of isolation demonstrates that prosperity and technology isolate people, rather than bringing them together.

UNIT FEATURES

Reading Informational Materials

These selections will help students learn to analyze and evaluate informational texts, such as workplace documents, technical directions, and consumer materials. They will expose students to the organization and features unique to nonnarrative texts.

In this unit, the focus is on Critical Commentary. An excerpt from "On Social Plays" is on p. 1339.

66 *Sometimes I can see the future stretched out in front of me—just as plain as day. The future hanging over there at the edge of my days. Just waiting for me.* 99

— Lorraine Hansberry

ASSESSMENT RESOURCES

The following resources can be used to assess students' knowledge and skills.

Selection Assessment

📖 **Selection Support:** Skills Development Workbook

📖 **Formal Assessment**

📖 **Open Book Tests**

📖 **Performance Assessment and Portfolio Management**

📖 **Extension Activities**

Assessing Student Progress

Listed below are the tools that are available to measure the degree to which students meet the unit objectives.

Informal Assessment

The questions in the Review and Assess sections are a first level of response to the concepts and skills presented within the selections. Students' responses are a brief, informal measure of their grasp of the material. These responses can indicate where further instruction and practice are needed. Then follow up with the practice pages in the **Selection Support: Skills Development Workbook.**

Formal Assessment

The **Formal Assessment** booklet contains Selection Tests and Unit Tests.

- Selection Tests measure comprehension and skills acquisition for each selection or group of selections.
- Each Unit Test provides students with thirty multiple-choice questions and five essay questions designed to assess students' knowledge of the literature and skills taught in the unit.

The **Open Book Tests** ask students to demonstrate their ability to synthesize and communicate information from selections or groups of selections.

To assess student writing, you will find rubrics and scoring models in the **Performance Assessment and Portfolio Management** booklet. In this booklet you will also find scoring rubrics for listening and speaking activities.

Alternative Assessment

The **Extension Activities** booklet contains writing activities, listening and speaking activities, and research and technology activities that are appropriate for students with different ability levels. You may also use these activities as an alternative measurement of students' growth.

Using the Timeline

The Timeline can serve a number of instructional purposes, as follows:

Getting an Overview

Use the Timeline to help students get a quick overview of themes and events of the period. This approach will benefit all students but may be especially helpful for Visual/Spatial Learners, English Learners, and Less Proficient Readers. (For strategies in using the Timeline as an overview, see the bottom of this page.)

Thinking Critically

Questions are provided on the facing page. Use these questions to have students review the events, discuss their significance, and examine the *so what* behind the *what happened.*

Connecting to Selections

Have students refer to the Timeline when they begin to read individual selections. By consulting the Timeline regularly, they will gain a better sense of the period's chronology. In addition, they will appreciate what was occurring in the world that gave rise to these works of literature.

Projects

Students can use the Timeline as a launching pad for projects like these:

- **Timeline Follow-up** Have students bring the Timeline up-to-date by drawing an additional column in their notebooks and entering significant new American and world events. These can include new works of literature, scientific achievements, and political events.

- **Oral Reports** Have students choose an item on the Timeline and report to the class on some of its effects. For example, students might report on public reaction to the Vietnam Veterans Memorial, which was dedicated in 1982.

Timeline 1946–Present

1945   1955   1965

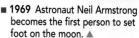
American Events

- **1945** United States grants independence to the Philippines.
- **1949** *Death of a Salesman* by Arthur Miller is first produced.
- **1952** Ralph Ellison publishes *Invisible Man.* ▼
- **1954** Supreme Court rules public school segregation to be unconstitutional.

- **1955** Flannery O'Connor publishes *A Good Man Is Hard to Find.* ▼

- **1959** Alaska and Hawaii admitted to the Union as the 49th and 50th states.
- **1961** Joseph Heller publishes *Catch-22.*
- **1962** Environmental protection movement spurred by Rachel Carson's book *Silent Spring.*
- **1963** President John F. Kennedy assassinated in Dallas.

- **1966** *Ariel,* Sylvia Plath's last collection of poems, appears.
- **1968** Martin Luther King, Jr., civil rights leader, murdered in Memphis.
- **1969** Astronaut Neil Armstrong becomes the first person to set foot on the moon. ▲
- **1972** Last U.S. combat troops leave Vietnam; peace pact signed in 1973. ▶

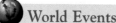
World Events

- **1947** India-Pakistan: India and Pakistan granted independence from Great Britain.
- **1948** Israel: United Nations establishes state of Israel.
- **1948** Germany: Soviet Union blockades Allied sectors of Berlin.
- **1950** England: Doris Lessing publishes *The Grass Is Singing.*
- **1954** England: *Lord of the Flies* by William Golding appears.

- **1956** Argentina: Jorge Luis Borges publishes *Extraordinary Tales.*
- **1957** Ghana: Ghana emerges as independent nation.
- **1957** USSR: *Doctor Zhivago* by Boris Pasternak appears.
- **1959** Germany: East Germany builds Berlin Wall.
- **1961** Cuba: Fidel Castro comes to power.
- **1962** USSR: *One Day in the Life of Ivan Denisovich* by Alexander Solzhenitsyn appears.

- **1967** Israel: Israel gains territory from Arab states in Six-Day War.
- **1969** Northern Ireland: Long period of violence begins between Catholics and Protestants.
- **1972** China: Nixon makes historic visit to China. ▼

958 ◆ *Prosperity and Protest (1946–Present)*

American and World Events

- ■ **1980** Ronald Reagan elected president.
- ■ **1982** Vietnam Veterans Memorial dedicated in Washington, D.C. ▼

CHARLES J GIBILTERRA Jr · LAWRENCE F GREER · WAYNE D GROAT
DAVID F HEISER · DOUGLAS E HOFFMAN · HOMER W HOLLISTER
E L JACKSON · RANDALL E JENKINS · CARL R KECK · ASA MARTIN Jr
LARRY W NEILL · ARTHUR A CALLISTER · RAYMOND NITO RIVERA
ROMERO · PAUL C RUDY · THEODORE M RUSH · RONALD SABIN
JOHN E SENOR · KENNETH H SHELLEMAN · LEONARD D SMITH Jr
A TRESSLER Jr · JAMES B WHITE · RAY M WILLIAMS · JERRY R DAVIS
ISIAH BARNES Jr · RONALD G BAUGHMAN · DONALD C BERRY
O CASSIDY · THOMAS CLARK · OTIS L DARDEN · ALVIN J DERRICK
ANT · GORDON D GARDNER · GARY LEE GLEAR · DENNIS J GULLA
NSEN · LESLIE A JERSTAD · LESTER JOHNSON Jr · WILLIAM R LARKIN
· MICHAEL A MASSONE · WILLIAM H MILLER · RICKEY C C McCOY
MUSSEN · JOHN R REBITS · ROBERT E SHERLOCK · JAMES E SKIPPER
MPLE · JOHN T WALLS · DENNIS R WHICKER · DAVID R AUGUSTUS
HALE A BARNES · ROBERT E BEAUMONT · BENJAMIN H BINEGAR Jr
H BRUBAKER Jr · LEE E BURNSOR · JIMMY O CALL · JAMES D CAMP
· ANTHONY A BARBARINO · JOHN A DURHAM · ROBERT L EATON
J GILDOW · OTIS GREEN · GREGORY J NICCOLI · ANTHONY A KOSTER
· ANTHONY L QUINN · HAROLD R RICHARDSON · JUAN RIVERA
· GERALD L THOMAS · HOUSTON F THOMAS · JAMES W TUCK Jr
WALKER · FRANKIE R WILLIAMS · RAY L GOOD · WILLIAM E BOEHM
BURKHART · JAMES L CLARK · LOUIS E CULVER · JAMES V DORSEY Jr
D · BRUCE B BERNSTEIN · ALVIN GORDON Jr · GERALD J JOHNSON
· GARY R HALEY · ROBERT W HAMLIN · TIMOTHY M HARRINGTON

- ■ **1979** India: Mother Teresa wins Nobel Prize for Peace.
- ■ **1979** Vietnam: Hundreds of thousands of "boat people" flee Vietnam.
- ■ **1979** Trinidad: V. S. Naipaul publishes *A Bend in the River.*
- ■ **1979** England: Margaret Thatcher becomes British prime minister.
- ■ **1981** Poland: Polish trade union movement, Solidarity, suppressed.

- ■ **1987** President Reagan and Soviet leader Mikhail Gorbachev sign the INF treaty, agreeing to ban short-range and medium-range nuclear missiles. ▲
- ■ **1988** George Bush elected president.
- ■ **1990** Congress passes the Americans With Disabilities Act, prohibiting discrimination against people with disabilities.
- ■ **1992** Bill Clinton elected president.
- ■ **1993** Toni Morrison wins Nobel Prize for Literature.

- ■ **1986** USSR: Chernobyl nuclear disaster spreads radioactive cloud across Eastern Europe.
- ■ **1989** Eastern Europe: Berlin Wall comes down.
- ■ **1989** China: Pro-democracy demonstrations violently suppressed at Tiananmen Square.
- ■ **1991** Middle East: Unified forces led by U.S. defeat Iraq in Persian Gulf War.
- ■ **1994** South Africa: Nelson Mandela becomes the first democratically elected president.

- ■ **1995** Amy Tan publishes her third novel, *The Hundred Secret Senses.*
- ■ **1996** Summer Olympic Games held in Atlanta, Georgia.
- ■ **1997** Frank McCourt's autobiography *Angela's Ashes* wins Pulitzer Prize.
- ■ **2000** George W. Bush defeats Al Gore in an extremely close and controversial presidential election.
- ■ **2001** Novelist and short story writer Eudora Welty dies.
- ■ **2001** Hijacked planes crash into the World Trade Center in New York and the Pentagon in Washington, D.C., on the same day. Thousands of lives are lost.

- ■ **1997** China: Hong Kong returns to Chinese rule, ending British rule. ▼

- ■ **1999** Conflict between Albanians and Serbs in Kosovo leads to a war between Serbia and NATO forces. Then, a peace agreement is signed.
- ■ **2001** Serbia: Serbian leader Slobodan Milosevic is arrested.

Analyzing the Timeline

1. **(a)** When did the Supreme Court rule that public school segregation is unconstitutional? **(b)** What is the relationship between that ruling and the civil rights movement of the 1950s and 1960s?
   Answer: (a) The Supreme Court ruling was in 1954. **(b)** Many students will realize that the Brown decision prompted further efforts to integrate schools.

2. **(a)** Name two important public figures who were assassinated during this period. **(b)** What do these events suggest about the decade in which they occurred?
   Answer: (a) John F. Kennedy was assassinated in 1963, and Martin Luther King, Jr. in 1968. **(b)** They suggest that the decade of the 1960s was turbulent.

3. **(a)** Identify two important political events occurring in Eastern Europe in the 1980s. **(b)** Taken together, what story do these events tell about Soviet control of Eastern Europe?
   Answer: (a) In 1981, the Polish trade union movement, Solidarity, was suppressed. In 1989, the Berlin Wall came down. **(b)** The first event suggests that the Soviet Union was having trouble with protest movements. The second suggests that the Soviet Union was coming apart.

4. **(a)** How long after the end of the Vietnam War was the Vietnam Veterans Memorial dedicated? **(b)** Do you think the dedication of the memorial meant that arguments over the war were finally coming to an end?
   Answer: (a) The Vietnam Veterans Memorial was dedicated in 1982, nine years after the peace pact was signed in 1973. **(b)** Some students may speculate that the dedication of a monument meant that some sense of conciliation had been reached. Others may point out that to this day, people disagree about the Vietnam War.

5. What recent events from 2001 and after could be possible entries in a timeline like this one?
   Possible response: The events that students choose should be important turning points, firsts, or milestones in the fields of politics, literature, science, music, or art.

continued

Answers continued

▶**Critical Viewing**

1. What is the mood of the image of the Vietnam Veterans Memorial (1982)? **[Interpret]**
   Possible response: Students may say that the names of the dead overpower the image of the soldier and that the image has a somber, sad mood.

2. **(a)** What is unusual about the flags in the 1987 photo featuring U.S. President Reagan and Soviet leader Gorbachev? **[Make Connections] (b)** How does this add to the moment as the men sign a treaty to ban certain nuclear missiles? **[Assess]**
   Possible response: **(a)** Each leader is sitting in front of the flag of the other's country. **(b)** It suggests that they are not enemies.

3. What are the benefits of using a symbol like the one on the "Handicapped Parking Only" sign (1990)? What are the disadvantages of such a symbol? **[Evaluate]**
   Possible response: Such a symbol can be understood in areas where a number of languages are spoken; however, it suggests that all people with disabilities travel in wheelchairs.

Prosperity and Protest
(1946–Present)

Looking to the future is a natural part of the human experience. Much of the technology that has become widespread since 1945—television and computers in particular—shows us a brighter future. The new technology often makes life easier. Paradoxically, it also introduces complexities that were unknown in earlier days.

The years from the end of World War II to the present day have been a time of change. Great strides have been made in civil rights and women's rights. Popular entertainment has changed dramatically, not just in presentation (for example, from radio to television, from phonograph records to CDs) but also in style (for example, from big bands to rock music and hip-hop). These changes and others have had an effect on American literature.

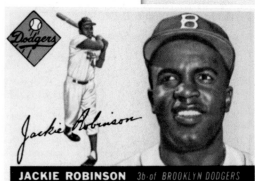

JACKIE ROBINSON 3b-of BROOKLYN DODGERS

▲ Critical Viewing
African Americans could not play baseball in the major leagues until Jackie Robinson broke the color barrier in 1947. What effects—both in sports and in society—did Robinson's breakthrough have? **[Analyze Cause and Effect]**

Historical Background

The United States emerged from World War II as the most powerful nation on Earth. Proud of their role in the Allied victory, Americans now wanted life to return to normal. Soldiers came home, the rationing of scarce goods ended, and the nation prospered. Despite postwar jubilation, however, the dawn of the nuclear age and the dominance of the Soviet Union throughout Eastern Europe meant that nothing would be the same again.

In 1945, the United Nations was created amid high hopes that it would prevent future wars. Nonetheless, the Cold War between the Soviet Union and the West began as soon as World War II ended. It was in Asia, however, that the first armed conflict came. In 1950, President Harry S. Truman sent American troops to help anticommunist South Korean forces turn back a North Korean invasion.

From Quiet Pride to Activism Americans of the 1950s are sometimes referred to as "the Silent Generation." Many of them had lived through both the Great Depression and World War II. When peace finally arrived, they were glad to adopt a quiet, somewhat complacent attitude. They greatly admired President Dwight D. Eisenhower, one of America's wartime heroes.

In October 1957, the Soviet Union launched *Sputnik*, the first artificial satellite to orbit Earth. This Soviet space triumph spurred many people to call

---

for changes in American science and education. President John F. Kennedy, elected in 1960, promised to "get the nation moving again." He had little time to do so, however, before his assassination in 1963.

After Kennedy's assassination came an escalating and increasingly unpopular war in Vietnam. A wave of protest followed. Gone were the calm of the Eisenhower years and the high hopes of Kennedy's brief administration. In their place came idealistic but strident demands for rapid change: greater "relevance" in education, more progress on civil rights, an immediate end to the Vietnam War. It was a time of crisis and confrontations, but it brought a great deal of genuine progress.

Real and lasting gains were made in civil rights after World War II. Segregation in the public schools was outlawed by the Supreme Court in 1954. Tragedy struck in 1968, however, when civil rights leader Martin Luther King, Jr., was assassinated in Memphis, Tennessee. Riots broke out in many cities across the nation.

Point /Counterpoint

The Dropping of the Atomic Bomb on Japan—Inevitable or Unjustifiable?

Was the dropping of the atomic bomb on Japan, an act that introduced the nuclear age, an inevitable event or an unjustifiable decision? Two equally distinguished historians disagree on this important question.

Inevitable Event

"Conceivably, as many would later argue, the Japanese might have surrendered before November and the scheduled invasion. Conceivably, they could have been strangled by naval blockade, forced to surrender by continued fire bombing, with its dreadful toll. . . . But no one close to Truman was telling him not to use the new weapon. General Marshall fully expected the Japanese to fight on even if the bomb were dropped. . . . That it might make the invasion unnecessary was too much to expect. . . . 'Truman made no decision because there was no decision to be made,' recalled George Elsey. . . . 'He could no more have stopped it than a train moving down a track. . . .'"

—*Truman*, David McCullough

Unjustifiable Decision

"The use of the atomic bomb was not really needed to produce this result [the surrender of Japan and the long-awaited end of the war]. With nine-tenths of Japan's shipping sunk or disabled, her air and sea forces crippled, her industries wrecked, and her people's food supplies shrinking fast, her collapse was already certain—as Churchill said.

"The U.S. Strategic Bombing Survey report emphasized this point, while adding: '. . . it seems clear that, even without the atomic bombing attacks, air supremacy could have exerted sufficient pressure to bring about unconditional surrender and obviate the need for invasion.'"

—*History of the Second World War*, B. H. Liddell Hart

Underscore that nuclear weapons—even the first atomic bombs, which were less powerful than today's weapons of mass destruction—proved to be a fearsome force in the modern world. The atomic bombing of Japan can now be seen as heralding in an age of unprecedented fear and anxiety. Then, ask the following questions.

1. What do the two viewpoints have in common? In what ways are they different?
   Possible response: Both viewpoints assume that Japan would ultimately have surrendered whether the bombs were dropped or not. They are different, however, because McCullough states that the surrender was not imminent, while Hart suggests that it was. Also, McCullough's focus is on President Truman, while Hart's is on Japan's condition.

2. Is it possible that both historians are correct? Explain.
   Possible response: Students should notice that Hart argues that Truman *should* have stopped the bombing, while McCullough argues that Truman *could not* have stopped it. Based on these excerpts, then, it is possible that both historians are correct.

3. Identify any effects of the bombing you see in today's world. How might the world be different if it had not happened?
   Possible response: Students may point to the ongoing issues of nuclear weapons and their proliferation as a long-term effect of the bombing—the fears and uncertainties that the bombings gave birth to still plague the world. Others may suggest, however, that the weapons would still exist and pose the same threat even if they had never been used in war.

CUSTOMIZE INSTRUCTION FOR UNIVERSAL ACCESS

For Less Proficient Readers	For English Learners	For Advanced Readers
Have students brainstorm to list issues and trends of contemporary life. After they have developed this framework of prior knowledge, have them look for evidence of these issues and trends in "Prosperity and Protest."	Encourage students to consider key issues and trends of their first cultures in the present. Discuss how these issues and trends compare and contrast with those in contemporary America. Then, as they read "Prosperity and Protest," instruct them to find parallels between their own cultures and that of contemporary America.	Instruct students to create flowcharts that illustrate how American issues and trends evolved from 1946 until the present, becoming the issues and trends that dominate contemporary American society.

Historical Background

Comprehension Check

1. What international organization was created in 1945? Briefly describe this organization's chief goal.

Answer: The United Nations was founded in 1945. Its goal was to prevent future wars.

2. Why are Americans of the 1950s sometimes referred to as "the Silent Generation"?

Answer: Having lived through the Great Depression and World War II, they were glad to live quietly.

3. In what ways did the 1960s differ from the 1950s?

Answer: The 1960s—which saw the assassinations of Kennedy and King and protests against the Vietnam War—were years of crisis and confrontation. The 1950s were characterized by a greater acceptance of things as they were.

4. In the years after World War II, what new medium changed the leisure habits of Americans?

Answer: Television changed the leisure habits of Americans.

5. What type of regions grew most rapidly as a result of the automobile?

Answer: The automobile made possible explosive suburban growth.

Critical Thinking

1. In what ways would America be different without cars and televisions? **[Speculate]**

Possible response: Students may say that more people might travel by public transportation and that there might be more extensive rail lines connecting cities. Also, people might create more of their own entertainment.

2. Is it accurate to describe this era as one of protest? **[Evaluate]**

Possible response: Students who agree will point out the civil rights movement, the women's movement, and the Vietnam War protests. Other students may distinguish among decades, pointing to the 1960s as a time of protest, with various movements continuing past that decade.

continued

Literature of the Period

Variety and Promise The turbulence of contemporary times has contributed to the development of a looseknit variety of approaches known as Postmodernism. Listed here are some of the general ways in which Postmodernism tends to differ from its precursor, Modernism.

Modernism
- Viewed the massive casualties of World War I as undercutting pretensions to rationality and civilization
- Influenced by Freud's studies of the unconscious and a new interest in the art of primitive peoples
- Loss of trust in rationality, balanced by a newfound trust in the artist's ability to glean meaning from the irrational
- Confidence that the work of art is a unique and powerful creation with its own individual aura or atmosphere
- Tendency to view the work of art as a perfected product rather than as an incomplete and ongoing process
- Some confidence in the truth of the Renaissance notion that a great work of art is immortal and ensures immortality for its author
- Belief that "high" culture and "low" culture are separated by a meaningful dividing line and that a work of fine art is inherently superior to a cartoon

Postmodernism
- Viewed World War II, with the Holocaust and the dropping of the A-bomb, as undercutting assumptions of life's meaning
- Influenced by studies of media and language and by the explosive growth of information technology
- Some loss of trust in the artist's ability to access the irrational and return with a sense of renewal and greater meaning
- Less confidence that the work of art is unique, coupled with a sense that culture endlessly duplicates and copies itself
- Greater interest in the work of art as a process that reflects on its own making as it evolves
- Loss of confidence in the Renaissance notion that a great work of art is immortal and ensures immortality for its author
- Loss of belief in the meaningful dividing line between "high" culture and "low" culture, so that in Pop Art, the subject matter of fine art can be a cartoon

In the spirit of Postmodernism, some writers have explored new literary forms and techniques, composing works from dialogue alone, creating works that blend fiction and nonfiction, and experimenting with the physical appearance of their work. Still other writers, using more traditional forms, have focused on capturing the essence of contemporary life in the content of their works, addressing the impersonal and commercial nature of today's world.

Critical Thinking continued

3. What is the single most important development of this era? Explain. **[Support]**

Possible response: Students should justify the importance of whatever issue or trend they choose to emphasize. For example, students might point to the civil rights movement as an attempt to fulfill the founders' promise of equality for all.

A Quest for Stability The upheavals of the 1960s brought a conservative reaction. Many Americans longed for a return to "the good old days." President Richard M. Nixon, elected in 1968, promised to end the Vietnam War and to restore order in the nation. Nixon's achievements were soon overshadowed by the Watergate affair—the burglarizing of Democratic Party headquarters under the direction of Nixon government officials. This scandal forced his resignation from the presidency in 1974.

Civil rights activism continued during the 1970s, and another movement attracted growing attention—the women's liberation movement. Although women had earned the right to vote in 1920, discrimination still existed. Women received lower pay than men did for the same jobs, and promotion was more difficult. Betty Friedan's *The Feminine Mystique*, published in 1963, called for change. The women's movement grew steadily throughout the 1970s.

After Jimmy Carter's one-term presidency in the late 1970s, the nation sent Ronald Reagan to the White House. A former film star and governor of California, Reagan proved a popular and persuasive president. His reelection in 1984 was one of the biggest landslide victories in American history. In 1988, George Bush, Reagan's vice president, was elected to the presidency. Seeking reelection in 1992, Bush faced a tough fight against high unemployment, a recession, growing dissatisfaction with government, and his youthful opponent. Democrat Bill Clinton and his running mate, Al Gore—the youngest ticket in American history—won the election. Despite the 1994 elections that voted many Democratic Congress members out of office, Clinton won reelection in 1996. However, in 2000, Al Gore lost to George Bush's son, George W. Bush, in an election that was extremely controversial.

The Changing Scene Commercial television was still in its infancy at the end of World War II, but it was on the verge of spectacular growth. Over the next few years, television changed the leisure habits of Americans.

The postwar period was a time of explosive suburban growth, made possible by the automobile. At first, most suburban homeowners worked in a city and commuted to their jobs by train, bus, or car. Then, major corporations began establishing suburban headquarters, and workers could live nearby or commute short distances from one suburb to another. Even more recently, advanced technology has allowed people to "telecommute," or work in home offices and stay connected by Internet, phone, and fax.

The world has changed dramatically since 1945, and it is still changing. One of the most dramatic examples is the development of the Internet in a few short years from a military and scientific communication system to a global information network. The changes have had an impact on the literature of the time, although this impact has not always been obvious.

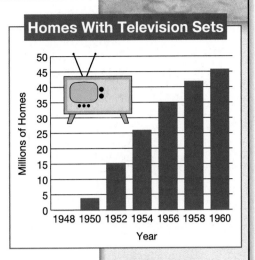

Homes With Television Sets

▲ Critical Viewing
Before 1950, television was a novelty. By the end of the decade, however, television sets were a common feature in American homes. What factors might have influenced the steady rise in television ownership? **[Draw Conclusions]**

Introduction ◆ 963

Background

Postmodernism

Postmodernism involved a significant change of focus for American literature, away from the certainty of carefully crafted art and towards the process of creating. This shift is reflected in the literary scholarship of the time. Drawing on and responding to the ideas of such European critics as Jacques Derrida and Michel Foucault, such American *deconstructionists* as Paul de Man and J. Hillis Miller turned their attention to the uncertainties of language and literature. Some other critics examined historical contexts of literature; still others took literary criticism into political directions. Postmodernism in literary criticism may be as varied as in literature itself.

Background

Postmodern Architecture

Postmodernism was not limited to literature. The movement flourished in other arts, including architecture. Modernist architecture had been simple, pure, and even utopian; postmodern architecture rebelled against this. Architectural postmodernism emerged in the United States, when modernist apartment buildings in St. Louis, Missouri, were demolished in 1972. The postmodern buildings drew on commercial architecture and art, as well as incorporating historical references. Robert Venturi was a major critic of modernist architecture, and he and his partner, John Rauch, were leading proponents of the new style, building houses in New York and Colorado.

▶Critical Viewing

Possible response: The steady rise in television ownership might have resulted from falling prices, improving technology, increased advertising, and appealing programs.

✳ ENRICHMENT: Social Studies

The Civil Rights Movement

After scoring major legal victories through the 1950s, including the famous decision in the *Brown v. Board of Education* case (see the note on p. 960), the civil rights movement gained support in the 1960s. African Americans and others attempted to end segregation and secure voting rights in the South. This battle was hard fought and sometimes violent, but it began to produce results by the mid-1960s. With desegregation progressing, the movement began to focus on economic injustice in cities.

Martin Luther King, Jr., was perhaps the most important leader in the civil rights movement. Both his father and grandfather were ministers, and he followed in their footsteps. He was also influenced by the teachings of the Indian leader Mohandas Gandhi, who believed that strong foes could be vanquished through nonviolence.

Ask students why King chose a nonviolent approach. Possible response: It is morally preferable to avoid violence. Also, when you are in the minority, it makes strategic sense to appeal to people's better instincts.

Answer: In 1950, the ratio of women's income to men's was about $800 to $1200, or 2/3. In 1975, the ratio was $4000 to $6500, which is less than 2/3. Although the ratios seem to remain relatively constant, the difference between men's and women's income in 1950 was $400, while the difference grew to $2500 in 1975.

Background

Southern Writers

The South experienced a literary awakening between the world wars, in the heyday of Nobel Prize–winner William Faulkner. Writers emerging in the region after World War II inherited Faulkner's legacy. Flannery O'Connor was among the most prominent southern writers of the period. O'Connor captured southern social mores in richly detailed short stories. Students can find O'Connor's "The Life You Save May Be Your Own" on p. 973. Students may wish to compare her work with that of another southern writer, Eudora Welty. Welty's "A Worn Path" appears in Unit 5 on p. 820.

Background

Post-War Writers

A number of the new American writers who emerged after World War II brought absurdity, dark humor, and grim fantasy into their work. Such novelists as Joseph Heller and Kurt Vonnegut, Jr., portrayed the war in unrealistic terms, using absurdism to respond to its horrors. The atomic bomb and the rapidly escalating nuclear arms race that it heralded drove more American writers toward black humor and fantasy. These styles and concerns are reflected in the absurdist fables of Thomas Pynchon.

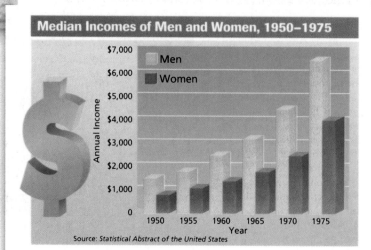

Median Incomes of Men and Women, 1950–1975
Source: Statistical Abstract of the United States

◄ **Critical Viewing** Between 1950 and 1975, women's incomes continued to lag behind men's earnings, partly because many low-paying fields such as nursing and teaching were traditionally considered "women's work." Did the income gap increase or decrease between 1950 and 1975? **[Analyze]**

Authors for a New Era Although contemporary writers have produced a wide variety of impressive works, it is all but impossible to predict which writers will achieve lasting fame and which will not. Time is needed to certify greatness. Modern readers and critics have their favorites, of course. Some of them will undoubtedly become part of America's enduring literary legacy.

Every writer owes a debt to those writers who have gone before. In that sense, literature is cumulative. The earliest American literature, except for that of the Native Americans, was based on European models. Writers in the United States today can look to a rich heritage of their own. Contemporary novelists are well aware of Nathaniel Hawthorne, Mark Twain, Ernest Hemingway, and William Faulkner. Short-story writers know Edgar Allan Poe, Willa Cather, and Eudora Welty. Poets study Emily Dickinson, Walt Whitman, and Langston Hughes. Playwrights are familiar with Eugene O'Neill and Thornton Wilder.

Renowned contemporary novelists include Carson McCullers, Norman Mailer, Bernard Malamud, John Updike, Flannery O'Connor, Joyce Carol Oates, Anne Tyler, and Alice Walker. Many of these novelists have written short stories as well. Flannery O'Connor and John Updike are modern masters of the short-story form. Other writers, such as Donald Barthelme and Ann Beattie, have written novels but are better known for their short stories. Isaac Bashevis Singer, a Polish-born New Yorker who wrote in Yiddish, was famous for both his novels and his short stories. He won the Nobel Prize for Literature in 1978. John Cheever, a respected novelist, won the Pulitzer Prize for Fiction in 1979 for his collected short stories, many of which concern suburban life.

Just as Realism and Romanticism have tended to merge in recent literature, so, curiously, have fiction and nonfiction. Truman Capote's *In Cold Blood*, published in 1966, was billed as a "nonfiction novel." Capote, primarily a novelist and short-story writer, used fictional techniques to analyze a real and

---

✳ ENRICHMENT: Humanities Connection

The Music of Aaron Copland

Tell students that Aaron Copland (1900–1990) is widely regarded as America's greatest composer. His works range from jazz- and blues-influenced compositions to orchestral pieces to ballets reflecting the influence of folk music.

Appalachian Spring, a ballet composed in 1944, is one of Copland's most popular works. It tells the story of a "pioneer celebration of Spring in a newly built farmhouse in Pennsylvania in the early 1800s." In one movement, Copland celebrates a young couple's new

life together. Based on the Shaker hymn "Simple Gifts," the movement is a theme with variations, the theme being introduced by a solo clarinet and each variation becoming more elaborate.

If possible, find a recording of *Appalachian Spring* and play an excerpt for students—possibly the "Simple Gifts" movement described above. Have students discuss what is specifically American about this work. Guide them to recognize that the melodies come from old American songs.

seemingly senseless crime. Later authors, such as E. L. Doctorow in his novel *Ragtime*, combined historical figures with purely fictional characters. This technique has aroused some controversy.

Increasing attention has been paid recently to the place of nonfiction in the literary hierarchy. The essay has always been considered an important literary form, and some outstanding essays are published every year. James Baldwin and John McPhee are accomplished essayists. Among the many notable longer works of nonfiction are Paul Theroux's *The Great Railway Bazaar*, N. Scott Momaday's *The Names*, and Barry Lopez's *Arctic Dreams*.

Poetry Within the Tradition A number of the famed prewar poets continued to publish extensively after the war. Robert Frost, Marianne Moore, Wallace Stevens, E. E. Cummings, William Carlos Williams, and Ezra Pound all produced major collections of their works.

During the late 1940s and the 1950s, many poets starting out in the shadow of these great names were content to work within the technical boundaries established in the earlier part of the century. Nevertheless, poets like Theodore Roethke and Elizabeth Bishop created important and memorable work. Roethke, a master of poetic rhythm, was deeply influenced by his father, a strong-willed greenhouse owner in Saginaw, Michigan. The best of Roethke's poems recall his childhood life in and around the greenhouse. Bishop's poems are beautifully crafted, with precise and memorable descriptions that sometimes suggest realities beyond the physical.

Art in the Historical Context

California Artist Wayne Thiebaud

After World War II, Abstract Expressionists like Jackson Pollock inaugurated Postmodernist painting with works that seemed to be "about" their own making and whose swirls and shapes represented an inner rather than an outer reality. In California, however, a group of painters admired the energy of abstract work but wanted to use it in depicting what critic Donald Goddard called "California scenes filled with California light."

One of these artists was Wayne Thiebaud, a former cartoonist and designer. In his earlier work, Thiebaud demonstrated a fascination with such objects as shoes, ties, and ice cream cones. These paintings influenced the movement known as Pop Art. In later works, Thiebaud depicted landscapes. His San Francisco landscapes, like this one, render cityscapes in abstract terms but also capture "California light" and, in the roller-coaster swoop of a hill, convey a sense of surprise.

▶ **Critical Viewing** Which specific features in this painting suggest that Thiebaud was influenced by painters who use only abstract forms? Explain. **[Analyze]**

Corner Apartments (Down 18th Street), 1980, Wayne Thiebaud, at Hirshhorn Museum, Smithsonian Institution

Background
Art

Corner Apartments (Down 18th Street), by Wayne Thiebaud

Thiebaud was born in Arizona in 1920. After working at a wide range of different jobs, including three years in the Air Force painting murals for the military, he began a career as an artist in 1947.

Thiebaud is best known in California, where he had his first solo exhibition in 1951. He has studied and taught at California universities. Although his most famous work captures such subjects as cakes and pastries in bright, striking colors, he has also painted a number of cityscapes such as this one.

▶**Critical Viewing**

The tall geometric shapes of the buildings echo those of the roads and emphasize the formal, abstract qualities of these structures rather than their realistic details.

✷ ENRICHMENT: Humanities Connection

Rock and Roll

Tell students that after World War II, the United States entered a period of economic prosperity and rapid change. In what is popularly referred to as "The Baby Boom," the population expanded dramatically, altering the age balance of the American people. Making up an increasingly large percentage of the population, American teenagers became a major social and economic force.

The emerging economic importance of young Americans prompted major changes in popular entertainment. Among these was the development of rock-and-roll, a rebellious new type of music. "Rock Around the Clock," released in 1955 by Bill Haley and the Comets, was one of the earliest rock-and-roll hits.

If possible, find a recording of "Rock Around the Clock" and play it for students. Then, ask them how the song expresses the rebelliousness of early rock-and-roll.

Possible response: Its quick, insistent rhythms and lyrics advocating all-night dancing are rebellious.

Tell students that poetry experienced a renaissance in the 1990s, with many Americans becoming more aware of this art form. Signs of this renaissance include the broadcast of Bill Moyers's television show about poets and poetry, *The Language of Life*; the increasing popularity of poetry readings, including contests known as poetry slams; and the activism of poetry organizations like Poets House in New York, with its archive of literary magazines, schedule of readings, and outreach program for libraries and high schools.

Tell students that poetry often appears in small literary magazines before it is collected and published in books. Explain that thousands of these magazines are published throughout the country, including *Beloit Poetry Journal* (Maine), *Atlanta Review* (Georgia), *Threepenny Review* (California), and *Descant* (Texas), to name just a few. There is even a poetry magazine on the Internet, *Poetry Daily*, featuring a new poem each day.

Background

Art

Show students the Asian Women United Commemorative Quilt, on Transparency 11 in **Fine Art Transparencies, Volume 1**. Use the image to help students appreciate that diversity and the assertion of ethnic identity have been issues in the visual arts as well as in literature.

A Living Tradition

A. R. Ammons, Emersonian Postmodernist

A. R. Ammons, a North Carolinian, brought the verve of Southern speech to poetry. In a long, outrageous poem humorously entitled *Garbage* (1993), Ammons takes trash—or the reprocessing of it—as a symbol of our times. Unlike Modernists who strove to create poems as perfect, well-constructed artifacts, Ammons, in good Postmodernist style, creates a talky, sprawling, shifting poem that is itself like a trash heap and that considers, among so many other things, its own making.

Emerson might have blinked and rubbed his eyes hard if he could have read this poem. However, he also might have recognized in it his own, distinctly American belief in renewal. He wrote in his essay "Compensation": "And such should be the outward biography of man in time, a putting off of dead circumstances day by day, as he renews his raiment day by day. . . ."

from *Garbage* by A. R. Ammons

garbage has to be the poem of our time because
garbage is spiritual, believable enough

to get our attention, getting in the way, piling
up, stinking, turning brooks brownish and

creamy white: what else deflects us from the
errors of our illusionary ways . . .

     *   *   **

. . . here the driver knows,

where the consummations gather, where the disposal
flows out of form, where the last translations

cast away their immutable bits and scraps,
flits of steel, shivers of bottle and tumbler,

here is the gateway to beginning, here the portal
of renewing change . . .

New Directions in Poetry However, some poets challenged the boundaries of the art. Allen Ginsberg and A.R. Ammons, inspired by the work of William Carlos Williams, wrote bolder, more sprawling poems. In a Postmodernist spirit, Ginsberg's *Howl* and Ammons's *Tape for the Turn of the Year* and *Garbage* engaged powerfully with contemporary realities, dramatic and mundane alike. They dared to take in more confusion and chaos, even at the expense of their own apparent "perfection" as works of art.

The Literature of Personal and Group Identity Robert Lowell, a great-nephew of the poet James Russell Lowell, began his career in the postwar years as a creator of powerful, though traditional, poems. However, in the late 1950s, he began to reread William Carlos Williams. The result was *Life Studies*, a breakthrough book in which Lowell abandoned tight, traditional forms and opened his work to the frustrations and confusions of his own personal and family history. Lowell was followed by others who revealed personal secrets, like Anne Sexton and Sylvia Plath. Rightly or wrongly, they were dubbed "confessional poets."

The tumultuous 1960s brought great changes in behavior and awareness—the civil rights movement, the protests against the Vietnam War, and the women's movement are three examples—that affected the subject matter of all literature. In poetry, as in fiction, these changes inspired a movement that encouraged the proud assertion and passionate exploration of personal, ethnic, and racial identity. It is important to realize, however, that this flowering of work that began in the 1960s, and still continues, had its roots in earlier decades. For example, African American poet Rita Dove, who won a Pulitzer Prize for *Thomas and Beulah* in 1986, could certainly acknowledge a debt to Robert Hayden and to Gwendolyn Brooks, who in 1950, became the first African American writer to win a Pulitzer Prize for her book *Annie Allen*.

Other writers in this rainbow movement are Native Americans N. Scott Momaday, also a Pulitzer Prize winner, and Joy Harjo; Asian Americans Maxine Hong Kingston, Amy Tan, and Garret Hongo; and Latino and Latina writers Martín Espada, Sandra Cisneros, and Julia Alvarez. Adrienne Rich, strongly influenced by the women's movement, began changing her poetry in mid-career, loosening her formal structures and dealing with previously unexpressed conflicts and aspirations of women.

These and other writers are proving that, in literature as in society, America's strength lies in its diversity. Although it is too early to assess their achievements, it seems likely that some of the works they are producing today will become the classics of tomorrow.

Beyond the Horizon

One of the features of literary evolution is its unpredictability: No one knows in which direction it will develop next. Of this, however, we can be reasonably sure: The novel is not dead, as some were proclaiming in the 1950s and 1960s. Poetry is not dead, nor is the short story. Literature has great resilience. While it may be profoundly influenced by other media—radio, television, film—it has not been replaced by them. Indeed, for sheer technical virtuosity, there has probably never been a more impressive group of American writers at work than at the present time.

▼ **Critical Viewing**
In a few short years, the Internet has become an accepted part of American life. What benefits does it offer and what problems, if any, does it pose? **[Make a Judgment]**

Introduction ◆ 967

▶**Critical Viewing**
Possible response: Students will likely be familiar with many of the benefits of the Internet, such as easy long-distance communication and its value as a research tool and entertainment medium. Some students may say that people find the Internet a cause for concern because children can use it to access information that their parents might not want them to see. Others may point to issues such as problems in retaining control of intellectual property.

Literature of the Period
Comprehension Check

1. In what way does the literature of this era differ from that written in the earlier part of the twentieth century?
   Answer: Our time has not seen a literary revolution of the kind that occurred in the 1920s.

2. What new type of book did Truman Capote create?
   Answer: He created the nonfiction novel, which blends fiction and fact.

3. Name three important fiction writers from this era.
   Answer: Important fiction writers include Carson McCullers, Norman Mailer, Bernard Malamud, John Updike, Flannery O'Connor, Joyce Carol Oates, and Alice Walker, among others.

4. What important contemporary poet was a descendant of a well-known nineteenth-century poet?
   Answer: Robert Lowell was a great-nephew of James Russell Lowell.

5. What type of prose has received increased attention in recent years?
   Answer: Nonfiction and the essay have received increased attention.

Critical Thinking

1. What trends in the history of this era explain the greater diversity among authors? **[Analyze Cause and Effect]**
   Possible response: Students may point out that this was an era of protest, in which various groups asserted their identities and claimed their rights. The increased diversity among authors represents a literary reflection of these times.

continued

Critical Thinking continued

2. Why do you think that the turbulence of this era did not foster a literary revolution of the kind that occurred in the 1920s? **[Speculate]**
   Possible response: Students may argue that issues of identity and self-assertion took precedence over literary experimentation.

3. Do you think that advances in computer technology will eventually lead to the disappearance of books? In other words, will literature be written for the screen? **[Analyze Cause and Effect]**

Possible response: Some students may feel that the book is a resilient medium that will co-exist with computers. Other, more technologically oriented students may believe that the computer is bringing about an information revolution comparable to that created by the invention of printed books in 1450. In any case, students should support their answers with facts and examples.

1. At what time in American history have the most words been added to the language? Support your answer. **[Support]**
Possible response: Students may respond that more words are added in the present than at any other time. The essay mentions that 5,000 words are added per year, and science and technology are advancing more dramatically now than ever.

2. What current developments in American society do you think will produce many new words in the future? Explain. **[Speculate]**
Possible response: Students may point to any of a number of technological or medical developments in progress. Rapidly advancing communication technology is a likely response, as is the field of medications for mental health. Students should support their responses with examples.

Activities

1. *Home page* is constructed from the English words *home*, from the Old English, and *page*, from the Latin. *Inkjet* is put together from *ink*, from the Medieval English, and *jet*, from the French word *jeter*, "to throw." *Laptop* is put together from *lap*, from the Old English word for a folding part of a garment, and *top*, from the Old English for a tuft of hair.

2. *Black hole* is formed from the English words *black*, from the Old English for "burn," and *hole*, from the Old English for "hollow." *Camcorder* is formed from *camera*, from the Latin word for "vault," and *recorder*, from the Latin word for "remember." *Supercluster* is formed from *super*, from the Latin for "above," and *cluster*, from Medieval English.

THE DEVELOPMENT OF AMERICAN ENGLISH
Brave New Words

BY RICHARD LEDERER

The history of a living language like English is a history of constant change. Language is like a tree that sheds its leaves and grows new ones so that it may live on. New words, like new leaves, are essential to a living, healthy vocabulary.

A language draws its nutrients from the environment in which its speakers live. This growth is not new to English. Throughout history, as English speakers and writers have met with new objects, experiences, and ideas, they have needed new words to describe them. Nowadays, an average of 5,000 new words enter our language each year!

In almost every case, we cobble these new words from already existing word-making materials called morphemes. Morphemes are prefabricated bits of meaning from which words are made.

The Anglo-Saxons, who were the earliest speakers of our language, used a vivid term to describe the great wealth of English. They called it *word-hoard*. This stock of words grows considerably with each new development in science, medicine, and technology.

One of the major technologies of our lives is the computer. As the wonders of the computer have unfolded, we have acquired a new *user-friendly* (a compound composed of Latin and Anglo-Saxon word parts) vocabulary by piecing together morphemes from Latin, Greek, and early English.

We English speakers needed a name for the system of networks that connects computers around the world. So we combined the Latin prefix *inter*, "together," with the Anglo-Saxon word for a mesh fabric, and — presto! — we came up with the *Internet*. Then, we required a name for the complete set of documents on all Internet servers. So we mixed three Anglo-Saxon words into — ta da! — the World Wide Web.

The growing study of life on other worlds we have labeled astrobiology or exobiology, from the Greek word parts *astro* ("star") and *exo* ("outer") + *bio* ("life") + *logy* ("study of").

We have been aware of genes for more than a century, but only recently have scientists studied whole sets of genes and their interactions. The entire chomosomal makeup of an organism we now call the *genome* — a blend of two Greek words, *gen(e)* and *(chromos)ome*. The same blend names the field — *genomics*.

Over the past few decades, we have acquired countless new words for the brave new worlds of science, technology, and medicine. Scientific and medical breakthroughs seem to make the headlines almost every day, but our English "word-hoard" will never run out of prefixes, suffixes, and roots to identify these new concepts.

ACTIVITIES

1. Identify the word parts and original languages of these computer terms: *home page*, *inkjet*, and *laptop*.
2. Identify the word parts and original languages of these scientific terms: *black hole*, *camcorder*, and *supercluster*.

Literature Confronts the Everyday

Television Moon, 1978-79, Alfred Leslie, Wichita Art Museum, Wichita, Kansas

Selection Planning Guide

The writers whose work appears in this section reveal the variety of angles from which one can view everyday events. Both O'Connor's "The Life You Save May Be Your Own" and Malamud's "The First Seven Years" ask readers to consider the level of honesty between strangers, acquaintances, and co-workers. Updike's "The Brown Chest" presents the objects a family treasures, and Walker's "Everyday Use" challenges students to decide the value of such family heirlooms. Essays by Nye and Harjo reveal that ordinary happenings can be momentous. Finally, poetry by Cervantes, Espada, Ortiz, Chang, and Hongo suggests the filter that ethnicity and personal experience bring to the daily tasks of living.

Background

Art

***Television Moon, 1978–1979,* by Alfred Leslie**

Like the writers of this period, Alfred Leslie has chosen an ordinary subject for this still life, adding significance to an otherwise mundane piece of furniture. Leslie converts the broad landscapes of earlier American artists into a limited, dim rendering shown on a television screen. Instead of facing the frontier through rugged exploration, citizens can now passively examine the landscape without leaving their armchairs.

Link the art to the theme of Part 1, "Literature Confronts the Everyday," with the following questions:

1. What might the artist be saying about America by focusing on the mundane items shown in this painting?
   Possible response: Americans are caught up in daily trivia and material goods, rather than focusing on more important issues.

2. Would this painting be a good one to include in a time capsule to show future generations? Explain.
   Possible response: Students who say "yes" might point to the way the painting accurately records the television at the center of many American lives; students who say "no" might argue that the painting overemphasizes the trivial, that other things not shown here are more important to Americans.

TOMIZE INSTRUCTION FOR UNIVERSAL ACCESS

n assigning the selections in this part, keep in mind these factors:

Life You Save May Be Your Own"
- ccessible story will appeal to almost all students

First Seven Years"
- harming piece will spark discussions about ndependence

thorne," "Gold Glade," "The Light Comes ter," "The Adamant"
- bstract concepts may make these poems diffi- ult for less proficient readers.

from *The Names,* "Mint Snowball," "Suspended"
- Three brief selections will appeal to students of all levels.
- Musical/rhythmic learners may especially relate to "Suspended."

"Everyday Use"
- Interpersonal learners will find sympathetic characters that bring the conflict in this story to life.

969

The Life You Save May Be Your Own

Lesson Objectives

1. **To analyze and respond to literary elements**
   - Literary Analysis: Grotesque Characters
   - Connecting Literary Elements: Direct and Indirect Characterization

2. **To read, comprehend, analyze, and critique a short story**
   - Reading Strategy: Making Predictions
   - Reading Check questions
   - Review and Assess questions
   - Assessment Practice (ATE)

3. **To develop word analysis skills, fluency, and systematic vocabulary**
   - Vocabulary Development Lesson: Latin Word Root: -sol-

4. **To understand and apply written and oral language conventions**
   - Spelling Strategy
   - Grammar and Style Lesson: Subjunctive Mood

5. **To understand and apply appropriate writing and research strategies**
   - Writing Lesson: Deposition
   - Extension Activity: Body Language Presentation

6. **To understand and apply listening and speaking strategies**
   - Extension Activity: Readers Theatre

STEP-BY-STEP TEACHING GUIDE	PACING GUIDE
PRETEACH	
Motivate Students and Provide Background	
Use the Motivation activity (ATE p. 970)	5 min.
Read and discuss author and background features (SE/ATE pp. 970, 973) [A]	10 min.
Introduce the Concepts	
Introduce the Literary Analysis and Reading Strategy (SE/ATE p. 971) [A]	15 min.
Pronounce the vocabulary words and read their definitions (SE p. 971)	5 min.
TEACH	
Monitor Comprehension	
Informally monitor comprehension by circulating while students read independently or in groups [A]	45 min.
Monitor students' comprehension with the Reading Check notes (SE/ATE pp. 973, 975, 977, 979, 981)	as students read
Develop vocabulary with Vocabulary notes (SE pp. 973, 975, 977, 980,982)	as students read
Develop Understanding	
Develop students' understanding of grotesque characters with the Literary Analysis annotations (SE pp. 974, 976, 978, 979, 980; ATE pp. 973,974,976,978,979, 980) [A]	10 min.
Develop students' ability to make predictions about events in the reading by using the Reading Strategy annotations (SE pp. 975, 976, 979, 980; ATE pp. 975, 976, 979, 980)	5 min.
ASSESS	
Assess Mastery	
Assess students' mastery of the Reading Strategy and Literary Analysis by having them answer the Review and Assess questions (SE/ATE p. 983)	15 min.
Use one or more of the print and media Assessment Resources (ATE p. 985) [A]	up to 45 min.
EXTEND	
Apply Understanding	
Have students complete the Vocabulary Development Lesson and the Grammar and Style Lesson (SE p. 984) [A]	20 min.
Apply students' ability to use transitions to show cause and effect by using the Writing Lesson (SE/ATE, p. 985) [A]	45 min.
Apply students' understanding using one or more of the Extension Activities (SE p. 985)	20–90 min.

[A] ACCELERATED INSTRUCTION:
Use the strategies and activities identified with an [A].

UNIVERSAL ACCESS
- ● = Below Level Students
- ▲ = On-Level Students
- ■ = Above Level Students

Time and Resource Manager

Reading Level: Average
Average Number of Instructional Days: 4

RESOURCES		
PRINT	**TRANSPARENCIES**	**TECHNOLOGY**
• **Beyond Literature,** Career Connection: Human Resources Interview, p. 55 ▲ ■		• **Interest Grabber Video,** Tape 6 ● ▲ ■
• **Selection Support Workbook:** ● ▲ ■ Literary Analysis, p. 245 Reading Strategy, p. 244 Build Vocabulary, p. 242	• **Literary Analysis and Reading Transparencies,** pp. 113 and 114 ● ▲ ■	
		• **Listening to Literature** ● ▲ ■ Audiocassettes, Side 33 Audio CDs, CD 19
• **Literatura en español** ● ▲ • **Literary Analysis for Enrichment** ■		
• **Formal Assessment:** Selection Test, pp. 248–250 ● ▲ ■ • **Open Book Test,** pp. 163–165 ● ▲ ■ • **Performance Assessment and Portfolio Management,** p. 20 ● ▲ ■ • **PRENTICE HALL ASSESSMENT SYSTEM** ● ▲ ■	• **PRENTICE HALL ASSESSMENT SYSTEM** ● ▲ ■ Skills Practice Answers and Explanations on Transparencies	• **Test Bank Software** ● ▲ ■ • **Got It! Assessment Videotapes,** Tape 5 ● ▲
• **Selection Support Workbook:** ● ▲ ■ Grammar and Style, p. 243 • **Writing and Grammar,** Ruby Level ● ▲ ■ • **Extension Activities,** p. 55 ● ▲ ■	• **Daily Language Practice Transparencies** ● ▲	• **Writing and Grammar iText CD-ROM** ● ▲ ■ **Take It to the Net** www.phschool.com

BLOCK SCHEDULING: Use one 90-minute class period to preteach the selection and have students read it. Use a second 90-minute class period to assess students' mastery of skills and have them complete one of the Extension Activities.

Motivation

The title of this story is a slogan that once commonly appeared on American highways. Such slogans—like this story—challenge readers' consciences and try to raise their moral standards. To spark students' interest in the story, post the title along with other common slogans, such as anti-drug or safety belt warnings. Discuss the motives to which these slogans appeal. Invite students to predict what this story may reveal about human nature.

▣ Interest Grabber Video

As an alternative, play "Flannery O'Connor" on Tape 6 to engage students' interest.

❶ Background

More About the Author

In 1954, "The Life You Save May Be Your Own" won an O. Henry award for being one of the best short stories of the year. Flannery O'Connor was to win this award four more times—for "A Circle in the Fire," *Everything That Rises Must Converge*, "Greenleaf," and "Revelation." Like "The Life You Save," these stories share rural Southern settings, grotesque characters, moments of epiphany, religious symbols, and profound irony.

Prepare to Read

❶ The Life You Save May Be Your Own

Flannery O'Connor (1925–1964)

Flannery O'Connor's work reflects her intense commitment to her personal beliefs. In her exaggerated, tragic, and at times shockingly violent tales, she forces readers to confront such human faults as hypocrisy, insensitivity, self-centeredness, and prejudice. Many of her stories revolve around death and exhibit a dark sense of humor. Some critics have objected to the presence of such comic doom in her fiction, but O'Connor felt that she was portraying the world accurately. She once said, "People are always complaining that the modern novelist has no hope and that the picture he paints of the world is unbearable. The only answer to this is that people without hope do not write novels."

The Habit of Art Born in Savannah, Georgia, Flannery O'Connor was raised in the small Georgia town of Milledgeville. She earned her undergraduate degree from Georgia State College for Women and then left her home state to attend the celebrated University of Iowa Writers' Workshop. While still in graduate school, she published her first short story, "Geranium."

In 1950, O'Connor became ill with lupus, a serious disease that restricted her independence. She moved back to the family farm outside Milledgeville, where she lived with her mother. "I have never been anywhere but sick," she wrote. "In a sense, sickness is a place more instructive than a trip to Europe." Despite her illness, O'Connor committed herself not only to her writing but also to "the habit of art," an enlivened way of thinking and seeing. In 1952, at the age of twenty-seven, she published her first novel, *Wise Blood*, the story of a violent rivalry among members of a fictional religious sect in the South. In 1955, she published her first collection of stories, *A Good Man Is Hard to Find*. It was followed by a second novel, *The Violent Bear It Away* (1960), and *Everything That Rises Must Converge* (1965), another collection of short stories.

A Triumphant Spirit Throughout most of her adult life, O'Connor lived with physical pain and the awareness that she would probably die young. Despite her condition, she often seemed joyous, entertaining friends at home and painting watercolors of the peacocks that she and her mother raised on the farm. Still, her disease set her apart from other people, and O'Connor felt a deep sense of kinship with eccentrics and outsiders. In her fiction, she often portrays those who are outcast or suffering. Many of her characters are social misfits or people who are physically or mentally challenged. Although she paints these characters in an unsentimental way, O'Connor brings to their stories an underlying sense of sympathy, which reflects both her own physical problems and her strong Catholic faith.

Religious Faith Flannery O'Connor was raised as a devout Catholic in a region of the American South that was predominantly Protestant. She considered herself a religious writer in a world that had abandoned true religious values. In an effort to point out the spiritual failings of the modern world, O'Connor often highlights characters with powerfully stated convictions but dubious moral and intellectual capabilities. "The Life You Save May Be Your Own" is a typical O'Connor work. In its grim depiction of a group of outcasts with sharply exaggerated physical characteristics and personality traits, the story conveys shrewd insights, a powerful moral message, and an urgent sense of the tragic realities of life in the modern world.

TEACHING RESOURCES

The following resources can be used to enrich or extend the instruction for pp. 970–971.

Motivation

▣ **Interest Grabber Video,** Tape 6

Background

📖 **Beyond Literature,** p. 55 ▪

🖼 **Take It to the Net**
Visit www.phschool.com for Background and hotlinks for "The Life You Save May Be Your Own."

Literary Analysis

🖼 **Literary Analysis and Reading Transparencies,** Grotesque Characters, p. 110 ▪

Reading

📖 **Selection Support:** Reading Strategy, p. 244; Build Vocabulary, p. 242

🖼 **Literary Analysis and Reading Transparencies,** Making Predictions, p. 109

▪ BLOCK SCHEDULING: Resources marked with this symbol provide varied instruction during 90-minute blocks.

Preview

Connecting to the Literature

In this story, a stranger appears at a remote farm where an elderly widow lives alone with her unmarried daughter. The woman must decide whether or not to trust the drifter. Similar decisions confront all of us as strangers enter our lives as potential friends or enemies.

❷ Literary Analysis

Grotesque Characters

The word *grotesque* in literature does not mean ugly or disgusting, as it sometimes does in popular speech. In literature, the **grotesque character** is one who has become bizarre or twisted, usually through some kind of obsession. Grotesque traits may be expressed in a character's physical appearance. Or, they may be hidden, visible only in a character's actions and emotions. In this story, all of the characters can be classified as grotesques. As you read, look for examples of absurd or extreme behavior, distortions, and striking incongruities that combine to create images of the grotesque.

Connecting Literary Elements

Writers create portraits of characters through **characterization**—the revelation of personality. There are two methods of characterization. With **direct characterization,** the writer simply tells the reader what a character is like. With **indirect characterization,** characters' traits are revealed

- through the character's words, thoughts, and actions.
- through descriptions of the character's appearance or background.
- through what other characters say about him or her.
- through the ways in which other characters react or respond.

Use a chart like the one shown to examine O'Connor's use of indirect characterization in portraying the cast of grotesque characters in this story.

❸ Reading Strategy

Making Predictions

When you find yourself wondering how a series of events will unfold, pause and **predict** what will happen. Predict outcomes by looking back and weighing what you have read. Pay heed to hints the author has dropped, and measure these against your own understanding of human behavior.

Vocabulary

desolate (des′ ə lit) *adj.* forlorn; wretched (p. 973)

listed (list′ id) *v.* tilted; inclined (p. 973)

ominous (äm′ ə nəs) *adj.* threatening; sinister (p. 975)

ravenous (rav′ ə nəs) *adj.* extremely eager (p. 977)

morose (mə rōs′) *adj.* gloomy; sullen (p. 980)

guffawing (gə fô′ iŋ) *adj.* laughing in a loud, coarse manner (p. 982)

Shiftlet

Physical Appearance   One-armed
Words
Thoughts
Actions
How others react
What others say

---

❷ Literary Analysis

Grotesque Characters

- Go over the definition of grotesque characters with students.

  Remind them that in literature, *grotesque* has a meaning different from what it means in popular speech.

- Ask students to discuss the effects a writer might achieve with grotesque characters. Why might someone want to people a story with grotesque rather than more realistic characters? Have students share their ideas. Encourage them to cite examples from their reading.

- As students read, have them try to identify what makes each character in this story grotesque. Have them consider also whether the characters, in spite of being grotesque, are believable.

❸ Reading Strategy

Making Predictions

- Write the word *predict* on the chalkboard, drawing a vertical line between the prefix *pre-* and the root *dict.* Explain that *predict* comes from two Latin words and literally means "say before." When you predict, you state what will happen before it happens.

- Make sure students understand that a prediction is not a wild guess; it is based on details about the plot and characters. As students read, have them note details in the story that help them predict its outcome.

- Challenge students to pause at the end of every page or two of the story to predict what may come next. Remind them to identify details in the story that support these predictions.

Vocabulary Development

- Pronounce each vocabulary word for students and read the definitions as a class. Have students, identify any words with which they are already familiar.

 E-Teach

Visit E-Teach at www.phschool.com for teachers' essays on how to teach, with questions and answers.

CUSTOMIZE INSTRUCTION FOR UNIVERSAL ACCESS

For Less Proficient Readers	For English Learners	For Advanced Readers
Have students pause every so often in their reading to discuss the main characters with partners. Have them focus on which aspects of each character seem grotesque and why.	Have students make word webs for each character. On the web's rays, they can write down physical characteristics and personality traits. Students can then discuss the characters with partners, identifying what makes each character grotesque.	Have students discuss what effect O'Connor's main characters might have had on the reader if they did the same things but were less grotesque in manner and appearance. Would readers identify with them more? Sympathize with them more? Like them better?

Step-by-Step Teaching Guide for pp. 972–982

CUSTOMIZE INSTRUCTION
For Visual/Spatial Learners

Encourage students to pay close attention to the details of the setting. Discuss how these details reflect the events in the story. For example, how do they suggest the decay in the characters' morality?

❶ About the Selection

This story of grotesque characters obsessed with outmaneuvering one another becomes a morality tale about the spiritual desert facing those who behave immorally. Mr. Shiftlet and Mrs. Lucynell Crater appear to be good people who denounce the moral deterioration of the world. They are motivated by goals that are not outwardly evil: Shiftlet wants a car, and Mrs. Crater wants a husband for her daughter, who is mentally retarded, deaf, and mute. As they plot to achieve their goals, they show that they are willing to sacrifice both human decency and the younger Lucynell's future. Their hypocrisy comes at a high price.

❷ Background

Art

Deep Fork Overlook by Joan Marron-LaRue

Joan Marron-La Rue grew up in rural Oklahoma. Interested in painting from early childhood, she worked in fashion design, for a time and later studied with various master painters. *Deep Fork Overlook* was a cover illustration for a poetry anthology written by students of Central State University. LaRue once lived down the road from the gas station and barn it depicts.

Use this question for discussion.

What elements in this painting suggest the time period of the story?

Answer: The old truck and barn, the antiquated gas pumps, and the wandering chickens suggest both the Depression time period and the rural setting.

Deep Fork Overlook, Joan Marron-LaRue

❸ ▲ **Critical Viewing** Why might an automobile be so valuable in a rural area like the one in this story? **[Draw Conclusions]**

972 ◆ *Prosperity and Protest (1946–Present)*

TEACHING RESOURCES

The following resources can be used to enrich or extend the instruction for pp. 972–982.

Literary Analysis

📖 **Selection Support:** Literary Analysis, p. 245

Reading

🎧 **Listening to Literature Audiocassettes,** Side 33 ▪

💿 **Listening to Literature Audio CDs,** CD 19 ▪

▪ **BLOCK SCHEDULING:** Resources marked with this symbol provide varied instruction during 90-minute blocks.

The Life You Save May Be Your Own

Flannery O'Connor

Background

Gothic literature, a genre of fiction that developed in Britain in the late 1700s, features horror and violence. Traditional gothic tales are often set against dramatic, gloomy backdrops—remote castles, deserted fortresses, and the like. Such literature acknowledges evil as a real force and ascribes to some characters a dark side that lures them to violent or wicked acts. Flannery O'Connor borrowed some devices from Gothic fiction, such as a foreboding atmosphere and grotesque characters, but she set her stories in an unremarkable American landscape. The story you are about to read is a perfect example of her exploration of the gothic under the familiar sunlight of the American South.

The old woman and her daughter were sitting on their porch when Mr. Shiftlet came up their road for the first time. The old woman slid to the edge of her chair and leaned forward, shading her eyes from the piercing sunset with her hand. The daughter could not see far in front of her and continued to play with her fingers. Although the old woman lived in this <u>desolate</u> spot with only her daughter and she had never seen Mr. Shiftlet before, she could tell, even from a distance, that he was a tramp and no one to be afraid of. His left coat sleeve was folded up to show there was only half an arm in it and his gaunt figure <u>listed</u> slightly to the side as if the breeze were pushing him. He had on a black town suit and a brown felt hat that was turned up in the front and down in the back and he carried a tin tool box by a handle. He came on, at an amble, up her road, his face turned toward the sun which appeared to be balancing itself on the peak of a small mountain.

The old woman didn't change her position until he was almost into her yard; then she rose with one hand fisted on her hip. The daughter, a large girl in a short blue organdy dress, saw him all at once and jumped up and began to stamp and point and make excited speechless sounds.

Mr. Shiftlet stopped just inside the yard and set his box on the ground and tipped his hat at her as if she were not in the least afflicted; then he turned toward the old woman and swung the hat all the way off. He had long black slick hair that hung flat from a part in the middle to beyond the tips of his ears on either side. His face descended in forehead for more than half its length and ended suddenly with his features just balanced over a jutting steel-trap jaw.

desolate (des′ ə lit) *adj.* forlorn; wretched

listed (list′ id) *v.* tilted; inclined

✓ Reading Check

In this opening scene, who does the old woman notice coming up her road?

The Life You Save May Be Your Own ◆ 973

---

❸ ▶ Critical Viewing

Answer: There is probably no other means of transportation. A car is needed for emergencies and for hauling any heavy items like groceries from town.

❹ Vocabulary Development

The Latin Root –sol–

- Draw students' attention to the word *desolate* in the first paragraph.
- Explain that the root *–sol–* means "alone." Challenge students to use their knowledge of this root to define the word *desolate*.
  Answer: A *desolate* place is one that is abandoned, or left alone.

❺ Literary Analysis

Grotesque Characters

- Ask students whether any aspects of Shiftlet seem grotesque. If so, what are they?
  Answer: He has only one whole arm and he doesn't stand up quite straight. His forehead is very long, and his features are all squashed together below it.
- Then, ask: Does the daughter seem grotesque in any way? If so, how?
  Answer: She apparently can't speak normally, and she is wearing a too-short dress. If the woman is old, the daughter must not be very young, but she is described as "a large girl"; it makes her seem like a parody of a child.

▶ **Monitor Progress** As students continue reading, have them think about what words and actions make each character grotesque.

❻ ✓ Reading Check

Answer: She sees a man—a tramp with one arm—whom she soon learns is named Shiftlet.

CUSTOMIZE INSTRUCTION FOR UNIVERSAL ACCESS

For English Learners

The dialect in this story, with its double negatives, missing verbs, and slang idioms, may challenge some students' comprehension. Explain that it represents the everyday speech of uneducated Americans from the rural South. Have students choose partners with whom to read Mrs. Crater and Shiftlet's conversations aloud. Students can discuss any expressions they don't understand and try to work out their meaning. Tell them to use context clues and pay attention to the sense of the entire conversation. After partners work through the dialogue together, have the whole class gather to help one another resolve any questions that remain.

Literary Analysis
Grotesque Characters
What exaggerated traits
do you perceive in this
description of the three
characters?

➐ Literary Analysis

Grotesque Characters

- Ask students to give their reactions to the three characters at this point in the story.
  Possible answers: All three seem bizarre and unattractive. The old woman and the tramp seem suspicious of one another. The tramp doesn't seem as harmless as the old woman thinks he is.

- Then, ask the first Literary Analysis question on p. 974: What exaggerated traits do you perceive in this description of the three characters?
  Answer: The old woman's smallness is exaggerated in the phrase "size of a cedar fence post." Mr. Shiftlet is again described as crooked. The colors associated with the daughter are overly bright.

➑ Literary Analysis

Grotesque Characters

- Point out that Shiftlet does not answer any of Mrs. Crater's questions directly. Ask students what this suggests about his character.
  Answer: Mr. Shiftlet is being intentionally evasive, perhaps because he wishes to hide something unsavory in his past.

- Ask the second Literary Analysis question on page 974: What personality traits are suggested by this description of Mr. Shiftlet's "pale sharp glance"?
  Answer: The description suggests that Shiftlet's character is ultimately transparent and without substance, and that he is possibly dangerous.

He seemed to be a young man but he had a look of composed dissatisfaction as if he understood life thoroughly.

"Good evening," the old woman said. She was about the size of a cedar fence post and she had a man's gray hat pulled down low over her head.

➐ The tramp stood looking at her and didn't answer. He turned his back and faced the sunset. He swung both his whole and his short arm up slowly so that they indicated an expanse of sky and his figure formed a crooked cross. The old woman watched him with her arms folded across her chest as if she were the owner of the sun, and the daughter watched, her head thrust forward and her fat helpless hands hanging at the wrists. She had long pink-gold hair and eyes as blue as a peacock's neck.

He held the pose for almost fifty seconds and then he picked up his box and came on to the porch and dropped down on the bottom step. "Lady," he said in a firm nasal voice, "I'd give a fortune to live where I could see me a sun do that every evening."

"Does it every evening," the old woman said and sat back down. The daughter sat down too and watched him with a cautious sly look as if he were a bird that had come up very close. He leaned to one side, rooting in his pants pocket, and in a second he brought out a package of chewing gum and offered her a piece. She took it and unpeeled it and began to chew without taking her eyes off him. He offered the old woman a piece but she only raised her upper lip to indicate she had no teeth.

Mr. Shiftlet's pale sharp glance had already passed over everything in the yard—the pump near the corner of the house and the big fig tree that three or four chickens were preparing to roost in—and had moved to a shed where he saw the square rusted back of an automobile. "You ladies drive?" he asked.

"That car ain't run in fifteen year," the old woman said. "The day my husband died, it quit running."

"Nothing is like it used to be, lady," he said. "The world is almost rotten."

"That's right," the old woman said. "You from around here?"

"Name Tom T. Shiftlet," he murmured, looking at the tires.

➑ "I'm pleased to meet you," the old woman said. "Name Lucynell Crater and daughter Lucynell Crater. What you doing around here, Mr. Shiftlet?"

He judged the car to be about a 1928 or '29 Ford. "Lady," he said, and turned and gave her his full attention, "lemme tell you something. There's one of these doctors in Atlanta that's taken a knife and cut the human heart—the human heart," he repeated, leaning forward, "out of a man's chest and held it in his hand," and he held his hand out, palm up, as if it were slightly weighted with the human heart, "and studied it like it was a day-old chicken, and lady," he said, allowing a long significant pause in which his head slid forward and his clay-colored eyes brightened, "he don't know no more about it than you or me."

Literary Analysis
Grotesque Characters
and Characterization
What personality traits
are suggested by this
description of Mr. Shiftlet's
"pale sharp glance"?

"That's right," the old woman said.

"Why, if he was to take that knife and cut into every corner of it, he still wouldn't know no more than you or me. What you want to bet?"

"Nothing," the old woman said wisely. "Where you come from, Mr. Shiftlet?"

He didn't answer. He reached into his pocket and brought out a sack of tobacco and a package of cigarette papers and rolled himself a cigarette, expertly with one hand, and attached it in a hanging position to his upper lip. Then he took a box of wooden matches from his pocket and struck one on his shoe. He held the burning match as if he were studying the mystery of flame while it traveled dangerously toward his skin. The daughter began to make loud noises and to point to his hand and shake her finger at him, but when the flame was just before touching him, he leaned down with his hand cupped over it as if he were going to set fire to his nose and lit the cigarette.

He flipped away the dead match and blew a stream of gray into the evening. A sly look came over his face. "Lady," he said, "nowadays, people'll do anything anyways. I can tell you my name is Tom T. Shiftlet and I come from Tarwater, Tennessee, but you never have seen me before: how you know I ain't lying? How you know my name ain't Aaron Sparks, lady, and I come from Singleberry, Georgia, or how you know it's not George Speeds and I come from Lucy, Alabama, or how you know I ain't Thompson Bright from Toolafalls, Mississippi?"

"I don't know nothing about you," the old woman muttered, irked.

"Lady," he said, "people don't care how they lie. Maybe the best I can tell you is, I'm a man; but listen lady," he said and paused and made his tone more <u>ominous</u> still, "what is a man?"

The old woman began to gum a seed. "What you carry in that tin box, Mr. Shiftlet?" she asked.

"Tools," he said, put back. "I'm a carpenter."

"Well, if you come out here to work, I'll be able to feed you and give you a place to sleep but I can't pay. I'll tell you that before you begin," she said.

There was no answer at once and no particular expression on his face. He leaned back against the two-by-four that helped support the porch roof. "Lady," he said slowly, "there's some men that some things mean more to them than money." The old woman rocked without comment and the daughter watched the trigger that moved up and down in his neck. He told the old woman then that all most people were interested in was money, but he asked what a man was made for. He asked her if a man was made for money, or what. He asked her what she thought she was made for but she didn't answer, she only sat rocking and wondered if a one-armed man could put a new roof on her garden house. He asked a lot of questions that she didn't answer. He told her that he was twenty-eight years old and had lived a varied life. He had been a gospel singer, a foreman on the railroad, an assistant in an undertaking parlor, and he come over the radio for three months with Uncle Roy and his Red Creek Wranglers. He said he had

Reading Strategy
Making Predictions
In what ways might Mr. Shiftlet's speech about lying be a clue to later events?

ominous (ăm´ ə nəs) *adj.* threatening; sinister

⑩ ✔ Reading Check

In what ways does young Lucynell try to communicate? Can she speak?

The Life You Save May Be Your Own ◆ 975

❾ Reading Strategy
Making Predictions

- Ask students whether they think Shiftlet will accept the old woman's offer to work in exchange for room and board? Why do they think so?
  Answer: Hints on p. 974 suggest that he is interested in her car. He probably will take the job she offers.

- Ask the Reading Strategy question on p. 975: In what way might Mr. Shiftlet's speech about lying be a clue to later events?
  Answer: Students might predict that Mr. Shiftlet will be dishonest, as a function of his duplicity thus far and the way he almost dares Lucynell to disbelieve him.

⑩ ✔ Reading Check

Answer: She communicates by gestures. She can "make loud noises" but does not speak in words.

CUSTOMIZE INSTRUCTION FOR UNIVERSAL ACCESS

For Advanced Readers

Have students analyze the religious imagery and symbolism in this story. References include "his figure formed a crooked cross," "I'm a carpenter," "the monks of old slept in their coffins," and "She looks like an angel of Gawd." Have students work together to interpret these allusions and discuss their effect on the story's themes and its overall impact. Students can write essays based on their discussions and analysis.

Grotesque Characters and Characterization

- Ask students what the question "Are you married or are you single?" reveals about the old woman's plans.
  Answer: She may hope to marry him to Lucynell and get him to stay at the house permanently.

- Then, ask the Literary Analysis question on p. 976: What does this dialogue about her daughter reveal about the old woman?
  Answer: The old woman seems to be focusing on and possibly exaggerating Lucynell's abilities in order to make her seem more attractive to Mr. Shiftlet.

⓬ Reading Strategy

Making Predictions

- After students read the bracketed passage, ask them why they think Shiftlet is working so hard and capably. What does he hope to gain?
  Answer: He wants the old woman to trust him enough to let him have the car.

- Then, ask the Reading Strategy question on p. 976: What prediction can you make about Mr. Shiftlet based on his capable performance in his work?
  Possible answer: Mr. Shiftlet probably will not stay around long because he can take care of himself; he does not need the Craters' food or shelter. He might leave after getting what he wants.

fought and bled in the Arm Service of his country and visited every foreign land and that everywhere he had seen people that didn't care if they did a thing one way or another. He said he hadn't been raised thataway.

A fat yellow moon appeared in the branches of the fig tree as if it were going to roost there with the chickens. He said that a man had to escape to the country to see the world whole and that he wished he lived in a desolate place like this where he could see the sun go down every evening like God made it to do.

"Are you married or are you single?" the old woman asked.

There was a long silence. "Lady," he asked finally, "where would you find you an innocent woman today? I wouldn't have any of this trash I could just pick up."

The daughter was leaning very far down, hanging her head almost between her knees watching him through a triangular door she had made in her overturned hair; and she suddenly fell in a heap on the floor and began to whimper. Mr. Shiftlet straightened her out and helped her get back in the chair.

"Is she your baby girl?" he asked.

"My only," the old woman said "and she's the sweetest girl in the world. I would give her up for nothing on earth. She's smart too. She can sweep the floor, cook, wash, feed the chickens, and hoe. I wouldn't give her up for a casket of jewels."

"No," he said kindly, "don't ever let any man take her away from you."

"Any man come after her," the old woman said, "'ll have to stay around the place."

Mr. Shiftlet's eye in the darkness was focused on a part of the automobile bumper that glittered in the distance. "Lady," he said, jerking his short arm up as if he could point with it to her house and yard and pump, "there ain't a broken thing on this plantation that I couldn't fix for you, one-arm jackleg or not. I'm a man," he said with a sullen dignity, "even if I ain't a whole one. I got," he said, tapping his knuckles on the floor to emphasize the immensity of what he was going to say, "a moral intelligence!" and his face pierced out of the darkness into a shaft of doorlight and he stared at her as if he were astonished himself at this impossible truth.

The old woman was not impressed with the phrase. "I told you you could hang around and work for food," she said, "if you don't mind sleeping in that car yonder."

"Why listen, lady, " he said with a grin of delight, "the monks of old slept in their coffins!"

"They wasn't as advanced as we are," the old woman said.

 The next morning he began on the roof of the garden house while Lucynell, the daughter, sat on a rock and watched him work. He had not been around a week before the change he had made in the place was apparent. He had patched the front and back steps, built a new hog pen, restored a fence, and taught Lucynell, who was completely

Reading Strategy
Making Predictions
What prediction can you make about Mr. Shiftlet based on his capable performance in his work?

☀ **ENRICHMENT: History Connection**

The Great Depression

This story is set during the Great Depression of the 1930s. Jobs were so scarce that many men became drifters like Shiftlet. They wandered from place to place, often covering thousands of miles in their search for work. Drifters often hitched rides aboard slow-moving freight trains rather than walking from one city to another. Money was so hard to come by that many drifters would have welcomed Mrs. Crater's offer of room and board in exchange for work. When World War II began, many drifters and other unemployed men joined the armed services, with its steady paycheck. The war also created thousands of jobs for those who did not go overseas to fight.

Black Walnuts, 1945, Joseph Pollet, Oil on canvas, 30" x 40", Collection of Whitney Museum of American Art, Purchase, Gift of Gertrude Vanderbilt Whitney, by exchange

deaf and had never said a word in her life, to say the word "bird." The big rosy-faced girl followed him everywhere, saying "Burrttddt ddbir-rrttdt," and clapping her hands. The old woman watched from a distance, secretly pleased. She was <u>ravenous</u> for a son-in-law.

Mr. Shiftlet slept on the hard narrow back seat of the car with his feet out the side window. He had his razor and a can of water on a crate that served him as a bedside table and he put up a piece of mirror against the back glass and kept his coat neatly on a hanger that he hung over one of the windows.

In the evenings he sat on the steps and talked while the old woman and Lucynell rocked violently in their chairs on either side of him. The old woman's three mountains were black against the dark blue sky and were visited off and on by various planets and by the moon after it had left the chickens. Mr. Shiftlet pointed out that the reason he had improved this plantation was because he had taken a personal interest in it. He said he was even going to make the automobile run.

He had raised the hood and studied the mechanism and he said he could tell that the car had been built in the days when cars were really built. You take now, he said, one man puts in one bolt and another man puts in another bolt and another man puts in another bolt so that it's a man for a bolt. That's why you have to pay so much for a car: you're paying all those men. Now if you didn't have to pay

⑭ ▲ Critical Viewing
Which aspects of the story are reflected in this painting? **[Connect]**

ravenous (rav´ ə nəs) *adj.* extremely eager

⑮ ☑ Reading Check
For what is the old woman "ravenous"?

The Life You Save May Be Your Own ◆ 977

⑬ Background
Art

Black Walnuts by Joseph Pollet

Swiss-American painter Joseph Pollet studied at the Art Students' League in New York, under American realist painter John Sloan.

Black Walnuts shows both Sloan's influence—a highly realistic stop-action quality that conveys a great deal of emotion—and the general focus of painting during the Depression: capturing everyday American images for American viewers.

Use these questions for discussion:

1. How does the mood of this painting compare with that of the story? Answer: The painting has a happier, brighter mood than the story does.

2. Do you think the story characters would fit in the painting's setting? Why or why not? Answer: They would fit into the setting because it is rural; however, they would not belong in the sense that the scene is one of purity and goodness, while the characters— as students will see—are morally bankrupt.

⑭ ► Critical Viewing

Answer: Students should notice the rural setting and general air of dilapidation, the large tree, the shed, and the old car.

⑮ ☑ Reading Check

Answer: The old woman is ravenous for a son-in-law.

CUSTOMIZE INSTRUCTION FOR UNIVERSAL ACCESS

For Gifted/Talented Students

Tell students that Flannery O'Connor liked to employ her biting sense of irony in playing off of Southern manners. For instance, Tom Shiftlet mouths the platitudes of what she called elsewhere "good country people." We see this when he says to Lucynell Crater that "Nothing is like it used to be, lady…The world is almost rotten." The humor of his words comes from his timing—he offers this morally charged declaration after being told that the Craters' car stopped running years back. Encourage students to be aware of similar ironies in stereotypes and mannerisms.

⑯ Literary Analysis

Grotesque Characters

• Have students consider what Shiftlet's reaction to Mrs. Crater suggests about his character. Answer: He knows what Mrs. Crater is up to. He turns his attention to the car immediately after she makes the suggestion, showing that he hopes to get the car running and leave the place as soon as possible.

• Finally, ask the first Literary Analysis question on p. 978: In what way does Mrs. Crater's suggestion about teaching Lucynell reveal her obsession? Answer: She wants to force Shiftlet to speak endearingly to Lucynell.

⑰ Literary Analysis

Grotesque Characters

• Have a student read aloud the bracketed passage. Then, point out that Mr. Shiftlet's thoughts are on the car during his conversation about young Lucynell.

• Ask students the second Literary Analysis question on p. 978: What does Mr. Shiftlet's remark about the car reveal about his obsession? Answer: It reveals that he cares more about the car than about the girl. He wants to repair it as much as possible while Mrs. Lucynell is footing the bill.

but one man, you could get you a cheaper car and one that had had a personal interest taken in it, and it would be a better car. The old woman agreed with him that this was so.

Mr. Shiftlet said that the trouble with the world was that nobody cared, or stopped and took any trouble. He said he never would have been able to teach Lucynell to say a word if he hadn't cared and stopped long enough.

"Teach her to say something else," the old woman said.

"What you want her to say next?" Mr. Shiftlet asked.

The old woman's smile was broad and toothless and suggestive. **⑯** "Teach her to say 'sugarpie,'" she said.

Mr. Shiftlet already knew what was on her mind.

The next day he began to tinker with the automobile and that evening he told her that if she would buy a fan belt, he would be able to make the car run.

The old woman said she would give him the money. "You see that girl yonder?" she asked, pointing to Lucynell who was sitting on the floor a foot away, watching him, her eyes blue even in the dark. "If it was ever a man wanted to take her away, I would say, 'No man on earth is going to take that sweet girl of mine away from me!' but if he was to say, 'Lady, I don't want to take her away, I want her right here,' I would say, 'Mister, I don't blame you none. I wouldn't pass up a chance to live in a permanent place and get the sweetest girl in the world myself. You ain't no fool,' I would say."

"How old is she?" Mr. Shiftlet asked casually.

"Fifteen, sixteen," the old woman said. The girl was nearly thirty but because of her innocence it was impossible to guess.

"It would be a good idea to paint it too," Mr. Shiftlet remarked. "You don't want it to rust out."

"We'll see about that later," the old woman said.

The next day he walked into town and returned with the parts he needed and a can of gasoline. Late in the afternoon, terrible noises issued from the shed and the old woman rushed out of the house, **⑰** thinking Lucynell was somewhere having a fit. Lucynell was sitting on a chicken crate, stamping her feet and screaming, "Burrddtt! bddurrddttt!" but her fuss was drowned out by the car. With a volley of blasts it emerged from the shed, moving in a fierce and stately way. Mr. Shiftlet was in the driver's seat, sitting very erect. He had an expression of serious modesty on his face as if he had just raised the dead.

That night, rocking on the porch, the old woman began her business, at once. "You want you an innocent woman, don't you?" she asked sympathetically. "You don't want none of this trash."

"No'm, I don't," Mr. Shiftlet said.

"One that can't talk," she continued, "can't sass you back or use foul language. That's the kind for you to have. Right there," and she pointed to Lucynell sitting crosslegged in her chair, holding both feet in her hands.

Literary Analysis
Grotesque Characters
In what way does Mrs. Crater's suggestion about teaching Lucynell reveal her obsession?

Literary Analysis
Grotesque Characters
What does Mr. Shiftlet's remark about the car reveal about his obsession?

"That's right," he admitted. "She wouldn't give me any trouble."

"Saturday," the old woman said, "you and her and me can drive into town and get married."

Mr. Shiftlet eased his position on the steps.

"I can't get married right now," he said. "Everything you want to do takes money and I ain't got any."

"What you need with money?" she asked.

"It takes money," he said. "Some people'll do anything anyhow these days, but the way I think, I wouldn't marry no woman that I couldn't take on a trip like she was somebody. I mean take her to a hotel and treat her. I wouldn't marry the Duchesser Windsor," he said firmly, "unless I could take her to a hotel and giver something good to eat.

"I was raised thataway and there ain't a thing I can do about it. My old mother taught me how to do."

"Lucynell don't even know what a hotel is," the old woman muttered. "Listen here, Mr. Shiftlet," she said, sliding forward in her chair, "you'd be getting a permanent house and a deep well and the most innocent girl in the world. You don't need no money. Lemme tell you something: there ain't any place in the world for a poor disabled friendless drifting man."

The ugly words settled in Mr. Shiftlet's head like a group of buzzards in the top of a tree.

He didn't answer at once. He rolled himself a cigarette and lit it and then he said in an even voice, "Lady, a man is divided into two parts, body and spirit."

The old woman clamped her gums together.

"A body and a spirit," he repeated. "The body, lady, is like a house: it don't go anywhere; but the spirit, lady, is like a automobile: always on the move, always . . ."

"Listen, Mr. Shiftlet," she said, "my well never goes dry and my house is always warm in the winter and there's no mortgage on a thing about this place. You can go to the courthouse and see for yourself. And yonder under that shed is a fine automobile." She laid the bait carefully. "You can have it painted by Saturday. I'll pay for the paint."

In the darkness, Mr. Shiftlet's smile stretched like a weary snake waking up by a fire. After a second he recalled himself and said, "I'm only saying a man's spirit means more to him than anything else. I would have to take my wife off for the weekend without no regards at all for cost. I got to follow where my spirit says to go."

"I'll give you fifteen dollars for a weekend trip," the old woman said in a crabbed voice. "That's the best I can do."

"That wouldn't hardly pay for more than the gas and the hotel," he said. "It wouldn't feed her."

"Seventeen-fifty," the old woman said. "That's all I got so it isn't any use you trying to milk me. You can take a lunch."

Mr. Shiftlet was deeply hurt by the word "milk." He didn't doubt that she had more money sewed up in her mattress but he had already told her he was not interested in her money. "I'll make that

Literary Analysis
Grotesque Characters and Characterization
What is revealed about Mr. Shiftlet and the old woman in this exchange about marriage and money?

Reading Strategy
Making Predictions
What predictions about Mr. Shiftlet can you make based on his discussion of body and spirit?

 Reading Check
What does Mr. Shiftlet do with the old car?

The Life You Save May Be Your Own ◆ 979

⓲ Literary Analysis

Grotesque Characters and Characterization

- Read aloud the bracketed passage to students. Have students pay attention to the information they learn about Shiftlet and the old woman from their conversation.

- Ask the Literary Analysis question on p. 979: What is revealed about Mr. Shiftlet and the old woman in this exchange about marriage and money?
  Answer: Each is trying to get what he or she wants from the other, while giving up as little as possible.

- Then, ask students to describe the part that Lucynell plays in this discussion. Have students consider what the others' attitude toward Lucynell in this passage reveals about them.
  Answer: Lucynell's future is decided for her without her input. The others regard her as property, or as a pawn in a chess game. She is simply a bargaining chip to both of them.

⓳ Reading Strategy

Making Predictions

- Have students read the bracketed passage to themselves. Then, have them explain in their own words what Shiftlet says in this passage.

- Ask the Reading Strategy question on p. 979: What prediction about Mr. Shiftlet can you make based on his discussion of body and spirit?
  Answer: Like the spirit, he will soon be "on the move."

▶ **Monitor Progress** Ask students what they think will happen to Lucynell once she is alone with Shiftlet.
  Possible answers: He has been kind to her up to this point, so he probably won't hurt her. However, if he has the car, he will no longer have any motivation to impress Mrs. Crater by treating her daughter well.

⓴ ☑ Reading Check

Answer: Shiftlet repairs and paints it.

Making Predictions

- Have students read the bracketed passage. Remind them that they can use details from a story to make predictions about future events.

- Then, ask the Reading Strategy question on p. 980: Based on this speech about his dissatisfaction, what do you predict will happen to the newlyweds?
  Possible answers: It is clear from his words that the ceremony was meaningless to Shiftlet. Based on this, we can predict that he does not feel bound to Lucynell and may harm or leave her.

▶ Monitor Progress Challenge students to predict how the story will end. Have them give reasons for their predictions. At the end of the story, discuss whether anyone came close to predicting the story's actual end.

❷② Literary Analysis

Grotesque Characters

- Ask the Literary Analysis question on p. 980: Why is the old woman upset as she parts from her daughter?
  Possible answers: She has some genuine feelings for her daughter. She is suddenly afraid of what Shiftlet may do to Lucynell.

- Then, ask students whether the old woman really believes that Shiftlet "would do right" to her daughter. Possible answer: Students might say that the old woman is trying to convince herself that this is true.

---

do," he said and rose and walked off without treating with her further.

On Saturday the three of them drove into town in the car that the paint had barely dried on and Mr. Shiftlet and Lucynell were married in the Ordinary's office while the old woman witnessed. As they came out of the courthouse, Mr. Shiftlet began twisting his neck in his collar. He looked morose and bitter as if he had been insulted while someone held him. "That didn't satisfy me none," he said. "That was just something a woman in an office did, nothing but paper work and blood tests. What do they know about my blood? If they was to take my heart and cut it out," he said, "they wouldn't know a thing about me. It didn't satisfy me at all."

"It satisfied the law," the old woman said sharply.

"The law," Mr. Shiftlet said and spit. "It's the law that don't satisfy me."

He had painted the car dark green with a yellow band around it just under the windows. The three of them climbed in the front seat and the old woman said, "Don't Lucynell look pretty? Looks like a baby doll." Lucynell was dressed up in a white dress that her mother had uprooted from a trunk and there was a Panama hat on her head with a bunch of red wooden cherries on the brim. Every now and then her placid expression was changed by a sly isolated little thought like a shoot of green in the desert.

"You got a prize!" the old woman said.

Mr. Shiftlet didn't even look at her. They drove back to the house to let the old woman off and pick up the lunch. When they were ready to leave, she stood staring in the window of the car, with her fingers clenched around the glass. Tears began to seep sideways out of her eyes and run along the dirty creases in her face. "I ain't ever been parted with her for two days before," she said.

Mr. Shiftlet started the motor.

"And I wouldn't let no man have her but you because I seen you would do right. Goodbye, Sugarbaby," she said, clutching at the sleeve of the white dress. Lucynell looked straight at her and didn't seem to see her there at all. Mr. Shiftlet eased the car forward so that she had to move her hands.

The early afternoon was clear and open and surrounded by pale blue sky. Although the car would go only thirty miles an hour, Mr. Shiftlet imagined a terrific climb and dip and swerve that went entirely to his head so that he forgot his morning bitterness. He had always wanted an automobile but he had never been able to afford one before. He drove very fast because he wanted to make Mobile by nightfall.

Occasionally he stopped his thoughts long enough to look at Lucynell in the seat beside him. She had eaten the lunch as soon as they were out of the yard and now she was pulling the cherries off the hat one by one and throwing them out the window. He became depressed in spite of the car. He had driven about a hundred miles when he decided that she must be hungry again and at the next small town they came to, he stopped in front of an aluminum-painted

morose (mə rōs´) adj. gloomy; sullen

Reading Strategy
Making Predictions
Based on this speech about his dissatisfaction, what do you predict will happen to the newlyweds?

Literary Analysis
Grotesque Characters
Why is the old woman upset as she parts from her daughter?

eating place called The Hot Spot and took her in and ordered her a plate of ham and grits. The ride had made her sleepy and as soon as she got up on the stool, she rested her head on the counter and shut her eyes. There was no one in The Hot Spot but Mr. Shiftlet and the boy behind the counter, a pale youth with a greasy rag hung over his shoulder. Before he could dish up the food, she was snoring gently.

"Give it to her when she wakes up," Mr. Shiftlet said. "I'll pay for it now." The boy bent over her and stared at the long pink-gold hair and the half-shut sleeping eyes. Then he looked up and stared at Mr. Shiftlet. "She looks like an angel of Gawd," he murmured.

"Hitchhiker," Mr. Shiftlet explained. "I can't wait. I got to make Tuscaloosa."

The boy bent over again and very carefully touched his finger to a strand of the golden hair and Mr. Shiftlet left.

He was more depressed than ever as he drove on by himself. The late afternoon had grown hot and sultry and the country had flattened out. Deep in the sky a storm was preparing very slowly and without thunder as if it meant to drain every drop of air from the earth before it broke. There were times when Mr. Shiftlet preferred not to be alone. He felt too that a man with a car had a responsibility to others and he kept his eye out for a hitchhiker. Occasionally he saw a sign that warned: "Drive carefully. The life you save may be your own."

The narrow road dropped off on either side into dry fields and here and there a shack or a filling station stood in a clearing. The sun began to set directly in front of the automobile. It was a reddening ball that through his windshield was slightly flat on the bottom and top. He saw a boy in overalls and a gray hat standing on the edge of the road and he slowed the car down and stopped in front of him. The boy didn't have his hand raised to thumb the ride, he was only standing there, but he had a small cardboard suitcase and his hat was set on his head in a way to indicate that he had left somewhere for good. "Son," Mr. Shiftlet said, "I see you want a ride."

The boy didn't say he did or he didn't but he opened the door of the car and got in, and Mr. Shiftlet started driving again. The child held the suitcase on his lap and folded his arms on top of it. He turned his head and looked out the window away from Shiftlet. Mr. Shiftlet felt oppressed. "Son," he said after a minute, "I got the best old mother in the world so I reckon you only got the second best."

The boy gave him a quick dark glance and then turned his face back out the window.

"It's nothing so sweet," Mr. Shiftlet continued, "as a boy's mother. She taught him his first prayers at her knee, she give him love when no other would, she told him what was right and what wasn't, and she seen that he done the right thing. Son," he said, "I never rued a

The American Experience

23 Southern Regionalism

While writers have the capacity to invent whole new worlds, they are human beings who are influenced by their environments. Regional writers are those who use specific geographical areas—usually their home turf—as settings. Yet regionalists do more than simply set their fiction in familiar locales; they incorporate the distinct culture of an area, including characteristic speech patterns, customs, beliefs, history, and folklore into the very fabric of their stories. This marriage of place, sensibility, and style goes beyond mere reporting to present a sophisticated treatment of the culture of a region. With the best regional writers, local detail helps to create stories of universal impact. You need not be from the American South to appreciate the work of such great Southern regional writers as Flannery O'Connor, Truman Capote, Carson McCullers, Tennessee Williams, William Faulkner, Eudora Welty, or Robert Penn Warren.

24 Reading Check

What does Mr. Shiftlet do when Lucynell falls asleep at The Hot Spot?

23 Background

Southern Regionalism

Though accents vary throughout the American South, the region as a whole is known for its distinctive cadences and patterns of speech. These unique qualities were influenced by a number of circumstances. In the small towns of this agricultural region, people entertained themselves with storytelling and long chatting sessions. They heard only one another's voices; few outsiders came through.

The strong religious current in the southern states, sometimes referred to as the "Bible Belt," helped infuse the cadences of the King James Bible into Southern speech. In the years following the Civil War, Southerners struggled to retain a semblance of their pre-war lives. People preserved their speech patterns, which varied with social position, as a way of associating themselves with a particular social group.

24 Reading Check

Answer: He leaves money to pay for her meal and then abandons her.

CUSTOMIZE INSTRUCTION FOR UNIVERSAL ACCESS

For Special Needs Students	For Advanced Readers
Discuss with students why Mr. Shiftlet leaves Lucynell in the diner. Help students determine that Shiftlet married her only in order to get the car and the honeymoon money; now that he has both, he no longer needs Lucynell.	To encourage these students to respond thoughtfully to the story, initiate an analysis of Mr. Shiftlet's motivations throughout the story. Discuss whether he had always planned to abandon young Lucynell, or whether he was in fact willing to live with the Craters if only to gain access to the car.

Answers for p. 982

Review and Assess

1. Students will probably say that they are exaggerated and bizarre. They may recognize common character traits such as selfishness.

2. **(a)** She notices that he has only one arm and she thinks he is harmless. **(b)** He wants the car. **(c)** She doesn't seem aware that he is essentially untrustworthy.

3. **(a)** She points out that Lucynell is innocent and that she will never talk back or argue. **(b)** He wants the car and the money that Mrs. Crater agrees to give them for a honeymoon.

4. **(a)** He prays for the Lord to "break forth and wash this slime from the earth." **(b)** The rainstorm threatens to wash Shiftlet from the earth. **(c)** It suggests that people will ultimately pay for their hypocrisy.

5. Since Lucynell is disabled, she would be helpless if her mother died without making some arrangement for her future. Lucynell's limited reactions to Shiftlet are positive. The mother is justified on these grounds.

---

day in my life like the one I rued when I left that old mother of mine."

The boy shifted in his seat but he didn't look at Mr. Shiftlet. He unfolded his arms and put one hand on the door handle.

"My mother was a angel of Gawd," Mr. Shiftlet said in a very strained voice. "He took her from heaven and giver to me and I left her." His eyes were instantly clouded over with a mist of tears. The car was barely moving.

The boy turned angrily in the seat. "You go to the devil!" he cried. "My old woman is a flea bag and yours is a stinking pole cat!" and with that he flung the door open and jumped out with his suitcase into the ditch.

Mr. Shiftlet was so shocked that for about a hundred feet he drove along slowly with the door still open. A cloud, the exact color of the boy's hat and shaped like a turnip, had descended over the sun, and another, worse looking, crouched behind the car. Mr. Shiftlet felt that the rottenness of the world was about to engulf him. He raised his arm and let it fall again to his breast. "Oh Lord!" he prayed. "Break forth and wash the slime from this earth!"

The turnip continued slowly to descend. After a few minutes there was a <u>guffawing</u> peal of thunder from behind and fantastic raindrops, like tin-can tops, crashed over the rear of Mr. Shiftlet's car. Very quickly he stepped on the gas and with his stump sticking out the window he raced the galloping shower into Mobile.

guffawing (gə fô´ iŋ) *adj.* laughing in a loud, coarse manner

---

Review and Assess

Thinking About the Selection

1. **Respond:** How did you react to the people in this story? In what way, if any, do they remind you of people you have met?

2. **(a) Recall:** What is Mrs. Crater's first reaction to Shiftlet when she sees him from a distance as the story begins? **(b) Infer:** What object on the Crater farm does Mr. Shiftlet want? **(c) Analyze:** What clues about Mr. Shiftlet's true character does Mrs. Crater seem to not notice?

3. **(a) Recall:** What arguments does Mrs. Crater use to persuade Shiftlet to marry Lucynell? **(b) Interpret:** What factors cause Shiftlet to agree to the marriage?

4. **(a) Recall:** What prayer does Shiftlet offer at the end of the story? **(b) Analyze:** What is ironic about the way in which his prayer is answered? **(c) Generalize:** What does this event suggest about those whose behavior contradicts their professed beliefs?

5. **Make a Judgment:** When Mrs. Crater decides to marry Lucynell to Shiftlet, the girl seems to have no control over her fate. Do Mrs. Crater's actions have any moral justification? Explain.

ASSESSMENT PRACTICE: Reading Comprehension

Punctuation   (For more practice, see Test Preparation Workbook, p. 58.)

Many tests require students to recognize errors in punctuation. Use the following sample test item to help students practice this skill.

"The Life You Save May Be Your Own" is the story of a drifter who meets a woman and her daughter. In the course of the story; the daughter is treated as if she were a piece of property.

Which punctuation mark above is incorrect?

A quotation marks around story title

B period after the word *daughter*

C semicolon after the word *story*

D period after the word *property*

The semicolon should be replaced by a comma. The correct answer is *C.*

Review and Assess

Literary Analysis

Grotesque Characters

1. Note two uses of physical description that create an exaggerated or **grotesque** effect for (a) Mrs. Crater, (b) Mr. Shiftlet, and (c) Lucynell.
2. Use a chart like the one shown to examine Mrs. Crater and Mr. Shiftlet. (a) What primary goal or obsession controls each character? (b) What actions does each undertake as a result of the obsession?

3. (a) In what ways are these characters exaggerated? (b) In what ways are they realistic?

Connecting Literary Elements

4. How does the narrator's observation that Mr. Shiftlet's figure "formed a crooked cross" contribute to his **characterization**?
5. What does Mr. Shiftlet's name suggest about his character?
6. (a) What is the cause of Lucynell's innocence? (b) What does the story suggest about the fate of such innocence?

Reading Strategy

Making Predictions

7. (a) What **predictions** did you make about Mr. Shiftlet's actions concerning Mrs. Crater and Lucynell when he first appeared? (b) What actually happened?
8. (a) What predictions did you make when Mr. Shiftlet departed with Lucynell after their wedding? (b) What actually happened?
9. In what ways do the story's actual events surprise the reader?

Extend Understanding

10. **Social Studies Connection:** In today's world, what educational opportunities or living situations might be available to a mentally challenged woman like Lucynell?

Quick Review

Grotesque characters become ludicrous or bizarre through their obsession with an idea, an assumption, or a value.

Characterization is the art of revealing character. With **direct characterization,** the writer simply states what a character is like. With **indirect characterization,** the writer reveals characters through their words, thoughts, actions, physical appearance, and by what other characters say and how they react.

To **make predictions,** use information from the text to anticipate how events will unfold later in the story.

 Take It to the Net
www.phschool.com
Take the interactive self-test online to check your understanding of the selection.

The Life You Save May Be Your Own ◆ 983

ENRICHMENT: Further Reading

Other Works by Flannery O'Connor

The Complete Stories

The Violent Bear It Away

Wise Blood

 Take It to the Net
Visit www.phschool.com for more information on Flannery O'Connor.

---

❶ Vocabulary Development

Word Analysis

1. Solitaire is played by a single person.
2. A soliloquy involves one actor.
3. A pilot would not have a co–pilot on a solo flight.
4. Yes, a person who likes to be alone enjoys solitude.

Concept Development: Context

1. With peeling paint and sagging window sashes, the cottage had a desolate appearance.
2. correct
3. correct
4. Having had no time to eat lunch, we were ravenous long before dinner.
5. Your morose reaction shows that your thoughts are gloomy.
6. correct

Spelling Strategy

1. shallower
2. glowing
3. withdrawal
4. hallowed

❷ Grammar and Style Lesson

1. were
2. pay
3. rents
4. try
5. tastes

Writing Application

Have partners check one another's sentences to make sure they used the subjective verb form correctly.

Integrate Language Skills

❶ Vocabulary Development Lesson

Word Analysis: Latin Root -sol-

The Latin word root -sol-, meaning "alone," builds the meaning of these words:

   a. *desolate*: isolated, uninhabited
   b. *solitary*: alone, without company
   c. *soloist*: one who performs by him- or herself

Use your knowledge of the Latin root -sol- to answer the following questions.

1. Is *solitaire* a game played by a single person or by a group of players?
2. In a *soliloquy*, do two actors have an exchange or does one actor address the audience?
3. Would a pilot have a co-pilot on a *solo* flight?
4. Would a person who usually loves to take long walks alone enjoy the state of *solitude*?

❷ Grammar and Style Lesson

Subjunctive Mood

The **subjunctive mood** is any verb form indicating possibility, supposition, or desire.

- If a verb expresses a condition contrary to fact, use the past-tense form *were*.
- If a verb demands, recommends, or suggests, use the third-person singular verb form without the usual -s, -es, or -ies ending. Look at these examples:

> **Contrary to fact:** Mr. Shiftlet talked as if he *were* an ethical person.
>
> **Demands/suggests:** Mrs. Crater suggested that Shiftlet *marry* her daughter.

W̶G *Prentice Hall Writing and Grammar Connection: Chapter 21, Section 3*

984 ◆ *Prosperity and Protest (1946–Present)*

Concept Development: Context

For each sentence, indicate whether the word in italics is used correctly. If it is used incorrectly, write a new correct sentence.

1. With fresh paint and flower boxes, the cottage had a *desolate* appearance.
2. The rickety fence *listed* in the strong winds.
3. In an *ominous* voice, the jury foreperson read the guilty verdict.
4. After a huge dinner, we were *ravenous*.
5. Your *morose* reaction shows your happiness.
6. He was *guffawing* at the comic's antics.

Spelling Strategy

When you add a suffix to a word that ends in *w*, never double the *w*. For each word below, create a new word by adding the given suffix.

1. *-er* to shallow   3. *-al* to withdraw
2. *-ing* to glow   4. *-ed* to hallow

Practice Determine whether the subjunctive mood is needed in each example. Then, write the correct form of the verb in parentheses to complete each sentence.

1. I wouldn't trust that broker, if I (be) you.
2. He requires that customers (pay) in cash.
3. Every summer, she (rent) a cottage.
4. He asks that each one (try) a sample.
5. The sample usually (taste) good.

Writing Application Write two different sentences using the subjunctive mood. For the first, express a condition contrary to fact. For the second, suggest a preferred course of action.

TEACHING RESOURCES

The following resources can be used to enrich or extend the instruction for pp. 984–985.

Vocabulary

📖 **Selection Support:** Build Vocabulary, p. 242
📖 **Vocabulary and Spelling Practice Book** (Use this booklet for skills enrichment)

Grammar

📖 **Selection Support:** Grammar and Style, p. 243
W̶G **Writing and Grammar,** Ruby Level, p. 548
📄 **Daily Language Practice Transparencies** ▪

Writing

W̶G **Writing and Grammar,** Ruby Level, p. 204 ▪
💿 **Writing and Grammar iText CD-ROM**

▪ **BLOCK SCHEDULING:** Resources marked with this symbol provide varied instruction during 90-minute blocks.

❸ Writing Lesson

Deposition

A deposition is a witness's formal, written testimony—a legal first-person recounting of events. Imagine that Mr. Shiftlet has been accused of stealing Mrs. Crater's car and of abandoning Lucynell. As a witness, write a deposition that may be used against him.

Prewriting   List Mr. Shiftlet's statements and actions and the effects you know or imagine they had. Locate quotations from the story that support your testimony.

Drafting   Begin by explaining, in objective detail, what Mr. Shiftlet did. Establish clear transitions that show cause and effect. Include relevant quotations to back up your statements. Finally, end by explaining why you believe that Mr. Shiftlet's actions were criminal.

Revising   Be sure that you have described events in a clear and logical way. Add any transition words necessary to clarify causes and effects.

Model: Revising to Show Cause and Effect

At The Hot Spot, Mr. Shiftlet paid in advance for Lucynell's

     , so that

meal ˄ he could leave her without arousing suspicion. He said

        thus

that she was just a hitchhiker,˄ justifying his leaving without her.

> Transition words like *thus* and *so that* clarify cause and effect.

W̶G *Prentice Hall Writing and Grammar Connection: Chapter 10, Section 4*

❹ Extension Activities

Listening and Speaking In a small group, conduct a **Readers Theatre** of the story.

- Name three students to be the narrator, Mrs. Crater, and Mr. Shiftlet.
- Have a fourth student act out Lucynell as the narrator describes her.

Follow your presentation with a discussion in which audience members comment on the author's use of stylistic devices to advance character and motive. **[Group Activity]**

Research and Technology People's posture or gestures may "speak" louder than their words. Conduct library and Internet research to prepare a **body language presentation.** Describe how body language reveals character. Link your findings to the selection and provide simple demonstrations to illustrate your main points.

 **Take It to the Net**   www.phschool.com

Go online for an additional research activity using the Internet.

The Life You Save May Be Your Own ◆ 985

Lesson Support for p. 985

❸ Writing Lesson

- Remind students that a deposition should give facts only, not opinions.
- Explain to students that depositions should describe only scenes and actions that the writer actually witnessed.
- Make sure students revise to show the causal relationships between events. Have students suggest other words and phrases that they can use to clarify these relationships.
- Use the Cause-and-Effect essay rubric on p. 20 or **Performance Assessment and Portfolio Management** to evaluate students' work.

❹ Listening and Speaking

- Students might choose an excerpt from the story, rather than the whole text, so their presentations will be of manageable length.
- If necessary, a fifth student can take on the roles of the boy in the diner and the hitchhiker.
- Encourage students to adjust the tone, volume, and speed of their words to accurately reflect the character they are portraying

CUSTOMIZE INSTRUCTION for Universal Access

To address different learning styles, use the following activities suggested in the **Extension Activities** booklet, p. 55.

For Intrapersonal Learners, use Activity 5.

For Verbal/Linguistic Learners, use Activity 6.

For Visual/Spatial Learners, use Activity 7.

ASSESSMENT RESOURCES

The following resources can be used to assess students' knowledge and skills.

Selection Assessment
- **Formal Assessment,** pp. 248–250
- **Open Book Test,** pp. 163–165
- **Got It! Assessment Videotapes,** Tape 5
- **Test Bank Software**

Take It to the Net
Visit www.phschool.com for self-tests and additional questions on "The Life You Save May Be Your Own."

Writing Rubric
- **Performance Assess. and Portfolio Mgmt.,** p.20

PRENTICE HALL ASSESSMENT *SYSTEM*
- **Workbook**
- **Skill Book**
- **Transparencies**
- **CD-ROM**

The First Seven Years

Lesson Objectives

1. **To analyze and respond to literary elements**
   - Literary Analysis: Epiphany
   - Connecting Literary Elements: Internal and External Conflict
2. **To read, comprehend, analyze, and critique poetry**
   - Reading Strategy: Identifying With Characters
   - Reading Check questions
   - Review and Assess questions
3. **To develop word analysis skills, fluency, and systematic vocabulary**
   - Vocabulary Development Lesson: Latin Word Roots: *-litera-*
4. **To understand and apply written and oral language conventions**
   - Spelling Strategy
   - Grammar and Style Lesson: Usage: *who* and *whom*
   - Assessment Practice (ATE)
5. **To understand and apply appropriate writing and research strategies**
   - Writing Lesson: Personality Profile
   - Extension Activity: Cultural Research
6. **To understand and apply listening and speaking strategies**
   - Extension Activity: Presentation

STEP-BY-STEP TEACHING GUIDE	PACING GUIDE
PRETEACH	
Motivate Students and Provide Background	
Use the Motivation activity (ATE p. 986)	5 min.
Read and discuss author and background features (SE/ATE pp. 986, 988)	5 min.
Introduce the Concepts	
Introduce the Literary Analysis and Reading Strategy (SE/ATE p. 987)	15 min.
Pronounce the vocabulary words and read their definitions (SE p. 987)	5 min.
TEACH	
Monitor Comprehension	
Informally monitor comprehension by circulating while students read independently or in groups	30 min.
Monitor students' comprehension with the Reading Check notes (SE/ATE pp. 989, 991, 993, 995)	as students read
Develop vocabulary with Vocabulary notes (SE pp. 988, 989, 991, 994; ATE p. 989)	as students read
Develop Understanding	
Develop students' understanding of epiphany with the Literary Analysis annotations (SE pp. 989, 990, 991, 993, 994, 995, 996; ATE pp. 989, 990, 991, 993, 994, 995, 996)	5 min.
Develop students' ability to identify with characters in the selection by using the Reading Strategy annotations (SE pp. 990, 995; ATE pp. 990, 992, 995)	5 min.
ASSESS	
Assess Mastery	
Assess students' mastery of the Reading Strategy and Literary Analysis by having them answer the Review and Assess questions (SE/ATE p. 997)	15 min.
Use one or more of the print and media Assessment Resources (ATE p. 999)	up to 45 min.
EXTEND	
Apply Understanding	
Have students complete the Vocabulary Development Lesson and the Grammar and Style Lesson (SE p. 998)	20 min.
Apply students' ability to elaborate for information in their writing by using the Writing Lesson (SE/ATE p. 999)	45 min.
Apply students' understanding using one or more of the Extension Activities (SE p. 999)	20–90 min.

A **ACCELERATED INSTRUCTION:**
Use the strategies and activities identified with an **A**.

UNIVERSAL ACCESS
● = Below Level Students
▲ = On-Level Students
■ = Above Level Students

Time and Resource Manager

Reading Level: Average
Average Number of Instructional Days: 4

PRINT	TRANSPARENCIES	TECHNOLOGY
RESOURCES		
• **Beyond Literature,** Workplace Skills: Conflict Resolution, p. 56 ▲ ■		• **Interest Grabber Video,** Tape 6 ● ▲ ■
• **Selection Support Workbook:** ● ▲ ■ Literary Analysis, p. 249 Reading Strategy, p. 248 Build Vocabulary, p. 246	• **Literary Analysis and Reading Transparencies,** pp. 111 and 112 ● ▲ ■	
• **Adapted Reader's Companion** ● • **Reader's Companion** ●		• **Listening to Literature** ● ▲ ■ Audiocassettes, Side 34 Audio CDs, CD 19
• **English Learner's Companion** ● ▲ • **Literatura en español** ● ▲ • **Literary Analysis for Enrichment** ■		
• **Formal Assessment:** Selection Test, pp. 251–253 ● ▲ ■ • **Open Book Test,** pp. 166–168 ● ▲ ■ • **Performance Assessment and Portfolio Management,** p. 16 ● ▲ ■ • **PRENTICE HALL ASSESSMENT SYSTEM** ● ▲ ■	• **PRENTICE HALL ASSESSMENT SYSTEM** ● ▲ ■ Skills Practice Answers and Explanations on Transparencies	• **Test Bank Software** ● ▲ ■ • **Got It! Assessment Videotapes,** Tape 5 ● ▲
• **Selection Support Workbook:** ● ▲ ■ Grammar and Style, p. 247 • **Writing and Grammar,** Ruby Level ● ▲ ■ • **Extension Activities,** p. 56 ● ▲ ■	• **Daily Language Practice Transparencies** ● ▲ • **Writing Models and Graphic Organizers on Transparencies,** pp. 9–12 ● ▲ ■	• **Writing and Grammar iText CD-ROM** ● ▲ ■ **Take It to the Net** www.phschool.com

BLOCK SCHEDULING: Use one 90-minute class period to preteach the selection and have students read it. Use a second 90-minute class period to assess students' mastery of skills and have them complete one of the Extension Activities.

986b

Motivation

Write the following statements on the chalkboard:

I want you to have all the things I never had.

I want you to make something of yourself.

I only want what's best for you.

Ask students to respond to these statements. Do they sound familiar? Who might be the speaker? Who is the "you" being addressed? Explain that these are aspirations that parents commonly have for their children. Tell students that they are about to read a story of a father who has ambitious dreams for his daughter's future that, unfortunately for him, she does not share.

📼 Interest Grabber Video

As an alternative, play "If the Shoe Fits" on Tape 6 to engage students' interest.

❶ Background

More About the Author

Bernard Malamud began publishing fiction in the 1950s, one of a generation of gifted Jewish writers that included Saul Bellow, Norman Mailer, and Isaac Bashevis Singer. Among these, Malamud has been praised for the accessibility of his style and themes. The author himself, in speaking of the value of ordinary narrative forms, said, "The human race needs the novel. . . . Those who say the novel is dead can't write them."

Malamud's place among writers of his generation is further defined by his moral vision. The characters in his fiction often seem to struggle against base instincts in an attempt to lead better, more virtuous lives.

Prepare to Read

❶ The First Seven Years

Bernard Malamud (1914–1986)

"I write . . . to explain life to myself and to keep me related to men," Bernard Malamud once commented when describing his life's work. He was a writer who possessed a strong social and political conscience, though he often insisted publicly that he was only interested in "the story." He explored the power of art to liberate people, always believing that "the purpose of freedom is to create it for others."

Childhood of Two Cultures Bernard Malamud was born in Brooklyn, New York, the son of Russian immigrants. His father was a grocer who, like so many immigrants, worked diligently to forge a better life for his family. According to his own account, Malamud's boyhood was "comparatively happy." He grew up hearing the constant mingling of Yiddish and English—an experience that contributed to his fine ear for the rhythms of spoken dialogue. Through his family's attention to Jewish culture, he developed a taste for Manhattan's Second Avenue Yiddish Theater, where two of his mother's relatives sometimes performed. A favored boyhood pastime was listening to his father recount tales of Jewish life in pre-Revolutionary Russia. Young Bernard began to display his father's gift for telling stories when, recovering from pneumonia at age nine, he spent hours in the back room of the family store writing down the stories he had composed to tell his friends.

A Literary Range Malamud attended City College of New York and Columbia University and began publishing stories in a number of well-known magazines. Despite his strong connection to Yiddish folk tales—many of Malamud's stories are drawn from this oral tradition—his work depicts a broad range of settings and characters. From the gifted baseball player in *The Natural* (1952), Malamud's first novel, to the handyman living in czarist Russia in the Pulitzer Prize-winning *The Fixer* (1966), all of his characters come across as real and accessible, with universal hopes and concerns.

Malamud's other novels include *The Assistant* (1957), *A New Life* (1961), *The Tenants* (1971), and *Dubin's Lives* (1979). He also wrote numerous short stories, many of which were published in *The Magic Barrel* (1958), which won the National Book Award.

Capturing Life's Lessons In much of his writing, Malamud uses Jewish characters to represent all of humanity, capturing their attempts to maintain a link to their cultural heritage while trying to cope with modern realities. While some of his characters achieve success, others experience disappointment. By portraying failure as well as triumph, Malamud reveals the essence of the human experience and creates a delicate balance between tragedy and comedy. Some of his stories amuse readers as the characters try to negotiate between fulfilling their ideals and meeting the practical demands of their lives.

A Touch of Magic Malamud often tells his stories in spare, compressed prose, sprinkled with flashes of highly charged metaphorical language. He allows magical events to happen in gloomy city neighborhoods, and gives his hard-working characters unexpected flashes of passion. Other Malamud stories move readers to sadness as characters struggle courageously within tragic circumstances. "The First Seven Years" depicts a Polish immigrant's desire to see his daughter achieve a better life. His notion of that life, however, is not the same as hers.

TEACHING RESOURCES

The following resources can be used to enrich or extend the instruction for pp. 986–987.

Motivation

📼 **Interest Grabber Video**, Tape 6

Background

📖 **Beyond Literature**, p. 56 ■

Take It to the Net
Visit www.phschool.com for background and hotlinks for "The First Seven Years."

Literary Analysis

▨ **Literary Analysis and Reading Transparencies**, Epiphany, p. 111 ■

Reading

📖 **Selection Support:** Reading Strategy, p. 248; Build Vocabulary, p. 246

▨ **Literary Analysis and Reading Transparencies**, Identifying with Characters, p. 112

 **BLOCK SCHEDULING:** Resources marked with this symbol provide varied instruction during 90-minute blocks.

Preview

Connecting to the Literature

When parents or teachers push you to study hard, learn a skill, or practice an instrument, they hope to help you achieve a better life. Similarly, the father in this story pushes his daughter in a certain direction in the hope that she will find happiness. However, her idea of happiness does not match his.

❶ Literary Analysis

Epiphany

In a traditional short story, the plot moves toward resolution, a point at which the conflict is untangled and the outcome of the action becomes clear. However, many twentieth-century writers turned away from such traditional plot structures. These writers constructed plots that move toward an **epiphany,** a moment when a character has a flash of insight that may alter the nature of the conflict without resolving it. In this story, the main character experiences an epiphany that requires him to reexamine long-held assumptions.

Connecting Literary Elements

Conflict, a struggle between opposing forces, is a key element of narrative literature because most plots develop from conflict. There are two main types of conflict:

- **Internal conflict** takes place within a character and involves a person's struggle with ideas, beliefs, or attitudes.
- **External conflict** takes place between a character and an outside force, such as society, nature, or an enemy.

As you read this story, think about the conflicts each character experiences. Use a chart like the one shown to examine the conflicts, and categorize them as either internal or external.

External

1. with Sobel
2.

↕

Feld's Conflicts

↕

Internal

1.
2.

❶ Reading Strategy

Identifying With Characters

When you **identify with characters,** you connect their thoughts, feelings, circumstances and actions to your own experience. Identifying with characters allows you to get more emotionally involved in your reading.

Vocabulary

diligence (dil´ ə jəns) *n.* constant, careful effort; perseverance (p. 988)

connivance (kə nī´ vəns) *n.* secret cooperation (p. 989)

illiterate (i lit´ ər it) *adj.* unable to read or write (p. 989)

unscrupulous (un skro͞o´ pyə ləs) *adj.* unethical; unprincipled (p. 991)

repugnant (ri pug´ nənt) *adj.* offensive; disagreeable (p. 991)

discern (di surn´) *v.* to perceive or recognize; make out clearly (p. 994)

The First Seven Years ◆ 987

❷ Literary Analysis

Epiphany

- Explain to students that an epiphany is literally a manifestation, or appearance, of divinity. In literary use, the term is broadened to mean an appearance of sudden understanding.

- Challenge students to recall epiphanies in other works they have read this year.

- Tell students to look for the epiphanies experienced by the characters in "The First Seven Years."

❸ Reading Strategy

Identifying With Characters

- To identify with a character means to feel a sense of comradeship with him or her—to understand and sympathize with the character's feelings.

- Point out that it is often easiest to identify with the character from whose point of view the story is told, because this character shares his or her thoughts and feelings openly with the reader.

- As students read, have them try to put themselves in Feld's place. How would they feel if they wanted only the best for their daughter, only to have her refuse her opportunities?

- Encourage students to keep journals with them as they read. They can note a character's reactions to a given situation and compare these reactions to what they might think and do in the same circumstances.

Vocabulary Development

- Pronounce each vocabulary word for students, and read the definitions as a class. Have students identify any words with which they are already familiar.

 E-Teach

Visit E-Teach at www.phschool.com for teachers' essays on how to teach, with questions and answers.

CUSTOMIZE INSTRUCTION FOR UNIVERSAL ACCESS

For Special Needs Students	For Less Proficient Readers	For English Learners
Have students read the adapted version of "The First Seven Years" in the **Adapted Reader's Companion.** This version provides basic-level instruction in an interactive format with questions and write-on lines. Completing the adapted version will prepare students to read the selection in the Student Edition.	Have students read "The First Seven Years" in the **Reader's Companion.** This version provides basic-level instruction in an interactive format with questions and write-on lines. After students finish the selection in **Reader's Companion,** have them complete the questions and activities in the Student Edition.	Have students read the adapted version of "The First Seven Years" in the **English Learner's Companion.** This version provides basic-level instruction in an interactive format with questions and write-on lines. Completing the adapted version will prepare students to read the selection in the Student Edition.

CUSTOMIZE INSTRUCTION
For Musical/Rhythmic Learners

Explain that Feld's manner of speaking indicates a Yiddish accent characterized by a musical quality and an uprising tone at the end of each sentence. To help musical/rhythmic learners appreciate Feld's speech patterns, play the recording of this selection on **Listening to Literature** Audiocassette Side 34 or CD 19.

❶ About the Selection

This poignant story portrays the potentially tragic results that can occur as parents struggle to let go of their maturing children. The main character, the shoemaker Feld, loves his only child, Miriam, with a fierce and ambitious love. Wanting an easier life for her than the immigrant trials of his own young adulthood, Feld plots what he believes will be an advantageous relationship with a young accounting student, Max. When Sobel, Feld's assistant, hears Feld and Max talking about Miriam, he flees the store. After her second date with Max, Miriam reports that the aspiring CPA is a soulless bore. Circumstance forces Feld to swallow his pride and visit Sobel, who reveals that he has worked for the shoemaker for five years solely out of love for Miriam. Feld, devastated, relinquishes his plans for his daughter's brilliant future as he agrees to let the apprentice ask for Miriam's hand in marriage in two years. Feld discovers the hard way that emotions cannot be dictated and that children must choose their own path in life.

❷ ▶ Critical Viewing

Answer: Students should realize that the setting is a commercial section of a fairly large city. The automobiles in the photograph reveal that the story is probably set in the first half of the twentieth century. The prominent shoe repair sign suggests that the story involves a shoemaker.

The First Seven Years
Bernard Malamud

Background

This story takes place in the 1950s, a prosperous decade in the United States. Both the Great Depression and World War II had ended and the baby boom was in full swing. People were upwardly mobile; if they worked hard, they were virtually assured that their status in society would improve. Parents labored for wealth so that their children would have easier lives, yet some children took material comfort for granted. They became more interested in matters of the spirit. Malamud's story explores the gap in values that sometimes occurred between children of the 1950s and their parents.

Feld, the shoemaker, was annoyed that his helper, Sobel, was so insensitive to his reverie that he wouldn't for a minute cease his fanatic pounding at the other bench. He gave him a look, but Sobel's bald head was bent over the last[1] as he worked and he didn't notice. The shoemaker shrugged and continued to peer through the partly frosted window at the nearsighted haze of falling February snow. Neither the shifting white blur outside, nor the sudden deep remembrance of the snowy Polish village where he had wasted his youth could turn his thoughts from Max the college boy, (a constant visitor in the mind since early that morning when Feld saw him trudging through the snowdrifts on his way to school) whom he so much respected because of the sacrifices he had made throughout the years—in winter or direst heat—to further his education. An old wish returned to haunt the shoemaker: that he had had a son instead of a daughter, but this blew away in the snow for Feld, if anything, was a practical man. Yet he could not help but contrast the diligence of the boy, who was a peddler's son, with Miriam's unconcern for an education. True, she was always with a book in her hand, yet when the opportunity arose for a college education, she had said no she would rather find a job. He had begged her to go, pointing out how many fathers could not afford to send their children to college, but she said she wanted to be independent. As for education, what was it, she asked, but books,

❷ ▲ Critical Viewing
What does this image reveal about the setting of the story? **[Predict]**

diligence (dil′ ə jəns) *n.* constant, careful effort; perseverance

---

1. **last** *n.* block shaped like a person's foot, on which shoes are made or repaired.

TEACHING RESOURCES

The following resources can be used to enrich or extend the instruction for pp. 988–996.

Literary Analysis

📖 **Writing Models and Graphic Organizers on Transparencies,** pp. 9–12 ■

📖 **Selection Support:** Literary Analysis, p. 249

Reading

📖 **Adapted Reader's Companion**

📖 **English Learner's Companion**

🎧 **Listening to Literature Audiocassettes,** Side 34 ■

💿 **Listening to Literature Audio CDs,** CD 19 ■

■ **BLOCK SCHEDULING:** Resources marked with this symbol provide varied instruction during 90-minute blocks.

which Sobel, who diligently read the classics, would as usual advise her on. Her answer greatly grieved her father.

A figure emerged from the snow and the door opened. At the counter the man withdrew from a wet paper bag a pair of battered shoes for repair. Who he was the shoemaker for a moment had no idea, then his heart trembled as he realized, before he had thoroughly discerned the face, that Max himself was standing there, embarrassedly explaining what he wanted done to his old shoes. Though Feld listened eagerly, he couldn't hear a word, for the opportunity that had burst upon him was deafening.

He couldn't exactly recall when the thought had occurred to him, because it was clear he had more than once considered suggesting to the boy that he go out with Miriam. But he had not dared speak, for if Max said no, how would he face him again? Or suppose Miriam, who harped so often on independence, blew up in anger and shouted at him for his meddling? Still, the chance was too good to let by: all it meant was an introduction. They might long ago have become friends had they happened to meet somewhere, therefore was it not his duty—an obligation—to bring them together, nothing more, a harmless <u>connivance</u> to replace an accidental encounter in the subway, let's say, or a mutual friend's introduction in the street? Just let him once see and talk to her and he would for sure be interested. As for Miriam, what possible harm for a working girl in an office, who met only loud-mouthed salesmen and <u>illiterate</u> shipping clerks, to make the acquaintance of a fine scholarly boy? Maybe he would awaken in her a desire to go to college; if not—the shoemaker's mind at last came to grips with the truth—let her marry an educated man and live a better life.

When Max finished describing what he wanted done to his shoes, Feld marked them, both with enormous holes in the soles which he pretended not to notice, with large white-chalk x's, and the rubber heels, thinned to the nails, he marked with o's, though it troubled him he might have mixed up the letters. Max inquired the price, and the shoemaker cleared his throat and asked the boy, above Sobel's insistent hammering, would he please step through the side door there into the hall. Though surprised, Max did as the shoemaker requested, and Feld went in after him. For a minute they were both silent, because Sobel had stopped banging, and it seemed they understood neither was to say anything until the noise began again. When it did, loudly, the shoemaker quickly told Max why he had asked to talk to him.

"Ever since you went to high school," he said, in the dimly-lit hallway, "I watched you in the morning go to the subway to school, and I said always to myself, this is a fine boy that he wants so much an education."

"Thanks," Max said, nervously alert. He was tall and grotesquely thin, with sharply cut features, particularly a beak-like nose. He was wearing a loose, long slushy overcoat that hung down to his ankles,

Literary Analysis
Epiphany and Conflict Is Feld's conflict in speaking to Max primarily internal or external? Explain.

connivance (kə nī′ vəns) *n.* secret cooperation

illiterate (i lit′ ər it) *adj.* unable to read or write

☑Reading Check ❺
What hope does Feld hold for his daughter Miriam and the college boy Max?

The First Seven Years ◆ 989

- Ask students whom they identify with in this scene, Max or Feld. Have them explain their answers. Possible answers: Students might identify with Feld because they probably know how hard it can be to ask for something they truly want; other students may identify with Max because it can be embarrassing to have someone make such a request; also, it can be hard to say no.

- Have students consider what they would have charged Max for the repair job. Why? Possible answer: Students might say that they would have charged the regular price because this is the appropriate thing to do. Charging nothing would have seemed like a bribe.

- Then, ask the Reading Strategy question on p. 990: How do you think Feld feels during this exchange with Max? Why? Answer: He is nervous and embarrassed because he wants so much to succeed in bringing the two young people together.

❼ Literary Analysis

Epiphany and Conflict

- Ask students why Sobel reacts as he does. Have them look back in the story for a clue. Answer: Sobel lends Miriam books, which suggests that the two have a friendship. Sobel may be jealous; he may want to date Miriam himself.

- Then, ask the Literary Analysis question on p. 990: What do Sobel's actions and Feld's reactions suggest about a conflict between the two men? Answer: Sobel is upset that Feld has not considered him as a potential husband for Miriam.

looking like a rug draped over his bony shoulders, and a soggy, old brown hat, as battered as the shoes he had brought in.

"I am a business man," the shoemaker abruptly said to conceal his embarrassment, "so I will explain you right away why I talk to you. I have a girl, my daughter Miriam—she is nineteen—a very nice girl and also so pretty that everybody looks on her when she passes by in the street. She is smart, always with a book, and I thought to myself that a boy like you, an educated boy—I thought maybe you will be interested sometime to meet a girl like this." He laughed a bit when he had finished and was tempted to say more but had the good sense not to.

Max stared down like a hawk. For an uncomfortable second he was silent, then he asked, "Did you say nineteen?"

"Yes."

"Would it be all right to inquire if you have a picture of her?"

"Just a minute." The shoemaker went into the store and hastily returned with a snapshot that Max held up to the light.

❻ "She's all right," he said.

Feld waited.

"And is she sensible—not the flighty kind?"

"She is very sensible."

After another short pause, Max said it was okay with him if he met her.

"Here is my telephone," said the shoemaker, hurriedly handing him a slip of paper. "Call her up. She comes home from work six o'clock."

Max folded the paper and tucked it away into his worn leather wallet.

"About the shoes," he said. "How much did you say they will cost me?"

"Don't worry about the price."

"I just like to have an idea."

"A dollar—dollar fifty. A dollar fifty," the shoemaker said.

At once he felt bad, for he usually charged two twenty-five for this kind of job. Either he should have asked the regular price or done the work for nothing.

❼ Later, as he entered the store, he was startled by a violent clanging and looked up to see Sobel pounding with all his might upon the naked last. It broke, the iron striking the floor and jumping with a thump against the wall, but before the enraged shoemaker could cry out, the assistant had torn his hat and coat from the hook and rushed out into the snow.

So Feld, who had looked forward to anticipating how it would go with his daughter and Max, instead had a great worry on his mind. Without his temperamental helper he was a lost man, especially since it was years now that he had carried the store alone. The shoemaker had for an age suffered from a heart condition that threatened collapse if he dared exert himself. Five years ago, after an attack, it had appeared as

Reading Strategy

Identifying With Characters How do you think Feld feels during this exchange with Max? Why?

Literary Analysis

Epiphany and Conflict What do Sobel's actions and Feld's reactions suggest about a conflict between the two men?

✳ ENRICHMENT: History Connection

America's Immigrants

This story is about Polish immigrants to the United States. The Poles are just one of many groups whose members left their homelands to seek better lives in America. For example, a huge immigration surge occurred in the mid-1800s as Irish, Chinese, and Germans—along with many others—fled economic or political difficulties. Additional immigration waves have swelled America's population since that time, whether comprising Russian Jews escaping mob attacks in the late 1870s or Vietnamese seeking

freedom from a changing government in the late 1980s.

Immigrants often settle first in coastal cities, straining the urban infrastructure. During the nineteenth and early twentieth centuries, large numbers of newcomers were forced to live in dark and dreary tenement house apartments, which often lacked windows, indoor plumbing, and fire escapes. Many new Americans arrived with limited financial resources, and even more limited English.

though he would have either to sacrifice his business upon the auction block and live on a pittance thereafter, or put himself at the mercy of some <u>unscrupulous</u> employee who would in the end probably ruin him. But just at the moment of his darkest despair, this Polish refugee, Sobel, appeared one night from the street and begged for work. He was a stocky man, poorly dressed, with a bald head that had once been blond, a severely plain face and soft blue eyes prone to tears over the sad books he read, a young man but old—no one would have guessed thirty. Though he confessed he knew nothing of shoemaking, he said he was apt and would work for a very little if Feld taught him the trade. Thinking that with, after all, a landsman,[2] he would have less to fear than from a complete stranger, Feld took him on and within six weeks the refugee rebuilt as good a shoe as he, and not long thereafter expertly ran the business for the thoroughly relieved shoemaker.

Feld could trust him with anything and did, frequently going home after an hour or two at the store, leaving all the money in the till, knowing Sobel would guard every cent of it. The amazing thing was that he demanded so little. His wants were few; in money he wasn't interested—in nothing but books, it seemed—which he one by one lent to Miriam, together with his profuse, queer written comments, manufactured during his lonely rooming house evenings, thick pads of commentary which the shoemaker peered at and twitched his shoulders over as his daughter, from her fourteenth year, read page by sanctified page, as if the word of God were inscribed on them. To protect Sobel, Feld himself had to see that he received more than he asked for. Yet his conscience bothered him for not insisting that the assistant accept a better wage than he was getting, though Feld had honestly told him he could earn a handsome salary if he worked elsewhere, or maybe opened a place of his own. But the assistant answered, somewhat ungraciously, that he was not interested in going elsewhere, and though Feld frequently asked himself what keeps him here? why does he stay? he finally answered it that the man, no doubt because of his terrible experiences as a refugee, was afraid of the world.

After the incident with the broken last, angered by Sobel's behavior, the shoemaker decided to let him stew for a week in the rooming house, although his own strength was taxed dangerously and the business suffered. However, after several sharp nagging warnings from both his wife and daughter, he went finally in search of Sobel, as he had once before, quite recently, when over some fancied slight—Feld had merely asked him not to give Miriam so many books to read because her eyes were strained and red—the assistant had left the place in a huff, an incident which, as usual, came to nothing for he had returned after the shoemaker had talked to him, and taken his seat at the bench. But this time, after Feld had plodded through the snow to Sobel's house—he had thought of sending Miriam but the idea became <u>repugnant</u> to him—the burly landlady at the door

2. **landsman** *n.* fellow countryman.

unscrupulous (un skro͞op′ yə les) *adj.* unethical; unprincipled

Literary Analysis
Epiphany and Conflict
What are some of the conflicts Feld experiences in regard to Sobel?

repugnant (ri pug′ nənt) *adj.* offensive; disagreeable

 **Reading Check** ❾
Under what circumstances did Sobel begin working for Feld?

❽ **Literary Analysis**
Epiphany and Conflict

- Read aloud the bracketed passage to students. Have them look for signs of conflict between Feld and Sobel.
- Ask the Literary Analysis question on p. 991: What are some of the conflicts Feld experiences in regard to Sobel?
  Answer: Feld feels guilty for paying Sobel less than he could earn elsewhere. He is thankful that Sobel stays with him, but he is puzzled by his reasons.
- Challenge students to guess why Sobel stays with Feld. Ask them to think about whether Feld senses why Sobel stays and refuses to acknowledge it, even to himself.
  Answer: Sobel stays so that he can see Miriam every day. Since Feld wants Miriam to marry an educated man, he doesn't want to see that Sobel cares for her.

❾ **Reading Check**
Answer: When Feld needed to find an assistant because of his weak heart, Sobel appeared and asked for a job.

- Have students read the bracketed passage, and discuss with them Feld's hopes for the date between Miriam and Max.

- To help them identify with the characters, ask students to consider experiences they have had with dates arranged by others. How do they think Max and Miriam's date is likely to turn out? Possible answers: Students may mention disastrous arranged dates or their surprise at successful arrangements. They will likely speculate that the date between Max and Miriam will not go well.

informed him in a nasal voice that Sobel was not at home, and though Feld knew this was a nasty lie, for where had the refugee to go? still for some reason he was not completely sure of—it may have been the cold and his fatigue—he decided not to insist on seeing him. Instead he went home and hired a new helper.

Having settled the matter, though not entirely to his satisfaction, for he had much more to do than before, and so, for example, could no longer lie late in bed mornings because he had to get up to open the store for the new assistant, a speechless, dark man with an irritating rasp as he worked, whom he would not trust with the key as he had Sobel. Furthermore, this one, though able to do a fair repair job, knew nothing of grades of leather or prices, so Feld had to make his own purchases: and every night at closing time it was necessary to count the money in the till and lock up. However, he was not dissatisfied, for he lived much in his thoughts of Max and Miriam. The college boy had called her, and they had arranged a meeting for this coming Friday night. The shoemaker would personally have preferred Saturday, which he felt would make it a date of the first magnitude, but he learned Friday was Miriam's choice, so he said nothing. The day of the week did not matter. What mattered was the aftermath. Would they like each other and want to be friends? He sighed at all the time that would have to go by before he knew for sure. Often he was tempted to talk to Miriam about the boy, to ask whether she thought she would like his type—he had told her only that he considered Max a nice boy and had suggested he call her—but the one time he tried she snapped at him—justly—how should she know?

At last Friday came. Feld was not feeling particularly well so he stayed in bed, and Mrs. Feld thought it better to remain in the bedroom with him when Max called. Miriam received the boy, and her parents could hear their voices, his throaty one, as they talked. Just before leaving, Miriam brought Max to the bedroom door and he stood there a minute, a tall, slightly hunched figure wearing a thick, droopy suit, and apparently at ease as he greeted the shoemaker and his wife, which was surely a good sign. And Miriam, although she had worked all day, looked fresh and pretty. She was a large-framed girl with a well-shaped body, and she had a fine open face and soft hair. They made, Feld thought, a first-class couple.

Miriam returned after 11:30. Her mother was already asleep, but the shoemaker got out of bed and after locating his bathrobe went into the kitchen, where Miriam, to his surprise, sat at the table, reading.

"So where did you go?" Feld asked pleasantly.

"For a walk," she said, not looking up.

"I advised him," Feld said, clearing his throat, "he shouldn't spend so much money."

"I didn't care."

The American Experience

The Rooming House

In this story, Sobel lives in a rooming house. Though rooming houses still exist today, up until the mid-twentieth century, they were a far more common form of shelter. Sometimes called boarding houses, rooming houses were inexpensive places to live. The roomer—or boarder— paid the owner a weekly fee for a bedroom, with access to a shared bathroom. The fee also covered meals, typically served family style. This setting was well suited to those with small incomes, new immigrants, and single people. Because they brought together strangers from all walks of life, rooming houses provided a rich setting for writers. They figure in some famous works of literature, including the short story "Tea-Time for Stout-Hearted Ladies" by Jean Stafford and, more recently, Frank McCourt's memoir *'Tis*.

✳ ENRICHMENT: Community Connection

Local Business

The main drama of this story takes place in a shoe repair shop, where people like Feld and Max have become acquainted while transacting routine business. Have students analyze the kinds of interactions they have had with businesses in your community. Have they worked in local businesses? Are they acquainted with any proprietors or workers? Then, discuss how local business owners participate in the community. Do they live locally? What, if any, role do they play in community decisions?

The shoemaker boiled up some water for tea and sat down at the table with a cupful and a thick slice of lemon.

"So how," he sighed after a sip, "did you enjoy?"

"It was all right."

He was silent. She must have sensed his disappointment, for she added, "You can't really tell much the first time."

"You will see him again?"

Turning a page, she said that Max had asked for another date.

"For when?"

"Saturday."

"So what did you say?"

"What did I say?" she asked, delaying for a moment—"I said yes."

Afterwards she inquired about Sobel, and Feld, without exactly knowing why, said the assistant had got another job. Miriam said nothing more and began to read. The shoemaker's conscience did not trouble him; he was satisfied with the Saturday date.

During the week, by placing here and there a deft question, he managed to get from Miriam some information about Max. It surprised him to learn that the boy was not studying to be either a doctor or lawyer but was taking a business course leading to a degree in accountancy. Feld was a little disappointed because he thought of accountants as bookkeepers and would have preferred "a higher profession." However, it was not long before he had investigated the subject and discovered that Certified Public Accountants were highly respected people, so he was thoroughly content as Saturday approached. But because Saturday was a busy day, he was much in the store and therefore did not see Max when he came to call for Miriam. From his wife he learned there had been nothing especially revealing about their meeting. Max had rung the bell and Miriam had got her coat and left with him—nothing more. Feld did not probe, for his wife was not particularly observant. Instead, he waited up for Miriam with a newspaper on his lap, which he scarcely looked at so lost was he in thinking of the future. He awoke to find her in the room with him, tiredly removing her hat. Greeting her, he was suddenly inexplicably afraid to ask anything about the evening. But since she volunteered nothing he was at last forced to inquire how she had enjoyed herself. Miriam began something noncommittal but apparently changed her mind, for she said after a minute, "I was bored."

When Feld had sufficiently recovered from his anguished disappointment to ask why, she answered without hesitation, "Because he's nothing more than a materialist."

"What means this word?"

"He has no soul. He's only interested in things."

He considered her statement for a long time but then asked, "Will you see him again?"

"He didn't ask."

"Suppose he will ask you?"

"I won't see him."

Literary Analysis
Epiphany and Conflict
What does this conversation suggest are some of Miriam's conflicts with her father?

Literary Analysis
Epiphany and Conflict
Why do you think Feld was "suddenly inexplicably afraid to ask anything about the evening"?

✔ Reading Check ⓭
What is Miriam's reaction to her first date with Max?

The First Seven Years ◆ 993

⓫ Literary Analysis
Epiphany and Conflict

- Ask the Reading Strategy question on p. 993: What does this conversation suggest are some of Miriam's conflicts with her father?
  Answer: Miriam seems more interested in Sobel than in Max. In addition, Miriam's answers are curt, which suggests that she does not want her father interfering in her personal life.

- Ask: Why do you think Miriam says nothing further about Sobel?
  Possible answers: She may be hurt by Sobel's having left without saying goodbye. She may sense that her father would not react well to her interest in Sobel.

⓬ Literary Analysis
Epiphany and Conflict

- After students have read the bracketed passage, ask them to restate the action in their own words.

- Ask the Literary Analysis question on p. 993: Why do you think Feld was "suddenly inexplicably afraid to ask anything about the evening"?
  Answer: Feld knows instinctively that the evening did not go well. He is afraid that if he asks questions, Miriam will confirm his fear.

- Ask students why Miriam decides to be honest about her reaction to Max.
  Answer: She knows that this will save her from having to see him again. She hopes that honesty now will prevent arguments in the future.

- Finally, ask: What does Miriam's reaction to Max suggest about a conflict between her values and Feld's?
  Answer: Feld wants Miriam to have material comforts; Miriam does not care as much about such things.

⓭ ✔ Reading Check

Answer: Miriam is unenthusiastic, but she agrees to see him again.

CUSTOMIZE INSTRUCTION FOR UNIVERSAL ACCESS

For Special Needs Students

Read aloud the descriptions of Max and Miriam. Ask students to compare and contrast the two characters' appearances—allow them to draw pictures, if necessary. What impression of each character is suggested by the comparison? Why is Feld's description of the couple ironic?

Students should see that Max appears physically unattractive—"droopy"—while Miriam is "fresh and pretty." Ironically, though Feld describes the two as a "first-class couple," readers can see that they are obviously ill suited to each other.

Encourage students to be aware of characters' physical descriptions when they read. These details often provide insights into the characters and the plot.

• As students read this passage, have them identify the conflicts that Feld experiences.

• Then, ask the Literary Analysis question on p. 994: What many conflicts does Feld experience in this passage? Which are internal and which are external?
Answer: Internal conflicts include Feld's illness, his pride versus his need to apologize to Sobel and ask him to return, and his inability to understand Sobel. External conflicts include Feld's disagreement with Miriam about going for Sobel and his struggle to climb the stairs.

▶ Monitor Progress Ask students what conflicts they think Sobel feels at seeing Feld again and hearing his request.
Answer: Sobel probably resents Feld's failure to value and respect him. He does not want to return to the store, but he does want to see Miriam again.

He did not argue; however, as the days went by he hoped increasingly she would change her mind. He wished the boy would telephone, because he was sure there was more to him than Miriam, with her inexperienced eye, could <u>discern</u>. But Max didn't call. As a matter of fact he took a different route to school, no longer passing the shoemaker's store, and Feld was deeply hurt.

Then one afternoon Max came in and asked for his shoes. The shoemaker took them down from the shelf where he had placed them, apart from the other pairs. He had done the work himself and the soles and heels were well built and firm. The shoes had been highly polished and somehow looked better than new. Max's Adam's apple went up once when he saw them, and his eyes had little lights in them.

"How much?" he asked, without directly looking at the shoemaker.

"Like I told you before," Feld answered sadly. "One dollar fifty cents."

Max handed him two crumpled bills and received in return a newly-minted silver half dollar.

He left. Miriam had not been mentioned. That night the shoemaker discovered that his new assistant had been all the while stealing from him, and he suffered a heart attack.

Though the attack was very mild, he lay in bed for three weeks. Miriam spoke of going for Sobel, but sick as he was Feld rose in wrath against the idea. Yet in his heart he knew there was no other way, and the first weary day back in the shop thoroughly convinced him, so that night after supper he dragged himself to Sobel's rooming house.

⓮ He toiled up the stairs, though he knew it was bad for him, and at the top knocked at the door. Sobel opened it and the shoemaker entered. The room was a small, poor one, with a single window facing the street. It contained a narrow cot, a low table and several stacks of books piled haphazardly around on the floor along the wall, which made him think how queer Sobel was, to be uneducated and read so much. He had once asked him, Sobel, why you read so much? and the assistant could not answer him. Did you ever study in a college someplace? he had asked but Sobel shook his head. He read, he said, to know. But to know what, the shoemaker demanded, and to know, why? Sobel never explained, which proved he read much because he was queer.

Feld sat down to recover his breath. The assistant was resting on his bed with his heavy back to the wall. His shirt and trousers were clean, and his stubby fingers, away from the shoemaker's bench, were strangely pallid. His face was thin and pale, as if he had been shut in this room since the day he had bolted from the store.

"So when you will come back to work?" Feld asked him.

To his surprise, Sobel burst out, "Never."

discern (di surn´) *v.* to perceive or recognize; make out clearly

Literary Analysis
Epiphany and Conflict
What conflicts does Feld experience in this passage? Which are internal, and which are external?

▼ **Critical Viewing**
Which item mentioned in the story is shown in this photograph? **[Connect]**

✷ **ENRICHMENT: Literature Connection**

Jacob and Rachel

"The First Seven Years" echoes the Biblical story of Jacob, Leah, and Rachel (Genesis 29–31). Like Sobel, Jacob falls in love with a young girl (Rachel) and agrees to work for her father Laban for seven years if, at the end of that time, Laban will allow them to marry. Laban agrees, but the morning after the wedding, Jacob discovers that Leah, Rachel's older sister, has taken Rachel's place. Laban explains that it would not be proper for the younger sister to be married before the older. Jacob agrees to serve Laban for another seven years if he can take Rachel as his second wife. Rachel eventually bears Joseph, Jacob's favorite son.

Jumping up, he strode over to the window that looked out upon the miserable street. "Why should I come back?" he cried.

"I will raise your wages."

"Who cares for your wages!"

The shoemaker, knowing he didn't care, was at a loss what else to say.

"What do you want from me, Sobel?"

"Nothing."

"I always treated you like you was my son."

Sobel vehemently denied it. "So why you look for strange boys in the street they should go out with Miriam? Why you don't think of me?"

The shoemaker's hands and feet turned freezing cold. His voice became so hoarse he couldn't speak. At last he cleared his throat and croaked, "So what has my daughter got to do with a shoemaker thirty-five years old who works for me?"

"Why do you think I worked so long for you?" Sobel cried out. "For the stingy wages I sacrificed five years of my life so you could have to eat and drink and where to sleep?"

"Then for what?" shouted the shoemaker.

"For Miriam," he blurted—"for her."

The shoemaker, after a time, managed to say, "I pay wages in cash, Sobel," and lapsed into silence. Though he was seething with excitement, his mind was coldly clear, and he had to admit to himself he had sensed all along that Sobel felt this way. He had never so much as thought it consciously, but he had felt it and was afraid.

"Miriam knows?" he muttered hoarsely.

"She knows."

"You told her?"

"No."

"Then how does she know?"

"How does she know?" Sobel said, "because she knows. She knows who I am and what is in my heart."

Feld had a sudden insight. In some devious way, with his books and commentary, Sobel had given Miriam to understand that he loved her. The shoemaker felt a terrible anger at him for his deceit.

"Sobel, you are crazy," he said bitterly. "She will never marry a man so old and ugly like you."

Sobel turned black with rage. He cursed the shoemaker, but then, though he trembled to hold it in, his eyes filled with tears and he broke into deep sobs. With his back to Feld, he stood at the window, fists clenched, and his shoulders shook with his choked sobbing.

Watching him, the shoemaker's anger diminished. His teeth were on edge with pity for the man, and his eyes grew moist. How strange and sad that a refugee, a grown man, bald and old with his miseries, who had by the skin of his teeth escaped Hitler's incinerators,[3] should fall in

---

3. **Hitler's incinerators** During World War II, millions of Jews were murdered by the Nazis under the direction of German dictator Adolf Hitler (1889–1945).

Reading Strategy
Identifying With Characters Put yourself in Sobel's position. Why is he so angry with Feld?

Literary Analysis
Epiphany How can you tell that Feld is having an epiphany?

✔ Reading Check ⑰
How does Sobel feel about Miriam? In what way has he expressed his feelings?

The First Seven Years ◆ 995

---

⑱ Literary Analysis

Epiphany and Conflict

- After students read the bracketed passage, ask them what Feld means when he says that Miriam's life will be "ugly" if she marries Sobel. **Answer:** Feld means that Miriam will have no hope of attaining the material comforts that he wished for her.

- Then, ask the Literary Analysis question on p. 996: What realization brings Feld such a strong feeling of sorrow? **Answer:** Feld realizes that if his daughter marries Sobel, her future will be bleak. His dreams for his daughter have been crushed.

Answers for p. 996

Review and Assess

Answers

1. Students may admire Feld for seeking a better life for his daughter, while others may sympathize with Miriam.

2. **(a)** He sees Max trudging through the snow to school. **(b)** Feld admires Max's college education and the comfortable future he thinks it will bring him.

3. **(a)** Max represents the possibility of a better, more comfortable life. **(b)** Miriam says that Max cares only for material things; Max seems to want these things for himself, while Feld wants them for his daughter.

4. **(a)** She is disappointed and shows no interest in future dates. **(b)** Miriam likes and respects Sobel and she finds Max materialistic and dull.

5. **(a)** He is a refugee from Poland. **(b)** Sobel has known hardship and sorrow. To Feld, he represents a lifetime of hardship, which he has hoped his daughter could avoid.

6. **(a)** Education represents the opportunity for a better life than their own. **(b)** Sobel views education as an opportunity to expand his knowledge and understanding of the world. Feld and Max look on education as a means of making money.

7. Some students will say that Feld had the right as Miriam's parent; others will say he should have stayed out of her love life.

---

love, when he had got to America, with a girl less than half his age. Day after day, for five years he had sat at his bench, cutting and hammering away, waiting for the girl to become a woman, unable to ease his heart with speech, knowing no protest but desperation.

"Ugly I didn't mean," he said half aloud.

Then he realized that what he had called ugly was not Sobel but Miriam's life if she married him. He felt for his daughter a strange and gripping sorrow, as if she were already Sobel's bride, the wife, after all, of a shoemaker, and had in her life no more than her mother had had. And all his dreams for her—why he had slaved and destroyed his heart with anxiety and labor—all these dreams of a better life were dead.

The room was quiet. Sobel was standing by the window reading, and it was curious that when he read he looked young.

"She is only nineteen," Feld said brokenly. "This is too young yet to get married. Don't ask her for two years more, till she is twenty-one, then you can talk to her."

Sobel didn't answer. Feld rose and left. He went slowly down the stairs but once outside, though it was an icy night and the crisp falling snow whitened the street, he walked with a stronger stride.

But the next morning, when the shoemaker arrived, heavy-hearted, to open the store, he saw he needn't have come, for his assistant was already seated at the last, pounding leather for his love.

⑱

Literary Analysis
Epiphany and Conflict
What realization brings Feld such a strong feeling of sorrow?

Review and Assess

Thinking About the Selection

1. **Respond:** Which ambitions for Miriam's future seem more worthy to you—Feld's or Miriam's? Explain.

2. **(a) Recall:** Under what circumstances does Feld first notice Max? **(b) Interpret:** Why is Max so appealing to Feld?

3. **(a) Recall:** To Feld, what values does Max seem to embody? **(b) Interpret:** Does Max really share Feld's values? Explain.

4. **(a) Recall:** How does Miriam react to her second date with Max? **(b) Compare and Contrast:** Explain the differences between Miriam's feelings for Max and her feelings for Sobel.

5. **(a) Recall:** What is Sobel's background? **(b) Speculate:** In what ways do the events of history that Sobel experienced add to his characterization?

6. **(a) Interpret:** What does education represent to Feld and Max? **(b) Compare and Contrast:** How does Sobel's love of reading compare with both Feld's and Max's feelings about education?

7. **Make a Judgment:** Do you think Feld was right to interfere in Miriam's life? Explain.

ASSESSMENT PRACTICE: Writing Skills

Punctuation   **(For more practice, see Test Preparation Workbook, p. 59.)**

Many tests require students to recognize errors in punctuation. Use the following sample test item to help students practice this skill.

Feld is a <u>shoemaker. Who emigrated</u> from Poland to America.

Which choice below corrects the error in the underlined phrase?

A shoemaker who emigrated

B shoemaker—who emigrated

C shoemaker; who emigrated

D correct as is

No punctuation is necessary between *shoemaker* and *who*. The correct answer is *A*.

Review and Assess

Literary Analysis

Epiphany

1. Use a chart like the one shown to examine the **epiphanies** the characters experience in this story.

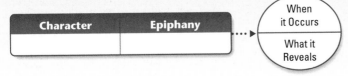

Character	Epiphany

⋯▸ When it Occurs / What it Reveals

2. What new ideas does Feld's epiphany introduce that challenge the values he has always held?
3. In what ways might Feld's epiphany (a) change his thinking in the future? (b) affect his attitude toward Miriam? (c) affect his attitude toward Sobel?

Connecting Literary Elements

4. (a) With what external **conflicts** does Feld struggle? (b) What internal conflicts trouble him? (c) Which conflicts affect Feld the most?
5. (a) What external conflicts does Sobel face? (b) What internal conflicts trouble him?
6. (a) What image of Sobel begins the story? (b) What image of Sobel ends it? (c) What meaning do you find in the relationship of the beginning of the story to its ending?
7. (a) At the end of this story, have the characters' situations changed? (b) If so, in what ways? If not, how might they change in the future?

Reading Strategy

Identifying With Characters

8. (a) Choose a character from "The First Seven Years" and list as many connections as possible to your own experience. (b) Imagine yourself in the character's situation. How would you feel? What actions might you take?

Extend Understanding

9. **Social Studies Connection:** For generations, many skilled trades in the United States, such as shoemaking, baking, stone cutting, or woodworking, have attracted immigrant workers. Why do you think this has so often been the case?

Quick Review

An **epiphany** is a sudden revelation or flash of insight.

A **conflict** is a struggle between opposing forces. **Internal conflict** takes place within the character and is characterized by the person's struggle with ideas. **External conflict** takes place between a character and an outside force, such as society, nature, or an enemy.

To **identify with characters,** connect their thoughts, feelings, circumstances, and actions to your own experience.

 Take It to the Net
www.phschool.com
Take the interactive self-test online to check your understanding of the selection.

The First Seven Years ◆ 997

Answers for p. 997

Review and Assess

1. **Possible answers:** Feld realizes that Sobel truly loves Miriam. He realizes what the past five years must have been like for Sobel.

2. Feld realizes that people may have other things to offer than material success.

3. **(a)** He may try harder to see situations from other people's points of view. **(b)** He may have learned that she has to make her own decisions. **(c)** He will probably treat Sobel with greater respect and understanding.

4. **(a)** He struggles to succeed in his business and provide for his family. **(b)** His pride and his need for help come into conflict after his heart attack. He struggles with the differences between his goals and Miriam's. **(c)** The greatest conflict is the one between his desires for Miriam's future, and Miriam's own desires for her life.

5. **(a)** He doesn't earn much money. **(b)** He loves Miriam but fears that his age and his low salary will prevent him from being with her.

6. **(a)** Sobel is pounding on the last in the shoe shop. **(b)** The same image ends the story. **(c)** It echoes the constancy of Sobel's love for Miriam, and his determination to wait for her.

7. **(a)** By the end of the story, all the characters' situations have changed. **(b)** Feld has had to abandon his dreams for his daughter; Sobel will have to wait two years, but he has gained permission to ask for Miriam's hand in marriage; Miriam does not know it yet, but she will be able to pursue her love for Sobel.

8. **(a)** Answers will vary depending on students' experiences. **(b)** **Sample answer:** A student in Miriam's situation might act just as she does: be polite to the interfering parent, but stick to his or her own goals and plans.

9. Some immigrant workers may have continued trades in the U.S. that they practiced in their countries of origin. However, for

continued

Answers continued

many immigrants, the trades were attractive because they did not usually require formal schooling or fluency in English and they provided reasonable pay.

Answers for p. 998

❶ Vocabulary Development

Word Analysis

1. having to do with letters
2. exactly as the letters say
3. the repetition of sounds from a letter or letters, used to create a particular effect in writing
4. the ability to read

Spelling Strategy

1. intelligent
2. originality
3. injustice
4. adjudicate

Concept Development: Context

1. illiterate
2. repugnant
3. diligence
4. unscrupulous
5. discern
6. connivance

❷ Grammar and Style

1. who (subject)
2. who (subject)
3. who (subject)
4. whom (direct object)
5. who (subject)

Writing Application

Have partners check each other's sentences to make sure they have used *who* and *whom* correctly.

Integrate Language Skills

❶ Vocabulary Development Lesson

Word Analysis: Latin Root -litera-

The root -*litera*- comes from the Latin word *littera*, which means "letter." Write a definition for each of the following words containing the root -*litera*-. Then, check your definitions against those in a dictionary.

1. literary
2. literal
3. alliteration
4. literacy

Spelling Strategy

When you hear the *j* sound in the middle of a word, that sound is often produced by the letter *g*, as in *diligence*. In your notebook, spell each word below by adding the letter that forms the *j* sound.

1. intelli__ent
2. ori__inality
3. in__ustice
4. ad__udicate

Concept Development: Context

Review the vocabulary list on p. 987. Then, select the word you might find in each of these newspaper articles.

1. "Reading Rate Declines Among Adults"
2. "Residents Complain of Dump's Disagreeable Smell"
3. "Hard-Working Teens Turn Vacant Lot Into Garden"
4. "Dishonorable Band of Thieves Gets Nabbed"
5. "Girl of Ten Recognizes Error in Mayor's Speech"
6. "Five Executives Caught Plotting a Takeover"

❷ Grammar and Style Lesson

Usage: *who* and *whom*

The correct use of *who* and *whom* helps an author clarify which character is being described. **Who,** like *he* or *she*, is used as a subject or subject complement. **Whom,** like *him* or *her*, is used as a direct object or as an object of the preposition. Study these examples:

> **Subject:** The diligence of the boy, *who* was a poor man's son, was inspiring. (*Who* serves as the subject of the adjective clause *who was . . . son.*)
>
> **Object:** Max, the college boy, *whom* he so much respected, was not a deep thinker. (*Whom* serves as the direct object of *respected.*)

Practice Identify which word—*who* or *whom*—correctly completes each sentence. Then, identify the word's function in the sentence.

1. She knows ___?___ I am . . .
2. Feld, ___?___ had looked forward to hearing about Max, was too nervous to ask.
3. There was little hope for a girl ___?___ met only loud-mouthed salesmen.
4. He had to open the store for the assistant, ___?___ he would not trust with the key.
5. He called Sobel, ___?___ he expected would be eagerly waiting.

Writing Application Write two sentences using *who* and *whom* correctly. In the first sentence, use the word that functions as a subject. In the second, use the word that functions as an object.

W̶G̶ *Prentice Hall Writing and Grammar Connection: Chapter 22, Section 2*

TEACHING RESOURCES

The following resources can be used to enrich or extend the instruction for pp. 998–999.

Vocabulary

📖 **Selection Support:** Build Vocabulary, p. 246

📖 **Vocabulary and Spelling Practice Book** (Use this booklet for skills enrichment.) ▪

Grammar

📖 **Selection Support:** Grammar and Style, p. 247

W̶G̶ **Writing and Grammar,** Ruby Level, p. 572

🖥 **Daily Language Practice Transparencies**

Writing

W̶G̶ **Writing and Grammar,** Ruby Level, p. 100 ▪

💿 **Writing and Grammar iText CD-ROM**

🖥 **BLOCK SCHEDULING:** Resources marked with this symbol provide varied instruction during 90-minute blocks.

Writing Lesson

Personality Profile

Malamud creates a believable and engaging character in Feld, the shoemaker. Suppose you are developing a television show based on "The First Seven Years." Write a personality profile of Feld to be used by your producers.

Prewriting	Before Feld's television character can be fully crafted, actors and producers need to know what he looks like and how he behaves. Use a cluster diagram like the one shown to jot down physical characteristics and personal qualities you observe in Feld.

Model: Clustering to Generate Details

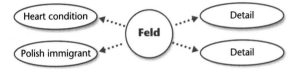

Drafting	Begin with an informative detail or image of Feld. Expand your profile in layers, referring to your cluster diagram as needed.
Revising	Have a classmate create a new cluster diagram based on your profile. Compare it to your prewriting diagram to discover key information you may have omitted.

Prentice Hall Writing and Grammar Connection: Chapter 6, Section 2

Extension Activities

Listening and Speaking Review the story to find details about Sobel's past, and create a **presentation** explaining how his past affected his personality, values, and decisions. Use these tips to prepare:

- Estimate Sobel's date of birth and possible birthplace.
- Conduct historical research to identify events Sobel experienced and include information from nonfiction accounts of those events.

Following your presentation, lead a class discussion about the issues raised by Sobel's life.

Research and Technology Using a variety of sources, including the Internet, conduct **cultural research** on a present-day society that adheres to the tradition of arranged marriages. Prepare a multimedia report, including text, quotations, images, and sound. In your report, balance the positive and negative aspects of such a tradition.

 **Take It to the Net** www.phschool.com

Go online for an additional research activity using the Internet.

The First Seven Years ◆ 999

❸ Writing Lesson

- Remind students that since the story is written from Feld's point of view, they have a good idea of what he thinks and feels. The of profiles they write should reflect this.
- Remind students to consider the way other characters react to Feld. What would Miriam say about him? How does Sobel feel about him?
- As an example, show students the Description and Observational Writing model on pp. 9–12 of **Writing Models and Graphic Organizers on Transparencies.**
- Use the Decription rubric on p. 16 of **Performance Assessment and Portfolio Management** to assess students' work.

❹ Listening and Speaking

- Students should start by summarizing what they know of Sobel's history, characteristics, and values.
- Remind students that Sobel fled Poland because of Nazi persecution. They might focus their research on the German occupation of Poland during World War II.
- Students may want to work with partners on this activity.

CUSTOMIZE INSTRUCTION for Universal Access

To address different learning styles, use the following activities suggested in the **Extension Activities** booklet, p. 56.

For Logical/Mathematical Learners, use Activity 5.

For Verbal/Linguistic Learners, use Activities 6 and 7.

For Visual/Spatial Learners, use Activity 7.

The Brown Chest

Lesson Objectives

1. **To analyze and respond to literary elements**
   - Literary Analysis: Atmosphere
   - Connecting Literary Elements: Precise Word Choice
2. **To read, comprehend, analyze, and critique a short story**
   - Reading Strategy: Breaking Down Long Sentences
   - Reading Check questions
   - Review and Assess questions
3. **To develop word analysis skills, fluency, and systematic vocabulary**
   - Vocabulary Development Lesson: Latin Word Root: *-sim-*
4. **To understand and apply written and oral language conventions**
   - Spelling Strategy
   - Grammar and Style Lesson: Adverb Clauses
   - Assessment Practice (ATE)
5. **To understand and apply appropriate writing and research strategies**
   - Writing Lesson: Analysis of a Symbol
   - Extension Activity: Feature Article on Fashions
6. **To understand and apply listening and speaking strategies**
   - Extension Activity: Conversation

STEP-BY-STEP TEACHING GUIDE	PACING GUIDE
PRETEACH	
Motivate Students and Provide Background	
Use the Motivation activity (ATE p. 1000)	5 min.
Read and discuss author and background features (SE/ATE p. 1000, 1002) 🅰	5 min.
Introduce the Concepts	
Introduce the Literary Analysis and Reading Strategy (SE/ATE p. 1001) 🅰	15 min.
Pronounce the vocabulary words and read their definitions (SE p. 1001)	5 min.
TEACH	
Monitor Comprehension	
Informally monitor comprehension by circulating while students read independently or in groups 🅰	20 min.
Monitor students' comprehension with the Reading Check notes (SE/ATE pp. 1003, 1005, 1007)	as students read
Develop vocabulary with Vocabulary notes (SE pp. 1004, 1005, 1006, 1007; ATE p. 1005)	as students read
Develop Understanding	
Develop students' understanding of atmosphere with the Literary Analysis annotations (SE pp. 1002, 1004, 1005, 1006; ATE pp. 1002, 1004, 1005, 1006) 🅰	5 min.
Develop students' ability to break down long sentences by using the Reading Strategy annotation (ATE p. 1003)	5 min.
ASSESS	
Assess Mastery	
Assess students' mastery of the Reading Strategy and Literary Analysis by having them answer the Review and Assess questions (SE/ATE p. 1009)	15 min.
Use one or more of the print and media Assessment Resources (ATE p. 1011) 🅰	up to 45 min.
EXTEND	
Apply Understanding	
Have students complete the Vocabulary Development Lesson and the Grammar and Style Lesson (SE p. 1010) 🅰	20 min.
Apply students' ability to use clear and logical organization in their writing by using the Writing Lesson (SE/ATE p. 1011) 🅰	45 min.
Apply students' understanding using one or more of the Extension Activities (SE p. 1011)	20–90 min.

 ACCELERATED INSTRUCTION:
Use the strategies and activities identified with an 🅰.

UNIVERSAL ACCESS
● = Below Level Students
▲ = On-Level Students
■ = Above Level Students

Time and Resource Manager

RESOURCES		
PRINT 📖	**TRANSPARENCIES**	**TECHNOLOGY** 💿 🎧 📼
• **Beyond Literature,** Cultural Connection: Family History, p. 57 ▲ ■		• **Interest Grabber Video,** Tape 6 ● ▲ ■
• **Selection Support Workbook:** ● ▲ ■ Literary Analysis, p. 253 Reading Strategy, p. 252 Build Vocabulary, p. 250	• **Literary Analysis and Reading Transparencies,** pp. 113 and 114 ● ▲ ■	
		• **Listening to Literature** ● ▲ ■ Audiocassettes, Side 34 Audio CDs, CD 19
• **Literatura en español** ● ▲ • **Literary Analysis for Enrichment** ■		
• **Formal Assessment:** Selection Test, pp. 254–256 ● ▲ ■ • **Open Book Test,** pp. 169–171 ● ▲ ■ • **Performance Assessment and Portfolio Management,** pp. 23, 30 ● ▲ ■ • **PRENTICE HALL ASSESSMENT** SYSTEM ● ▲ ■	• **PRENTICE HALL ASSESSMENT** SYSTEM ● ▲ ■ Skills Practice Answers and Explanations on Transparencies	• **Test Bank Software** ● ▲ ■ • **Got It! Assessment Videotapes,** Tape 5 ● ▲
• **Selection Support Workbook:** ● ▲ ■ Grammar and Style, p. 251 • **Writing and Grammar,** Ruby Level ● ▲ ■ • **Extension Activities,** p. 57 ● ▲ ■	• **Daily Language Practice Transparencies** ● ▲ • **Writing Models and Graphic Organizers on Transparencies,** pp. 9–12 ● ▲ ■	• **Writing and Grammar iText CD-ROM** ● ▲ ■ *Take It to the Net* www.phschool.com

BLOCK SCHEDULING: Use one 90-minute class period to preteach the selection and have students read it. Use a second 90-minute class period to assess students' mastery of skills and have them complete one of the Extension Activities.

Step-by-Step Teaching Guide for pp. 1000–1001

Motivation

To engage students' interest in the story, have them bring in or describe items that hold special memories for them or for their families. Have students explain why these items are special treasures. Explain that this story deals with a chest filled with such items.

▭ Interest Grabber Videotapes

As an alternative, play "John Updike" on Tape 6 to engage student interest.

❶ Background

More About the Author

The New Yorker published "Friends From Philadelphia," Updike's first story, in 1954. Since then Updike has published several collections of poetry, which have sometimes been received as insubstantial light entertainment. Even his critics acknowledge, however, that his style has developed over time; although humorous word-play and elaborate rhyme schemes have continued to be part of that style, Updike's subject matter and tone have grown progressively more serious and introspective. Early poems are merely funny and stylish; later poems tell stories of the poet's life and meditate on such subjects as death.

Updike finds plenty of inspiration in the everyday world. Many of his early poems were inspired by advertisements and articles in *The New Yorker*; he found them a never-failing source of entertainment and silliness. Titles like "Duet, with Muffled Brake Drums" and "Tao in the Yankee Stadium Bleachers" reflect this focus on everyday life.

Prepare to Read

❶ The Brown Chest

John Updike (b. 1932)

John Updike's fiction spins the gold of insight from the straw of everyday experience. Through his depictions of ordinary situations and everyday events, Updike explores some of the most important issues of our time and offers glimpses of the underlying significance of everyday life in contemporary America. Updike transfigures outwardly ordinary people, places, objects, and events with flashes of insight, grief, and love. His short stories, novels, plays, and poems have given shape to the lives of many Americans—children and adults, rich and poor, ordinary and gifted.

An Only Child John Updike was born and raised in Shillington, Pennsylvania. His father was a high-school teacher and his mother a writer who published a novel, *Enchanted*, in 1971. Updike thinks his experience as an only child helped to nurture his artistic temperament: "I'm sure that my capacities to fantasize and to make coherent fantasies, to have patience to sit down day after day and to whittle a fantasy out of paper, all that relates to being an only child." The young Updike coped with numerous personal drawbacks. For one thing, he suffered from intense bouts of hay fever and psoriasis, a painful skin disease. For another, he stammered.

A Fine Artist Updike excelled in drawing as well as writing. In his early years, he focused his hopes on a career as a cartoonist, following in the path of James Thurber. As he matured, his interest shifted toward writing, and by age eighteen, he had decided to pursue a career as a writer. After graduating from Harvard, where he edited the *Harvard Lampoon*, Updike studied for a year in England at the Ruskin School of Drawing and Fine Art. When he returned to the United States,

he became a staff writer for *The New Yorker* magazine, where James Thurber and E. B. White had made names for themselves earlier. *The New Yorker* published many of his short stories as well as his poems and literary criticism.

The Personal and the Global Updike has received wide acclaim for his many novels, as well as for volumes of poetry, criticism, and short stories. His thematic concerns are broad: Four novels featuring a character called Harry "Rabbit" Angstrom magnify the meaning of everyday moments. Novels such as *The Coup* (1978), *Brazil* (1994), and *In the Beauty of the Lilies* (1996) use a wider lens to examine how historical and political issues have affected people across the globe. Updike is also a master of the short story form, which is ideal for capturing flashes of insight into ordinary existence. Many of his stories, like his novels, are set in suburban America, which he often uses as a symbol of detachment from worldly concerns.

Updike's many honors include the National Book Award, and two Pulitzer Prizes for fiction. Of Updike, literary critic David Thorburn has written, "His steady productiveness has brought him a substantial and international audience, whose loyalty has nourished his faith in the traditional literary genres, and especially his belief in the power of realistic fiction to illuminate contemporary life." Updike has had a great influence on the generation of writers who were born after him. Some follow his tradition, while others rebel against his studied naturalism.

In the story "The Brown Chest," a man sifts through his family's accumulated belongings, focusing again and again on a chest filled with objects that call up memories. Set in rural and suburban locales, written with impeccable style, and expressing the extraordinary within the ordinary, it is vintage Updike.

TEACHING RESOURCES

The following resources can be used to enrich or extend the instruction for pp. 1000–1001.

Motivation
▭ **Interest Grabber Video,** Tape 6

Background
▭ **Beyond Literature,** p. 57 ▭

▭ *Take It to the Net*
Visit www.phschool.com for Background and hotlinks for "The Brown Chest."

Literary Analysis
▭ **Literary Analysis and Reading Transparencies,** Atmosphere, p. 114 ▭

Reading
▭ **Selection Support:** Reading Strategy, p. 252; Build Vocabulary, p. 250

▭ **Literary Analysis and Reading Transparencies,** Breaking Down Long Sentences, p. 113

▭ **BLOCK SCHEDULING:** Resources marked with this symbol provide varied instruction during 90-minute blocks.

Preview

Connecting to the Literature

Whether it is a drawer stuffed with old Scout badges or a box holding valentines from the third grade, most of us have a place to keep things we cannot bear to throw away. In this story, a chest full of family mementos becomes an emotional touchstone for a man's entire life.

❷ Literary Analysis

Atmosphere

In literature, **atmosphere** refers to the emotional quality of the world the author creates. Atmosphere arises from descriptions, especially those of the setting, and mirrors the emotions of the characters. In this story, descriptions of the brown storage chest create an atmosphere that varies as the main character's life develops. As you read, note how the story's atmosphere changes to reflect the main character's thoughts and feelings.

Connecting Literary Elements

Updike's ability to choose the best possible word to convey his meaning contributes to the power and beauty of his prose. For example, note the clarity of the image he creates with the words in italics:

> She spoke only to Gordon, as if a *pane of shyness* protected her from his *hoary* father . . .

As you read, notice other examples of Updike's **precise word choices,** and analyze how each one helps create atmosphere and meaning.

❸ Reading Strategy

Breaking Down Long Sentences

Updike tends to use long sentences that might be difficult to follow. To help your understanding, **break down long sentences** into their component parts. Use the punctuation—dashes, commas, parentheses, colons, and semi-colons—to divide the sentence into manageable sections, as in the example shown. Then, summarize the meaning of the sentence.

Vocabulary

mottled (mät′ ′ld) *adj.* blotched or streaked (p. 1004)

assimilate (ə sim′ ə lāt′) *v.* to absorb or incorporate (p. 1005)

unfathomable (un fath′ əm ə bəl) *adj.* unable to be understood (p. 1006)

egregious (ē grē′ jəs) *adj.* outstanding for undesirable qualities; remarkably bad (p. 1006)

proprietorial (prō prī′ ə tôr′ ē əl) *adj.* like someone who owns something (p. 1007)

evanescent (ev′ ə nes′ ənt) *adj.* short-lived; tending to fade or disappear (p. 1008)

> **Sentence in Sections**
>
> • These pieces that his infant eyes had grazed,
> • and that had framed his parents' lives,
> • seemed sadly shabby now, . . .
> • useless used furniture he had lacked the courage to discard.
>
> ⇩
>
> **Summary**

The Brown Chest ◆ 1001

❷ Literary Analysis

Atmosphere

- Write the word *atmosphere* on the chalkboard. Ask students what this word means to them. Explain that the atmosphere of a story is the mood it arouses in the reader.

- Have students think about the effect of the descriptive details Updike includes in his story.

- Encourage students to watch for details as they read, and think about how descriptive details draw them into the story.

❸ Reading Strategy

Breaking Down Long Sentences

- Explain that when sentences contain many clauses and details, readers can lose track of what the writer is saying. Have students look at the story's third sentence (page 1002). This sentence contains several clauses and descriptive details which may confuse readers' understanding of the main point.

- Challenge students to identify the main subject of the sentence (front) and the main actions taken by the subject (had, held). Once they have established the main idea of the sentence, students can then examine the details that give them further description and information.

- Encourage students to practice this strategy as they encounter confusing sentences in "The Brown Chest."

Vocabulary Development

- Pronounce each vocabulary word for students, and read the definitions as a class. Have students identify any words with which they are already familiar.

CUSTOMIZE INSTRUCTION FOR UNIVERSAL ACCESS

For Less Proficient Readers	For English Learners	For Advanced Readers
As students read, have them note difficult sentences. Have them identify the main subject(s) and verb(s) of each sentence, then add on details from the dependent and independent clauses until they have mastered each sentence.	Have students work with partners to paraphrase and summarize long sentences. The vocabulary of this story is relatively simple, but students may have trouble with the long sentences. Remind students to locate the subject and verb of each sentence to help their comprehension.	Have students discuss the effect of Updike's long sentences. Have them experiment with breaking some of the sentences down into shorter ones. Now have students compare the original with the rewritten sentences. Which effect do you prefer? Why?

 E-Teach

Visit E-Teach at www.phschool.com for teachers' essays on how to teach, with questions and answers.

Step-by-Step Teaching Guide for pp. 1002–1008

CUSTOMIZE INSTRUCTION
For Verbal/Linguistic Learners
Challenge students to identify sensory images in the story, listing words and phrases under the headings *sight*, *hearing*, *smell*, *taste*, and *touch*. Have students gather for a group discussion of how these words and phrases evoke the main character's emotional responses. Have students describe the effect the details have on the reader.

❶ About the Selection

Like many of us, the family in this story has imbued certain objects with special importance. Stored in a brown chest, which makes its way from home to home as the family moves over the years, these objects trace the family's history. As the main character grows from childhood to middle age, his feelings about the trunk and its freight of memory change from mixed fascination and revulsion to exasperation, as it becomes a white elephant. Finally, the chest acquires new meaning, as he shares its contents with his son and his son's fiancée —a new generation of family will continue the story, and add more history to the chest.

❷ Literary Analysis

Atmosphere

- Point out to students that Updike describes distinct atmospheres within the house. Ask students to identify the qualities that create each different atmosphere.
  Answer: Human activity creates a cheerful atmosphere in part of the house. Deserted, dark corners create a scary atmosphere in out-of-the-way places like the attic.

- Then, ask the Literary Analysis question on page 1002: What does the word "swish" add to this description of the street?
  Answer: It gives the street a busy, cheerful quality.

The Brown Chest
John Updike

Background

The chest in Updike's story is a kind of time capsule of the early twentieth century. It contains auburn curls from a haircut in 1919, recalling the bobbed styles that were popular after World War I. The 1925 wedding dress probably had a short hem in front and a long one in back. The photograph of the main character's father as a college football player in the early 1920s probably shows him wearing a leather helmet that provided much less protection than synthetic helmets do today. During the period profiled by the items in the chest, there was no videotape to help future generations grasp what life was like. As a result, these family mementos provide one of the few means of gaining insight into the past.

I n the first house he lived in, it sat up on the second floor, a big wooden chest, out of the way and yet not. For in this house, the house that he inhabited as if he would never live in any other, there were popular cheerful places, where the radio played and the legs of grown-ups went back and forth, and there were haunted bad places, like the coal bin behind the furnace, and the attic with its spiders and smell of old carpet, where he would never go without a grown-up close with him, and there were places in between, that were out of the main current but were not menacing, either, just neutral, and neglected. The entire front of the house had this neglected quality, with its guest bedroom where guests hardly ever stayed; it held a gray-painted bed with silver moons on the headboard and corner posts shaped at the top like mushrooms, and a little desk by the window where his mother sometimes, but not often, wrote letters and confided sentences to her diary in her tiny backslanting hand. If she had never done this, the room would have become haunted, even though it looked out on the busy street with its telephone wires and daytime swish of cars; but the occasional scratch of her pen

Literary Analysis
Atmosphere and Precise Word Choices What does the word "swish" add to this description of the street?

TEACHING RESOURCES

The following resources can be used to enrich or extend the instruction for pp. 1002–1008.

Literary Analysis

📖 **Writing Models and Graphic Organizers on Transparencies,** pp. 9–12 ▪

📖 **Selection Support:** Literary Analysis, p. 253

Reading

🎧 **Listening to Literature Audiocassettes,** Side 34 ▪

💿 **Listening to Literature Audio CDs,** CD 19 ▪

▪ **BLOCK SCHEDULING:** Resources marked with this symbol provide varied instruction during 90-minute blocks.

exerted just enough pressure to keep away the frightening shadows, the sad spirits from long ago, locked into events that couldn't change.

Outside the guest-bedroom door, the upstairs hall, having narrowly sneaked past his grandparent's bedroom's door, broadened to be almost a room, with a window all its own, and a geranium on the sill shedding brown leaves when the women of the house forgot to water it, and curtains of dotted swiss[1] he could see the telephone wires through, and a rug of braided rags shaped like the oval tracks his Lionel train[2] went around and around the Christmas tree on, and, to one side, its front feet planted on the rag rug, with just enough space left for the attic door to swing open, the chest.

It was big enough for him to lie in, but he had never dared try. It was painted brown, but in such a way that the wood grain showed through, as if paint very thinned with turpentine had been used. On the side, wavy stripes of paint had been allowed to run, making dribbles like the teeth of a big wobbly comb. The lid on its brown had patches of yellow freckles. The hinges were small and black, and there was a keyhole that had no key. All this made the chest, simple in shape as it was, strange, and ancient, and almost frightening. And when he, or the grown-up with him, lifted the lid of the chest, an amazing smell rushed out—deeply sweet and musty, of mothballs and cedar, but that wasn't all of it. The smell seemed also to belong to the

---

1. **dotted swiss** sheer fabric covered in woven dots.
2. **Lionel train** The Lionel Company is a famous manufacturer of model trains, which were a very popular hobby during Updike's youth.

3 ▲ **Critical Viewing**
What qualities does this chest share with the one depicted in the story? **[Connect]**

5 ☑ **Reading Check**
What object in the upstairs hallway seems "strange and ancient" to the boy?

The Brown Chest ◆ 1003

---

3 ▶ **Critical Viewing**
Answer: Students may say that the chest shown is large, brown, and old.

4 **Reading Strategy**
Breaking Down Long Sentences
- Challenge students to find the subject and verb of this sentence.
  Answer: subject: hall; verb: broadened
- Then, have students briefly paraphrase the sentence.
  Answer: The upstairs hall broadened to be almost a small room, and contained a window with a geranium and curtains, a braided rag rug, and the chest beside the door to the attic.

▶ **Monitor Progress** Ask students to describe the effect of the sentence as Updike wrote it. Why would he make his description so long and involved?
Answer: He wants to include every visual detail of the hallway so readers can see it. He is writing from the point of view of the child; the sentence reflects the ease with which a child is distracted from the main point by details like the curtains and the rag rug.

5 ☑ **Reading Check**
Answer: The object is a big wooden chest.

CUSTOMIZE INSTRUCTION FOR UNIVERSAL ACCESS

For Special Needs Students	For Advanced Readers
Have students read the story with partners, pausing at the end of each page or two to discuss the story. Each partner should make sure that the other can identify the setting and the main character's age and explain what happens during this section of the story.	Point out the boy's negative reaction to the chest and the emotions it evokes. How do students feel about objects or stories from their families' histories, about spending time with older relatives or acquaintances, or about collecting or interacting with elements of their community's past? Students may respond privately in journals.

1003

The New Yorker is noted not only as a forum for the best new fiction and poetry, but as a source for detailed coverage of current events. During World War II, the magazine was famous for the reports of its foreign correspondents. Long articles by noted writers such as A. J. Liebling, Janet Flanner, Mollie Panter-Downes, and Rebecca West described details of the London blitz, the German occupation of Paris, and the terrors and hardships being endured all over Europe. *The New Yorker's* war reports culminated in 1945 with *Hiroshima* by John Hersey. *Hiroshima* narrates the day of the atomic bombing and its aftermath from the points of view of six survivors. *The New Yorker* devoted nearly an entire issue to this long report, one of the most famous articles ever to appear in the pages of any magazine. Students will read an excerpt from *Hiroshima* in Unit 6.

⑦ **Literary Analysis**

Atmosphere

• Ask students how they would describe the atmosphere of the new house. What details gives it this atmosphere?
  Answer: The boy finds the atmosphere somewhat threatening. He doesn't like being isolated in a country place where neighbors are few and far away. He likes being around people.

• Then, ask the Literary Analysis question on page 1004: What specific word choices help to paint a clear picture of the boy's discomfort in the country?
  Answer: *Country space frightened him, dead trees were allowed to topple and slowly rot, spaces where he felt nobody had ever been*

▶ Monitor Progress Have students consider how the boy's fear of solitary places relates to his feelings about the brown chest.
  Answer: The chest is kept in an out-of-the-way place in the house where people don't spend a lot of time. The boy describes these quiet places as "haunted bad places." The chest frightens him because of its association with the quiet parts of the house.

contents—lace tablecloths and wool blankets on top, but much more underneath. The full contents of the chest never came quite clear, perhaps because he didn't want to know. His parents' college diplomas seemed to be under the blankets, and other documents going back still farther, having to do with his grandparents, their marriage, or the marriage of someone beyond even them. There was a folded old piece of paper with drawn-on hearts and designs and words in German. His mother had once tried to explain the paper to him, but he hadn't wanted to listen. A thing so old disgusted him. And there were giant Bibles, and squat books with plush covers and a little square <u>mottled</u> mirror buried in the plush of one. These books had fat pages edged in gold, thick enough to hold, on both sides, stiff brown pictures, often oval, of dead people. He didn't like looking into these albums, even when his mother was explaining them to him. The chest went down and down, into the past, and he hated the feeling of that well of time, with its sweet deep smell of things unstirring, waiting, taking on the moldy flavor of time, not moving unless somebody touched them.

Then everything moved: the moving men came one day and everything in the house that had always been in a certain place was swiftly and casually uplifted and carried out the door. In the general upheaval the week before, he had been shocked to discover, glancing in, that at some point the chest had come to contain drawings he had done as a child, and his elementary-school report cards, and photographs—studio photographs lovingly mounted in folders of dove-gray cardboard with deckle edges[3]—of him when he was five. He was now thirteen.

The new house was smaller, with more outdoors around it. He liked it less on both accounts. Country space frightened him, much as the coal bin and the dark triangles under the attic eaves had— spaces that didn't have enough to do with people. Fields that were plowed one day in the spring and harvested one day in the fall, woods where dead trees were allowed to topple and slowly rot without anyone noticing, brambled-around spaces where he felt nobody had ever been before he himself came upon them. Heaps and rows of overgrown stones and dumps of rusty cans and tinted bottles indicated that other people in fact had been here, people like those who had posed in their Sunday clothes in the gilded albums, but the traces they left weren't usable, the way city sidewalks and trolley-car tracks were usable. His instinct was to stay in the little thick-walled country house, and read, and eat sandwiches he made for himself of raisins and peanut butter, and wait for this phase of his life to pass. Moving from the first house, leaving it behind, had taught him that a life had phases.

The chest, on that day of moving, had been set in the new attic, which was smaller than the other, and less frightening, perhaps

---

3. **deckle edges** rough edges of paper, often regarded as decorative.

The *American* **Experience**

⑥ **The New Yorker** *Magazine*
  John Updike has had a career-long association with *The New Yorker*. Founded in 1925, the magazine has done more to shape the evolution of the American short story than any other single publication. Throughout its history, *The New Yorker* has hired and published some of America's most prominent writers, notably Dorothy Parker, E. B. White, James Thurber, and John Updike. Updike began his career with *The New Yorker* in 1955, when he became a staff writer. Though he left the staff after two years, he has continued to publish reviews, stories, and essays in its pages ever since. Today, nearly every major writer in the English language, from Eudora Welty to Toni Morrison to Stephen King, publishes in *The New Yorker*.

because gaps in the cedar-shingled roof let dabs of daylight in. When the roof was being repaired, the whole space was thrown open to the weather, and it rained in, on all the furniture there was no longer room for, except up here or in the barn. The chest was too important for the barn; it perched on the edge of the attic steps, so an unpainted back he had never seen before, of two very wide pale boards, became visible. At the ends of each board were careless splashes of the thin brown paint—stain, really—left by the chestmaker when he had covered the sides.

The chest's contents, unseen, darkened in his mind. Once in a great while his mother had to search in there for something, or to confide a treasure to its depths, and in those moments, peeking in, he was surprised at how full the chest seemed, fuller than he remembered, of dotted-swiss curtains and crocheted lap rugs and photographs in folders of soft cardboard, all smelling of camphor and cedar. There the chest perched, an inch from the attic stairwell, and there it stayed, for over forty years.

Then it moved again. His children, adults all, came from afar and joined him in the house, where their grandmother had at last died, and divided up the furniture—some for them to carry away, some for the local auctioneer to sell, and some for him, the only survivor of that first house, with its long halls and haunted places, to keep and to <u>assimilate</u> to his own house, hundreds of miles away.

Two of the three children, the two that were married, had many responsibilities and soon left; he and his younger son, without a wife and without a job, remained to empty the house and pack the U-Haul van they rented. For days they lived together, eating takeout food, poisoning mice and trapping cats, moving from crowded cellar to jammed attic like sick men changing position in bed, overwhelmed by decisions, by accumulated possessions, now and then fleeing the house to escape the oppression of the past. He found the iron scales, quite rusted by the cellar damp, whereon his grandmother used to weigh out bundles of asparagus against a set of cylindrical weights. The weights were still heavy in his hand, and left rust stains on his palm. He studied a tin basin, painted in a white-on-gray spatter-pattern that had puzzled him as a child with its apparent sloppiness, and he could see again his grandfather's paper-white feet soaking in suds that rustled as the bubbles popped one by one.

The chest, up there in the attic along with old rolled carpets and rocking chairs with broken cane seats, stacked hatboxes from the Thirties and paperback mysteries from the Forties, was too heavy to lift, loaded as it was. He and his younger son took out layers of blankets and plush-covered albums, lace tablecloths and linen napkins; they uncovered a long cardboard box labelled in his mother's handwriting "Wedding Dress 1925," and, underneath that, rumpled silk dresses that a small girl might have worn when the century was young, and patent-leather baby shoes, and a gold-plated horseshoe, and faithful notations of the last century's weather kept by his grandfather's

8 **assimilate** (ə sim′ ə lāt′) v. to absorb or incorporate

Literary Analysis
Atmosphere What adjectives might you use to describe the atmosphere in this paragraph about emptying the house? Which words contribute to that atmosphere?

10 ☑**Reading Check**
Where does the chest go when the family moves?

The Brown Chest ◆ 1005

- Call students' attention to the word *assimilate*, and to its definition. Let students know that the Latin word root *-sim-* means "same."

- Ask students to volunteer other words containing this root, and list them on the chalkboard. Possibilities include: *similar, similarity, simultaneous, simile, dissimulate*

- Next, have students look up the meanings of these words in a dictionary.

9 Literary Analysis

Atmosphere

- Read aloud the bracketed passage to students. Have them identify the atmosphere of this passage.

- Then, ask the Literary Analysis question on page 1005: What adjectives might you use to describe the atmosphere in this paragraph about emptying the house? What words contribute to that atmosphere?
  Answer: Words like *poisoning, sick, oppression, rusted, damp,* and *stains* create an atmosphere of aging and decay.

- Finally, ask students how the sight of the weights and the tin basin affects the man. Why does he find the past oppressive?
  Answer: They bring back vivid memories of his grandparents. He doesn't like thinking about the past because it makes him think about death and endings.

10 ☑**Reading Check**
Answer: The chest is put in the attic.

CUSTOMIZE INSTRUCTION FOR UNIVERSAL ACCESS

For Less Proficient Readers	For Advanced Readers
To help students appreciate the built-up layers of detail that provide the story's atmosphere, have students make lists of the objects in the attic and in the chest. Then, have students make observations in their own homes, and write a descriptive passage like Updike's. You may wish to use the Writing Process Model for Descriptive and Observational Writing, pp. 9–12 in **Writing Models and Graphic Organizers on Transparencies.**	Have students form a small reading group in which to explore more of Updike's short fiction. Students can choose one or two stories, read them independently, and gather for a group discussion of the stories. Students can consider themes and motifs these stories have in common with "The Brown Chest." They should also look for common aspects of diction and style.

- Have students read the bracketed passage, recording any details they can use to help them describe the atmosphere.

- Then, ask the Literary Analysis question on page 1006: What is the atmosphere of this passage listing the contents of the chest? **Answer:** The atmosphere is haunted by ghosts. The man looks at the items and learns about the days when his parents were young, long before he was born.

12 Critical Thinking

Connect

- Remind students that on page 1005, the narrator looks at kitchen weights and recalls vivid memories of his grandmother. Ask: Why does he think of this again when he gives his son wrong directions? **Answer:** He saw the weights recently and they remain in his mind. He realizes that a proper balance is restored when he turns out to be just as prone to mistakes as his son.

- Then, ask students how the fact that Gordon is named for his grandfather connects to the theme of the story. **Answer:** A family name is like an item saved in the brown chest. Like the locks of hair and photographs saved in the chest, a name is something to be kept in the family to remember a person by.

father in limp diaries bound in red leather, and a buggy-whip. A little box labelled in his mother's handwriting "Haircut July 1919" held, wrapped in tissue paper, coils of auburn hair startlingly silky to the touch. There were stiff brown photographs of his father's college football team, his father crouching at right tackle in an unpadded helmet, and of a stageful of posing young people among whom he finally found his mother, wearing a flimsy fairy dress and looking as if she had been crying. And so on and on, until he couldn't bear it and asked his son to help him carry the chest, half unemptied, down the narrow attic stairs whose bare wooden treads had been troughed[4] by generations of use, and then down the slightly broader stairs carpeted decades ago, and out the back door to the van. It didn't fit; they had to go back to the city ten miles away to rent a bigger van. Even so, packing everything in was a struggle. At one point, exasperated and anxious to be gone, his broad-backed son, hunched in the body of the U-Haul van, picked up the chest single-handed, and inverted it, lid open, over some smaller items to save space. The old thin-painted wood gave off a sharp *crack*, a piercing quick cry of injury.

The chest came to rest in his barn. He now owned a barn, not a Pennsylvania barn with stone sides and pegged oak beams but a skimpier, New England barn, with a flat tarred roof and a long-abandoned horse stall. He found the place in the chest lid, near one of the little dark hinges, where a split had occurred, and with a few carefully driven nails repaired the damage well enough. He could not blame the boy, who was named Gordon, after his paternal grandfather, the one-time football player crouching for his picture in some sunny autumn when Harding[5] was President. On the drive north in a downpour, Gordon had driven the truck, and his father tried to read the map, and in the dim light of the cab failed, and headed him the wrong way out of Westchester County, so they wound up across the Hudson River, amid blinding headlights, on an unfathomable, exitless highway. After that egregious piece of guidance, he could not blame the boy for anything, even for failing to get a job while concentrating instead on perfecting his dart game in the fake pubs of Boston. In a way not then immediately realized, the map-reading blunder righted the balance between them, himself and his son, as when under his grandmother's gnarled hands another stalk of asparagus would cause the tray holding the rusty cylindrical weights to rise with a soft *clunk*.

They arrived an hour late, after midnight. The unloading, including the reloading of the righted chest, all took place by flashlight, hurriedly, under the drumming sound of rain on the flat roof.

Now his barn felt haunted. He could scarcely bear to examine his inherited treasure, the chairs and cabinets and chinaware and faded best-sellers and old-fashioned bridge lamps clustered in a corner

---

4. **troughed** (trôf´ d) *v.* worn into troughs or grooves.
5. **Harding** Warren G. Harding (1865–1923), twenty-ninth president of the United States, from 1921 to 1923.

unfathomable (un fath´ əm ə bəl) *adj.* unable to be understood

egregious (ē grē´ jəs) *adj.* outstanding for undesirable qualities; remarkably bad

beyond the leaf-mulcher and the snow-blower and the rack of motorcycle tires left by the youngest son of the previous owner of the barn. He was the present owner. He had never imagined, as a child, owning so much. His wife saw no place in their house for even the curly-maple[6] kitchen table and the walnut corner cupboard, his mother's pride. This section of the barn became, if not as frightening as the old coal bin, a place he avoided. These pieces that his infant eyes had grazed, and that had framed his parents' lives, seemed sadly shabby now, cheap in their time, most of them, and yet devoid of antique value: useless used furniture he had lacked the courage to discard.

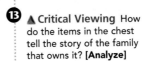

So he was pleased, one winter day, two years after their wayward drive north, to have Gordon call and ask if he could come look at the furniture in the barn. He had a job, he said, or almost, and was moving into a bigger place, out from the city. He would be bringing a friend, he vaguely added. A male friend, presumably, to help him lift and load what he chose to take away.

But the friend was a female, small and exquisite, with fascinating large eyes, the whites white as china, and a way of darting back and forth like a hummingbird, her wings invisible. "Oh," she exclaimed, over this and that, explaining to Gordon in a breathy small voice how this would be useful, and that would fit right in. "Lamps!" she said. "I love lamps."

"You see, Dad," the boy explained, the words pronounced softly yet in a manner so momentous that it seemed to take all the air in the barn to give them utterance, "Morna and I are planning to get married."

"Morna"—a Celtic name, fittingly elfin. The girl was magical, there in the cold barn, emitting puffs of visible breath, moving through the clutter with quick twists of her denim-clad hips and graceful stabs of her narrow white hands. She spoke only to Gordon, as if a pane of shyness protected her from his hoary[7] father—at this late phase of his life a kind of ogre, an ancestral, proprietorial figure full of potency and ugliness. "Gordon, what's this?" she asked.

The boy was embarrassed, perhaps by her innocent avidity.[8] "Tell her, Dad."

---

6. **curly-maple** maple wood with a pronounced wavy grain.
7. **hoary** (hôr´ ē) *adj.* ancient; old.
8. **avidity** (ə vid´ ə tē) *n.* eagerness.

---

⑬ ▲ Critical Viewing How do the items in the chest tell the story of the family that owns it? **[Analyze]**

proprietorial (prō prī´ ə tôr´ ē əl) *adj.* like someone who owns something

⑭ ✔ Reading Check
What part of the man's property feels "haunted"? Why?

The Brown Chest ◆ 1007

---

⑬ Critical Viewing
Answer: They reflect the important moments in people's lives, such as graduations and weddings. They show how people looked at different times, what they wore, where they traveled, and so on.

⑭ ✔ Reading Check
Answer: The parts of his property where he stores the chest, old furniture, or other reminders of the past.

CUSTOMIZE INSTRUCTION FOR UNIVERSAL ACCESS

For Less Proficient Readers	For Advanced Readers
Have students work together to make time lines of the story's main events. Have them look for clues and information about the passage of time so that they can list the story's main events in chronological order and indicate the appropriate intervals of time. Then, ask students to identify how the man's point of view about the chest changes as time passes.	Have students analyze the fairy-tale images and allusions that Updike begins using when Morna enters the story on page 1007. Have students gather in a small group to discuss why Updike introduces this fairy-tale motif. Have them consider whether and in what way this motif relates to the brown chest, its contents, and the man's feelings about the chest.

1. Answers will vary. Students should choose objects that are relevant to important moments in their lives.

2. **(a)** He is afraid of it. **(b)** He eventually comes to realize that the contents of the chest represent his family and its history, and that family is not something from the past but something that will last indefinitely into the future.

3. **(a)** The chest holds old papers and books, items from his grandparents' and parents' pasts. **(b)** They are stored in the chest. **(c)** The chest stands for the importance of family.

4. **(a)** The man makes a mistake when giving his son directions. **(b)** He realizes that he is as fallible as his son, whom he was previously prone to criticize.

5. **(a)** Her hair is auburn. **(b)** The chest contains locks of the man's mother's auburn hair. **(c)** Her presence and the forthcoming marriage suggest that the family will continue into the future.

6. **(a)** About fifty years **(b)** Students may say that the few and specific references to the passage of time are skillfully done.

"Our old guest bed." Which he used to lie diagonally across, listening to his mother's pen scratch as her diary tried to hold fast her days. Even then he knew it couldn't be done.

"We could strip off the ghastly gray, I guess," the boy conceded, frowning in the attempt to envision it and the work involved. "We *have* a bed," he reminded her.

"And this?" she went on, leaving the bed hanging in a realm of future possibility. Her headscarf had slipped back, exposing auburn hair glinting above the vapor of her breath, in <u>evanescent</u> present time.

She had paused at the chest. Her glance darted at Gordon, and then, receiving no response, at the present owner, looking him in the eyes for the first time. The ogre smiled. "Open it."

"What's in it?" she asked.

He said, "I forget, actually."

Delicately but fearlessly, she lifted the lid, and out swooped, with the same vividness that had astonished and alarmed his nostrils as a child, the sweetish deep cedary smell, undiminished, cedar and camphor and paper and cloth, the smell of family, family without end.

evanescent (ev´ ə nes´ ənt) *adj.* short-lived; tending to fade or disappear

---

Review and Assess

Thinking About the Selection

1. **Respond:** The brown chest clearly has had a profound effect upon the man in the story. What object or objects in your life have emotional power over you, and why?

2. **(a) Recall:** What are the boy's earliest impressions of the chest? **(b) Interpret:** In what ways does his attitude toward the chest change over time?

3. **(a) Recall:** What mementos does the chest hold early in the man's life? **(b) Infer:** What happens to some mementos of the man's childhood? **(c) Draw Conclusions:** What vision of life does the chest embody?

4. **(a) Recall:** What event "righted the balance" between the man and his son? **(b) Analyze:** Why does that event cause the man to reevaluate his feelings toward his son?

5. **(a) Recall:** What does the man notice about Morna's hair toward the story's end? **(b) Connect:** What connection does this detail establish between Morna and the chest? **(c) Generalize:** What is suggested by Morna's presence about the enduring nature of family?

6. **(a) Recall:** How much time passes in the story? **(b) Evaluate:** How well does Updike succeed in showing the passage of time within the confines of the short-story format?

ASSESSMENT PRACTICE: Writing Skills

Punctuation, Usage, and Sentence Structure   (For more practice, see Test Preparation Workbook, p. 60.)

Many tests require students to choose the best way to improve a sentence. Use the following sample test item to give students practice at this skill.

Looking through the chest, old and unused things repulse the boy.

Which of the following changes will correct the sentence?

A Change the comma to a semicolon.

B Change "Looking through the chest" to "As he looks through the chest."

C Change "repulse the boy" to "are repulsed by the boy."

D Delete the comma.

The correct answer is *B*; this is the only change that will correct the dangling modifier.

Review and Assess

Literary Analysis

Atmosphere

1. What **atmosphere** is created by the description of the chest in the upstairs hallway when the boy is young?
2. (a) What atmosphere is suggested by the phrase "the oppression of the past"? (b) What details does Updike use to illustrate that phrase?
3. (a) Describe the changes in the atmosphere that occur when Morna enters the story. (b) To what do you attribute these changes? (c) What might Morna represent to the main character?

Connecting Literary Elements

4. In the opening paragraphs, what **precise word choices** heighten the sense of neglect in the unused rooms of the house?
5. Use a chart like the one shown to analyze specific details that appeal to the senses in Updike's first description of the chest.

6. (a) On page 1007, what references to fairy tale creatures does Updike use to contrast the main character and Morna? (b) In what ways are Updike's word choices particularly apt?

Reading Strategy

Breaking Down Long Sentences

7. Select a long sentence from the story. (a) Use the punctuation marks to break the sentence into meaningful sections. (b) What action or actions are being performed in the sentence?
8. (a) Rewrite the sentence as a series of short sentences. (b) Compare the benefits of long sentences with those of short sentences.

Extend Understanding

9. **Humanities Connection:** (a) In what ways has technology affected people's ability to hold onto the past? (b) What are the benefits and drawbacks of these technological advances?

Quick Review

Atmosphere is the emotional quality of the world the author creates in a piece of writing.

Precise word choices involve the selection of the most appropriate, vivid, and specific words to create a desired effect.

To **break down long sentences,** use punctuation marks to separate sentences into component parts.

 Take It to the Net
www.phschool.com
Take the interactive self-test online to check your understanding of the selection.

The Brown Chest ◆ 1009

ENRICHMENT: Further Reading

Other Works by John Updike

Hugging the Shore

Problems and Other Stories

Rabbit, Run

Trust Me

 Take It to the Net
Visit www.phschool.com for more information on John Updike

Answers for p. 1009

Review and Assess

1. The description suggests a haunted atmosphere.
2. (a) The phrase suggests a desire to escape. (b) Details that stress this oppression include the references to the crowded attic and jammed cellar.
3. (a) From Morna's entrance to the end, the story is full of references to fairy-tales: her name is "elfin," she is "magical," she has "invisible wings," the father is compared to an ogre. (b) She seems to be associated with the future, not weighed down with the past. (c) She seems to be a kind of good fairy who breaks the spell of the past.
4. *out of the way and yet not, haunted bad places, smell of old carpet, neglected, frightening shadows*
5. Sight: brown color with wood grain showing through, yellow freckles, black hinges. Smell: sweet and musty, mothballs and cedar. Taste: moldy flavor of time.
6. (a) She is described as a fairy, he as an ogre. (b) A fairy is delicate and lovely like Morna; an ogre is big and gruff like the father.
7. Sample answer: page 1004, sentence beginning "In the general upheaval" (a) Check students' answers. (b) The boy glances in the chest and is shocked to see his drawings, report cards, and school photos.
8. (a) The boy glanced into the chest. He was shocked to see his own drawings. He also saw report cards. He saw school photographs in folders of dove-gray cardboard. The photos showed him at the age of five. (b) Long sentences allow a writer to develop an idea in a single flow from start to finish. Short sentences may be choppy; the thought has to keep stopping and starting.
9. (a) People can make videotapes of family events and vacations. (b) Benefits: People can see moving pictures of their relatives and hear them speak. Drawbacks: videotape may not be as durable as items like photographs or old dresses.

❶ Vocabulary Development

Word Analysis

1. b
2. c
3. a

Spelling Strategy

1. kilograms
2. antiwar

Fluency: Word Choice

1. unfathomable
2. mottled
3. proprietorial
4. evanescent
5. assimilate
6. egregious

❷ Grammar and Style Lesson

1. because Updike is beloved by readers; verb
2. although years have passed since he lived in Pennsylvania; verb
3. whenever he opened the chest; verb
4. after the chest was moved; adjective
5. as Updike entered the lecture hall; verb

Writing Application

Have partners check one another's paragraphs and use Writing and Grammar to resolve any differences of opinion.

Integrate Language Skills

❶ Vocabulary Development Lesson

Word Analysis: Latin Root -sim-

The Latin word root -sim- means "the same." Match the word containing the root -sim- in the left column with its definition in the right column.

1. simultaneous
2. simulation
3. similar

a. alike or comparable
b. occuring at nearly the same moment
c. a close copy or replica

Spelling Strategy

When adding a prefix to a word, do not change the spelling—for example, un- + fathomable forms unfathomable. Complete the words in the sentences below by affixing the prefix that makes sense. Use anti- or kilo-.

1. The chest weighs fifty ___grams.
2. The ___war candidate won the election.

Fluency: Word Choice

Replace the italicized word or phrase in each sentence with the appropriate word from the vocabulary list on page 1001.

1. The boy found the adults' attachment to the chest *impossible to figure out*.
2. The covers of the old books were *spotted*.
3. The man had an *ownerlike* interest in the chest.
4. His joy in the chest was *likely to disappear soon*.
5. He couldn't *incorporate* the old chest into his modern life.
6. If he had made any *outstandingly bad* errors, there was no evidence of them.

❷ Grammar and Style Lesson

Adverb Clauses

Adverb clauses are subordinate clauses that modify verbs, adjectives, or adverbs by telling where, when, in what way, to what extent, under what condition, or why. Adverb clauses begin with conjunctions like *when, where, as if, if, because, in,* and *so*.

> **Modifying Verb:** The Louisiana territory <u>entered</u> the Union *after Jefferson negotiated the purchase*.
>
> **Modifying Adjective:** *Whenever the soldier told stories of battle*, the children were <u>amazed</u>.
>
> **Modifying Adverb:** The story was <u>longer</u> *than the one yesterday was*.

Adverb clauses allow writers to quickly link events in a single sentence.

Practice Identify the adverb clause in each sentence and tell whether it modifies a verb, adjective, or adverb.

1. Because Updike is beloved by readers, he receives much fan mail.
2. Although years have passed since he lived in Pennsylvania, he still has vivid memories.
3. The boy in the story felt the weight of the past whenever he opened the chest.
4. After the chest was moved, it seemed less frightening.
5. The audience applauded madly as Updike entered the lecture hall.

Writing Application Write a paragraph describing a vivid memory. Use three sentences containing adverb clauses.

𝒲𝐆 *Prentice Hall Writing and Grammar Connection: Chapter 19, Section 3*

TEACHING RESOURCES

The following resources can be used to enrich or extend the instruction for pp. 1010–1011.

Vocabulary

📖 **Selection Support:** Build Vocabulary, p. 250

📖 **Vocabulary and Spelling Practice Book** (Use this booklet for skills enrichment.) ▪

Grammar

📖 **Selection Support:** Grammar and Style, p. 251

𝒲𝐆 **Writing and Grammar,** Ruby Level, p. 454

🖌 **Daily Language Practice Transparencies**

Writing

𝒲𝐆 **Writing and Grammar,** Ruby Level, p. 309 ▪

💿 **Writing and Grammar iText CD-ROM**

▪ **BLOCK SCHEDULING:** Resources marked with this symbol provide varied instruction during 90-minute blocks.

❸ Writing Lesson

Analysis of a Symbol

John Updike's story "The Brown Chest" uses a single symbol—the storage chest—as a lens through which to view a man's life. The chest means different things to the main character as he grows from boyhood to maturity. Write an essay analyzing the symbolic meaning of the chest at different points in the main character's life.

Prewriting	Review the story, and take notes about the main character's feelings about the chest as his life progresses. Identify quotes you can use to support each part of your analysis.
Drafting	Introduce the story and author, and give a brief summary of the plot. Then, state the main idea you will develop. Determine an organizational strategy to give order to your ideas.
Revising	Review your essay, and highlight any sections that seem out of order. Reorder those sections for logic and clarity.

Model: Revising for Clear Organization

To his young mind, the chest holds ghosts—all those who are dead and gone.

As a child, the man in John Updike's story is frightened by the brown chest. As a man, he values the past.

Exploring ideas in chronological order creates a clear organization.

 Prentice Hall Writing and Grammar Connection: Chapter 14, Section 3

❹ Extension Activities

Listening and Speaking With another student, role-play a **conversation** between Gordon and Morna on their way home from visiting the barn. Use these tips to prepare:

- Note each character's response both to the items in the barn and to Gordon's father.

- Create a voice for each character that reflects his or her portrayal in the story.

Make sure that each character has equal time to exchange distinct impressions of the visit. [Group Activity]

Research and Technology Using a variety of sources, including the Internet, conduct research and create a **feature article on fashions** of the 1920s. Illustrate the article with photos, drawings, images of magazine covers, or other graphics. Identify major fashion trend-setters of the period, and note connections between fashion and the social atmosphere of the time.

Take It to the Net www.phschool.com

Go online for an additional research activity using the Internet.

❸ Writing Lesson

- Students may want to divide their analysis into four sections, discussing the chest's symbolic value to the boy in the first house, in the second house, to the man in the attic, and in the barn.

- Remind students to identify specific details that support their arguments.

- Use the Response to Literature rubric in **Performance Assessment and Portfolio Management**, p. 23, to evaluate students' profiles.

❹ Listening and Speaking

- Remind students to think about how Gordon and Morna react to the chest.

- You may want to have all student pairs carry out this activity at once, or give students time to rehearse and perform their dialogue for the class.

- Have students use the Peer Assessment form for Delivering a Speech, p. 30, in **Performance Assessment and Portfolio Management**.

CUSTOMIZE INSTRUCTION
For Universal Access

To address different learning styles, use the following activities suggested in the **Extension Activities** booklet, p. 57.

For Intrapersonal Learners, use Activity 5.

For Visual/Spatial Learners, use Activity 6.

For Interpersonal Learners, use Activity 7.

ASSESSMENT RESOURCES

The following resources can be used to assess students' knowledge and skills.

Selection Assessment

- **Formal Assessment,** pp. 254–256
- **Open Book Test,** pp. 169–171
- **Got It! Assessment Videotapes,** Tape 6
- **Test Bank Software**
- **Take It to the Net**
  Visit www.phschool.com for self-tests and additional questions on "The Brown Chest."

Writing Rubric

- **Performance Assess. and Portfolio Mgmt.,** p. 23

Listening and Speaking Rubric

- **Performance Assess. and Portfolio Mgmt.,** p. 30

PRENTICE HALL ASSESSMENT SYSTEM

- **Workbook**
- **Skill Book**
- **Transparencies**
- **CD-ROM**

Hawthorne ✦ Gold Glade ✦ Traveling Through the Dark ✦ The Light Comes Brighter ✦ The Adamant

Lesson Objectives

1. **To analyze and respond to literary elements**
   - Literary Analysis: Style and Diction
   - Comparing Literary Works
2. **To read, comprehend, analyze, and critique poetry**
   - Reading Strategy: Paraphrasing
   - Reading Check Questions
   - Review and Assess Questions
3. **To develop word analysis skills, fluency, and systematic vocabulary**
   - Vocabulary Development Lesson: Related Words: *exhaust*
4. **To understand and apply written and oral language conventions**
   - Spelling Strategy
   - Grammar and Style Lesson: Subject and Verb Agreement
   - Assessment Practice (ATE)
5. **To understand and apply appropriate writing and research strategies**
   - Writing Lesson: Critical Response
   - Extension Activity: Oral Presentation
6. **To understand and apply listening and speaking strategies**
   - Extension Activity: Evaluation

STEP-BY-STEP TEACHING GUIDE	PACING GUIDE
PRETEACH	
Motivate Students and Provide Background	
Use the Motivation activity (ATE p. 1012)	5 min.
Read and discuss author and background features (SE/ATE p. 1012) **A**	5 min.
Introduce the Concepts	
Introduce the Literary Analysis and Reading Strategy (SE/ATE p. 1013) **A**	15 min.
Pronounce the vocabulary words and read their definitions (SE p. 1013)	5 min.
TEACH	
Monitor Comprehension	
Informally monitor comprehension by circulating while students read independently or in groups **A**	30 min.
Monitor students' comprehension with the Reading Check notes (SE/ATE pp. 1015, 1017)	as students read
Develop vocabulary with Vocabulary notes (SE pp. 1016, 1017,1020,1021; ATE p. 1020)	as students read
Develop Understanding	
Develop students' understanding of style and diction with the Literary Analysis annotations (SE/ATE pp. 1014, 1016–1019, 1021) **A**	10 min.
Develop students' ability to use paraphrasing by using the Reading Strategy annotations (SE/ATE pp. 1015, 1021)	5 min.
ASSESS	
Assess Mastery	
Assess students' mastery of the Reading Strategy and Literary Analysis by having them answer the Review and Assess questions (SE/ATE p. 1023)	15 min.
Use one or more of the print and media Assessment Resources (ATE p. 1025) **A**	up to 45 min.
EXTEND	
Apply Understanding	
Have students complete the Vocabulary Development Lesson and the Grammar and Style Lesson (SE p. 1024) **A**	20 min.
Apply students' ability to use suitable criteria to judge literary works by using the Writing Lesson (SE/ATE p. 1025) **A**	45 min.
Apply students' understanding using one or more of the Extension Activities (SE p. 1025)	20–90 min.

A **ACCELERATED INSTRUCTION:**
Use the strategies and activities identified with an **A**.

UNIVERSAL ACCESS
● = Below Level Students
▲ = On-Level Students
■ = Above Level Students

Time and Resource Manager

Reading Level: Challenging, Challenging, Average, Challenging, Easy
Average Number of Instructional Days: 3

RESOURCES

PRINT 📖	TRANSPARENCIES 🎞	TECHNOLOGY 💿 🎧 📼
• **Beyond Literature,** Community Connection: Community Identity, p. 58 ▲ ■		• **Interest Grabber Video,** Tape 6 ● ▲ ■
• **Selection Support Workbook:** ● ▲ ■ Literary Analysis, p. 257 Reading Strategy, p. 256 Build Vocabulary, p. 254	• **Literary Analysis and Reading Transparencies,** pp. 115 and 116 ● ▲ ■	
		• **Listening to Literature** ● ▲ ■ Audiocassettes, Side 35 Audio CDs, CD 20
• **Literatura en español** ● ▲ • **Literary Analysis for Enrichment** ■		
• **Formal Assessment:** Selection Test, pp. 257–259 ● ▲ ■ • **Open Book Test,** pp. 172–174 ● ▲ ■ • **Performance Assessment and Portfolio Management,** p. 23 ● ▲ ■ **PRENTICE HALL ASSESSMENT SYSTEM** ● ▲ ■	**PRENTICE HALL ASSESSMENT SYSTEM** ● ▲ ■ Skills Practice Answers and Explanations on Transparencies	• **Test Bank Software** ● ▲ ■ • **Got It! Assessment Videotapes,** Tape 5 ● ▲
• **Selection Support Workbook:** ● ▲ ■ Grammar and Style, p. 255 • **Writing and Grammar,** Ruby Level ● ▲ ■ • **Extension Activities,** p. 58 ● ▲ ■	• **Daily Language Practice Transparencies** ● ▲ • **Writing Models and Graphic Organizers on Transparencies,** pp. 37–40 ● ▲ ■	• **Writing and Grammar iText CD-ROM** ● ▲ ■ 💻 *Take It to the Net* www.phschool.com

BLOCK SCHEDULING: Use one 90-minute class period to preteach the selection and have students read it. Use a second 90-minute class period to assess students' mastery of skills and have them complete one of the Extension Activities.

Step-by-Step Teaching Guide for pp. 1012–1013

Motivation

Introduce students to the poetry by asking what inspires strong emotions or awe in them. You might show students some photographs of natural and man-made wonders as a stimulus. Ask how the emotions awakened by these images might take root in poetic form. Urge students to read on for the answer four poets give.

▣ Interest Grabber Videotapes

As an alternative, play "William Stafford" on Tape 6 to engage student interest.

❶ Background

More About the Author

Robert Lowell was deeply concerned not only with his own well-being but also with that of others. He was imprisoned as a conscientious objector during the Second World War, and actively protested America's involvement in Vietnam. For much of his life, Lowell suffered from severe depression, for which he was hospitalized; he often used mental illness in his poetry as a symbol of sickness in society.

Aside from winning three Pulitzer Prizes, Robert Penn Warren was appointed the first poet laureate of the United States in 1985.

Theodore Roethke was an acclaimed teacher of poetry. His pupils included James Wright, David Wagoner, and Richard Hugo. He advised his beginning students to "write like someone else": many critics believe that he followed his own advice too faithfully.

William Stafford's writings have won numerous awards, and he served as the Consultant in Poetry for the Library of Congress.

Prepare to Read

❶ Hawthorne ◆ Gold Glade ◆ Traveling Through the Dark ◆
The Light Comes Brighter ◆ The Adamant

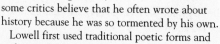

Robert Lowell (1917–1977)

Robert Lowell was born into one of America's oldest, most prominent families, which included the poets James Russell Lowell and Amy Lowell; Josiah Winslow, a governor of the Plymouth colony; and John Stark, a Revolutionary War general. Lowell found his ancestry to be embarrassing at best, and some critics believe that he often wrote about history because he was so tormented by his own.

Lowell first used traditional poetic forms and techniques, but in the late 1950s he began writing freer, more direct poems in what came to be called the "confessional" mode. His volume *Life Studies* (1959) launched a school of confessional poetry that included Sylvia Plath, John Berryman, and Anne Sexton.

Robert Penn Warren (1905–1989)

Among the most versatile, prolific, and distinguished writers of our time, Robert Penn Warren won the first of his three Pulitzer Prizes for *All the King's Men* (1946), a fictional study of a Southern politician (based on Louisiana Governor Huey Long). Warren's poetry collections include *Promises* (1957) and *Now and Then: Poems* (1978). Although Warren consistently used Southern settings and characters in his writing, he treated universal themes, such as the love of the land that fills the poem "Gold Glade."

Theodore Roethke (1908–1963)

Theodore Roethke (ret′ kē) was born in Saginaw, Michigan, where his family owned several large commercial greenhouses. As a boy, Roethke was a passionate observer of the plants that grew in the greenhouses. These observations later provided him with ideas for many of his poems.

Throughout his life, Roethke found it difficult to relate to other people. He found a refuge, though, in nature and poetry. At age thirty-three, Roethke published his first volume of poetry, launching a career as one of the most acclaimed poets of his day. He won the Pulitzer Prize for *The Waking* (1953) and the National Book Award for *The Far Field* (1964).

William Stafford (1914–1993)

William Stafford spent key parts of his life in Kansas, Iowa, and Oregon. These regions influenced his poetry, both in its content and in its serene, unadorned language. A believer in the sanctity of life, Stafford served in World War II as a conscientious objector. Focusing on such subjects as the threat of nuclear war and the beauty of nature, Stafford wrote of his fear that modern technology would someday destroy the wilderness. He did not publish his first volume of verse, *West of Your City* (1960), until he was forty-six, after years of working in the U.S. Forest Service.

1012 ◆ *Prosperity and Protest (1946–Present)*

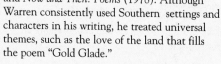

TEACHING RESOURCES

The following resources can be used to enrich or extend the instruction for pp. 1012–1013.

Motivation

▣ **Interest Grabber Video,** Tape 6

Background

▣ **Beyond Literature,** p. 58 ▣

▣ **Take It to the Net**
Visit www.phschool.com for Background and hotlinks for the selections.

Literary Analysis

▣ **Literary Analysis and Reading Transparencies,** Style and Diction, p. 116 ▣

Reading

▣ **Selection Support:** Reading Strategy, p. 256; Build Vocabulary, p. 254

▣ **Literary Analysis and Reading Transparencies,** Paraphrasing, p. 115

▣ **BLOCK SCHEDULING:** Resources marked with this symbol provide varied instruction during 90-minute blocks.

Preview

Connecting to the Literature

Sometimes, when you least expect it, you make the most surprising discoveries about yourself and the world around you. In a similar way, the four poets whose work follows make discoveries in unexpected places.

Literary Analysis

Style and Diction

A writer's **style** is the manner in which he or she puts ideas into words. Style generally concerns *form* rather than *content*. In poetry, style is determined by a poet's use of these elements:

- Tone
- Sound devices
- Symbolism
- Rhythm
- The length and arrangement of lines
- Figurative language
- Punctuation and capitalization

Another important aspect of style is **diction,** or word choice. As you read these poems, note the ways in which each poet's style and diction not only reflect varying degrees of formality but also help establish a unique voice.

Comparing Literary Works

In his poem "Hawthorne," Robert Lowell describes a young Nathaniel Hawthorne as "meditating" about the "true/and insignificant." For Lowell, part of Hawthorne's greatness lies in his search for truth within the ordinary—the insignificant, rather than the grand. With this idea in mind, examine how Lowell might have felt about the other poems that appear here. Explore whether or not they begin in meditations upon the "true and insignificant," or in ideas that are more lofty and abstract.

Reading Strategy

Paraphrasing

Some poems contain passages that are especially difficult to understand because of unusual vocabulary, complex sentences, or the ambiguities of poetic language. To improve your comprehension, **paraphrase,** or restate in your own words, any difficult passages you encounter. As you read these poems, use a chart like the one shown to aid your understanding.

Roethke's Words

Soon field and wood will wear an April look.

Paraphrase

Soon it will be spring.

Vocabulary

brooding (brōōd´ in) *v.* pondering in a troubled or mournful way (p. 1016)

furtive (fur´ tiv) *adj.* sneaky; stealthy (p. 1016)

meditation (med´ ə tā´ shən) *n.* deep thought or solemn reflection (p. 1016)

declivity (dē kliv´ ə tē) *n.* downward slope (p. 1017)

exhaust (eg zôst´) *n.* discharge of used steam or gas from an engine (p. 1020)

vestiges (ves´ tij iz) *n.* traces (p. 1021)

Hawthorne / Gold Glade / Traveling Through the Dark / The Light Comes Brighter / The Adamant ◆ 1013

---

❷ Literary Analysis

Style and Diction

- Point out that both style and diction have to do with the choices a writer makes. Write the following sentences on the board, pointing out that each gives the same information. Students can compare and contrast the styles and diction of the two sentences. *The right fielder hit a home run. Flexing mighty arms, the batter swung powerfully and smashed the ball over the fences.*

- Have students try to characterize the style and diction of some of the poets they have read earlier this year. **Sample answers:** T.S. Eliot: elevated style, sophisticated and formal diction. Carl Sandburg: plain style, colloquial and informal diction.

- As students read the poems in this group, have them try to characterize the style and diction of each poet.

❸ Reading Strategy

Paraphrasing

- A good first step in paraphrasing poetry is to write out complete sentences, ignoring line breaks and the capital letters at the start of lines. Students will have an easier time paraphrasing when they can see where the sentences end.

- Remind students that paraphrasing and summarizing are not the same. A paraphrase should restate the original idea without leaving out any details.

Vocabulary Development

Pronounce each vocabulary word for students, and read the definitions as a class. Have students identify any words with which they are already familiar.

CUSTOMIZE INSTRUCTION FOR UNIVERSAL ACCESS

For Less Proficient Readers	For English Learners	For Advanced Readers
Have students note at least two words in each poem that strike them as especially effective. Have them try the exercise of substituting synonyms for these words. Have them write brief essays explaining why the poet's choices seem more effective than others.	Students can note two new or unfamiliar words in each poem. Have students look up each word's definition and origin. Students can then exchange word lists with partners and work together until both have learned all the new words.	Have students characterize the diction of each of the poems in this group. Interested students might each choose one poem and write a short essay analyzing the poet's word choices.

 E-Teach

Visit E-Teach at www.phschool.com for teachers' essays on how to teach, with questions and answers.

Step-by-Step Teaching Guide for pp. 1014–1022

CUSTOMIZE INSTRUCTION
For Visual Learners

Have students consider the visual impact of each poem's images. Students can choose any two poems and write brief essays comparing and contrasting how each poet uses words to create visual images. Do the poets create similar images? Do they use similar techniques to create widely different images? How would students illustrate these poems if they had the opportunity?

❶ About the Selections

Four of these poems describe different aspects of America: an old New England town, a forest glade in autumn, an unexpected highway encounter with a dead doe, and the breaking of dawn late in winter. The fifth poem comments on the endurance of truth.

❷ Literary Analysis
Style and Diction

- Read aloud the bracketed stanza to students. Ask them to pay attention to the repeated sound of the letter *l*.

- Then, ask the Literary Analysis question on p. 1014: What do you notice about the poet's use of the "l" sound in his choice of words? What is the effect?
  Answer: The first 8 lines contain a total of 15 "l" sounds. The effect is lilting and lazy. It seems to echo the winding curves of the main street.

- Ask students what impression of Salem these first eight lines give the reader. Which words and phrases create this impression?
  Answer: The town seems deserted; the poem doesn't mention any people walking along the street. *Gallows Hill, yellow drain, unhealthy,* and *old dog* suggest a ghost town; a place that is drained of life. *You'll walk to no purpose.*

❶ Hawthorne

Robert Lowell

❷
Follow its lazy main street lounging
from the alms house to Gallows Hill[1]
along a flat, unvaried surface
covered with wooden houses
5   aged by yellow drain
like the unhealthy hair of an old dog.
You'll walk to no purpose
in Hawthorne's Salem.

Literary Analysis
Style and Diction What do you notice about the poet's use of the 'l' sound in his choice of words? What is the effect?

---

1. **Gallows Hill** hill in Salem, Massachusetts, where nineteen people who were accused of practicing witchcraft were hanged.

TEACHING RESOURCES

The following resources can be used to enrich or extend the instruction for pp. 1014–1022.

Literary Analysis

📘 **Writing Models and Graphic Organizers on Transparencies,** p. 37–40 ▪

📖 **Selection Support:** Literary Analysis, p. 257

Reading

🎧 **Listening to Literature Audiocassettes,** Side 35 ▪

💿 **Listening to Literature Audio CDs,** CD 20

▪ **BLOCK SCHEDULING:** Resources marked with this symbol provide varied instruction during 90-minute blocks.

◀ **Critical Viewing** ❸
What does this scene suggest about the port of Salem? In what ways is the painting similar to Lowell's description of the town? In what ways is it different? **[Compare and Contrast]**

Crowninshield's Wharf, George Ropes, Peabody Museum of Salem

❹   I cannot resilver the smudged plate.[2]

10   I drop to Hawthorne, the customs officer,[3]
    measuring coal and mostly trying to keep warm—
    to the stunted black schooner,
    the dismal South-end dock,
    the wharf-piles with their fungus of ice.
15   On State Street[4]
    a steeple with a glowing dial-clock
    measures the weary hours,
    the merciless march of professional feet.

    Even this shy distrustful ego
20   sometimes walked on top of the blazing roof,
    and felt those flashes
    that char the discharged cells of the brain.

    Look at the faces—
    Longfellow, Lowell, Holmes and Whittier!

---

2. **resilver . . . plate** Early photographs were taken on a metal plate coated with silver.
3. **customs officer** Nathaniel Hawthorne worked as a customs officer in Salem.
4. **State Street** street in the business district of Boston.

 **Reading Check** ❺

Why does the town of Salem remind the speaker of Nathaniel Hawthorne?

Hawthorne ◆ *1015*

Answer: The scene suggests that the port is thriving. The bright blue of sky and water contrast with the poem's mention of "yellow drain." The flags and tall ships suggest a busy place; in the poem, the town seems deserted.

❹ Reading Strategy

Paraphrasing

- Challenge students to paraphrase line 9. The footnote at the bottom of the page should give them some help.
  Answer: Once the photographic plate is damaged, I can't repair it.

- Ask students to explain the metaphor in this line. To what is the speaker comparing the "smudged plate"?
  Answer: The speaker feels that Salem is the "smudged plate." It is no longer the bustling port of its former days; it is a tired and decayed town. The speaker cannot bring it back to its former liveliness.

▶ Monitor Progress Have students give their opinion of this metaphor.
Answer: Students should say that the metaphor is striking and original. The impossibility of repairing a smudged photographic plate makes the impossibility of restoring the town very clear and vivid.

❺ ✔ Reading Check

Answer: Hawthorne lived and wrote in Salem. He worked in its customs office. Students may remember from the Hawthorne biography in their textbooks that his ancestor played a key role in the Salem witchcraft trials.

CUSTOMIZE INSTRUCTION FOR UNIVERSAL ACCESS

For Special Needs Students	For Gifted/Talented Students
Remind students that the end of a line of poetry is often not the end of the sentence or complete thought. Remind students to note the punctuation, rather than the end of a line, so that they will get the sense of the poems they read. Have them consider the effect of such literary elements as alliteration and sound effects on the reader.	Invite students to create a visual interpretation of one of the poems in a painting or collage. Encourage students to list descriptive terms that they can use as cues to creating the scene. For example, students who choose "Hawthorne," could list visual elements such as "wooden houses aged by yellow drain," "stunted black schooner," and "wharf piles with their fungus of ice," and incorporate them into their compositions.

❻ Literary Analysis

Style and Diction

• Read aloud the bracketed stanza to students. Ask them what image of Hawthorne's personality the speaker creates. How does Lowell's diction make Hawthorne's description distinct?
Answer: Lowell uses terms such as "golden General Custer scalp," and "touched with fire" to make Hawthorne seem young and vital, unlike the "grizzled," or gray-haired, other poets.

• Then, ask students to describe the effect that this description of Hawthorne has on the reader.
Answer: Hawthorne seems like a symbol of Salem's past. Salem was once a young, energetic town; now it is desolate. Hawthorne was once a young, Romantic poet; now he is dead, just a portrait on a wall.

Answers for p. 1016

Review and Assess

1. Students should support their answers.

2. **(a)** a walk down Salem's main street **(b)** Gallows Hill; flat, unvaried surface; aged by yellow drain; unhealthy; old dog; no purpose

3. **(a)** trying to keep warm in the Customs House **(b)** The "merciless march" suggests that they are cold and unfeeling.

4. **(a)** a glowing "dial-clock measures the weary hours"; **(b)** Time goes relentlessly forward. The clock can never be turned back.

5. **(a)** Hawthorne **(b)** The image suggests that Hawthorne took risks and was passionate, brilliant, and insightful. **(c)** Hawthorne is young and the others are old.

6. **(a)** Lowell apparently respects and admires Hawthorne. **(b)** Have students support their answers in detail.

---

25   Study the grizzled silver of their beards.
Hawthorne's picture,
however, has a blond mustache
❻   and golden General Custer[5] scalp.
He looks like a Civil War officer.
30   He shines in the firelight. His hard
survivor's smile is touched with fire.

Leave him alone for a moment or two,
and you'll see him with his head
bent down, brooding, brooding,
35   eyes fixed on some chip,
some stone, some common plant,
the commonest thing,
as if it were the clue.
The disturbed eyes rise,
40   furtive, foiled, dissatisfied
from meditation on the true
and insignificant.

---

5. General Custer George Armstrong Custer (1839–1876), Civil War general

brooding (brood´ iŋ) v. pondering in a troubled or mournful way

furtive (fur´ tiv) adj. sneaky; stealthy

meditation (med´ ə tā´ shən) n. deep thought or solemn reflection

---

Review and Assess

Thinking About the Selection

1. **Respond:** What is your opinion of Nathaniel Hawthorne, based on the way he is portrayed in this poem?

2. **(a) Recall:** What action is described in the first stanza? **(b) Interpret:** Which images in the first stanza contribute to the impression of Salem as a stagnant, decaying town?

3. **(a) Recall:** What does the speaker imagine Hawthorne doing in the third stanza? **(b) Interpret:** What image of professional people is created by the images in that stanza?

4. **(a) Recall:** Which words in lines 15–17 convey an image of the passage of time? **(b) Interpret:** What impression of time is suggested by this image?

5. **(a) Infer:** Who is the "shy, distrustful ego"? **(b) Analyze:** What is the significance of the image of this person walking "on top of the blazing roof"? **(c) Compare and Contrast:** Based on lines 23–31, how does the speaker view Hawthorne in comparison to his literary contemporaries?

6. **(a) Speculate:** In what ways has Hawthorne served as a literary landmark for Lowell? **(b) Extend:** Think of your own field of interest. Who would serve as a landmark for you? Explain.

Gold Glade

Robert Penn Warren

Background

Following an English tradition dating back to 1616, the Library of Congress named Robert Penn Warren as the first Poet Laureate of the United States in 1985. Since then, some of America's best and brightest literary talents have held the title of Poet Laureate. Unlike their British counterparts, American poets laureate are under no obligation to write poems to commemorate special occasions. Though they receive a sizable stipend and an office in the Library of Congress for the duration of the one-year term, poets laureate are free to continue writing (or not writing) as they choose.

Wandering, in autumn, the woods of boyhood,
Where cedar, black, thick, rode the ridge,
Heart aimless as rifle, boy-blankness of mood,
I came where ridge broke, and the great ledge,
5 Limestone, set the toe high as treetop by dark edge

Of a gorge, and water hid, grudging and grumbling,
And I saw, in mind's eye, foam white on
Wet stone, stone wet-black, white water tumbling,
And so went down, and with some fright on
10 Slick boulders, crossed over. The gorge-depth drew night on,
But high over high rock and leaf-lacing, sky
Showed yet bright, and declivity wooed
My foot by the quietening stream, and so I
Went on, in quiet, through the beech wood:
15 There, in gold light, where the glade gave, it stood.

Literary Analysis
Style and Diction In the very first stanza, what do you notice about the poet's innovative diction?

declivity (dē kliv′ ə tē) *n.* downward slope

8 ✔ **Reading Check**
Where is the speaker wandering?

Gold Glade ◆ 1017

❾ Literary Analysis

Style and Diction

- Point out that the poem has a regular rhyme scheme. Ask students to identify the rhyme scheme and describe its effect on the poem.
  Answer: The rhyme scheme is *ababb*. It is the only fixed element in the poem; the lines are all of different lengths and the rhythm is irregular. Students may say that the rhyme scheme gives the poem a stately, rhythmic sound that matches the poet's reverent tone.

- Then, ask the Literary Analysis question on p. 1018: Which words in this stanza (lines 16–20) are repeated? What is the effect?
  Possible answers: The word *gold* is used four times; *fall* is used three times. Effect: readers can visualize the gold leaves falling from the trees.

Answers for p. 1018

Review and Assess

1. Make sure students offer similarities and differences as they compare their memories with those of the speaker.

2. **(a)** a great shagbark (hickory tree) **(b)** human suffering and grief **(c)** The glade's beauty made it seem eternal, untouched by time or human suffering.

3. **(a)** line 26 **(b)** The tone becomes prosaic, everyday—the reader becomes aware that the glade and great tree are only an uncertain memory.

4. **(a)** The images appeal to sight and hearing. **(b)** He feels awe and reverence for the hickory tree's beauty. **(c)** He means that the gold and light seem to be eternal, even sacred.

5. **(a)** It represents beauty and eternity. **(b)** The glade seems real; it is described in detail and realistically but the speaker is ambivalent about whether it is only a haunting image or a real place. **(c)** Students should say yes; the speaker remembers the beauty of the place and the feelings it evoked, but finds that the specifics connected with the memory fade and waver, as often happens with memories.

The glade was geometric, circular, gold,
No brush or weed breaking that bright gold of leaf-fall.
In the center it stood, absolute and bold
Beyond any heart-hurt, or eye's grief-fall.
20 Gold-massy in air, it stood in gold light-fall,

No breathing of air, no leaf now gold-falling,
No tooth-stitch of squirrel, or any far fox bark,
No woodpecker coding, or late jay calling.
Silence: gray-shagged, the great shagbark[1]
25 Gave forth gold light. There could be no dark.

But of course dark came, and I can't recall
What county it was, for the life of me.
Montgomery, Todd, Christian—I know them all.
Was it even Kentucky or Tennessee?
30 Perhaps just an image that keeps haunting me.

No, no! in no mansion under earth,
Nor imagination's domain of bright air,
But solid in soil that gave it its birth,
It stands, wherever it is, but somewhere.
35 I shall set my foot, and go there.

---

1. **shagbark** hickory tree.

Review and Assess

Thinking About the Selection

1. **Respond:** What are some of your memories of autumn? In what ways do they compare to the speaker's memories?

2. **(a) Recall:** What majestic thing does the speaker find in the center of the glade? **(b) Define:** What are "heart-hurt" and "grief-fall"? **(c) Analyze:** Why is the glade "beyond" those things?

3. **(a) Recall:** Where does the action of the poem shift from past to present? **(b) Interpret:** Describe the change in tone that occurs at that point.

4. **(a) Interpret:** In lines 21–25, what are the dominant sensory impressions? **(b) Deduce:** What emotions does the speaker seem to feel in that stanza? **(c) Analyze:** What does the speaker mean by saying, "There could be no dark"?

5. **(a) Interpret:** What does the gold glade represent to the speaker? **(b) Speculate:** Is the glade a real place to which the speaker could actually return? Explain. **(c) Evaluate:** Is this poem an accurate portrayal of memory? Explain.

Literary Analysis
Style and Diction
Which words in this stanza are repeated? What is the effect?

Traveling Through the Dark

William Stafford

- Draw students' attention to the bracketed passage. Ask how they would characterize William Stafford's diction in this poem. How do they think it differs from Robert Lowell's, for example? Possible answer: Students may observe that Stafford's diction is much more like ordinary speech.

- Ask students to identify the stylistic techniques that Stafford uses to craft poetry in this piece. Answer: Students should note that Stafford uses highly original line arrangement and sentence rhythms, punctuation, and capitalization to create the poem, rather than the more traditional techniques of rhyme and meter.

⑩
Traveling through the dark I found a deer
dead on the edge of the Wilson River road.
It is usually best to roll them into the canyon:
that road is narrow; to swerve might make more dead.

Traveling Through the Dark ◆ 1019

CUSTOMIZE INSTRUCTION FOR UNIVERSAL ACCESS

For Special Needs Students	For Advanced Readers
Have students work together to answer the questions on pages 1016, 1018, and 1020. They can meet in a small group afterwards to compare answers. If there is significant disagreement, have students identify words, phrases, and lines from the poems that support their interpretations.	Point out to students the moral and medical dilemma facing the speaker when he realizes the fawn is still alive. Have students speculate about the speaker's chain of thought as he knelt beside the dead deer—why do they think the speaker acted in this way? Challenge students to develop alternative courses of action the speaker might have considered to try to save the fawn. How practical and successful might these be?

Analyze and Connect

- Ask students how they feel the mood of the poem is affected by the time of day in which it is set. Possible answer: Students may observe that nighttime and the resulting lighting from the car's lights creates a mood of loneliness, isolation, and danger.

- Draw students' attention to the image of the warm, still-living fawn within the belly of the dead deer. Ask students to look for a parallel image in the poem. Answer: Students should link the image with that of the warm engine purring beneath the hood of the car.

⓬ Vocabulary Development

Related Words: exhaust

- Point out that the word exhaust in this line is a noun meaning "fumes from an engine." Ask students to define the verb exhaust in a different way. Answer: to tire out

- Ask what effect this second meaning of exhaust has on this line of poetry. Answer: The word exhaust might suggest the speaker's fatigue, or how the doe must have felt as her life ebbed away. It adds emotion to the scene.

Answers for p. 1020

Review and Assess

1. Students might ask whether this incident really occurred.

2. (a) on the edge of the road (b) She was probably hit by a car or truck, since she's in the road.

3. (a) The doe is carrying a fawn. (b) His impulse is to try to save the fawn.

4. (a) The words "aimed" and "purred" suggest that the car is alive. (b) The car is cold on the outside, like the dead doe, but has a warm, purring engine.

5. (a) The speaker weighs motorists' safety against the life of the fawn. (b) The speaker can't clearly see what he should do and is thus literally and metaphorically "travelling in the dark."

continued

---

5 By glow of the tail-light I stumbled back of the car
and stood by the heap, a doe, a recent killing;
she had stiffened already, almost cold.
I dragged her off; she was large in the belly.

My fingers touching her side brought me the reason—
10 her side was warm; her fawn lay there waiting,
alive, still, never to be born.
Beside that mountain road I hesitated.

The car aimed ahead its lowered parking lights;
under the hood purred the steady engine.
15 I stood in the glare of the warm <u>exhaust</u> turning red;
around our group I could hear the wilderness listen.

I thought hard for us all—my only swerving—,
then pushed her over the edge into the river.

exhaust (eg zôst') *n.* discharge of used steam or gas from an engine

Review and Assess

Thinking About the Selection

1. **Respond:** If you could meet him, what would you say to William Stafford about this poem?

2. **(a) Recall:** Where does the speaker find the dead deer? **(b) Speculate:** How do you think the deer met her fate?

3. **(a) Recall:** What discovery does the speaker make when he examines the deer more closely? **(b) Infer:** Why does the speaker hesitate upon making this discovery?

4. **(a) Interpret:** With what details does the speaker personify his car in the fourth stanza? **(b) Connect:** In what ways does the speaker's description of the car echo his discovery about the deer?

5. **(a) Deduce:** What factors does the speaker weigh in his decision about what to do with the deer? **(b) Analyze:** In what ways does the title reflect the speaker's moral dilemma?

6. **(a) Make a Judgment:** Do you think the speaker makes the proper decision? Explain. **(b) Interpret:** What details in the poem suggest the speaker's emotion or attitude about what he has done? Explain.

7. **Generalize:** What does this poem reveal about the relationship between humanity and nature in the modern world?

Answers continued

6. **(a)** Possible answers: Yes, because there was no practical way to save the fawn. No, the speaker didn't even try to save the fawn. **(b)** *The speaker* hesitates and "swerves."

7. Human beings are taking up more space than ever, and animals like deer are threatened.

The Light Comes Brighter
Theodore Roethke

The light comes brighter from the east; the caw
Of restive crows is sharper on the ear.
A walker at the river's edge may hear
A cannon crack announce an early thaw. **14**

5 The sun cuts deep into the heavy drift,
Though still the guarded snow is winter-sealed,
At bridgeheads buckled ice begins to shift,
The river overflows the level field.

Once more the trees assume familiar shapes,
10 As branches loose last <u>vestiges</u> of snow.
The water stored in narrow pools escapes
In rivulets; the cold roots stir below.

Soon field and wood will wear an April look,
The frost be gone, for green is breaking now;
15 The ovenbird[1] will match the vocal brook,
The young fruit swell upon the pear-tree bough.

And soon a branch, part of a hidden scene,
The leafy mind, that long was tightly furled,
Will turn its private substance into green,
20 And young shoots spread upon our inner world.

---

1. ovenbird common name for any of the many birds that build a domelike nest on the ground.

Literary Analysis
Style and Diction What do you notice about the rhythm, length, and arrangements of lines in this poem?

vestiges (ves′ tij iz) *n.* traces

☑ **Reading Check**
What seasonal process does this poem describe?

The Light Comes Brighter ◆ 1021

15 Reading Strategy

Paraphrasing

- To help students answer the Reading Strategy question on p. 1022, draw their attention to Roethke's diction, or choice of words and phrases.

- Let students know that the word *sledge* in the poem signifies a sledgehammer, a large hammer usually wielded with two hands.

- Ask students to speculate about what it might mean for something to "crush to stone." **Possible answer:** The poet may mean that thought cannot be ground up or pulverized like gravel.

Answers for p. 1022

Review and Assess

1. Possible response: "Light" makes the stronger impression because it describes a familiar phenomenon; "Adamant" because of its strong vocabulary and powerful imagery.

2. **(a)** the change from winter into spring **(b)** the "cannon crack" of the early thaw, the sun "cutting deep" into the snowdrifts

3. **(a)** *inner* **(b)** The inner creative process is fueled by the creativity of the external world in the form of nature.

4. **(a)** crush to stone, sledge drops, shafts, teeth of knitted gears, hammer's weight, tool can chip no flake **(b)** The poem describes powerful machinery, but not even such machinery can damage truth. **(c)** Students should support their answers.

5. Optimistic; he believes that truth can't be destroyed.

The Adamant

Theodore Roethke

Thought does not crush to stone.
The great sledge drops in vain.
Truth never is undone;
Its shafts remain.

5   The teeth of knitted gears
Turn slowly through the night,
15 But the true substance bears
The hammer's weight.

Compression cannot break
10 A center so congealed;
The tool can chip no flake:
The core lies sealed.

Reading Strategy
Paraphrasing How might you paraphrase the opening two lines of this poem?

Review and Assess

Thinking About the Selections

1. **Respond:** Which of these poems made a stronger impression on you? Why?

2. **(a) Recall:** In "The Light Comes Brighter," what change of seasons is described? **(b) Distinguish:** Identify two images that suggest that change involves action and even violence.

3. **(a) Recall:** In the final line, what adjective does the poet use to describe the "world"? **(b) Analyze:** What do you think the poet is saying about the creative process?

4. **(a) Interpret:** In "The Adamant," which words and phrases suggest industrial machinery? **(b) Analyze:** In what ways does this imagery emphasize the indestructibility of truth? **(c) Speculate:** Why might truth be indestructible?

5. **Make a Judgment:** Does Roethke demonstrate an optimistic or a pessimistic outlook in "The Adamant"? Explain.

ASSESSMENT PRACTICE: Writing Skills

Grammar and Usage	(For more practice, see Test Preparation Workbook, p. 61.)

Many tests require students to complete sentences with the correct form of a verb. Use the following sample test item to give students practice at this skill.

In 1946, Robert Penn Warren published *All the King's Men* and _____ the Pulitzer Prize.

Choose the correct form of the verb.

A wins

B had won

C won

D has won

Since *published* is in the past tense and both events happened during the same year, the other verb in the sentence must also be past tense. The correct answer is *C*.

Review and Assess

Literary Analysis
Style and Diction

1. Do the **style** and organization of Lowell's poem "Hawthorne" adhere to a traditional poetic form? Explain.

2. (a) What formal structure does Roethke use in his poem "The Light Comes Brighter"? (b) Why would such an orderly structure make sense for this poem?

3. (a) In "Gold Glade," which letter sounds does Warren use most to create alliteration—the repetition of initial consonants? (b) What is the effect?

4. (a) Use a chart like the one shown to analyze each poet's **diction**. (b) How does diction help to create a distinct voice in each poem?

Poet	Formal or Informal	Plain or Ornate	Abstract or Concrete	Effect
Stafford	informal	plain	concrete	casual, familiar

Comparing Literary Works

5. (a) Which of these poems describe everyday life? Explain. (b) What grand or important ideas, if any, do the poets discover through the lens of ordinary experience?

6. (a) Which of these poems attempts to define an abstract idea? Explain. (b) What details do the poets use to give form to their ideas?

7. Which of these poems best expresses Lowell's idea that the "true and insignificant" is the subject of great poetry? Explain your choice.

Reading Strategy
Paraphrasing

8. Paraphrase each of the following passages: (a) "Gold Glade," lines 16–20; (b) "The Adamant," lines 5–8.

9. For each, explain whether the paraphrase helped you to see something that was previously unclear.

Extend Understanding

10. **Social Studies Connection:** (a) What aspects of a city like Salem stay constant over time? (b) What aspects change?

Hawthorne / Gold Glade / Traveling Through the Dark / The Light Comes Brighter / The Adamant ◆ 1023

Quick Review

Style is the manner in which a writer puts ideas into words. **Diction** is a writer's word choice.

To clarify the meaning of a difficult passage, **paraphrase** it—restate it in your own words.

 Take It to the Net
www.phschool.com
Take the interactive self-test online to check your understanding of these selections.

Answers for p. 1024

❶ Vocabulary Development

Related Words

1. exhaustion
2. exhausted
3. inexhaustible

Concept Development: Synonyms

1. d
2. f
3. e
4. a
5. c
6. b

Spelling Strategy

1. footing
2. wooden
3. rootless

❷ Grammar and Style

1. water escapes
2. walkers hear
3. teeth turn
4. fingers reveal
5. mind turns

Writing Application

Sample answers:

1. The many leaves beyond the rake rustle in the breeze.
2. His troubled heart, churning in pain, awakened her compassion.
3. My fingers touching her side felt the steady beat of her heart.
4. The water stored in narrow pools shimmered in the moonlight.

Integrate Language Skills

❶ Vocabulary Development Lesson

Related Words: *exhaust*

As a noun, the word *exhaust* means "the discharge of used steam or gas from an engine." *Exhaust* may also function as a verb meaning "to empty completely" or "to tire out." Other words related to *exhaust* include the following:

inexhaustible   exhausted   exhaustion

Complete each of the following sentences with one of the related words listed above.

1. The ____?____ I felt was due to lack of sleep.
2. The marathon runner had become completely ____?____.
3. A fit athlete, her energy level was usually ____?____.

❷ Grammar and Style Lesson

Subject and Verb Agreement

Subjects and verbs must agree in number, even if the verb is separated from its subject by intervening words. Study this example from "The Light Comes Brighter:"

Example: ... the <u>caw</u> / Of restive crows <u>is</u> sharper on the ear.

The singular verb *is* agrees with the singular subject *caw*, not with the plural noun *crows*, which is not the subject of its clause.

Practice Identify the subject in each of the following sentences. Then, choose the correct form of the verb in parentheses.

1. The water (escapes, escape) in rivulets.

𝒲𝒢 *Prentice Hall Writing and Grammar Connection: Chapter 23, Section 1*

1024 ◆ Prosperity and Protest (1946–Present)

Concept Development: Synonyms

Select the word in the second column that is the best synonym for each word in the first column.

1. brooding   a. slope
2. furtive   b. fumes
3. meditation   c. traces
4. declivity   d. worrying
5. vestiges   e. pensiveness
6. exhaust   f. sneaky

Spelling Strategy

When adding a suffix to a word that ends in one consonant preceded by two vowels, do not double the final consonant: *brood* becomes *brooding*. Add the given suffix to each of these words.

1. *-ing* to foot 2. *-en* to wood 3. *-less* to root

2. Walkers at the river's edge (hears, hear) a cannon crack.
3. The teeth of knitted gears (turns, turn) slowly through the night.
4. My fingers touching her side (reveals, reveal) the reason.
5. The leafy mind, that was tightly furled, (turns, turn) its private substance into green.

Writing Application For each of the following fragments add a verb that agrees in number with the subject, and complete the sentence.

1. The many leaves beyond the rake . . .
2. His troubled heart, churning in pain . . .
3. My fingers touching her side . . .
4. The water stored in narrow pools . . .

TEACHING RESOURCES

The following resources can be used to enrich or extend the instruction for pp. 1024–1025.

Vocabulary

📖 **Selection Support:** Build Vocabulary, p. 254

📖 **Vocabulary and Spelling Practice Book** (Use this booklet for skills enrichment.) ▪

Grammar

📖 **Selection Support:** Grammar and Style, p. 255

𝒲𝒢 **Writing and Grammar,** Ruby Level, p. 584

📄 **Daily Language Practice Transparencies**

Writing

𝒲𝒢 **Writing and Grammar,** Ruby Level, p. 309 ▪

💿 **Writing and Grammar iText CD-ROM**

▪ **BLOCK SCHEDULING:** Resources marked with this symbol provide varied instruction during 90-minute blocks.

Writing Lesson

Critical Response

On the art of writing poetry, Robert Lowell once said, "In life we speak with many false voices; occasionally, if we are lucky, we find a true one in our poems." Choose one of these poems and write an essay in which you discuss whether or not it achieves a "true" voice.

Prewriting   Select the poem that you like the most. Reread it, taking notes about its message, imagery, and style. Assess why the poem speaks to you. Based on your assessment, create a list of criteria for a poem that has a "true" voice.

Model: Identifying Criteria

Judging from my reading of "Traveling Through the Dark,"

a true voice

- deals with a moral question
- uses plain words, but in a beautiful way
- is not heroic

A list of criteria lays the foundation for the development of ideas in an essay.

Drafting   Begin by identifying the poem you have selected, and briefly describe its subject. Then, introduce your criteria. Use body paragraphs to explain how each of your criteria apply to the poem.

Revising   Review your essay, and make sure that each body paragraph clearly speaks to one item on your list of criteria.

Prentice Hall Writing and Grammar Connection: Chapter 14, Section 3

Extension Activities

Listening and Speaking   Watch the film based on Robert Penn Warren's novel "All the King's Men." Then, prepare an **evaluation** of the film. To prepare, keep these tips in mind:

- Offer a brief summary of the story.
- Evaluate how effectively the film expresses ideas visually.

As you work, pay close attention to strategies the filmmakers use to shape viewers' perceptions of events and characters. [**Group Activity**]

Research and Technology   Conduct library and Internet research to learn more about Robert Lowell and confessional poetry. Prepare and give an **oral presentation** in which you share your findings on the confessional poets and their work. Recite two or three of the poems you like best.

 Take It to the Net   www.phschool.com

Go online for an additional research activity using the Internet.

Hawthorne / Gold Glade / Traveling Through the Dark / The Light Comes Brighter / The Adamant ◆ 1025

❸ Writing Lesson

- Encourage students to read their chosen poems several times. Repeated reading often leads to greater understanding of a literary work.
- Encourage students to paraphrase their chosen poems. This will help clarify any ideas that seem difficult or obscure.
- You may wish to use Writing Process Model 7, Interpreting a Work of Literature, pp. 37–40 in **Writing Models and Graphic Organizers on Transparencies.**
- Use the Response to Literature rubric in **Performance assessment and Portfolio Management,** p. 23, to assess students' critical responses.

❹ Listening and Speaking

- Students may want to view the film as a group and discuss it afterwards.
- As an extension, interested students may want to try reading the novel on which the film was based.
- Have students use the Peer Assessment form for Delivering a Speech, p. 30, in **Performance Assessment and Portfolio Management.**

CUSTOMIZE INSTRUCTION
For Universal Access

To address different learning styles, use the following activities suggested in the **Extension Activities** booklet, p. 58.

For Visual/Spatial Learners, use Activities 5 and 6.

For Musical/Rhythmic Learners, use Activity 6.

For Verbal/Linguistic and Bodily/Kinesthetic Learners, use Activity 7.

ASSESSMENT RESOURCES

The following resources can be used to assess students' knowledge and skills.

Selection Assessment

- 📖 **Formal Assessment,** pp. 257–259
- 📖 **Open Book Test,** pp. 172–174
- 📼 **Got It! Assessment Videotapes,** Tape 5
- 💿 **Test Bank Software**

📖 *Take It to the Net*
Visit www.phschool.com for self-tests and additional questions on the selections.

Writing Rubric

- 📖 **Performance Assess. and Portfolio Mgmt.,** p. 23

Listening and Speaking Rubric

- 📖 **Performance Assess. and Portfolio Mgmt.,** p. 30

PRENTICE HALL ASSESSMENT SYSTEM

- 📖 **Workbook**
- 📖 **Skill Book**
- 📖 **Transparencies**
- 💿 **CD-ROM**

Average Waves in Unprotected Waters

Lesson Objectives

1. **To analyze and respond to literary elements**
   - Literary Analysis: Foreshadowing
   - Connecting Literary Elements: Suspense
2. **To read, comprehend, analyze, and critique a short story**
   - Reading Strategy: Putting Events in Order
   - Reading Check questions
   - Review and Assess questions
3. **To develop word analysis skills, fluency, and systematic vocabulary**
   - Vocabulary Development Lesson: Latin Prefix: *trans-*
4. **To understand and apply written and oral language conventions**
   - Spelling Strategy
   - Grammar and Style Lesson: Correct Use of Adjectives and Adverbs
   - Assessment Practice (ATE)
5. **To understand and apply appropriate writing and research strategies**
   - Writing Lesson: Social Worker's Report
   - Extension Activity: Fact-Finding Research Report
6. **To understand and apply listening and speaking strategies**
   - Extension Activity: Political Speech

STEP-BY-STEP TEACHING GUIDE	PACING GUIDE
PRETEACH	
Motivate Students and Provide Background	
Use the Motivation activity (ATE p. 1026)	5 min.
Read and discuss author and background features (SE/ATE pp. 1026, 1029) **A**	5 min.
Introduce the Concepts	
Introduce the Literary Analysis and Reading Strategy (SE/ATE p. 1027) **A**	15 min.
Pronounce the vocabulary words and read their definitions (SE p. 1027)	5 min.
TEACH	
Monitor Comprehension	
Informally monitor comprehension by circulating while students read independently or in groups **A**	25 min.
Monitor students' comprehension with the Reading Check notes (SE/ATE pp. 1029, 1031, 1033, 1035,)	as students read
Develop vocabulary with Vocabulary notes (SE pp. 1030, 1031, 1032; ATE p. 1031)	as students read
Develop Understanding	
Develop students' understanding of foreshadowing with the Literary Analysis annotations (SE pp. 1029, 1030, 1032, 1034, 1035; ATE pp. 1028, 1029, 1030, 1032, 1033, 1034, 1035) **A**	5 min.
Develop students' ability to order events in the story by using the Reading Strategy annotations (SE p. 1031; ATE pp. 1030, 1031)	5 min.
ASSESS	
Assess Mastery	
Assess students' mastery of the Reading Strategy and Literary Analysis by having them answer the Review and Assess questions (SE/ATE p. 1037)	15 min.
Use one or more of the print and media Assessment Resources (ATE p. 1039) **A**	up to 45 min.
EXTEND	
Apply Understanding	
Have students complete the Vocabulary Development Lesson and the Grammar and Style Lesson (SE p. 1038) **A**	20 min.
Apply students' ability to use transitions to show cause and effect by using the Writing Lesson (SE/ATE p. 1039) **A**	45 min.
Apply students' understanding using one or more of the Extension Activities (SE p. 1039)	20–90 min.

 ACCELERATED INSTRUCTION:
Use the strategies and activities identified with an **A**.

UNIVERSAL ACCESS
- ● = Below Level Students
- ▲ = On-Level Students
- ■ = Above Level Students

Time and Resource Manager

RESOURCES		
PRINT 📖	**TRANSPARENCIES** 📄	**TECHNOLOGY** 💿 🎧 📼
• **Beyond Literature,** Humanities Connection: Art, p. 59 ▲ ■		• **Interest Grabber Video,** Tape 6 ● ▲ ■
• **Selection Support Workbook:** ● ▲ ■ Literary Analysis, p. 261 Reading Strategy, p. 260 Build Vocabulary, p. 258	• **Literary Analysis and Reading Transparencies,** pp. 117 and 118 ● ▲ ■	
		• **Listening to Literature** ● ▲ ■ Audiocassettes, Side 35 Audio CDs, CD 20
• **Literatura en español** ● ▲ • **Literary Analysis for Enrichment** ■		
• **Formal Assessment:** Selection Test, pp. 260–262 ● ▲ ■ • **Open Book Test,** pp. 175–177 ● ▲ ■ • **Performance Assessment and Portfolio Management,** p. 20 ● ▲ ■ • **PRENTICE HALL** ASSESSMENT *SYSTEM* ● ▲ ■	• **PRENTICE HALL** ASSESSMENT *SYSTEM* ● ▲ ■ Skills Practice Answers and Explanations on Transparencies	• **Test Bank Software** ● ▲ ■ • **Got It! Assessment Videotapes,** Tape 5 ● ▲
• **Selection Support Workbook:** ● ▲ ■ Grammar and Style, p. 259 • **Writing and Grammar,** Ruby Level ● ▲ ■ • **Extension Activities,** p. 59 ● ▲ ■	• **Daily Language Practice Transparencies** ● ▲ • **Writing Models and Graphic Organizers on Transparency,** pp. 91–93 ● ▲ ■	• **Writing and Grammar iText CD-ROM** ● ▲ ■ 💻 *Take It to the Net* www.phschool.com

BLOCK SCHEDULING: Use one 90-minute class period to preteach the selection and have students read it. Use a second 90-minute class period to assess students' mastery of skills and have them complete one of the Extension Activities.

Step-by-Step Teaching Guide for pp. 1026–1027

Motivation

Students may find this story of ambivalence in the face of seemingly unavoidable change both touching and depressing. Involve them in considering the range of human reactions to change by presenting the following dramatization. Ask the school principal to announce to your class an impending major change—for example, relocating the school, the retirement of a popular teacher, or cancelation of the athletic program. Ask students to identify both positive and negative reactions to the proposed change. Lead from this discussion of change to the story, in which the main character experiences emotional extremes when facing an important life change.

▣ Interest Grabber Video

As an alternative, play "Adapting to Change" on Tape 6 to engage student interest

❶ Background

More About the Author

Author Anne Tyler is celebrated for her sensitive ear for dialogue and her lifelike contemporary characters with whom readers can relate. Tyler's themes are human experiences—relationships between husbands and wives, parents and children, siblings; the meaning of love; the nature of identity; impermanence and change.

Tyler, who strives to make each novel an "extremely believable lie," hopes to be known as a writer of serious, not necessarily important, books, ones that have "layers and layers and layers, like life does."

Prepare to Read

Average Waves in Unprotected Waters

❶ Anne Tyler (b. 1941)

As the wife of a child psychiatrist and the mother of two daughters, Anne Tyler has for years successfully juggled the demands of family life while maintaining her commitment to writing. She works at home in her starkly plain study, seated on a daybed. She pens her fiction in longhand so that, as she explains it, she can hear her characters speak. During occasional bouts of insomnia, she records her ideas in boxes of index cards.

Everyday People Tyler, who has remained a private person despite her fame, lives in Baltimore, Maryland, a city that provides a strong setting for her work. Many of her stories focus on the loneliness and isolation of ordinary middle-class people.

Young Talent Born in Minneapolis, Tyler spent most of her early childhood in Quaker communes in the Midwest and South. This experience, she recalls, was helpful to her as a writer because it enabled her to look "at the normal world with a certain amount of distance and surprise." After attending high school in Raleigh, North Carolina, she enrolled at Duke University to study Russian when she was sixteen. After graduating from college, she worked as a bibliographer at Duke and then moved to Montreal, Canada, where she held a job as a librarian at McGill University.

Tyler began her writing career with a series of short stories, few of which were published. Then, at age twenty-four, she published her first work, the novel *If Morning Ever Comes*. The book depicts a young man who returns home and attempts to find his identity amid overpowering family expectations. Since then Tyler has produced a string of novels to ever-increasing acclaim. Among them are *Dinner at the Homesick Restaurant* (1982); *The Accidental Tourist* (1985), which was made into a film in 1988; *Breathing Lessons* (1988), winner of the 1989 Pulitzer Prize for Fiction; *A Patchwork Planet* (1998); and *Back When We Were Grown Ups* (2000). Tyler has also published numerous short stories in literary magazines like *The New Yorker*.

Serious Fiction When Tyler works on a novel, she follows a pattern. First, she writes out a draft in longhand. She then reads the draft to "find out what it means." She revises the draft to enhance "the subconscious intentions" she has discovered in the work. Tyler keeps the goal of writing "serious fiction" firmly in sight. Her characters are not fictionalized versions of people from her own life; instead, they are products of a fertile imagination that are drawn with her gift for fine, realistic detail.

Eccentrics Tyler has a flair for creating eccentric people in improbable yet touching plots. Her compassion, wit, and use of the precise details of domestic life flavor her tales of relationships and family dynamics. Her overall theme may be seen as the persistent endurance of the human spirit in the face of the inevitable struggles and strains of daily life.

"Average Waves in Unprotected Waters," which was first published in *The New Yorker* in 1977, displays Tyler's ability to create well-developed, realistic characters and to evoke an emotional response through an unsentimental portrayal of the characters' tragic lives.

TEACHING RESOURCES

The following resources can be used to enrich or extend the instruction for pp. 1026–1027.

Motivation
▣ **Interest Grabber Video**, Tape 6

Background
📖 **Beyond Literature**, p. 59 ▣

🖥 *Take It to the Net*
Visit www.phschool.com for Background and hotlinks for the poems.

Literary Analysis
📄 **Literary Analysis and Reading Transparencies,** Foreshadowing, p. 118 ▣

Reading
📖 **Selection Support:** Reading Strategy, p. 260; Build Vocabulary, p. 258

📄 **Literary Analysis and Reading Transparencies,** Putting Events in Order, p. 117

▣ **BLOCK SCHEDULING:** Resources marked with this symbol provide varied instruction during 90-minute blocks.

Preview

Connecting to the Literature

A family move, a transfer to a new school—these events can present both problems and challenges. In this story, the main character faces the reality that a painful change in her life just may be for the better.

② Literary Analysis

Foreshadowing

Foreshadowing is the use of details or clues that hint at what will occur later in a plot or suggest a certain outcome. Foreshadowing builds suspense because it makes the reader wonder what will happen next or how the story will end, as this passage demonstrates:

> Maybe she felt to blame that he was going. But she'd done the best she could: babysat him all these years and only given up when he'd grown too strong and wild to manage.

As you read, notice how Tyler's use of foreshadowing keeps you guessing about the story's outcome.

Connecting Literary Elements

An effective use of foreshadowing can heighten the suspense for readers and pique their interest to read further. **Suspense** is a feeling of growing uncertainty about the outcome of events in a literary work. Writers create suspense by raising questions in readers' minds. Because most people are curious or concerned, they keep reading to find out what will happen next. As you read, notice how the suspense makes you anxious to learn the outcome.

③ Reading Strategy

Putting Events in Order

Most stories are written in chronological order—the order in which events happen in real time. Sometimes, however, the writer interrupts the sequence to present a flashback—a scene or an event from an earlier time. As you read Tyler's story, **put the events in order** by noting the sequence in which they actually occurred. Create a chain-of-events diagram like the one shown to record the events in order, from the earliest to the latest.

Order of Events

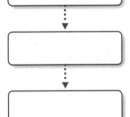

Vocabulary Development

orthopedic (ôr´ thō pē´ dik) *adj.* correcting posture or other disorders of the skeletal system (p. 1030)

transparent (trans per´ ənt) *adj.* capable of being seen through (p. 1031)

stocky (stäk´ ē) *adj.* solidly built; sturdy (p. 1031)

staunch (stônch) *adj.* strong; unyielding (p. 1032)

viper (vī´pər) *n.* type of snake; a malicious person (p. 1032)

---

② Literary Analysis

Foreshadowing

- Explain to students that they will focus on foreshadowing, clues to events that will occur later in the story, as they read "Average Waves in Unprotected Waters."

- Draw students' attention to the example of foreshadowing. Have them consider how foreshadowing builds suspense.

- Go over the Foreshadowing transparency in **Literary Analysis and Reading Transparencies**, p. 118, with students. Cover the second column. Have students pick out the words in each example that signal foreshadowing and speculate about how each example might heighten the suspense.

③ Reading Strategy

Putting Events in Order

- Reiterate to students that most stories are written in chronological order. Tell students that strict chronological order in a story may be interrupted by a flashback or flash forward, a memory of an action that has already taken place or one that is yet to come.

- On the board, draw a chart like the one on p. 1027 and have volunteers tell a few events from a common fairy tale in the order that they occurred.

- Ask students to use a chart like this one to record the main events in "Average Waves in Unprotected Waters" in chronological order. Caution them to watch out for flashbacks.

Vocabulary Development

- Pronounce each vocabulary word for students, and read the definitions as a class. Have students identify any words with which they are already familiar.

 E-Teach

Visit E-Teach at www.phschool.com for teachers' essays on how to teach, with questions and answers.

CUSTOMIZE INSTRUCTION FOR UNIVERSAL ACCESS

For Less Proficient Readers	For English Learners	For Advanced Readers
At the start of the story, Tyler gives only clues about the challenge Bet faces. Encourage these students to read on, despite any early confusion, as the situation will ultimately become clear. For extra support, have students listen to the story on the **Listening to Literature** audiocassette or CD before they read it independently.	As students read the story, have them note confusing words and phrases. Figurative language, idiomatic expressions, and uncommon syntax may cause problems. Discuss the phrases students have noted. Then, have students read on, continuing to note and discuss problem passages.	Draw students' attention to the challenge Tyler faces in truthfully and respectfully portraying a mentally challenged boy. Have them identify Tyler's characterization techniques, such as direct and indirect characterization, as they read the story independently.

Step-by-Step Teaching Guide for pp. 1028–1036

CUSTOMIZE INSTRUCTION
For Musical/Rhythmic Learners

Point out the care with which Bet modulates her tone of voice, sure that it will reveal too much of her feelings to Arnold. As Bet, have students read portions of the text aloud, listening for the intonations that might signal to Arnold that something is amiss.

❶ About the Selection

In this story, readers meet Bet, a woman torn apart emotionally by the difficult decision she has made about the care of her mentally challenged son, Arnold. As Bet accompanies Arnold to his new home, guiding him and helping him negotiate the obstacles of travel, she recalls the events that have brought her to this point. Readers learn of the gritty perseverance that has enabled her to endure the catastrophic events of her life, which have washed over her like "average waves in unprotected waters." As Bet leaves her son behind in a mental hospital, she is torn with ambivalent feelings of guilt and relief as she realizes that she will no longer participate in the daily agonies of caring for Arnold.

❷ Literary Analysis
Foreshadowing

- Point out that the bracketed passage is an example of foreshadowing.

- Ask whether the event coming up is likely to be pleasant or unpleasant.
  Answer: Most students will believe that the event will be unpleasant because the boy seems upset.

- Have students answer the Literary Analysis question on p. 1029: What details in this paragraph hint that something unusual, or even unpleasant, may be ahead?
  Answer: Details include the following: The boy and his mother are up before daylight. The boy won't eat. He seems upset.

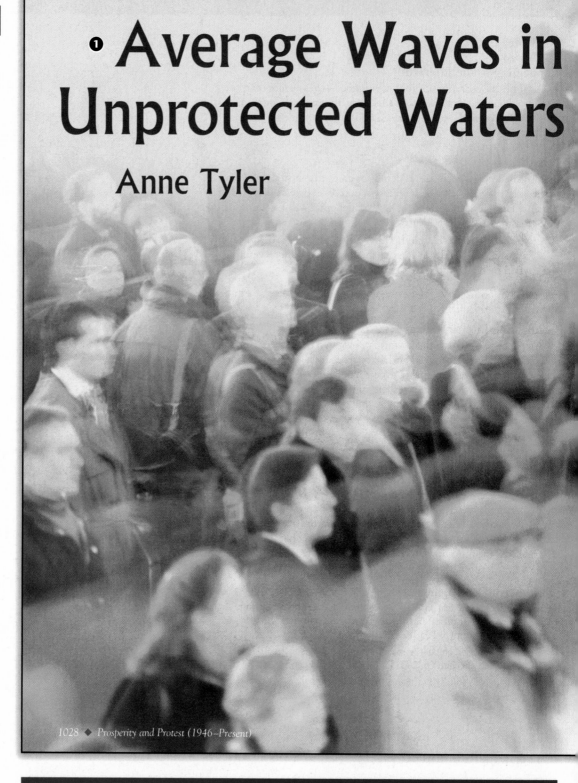

❶ Average Waves in Unprotected Waters

Anne Tyler

1028 ◆ *Prosperity and Protest (1946–Present)*

TEACHING RESOURCES

The following resources can be used to enrich or extend the instruction for pp. 1028–1036.

Literary Analysis

📖 **Selection Support:** Literary Analysis, p. 261 ▪

Reading

🎧 **Listening to Literature Audiocassettes,** Side 35 ▪

💿 **Listening to Literature Audio CDs,** CD 20 ▪

▪ **BLOCK SCHEDULING:** Resources marked with this symbol provide varied instruction during 90-minute blocks.

Background

The decision to institutionalize a child is an extremely difficult one. In this story, Anne Tyler explores a single mother's attempts to care for a severely mentally challenged child. When this story was written in the mid-1970s, a single parent may have felt she had few other options available to her. Then, as now, the cost of private care was so high that many patients were placed in state-run or charitable hospitals where lack of funding sometimes resulted in grim conditions, outdated equipment, and an inadequate staff. Fortunately, an array of educational, medical, and counseling programs for children with special needs today makes it possible for many of them who might once have been institutionalized to remain at home.

As soon as it got light, Bet woke him and dressed him, and then she walked him over to the table and tried to make him eat a little cereal. He wouldn't, though. He could tell something was up. She pressed the edge of the spoon against his lips till she heard it click on his teeth, but he just looked off at a corner of the ceiling—a knobby child with great glassy eyes and her own fair hair. Like any other nine-year-old, he wore a striped shirt and jeans, but the shirt was too neat and the jeans too blue, unpatched and unfaded, and would stay that way till he outgrew them. And his face was elderly—pinched, strained, tired—though it should have looked as unused as his jeans. He hardly ever changed his expression.

She left him in his chair and went to make the beds. Then she raised the yellowed shade, rinsed a few spoons in the bathroom sink, picked up some bits of magazines he'd torn the night before. This was a rented room in an ancient, crumbling house, and nothing you could do to it would lighten its cluttered look. There was always that feeling of too many lives layered over other lives, like the layers of brownish wallpaper her child had peeled away in the corner by his bed.

She slipped her feet into flat-heeled loafers and absently patted the front of her dress, a worn beige knit she usually saved for Sundays. Maybe she should take it in a little; it hung from her shoulders like a sack. She felt too slight and frail, too wispy for all she had to do today. But she reached for her coat anyhow, and put it on and tied a blue kerchief under her chin. Then she went over to the table and slowly spun, modeling the coat. "See, Arnold?" she said. "We're going out."

Arnold went on looking at the ceiling, but his gaze turned wild and she knew he'd heard.

⑤ ◀ Critical Viewing How might this busy scene at a train station represent the isolation or alienation Bet feels in this story? **[Connect]**

Literary Analysis ②
Foreshadowing What details in this paragraph hint that something unusual, or even unpleasant, may lie ahead?

③

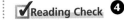
✔ Reading Check ④
What is Arnold's reaction as his mother busily prepares to leave the house?

❸ Literary Analysis
Foreshadowing

- Ask students to identify the foreshadowing in the passage.
  Answer: Bet wears a dress she usually wears only on Sunday, and she feels too frail for all she has to do this day.
- Point out to students that the foreshadowing indicates the importance of an upcoming journey.

▶ Monitor Progress Have students who can't identify the foreshadowing or speculate about its possible implications consider why the author included the information. Remind them that authors have a purpose for all the details they include. Good readers will wonder why the author decided to have Bet wear her Sunday dress on a weekday. They will realize that the Sunday dress suggests that Bet faces a day of great importance.

❹ ✔ Reading Check

Answer: Arnold is upset. He refuses to eat and gazes about wildly.

❺ ▶ Critical Viewing

Possible response: It is said that people feel most alone in a crowd. No matter how many people Bet is surrounded by, she will always be lonely for her son.

CUSTOMIZE INSTRUCTION FOR UNIVERSAL ACCESS

For Special Needs Students	For Gifted/Talented Students	For Advanced Readers
To help students gain some insight into the two characters, ask them to list adjectives to describe Arnold and Bet. Then, have small groups of students discuss these questions: What are Bet's feelings toward Arnold? How does her son feel about her?	Ask students to think of songs and poems that capture the feeling they get from reading this page. Ask students to gather in small groups to share their songs and poems. Then, have them discuss the emotions this page arouses and the devices the author uses to evoke these emotions.	Ask students to gather in small groups to discuss the beginning of the story. What mood or tone does the author establish in the first paragraph? How does she accomplish this task? In what ways do the figurative language and the point of view contribute to the emotional content of this page?

❻ Literary Analysis

Foreshadowing

- Remind students that foreshadowing builds suspense by hinting at what might happen next.

- Read the bracketed passage aloud, and ask students to describe Mrs. Puckett's behavior. **Answer:** Mrs. Puckett waits outside her door with tear-filled eyes and quavering voice, and makes Arnold peanut butter cookies.

- Then, have students answer the Literary Analysis question on p. 1030: What does Mrs. Puckett's behavior hint about the events to come? **Answer:** Mrs. Puckett is distressed; her behavior indicates she is worried about what will happen to Arnold.

❼ Reading Strategy

Putting Events in Order

- Ask students to identify when in the chronology of the story the bracketed passage occurs. **Answer:** Mrs. Puckett had cared for Arnold from early childhood until recently.

- Ask: How does inserting this information about past events help clarify the current situation? **Answer:** The reference to the change in Arnold's behavior explains why his mother feels she must make new arrangements for his care.

❽ Critical Thinking

Predict

- Have students predict where Bet and Arnold are going.

- Have students give reasons for their predictions. Remind them that they should base their ideas on details about the characters and the plot. **Answer:** Many students will predict that Arnold is going to some sort of institution because his mother can no longer care for him.

She fetched his jacket from the closet—brown corduroy, with a hood. It had set her back half a week's salary. But Arnold didn't like it; he always wanted his old one, a little red duffel coat he'd long ago outgrown. When she came toward him, he started moaning and rocking and shaking his head. She had to struggle to stuff his arms in the sleeves. Small though he was, he was strong, wiry; he was getting to be too much for her. He shook free of her hands and ran over to his bed. The jacket was on, though. It wasn't buttoned, the collar was askew, but never mind; that just made him look more real. She always felt bad at how he stood inside his clothes, separate from them, passive, unaware of all the buttons and snaps she'd fastened as carefully as she would a doll's.

She gave a last look around the room, checked to make sure the hot plate was off, and then picked up her purse and Arnold's suitcase. "Come along, Arnold," she said.

He came, dragging out every step. He looked at the suitcase suspiciously, but only because it was new. It didn't have any meaning for him. "See?" she said. "It's yours. It's Arnold's. It's going on the train with us."

But her voice was all wrong. He would pick it up, for sure. She paused in the middle of locking the door and glanced over at him fearfully. Anything could set him off nowadays. He hadn't noticed, though. He was too busy staring around the hallway, goggling at a freckled, walnut-framed mirror as if he'd never seen it before. She touched his shoulder. "Come, Arnold," she said.

They went down the stairs slowly, both of them clinging to the sticky mahogany railing. The suitcase banged against her shins. In the entrance hall, old Mrs. Puckett stood waiting outside her door—a huge, soft lady in a black crepe dress and <u>orthopedic</u> shoes. She was holding a plastic bag of peanutbutter cookies, Arnold's favorites. There were tears in her eyes. "Here, Arnold," she said, quavering. Maybe she felt to blame that he was going. But she'd done the best she could: babysat him all these years and only given up when he'd grown too strong and wild to manage. Bet wished Arnold would give the old lady some sign—hug her, make his little crowing noise, just take the cookies, even. But he was too excited. He raced on out the front door, and it was Bet who had to take them. "Well, thank you, Mrs. Puckett," she said. "I know he'll enjoy them later."

"Oh, no . . ." said Mrs. Puckett, and she flapped her large hands and gave up, sobbing.

They were lucky and caught a bus first thing. Arnold sat by the window. He must have thought he was going to work with her; when they passed the red-and-gold Kresge's sign, he jabbered and tried to stand up. "No, honey," she said, and took hold of his arm. He settled down then and let his hand stay curled in hers awhile. He had very small, cool fingers, and nails as smooth as thumbtack heads.

At the train station, she bought the tickets and then a pack of Wrigley's spearmint gum. Arnold stood gaping at the vaulted ceiling,

orthopedic (ôr´ thō pē´ dik) *adj.* correcting posture or other disorders of the skeletal system

Literary Analysis
Foreshadowing What does Mrs. Puckett's behavior hint about the events to come?

CUSTOMIZE INSTRUCTION FOR UNIVERSAL ACCESS

For Gifted/Talented Students	For Advanced Readers
Have students do some research to find out what resources are available in their community to help support parents, especially single parents, who are caretakers of children with mental disabilities similar to Arnold's. Then, have them write a dialogue between Bet and a social worker who has been assigned to help her find the best ways to take care of her son and make the most of his potential for learning. Have students perform their dialogues for the rest of the class.	Have students research the mainstreaming of mentally and physically disabled students into general classrooms. Have them consider such questions as when and why mainstreaming began and what the goal of mainstreaming is. Have students write about or discuss the benefits and liabilities of mainstreaming. Urge students to suggest ways that mainstreaming could be modified to work even better than it now does.

with his head flopped back and his arms hanging limp at his sides. People stared at him. She would have liked to push their faces in. "Over here, honey," she said, and she nudged him toward the gate, straightening his collar as they walked.

He hadn't been on a train before and acted a little nervous, bouncing up and down in his seat and flipping the lid of his ashtray and craning forward to see the man ahead of them. When the train started moving, he crowed and pulled at her sleeve. "That's right, Arnold. Train. We're taking a trip," Bet said. She unwrapped a stick of chewing gum and gave it to him. He loved gum. If she didn't watch him closely, he sometimes swallowed it—which worried her a little because she'd heard it clogged your kidneys; but at least it would keep him busy. She looked down at the top of his head. Through the blond prickles of his hair, cut short for practical reasons, she could see his skull bones moving as he chewed. He was so thin-skinned, almost <u>transparent</u>; sometimes she imagined she could see the blood traveling in his veins.

When the train reached a steady speed, he grew calmer, and after a while he nodded over against her and let his hands sag on his knees. She watched his eyelashes slowly drooping—two colorless, fringed crescents, heavier and heavier, every now and then flying up as he tried to fight off sleep. He had never slept well, not ever, not even as a baby. Even before they'd noticed anything wrong, they'd wondered at his jittery, jerky catnaps, his tiny hands clutching tight and springing open, his strange single wail sailing out while he went right on sleeping. Avery said it gave him the chills. And after the doctor talked to them Avery wouldn't have anything to do with Arnold anymore—just walked in wide circles around the crib, looking stunned and sick. A few weeks later, he left. She wasn't surprised. She even knew how he felt, more or less. Halfway, he blamed her; halfway, he blamed himself. You can't believe a thing like this will just fall on you out of nowhere.

She'd had moments herself of picturing some kind of evil gene in her husband's ordinary, <u>stocky</u> body—a dark little egg like a black jelly bean, she imagined it. All his fault. But other times she was sure the gene was hers. It seemed so natural; she never could do anything as well as most people. And then other times she blamed their marriage. They'd married too young, against her parents' wishes. All she'd wanted was to get away from home. Now she couldn't remember why. What was wrong with home? She thought of her parents' humped green trailer, perched on cinder blocks near a forest of masts in Salt Spray, Maryland. At this distance (parents dead, trailer rusted to bits, even Salt Spray changed past recognition), it seemed to her that her old life had been beautifully free and spacious. She closed her eyes and saw wide gray skies. Everything had been ruled by the sea. Her father (who'd run a fishing boat for tourists) couldn't arrange his day till he'd heard the marine forecast—the wind, the tides, the small-craft warnings, the height of average waves in unprotected waters. He loved to fish, offshore and on, and he swam every chance he could get. He'd tried to teach her to bodysurf, but it hadn't worked out.

transparent (trans per′ ənt) *adj.* capable of being seen through

stocky (stäk′ ē) *adj.* solidly built; sturdy

Reading Strategy
Putting Events in Order
What clues tell you that Bet is recalling the past?

✔**Reading Check** ⓫

How did Arnold's father react to his son's condition?

Average Waves in Unprotected Waters ◆ 1031

---

❾ Vocabulary Development

Latin Prefix *trans-*

- Call students' attention to the word *transparent*. Tell them that the prefix *trans-* means "across," "over," or "through." *Transparent* means "able to be seen through."

- Have volunteers suggest other words with the prefix *trans-* and explain what each word means. Write the words on the board. Answer: Words with the prefix *trans-* include, among many others, *transfix, transcend, transcribe, transfer, translate, transportation,* and *transit.*

❿ Reading Strategy

Putting Events in Order

- Have a volunteer read the bracketed passage aloud. Then, ask the Reading Strategy question on p. 1031: What clues tell you that Bet is recalling the past? Answer: Clues include Arnold's sleep habits, which remind Bet of how Arnold slept as a baby. Moreover, Bet is described as "picturing" events from the past. Bet lets memories of those times propel her further into her own childhood.

- Make sure that students realize that the flashback begins with Arnold's childhood, then moves to Bet's childhood, and finally explores her marriage to Avery.

▶ **Monitor Progress** Ask students to suggest some reasons why Bet might recall events out of chronological order. Answer: Students may point out that thinking of Arnold's childhood naturally leads Bet to contrast it with her own childhood. The memory of her father then leads to memories of Arnold's father.

⓫ ✔Reading Check

Answer: Avery left his baby and wife a few weeks after they learned that the baby had a mental disability.

⑫ Critical Thinking

Connect

- Ask students whether they think Bet's habit of enduring is a good and useful one.
  Possible answers: Some students will believe that Bet's stoicism is useful since she can't change Arnold's condition; many students will believe Bet could do more for Arnold and herself if she were more assertive.

- Have students identify an episode from Bet's childhood that demonstrates this character trait.
  Answer: Bet demonstrates her stoic endurance when she lets the waves slam into her rather than attempting to bodysurf.

⑬ Literary Analysis

Foreshadowing and Suspense

- Ask students what details and phrases clue them in to the threatening tone of the bracketed passage.
  Possible response: The conductor "lurched down the aisle, plucking pink tickets"; the lady's coat has a "fox fur piece biting its own tail," her muscles twitch; she waves a "spidery hand."

- Then, ask the Literary Analysis question on p. 1032: In what ways does this scene raise questions in your mind and create suspense?
  Answer: The scene is suspenseful because the reader has no idea whether the woman is going to pay for her ticket or be put off the train.

There was something about the breakers: she just gritted her teeth and stood <u>staunch</u> and let them slam into her. As if standing staunch were a virtue, really. She couldn't explain it. Her father thought she was scared, but it wasn't that at all.

She'd married Avery against their wishes and been sorry ever since—sorry to move so far from home, sorrier when her parents died within a year of each other, sorriest of all when the marriage turned grim and cranky. But she never would have thought of leaving him. It was Avery who left; she would have stayed forever. In fact, she did stay on in their apartment for months after he'd gone, though the rent was far too high. It wasn't that she expected him back. She just ⑫ took some comfort from enduring.

Arnold's head snapped up. He looked around him and made a gurgling sound. His chewing gum fell onto the front of his jacket. "Here, honey," she told him. She put the gum in her ashtray. "Look out the window. See the cows?"

He wouldn't look. He began bouncing in his seat, rubbing his hands together rapidly.

"Arnold? Want a cookie?"

If only she'd brought a picture book. She'd meant to and then forgot. She wondered if the train people sold magazines. If she let him get too bored, he'd go into one of his tantrums, and then she wouldn't be able to handle him. The doctor had given her pills just in case, but she was always afraid that while he was screaming he would choke on them. She looked around the car. "Arnold," she said, "see the . . . see the hat with feathers on? Isn't it pretty? See the red suitcase? See the, um . . ."

The car door opened with a rush of clattering wheels and the conductor burst in, singing "Girl of my dreams, I love you." He lurched down the aisle, plucking pink tickets from the back of each seat. Just across from Bet and Arnold, he stopped. He was looking down at a tiny black lady in a purple coat, with a fox fur piece biting its own tail around her neck. "You!" he said.

The lady stared straight ahead.

"You, I saw you. You're the one in the washroom."

⑬ A little muscle twitched in her cheek.

"You got on this train in Beulah, didn't you. Snuck in the washroom. Darted back like you thought you could put something over on me. I saw that bit of purple! Where's your ticket gone to?"

She started fumbling in a blue cloth purse. The fumbling went on and on. The conductor shifted his weight.

"Why!" she said finally. "I must've left it back in my other seat."

"What other seat?"

"Oh, the one back . . ." She waved a spidery hand.

The conductor sighed. "Lady," he said, "you owe me money."

"I do no such thing!" she said. "Viper! Monger! Hitler!"[1] Her voice screeched up all at once; she sounded like a parrot. Bet winced and

---

1. **Hitler** German dictator Adolf Hitler (1889–1945).

1032 ◆ Prosperity and Protest (1946–Present)

staunch (stônch) *adj.* strong; unyielding

Literary Analysis
Foreshadowing and Suspense In what ways does this scene raise questions in your mind and create suspense?

viper (vī′pər) *n.* type of snake; a malicious person

 ENRICHMENT: Career Connection

Specialized Skills

Several characters in the story—the narrator, Mrs. Puckett, and the nurse—must care for a young, mentally challenged boy. Challenge students to brainstorm for a list of skills a caregiver would need to care for the mentally challenged properly and kindly. Discuss how interested students might acquire these skills. Does your community offer training classes, or does a local hospital offer internships? Then, discuss whether these skills might be useful in other workplace or family situations.

felt herself flushing, as if *she* were the one. But then at her shoulder she heard a sudden, rusty clang, and she turned and saw that Arnold was laughing. He had his mouth wide open and his tongue curled, the way he did when he watched "Sesame Street." Even after the scene had worn itself out, and the lady had paid and the conductor had moved on, Arnold went on chortling and la-la-ing, and Bet looked gratefully at the little black lady, who was settling her fur piece fussily and muttering under her breath.

From the Parkinsville Railroad Station, which they seemed to be tearing down or else remodeling—she couldn't tell which—they took a taxicab to Parkins State Hospital. "Oh, I been out there many and many a time," said the driver. "Went out there just the other—"

But she couldn't stop herself; she had to tell him before she forgot. "Listen," she said, "I want you to wait for me right in the driveway. I don't want you to go on away."

"Well, fine," he said.

"Can you do that? I want you to be sitting right by the porch or the steps or whatever, right where I come out of, ready to take me back to the station. Don't just go off, and—"

"I *got* you, I got you," he said.

She sank back. She hoped he understood.

Arnold wanted a peanut-butter cookie. He was reaching and whimpering. She didn't know what to do. She wanted to give him anything he asked for, anything; but he'd get it all over his face and arrive not looking his best. She couldn't stand it if they thought he was just ordinary and unattractive. She wanted them to see how small and neat he was, how somebody cherished him. But it would be awful if he went into one of his rages. She broke off a little piece of cookie from the bag. "Here," she told him. "Don't mess, now."

He flung himself back in the corner and ate it, keeping one hand flattened across his mouth while he chewed.

The hospital looked like someone's great, pillared mansion, with square brick buildings all around it. "Here we are," the driver said.

"Thank you," she said. "Now you wait here, please. Just wait till I get—"

"*Lady*," he said. "I'll wait."

She opened the door and nudged Arnold out ahead of her. Lugging the suitcase, she started toward the steps. "Come on, Arnold," she said.

He hung back.

"Arnold?"

Maybe he wouldn't allow it, and they would go on home and never think of this again.

But he came, finally, climbing the steps in his little hobbled way. His face was clean, but there were a few cookie crumbs on his jacket. She set down the suitcase to brush them off. Then she buttoned all his buttons and smoothed his shirt collar over his jacket collar before she pushed open the door.

Literary Analysis
Foreshadowing and Suspense What questions does Bet's request raise in your mind?

✓**Reading Check** ⑯
What instruction does Bet give the taxicab driver?

Average Waves in Unprotected Waters ◆ 1033

---

⑭ **Literary Analysis**
Foreshadowing and Suspense

- Ask a volunteer to read the bracketed passage aloud.
- Ask students what words they might use to characterize Bet in this passage.
  Possible responses: Students might say that Bet is nervous, unsure, paranoid or panic-stricken.
- Then, ask the Literary Analysis question on p. 1033: What is suspenseful about Bet's request?
  Answer: The urgency of Bet's request makes the reader wonder what might happen at the hospital that would make her want to leave in a hurry. It also makes the reader ask what would happen if the taxi driver were to leave before Bet was through with her business at the hospital.

⑮ **Critical Thinking**
Draw Conclusions

- Discuss with students Bet's state of mind at this point in the story. What conclusions can they draw from her thought that Arnold might refuse to get out of the taxicab and go into the hospital?
  Answer: Students may conclude that Bet is conflicted about taking Arnold to the hospital. If he refuses to cooperate, she will be relieved of responsibility for making this difficult decision.
- Ask students how much control Bet feels she has over her life. Have them support their responses with examples from the story.
  Answer: Students should recognize a pattern of passive endurance in Bet dating from the incident with the waves and including her response to Avery's departure.

⑯ ✓**Reading Check**
Answer: Bet tells the taxi driver to wait for her in the driveway of the hospital.

🅱 Literary Analysis

Foreshadowing and Suspense

- Have students read the bracketed passage.

- Ask students to answer the Literary Analysis question on p. 1034: Why does the mundane smell of disinfectant create suspense?
  Answer: Since smells sometimes cause Arnold to have a temper tantrum, the reader wonders whether the smell of disinfectant will have this effect on the boy and whether he will realize that he is in a mental health facility.

🅱 Critical Thinking

Evaluate

- Ask students why the hospital might want visitors to wait six months before visiting new patients.
  Answer: The hospital believes new patients will accept their new home more easily if they are not reminded of their former lives.

- Ask students whether they agree or disagree with the hospital's policy.
  Possible answers: Some students will agree for the reason cited above; other students will think that this policy is cruel and will make patients believe that their families no longer care about them.

🅱 Critical Thinking

Analyze

- Have students describe the nurse's attitude toward Bet and Arnold.
  Answer: Students may say that the nurse seems emotionally uninvolved.

- Ask students to explain why the nurse might have this attitude.
  Answer: The nurse has seen relatives say good-bye and leave their loved ones in the hospital many times before. She would be too upset to do her work well if she got involved emotionally with every patient.

In the admitting office, a lady behind a wooden counter showed her what papers to sign. Secretaries were clacketing typewriters all around. Bet thought Arnold might like that, but instead he got lost in the lights—chilly, hanging ice-cube-tray lights with a little flicker to them. He gazed upward, looking astonished. Finally a flat-fronted nurse came in and touched his elbow. "Come along, Arnold. Come, Mommy. We'll show you where Arnold is staying," she said.

They walked back across the entrance hall, then up wide marble steps with hollows worn in them. Arnold clung to the banister. There was a smell Bet hated, pine-oil disinfectant, but Arnold didn't seem to notice. You never knew; sometimes smells could just put him in a state.

The nurse unlocked a double door that had chicken-wired windows. They walked through a corridor, passing several fat, ugly women in shapeless gray dresses and ankle socks. "Ha!" one of the women said, and fell giggling into the arms of a friend. The nurse said, "*Here* we are." She led them into an enormous hallway lined with little white cots. Nobody else was in it; there wasn't a sign that children lived here except for a tiny cardboard clown picture hanging on one vacant wall. "This one is your bed, Arnold," said the nurse. Bet laid the suitcase on it. It was made up so neatly, the sheets might have been painted on. A steely-gray blanket was folded across the foot. She looked over at Arnold, but he was pivoting back and forth to hear how his new sneakers squeaked on the linoleum.

"Usually," said the nurse, "we like to give new residents six months before the family visits. That way they settle in quicker, don't you see." She turned away and adjusted the clown picture, though as far as Bet could tell it was fine the way it was. Over her shoulder, the nurse said, "You can tell him goodbye now, if you like."

"Oh," Bet said. "All right." She set her hands on Arnold's shoulders. Then she laid her face against his hair, which felt warm and fuzzy. "Honey," she said. But he went on pivoting. She straightened and told the nurse, "I brought his special blanket."

"Oh, fine," said the nurse, turning toward her again. "We'll see that he gets it."

"He always likes to sleep with it; he has ever since he was little."

"All right."

"Don't wash it. He hates if you wash it."

"Yes. Say goodbye to Mommy now, Arnold."

"A lot of times he'll surprise you. I mean there's a whole lot to him. He's not just—"

"We'll take very good care of him, Mrs. Blevins, don't worry."

"Well," she said. " 'Bye, Arnold."

She left the ward with the nurse and went down the corridor. As the nurse was unlocking the doors for her, she heard a single, terrible scream, but the nurse only patted her shoulder and pushed her gently on through.

In the taxi, Bet said, "Now, I've just got fifteen minutes to get to the station. I wonder if you could hurry?"

1034 ◆ *Prosperity and Protest (1946–Present)*

Literary Analysis
Foreshadowing and Suspense Why does the mundane smell of disinfectant create suspense?

Literary Analysis
Foreshadowing and Suspense What actions do you anticipate after Arnold's scream?

CUSTOMIZE INSTRUCTION FOR UNIVERSAL ACCESS

For Gifted/Talented Students	For Advanced Readers
Invite these students to role-play the scene between Bet and the nurse. Ask students playing Bet how the nurse's behavior makes them feel. Discuss with those playing the nurse the conflicting emotions they may feel about taking on the care of another child with severe problems.	Have students research the changes in treatment for people with schizophrenia, bipolar disorder, and other mental illnesses that have taken place in the last forty or fifty years. Encourage students to conduct direct research by interviewing health care providers. Ask students to consider whether the enormous changes in the approach to treatment have been helpful for most mentally ill people.

Girl Looking at Landscape, 1957, Richard Diebenkorn, oil on canvas, 59 x 60 3/8 inches, (149.9 x 153.4 cm), Gift of Mr. and Mrs. Alan H. Temple, 61.49, Collection of Whitney Museum of American Art, photograph by Geoffrey Clements, N.Y., Photograph copyright © 1997; Whitney Museum of American Art

21 ▲ **Critical Viewing** Bet probably experienced a range of emotions after leaving the hospital. Which of her possible emotions are reflected in this painting? **[Interpret]**

"Sure thing," the driver said.

She folded her hands and looked straight ahead. Tears seemed to be coming down her face in sheets.

Once she'd reached the station, she went to the ticket window. "Am I in time for the twelve-thirty-two?" she asked.

"Easily," said the man. "It's twenty minutes late."

"What?"

"Got held up in Norton somehow."

"But you can't!" she said. The man looked startled. She must be a sight, all swollen-eyed and wet-cheeked. "Look," she said, in a lower voice. "I figured this on purpose. I chose the one train from Beulah that would let me catch another one back without waiting. I do not want to sit and wait in this station."

 ✔Reading Check

What is the physical appearance of Arnold's hospital room?

20 **Literary Analysis**

Foreshadowing and Suspense

- Have a volunteer read the bracketed passage aloud.
- Ask students what words Tyler uses to heighten the suspense. **Answer:** The use of the adjectives *single* and *terrifying* to characterize the scream heightens the suspense.
- Ask students the second Literary Analysis question on p. 1034: What action do you anticipate after Arnold's scream? **Answer:** Most students will believe that Arnold will have a severe temper tantrum after he screams, and may hurt himself and/or others.

21 ▶ **Critical Viewing**

Answer: Many students will suggest that this painting reflects Bet's sadness over leaving her son. This emotion is conveyed by the posture of the slumped, still figure of the woman.

22 **✔Reading Check**

Answer: Arnold's bed is in a long hallway with many small cots in it. The cot to which Arnold is assigned is made up neatly and has a gray blanket folded at the foot. The only indication that children live there is a picture of a clown.

ENRICHMENT: Art Connection

Girl Looking at Landscape, 1957, by Richard Diebenkorn

Richard Diebenkorn (1922–1993) was educated in California and New Mexico and migrated to New York in the 1940s, the heyday of abstract expressionism. Throughout his career, Diebenkorn switched from abstract to figurative works, such as *Girl Looking at Landscape*, and back again. Known for luscious color and underlying geometric rigor, Diebenkorn was influenced by many, including painters Edward Hopper, Paul Cezanne, and Henri Matisse.

Ask students how the painting symbolizes Bet's relationship to the world. **Answer:** Like Bet, the girl in the painting is an observer of, rather than a participant in, the world around her.

Review and Assess

1. Possible answer: Most students will disapprove of Bet's new outlook on life because it indicates she has given up. Students may say that it is unlikely that Bet will maintain this attitude.

2. **(a)** Bet is taking Arnold to the Parkins State Hospital, a mental hospital. **(b)** Bet can no longer care for Arnold adequately at home. **(c)** Arnold seems to suspect something is amiss. He is upset and uneasy, constantly on the verge of a temper tantrum.

3. **(a)** She grew up in a trailer and married at a young age to get away from home. Her husband left her when Arnold was still an infant. **(b)** Bet takes pride in enduring. She does little to change the flow of events.

4. **(a)** Bet wants to escape from the hospital as soon as possible because she feels guilty about leaving Arnold there. **(b)** Students may say that Bet is not sure she is doing the right thing and wants to get away before she can change her mind.

5. **(a)** Bet will no longer participate in the daily care for Arnold that had been the center of her life. **(b)** The title refers to those events in life that can catch a person off guard, such as Bet's son's condition and her husband's leaving the family.

6. Possible answer: Many students will feel that Bet did the only thing she could do under the circumstances. Students should realize that there were not as many options for high-quality care available at that time, particularly for those who, like Bet, lacked financial resources.

"Twenty *minutes*, lady. That's all it is."

"What am I going to do?" she asked him.

He turned back to his ledgers.

She went over to a bench and sat down. Ladders and scaffolding towered above her, and only ten or twelve passengers were dotted through the rest of the station. The place looked bombed out—nothing but a shell. "Twenty minutes!" she said aloud. "What am I going to do?"

Through the double glass doors at the far end of the station, a procession of gray-suited men arrived with briefcases. More men came behind them, dressed in work clothes, carrying folding chairs, black trunklike boxes with silver hinges, microphones, a wooden lectern, and an armload of bunting. They set the lectern down in the center of the floor, not six feet from Bet. They draped the bunting across it—an arc of red, white, and blue. Wires were connected, floodlights were lit. A microphone screeched. One of the workmen said, "Try her, Mayor." He held the microphone out to a fat man in a suit, who cleared his throat and said, "Ladies and gentlemen, on the occasion of the expansion of this fine old railway station—"

"Sure do get an echo here," the workman said. "Keep on going."

The Mayor cleared his throat again. "If I may," he said, "I'd like to take about twenty minutes of your time, friends."

He straightened his tie. Bet blew her nose, and then she wiped her eyes and smiled. They had come just for her sake, you might think. They were putting on a sort of private play. From now on, all the world was going to be like that—just something on a stage, for her to sit back and watch.

Review and Assess

Thinking About the Selection

1. **Respond:** What do you think of Bet's new outlook? Explain.

2. **(a) Recall:** Where is Bet taking Arnold? **(b) Recall:** Why is she taking him there? **(c) Interpret:** Does Arnold seem to suspect anything different? Support your answer.

3. **(a) Summarize:** Summarize what you learn about Bet's childhood and marriage. **(b) Connect:** How does Bet's behavior while her father teaches her to bodysurf relate to her behavior later in life?

4. **(a) Infer:** Why does Bet insist that the cab driver wait for her outside the hospital? **(b) Draw Conclusions:** What does this action reveal about Bet's needs and fears?

5. **(a) Analyze:** What is the meaning of the story's final sentence? **(b) Connect:** How does the story's title relate to its meaning?

6. **Take a Position:** Do you think that most people today would act as Bet did if they were in her place? Why or why not?

✎ ASSESSMENT PRACTICE: Writing Skills

Grammar and Usage (For more practice, see Test Preparation Workbook, p. 62.)

The writing sections of tests often require students to choose the correct word or group of words to complete a sentence. Use the following sample item to show students how to recognize correct and incorrect grammar and choose the correct word to complete a sentence.

A writer who wishes to create serious fiction should be willing to revise _____ work as many times as necessary.

Choose the word or group of words that belong in the blank.

A their   **C** him or her

B they're   **D** his or her

A is plural, whereas the antecedent is singular. *B* is not a possessive pronoun, but a contraction meaning "they are." *C* is not possessive. *D* is both singular and possessive, and is therefore the correct answer.

Review and Assess

Literary Analysis

Foreshadowing

1. How does Arnold's reluctance to cooperate with his mother at the beginning of the story **foreshadow** the story's main event?
2. Using a chart like the one shown, find three other examples of foreshadowing from the story, and analyze their effect on the reader.

Foreshadowing	...	Effect on Reader

3. Would the story be less effective if Tyler did not use foreshadowing? Explain.

Connecting Literary Elements

4. How does Tyler's use of foreshadowing help to build **suspense**?
5. In what ways does Bet's concern that the cab driver may not wait for her create suspense?
6. (a) What is suspenseful about the train being delayed twenty minutes? (b) Did you anticipate a different ending? Explain.
7. (a) Note three points in the story where you felt the greatest suspense. (b) List the questions each of these moments raised in your mind. (c) In what ways were those questions answered?
8. At what point in the story does the suspense end? Why?

Reading Strategy

Putting Events in Order

9. State the main events and details of the story in chronological order.
10. (a) What flashback does Bet have? (b) What prompts this flashback, and what causes it to end?
11. (a) What does this flashback add to your understanding of the story? (b) Do you think the story would suffer without it? Why or why not?

Extend Understanding

12. **Career Connection:** Bet entrusts the life of her son to others. What qualities would you look for in a caregiver for children like Arnold who are mentally challenged?

Average Waves in Unprotected Waters ◆ 1037

Quick Review

Foreshadowing is the placement of hints or clues in a narrative to suggest later events.

Suspense is a feeling of growing uncertainty about the outcome of events in a literary work.

A **flashback** is a scene or an event from an earlier time that interrupts the chronological presentation of events.

To **put events in order,** note the sequence in which they occur in real time.

 Take It to the Net
www.phschool.com
Take the interactive self-test online to check your understanding of the selection.

Answers continued

and the history of her childhood and marriage. **(b)** The flashback is prompted by remembering, as Arnold falls asleep, that he has never slept well; it ends when Arnold's head snaps up.

11. **(a)** The flashback sheds new light on Bet's personality and circumstances. **(b)** Without it, the story would suffer because of the insight the flashback provides.

12. Students are likely to mention such qualities as patience and knowledge about patients' conditions.

Answers for p. 1037

Review and Assess

1. Arnold senses that something unsettling is going to happen to him.

2. **Foreshadowing:** Descriptions of Arnold in the opening paragraph **Effect on Reader:** The reader becomes concerned about Arnold. **Foreshadowing:** Arnold eyes the suitcase suspiciously. **Effect on Reader:** The reader wonders where Arnold is going. **Foreshadowing:** Bet's nervousness **Effect on Reader:** The reader suspects that the change will be bad.

3. The story would be less effective because the foreshadowing gives the reader a sense of suspenseful anticipation; without it, the flashbacks would have less significance and the story itself would probably have less appeal.

4. Foreshadowing helps increase the reader's interest in learning the purpose of the trip.

5. The reader becomes concerned about the effect on Bet if the cab driver does not wait.

6. **(a)** The delay is suspenseful because the reader is not sure whether Bet can gain some equanimity about her decision. **(b)** The ending is fitting because Bet's behavior follows the pattern she has established in her life.

7. **(a), (b),** and **(c)** Students' answers should be supported by references to the story.

8. The suspense ends in the last paragraph when the reader becomes convinced that Bet will not change her mind about Arnold and finds out her plan for the future.

9. Bet's father tried unsuccessfully to teach her to bodysurf. She married Avery against her parents' wishes. Her parents died. She and Avery had Arnold and learned about his condition. Avery deserted the family. Bet took Arnold to a state hospital where he would remain. When she returned to the train station, she learned the train was delayed. The mayor came to give a speech, and she watched.

10. **(a)** She flashes back to Arnold as a baby, her husband's desertion,

continued

❶ Vocabulary Development

Word Analysis

1. *Transcribe* means to make a copy, or write something over.
2. *Transcontinental* means across a continent.
3. *Transportation* is the act of carrying something across or over.
4. *Transplant* is to replant or plant something over.

Spelling Strategy

1. childhood
2. kindness
3. resistance

Fluency

1. a
2. c
3. b
4. b
5. a

❷ Grammar and Style

1. suspiciously (modifies *stared*)
2. pathetic (modifies *Arnold*)
3. well (modifies *behaved*)
4. carefully (modifies *chewed*)
5. awful (modifies *hospital*)
6. bad (modifies *she*)

Writing Application

Remind students to use adverbs to modify action verbs, and to use adjectives after linking verbs if the modifier describes the subject.

Integrate Language Skills

❶ Vocabulary Development Lesson

Word Analysis: Latin Prefix *trans-*

The Latin prefix *trans-* means "across," "over," or "through." Something *transparent* is clear enough to be seen through. Explain how the meaning of the prefix relates to the meaning of each word.

1. transcribe
2. transcontinental
3. transportation
4. transplant

Spelling Strategy

To add a suffix to a word ending in two consonants, retain both consonants. For example, *bunt + ing = bunting* and *thank + ful = thankful*. Using this rule, add a suffix to each word.

1. Bet thought back on her child_____.
2. Treat everyone with kind_____.
3. Arnold offered resist_____ to his mother.

❷ Grammar and Style Lesson

Correct Use of Adjectives and Adverbs

Adjectives modify nouns or pronouns; **adverbs** modify verbs, adjectives, or other adverbs.

Always use an adjective, not an adverb, after linking verbs such as *be, am, is,* or *seem* if the modifier describes the subject.

Always use an adverb, never an adjective, to modify an action verb.

In the following examples, the verbs are underlined and the modifiers are in italics.

> **Adverb:** She <u>could</u> never <u>do</u> anything as *well* as most people. (modifies the verb *could do*)
>
> **Adjective:** The collar <u>was</u> *askew*. (modifies the noun *collar*)

W̶G *Prentice Hall Writing and Grammar Connection: Chapter 17, Section 3*

1038 ◆ Prosperity and Protest (1946–Present)

Fluency: Sentence Completion

Review the words in the vocabulary list on page 1027. Then, choose the letter of the word or phrase that best completes each of the following statements.

1. Something *transparent* might be made of (a) glass, (b) wool, (c) stainless steel.
2. A *stocky* person looks (a) bored, (b) rich, (c) sturdy.
3. A *staunch* ally (a) betrays you, (b) always stands by you, (c) abandons you.
4. *Orthopedic* shoes (a) make you look taller, (b) correct your posture, (c) cost less than most other shoes.
5. A *viper* might (a) bite you, (b) sing to you, (c) shake your hand.

Practice For each item, choose the correct modifier and identify the word it modifies.

1. Arnold stared (suspicious, suspiciously).
2. Sometimes Arnold looked (pathetic, pathetically) in his neatly buttoned clothes.
3. Arnold usually behaved (good, well).
4. Arnold chewed his gum (careful, carefully).
5. The hospital smelled (awful, awfully).
6. After Bet left Arnold there, she felt very (bad, badly).

Writing Application Write two sentences for each modifier given. Construct one sentence so that the modifier serves as an adjective, and the other so that the modifier serves as an adverb.

1. early
2. lone / lonely

TEACHING RESOURCES

The following resources can be used to enrich or extend the instruction for pp. 1038–1039.

Vocabulary

📖 **Selection Support:** Build Vocabulary, p. 258

📖 **Vocabulary and Spelling Practice Book**
(Use this booklet for skills enrichment.)

Grammar

📖 **Selection Support:** Grammar and Style, p. 259

W̶G **Writing and Grammar,** Ruby Level, p. 380

💾 **Daily Language Practice Transparencies** ▪

Writing

W̶G **Writing and Grammar,** Ruby Level, p. 204 ▪

💿 **Writing and Grammar iText CD-ROM**

💾 **Writing Models and Graphic Organizers on Transparencies,** pp. 91–93

BLOCK SCHEDULING: Resources marked with this symbol provide varied instruction during 90-minute blocks.

Writing Lesson

Social Worker's Report

Imagine that you are the social worker assigned to Bet and Arnold's case. Write a report explaining Arnold's condition and summarizing the events that led to Bet's decision to have her son institutionalized.

Prewriting Scan the story for details that indicate that Bet can no longer care for Arnold. Categorize the information into causes and effects to show how each detail contributes to Bet's decision.

Model: Listing Causes and Effects

Causes	Effects
1. Arnold cannot dress or feed himself.	1. He requires a lot of care.
2. He is getting bigger and stronger.	2. "He was getting to be too much for her."

Drafting Build your report on the information you gathered. Use clear transitions to show cause-and-effect and other relationships. Work to maintain the objective tone of an effective social worker.

Revising Read your report as though you were a supervisor reviewing the case for the first time. Make sure the draft includes sufficient details to support the conclusion. Check that your facts are accurate, your word choice is precise, and that you establish clear cause-and-effect relationships.

Prentice Hall Writing and Grammar Connection: Chapter 10, Section 4

Extension Activities

Listening and Speaking Imagine that the subject of the mayor's speech was the need for more funding and improved care at state-run institutions. Prepare and present a **political speech** he might give using Arnold's case to support his points. Consider these ideas in your speech:

- The benefits for the needy children
- The expertise of health care professionals
- The humanitarian effort

Present the speech to the class.

Research and Technology With a group, research autism, Down's syndrome, or another childhood condition that causes severe mental or emotional challenges. Check the Internet or the library for information. Present your findings in a medical **research report.** [Group Activity]

 Take It to the Net www.phschool.com

Go online for an additional research activity using the Internet.

Average Waves in Unprotected Waters ◆ 1039

❸ Writing Lesson

- Review the model on p. 1039. Have students add other effects caused by Arnold's behavior. Ask students to make a similar chart to list all the causes and effects having to do with Arnold's condition. Students might wish to record their notes in the Cause-and-Effect Organizer on pp. 91–93 of **Writing Models and Graphic Organizers on Transparencies.**

- Discuss the form a social worker's report on Bet and Arnold's case would take. Remind students first to describe Arnold's condition and then to summarize the events that led to Bet's decision.

- Use the Writing Lesson to guide students in writing their reports.

- Use the Cause-and-Effect Essay rubric in **Performance Assessment and Portfolio Management**, p. 20, to evaluate students' reports.

❹ Research and Technology

- Suggest that students try to interview an expert on the condition they have chosen as the subject of their paper. Students should do as much research as possible before the interview, so their questions can be focused and on target. If possible, they should tape the interview.

- Urge students to make formal or informal outlines to organize the information they have gathered.

- Encourage students to include charts, graphs, and diagrams to make the information in their report clear.

CUSTOMIZE INSTRUCTION
For Universal Access

To address different learning styles, use the activities suggested in the Extension Activities booklet, p. 59.

For Interpersonal and Verbal/Linguistic Learners, use Activity 5.

For Bodily/Kinesthetic and Logical/Mathematical Learners, use Activity 6.

For Visual/Spatial Learners, use Activity 7.

ASSESSMENT RESOURCES

The following resources can be used to assess students' knowledge and skills.

Selection Assessment
- **Formal Assessment**, pp. 260–262
- **Open Book Test**, pp. 175–177
- **Test Bank Software**
- **Got It! Assessment Videotapes**, Tape 5

Take It to the Net
Visit www.phschool.com for self-tests and additional questions on "Average Waves in Unprotected Waters."

Writing Rubric
- **Performance Assess. and Portfolio Mgmt.**, p. 20

PRENTICE HALL
ASSESSMENT SYSTEM
- **Workbook**
- **Skill Book**
- **Transparencies**
- **CD-ROM**

from The Names ✦ Mint Snowball ✦ Suspended

Lesson Objectives

1. **To analyze and respond to literary elements**
   - Literary Analysis: Anecdote
   - Comparing Literary Works:

2. **To read, comprehend, analyze, and critique nonfiction**
   - Reading Strategy: Relating to Your Own Experiences
   - Reading Check questions
   - Review and Assess questions

3. **To develop word analysis skills, fluency, and systematic vocabulary**
   - Vocabulary Development Lesson: Latin Prefix: *con-*

4. **To understand and apply written and oral language conventions**
   - Spelling Strategy
   - Grammar and Style Lesson: Elliptical Clauses
   - Assessment Practice (ATE)

5. **To understand and apply appropriate writing and research strategies**
   - Writing Lesson: Reflective Essay
   - Extension Activity: Class Anthology

6. **To understand and apply listening and speaking strategies**
   - Extension Activity: Musical Analysis

STEP-BY-STEP TEACHING GUIDE	PACING GUIDE
PRETEACH	
Motivate Students and Provide Background	
Use the Motivation activity (ATE p. 1040)	5 min.
Read and discuss author and background features (SE/ATE pp. 1040, 1042)	5 min.
Introduce the Concepts	
Introduce the Literary Analysis and Reading Strategy (SE/ATE p. 1041) A	15 min.
Pronounce the vocabulary words and read their definitions (SE p. 1041)	5 min.
TEACH	
Monitor Comprehension	
Informally monitor comprehension by circulating while students read independently or in groups A	25 min.
Monitor students' comprehension with the Reading Check notes (SE/ATE pp. 1043, 1045, 1047, 1049)	as students read
Develop vocabulary with Vocabulary notes (SE pp. 1043, 1047, 1048, 1049, 1050; ATE pp. 1043, 1047)	as students read
Develop Understanding	
Develop students' understanding of anecdotes with the Literary Analysis annotations (SE p. 1044; ATE p. 1044) A	5 min.
Develop students' ability to relate the reading to their own experiences by using the Reading Strategy annotations (SE p. 1042; ATE pp. 1042, 1044, 1045, 1047)	5 min.
ASSESS	
Assess Mastery	
Assess students' mastery of the Reading Strategy and Literary Analysis by having them answer the Review and Assess questions (SE/ATE p. 1051)	15 min.
Use one or more of the print and media Assessment Resources (ATE p. 1053) A	up to 45 min.
EXTEND	
Apply Understanding	
Have students complete the Vocabulary Development Lesson and the Grammar and Style Lesson (SE p. 1052) A	20 min.
Apply students' ability to add emotional depth to in their writing through elaboration by using the Writing Lesson (SE/ATE p. 1053) A	45 min.
Apply students' understanding using one or more of the Extension Activities (SE p. 1053)	20–90 min.

A ACCELERATED INSTRUCTION:
Use the strategies and activities identified with an A.

UNIVERSAL ACCESS
● = Below Level Students
▲ = On-Level Students
■ = Above Level Students

Time and Resource Manager

Reading Level: Easy, Easy, Easy
Average Number of Instructional Days: 4

RESOURCES

PRINT	TRANSPARENCIES	TECHNOLOGY
• **Beyond Literature,** Cross-Curricular Connection: Science, p. 60 ▲ ■		• **Interest Grabber Video,** Tape 6 ● ▲ ■
• **Selection Support Workbook:** ● ▲ ■ Literary Analysis, p. 265 Reading Strategy, p. 264 Build Vocabulary, p. 262	• **Literary Analysis and Reading Transparencies,** pp. 119 and 120 ● ▲ ■	
		• **Listening to Literature** ● ▲ ■ Audiocassettes, Sides 35 and 36 Audio CDs, CD 20
• **Literatura en español** ● ▲ • **Literary Analysis for Enrichment** ■	• **Fine Art Transparencies, Volume 1,** Art Transparency 9 ● ▲ ■	
• **Formal Assessment:** Selection Test, pp. 263–265 ● ▲ ■ • **Open Book Test,** pp. 178–180 ● ▲ ■ • **Performance Assessment and Portfolio Management,** p. 11 ● ▲ ■ • **PRENTICE HALL ASSESSMENT SYSTEM** ● ▲ ■	• **PRENTICE HALL ASSESSMENT SYSTEM** ● ▲ ■ Skills Practice Answers and Explanations on Transparencies	• **Test Bank Software** ● ▲ ■ • **Got It! Assessment Videotapes,** Tape 5 ● ▲
• **Selection Support Workbook:** ● ▲ ■ Grammar and Style, p. 263 • **Writing and Grammar,** Ruby Level ● ▲ ■ • **Extension Activities,** p. 60 ● ▲ ■	• **Daily Language Practice Transparencies** ● ▲ • **Writing Models and Graphic Organizers on Transparencies,** pp. 5–8 ● ▲ ■	• **Writing and Grammar iText CD-ROM** ● ▲ ■ *Take It to the Net* www.phschool.com

BLOCK SCHEDULING: Use one 90-minute class period to preteach the selection and have students read it. Use a second 90-minute class period to assess students' mastery of skills and have them complete one of the Extension Activities.

PRETEACH

Step-by-Step Teaching Guide for pp. 1040–1041

Motivation

In preparation for reading these essays, ask students to find a piece of music that is especially meaningful to them. Invite students to bring recordings to class and, in small groups, share the feelings or memories that the music evokes. Alternatively, you might play segments of music and ask the class to respond. Consider using music that will evoke childhood memories: the sound of the ice cream truck, music from "A Charlie Brown Christmas," or a lullaby.

▣ Interest Grabber Video

As an alternative, play "N. Scott Momaday" on Tape 6 to engage student interest.

❶ Background

More About N. Scott Momaday

N. Scott Momaday has spent a good part of his life trying to safeguard the oral tradition and other aspects of Indian culture. He is the chairman and founder of the Buffalo Trust, a nonprofit organization founded to preserve and return their heritage to Native Americans. Momaday, a professor of English at the University of Arizona at Tucson and a consultant for the National Endowment for the Humanities and the National Endowment for the Arts since 1970, has this to say about his interest in preserving the oral tradition:

> My father was a great storyteller and he knew many stories from the Kiowa oral tradition...But it was only after I became an adult that I understood how fragile they are, because they exist only by word of mouth, always just one generation away from extinction. That's when I began writing down the tales my father and others had told me.

Prepare to Read

from The Names ◆ Mint Snowball ◆
❶ Suspended

N. Scott Momaday (b. 1934)

A member of the Kiowa nation, N. Scott Momaday was born in Lawton, Oklahoma. As a child, he often visited his grandparents, whose home was a meeting place for elderly Kiowas. Momaday describes these people as being "made of lean leather."

Inspired by his boyhood experiences, Momaday devoted himself to preserving his Kiowa heritage. After receiving his doctorate from Stanford University, Momaday wrote his first book, *House Made of Dawn* (1969), a novel about a young Native American torn between his roots and white society. The book earned Momaday a Pulitzer Prize. In the mid-1960s, the author made a pilgrimage to his grandmother's grave in western Oklahoma. He wrote about that experience in his best-known work, *The Way to Rainy Mountain* (1969), a collection of personal anecdotes and retellings of Kiowa myths and legends.

Momaday has since published poetry, essays, anecdotes, and retellings of Kiowa legends. His work provides the reader with a deeper understanding of Native American culture, both past and present.

Naomi Shihab Nye (b. 1952)

Arab American poet Naomi Shihab Nye spent her teenage years in Jerusalem, far from the cities of St. Louis, Missouri, and San Antonio, Texas, where she had been a child. Her father had emigrated from Palestine and settled in St. Louis, Missouri, where he and his wife operated stores specializing in imported goods. When Naomi was fourteen, the family moved back to Jerusalem to be near her father's Arab relatives. Nye says the family's years in Jerusalem enabled her to discover her heritage.

In addition to publishing award-winning volumes of poetry, Nye has also created picture books for children. This versatile writer, whose work is built on the sturdy foundation of everyday experiences, believes that "the primary source of poetry has always been local life, random characters met on the streets, our own ancestry sifting down to us through small essential daily tasks."

Joy Harjo (b. 1951)

The influence of Joy Harjo's Native American Creek (or Muscogee) and Cherokee heritage is evident in many aspects of her life, including her writing. Born in Tulsa, Oklahoma, Harjo became interested in dance and joined a troupe of Native American dancers when she was a teenager. Her essay "Suspended" demonstrates music's ability to become a transport, a vehicle through which Harjo can connect her cultural heritage to her creative and everyday world.

Harjo attended the Institute of American Indian Arts, the University of New Mexico, and the Writers' Workshop of the University of Iowa. In addition to publishing books of poetry and prose, Harjo has also written film scripts and taught at the state universities of California, New Mexico, and Montana.

1040 ◆ Prosperity and Protest (1946–Present)

TEACHING RESOURCES

The following resources can be used to enrich or extend the instruction for pp. 1040–1041.

Motivation
▣ **Interest Grabber Video**, Tape 6

Background
📖 **Beyond Literature,** p. 60

Take It to the Net
Visit www.phschool.com for Background and hotlinks for the selections.

Literary Analysis
📄 **Literary Analysis and Reading Transparencies,** Anecdote, p. 120 ▣

Reading
📖 **Selection Support:** Reading Strategy, p. 264; Build Vocabulary, p. 262

📄 **Literary Analysis and Reading Transparencies,** Relating to Your Own Experiences, p. 119

▣ **BLOCK SCHEDULING:** Resources marked with this symbol provide varied instruction during 90-minute blocks.

Preview

Connecting to the Literature

Watching home videos or flipping through family photos may bring back special memories of a treasured toy, a long-forgotten friend, or a special occasion. As you read these selections, think about childhood experiences that helped form your sense of self.

Literary Analysis

Anecdote

An **anecdote** is a short account of an amusing or interesting event. People tell anecdotes all the time, mostly for entertainment. Essayists recount anecdotes to make a point, make generalizations, or illustrate conclusions, as in this example from "Mint Snowball":

> Perhaps the clue to my entire personality connects to the lost Mint Snowball. I have always felt out-of-step with my environment, disjointed in the modern world.

Identify the anecdotes in these essays and the generalizations or conclusions they inspire. Use a chart like the one shown to help you.

Comparing Literary Works

These essays describe **rites of passage**—events that mark personal transitions that have cultural significance. Momaday and Harjo write about unique experiences while Nye describes a lost recipe that was a link to her cultural heritage. As you read, compare how the experiences of the writers created in them a new awareness of self and the world around them.

Reading Strategy

Relating to Your Own Experiences

Many common experiences know no cultural boundaries. If you have ever taken a journey, yearned for the past, or experienced an inner awakening, you can find a connection between your experiences and the ones expressed in these selections. **Relating to your own experiences** will increase your understanding and enjoyment of the essays.

Vocabulary Development

supple (sup´ əl) *adj.* able to bend and move easily and nimbly (p. 1043)

concocted (kən käkt´ əd) *v.* made by combining various ingredients (p. 1047)

flamboyant (flam boi´ ənt) *adj.* too extravagant (p. 1047)

elixir (i liks´ ər) *n.* supposed remedy for all ailments (p. 1047)

permeated (pur´ mē āt´ id) *adj.* penetrated and spread through (p. 1047)

replicate (rep´ li kāt´) *v.* duplicate (p. 1048)

revelatory (rev´ ə lə tôr´ ē) *adj.* revealing; disclosing (p. 1049)

confluence (kän´ floo əns) *n.* a flowing together (p. 1050)

Anecdote

⋮
↓

Generalization

❷ Literary Analysis

Anecdote

- Ask students to pay particular attention to the anecdotes, short accounts of amusing or interesting events, as they read these three essays. Ask them to think about the purposes the anecdotes serve.

- Have a volunteer read the generalization Naomi Shihab Nye drew from the anecdote she shares in her essay, "Mint Snowball."

- Tell students to use a chart similar to the one on this page to record the anecdotes they relate in their essays and the generalizations they drew from these anecdotes.

- Tell students that the authors may state the generalizations they drew from the experiences they describe, as did Naomi Shihab Nye, or students may have to infer generalizations.

❸ Reading Strategy

Relating to Your Own Experiences

- Discuss with students the essential similarities among human experiences despite cultural differences.

- Urge students to compare their own experiences with the authors' as they read these essays. Remind them that such comparisons will increase their understanding and enjoyment of the essays.

Vocabulary Development

Pronounce each vocabulary word for students, and read the definitions as a class. Have students identify any words with which they are already familiar.

CUSTOMIZE INSTRUCTION FOR UNIVERSAL ACCESS

For Less Proficient Readers	For English Learners	For Advanced Readers
Less proficient readers may need help figuring out the sentence fragments in these essays. Encourage students to paraphrase to complete the fragments, using information from the context, before reading on. Provide a few examples from the essays before having students continue paraphrasing on their own.	Point out the first-person voice to students, explaining how this voice affects verb forms. Pair students with native speakers of English to read and discuss the essays paragraph by paragraph.	Ask students to explain the connections between the essays in this section and the authors' cultural backgrounds. Urge students to research the culture and setting of each essay and to exchange information with one another.

 E-Teach

Visit E-Teach at www.phschool.com for teachers' essays on how to teach, with questions and answers.

CUSTOMIZE INSTRUCTION
For Interpersonal Learners

These students will benefit from a dramatic reading or a *role-play of the* story anecdotes. Encourage small groups to participate, using voice, gesture, and pantomime to create realistic effects.

❶ About the Selection

In reading this essay, students will travel with a young Kiowa boy on a journey of discovery and personal growth. The speaker, presumably young Momaday, recounts his travels on the horse he receives as a thirteenth-birthday gift. As he journeys across his southwestern homelands, the boy recognizes how his physical journey is intertwined with a spiritual journey toward connection with his Kiowa heritage.

❷ Critical Thinking

Analyze

- Have a volunteer read the bracketed passage.

- Ask students what details they learn about Kiowa culture from the paragraph.
  Answer: Kiowas lived on the Great Plains; horses were an important element of Kiowa life and folklore.

- Discuss what these details imply about Kiowa values.
  Answer: Values mentioned might include closeness with nature and an emphasis on bravery.

❸ Reading Strategy

Relating to Your Own Experience

- Ask whether any students are pet owners. Have students discuss their feelings for their pets.

- Have students answer the Reading Strategy question on p. 1042: Have you ever had great affection for a pet that can help you to relate to this experience? Explain.
  Possible response: Make sure students use concrete examples to explain how their experiences relate to Momaday's.

from
The Names
❶

N. Scott Momaday

Background

If you were asked to name a literary form associated with personal, creative expression, the essay might not be your immediate response. However, the essay's flexibility provides an excellent arena for personal expression. Although they are a form of nonfiction, essays can be as moving, entertaining, and enriching as your favorite piece of fiction. In each of the three essays that follow, the writer uses a vivid memory as the springboard to an analysis of her or his identity.

I sometimes think of what it means that in their heyday—in 1830, say—the Kiowas owned more horses *per capita* than any other tribe on the Great Plains, that the Plains Indian culture, the last culture to evolve in North America, is also known as "the horse culture" and "the centaur[1] culture," that the Kiowas tell the story of a horse that died of shame after its owner committed an act of cowardice, that I am a Kiowa, that therefore there is in me, as there is in the Tartars,[2] an old, sacred notion of the horse. I believe that at some point in my racial life, this notion must needs be expressed in order that I may be true to my nature. ❷

It happened so: I was thirteen years old, and my parents gave me a horse. It was a small nine-year-old gelding of that rare, soft color that is called strawberry roan. This my horse and I came to be, in the course of our life together, in good understanding, of one mind, a true story and history of that large landscape in which we made the one entity of whole motion, one and the same center of an intricate, pastoral composition, evanescent,[3] ever changing. And to this my horse I gave the name Pecos.

On the back of my horse I had a different view of the world. I could see more of it, how it reached away beyond all the horizons I had ever

Reading Strategy ❸
Relating to Your Own Experiences Have you ever had great affection for a pet that can help you to relate to this experience? Explain.

---

1. **centaur** (sen´ tôr) *adj.* pertaining to a mythical creature with the head and upper body of a man and the lower body of a horse.
2. **Tartars** (tär´ tərz) *n.* nomadic Turkish peoples who took part in the invasions of Eastern Europe during the Middle Ages.
3. **evanescent** (ev´ ə nes´ ənt) *adj.* transient; tending to fade from sight.

TEACHING RESOURCES

The following resources can be used to enrich or extend the instruction for pp. 1042–1050.

Literary Analysis

📖 **Selection Support:** Literary Analysis, p. 265 ▪

Reading

🎧 **Listening to Literature Audiocassettes,** Sides 35 and 36 ▪

💿 **Listening to Literature Audio CDs,** CD 20 ▪

Extention

🖼 **Fine Art Transparencies,** Volume 1, Art Transparency 9
Introduce "Suspended" by showing Art Transparency 9. Invite students to comment on Beasley's vibrant depiction of jazz musicians and to share what they already know about jazz.

▪ **BLOCK SCHEDULING:** Resources marked with this symbol provide varied instruction during 90-minute blocks.

Passion of Paints, Bob Peters

seen; and yet it was more concentrated in its appearance, too, and more accessible to my mind, my imagination. My mind loomed upon the farthest edges of the earth, where I could feel the full force of the planet whirling into space. There was nothing of the air and light that was not pure exhilaration, and nothing of time and eternity. Oh, Pecos, *un poquito mas!* Oh, my hunting horse! Bear me away, bear me away!

It was appropriate that I should make a long journey. Accordingly I set out one early morning, traveling light. Such a journey must begin in the nick of time, on the spur of the moment, and one must say to himself at the outset: Let there be wonderful things along the way; let me hold to the way and be thoughtful in my going; let this journey be made in beauty and belief.

I sang in the sunshine and heard the birds call out on either side. Bits of down from the cottonwoods drifted across the air, and butter-flies fluttered in the sage. I could feel my horse under me, rocking at my legs, the bobbing of the reins to my hand; I could feel the sun on my face and the stirring of a little wind at my hair. And through the hard hooves, the slender limbs, the supple shoulders, the fluent back of my horse I felt the earth under me. Everything was under me, buoying me up; I rode across the top of the world. My mind soared; time and again I saw the fleeting shadow of my mind moving about me as it went winding upon the sun.

When the song, which was a song of riding, was finished, I had Pecos pick up the pace. Far down on the road to San Ysidro

▲ **Critical Viewing** ❻
Using the third paragraph of the essay as a guide, how do you think Momaday would describe this painting? **[Hypothesize]**

supple (sup´ əl) *adj.* able to bend and move easily and nimbly

☑ **Reading Check** ❼
What is Momaday's idea of a great journey?

from The Names ◆ 1043

Relating to Your Own Experiences

- Have students discuss the reasons Momaday was ashamed to admit that he had made a bad bargain in exchanging horses.
  Possible response: People often don't like to admit that they have made a mistake.

- Then, have students think about decisions they made that they later regretted. Encourage volunteers to give examples.

- Ask students whether they were ashamed to admit their mistakes and to give reasons for their reactions.

  ▶ Monitor Progress Have students compare their experiences and reactions to Momaday's.

❾ Literary Analysis

Anecdote

- Have students discuss the attraction that Pasqual's horse might have had for the boy.
  Possible responses: The boy was curious about the horse. The horse was half wild and would be a challenge to ride.

  ▶ Monitor Progress Ask what Pasqual's goal was when he began praising the horse.
  Answer: Pasqual was probably hoping that the boy would want to trade horses, possibly to show up his friend as unable to ride the stallion.

- Ask students why they think the narrator fell for Pasqual's smooth talk.
  Possible response: He felt challenged to prove something; he was intrigued by the wildness of the stallion.

- Have students answer the Literary Analysis question on p. 1044: What do you think Momaday means by "wiser and better mounted?"
  Answer: The boy has come to appreciate the virtues of his horse, which is much more comfortable to ride than Pasqual's horse is.

I overtook my friend Pasqual Fragua. He was riding a rangy, stiff-legged black and white stallion, half wild, which horse he was breaking for the rancher Cass Goodner. The horse skittered and blew as I drew up beside him. Pecos began to prance, as he did always in the company of another horse. "Where are you going?" I asked in the Jemez language. And he replied, "I am going down the road." The stallion was hard to manage, and Pasqual had to keep his mind upon it; I saw that I had taken him by surprise. "You know," he said after a moment, "when you rode up just now I did not know who you were." We rode on for a time in silence, and our horses got used to each other, but still they wanted their heads.[4] The longer I looked at the stallion the more I admired it, and I suppose that Pasqual knew this, for he began to say good things about it: that it was a thing of good blood, that it was very strong and fast, that it felt very good to ride it. The thing was this: that the stallion was half wild, and I came to wonder about the wild half of it; I wanted to know what its wildness was worth in the riding. "Let us trade horses for a while," I said, and, well, all right, he agreed. At first it was exciting to ride the stallion, for every once in a while it pitched and bucked and wanted to run. But it was heavy and raw-boned and full of resistance, and every step was a jolt that I could feel deep down in my bones. I saw soon enough that I had made a bad bargain, and I wanted my horse back, but I was ashamed to admit it. There came a time in the late afternoon, in the vast plain far south of San Ysidro, after thirty miles, perhaps, when I no longer knew whether it was I who was riding the stallion or the stallion who was riding me. "Well, let us go back now," said Pasqual at last. "No. I am going on; and I will have my horse back, please," I said, and he was surprised and sorry to hear it, and we said goodbye. "If you are going south or east," he said, "look out for the sun, and keep your face in the shadow of your hat. *Vaya con Dios.*"[5] And I went on my way alone then, wiser and better mounted, and thereafter I held on to my horse. I saw no one for a long time, but I saw four falling stars and any number of jackrabbits, roadrunners, and coyotes, and once, across a distance, I saw a bear, small and black, lumbering in the ravine. The mountains drew close and withdrew and drew close again, and after several days I swung east.

Now and then I came upon settlements. For the most part they were dry, burnt places with Spanish names: Arroyo Seco, Las Piedras, Tres Casas. In one of these I found myself in a narrow street between high adobe walls. Just ahead, on my left, was a door in the wall. As I approached the door was flung open, and a small boy came running out, rolling a hoop. This happened so suddenly that Pecos shied very sharply, and I fell to the ground, jamming the thumb of my left hand. The little boy looked very worried and said that he was sorry to have caused such an accident. I waved the matter off, as if it were nothing;

---

4. **. . . they wanted their heads** The horses wanted to be free of the control of the reins.
5. **Vaya con Dios** (vī yə kən dē′ ōs) "Go with God" (Spanish).

Literary Analysis
❾ Anecdote What do you think Momaday means by the phrase "wiser and better mounted"?

⚜ **ENRICHMENT: Social Studies Connection**

The Kiowa

The Kiowa are a Native American people of the southern Great Plains. A fierce tribe of expert horsemen, the Kiowa were one of the last Plains Indian tribes to capitulate to the U.S. government.

The Kiowa were in many ways typical of nomadic Plains tribes. They hunted buffalo on horseback, did no farming, and lived in skin tepees supported by three poles. The Kiowa society had a warrior tradition; exploits in war enabled members to rise in rank.

The Kiowa believed that dreams and visions gave them supernatural powers. They came close to a written language in their twice yearly recording of events using pictographs on animal skins.

At the time of the 1990 census, there were 9,421 Kiowa. Most of them live in Southwestern Oklahoma, where their people have shared a reservation with the Comanche since 1868.

but as a matter of fact my hand hurt so much that tears welled up in my eyes. And the pain lasted for many days. I have fallen many times from a horse, both before and after that, and a few times I fell from a running horse on dangerous ground, but that was the most painful of them all.

In another settlement there were some boys who were interested in racing. They had good horses, some of them, but their horses were not so good as mine, and I won easily. After that, I began to think of ways in which I might even the odds a little, might give some advantage to my competitors. Once or twice I gave them a head start, a reasonable head start of, say, five or ten yards to the hundred, but that was too simple, and I won anyway. Then it came to me that I might try this: we should all line up in the usual way, side by side, but my competitors should be mounted and I should not. When the signal was given I should then have to get up on my horse while the others were breaking away; I should have to mount my horse during the race. This idea appealed to me greatly, for it was both imaginative and difficult, not to mention dangerous; Pecos and I should have to work very closely together. The first few times we tried this I had little success, and over a course of a hundred yards I lost four races out of five. The principal problem was that Pecos simply could not hold still among the other horses. Even before they broke away he was hard to manage, and when they were set running nothing could hold him back, even for an instant. I could not get my foot in the stirrup, but I had to throw myself up across the saddle on my stomach, hold on as best I could, and twist myself into position, and all this while racing at full speed. I could ride well enough to accomplish this feat, but it was a very awkward and inefficient business. I had to find some way to use the whole energy of my horse, to get it all into the race. Thus far I had managed only to break his motion, to divert him from his purpose and mine. To correct this I took Pecos away and worked with him through the better part of a long afternoon on a broad reach of level ground beside an irrigation ditch. And it was hot, hard work. I began by teaching him to run straight away while I ran beside him a few steps, holding on to the saddle horn, with no pressure on the reins. Then, when we had mastered this trick, we proceeded to the next one, which was this: I placed my weight on my arms, hanging from the saddle horn, threw my feet out in front of me, struck them to the ground, and sprang up against the saddle. This I did again and again, until Pecos came to expect it and did not flinch or lose his stride. I sprang a little higher each time. It was in all a slow process of trial and error, and after two or three hours both Pecos and I were covered with bruises and soaked through with perspiration. But we had much to show for our efforts, and at last the moment came

Literature in context — Mythology Connection

The Centaur

In the first paragraph of this essay, N. Scott Momaday refers to the Plains Indian culture as "the centaur culture." In alluding to that mythical creature with the upper body of a man and the lower body of a horse, Momaday indirectly places his discussion within the larger context of legend and cultural history. According to Greek legend, centaurs like the one shown here were a race of wild, lawless, inhospitable beings who dwelled in the mountains of Thessaly, in northern Greece. However, one centaur, Chiron, taught many Greek heroes and was well known for his wisdom and for his knowledge of medicine.

 Reading Check

Why were Momaday and Pecos training together?

from *The Names* ◆ 1045

⑩ Background

Mythology Connection

One Greek legend describes Chiron as the first centaur. According to the myth, Chiron was originally a Titan—the son of Chronos and the sea nymph Philyra—and received the half-man/half-horse form as punishment from Apollo (Greek god of light and reason) because Chiron was bold enough to declare war on the young Olympians.

Chiron was said to have been educated by the gods, and in his wilderness surroundings instructed mythical heroes such as Achilles, Jason, and Acteon.

⑪ Reading Strategy

Relating to Your Own Experiences

• Have students discuss Momaday's motivation for wanting to give an advantage to his competitors in horse races.
  Possible response: Momaday was winning all the time and grew bored.

• Ask students whether they would feel the same way Momaday did.
  Answer: Many students will agree that winning constantly would eventually become dull.

• Have volunteers discuss situations in their lives in which they either sought out or avoided competition, and ask them to explain their reasons.

⑫ ✔ Reading Check

Answer: Momaday and Pecos were training together so that the horse would get used to being mounted while a race was in progress.

CUSTOMIZE INSTRUCTION FOR UNIVERSAL ACCESS

For Less Proficient Readers	Gifted/Talented Students	For Advanced Readers
Help students understand the process through which Momaday trained Pecos not to break stride as the author ran alongside him and leaped into the saddle. Discuss the training process with students. Write each step on the board. You may have students sketch the actions as you describe them.	Have students write a journal entry in which they describe a time when they successfully mastered a goal. What lessons did they learn from working hard to meet a challenge? When they finish, have students discuss their answers.	Have students research horse-training techniques. After they learn about some of the latest and most effective training techniques, are, ask them to evaluate the methods Momaday used to train Pecos.

Review and Assess

1. Most students will choose animals with which they have had contact or wild animals such as the bald eagle or lion that hold symbolic significance.

2. **(a)** After he was given a horse at age thirteen, the feeling of exhilaration on horseback was so strong that he felt compelled to make a journey. **(b)** The journey was a rite of passage for him, and completing it successfully made him feel accomplished and close to nature and his Kiowa heritage.

3. **(a)** He trades his horse for Pasqual's. **(b)** He is motivated by curiosity and admiration for the half wild horse.

4. **(a)** He meets a friend and trades horses; he hurts his hand; he travels through many settlements and experiences the beauty of nature; he becomes involved in horse racing. **(b)** Since horses are an important element of Kiowa culture, this journey on horseback connects him with his heritage.

5. **(a)** Possible response: Pecos allows himself to be trained. **(b)** Pecos worked hard but was treated fairly and with appreciation. **(c)** Momaday probably became involved in activities for which he could not use a horse, or lived in places where he could not have a horse.

6. Possible responses include compassion, patience, perseverance, courage, and the value of friendship.

when we must put the whole performance together. I had not yet leaped into the saddle, but I was quite confident that I could now do so; only I must be sure to get high enough. We began this dress rehearsal then from a standing position. At my signal Pecos lurched and was running at once, straight away and smoothly. And at the same time I sprinted forward two steps and gathered myself up, placing my weight precisely at my wrists, throwing my feet out and together, perfectly. I brought my feet down sharply to the ground and sprang up hard, as hard as I could, bringing my legs astraddle of my horse—and everything was just right, except that I sprang too high. I vaulted all the way over my horse, clearing the saddle by a considerable margin, and came down into the irrigation ditch. It was a good trick, but it was not the one I had in mind, and I wonder what Pecos thought of it after all. Anyway, after a while I could mount my horse in this way and so well that there was no challenge in it, and I went on winning race after race.

I went on, farther and farther into the wide world. Many things happened. And in all this I knew one thing: I knew where the journey was begun, that it was itself a learning of the beginning, that the beginning was infinitely worth the learning. The journey was well undertaken, and somewhere in it I sold my horse to an old Spanish man of Vallecitos. I do not know how long Pecos lived. I had used him hard and well, and it may be that in his last days an image of me like thought shimmered in his brain.

Review and Assess

Thinking About the Selection

1. **Respond:** What kind of animal seems "sacred" or special in some way to you? Why?

2. **(a) Recall:** What inspires Momaday's decision to take a journey? **(b) Draw Conclusions:** What do you think such a journey meant to him, and how did it make him feel?

3. **(a) Recall:** What does Momaday trade with Pasqual? **(b) Analyze:** What motivates him to make this trade?

4. **(a) Recall:** What does Momaday see and do on his journey? **(b) Draw Conclusions:** Why is it significant that his first long journey was on horseback?

5. **(a) Support:** Provide one detail that shows that Pecos was an extremely good horse. **(b) Infer:** What does the writer mean when he says that he "had used him hard and well"? **(c) Draw Conclusions:** Why do you suppose Momaday sold the horse?

6. **Apply:** What life lesson have you learned that was "infinitely worth the learning"?

✹ ENRICHMENT: Social Studies Connection

Horses and Plains Indians

Plains Indians have not always had horses. There were no horses in North America until some were left behind in the 1540s by the expeditions of Spanish explorers Coronado and DeSoto. But Indians didn't ride or use horses until much later.

In the 1600s, Pueblo and Navaho Indians learned to train and ride horses at Spanish missions in New Mexico, but were not allowed to own the animals. In 1680, Pueblo Indians revolted against the Spanish and drove them back to Old Mexico, where they stayed for over a decade. The Spanish left behind many horses, which the Indians used. Soon the Pueblo Indians began selling and trading horses to other Indians such as the Kiowa and Comanche. Soon after, horses spread across the Southern Plains very quickly.

Mint Snowball

Naomi Shihab Nye

My great-grandfather on my mother's side ran a drugstore in a small town in central Illinois. He sold pills and rubbing alcohol from behind the big cash register and creamy ice cream from the soda fountain. My mother remembers the counter's long polished sweep, its shining face. She twirled on the stools. Dreamy fans. Wide summer afternoons. Clink of nickels in anybody's hand. He sold milkshakes, cherry cokes, old fashioned sandwiches. What did an old fashioned sandwich look like? Dark wooden shelves. Silver spigots on chocolate dispensers.

My great-grandfather had one specialty: a Mint Snowball which he invented. Some people drove all the way in from Decatur just to taste it. First he stirred fresh mint leaves with sugar and secret ingredients in a small pot on the stove for a very long time. He <u>concocted</u> a <u>flamboyant</u> <u>elixir</u> of mint. Its scent clung to his fingers even after he washed his hands. Then he shaved ice into tiny particles and served it mounted in a glass dish. <u>Permeated</u> with mint syrup. Scoops of rich vanilla ice cream to each side. My mother took a bite of minty ice and ice cream mixed together. The Mint Snowball tasted like winter. She closed her eyes to see the Swiss village my great-grandfather's parents came from. Snow frosting the roofs. Glistening, dangling spokes of ice.

Before my great-grandfather died, he sold the recipe for the mint syrup to someone in town for one hundred dollars. This hurt my

concocted (kən käkt´ əd) *v.* made by combining various ingredients

flamboyant (flam boi´ ənt) *adj.* too extravagant

elixir (il iks´ ər) *n.* supposed remedy for all ailments

permeated (pʉr´ mē āt´ id) *adj.* penetrated and spread through

⑯ ✓ Reading Check
Describe Nye's great-grandfather's specialty.

Mint Snowball ◆ 1047

CUSTOMIZE INSTRUCTION FOR UNIVERSAL ACCESS

For Less Proficient Readers	For English Learners	For Advanced Readers
Explain that the text break in this essay indicates a shift in focus. Prior to the break, the essay describes an earlier time. After the break, Nye jumps forward in time to focus on her own personal experiences.	Students may be unfamiliar with the soda fountains once found in old-fashioned drugstores. Explain the words and phrases the author uses to describe her great-grandfather's store, such as milkshakes, cherry cokes, and silver spigots.	Have students discuss the effect of memories and family stories on children's personalities. Ask students to talk about experiences they had early in their lives, as well as stories they heard from relatives, that affected them.

Review and Assess

1. **Possible response:** Students may feel out of step with some aspects of the modern world, such as the pace of life, the many choices, and the emphasis on physical appearance.

2. **(a)** Nye's mother describes the drugstore and the Mint Snowball. **(b)** The cold, minty taste reminds Nye's mother of Switzerland.

3. **(a)** Nye's great-grandfather sold the recipe. **(b)** Nye's mother came close to duplicating the recipe. **(c)** It was impossible to replicate the recipe because it contained ingredients that had never been identified.

4. **(a)** The author longs for old-fashioned things that have been lost, such as the recipe for the Mint Snowball. **(b)** The author feels that many of the possible futures that she and members of her family might have had have been lost.

5. **(a)** A wistful longing is expressed in the last paragraph. **(b)** Details include images of her great-grandfather and her mother in the drugstore and descriptions of mint and ice.

6. Most students will believe that the image of the dessert captures a past time successfully because it is described in such loving detail and has had such a great effect on the author.

grandfather's feelings. My grandfather thought he should have inherited it to carry on the tradition. As far as the family knew, the person who bought the recipe never used it. At least not in public. My mother had watched my grandfather make the syrup so often she thought she could <u>replicate</u> it. But what did he have in those little unmarked bottles? She experimented. Once she came close. She wrote down what she did. Now she has lost the paper.

replicate (rep′ li kāt) v. duplicate

Perhaps the clue to my entire personality connects to the lost Mint Snowball. I have always felt out-of-step with my environment, disjointed in the modern world. The crisp flush of cities makes me weep. Strip centers, Poodle grooming and Take-out Thai. I am angry over lost department stores, wistful for something I have never tasted or seen.

Although I know how to do everything one needs to know—change airplanes, find my exit off the interstate, charge gas, send a fax—there is something missing. Perhaps the stoop of my great-grandfather over the pan, the slow patient swish of his spoon. The spin of my mother on the high stool with her whole life in front of her, something fine and fragrant still to happen. When I breathe a handful of mint, even pathetic sprigs from my sunbaked Texas earth, I close my eyes. Little chips of ice on the tongue, their cool slide down. Can we follow the long river of the word "refreshment" back to its spring? Is there another land for me? Can I find any lasting solace in the color green?

Review and Assess

Thinking About the Selection

1. **Respond:** Do you feel out of step with the modern world or in tune with it? Explain your feelings.

2. **(a) Recall:** Whose memory provides the description of the drugstore and of the Mint Snowball? **(b) Connect:** Why does this memory evoke the country from which her ancestors came?

3. **(a) Recall:** What happened to the original Mint Snowball recipe? **(b) Recall:** Which family member comes close to duplicating the recipe? **(c) Infer:** Why do you think it was impossible to replicate?

4. **(a) Interpret:** What connection is made between the Mint Snowball and the author's life? **(b) Infer:** What does Nye consider lost as a result of the vanished recipe?

5. **(a) Analyze:** What is the mood of the final paragraph of the essay? **(b) Analyze:** Which details create that mood?

6. **Evaluate:** Does the image of this family dessert successfully capture a time long passed? Explain.

CUSTOMIZE INSTRUCTION FOR UNIVERSAL ACCESS

For Gifted/Talented Students

Have students make a mural showing the soda fountain the author's great-grandfather owned. First, students should reread the first two paragraphs of the essay and list every detail that describes the soda fountain. Then, they should gather visual resources, illustrations, and photographs of old-time soda fountains. They will then be ready to draw some preliminary sketches of the soda fountain based on their notes, photos, and illustrations, striving to make their sketches as accurate as possible. After they choose sketches they like, students can refer to them as they make a mural of a life-size soda fountain, on large sheets of paper.

SUSPENDED

Joy Harjo

Getting Down, Joseph Holston

◀ **Critical Viewing** ⑲
Does this illustration of a jazz musician effectively convey Harjo's belief that jazz is "a way to speak beyond the confines of ordinary language"? Explain. **[Evaluate]**

Once I was so small that I could barely peer over the top of the backseat of the black Cadillac my father polished and tuned daily; I wanted to see everything. It was around the time I acquired language, or even before that time, when something happened that changed my relationship to the spin of the world. My concept of language, of what was possible with music was changed by this <u>revelatory</u> moment. It changed even the way I looked at the sun. This suspended integer of time probably escaped ordinary notice in my parents' universe, which informed most of my vision in the ordinary world. They were still omnipresent gods. We were driving somewhere in Tulsa, the northern border of the Creek Nation.[1] I don't know where we were going or

revelatory (rev' ə lə tôr' ē) *adj.* revealing; disclosing

⑳ ☑ **Reading Check**
At what stage of Harjo's life does this narrative take place?

---

1. **Creek Nation** nation of Native American peoples, mainly Muscogean, formerly of Georgia and Alabama. Most now live in Oklahoma and Florida.

Suspended ◆ 1049

---

⑰ ▶ **About the Selection**

This essay illustrates how a single sensory experience can radically change a person's life. The speaker recalls a critical moment in which the glory of jazz reached her pre-verbal childhood mind. Blended with the heat of the day and the scent of her father's aftershave, the music became a catalyst, a medium through which the author could suddenly connect her creative dream world to everyday existence.

⑱ ▶ **Background**

Art

Getting Down, by Joseph Holston

This painting—gouache on paper—illustrates an African American jazz musician, like Miles Davis, whom the speaker in the story hears on the radio.

Joseph Holston was born in Washington, D.C. Self-taught during a career in advertising art, he also studied with Marcus Blahove and Richard Goetz. Encouraged by Harlem Renaissance artists Lois Mailou Jones and James Wells, Holston developed a cubist abstractionist style in both his paintings and prints. *Getting Down*, with its fragmented forms and emphasis on line, tone, and shadow, illustrates that style.

Use this question for discussion:

How might the speaker respond to this painting?
Possible response: She would likely enjoy it as a bridge between reality—the musician and his instrument—and visual art—the play of shadow and form.

⑲ ▶ **Critical Viewing**

Answer: Students may say that the painting conveys emotions such as excitement, moodiness, and pleasure without words in a fashion similar to the way jazz communicates these emotions without words.

⑳ ☑ **Reading Check**

Answer: Harjo writes about an incident that happened when she was very young, at about the time she learned to speak.

CUSTOMIZE INSTRUCTION FOR UNIVERSAL ACCESS

For Special Needs Students	For Less Proficient Readers	For English Learners
This short essay can be challenging because of its complex syntax and vocabulary. Have students listen to the essay on the **Listening to Literature** audiocassette or CD. Then, have them discuss the essay and use the Got It! Assessment Videotape to test their comprehension.	Ask students to listen to the essay on the **Listening to Literature** audiocassette or CD before they read it on their own. Ask students to form pairs to read and discuss the essay together paragraph by paragraph.	Guide students through the essay and have them listen to it on the **Listening to Literature** audiocassette or CD before they attempt to read it on their own. You may want to pair English learners with students whose first language is English and have pairs read and discuss the essay together.

1. Students may recall experiences from their early childhood. Encourage them to think about why words cannot always sufficiently communicate a past event.

2. **(a)** Harjo's experience took place in the summer. **(b)** She describes the boiling hot sun and her attempts to get a breeze.

3. **(a)** Harjo describes her father as a "handsome god" who dresses impeccably and smells like aftershave. **(b)** These details reveal her affection and respect for her father.

4. **(a)** She hears a trumpet playing jazz on the car radio. **(b)** It teaches her that music can speak in ways that reach beyond words.

5. Growing up means losing childhood innocence and becoming aware of people's failings and the finite nature of life.

6. The essay suggests that everyone's inner world is unique and that different experiences are important to people in indescribable ways.

where we had been, but I know the sun was boiling the asphalt, the car windows open for any breeze as I stood on tiptoes on the floor-board behind my father, a handsome god who smelled of Old Spice, whose slick black hair was always impeccably groomed, his clothes perfectly creased and ironed. The radio was on. I loved the radio, jukeboxes or any magic thing containing music even then.

I wonder now what signaled this moment, a loop of time that on first glance could be any place in time. I became acutely aware of the line the jazz trumpeter was playing (a sound I later associated with Miles Davis). I didn't know the word jazz or trumpet, or the concepts. I don't know how to say it, with what sounds or words, but in that <u>confluence</u> of hot southern afternoon, in the breeze of aftershave and humidity, I followed that sound to the beginning, to the place of the birth of sound. I was suspended in whirling stars, a moon to which I'd traveled often by then. I grieved my parents' failings, my own life which I saw stretched the length of that rhapsody.

My rite of passage into the world of humanity occurred then, via jazz. The music made a startling bridge between familiar and strange lands, an appropriate vehicle, for though the music is predominantly west African in concept, with European associations, jazz was influenced by the Creek (or Muscogee) people, for we were there when jazz was born. I recognized it, that humid afternoon in my formative years, as a way to speak beyond the confines of ordinary language. I still hear it.

confluence (kän′ flōō əns) *n.* a flowing together

Review and Assess

Thinking About the Selection

1. **Respond:** Can you recall a personal experience that was important in your life but is difficult for you to analyze or describe?

2. **(a) Recall:** During what season did Harjo's experience take place? **(b) Support:** How do you know?

3. **(a) Recall:** Describe the appearance of Harjo's father. **(b) Analyze:** Which details of her description reveal the way she feels about her father?

4. **(a) Recall:** What kind of music was playing on the car radio? **(b) Draw Conclusions:** What did the music teach Harjo about communication?

5. **Deduce:** How does Harjo suggest that growing up involves sadness and disillusion?

6. **Apply:** What does this essay suggest about the mysterious workings of every person's inner world?

⬥ ASSESSMENT PRACTICE: Writing Skills

Sentence Structure   (For more practice, see Test Preparation Workbook, p. 63.)

Standardized tests often require students to choose the best way to correct the structure of a sentence. Use the sample test item below to demonstrate.

If you don't know much about horses, riding one can be quite dangerous. <u>A horse can easily throw an inexperienced rider, this can cause serious injury.</u>

Choose the best way to write the underlined section of the passage.

A A horse can easily throw an inexperienced

rider, can cause serious injury.

B A horse can easily throw an inexperience rider, causing serious injury.

C A horse, easily throwing an inexperienced rider, causing serious injury.

D Correct as is.

B is the best answer; it is the only complete sentence that is correctly structured and punctuated.

Review and Assess

Literary Analysis

Anecdote

1. (a) Identify two **anecdotes** in Momaday's essay. (b) What connects these anecdotes to the theme introduced in the opening paragraph?
2. In what ways is the lost recipe significant in Nye's life and in the development of her personality?
3. (a) Describe the way in which Harjo's experience of jazz affected her in a single moment. (b) How did the experience change her life?

Comparing Literary Works

4. What **rite of passage** did Momaday experience through his journey and the later selling of his horse?
5. Explain the significance of Harjo's statement, "My rite of passage into the world of humanity occurred then . . ."
6. Nye feels a great loss over her inability to recreate the Mint Snowball. If she still had the recipe, how might it have served as a rite of passage for her?
7. When a person experiences a rite of passage, he or she learns an adult truth about life and leaves childhood behind. What truths about life do each of these authors learn? Support your answer.

Reading Strategy

Relating to Your Own Experiences

8. Use a chart like the one shown to note the relationships you can find between these selections and your own experiences.

Writer's Experience	My Experience	How They Relate

9. Which writer's experiences or reflections were most accessible to you? Why?

Extend Understanding

10. **Literature Connection:** Relate "The Mint Snowball" to another literary work that expresses the theme of yearning for a way of life that is long gone. How are they similar? How do they differ?

from The Names / Mint Snowball / Suspended ◆ 1051

Quick Review

An **anecdote** is a short account of an amusing or interesting event or experience.

A **rite of passage** is a significant event in a person's life that marks a transition.

To **relate to your own experiences,** connect your personal situations, emotions, attitudes, and behaviors with those of the writers.

 Take It to the Net
www.phschool.com
Take the interactive self-test online to check your understanding of these selections.

Answers for p. 1051
Review and Assess

1. **(a)** Possible response: Two anecdotes include Momaday's trading horses with Pasqual and training his horse Pecos. **(b)** Both anecdotes demonstrate the importance of horses to people of Kiowa descent.

2. The lost recipe contributes to Nye's wistfulness and longing for things that have been lost in modern society.

3. **(a)** Harjo was fascinated and transported, and she experienced a "rite of passage." **(b)** The experience made her realize that there are worlds beyond what she knew and that connected her with all of humankind.

4. Momaday tested himself physically and tested his courage on his journey. His courage was again tested as he moved out into the world after selling his horse.

5. Harjo understands that feelings beyond words connect her with the rest of humanity.

6. The recipe might have connected Nye to her great-grandfather and, through him, to other relatives whom she never knew.

7. Possible response: Momaday's rite of passage is most traditional because he tests his physical strength and courage. Nye's rite of passage is the most subtle, because for most people losing a recipe is an insignificant event. Harjo's rite of passage may be the most powerful, because she was so dramatically changed from it and because she still experiences the feelings she had during the experience.

8. Many students will relate physical challenges and experiences with music and art.

9. Many students will find Harjo's experience with music most accessible because of the accessibility of various kinds of music.

10. Students might connect "Mint Snowball" to accounts of Native American or pioneer life in America.

☀ ENRICHMENT: Further Reading

Other Works by the Authors

Works by N. Scott Momaday
House Made of Dawn
The Way to Rainy Mountain
The Gourd Dancer

Works by Naomi Shihab Nye
Different Ways to Pray
Hugging the Jukebox
Yellow Glove

Works by Joy Harjo
Secrets from the Center of the World
In Mad Love and War
The Last Song

 Take It to the Net
Visit www.phschool.com for more information on the authors.

Answers for p. 1052

❶ Vocabulary Development

Word Analysis

1. conference: conferring with
2. congregated: got together with
3. concocted: made by putting ingredients together
4. conform: go along with

Spelling Strategy

1. reluctant
2. deference
3. descendant

Concept Development

1. a
2. a
3. a
4. a
5. b
6. b
7. b
8. a

❷ Grammar

1. Pecos ran faster <u>than the other horses</u> [ran].
2. Momaday thought the stallion was better <u>than his own horse</u> [was].
3. Nye's great-grandfather sold the recipe [that] <u>he invented</u>.
4. Harjo recalls hearing the music in the car more vividly <u>than she does</u> [recall] <u>any other early experience</u>.
5. She noticed more <u>than she had</u> [noticed] <u>before</u>.

Writing Application

The two sentences students write must contain elliptical clauses. Make sure students understand that elliptical clauses are clauses in which one or more words are omitted because they are understood.

Integrate Language Skills

❶ Vocabulary Development Lesson

Word Analysis: Latin Prefix *con-*

The Latin prefix *con-* means "with" or "together." Combined with *fluence*, it produces *confluence*, meaning "flowing together." Define each of the following words, using "with" or "together."

1. conference   3. concocted
2. congregated   4. conform

Spelling Strategy

Many words end in *-ent* or *-ence*, such as *dependent* and *dependence*. However, there are exceptions, such as *flamboyant* and *flamboyance*, which end in *-ant* or *-ance*. In your notebook, complete the spelling of words in each sentence.

1. He was reluct____ to ride on the horse.
2. She showed defer____ to her grandfather.
3. She was a descend____ of the pilgrims.

Concept Development: Analogies

Select the word that best completes the analogy.

1. comfortable : chair :: supple : ____?____
   (a) dancer (b) flexible
2. stitched : clothing :: concocted : ____?____
   (a) potion (b) scientist
3. shy : timid :: flamboyant : ____?____
   (a) showy (b) nervous
4. treatment : disease :: elixir : ____?____
   (a) ailment (b) doctor
5. spread : rumor :: permeated : ____?____
   (a) filled (b) odor
6. design : create :: replicate : ____?____
   (a) count (b) copy
7. illuminating : lamp :: revelatory : ____?____
   (a) celebration (b) news
8. join : split :: confluence : ____?____
   (a) divergence (b) river

❷ Grammar and Style Lesson

Elliptical Clauses

The term *elliptical* comes from the word *ellipsis*, meaning "omission." In an **elliptical clause,** one or more words are omitted because they are understood. An elliptical clause is only understood if the context makes clear what the missing elements are—for example, in many cases, the word *that* is omitted.

> **Examples:** Her mother enjoyed the dessert *more than* [. . .] *any other.* (*she enjoyed* is understood)
>
> I hoped [. . .] *she would like it.* (*that* is understood)

Practice Copy each sentence, underline the elliptical clause, and write the understood word(s).

1. Pecos ran faster than the other horses.
2. Momaday thought the stallion was better than his own horse.
3. Nye's great-grandfather sold the recipe he invented.
4. Harjo recalls hearing the music in the car more vividly than she does any other early experience.
5. She noticed more than she had before.

Writing Application Write two sentences containing elliptical clauses.

𝒲𝒢 *Prentice Hall Writing and Grammar Connection: Chapter 22, Section 2*

TEACHING RESOURCES

The following resources can be used to enrich or extend the instruction for pp. 1052–1053.

Vocabulary

📖 **Selection Support:** Build Vocabulary, p. 262

📖 **Vocabulary and Spelling Practice Book**
(Use this booklet for skills enrichment.)

Grammar

📖 **Selection Support:** Grammar and Style, p. 263

𝒲𝒢 **Writing and Grammar,** Ruby Level, p. 572

📱 **Daily Language Practice Transparencies**

Writing

𝒲𝒢 **Writing and Grammar,** Ruby Level, p. 56 ■

💿 **Writing and Grammar iText CD-ROM**

📱 **Writing Models and Graphic Organizers on Transparencies,** pp. 5–8

■ **BLOCK SCHEDULING:** Resources marked with this symbol provide varied instruction during 90-minute blocks.

Writing Lesson

Reflective Essay

Each of these writers shares a moment from the past and reflects on its importance. Choose a significant event and write a reflective essay exploring its meaning.

Prewriting   Brainstorm for a list of events that affected you earlier. For each, write two or three reasons why the event was significant. Decide which one you will write about.

Drafting   After describing the event or experience, provide the insight to explain its effect on you. Include details that build the emotional impact of your insight.

Model: Elaborating to Add Emotional Depth

It was during my aunt's visit in the summer of 1996 that I discovered my pride in my Native American heritage. Through her stories about my grandparents and their struggles, I finally learned to celebrate what makes my life different instead of trying to hide it.

Words like *proud, finally,* and *celebrate* relate the symbolic meaning of the event.

Revising   Ask a classmate to read your draft to see if he or she can identify with your experience. Then, revise your draft, adding elaboration to ensure that readers will understand the importance of the event and the feelings it inspired in you.

 *Prentice Hall Writing and Grammar Connection: Chapter 4, Section 3*

Extension Activities

Listening and Speaking   A line of jazz gave Joy Harjo a new vision of the world. Listen to a piece of music that does the same for you. Then, using these tips, conduct a **musical analysis,** explaining the music's effect on you:

- Describe the images that are evoked by the melody.
- If there are any lyrics, connect them with your own experiences.

Play the music for your class and discuss your feelings about it.

Research and Technology   Like music, photography also has the power to evoke memory. With a group, create a word-processed **class anthology** of photographs and memories. Include personal photographs with anecdotal notes. Provide an introduction to the anthology, and illustrations or art to enhance your booklet. [**Group Activity**]

 *Take It to the Net*   www.phschool.com

Go online for an additional research activity using the Internet.

from The Names / Mint Snowball / Suspended ◆ 1053

ASSESSMENT RESOURCES

The following resources can be used to assess students' knowledge and skills.

Selection Assessment
- **Formal Assessment,** pp. 263–265
- **Open Book Test,** pp. 178–180
- **Test Bank Software**
- **Got It! Assessment Videotapes,** Tape 5

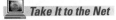 *Take It to the Net*
Visit www.phschool.com for self-tests and additional questions on the selections.

Writing Rubric
- **Performance Assess. and Portfolio Mgmt.,** p. 11

PRENTICE HALL
ASSESSMENT *SYSTEM*
- **Workbook**
- **Skill Book**
- **Transparencies**
- **CD-ROM**

Lesson Support for p. 1053

❸ Writing Lesson

- Review the prewriting, drafting, and revising steps that students will undertake as they write their reflective essays. Remind students that they will want to give at least two reasons why the event they chose is significant.

- As a model, show students the Reflective Essay on pp. 5–8 of **Writing Models and Graphic Organizers on Transparencies**.

- Use the Reflective Composition rubric in **Performance Assessment and Portfolio Management**, p. 11, to evaluate students' essays.

❹ Research and Technology

- Suggest that students work in groups of at least five to produce their class anthologies.

- Each student in the group should take on a task: choosing and assembling the photographs, writing the introduction, editing copy, illustrating, and assembling the anthology.

- When the students are done with their booklets, have them present their work to the rest of the class. You may wish to display the booklets so students can view them on their own time.

CUSTOMIZE INSTRUCTION
For Universal Access

To address different learning styles, use the activities suggested in the **Extension Activities** booklet, p. 60.

- For Visual/Spatial and Interpersonal Learners, use Activity 5.
- For Logical/Mathematical and Verbal/Linguistic Learners, use Activity 6.
- For Bodily/Kinesthetic and Logical/Mathematical Learners, use Activity 7.

Everyday Use

Lesson Objectives

1. To analyze and respond to literary elements
- Literary Analysis: Character's Motivation
- Connecting Literary Elements: Point of View

2. To read, comprehend, analyze, and critique a short story
- Reading Strategy: Contrasting Characters
- Reading Check Questions
- Review and Assess Questions
- Assessment Practice (ATE)

3. To develop word analysis skills, fluency, and systematic vocabulary
- Vocabulary Development Lesson: Latin Root: -doc-, -doct-

4. To understand and apply written and oral language conventions
- Spelling Strategy
- Grammar and Style Lesson: Sentence Fragments

5. To understand and apply appropriate writing and research strategies
- Writing Lesson: Review of a Short Story
- Extension Activity: African Languages Presentation

6. To understand and apply listening and speaking strategies
- Extension Activity: Television Talk Show

STEP-BY-STEP TEACHING GUIDE	PACING GUIDE
PRETEACH	
Motivate Students and Provide Background	
Use the Motivation activity (ATE p. 1054)	5 min.
Read and discuss author and background features (SE/ATE p. 1054)	5 min.
Introduce the Concepts	
Introduce the Literary Analysis and Reading Strategy (SE/ATE p. 1055)	15 min.
Pronounce the vocabulary words and read their definitions (SE p. 1055)	5 min.
TEACH	
Monitor Comprehension	
Informally monitor comprehension by circulating while students read independently or in groups	30 min.
Monitor students' comprehension with the Reading Check notes (SE/ATE pp. 1059, 1060, 1061)	as students read
Develop vocabulary with Vocabulary notes (SE pp. 1059, 1060, 1061; ATE p. 1061)	as students read
Develop Understanding	
Develop students' understanding of character's motivation with the Literary Analysis annotations (SE pp. 1057–1060; ATE pp.1057–1060)	5 min.
Develop students' ability to contrast characters by using the Reading Strategy annotations (SE pp. 1057, 1058, 1063; ATE pp. 1057, 1062, 1063)	5 min.
ASSESS	
Assess Mastery	
Assess students' mastery of the Reading Strategy and Literary Analysis by having them answer the Review and Assess questions (SE/ATE p. 1065)	15 min.
Use one or more of the print and media Assessment Resources (ATE p. 1067)	up to 45 min.
EXTEND	
Apply Understanding	
Have students complete the Vocabulary Development Lesson and the Grammar Lesson (SE p. 1066)	20 min.
Apply students' ability to use precise details by using the Writing Lesson (SE/ATE p. 1067)	45 min.
Apply students' understanding using one or more of the Extension Activities (SE p. 1067)	20–90 min.

A **ACCELERATED INSTRUCTION:**
Use the strategies and activities identified with an **A**.

UNIVERSAL ACCESS
● = Below Level Students
▲ = On-Level Students
■ = Above Level Students

Time and Resource Manager

RESOURCES

PRINT	TRANSPARENCIES	TECHNOLOGY
• **Beyond Literature,** Cross-Curricular Connection: Art, p. 61 ▲ ■		• **Interest Grabber Video,** Tape 6 ● ▲ ■
• **Selection Support Workbook:** ● ▲ ■ Literary Analysis, p. 269 Reading Strategy, p. 268 Build Vocabulary, p. 266	• **Literary Analysis and Reading Transparencies,** pp. 121 and 122 ● ▲ ■	
• **Adapted Reader's Companion** ● • **Reader's Companion** ●		• **Listening to Literature** ● ▲ ■ Audiocassettes, Side 36 Audio CDs, CD 20
• **English Learner's Companion** ● ▲ • **Literatura en español** ● ▲ • **Literary Analysis for Enrichment** ■	• **Fine Art on Transparencies,** Volume 1, Transparency 11	
• **Formal Assessment:** Selection Test, p. 266 ● ▲ ■ • **Open Book Test,** p. 181 ● ▲ ■ • **Performance Assessment and Portfolio Management,** pp. 13, 23 ● ▲ ■ • *PRENTICE HALL* **ASSESSMENT** *SYSTEM* ● ▲ ■	• *PRENTICE HALL* **ASSESSMENT** *SYSTEM* ● ▲ ■ Skills Practice Answers and Explanations on Transparencies	• **Test Bank Software** ● ▲ ■ • **Got It! Assessment Videotapes,** Tape 5 ● ▲
• **Selection Support Workbook:** ● ▲ ■ Grammar and Style, p. 267 • **Writing and Grammar,** Ruby Level ● ▲ ■ • **Extension Activities,** p. 61 ● ▲ ■	• **Daily Language Practice Transparencies** ● ▲ • **Writing Models and Graphic Organizers on Transparencies,** p. 37 ● ▲ ■	• **Writing and Grammar iText CD-ROM** ● ▲ ■ *Take It to the Net* www.phschool.com

BLOCK SCHEDULING: Use one 90-minute class period to preteach the selection and have students read it. Use a second 90-minute class period to assess students' mastery of skills and have them complete one of the Extension Activities.

Step-by-Step Teaching Guide
for pp. 1054–1055

Motivation

Ask students to bring to class, or be prepared to discuss, mementos that represent their heritage. These items might be anything from a treasured photograph or great-grandfather's watch to a china teapot that has been in the family for generations. Ask students how their families use or display these items: Are they tucked away in storage or display cabinets, or do their families use them regularly? Is the risk of damaging the objects outweighed by the pleasure of seeing and using them regularly? Tell students that the story they are about to read poses the question of whether such family heirlooms belong in "everyday use."

▣ Interest Grabber Video

As an alternative, you may wish to play " 'Everyday Use': An Interview with Alice Walker" on Tape 5 to engage student interest.

❶ Background

More About the Author

Alice Malsenior Walker was the eighth and youngest child of poor sharecroppers, Minnie Tallulah Grant Walker and Willie Lee Walker. Her family was rich in spirit, love, and family pride. Walker often heard stories about her father's great-great-great grandmother, Mary Poole—who was a slave forced to walk from Virginia to Georgia carrying two babies—and her mother's grandmother Tallulah, who was mostly Cherokee Indian.

Walker remembered her heritage throughout her years of education at Spelman College and Sarah Lawrence College, her participation in the civil rights movement, and her career as a novelist and poet. Strong women and love of the earth are recurring themes in Walker's work.

Prepare to Read

❶ Everyday Use

Alice Walker (b. 1944)

Born in Eatonton, Georgia, Alice Walker was the eighth and youngest child in a family of sharecroppers. Of her childhood, Walker writes, "It was great fun being cute. But then, one day, it ended."

The self-confidence of her childhood was challenged by an accident with a BB gun that scarred and nearly blinded her. Eight years old when the accident happened, Walker reports that she did not lift her head for six years. It was during this time of self-imposed isolation that she indulged her passion for reading. It was not until the family could afford surgery that Walker finally had the scar tissue on her eye removed. With that surgery, her self-confidence returned.

Civil Rights Walker became one of the most popular students in her high school and graduated as both class valedictorian and prom queen. She attended Spelman College, an elite college for African American women in Atlanta. While at Spelman, Walker became deeply involved in the civil rights movement. In August 1963, she traveled to Washington, D.C., to take part in the March on Washington for Jobs and Freedom. The guest speaker that day was Dr. Martin Luther King. Unable to see him through the crowd, Walker perched in a tree to get a better view. From there, she heard Dr. King deliver his famous "I Have a Dream" address.

After two years at Spelman, Walker learned that she had won a scholarship for full tuition to Sarah Lawrence College in Bronxville, New York. Although she was reluctant to leave Spelman and her civil rights activities, Walker's teachers persuaded her to accept the offer.

From Prom Queen to Poet At Sarah Lawrence, Walker studied under famed poets Muriel

Rukeyser and Jane Cooper, who encouraged her and nurtured her talent. Walker's first collection of poetry, *Once* (1968), was written while she was a student at Sarah Lawrence.

After graduating from Sarah Lawrence, Walker moved to Mississippi to continue her work in the civil rights movement. During this period, she also taught African American studies at Jackson State University, where she was a writer-in-residence.

Cultural Pride Much of Alice Walker's fiction—novels including *The Third Life of Grange Copeland* (1970) and story collections including *In Love and Trouble* (1973) and *You Can't Keep a Good Woman Down* (1981)—delves into the lives of African American women and their experiences throughout history and in the modern world.

Walker's fiction and essays reflect a pride in her personal heritage and the culture of her people. She draws inspiration from the creative efforts of countless African American artists who, long ago, survived the oppression of slavery. In looking at today's world, Walker explores the connections between sexism and racism and the effects of both on individuals and their relationships.

The Color Purple With the publication of *The Color Purple* in 1982, Walker shot to international fame. The novel portrays women who are oppressed by the abusive men in their lives, but go on to find inner strength and personal dignity. Awarded both a Pulitzer Prize and a National Book Award, the book was later adapted into a successful motion picture. Walker took an active role in the making of the film, and received a hero's welcome at its premier in her home town of Eatonton.

"Everyday Use" explores Walker's maternal heritage, describing the creative legacy of "ordinary" black southern women. The title essay of Walker's *In Search of Our Mothers' Gardens* can be considered the nonfiction counterpart of "Everyday Use."

TEACHING RESOURCES

The following resources can be used to enrich or extend the instruction for pp. 1054–1055

Motivation
▣ **Interest Grabber Video,** Tape 5

Background
📖 **Beyond Literature,** p. 61

🖥 *Take It to the Net*
Visit www.phschool.com for Background and hotlinks for the poems.

Literary Analysis
▨ **Literary Analysis and Reading Transparencies,** Character's Motivation, p. 122 ▪

Reading
📖 **Selection Support:** Reading Strategy, p. 268; Build Vocabulary, p. 266

▨ **Literary Analysis and Reading Transparencies,** Contrasting Characters, p. 121

■ **BLOCK SCHEDULING:** Resources marked with this symbol provide varied instruction during 90-minute blocks.

Preview

Connecting to the Literature

Time and new experiences can create divisions between people—even close relatives. In this story, distance and the passage of time lead a mother and her daughter to two very different views of the world.

Literary Analysis

Character's Motivation

To truly know a character, you have to understand that **character's motivation,** the reasons behind his or her thoughts, actions, and speech. Characters may be motivated by their values, experiences, needs, or dreams. These lines of "Everyday Use" are clues to the narrator's motivation.

> Maggie will be nervous until her sister goes . . . She thinks her sister has held life always in the palm of one hand, that "no" is a word the world never learned to say to her.

This quotation suggests that the narrator is motivated, at least in part, by feelings of love and protectiveness for Maggie. As you read, ask yourself:

- Why is this character doing or saying this?
- What need or goal does she hope to satisfy?

Connecting Literary Elements

"Everyday Use" is written in the **first-person point of view,** featuring a narrator who is a character in the story. When a story is told from the first-person point of view, the narrator's motivations may be easily understood. As you read, examine the thoughts and feelings of the narrator to understand her actions in the story.

Reading Strategy

Contrasting Characters

As this story opens, you learn that two sisters and their life experiences are quite different. By **contrasting characters,** or identifying the ways in which they differ, you can uncover the major conflict in the story. Use a Venn diagram like the one shown to note the personalities and details in behavior and speech that separate Dee from Maggie. Consider the ways their experiences have shaped their differences.

Vocabulary Development

furtive (fur´ tiv) *adj.* sneaky (p. 1059)

lye (lī) *n.* strong alkaline solution used in cleaning and making soap (p. 1059)

oppress (ə pres´) *v.* keep down by cruel or unjust use of power or authority (p. 1060)

doctrines (däk´ trinz) *n.* religious beliefs or principles (p. 1061)

Dee

Maggie

Everyday Use ◆ 1055

---

❷ Literary Analysis

Character's Motivation

- Reiterate to students that to understand fictional characters, readers must notice clues to their motivation, the causes that underlie the characters' behavior.

- Have a volunteer read the quotation from "Everyday Use" on p. 1055. Discuss with students what these few words reveal about the narrator's values and beliefs.

- Explain that because the story is written in the first-person point of view, readers learn a great deal about the motivation of the narrator, the mother of the two other main characters, Maggie and Dee.

- Remind students that all the details that Walker provides about her characters are important to fully understanding them. Urge students to keep questions such as the following in mind as they read: Why do characters behave as they do? What is important to them? What are their values, beliefs, fears, and joys?

❸ Reading Strategy

Contrasting Characters

- Refer students to The Venn diagram, on p. 1055.

- Remind students that the overlapping portion of the Venn diagram indicates those traits that are shared by both characters. The parts of the circles that don't overlap indicate contrasting traits.

- Ask students to use a similar Venn diagram to track the similarities and differences between Maggie and Dee as they read "Everyday Use."

Vocabulary Development

- Pronounce each vocabulary word for students, and read the definitions as a class. Have students identify any words with which they are already familiar.

 E-Teach

Visit E-Teach at www.phschool.com for teachers' essays on how to teach, with questions and answers.

CUSTOMIZE INSTRUCTION
For Visual/Spatial Learners

Have students search in books, magazines, or web sites for examples of slave-era and contemporary African American quilts or other folk arts. Students can use the examples they locate to help them visualize the items that are so pivotal to the story.

❶ About the Selection

In this short story, a mother and daughter struggle to make themselves known to each other across the considerable chasm that time and change have created between them. Educated and self-assured, Dee, who now uses the African name Wangero, visits her rural Georgia childhood home. She has returned after a long absence, ostensibly to reintroduce herself to her cultural heritage, but also to display her spiritual growth to the mother and sister she has left behind. As Dee tries to extract some material trappings of her African American heritage from the house, her mother and sister discover their own personal brand of cultural pride.

❷ ▶ Critical Viewing

Answer: The pieces stitched together to make the quilts are remnants of the family's clothing. The quilt patterns may be traditional and handed down from generation to generation.

❶

Everyday Use
Alice Walker

Background

In this story, the character Dee, the narrator's daughter, is interested in a butter churn and a quilt—two homely artifacts that reveal her family's history. Today, such home-crafted pieces are celebrated for their beauty, but most folk art was originally created for utilitarian purposes. People took pride in creating items that were attractive as well as useful. The quilt in this story is an especially important symbol. Like most folk art, quilts served many purposes: keeping people warm, recycling worn-out clothing, providing a focal point for social gatherings of women, and preserving precious bits of family history for future generations. The differing ways in which each character regards the quilt become a critical point of division in this story.

❷

▲ Critical Viewing
In what ways can quilts like these and the ones described in "Everyday Use" represent people's lives? **[Connect]**

1056 ◆ *Prosperity and Protest (1946–Present)*

TEACHING RESOURCES

The following resources can be used to enrich or extend the instruction for pp. 1056–1064.

Literary Analysis
📖 **Selection Support:** Literary Analysis, p. 269 ▪

Reading
📖 **Adapted Reader's Companion**
📖 **Reader's Companion**
📖 **English Learner's Companion**
🎧 **Listening to Literature Audiocassettes,** Side 36 ▪

💿 **Listening to Literature Audio CDs,** CD 20 ▪

Extension
📄 **Fine Art Transparencies,** Volume 1, Transparency 11

▪ **BLOCK SCHEDULING:** Resources marked with this symbol provide varied instruction during 90-minute blocks.

I will wait for her in the yard that Maggie and I made so clean and wavy yesterday afternoon. A yard like this is more comfortable than most people know. It is not just a yard. It is like an extended living room. When the hard clay is swept clean as a floor and the fine sand around the edges lined with tiny, irregular grooves, anyone can come and sit and look up into the elm tree and wait for the breezes that never come inside the house.

Maggie will be nervous until after her sister goes: she will stand hopelessly in corners, homely and ashamed of the burn scars down her arms and legs, eyeing her sister with a mixture of envy and awe. She thinks her sister has held life always in the palm of one hand, that "no" is a word the world never learned to say to her.

Reading Strategy
Contrasting Characters
What contrasts do you learn about Maggie and her sister from the narrator's comments in this passage?

You've no doubt seen those TV shows where the child who has "made it" is confronted, as a surprise, by her own mother and father, tottering in weakly from backstage. (A pleasant surprise, of course: What would they do if parent and child came on the show only to curse out and insult each other?) On TV mother and child embrace and smile into each other's faces. Sometimes the mother and father weep, the child wraps them in her arms and leans across the table to tell how she would not have made it without their help. I have seen these programs.

Sometimes I dream a dream in which Dee and I are suddenly brought together on a TV program of this sort. Out of a dark and soft-seated limousine I am ushered into a bright room filled with many people. There I meet a smiling, gray, sporty man like Johnny Carson who shakes my hand and tells me what a fine girl I have. Then we are on the stage and Dee is embracing me with tears in her eyes. She pins on my dress a large orchid, even though she has told me once that she thinks orchids are tacky flowers.

In real life I am a large, big-boned woman with rough, man-working hands. In the winter I wear flannel nightgowns to bed and overalls during the day. I can kill and clean a hog as mercilessly as a man. My fat keeps me hot in zero weather. I can work outside all day, breaking ice to get water for washing; I can eat pork liver cooked over the open fire minutes after it comes steaming from the hog. One winter I knocked a bull calf straight in the brain between the eyes with a sledge hammer and had the meat hung up to chill before nightfall. But of course all of this does not show on television. I am the way my daughter would want me to be: a hundred pounds lighter, my skin like an uncooked barley pancake. My hair glistens in the hot bright lights. Johnny Carson has much to do to keep up with my quick and witty tongue.

4

Literary Analysis
Character's Motivation
What do you think motivates the narrator to feel this way about herself in her dream?

☑ **Reading Check** **5**

Who are Maggie and her mother waiting to welcome?

❸ Reading Strategy
Contrasting Characters

- Have a volunteer read the second paragraph of the story.
- If Maggie is *homely*, ask students what word would best describe Dee.
  Possible response: Attractive, pretty or sophisticated
- Have students answer the Reading Strategy question on p. 1057: What contrasts do you learn about Maggie and her sister from the narrator's comments in this passage?
  Answer: Dee, is beautiful, self-assured, and lucky; Maggie has been unlucky; she is physically and consequently, emotionally scarred, and lacking in self-confidence.

❹ Literary Analysis
Character's Motivation

- Ask students to describe the narrator, both physically and psychologically.
  Possible response: She is a big, strong woman who can handle difficult farm tasks, like slaughtering a hog or cow—jobs usually reserved for men. She can take care of herself and her family, and seems confident in her abilities.
- Ask students the Literary Analysis question on p. 1057: What do you think motivates the character to feel this way about herself in her dream?
  Answer: The narrator's motivation probably comes from her desire to please her daughter Dee.

❺ ☑ Reading Check

Answer: Maggie and her mother are waiting for Maggie's older sister Dee.

CUSTOMIZE INSTRUCTION FOR UNIVERSAL ACCESS

For Special Needs Students	For Gifted/Talented Students	For Advanced Readers
Help students build some of the background they will need to understand the narrator's dream. Explain that the television show to which she refers is *This Is Your Life*, which aired during the 1950s. The program reunited celebrities with surprise visitors from their past.	Explain that the television show described in the narrator's dream is *This Is Your Life*, which aired during the 1950s. Ask students to act out the narrator's dream scene from the television show.	Explain that the television show described in this part of the story is *This Is Your Life*, which aired during the 1950s. Have students research the show and write about its importance to popular culture at the time.

Character's Motivation and First-Person Point of View

- Have a volunteer read the bracketed passage aloud.

- Remind students that descriptions told from the first-person point of view can be very powerful because they serve as eyewitness accounts, both observed and experienced.

- Ask students why the narrator is moved to remember details of the night the fire burned down her house and injured Maggie.
  Possible response: The narrator is thinking about the differences between Maggie and Dee, and Dee's light beautiful skin emphasizes Maggie's suffering.

- Have students answer the Literary Analysis question on p. 1058: What does the narrator's memory of the fire reveal about her point of view towards her two daughters?
  Answer: The narrator feels pity for Maggie and anger toward Dee.

❼ Reading Strategy

Contrasting Characters

- Have students reread the last paragraph on p. 1057 in which the narrator describes herself.

- Then, read the bracketed passage aloud.

- Ask the Reading Strategy question on p. 1058: What contrasts between herself and Dee does the narrator describe?
  Answer: The narrator is large, uninterested in fashion, strong in both mind and body, and compassionate. She sees Dee as stylish, pretty, determined, and strong-minded but also self-centered.

But that is a mistake. I know even before I wake up. Who ever knew a Johnson with a quick tongue? Who can even imagine me looking a strange white man in the eye? It seems to me I have talked to them always with one foot raised in flight, with my head turned in whichever way is farthest from them. Dee, though. She would always look anyone in the eye. Hesitation was no part of her nature.

"How do I look, Mama?" Maggie says, showing just enough of her thin body enveloped in pink skirt and red blouse for me to know she's there, almost hidden by the door.

"Come out into the yard," I say.

Have you ever seen a lame animal, perhaps a dog run over by some careless person rich enough to own a car, sidle up to someone who is ignorant enough to be kind to him? That is the way my Maggie walks. She has been like this, chin on chest, eyes on ground, feet in shuffle, ever since the fire that burned the other house to the ground.

Dee is lighter than Maggie, with nicer hair and a fuller figure. She's a woman now, though sometimes I forget. How long ago was it that the other house burned? Ten, twelve years? Sometimes I can still hear the flames and feel Maggie's arms sticking to me, her hair smoking and her dress falling off her in little black papery flakes. **❻** Her eyes seemed stretched open, blazed open by the flames reflected in them. And Dee. I see her standing off under the sweet gum tree she used to dig gum out of; a look of concentration on her face as she watched the last dingy gray board of the house fall in toward the red-hot brick chimney. Why don't you do a dance around the ashes? I'd want to ask her. She had hated the house that much.

I used to think she hated Maggie, too. But that was before we raised the money, the church and me, to send her to Augusta to school. She used to read to us without pity; forcing words, lies, other folks' habits, whole lives upon us two, sitting trapped and ignorant underneath her voice. She washed us in a river of make-believe, burned us with a lot of knowledge we didn't necessarily need to know. Pressed us to her with the serious way she read, to shove us away at just the moment, like dimwits, we seemed about to understand.

Dee wanted nice things. A yellow organdy dress to wear to her graduation from high school; black pumps to match a green suit she'd made from an old suit somebody gave me. She was determined to stare down any disaster in her efforts. Her eyelids would not flicker for minutes at a time. Often I fought off the temptation **❼** to shake her. At sixteen she had a style of her own, and knew what style was.

I never had an education myself. After second grade the school was closed down. Don't ask me why: in 1927 colored asked fewer questions than they do now. Sometimes Maggie reads to me. She stumbles along good-naturedly but can't see well. She knows she is not bright. Like good looks and money, quickness passed her by. She will marry John

Literary Analysis
Character's Motivation and First-Person Point of View What does the narrator's memory of the fire reveal about her point of view toward her two daughters?

Reading Strategy
Contrasting Characters What contrasts between herself and Dee does the narrator describe?

☀ ENRICHMENT: Social Studies Connection

TV Shows

The story's narrator alludes to several popular television shows that were a well-established feature of American popular culture in the mid-to-late-twentieth century. The television show *This Is Your Life* ran from 1952 to 1961. Hosted by Ralph Edwards, the show staged reunions between celebrities and influential people from various phases of their lives. The narrator also mentions Johnny Carson, who hosted late-night television's *Tonight Show* from 1962 until 1992. With wry humor, Carson interviewed celebrities from various walks of life, with the emphasis on comedy and show business.

Thomas (who has mossy teeth in an earnest face) and then I'll be free to sit here and I guess just sing church songs to myself. Although I never was a good singer. Never could carry a tune. I was always better at a man's job. I used to love to milk till I was hooved in the side in '49. Cows are soothing and slow and don't bother you, unless you try to milk them the wrong way.

I have deliberately turned my back on the house. It is three rooms, just like the one that burned, except the roof is tin; they don't make shingle roofs any more. There are no real windows, just some holes cut in the sides, like the portholes in a ship, but not round and not square, with rawhide holding the shutters up on the outside. This house is in a pasture, too, like the other one. No doubt when Dee sees it she will want to tear it down. She wrote me once that no matter where we "choose" to live, she will manage to come see us. But she will never bring her friends. Maggie and I thought about this and Maggie asked me, "Mama, when did Dee ever *have* any friends?"

She had a few. Furtive boys in pink shirts hanging about on wash-day after school. Nervous girls who never laughed. Impressed with her they worshiped the well-turned phrase, the cute shape, the scalding humor that erupted like bubbles in lye. She read to them.

When she was courting Jimmy T she didn't have much time to pay to us, but turned all her faultfinding power on him. He *flew* to marry a cheap city girl from a family of ignorant flashy people. She hardly had time to recompose herself.

When she comes I will meet—but there they are!

Maggie attempts to make a dash for the house, in her shuffling way, but I stay her with my hand. "Come back here," I say. And she stops and tries to dig a well in the sand with her toe.

It is hard to see them clearly through the strong sun. But even the first glimpse of leg out of the car tells me it is Dee. Her feet were always neat-looking, as if God himself had shaped them with a certain style. From the other side of the car comes a short, stocky man. Hair is all over his head a foot long and hanging from his chin like a kinky mule tail. I hear Maggie suck in her breath. "Uhnnnh," is what it sounds like. Like when you see the wriggling end of a snake just in front of your foot on the road. "Uhnnnh."

Dee next. A dress down to the ground, in this hot weather. A dress so loud it hurts my eyes. There are yellows and oranges enough to throw back the light of the sun. I feel my whole face warming from the heat waves it throws out. Earrings gold, too, and hanging down to her shoulders. Bracelets dangling and making noises when she moves her arm up to shake the folds of the dress out of her armpits. The dress is loose and flows, and as she walks closer, I like it. I hear Maggie go "Uhnnnh" again. It is her sister's hair. It stands straight up like the wool on a sheep. It is black as night and around the edges are two long pigtails that rope about like small lizards disappearing behind her ears.

furtive (fur′ tiv) *adj.* sneaky

lye (li) *n.* strong alkaline solution used in cleaning and making soap

Literary Analysis
Character's Motivation
What motivates Maggie to try to run for the house?

⓫

☑**Reading Check**

What traumatic event occurred in the lives of the mother and her daughters?

Everyday Use ◆ 1059

- Have a volunteer read the bracketed passage aloud.

- Then, ask the Literary Analysis question on p. 1060: Why does Dee take so many photographs? Possible response: Dee takes numerous photographs of the house, its surroundings, and her relatives as a reminder of her "heritage." In doing so, she diminishes her family by portraying them and their home as quaint. She may be gathering pictures to show her friends because she does not plan to return again soon.

⑬ Literary Analysis

Character's Motivation

- Discuss with students the reasons behind Dee's decision to change her name. What do they think of this decision? Possible answer: Students may say that Dee's name change reinforces her African heritage but distances her from her immediate family.

- Then, discuss the narrator's reaction to the name change. Ask: Does the narrator understand Dee's perspective? Does she approve? Answer: Most students will believe that her mother does understand but that she does not approve.

▶ Monitor Progress Ask students what feelings and thoughts may motivate the narrator's behavior in this discussion with her daughter. Answer: Most students will believe that the narrator is deliberately "playing dumb" by pretending not to understand that the family name ultimately derives from the days of slavery. She does this to irritate her daughter and to make the point that wherever the name came from, it has become their own, and she is proud of it.

"Wa-su-zo-Tean-o!"[1] she says, coming on in that gliding way the dress makes her move. The short stocky fellow with the hair to his navel is all grinning and he follows up with "Asalamalakim,[2] my mother and sister!" He moves to hug Maggie but she falls back, right up against the back of my chair. I feel her trembling there and when I look up I see the perspiration falling off her chin.

"Don't get up," says Dee. Since I am stout it takes something of a push. You can see me trying to move a second or two before I make it. She turns, showing white heels through her sandals, and goes back to the car. Out she peeks next with a Polaroid. She stoops down quickly and lines up picture after picture of me sitting there in front of the house with Maggie cowering behind me. She never takes a ⑫ shot without making sure the house is included. When a cow comes nibbling around the edge of the yard she snaps it and me and Maggie and the house. Then she puts the Polaroid in the back seat of the car, and comes up and kisses me on the forehead.

Meanwhile Asalamalakim is going through motions with Maggie's hand. Maggie's hand is as limp as a fish, and probably as cold, despite the sweat, and she keeps trying to pull it back. It looks like Asalamalakim wants to shake hands but wants to do it fancy. Or maybe he don't know how people shake hands. Anyhow, he soon gives up on Maggie.

"Well," I say. "Dee."

"No, Mama," she says. "Not 'Dee,' Wangero Leewanika Kemanjo!"

"What happened to 'Dee'?" I wanted to know.

"She's dead," Wangero said. "I couldn't bear it any longer, being named after the people who <u>oppress</u> me."

"You know as well as me you was named after your aunt Dicie," I ⑬ said. Dicie is my sister. She named Dee. We called her "Big Dee" after Dee was born.

"But who was *she* named after?" asked Wangero.

"I guess after Grandma Dee," I said.

"And who was she named after?" asked Wangero.

"Her mother," I said, and saw Wangero was getting tired. "That's about as far back as I can trace it," I said. Though, in fact, I probably could have carried it back beyond the Civil War through the branches.

"Well," said Asalamalakim, "there you are."

"Uhnnnh," I heard Maggie say.

"There I was not," I said, "before 'Dicie' cropped up in our family, so why should I try to trace it that far back?"

He just stood there grinning, looking down on me like somebody inspecting a Model A car. Every once in a while he and Wangero sent eye signals over my head.

"How do you pronounce this name?" I asked.

---

1. **Wa-su-zo-Tean-o** (wä sōō zō tēn′ ō) African greeting.
2. **Asalamalakim** *Salaam aleikhim* (sə läm′ ä lī′ kēm′) Islamic greeting meaning "Peace be with you."

Literary Analysis
Character's Motivation
Why does Dee take so many photographs?

oppress (ə pres′) *v.* keep down by cruel or unjust use of power or authority

---

✷ ENRICHMENT: Social Studies Connection

African American Identity and Islam

In the 1960s and early 1970s, as part of their quest for an African American identity, some African Americans began to emphasize their links to their African ancestry. They celebrated their cultural heritage, dressed in African clothing, and wore their hair in the natural "afro" style. Some took African or Arabic names, rejecting the names acquired through their American slave ancestry, and some became Muslims.

African Americans who converted to Islam followed the teachings of Mohammed established in the seventh century and expressed in the Koran, the Muslim holy book. The Koran forbids usury, games of chance, and the consumption of pork and alcohol. Practicing Muslims believe in a single God, pray five times a day facing Mecca, donate to charity, fast during Ramadan, and make a pilgrimage to Mecca once in their lifetime.

"You don't have to call me by it if you don't want to," said Wangero.

"Why shouldn't I?" I asked. "If that's what you want us to call you, we'll call you."

"I know it might sound awkward at first," said Wangero.

"I'll get used to it," I said. "Ream it out again."

Well, soon we got the name out of the way. Asalamalakim had a name twice as long and three times as hard. After I tripped over it two or three times he told me to just call him Hakim-a-barber. I wanted to ask him was he a barber, but I didn't really think he was, so I didn't ask.

"You must belong to those beef-cattle people down the road," I said. They said "Asalamalakim" when they met you, too, but they didn't shake hands. Always too busy: feeding the cattle, fixing the fences, putting up salt-lick shelters, throwing down hay. When the white folks poisoned some of the herd the men stayed up all night with rifles in their hands. I walked a mile and a half just to see the sight.

Hakim-a-barber said, "I accept some of their <u>doctrines</u>, but farming and raising cattle is not my style." (They didn't tell me, and I didn't ask, whether Wangero (Dee) had really gone and married him.)

We sat down to eat and right away he said he didn't eat collards[3] and pork was unclean. Wangero, though, went on through the chitlins[4] and corn bread, the greens and everything else. She talked a blue streak over the sweet potatoes. Everything delighted her. Even the fact that we still used the benches her daddy made for the table when we couldn't afford to buy chairs.

"Oh, Mama!" she cried. Then turned to Hakim-a-barber. "I never knew how lovely these benches are. You can feel the rump prints," she said, running her hands underneath her and along the bench. Then she gave a sigh and her hand closed over Grandma Dee's butter dish. "That's it!" she said. "I knew there was something I wanted to ask you if I could have." She jumped up from the table and went over in the corner where the churn stood, the milk in it clabber by now. She looked at the churn and looked at it.

"This churn top is what I need," she said. "Didn't Uncle Buddy whittle it out of a tree you all used to have?"

"Yes," I said.

"Uh huh," she said happily. "And I want the dasher, too."

"Uncle Buddy whittle that, too?" asked the barber.

---

3. **collards** (käl´ erdz) *n.* leaves of the collard plant, often referred to as "collard greens."
4. **chitlins** (chit´ lenz) *n.* chitterlings, a pork dish popular among southern African Americans.

doctrines (däk´ trinz) *n.* religious beliefs or principles

16

✔**Reading Check**

Why has Dee changed her name?

14 Critical Thinking

Infer

- Invite a volunteer to read the bracketed passage aloud.
- Ask students what the narrator thinks of her Muslim neighbors down the road. Why does she call them "beef-cattle people"? **Answer:** She thinks they are enterprising but not neighborly. Thus, they are "beef-cattle people," who would rather spend time with their herd than say hello. However, she admires their ability to defend themselves against white people who threaten them.

15 Vocabulary Development

The Latin Root -doc- / -doct-

- Draw students' attention to the word *doctrines* and read its definition.
- Explain that the Latin root *-doc-* or *-doct-* means "teach."
- Give an example of a word with this Latin root and ask students to think of some others.
- **Possible answers:** *doctrinaire, doctor, doctorate, document, docudrama,* and *indoctrinate*
- Finally, have students choose three words from the list and construct sentences with them.

16 ✔ Reading Check

Answer: Dee says she has changed her name because she no longer wanted to use a name given to her by the oppressor. The reader may suspect that she has also changed her name because it was a fashionable thing to do among a select group of African Americans at the time.

CUSTOMIZE INSTRUCTION FOR UNIVERSAL ACCESS

For English Learners	For Gifted/Talented Students
Students who are learning English may have had the experience of being treated as though they were stupid because their grasp of English was limited. Have students discuss this problem and compare their feelings with the feelings of the mother and Maggie. What advice would students give Hakim-a-barber to help him get along better with the narrator and Maggie? Note students' suggestions on the chalkboard and have them use your notes to write a letter of advice to Hakim-a-barber.	Have students gather in small groups to describe the behavior of Hakim-a-barber toward Maggie and her mother. Ask the groups to discuss the reasons why Maggie and her mother don't like him very much. Urge students to compare his behavior with that of people they have known. Then, ask students to work together to write Hakim-a-barber a letter of advice about getting along with people who are different from him.

Answer: Students are likely to say that the young girl's shy glance and poor clothing are similar to their mental image of Maggie. Some students may believe that the girl's glance and posture are more self-confident than Maggie's would be.

⑱ **Reading Strategy**

Contrasting Characters

• Ask students to describe what the two sisters do after dinner.
Answer: Dee goes through her mother's trunk. Maggie starts washing the dinner dishes.

• Invite students to explain what this difference in behavior reveals about the sisters' personalities.
Answer: Dee immediately thinks about getting what she wants. Maggie thinks first about helping out. Maggie "hanging back" in the kitchen also demonstrates her shyness.

⑲ **Critical Thinking**

Analyze

• Ask students what event is described in this sentence.
Answer: Maggie drops something in the kitchen and slams the door.

• Invite students to explain why Maggie did this.
Answer: Maggie was upset at the prospect of Dee getting the quilts.

• Ask students to explain what this behavior reveals about Maggie.
Answer: Maggie cannot express her feelings directly, but she is angry.

Dee (Wangero) looked up at me.

"Aunt Dee's first husband whittled the dash," said Maggie so low you almost couldn't hear her. "His name was Henry, but they called him Stash."

"Maggie's brain is like an elephant's," Wangero said, laughing. "I can use the churn top as a centerpiece for the alcove table," she said, sliding a plate over the churn, "and I'll think of something artistic to do with the dasher."

When she finished wrapping the dasher the handle stuck out. I took it for a moment in my hands. You didn't even have to look close to see where hands pushing the dasher up and down to make butter had left a kind of sink in the wood. In fact, there were a lot of small sinks; you could see where thumbs and fingers had sunk into the wood. It was beautiful light yellow wood, from a tree that grew in the yard where Big Dee and Stash had lived.

⑱ After dinner Dee (Wangero) went to the trunk at the foot of my bed and started rifling through it. Maggie hung back in the kitchen over the dishpan. Out came Wangero with two quilts. They had been pieced by Grandma Dee and then Big Dee and me had hung them on the quilt frames on the front porch and quilted them. One was in the Lone Star pattern. The other was Walk Around the Mountain. In both of them were scraps of dresses Grandma Dee had worn fifty and more years ago. Bits and pieces of Grandpa Jarrell's Paisley shirts. And one teeny faded blue piece, about the size of a penny matchbox, that was from Great Grandpa Ezra's uniform that he wore in the Civil War.

"Mama," Wangero said sweet as a bird. "Can I have these old quilts?"

⑲ I heard something fall in the kitchen, and a minute later the kitchen door slammed.

"Why don't you take one or two of the others?" I asked. "These old things was just done by me and Big Dee from some tops your grandma pieced before she died."

Look at the expression on this young girl's face and the clothing she is wearing. Compare and contrast them with your perception of Maggie. **[Compare and Contrast]**

❋ ENRICHMENT: Social Studies Connection

African American Quilts

Enslaved African American women became expert quilters during slavery times, using their master's fabrics and patterns to make quilts for their masters use.

After the Civil War, black women continued to create quilts, but now did so for their own families. They used scraps of clothing and feed sacks—whatever fabric was available. Few examples of these quilts remain because the quilts were used until they wore out. Many everyday quilts were made of fabric strips, the "string" technique, a quick and efficient quilting method.

African American women also made story quilts that used appliqué over fabric to create pictures that tell stories. No one knows how common these quilts were, but story quilt techniques have been handed down through the generations. Today, many African American women still make story quilts.

"No," said Wangero. "I don't want those. They are stitched around the borders by machine."

"That'll make them last better," I said.

"That's not the point," said Wangero. "These are all pieces of dresses Grandma used to wear. She did all this stitching by hand. Imagine!" She held the quilts securely in her arms, stroking them.

"Some of the pieces, like those lavender ones, come from old clothes her mother handed down to her," I said, moving up to touch the quilts. Dee (Wangero) moved back just enough so that I couldn't reach the quilts. They already belonged to her.

"Imagine!" she breathed again, clutching them closely to her bosom.

"The truth is," I said, "I promised to give them quilts to Maggie, for when she marries John Thomas."

She gasped like a bee had stung her.

"Maggie can't appreciate these quilts!" she said. "She'd probably be backward enough to put them to everyday use."

"I reckon she would," I said. "God knows I been saving 'em for long enough with nobody using 'em. I hope she will!" I didn't want to bring up how I had offered Dee (Wangero) a quilt when she went away to college. Then she had told me they were old-fashioned, out of style.

"But they're *priceless*!" she was saying now, furiously; for she has a temper. "Maggie would put them on the bed and in five years they'd be in rags. Less than that!"

"She can always make some more," I said. "Maggie knows how to quilt."

Dee (Wangero) looked at me with hatred. "You just will not understand. The point is these quilts, *these quilts*!"

"Well," I said, stumped. "What would *you* do with them?"

"Hang them," she said. As if that was the only thing you *could* do with quilts.

Maggie by now was standing in the door. I could almost hear the sound her feet made as they scraped over each other.

"She can have them, Mama," she said, like somebody used to never winning anything, or having anything reserved for her.

"I can 'member Grandma Dee without the quilts."

I looked at her hard. She had filled her bottom lip with checker-berry snuff and it gave her face a kind of dopey, hangdog look. It was Grandma Dee and Big Dee who taught her how to quilt herself. She stood there with her scarred hands hidden in the folds of her skirt.

Reading Strategy
Contrasting Characters
In what way does the dispute over the quilts reveal differences between the two sisters?

21

☑**Reading Check**

Why does Dee think Maggie should not have the quilts?

Everyday Use ◆ 1063

20 **Reading Strategy**
Contrasting Characters

- Ask students to discuss Dee's behavior after she retrieves the quilts from the trunk. Why does she act as though the quilts already belong to her?
  Answer: Dee is very self-confident and self-centered. She is accustomed to getting what she wants.
- Then, ask the Reading Strategy question on p. 1063: In what way does the dispute over the quilts reveal differences between the two sisters?
  Answer: The dispute reveals Maggie's practical unassuming nature and Dee's quest for the latest in fashion. Dee will fight as hard as she can to acquire the quilts; Maggie is willing to give them up without a battle because she doesn't expect to get things she wants.

21 ☑**Reading Check**

Answer: Dee thinks Maggie should not have the quilts because Maggie does not appreciate their artistic and historical value. Dee believes that Maggie will use the quilts every day and quickly wear them out.

CUSTOMIZE INSTRUCTION FOR UNIVERSAL ACCESS

For Gifted/Talented Students	For Advanced Readers
Invite students to work together to make a story quilt. Each student should design a quilt square that represents him or herself. Students should then choose a design that says something about them: what they like, what is important to them, how they see themselves, and so on. Each student should appliqué the design on a quilt square. After all the squares are complete, an adult volunteer can stitch the squares together and add stuffing and a backing.	Have students research quilting techniques and designs. Suggest that they focus particularly on quilts made by African American women. Ask students to make presentations to the rest of the class in which they display photographs or actual examples of the various techniques and designs. If possible, encourage students to invite a quilt maker to class for a lecture demonstration.

Review and Assess

1. Many students will feel upset that Dee treated her mother and sister in such a thoughtless, high-handed, and condescending fashion.

2. **(a)** Maggie was burned in a fire. **(b)** Maggie was upset at losing her home; Dee seemed glad to see it go.

3. **(a)** Dee asks for a churn top, dasher, and two quilts. **(b)** She intends to display them as art objects. **(c)** She hated both these items and her heritage when she lived with them.

4. **(a)** The quilts symbolize the experiences and shared heritage of the women's family. **(b)** For Dee, the quilts are a quaint reminder of a heritage she has left behind; for Maggie, the quilts are part of a living heritage to be used and enjoyed in her daily life.

5. Dee's main purpose in visiting her childhood home seems to have been to show it to her friend and to gather keepsakes to take away.

6. Many students will believe that Dee's behavior was so offensive that her mother should not have given her anything. Other students will say that Dee's mother should have given her some family heirlooms, but not the ones she had already promised to Maggie.

She looked at her sister with something like fear but she wasn't mad at her. This was Maggie's portion. This was the way she knew God to work.

When I looked at her like that something hit me in the top of my head and ran down to the soles of my feet. Just like when I'm in church and the spirit of God touches me and I get happy and shout. I did something I never had done before: hugged Maggie to me, then dragged her on into the room, snatched the quilts out of Miss Wangero's hands and dumped them into Maggie's lap. Maggie just sat there on my bed with her mouth open.

"Take one or two of the others," I said to Dee.

But she turned without a word and went out to Hakim-a-barber.

"You just don't understand," she said, as Maggie and I came out to the car.

"What don't I understand?" I wanted to know.

"Your heritage," she said. And then she turned to Maggie, kissed her, and said, "You ought to try to make something of yourself, too, Maggie. It's really a new day for us. But from the way you and Mama still live you'd never know it."

She put on some sunglasses that hid everything above the tip of her nose and her chin.

Maggie smiled; maybe at the sunglasses. But a real smile, not scared. After we watched the car dust settle I asked Maggie to bring me a dip of snuff. And then the two of us sat there just enjoying, until it was time to go in the house and go to bed.

Review and Assess

Thinking About the Selection

1. **Respond:** How did you feel about Dee's behavior on her visit home? Explain.

2. **(a) Recall:** How was Maggie injured? **(b) Compare and Contrast:** How did Maggie and Dee each react to that dramatic experience?

3. **(a) Recall:** What objects does Dee ask to have? **(b) Recall:** What does Dee intend to do with the items she requests? **(c) Interpret:** What is ironic about her request for these objects and her professed interest in her heritage?

4. **(a) Interpret:** What do the quilts symbolize? **(b) Compare and Contrast:** In what ways do the quilts hold different meanings for Dee and for Maggie?

5. **Infer:** What seems to have been Dee's main purpose in visiting her home?

6. **Take a Position:** Should Dee's mother have given some of the family heirlooms to Dee? Why or why not?

✎ ASSESSMENT PRACTICE: Writing Skills

Grammar and Usage (For more practice, see **Test Preparation Workbook**, p. 64.)

The writing sections of some tests often require students to choose the correct word or group of words to complete a sentence. Use the following sample item to demonstrate.

The pieces of the unfinished quilt _____ scattered on the floor.

Choose the word that belongs in the blank.

A lay

B lied

C laid

D lain

B is the past tense of the word *lie*, meaning "to tell an untruth"; *C* is the past tense of the transitive verb *lay*; *D* is the past participle of *lie*; *A* is the simple past tense of *lie*, meaning "to rest or recline," and is therefore the correct answer.

Review and Assess

Literary Analysis

Character's Motivation

1. What appears to **motivate** Dee's interest in her heritage?
2. (a) List three personality traits that enable Dee to return home after a long absence and assume she may take things from the house. (b) Give three examples that reveal Maggie's character.
3. What does the narrator's act of snatching the quilts from Dee reveal about her personal values?
4. Explain Dee's complex motivations when she uses the word "heritage" and describes Maggie as "backward."

Connecting Literary Elements

5. Using a chart like the one shown, analyze the narrator's feelings toward Dee and Maggie.

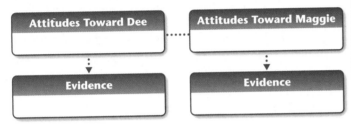

6. (a) What is your attitude toward each sister? (b) How does Walker's choice of narrator influence your response?
7. In what ways might the story change if it were told by Dee? Explain.

Reading Strategy

Contrasting Characters

8. How do Maggie and Dee differ (a) physically, (b) intellectually, and (c) emotionally?
9. (a) What does each sister know about her heritage? (b) To what extent does each sister think it is important to incorporate knowledge of her African heritage into her daily life?

Extend Understanding

10. **Cultural Connection:** What message does the story convey about family relationships and the meaning of heritage?

Quick Review

A **character's motivations** are the reasons for his or her thoughts, feelings, actions, and speech.

A story using the **first-person point of view** is told from the vantage point of a narrator who is involved in the action and who uses the first-person pronoun "I."

To **contrast characters,** identify the ways in which they differ.

 Take It to the Net
www.phschool.com
Take the interactive self-test online to check your understanding of the selection.

☀ **ENRICHMENT: Further Reading**

Other Works by Alice Walker

The Color Purple

In Love and Trouble

In Search of Our Mothers' Gardens: Womanist Prose

The Third Life of Grange Copeland

You Can't Keep a Good Woman Down

 Take It to the Net
Visit www.phschool.com for more information on the author.

Answers for p. 1065

Review and Assess

1. Possible response: A desire to keep up with the fashionable trend of connecting with one's African American heritage seems to motivate Dee's interest.

2. **(a)** Personality traits include self-confidence, lack of sensitivity to others, and selfishness. **(b)** Maggie's hanging back to avoid meeting the visitors; Maggie's cleaning up after dinner; Maggie's willingness to give up the quilts.

3. The narrator can be pushed only so far. When Maggie is being hurt once again, she defends her.

4. Dee has turned her back on her family but pretends to value her heritage.

5. Attitudes Toward Dee: Dislike; Evidence: Dee's happiness at seeing their house burn, treating her mother and sister as if they were stupid. Attitudes Toward Maggie: Pity; Evidence: Descriptions of Maggie's burns and her cringing posture.

6. **(a)** Most students will dislike Dee and feel sorry for Maggie. **(b)** The mother has ambivalent feelings about Dee but she loves Maggie. These feelings influence the reader's perceptions of the characters.

7. Dee might be a far more sympathetic character and might present details of her experiences growing up that alter readers' perceptions of her and her family.

8. **(a)** Dee is prettier and more stylish than Maggie. **(b)** Dee has had a much better formal education than Maggie has had and is much more quick-witted than her sister. **(c)** Dee is more self-confident and less sensitive than Maggie is.

9. **(a)** Dee has learned about her heritage from books; Maggie from everyday life. **(b)** To Dee, her heritage is something to be studied; for Maggie, it is something to be lived.

10. Many students will comment on the importance of maintaining close family relationships and appreciating everyday aspects of one's heritage.

❶ Vocabulary Development

Word Analysis

1. documentary
2. docile
3. indoctrinate
4. documents

Concept Development

1. lye
2. oppress
3. furtive
4. doctrines

Spelling Strategy

1. distressing
2. willing
3. obsessive

❷ Grammar and Style

1.-3., 5. Students may say that these fragments are missing a verb, or both a subject and verb. Either answer is acceptable.

In fragment 4, there is no subject or verb. In fragment 5, there is no verb.

Possible responses:

1. Her friends were furtive boys in pink shirts hanging about on washday.
2. Her friends were nervous girls who never laughed.
3. Her earrings were gold, too, and hanging down to her shoulder.
4. They were always too busy: feeding the cattle, fixing the fences, putting up salt-lick shelters.
5. Your heritage is important to you.

Writing Application

The dialogue must be among characters from "Everyday Use" and include sentence fragments.

Integrate Language Skills

❶ Vocabulary Development Lesson

Word Analysis: Latin Root -doc- / -doct-

The word *doctrines*, meaning "teachings, ideas, or beliefs," includes the Latin root *-doc- / -doct-,* meaning "teach." By combining this information with context clues, choose the best word to complete each sentence.

documents indoctrinate docile documentary

1. We watched a ___?___ on the history of quilt-making in America.
2. A ___?___ learner is one who accepts without question anything he or she is taught.
3. The political leader worked to ___?___ his followers by repeating his ideology every day.
4. Immigrants were asked to show ___?___ to prove their citizenship in their original country.

Concept Development: Analogies

Complete each analogy using a word from the vocabulary list on page 1055.

1. *Flour* is to *pie crust* as ___?___ is to *soap*.
2. *Encourage* is to *coach* as ___?___ is to *dictator*.
3. *Competitive* is to *athlete* as ___?___ is to *prowler*.
4. *Moral* is to *lesson* as ___?___ is to *belief*.

Spelling Strategy

To add a suffix to a word ending in two consonants, retain both consonants and add the suffix: *oppress + -ive = oppressive.* Add a suffix to each of the words below and write a sentence for each.

1. distress   2. will   3. obsess

❷ Grammar and Style Lesson

Sentence Fragments

A sentence expresses a complete thought with a subject and a verb. **Sentence fragments** are parts of sentences incorrectly punctuated as though they were complete. The fragment in this example lacks a subject:

Example: Never could carry a tune. (missing a subject: *Who?*)

Although it was a quilt made by my mother. (does not express a complete thought)

While fragments are not acceptable in formal writing, writers do use them to imitate the way people speak.

Practice Explain why each example is a sentence fragment, and identify the missing sentence part. Rewrite each fragment as a complete sentence.

1. Furtive boys in pink shirts hanging about on washday after school.
2. Nervous girls who never laughed.
3. Earrings gold, too, and hanging down to her shoulder.
4. Always too busy: feeding the cattle, fixing the fences, putting up salt-lick shelters.
5. Your heritage.

Writing Application Write a dialogue between characters from "Everyday Use." Incorporate fragments to capture speech patterns.

$\mathcal{W}_G$ *Prentice Hall Writing and Grammar Connection: Chapter 20, Section 4*

TEACHING RESOURCES

The following resources can be used to enrich or extend the instruction for pp. 1066–1067

Vocabulary

📖 **Selection Support:** Build Vocabulary, p. 266
📖 **Vocabulary and Spelling Practice Book** (Use this booklet for skills enrichment.)

Grammar

📖 **Selection Support:** Grammar and Style, p. 267 ▪
$\mathcal{W}_G$ **Writing and Grammar,** Ruby Level, p. 492
📖 **Daily Language Practice Transparencies** ▪

Writing

$\mathcal{W}_G$ **Writing and Grammar,** Ruby Level, p. 309
💿 **Writing and Grammar iText CD-ROM**
📖 **Writing Models and Graphic Organizers on Transparencies,** p. 37 ▪

▪ **BLOCK SCHEDULING:** Resources marked with this symbol provide varied instruction during 90-minute blocks.

❸ Writing Lesson

Review of a Short Story

Write a critical review of "Everyday Use," explaining whether you think the story is effective. Note your reactions to the story and explain whether the characters are believable and interesting. Consider the story's message, and express your opinion about its importance.

Prewriting   Review the story and list your responses, both positive and negative. Beside each item, note the page numbers of appropriate examples. Review your chart, and summarize your opinion in a sentence or two.

Drafting   Begin by stating your overall opinion of the story. Then, present a series of paragraphs in which you support your ideas with details.

Revising   Evaluate your draft to replace weak modifiers with precise adjectives and adverbs that capture your reactions. Be sure your writing is accurate by checking that you have copied all quotations exactly.

Model: Revising to Add Precise Details

genuine

Dee, as Wangero, appeared ~~nice~~, but she was ~~really~~

~~quite~~ insincere. She was not at all interested in ~~the~~

her heritage

~~things~~, but rather in appearances.

> Replacing weak modifiers with specific words makes writing more precise and interesting. Words like *really* do not add meaning to the work.

 Prentice Hall Writing and Grammar Connection: Chapter 14, Section 3

❹ Extension Activities

Listening and Speaking With a partner, dramatize the narrator's dream of a **television talk show** reunion with Dee. Consider these techniques:

- Use appropriate dialogue for the scene.
- Create skillful and artistic staging.
- Make your characters interesting and believable.

After rehearsing to achieve command of your text, present the dramatization to your class. **[Group Activity]**

Research and Technology The names *Wangero* and *Hakim-a-barber* come from one of the more than 800 languages spoken in Africa today. Conduct research on one of the four major language families. Create an **African languages presentation,** including audio and videotapes and maps of the region, to your class.

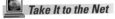 **Take It to the Net**   www.phschool.com

Go online for an additional research activity using the Internet.

ASSESSMENT RESOURCES

The following resources can be used to assess students' knowledge and skills.

Selection Assessment
- 📖 **Formal Assessment,** p. 266
- 📖 **Open Book Test,** p. 181
- 📼 **Got It! Assessment Videotapes,** Tape 5
- 💿 **Test Bank Software**
- 💻 **Take It to the Net**
  Visit www.phschool.com for self-tests and additional questions on "Average Waves in Unprotected Waters."

Writing Rubric
- 📖 **Performance Assess. and Portfolio Mgmt.,** p. 23

Research Rubric
- 📖 **Performance Assess. and Portfolio Mgmt.,** p. 13

PRENTICE HALL ASSESSMENT SYSTEM
- 📖 **Workbook**
- 📖 **Skill Book**
- 🖼️ **Transparencies**
- 💿 **CD-ROM**

---

❸ Writing Lesson

- Read a brief book review to students and discuss it with the class. What evidence did the writer of the review provide to back up his or her opinions of the book?

- Explain that regardless of their opinion of the story, their reviews of "Everyday Use" must offer well-supported reasons and examples from the story.

- Use the Writing Lesson instruction as well as Writing Process Model 7 in **Writing Models and Graphic Organizers on Transparencies,** p. 37, to guide students in writing their reviews.

- Use the Response to Literature rubric in **Performance Assessment and Portfolio Management,** p. 23, to evaluate students' reviews.

❹ Research and Technology

- Suggest that students work in small groups to research an African language and present their findings.

- Each group member should check at least one source for information.

- If possible, encourage students to tape native speakers of the language they are researching. If this is not possible, they may be able to locate sound clips on the Internet to share during their presentations.

- Use the Multimedia Presentation rubric in **Performance Assessment and Portfolio Management,** p. 13, to assess students' presentations.

CUSTOMIZE INSTRUCTION
For Universal Access

To address different learning styles, use the activities suggested in the Extension Activities booklet, p. 61.

For Verbal/Linguistic and Logical/Mathematical Learners, use Activity 5.

For Visual/Spatial Learners, use Activity 6.

For Interpersonal and Verbal/Linguistic Learners, use Activity 7.

from The Woman Warrior

Lesson Objectives

1. **To analyze and respond to literary elements**
   - Literary Analysis: Memoirs
   - Connecting Literary Elements: Limited Third-Person Point of View
2. **To read, comprehend, analyze, and critique a short story**
   - Reading Strategy: Applying Background Information
   - Reading Check Questions
   - Review and Assess Questions
3. **To develop word analysis skills, fluency, and systematic vocabulary**
   - Vocabulary Development Lesson: Latin Root: *-aud-*
4. **To understand and apply written and oral language conventions**
   - Spelling Strategy
   - Grammar and Style Lesson: Punctuating a Quotation Within a Quotation
   - Assessment Practice (ATE)
5. **To understand and apply appropriate writing and research strategies**
   - Writing Lesson: Character Analysis
   - Extension Activity: Immigration Report
6. **To understand and apply listening and speaking strategies**
   - Extension Activity: Panel Discussion

STEP-BY-STEP TEACHING GUIDE	PACING GUIDE
PRETEACH	
Motivate Students and Provide Background	
Use the Motivation activity (ATE p. 1068)	5 min.
Read and discuss author and background features (SE/ATE pp. 1068, 1070) **A**	5 min.
Introduce the Concepts	
Introduce the Literary Analysis and Reading Strategy (SE/ATE p. 1069) **A**	15 min.
Pronounce the vocabulary words and read their definitions (SE p. 1069)	5 min.
TEACH	
Monitor Comprehension	
Informally monitor comprehension by circulating while students read independently or in groups **A**	15 min.
Monitor students' comprehension with the Reading Check notes (SE/ATE pp. 1071, 1073, 1075)	as students read
Develop vocabulary with Vocabulary notes (SE pp. 1071, 1072, 1074, 1075; ATE p. 1074)	as students read
Develop Understanding	
Develop students' understanding of memoir with the Literary Analysis annotations (SE p. 1071; ATE p. 1071) **A**	5 min.
Develop students' ability to apply background information when they read by using the Reading Strategy annotations (SE pp. 1071, 1072; ATE pp. 1070, 1072)	5 min.
ASSESS	
Assess Mastery	
Assess students' mastery of the Reading Strategy and Literary Analysis by having them answer the Review and Assess questions (SE/ATE p. 1077)	15 min.
Use one or more of the print and media Assessment Resources (ATE p. 1079) **A**	up to 45 min.
EXTEND	
Apply Understanding	
Have students complete the Vocabulary Development Lesson and the Grammar and Style Lesson (SE p. 1078) **A**	20 min.
Apply students' ability to revise to provide support by using the Writing Lesson (SE/ATE p. 1079) **A**	45 min.
Apply students' understanding using one or more of the Extension Activities (SE p. 1079)	20–90 min.

 ACCELERATED INSTRUCTION:
Use the strategies and activities identified with an **A**.

UNIVERSAL ACCESS
● = Below Level Students
▲ = On-Level Students
■ = Above Level Students

Time and Resource Manager

RESOURCES		
PRINT	**TRANSPARENCIES**	**TECHNOLOGY**
• **Beyond Literature,** Career Connection: Memoir Writing, p. 62 ▲ ■		• **Interest Grabber Video,** Tape 6 ● ▲ ■
• **Selection Support Workbook:** ● ▲ ■ Literary Analysis, p. 273 Reading Strategy, p. 272 Build Vocabulary, p. 270	• **Literary Analysis and Reading Transparencies,** pp. 123 and 124 ● ▲ ■	
		• **Listening to Literature** ● ▲ ■ Audiocassettes, Side 36 Audio CDs, CD 20
• **Literatura en español** ● ▲ • **Literary Analysis for Enrichment** ■		
• **Formal Assessment:** Selection Test, pp. 269–271 ● ▲ ■ • **Open Book Test,** pp. 184–186 ● ▲ ■ • **Performance Assessment and Portfolio Management,** p. 23 ● ▲ ■ • PRENTICE HALL ASSESSMENT SYSTEM ● ▲ ■	• PRENTICE HALL ASSESSMENT SYSTEM ● ▲ ■ Skills Practice Answers and Explanations on Transparencies	• **Test Bank Software** ● ▲ ■ • **Got It! Assessment Videotapes,** Tape 5 ● ▲
• **Selection Support Workbook:** ● ▲ ■ Grammar and Style, p. 271 • **Writing and Grammar,** Ruby Level ● ▲ ■ • **Extension Activities,** p. 62 ● ▲ ■	• **Daily Language Practice Transparencies** ● ▲ • **Writing Models and Graphic Organizers on Transparencies,** pp. 83–85 ● ▲ ■	• **Writing and Grammar iText CD-ROM** ● ▲ ■ *Take It to the Net* www.phschool.com

BLOCK SCHEDULING: Use one 90-minute class period to preteach the selection and have students read it. Use a second 90-minute class period to assess students' mastery of skills and have them complete one of the Extension Activities.

Motivation

In reading this memoir, students will experience the excitement, impatience, and surprise of a long-awaited family reunion. Engage student interest with the following activity. Provide childhood pictures of yourself and other teachers, or ask students to contribute their own baby photos. Challenge the class to match up the photos with the correct people. How difficult might it be to recognize someone who has changed this much? What feelings might such a reunion produce in both parties?

▣ Interest Grabber Video

As an alternative, play "Maxine Hong Kingston" on Tape 6 to engage student interest.

❶ Background

More About the Author

Writing has long been central to Maxine Hong Kingston's life. She explains, "My writing is an ongoing function, like breathing or eating. . . . I have the habit of writing things down. Anything. And then some of it falls into place. . . ."

In 1976, while Kingston was teaching creative writing at the Mid-Pacific Institute, she published *The Woman Warrior*. In this book, her first, she weaves folklore and autobiography to give the popular topic of mother-daughter relationships an exotic setting and a unique voice. By the end of the memoir, the shy Kingston has broken her silence to carry on the Chinese oral tradition through her writing.

Prepare to Read

❶ *from* The Woman Warrior

Maxine Hong Kingston (b. 1940)

"I was born to be a writer," Maxine Hong Kingston once told an interviewer. "In the midst of any adventure, a born writer has a desire to hurry home and put it into words."

Crossing Cultures Although Kingston was born in America, she did not begin describing her adventures in English until she was nearly ten because the language spoken at home was Say Yup, a Chinese dialect spoken around Canton, now known as Guangzhou, China. Kingston's parents came from a village near Canton. Her father left first for "the Golden Mountain" of America and settled in New York City. His training as a poet and calligrapher was unmarketable in the United States, so he earned a living working in the laundry business. Kingston's mother, who was trained as a midwife, used the money her husband sent home to run a clinic in their native village. She did so until 1939, when she escaped war-torn China and joined her husband. Not long afterward, the couple resettled in Stockton, California, where Maxine Hong was born.

Building a Love for Story Young Maxine, whose Chinese name is Ting Ting, was a shy and quiet girl who repeated kindergarten because she spoke very little English. While at home, however, she listened intently to the stories told by family members and friends; this love of storytelling later influenced her writing style as Kingston developed her "talk stories." By the time she was nine years old, she mastered English and began writing poetry. Soon, she began to earn straight A's in school.

Kingston won a scholarship to the University of California at Berkeley, which she attended in the 1960s during its heyday as a center of intellectual activity and political activism. There, she met Earll Kingston and married him in 1962. After graduation, the Kingstons supported themselves as teachers while pursuing success in their chosen fields—Earll in acting, Maxine in writing. They lived in Hawaii for many years but returned to the mainland with their son, settling in Oakland, California.

A Bestseller Kingston shot to success with her first and best-known book, *The Woman Warrior: Memoirs of a Girlhood Among Ghosts.* The subtitle refers to the pale "ghosts" of white America as well as the "ghosts" of the narrator's ancestors in China. *The Woman Warrior*, a unique blend of folklore, myth, feminism, and autobiography, won the National Book Critics' Circle Award in 1976. The major focus of the book is on Brave Orchid—Kingston's mother. Brave Orchid tells her daughter about China and the female members of their family through her talk stories—a blend of truth and fiction, tales of ancient heroes, family secrets, and important cultural traditions and values passed from generation to generation.

Kingston earned the National Book Critics' Circle Award a second time in 1980 for *China Men*. In 1989, she published the novel *Tripmaster Monkey*. A slow, methodical writer, Kingston labors over numerous revisions to her books. For at least eight years, she has been working on her next book, tentatively titled *The Fifth Book of Peace*.

TEACHING RESOURCES

The following resources can be used to enrich or extend the instruction for pp. 1068–1069.

Motivation
▣ **Interest Grabber Video**, Tape 6

Background
▣ **Beyond Literature**, p. 62 ▪

▣ **Take It to the Net**
Visit www.phschool.com for background and hotlinks for the selection.

Literary Analysis
▣ **Selection Support:** Literary Analysis, p. 273 ▪
▣ **Literary Analysis and Reading Transparencies,** Memoirs, p. 124

Reading
▣ **Literary Analysis and Reading Transparencies,** Applying Background Information, p. 123

▪ **BLOCK SCHEDULING:** Resources marked with this symbol provide varied instruction during 90-minute blocks.

Preview

Connecting to the Literature

At some point in your life, you have probably felt that your older relatives view the world quite differently than you do. In families whose adults and children were born in different countries, these differences can be especially pronounced, as they are in this selection.

Literary Analysis

Memoirs

Most **memoirs** are first-person nonfiction narratives that recount historically or personally significant events in which the writer was a participant or an eyewitness. The following excerpt from Kingston's memoir blends the historical and the personal:

> To while away time, she and her niece talked about the Chinese passengers. These new immigrants had it easy. On Ellis Island the people were thin after forty days at sea and had no fancy luggage.

Kingston skillfully incorporates details of culture and time period into an account of a memorable day in her life.

Connecting Literary Elements

Memoirs are, by definition, acts of memory—accounts of individual experience told in the first person point of view. In most memoirs, the writer uses "I" to narrate events. Kingston, however, defies convention by using the **limited third-person point of view**—the story is related by a narrator who uses the pronoun "she" to describe herself. This unusual use of point of view helps to blur the line between fact and fiction. As you read, think about why Kingston made this choice.

Reading Strategy

Applying Background Information

Background information given in a book jacket, an introduction, or footnote can help you fully appreciate a literary work. In this textbook, you can gain such information from the author biography, the Prepare to Read pages, and the Background. As you read, record the information you learn from these features in a chart like the one shown.

Vocabulary Development

hysterically (hi ster′ i klē) *adv.* in a highly emotional manner (p. 1071)

encampment (en kamp′ mənt) *n.* place where a person has set up camp (p. 1072)

inaudibly (in ôd′ ə blē) *adv.* in a manner that cannot be heard (p. 1074)

gravity (grav′ i tē) *n.* seriousness (p. 1075)

oblivious (ə bliv′ ē əs) *adj.* lacking all awareness (p. 1075)

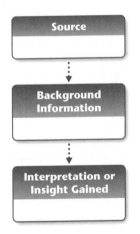

from The Woman Warrior ◆ 1069

---

❷ Literary Analysis

Memoirs

- Remind students that traditional memoirs are accounts of people's personal experiences and observations. Kingston incorporates folklore and history into her memoir, *The Woman Warrior.*

- Discuss the information under Connecting Literary Elements with students. Make sure they understand that though memoirs are usually told from the first-person point of view, *The Woman Warrior* uses the limited third-person point of view. Readers gain access to the thoughts and feelings of Brave Orchid; to learn about the other characters, readers must observe their words and actions.

- Use the Memoirs transparency in **Literary Analysis and Reading Transparencies**, p. 124, to compare traditional memoirs with *The Woman Warrior.*

❸ Reading Strategy

Applying Background Information

- Encourage students to activate relevant background information as they read the excerpt from *The Woman Warrior*, including the information in their textbook about Maxine Hong Kingston.

- Ask students to use a chart like the one on this page to track some of the sources of the background information they used to gain greater insight into the selection.

Vocabulary Development

- Pronounce each vocabulary word for students, and read the definitions as a class. Have students identify any words with which they are already familiar.

PATCHES FOR "THE WOMAN WARRIOR"

For Less Proficient Readers	For English Learners	For Advanced Readers
Brave Orchid's description of American culture includes contextual references some readers may find confusing. Encourage less proficient readers to pause as necessary and carefully read the explanatory footnotes.	Explain that the memoir focuses on the experiences of a Chinese American woman for whom English is also a second language. Her thoughts are sometimes stated awkwardly. Urge students to study context as they decipher any confusing passages.	Comparison and contrast can help students appreciate the cultural dualities presented in this memoir. Have students identify elements about both Chinese and American culture, as seen through Brave Orchid's eyes. What does the comparison reveal about Brave Orchid?

 E-Teach

Visit E-Teach at www.phschool.com for teachers' essays on how to teach, with questions and answers.

Step-by-Step Teaching Guide for pp. 1070–1076

CUSTOMIZE INSTRUCTION
For Verbal/Linguistic Learners

To understand and appreciate Brave Orchid's personality and behavior, students will benefit from hearing her words and thoughts read aloud. Have students take turns reading the selection aloud, or have them listen to it on the **Listening to Literature** audiocassette or CD before they read it on their own.

❶ About the Selection

This memoir captures the strange distortion that passing time can create. When the main character, Brave Orchid, arrives at the airport to meet the sister she has not seen for thirty years, she brings along the unique perspective of her memories —sure that she and Moon Orchid remain unchanged by time. Determined as well to resist the effects of the alien American culture in which she now lives, Brave Orchid evokes the universal struggle between tradition and change.

❷ ▶ Critical Viewing

Answer: The China that Brave Orchid remembers probably had few automobiles, and the inhabitants probably wore more traditional clothing.

❸ Reading Strategy

Applying Background Information

- Ask students why authors and editors use footnotes.
  Possible answer: Footnotes are used to clarify phrases and words, and to cite sources. They enrich the reader's enjoyment of a story by providing helpful background information.

- Ask students: What does the footnoted information suggest about Moon Orchid's life since she and Brave Orchid last saw each other?
  Answer: Moon Orchid has probably had a difficult life and has had to adapt to many changes. She may have immigrated to Hong Kong before traveling to the United States.

❶

from # The Woman Warrior
Maxine Hong Kingston

❷

▲ **Critical Viewing**
Do you think this scene at a chaotic Beijing intersection might represent the China Brave Orchid remembers? Why or why not? **[Compare]**

Background

The *Woman Warrior* is an innovative memoir that attempts to capture the experience of growing up in a bicultural world—part Chinese, part American. To accomplish her purpose, Kingston mingles the narrative with "talk stories," tales full of magical events that she heard as a girl from her mother, Brave Orchid. The subtitle of the book, *Memoir of a Girlhood Among Ghosts*, refers both to white America, whose pale inhabitants remind Brave Orchid of ghosts, and to the family's ancestors in China. In this excerpt, Brave Orchid reunites with her sister, one of the ghosts of her past.

When she was about sixty-eight years old, Brave Orchid took a day off to wait at San Francisco International Airport for the plane that was bringing her sister to the United States. She had not seen Moon Orchid for thirty years. She had begun this waiting at home, getting up a half-hour before Moon Orchid's plane took off in Hong Kong.[1] Brave Orchid would add her will power to the forces that keep an airplane up. Her head hurt with the concentration. The plane had to be light, so no matter how tired she felt, she

❸ 1. **took off in Hong Kong** After mainland China fell to the Communists in the late 1940's, many native Chinese fled first to Hong Kong (a British colony until 1997) before emigrating to the United States.

1070 ◆ Prosperity and Protest (1946–Present)

TEACHING RESOURCES

The following resources can be used to enrich or extend the instruction for pp. 1070–1076.

Literary Analysis

📖 **Selection Support:** Literary Analysis, p. 273

Reading

🎧 **Listening to Literature Audiocassettes,** Side 36

💿 **Listening to Literature Audio CDs,** CD 20

🔲 **BLOCK SCHEDULING:** Resources marked with this symbol provide varied instruction during 90-minute blocks.

dared not rest her spirit on a wing but continuously and gently pushed up on the plane's belly. She had already been waiting at the airport for nine hours. She was wakeful.

Next to Brave Orchid sat Moon Orchid's only daughter, who was helping her aunt wait. Brave Orchid had made two of her own children come too because they could drive, but they had been lured away by the magazine racks and the gift shops and coffee shops. Her American children could not sit for very long. They did not understand sitting; they had wandering feet. She hoped they would get back from the pay TV's or the pay toilets or wherever they were spending their money before the plane arrived. If they did not come back soon, she would go look for them. If her son thought he could hide in the men's room, he was wrong.

"Are you all right, Aunt?" asked her niece.

"No, this chair hurts me. Help me pull some chairs together so I can put my feet up."

She unbundled a blanket and spread it out to make a bed for herself. On the floor she had two shopping bags full of canned peaches, real peaches, beans wrapped in taro leaves,[2] cookies, Thermos bottles,[3] enough food for everybody, though only her niece would eat with her. Her bad boy and bad girl were probably sneaking hamburgers, wasting their money. She would scold them.

Many soldiers and sailors sat about, oddly calm, like little boys in cowboy uniforms. (She thought "cowboy" was what you would call a Boy Scout.) They should have been crying <u>hysterically</u> on their way to Vietnam.[4] "If I see one that looks Chinese," she thought, "I'll go over and give him some advice." She sat up suddenly; she had forgotten about her own son, who was even now in Vietnam. Carefully she split her attention, beaming half of it to the ocean, into the water to keep him afloat. He was on a ship. He was in Vietnamese waters. She was sure of it. He and the other children were lying to her. They had said he was in Japan, and then they said he was in the Philippines. But when she sent him her help, she could feel that he was on a ship in Da Nang.[5] Also she had seen the children hide the envelopes that his letters came in.

"Do you think my son is in Vietnam?" she asked her niece, who was dutifully eating.

"No. Didn't your children say he was in the Philippines?"

"Have you ever seen any of his letters with Philippine stamps on them?"

"Oh, yes. Your children showed me one."

---

2. **taro** (te´ rō) **leaves** leaves of an edible tuberous plant widely eaten in Asia.
3. **Thermos** (thur´ mes) **bottles** insulated containers for holding liquids and keeping them warm or cold.
4. **Vietnam** southeast Asian nation where, in the late 1960s when this selection takes place, the U.S. had joined the conflict known as the Vietnam War (1954–1975).
5. **Da Nang** (da nan) city in central Vietnam that was the site of an important U.S. military base during the Vietnam War; also spelled Danang.

from *The Woman Warrior* ◆ 1071

Literary Analysis

Memoirs Whose impressions are described in this passage about "her American children"?

hysterically (hi ster´ i klē) *adv.* in a highly emotional manner

Reading Strategy

Applying Background Information How do footnotes 4 and 5 help to clarify this passage?

⑥ ✔Reading Check

Who is Brave Orchid waiting to meet?

---

❹ Literary Analysis

Memoirs

- Have a volunteer read the bracketed passage aloud.
- Ask the Literary Analysis question on p. 1071: Whose impressions are described in this passage about "her American children"?
  Answer: Brave Orchid's impressions are described in this passage.

▶ Monitor Progress Ask students what Brave Orchid's musings reveal about her impression of American values.
Answer: Brave Orchid seems to believe that American children are restless, impatient, and wasteful.

❺ Reading Strategy

Applying Background Information

- After students read the bracketed passage, ask them to write down questions about it.
  Possible answers: Why were the soldiers being shipped to Vietnam? Where is Da Nang? Why does Brave Orchid believe that her son is in Da Nang?
- Ask students the Reading Strategy question on this page: How do footnotes 4 and 5 help to clarify this passage?
  Answer: The footnotes explain why the boys "should have been crying": They were on their way to the Vietnam War. The footnotes also provide information about Da Nang, which is where Brave Orchid believes her son has been stationed.

❻ ✔Reading Check

Answer: Brave Orchid is waiting to meet her sister, Moon Orchid, whom she has not seen for thirty years.

- Ask students the Reading Strategy
question on p. 1072: What
information in footnote 8 helps to
clarify this passage?
Answer: To understand Brave
Orchid's comparison of "old
immigrants" and "new
immigrants," readers need to
know that Ellis Island is where
many "old immigrants" arrived in
the United States.

- Then, ask students to apply
background knowledge to explain
why Brave Orchid, who lives in
California, would be familiar with
Ellis Island.
Answer: Students should recall
from the author information on p.
1068 that the author's mother,
upon whom Brave Orchid is based,
was an immigrant who arrived in
New York City. She would
therefore have passed through
Ellis Island.

"I wouldn't put it past them to send the letters to some Filipino they know. He puts Manila[6] postmarks on them to fool me."

"Yes, I can imagine them doing that. But don't worry. Your son can take care of himself. All your children can take care of themselves."

"Not him. He's not like other people. Not normal at all. He sticks erasers in his ears, and the erasers are still attached to the pencil stubs. The captain will say, 'Abandon ship,' or 'Watch out for bombs,' and he won't hear. He doesn't listen to orders. I told him to flee to Canada,[7] but he wouldn't go."

She closed her eyes. After a short while, plane and ship under control, she looked again at the children in uniforms. Some of the blond ones looked like baby chicks, their crew cuts like the downy yellow on baby chicks. You had to feel sorry for them even though they were Army and Navy Ghosts.

Suddenly her son and daughter came running. "Come, Mother. The plane's landed early. She's here already." They hurried, folding up their mother's <u>encampment</u>. She was glad her children were not useless. They must have known what this trip to San Francisco was about then. "It's a good thing I made you come early," she said.

Brave Orchid pushed to the front of the crowd. She had to be in front. The passengers were separated from the people waiting for them by glass doors and walls. Immigration Ghosts were stamping papers. The travellers crowded along some conveyor belts to have their luggage searched. Brave Orchid did not see her sister anywhere. She stood watching for four hours. Her children left and came back. "Why don't you sit down?" they asked.

"The chairs are too far away," she said.

"Why don't you sit on the floor then?"

No, she would stand, as her sister was probably standing in a line she could not see from here. Her American children had no feelings and no memory.

❼ To while away time, she and her niece talked about the Chinese passengers. These new immigrants had it easy. On Ellis Island[8] the people were thin after forty days at sea and had no fancy luggage.

"That one looks like her," Brave Orchid would say.

"No, that's not her."

Ellis Island had been made out of wood and iron. Here everything was new plastic, a ghost trick to lure immigrants into feeling safe and spilling their secrets. Then the Alien Office could send them right back. Otherwise, why did they lock her out, not letting her help her sister answer questions and spell her name? At Ellis Island when the ghost asked Brave Orchid what year her husband had cut off his

encampment (en kamp´ ment) *n.* place where a person has set up camp

Reading Strategy
Applying Background
Information What
information in footnote 8
helps to clarify this
passage?

---

6. **Manila** (mə nil´ ə) capital of the Philippines.
7. **flee to Canada** During the Vietnam War era, thousands of Americans fled to Canada to escape the military draft, even though such draft dodgers were subject to prosecution upon returning to the U.S.
8. **Ellis Island** island in the harbor off New York City that was the chief U.S. immigration station from 1892 to 1943.

ENRICHMENT: Literature Connection

Literary Criticism For Advanced Readers

The critic *Sharon Wong* reviewed Kingston's work: "In this beautifully written collection of interrelated reminiscences, Kingston tells the story of a Chinese American woman searching for her past to explain her present…Kingston grows painfully aware that she cannot accept the old values, yet she is somehow saddened by her loss."

Use this question to discuss Wong's review.

How does Kingston use the characters to reveal the conflict within her?

Answer: The two sisters have changed and seem to disapprove of each other; they might be compared as the products of two cultures.

pigtail, a Chinese who was crouching on the floor motioned her not to talk. "I don't know," she had said. If it weren't for that Chinese man, she might not be here today, or her husband either. She hoped some Chinese, a janitor or a clerk, would look out for Moon Orchid. Luggage conveyors fooled immigrants into thinking the Gold Mountain was going to be easy.

Brave Orchid felt her heart jump—Moon Orchid. "There she is," she shouted. But her niece saw it was not her mother at all. And it shocked her to discover the woman her aunt was pointing out. This was a young woman, younger than herself, no older than Moon Orchid the day the sisters parted. "Moon Orchid will have changed a little, of course," Brave Orchid was saying. "She will have learned to wear western clothes." The woman wore a navy blue suit with a bunch of dark cherries at the shoulder.

"No, Aunt," said the niece. "That's not my mother."

"Perhaps not. It's been so many years."

Yes, it is your mother. It must be. Let her come closer, and we can tell. Do you think she's too far away for me to tell, or is it my eyes getting bad?"

"It's too many years gone by," said the niece.

Brave Orchid turned suddenly—another Moon Orchid, this one a neat little woman with a bun. She was laughing at something the person ahead of her in line said. Moon Orchid was just like that, laughing at nothing. "I would be able to tell the difference if one of them would only come closer," Brave Orchid said with tears, which she did not wipe. Two children met the woman with the cherries, and she shook their hands. The other woman was met by a young man. They looked at each other gladly, then walked away side by side.

Up close neither one of those women looked like Moon Orchid at all. "Don't worry, Aunt," said the niece. "I'll know her."

"I'll know her too. I knew her before you did."

The niece said nothing, although she had seen her mother only five years ago. Her aunt liked having the last word.

Finally Brave Orchid's children quit wandering and drooped on a railing. Who knew what they were thinking? At last the niece called out, "I see her! I see her! Mother! Mother!" Whenever the doors parted, she shouted, probably embarrassing the American cousins, but she didn't care. She called out, "Mama! Mama!" until the crack in the sliding doors became too small to let in her voice. "Mama!" What a strange word in an adult voice. Many people turned to see what adult was calling, "Mama!" like a child. Brave Orchid saw an old, old woman jerk her head up, her little eyes blinking confusedly, a woman whose nerves leapt toward the sound anytime she heard "Mama!" Then she relaxed to her own business again. She was a tiny, tiny lady, very thin, with little fluttering hands, and her hair was in a gray knot. She was dressed in a gray wool suit; she wore pearls around

New American Voices

During the 1970s, two vigorous social movements—feminism and multiculturalism—had a major impact on American literature. For the first time, the writings of minority women began to appear in the mainstream press. In 1970, African American author Toni Cade Bambara published an influential anthology of fiction, nonfiction, and poetry entitled *The Black Woman*. In that same year, Toni Morrison, who would later win the 1993 Nobel Prize for literature, published her first novel, *The Bluest Eye*. When Maxine Hong Kingston's *The Woman Warrior* appeared in 1976, it represented yet another utterly new voice. In the decades to follow, these writings influenced the work of younger minority women, including Julia Alvarez, Sandra Cisneros, Amy Tan, and Gish Jen. Thus, a new sub-genre emerged, giving voice to women of all backgrounds and enriching the landscape of American literature.

☑ Reading Check

How does Moon Orchid's physical appeerence compare with those of the women Brave Orchid mistakes for her sister?

from The Woman Warrior ◆ 1073

❽ **Background**

Amy Tan

Like Maxine Hong Kingston, Amy Tan is a Chinese American and a Californian. Writing in the wake of Kingston's success, Tan has published numerous short stories, essays, and novels. Her first novel, *The Joy Luck Club* (1989), received critical acclaim and was made into a film in 1993.

In her work, Tan, like Kingston, explores the cultural implications of being a Chinese American. Her characters often struggle to understand and reconcile threads of the two disparate cultures.

❾ **Critical Thinking**

Interpret

- Have a volunteer recall what the phrase "Gold Mountain" means.
  Answer: "Gold Mountain" is a term the Chinese immigrants used for the United States.

- Ask students to explain what this term implies about the immigrants' view of the United States.
  Answer: The term implies that the immigrants expected to find great wealth in their new home.

- Ask why Brave Orchid thinks that luggage conveyors fooled immigrants into thinking that life in America was going to be easy.
  Answer: Because the conveyors transported her luggage without her having to expend any energy, Brave Orchid was fooled into thinking all the other difficult parts of her new life would be taken care of as easily.

❿ **☑ Reading Check**

Answer: Moon Orchid is small, thin, and much older than the women for whom Brave Orchid mistakes her.

CUSTOMIZE INSTRUCTION FOR UNIVERSAL ACCESS

For Less Proficient Readers	For Gifted/Talented Students	For Advanced Readers
Have students make a chart on which to record the feelings of the characters as they wait for Moon Orchid to arrive. How are the niece's feelings different from those of her cousins? What conflicting feelings might Brave Orchid have?	Have students perform a reader's theater presentation of pp. 1072–1073. Volunteers should take the parts of the narrator, the niece, and Brave Orchid. Urge students to consider the characters' feelings as they decide how to interpret their parts.	Have students analyze in detail Brave Orchid's feelings at this point in the story. What might be some of her hopes and fears about her sister? Why does she seem unable to realize that Moon Orchid is quite old? Ask students to discuss their ideas with classmates and then record them in writing.

Latin Root –aud-

- Write *inaudibly* on the board and circle the root -aud-. Tell students that -aud- is a Latin root that means "hearing" or "sound."

- Have students give other examples of words with this root. Write their suggestions on the board and circle the root -aud-. Some words with -aud- include the following: *auditory, audience, audition, audiotape,* and *auditorium.*

- Finally, have students explain how the root -aud- helps them understand the meaning of three words on the list.

❶❷ ►Critical Viewing

Answer: In Hong Kong, nearly 98 per cent of the population is ethnic Han Chinese; in 1990, about 30 per cent of San Francisco's population was of Asian descent. In San Francisco, Moon Orchid will probably experience a wider variety of cultures and values than she did in Hong Kong.

her neck and in her earlobes. Moon Orchid *would* travel with her jewels showing. Brave Orchid momentarily saw, like a larger, younger outline around this old woman, the sister she had been waiting for. The familiar dim halo faded, leaving the woman so old, so gray. So old. Brave Orchid pressed against the glass. *That* old lady? Yes, that old lady facing the ghost who stamped her papers without questioning her was her sister. Then, without noticing her family, Moon Orchid walked smiling over to the Suitcase Inspector Ghost, who took her boxes apart, pulling out puffs of tissue. From where she was, Brave Orchid could not see what her sister had chosen to carry across the ocean. She wished her sister would look her way. Brave Orchid thought that if she were entering a new country, she would be at the windows. Instead Moon Orchid hovered over the unwrapping, surprised at each reappearance as if she were opening presents after a birthday party.

"Mama!" Moon Orchid's daughter kept calling. Brave Orchid said to her children, "Why don't you call your aunt too? Maybe she'll hear us if all of you call out together." But her children slunk away. Maybe that shame-face they so often wore was American politeness.

"Mama!" Moon Orchid's daughter called again, and this time her mother looked right at her. She left her bundles in a heap and came running. "Hey!" the Customs Ghost yelled at her. She went back to clear up her mess, talking <u>inaudibly</u> to her daughter all the while. Her daughter pointed toward Brave Orchid. And at last Moon Orchid looked at her—two old women with faces like mirrors.

inaudibly (in ôd′ə blē) *adv.* in a manner that cannot be heard

▼ Critical Viewing ❶❷
How might life in the city of San Francisco, shown in this image, compare or contrast with life in Hong Kong from where Moon Orchid has just arrived? **[Compare and Contrast]**

1074 ◆ *Prosperity and Protest (1946–Present)*

✷ ENRICHMENT: Geography Connection

Hong Kong

Hong Kong has been an administrative region of China since 1997, when it passed to Chinese sovereignty from Britain. The British control of Hong Kong began in 1842, when China was forced to cede it after the First Opium War.

The government of Hong Kong is headed by a chief executive who is selected by a committee appointed by China. Members of a Legislative Council, whose members assist the chief executive in making policy

decisions, are elected by the people of Hong Kong.

Hong Kong consists of a mainland portion, which is located on the southeastern coast of China, and about 235 islands. The total area is only 422 square miles. The city of Hong Kong, also known as Victoria, is located on Hong Kong Island and is home to both the government offices and the central business district.

Their hands reached out as if to touch the other's face, then returned to their own, the fingers checking the grooves in the forehead and along the sides of the mouth. Moon Orchid, who never understood the <u>gravity</u> of things, started smiling and laughing, pointing at Brave Orchid. Finally Moon Orchid gathered up her stuff, strings hanging and papers loose, and met her sister at the door, where they shook hands, <u>oblivious</u> to blocking the way.

"You're an old woman," said Brave Orchid.

"Aiaa. *You're* an old woman."

"But *you* are really old. Surely, you can't say that about me. I'm not old the way you're old."

"But you really are old. You're one year older than I am."

"Your hair is white and your face all wrinkled."

"You're so skinny."

"You're so fat."

"Fat women are more beautiful than skinny women."

The children pulled them out of the door-way. One of Brave Orchid's children brought the car from the parking lot, and

gravity (grav´ i tē) *n.* seriousness

oblivious (ə bliv´ ē əs) *adj.* lacking all awareness

☑ **Reading Check**

Why is the reunion between Brave Orchid and her sister delayed?

from *The Woman Warrior* ◆ 1075

⓭ **Critical Thinking**

Infer

• Have two volunteers read the dialogue between Brave Orchid and Moon Orchid.

• Ask students what they can infer about Brave Orchid and Moon Orchid's relationship from the dialogue on this page.
Answer: Brave Orchid and Moon Orchid do not openly demonstrate their affection for one another, as shown by their formal handshake. However, they do talk to each other in a blunt and open manner.

⓮ ☑ **Reading Check**

Answer: The reunion is delayed as Moon Orchid waits to enter the terminal, passes through customs, and has her luggage examined.

CUSTOMIZE INSTRUCTION FOR UNIVERSAL ACCESS

For English Learners	For Gifted/Talented Students	For Advanced Readers
Point out that the three main characters in the memoir are all women. In describing them, Kingston frequently uses the pronouns *her* and *she*. To avoid confusion, suggest that students replace pronouns with proper nouns to clarify which character is being described.	Have students invent and perform a dialogue between Brave Orchid and Moon Orchid in which the two women say what's really on their minds, without the constraints of custom and habit. Have the audience determine whether the dialogue is convincing, and why.	Challenge students to create, from their own knowledge or research, additional footnotes to explain Brave Orchid's references to American culture and to the events of the memoir's historical setting (the late 1960s).

Review and Assess

1. Students should be prepared to explain their responses.

2. **(a)** Family members include Brave Orchid, who is anxiously awaiting her sister's arrival; Brave Orchid's niece, who is attentive to her aunt and keeps her company; and Brave Orchid's children, who restlessly roam the airport. **(b)** Brave Orchid has not embraced American culture the way her children have.

3. **(a)** Brave Orchid attempts to keep her sister's plane in the air and her son's ship afloat. **(b)** She seems to be a reserved, dignified woman who clings to traditional Chinese values and customs.

4. **(a)** Brave Orchid cannot believe how old her sister has grown. **(b)** Possible response: They fall back into old habits, bickering with one another as they did in their youth.

5. **(a)** Brave Orchid seems to feel that they are inferior to China and its culture. **(b)** It suggests that immigrants struggle to hold on to their cultural heritage while making their way in a new culture. Their children are often caught between the old and new cultures, and may feel that they do not fully belong in either.

6. Students may suggest that Kingston succeeds in showing how Brave Orchid is still staunchly Chinese in her attitudes and behavior. They may cite Brave Orchid's supply of Chinese foods, her insistence on standing for hours as her sister goes through customs, and the way she formally shakes her sister's hand when they finally meet.

---

the other heaved the luggage into the trunk. They put the two old ladies and the niece in the back seat. All the way home—across the Bay Bridge,[9] over the Diablo hills,[10] across the San Joaquin River[11] to the valley, the valley moon so white at dusk—all the way home, the two sisters exclaimed every time they turned to look at each other, "Aiaa! How old!"

Brave Orchid forgot that she got sick in cars, that all vehicles but palanquins[12] made her dizzy. "You're so old," she kept saying. "How did you get so old?"

Brave Orchid had tears in her eyes. But Moon Orchid said, "You look older than I. You *are* older than I," and again she'd laugh. "You're wearing an old mask to tease me." It surprised Brave Orchid that after thirty years she could still get annoyed at her sister's silliness.

---

9. **Bay Bridge** one of the bridges across San Francisco Bay.
10. **Diablo** (dē äb´ lō) **hills** hills outside San Francisco.
11. **San Joaquin** (wô kēn´) **River** river of central California; its valley is one of the state's richest agricultural areas.
12. **palanquins** (pal´ ən kēnz´) hand-carried covered litters once widely used to transport people in China and elsewhere in eastern Asia.

Review and Assess

Thinking About the Selection

1. **Respond:** With which character do you identify the most? Why?

2. **(a) Recall:** Identify the family members waiting for Moon Orchid at the airport, and briefly describe each one's behavior. **(b) Interpret:** What do Brave Orchid's thoughts about her children's behavior reveal about her?

3. **(a) Recall:** What two things does Brave Orchid try to keep safe by applying her willpower? **(b) Connect:** What does this behavior reveal about Brave Orchid's worldview?

4. **(a) Interpret:** What is Brave Orchid's main impression when she finally sees Moon Orchid? **(b) Draw Conclusions:** When the two sisters finally meet, why do they speak to each other as they do?

5. **(a) Infer:** What seems to be Brave Orchid's attitude toward America and American culture? **(b) Apply:** What does this selection suggest about the conflicts that face immigrants and the children of immigrants in America?

6. **Evaluate:** Do you think Kingston succeeds in evoking the lives of people from very different cultures? Explain your answer.

ASSESSMENT PRACTICE: Writing Skills

Punctuation   (For more practice, see Test Preparation Workbook, p. 65.)

Many tests require students to identify the type of error in a sentence. Use the following sample test item to demonstrate.

Immigrants who arrived at Ellis Island had often spent months at sea; and were thin and weak by the time they landed.

Read the passage and decide which type of error, if any, appears in the underlined section.

A Spelling error

B Capitalization error

C Punctuation error

D No error

C is the correct answer. The underlined section contains a semicolon separating two parts of a compound predicate. Remind students that semicolons are used to separate independent clauses.

Review and Assess

Literary Analysis

Memoirs

1. Using a chart like the one shown, list details to show how this **memoir** incorporates historical details with personal ones.

Historical Details	Personal Details

2. (a) Cite two memories Brave Orchid has while waiting at the airport. (b) Are these memories typical features of a memoir? Why or why not?

3. Explain how a memoir such as Kingston's could be meaningful to many women growing up in a bicultural world.

Connecting Literary Elements

4. Whose impressions provide the **third-person limited narration** of this excerpt?

5. Brave Orchid is Kingston's mother. (a) What role does Kingston herself play in this excerpt? (b) What techniques more commonly found in fiction does Kingston use to create her mother as a literary character?

6. How might Brave Orchid's story have been different if the narrative had been written with her voice, using *I* instead of *she*? Explain.

Reading Strategy

Applying Background Information

7. (a) From what province in China might Moon Orchid be coming? (b) What evidence did you use to draw your conclusion?

8. What does the narrator mean by (a) Army and Navy Ghosts? (b) Customs Ghosts?

9. (a) Where might the family be headed in the last paragraphs? (b) How do you know?

Extend Understanding

10. **Social Studies Connection:** Immigration brings with it the timeless struggle between tradition and change. Choose a culture—your own or another—and discuss the conflicts that people of this culture are likely to face when they come to live in America.

from *The Woman Warrior* ◆ 1077

✹ ENRICHMENT: Further Reading

Other Works by Maxine Hong Kingston

China Men

Tripmaster Monkey

 Take It to the Net

Visit www.phschool.com for more information on the author.

Quick Review

Memoirs are usually first-person nonfiction narratives that recount historically or personally significant events in which the writer was a participant or an eyewitness.

Narratives using the **limited third-person point of view** relate the inner thoughts and feelings of only one character.

When you **apply background information,** you read information in book jackets, forewords, introductions, and footnotes to gain better understanding of the text.

 Take It to the Net
www.phschool.com
Take the interactive self-test online to check your understanding of the selection.

Answers for p. 1077

Review and Assess

1. Historical detail: Vietnam War Brave Orchid's son is in the Navy. Historical detail: Ellis Island was the chief immigration station of the U.S. Personal detail: Brave Orchid came through Ellis Island. Historical detail: Chinese men wore pigtails. Personal detail: Brave Orchid is asked when her husband cut off his pigtail.

2. **(a)** She remembers entering the U.S. through Ellis Island. She remembers telling her son to go to Canada rather than be drafted. **(b)** The memories are not typical in that they recall events in which the writer was not directly involved. The memories are, on the other hand, personally significant to the subject of the memoir, Brave Orchid—a typical feature of the events recounted in memoirs.

3. The struggle to hold onto one culture while embracing another is probably typical of many women growing up in a bicultural world.

4. The narrator's impressions provide the third-person limited narration for the selection.

5. **(a)** Kingston plays the role of the narrator. **(b)** Kingston imagines not only Brave Orchid's actions, but her thoughts and emotions, as if she were a literary character that Kingston had created.

6. The reader would have known more about the reasons Brave Orchid acted as she did, but would not have been sure whether she was relating events accurately.

7. **(a)** Moon Orchid is probably coming from Canton. **(b)** The author's biography reveals that her family came from this region.

8. **(a)** The narrator means white soldiers and sailors. **(b)** The narrator means white customs officers.

9. **(a)** They are probably heading to Stockton, California. **(b)** The author's biography reveals that her family relocated to this area.

10. Many students will comment on differences in values between American culture and the culture they choose.

Answers for p. 1078

❶ Vocabulary Development

Word Analysis

1. Sound is recorded and played back on an audiocassette.
2. *Auditory* describes something that relates to hearing.
3. An auditorium is where one hears musical or theatrical performances.
4. An audition is a chance to be heard.

Spelling Strategy

1. suddenly
2. hysterically

Fluency: Sentence Completion

1. encampment
2. Oblivious
3. inaudibly
4. hysterically
5. gravity

❷ Grammar and Style Lesson

"My sister wrote, 'I am coming to America,'" Brave Orchid told her family. "She asked, 'Will you be able to pick me up?' I told her, 'Yes, I will leave my house before your plane takes off from Hong Kong.' Do you think she knows I am excited?"

Writing Application

The paragraph must include properly punctuated quotations within quotations.

Integrate Language Skills

❶ Vocabulary Development Lesson

Word Analysis: Latin Root -aud-

The Latin word root *-aud-* indicates "hearing" or "sound." The adverb *inaudibly* means "in a tone too low to be heard." Explain how the meaning of the root is connected to each of these words.

1. audiocassette
2. auditory
3. auditorium
4. audition

Spelling Strategy

When adding the suffix *-ly* or *-less* to a word ending in *l*, or when adding *-ness* to a word ending in *n*, keep all the letters of the base word. For example, *tail* becomes *tailless*.

Add *-ly*, *-less*, or *-ness* to each word in italics to create a new word that fits the clue.

1. happening all of a *sudden*
2. with *hysterical* feelings

Fluency: Sentence Completion

Review the vocabulary list on page 1069. Then, copy each sentence, replacing the blank with the appropriate word.

1. We left our homey ____?____ and hiked up the mountain.
2. ____?____ to the clock, she worked on into the night.
3. When she replied ____?____, I asked her to speak up.
4. The boy yelled ____?____ when he thought he was lost.
5. The ____?____ of the situation silenced all bickering.

❷ Grammar Lesson

Punctuating a Quotation Within a Quotation

For clarity, use single quotation marks to enclose a quotation within a quotation.

> **Example:** "The captain will say, 'Abandon ship,' or 'Watch out for bombs,' and he won't hear."

Remember to also place commas and periods inside closing quotation marks, but keep colons and semicolons outside. Question marks and exclamation points can be placed either inside or outside the quotation marks, depending on the words to which they apply.

Practice Copy this paragraph about the characters in *The Woman Warrior*, adding all the missing single quotation marks.

"My sister wrote, I am coming to America," Brave Orchid told her family. "She asked, Will you be able to pick me up? I told her, Yes, I will leave my house before your plane takes off from Hong Kong. Do you think she knows I am excited?"

Writing Application Write a second paragraph in which Brave Orchid quotes her sister. Use single quotation marks to indicate quotations within quotations. Punctuate according to the rules that apply.

W̶G Prentice Hall Writing and Grammar Connection: Chapter 27, Section 4

TEACHING RESOURCES

The following resources can be used to enrich or extend the instruction for pp. 1078–1079.

Vocabulary

- 📓 **Selection Support,** Build Vocabulary, p. 270
- 📓 **Vocabulary and Spelling Practice Book** (Use this booklet for skills enrichment.)

Grammar

- 📓 **Selection Support:** Grammar and Style, p. 271 ■
- W̶G **Writing and Grammar,** Ruby Level, p. 726
- 📖 **Daily Language Practice Transparencies** ■

Writing

- W̶G **Writing and Grammar,** Ruby Level, p. 800
- ◉ **Writing and Grammar iText CD-ROM**
- 📖 **Writing Models and Graphic Organizers on Transparencies,** pp. 83–85 ■

 BLOCK SCHEDULING: Resources marked with this symbol provide varied instruction during 90-minute blocks.

❸ Writing Lesson

Character Analysis

In an essay, analyze Brave Orchid's character. Identify three or four of her personality traits, and connect them to her background and behavior. Cite appropriate supporting examples from the selection.

Prewriting	List Brave Orchid's character traits, using such words as *bossy* or *nervous*. Next to each trait, note the background, attitudes, and behaviors connected with them. Then, select the traits you will write about.
Drafting	In the first paragraph of your essay, introduce Brave Orchid and *The Woman Warrior*. Include information about where she was born, her culture, her emigration to America, and her character. In the body paragraphs of your essay, address each one of those elements.
Revising	Highlight Brave Orchid's character traits and be sure you have connected them with her behaviors. To do so, cite examples from the selection.

Model: Revising to Provide Support

Because of her hard life, Brave Orchid was skeptical about American conveniences. *For example, she felt that the luggage conveyors at American airports fooled immigrants into thinking life would be much easier here.*

> Added information from the selection supports a specific idea.

 Prentice Hall Writing and Grammar Connection: Chapter 28, Section 3

❹ Extension Activities

Listening and Speaking When *The Woman Warrior* won a 1976 award for nonfiction, many debated whether or not it fit that category. Hold a **panel discussion** to address the issue. Use the following tips:

- Identify criteria to determine whether the work fits the definition of nonfiction.
- Quote Kingston's own comments on the topic.

Present the discussion, inviting questions from classmates. **[Group Activity]**

Research and Technology Conduct research to prepare a written **immigration report** about the arrival of Chinese immigrants in the United States. Find at least two historical records to analyze. Supplement your report with a chart of statistical information. Present your findings to your class.

Take It to the Net www.phschool.com

Go online for an additional research activity using the Internet.

---

❸ Writing Lesson

- Briefly discuss a favorite character from literature with students. What were the character's outstanding traits? How did the character demonstrate these traits?

- Lead students into a discussion of Brave Orchid. Remind students to support their descriptions of Brave Orchid with specific examples from the selection.

- Students might want ot use the Analysis Map, pp. 83–85 of **Writing Models and Graphic Organizers on Transparencies**, to record their ideas about Brave Orchid.

- Use the Writing Lesson to guide students in writing their character analyses.

- Use the Response to Literature rubric in **Performance Assessment and Portfolio Management**, p. 23, to assess students' analyses.

❹ Research and Technology

- Suggest that students work in small groups to complete their projects.

- Encourage students to use the Internet as a source of up-to-date information. However, stress to students that they must evaluate Internet sources carefully. Information from the official Ellis Island Web site, for example, may be presumed to be reliable. Information from an individual's Web site, on the other hand, should be corroborated. Urge students to corroborate statistics from at least three sources before considering them reliable.

CUSTOMIZE INSTRUCTION
For Universal Access

To address different learning styles, use the activities suggested in the **Extension Activities** booklet, p. 62.

For Verbal/Linguistic and Visual/Spatial Learners use Activity 5. For Verbal/Linguistic Learners, use Activity 6.

For Interpersonal and Visual/Spatial Learners, use Activity 7.

ASSESSMENT RESOURCES

The following resources can be used to assess students' knowledge and skills.

Selection Assessment
- 📖 **Formal Assessment**, pp. 269–271
- 📖 **Open Book Test**, pp. 184–186
- 📼 **Got It! Assessment Videotapes**, Tape 5
- 💿 **Test Bank Software**

📖 **Take It to the Net**
Visit www.phschool.com for self-tests and additional questions on *The Woman Warrior*.

Writing Rubric
- 📖 **Performance Assessment and Portfolio Management**, p. 23

PRENTICE HALL ASSESSMENT SYSTEM
- 📖 Workbook
- 📖 Skill Book
- 📄 Transparencies
- 💿 CD-ROM

Antojos

Lesson Objectives

1. **To analyze and respond to literary elements**
   - Literary Analysis: Plot
   - Connecting Literary Elements: Flashback

2. **To read, comprehend, analyze, and critique a short story**
   - Reading Strategy: Identifying With a Character
   - Reading Check Questions
   - Review and Assess Questions

3. **To develop word analysis skills, fluency, and systematic vocabulary**
   - Vocabulary Development Lesson: Words From Spanish

4. **To understand and apply written and oral language conventions**
   - Spelling Strategy
   - Grammar and Style Lesson: Absolute Phrases
   - Assessment Practice (ATE)

5. **To understand and apply appropriate writing and research strategies**
   - Writing Lesson: New Version of the Story
   - Extension Activity: Multimedia Report

6. **To understand and apply listening and speaking strategies**
   - Extension Activity: Cause–and–Effect Flowchart

STEP-BY-STEP TEACHING GUIDE	PACING GUIDE
PRETEACH	
Motivate Students and Provide Background	
Use the Motivation activity (ATE p. 1080)	5 min.
Read and discuss author and background features (SE/ATE pp. 1080, 1083) [A]	10 min.
Introduce the Concepts	
Introduce the Literary Analysis and Reading Strategy (SE/ATE p. 1081) [A]	15 min.
Pronounce the vocabulary words and read their definitions (SE p. 1081)	5 min.
TEACH	
Monitor Comprehension	
Informally monitor comprehension by circulating while students read independently or in groups [A]	30 min.
Monitor students' comprehension with the Reading Check notes (SE/ATE pp. 1083, 1085, 1087, 1089, 1091)	as students read
Develop vocabulary with Vocabulary notes (SE pp. 1084, 1086–1089, 1091; ATE p. 1088)	as students read
Develop Understanding	
Develop students' understanding of plot with the Literary Analysis annotations (SE/ATE pp. 1083, 1084, 1088, 1089, 1091) [A]	5 min.
Develop students' ability to identify with a character by using the Reading Strategy annotations (SE/ATE pp. 1084, 1086, 1088, 1089, 1090, 1091)	5 min.
ASSESS	
Assess Mastery	
Assess students' mastery of the Reading Strategy and Literary Analysis by having them answer the Review and Assess questions (SE/ATE p. 1093)	15 min.
Use one or more of the print and media Assessment Resources (ATE p. 1095) [A]	up to 45 min.
EXTEND	
Apply Understanding	
Have students complete the Vocabulary Development Lesson and the Grammar and Style Lesson (SE p. 1094) [A]	20 min.
Apply students' ability to use details to create a vivid portrayal by using the Writing Lesson (SE/ATE p. 1095) [A]	45 min.
Apply students' understanding using one or more of the Extension Activities (SE p. 1095)	20–90 min.

 ACCELERATED INSTRUCTION:
Use the strategies and activities identified with an [A].

UNIVERSAL ACCESS
● = Below Level Students
▲ = On-Level Students
■ = Above Level Students

Time and Resource Manager

Reading Level: Easy
Average Number of Instructional Days: 4

PRINT 📖	**TRANSPARENCIES**	**TECHNOLOGY** 💿 🎧
• **Beyond Literature,** Cross-Curricular Connection: World Languages, p. 63 ▲ ■		• **Interest Grabber Video,** Tape 6 ● ▲ ■
• **Selection Support Workbook:** ● ▲ ■ Literary Analysis, p. 277 Reading Strategy, p. 276 Build Vocabulary, p. 274	• **Literary Analysis and Reading Transparencies,** pp. 125 and 126 ● ▲ ■	
• **Authors In Depth,** The American Experience, p. 179 ■		• **Listening to Literature** ● ▲ ■ Audiocassettes, Side 37 Audio CDs, CD 21
• **Literatura en español** ● ▲ • **Literary Analysis for Enrichment** ■		
• **Formal Assessment:** Selection Test, pp. 272–274 ● ▲ ■ • **Open Book Test,** pp. 187–189 ● ▲ ■ • **Performance Assessment and Portfolio Management,** p. 15 ● ▲ ■ • (ASSESSMENT SYSTEM) ● ▲ ■	(PRENTICE HALL ASSESSMENT SYSTEM) ● ▲ ■ Skills Practice Answers and Explanations on Transparencies	• **Test Bank Software** ● ▲ ■ • **Got It! Assessment Videotapes,** Tape 5 ● ▲
• **Selection Support Workbook:** ● ▲ ■ Grammar and Style, p. 275 • **Writing and Grammar,** Ruby Level ● ▲ ■ • **Extension Activities,** p. 63 ● ▲ ■	• **Daily Language Practice Transparencies** ● ▲ • **Writing Models and Graphic Organizers on Transparencies,** pp. 17–23 ● ▲ ■	• **Writing and Grammar iText CD-ROM** ● ▲ ■ 💻 *Take It to the Net* www.phschool.com

BLOCK SCHEDULING: Use one 90-minute class period to preteach the selection and have students read it. Use a second 90-minute class period to assess students' mastery of skills and have them complete one of the Extension Activities.

Step-by-Step Teaching Guide for pp. 1080–1081

Motivation

Like a travel diary, this story of a young woman's journey to her homeland is immediate and engaging. To entice travelers to visit particular places, travel agents often show photographs and excerpt travel diaries. Invite your students into the world of the Dominican Republic by displaying some photos of the region and travel advertisements. Write these passages on the board:

"She hadn't had her favorite *antojo*, guavas, since her last trip seven years ago."

"She ate right on the spot, relishing the slightly bumpy feel of the skin in her hand, devouring the crunchy, sweet, white meat."

Ask students to describe journeys they have taken and identify moments they found enjoyable.

■ Interest Grabber Video

As an alternative, play "Julia Alvarez on Coming to America" on Tape 6 to engage student interest.

❶ Background

More About the Author

Reared in a Spanish-speaking home, as a girl Julia Alvarez failed English classes again and again. How ironic that she is now a fluent and successful writer of novels and poetry in English!

Alvarez's work draws heavily on her own experiences and those of her family as she explores themes of family expectations conflicting with personal ambitions and the difficulties of living in two cultures. When interviewer Marny Requa asked her whether it was inspiring to have a foot in both Anglo and Latino cultures, Alvarez replied," . . . It was a burden because I felt torn—I wanted to be part of the other . . . Now I see the richness. Part of what I want to show with my work is that complexity, that richness. I don't want it to be simplistic and either/or."

Prepare to Read

❶ Antojos

Julia Alvarez
(b. 1950)

Julia Alvarez was born in New York City but raised in the Dominican Republic. When her father's involvement in a plot to overthrow that country's dictator, Rafael Trujillo, was uncovered, the family was forced to flee to the United States. It was 1960. When Alvarez arrived in the United States, she spoke only Spanish and had few friends. "I came into English as a ten-year-old from the Dominican Republic, and I consider this radical uprooting from my culture, my native language, my country, the reason I began writing," Alvarez once explained.

Writing to Ease the Pain While moving to a new country changed her life forever, Alvarez quickly found her voice as a writer. She said, "I landed, not in the United States, but in the English language. That became my new home . . . which you never had to lose, because it was a portable homeland." As a young adult, Alvarez found that writing helped her deal with the pain of adjustment to a new culture and language. "In high school, I fell in love with how words can make you feel complete in a way that I hadn't felt complete since leaving the island," she said. Alvarez found herself turning more and more to writing "as the one place where I felt I belonged and could make sense of myself, my life, all that was happening to me."

After graduating from college, where she was awarded several poetry prizes, Alvarez earned a masters degree in creative writing at Syracuse University. She went on to join the Kentucky Arts Commission's poetry-in-the-schools program. For two years, she traveled around Kentucky teaching poetry. She then held a variety of teaching jobs before settling in Vermont as a Professor of English at Middlebury College.

Writing to Understand For Alvarez, writing "is happening all the time. When you go outside and you see the way a blade of grass bends in the breeze—when you're a writer, you're thinking about how that's happening." She also says that writing "is a way to understand yourself. You learn how you feel about things, but you're also making your little statement about things, and that makes you feel a little bit more powerful."

Alvarez's poetry often focuses on her personal experiences and on details of daily life as well as her Caribbean heritage. She has published two volumes of poetry, *Homecoming* (1984) and *The Other Side* (1995).

A Storytelling Tradition After *Homecoming* was published, Alvarez began to focus on a new area of writing: fiction. "My own island background was steeped in a tradition of storytelling that I wanted to explore in prose," Alvarez explained. The move to prose proved fruitful, for Alvarez has won fame for three novels rooted in Hispanic American tradition: *How the García Girls Lost Their Accents* (1991), *In the Time of the Butterflies* (1994), and *¡Yo!* (1997). Her fiction, like her poetry, can be viewed as semi-autobiographical, dealing with both the immigrant experience and her own bicultural identity.

As the story "Antojos" illustrates, Alvarez has also shown that she is a talented short-story writer. Like her novels, "Antojos" relates the story of a Dominican woman who has settled in the United States. The story captures what happens when she revisits her homeland and confronts the culture she had left behind.

1080 ◆ *Prosperity and Protest (1946–Present)*

TEACHING RESOURCES

The following resources can be used to enrich or extend the instruction for pp. 1080–1081.

Motivation

■ Interest Grabber Video, Tape 6

Background

📖 **Beyond Literature,** p. 63

 Take It to the Net
Visit www.phschool.com for background and hotlinks for the selection.

Literary Analysis

 Literary Analysis and Reading Transparencies, Plot, p. 126

Reading

📖 **Selection Support:** Reading Strategy, p. 276; Build Vocabulary, p. 274

 **Literary Analysis and Reading Transparencies,** Identifying With a Character, p. 125

■ BLOCK SCHEDULING: Resources marked with this symbol provide varied instruction during 90-minute blocks.

Preview

Connecting to the Literature

If you have ever felt vulnerable in the presence of strangers whose motives might be questionable, you will understand how the main character in this story feels. Read to discover if her fears are justified.

Literary Analysis
Plot

Plot is the sequence of events in a literary work. In most narrative literature, the plot involves characters and a central conflict. Most plots follow a specific sequence, often referred to as the dramatic arc:

- **Exposition:** The basic situation is introduced.
- **Inciting incident:** The central conflict or struggle is revealed.
- **Development:** The conflict increases in intensity.
- **Climax:** The conflict reaches its most intense point.
- **Denouement:** Information is given about events that occur after the climax.
- **Resolution:** The story ends with details that reveal insight.

Plot events that lead up to the climax comprise the rising action. The events that follow the climax comprise the falling action.

Connecting Literary Elements

A **flashback** is an interruption in the chronological presentation of events in a story. Writers use flashbacks to highlight a scene or event from an earlier time, thus providing valuable information about the characters' backgrounds, personalities, and motives. When you come to a flashback in "Antojos," consider what it reveals about the character and her situation.

Reading Strategy
Identifying With a Character

You can often understand literature better if you **identify with a character** who appears in the work. Think about what you and the character have in common. For example, as you read "Antojos," note qualities you share with the main character, Yolanda. List similarities in a chart like the one shown.

Vocabulary Development

dissuade (di swād') *v.* convince someone not to do something (p. 1084)

loath (lōth) *adj.* reluctant (p. 1086)

appease (ə pēz') *v.* satisfy (p. 1087)

machetes (mə shet' ēz) *n.* large heavy knives with broad blades (p. 1088)

collusion (kə lōō' zhən) *n.* secret agreement; conspiracy (p. 1089)

docile (däs' əl) *adj.* easy to direct or manage; obedient (p. 1089)

enunciated (ē nun' sē āt' əd) *v.* pronounced; stated precisely (p. 1091)

Yolanda	Me
Background	
Personality	
Attitudes	
Motives	
Behavior	

Antojos ◆ 1081

---

❷ Literary Analysis
Plot

- Tell students to focus on the dramatic arc of the plot, the rising action before the climax and the falling action after it, as they read "Antojos." They should decide whether the story includes all the classic stages and follows the plot order of exposition, inciting incident, development, climax, denouement and resolution.

- Go over each stage in the plot sequence from exposition to resolution. Have a volunteer define the term for each stage of the plot and give an example from his or her reading, preferably from a work that the class has read together.

- Mention that "Antojos" includes several flashbacks, interruptions in the chronological order of events. Ask students to note at which junctures in the story the flashbacks occur.

❸ Reading Strategy
Identifying With a Character

- Explain that the main character, Yolanda, is a young woman who has returned to the Dominican Republic for a visit after living in the United States for many years. Might she be similar in any way to themselves?

- Draw students' attention to the chart on p. 1081. Ask them to create a similar chart on which to record any similarities they discover between Yolanda and themselves as they read the story.

Vocabulary Development

- Pronounce each vocabulary word for students, and read the definitions as a class. Have students identify any words with which they are already familiar.

CUSTOMIZE INSTRUCTION FOR UNIVERSAL ACCESS

For Less Proficient Readers	For English Learners	For Advanced Readers
Before students begin reading the story, have them listen to the story on audiotape or CD. Then, review the footnoted Spanish words and the rest of the footnoted vocabulary with them. Students might also benefit from seeing pictures of the fruit mentioned in the story, especially the guava, which is the character's favorite *antojo*.	Have students listen to the story on audiotape or CD before they read it. Students whose first language is Spanish may be able to help their classmates understand both the Spanish words in the story and the point of view of the main character, her aunts, and the campesinos she meets on the road.	Have students analyze the language the various characters in the story use. Ask students to answer this question: What assumptions can readers make about the characters from the way they speak?

 E-Teach

Visit E-Teach at www.phschool.com for teachers' essays on how to teach, with questions and answers.

Step-by-Step Teaching Guide for pp. 1082–1092

CUSTOMIZE INSTRUCTION
For Visual/Spatial Learners
Have students make maps of Yolanda's journey. The purpose of the maps is not to record Yolanda's exact route, but to visualize the various settings through which she passes.

❶ About the Selection
If students have ever taken a journey of any significant length alone, they will recognize the mix of confidence, anticipation, and fear that the main character, Yolanda, experiences in this story. Yolanda has returned to her Caribbean Island homeland intent on demonstrating her adult independence from the family. As she travels through the countryside, aware of the region's unpredictable political climate, Yolanda must decide whom to trust and whom to fear. By facing some risks and making choices, she begins to consider how high a price she is willing to pay for her independence.

❷ ▶Critical Viewing
Answer: The painting shows an abundant and beautiful arrangement of fruit: colorful, ripe, and inviting. In a similar way, Yolanda thinks of guavas as inviting, craving them all the more since it has been so long since she has eaten them in her homeland.

❶

Antojos ¹

JULIA ALVAREZ

Fruit Vendor, 1951, Olga Costa, Museo de Arte Moderno, Mexico

❷ ▲**Critical Viewing** What elements of this artist's portrayal of fruit mirror Yolanda's feelings about guavas? **[Compare]**

1. **Antojos** (än tō´ hōs) Spanish for "cravings." The story explores the additional connotations of the word.

1082 ◆ *Prosperity and Protest (1946–Present)*

TEACHING RESOURCES

The following resources can be used to enrich or extend the instruction for pp. 1082–1092.

Literary Analysis
📖 **Selection Support:** Literary Analysis, p. 126

Reading
🎧 **Listening to Literature Audiocassettes,** Side 37 ■

💿 **Listening to Literature Audio CDs,** CD 21 ■

■ **BLOCK SCHEDULING:** Resources marked with this symbol provide varied instruction during 90-minute blocks.

Background

Alvarez's homeland, the Dominican Republic, won independence in 1844 after a successful rebellion against Haitian rule. Since then, however, the country has suffered through several dictatorships and frequent foreign domination. One of the most ruthless dictators was Rafael Trujillo, who ruled the country from 1930 until he was assassinated in 1961. Julia Alvarez's father was part of the underground movement against Trujillo, and it was this involvement that forced the Alvarez family to flee the country. Three months after the family left, three of her father's co-conspirators were killed. Alvarez's emigration experience and her feelings of displacement and exile have influenced much of her writing, including the story that appears here.

For the first time since Yolanda had reached the hills, there was a shoulder on the left side of the narrow road. She pulled the car over out of a sense of homecoming: every other visit she had stayed with her family in the capital.

Once her own engine was off, she heard the sound of another motor, approaching, a pained roar as if the engine were falling apart. She made out an undertow of men's voices. Quickly, she got back into the car, locked the door, and pulled off the shoulder, hugging her right side of the road.

—Just in time too. A bus came lurching around the curve, obscuring her view with a belching of exhaust, the driver saluting or warning with a series of blasts on his horn. It was an old army bus, the official name brushed over with paint that didn't quite match the regulation gray. The passengers saw her only at the last moment, and all up and down her side of the bus, men poked out of the windows, hooting and yelling, waving purple party flags, holding out bottles and beckoning to her. She speeded up and left them behind, the small compact climbing easily up the snakey highway, its well-oiled hum a gratifying sound after the hullabaloo of the bus.

She tried the radio again, but all she could tune to was static even here on the summit hills. She would have to wait until she got to the coast to hear news of the hunger march in the capital. Her family had been worried that trouble would break out, for the march had been scheduled on the anniversary of the failed revolution nineteen years ago today. A huge turnout was expected. She bet that bus she had just passed had been delayed by breakdowns on its way to the capital. In fact, earlier on the road when she had first set out, Yolanda had passed buses and truckloads of men, drinking and shouting slogans. It crossed her mind that her family had finally agreed to loan her a car because they knew she'd be far safer on the north coast than in the capital city where revolutions always broke out.

The hills began to plane out into a high plateau, the road widening. Left and right, roadside stands began appearing. Yolanda slowed

Literary Analysis

Plot In this opening paragraph, what do you learn about the story's basic situation, including the character and setting?

⑤ ✔ **Reading Check**
What political event is occurring in the city as Yolanda drives into the hills?

Antojos ◆ 1083

---

❸ Background

Art

Fruit Vendor, by Olga Costa
This painting vividly illustrates a fruit stand similar to those Yolanda passes in the story.

The artist, Olga Costa, was born in Leipzig, Germany, but has been a resident of Mexico since 1945. Largely self-taught, Costa's realistic style has been exhibited countless times during her years in Mexico and was ultimately honored by Mexico's National Art Prize in 1990.

Use this question for discussion:

• What elements of the painting capture the sensory images of the story setting?
Possible response: The bright colors, bountiful quantities, and tropical nature of the fruits all reflect the vivid sensory images of the story setting.

❹ Literary Analysis

Plot

• Read the opening paragraph aloud.

• Ask students the Literary Analysis question on p. 1083: In this opening paragraph, what do you learn about the story's basic situation, including the character and setting?
Answer: Yolanda is an adult woman who is on a visit but not staying with her family in the capital city as she usually does. She has been driving a car on a narrow road in the hills, and her feelings have caused her to pull the car over to the side of the road.

❺ ✔ Reading Check
Answer: People are going on a hunger march in the capital city as Yolanda is driving through the hills.

CUSTOMIZE INSTRUCTION FOR UNIVERSAL ACCESS

For Advanced Readers

Suggest that students read additional works by Julia Alvarez. Provide students with titles listed in the Enrichment box, ATE p. 1093. You may wish to use **Authors in Depth**, The American Experience, which contains the following selections:

from How the García Girls Lost Their Accents,
(fiction, p. 179)
Papi Working (poem, p.180)
Storm Windows (poem, p. 181)
Writing Matters (nonfiction, p. 182)

After students have read these or other works by Alvarez, have them form discussion groups in which they compare and contrast the selections they have read. Suggest criteria for comparison, such as setting, theme, and characters. To extend the activity, have volunteers present tp the class brief oral reports on their favorite Alvarez selections.

Plot and Flashback

- Have a volunteer read the passage aloud.

- Remind students that a flashback is a break in the chronological presentation of events in a story. Then, ask them why writers use flashbacks.
  Answer: Writers use flashbacks to provide important background information about characters.

- Have students answer the Literary Analysis question on p. 1084: What information about Yolanda and her family is conveyed in this flashback?
  Answer: Yolanda and her aunts are quite wealthy. They don't see each other very often.

Monitor Progress Ask students to discuss the relationship between Yolanda and her aunts revealed in this passage. How does Yolanda feel about her aunts? How do they feel about her?
Answer: The relationship is cordial on both sides, but the aunts think that Yolanda is too "American," and Yolanda is slightly exasperated by her aunts, who in her opinion lead overly sheltered lives.

❼ Reading Strategy

Identifying With a Character

- Ask students why Yolanda wants to head off by herself.
  Possible response: Yolanda wants to be an independent adult.

Monitor Progress Ask students whether they think Yolanda's behavior is universal. How often and under what circumstances have they felt the way Yolanda feels?
Answer: Most students will feel that Yolanda's behavior is typical of young adults and will be able to provide plenty of similar examples from their own lives.

down and kept an eye out for guavas, supposedly in season this far north. Piled high on wooden stands were fruits she hadn't seen in so many years: pinkish-yellow mangoes, and tamarind pods oozing their rich sap, and small cashew fruits strung on a rope to keep them from bruising each other. There were little brown packets of roasted cashews and bars of milk fudge wrapped in waxed paper and tied with a string, the color of which told what filling was inside the bar. Strips of meat, buzzing with flies, hung from the windows of butcher stalls. An occasional display of straw hats and baskets and hammocks told that tourists sometimes did pass by here. Looking at the stores spread before her, it was hard to believe the poverty the organizers of the march kept discussing on the radio. There seemed to be plenty here to eat—except for guavas.

In the capital, her aunts had plied her with what she most craved after so many years away. "Any little *antojo*, you must tell us!" They wanted to spoil her, so she'd stay on in her nativeland before she forgot where she had come from. "What exactly does it mean, *antojo*?" Yolanda asked. Her aunts were proven right: After so many years away, their niece was losing her Spanish.

"An *antojo*—" The aunts exchanged quizzical looks. "How to put it? An *antojo* is like a craving for something you have to eat."

A cousin blew out her cheeks. "Calories."

An *antojo*, one of the older aunts continued, was a very old Spanish word from before "your United States was thought of," she added tartly. In the countryside some *campesinos*[2] still used the word to mean possession by an island spirit demanding its due.

Her island spirit certainly was a patient soul, Yolanda joked. She hadn't had her favorite *antojo*, guavas, since her last trip seven years ago. Well, on this trip, her aunts promised, Yoyo could eat guavas to her heart's content. But when the gardener was summoned, he wasn't so sure. Guavas were no longer in season, at least not in the hotter lowlands of the south. Maybe up north, the chauffeur could pick her up some on his way back from some errand. Yolanda took this opportunity to inform her aunts of her plans: she could pick the guavas herself when she went up north in a few days.

—She was going up north? By herself? A woman alone on the road! "This is not the States." Her old aunts had tried to <u>dissuade</u> her. "Anything can happen." When Yolanda challenged them, "What?" they came up with boogeymen stories that made her feel as if she were talking to china dolls.[3] Haitian hougans[4] and Communist kidnappers. "And Martians?" Yolanda wanted to tease them. They had led such sheltered lives, riding from one safe place to another in their air-conditioned cars.

---

2. **campesinos** (käm´ pe sē´ nōs) "poor farmers; simple rural dwellers" (Spanish).
3. **china dolls** old-fashioned, delicate dolls made of fragile high-quality porcelain or ceramic ware.
4. **Haitian hougans** (o͞o gänz´) voodoo priests or cult leaders.

Literary Analysis
Plot and Flashback What information about Yolanda and her family is conveyed in this flashback?

dissuade (di swād´) *v.* convince someone not to do something

---

The Guava

The guava is a tropical fruit native to Central and South America that grows on trees and shrubs. It belongs to the genus Psidium. There are several species of guava: the common guava, the cattley, the cás, the guisaro, and the Brazilian guava. The fruit referred to as the pineapple guava is actually a feijoa.

The guava that Yolanda craves is the common guava. The tree of the common guava has four-petal white flowers. The three-inch-long yellow-skinned guava fruit is round to pear shaped. The flesh can be pink, white, or yellow. Some people don't care for the strong smell of guava pulp or the multitude of small, hard seeds.

Guavas are very healthful fruit loaded with vitamins A, B, and C. People eat guavas right off the tree or sliced with sugar and cream. These fruits are also made into jams, jellies, and preserves.

She had left the fruit stands behind her and was approaching a compound very much like her family's in the capital. The underbrush stopped abruptly at a high concrete wall, topped with broken bottle glass. Parked at the door was a chocolate brown Mercedes. Perhaps the owners had come up to their country home for the weekend to avoid the troubles in the capital?

Just beyond the estate, Yolanda came upon a small village—ALTAMIRA in rippling letters on the corrugated tin roof of the first little house. It was a little cluster of houses on either side of the road, a good place to stretch her legs before what she'd heard was a steep and slightly (her aunts had warned "very") dangerous descent to the coast. Yolanda pulled up at a cantina, the thatched roof held up by several posts. Instead of a menu, there was a yellowing, grimy poster for Palmolive soap tacked on one of the posts with a picture of a blonde woman under a spraying shower, her head thrown back in seeming ecstasy, her mouth opened in a wordless cry. ("Palmolive"? Yolanda wondered.) She felt even thirstier and grimier looking at this lathered beauty after her hot day on the road.

An old woman emerged at last from a shack behind the cabana, buttoning up a torn housedress, and followed closely by a little boy, who kept ducking behind her whenever Yolanda smiled at him. Asking him his name just drove him further into the folds of the old woman's skirt.

"You must excuse him, Doña,"[5] she apologized. "He's not used to being among people." But Yolanda knew the old woman meant, not the people in the village, but the people with money who drove through Altamira to the beaches on the coast. "Your name," the old woman repeated, as if Yolanda hadn't asked him in Spanish. The little boy mumbled at the ground. "Speak up!" the old woman scolded, but her voice betrayed pride when she spoke up for him. "This little know-nothing is Jose Duarte Sanchez y Mella Garcia."

Yolanda laughed. Not only were those a lot of names for such a little boy, but they certainly were momentous: the surnames of the three liberators of the country!

"Can I serve the Doña in any way?" the woman asked. Yolanda gave the tree line beyond the woman's shack a glance. "You think you might have some guavas around?"

The old woman's face scrunched up. "Guavas?" she murmured and thought to herself a second. "Why, they're all around, Doña. But I can't say as I've seen any."

---

5. **Doña** (dō´ nyä) "Madam" (Spanish)

History Connection

The Dominican Republic

Located in the West Indies, and occupying an area of 18,800 square miles, the Dominican Republic takes up the eastern two thirds of the island of Hispaniola. The country is bounded on the north by the Atlantic Ocean; on the east, by the Mona Passage, which separates it from Puerto Rico; on the south, by the Caribbean Sea; and on the west, by Haiti.

In Alvarez's story, Yolanda begins her journey in Santo Domingo, the capital city. Located on the country's southern coast, Santo Domingo was founded in 1496, four years after Christopher Columbus landed on the island. Yolanda's journey takes her into the Cordillera Central Range, which includes Pico Duarte, the highest mountain in the Caribbean at a height of 3,175 meters (over 10,000 feet). The slopes of many of these mountains are covered with dense semi-tropical forests, like those in which Yolanda searches for guavas.

 Reading Check

Who does Yolanda meet at the roadside cantina?

Antojos ◆ 1085

❽ **Background**

Geography Connection

The Dominican Republic is a country of the West Indies that occupies the eastern two-thirds of the Island of Hispaniola.

The capital of the Dominican Republic, Santo Domingo, is on the southern coast of the country. To reach the northern part of the Dominican Republic from the capital city, Yolanda would have had to drive across the Cordillera Central, a highland area containing the West Indies's highest mountain, the Pico Duarte, which is 10,417 ft. (3,175 m) high.

Though the transportation system in the Dominican Republic is generally considered adequate, the mountainous center of the country is challenging to motorists. Traveling through the mountains is slow, though scenic. In fact, the name of the village where Yolanda stops—Altamira—can be translated as "View from Above."

❾ **Critical Thinking**

Infer

• Ask students what evidence indicates that the owners of the compound are of the same social class as Yolanda's family.
Answer: They have a compound similar to her family's compound in the capital city.

• Have students speculate about why rich families lived in compounds surrounded by high walls topped by broken glass.
Answer: Rich families wanted to protect themselves against political unrest and thievery.

❿ **Reading Check**

Answer: Yolanda meets an old woman and a little boy.

CUSTOMIZE INSTRUCTION FOR UNIVERSAL ACCESS

For Less Proficient Readers	For Gifted/Talented Students	For Advanced Readers
Help students clarify the settings and characters introduced on this page by listing where Yolanda is, what she sees, and whom she sees. Write the headings *Where, What,* and *Whom* on the board and have volunteers fill in the information, or ask them to do this independently using their notebooks.	Have students discuss where Yolanda is at this point in the story and what and whom she sees there. Then, have students draw illustrations of the cantina and the people Yolanda meets there. Urge students to refer to the text in order to include as many accurate details as possible in their illustrations.	Have students analyze the settings and characters introduced on this page. For each concrete detail the author provides, have students speculate about why the author included that detail and what conclusions readers can draw from it.

Identifying With a Character

- Ask a volunteer to explain why Yolanda becomes irritated when the woman tries to discourage her from going with the boys to pick guavas.
  Answer: Yolanda feels overprotected by the old woman. She feels that the old woman, much like Yolanda's family, is keeping her from exploring her country.

- Then, ask the Reading Strategy question on p. 1086: Can you identify with Yolanda's feelings as she responds to the old woman? Why or why not?
  Answer: Most students will identify with Yolanda's feelings. Teenagers often experience constraints imposed by their families on their growing independence.

12 Critical Thinking

Analyze/Predict

- Ask students to explain why the boys are so excited about going for a ride in Yolanda's car.
  Answer: The boys probably have few chances to ride in cars. It is unlikely that their families own cars.

- Have students speculate about what might happen as Yolanda and the boys ride off together in her car to look for guavas.
  Possible response: Students may predict that they will have some kind of problem to provide an inciting incident in the plot.

13 ▶ Critical Viewing

Answer: Since the people shown in the photograph are peasants, they have more in common with the people Yolanda meets in the mountains than with her wealthy family back in the capital city.

1086

"With your permission—" Jose Duarte had joined a group of little boys who had come out of nowhere and were milling around the car, boasting how many automobiles they had ridden in. At Yolanda's mention of guavas, he sprung forward, pointing across the road towards the summit of the western hills. "I know where there's a whole grove of them." Behind him, his little companions nodded.

"Go on, then!" His grandmother stamped her foot as if she were scatting a little animal. "Get the Doña some."

A few boys dashed across the road and disappeared up a steep path on the hillside, but before Jose could follow, Yolanda called him back. She wanted to go along too. The little boy looked towards his grandmother, unsure of what to think. The old woman shook her head. The Doña would get hot, her nice clothes would get all dirty. Jose would get the Doña as many guavas as she was wanting.

11

"But they taste so much better when you've picked them yourself," Yolanda's voice had an edge, for suddenly, it was as if the woman had turned into the long arm of her family, keeping her away from seeing her country on her own.

The few boys who had stayed behind with Jose had congregated around the car. Each one claimed to be guarding it for the Doña. It occurred to Yolanda that there was a way to make this a treat all the way around. "What do you say we take the car?"

12

"*Sí, Sí, Sí,*"[6] the boys screamed in a riot of excitement.

The old woman hushed them but agreed that was not a bad idea if the Doña insisted on going. There was a dirt road up ahead she could follow a ways and then cross over onto the road that was paved all the way to the coffee barns. The woman pointed south in the direction of the big house. Many workers took that short cut to work.

They piled into the car, half a dozen boys in the back, and Jose as co-pilot in the passenger seat beside Yolanda. They turned onto a bumpy road off the highway, which got bumpier and bumpier, and climbed up into wilder, more desolate country. Branches scraped the sides and pebbles pelted the underside of the car. Yolanda wanted to turn back, but there was no room to maneuver the car around. Finally, with a great snapping of twigs and thrashing of branches across the windshield, as if the countryside were <u>loath</u> to release them, the car burst forth onto smooth pavement and the light of day. On either side of the road were groves of guava trees. Among them, the boys who had gone ahead on foot were already pulling down branches and shaking loose a rain of guavas. The fruit was definitely in season.

For the next hour or so, Yolanda and her crew scavenged the grove, the best of the pick going into the beach basket Yolanda had gotten out of the trunk, with the exception of the ones she ate right on the spot, relishing the slightly bumpy feel of the skin in her hand, devouring the crunchy, sweet, white meat. The boys watched her, surprised by her odd hunger.

---

6. *Sí, Sí, Sí* (sē) "Yes, Yes, Yes" (Spanish).

Reading Strategy
Identifying With a Character Can you identify with Yolanda's feelings as she responds to the old woman? Why or why not?

loath (lōth) *adj.* reluctant

13

▶ **Critical Viewing**
Do you think the people in this picture have more in common with Yolanda and her family or with the people she meets in the mountains? Explain. **[Analyze]**

Yolanda and Jose, partners, wandered far from the path that cut through the grove. Soon they were bent double to avoid getting entangled in the thick canopy of branches overhead. Each addition to the basket caused a spill from the stash already piled high above the brim. Finally, it was a case of abandoning the treasure in order to cart some of it home. With Jose hugging the basket to himself and Yolanda parting the wayward branches in front of them, they headed back toward the car.

When they finally cleared the thicket of guava branches, the sun was low on the western horizon. There was no sign of the other boys. "They must have gone to round up the goats," Jose observed.

Yolanda glanced at her watch: it was past six o'clock. She'd never make the north coast by nightfall, but at least she could get off the dangerous mountain roads while it was still light. She hurried Jose back to the car, where they found a heap of guavas the other boys had left behind on the shoulder of the road. Enough guavas to appease even the greediest island spirit for life!

They packed the guavas in the trunk quickly and climbed in, but the car had not gone a foot before it lurched forward with a horrible hobble. Yolanda closed her eyes and laid her head down on the wheel, then glanced over at Jose. The way his eyes were searching

appease (ə pēz′) v. satisfy

 Reading Check

What do Jose and his friends help Yolanda to gather?

Antojos ◆ 1087

⓮ **Critical Thinking**

Infer

- Ask students to name the likeliest reason for Yolanda's car lurching "with a horrible hobble."
  Answer: Yolanda's car probably has a flat tire.

- Ask what motivates Yolanda to close her eyes and rest her head on the wheel.
  Answer: Yolanda is upset and discouraged.

- Discuss with students what they would do if they found themselves in a similar situation. What would they advise Yolanda to do?
  Answer: Suggestions may include changing the tire with Jose's help, waiting in the car for help, and hiking out with Jose to look for help.

⓯ **Reading Check**

Answer: Jose and his friends help Yolanda gather guavas.

⑯ Literary Analysis

Plot

- Ask students the Literary Analysis question on p. 1088: What elements of the setting serve to intensify Yolanda's conflict? **Answer:** The bad road and the rapidly setting sun intensify Yolanda's conflict.

- Ask students to discuss the relationship between setting and plot. **Answer:** Students should understand that the setting and plot are interwoven. If the setting in this story had not turned threatening, for example, there would have been less difficulty for the main character to face.

⑰ Reading Strategy

Identifying With a Character

- Have a volunteer read the bracketed passage aloud.

- Then, ask the Reading Strategy question on p. 1088: What is Yolanda feeling as she waits for Jose? Do you think you would react with similar emotions if you were in her situation? Explain. **Answer:** Yolanda is enjoying the beauty and sense of connectedness she feels in the countryside, a feeling she has missed while living in the United States. Most students will say that they would not feel as Yolanda does; they would be too worried about being in a potentially dangerous situation.

⑱ Vocabulary Development

Words From Spanish

- Have a volunteer read aloud the definition of *machete* in the margin. Point out that *machete* comes from the Spanish word for sledgehammer.

- Remind students that we use many words that come from Spanish, such as *hammock*, as well as words that are Spanish, such as, *Latino*.

- Encourage students to note other Spanish words and words that came from Spanish as they read. Explain that English has borrowed more words from other languages—French, German, Yiddish, Italian, and many others—than has any other language.

---

the inside of the car for a clue as to what could have happened, she could tell he didn't know how to change a flat tire either.

⑯ It was no use regretting having brought the car up that bad stretch of road. The thing to do now was to act quickly. Soon the sun would set and night would fall swiftly, no lingering dusk as in the States. She explained to Jose that they had a flat tire and had to hike back to town and send for help down the road to the big house. Whoever tended to the brown Mercedes would know how to change the tire on her car.

"With your permission," Jose offered meekly. He pointed down the paved road. "This goes directly to the big house." The Doña could just wait in the car and he would be back in no time with someone from the Miranda place.

She did not like the idea of staying behind in the car, but Jose could probably go and come back much quicker without her. "All right," she said to the boy. "I'll tell you what." She pointed to her watch. It was almost six thirty. "If you're back by the time this hand is over here, I'll give you"—she held up one finger "a dollar." The boy's mouth fell open. In no time, he had shot out of his side of the car and was headed at a run toward the Miranda place. Yolanda climbed out as well and walked down a pace, until the boy had disappeared in one of the turnings of the road.

⑰ Suddenly, the countryside was so very quiet. She looked up at the purple sky. A breeze was blowing through the grove, rustling the leaves, so they whispered like voices, something indistinct. Here and there a light flickered on the hills, a *campesino* living out his solitary life. This was what she had been missing without really knowing that she was missing it all these years. She had never felt at home in the States, never, though she knew she was lucky to have a job, so she could afford her own life and not be run by her family. But independence didn't have to be exile. She could come home, home to places like these very hills, and live here on her own terms.

Heading back to the car, Yolanda stopped. She had heard footsteps in the grove. Could Jose be back already? Branches were being thrust aside, twigs snapped. Suddenly, a short, dark man, and then a slender, light-skin man emerged from a footpath on the opposite side of the grove from the one she and Jose had scavenged. They wore ragged work clothes stained with patches of sweat; their faces were drawn and tired.

⑱ Yolanda's glance fell on the machetes that hung from their belts.

The men's faces snapped awake from their stupor at the sight of her. They looked beyond her at the car. "Yours?" the darker man spoke first. It struck her, even then, as an absurd question. Who else's would it be here in the middle of nowhere?

"Is there some problem?" the darker man spoke up again. The taller one was looking her up and down with interest. They were now both in front of her on the road, blocking her escape. Both—she had looked them up and down as well—were strong and quite capable of catching her if she made a run for the Miranda's. Not that she could have moved, for her legs seemed suddenly to have been hammered

1088 ◆ *Prosperity and Protest (1946–Present)*

Literary Analysis
Plot What elements of the setting serve to intensify Yolanda's conflict?

Reading Strategy
Identifying With a Character What is Yolanda feeling as she waits for Jose? Do you think you would react with similar emotions if you were in her situation? Explain.

machetes (mə shet´ ēz) *n.* large heavy knives with broad blades

---

✹ ENRICHMENT: Social Studies Connection

People of the Dominican Republic

The people of the Dominican Republic are mostly mulatto (of mixed European and African descent). The original Indian inhabitants of the island of Hispaniola, of which the Dominican Republic occupies the eastern part, were long ago decimated by disease, warfare, and the ravages of slavery. Spanish is the dominant language of the Dominican Republic, and most of the inhabitants are Roman Catholic. The original Spanish colonizers of the Dominican Republic were joined in the 1800s and 1900s by East Asians and immigrants from France, England, and Germany. Small numbers of Jews, Middle Easterners, and Japanese also emigrated to the Dominican Republic during this time.

into the ground beneath her. She thought of explaining that she was just out for a drive before dinner at the big house, so that these men would think someone knew where she was, someone would come looking for her if they tried to carry her off. But she found she could not speak. Her tongue felt as if it'd been stuffed in her mouth like a rag to keep her quiet.

The men exchanged a look—it seemed to Yolanda of collusion. Then the shorter, darker one spoke up again, "Señorita,[7] are you all right?" He peered at her. The darkness of his complexion in the growing darkness of the evening made it difficult to distinguish an expression. He was no taller than Yolanda, but he gave the impression of being quite large, for he was broad and solid, like something not yet completely carved out of a piece of wood. His companion was tall and of a rich honey-brown color that matched his honey-brown eyes. Anywhere else, Yolanda would have found him extremely attractive, but here on a lonely road, with the sky growing darker by seconds, his good looks seemed dangerous, a lure to catch her off her guard.

"Can we help you?" the shorter man repeated.

The handsome one smiled knowingly. Two long, deep dimples appeared like gashes on either side of his mouth. "*Americana,*" he said to the other in Spanish, pointing to the car. "She doesn't understand."

The darker man narrowed his eyes and studied Yolanda a moment. "*Americana?*" he asked her as if not quite sure what to make of her.

She had been too frightened to carry out any strategy, but now a road was opening before her. She laid her hand on her chest—she could feel her pounding heart—and nodded. Then, as if the admission itself loosened her tongue, she explained in English how it came that she was on a back road by herself, her craving for guavas, her never having learned to change a flat. The two men stared at her, uncomprehendingly, rendered docile by her gibberish. Strangely enough, it soothed her to hear herself speaking something they could not understand. She thought of something her teacher used to say to her when as a young immigrant girl she was learning English, "Language is power." It was her only defense now.

Yolanda made the motions of pumping. The darker man looked at the other, who had shown better luck at understanding the foreign lady. But his companion shrugged, baffled as well. "I'll show you," Yolanda waved for them to follow her. And suddenly, as if after pulling and pulling at roots, she had finally managed to yank them free of the soil they had clung to, she found she could move her own feet forward to the car.

The small group stood staring at the sagging tire a moment, the two men kicking at it as if punishing it for having failed the Señorita. They squatted by the passenger's side, conversing in low tones. Yolanda led them to the rear of the car, where the men lifted the spare out of its sunken nest—then set to work, fitting the interlocking pieces of the

---

7. **Señorita** (se´ ny ō rē´ tä) "Miss" (Spanish).

collusion (kə lōō´ zhən) *n.* secret agreement; conspiracy

Literary Analysis
Plot In what ways is Yolanda's conflict growing more intense and complex?

docile (däs´ əl) *adj.* easy to direct or manage; obedient

 ✔Reading Check
What does Yolanda pretend when she is approached by the two men?

Antojos ◆ 1089

19 Literary Analysis
Plot

- Have students identify Yolanda's predominant emotion in the bracketed passage.
  Answer: Yolanda's predominant emotion is fear.

- Then, ask the Literary Analysis question on p. 1089: In what ways is Yolanda's conflict growing more intense and complex?
  Answer: Her conflict is more intense because she is unable to follow her normal instincts. Her feelings are complicated by finding the man attractive yet fearing him.

20 Reading Strategy
Identifying With a Character

- Have students discuss the phrase "language is power." What does it mean? Do they agree?
  Possible response: The person whose language dominates defines the terms of debate. Language can be used to wound and manipulate, and in many ways language may be a more powerful tool than a weapon.

- Have students give examples of the power of language.
  Possible response: Students may mention instances in which someone's words made them feel either awful or great.

21 ✔Reading Check
Answer: Yolanda pretends she is an American who doesn't speak Spanish.

CUSTOMIZE INSTRUCTION FOR UNIVERSAL ACCESS		
For Special Needs Students	**For Less Proficient Readers**	**For Advanced Readers**
Students may understand the story better by discussing the swings of emotions Yolanda displays on pp. 1088 and 1089. Ask students how Yolanda feels in the fourth full paragraph on p. 1088. What happens shortly after that to change her mood?	Have students chart the trajectory of Yolanda's emotions that the author describes on pp. 1088 and 1089. If necessary, prompt students with questions such as the following: How does Yolanda feel as she walks outside the car? How do her feelings change when she sees the men? Why is Yolanda afraid of the men? Are her fears rational?	Have students trace the arc of Yolanda's emotions as they are revealed on pp. 1088 and 1089. Then, ask students to imagine the point of view of the men she encounters on the path. How did they feel when they saw Yolanda and listened to her speak in English? What is the meaning of the looks they shoot at each other?

Answer: The boys seem slightly awe-stricken and overwhelmed, yet interested in the photographer, which is similar to Jose's reaction to Yolanda in the story.

23 Reading Strategy

Identifying With a Character

• Have students speculate about how Yolanda is feeling now that the men are fixing her tire and one of them has injured his hand. Which sentence gives a clue about her feeling?
Answer: Yolanda is probably feeling guilty about her suspicions about the men. The sentence that gives readers a clue about her feelings is the following: "She had been sure that if any blood were going to be spilled tonight, it would be hers."

• Ask students to think of similar situations in their lives in which they made an assumption about someone that turned out to be faulty. How did they feel when that happened? What did they learn from the incident?

jack, unpacking the tools from the deeper hollows of the trunk. They laid their machetes down on the side of the road, out of the way. Yolanda turned on the headlights to help them see in the growing darkness. Above the small group, the sky was purple with twilight.

There was a problem with the jack. It squeaked and labored, but the car would not rise. The shorter man squirmed his way underneath and placed the mechanism deeper under the bowels of the car. There, he pumped vigorously, his friend bracing him by holding him down by the ankles. Slowly, the car rose until the wheel hung suspended. When the man came out from under the car, his hand was bloody where his knuckles had scraped against the pavement.

Yolanda pointed to the man's hand. She had been sure that if any blood were going to be spilled tonight, it would be hers. She offered him the towel she kept draped on her car seat to absorb her perspiration. But he waved it away and sucked his knuckles to make the bleeding stop.

Once the flat had been replaced with the spare, the two men lifted the deflated tire into the trunk and put away the tools. They handed Yolanda her keys. There was still no sign of Jose and the Miranda's.

1090 ◆ Prosperity and Protest (1946–Present)

22 ▲ Critical Viewing
In what ways might these boys' reactions to the photographer taking their picture be similar to Jose's reaction to Yolanda in the story? **[Connect]**

Raising Mangoes

The tropical climate of the Dominican Republic is well suited to growing fruits such as guavas, mangoes, tamarind pods, and cashew nuts. In fact, mangoes are one of the nation's major agricultural products. Like many tropical fruits, mangoes are evergreen while also sensitive to cold temperatures. Grown widely in India and other parts of Asia, as well as tropical parts of Central and South America, mangoes range from plum-size to almost five pounds. A reddish-yellow to green skin covers orange-yellow flesh and a single large stone. Mangoes contain vitamins A, C, and D. Unfortunately, they are highly perishable and therefore difficult and expensive to transport.

If possible, offer students the opportunity to taste a mango. Otherwise, display pictures of the fruit and some foods prepared with it. Discuss how its succulence suggests the tropical setting of the story.

Yolanda was relieved. As she had waited, watching the two men hard at work, she had begun to dread the boy's return with help. The two men would realize she spoke Spanish. It was too late to admit that she had tricked them, to explain she had done so only because she thought her survival was on the line. The least she could do now was to try and repay them, handsomely, for their trouble.

"I'd like to give you something," she began reaching for the purse she'd retrieved from the trunk. The English words sounded hollow on her tongue. She rolled up a couple of American bills and offered them to the men. The shorter man held up his hand. Yolanda could see where the blood had dried dark streaks on his palm. "No, no, Señorita. *Nuestro placer.*"[8] Our pleasure.

Yolanda turned to the other man, who had struck her as more pliant than his sterner companion. "Please," she urged the bills on him. But he too looked down at the ground with the bashfulness she had observed in Jose of country people not wanting to offend. She felt the poverty of her response and stuffed the bills quickly into his pocket.

The two men picked up their machetes and raised them to their shoulders like soldiers their guns. The tall man motioned towards the big house. "*Directo, directo,*"[9] he <u>enunciated</u> the words carefully. Yolanda looked in the direction of his hand. In the faint light of what was left of day, she could barely make out the road ahead. It was as if the guava grove had overgrown into the road and woven its mat of branches so securely and tightly in all directions, she would not be able to escape.

But finally, she was off! While the two men waited a moment on the shoulder to see if the tire would hold, Yolanda drove a few yards, poking her head out the window before speeding up. "*Gracias!*"[10] she called, and they waved, appreciatively, at the foreign lady making an effort in their native tongue. When she looked for them in her rear-view mirror, they had disappeared into the darkness of the guava grove.

Just ahead, her lights described the figure of a small boy: Jose was walking alone, listlessly, as if he did not particularly want to get to where he was going.

Yolanda leaned over and opened the door for him. The small overhead light came on; she saw that the boy's face was streaked with tears.

"Why, what's wrong, Jose?"

The boy swallowed hard. "They would not come. They didn't believe me." He took little breaths between words to keep his tears at bay. He had lost his chance at a whole dollar. "And the guard, he said if I didn't stop telling stories, he was going to whip me."

"What did you tell him, Jose?"

"I told him you had broken your car and you needed help fixing it."

---

8. *Nuestro placer* (nōō es´ trō plä ser´) "Our pleasure" (Spanish).
9. *Directo, directo* (dē rek´ tō) "Straight, straight" (Spanish).
10. *Gracias* (grä´ sē äs) "Thank you" (Spanish).

Literary Analysis

Plot Is Yolanda's problem fully addressed now that the men have fixed her tire? What is still unresolved?

enunciated (ē nun´ sē āt´ əd) *v.* pronounced; stated precisely

✔Reading Check
What do the two men do to help Yolanda?

Antojos ◆ *1091*

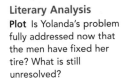
❷❹ Literary Analysis
Plot

- Read the bracketed passage aloud, and have students identify Yolanda's primary emotion.
  Answer: Though all her problems aren't solved, Yolanda is overwhelmingly relieved that the men haven't harmed her and have fixed the flat tire on her car.

▶ Monitor Progress Ask the Literary Analysis question on p. 1091: Is Yolanda's problem fully addressed now that the men have fixed her tire? What is unresolved?
  Answer: Students should understand that Yolanda has sent Jose to get help from the Mirandas. If he returns before the men leave, they will know that she speaks Spanish. If he doesn't return, Yolanda will have to worry about what happened to him.

❷❺ Reading Strategy
Identifying With a Character

- Ask students to explain why such poor men have turned down an offer of money for changing the tire.
  Answer: The men don't think it's proper to take money for performing a good deed.

- Why is Yolanda embarrassed?
  Answer: She realizes that offering money for the men's politeness could be considered insulting to them.

- Ask students whether they have made a similar *faux pas*, perhaps with people they didn't know well or in an unfamiliar situation. How did they feel? What did they learn?
  Answer: Many students will be able to relate to Yolanda's social gaffe and her feelings of embarrassment.

❷❻ ✔Reading Check
Answer: The men change the tire on Yolanda's car.

CUSTOMIZE INSTRUCTION FOR UNIVERSAL ACCESS

For Special Needs Students	For Gifted/Talented Readers
To help students understand the characters' motivations, have them analyze the charcaters' behavior on pp. 1090 and 1091. Have students make a chart with the headings *Yolanda*, *The Campesinos*, and *Jose*. Along the side of the chart, ask them to write What the Character(s) Do(es) and Why the Character(s) Do(es) It. As they read these pages, students can fill in the chart. After completing their charts, students should discuss them. You may want to draw a similar chart on the board and fill in an item or two to provide a model.	Have students discuss the characters' various motivations and behavior in this part of the story. Then, have each student take the part of Yolanda, Jose, or one of the two campesinos. Have them get together in groups for a heart-to-heart chat. The characters should tell each other what lies behind their behavior—what they truly think and why they are behaving as they are.

ASSESS

Answers for p. 1092

Review and Assess

1. Some students might be surprised that the campesinos didn't harm Yolanda, given her aunt's worries. Other students may be surprised by Yolanda's shame at her behavior and Jose's distress at not being believed.

2. **(a)** Her aunts tell Yolanda anything could happen, such as attacks by Haitian hougans and kidnappings by Communists. **(b)** Yolanda does encounter campesinos in a remote area, though no harm comes to her.

3. **(a)** Her aunts are concerned and upset. **(b)** Yolanda has led a less sheltered life than her aunts; she is more adventurous and is not concerned about traveling on her own. **(c)** Yolanda is from a different generation than her aunts and has lived on her own in the United States.

4. **(a)** *Antojos* are cravings for certain foods. **(b)** The title emphasizes the theme of longing for connection with one's heritage.

5. **(a)** Jose is delighted with the promise of a dollar. **(b)** A segment of the population in the Dominican Republic is not making a living wage. **(c)** The issue of social and economic inequity is central to the story, defining the characters' behavior and underlying the assumptions they make about one another.

6. **(a)** Yolanda is afraid of the men, though she acknowledges that under different circumstances, she would find one of the men attractive. **(b)** Yolanda thinks she will be safer if she pretends to be an American who does not speak Spanish.

7. **(a)** Yolanda learns that the campesinos are more complex and sensitive than her simplistic view of them had led her to believe. **(b)** Many students will believe that Yolanda might make light of her experiences to her family because she would not want her family to believe that their fears had been justified.

1092

She should have gone along with Jose to the Miranda's. Given all the trouble in the country, they would be suspicious of a boy coming to their door at nightfall with some story about a lady on a back road with a broken car. "Don't you worry, Jose," Yolanda patted the boy. She could feel the bony shoulder through the thin fabric of his worn shirt. "You can still have your dollar. You did your part."

But the shame of being suspected of lying seemed to have obscured any immediate pleasure he might feel in her offer. Yolanda tried to distract him by asking what he would buy with his money, what he most craved, thinking that on a subsequent trip, she might bring him his little *antojo*. But Jose Duarte Sanchez y Mella said nothing, except a bashful thank you when she left him off at the cantina with his promised dollar. In the glow of the headlights, Yolanda made out the figure of the old woman in the black square of her doorway, waving good-bye. Above the picnic table on a near post, the Palmolive woman's skin shone; her head was thrown back, her mouth opened as if she were calling someone over a great distance.

Review and Assess

Thinking About the Selection

1. **Respond:** Did this story surprise you in any way? Explain.

2. **(a) Recall:** What warnings do her aunts give Yolanda before she starts on her journey? **(b) Interpret:** How do these warnings anticipate, or foreshadow, Yolanda's experiences on her trip?

3. **(a) Recall:** With what emotions do her aunts react to Yolanda's announcement that she plans to drive north on her own? **(b) Compare and Contrast:** In what ways is Yolanda different from her aunts? **(c) Speculate:** What factors might account for the differences between Yolanda and her aunts?

4. **(a) Recall:** What are *antojos*? **(b) Connect:** What theme does the title of the story stress?

5. **(a) Recall:** How does the boy Jose react to Yolanda's promise of a dollar? **(b) Infer:** What is suggested about the country's political situation by the idea of a "hunger march" taking place in the capital? **(c) Analyze:** What role do issues of money and social inequity play in this story?

6. **(a) Interpret:** When Yolanda first sees the two men what emotions does she experience? **(b) Analyze:** Why does Yolanda pretend not to speak Spanish?

7. **(a) Evaluate:** Does Yolanda learn or grow in the story? Explain. **(b) Speculate:** How might Yolanda describe her experiences to her family when she returns from her trip?

1092 ◆ Prosperity and Protest (1946–Present)

ASSESSMENT PRACTICE: Writing Skills

Grammar and Usage (For more practice, see **Test Preparation Workbook**, p.66.)

The writing sections of many tests require students to recognize and correct errors in grammar. Use the following sample test item to give students practice in this skill.

The latest sales reports indicate that the popularity of guavas are growing in the United States.

Chose the best way to rewrite the underlined section of the passage. If the underlined section needs no change, choose "Correct as is."

A of guavas were growing

B of guavas is growing

C of guavas was growing

D Correct as is

A and *C* are in the past tense, while the passage refers to the present. The plural verb *are* does not agree with the singular subject *popularity*, so *D* is incorrect. The correct choice is *B*.

Review and Assess

Literary Analysis

Plot

1. Use a chart like the one shown to analyze the **plot** and answer the following questions: (a) What events in the story form the rising action? (b) What events form the falling action? (c) What is the story's main conflict? (d) How does it resolve?

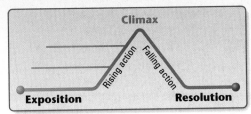

2. In what ways does the story's central conflict mirror other, deeper conflicts that may not be so easily resolved?

Connecting Literary Elements

3. (a) What does the **flashback** to Yolanda's visit with her aunts reveal about her family's social and economic circumstances? (b) What does the flashback reveal about Yolanda's reasons for traveling north?

4. (a) How else might Alvarez have conveyed the information given in the flashback? (b) Is her use of flashback more or less effective than another technique might be? Explain.

Reading Strategy

Identifying With a Character

5. (a) Examine Yolanda's attitudes and behavior toward her aunts, Jose, and the two men who approach her. (b) Do you **identify** with Yolanda in her dealings with these people? Explain.

6. (a) What information about the country's political turmoil adds to the weight of Yolanda's feelings about the two men? (b) How might her aunts' feelings about solo travel have affected Yolanda?

Extend Understanding

7. **Cultural Connection:** How might it feel to return to one's country of origin after a long absence? Respond from your own experience, or interview a family member, friend, or neighbor to find out.

Quick Review

Plot is the sequence of events in narrative writing. The sequence of a plot follows these stages: the **exposition**, when the basic situation is introduced; the **inciting incident**, when the conflict is revealed; the **development**, when the conflict intensifies; the **climax**, when the conflict reaches its most intense point; the **denouement**, when information about events that occur after the climax are revealed; and the **resolution**, when the conflict is resolved and changes or insights are noted.

A **flashback** is an interruption in the chronological narrative that is used to present a scene or an event from an earlier time.

To **identify with a character**, think about character traits and experiences you share.

 Take It to the Net
www.phschool.com

Take the interactive self-test online to check your understanding of the selection.

Antojos ◆ 1093

ENRICHMENT: Further Reading

Other Works by Julia Alvarez

Homecomings

The Other Side

How the García Girls Lost Their Accents

In the Time of Butterflies

¡Yo!

Take It to the Net
Visit www.phschool.com for more information on Julia Alvarez.

---

❶ Concept Development

Words From Spanish

1. guava
2. canteen
3. In the story, people live in a village comprised of *cabanas*, or small shacks.

Concept Development

1. synonyms
2. antonyms
3. antonyms
4. synonyms
5. synonyms
6. antonyms
7. antonyms

Spelling Strategy

1. skated
2. defining
3. captured

❷ Grammar and Style

1. It was an old army bus, <u>the official name brushed over with paint</u>.
2. She speeded up and left them behind, <u>the small compact climbing easily</u>.
3. Yolanda pulled at a cantina, <u>the thatched roof held up by several posts</u>.
4. Yolanda and her crew scavenged the grove, <u>the best of the pick going into the basket</u>.
5. The small group stared at the sagging tire, <u>the two men kicking it</u>.

Writing Application

Students must include three or more absolute phrases in their descriptions of childhood memories.

Integrate Language Skills

❶ Vocabulary Development Lesson

Concept Development: Words From Spanish

Many words, such as *machete*, *tortilla*, and *sombrero*, come to English directly from Spanish. Use the story context to help you answer these questions about three other Spanish words.

1. Which English word used in the story probably comes from *guayaba*, the Spanish name for the same tropical fruit?

2. *Cantina*, from the Spanish for "bar" or "tavern," is related to an Italian word for "wine cellar." Which English word probably has a similar origin?

3. In English, a *cabana* or *cabaña* is usually a small building at a swimming pool or beach. Is that the word's meaning on page 1085 in the story? Explain.

Concept Development: Synonyms or Antonyms

Classify each of the following pairs of words as either synonyms or antonyms.

1. dissuade, discourage
2. loath, eager
3. appease, arouse
4. machetes, knives
5. collusion, plotting
6. docile, cantankerous
7. enunciated, slurred

Spelling Strategy

For words ending in silent *e*, drop the *e* before adding a suffix beginning with a vowel (*enunciate* +-*ed* = *enunciated*). Correctly add the indicated suffix to each word listed.

1. skate (-*ed*)   2. define (-*ing*)   3. capture (-*ed*)

❷ Grammar and Style Lesson

Absolute Phrases

An **absolute phrase** consists of a noun or noun phrase modified by a participle or participial phrase. Though it modifies the clause to which it is attached, it is not part of the subject or predicate and is set off from the rest of the sentence by commas.

> **Example:** A bus came lurching around the curve, *the driver saluting*.

Practice Identify the absolute phrases in the following sentences.

1. It was an old army bus, the official name brushed over with paint.

2. She speeded up and left them behind, the small compact climbing easily.
3. Yolanda pulled up at a cantina, the thatched roof held up by several posts.
4. Yolanda and her crew scavenged the grove, the best of the pick going into the basket.
5. The small group stared at the sagging tire, the two men kicking it.

Writing Application Write a one-paragraph description of an important childhood memory. Include at least three absolute phrases in your account to add descriptive detail.

W̶G̶ Prentice Hall Writing and Grammar Connection: Chapter 19, Section 2

TEACHING RESOURCES

The following resources can be used to enrich or extend the instruction for pp. 1094–1095.

Vocabulary

📖 **Selection Support:** Build Vocabulary, p. 224 ▪
📖 **Vocabulary and Spelling Practice Book** (Use this booklet for skills enrichment.)

Grammar

📖 **Selection Support:** Grammar and Style, p. 275 ▪
W̶G̶ **Writing and Grammar,** Ruby Level, p. 442
📖 **Daily Language Practice Transparencies** ▪

Writing

W̶G̶ **Writing and Grammar,** Ruby Level, p. 82
📖 **Writing Models and Graphic Organizers on Transparencies,** pp. 17–23
💿 **Writing and Grammar iText CD-ROM**

❸ Writing Lesson

New Version of the Story

In both literature and life, stories are shaped by the points of view of those who tell them. For example, in this story you see events and people through Yolanda's eyes. You can only speculate about the thoughts of the people she encounters. Write a new version of the story from the point of view of one of the men who changes Yolanda's tire.

Prewriting   Choose the character whose point of view you will use and reread the story considering that perspective. Note details to incorporate and develop. Then, write a brief outline of your new version.

Drafting   Write the story from the new point of view you have selected. Use sensory details, flashbacks, and dialogue to provide background and flesh out the character's world.

> **Model: Using Details to Create A Vivid Portrayal**
>
> Paulo saw a small, white car stuck in the foliage. The tire was busted, and a lady stood there. Her eyes were nervous and black. She reminded Paulo of a cornered chihuahua, and he thought she might bite. He laughed at the thought. "How can we help you, Doña?" he asked.
>
> The inclusion of dialogue and a character's inner thoughts add to the vividness of a narrative.

Revising   Reread your story, and look for points where you may have strayed from the perspective you have chosen. Delete details the character might not know, and add information to strengthen your use of point of view.

Prentice Hall Writing and Grammar Connection: Chapter 5, Section 4

❹ Extension Activities

Listening and Speaking Create a **cause-and-effect flowchart** that examines the series of decisions each character makes. Use the flowchart as the basis for a class presentation. Use these tips to prepare:

- Diagram the characters' choices in each situation.
- Note how the decisions made by Yolanda and other characters affect the plot.

After your presentation, lead a discussion about the conflicts and decisions portrayed in this story.

Research and Technology Work with several classmates to prepare a **multimedia report** about the Dominican Republic. Choose one area to research—for example, geography or economics. Add music and images, and report your findings in a presentation. **[Group Activity]**

 Take It to the Net   www.phschool.com

Go online for an additional research activity using the Internet.

Antojos ◆ 1095

Lesson Support for p. 1095

❸ Writing Lesson

- To prepare them to write a new version of "Antojos," have students reread the part of the story in which the campesinos appear. Remind students to jot down relevant details.

- Use the Writing Lesson to guide students in preparing to write and draft their versions of the stories. Remind them to use sensory details, flashbacks, and dialogue. You may wish to use the Writing Model for Story, pp. 17–23 in **Writing Models and Graphic Organizer on Transparencies,** to help students draft their versions.

- Use the drafting model to provide an example for students. Urge students to revise their stories to add details or dialogue to make the character come alive.

- Use the Short Story rubric in **Performance Assessment and Portfolio Management,** p. 15, to evaluate students' stories.

❹ Research and Technology

- Suggest that students work in small groups to research the Dominican Republic.

- Have group members choose a topic for their group, such as geography, demographics, or the economy.

- Make sure that each student in the group contributes to the presentation, either by doing research, writing, or preparing one of the elements of the presentation.

CUSTOMIZE INSTRUCTION
For Universal Access

To address different learning styles, use the activities suggested in the **Extension Activities** booklet, p. 63.

For Interpersonal Learners, use Activity 5.

For Verbal/Linguistic and Bodily/Kinesthetic Learners, use Activity 6.

For Visual/Spatial and Logical/Mathematical Learners, use Activity 7.

ASSESSMENT RESOURCES

The following resources can be used to assess students' knowledge and skills.

Selection Assessment

- Formal Assessment, pp. 272–274
- Open Book Test, pp. 187–189
- Got It! Assessment Videotapes
- Test Bank Software

Take It to the Net
Visit www.phschool.com for self-tests and additional questions on "Antojos."

Writing Rubric

- Performance Assess. and Portfolio Mgmt., p. 15

PRENTICE HALL
ASSESSMENT SYSTEM

- Workbook
- Skill Book
- Transparencies
- CD-ROM

Freeway 280 ✦ Who Burns for the Perfection of Paper ✦ Most Satisfied by Snow ✦ Hunger in New York City ✦ What For

Lesson Objectives

1. **To analyze and respond to literary elements**
   - Literary Analysis: Voice
   - Comparing Literary Works
2. **To read, comprehend, analyze, and critique poetry**
   - Reading Strategy: Summarizing
   - Reading Check Questions
   - Review and Assess Questions
3. **To develop word analysis skills, fluency, and systematic vocabulary**
   - Vocabulary Development Lesson: Greek Prefix: *auto-*
4. **To understand and apply written and oral language conventions**
   - Spelling Strategy
   - Grammar and Style Lesson: Participial Phrases
   - Assessment Practice (ATE)
5. **To understand and apply appropriate writing and research strategies**
   - Writing Lesson: Comparison-and-Contrast Essay
   - Extension Activity: Anthology
6. **To understand and apply listening and speaking strategies**
   - Extension Activity: Interview

STEP-BY-STEP TEACHING GUIDE	PACING GUIDE
PRETEACH	
Motivate Students and Provide Background	
Use the Motivation activity (ATE p. 1096)	5 min.
Read and discuss author and background features (SE/ATE pp. 1096, 1098) **A**	10 min.
Introduce the Concepts	
Introduce the Literary Analysis and Reading Strategy (SE/ATE p. 1097) **A**	15 min.
Pronounce the vocabulary words and read their definitions (SE p. 1097)	5 min.
TEACH	
Monitor Comprehension	
Informally monitor comprehension by circulating while students read independently or in groups **A**	25 min.
Develop vocabulary with Vocabulary notes (SE pp. 1100, 1101, 1102, 1103, 1104; ATE p. 1102)	as students read / as students read
Develop Understanding	
Develop students' understanding of voice with the Literary Analysis annotations (SE pp. 1104, 1105; ATE pp. 1098, 1104) **A**	5 min.
Develop students' ability to summarize by using the Reading Strategy annotations (SE pp. 1102, 1104; ATE pp. 1100, 1102, 1104)	5 min.
ASSESS	
Assess Mastery	
Assess students' mastery of the Reading Strategy and Literary Analysis by having them answer the Review and Assess questions (SE/ATE p. 1106)	15 min.
Use one or more of the print and media Assessment Resources (ATE p. 1108) **A**	up to 45 min.
EXTEND	
Apply Understanding	
Have students complete the Vocabulary Development Lesson and the Grammar and Style Lesson (SE p. 1107) **A**	20 min.
Apply students' ability to elaborate for a stronger statement by using the Writing Lesson (SE/ATE p. 1108) **A**	45 min.
Apply students' understanding using one or more of the Extension Activities (SE p. 1108)	20–90 min.

 ACCELERATED INSTRUCTION:
Use the strategies and activities identified with an **A**.

UNIVERSAL ACCESS
● = Below Level Students
▲ = On-Level Students
■ = Above Level Students

Time and Resource Manager

Reading Level: Challenging, Easy, Average, Average, Challenging
Average Number of Instructional Days: 4

PRINT 📝	TRANSPARENCIES	TECHNOLOGY 💿 🎧
	RESOURCES	
• **Beyond Literature,** Cross-Curricular Connection: Social Studies, p. 64 ▲ ■		• **Interest Grabber Video,** Tape 6 ● ▲ ■
• **Selection Support Workbook:** ● ▲ ■ Literary Analysis, p. 281 Reading Strategy, p. 280 Build Vocabulary, p. 278	• **Literary Analysis and Reading Transparencies,** pp. 127 and 128 ● ▲ ■	
• **Adapted Reader's Companion** ● • **Reader's Companion** ●		• **Listening to Literature** ● ▲ ■ Audiocassettes, Side 37 Audio CDs, CD 21
• **English Learner's Companion** ● ▲ • **Literatura en español** ● ▲ • **Literary Analysis for Enrichment** ■		
• **Formal Assessment:** Selection Test, pp. 275–277 ● ▲ ■ • **Open Book Test,** pp. 190–192 ● ▲ ■ • **Performance Assessment and Portfolio Management,** p. 19 ● ▲ ■ • ⬤ PRENTICE HALL **ASSESSMENT** *SYSTEM* ● ▲ ■	• ⬤ PRENTICE HALL **ASSESSMENT** *SYSTEM* ● ▲ ■ Skills Practice Answers and Explanations on Transparencies	• **Test Bank Software** ● ▲ ■ • **Got It! Assessment Videotapes,** Tape 5 ● ▲
• **Selection Support Workbook:** ● ▲ ■ Grammar and Style, p. 297 • **Writing and Grammar,** Ruby Level ● ▲ ■ • **Extension Activities,** p. 64 ● ▲ ■	• **Daily Language Practice Transparencies** ● ▲ • **Writing Models and Graphic Organizers on Transparencies,** p. 87 ● ▲ ■	• **Writing and Grammar iText CD-ROM** ● ▲ ■ 💻 *Take It to the Net* www.phschool.com

BLOCK SCHEDULING: Use one 90-minute class period to preteach the selection and have students read it. Use a second 90-minute class period to assess students' mastery of skills and have them complete one of the Extension Activities.

Step-by-Step Teaching Guide
for pp. 1096–1097

Motivation

As students question and define their own identities in relation to their cultural heritages, they will find these poems—statements of cultural pride and definition—intensely relevant. Begin a discussion of this topic by displaying a selection of advertisements featuring people of various ethnicities and cultures. Ask students to discuss why the advertisers chose to use these models. Discuss as a class the growing role of cultural identity in America's multicultural society.

▣ Interest Grabber Video

As an alternative, play "Martín Espada on Sensory Language" on Tape 6 to engage student interest.

❶ Background

More About the Authors

Lorna Dee Cervantes is also co-editor of *Red Dirt*, a cross-cultural poetry journal, and her work has been included in many anthologies. In 1995, she received a Lila Wallace-Reader's Digest Writers' Award.

Martín Espada's work has appeared in the *New York Times Book Review*, *Harper's*, *The Nation*, and *The Best American Poetry*. He has received the Pen/Revson Award, Paterson Poetry Prize, two NEA fellowships, and the National Book Award.

Diana Chang received a John Hay Whitney Foundation Fellowship in order to complete her first novel, *The Frontiers of Love* (1956). She is a charter life member of the International Society of Poets and The Library of Congress.

Simon Ortiz's books of poetry include *Going for Rain* (1976), *Woven Stone* (1992), and *After and Before the Lightning* (1994).

Garrett Hongo's *The River of Heaven* was the Lamont Poetry Selection of the Academy of American Poets and a finalist for the Pulitzer Prize in 1988. He has also received fellowships from the National Endowment for the Arts and the Rockefeller Foundation.

Prepare to Read

❶ Freeway 280 ◆ Who Burns for the Perfection of Paper ◆ Most Satisfied by Snow ◆ Hunger in New York City ◆ What For

Lorna Dee Cervantes (b. 1954)

California native Lorna Dee Cervantes has been writing poetry since she was eight years old. A committed feminist and Hispanic rights activist, she founded her own small press in 1976 "to broaden not only the horizons but also the definitions of what was Chicana literature." Cervantes published her own first book of poetry, *Emplumada*, in 1981. She also established the literary magazine *Mango* to help nurture other Hispanic American writers. Despite her commitment to the Chicano community, she writes in English to give her work a greater political reach.

Martín Espada (b. 1957)

Not many lawyers pursue simultaneous careers as poets, but, until 1993, Martín Espada was an exception. Espada's creativity was inspired by his father, a talented photographer based in Brooklyn, New York. Father and son worked together on a 1981 photo documentary called *The Puerto Rican Diaspora Documentary Project*. A year later, Espada published his first volume of poetry, *The Immigrant Iceboy's Bolero*. He now teaches poetry at the University of Massachusetts at Amherst.

Diana Chang (b. 1934)

Born in New York City, Diana Chang spent most of her childhood in China. She returned to the United States after World War II and attended Barnard College in New York. In addition to writing poetry, she has written several novels, including *The Frontiers of Love* (1993). Chang's spare, introspective poetry, collected in volumes such as *What Matisse Is After* (1984), shows the influence of traditional Asian verse forms. She has also translated Asian writings into English. Perhaps due to the many views and voices in her experience, Chang's work "moves beyond ethnicity" to examine "identity and self."

Simon Ortiz (b. 1941)

A native of the Acoma Pueblo in New Mexico, Simon Ortiz grew up steeped in the oral tradition of his people. Writing came naturally to him, and in 1980 he was honored at a White House "Salute to Poetry and American Poets." Ortiz has published more than a dozen books of poetry and prose, including *Men on the Moon: Collected Short Stories* (1999) and *From Sand Creek* (2000). He edits the literary magazine *Wanbli Ho*.

Garrett Hongo (b. 1951)

One of the stars among contemporary Asian American poets, Garrett Hongo is a fourth-generation Japanese American who spent his early childhood in Hawaii. His father, an electrical technician, figures prominently in Hongo's poems and is profiled in his book *Volcano: A Memoir of Hawaii* (1995). Hongo has won numerous awards, including fellowships from the Thomas Watson and Guggenheim foundations. Among Hongo's other works are *Yellow Light* (1982) and *The River of Heaven* (1988).

1096 ◆ *Prosperity and Protest (1946–Present)*

TEACHING RESOURCES

The following resources can be used to enrich or extend the instruction for pp. 1096–1097.

Motivation
▣ **Interest Grabber Video,** Tape 6

Background
📖 **Beyond Literature,** p. 64

💻 *Take It to the Net*
Visit www.phschool.com for Background and hotlinks for the poems.

Literary Analysis
▤ **Literary Analysis and Reading Transparencies,** Voice, p. 128 ▣

Reading
▤ **Literary Analysis and Reading Transparencies,** Summarizing, p. 127

📖 **Selection Support:** Reading Strategy, p. 280; Build Vocabulary, p. 278 ▣

▣ **BLOCK SCHEDULING:** Resources marked with this symbol provide varied instruction during 90-minute blocks.

Preview

Connecting to the Literature

The poets whose work appears here represent some of the many distinct cultural groups that make up the American fabric. As you read, think about the role that family and cultural heritage plays in your life.

❷ Literary Analysis

Voice

Just as each person has a distinctive way of speaking, every poet has a unique **voice**, or literary personality. A poet's voice is based on word choice, tone, sound devices, rhyme (or its absence), pace, attitude, and even the patterns of vowels and consonants. Consider these examples:

Cervantes: Viejitas come here with paper bags to gather greens . . .
Chang: Against my windows, / fog knows / what to do, too

As you read these poems, note the distinctive voice each one reveals.

Comparing Literary Works

Issues of cultural and personal **alienation** are a common theme in American poetry of the late twentieth century. Alienation is the feeling of being separate, or detached from a group. Feelings of alienation arise from internal sources, such as questions of personal identity, or from external sources, such as clashes between cultures. As you read these poems, think about the poet's relationship to his or her subject, and whether or not it expresses acceptance or the more difficult feelings of alienation.

❸ Reading Strategy

Summarizing

Sometimes, you can understand a poem better if you briefly restate the main points in a **summary.** A summary should match these criteria:

- It includes content from the beginning, middle, and end.
- It is concise—no longer than a single sentence.
- It is precise, clearly conveying the poem's essence.

Use a chart like the one shown to create summaries of each poem.

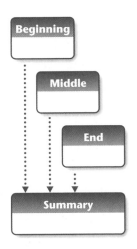

Vocabulary

crevices (krev´ is iz) *n.* narrow cracks or splits (p. 1100)

pervade (pər vād´) *v.* to spread throughout (p. 1101)

automation (ôt´ ə mā´ shən) *n.* manufacturing conducted with partly or fully self-operating machinery (p. 1102)

liturgy (lit´ ər jē) *n.* public religious ceremonies; religious ritual (p. 1103)

conjure (kun´ jər) *v.* to summon by magic or as if by magic; to call forth (p. 1103)

calligraphy (kə lig´ rə fē) *n.* artistic handwriting (p. 1104)

trough (trôf) *n.* a low point of a wave (p. 1104)

❷ Literary Analysis

Voice

- As they read the four poems, students will think about how each poet's culture and heritage is reflected in his or her work. Are the poets integrated into their culture, or do they seem alienated?

- Encourage students to read the poems carefully and repeatedly, considering as they read each one how they would describe the poet's voice, or literary personality.

- Discuss the elements that make up a poet's voice, and have volunteers compare the voice reflected in the two examples on this page.

- Use the Voice transparency on p. 128 of **Literary Analysis and Reading Transparencies** to show students a model of an analysis of voice in a poem.

❸ Reading Strategy

Summarizing

- Remind students that summaries are concise statements that contain the essential ideas of a selection. Mention that attempting to write a summary can help students realize whether or not they understood what they read.

- Have students write a one-sentence summary of each of the four poems. To help them write the summaries, they should copy the chart shown on p. 1097 and use it to make sure they include information from the beginning, middle, and end of each poem.

Vocabulary Development

- Pronounce each vocabulary word for students, and read the definitions as a class. Have students identify any words with which they are already familiar.

CUSTOMIZE INSTRUCTION FOR UNIVERSAL ACCESS

For Less Proficient Readers	For English Learners	For Advanced Readers
Encourage students to listen to each poem on audiotape or CD before they read it. Poetic syntax may be challenging to less proficient readers. To help students understand the meaning of the poems, encourage them to punctuate or rewrite part or all of the poems in sentence form.	Encourage students to listen to each poem on audiotape or CD before they read it. Understanding the specific cultural references in these poems may add a level of difficulty that challenges students learning English. Remind students to read the footnotes carefully.	Analyzing the figurative language can help more advanced readers appreciate the literary style of these poems. Urge students to listen to the poems on audiotape or CD before they read them, enjoying the sound and the meaning of each one. As they listen, and later as they read each poem, ask them to pay particular attention to figurative language.

 E-Teach

Visit E-Teach at www.phschool.com for teachers' essays on how to teach, with questions and answers.

Step-by-Step Teaching Guide for pp. 1098–1105

CUSTOMIZE INSTRUCTION
For Visual/Spatial Learners

Encourage these students to respond freely to the illustrations that accompany the poems. Challenge them to make predictions about the content and mood of the poems based on the illustrations.

❶ About the Selection

"Freeway 280" demonstrates how the bonds of cultural heritage and childhood experiences help shape adult identities. In "Freeway 280," the speaker traces the path of her own rediscovered cultural identity by blending Spanish and English and focusing on the endurance of nature despite human interference.

❷ Literary Analysis

Voice

• Read aloud the first stanza to students. Ask students to respond to the stanza. How would they describe its voice?
Answer: The voice has a tone of wistfulness and regret.

• Then, ask students to identify a device that the poet uses that contributes to this tone.
Answer: Many students will cite the use of Spanish words.

❸ Background

Art

Untitled by Peter Malone

This painting creates a relatively accurate physical representation of a real place through the colors and images of the artist's personal experience.

Use this question for discussion:

• How might the poem's speaker characterize the place depicted in the painting?
Answer: The speaker might characterize it first as a means of escape from her Chicano community, but later as a symbol of outside interference with her community.

---

❶ Freeway 280
Lorna Dee Cervantes

Background

The poems you are about to read reflect the cultural roots of their authors. Cervantes writes of her Chicana heritage in a familiar California setting, a barrio near a freeway. Espada recalls the harsh physical labor of an after-school job. Ortiz describes how life in New York City prompts a hunger for his southwestern home. Chinese American writer Chang offers a poem whose subject and style are reminiscent of Asian verse. Hongo's poem draws on his heritage as one of many Japanese Americans in Hawaii, some of whom practice the Buddhist faith of their ancestors.

❸

❷
Las casitas[1] near the gray cannery,
nestled amid wild abrazos[2] of climbing roses
and man-high red geraniums
are gone now. The freeway conceals it
5   all beneath a raised scar.

But under the fake windsounds of the open lanes,
in the abandoned lots below, new grasses sprout,
wild mustard remembers, old gardens
come back stronger than they were,
10 trees have been left standing in their yards.
Albaricoqueros, cerezos, nogales . . .[3]

---

1. **Las casitas** (läs kä sē´ täs) "The little houses" (Spanish).
2. **abrazos** (ä brä´ sōs) "hugs" (Spanish).
3. **Albaricoqueros, cerezos, nogales** (äl bär´ rē kō ker´ ōs, se rē´ sōs, nō gä´ les) "Apricot trees, cherry trees, walnut trees" (Spanish).

1098 ◆ *Prosperity and Protest (1946–Present)*

▲ **Critical Viewing** ❹
Is the red light in this painting suited to the ideas in Cervantes' poem? Why or why not? **[Connect]**

TEACHING RESOURCES

The following resources can be used to enrich or extend the instruction for pp. 1098–1105.

Literary Analysis

📖 **Selection Support:** Literary Analysis, p. 281 ▪

Reading

🎧 **Listening to Literature Audiocassettes,** Side 37 ▪

💿 **Listening to Literature Audio CDs,** CD 21 ▪

▪ **BLOCK SCHEDULING:** Resources marked with this symbol provide varied instruction during 90-minute blocks.

Viejitas[4] come here with paper bags to gather greens.
Espinaca, verdolagas, yerbabuena . . .[5]

I scramble over the wire fence
15 that would have kept me out.
Once, I wanted out, wanted the rigid lanes
to take me to a place without sun,
without the smell of tomatoes burning
on swing shift in the greasy summer air.

20 Maybe it's here
en los campos extraños de esta ciudad[6]
where I'll find it, that part of me
mown under
like a corpse
25 or a loose seed.

---

4. **Viejitas** (bye hē´ täs) "Old women" (Spanish).
5. **Espinaca, verdolagas, yerbabuena** (es pē nä´ kä, ber thō lä´ gäs, yer´ bä bwe´ nä) "Spinach, purslane, peppermint" (Spanish).
6. **en los campos extraños de esta ciudad** (en lōs käm´ pōs es trä´ nyōs de es´ tä syōō däd´) "In the strange fields of this city" (Spanish).

Review and Assess

Thinking About the Selection

1. **Respond:** In what way does the author's use of both Spanish and English affect your response to this poem? Explain.

2. **(a) Recall:** In the first stanza, which buildings does the speaker say are now gone? **(b) Classify:** What sort of neighborhood once stood at the site of the freeway? **(c) Interpret:** In what way is Freeway 280 like a scar?

3. **(a) Recall:** In lines 14–19, what does the speaker do? **(b) Interpret:** How do the speaker's actions represent a change in attitude toward this neighborhood?

4. **(a) Connect:** In lines 24–25, what does the speaker liken to a "corpse" and a "loose seed"? **(b) Interpret:** In your own words, what do you think the speaker is seeking? **(c) Analyze:** What details in lines 7–10 imply that the "loose seed" will take root?

5. **(a) Analyze:** What aspects of this poem challenge the idea that speed and progress are always beneficial? **(b) Take a Position:** Do you agree or disagree with the poet's position? Explain.

Freeway 280 ◆ 1099

❺ Who Burns for the Perfection of Paper

Martín Espada

At sixteen, I worked after high school hours
at a printing plant
that manufactured legal pads:
Yellow paper
5   stacked seven feet high
and leaning
as I slipped cardboard
between the pages,
then brushed red glue
10 up and down the stack.
No gloves: fingertips required
for the perfection of paper,
smoothing the exact rectangle.
Sluggish by 9 PM, the hands
15 would slide along suddenly sharp paper,
and gather slits thinner than the crevices
of the skin, hidden.
Then the glue would sting,
hands oozing
20 till both palms burned
at the punchclock.

Ten years later, in law school,
I knew that every legal pad
was glued with the sting of hidden cuts,
25 that every open lawbook
was a pair of hands
upturned and burning.

crevices (krev´ is iz) n. narrow cracks or splits

1100 ◆ Prosperity and Protest (1946–Present)

✦ ENRICHMENT: Social Studies Connection

Child Labor

The International Labor Organization estimates that at least 250 million children between the ages of five and fourteen work, about half of them full-time. Most working children, about 62% of them, are in Asia. About 32% are in Africa, and most of the rest are in Latin America and the Caribbean.

The majority of child laborers work in agriculture. Other children work in service industries and small-scale manufacturing, which is rarely covered by national laws. Many children who work are exposed to harmful pesticides and toxic substances such as asbestos and mercury. No one knows exactly how many tens of millions of children are working in unhealthful, dangerous conditions. Of course, most children who are working are not going to school. An estimated 145 million children between the ages of six and eleven do not attend school.

MOST SATISFIED BY SNOW
Diana Chang

Against my windows,
fog knows
what to do, too

Spaces pervade
5   us, as well

But occupied by snow,
I see

Matter
matters

10 I, too,
flowering

❼ ▲ Critical Viewing
In what ways does this image of trees relate to the last two lines of the poem? [Connect]

pervade (per vād´) v. to spread throughout

Review and Assess

Thinking About the Selections

1. **Respond:** In what ways were you surprised by these poems?

2. **(a) Recall:** In "Who Burns for the Perfection of Paper," what was the speaker's first experience with legal pads?
   (b) Recall: What were the speaker's later job with legal pads?
   (c) Interpret: What did the speaker learn from the first job?

3. **(a) Recall:** What word does the speaker use twice to describe cuts on the hands? **(b) Interpret:** What role does the idea of anonymity play in this poem?

4. **(a) Classify:** In "Most Satisfied by Snow," the speaker observes two kinds of weather. What are they?
   (b) Compare and Contrast: What differences between these two types of weather does the poem highlight?

5. **(a) Interpret:** What might the speaker mean by the comment that "spaces pervade us"? **(b) Interpret:** What is the relationship of "matter" to these "spaces"?

Most Satisfied By Snow ◆ 1101

CUSTOMIZE INSTRUCTION FOR UNIVERSAL ACCESS

For Less Proficient Readers	For Gifted/Talented Students	For Advanced Readers
Help students relate to "Who Burns for the Perfection of Paper" by discussing jobs they have held. What were the most difficult parts of those jobs?	Help students relate to "Who Burns for the Perfection of Paper" by discussing jobs they have held. What were the most difficult parts of those jobs? Have students pantomime doing various jobs and ask classmates to guess which jobs they are acting out and how they feel about doing the work.	Help students relate to "Who Burns for the Perfection of Paper" by discussing jobs they have held. What were the most difficult parts of those jobs? Ask students to research child labor practices in the United States and list some suggestions for improving the lives of children who work.

The speaker in "Hunger in New York City" acknowledges a longing for his home, where nature is more accessible, and draws on memories of a closer connection to the earth to satisfy his longing.

❾ ▶ Critical Viewing
Answer: The poem and photograph both convey sadness and longing.

❿ Vocabulary Development
Greek Prefix auto–
• Draw students' attention to the definition of the word automation in the margin. Have a volunteer read the definition.
• Tell students that the prefix auto– means "self." Have them explain how the prefix relates to the meaning of automation.
Answer: Automation is self-operated machinery.

⓫ Reading Strategy
Summarizing
• Have a volunteer read aloud the last stanza of the poem. Ask students to identify the main idea of this stanza.
• Then, ask students the Reading Strategy question on p. 1102: Summarize the final stanza to determine what it reveals about the speaker's struggle.
Answer: The speaker nurtures and heals himself by communing with nature.

❽ Hunger in New York City

Simon Ortiz

Hunger crawls into you
from somewhere out of your muscles
or the concrete or the land
or the wind pushing you.

5   It comes to you, asking
for food, words, wisdom, young memories
of places you ate at, drank cold spring water,
or held somebody's hand,
or home of the gentle, slow dances,
10   the songs, the strong gods, the world
you know.

That is, hunger searches you out.
It always asks you,
How are you, son? Where are you?
15   Have you eaten well?
Have you done what you as a person
of our people is supposed to do?

And the concrete of this city,
the oily wind, the blazing windows,
20   the shrieks of <u>automation</u> cannot,
truly cannot, answer for that hunger
although I have hungered,
truthfully and honestly, for them
to feed myself with.

25   So I sang to myself quietly:
I am feeding myself
with the humble presence
of all around me;
I am feeding myself
30   with your soul, my mother earth;
make me cool and humble.
Bless me.

1102 ◆ *Prosperity and Protest (1946–Present)*

❾ ▲ Critical Viewing
What words would you use to describe the emotions conveyed by both the poem and this photograph? [Interpret]

automation (ôt′ ə mā′ shən) *n.* manufacturing conducted with partly or fully self-operating machinery

Reading Strategy
Summarizing Summarize the final stanza to determine what it reveals about the speaker's struggle.

What For

GARRETT HONGO

At six I lived for spells:
how a few Hawaiian words could call
up the rain, could hymn like the sea
in the long swirl of chambers
5   curling in the nautilus of a shell,[1]
how Amida's[2] ballads of the Buddhaland
in the drone of the priest's <u>liturgy</u>
could <u>conjure</u> money from the poor
and give them nothing but mantras,[3]
10 the strange syllables that healed desire.

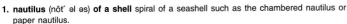

1. **nautilus** (nôt´ əl əs) **of a shell** spiral of a seashell such as the chambered nautilus or paper nautilus.
2. **Amida's** (ä mēd ä) referring to Amida, the great savior worshiped by members of the Pure Land sect of Buddhism popular in eastern Asia.
3. **mantras** (män´ trəz) sacred words repeated in prayers, hymns, or chants.

▲ **Critical Viewing** In the poem's final stanza, in what way does the poet use the image of the fragrant plumeria flower to communicate his desire to heal his father's pain? **[Analyze]**

liturgy (lit´ ər jē) *n.* public religious ceremonies; religious ritual

conjure (kän´ jər) *v.* to summon by magic or as if by magic; to call forth

What For ◆ 1103

⓬ About the Selection

In this poem, the speaker recalls childhood moments of waiting patiently for his father to come home from a physically demanding job and the fervent wish to use the power of his Japanese and Hawaiian heritage to ease his father's pain.

⓭ ▶Critical Viewing

Answer: The plumeria flower is particularly fragrant, and the speaker equates the sweet smell of the flower with sweet words that he wishes could cure his father's aches and pains.

⓮ Critical Thinking

Infer

• Read aloud the bracketed stanza to students. Have them clarify what the speaker means by "spells." Have them point out other words in the stanza that support their responses, such as *liturgy, conjure,* and *mantras.*

• Then, ask students to decide what makes spells so powerful to the speaker.
Answer: The speaker seems most impressed by the way words are used in spells to affect natural forces and people.

Summarizing

- Have students read lines 24–40 to themselves. As they read, instruct them to record all the details that relate to the father's daily experience.

- Then, ask them the Reading Strategy question on p. 1104: Summarize the father's daily experience.
  Answer: The father works hard at a physically demanding job that is destroying his health and leaves him too tired at the end of a day to play with his child.

▶ Monitor Progress Ask students how they decided what information to include in the summary.
Answer: Students should understand that the important points in a passage should be included in a summary: in this case, the physical demands of the father's job and the effect his job has on him.

⑯ Literary Analysis

Voice

- Read aloud the bracketed stanza to students. Have students close their eyes as you read, and ask them to think about the effects of the speaker's words on them.

- Then, ask them the Literary Analysis question on p. 1004: In what way would you describe the speaker's voice in lines 41–46?
  Answer: The speaker's voice is straightforward and clear, as would be typical of a child. The speaker's longing is expressed in the first two words in the stanza: "I wanted." The poet uses two figures of speech in this stanza, a metaphor comparing hearing to crystal chimes and a simile comparing crystal chimes to "fins of glass."

⑰ Literary Analysis

Voice and Alienation

- Ask students to restate the meaning of the last stanza in their own words.

- Then, have students respond to the Literary Analysis question on p. 1105: What is the speaker's desire in the last stanza of this poem?
  Answer: The speaker wants to be able to cure his father through the power of words.

I lived for stories about the war
my grandfather told over *hana* cards,[4]
slapping them down on the mats
with a sharp Japanese *kiai*.[5]

15 I lived for songs my grandmother sang
stirring curry into a thick stew,
weaving a <u>calligraphy</u> of Kannon's[6] love
into grass mats and straw sandals.

I lived for the red volcano dirt
20 staining my toes, the salt residue
of surf and sea wind in my hair,
the arc of a flat stone skipping
in the hollow <u>trough</u> of a wave.

I lived a child's world, waited
25 for my father to drag himself home,
dusted with blasts of sand, powdered rock,
and the strange ash of raw cement,
his deafness made worse by the clang
of pneumatic drills,[7] sore in his bones
30 from the buckings of a jackhammer.

⑮ He'd hand me a scarred lunchpail,
let me unlace the hightop G.I. boots,[8]
call him the new name I'd invented
that day in school, write it for him
35 on his newspaper. He'd rub my face
with hands that felt like gravel roads,
tell me to move, go play, and then he'd
walk to the laundry sink to scrub,
rinse the dirt of his long day
40 from a face brown and grained as koa wood.[9]

⑯ I wanted to take away the pain
in his legs, the swelling in his joints,
give him back his hearing,
clear and rare as crystal chimes,
45 the fins of glass that wrinkled
and sparked the air with their sound.

calligraphy (kə lig′ rə fē) *n.* artistic handwriting

trough (trôf) *n.* a low point of a wave

Reading Strategy
Summarizing Summarize the father's daily experience.

Literary Analysis
Voice In what way would you describe the speaker's voice in lines 41–46?

---

4. *hana* (hä′ nä) **cards** cards with flower patterns that players try to pair up in a popular Japanese card game. *Hana* is Japanese for "flower."
5. *kiai* (kē ī′) Japanese word for the sound made by slapping down *hana* cards.
6. **Kannon's** (kä′ nənz) referring to an enlightened savior of Japanese Buddhism who, out of infinite compassion and mercy, forgoes the heavenly state of nirvana in order to save others.
7. **pneumatic** (nōō mat′ ik) **drills** air drills used in construction.
8. **hightop G.I. boots** army boots.
9. **koa** (kō′ ə) **wood** grainy wood of the Hawaiian acacia tree.

1104 ◆ *Prosperity and Protest (1946–Present)*

✸ ENRICHMENT: Science Connection

Noise Pollution

Noise pollution has been an unwanted side effect of the growth and development of cities and transportation systems.

The intensity of sound is commonly measured in logarithmic units called decibels. A change from a level of 10 decibels to 20 decibels represents a 100% increase in sound. Steady noise at 80 decibels is annoying, but steady exposure to 90 decibels or more—which is what the speaker's father experi-enced using a pneumatic drill—is dangerous. Besides causing hearing loss, such loud noises may have other bad effects on health and productivity at work.

Many large cities have tried to limit noise pollution—especially at airports—with limited success.

I wanted to heal the sores that work
and war had sent to him,
let him play catch in the backyard
50   with me, tossing a tennis ball
past papaya trees without the shoulders
of pain shrugging back his arms.

I wanted to become a doctor of pure magic,
to string a necklace of sweet words
55   fragrant as pine needles and plumeria,[10]
fragrant as the bread my mother baked,
place it like a lei of cowrie shells[11]
and *pikake*[12] flowers around my father's neck,
and chant him a blessing, a sutra.[13]

---

10. **plumeria** (plōō mer′ ē ə) tropical tree bearing flowers known for their fragrance.
11. **lei** (lā) **of cowrie** (kou′ rē) **shells** garland made of brightly colored seashells found in the South Pacific.
12. *pikake* (pē kä′ kä) Hawaiian word for jasmine, a fragrant flowering shrub.
13. **sutra** (sōō′ trə) one of the sacred texts or scriptures of Buddhism.

Literary Analysis
Voice and Alienation
What is the speaker's desire in the last stanza of this poem?

Review and Assess

Thinking About the Selections

1. **Respond:** Do you think the speaker of "What For" had a happy childhood? Why or why not?

2. **(a) Recall:** In "Hunger in New York City," what four questions does hunger ask? **(b) Analyze:** What kind of hunger does the speaker mean?

3. **(a) Interpret:** What key words does the speaker use to paint a harsh portrait of New York City?
   (b) Compare and Contrast: In what ways is the city unlike the world the speaker has known—the world of his home?

4. **(a) Recall:** In the first four stanzas of "What For," what forms of communication did the speaker live for? **(b) Infer:** What do these forms of communication suggest about the child's relationship to adults?

5. **(a) Deduce:** From where did the father "drag himself home" each day? **(b) Analyze:** What values are expressed in the father's behavior?

6. **(a) Classify:** In what ways does the landscape of the poem change in the fifth stanza? **(b) Interpret:** Is this shift connected to the child's wish for the father in the final stanza? Explain.

7. **Evaluate:** Evaluate the title's relationship to the content of the poem. Is the title an effective one? Explain.

✎ ASSESSMENT PRACTICE: Writing Skills

Sentence Structure   **(For more practice, see Test Preparation Workbook, p. 67.)**

Many tests require students to identify correctly written sentences that should be combined. Use the following sample item to demonstrate.

   Poets often do other work. They work to support themselves. Among the members of most professions, you can find a poet or two.

   Chose the best way to write the underlined section. If the underlined section needs no change, choose "Correct as is."

A Poets often do other work to support themselves.

B Poets often do other work, or they work to support themselves.

C Among the members of most professions, poets work to support themselves.

D Correct as is.

   Students should recognize that choice *A* combines two choppy sentences, but maintains the sense of both.

1. Many students will feel that the speaker had a fairly happy childhood, but that he was sad about his father's aches and pains and his inability to spend much time with the speaker.

2. **(a)** Hunger asks these questions: How are you? Where are you? Have you eaten well? Have you done what you are supposed to do? **(b)** The hunger is for a connection to a person's cultural heritage and to nature.

3. **(a)** The poet uses the words "Concrete," "oily wind," "blazing windows," and "shrieks of automation" to describe New York City. **(b)** New York City is unlike the speaker's home because it holds no memories of the speaker's cultural heritage and connectedness with nature.

4. **(a)** The speaker lived for spells, stories, songs, and volcanic dirt. **(b)** Significant adults were very important to the child.

5. **(a)** He dragged himself home from work. **(b)** The behavior of the speaker's father expresses the values of working hard and not complaining or discussing difficulties.

6. **(a)** The landscape shifts from the speaker's world to his father's. **(b)** Yes, this shift permits readers to appreciate how hard the father works and how exhausted he is so that the speaker's wish in the last stanza makes sense.

7. The title asks a question that the poem answers by listing the things for which the speaker lived as a boy and describing how the father works to support the family. Most students will think that the title is effective because it addresses the central concerns of the poem.

Review and Assess

1. **(a)** Possible response for "Freeway 280": Adjective: yearning; Evidence: the speaker is looking for something. **(b)** Another adjective would be *remorseful*.

2. **(a)** The poets' descriptions of customs and their use of their first languages reflect their cultural background. **(b)** The poets' descriptions of physical labor reflect their working class backgrounds. Ortiz's longing for a connection with nature reflects the importance of nature to his heritage. The form of Chang's poem as well as her contemplation of nature may reflect her heritage.

3. **(a)** Cervantes and Ortiz express alienation. **(b)** Cervantes is alienated from her childhood, Ortiz from the earth.

4. **(a)** These settings are all products of an industrial society. **(b)** The freeway brings a way out to Cervantes; it deprives her of a connection with her past. The plant lets Espada earn money. It deprives him of the time to do other things. The city deprives Ortiz of his connection to nature. It presumably supplies him with a job and housing. The construction site deprives the speaker's father of his health. It permits him to earn a living.

5. Cervantes is searching for a connection to her past. Espada has not forgotten his background as he strives to get ahead. Hongo appreciates the sacrifices his family has made for him.

6. **(a)** The speaker relies on memories of a closer connection to nature for comfort. The speaker appreciates the labor of ordinary workers because he remembers his own efforts. **(b)** Rhyme, meter, and figurative language are lost.

7. **(a)** The speaker remembers the stories and songs that he heard, as well as his interaction with nature. **(b)** The speaker remembers the toll hard work took on his father and how he wished he could heal him. **(c)** The summaries reveal that the poem is divided roughly in half.

8. Students may mention various holiday celebrations, foods, dress, and other customs.

1106

Review and Assess

Literary Analysis

Voice

1. (a) Use a chart like the one shown to select the adjective that best describes each poet's **voice.** (b) Then, choose another adjective that additionally characterizes each poet's voice.

Adjectives: angry, meditative, remorseful, yearning, reverent

Poet	Voice	Evidence	⋯▶	Additional Adjectives

2. (a) What aspects of Hongo's and Cervantes's voices reflect their respective cultures? (b) In what ways do the voices of the other poets reflect their cultural backgrounds?

Comparing Literary Works

3. (a) Which of these poets express **alienation**? (b) In each case, what is the cause of that alienation?

4. (a) What traits do the freeway, the printing plant, the urban setting, and the construction site share? (b) What does each bring to the speakers in these poems? What does each take away?

5. Simon Ortiz notes that the "hunger" asks "Have you done what you as a person / of our people is supposed to do?" How does this question apply to the poems by Cervantes, Espada, and Hongo?

Reading Strategy

Summarizing

6. (a) Write a **summary** of "Hunger in New York City" and "Who Burns for the Perfection of Paper." (b) What poetic effects and meanings are lost in the summaries?

7. (a) Write a summary of stanzas 1–4 of "What For." (b) Write a summary of stanzas 5–8. (c) What do these summaries reveal to you about the poem's structure?

Extend Understanding

8. **Cultural Connection:** What aspects of American popular culture reflect the country's growing diversity?

Quick Review

Voice is a poet's distinctive literary personality, created by word choice, tone, sound devices, rhyme, pace, and attitude.

Alienation, a sense of detachment or separation from a group, is a common theme in American literature of the twentieth century.

To **summarize,** briefly restate the main points of a poem in a concise way.

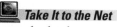 **Take It to the Net**
www.phschool.com
Take the interactive self-test online to check your understanding of these selections.

☀ **ENRICHMENT: Further Reading**

Other Works by the Authors

Works by Lorna Dee Cervantes
Emplumada

Works by Martín Espada
Trumpets from the Islands of their Eviction

Works by Diana Chang
The Frontiers of Love

Works by Simon Ortiz
Homecomings

Works by Garrett Hongo
Yellow Light

 **Take It to the Net**
Visit www.phschool.com for more information on the authors.

Integrate Language Skills

Vocabulary Development Lesson

Word Analysis: Greek Prefix *auto-*

Explain how the meaning of *auto-*, defined as "self," is expressed in each of the following words:

1. automobile
2. autopilot
3. autograph
4. autobiography
5. automatic
6. autocratic

Spelling Strategy

The *shun* sound in a suffix is usually formed by the letters *sion* or *tion*, as in percus*sion* or auto*mation*. Add the suffix *-sion* or *-tion* to change each of the following verbs into a noun.

1. fascinate
2. extend
3. intervene
4. devote

Fluency: Definitions

Choose the definition that best matches each numbered word.

1. trough (a) high point of a wave, (b) low point of a wave, (c) surf
2. conjure (a) quickly follow, (b) harshly criticize, (c) magically summon
3. calligraphy (a) bright tapestry, (b) intricate hairdo, (c) artistic handwriting
4. liturgy (a) a religious ritual, (b) dinner menu, (c) architectural blueprint
5. automation (a) electrification, (b) mechanization, (c) termination
6. crevices (a) gorges, (b) rivers, (c) narrow cracks
7. pervade (a) spread, (b) withdraw, (c) request

Grammar and Style Lesson

Participial Phrases

A **participial phrase** is a participle—a verb form that can be used as an adjective—and the words that modify or complete it. The entire phrase works as an adjective to modify a noun or a pronoun.

> **Present Participle:** My hands, *smoothing the exact rectangle*, would slide along the paper. (modifies *hands*)
>
> **Past Participle:** *Reminded of the experience*, he winced. (modifies *he*)

Practice Identify the participial phrase in each sentence. Determine the noun or pronoun it modifies.

1. Seeking an after-school job, I found one at a printing plant.
2. I worked hard, slipping cardboard between the papers.
3. Cut by sharp edges, my hands were often stinging.
4. The glue, oozing over them, made the stinging worse.
5. I can still visualize my hands, upturned in pain.

Writing Application Write a paragraph about a place you know or can picture, using the following participial phrases:

1. nestled among climbing roses
2. sitting beside the freeway
3. abandoned in the open lots

$\mathcal{WG}$ *Prentice Hall Writing and Grammar Connection: Chapter 19, Section 2*

Freeway 280 / Who Burns for the Perfection of Paper / Most Satisfied by Snow / Hunger in New York City / What For ◆ 1107

❸ Writing Lesson

- Discuss with students the views of childhood portrayed in "Freeway 280" and "What For."

- Explain that students will write comparisons of the messages about childhood in these poems and the means the poets use to relay their messages.

- Remind students that they are to take notes on the language, meaning, and structure of both poems and then compare the two poems. They might want to record their notes in the Comparison-and-Contrast organizer on p. 87 of **Writing Models and Graphic Organizers on Transparencies.**

- Go over the model with students so that they understand how to revise their own work to make the modifiers as precise as possible.

- Use the Comparison-and-Contrast Essay rubric on p. 19 of **Performance Assessment and Portfolio Management** to evaluate students' work.

❹ Listening and Speaking

- Suggest that students work in small groups to interview someone about his or her heritage.

- Have students find out as much as they can beforehand about the person's background so that their interviews can be as focused as possible. Remind students to let the interviewee talk—silence while the person considers a question is fine.

CUSTOMIZE INSTRUCTION
For Universal Access

To address different learning styles, use the activities suggested in the **Extension Activities** booklet, p. 64.

- For Verbal/Linguistic and Visual/Spatial Learners, use Activity 5.

- For Verbal/Linguistic Learners, use Activity 6.

- For Visual/Spatial Learners, use Activity 7.

---

❸ Writing Lesson

Comparison-and-Contrast Essay

The poems by Cervantes and Hongo present childhood in distinctly different ways. In a comparison-and-contrast essay, evaluate the sensory images each poet uses to generate a vivid sense of childhood. Compare and contrast the nature of the wisdom each speaker gains in adulthood.

Prewriting   Reread each poem and take notes about its language, meaning, and structure. Decide why each poem is effective on its own, and then compare the two.

Drafting   Introduce the poets and summarize the poems. Then, state your main ideas about the way each poem portrays childhood. As you draft, include modifiers that clearly express praise or criticism.

Revising   Review your essay to make sure you have expressed your points about each poem with conviction. Identify any weak or unclear modifiers and replace them with stronger choices.

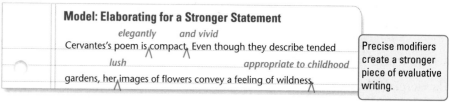

Model: Elaborating for a Stronger Statement

Cervantes's poem is compact. Even though they describe tended gardens, her images of flowers convey a feeling of wildness.

elegantly   *and vivid*   *lush*   *appropriate to childhood*

Precise modifiers create a stronger piece of evaluative writing.

Prentice Hall Writing and Grammar Connection: Chapter 14, Section 4

❹ Extension Activities

Listening and Speaking You probably know someone whose life centers around his or her cultural heritage. With a classmate, conduct an **interview** with such a person. To prepare, use the following tips:

- Develop questions to establish the subject's background and personal history.

- Create a list of suitable follow-up questions.

Videotape or record the interview to share with classmates. **[Group Activity]**

Research and Technology Locate and gather Asian poetry in English translation, using library or Internet resources. Create an **anthology** of these poems. In a brief introduction to your anthology, explain how Diana Chang's "Most Satisfied by Snow" demonstrates the influence of Asian verse.

 **Take It to the Net**   www.phschool.com

Go online for an additional research activity using the Internet.

ASSESSMENT RESOURCES

The following resources can be used to assess students' knowledge and skills.

Selection Assessment

- 📖 **Formal Assessment**, p. 275
- 📖 **Open Book Test**, p. 190
- 📼 **Got It! Assessment Videotapes**, Tape 6
- 💿 **Test Bank Software**
- 💻 *Take It to the Net*
  Visit www.phschool.com for self–tests and additional questions on the selections.

Writing Rubric

- 📖 **Performance Assessment and Portfolio Management.**, p. 19

PRENTICE HALL ASSESSMENT SYSTEM

- 📖 **Workbook**
- 📖 **Skill Book**
- 📇 **Transparencies**
- 💿 **CD-ROM**

Focus on Literary Forms: Essay

My Mother's Book of Life, Lee Lawson

...alytic, expository, satiric, or personal, the essay has been used for centuries to express ideas that range from personal ...tion to national revolution. In the busy modern world, ...s have embraced the essay form, which presents ideas ...mited space. From comedy to personal triumph, the ...s in this section demonstrate the flexibility of the form.

Focus on Literary Forms: Essay ◆ 1109

Selection Planning Guide

The selections in this section offer students a sampling of a wide range of styles and subjects. Carson McCullers's analytical essay from "The Mortgaged Heart" addresses the issue of loneliness. Safire's expository essay "Onomatopoeia" presents an interesting segment of language. Frazier's satirical "Coyote v. Acme" takes a humorous look at the court system. Reflective essays by Cisneros, Dove, and Tan address each author's thoughts about life.

Background

Art

My Mother's Book of Life, 1987, by Lee Lawson

Encourage students to contrast this painting with *Television Moon* (p. 969), which introduced Part 1. Help them to see not only the difference in subject matter—a real moon, as opposed to a televised one, along with a human being reading—but also the differences in style. This painting has visible texture, which softens the edges of the images, as opposed to the hard, almost photographic quality of *Television Moon*.

Use these questions for discussion:

1. What mood would you say this painting creates, and how? Possible answer: The painting creates a quiet, reflective, tender mood through the use of soft colors and interesting textures and through its title.

2. An essay is a highly personal form of literature, directly expressing the author's thoughts, feelings, and opinions. What do you feel this painting reveals about its creator? Possible answer: The artist expresses love for a mother who cherished books and natural beauty.

INSTRUCTION FOR UNIVERSAL ACCESS

...the selections in this part, keep in mind these factors:

...ged Heart"
- ...alysis of an abstract concept

...e, humorous essay about unusual
- ...nliven everyday speech

...comical "opening argument" in a
- ...ght by Wile E. Coyote against the com-...nich he frequently makes purchases

"Straw Into Gold"
- An inspirational essay about overcoming obstacles and finding success

"For the Love of Books"
- An accessible, short essay describing a poet laureate's childhood passion for reading

"Mother Tongue"
- Students who are learning English may relate strongly to this essay.

from The Mortgaged Heart ✦ Onomatopoeia ✦ Coyote v. Acme

Lesson Objectives

1. **To analyze and respond to literary elements**
   - Literary Analysis: Essay
   - Comparing Literary Works
2. **To read, comprehend, analyze, and critique nonfiction**
   - Reading Strategy: Identifying Line of Reasoning
   - Reading Check Questions
   - Review and Assess Questions
3. **To develop word analysis skills, fluency, and systematic vocabulary**
   - Vocabulary Development Lesson: Latin Root: -ten-
4. **To understand and apply written and oral language conventions**
   - Spelling Strategy
   - Grammar and Style Lesson: Pronouns With Appositives
   - Assessment Practice (ATE)
5. **To understand and apply appropriate writing and research strategies**
   - Writing Lesson: Analytical Essay
   - Extension Activity: Essay
6. **To understand and apply listening and speaking strategies**
   - Extension Activity: Opening Statement

STEP-BY-STEP TEACHING GUIDE	PACING GUIDE
PRETEACH	
Motivate Students and Provide Background	
Use the Motivation activity (ATE p. 1110)	5 min.
Read and discuss author and background features (SE/ATE pp. 1110, 1116, 1118) [A]	10 min.
Introduce the Concepts	
Introduce the Literary Analysis and Reading Strategy (SE/ATE p. 1111) [A]	15 min.
Pronounce the vocabulary words and read their definitions (SE p. 1111)	10 min.
TEACH	
Monitor Comprehension	
Informally monitor comprehension by circulating while students read independently or in groups [A]	30 min.
Monitor students' comprehension with the Reading Check notes (SE/ATE pp. 1113, 1119, 1121)	as students read
Develop vocabulary with Vocabulary notes (SE pp. 1112, 1113, 1118, 1119, 1120, 1121; ATE p. 1121)	as students read
Develop Understanding	
Develop students' understanding of the essay form with the Literary Analysis annotations (SE/ATE pp. 1112, 1116, 1120, 1122) [A]	5 min.
Develop students' ability to identify a writer's line of reasoning by using the Reading Strategy annotations (SE/ATE pp. 1113, 1119)	5 min.
ASSESS	
Assess Mastery	
Assess students' mastery of the Reading Strategy and Literary Analysis by having them answer the Review and Assess questions (SE/ATE p. 1123)	15 min.
Use one or more of the print and media Assessment Resources (ATE p. 1125) [A]	up to 45 min.
EXTEND	
Apply Understanding	
Have students complete the Vocabulary Development Lesson and the Grammar and Style Lesson (SE p. 1124) [A]	20 min.
Apply students' ability to use transitions by using the Writing Lesson (SE/ATE p. 1125) [A]	45 min.
Apply students' understanding using one or more of the Extension Activities (SE p. 1125)	20–90 min.

[A] ACCELERATED INSTRUCTION:
Use the strategies and activities identified with an [A].

UNIVERSAL ACCESS
- ● = Below Level Students
- ▲ = On-Level Students
- ■ = Above Level Students

Time and Resource Manager

Reading Level: Challenging, Easy, Average
Average Number of Instructional Days: 4

RESOURCES		
PRINT 📖	**TRANSPARENCIES** 🔖	**TECHNOLOGY** 💿 🎧 📼
• **Beyond Literature,** Cross-Curricular Connection: Social Studies, p. 65 ▲ ■		• **Interest Grabber Video,** Tape 6 ● ▲ ■
• **Selection Support Workbook:** ● ▲ ■ Literary Analysis, p. 285 Reading Strategy, p. 284 Build Vocabulary, p. 282	• **Literary Analysis and Reading Transparencies,** pp. 129 and 130 ● ▲ ■	
		• **Listening to Literature** ● ▲ ■ Audiocassettes, Side 37 Audio CDs, CD 21
• **Literatura en español** ● ▲ • **Literary Analysis for Enrichment** ■		
• **Formal Assessment:** Selection Test, pp. 282–284 ● ▲ ■ • **Open Book Test,** pp. 193–195 ● ▲ ■ • **Performance Assessment and Portfolio Management,** p. 26 ● ▲ ■ • **ASSESSMENT SYSTEM** ● ▲ ■	• **ASSESSMENT SYSTEM** ● ▲ ■ Skills Practice Answers and Explanations on Transparencies	• **Test Bank Software** ● ▲ ■ • **Got It! Assessment Videotapes,** Tape 5 ● ▲
• **Selection Support Workbook:** ● ▲ ■ Grammar and Style, p. 283 • **Writing and Grammar,** Ruby Level ● ▲ ■ • **Extension Activities,** p. 65 ● ▲ ■	• **Daily Language Practice Transparencies** ● ▲	• **Writing and Grammar iText CD-ROM** ● ▲ ■ **Take It to the Net** www.phschool.com

BLOCK SCHEDULING: Use one 90-minute class period to preteach the selection and have students read it. Use a second 90-minute class period to assess students' mastery of skills and have them complete one of the Extension Activities.

PRETEACH

Step-by-Step Teaching Guide for pp. 1110–1111

Motivation

As you show a Roadrunner cartoon to the class, ask students to count the times Coyote meets with disaster. Ask students to draw a few conclusions about Coyote as a predator. (Students will probably decide he is incompetent.) Then, ask for student reaction to the cartoon. Point out that essays—like cartoons, movies, or advertisements—generate a variety of responses. Invite students to be open to the range of expression this genre, and this grouping, offers.

▣ Interest Grabber Video

As an alternative, you may wish to play "Play on Words" on Tape 6 to engage student interest.

❶ Background

More About the Authors

In all McCullers's works, which fit in the category of Southern gothic, characters suffer from physical and psychological problems, perhaps reflecting the author's own difficulties.

In addition to his "On Language" column, William Safire has published a number of books. His 1975 book, *Before the Fall*, describes the pre-Watergate White House. His *New Language of Politics* is considered the definitive study on the language of politics.

Ian Frazier has a great love for the American West. In an interview, he said of the West, "I'm afraid of people thinking, 'There's nothing out there anyway, so let's ruin it.' There's an idea of the Plains as the middle of nowhere, something to be contemptuous of. But it's really a heroic place."

Prepare to Read

❶ *from* The Mortgaged Heart ◆ Onomatopoeia ◆ Coyote v. Acme

Carson McCullers (1917–1967)

Carson McCullers, whose writing has been praised as a brilliant fusion of the compassionate and the grotesque, led a troubled life marked by serious health problems. She was raised in Columbus, Georgia, a town that later formed the backdrop for all her fiction. At the age of seventeen, she moved to New York and married Reeves McCullers three years later. While still in her twenties, she suffered a series of strokes that incapacitated her for long periods. In later years, partial paralysis confined her to a wheelchair, yet she still managed to type new manuscripts. Her loneliness and suffering are reflected in her novels, which include *The Heart Is a Lonely Hunter* (1940), *The Member of the Wedding* (1946), and *Clock Without Hands* (1961).

William Safire (b. 1929)

When it comes to questions about the use—and misuse—of the English language, few people have more answers or observations than William Safire. A political commentator and the author of the "On Language" column of *The New York Times*, Safire is one of the world's most widely read writers on language in America today. The 1978 Pulitzer Prize winner for distinguished commentary, Safire was once a political speech writer for the Nixon White House. His books include *On Language* (1980), *What's the Good Word?* (1982), *I Stand Corrected* (1984), *Take My Word for It* (1986), *You Could Look It Up* (1988), and *Coming to Terms* (1991). He has also written four novels, *Full Disclosure* (1977), *Freedom* (1987), *Sleeper Spy* (1995), and *Scandalmonger* (2000).

Ian Frazier (b. 1951)

Known for humorous essays and affectionate descriptions of rural America, Ian Frazier brings "an antic sense of fun" to much of his work. He does have a serious side, too. For example, his nonfiction book, *Great Plains* (1989), explores the history of the American West to discover its meaning for today's Americans. His book *On The Rez* (2000), an exploration of life for today's Oglala Sioux Indians, followed.

Frazier was born in Cleveland, Ohio, and now lives in New York City, where he works as a staff writer for *The New Yorker* magazine. His humorous and often ironic essays are collected in a series of nonfiction books, including *Dating Your Mom* (1986), *Nobody Better, Better Than Nobody* (1987), *Family* (1994), *Coyote v. Acme* (1996), and *Lamentations of the Father* (2000). "Coyote v. Acme" is typical of his work: a ludicrous premise packaged in serious style.

1110 ◆ Prosperity and Protest (1946–Present)

TEACHING RESOURCES

The following resources can be used to enrich or extend the instruction for pp. 1110–1111.

Motivation

▣ **Interest Grabber Video**, Tape 6

Background

📖 **Beyond Literature**, p. 65

💻 *Take It to the Net*
Visit www.phschool.com for background and hotlinks for the selections.

Literary Analysis

📄 **Literary Analysis and Reading Transparencies,** Essay, p. 130 ▣

Reading

📖 **Selection Support:** Reading Strategy, p. 284; Build Vocabulary, p. 282 ▣

📄 **Literary Analysis and Reading Transparencies,** Identifying Line of Reasoning, p. 129

 **BLOCK SCHEDULING:** Resources marked with this symbol provide varied instruction during 90-minute blocks.

Preview

Connecting to the Literature

Perhaps you explore subjects that matter to you, such as friendship or creativity, in a journal. Some writers use a more public form of writing—the essay—to discuss ideas they find important.

❷ Literary Analysis

Essay

An **essay** is a short piece of nonfiction in which a writer expresses a personal view on a topic. The many types of essays include

- the **analytical essay,** which breaks down and interprets various elements of a topic.
- the **expository essay,** which explains a topic.
- the **satirical essay,** which uses irony, ridicule, or sarcasm to comment on a topic.

Look for the elements in these essays that will help you decide how to classify each one.

Comparing Literary Works

Different from one another in topic and mood, these selections illustrate the flexibility of the essay form. Yet their greatest difference lies in the concept of **tone,** or the author's attitude toward the subject, characters, or audience. You can hear the tone—humorous, critical, or serious—in each writer's choice of words and details. As you read, note how each author's tone contributes to the structure and meaning of each essay.

❸ Reading Strategy

Identifying Line of Reasoning

When presenting an argument, an essayist offers a **line of reasoning** to convince readers of the soundness of his or her ideas. As you read these essays, identify the key points and note the reasons, facts, and examples that support them. Study the ways in which pieces of evidence are connected, noting any cause-and-effect relationships. Record each line of reasoning, and its evidence, in a chart like the one shown.

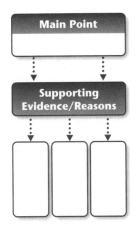

Vocabulary Development

pristine (pris′ tēn) *adj.* pure; uncorrupted (p. 1113)

corollary (kôr′ ə ler′ ē) *n.* easily drawn conclusion (p. 1113)

aesthetic (es thet′ ik) *adj.* pertaining to the study or theory of beauty (p. 1113)

maverick (mav′ ər ik) *n.* nonconformist (p. 1113)

contiguous (kən tig′ yōō əs) *adj.* bordering; adjacent (p. 1118)

precipitate (prē sip′ ə tit) *adj.* very sudden (p. 1119)

caveat (kā′ vē at′) *n.* formal notice; warning (p. 1120)

tensile (ten′ sil) *adj.* stretchable (p. 1121)

from The Mortgaged Heart / Onomatopoeia / Coyote v. Acme ◆ 1111

---

❷ Literary Analysis

Essay

- Tell students that they should label each essay one of the following: an analytical essay, an expository essay, or a satirical essay. As they read, they should compare the tone of the essays, and the author's attitude toward the subject, characters, and audience.

- Discuss the instruction under Literary Analysis on this page. If possible, select a model of each type of essay and read aloud several paragraphs from each one. Then, decide as a class how to classify each excerpt.

- Use the Essay transparency in **Literary Analysis and Reading Transparencies**, p. 130, to help clarify the differences among the three types of essays. Use this transparency again after students have read the essays so that they can find out whether they have categorized the essays correctly.

❸ Reading Strategy

Identifying Line of Reasoning

- Explain to students that they should use a chart similar to the one on this page to record the main points that the essayists make, as well as the evidence and the arguments they provide that support those points.

- Remind students that evidence can include reasons, facts, examples, and relationships of cause and effect.

Vocabulary Development

- Pronounce each vocabulary word for students, and read the definitions as a class. Have students identify any words with which they are already familiar.

CUSTOMIZE INSTRUCTION FOR UNIVERSAL ACCESS

For Less Proficient Readers	For English Learners	For Advanced Readers
All three essays contain specialized or challenging vocabulary. To help less proficient students, encourage them to read the essays with a dictionary at hand. Each time they can't figure out a word from context, they should pause to look it up.	The complex ideas, challenging language, and satirical tone of these essays will likely prove difficult for students who are learning English. Scan the essays for words students are unlikely to know, and assemble a more comprehensive list of vocabulary words than the one provided on p. 1111.	Comparative analysis can enable advanced readers to appreciate the differences in style among the three essays. Have students describe the diction, tone, and syntax of each essay and then link these elements to the essays' messages.

 E-Teach

Visit E-Teach at www.phschool.com for teachers' essays on how to teach, with questions and answers.

**CUSTOMIZE INSTRUCTION
For Musical/Rhythmic Learners**

Remind students that loneliness is a prime topic for songwriters. Many songs, in styles as varied as rock, jazz, and country and western, focus on the speaker's isolation. Invite students to share favorites, prompting them with classics such as The Beatles's "Eleanor Rigby."

❶ About the Selection

As young adults working to define their own place in the world, students will find "The Mortgaged Heart" both poignant and highly relevant. McCullers begins with the challenge of understanding American loneliness. She follows the path of human growth to track the development of Americans' sense of isolation and offers examples of real-life responses to loneliness. By analyzing this apparently ingrained element of the human experience and urging self-examination as a method for relief, McCullers offers hope to any reader who has ever felt like an outsider.

❷ Literary Analysis

Essay

• Remind students that an analytical essay attempts to explain a topic by breaking it down into parts.

• Read the bracketed section aloud, and ask students the Literary Analysis question on p. 1112: In what ways does the question about the nature of loneliness signal to the readers that this is an analytical essay?
Answer: The question deals with what *constitutes* a particular kind of loneliness: American loneliness. The question signals that McCullers is going to break down this notion and assess it from different angles.

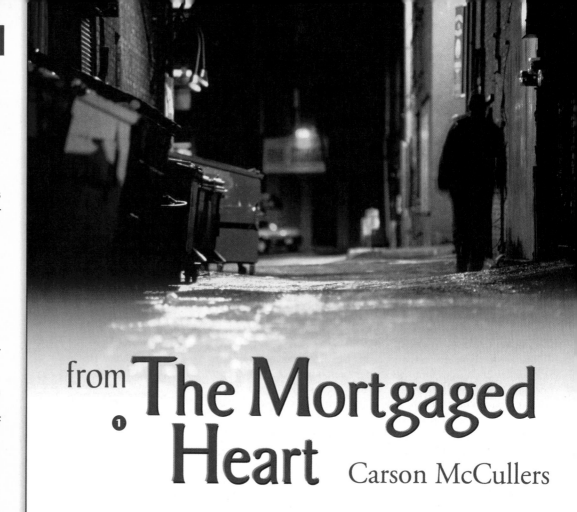

from The Mortgaged Heart

❶

Carson McCullers

❷ This city, New York—consider the people in it, the eight million of us. An English friend of mine, when asked why he lived in New York City, said that he liked it here because he could be so alone. While it was my friend's desire to be alone, the aloneness of many Americans who live in cities is an involuntary and fearful thing. It has been said that loneliness is the great American malady. What is the nature of this loneliness? It would seem essentially to be a quest for identity.

To the spectator, the amateur philosopher, no motive among the complex ricochets of our desires and rejections seems stronger or more enduring than the will of the individual to claim his identity and belong. From infancy to death, the human being is obsessed by these dual motives. During our first weeks of life, the question of identity shares urgency with the need for milk. The baby reaches for his toes, then

Literary Analysis
Essay In what ways does the question about the nature of loneliness signal to readers that this is an analytical essay?

1112 ◆ *Prosperity and Protest (1946–Present)*

TEACHING RESOURCES

The following resources can be used to enrich or extend the instruction for pp. 1112–1122.

Literary Analysis
📖 **Selection Support:** Literary Analysis, p. 285 ▪

Reading
🎧 **Listening to Literature Audiocassettes,**
Side 37 ▪

💿 **Listening to Literature Audio CDs,** CD 21 ▪

▪ **BLOCK SCHEDULING:** Resources marked with this symbol provide varied instruction during 90-minute blocks.

explores the bars of his crib; again and again he compares the difference between his own body and the objects around him, and in the wavering, infant eyes there comes a <u>pristine</u> wonder.

Consciousness of self is the first abstract problem that the human being solves. Indeed, it is this self-consciousness that removes us from lower animals. This primitive grasp of identity develops with constantly shifting emphasis through all our years. Perhaps maturity is simply the history of those mutations that reveal to the individual the relation between himself and the world in which he finds himself.

After the first establishment of identity there comes the imperative need to lose this new-found sense of separateness and to belong to something larger and more powerful than the weak, lonely self. The sense of moral isolation is intolerable to us.

In *The Member of the Wedding*[1] the lonely twelve-year-old girl, Frankie Addams, articulates this universal need: "The trouble with me is that for a long time I have just been an *I* person. All people belong to a *We* except me. Not to belong to a *We* makes you too lonesome."

Love is the bridge that leads from the *I* sense to the *We*, and there is a paradox about personal love. Love of another individual opens a new relation between the personality and the world. The lover responds in a new way to nature and may even write poetry. Love is affirmation; it motivates the *yes* responses and the sense of wider communication. Love casts out fear, and in the security of this togetherness we find contentment, courage. We no longer fear the age-old haunting questions: "Who am I?" "Why am I?" "Where am I going?"—and having cast out fear, we can be honest and charitable.

For fear is a primary source of evil. And when the question "Who am I?" recurs and is unanswered, then fear and frustration project a negative attitude. The bewildered soul can answer only: "Since I do not understand 'Who I am,' I only know what I am *not*." The <u>corollary</u> of this emotional incertitude is snobbism, intolerance and racial hate. The xenophobic[2] individual can only reject and destroy, as the xenophobic nation inevitably makes war.

The loneliness of Americans does not have its source in xenophobia; as a nation we are an outgoing people, reaching always for immediate contacts, further experience. But we tend to seek out things as individuals, alone. The European, secure in his family ties and rigid class loyalties, knows little of the moral loneliness that is native to us Americans. While the European artists tend to form groups or <u>aesthetic</u> schools, the American artist is the eternal <u>maverick</u>—not only from society in the way of all creative minds, but within the orbit of his own art.

Thoreau took to the woods to seek the ultimate meaning of his life. His creed was simplicity and his *modus vivendi*[3] the deliberate stripping

---

1. *The Member of the Wedding* novel and play by Carson McCullers.
2. **xenophobic** (zen′ ə fō′ bik) *adj.* afraid of strangers or foreigners.
3. *modus vivendi* (mō′ dəs vi ven′ dī) "manner of living" (Latin).

pristine (pris′ tēn) *adj.* pure; uncorrupted

Reading Strategy
Identifying Line of Reasoning What evidence does McCullers offer to support the connections between her ideas about identity and loneliness?

corollary (kôr′ ə ler′ ē) *n.* easily drawn conclusion

aesthetic (es thet′ ik) *adj.* pertaining to the study or theory of beauty

maverick (mav′ ər ik) *n.* nonconformist

☑ **Reading Check**
❺ According to McCullers, what is the bridge that leads from the sense of *I* to the sense of *We*?

from *The Mortgaged Heart* ◆ 1113

---

❸ **Reading Strategy**
Identifying Line of Reasoning
- Ask students to explain "the primitive grasp of identity."
  Answer: It is self-consciousness.
- Then, have students answer the Reading Strategy question on p. 1113: What evidence does McCullers offer to support the connections between her ideas about identity and loneliness? **Answer:** McCullers offers the example of a baby establishing his or her sense of self, and the separation that is implicit in self-awareness. McCullers explains that throughout their lives, humans are concerned with the desire to establish an individual identity and forge connections with others.

❹ **Reading Strategy**
Identifying Line of Reasoning
- Draw students' attention to this paragraph, in which McCullers introduces an element in her argument.
- Ask students to paraphrase the text and restate McCullers's position. **Possible response:** Love helps people reduce their loneliness by offering a bridge to others, by creating a positive lens through which to view the world, and by casting out fear.

❺ ☑ **Reading Check**
Answer: According to McCullers, love is the bridge that leads from the sense of *I* to the sense of *we*.

CUSTOMIZE INSTRUCTION FOR UNIVERSAL ACCESS

For Special Needs Students	For Less Proficient Readers	For Advanced Readers
Students may have difficulty identifying McCullers's arguments in this essay. Model this process with the help of the Identifying Line of Reasoning transparency in **Literary Analysis and Reading Transparencies**, p. 129.	Discuss with students the sorts of evidence and reasoning authors use to support their main points, such as definitions, examples, and logical arguments. Which of these kinds of evidence can students find on the first two pages of McCullers's essay?	Have students summarize McCullers's main points and list the evidence and reasons she uses to support them. Then, have students take a position: Do they agree or disagree with McCullers? Ask students to give logical reasons for their opinions and support their opinions with facts and examples.

Review and Assess

1. **Possible response:** Many students would like to talk to McCullers about her idea that love helps people move from concentrating on establishing their individual identify to forging connections with others.

2. **(a)** McCullers's friend likes New York because he can be alone there. **(b)** New York is a huge city crowded with people, so it seems paradoxical that the city is a place where people feel alone.

3. **(a)** "The great American malady" is loneliness. **(b)** She uses "moral" to imply conformity to accepted ideas of right and wrong. A child loses his or her moral isolation by learning the standards of family and society. Without the strict class structure of Europeans, Americans experience the "moral isolation" of deciding correct behavior themselves.

4. **(a)** McCullers believes that fear is the main cause of evil. **(b)** "Emotional incertitude," which begets xenophobia, is a consequence of evil. **(c)** McCullers believes that experiencing love leads from a concentration on the individual to thinking of oneself as part of a group, and thus being concerned with the fate of society.

5. **(a)** The main difference between Europeans and Americans is that Americans seek out things as individuals, whereas Europeans are secure in groups, such as families and classes. **(b)** An example of this difference is that European artists form schools, while the American artist is the "eternal maverick."

6. **(a)** The *I* sense is the sense of the individual. **(b)** The *We* sense is identifying with another person or people. **(c)** Love expands the sense of self from the individual to include the beloved.

7. **(a)** McCullers thinks that American individualism makes people lonely. **(b)** Students may state that positive aspects of American individualism include self-reliance and creative problem solving.

---

of external life to the Spartan[4] necessities in order that his inward life could freely flourish. His objective, as he put it, was to back the world into a corner. And in that way did he discover "What a man thinks of himself, that it is which determines, or rather indicates, his fate."

On the other hand, Thomas Wolfe turned to the city, and in his wanderings around New York he continued his frenetic and lifelong search for the lost brother, the magic door. He too backed the world into a corner, and as he passed among the city's millions, returning their stares, he experienced "That silent meeting [that] is the summary of all the meetings of men's lives."

Whether in the pastoral joys of country life or in the labyrinthine city, we Americans are always seeking. We wander, question. But the answer waits in each separate heart—the answer of our own identity and the way by which we can master loneliness and feel that at last we belong.

---

4. **Spartan** (spär´ tən) *adj.* characteristic of the people of ancient Sparta: hardy, stoical, severe, frugal.

Review and Assess

Thinking About the Selection

1. **Respond:** If you could meet Carson McCullers, which of the observations in this essay would you most like to discuss with her? Explain your reasons for choosing this observation.

2. **(a) Recall:** Why does McCullers's English friend like living in New York City? **(b) Interpret:** In what way is his explanation seemingly contradictory or paradoxical?

3. **(a) Recall:** According to McCullers, what is "the great American malady"? **(b) Analyze:** When McCullers describes this American malady, she speaks of *moral* isolation and *moral* loneliness. What does she mean by these terms?

4. **(a) Recall:** What is a primary source of evil? **(b) Analyze Cause and Effect:** What are the consequences of evil? **(c) Speculate:** According to McCullers, how might the personal experience of love change society?

5. **(a) Distinguish:** What does McCullers say is the main difference between Europeans and Americans? **(b) Interpret:** In what ways does she believe this difference is expressed?

6. **(a) Define:** What is the *I* sense? **(b) Define:** What is the *We* sense? **(c) Interpret:** According to McCullers, how does love lead from one to the other?

7. **(a) Evaluate:** In what ways does McCullers think American individualism hurts people? **(b) Take a Position:** Do you see any positive effects of our emphasis on individualism? Explain.

ENRICHMENT: Culture Connection

Thomas Wolfe

Thomas Wolfe (1900–1938) is best known for his classic American novel, *Look Homeward, Angel.* Wolfe grew up in Asheville, North Carolina, the setting of several of his plays and novels, and left for New York City as a young man.

Look Homeward, Angel was published in 1929. The novel, which has become an American classic, tells of the coming of age of Eugene Gant in the mountain town of Altamont. The thinly disguised autobiographical novel was an immediate success but caused quite a scandal in Wolfe's hometown of Asheville.

ONOMATOPOEIA

William Safire

Blam, 1962, Roy Lichtenstein

▲ **Critical Viewing** What meaning does the onomatopoeia *Blam* convey in this image? **[Analyze]**

❻ **About the Selection**
This expository essay explains the origin and meaning of *onomatopoeia*. As a linguistic tool, onomatopoeia—"words that are made by people making sounds like the action to be described"—has proved appealing to writers, both serious and commercial, as well as to readers and consumers, for centuries. In recounting some history and applications of onomatopoeia, Safire humorously confirms the extraordinary power of words and sounds to engage the human mind.

❼ **Background**
Art
Blam, 1962, by Roy Lichtenstein
This illustration depicts a cartoon character ejecting from an exploding airplane and features an onomatopoetic word—*BLAM.*

The artist, Roy Lichtenstein, was born and raised in New York City, where in his boyhood he was a fan of science and science fiction. He studied at the Art Students League and later with Hoyt Sherman at Ohio State University.

Use these questions for discussion:
1. How is the word *BLAM* an example of the onomatopoetic effects explained in this essay? Answer: It imitates the sound of the explosion as it might be heard in the viewer's ears.
2. According to the essay, why are words and images like those in the painting so enduring? Answer: They engage the human imagination through multiple senses.

❽ ▶**Critical Viewing**
Answer: *Blam* conveys the sound of the exploding plane.

Essay

- Based on the title and illustration, have students predict what the tone of the essay will be.
  Answer: Many students will predict that the tone of the essay will be light and amusing.

▶ **Monitor Progress** Read the bracketed passage aloud, and ask the Literary Analysis question on p. 1116: What kind of essay do you think Safire is writing? Explain.
Answer: Safire is writing an expository essay because the essay explains the origin of the word *onomatopoeia*.

❿ ▶ **Critical Viewing**

Answer: Most students will assign the words *zap* or *pow* to the image on this page because both words fit the image and are mentioned in the essay.

Background

The vocabulary of English is the largest of any language in the world. English readily incorporates new words from a wide variety of sources, including borrowing them from other languages. William Safire, a former Presidential speechwriter, describes another way in which English evolves. According to Safire, when we consider onomatopoeia—the figure of speech in which a word sounds like what it means—we discover that new words are not just based on what we experience, but on what we merely imagine.

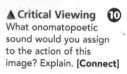

❾ The word *onomatopoeia* was used above, and it had better be spelled right or one usage dictator and six copy editors will get zapped. That word is based on the Greek for "word making"—the *poe* is the same as in *poetry*, "something made"—and is synonymous with *imitative* and *echoic*, denoting words that are made by people making sounds like the action to be described. (The *poe* in *onomatopoeia* has its own rule for pronunciation. Whenever a vowel follows *poe*, the *oe* combination is pronounced as a long *e: onomato-PEE-ia*. Whenever a consonant follows, as in *poetry* and *onomatopoetic*, pronounce the long *o* of Edgar Allan's name.)

Henry Peacham, in his 1577 book on grammar and rhetoric called *The Garden of Eloquence*, first used *onomatopoeia* and defined it as "when we invent, devise, fayne, and make a name intimating the sound of that it signifieth, as *hurlyburly*, for an uprore and tumultuous stirre." He also gave *flibergib* to "a gossip," from which we derive *flibbertigibbet*, and the long-lost *clapperclaw* and *kickle-kackle*.

Since Willard Espy borrowed the title of Peacham's work for his rhetorical bestiary in 1983, the author went beyond the usual examples of *buzz, hiss, bobwhite* and *babble*. He pointed out that one speculation about the origin of language was the *bow-wow theory*, holding that words originated in imitation of natural sounds of animals and thunder. (Proponents of the *pooh-pooh theory* argued that interjections like *ow!* and *oof!* started us all yakking toward language. Other theories— arrgh!—abound.)

Reaching for an alliterative onomatope, the poet Milton chose "melodious *murmurs;*" Edgar Allan Poe one-upped him with "the *tintinnabulation* of the bells." When carried too far, an obsession with words is called *onomatomania;* in the crunch (a word imitating the sound of an icebreaker breaking through ice) Gertrude Stein turned into an *onomatomaniac*.

▲ **Critical Viewing** ❿
What onomatopoetic sound would you assign to the action of this image? Explain. **[Connect]**

Literary Analysis
Essay What kind of essay do you think Safire is writing? Explain.

✹ ENRICHMENT: Culture Connection

Buck Rogers

Buck Rogers made his first appearance in a comic strip in *Amazing Stories* in the late 1920s. In 1934, the first Buck Rogers movie appeared—*Buck Rogers in the 25th Century*. In this 10-minute-long film, Buck and Wilma Deering battle the Tiger Men of Mars. The movie, with its cliffhanger ending that clearly indicated that the short film was the first in a series, was a great hit at the 1935 World's Fair in Chicago.

During the latter part of the 1930s, Buster Crabbe starred in twelve Buck Rogers serials. As in the comic book, Buck awakens in the 25th century and battles various villains, including the terrifying Killer Kane.

What makes a word like *zap* of particular interest is that it imitates an imaginary noise—the sound of a paralyzing ray gun. Thus we can see another way that the human mind creates new words: imitating what can be heard only in the mind's ear. The coinage filled a need for an unheard sound and—*pow!*—slammed the vocabulary right in the kisser. Steadily, surely, under the watchful eye of great lexicographers and with the encouragement of columnists and writers who ache for color in verbs, the creation of Buck Rogers's creator has blasted its way into the dictionaries. The verb will live long after superpowers agree to ban ray guns; no sound thunders or crackles like an imaginary sound turned into a new word.

Took me a while to get to the point today, but that is because I did not know what the point was when I started.

"I now zap all the commercials," says the merry Ellen Goodman. "I zap to the memory of white tornadoes past. I zap headaches, arthritis, bad breath and laundry detergent. I zap diet-drink maidens and hand-lotion mavens . . . Wiping out commercials could entirely and joyfully upend the TV industry. Take the word of The Boston Zapper."

Review and Assess

Thinking About the Selection

1. **Respond:** Had you ever noticed the connection between the onomatopoetic words Safire discusses and the sounds they describe?

2. **(a) Recall:** What is onomatopoeia? **(b) Classify:** What is the origin of this word?

3. **(a) Recall:** What is the *bow-wow theory* concerning the origin of language? **(b) Compare and Contrast:** Compare and contrast it with the *pooh-pooh theory* of language. **(c) Make a Judgment:** Do you think either of these terms is actually used by linguists? Explain.

4. **(a) Recall:** What does Safire find so interesting about the word *zap*? **(b) Analyze:** Why does he believe that this word will "live long after superpowers agree to ban ray guns"?

5. **(a) Infer:** Based on Safire's comment, what would you expect to find in Gertrude Stein's writing? **(b) Infer:** How do you think Safire views the use of onomatopoeia by writers?

6. **Evaluate:** Do you think Safire's humorous style is more or less effective than a factual explanation? Explain.

Review and Assess

1. Many students will have learned about onomatopoetic words in earlier grades and will have explored the connections between onomatopoetic words and the sounds they describe.

2. **(a)** Onomatopoeia is the use of words whose sounds suggest their meaning. **(b)** The word comes from the Greek for "word making."

3. **(a)** The "bow-wow theory" posits that words began as people imitated natural sounds. **(b)** The "pooh-pooh theory" holds that interjections started people on the path toward language. **(c)** Most students will say that these theories probably have more official or scholarly names that linguists use.

4. **(a)** Safire thinks *zap* is particularly interesting because the word imitates an imaginary noise. **(b)** He thinks that the word has enough power that it will live on.

5. **(a)** Based on Safire's comment, one would expect to find many onomatopoetic words in Stein's writing. **(b)** Safire seems to enjoy the use of onomatopoeia by writers.

6. Many students will find Safire's humorous style an appropriate and enjoyable way to learn about a topic such as onomatopoeia. Students may point out that the amusing examples Safire uses will help them remember the information he presents.

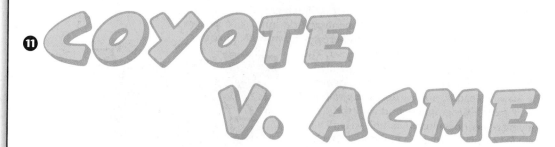

⓫ COYOTE V. ACME

Ian Frazier

Background

This essay is the fictional opening statement of a lawsuit by Mr. Wile E. Coyote, charging the Acme Company with the sale of defective merchandise. If these names sound familiar, you may have a childhood memory of watching Wile E. Coyote chase the Road Runner around the desert. The Warner Brothers cartoon "Road Runner and Coyote" made its debut in 1949; more than half a century later, both the coyote and the elusive bird are still going strong. Perhaps fifty years from now your grandchildren will be watching Coyote's ill-fated attempts—many involving Acme products—to capture the fleet-footed bird. As you read the essay, consider what Frazier is really satirizing—the cartoon character who is his subject or the legal profession.

⓬
In the United States District Court,
Southwestern District,
Tempe, Arizona
Case No. B19294,
Judge Joan Kujava, Presiding

WILE E. COYOTE, Plaintiff
—v.—
ACME COMPANY, Defendant

⓭
Opening Statement of Mr. Harold Schoff, attorney for Mr. Coyote: My client, Mr. Wile E. Coyote, a resident of Arizona and <u>contiguous</u> states, does hereby bring suit for damages against the Acme Company, manufacturer and retail distributor of assorted merchandise, incorporated in Delaware and doing business in every state, district, and territory. Mr. Coyote seeks compensation for personal injuries, loss of business income, and mental suffering caused as a direct result of the actions and/or gross negligence of said company, under Title 15 of the United States Code, Chapter 47, section 2072, subsection (a), relating to product liability.

contiguous (kən tig′ yoo əs) *adj.* bordering; adjacent

☀ **ENRICHMENT: Art Connection**

Animation

The animation techniques used to create cartoon figures such as Wile E. Coyote date back to 1908 when Frenchman Émile Cohl drew white matchstick figures on a black background. Later methods, such as those used by Walt Disney, were based on drawings either inked or painted onto clear plastic sheets. Repeated or unmoving elements could be reproduced on many sheets, while moving elements had to be redrawn in their new position for each image. When the many images were photographed and linked together, the elements appeared to be animated, or moving. Today's animation is often computer generated, saving a great deal of time and enhancing the range of possible effects.

Have students discuss why an animated character is so suited for the satirical essay Ian Frazier chose to write. How does the animation process lend itself to portraying exaggeration and irony?

Mr. Coyote states that on eighty-five separate occasions he has purchased of the Acme Company (hereinafter, "Defendant"), through that company's mail-order department, certain products which did cause him bodily injury due to defects in manufacture or improper cautionary labeling. Sales slips made out to Mr. Coyote as proof of purchase are at present in the possession of the Court, marked Exhibit A. Such injuries sustained by Mr. Coyote have temporarily restricted his ability to make a living in his profession of predator. Mr. Coyote is self-employed and thus not eligible for Workmen's Compensation.[1]

Mr. Coyote states that on December 13th he received of Defendant via parcel post one Acme Rocket Sled. The intention of Mr. Coyote was to use the Rocket Sled to aid him in pursuit of his prey. Upon receipt of the Rocket Sled Mr. Coyote removed it from its wooden shipping crate and, sighting his prey in the distance, activated the ignition. As Mr. Coyote gripped the handlebars, the Rocket Sled accelerated with such sudden and precipitate force as to stretch Mr. Coyote's forelimbs to a length of fifty feet. Subsequently, the rest of Mr. Coyote's body shot forward with a violent jolt, causing severe strain to his back and neck and placing him unexpectedly astride the Rocket Sled. Disappearing over the horizon at such speed as to leave a diminishing jet trail along its path, the Rocket Sled soon brought Mr. Coyote abreast of his prey. At that moment the animal he was pursuing veered sharply to the right. Mr. Coyote vigorously attempted to follow this maneuver but was unable to, due to poorly designed steering on the Rocket Sled and a faulty or nonexistent braking system. Shortly thereafter, the unchecked progress of the Rocket Sled brought it and Mr. Coyote into collision with the side of a mesa.[2]

Paragraph One of the Report of Attending Physician (Exhibit B), prepared by Dr. Ernest Grosscup, M.D., D.O., details the multiple fractures, contusions, and tissue damage suffered by Mr. Coyote as a result of this collision. Repair of the injuries required a full bandage around the head (excluding the ears), a neck brace, and full or partial casts on all four legs.

---

1. **Workmen's Compensation** form of disability insurance that provides income to workers who are unable to work due to injuries sustained on the job.
2. **mesa** (mā′ sə) *n.* small, high plateau with steep sides.

▲ **Critical Viewing** ⑮
Which word from the vocabulary list on page 1111 might be used to describe Coyote's bow? Explain. [**Connect**]

precipitate (prē sip′ ə tit) *adj.* very sudden

☑ **Reading Check**
For what three reasons does Mr. Coyote seek compensation from The Acme Company?

Coyote v. Acme ◆ 1119

⑭ **Background**
Art

Road Runner and Wile E. Coyote, by Chuck Jones, still-photo from animated film

This illustration shows the cartoon figure of Wile E. Coyote chasing his prey, the Road Runner, in a situation similar to the one in the essay.

Chuck Jones created the hilarious Road Runner cartoons, in which the obsessive and indefatigable Wile E. Coyote is forever chasing his nemesis, the Road Runner, with a notable lack of success. The duo first appeared in 1949 in "Fast and Furry-ous."

Jones, who has worked in animation for more than 60 years as a director, producer, and animator, studied at the Chouinard Art Institute in Los Angeles and eventually joined the animation team at Warner Bros. Jones stayed with the innovative animation company until it closed in the early 1960s. With colleagues, he came up with such cartoon favorites as Bugs Bunny, Tweety Pie, Sylvester, Daffy Duck, Elmer Fudd, Porky Pig, and Pepe Le Pew. In the 1960s, Jones founded his own animation company to create cartoons for television, the best-known being an adaptation of a Dr. Seuss classic, "How the Grinch Stole Christmas."

⑮ ▶ **Critical Viewing**
Answer: The vocabulary word *tensile* might be used to describe Coyote's bow.

⑯ **Reading Strategy**
Identifying Line of Reasoning
• Ask students to speculate about what purpose is served by the detailed description of exactly how the Rocket Sled did—or rather didn't—function.
Answer: This level of detail is needed to explain exactly how the Rocket Sled was supposed to work in order to support the claim of negligence.

▶ Monitor Progress Ask students how this evidence supports the accusation in the legal brief.
Answer: The Rocket Sled did not operate as it was supposed to.

⑰ ☑ **Reading Check**
Answer: Mr. Coyote seeks compensation from the Acme Company for injuries, loss of income, and mental suffering.

1119

- Read the passage aloud, and remind students that tone refers to the writer's attitude towards his or her subject, characters, and audience.

- Then, ask the Literary Analysis question on p. 1120: How would you describe the tone created by the use of legal language to describe the exaggerated events of the cartoon?
  Answer: The author creates a tone of hilarious absurdity through the use of dry legal language to describe the exaggerated, nonsensical events that take place in a cartoon.

⓲ Critical Thinking

Infer

- Ask students why preparers of legal briefs might use language that is hard to understand rather than simple, straightforward English.
  Answer: Students may think that using language that is difficult for laypeople to understand makes the legal claims seem more impressive. Legal language can distract people who are not used to reading it from the lack of evidence or the weakness of arguments.

- Have students explain how the word choices in this passage heighten the hilarity.
  Answer: The more elevated the language is, the further it is from matching the tone of the events in the cartoons.

Hampered by these injuries, Mr. Coyote was nevertheless obliged to support himself. With this in mind, he purchased of Defendant as an aid to mobility one pair of Acme Rocket Skates. When he attempted to use this product, however, he became involved in an accident remarkably similar to that which occurred with the Rocket Sled. Again, Defendant sold over the counter, without <u>caveat</u>, a product which attached powerful jet engines (in this case, two) to inadequate vehicles, with little or no provision for passenger safety. Encumbered by his heavy casts, Mr. Coyote lost control of the Rocket Skates soon after strapping them on, and collided with a roadside billboard so violently as to leave a hole in the shape of his full silhouette.

Mr. Coyote states that on occasions too numerous to list in this document he has suffered mishaps with explosives purchased of Defendant: the Acme "Little Giant" Firecracker, the Acme Self-Guided Aerial Bomb, etc. (For a full listing, see the Acme Mail Order Explosives Catalogue and attached deposition,[3] entered in evidence as Exhibit C.) Indeed, it is safe to say that not once has an explosive **⓱** purchased of Defendant by Mr. Coyote performed in an expected manner. To cite just one example: At the expense of much time and personal effort, Mr. Coyote constructed around the outer rim **⓲** of a butte[4] a wooden trough beginning at the top of the butte and spiraling downward around it to some few feet above a black X painted on the desert floor. The trough was designed in such a way that a spherical explosive of the type sold by Defendant would roll easily and swiftly down to the point of detonation indicated by the X. Mr. Coyote placed a generous pile of birdseed directly on the X, and then, carrying the spherical Acme Bomb (Catalogue #78–832), climbed to the top of the butte. Mr. Coyote's prey, seeing the birdseed, approached, and Mr. Coyote proceeded to light the fuse. In an instant, the fuse burned down to the stem, causing the bomb to detonate.

In addition to reducing all Mr. Coyote's careful preparations to naught, the premature detonation of Defendant's product resulted in the following disfigurements to Mr. Coyote:

1. Severe singeing of the hair on the head, neck, and muzzle.
2. Sooty discoloration.
3. Fracture of the left ear at the stem, causing the ear to dangle in the aftershock with a creaking noise.
4. Full or partial combustion of whiskers producing kinking, frazzling, and ashy disintegration
5. Radical widening of the eyes, due to brow and lid charring.

---

3. **deposition** (dep′ ə zish′ ən) *n.* legal term for the written testimony of a witness.
4. **butte** (byo͞ot) *n.* steep hill standing alone in a plain.

caveat (kā′ vē at′) *n.* formal notice; warning

Literary Analysis
Essay and Tone How would you describe the tone created by the use of legal language to describe the exaggerated events of a cartoon?

We come now to the Acme Spring-Powered Shoes. The remains of a pair of these purchased by Mr. Coyote on June 23rd are Plaintiff's Exhibit D. Selected fragments have been shipped to the metallurgical laboratories of the University of California at Santa Barbara for analysis, but to date no explanation has been found for this product's sudden and extreme malfunction. As advertised by Defendant, this product is simplicity itself: two wood-and-metal sandals, each attached to milled-steel springs of high <u>tensile</u> strength and compressed in a tightly coiled position by a cocking device with a lanyard release. Mr. Coyote believed that this product would enable him to pounce upon his prey in the initial moments of the chase, when swift reflexes are at a premium.

To increase the shoes' thrusting still further, Mr. Coyote affixed them by their bottoms to the side of a large boulder. Adjacent to the boulder was a path which Mr. Coyote's prey was known to frequent. Mr. Coyote put his hind feet in the wood-and-metal sandals and crouched in readiness, his right forepaw holding firmly to the lanyard release. Within a short time Mr. Coyote's prey did indeed appear on the path coming toward him. Unsuspecting, the prey stopped near Mr. Coyote, well within range of the springs at full extension. Mr. Coyote gauged the distance with care and proceeded to pull the lanyard release.

At this point, Defendant's product should have thrust Mr. Coyote forward and away from the boulder. Instead, for reasons yet unknown, the Acme Spring-Powered Shoes thrust the boulder away from Mr. Coyote. As the intended prey looked on unharmed, Mr. Coyote hung suspended in air. Then the twin springs recoiled, bringing Mr. Coyote to a violent feet-first collision with the boulder, the full weight of his head and forequarters falling upon his lower extremities.

The force of this impact then caused the springs to rebound, whereupon Mr. Coyote was thrust skyward. A second recoil and collision followed. The boulder, meanwhile, which was roughly ovoid in shape, had begun to bounce down a hillside, the coiling and recoiling of the springs adding to its velocity. At each bounce, Mr. Coyote came into contact with the boulder, or the boulder came into contact with Mr. Coyote, or both came into contact with the ground. As the grade was a long one, this process continued for some time.

The sequence of collisions resulted in systemic physical damage to Mr. Coyote, viz., flattening of the cranium, sideways displacement of the tongue, reduction of length of legs and upper body, and compression of vertebrae from base of tail to head. Repetition of blows along a vertical axis produced a series of regular horizontal folds in Mr. Coyote's body tissues—a rare and painful condition which caused Mr. Coyote to expand upward and contract downward alternately as he walked, and to emit an off-key accordion-like wheezing with every step.

tensile (ten´ sil) *adj.* stretchable

☑**Reading Check** ⑳
Have Acme products performed well for Mr. Coyote? Explain.

Coyote v. Acme ◆ 1121

⑲ **Vocabulary Development**
Latin Root –ten–
- Have a volunteer read the sentence in which the word *tensile* appears.
- Draw students' attention to the definition of *tensile* that appears in the margin.
- Point out that *tensile* begins with the Latin root *ten-*, which means "stretch tightly."
- Challenge students to think of other words with this root.
  Answer: Some examples include *tendon, tender, attenuate, extenuate, extend,* and *portend.*

⑳ **Reading Check**

Answer: Acme products have not performed well for Mr. Coyote. He has injured himself every time he has used an Acme product. In addition, Acme products have not helped him catch his prey, the Road Runner.

㉑ **Literary Analysis**
Essay
- Read the bracketed passage aloud.
- Ask the Literary Analysis question on p. 1122: What aspects of the legal and business professions does the line about "our trading partners" satirize?
  Answer: The line about "our trading partners" satirizes the United States' sensitivity to international opinion.

CUSTOMIZE INSTRUCTION FOR UNIVERSAL ACCESS

For Less Proficient Readers	For English Learners	For Gifted/Talented Students
To help students picture the sequence of events, encourage them to draw simple thumbnail sketches of what happened, step by step, to Mr. Coyote when he tried to use the Acme Spring-Powered Shoes.	To help students picture the sequence of events, help them "translate" the legal language into ordinary words and simplify the complex sentences. Then, have students make thumbnail sketches of the sequence of events when Mr. Coyote tried to use the Acme Spring-Powered Shoes.	Have students make a catalogue of Acme Company products. Ask students to list the products and to explain how each one functions.

Review and Assess

1. Most students will feel sorry for Wile E. Coyote, though they will laugh at his exploits. Some students will be unsympathetic because they will believe Wile E. Coyote deserved his fate.

2. **(a)** His forelimbs stretched 50 feet. **(b)** Things happen to Wile E. Coyote, such as his legs stretching 50 feet, that could never happen in real life.

3. **(a)** Wile E. Coyote buys Acme products frequently. The essay states that he has bought them 85 times. **(b)** The essay states that Wile E. Coyote has no other source of the goods he needs for his "work" trying to catch the Road Runner.

4. **(a)** Wile E. Coyote is trying to collect $38,750,000 in damages. **(b)** Many students will believe that Wile E. Coyote has misused Acme products and thus is not eligible for damages.

5. Most students will understand that Frazier is not only trying to be funny but is also satirizing the legal profession and frivolous product liability claims.

The distracting and embarrassing nature of this symptom has been a major impediment to Mr. Coyote's pursuit of a normal social life.

As the Court is no doubt aware, Defendant has a virtual monopoly of manufacture and sale of goods required by Mr. Coyote's work. It is our contention that Defendant has used its market advantage to the detriment of the consumer of such specialized products as itching powder, giant kites, Burmese tiger traps, anvils, and two-hundred-foot-long rubber bands. Much as he has come to mistrust Defendant's products, Mr. Coyote has no other domestic source of supply to which to turn. One can only wonder what our trading partners in Western Europe and Japan would make of such a situation, where a giant company is allowed to victimize the consumer in the most reckless and wrongful manner over and over again.

Mr. Coyote respectfully requests that the Court regard these larger economic implications and assess punitive damages in the amount of seventeen million dollars. In addition, Mr. Coyote seeks actual damages (missed meals, medical expenses, days lost from professional occupation) of one million dollars; general damages (mental suffering, injury to reputation) of twenty million dollars; and attorney's fees of seven hundred and fifty thousand dollars. Total damages: thirty-eight million seven hundred and fifty thousand dollars. By awarding Mr. Coyote the full amount, this Court will censure Defendant, its directors, officers, shareholders, successors, and assigns, in the only language they understand, and reaffirm the right of the individual predator to equal protection under the law.

Literary Analysis
Essay What aspects of the legal and business professions does the line about "our trading partners" satirize?

Review and Assess

Thinking About the Selection

1. **Respond:** As you read the attorney's statement, did you sympathize with Wile E. Coyote? Why or why not?

2. **(a) Recall:** What happens to Wile E. Coyote's forelimbs when he uses the Rocket Sled? **(b) Support:** What details in this essay suggest that Wile E. Coyote is a cartoon character?

3. **(a) Recall:** How often does Wile E. Coyote buy products from the Acme Company? **(b) Support:** Find evidence to explain why he maintains this relationship with Acme, despite the outcomes he has faced with their products.

4. **(a) Recall:** What action is Wile E. Coyote seeking from the court? **(b) Make a Judgment:** If you were a member of the jury in this case, what would your verdict be? Explain.

5. **Evaluate:** What do you believe was Frazier's purpose in writing this essay? Was he simply trying to be funny or was he making a point? Explain.

✎ ASSESSMENT PRACTICE: Writing Skills

Punctuation	(For more practice, see Test Preparation Workbook, p. 68.)

The writing sections of many tests require students to identify and correct punctuation errors. Use the following sample test item to give students practice in this skill.

A coyote could not possibly use the following <u>items! a rocket</u> sled, rocket skates, a bomb, and spring-powered shoes.

What is the BEST way to rewrite the underlined section of the passage.

A NO CHANGE   **C** items a rocket
B items: a rocket   **D** items. A rocket

An exclamation mark is not appropriate preceding a list, so *A* is incorrect. *C* does not provide the necessary punctuation between the clause and the list. *D* creates a sentence fragment. *B* is the correct answer because it uses a colon to introduce the list.

Review and Assess

Literary Analysis

Essay

1. (a) What type of **essay** is "The Mortgaged Heart"? (b) What aspects of loneliness does McCullers explore? (c) What is her main point?
2. (a) What is the main purpose of "Onomatopoeia"? (b) Give an example of an idea that Safire explains.
3. (a) In "Coyote v. Acme," in what ways does the use of humor convey a serious idea? (b) What is the main point of the essay?

Comparing Literary Works

4. (a) Use a chart like the one shown to analyze the first paragraph of each essay and determine the author's **tone**. (b) What attitude toward his or her subject is revealed in each author's tone?

Summary of first paragraph	Words/details that indicate tone		Tone
		...▶	

5. Both Safire's and Frazier's essays rely on humor, but of different kinds. In your own words, describe the kind of humor used in each essay.
6. Imagine these essays with different tones. What role does tone play in the overall effect of each one? Explain.

Reading Strategy

Identifying Line of Reasoning

7. In "The Mortgaged Heart," what supporting information does McCullers use to convince the reader that (a) loneliness stems from the quest for identity and (b) love is the means of overcoming loneliness? (c) Is her supporting evidence convincing?
8. (a) Summarize the attorney's case for Mr. Coyote in "Coyote v. Acme." (b) What is the connection between Exhibits A–D and the main points of the attorney's arguments?

Extend Understanding

9. **Social Studies Connection:** Do you think Americans today are likely to be more or less lonely than the early settlers? Explain the societal changes that prompted your answer.

from The Mortgaged Heart / Onomatopoeia / Coyote v. Acme ◆ 1123

Quick Review

In an **analytical essay,** writers explore and clarify a topic. In an **expository essay,** writers explain, or provide information about, a topic. In a **satirical essay,** writers use irony, ridicule, or sarcasm to comment on a topic.

A writer's **tone** reflects his or her attitude toward the topic, characters, or audience.

To **identify the line of reasoning,** note the author's main points and the connection between the supporting evidence.

 Take It to the Net

www.phschool.com

Take the interactive self-test online to check your understanding of these selections.

Answers continued

9. Some students may argue that Americans today are more likely to be lonely than early settlers because extended family may live far apart. Others may argue that Americans are less lonely because travel is easier and modes of communication quicker and more reliable.

Answers for p. 1123

Review and Assess

1. (a) "The Mortgaged Heart" is an analytical essay. (b) McCullers explores the development of a social consciousness from birth and American tendencies toward loneliness. (c) McCullers's main point is that everyone experiences the conflicting pulls of establishing self-identity and needing connection with others.

2. (a) The main purpose of "Onomatopoeia" is to explain what *onomatopoeia* means and to give examples of it. (b) Safire explains the "bow-wow theory," which posits that words began in imitation of natural sounds.

3. (a) "Coyote v. Acme" satirizes a product liability lawsuit. (b) The main point of the essay is that some product liability suits are frivolous.

4. (a) McCullers uses a philosophical question about loneliness to convey a serious tone. Safire uses casual language to convey a light-hearted tone. Frazier uses legal jargon to convey a satirical tone. (b) McCullers takes her subject very seriously. Safire provides useful and interesting information in a lighthearted way, and Frazier satirizes his subject.

5. Safire jokes openly in his essay. Frazier pretends to be serious, but his basic premise is absurd, resulting in a satire.

6. McCullers's serious tone encourages the reader to take her points seriously. Safire teaches through humor. Frazier makes his point through exaggeration.

7. (a) She describes a baby's growing self-identity. (b) She describes how loves change from identifying with the *I* to identifying with the *we*. (c) Most students will find her evidence convincing.

8. (a) Acme's products have malfunctioned, causing bodily harm and loss of employment to Mr. Coyote. (b) The exhibits are various kinds of documentation that support the attorney's contention.

continued

❶ Vocabulary Development

Word Analysis: Latin Root –ten–

Paragraphs about disastrous camping trips must include four of the following six words: *tension, tense, tent, extent, tendon, intensify.*

Spelling Strategy

1. athletic
2. basic
3. fantastic

Fluency: Definitions

1. c
2. f
3. a
4. h
5. d
6. g
7. b
8. e

❷ Grammar and Style

1. Loneliness is common among <u>us</u> Americans.
2. Love can help <u>you</u> and <u>me</u>.
3. Two students, <u>she</u> and Carlos, were tied for the best grades.
4. <u>We</u> cartoon lovers all know Wile E. Coyote.
5. He would like to gain sympathy amongst <u>us</u> predators.

Writing Application

Paragraphs must include at least three appositives.

Integrate Language Skills

❶ Vocabulary Development Lesson

Word Analysis: Latin Root *-ten-*

The word *tensile* contains the Latin root *-ten-*, meaning "to stretch tightly." Tensile springs would be "stretchable." The words below take their meaning from the root *-ten-*. Use at least four of the words to write a paragraph about a disastrous camping trip.

tension	tense	tent
extent	tendon	intensify

Spelling Strategy

When you add the suffix *-ic* to nouns ending in *e* or *y*, drop the final *e*, as in *aesthete + -ic = aesthetic*. Notice that the new word is an adjective. Add the suffix *-ic* to create the adjective form for each of the following words.

1. athlete   2. base   3. fantasy

Fluency: Definitions

Review the vocabulary list on page 1111. Then, choose the definition from the right column that best fits the word in the left column.

1.	precipitate	a.	share a common border
2.	tensile	b.	conclusion
3.	contiguous	c.	sudden, abrupt
4.	pristine	d.	formal warning
5.	caveat	e.	nonconformist
6.	aesthetic	f.	stretchable quality
7.	corollary	g.	sense of beauty
8.	maverick	h.	completely untouched

❷ Grammar and Style Lesson

Pronouns With Appositives

McCullers observes that ". . . we Americans are always seeking." Notice that the pronoun *we* is followed by the noun *Americans* and acts as the subject of the clause. When a **pronoun** is followed by an **appositive**—a noun that renames the pronoun—choose the correct pronoun by mentally dropping the appositive.

> **Subject:** We <u>players</u> had to win.
> (We had to win.)
>
> **Object:** It was up to us <u>players</u>.
> (It was up to us.)

Use *I, he, she, we,* or *they* to rename subjects and *me, him, her, us,* or *them* to rename objects.

Practice For each of the sentences below, choose the correct form of the pronoun in parentheses. Then, rewrite the complete sentence correctly.

1. Loneliness is common among (we, us) Americans.
2. Love can help (us, you) and (I, me).
3. Two students, (she, her) and Carlos, were tied for the best grades.
4. (We, Us) cartoon lovers all know Wile E. Coyote.
5. He would like to gain sympathy amongst (us, we) predators.

Writing Application Write a paragraph in which you describe a sporting event. Use the correct form of pronouns with appositives at least three times.

WG *Prentice Hall Writing and Grammar Connection: Chapter 19, Section 1*

TEACHING RESOURCES

The following resources can be used to enrich or extend the instruction for pp. 1124–1125.

Vocabulary

📖 **Selection Support:** Build Vocabulary, p. 282 🔲

📖 **Vocabulary and Spelling Practice Book**
(Use this booklet for skills enrichment.)

Grammar

📖 **Selection Support:** Grammar and Style, p. 283

WG **Writing and Grammar,** Ruby Level, p. 562 🔲

🔲 **Daily Language Practice Transparencies** 🔲

Writing

WG **Writing and Grammar,** Ruby Level, p. 37

💿 **Writing and Grammar iText CD-ROM**

🔲 **BLOCK SCHEDULING:** Resources marked with this symbol provide varied instruction during 90-minute blocks.

❸ Writing Lesson

Analytical Essay

Carson McCullers describes the American artist as "the eternal maverick." In an analytical essay, explore the origin and current meaning of the word. Then, explain why being a maverick is or is not a uniquely American quality.

Prewriting   Use a dictionary to trace the etymology of the word *maverick*. Compare the word's origins with its use today. Brainstorm for specific examples of people who demonstrate maverick traits.

Drafting   Include the quote from McCullers's essay in your introduction, and state whether or not you agree with it. Use your body paragraphs to explain the origin and meaning of *maverick*, and to cite evidence for agreeing or disagreeing with McCullers.

Revising   Review your essay and make sure you have clearly connected your ideas. Highlight transitional phrases you have used, and add any that may be needed.

Model: Using Transitions for Clarity

In comparison to the rest of the world, America is a young, brash country. *However,* we are not the only ones who value independent thinking. *For example,* Pablo Picasso was one of the great artists of the 20th century. He was a maverick, but he was not American.

> Transitional words and phrases help to establish a sound line of reasoning.

 *Prentice Hall Writing and Grammar Connection: Chapter 3, Section 2*

❹ Extension Activities

Listening and Speaking Working in groups as teams of attorneys defending the Acme Company, develop a response to the arguments presented in "Coyote v. Acme." Present your **opening statement** for the defense to the class. Use these tips to prepare:

- Respond to each of the main arguments presented in the essay.
- Appeal both to logic and to the emotions.

Present your opening statements using appropriate body language. **[Group Activity]**

Research and Technology View episodes of the Roadrunner cartoon. As you watch, evaluate the various ways the cartoon makers present events and communicate characters' motivations. Then, write a short **essay** analyzing the cartoon and discussing the expository methods you identified. Exchange your essay with classmates and discuss points of agreement and disagreement.

 **Take It to the Net**   www.phschool.com

Go online for an additional research activity using the Internet.

from The Mortgaged Heart / Onomatopoeia / Coyote v. Acme ◆ 1125

ASSESSMENT RESOURCES

The following resources can be used to assess students' knowledge and skills.

Selection Assessment

📖 **Formal Assessment,** pp. 282–284

📖 **Open Book Test,** pp. 193–195

📼 **Got It! Assessment Videotapes**

💿 **Test Bank Software**

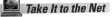 **Take It to the Net**

Visit www.phschool.com for self-tests and additional questions on the selections.

Listening and Speaking Rubric

📖 **Performance Assess. and Portfolio Mgmt.,** p. 26

PRENTICE HALL ASSESSMENT SYSTEM

📖 **Workbook**   📕 **Transparencies**

📖 **Skill Book**   💿 **CD-ROM**

❸ Writing Lesson

- Review the characteristics that make McCullers's essay "The Mortgaged Heart" an analytic essay: the breaking down of a subject into subtopics and the analysis of each subtopic.

- Use the Writing Lesson to guide students in planning and drafting their own analytical essays. Make sure that students have a dictionary that includes the origin of *maverick*.

- Remind students that they must include these features in their essay: the origin of *maverick*, a comparison of the original meaning of the word with its use today, the quotation by McCullers, a statement that explains whether they agree with it, and evidence that supports their point of view.

❹ Listening and Speaking

- Suggest that each group of students work its way through the plaintiff's brief, brainstorming for arguments to refute each point.

- Students should decide as a group which arguments are most convincing and use those in their opening statement.

- After preparing a draft of the statement, a group member should read it aloud to the rest of their group and have them critique it before it is revised.

- Encourage presenters to practice reading the opening statement several times so that they can maintain eye contact with the audience when they present it.

- Have students use the rubric for Critiquing Arguments, p. 26, in **Performance Assessment and Portfolio Management.**

CUSTOMIZE INSTRUCTION
For Universal Access

To address different learning styles, use the activities suggested in the **Extension Activities** booklet, p. 65.

- For Visual/Spatial and Logical/Mathematical Learners, use Activity 5.

- For Musical/Rhythmic and Intrapersonal Learners, use Activity 6.

- For Visual/Spatial and Logical/Mathematical Learners, use Activity 7.

Straw Into Gold ✦ For the Love of Books ✦ Mother Tongue

Lesson Objectives

1. **To analyze and respond to literary elements**
   - Literary Analysis: Reflective Essay
   - Comparing Literary Works
2. **To read, comprehend, analyze, and critique nonfiction**
   - Reading Strategy: Evaluating a Writer's Message
   - Reading Check questions
   - Review and Assess questions
3. **To develop word analysis skills, fluency, and systematic vocabulary**
   - Vocabulary Development Lesson: Latin root: *-scrib-, -script-*
4. **To understand and apply written and oral language conventions**
   - Spelling Strategy
   - Grammar and Style Lesson: Varying Sentence Structure
   - Assessment Practice (ATE)
5. **To understand and apply appropriate writing and research strategies**
   - Writing Lesson: Letter to the Author
   - Extension Activity: Team Report
6. **To understand and apply listening and speaking strategies**
   - Extension Activity: Speech

STEP-BY-STEP TEACHING GUIDE	PACING GUIDE
PRETEACH	
Motivate Students and Provide Background	
Use the Motivation activity (ATE p. 1126)	5 min.
Read and discuss author and background features (SE/ATE pp. 1126, 1128) 🅰	5 min.
Introduce the Concepts	
Introduce the Literary Analysis and Reading Strategy (SE/ATE p. 1127) 🅰	15 min.
Pronounce the vocabulary words and read their definitions (SE p. 1127)	5 min.
TEACH	
Monitor Comprehension	
Informally monitor comprehension by circulating while students read independently or in groups 🅰	45 min.
Monitor students' comprehension with the Reading Check notes (SE/ATE pp. 1129, 1131, 1133, 1137)	as students read
Develop vocabulary with Vocabulary notes (SE pp. 1130, 1137, 1138, 1139, 1140, 1141; ATE p. 1137)	as students read
Develop Understanding	
Develop students' understanding of the reflective essay with the Literary Analysis annotations (SE/ATE pp. 1128, 1130, 1131, 1134, 1136, 1137, 1138, 1140) 🅰	5 min.
Develop students' ability to evaluate a writer's message by using the Reading Strategy annotations (SE pp. 1131, 1134, 1138, 1140; ATE pp. 1130, 1131, 1132, 1134, 1138, 1139, 1140)	5 min.
ASSESS	
Assess Mastery	
Assess students' mastery of the Reading Strategy and Literary Analysis by having them answer the Review and Assess questions (SE/ATE p. 1142)	15 min.
Use one or more of the print and media Assessment Resources (ATE p. 1144) 🅰	up to 45 min.
EXTEND	
Apply Understanding	
Have students complete the Vocabulary Development Lesson and the Grammar and Style Lesson (SE p. 1143) 🅰	20 min.
Apply students' ability to revise to include precise language in their writing by using the Writing Lesson (SE/ATE p. 1144) 🅰	45 min.
Apply students' understanding using one or more of the Extension Activities (SE p. 1144)	20–90 min.

 ACCELERATED INSTRUCTION:
Use the strategies and activities identified with an 🅰.

UNIVERSAL ACCESS
- ● = Below Level Students
- ▲ = On-Level Students
- ■ = Above Level Students

Time and Resource Manager

RESOURCES

PRINT 📖	TRANSPARENCIES 🧴	TECHNOLOGY 💿 🎧 📼
• **Beyond Literature,** Career Connection: Writing, p. 66 ▲ ■		• **Interest Grabber Video,** Tape 6 ● ▲ ■
• **Selection Support Workbook:** ● ▲ ■ Literary Analysis, p. 289 Reading Strategy, p. 288 Build Vocabulary, p. 286	• **Literary Analysis and Reading Transparencies,** pp. 131 and 132 ● ▲ ■	
• **Adapted Reader's Companion** ● • **Reader's Companion** ● • **Authors In Depth,** The American Experience, p. 193 ■		• **Listening to Literature** ● ▲ ■ Audiocassettes, Side 38 Audio CDs, CD 22
• **English Learner's Companion** ● ▲ • **Literatura en español** ● ▲ • **Literary Analysis for Enrichment** ■		
• **Formal Assessment:** Selection Test, pp. 285–287 ● ▲ ■ • **Open Book Test,** pp. 196–198 ● ▲ ■ • **Performance Assessment and Portfolio Management,** p. 55 ● ▲ ■ • **PRENTICE HALL ASSESSMENT SYSTEM** ● ▲ ■	• **PRENTICE HALL ASSESSMENT SYSTEM** ● ▲ ■ Skills Practice Answers and Explanations on Transparencies	• **Test Bank Software** ● ▲ ■ • **Got It! Assessment Videotapes,** Tape 5 ● ▲
• **Selection Support Workbook:** ● ▲ ■ Grammar and Style, p. 287 • **Writing and Grammar,** Ruby Level ● ▲ ■ • **Extension Activities,** p. 66 ● ▲ ■	• **Daily Language Practice Transparencies** ● ▲ • **Writing Models and Graphic Organizers on Transparencies,** p. 80 ● ▲ ■	• **Writing and Grammar iText CD-ROM** ● ▲ ■ 💻 *Take It to the Net* www.phschool.com

BLOCK SCHEDULING: Use one 90-minute class period to preteach the selection and have students read it. Use a second 90-minute class period to assess students' mastery of skills and have them complete one of the Extension Activities.

Prepare to Read

❶ Straw Into Gold ◆ For the Love of Books ◆ Mother Tongue

Motivation

These essays offer a convincing mosaic of the many reasons people write and the myriad experiences that fan writers' imaginations. To interest students in the essays, ask students to bring or suggest a favorite title for a classroom library from each student's most recently enjoyed reading material. Urge students to be candid; all reading is worthwhile. Discuss what inspired these many writers to share their experiences, topics, and issues: what makes an idea worth writing about.

📼 Interest Grabber Video

As an alternative, play "An Interview with Rita Dove" on Tape 6 to engage student interest.

❶ Background

More About Sandra Cisneros

As a young girl in a large Mexican American family, Sandra Cisneros mourned her lack of a "normal" childhood like the one she saw on *Leave It to Beaver* and *Father Knows Best*. The Cisneros family moved frequently between Mexico City and Chicago. She had, as she says, "seven fathers," or six brothers and a father, and was lonely for a sister and female friends.

Her loneliness drove Cisneros into the library and motivated her to write. She began writing poetry in high school, but she didn't really take writing seriously until she took her first creative writing class in college. In college, she searched for her unique voice and developed a writing style that was deliberately different from that of her classmates.

In "Ghosts and Voices: Writing from Obsession," Cisneros writes, "If I were asked what it is I write about, I would have to say I write about those ghosts that haunt me, that will not let me sleep, of that which even memory does not like to mention."

Sandra Cisneros (b. 1954)
Sandra Cisneros was born in Chicago into a large Mexican American family. Because her family was poor, Cisneros moved frequently and lived for the most part in small, cramped apartments. To cope with these conditions, she retreated into herself and spent much of her time reading fairy tales and classic literature. She attended Loyola University in Chicago and the Writer's Workshop at the University of Iowa. During her college years, Cisneros met writers from many other backgrounds. At first uncomfortable about her family's struggles, she soon realized that her heritage provided her with something unique. Cisneros began writing about her childhood in a book of connected short stories. *The House on Mango Street* (1984) was a modest success. However, her later book, *Woman Hollering Creek* (1991), won critical acclaim and earned Cisneros widespread recognition. Of her desire to write about her family and community, Cisneros has said "I'm trying to write stories that haven't been written. I feel like a cartographer; I'm determined to fill a literary void."

Rita Dove (b. 1952)
Now a famous poet, Rita Dove's first writing efforts—at the age of nine or ten— were comic books with female superheroes. Dove was born in Akron, Ohio, to highly educated parents. Her father, Ray A. Dove, was the first African American chemist to work in the tire and rubber industry. Dove attended Miami University in Oxford, Ohio, and later the University of Iowa. She has published six volumes of poetry, including the Pulitzer Prize-winning *Thomas and Beulah* (1986) and the critically acclaimed *On the Bus with Rosa Parks* (1999). Dove has also written a play, a novel, and a collection of short stories. In 1993, she was appointed Poet Laureate of the United States, becoming the first African American and the youngest person ever to hold that position. "Every time I write a poem," Dove has said, "I try to imagine the reader—the reader that I was—curled up on the couch, at the moment of opening a book and absolutely having my world fall away and entering into another one."

Amy Tan (b. 1952)
As a child starting school, Amy Tan—the daughter of Chinese immigrants—would answer her mother's Chinese questions in English. Growing up in Oakland, California, Tan continued to embrace typical American values and ideas, which she assumed defined her identity. These assumptions were upended when the thirty-five-year old Tan visited China with her mother. There she came to appreciate her Chinese roots. At the time, she was leaving a successful career as a business writer to become a fiction writer. When she returned to the United States, she began *The Joy Luck Club* (1989), a novel about four Chinese American women and their mothers. The book made Tan a celebrity. Although she struggled terribly with writer's block—beginning and discarding six novels—Tan triumphed with her second novel, *The Kitchen God's Wife* (1991). Her third novel, *The Hundred Secret Senses*, was published in 1995, and her fourth, *The Bonesetter's Daughter*, appeared in 2001.

1126 ◆ Prosperity and Protest (1946–Present)

TEACHING RESOURCES

The following resources can be used to enrich or extend the instruction for pp. 1126–1127.

Motivation
📼 **Interest Grabber Videotapes**, Tape 6

Background
📖 **Beyond Literature**, p. 66

💻 *Take It to the Net*
Visit www.phschool.com for Background and hotlinks for the poems.

Literary Analysis
📄 **Literary Analysis and Reading Transparencies**, Reflective Essay, p. 132 📼

Reading
📖 **Selection Support**: Reading Strategy, p. 288; Build Vocabulary, p. 286

📄 **Literary Analysis and Reading Transparencies**, Evaluating a Writer's Message, p. 131

■ **BLOCK SCHEDULING**: Resources marked with this symbol provide varied instruction during 90-minute blocks.

Preview

Connecting to the Literature

Perhaps, like the writers of these essays when they were girls, you are not as confident as you would like to be. These writers discovered the world of books, and their love of reading led them to write. In writing, each found her own voice.

❷ Literary Analysis

Reflective Essay

An essay is a short piece of nonfiction in which a writer expresses a personal view of a topic. In a **reflective essay,** the writer uses an informal tone to describe personal experiences or pivotal events. In her essay Rita Dove focuses on her love of books:

> . . . always, I have been passionate about books. . . . I loved to feel their heft in my hand . . .

An essay writer often explores an experience in order to arrive at a deeper understanding of its significance. To help you track each writer's reflections, use a chart like the one shown.

Comparing Literary Works

Each of these three writers discusses her struggle to create her own true sense of **identity.** As you read, examine how each writer describes the role played by other people in her creation of a genuine sense of self. Determine if a true sense of identity is to be discovered among our companions, in the recesses of our own privacy, or in some combination of the two.

❸ Reading Strategy

Evaluating a Writer's Message

As a reader, your job is not only to get a writer's point, but also to decide what you think about it. When you **evaluate a writer's message,** you assess the validity of the writer's ideas and decide whether you agree or disagree with them. As you read these essays, identify and then evaluate the message of each writer.

Vocabulary Development

nomadic (nō mad´ ik) *adj.* wandering; leading the life of a nomad (p. 1130)

transcribed (tran skrībd´) *v.* wrote or typed a copy (p. 1137)

empirical (em pir´ i kəl) *adj.* derived from observation or experiment (p. 1138)

benign (bi nīn´) *adj.* not injurious or malignant; not cancerous (p. 1139)

semantic (sə man´ tik) *adj.* pertaining to meaning in language (p. 1140)

quandary (kwän´ də rē; kwän´ drē) *n.* state of uncertainty; dilemma (p. 1141)

nascent (nas´ ənt; nā´ sənt) *adj.* coming into existence; emerging (p. 1141)

Straw Into Gold / For the Love of Books / Mother Tongue ◆ 1127

---

❷ Literary Analysis

Reflective Essay

- Tell students that as they read the three essays, they will become familiar with the essay form called the reflective essay, in which a writer reflects on important life experiences.

- As they read, students should compare the writers' struggles to forge their own identity to their own. How closely can students relate to the writers' experiences and feelings and the conclusions they drew in their essays?

- Draw a chart on the board similar to the one on this page of the student book. Read the example from Rita Dove's essay and use it to fill in the chart as a model for the chart students will fill in as they read the essays. Under the heading Experiences, write "Loved to handle books." Under Feelings, write "Passion," and under Significance, write "Importance of books." Have the class decide as a group what to write under Understanding. (Answers should reflect the enormous influence her experiences with books have had on Rita Dove's life and career.)

❸ Reading Strategy

Evaluating a Writer's Message

- Urge students to make sure that they have read the essays carefully and feel confident that they have understood each writer's message before they attempt to evaluate it.

- Ask students to evaluate the message each of the three writers transmits in her essay. Remind students to support their opinions with reasoned arguments and examples from the text.

Vocabulary Development

- Pronounce each vocabulary word for students and read the definitions as a class. Have students identify any words with which they are already familiar.

 E-Teach

Visit E-Teach at www.phschool.com for teachers' essays on how to teach, with questions and answers.

CUSTOMIZE INSTRUCTION FOR UNIVERSAL ACCESS

For Less Proficient Readers	For English Learners	For Advanced Readers
Writing that contains specific contextual references that may be unfamiliar, in this case references to the writers' cultures, can challenge less proficient readers. Urge students to use footnotes, background information, and peer exchange to explain any confusing references.	Students learning English may relate closely to the authors' feelings of being outsiders in the dominant culture. Students may still need help with challenging vocabulary and sentence structure. Urge students to read all the footnotes and look up words they can't define from context in a dictionary. You may also want to have students listen to the essays on audiotape or CD.	Outlining can help students identify how the essay writers' cultural heritages have influenced their writing. Outlining will also be useful to students as they analyze the structure of each essay. Have students compare the three outlines. What do the outlines suggest about the influences of the three cultures and about each writer's style?

Invite students to demonstrate for the class a physical skill—analogous to the tortilla making in the story—they have recently mastered. As all students attempt the task, urge them to share their feelings about facing and managing challenges.

❶ About the Selection

This essay connects life experiences and a writer's imaginative powers. The essayist, Sandra Cisneros shares anecdotes about her childhood in a Mexican American family and her travels through Europe as a fledgling writer. In recounting some unexpected turns in her life, Cisneros highlights the contrast between her inner experience and the world's view of her and emphasizes strengths she had been surprised to discover in herself.

❷ Literary Analysis
Reflective Essay

- Ask a volunteer to read the bracketed passage aloud.

- Then, have students answer the Literary Analysis question on p. 1128: What aspects of the author's tone and word choice let you know right away that this is an informal, personal piece of writing?
  Answer: The informal tone is established by the use of sentence fragments and informal sentence openers, such as the word *so*.

- Remind students that reflective essays often describe seemingly insignificant events and draw universal conclusions from them.

- Ask: What event does the essayist mention? What problem crops up as a result?
  Answer: Cisneros mentions being invited to share a home-cooked dinner of Mexican food. Cisneros has been asked to make tortillas, but she doesn't know how.

▶ Monitor Progress Have students suggest a larger lesson that readers could learn from this incident.
Answer: Students are likely to suggest the following: People should not make assumptions based on others' cultural background.

1128

STRAW INTO GOLD: ❶
THE METAMORPHOSIS
OF THE EVERYDAY

Sandra Cisneros

Background

The term "essay" from the French *essai,* meaning "try," historically described an exploratory piece of writing that lacked finish. In 1597, Francis Bacon called his own *Essays* "grains of salt which will rather give an appetite than offend with satiety." Eventually, the essay lost its original "unfinished" sense and writers began to think of it as an elegant, logically reasoned, polished piece of writing. Today, the essay has become one of the most popular literary forms among writers and readers.

❷ When I was living in an artists' colony in the south of France, some fellow Latin-Americans who taught at the university in Aix-en-Provence[1] invited me to share a home-cooked meal with them. I had been living abroad almost a year then on an NEA[2] grant, subsisting mainly on French bread and lentils while in France so that my money could last longer. So when the invitation to dinner arrived, I accepted without hesitation. Especially since they had promised Mexican food.

What I didn't realize when they made this invitation was that I was supposed to be involved in preparing this meal. I guess they assumed I knew how to cook Mexican food because I was Mexican. They wanted specifically tortillas, though I'd never made a tortilla in my life.

It's true I had witnessed my mother rolling the little armies of dough into perfect circles, but my mother's family is from Guanajuato,[3] *provinciales,*[4] country folk. They only know how to make flour tortillas. My father's family, on the other hand, is chilango,[5] from Mexico City.

---

1. **Aix-en-Provence** (eks än prō väns´) city in southeastern France.
2. **NEA** National Endowment for the Arts.
3. **Guanajuato** (gwä´ nä hwä´ tō) state in central Mexico.
4. **provinciales** (prō bēn sē ä´ lās) "country folk" (Spanish).
5. **chilango** (chē län´ gō) "city folk" (Spanish).

1128 ◆ *Prosperity and Protest (1946–Present)*

Literary Analysis
Reflective Essay What aspects of the author's tone and word choice let you know right away that this is an informal, personal piece of writing?

TEACHING RESOURCES

The following resources can be used to enrich or extend the instruction for pp. 1128–1141.

Literary Analysis

📖 **Selection Support:** Literary Analysis, p. 289

Reading

🎧 **Listening to Literature Audiocassettes,** Side 38

💿 **Listening to Literature Audio CDs,** CD 22

Biography, 1988, Marina Gutierrez, Courtesy of the artist

❸ Background

Art

Biography, 1988, by Marina Gutierrez

The creator of the painting is Marina Gutierrez, a Contemporary Latin American artist (1954-   ). In titling this painting *Biography,* Gutierrez offers viewers a guiding hand through the painting's complexity, just as Sandra Cisneros points the way for readers of her "biography," each recognizing that a life and a personality is often more complex than it initially appears to be.

Use these questions for discussion:

1. Which objects in the painting suggest experiences mentioned in the essay?
   Possible response: The apartment building, red house, table with food, and open book all suggest aspects of Cisneros's life experiences.

2. How might each of the young women depicted in the painting represent aspects of Sandra Cisneros?
   Possible response: One might be her eleven-year-old self, one her intellectual/writer self, and one her proud Mexican American self.

❹ ▶ Critical Viewing

Answer: Students should note that Cisneros also pieces together a picture of her life experiences from a collection of anecdotes and incidents.

❺ Critical Thinking

Interpret

- Read the bracketed passage aloud.
- Ask students to suggest reasons why Cisneros does not tell her hosts that she does not know how to make tortillas.
  Answer: Students' responses should focus on Cisneros's personality. Cisneros is clearly a proud person who rises to a challenge. She had wanted to break down in tears and give up as she had wanted to when she had to write a critical essay for her MFA, but she didn't in either case.

❻ ✓ Reading Check

Answer: Cisneros was asked to prepare corn tortillas.

❹

▲ **Critical Viewing** This painting, titled *Biography,* challenges the viewer to piece together the experiences of a lifetime from a variety of small objects. What parallels can you draw between the picture and this essay? **[Connect]**

❻

✓**Reading Check**

What Mexican dish was Cisneros asked to prepare?

We ate corn tortillas but we didn't make them. Someone was sent to the corner tortilleria to buy some. I'd never seen anybody make corn tortillas. Ever.

Well, somehow my Latino hosts had gotten a hold of a packet of corn flour, and this is what they tossed my way with orders to produce tortillas. *Asi como sea.* Any ol' way, they said and went back to their cooking.

Why did I feel like the woman in the fairy tale who was locked in a room and ordered to spin straw into gold? I had the same sick feeling when I was required to write my critical essay for my MFA[6] exam—the only piece of noncreative writing necessary in order to get my graduate degree. How was I to start? There were rules involved here, unlike writing a poem or story, which I did intuitively. There was a step-by-step process needed and I had better know it. I felt as if making tortillas, or writing a critical paper for that matter, were tasks so impossible I wanted to break down into tears.

Somehow though, I managed to make those tortillas—crooked and burnt, but edible nonetheless. My hosts were absolutely ignorant when it came to Mexican food; they thought my tortillas were delicious. (I'm glad my mama wasn't there.) Thinking back and

6. **MFA** Master of Fine Arts.

CUSTOMIZE INSTRUCTION FOR UNIVERSAL ACCESS

For Special Needs Students	For English Learners	For Advanced Readers
Read aloud a version of the fairy tale *Rumplestiltskin* to refresh students' memory of the tale and make sure they understand the title and references to *Rumplestiltskin* in the body of the essay. Discuss why Cisneros felt like the miller's daughter in the tale when she was asked to make tortillas.	Students learning English may not be familiar with the fairy tale *Rumplestiltskin* and will be puzzled by the title and references to the fairy tale in the text of the essay. Read *Rumplestiltskin* aloud to students or have them listen to the story on an audiotape or CD. Then point out and discuss the references to the fairy tale in the essay.	Have a volunteer summarize the fairy tale *Rumplestiltskin* and suggest reasons Cisneros drew on this tale in her essay. Then ask students to make a chart that compares Cisneros with the miller's daughter in the fairytale.

Reflective Essay

- Have a volunteer read the bracketed passage aloud.

- Remind students that in a reflective essay, the writer uses a personal tone.

- Have students answer the Literary Analysis question on p. 1130: What words or phrases in this paragraph signal the fact that this is a reflective essay on a personal topic?

  Answer: Cisneros reflects on her heritage by describing herself as a Latina and an only daughter in a family of six brothers. She explains that in her culture women don't leave home until they get married. Words and phrases that suggest the reflective nature of the essay include *because I am a woman, an only daughter,* and *I crossed my father's threshold.*

❼ Reading Strategy

Evaluate Writer's Message

- Ask students to consider in what ways their heritage or culture defines the roles of men and women. How does their cultural heritage compare to Cisneros'?

- What aspects of Cisneros' background shaped her as a writer?
  Answer: Her family, her ethnicity, and her poverty all influenced Cisneros.

- Point out that many people have backgrounds in some ways similar to Cisneros', yet they don't become writers. Have students discuss what is unique about Cisneros.
  Answer: Students should understand that each person is influenced by his or her background in a unique way.

---

looking at that photograph documenting the three of us consuming those lopsided circles I am amazed. Just as I am amazed I could finish my MFA exam (lopsided and crooked, but finished all the same). Didn't think I could do it. But I did.

I've managed to do a lot of things in my life I didn't think I was capable of and which many others didn't think me capable of either.

❻ Especially because I am a woman, a Latina, an only daughter in a family of six men. My father would've liked to have seen me married long ago. In our culture, men and women don't leave their father's house except by way of marriage. I crossed my father's threshold with nothing carrying me but my own two feet. A woman whom no one came for and no one chased away.

To make matters worse, I had left before any of my six brothers had ventured away from home. I had broken a terrible taboo. Somehow, looking back at photos of myself as a child, I wonder if I was aware of having begun already my own quiet war.

❼ I like to think that somehow my family, my Mexicanness, my poverty all had something to do with shaping me into a writer. I like to think my parents were preparing me all along for my life as an artist even though they didn't know it. From my father I inherited a love of wandering. He was born in Mexico City but as a young man he traveled into the U.S. vagabonding. He eventually was drafted and thus became a citizen. Some of the stories he has told about his first months in the U.S. with little or no English surface in my stories in *The House on Mango Street* as well as others I have in mind to write in the future. From him I inherited a sappy heart. (He still cries when he watches the Mexican soaps—especially if they deal with children who have forsaken their parents.)

My mother was born like me—in Chicago but of Mexican descent. It would be her tough, streetwise voice that would haunt all my stories and poems. An amazing woman who loves to draw and read books and can sing an opera. A smart cookie.

When I was a little girl we traveled to Mexico City so much I thought my grandparents' house on La Fortuna, Number 12, was home. It was the only constant in our <u>nomadic</u> ramblings from one Chicago flat to another. The house on Destiny Street, Number 12, in the colonia Tepeyac,[7] would be perhaps the only home I knew, and that nostalgia for a home would be a theme that would obsess me.

My brothers also figured greatly in my art. Especially the oldest two; I grew up in their shadows. Henry, the second oldest and my favorite, appears often in poems I have written and in stories which at times only borrow his nickname, Kiki. He played a major role in my childhood. We were bunkbed mates. We were co-conspirators. We were pals. Until my oldest brother came back from studying in Mexico and left me odd-woman-out for always.

What would my teachers say if they knew I was a writer? Who would've guessed it? I wasn't a very bright student. I didn't much like

---

7. **colonia Tepeyac** (cô lō′ nēä tā pä′ yäc) district of Mexico City.

Literary Analysis
Reflective Essay What words or phrases in this paragraph signal that this is a reflective essay on a personal topic?

nomadic (nō mad′ ik) *adj.* wandering; leading the life of a nomad

---

✹ ENRICHMENT: Geography Connection

Mexico City

Mexico City, the capital of Mexico, is located in the central plateau of Mexico in the Valley of Mexico, which is ringed by mountains. The city was founded by Aztec Indians in the 1300s and called Tenochtitlan. It quickly became the center of the powerful Aztec empire.

Modern Mexico City is the center of Mexico's cultural, economic, and political life. Though overcrowded and plagued by water and air pollution as well as social unrest, Mexico City has beautiful parks and neighborhoods, important museums, and significant architecture.

Mexico City is one of the fastest growing areas in the world. About 17 million people live in the metropolitan area (nearly 10 million people live in Mexico City proper). Most of the people who live in Mexico City are mestizos, people of mixed Spanish and Indian heritage, and the vast majority of people who live in Mexico City (as in the rest of Mexico) are Roman Catholics.

school because we moved so much and I was always new and funny-looking. In my fifth-grade report card, I have nothing but an avalanche of C's and D's, but I don't remember being that stupid. I was good at art and I read plenty of library books and Kiki laughed at all my jokes. At home I was fine, but at school I never opened my mouth except when the teacher called on me, the first time I'd speak all day.

When I think how I see myself, it would have to be at age eleven. I know I'm thirty-two on the outside, but inside I'm eleven. I'm the girl in the picture with skinny arms and a crumpled shirt and crooked hair. I didn't like school because all they saw was the outside me. School was lots of rules and sitting with your hands folded and being very afraid all the time. I liked looking out the window and thinking. I liked staring at the girl across the way writing her name over and over again in red ink. I wondered why the boy with the dirty collar in front of me didn't have a mama who took better care of him.

I think my mama and papa did the best they could to keep us warm and clean and never hungry. We had birthday and graduation parties and things like that, but there was another hunger that had to be fed. There was a hunger I didn't even have a name for. Was this when I began writing?

In 1966 we moved into a house, a real one, our first real home. This meant we didn't have to change schools and be the new kids on the block every couple of years. We could make friends and not be afraid we'd have to say goodbye to them and start all over. My brothers and the flock of boys they brought home would become important characters eventually for my stories—Louie and his cousins, Meme Ortiz and his dog with two names, one in English and one in Spanish.

My mother flourished in her own home. She took books out of the library and taught herself to garden, producing flowers so envied we had to put a lock on the gate to keep out the midnight flower thieves. My mother is still gardening to this day.

This was the period in my life, that slippery age when you are both child and woman and neither, I was to record in *The House on Mango Street*. I was still shy. I was a girl who couldn't come out of her shell.

How was I to know I would be recording and documenting the women who sat their sadness on an elbow and stared out a window? It would be the city streets of Chicago I would later record, but from a child's eyes.

I've done all kinds of things I didn't think I could do since then. I've gone to a prestigious university, studied with famous writers, and taken away an MFA degree. I've taught poetry in the schools in Illinois and Texas. I've gotten an NEA grant and run away with it as far as my courage would take me. I've seen the bleached and bitter mountains of the Peloponnesus.[8] I've lived on a Greek island. I've been to Venice[9]

---

8. **Peloponnesus** (pel´ ə pə nē´ səs) peninsula forming the southeastern part of the Greek mainland.
9. **Venice** (ven´ is) seaport in northern Italy.

Straw Into Gold: The Metamorphosis of the Everyday ◆ 1131

Literary Analysis
Reflective Essay and Identity When she was a child, in what ways did Cisneros's inner life not communicate itself to those around her?

Reading Strategy
Evaluating a Writer's Message Why do you think Cisneros does not go into greater detail about the nature of her "hunger"?

❿

Reading Check
In Cisneros's culture, under what circumstances do women usually leave home?

❽ Literary Analysis
Reflective Essay and Identity
- Read the bracketed passage aloud.
- Have students answer the Literary Analysis question on p. 1131: When she was a child, in what ways did Cisneros's inner life not communicate itself to those around her?
Answer: Cisneros did not speak in school unless the teacher called on her. Her alertness, love of reading, talent for art, and sense of humor were not apparent to teachers and students at school. At home, Cisneros had longings she couldn't put a name to, so these feelings probably went unnoticed by her family.

❾ Reading Strategy
Evaluating a Writer's Message
- Read the bracketed passage aloud, and ask students what kinds of hunger is Cisneros discussing.
Answer: literal and figurative hunger
- Ask students the Reading Strategy question on p. 1131: Why do you think Cisneros does not go into greater detail about her "hunger"?
Answer: Cisneros probably cannot go into greater detail because as a child she could not name or understand this figurative or abstract "hunger."

❿ ✔Reading Check
Answer: In Cisneros's culture, women normally leave home only when they marry.

CUSTOMIZE INSTRUCTION FOR UNIVERSAL ACCESS

For Gifted/Talented Students	For Advanced Readers
Do students think that their interior selves remain hidden, or do their friends, family, and acquaintances have a pretty good idea of what they are really like? Invite students to describe and express their essential selves through a medium of their choice. They might create a work of art, such as a painting or piece of sculpture, do a dance or recite a monologue, or write a song, poem, or personal essay. Regardless of the medium they choose, students should keep in mind their goal of giving voice to the person that they are on the inside.	Do students believe that their own inner and outer selves are in sync? Invite students to assemble an anthology of poems or excerpts from memoirs, short stories, and other works of literature that discuss the writers' sense of self. If they like, students can invite contributions from their classmates and write selections themselves. Urge students to include an introduction to the anthology that describes the theme that unites the anthology and explains how it was put together.

⓫ Reading Strategy

Evaluating a Writer's Message

- Ask a volunteer to explain what the author means by "straw for the taking" and how imagination might spin straw into gold.
  Answer: The author means that the world of experience is open to the author and that any experiences can be material from which an author can draw.

- Ask students why Cisneros used these words.
  Answer: Students should recall the central metaphor of the fairy tale *Rumplestiltskin.*

- Then, ask students whether they agree with Cisneros's message.
  Answer: Many students will agree that any experience is valid subject matter for a writer.

Answers for p. 1132

Review and Assess

1. Cisneros is likely to be a person many students would want to meet because she has had many interesting experiences and is full of verve and spunk.

2. (a) Being asked to make tortillas brings to Cisneros's mind the woman who had to spin straw into gold. (b) She is trying to point out that people can use any of life's experiences. (c) Cisneros drew from her good and bad experiences to become a writer.

3. (a) Cisneros left home for a reason other than getting married. (b) The enemy in Cisneros's quiet war is traditional definitions of what women are supposed to do and be.

4. (a) Cisneros is eleven "on the inside." (b) At eleven, she appeared to be quiet and timid, with limited intelligence and imagination. Inside she is thoughtful, bright, observant, and rebellious.

5. (a) Traditional expectations for a Latina from a poor family were obstacles for Cisneros. (b) Cisneros's family acquired a home and stopped traveling so much. She went to college and took creative writing. She developed her own voice as a writer and drew on her experiences for subject matter.

continued

1132

---

twice. In Rapallo, I met Ilona once and forever and took her sad heart with me across the south of France and into Spain.

I've lived in Yugoslavia. I've been to the famous Nice[10] flower market behind the opera house. I've lived in a village in the pre-Alps[11] and witnessed the daily parade of promenaders.

I've moved since Europe to the strange and wonderful country of Texas, land of polaroid-blue skies and big bugs. I met a mayor with my last name. I met famous Chicana/o artists and writers and *politicos.*[12]

Texas is another chapter in my life. It brought with it the Dobie-Paisano Fellowship, a six-month residency on a 265-acre ranch. But most important Texas brought Mexico back to me.

Sitting at my favorite people-watching spot, the snaky Woolworth's counter across the street from the Alamo,[13] I can't think of anything else I'd rather be than a writer. I've traveled and lectured from Cape Cod to San Francisco, to Spain, Yugoslavia, Greece, Mexico, France, Italy, and finally today to Seguin, Texas. Along the way there is straw for the taking. With a little imagination, it can be spun into gold.

---

10. **Nice** (nēs) seaport and resort in southeastern France.
11. **pre-Alps** foothills of the Alps, a mountain range in south-central Europe.
12. **politicos** (pō lē′ tē cōs) "politicians" (Spanish).
13. **the Alamo** (al′ ə mō′) mission in San Antonio, Texas, that was the scene of a famous battle between Texans and Mexican troops in 1836.

Review and Assess

Thinking About the Selection

1. **Respond:** Does Cisneros seem to be someone you would like to meet? Why or why not?

2. (a) **Recall:** Which experience reminds Cisneros of the story of the woman who had to spin straw into gold? (b) **Interpret:** What point is she trying to make through this anecdote? (c) **Connect:** What connections does Cisneros draw between this anecdote and the rest of her essay?

3. (a) **Recall:** What was the taboo Cisneros broke when she left her family home? (b) **Analyze:** Who was the enemy in the "quiet war" Cisneros had begun?

4. (a) **Recall:** How old is Cisneros "on the inside"? (b) **Analyze:** In what ways does her description of herself at that age represent a divide between her inner sense of self and her external realities?

5. (a) **Distinguish:** Which obstacles stood in the way of Cisneros's becoming a writer? (b) **Analyze:** What circumstances contributed to her literary success?

6. (a) **Draw Conclusions:** What is the main point of the essay? Support your answer. (b) **Apply:** In what ways could you apply Cisneros's message to your own life?

Answers continued

6. (a) The main point of the essay is that writers draw on their life experiences ("straw") to make literature ("gold"). Cisneros demonstrates this with examples from her own life. (b) Students may comment on learning from one's life experiences.

For the Love of BOOKS
—Rita Dove

When I am asked: "What made you want to be a writer?" my answer has always been: "Books." First and foremost, now, then, and always, I have been passionate about books. From the time I began to read, as a child, I loved to feel their heft in my hand and the warm spot caused by their intimate weight in my lap; I loved the crisp whisper of a page turning, the musky odor of old paper and the sharp inky whiff of new pages. Leather bindings sent me into ecstasy. I even loved to gaze at a closed book and daydream about the possibilities inside—it was like contemplating a genie's lamp. Of course, my favorite fairy tale was *A Thousand and One Nights*—imagine buying your life with stories!— and my favorite cartoons were those where animated characters popped out of books and partied while the unsuspecting humans slept. In books, I could travel anywhere, be anybody, understand worlds long past and imaginary colonies in the future. My idea of a bargain was to go to the public library, wander along the bookshelves, and emerge with a chin-high stack of books that were mine, all mine, for two weeks—free of charge!

What I remember most about long summer days is browsing the bookshelves in our solarium to see if there were any new additions. I grew up with those rows of books; I knew where each one was shelved and immediately spotted newcomers. And after months had gone by and there'd be no new books, I would think: Okay, I guess I'll try this one—and then discover that the very book I had been avoiding because of a drab cover or small print was actually a wonderful read. Louis Untermeyer's *Treasury of Best Loved Poems* had a sickeningly sweet lilac and gold cover and was forbiddingly thick, but I finally pulled it

⑬ ✓ Reading Check
What made Dove want to be a writer?

For the Love of Books ◆ 1133

⑫ About the Selection
In this essay, Rita Dove vividly communicates her love of books and the critical influence that passion had on her decision to become a writer. As a young child, Rita adored books, not just reading them but holding them, smelling them, and turning their pages. As she matured to discover the magic of language and the places it could take her, Rita encountered many literary voices. When she met a real writer (poet John Ciardi), the possibility of living her adult life among these literary voices—and perhaps adding her own to theirs—became startlingly and wonderfully tangible.

⑬ ✓ Reading Check
Answer: Her passion for books made Dove want to be a writer.

CUSTOMIZE INSTRUCTION FOR UNIVERSAL ACCESS

For English Learners	For Gifted/Talented Students	For Advanced Readers
To help students appreciate Rita Dove's feelings about books and develop their English vocabulary, have students describe books. Ask them to close their eyes as they touch a book, lift it, smell it, and turn the pages. Then they should write as many adjectives as they can to describe the experience.	Have students interview several people who are passionate about a hobby, an academic discipline, an author, and so on. After students talk to people about their interests, have students choose a quotation from each person they interviewed, write the quotation at the top of a large sheet of paper, and illustrate the meaning of the quote.	Have students interview people who are passionate about a hobby, an academic discipline, an author or genre of writing, and so on. Ask students to use the interviews to write an article explaining what intrigues people about their passionate interests and tracing people's passions to experiences from their childhood.

⓮ Reading Strategy

Evaluating a Writer's Message

- Have a volunteer read the brack-eted passage aloud

- Then, ask students to recall the first time they read Shakespeare, and ask them if they enjoyed the experience? What was the most difficult aspect of reading Shakespeare?
  Possible response: Most students will say that they had a difficult time with Shakespeare's diction.

- Have students answer the Reading Strategy question on p. 1135: What point is Dove making about the value of reading when she notes that she did not understand every word she read?
  Answer: Readers can be thrilled by the language they read even though they may not understand every word. Imperfect understand-ing does not preclude enjoyment.

⓯ Literary Analysis

Reflective Essay and Identity

- Read the bracketed passage aloud.

- Ask the students the Literary Analysis Question on p. 1134: What sense of herself as a child does Dove's description of the boy in the story convey?
  Answer: Dove identifies with the "dreamy, mild, scatter-brained" boy in the story because she was shy and people who observed her had no idea of what she was really like.

off the shelf and discovered a cornucopia of emotional and linguistic delights, from "The Ballad of Barbara Fritchie," which I adored for its sheer length and rather numbing rhymes, to Langston Hughes's daz-zlingly syncopated "Dream Boogie." Then there was Shakespeare—daunting for many years because it was his entire oeuvre,[1] in matching wine-red volumes that were so thick they looked more like over-sized bouillon cubes than books, and yet it was that ponderous title—*The Complete Works of William Shakespeare*—that enticed me, because here was a lifetime's work—a lifetime!—in two compact, dense packages. I began with the long poem "The Rape of Lucrece" . . . I sampled a few sonnets, which I found beautiful but rather adult; and finally wandered into the plays—first *Romeo and Juliet*, then *Macbeth, Julius Caesar, A Midsummer Night's Dream, Twelfth Night*—enthralled by the language, by the fact that poetry was spinning the story. Of course I did not understand every single word, but I was too young to know that this was supposed to be difficult; besides, no one was waiting to test me on anything, so, free from pressure, I dove in.

At the same time, my brother, two years my senior, had become a science fiction buff, so I'd read his *Analog* and *Fantasy* and Science Fiction magazines after he was finished with them. One story particu-larly fascinated me: A retarded boy in a small town begins building a sculpture in his backyard, using old and discarded materials—coke bottles, scrap iron, string, and bottle caps. Everyone laughs at him, but he continues building. Then one day he disappears. And when the neighbors investigate, they discover that the sculpture has been dragged onto the back porch and that the screen door is open. Somehow the narrator of the story figures out how to switch on the sculpture: The back door frame begins to glow, and when he steps through it, he's in an alternate universe, a town the mirror image of his own—even down to the colors, with green roses and an orange sky. And he walks through this town until he comes to the main square, where there is a statue erected to—who else?—the village idiot.

I loved this story, the idea that the dreamy, mild, scatter-brained boy of one world could be the hero of another. And in a way, I identified with that village idiot because in real life I was painfully shy and awk-ward; the place where I felt most alive was between the pages of a book.

Although I loved books, for a long time I had no aspirations to be a writer. The possibility was beyond my imagination. I liked to write, however—and on long summer days when I ran out of reading mater-ial or my legs had fallen asleep because I had been curled up on the couch for hours on end, I made up my own stories. Most were aban-doned midway. Those that I did bring to a conclusion I neither showed to others nor considered saving.

My first piece of writing I thought enough of to keep was a novel called *Chaos*, which was about robots taking over the earth. I had

---

1. **oeuvre** (ĕ′ vrə) *n.* all the works, usually of a lifetime, of a particular writer, artist, or composer.

1134 ◆ *Prosperity and Protest (1946–Present)*

Reading Strategy
Evaluating a Writer's Message What point is Dove making about the value of reading when she notes that she did not understand every word she read?

Literary Analysis
Reflective Essay and Identity What sense of herself as a child does Dove's description of the boy in the story convey?

ENRICHMENT: Cultural Connection

Bookbinding

The art of bookbinding, which so enchanted young Rita Dove, began with the production of beautifully illu-minated, or decorated, bibles and other religious books used in worship services in churches. These magnificently adorned volumes sometimes included ivory carvings, jewels, gold leaf, or embroidery. Later, decorated leather bindings became the norm. These books were hand-bound with carefully tooled leather.

Today's books are usually machine bound, though

they can be quite beautiful. Some books have lettering or illustrations impressed into the fabric covering. Paper jackets, often incorporating paintings, illustra-tions, or stylized text, are contemporary examples of the bookbinder's art.

just entered third or fourth grade; the novel had forty-three chapters, and each chapter was twenty lines or less because I used each week's spelling list as the basis for each chapter, and there were twenty words per list. In the course of the year I wrote one installment per week, and I never knew what was going to happen next—the words led me, not the other way around.

At that time I didn't think of writing as an activity people admitted doing. I had no living role models—a "real" writer was a long-dead white male, usually with a white beard to match. Much later, when I was in eleventh grade, my English teacher, Miss Oechsner, took me to a book-signing in a downtown hotel. She didn't ask me if I'd like to go—she asked my parents instead, signed me and a classmate (who is now a professor of literature) out of school one day, and took us to meet a writer. The writer was John Ciardi, a poet who also had translated Dante's *Divine Comedy*, which I had heard of, vaguely. At that moment I realized that writers were real people and how it was possible to write down a poem or story in the intimate sphere of one's own room and then share it with the world.

Review and Assess

Thinking About the Selection

1. **Respond:** Would you have been friends with Rita Dove if you had known her as a child? Why or why not?

2. **(a) Recall:** Which emotion did Dove feel in the presence of an unopened book? **(b) Interpret:** For Dove, what traits did an unopened book and a genie's lamp share? **(c) Analyze:** What attitude toward the imagination is suggested by this simile?

3. **(a) Recall:** What books does Dove note most delighted her as a child? **(b) Interpret:** What point is Dove making about the imaginative life of a child through this catalog of her favorite literature?

4. **(a) Recall:** What happens in the science fiction story that Dove enjoys so much? **(b) Connect:** Why is the story especially meaningful to Dove?

5. **(a) Recall:** Which experience made Dove realize that she could be a "real" writer? **(b) Speculate:** Do you think Dove would have gone on to become a writer if she had not had that experience? Why or why not?

6. **Take a Position:** When Dove started reading Shakespeare, she did not know that it "was supposed to be difficult" and so she loved it. What does this statement suggest about our expectations when approaching challenges?

Answers for p. 1135

Review and Assess

1. Some students will respond that they would have been friends with Rita Dove because they were shy or shared her passion for books. Other students, who were more active and had other interests, will feel it unlikely that they would have been friends with Dove.

2. **(a)** Dove felt excitement and anticipation. **(b)** They were both entrees into magical worlds with endless possibilities. **(c)** The importance of the imagination is suggested by this simile.

3. **(a)** Books that delighted Dove included *A Thousand and One Nights*, *Treasury of Best Loved Poems*, and *The Complete Works of William Shakespeare*. **(b)** Dove is making the point that children's imaginative lives are unlimited.

4. **(a)** A retarded boy is appreciated for his creativity in an alternate universe. **(b)** Dove had an active and imaginative interior life that was not apparent to others.

5. **(a)** She met the poet John Ciardi. **(b)** Some students will believe that Dove would never have gone on to become a writer without a role model. Others will believe that she was so imaginative, she would somehow have found her way to writing.

6. The statement suggests that we can succeed at many challenging activities if we have self-confidence, and if we do not know that the challenges we face are considered difficult.

CUSTOMIZE INSTRUCTION FOR UNIVERSAL ACCESS

For Special Needs Students	For Less Proficient Readers	For Advanced Readers
Special needs students may find it very difficult to relate to someone such as Rita Dove who is so enamored of books and reading. Share some of your favorite childhood books with these students and talk about why the books are important to you. Encourage students to discuss their favorite books.	Share some favorite childhood books with students and have students recall some of their own favorites. Discuss together what qualities make some books so important to children. How unusual do students think Rita Dove's attitude toward books and reading was?	Ask advanced readers to gather in small groups to recall their favorite childhood books and discuss the reasons they loved them. Have students poll their classmates to find out their favorite books. Ask students to make a graph or chart that displays the results of the poll.

16 Mother Tongue

Amy Tan

I am not a scholar of English or literature. I cannot give you much more than personal opinions on the English language and its variations in this country or others.

I am a writer. And by that definition, I am someone who has always loved language. I am fascinated by language in daily life. I spend a great deal of my time thinking about the power of language—the way it can evoke an emotion, a visual image, a complex idea, or a simple truth. Language is the tool of my trade. And I use them all—all the Englishes I grew up with.

Recently, I was made keenly aware of the different Englishes I do use. I was giving a talk to a large group of people, the same talk I had already given to half a dozen other groups. The nature of the talk was about my writing, my life, and my book, *The Joy Luck Club.* The talk was going along well enough, until I remembered one major difference that made the whole talk sound wrong. My mother was in the room. And it was perhaps the first time she had heard me give a lengthy speech, using the kind of English I have never used with her. I was saying things like, "The

---

intersection of memory upon imagination" and "There is an aspect of my fiction that relates to thus-and-thus"—a speech filled with carefully wrought grammatical phrases, burdened, it suddenly seemed to me, with nominalized forms, past perfect tenses, conditional phrases, all the forms of standard English that I had learned in school and through books, the forms of English I did not use at home with my mother.

Just last week, I was walking down the street with my mother, and I again found myself conscious of the English I was using, the English I do use with her. We were talking about the price of new and used furniture and I heard myself saying this: "Not waste money that way." My husband was with us as well, and he didn't notice any switch in my English. And then I realized why. It's because over the twenty years we've been together I've often used the same kind of English with him, and sometimes he even uses it with me. It has become our language of intimacy, a different sort of English that relates to family talk, the language I grew up with.

So you'll have some idea of what this family talk I heard sounds like, I'll quote what my mother said during a recent conversation which I videotaped and then <u>transcribed</u>.

During this conversation, my mother was talking about a political gangster in Shanghai[1] who had the same last name as her family's, Du, and how the gangster in his early years wanted to be adopted by her family, which was rich by comparison. Later, the gangster became more powerful, far richer than my mother's family, and one day showed up at my mother's wedding to pay his respects. Here's what she said in part:

"Du Yusong having business like fruit stand. Like off the street kind. He is Du like Du Zong—but not Tsung-ming Island people. The local people call putong, the river east side, he belong to that side local people. That man want to ask Du Zong father take him in like become own family. Du Zong father wasn't look down on him, but didn't take seriously, until that man big like become a mafia. Now important person, very hard to inviting him. Chinese way, come only to show respect, don't stay for dinner. Respect for making big celebration, he shows up. Mean gives lots of respect. Chinese custom. Chinese social life that way. If too important won't have to stay too long. He come to my wedding. I didn't see, I heard it. I gone to boy's side, they have YMCA[2] dinner. Chinese age I was nineteen."

You should know that my mother's expressive command of English belies how much she actually understands. She reads the Forbes[3] report, listens to *Wall Street Week,*[4] converses daily with her stock-broker, reads all of Shirley MacLaine's[5] books with ease—all kinds

---

1. **Shanghai** (shaŋˈ hī´) seaport city in eastern China.
2. **YMCA** Young Men's Christian Association.
3. *Forbes* magazine of business and finance.
4. *Wall Street Week* weekly television program that reports business and investment news.
5. **Shirley MacLaine's** (mək lānz´) Shirley MacLaine is an American actress who has written several books.

Literary Analysis
Reflective Essay and Identity What division in her sense of identity does Tan experience while giving her lecture?

transcribed (tran skrībd´) *v.* wrote or typed a copy

㉑ ✔ **Reading Check**
How does Tan's language change when she gives her speech?

Mother Tongue ◆ 1137

---

⑲ Literary Analysis
Reflective Essay and Identity

- Have a student volunteer read the bracketed passage aloud.

- Ask students the Literary Analysis question on p. 1137: What division in her sense of identity does Tan experience while giving her lecture? **Answer:** Tan experiences a conflict between the formally educated aspect of herself that she developed in school and her at-home self, which she experiences with her mother.

- Ask students how the languages they speak at home are similar to or different from those they speak at school. **Possible response:** Most students will acknowledge a difference between private, family language and public, or formal language. These languages may be entirely different or simply subtle variations of English.

⑳ Vocabulary Development
The Latin Word Root -scrib-, -script-

- Read the sentence in which the word *transcribed* appears and have students define *transcribed*. Make sure that students understand that transcribing means copying out in full.

- Point out the root -scrib- appears in the word *transcribed* and that -scrib- and -script- are Latin word roots that mean "write."

- Invite students to think of other common words with this root. **Answer:** Some examples include *script, scripture, scribe,* and *scribble.*

㉑ ✔ **Reading Check**
Answer: Tan's language in her speech changes from informal to formal or standard English "with carefully wrought grammatical forms, past perfect tenses, conditional phrases, all the forms of standard English."

CUSTOMIZE INSTRUCTION FOR UNIVERSAL ACCESS

For Special Needs Students	For Less Proficient Readers	For English Learners
Have students read the adapted version of "Mother Tongue" in the **Adapted Reader's Companion**. This version provides basic-level instruction in an interactive format with questions and write-on lines. Completing the adapted version will prepare students to read the selection in the Student Edition.	Have students read "Mother Tongue" in the **Reader's Companion**. This version provides basic-level instruction in an interactive format with questions and write-on lines. After students finish the selection in **Reader's Companion,** have them complete the questions and activities in the Student Edition.	Have students read the adapted version of "Mother Tongue" in the **English Learner's Companion**. This version provides basic-level instruction in an interactive format with questions and write-on lines. Completing the adapted version will prepare students to read the selection in the Student Edition.

Reflective Essay

- Read the bracketed passage aloud.

- Have students state some of the "I" phrases that Tan uses in this passage.
  Answer: "I've been giving more thought . . . "; "I have described it . . . " "I wince when I say . . . "

- Then, ask the Literary Analysis question on p. 1138: What language in this paragraph reinforces the idea that the essay is reflective?
  Answer: The idea that the essay is reflective is reinforced by the personal language and Tan's reference to her mother's English to illustrate that language is often a reflection of identity. Tan explicitly states that she has been "giving more thought" to the English her mother speaks.

23 Reading Strategy

Evaluating a Writer's Message

- Have a volunteer read the bracketed passage aloud.

- Ask the Reading Strategy question on p. 1138: What point does Tan make through this anecdote bout speaking for her mother? Do you find her point valid? Explain.
  Answer: The author is making the point that people don't take those who speak fractured, or imperfect, English seriously. Tan herself was guilty of thinking that her mother's non-standard English reflected the quality of her mother's thinking.

- Have students speculate about how important the author's mother feels her lack of proper English is and explain why they hold that opinion.
  Answer: Many students will remark that the author's mother believes that her lack of formal English has been a hindrance because she calls on her daughter to help her in difficult situations. Still, the author's mother hasn't let her limited English stand in her way too much as demonstrated by her meeting with her stockbroker.

---

of things I can't begin to understand. Yet some of my friends tell me they understand 50 percent of what my mother says. Some say they understand 80 to 90 percent. Some say they understand none of it, as if she were speaking pure Chinese. But to me, my mother's English is perfectly clear, perfectly natural. It's my mother tongue. Her language, as I hear it, is vivid, direct, full of observation and imagery. That was the language that helped shape the way I saw things, expressed things, made sense of the world.

22 Lately, I've been giving more thought to the kind of English my mother speaks. Like others, I have described it to people as "broken," or "fractured" English. But I wince when I say that. It has always bothered me that I can think of no way to describe it other than "broken," as if it were damaged and needed to be fixed, as if it lacked a certain wholeness and soundness. I've heard other terms used, "limited English," for example. But they seem just as bad, as if everything is limited, including people's perceptions of the limited English speaker.

I know this for a fact, because when I was growing up, my mother's "limited" English limited my perception of her. I was ashamed of her English. I believed that her English reflected the quality of what she had to say. That is, because she expressed them imperfectly her thoughts were imperfect. And I had plenty of empirical evidence to support me: the fact that people in department stores, at banks, and at restaurants did not take her seriously, did not give her good service, pretended not to understand her, or even acted as if they did not hear her.

My mother has long realized the limitations of her English as well. When I was fifteen, she used to have me call people on the phone to pretend I was she. In this guise, I was forced to ask for information or even to complain and yell at people who had been rude to her. One time it was a call to her stockbroker in New York. She had cashed out her small portfolio and it just so happened we were going to go to New York the next week, our very first trip outside California. I had to get on the phone and say in an adolescent voice that was not very convincing, "This is Mrs. Tan."

And my mother was standing in the back whispering loudly, "Why he don't send me check, already two weeks late. So mad he lie to me, losing me money."

23 And then I said in perfect English, "Yes, I'm getting rather concerned. You had agreed to send the check two weeks ago, but it hasn't arrived."

Then she began to talk more loudly. "What he want, I come to New York tell him front of his boss, you cheating me?" And I was trying to calm her down, make her be quiet, while telling the stockbroker, "I can't tolerate any more excuses. If I don't receive the check immediately, I am going to have to speak to your manager when I'm in New York next week." And sure enough, the following week there we were in front of this astonished stockbroker, and I was sitting there red-faced and quiet, and my mother, the real Mrs. Tan, was shouting at his boss in her impeccable broken English.

Literary Analysis
Reflective Essay
What language in this paragraph reinforces the idea that the essay is reflective?

empirical (em pir´ i kəl) *adj.* derived from observation or experiment

Reading Strategy
Evaluating a Writer's Message What point does Tan make through this anecdote about speaking for her mother? Do you find her point valid? Explain.

✳ ENRICHMENT: SOCIAL SCIENCE CONNECTION

Attitudes Toward Chinese Americans

The Anti-Defamation League and the Committee of 100 (an organization of prominent Chinese Americans) released a poll in the spring of 2001 that examined Americans' attitudes toward Chinese Americans, though the poll found that most Americans do not distinguish between Chinese Americans and other Asian Americans.

According to the poll, 32% of Americans believe Chinese Americans are more loyal to China than to America. Thirty-four percent said that Chinese Americans have too much control over the high tech industry. Twenty-four percent of Americans do not approve of intermarriage between Chinese Americans and Americans of other backgrounds, and 23% said they would not vote for a Chinese American for President.

The ADL believes that Chinese Americans face a combination of racial and political prejudice, one that discussion and education can help overcome.

We used a similar routine just five days ago, for a situation that was far less humorous. My mother had gone to the hospital for an appointment, to find out about a benign brain tumor a CAT scan[6] had revealed a month ago. She said she had spoken very good English, her best English, no mistakes. Still, she said, the hospital did not apologize when they said they had lost the CAT scan and she had come for nothing. She said they did not seem to have any sympathy when she told them she was anxious to know the exact diagnosis, since her husband and son had both died of brain tumors. She said they would not give her any more information until the next time and she would have to make another appointment for that. So she said she would not leave until the doctor called her daughter. She wouldn't budge. And when the doctor finally called her daughter, me, who spoke in perfect English—lo and behold—we had assurances the CAT scan would be found, promises that a conference call on Monday would be held, and apologies for any suffering my mother had gone through for a most regrettable mistake.

I think my mother's English almost had an effect on limiting my possibilities in life as well. Sociologists and linguists probably will tell you that a person's developing language skills are more influenced by peers. But I do think that the language spoken in the family, especially in immigrant families which are more insular, plays a large role in shaping the language of the child. And I believe that it affected my results on achievement tests, IQ tests, and the SAT.[7] While my English skills were never judged as poor, compared to math, English could not be considered my strong suit. In grade school I did moderately well, getting perhaps B's, sometimes B-pluses, in English and scoring perhaps in the sixtieth or seventieth percentile on achievement tests. But those scores were not good enough to override the opinion that my true abilities lay in math and science, because in those areas I achieved A's and scored in the ninetieth percentile or higher.

This was understandable. Math is precise; there is only one correct answer. Whereas, for me at least, the answers on English tests were always a judgment call, a matter of opinion and personal experience. Those tests were constructed around items like fill-in-the-blank sentence completion, such as, "Even though Tom was

benign (bi nin′) *adj.* not injurious or malignant; not cancerous

6. **CAT scan** method used by doctors to diagnose brain disorders.
7. **SAT** Scholastic Aptitude Test; national college entrance exam.

25 ► **Critical Viewing** Is the language on these signs in San Francisco's Chinatown district the "mother tongue" to which Tan refers? Explain. **[Distinguish]**

Mother Tongue ◆ 1139

24 **Reading Strategy**
Evaluating a Writer's Message
• Read the bracketed passage aloud.
• Remind students of how Tan's mother felt about her limited English. Then, ask students to describe the effect Tan believes her mother's English has had on her own life.
  Answer: Tan feels that her mother's lack of English has lowered her own results on tests of language skills and caused people to assume that Tan's true abilities are in mathematics.

25 ► **Critical Viewing**
Answer: Students should recall that Tan describes her mother's "broken English," not Chinese, as her mother tongue.

CUSTOMIZE INSTRUCTION FOR UNIVERSAL ACCESS

For Special Needs Students	For Less Proficient Readers	For Advanced Readers
Discuss how the author's mother was treated by the stockbroker and the hospital staff. Use a graphic organizer such as the Problem/Solution organizer on p. 80 of **Writing Models and Graphic Organizers on Transparencies** to help students identify the mother's problem, the reasons for it, and possible solutions.	Ask students to use the Problem/Solution graphic organizer on p. 80 of **Writing Models and Graphic Organizers on Transparencies** to help students analyze the causes of the mother's problem and possible solutions for it. Ask students to use the information on the organizer to write a note of advice to the mother.	Ask students to use the Problem/Solution graphic organizer on p. 80 of **Writing Models and Graphic Organizers on Transparencies** to analyze why the broken English of the author's mother causes people to treat her so shabbily. Ask students to use their data on the graphic organizer to write a brief essay on this topic.

Reflective Essay and Identity

- Read the bracketed passage aloud.

- Then have students answer the Literary Analysis question on p. 1140: What conflict between her personal sensibilities and the values of a society does Tan highlight in this discussion of her struggles in English classes?

Answer: Tan's imagination felt limited by the choices she had to make on multiple-choice tests she took in English class because her model, her mother's English, was so imaginative and fluid and admitted so many possibilities.

27 Reading Strategy

Evaluating a Writer's Message

- Have a volunteer read the bracketed passage.

- Ask the Reading Strategy question on p. 1140: What point about defying expectations is Tan making? Do you agree with her?

Possible response: Because she is Chinese American, people expected Tan to go into a field that relies on logic and mathematics. Tan defied expectations by majoring in English, and she began to write after a boss told her that writing was her weakest skill.

- Ask students how Tan's behavior—defying expectations— relates to her mother's English.

Possible response: Much like Tan's behavior in the face of doubt and adversity, Tan's mother's limited English defied expectations by reinforcing imagination and engendering possibility for Tan.

_____, Mary thought he was _____." And the correct answer always seemed to be the most bland combinations of thoughts, for example, "Even though Tom was shy, Mary thought he was charming," with the grammatical structure "even though" limiting the correct answer to some sort of <u>semantic</u> opposites, so you wouldn't get answers like, "Even though Tom was foolish, Mary thought he was ridiculous." Well, according to my mother, there were very few limitations as to what Tom could have been and what Mary might have thought of him. So I never did well on tests like that.

The same was true with word analogies, pairs of words in which you were supposed to find some sort of logical, semantic relationship—for example, "_Sunset_ is to _nightfall_ as _____ is to _____." And here you would be presented with a list of four possible pairs, one of which showed the same kind of relationship: _red_ is to _stoplight_, _bus_ is to _arrival_, _chills_ is to _fever_, _yawn_ is to _boring_. Well, I could never think that way. I knew what the tests were asking, but I could not block out of my mind the images already created by the first pair, "_sunset_ is to _nightfall_"—and I would see a burst of colors against a darkening sky, the moon rising, the lowering of a curtain of stars. And all the other pairs of words—red, bus, stoplight, boring—just threw up a mass of confusing images, making it impossible for me to sort out something as logical as saying: "A sunset precedes nightfall" is the same as "a chill precedes a fever." The only way I would have gotten that answer right would have been to imagine an associative situation, for example, my being disobedient and staying out past sunset, catching a chill at night, which turns into feverish pneumonia as punishment, which indeed did happen to me.

I have been thinking about all this lately, about my mother's English, about achievement tests. Because lately I've been asked, as a writer, why there are not more Asian Americans represented in American literature. Why are there few Asian Americans enrolled in creative writing programs? Why do so many Chinese students go into engineering? Well, these are broad sociological questions I can't begin to answer. But I have noticed in surveys—in fact, just last week—that Asian students, as a whole, always do significantly better on math achievement tests than in English. And this makes me think that there are other Asian-American students whose English spoken in the home might also be described as "broken" or "limited." And perhaps they also have teachers who are steering them away from writing and into math and science, which is what happened to me.

Fortunately, I happen to be rebellious in nature and enjoy the challenge of disproving assumptions made about me. I became an English major my first year in college, after being enrolled as pre-med. I started writing nonfiction as a freelancer the week after I was told by my former boss that writing was my worst skill and I should hone my talents toward account management.

But it wasn't until 1985 that I finally began to write fiction. And at first I wrote using what I thought to be wittily crafted sentences,

semantic (sə man′ tik) _adj._ pertaining to meaning in language

Literary Analysis
Reflective Essay and Identity What conflict between her personal sensibilities and the values of society does Tan highlight in this discussion of her struggles in English classes?

Reading Strategy
Evaluating a Writer's Message What point about defying expectations is Tan making? Do you agree with her?

ENRICHMENT: Social Science Connection

Standardized Achievement Tests

In this essay Amy Tan describes difficulties she had with standardized tests. What are standardized tests and what do they measure? Some tests are criteria-based, that is they measure a body of knowledge. Others are norm-referenced. Norm-referenced tests compare a test-taker's score against the scores of people who have already taken the test.

Common norm-referenced tests include the California Achievement Test, Comprehensive Test of Basic Skills, Iowa Test of Basic Skills, Metropolitan

Achievement Test, and Stanford Achievement Test. Scores on norm-referenced tests are reported in percentile ranks. For example, if a student scored in the 75th percentile, the student had a higher score than 75% of the other students who took the test.

Should schools use tests that rank and sort students, rather than determine whether they have learned the material they have been taught? Norm-referenced tests are a continuing topic of debate in schools.

sentences that would finally prove I had mastery over the English language. Here's an example from the first draft of a story that later made its way into *The Joy Luck Club*, but without this line: "That was my mental quandary in its nascent state." A terrible line, which I can barely pronounce.

Fortunately, for reasons I won't get into today, I later decided I should envision a reader for the stories I would write. And the reader I decided upon was my mother, because these were stories about mothers. So with this reader in mind—and in fact she did read my early drafts—I began to write stories using all the Englishes I grew up with: the English I spoke to my mother, which for lack of a better term might be described as "simple"; the English she used with me, which for lack of a better term might be described as "broken"; my translation of her Chinese, which could certainly be described as "watered down"; and what I imagined to be her translation of her Chinese if she could speak in perfect English, her internal language, and for that I sought to preserve the essence, but neither an English nor a Chinese structure. I wanted to capture what language ability tests can never reveal: her intent, her passion, her imagery, the rhythms of her speech and the nature of her thoughts.

Apart from what any critic had to say about my writing, I knew I had succeeded where it counted when my mother finished reading my book and gave me her verdict: "So easy to read."

quandary (kwän´ dä rē) *n.* state of uncertainty; dilemma

nascent (nas´ ənt, nā´ sənt) *adj.* coming into existence; emerging

Review and Assess

Thinking About the Selection

1. **Respond:** Having read this essay, what are your feelings about Tan and her mother? Explain.

2. **(a) Recall:** What does Tan realize while speaking to an audience that includes her mother? **(b) Infer:** What circumstances account for Tan's having developed more than one "English"?

3. **(a) Recall:** According to Tan, in what ways do math skills differ from language skills? **(b) Interpret:** In what ways did Tan's sense of different "Englishes" prevent her from answering correctly on grammar tests?

4. **(a) Summarize:** Summarize one experience Tan had involving her mother's difficulty with Standard English.
   (b) Compare and Contrast: In what ways does Tan's sense of her mother's English differ from the perceptions of strangers?
   (c) Analyze: What influence has Tan's mother had on her daughter's writing? Support your answer.

5. **Speculate:** What would it be like to live in a place where a language barrier made it difficult for you to communicate with others? What actions might you take to overcome the barrier?

Mother Tongue ◆ 1141

✎ ASSESSMENT PRACTICE: Writing Skills

Identifying Errors

(For more practice, see Test Preparation Workbook, p. 69.)

The writing sections of many tests require students to identify the type of error, if any, present in a sentence or phrase. Use the following sample item to show students how to determine the type of error a passage contains.

> Many people have too different selves: the one they show to the outside world and the one they keep hidden.

> Which type of error, if any, appears in the underlined section of the passage?

A Spelling error   **C** Punctuation error
B Capitalization error   **D** No error

There are no capitalization errors or punctuation errors, but *too* should be spelled "two." The correct answer is *A*.

ASSESS

Answers for p. 1141

Review and Assess

1. Many students will admire both Tan and her mother because the mother fought prejudice against her poor English by continuing to demand what she wanted and needed and because Tan overcame her embarrassment at her mother's non-standard English and went on to achieve in an area in which people assumed she could not do well.

2. **(a)** Tan realizes she is using a kind of complex standard English that she would never use at home with her mother. **(b)** Tan had to use English her mother would understand at home and more formal English to succeed in school and in her profession.

3. **(a)** In math, there is one precise correct answer to a problem; language skills cannot be evaluated as precisely. **(b)** Tan sees too many possible answers and cannot figure out which of the many possibilities is considered "correct."

4. **(a)** The author's mother often asked that Tan pretend to be her own mother on the phone, because she spoke standard English. **(b)** Tan knows that her mother is bright and capable despite her fractured English. Strangers assume Tan's mother is stupid because of her limited English. **(c)** Tan's mother has provided an example of some of the many creative ways English may be used through her imaginative "broken" English.

5. Most students will state that they would dislike living in a place where a language barrier prevented them from communicating with other people. They would likely try to keep a sense of humor as they learned the native language as quickly and thoroughly as possible.

1. **(a)** Cisneros believes that people can transform their lives; she thinks that education, travel, and writing about a variety of experiences are very important. **(b)** The last paragraph confirms this idea as it describes the places her writing has taken her.

2. **(a)** Dove was a shy and awkward child. **(b)** Dove is grateful for the worlds she discovered in books.

3. Tan is no longer embarrassed by her mother's non-standard English, which doesn't indicate her mother's intelligence.

4. A reflective essay may provide the opportunity for a more logical, extended analysis of a personal experience.

5. **(a)** Both Dove and Cisneros were awkward youngsters who discovered books and writing. Cisneros became a writer almost as a reaction to people's expectations; Dove became a writer as a result of meeting a writer. **(b)** Both authors drew on childhood experiences in their essays.

6. All three authors had to fight against prejudice and feeling like outsiders. Through their reading and writing, they gained and strengthened their unique identities.

7. **(a)** Students should support their answers. **(b)** Writing has helped all three authors bridge the gap between their inner lives and their outward circumstances.

8. **(a) Author's Message:** Books are magical and transformative **Evidence For:** Dove describes several books and stories and her reactions to them. **Your Response:** Most students will believe that books transformed Dove's life. **(b) Author's Message:** Language abilities indicate nothing about intelligence. **Evidence For:** Tan's mother is intelligent and her English is expressive, though non-standard. **Your Response:** Most students will agree based on what they have learned about Tan's mother. **(c)** Students should explain their answers.

Continued

1142

Review and Assess

Literary Analysis

Reflective Essay

1. (a) What does Cisneros's list of accomplishments reveal about her values? (b) Does the last paragraph confirm or contradict that idea? Explain.

2. (a) What kind of child does Dove say she was? (b) How do you think Dove feels about her childhood?

3. In what ways has Tan's attitude toward her mother changed as she has grown older? Explain.

4. Based on these examples, why might an author use a **reflective essay** instead of fiction or poetry to explore a specific subject?

Comparing Literary Works

5. (a) Compare and contrast Dove's and Cisneros's childhoods and the paths each took to become writers. (b) In what ways do you think their backgrounds might be expressed in their fiction?

6. What evidence do you find in these essays that each writer struggled or sacrificed to create a true sense of **identity**?

7. (a) In what ways do these author's inner lives contrast—or conflict—with the outside world? (b) What role does writing play in the relationship between each writer's inner and outer life?

Reading Strategy

Evaluating a Writer's Message

8. Use a chart like the one shown to answer the following questions: (a) What does Dove believe about the power of books? (b) What does Tan's essay reveal about how language differences can lead to misconceptions? (c) For each essay, explain whether you do or do not agree with the author's message.

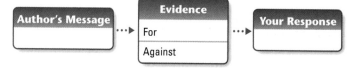

Extend Understanding

9. **Community Connection:** Amy Tan's mother struggled to communicate effectively in the United States. What services can a community provide to people with limited abilities in English?

9. A community can provide various social services and English language instruction.

Quick Review

A **reflective essay** explores the meaning of a writer's personal experiences or observations.

The struggle for a true sense of **identity**, which reflects a person's values, experiences, heritage, and interests, is often a shaping force in a writer's life and work.

To **evaluate a writer's message,** judge it critically and decide whether you do or do not agree with it.

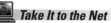

Take It to the Net
www.phschool.com
Take the interactive self-test online to check your understanding of these selections.

ENRICHMENT: Further Reading

Other Works by the Authors

Works by Sandra Cisneros
The House on Mango Street

Works by Rita Dove
Through the Ivory Gate

Works by Amy Tan
The Joy Luck Club

Take It to the Net

Visit www.phschool.com for more information on the authors.

Integrate Language Skills

Vocabulary Development Lesson

Word Analysis: Latin Root -scrib-, -script-

The word *transcribe*, which means "write out or type out in full," is formed from the Latin root *-scrib-*, which means "write." Using each pair of words below, write a sentence that demonstrates the meaning of this root.

1. scribble, child
2. prescription, doctor
3. inscription, trophy
4. author, manuscript

Spelling Strategy

When adding a suffix beginning with a vowel to words of more than one syllable ending with a single consonant, do not double the final consonant: *nomad + -ic = nomadic.* Often, however, when a word's final syllable has the accent, the final consonant is doubled: *regrettable.* Correctly add the indicated suffix to each word below.

1. benefit + *-ed*   2. refer + *-ing*   3. travel + *-er*

❷ Grammar and Style Lesson

Varying Sentence Structure

Simple sentences—those consisting of one independent clause—convey ideas concisely and directly. **Compound sentences** contain two or more independent clauses. **Complex sentences** contain an independent clause and one or more subordinate clauses. In this example, Sandra Cisneros follows a complex sentence with a simple one:

> **Example:** To make matters worse, I had left before any of my six brothers had ventured away from home. I had broken a terrible taboo.

W̶G Prentice Hall Writing and Grammar Connection: Chapter 20, Section 3

Fluency: Sentence Completions

Complete each sentence by filling in each blank with a vocabulary word from the list on page 1127.

1. The wandering tribe led a ___?___ life in the desert.
2. A person who loves language might pursue ___?___ studies.
3. The kindly old woman had a ___?___ influence on her children.
4. Her ___?___ social extroversion revealed itself before she could talk.
5. The archaeologist ___?___ the message that was carved on the wall of the tomb.
6. Having accepted two invitations, he found himself in a social ___?___.
7. Scientists use ___?___ evidence to prove or disprove a hypothesis.

Looking at Style Compare Amy Tan's first two paragraphs with the rest of her essay.

1. What do you notice about the sentence structure?
2. What affect does her choice of sentence structure have on the rhythm of her writing?
3. How does Tan's style relate to her message?

Writing Application Using a variety of sentence structures, write a paragraph in which you discuss the essay you enjoyed most. In your writing, explain your choice.

Straw Into Gold / For the Love of Books / Mother Tongue ◆ 1143

TEACHING RESOURCES

The following resources can be used to enrich or extend the instruction for pp. 1143–1144.

Vocabulary
- 📖 **Selection Support:** Build Vocabulary, p. 286 ▪
- 📖 **Vocabulary and Spelling Practice Book** (Use this booklet for skills enrichment.)

Grammar
- 📖 **Selection Support:** Grammar and Style, p. 287 ▪
- *W̶G* **Writing and Grammar,** Ruby Level, p. 487
- ▪ **Daily Language Practice Transparencies** ▪

Writing
- *W̶G* **Writing and Grammar,** Ruby Level, p. 311
- ▪ **Writing Models and Graphic Organizers on Transparencies,** p. 80 ▪
- 💿 **Writing and Grammar iText CD-ROM**

▪ **BLOCK SCHEDULING:** Resources marked with this symbol provide varied instruction during 90-minute blocks.

EXTEND

Answers for p. 1143

❶ Vocabulary Development

Word Analysis

Sentences should include word pairs in a way that demonstrates an understanding of the root *-scrib-* or *-script-*.

Spelling Strategy

1. benefited
2. referring
3. traveler

Fluency

1. The wandering tribe led a <u>nomadic</u> life in the desert.
2. A person who loves language might pursue <u>semantic</u> studies.
3. The kindly old woman had a <u>benign</u> influence on her children.
4. Her <u>nascent</u> social extroversion revealed itself before she could talk.
5. The archaeologist <u>transcribed</u> the message that was carved on the wall of the tomb.
6. Having accepted two invitations, he found himself in a social <u>quandary</u>.
7. Scientists use <u>empirical</u> evidence to prove or disprove a hypothesis.

❷ Grammar and Style

Looking at Style

1. The first two paragraphs are written in short, simple sentences.
2. The first two paragraphs present information bluntly and forcefully. The following paragraphs are more flowing.
3. The first two paragraphs may represent the simpler writing of a mother tongue. The next paragraphs are more fluent. Tan's message is about fluency and the ability to communicate with ease using different styles.

Writing Application

Students must use a variety of sentence structures in their paragraphs about the essay they enjoyed most.

❸ Writing Lesson

- To prepare students to write their letters to authors, choose one of the three essays and discuss what students liked and didn't like about it, as well as aspects of the essay that puzzled them. Summarize the students' comments in a list that you write on the board.

- Review the Writing Lesson with students to help them take notes for, draft, and revise their letters.

- Go over the writing model so that students gain practice in substituting stronger modifiers for weaker ones. Urge them to revise their own drafts to make their own writing more vivid and precise.

❹ Listening and Speaking

- Urge students to reread the essay by the author they have chosen. As they reread it, they should note the main points that they plan to include in their speech.

- Have students look over their notes and summarize the most important points on the index cards. Encourage them to write words and phrases rather than complete sentences so they are not tempted to read from the cards when they give the speech rather than referring to them from time to time.

- Ask students to practice their speeches for a classmate or two before they present them to the entire class.

- Have students use the Peer Assessment form for Persuasive, p. 55 in **Performance Assessment and Portfolio Management**.

CUSTOMIZE INSTRUCTION
For Universal Access

To address different learning styles, use the activities suggested in the **Extension Activities** booklet, p. 66.

For Intrapersonal and Bodily/Kinesthetic Learners, use Activity 5.

For Visual/Spatial and Interpersonal Learners, use Activity 6.

For Logical/ Mathematical and Verbal/Linguistic Learners, use Activity 7.

---

❸ Writing Lesson

Letter to the Author

Because they seem so personal and are written in a conversational style, these reflective essays invite response. Write a letter to the author of the essay you found most interesting. Explain what you liked, what you did not like, and ask any questions you might have.

Prewriting	Choose the essay you wish to discuss and reread it. Take notes about the author's message and style. List statements and images that you like, or that disturb you in some way.
Drafting	In your opening paragraph, state how much you enjoyed the essay and why. In the body paragraphs, go into greater detail, and ask any relevant questions. Consider drawing parallels to your own life.
Revising	Review your letter, and determine whether or not you have used the best language to communicate your thoughts. Highlight and replace any vague words with more specific ones.

Model: Revising to Include Precise Language

captured
I enjoyed the way you s̶t̶a̶t̶e̶d̶ your mother's English in

This example of her speech
the anecdote of the Shanghai gangster. I̶t̶ helped me to

incident
see my own prejudices. The p̶o̶i̶n̶t̶ with the stockbroker

described
you a̶d̶d̶e̶d̶ made your mother's struggle very clear.

> Replacing vague references with more accurate words and phrases more accurately conveys ideas.

WG Prentice Hall Writing and Grammar Connection: Chapter 14, Section 4

Extension Activities

❹ **Listening and Speaking** Write and deliver a **speech** that Cisneros, Dove, or Tan might present to aspiring young authors. Keep the following tips in mind as you prepare:

- List each main point on an index card for easy reference.
- Practice until you refer only occasionally to your index cards.

As you deliver your speech, speak slowly and clearly, maintaining eye contact with the audience.

Research and Technology Both Tan and Cisneros grew up with more than one language. In a group, research the ways in which multilingual environments affect the development of language skills. Then, deliver a **team report** arguing either for or against language studies for young children. [**Group Activity**]

 **Take It to the Net** www.phschool.com

Go online for an additional research activity using the Internet.

PART 3 · Social Protest

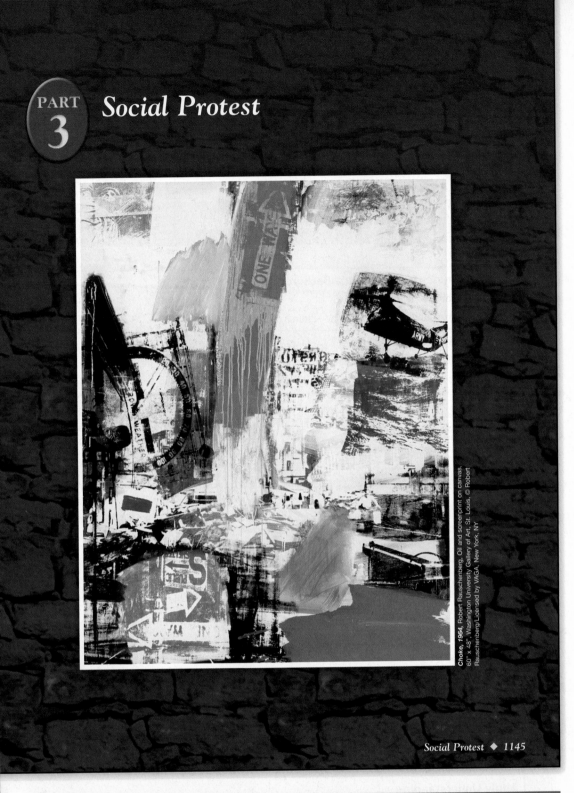

Choke, 1964, Robert Rauschenberg, Oil and screenprint on canvas. 60" x 48", Washington University, Gallery of Art, St. Louis. © Robert Rauschenberg/Licensed by VAGA, New York, NY

Selection Planning Guide

From Hersey's account of the bombing of Hiroshima to the dark themes of *The Crucible*, the selections in this section capture the mood of the second half of the twentieth century. Social protest threads through poems such as "Mirror," which questions society's emphasis on youth, and "Frederick Douglass," which assesses the progress African Americans have made toward equality. Writings by Yusef Komunyakaa and Tim O'Brien bring home the lessons of the Vietnam War.

Background

Art

Choke, 1964, by Robert Rauschenberg

Born in Texas in 1925, Robert Rauschenberg has been one of the leading experimental American artists of the late twentieth century. Rauschenberg studied art at Black Mountain College in North Carolina. After creating a series of all-white and all-black paintings, Rauschenberg invented what he called the "combine"—a collage incorporating actual objects into paintings. The work shown here uses another technique he developed in the early 1960s: combining images from media and other artifacts of everyday life in silk-screen prints.

Encourage students to identify as many images in this work as they can. For example, guide students to see the upside-down Public Shelter sign, the One Way sign, the grainy Army helicopter, and the Statue of Liberty.

Use these questions for discussion:

1. There are references to the military and bomb shelters in this work. Given that Rauschenberg created this image a few years after the Cuban Missile Crisis, what aspect of American life might he be protesting?
   Possible answer: He might be protesting the possibility of nuclear war or the power of the military.

2. The term *choke* means to clog something to the point of constriction or even suffocation. What aspects of American life might create such a feeling?
   Possible answer: This feeling might be created by the way people are bombarded by media images and information or the fear of nuclear war.

CUSTOMIZE INSTRUCTION FOR UNIVERSAL ACCESS

When assigning the selections in this part, keep in mind these factors:

"The Rockpile"
- Engaging short story about family relationships
- Dialect may pose challenges for some readers.

from *Hiroshima*
- A compelling story of four survivors of the atomic bomb
- Students may need some help keeping the narratives separate.

"Losses"; "Death of the Ball Turret Gunner"
- In simple language, these poems ask what becomes of human values in war.

"Frederick Douglass"; "Runagate Runagate"
- Accessible poems will appeal to most students.

"Ambush"
- Brief, accessible, high-interest story of a veteran's painful memories of war

The Crucible
- Powerful story of mass hysteria, guilt and innocence based on true historical events

The Rockpile

Lesson Objectives

1. **To analyze and respond to literary elements**
   - Literary Analysis: Setting
   - Connecting Literary Elements: Symbol

2. **To read, comprehend, analyze, and critique a short story**
   - Reading Strategy: Identifying Cause and Effect
   - Reading Check Questions
   - Review and Assess Questions
   - Assessment Practice (ATE)

3. **To develop word analysis skills, fluency, and systematic vocabulary**
   - Vocabulary Development Lesson: Latin Prefix: *mal-*

4. **To understand and apply written and oral language conventions**
   - Spelling Strategy
   - Grammar and Style Lesson: Restrictive and Nonrestrictive Adjective Clauses

5. **To understand and apply appropriate writing and research strategies**
   - Writing Lesson: Roy's Journal
   - Extension Activity: Illustrated Report

6. **To understand and apply listening and speaking strategies**
   - Extension Activity: Radio Play

STEP-BY-STEP TEACHING GUIDE	PACING GUIDE
PRETEACH	
Motivate Students and Provide Background	
Use the Motivation activity (ATE p. 1146)	5 min.
Read and discuss author and background features (SE/ATE p. 1146) [A]	5 min.
Introduce the Concepts	
Introduce the Literary Analysis and Reading Strategy (SE/ATE p. 1147) [A]	15 min.
Pronounce the vocabulary words and read their definitions (SE p. 1147)	5 min.
TEACH	Estimate how long it will take students
Monitor Comprehension	to read selection and discuss Reading and Vocab notes
Informally monitor comprehension by circulating while students read independently or in groups [A]	
Monitor students' comprehension with the Reading Check notes (SE/ATE pp. 1149, 1151, 1153, 1155)	as students read
Develop vocabulary with Vocabulary notes (SE pp. 1149, 1150, 1151, 1152, 1156; ATE p. 1156)	as students read
Develop Understanding	
Develop students' understanding of setting with the Literary Analysis annotations (SE pp. 1149, 1150, 1152; ATE pp. 1148, 1150, 1152) [A]	5 min.
Develop students' ability to analyze cause and effect by using the Reading Strategy annotations (SE pp. 1151, 1152, 1154, 1155; ATE pp. 1151, 1152, 1154, 1155)	5 min.
ASSESS	
Assess Mastery	
Assess students' mastery of the Reading Strategy and Literary Analysis by having them answer the Review and Assess questions (SE/ATE p. 1157)	15 min.
Use one or more of the print and media Assessment Resources (ATE p. 1159) [A]	up to 45 min.
EXTEND	
Apply Understanding	
Have students complete the Vocabulary Development Lesson and the Grammar Lesson (SE p. 1158) [A]	20 min.
Apply students' ability to develop a personal tone in their writing by using the Writing Lesson (SE/ATE p. 1159) [A]	45 min.
Apply students' understanding using one or more of the Extension Activities (SE p. 1159)	20–90 min.

 ACCELERATED INSTRUCTION:
Use the strategies and activities identified with an [A].

UNIVERSAL ACCESS
● = Below Level Students
▲ = On-Level Students
■ = Above Level Students

Time and Resource Manager

Reading Level: Average
Average Number of Instructional Days: 4

RESOURCES		
PRINT 📖	**TRANSPARENCIES** 🗂	**TECHNOLOGY** 💿 🎧 📼
• **Beyond Literature,** Community Connection: Emergency Services, p. 67 ▲ ■		• **Interest Grabber Videotapes,** Tape 6 ● ▲ ■
• **Selection Support Workbook:** ● ▲ ■ Literary Analysis, p. 293 Reading Strategy, p. 292 Build Vocabulary, p. 290	• **Literary Analysis and Reading Transparencies,** pp. 133 and 134 ● ▲ ■	
		• **Listening to Literature** ● ▲ ■ Audiocassettes, Side 38 Audio CDs, CD 22
• **Literatura en español** ● ▲ • **Literary Analysis for Enrichment** ■		
• **Formal Assessment:** Selection Test, p. 291 ● ▲ ■ • **Open Book Test,** p. 199 ● ▲ ■ • **Performance Assessment and Portfolio Management,** p. 31 ● ▲ ■ **PRENTICE HALL** ASSESSMENT *SYSTEM* ● ▲ ■	**PRENTICE HALL** ASSESSMENT *SYSTEM* ● ▲ ■ Skills Practice Answers and Explanations on Transparencies	• **Test Bank Software** ● ▲ ■ • **Got It! Assessment Videotapes,** Tape 6 ● ▲
• **Selection Support Workbook:** ● ▲ ■ Grammar and Style, p. 291 • **Writing and Grammar,** Ruby Level ● ▲ ■ • **Extension Activities,** p. 67 ● ▲ ■	• **Daily Language Practice Transparencies** ● ▲ • **Writing Models and Graphic Organizers on Transparencies,** pp. 41, 91 ● ▲ ■	• **Writing and Grammar iText CD-ROM** ● ▲ ■ 💻 *Take It to the Net* www.phschool.com

BLOCK SCHEDULING: Use one 90-minute class period to preteach the selection and have students read it. Use a second 90-minute class period to assess students' mastery of skills and have them complete one of the Extension Activities.

Motivation

Write the following statement on the board: "I am not my brother's keeper." Discuss its meaning with students. You might use some of the following questions to shape the discussion:

- To whom does the word *brother* refer?

- What does the word *keeper* mean in this context?

- When would someone be apt to make such a statement?

- Do you agree with the sentiments expressed by this statement? Why or why not?

Encourage students to keep this statement in mind as they read "The Rockpile" and to note which characters might agree with its meaning.

▣ Interest Grabber Video

As an alternative, you may wish to play "James Baldwin" on Tape 6 to engage student interest.

❶ Background

More About the Author

Much of James Baldwin's work reflects his experience growing up in Harlem. This New York City neighborhood has been a vital center of African American life and culture since southern blacks began migrating there in the 1910s. In the 1920s, it was the hub of the Harlem Renaissance, an African American literary and artistic movement. One of the leading writers of that movement was Baldwin's teacher, Countee Cullen.

When the Depression hit in the 1930s, the largely poor population of Harlem plunged even deeper into poverty. This was the Harlem in which Baldwin grew up. Despite economic hardship, however, Harlem's culture—its theaters, music and dance centers, and the churches where the young Baldwin preached —remained strong.

Prepare to Read

❶ The Rockpile

James Baldwin (1924–1987)

James Baldwin once told an interviewer that he "never had a childhood." Because his stepfather worked long hours as both a preacher and a factory hand, Baldwin was given much of the responsibility for raising his eight half brothers and half sisters. The only leisure activity he was able to pursue was reading. He explained, "As [my half brothers and half sisters] were born, I took them over with one hand and held a book with the other. . . . In this way I read *Uncle Tom's Cabin* and *A Tale of Two Cities* over and over again; in this way, in fact, I read just about everything I could get my hands on." Baldwin's early love for reading deepened his imagination, planting the seeds of inspiration for his later success as a writer.

A Harlem Childhood Baldwin was born in Harlem, the New York community that served as a cultural center for African Americans during the 1920s and 30s. Even as a young boy, it was clear that he had a gift for words. He published his first short story in a church newspaper when he was twelve years old. Despite his obvious gift, Baldwin's deeply religious parents disapproved of his interest in literature. At age fourteen, Baldwin followed their wishes and became a preacher, earning a degree of fame in churches around Harlem, but he continued to pursue his literary ambitions.

Baldwin was encouraged by African American poet Countee Cullen, who taught in his junior high school. With Cullen's support, he wrote poetry and worked on his school's literary magazine. Inspired by the success of Richard Wright's novel *Native Son*, which proved to him that an African American could have success as a writer, Baldwin eventually decided to abandon preaching and devote his life to writing.

The Road to "Writer" For several years, Baldwin worked at odd jobs while writing and reading in his spare time. He wrote book reviews and essays, which were published in several New York journals. Some of these articles were later collected in *Notes of a Native Son* (1955). When he was twenty-four, Baldwin won a fellowship that enabled him to travel to Europe and write. He lived in Paris for the next four years, where he completed his first novel, *Go Tell It on the Mountain* (1953). The novel marked the beginning of a distinguished literary career that included the novels *Giovanni's Room* (1956), *Another Country* (1962), *The Fire Next Time* (1963), and *Tell Me How Long the Train's Been Gone* (1968); a play set in the American South called *Blues for Mr. Charlie* (1964); a collection of short stories titled *Going to Meet the Man* (1965); and several successful collections of essays.

A Powerful Witness Baldwin once said, "One writes out of one thing only—one's own experience. Everything depends on how relentlessly one forces from this experience the last drop, sweet or bitter, it can possibly give." Baldwin's work bears powerful witness to his own experience as an African American. In his writing, he expresses the need for social justice as well as the universal desire for love. Because his books dig deeply into contemporary life, they are sometimes painful to read, but the pain is always tempered by hope, and by Baldwin's magnificent language. Of Baldwin's essays, the poet Langston Hughes once wrote, "He uses words like the sea uses waves, to flow and beat, advance and retreat, rise and take a bow in disappearing." In interviews throughout his life, Baldwin often repeated one phrase: "People can be better than they are." This simple idea is woven into everything he wrote.

TEACHING RESOURCES

The following resources can be used to enrich or extend the instruction for pp. 1146–1147.

Motivation

▣ **Interest Grabber Video**, Tape 6

Background

▢ **Beyond Literature**, p. 67

▣ **Take It to the Net**
   Visit www.phschool.com for Background and hotlinks for James Baldwin.

Literary Analysis

▢ **Selection Support:** Literary Analysis, p. 293

▢ **Literary Analysis and Reading Transparencies,** Setting, p. 134

Reading

▢ **Literary Analysis and Reading Transparencies,** Identifying Cause and Effect, p. 133

Preview

Connecting to the Literature

This story centers on a family living in a poor neighborhood where the setting itself presents a conflict. The children of the family are caught between two sources of danger—the street life they are forbidden to join and the tensions between their parents.

❷ Literary Analysis

Setting

The **setting** of a story is the time and place in which it occurs, and may include details about the weather, physical features of the landscape, and other elements of an environment. "The Rockpile" is set in Harlem during the 1930s. Life in that place and time was influenced by the difficult economic and social realities that people faced. As you read, think about how the setting helps to shape the characters' personalities and actions.

Connecting Literary Elements

A **symbol** is a person, place, or object that has a meaning in itself but also suggests a larger meaning. For example, in this story, the rockpile represents both failure in the community and conflict within the family.

> They fought on the rockpile. Sure footed, dangerous, and reckless, they rushed each other and grappled on the heights . . .

As you read, note the ways in which the rockpile is described, the characters associated with it, and the events that take place there. These details will help reveal the symbolic meaning of the rockpile.

❸ Reading Strategy

Identifying Cause and Effect

In this story, a child's disobedience reveals a complicated family dynamic. You will understand the characters in the story better if you **identify cause-and-effect** relationships among them. Use a chart like the one shown to determine the motives for characters' actions and their effects on others.

Vocabulary Development

intriguing (in trē´ gin) *adj.* interesting or curious (p. 1149)

benevolent (bə nev´ ə lənt) *adj.* kindly; charitable (p. 1150)

decorously (dek´ ə rəs lē) *adv.* characterized by or showing decorum and good taste (p. 1150)

latent (lāt´ 'nt) *adj.* present but invisible or inactive (p. 1150)

engrossed (en grōst´) *adj.* occupied wholly; absorbed (p. 1151)

jubilant (jōō´ bə lənt) *adj.* joyful and triumphant (p. 1151)

arrested (ə res´ tid) *adj.* stopped (p. 1152)

malevolence (mə lev´ ə ləns) *n.* malice; spitefulness (p. 1156)

perdition (pər dish´ ən) *n.* complete and irreparable loss; ruin (p. 1156)

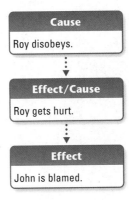

Cause

Roy disobeys.

Effect/Cause

Roy gets hurt.

Effect

John is blamed.

The Rockpile ◆ 1147

---

❷ Literary Analysis

Setting

- Explain to students that setting—the time and place in which a story occurs—can shape the characters of a literary work.

- Use the Setting transparency in **Literary Analysis and Reading Transparencies**, p. 134 to illustrate the various elements that make up the setting of "The Rockpile."

- Ask students to consider how a setting like the one described in the story might shape a young boy's personality.

- Instruct students as they read to take notes on the influence the setting has on the characters in "The Rockpile."

❸ Reading Strategy

Identifying Cause and Effect

- Be sure students understand that "cause and effect" refers to the causes of a character's actions, and the effects those actions have on others.

- As an example, suggest that if a student's younger sibling disobeys rules, he or she might get hurt. Write on the chalkboard: Cause: *Sibling disobeys*; Effect: *Sibling gets hurt.*

- Then, suggest that if the younger sibling gets hurt, parents might blame the student. Write on the chalkboard: Cause: *Sibling gets hurt*; Effect: *Student is blamed.*

- Point out that the chart on p. 1147 illustrates such a chain of cause and effects in "The Rockpile."

Vocabulary Development

- Pronounce each vocabulary word for students, and read the definitions as a class. Have students identify any words with which they are already familiar.

CUSTOMIZE INSTRUCTION FOR UNIVERSAL ACCESS

For Less Proficient Readers	For English Learners	For Advanced Readers
Students may need additional practice to master the Literary Analysis skill for this selection, setting. Be sure that they recognize that setting involves both time and place, contributes to the conflict, and helps shape the characters. Use **Selection Support Workbook**, p. 293, to help develop comprehension.	In order to fully appreciate the effects of a story's setting readers must carefully study the details in a text. Encourage students to read descriptive passages slowly, making note of any unfamiliar words. Have them look up such words, and then reread.	Setting plays a major role in this story. Suggest that students consider: What is the greatest danger that the characters face? Is it a danger posed by the setting, or by the other characters? Have students take notes to support their answers.

 E-Teach

Visit E-Teach at www.phschool.com for teachers' essays on how to teach, with questions and answers.

Step-by-Step Teaching Guide for pp. 1148–1156

CUSTOMIZE INSTRUCTION
For Verbal/Linguistic Learners

Baldwin's use of language reveals the influence of the evangelical church, where both he and his father preached. Call students' attention to the Literature in Context feature on p. 1154. Encourage students to find and listen to recordings of evangelical preachers, and identify resonances in Baldwin's prose. Students can make a presentation based on their findings.

❶ About the Selection

Family relationships are complicated, and family conflicts are studies in cause and effect. As students read this story about one family's response to a child's seemingly ordinary act of disobedience, they will see that the characters' actions have both obvious and underlying causes and both immediate and far-reaching effects. Tracing these strands will help students understand the forces of love, need, resentment, and fear that bind and divide Baldwin's fictional family.

❷ Literary Analysis

Setting

• Remind students that a story's setting—the time and place in which it occurs—can shape the characters in important ways.

• Have students read the bracketed passage. Then, ask the Literary Analysis question on p. 1149: What unique features of the rockpile are described in the opening paragraph?
Answer: It is "a mass of natural rock jutting out of the ground" in the middle of a city block.

• Ask students to keep these physical details about the rockpile in mind as they read.

1148   Prosperity and Protest (1946–Present)

TEACHING RESOURCES

The following resources can be used to enrich or extend the instruction for pp. 1148–1156.

Literary Analysis

📖 **Literary Analysis and Reading Transparencies,** p. 134

📖 **Writing Models and Graphic Organizers on Transparencies,** p. 91 ▪

Reading

📖 **Selection Support:** Reading Strategy, p. 292; Build Vocabulary, p. 290

🎧 **Listening to Literature Audiocassettes,** Side 38 ▪

💿 **Listening to Literature Audio CDs,** CD 22 ▪

▪ **BLOCK SCHEDULING:** Resources marked with this symbol provide varied instruction during 90-minute blocks.

The Rock Pile

James Baldwin

Background

Even though he spent most of his adult life in Europe, James Baldwin's impassioned voice is full of the rhythms and details of life in Harlem, the New York City neighborhood where he grew up. This story, about a struggling Harlem family, is a strong example of Baldwin's connection to the place that shaped him both as a writer and as a person.

Push to Walk, (collage 48" x 48"), Phoebe Beasley

Across the street from their house, in an empty lot between two houses, stood the rockpile. It was a strange place to find a mass of natural rock jutting out of the ground; and someone, probably Aunt Florence, had once told them that the rock was there and could not be taken away because without it the subway cars underground would fly apart, killing all the people. This, touching on some natural mystery concerning the surface and the center of the earth, was far too <u>intriguing</u> an explanation to be challenged, and it invested the rockpile, moreover, with such mysterious importance that Roy felt it to be his right, not to say his duty, to play there.

Other boys were to be seen there each afternoon after school and all day Saturday and Sunday. They fought on the rockpile. Sure footed, dangerous, and reckless, they rushed each other and grappled on the

Literary Analysis
Setting and Symbol
Which unique features of the rockpile are described in the opening paragraph?

intriguing (in trē´ gin) *adj.* interesting or curious

☑ **Reading Check**
Where is the rockpile located?

◄ **Critical Viewing** What details shown in this painting connect to Baldwin's story? [Connect]

The Rockpile ◆ 1149

---

⑥ Literary Analysis

Setting and Symbol

- Remind students that some elements of setting—such as the rockpile—can be symbols, a person, place, or object that has a meaning in itself but suggests a larger meaning.

- After students have read the first two paragraphs, be sure that they understand that the rockpile is a rock formation where children play—and where Roy and John are forbidden to go.

- Ask students the first part of the first Literary Analysis question on p. 1150: What does the rockpile represent to the neighborhood children?
  Possible response: The rockpile represents a mysterious, exciting, and dangerous place beyond the strict control of their parents.

- Then, ask the second part of the question: What does it represent to Roy's mother?
  Possible response: It represents the dangers from which she must protect her children.

▶ **Monitor Progress** Encourage students to discuss how the rockpile is likely to shape the events of the story. Have them write down their ideas and review them after completing the story.

⑦ Literary Analysis

Setting and Symbol

- Point out to students that actions and events, as well as places and objects, can be symbols with larger meanings.

- Have students read the bracketed passage. Then, ask them what the drowning reveals about the setting.
  Answer: There are many dangers for children in this neighborhood.

- Then, ask students the second Literary Analysis question on p. 1150: Can the tragedy of the boy's drowning in the river be seen as a symbol? If so, why?
  Possible response: Students may respond that it can be, because for Roy and John's mother it represents the dangers of the world outside their home.

---

heights, sometimes disappearing down the other side in a confusion of dust and screams and upended, flying feet. "It's a wonder they don't kill themselves," their mother said, watching sometimes from the fire escape. "You children stay away from there, you hear me?" Though she said "children" she was looking at Roy, where he sat beside John on the fire escape. "The good Lord knows," she continued, "I don't want you to come home bleeding like a hog every day the Lord sends." Roy shifted impatiently, and continued to stare at the street, as though in this gazing he might somehow acquire wings. John said nothing. He had not really been spoken to: he was afraid of the rockpile and of the boys who played there.

Each Saturday morning John and Roy sat on the fire escape and watched the forbidden street below. Sometimes their mother sat in the room behind them, sewing, or dressing their younger sister, or nursing the baby, Paul. The sun fell across them and across the fire escape with a high, benevolent indifference; below them, men and women, and boys and girls, sinners all, loitered; sometimes one of the church-members passed and saw them and waved. Then, for the moment that they waved decorously back, they were intimidated. They watched the saint, man or woman, until he or she had disappeared from sight. The passage of one of the redeemed made them consider, however vacantly, the wickedness of the street, their own latent wickedness in sitting where they sat; and made them think of their father, who came home early on Saturdays and who would soon be turning this corner and entering the dark hall below them.

But until he came to end their freedom, they sat, watching and longing above the street. At the end of the street nearest their house was the bridge which spanned the Harlem River[1] and led to a city called the Bronx; which was where Aunt Florence lived. Nevertheless, when they saw her coming, she did not come from the bridge, but from the opposite end of the street. This, weakly, to their minds, she explained by saying that she had taken the subway, not wishing to walk, and that, besides, she did not live in that section of the Bronx. Knowing that the Bronx was across the river, they did not believe this story ever, but, adopting toward her their father's attitude, assumed that she had just left some sinful place which she dared not name, as, for example, a movie palace.

In the summertime boys swam in the river, diving off the wooden dock, or wading in from the garbage-heavy bank. Once a boy, whose name was Richard, drowned in the river. His mother had not known where he was; she had even come to their house, to ask if he was there. Then, in the evening, at six o'clock, they had heard from the street a woman screaming and wailing; and they ran to the windows and looked out. Down the street came the woman, Richard's mother, screaming, her face raised to the sky and tears running down her face. A woman walked beside her, trying to make her quiet and trying

---

1. **Harlem River** river that separates Manhattan Island from the Bronx in New York City.

1150 ◆ Prosperity and Protest (1946–Present)

Literary Analysis
Setting and Symbol
What does the rockpile represent to the neighborhood children? What does it represent to Roy's mother?

benelovent (bə nev′ ə lənt) *adj.* kindly; charitable

decorously (dek′ ər əs lē) *adv.* characterized by or showing decorum and good taste

latent (lāt′ ənt) *adj.* present but invisible or inactive

Literary Analysis
Setting and Symbol Can the tragedy of the boy's drowning in the river be seen as a symbol? If so, of what?

✸ ENRICHMENT: Literature Connection

Countee Cullen

Countee Cullen, who taught and encouraged James Baldwin, was a leading writer of the Harlem Renaissance. Cullen grew up in Kentucky and moved to Harlem when he was fifteen. He received several important poetry awards while he was a college student at New York University and published *Color*, his first book of poetry, shortly before his graduation.

Cullen went on to earn a Masters degree at Harvard; to teach French and English in New York City's public schools; and to publish several more volumes of poetry, a novel, two collections of children's stories, and several plays. He is best known for his poems, which he often wrote in sonnet form, and in which he explored such themes as race, creativity, and spirituality.

Refer students to Cullen's poem "From the Dark Tower," on p. 936. After they read the poem, ask students how Countee Cullen and other Harlem Renaissance writers and artists might have influenced James Baldwin.

to hold her up. Behind them walked a man, Richard's father, with Richard's body in his arms. There were two white policemen walking in the gutter, who did not seem to know what should be done. Richard's father and Richard were wet, and Richard's body lay across his father's arms like a cotton baby. The woman's screaming filled all the street; cars slowed down and the people in the cars stared; people opened their windows and looked out and came rushing out of doors to stand in the gutter, watching. Then the small procession disappeared within the house which stood beside the rockpile. Then, *"Lord, Lord, Lord!"* cried Elizabeth, their mother, and slammed the window down.

One Saturday, an hour before his father would be coming home, Roy was wounded on the rockpile and brought screaming upstairs. He and John had been sitting on the fire escape and their mother had gone into the kitchen to sip tea with Sister McCandless. By and by Roy became bored and sat beside John in restless silence; and John began drawing into his schoolbook a newspaper advertisement which featured a new electric locomotive. Some friends of Roy passed beneath the fire escape and called him. Roy began to fidget, yelling down to them through the bars. Then a silence fell. John looked up. Roy stood looking at him.

"I'm going downstairs," he said.

"You better stay where you is, boy. You know Mama don't want you going downstairs."

"I be right *back*. She won't even know I'm gone, less you run and tell her."

"I ain't *got* to tell her. What's going to stop her from coming in here and looking out the window?"

"She's talking," Roy said. He started into the house.

"But Daddy's going to be home soon!"

"I be back before *that*. What you all the time got to be so *scared* for?" He was already in the house and he now turned, leaning on the windowsill, to swear impatiently, "I be back in *five* minutes."

John watched him sourly as he carefully unlocked the door and disappeared. In a moment he saw him on the sidewalk with his friends. He did not dare to go and tell his mother that Roy had left the fire escape because he had practically promised not to.

He started to shout, *Remember, you said five minutes!* but one of Roy's friends was looking up at the fire escape. John looked down at his schoolbook: he became <u>engrossed</u> again in the problem of the locomotive.

When he looked up again he did not know how much time had passed, but now there was a gang fight on the rockpile. Dozens of boys fought each other in the harsh sun: clambering up the rocks and battling hand to hand, scuffed shoes sliding on the slippery rock; filling the bright air with curses and <u>jubilant</u> cries. They filled the air, too, with flying weapons: stones, sticks, tin cans, garbage, whatever could be picked up and thrown. John watched in a kind of absent amazement—until he remembered that Roy was still downstairs, and that he was one of the

---

Reading Strategy
Identifying Cause and Effect What causes Roy to go down to the street?

engrossed (en grōst´) *adj.* occupied wholly; absorbed

jubilant (jōō´ bəl ənt) *adj.* joyful and triumphant

⑩ ✓ Reading Check
Does Roy obey the instructions his mother gives him regarding the rockpile?

The Rockpile ◆ 1151

---

❽ Reading Strategy
Identifying Cause and Effect

- Draw a chart on the board that consists of two boxes linked by an arrow, one labeled "Cause" and the other "Effect." Instruct students to copy it into their notebooks.
- Have students read the bracketed passage. Then, ask them the Reading Strategy question on p. 1151: What causes Roy to go down to the street?
- Ask students to write their answers on their cause-and-effect charts.
  Possible response: Cause: Roy's friends call him from the street. Effect: Roy goes to the rockpile.
- Use the Identifying Cause-and-Effect transparency in **Literary Analysis and Reading Transparencies**, p. 133 to show other causes for Roy's action.

❾ Critical Thinking
Infer

- Have students read the bracketed passage. Be sure they understand that Roy runs downstairs to see his friends although John urges him not to go.
- Ask students what inferences they can make about John's character, based on the argument he has with his brother Roy.
  Possible response: Students should recognize that John is the older brother, and is supposed to watch out for Roy. However, he is also less bold, and afraid that something bad will happen.

❿ ✓ Reading Check
Answer: Roy does not obey his mother; instead, he goes to play on the rockpile.

CUSTOMIZE INSTRUCTION FOR UNIVERSAL ACCESS

For Gifted/Talented Students	For Advanced Readers
Aunt Florence had offered one explanation of why the rockpile cannot be moved. Ask students to consider what other adults in Roy and John's neighborhood might have told the children about the rockpile. Challenge students to invent a series of alternative explanations to account for the rockpile's presence. They can present these explanations in a dramatic reading representing how the neighborhood children might perceive the rockpile.	Encourage students to begin to analyze the differences between Roy and John. Students should notice that Roy "tunes out" their mother's scolding and is rebellious and disobedient. John appears to be the opposite—he is afraid to misbehave. Students can use a Cause-and-Effect chart such as the one modeled in **Writing Models and Graphic Organizers on Transparencies**, p. 91 to examine these characteristics as causes of events and effects in a chain of circumstances.

⓫ Literary Analysis

Setting

- Remind students of the importance of setting—that it can have a direct impact on the lives of characters.

- Have students read the bracketed passage. Then, ask them to explain what happened to Roy on the rockpile.
  Answer: Roy joined in a rough game; he tore his shirt; he stood on top of the rockpile; a can hit him in the head, cutting him; he fell to the ground.

- Ask students the Literary Analysis question on p. 1152: What details of Roy's accident reflect the difficulties of life in this place?
  Possible response: The rowdiness, the presence of jagged tin cans, the lack of a safe place for children to play, and the danger of the rockpile all reflect the difficulties of life in this setting.

▶ **Monitor Progress** Encourage students to discuss how these details of the setting have shaped Roy's and John's personalities.

⓬ Reading Strategy

Identifying Cause and Effect

- Have students read the bracketed passage. Then, ask them the Reading Skills question on p. 1152: What causes Elizabeth to look "with apprehension" toward the clock?
  Possible response: Students should understand that both John and Elizabeth are frightened of the father who is expected home momentarily.

---

boys on the rockpile. Then he was afraid; he could not see his brother among the figures in the sun; and he stood up, leaning over the fire-escape railing. Then Roy appeared from the other side of the rocks; John saw that his shirt was torn; he was laughing. He moved until he stood at the very top of the rockpile. Then, something, an empty tin can, flew out of the air and hit him on the forehead, just above the eye. Immediately, one side of Roy's face ran with blood, he fell and rolled on

⓫ his face down the rocks. Then for a moment there was no movement at all, no sound, the sun, arrested, lay on the street and the sidewalk and the <u>arrested</u> boys. Then someone screamed or shouted; boys began to run away, down the street, toward the bridge. The figure on the ground, having caught its breath and felt its own blood, began to shout. John cried, "Mama! Mama!" and ran inside.

"Don't fret, don't fret," panted Sister McCandless as they rushed down the dark, narrow, swaying stairs, "don't fret. Ain't a boy been born don't get his knocks every now and again. *Lord!*" they hurried into the sun. A man had picked Roy up and now walked slowly toward them. One or two boys sat silent on their stoops; at either end of the street there was a group of boys watching. "He ain't hurt bad," the man said, "wouldn't be making this kind of noise if he was hurt real bad."

Elizabeth, trembling, reached out to take Roy, but Sister McCandless, bigger, calmer, took him from the man and threw him over her shoulder as she once might have handled a sack of cotton. "God bless you," she said to the man, "God bless you, son." Roy was still screaming. Elizabeth stood behind Sister McCandless to stare at his bloody face.

"It's just a flesh wound," the man kept saying, "just broke the skin, that's all." They were moving across the sidewalk, toward the house. John, not now afraid of the staring boys, looked toward the corner to see if his father was yet in sight.

Upstairs, they hushed Roy's crying. They bathed the blood away,

⓬ to find, just above the left eyebrow, the jagged, superficial scar. "Lord, have mercy," murmured Elizabeth, "another inch and it would've been his eye." And she looked with apprehension toward the clock. "Ain't it the truth," said Sister McCandless, busy with bandages and iodine.

"When did he go downstairs?" his mother asked at last.

Sister McCandless now sat fanning herself in the easy chair, at the head of the sofa where Roy lay, bound and silent. She paused for a moment to look sharply at John. John stood near the window, holding the newspaper advertisement and the drawing he had done.

"We was sitting on the fire escape," he said. "Some boys he knew called him."

"When?"

"He said he'd be back in five minutes."

"Why didn't you tell me he was downstairs?"

He looked at his hands, clasping his notebook, and did not answer.

"Boy," said Sister McCandless, "you hear your mother a-talking to you?"

Literary Analysis

Setting Which details of Roy's accident reflect the difficulties of life in this place?

arrested (ə rest′ id) *adj.* stopped

Reading Strategy

Identifying Cause and Effect What causes Elizabeth to look "with apprehension" toward the clock?

✳ ENRICHMENT: Social Studies Connection

Communities and Families

One of the problems that contributes to the conflict in this story is that John and Roy did not have a place outside the home where they could safely play. Many communities, however, provide programs and facilities for both children and teenagers, making such places as the rockpile less attractive. Local newspapers and community bulletins often offer information about such community resources. Interested students can explore the youth facilities and programs in their own community.

The other major source of conflict in the story lies within the family. Writers like James Baldwin delve into family problems and family dynamics as part of their creative work. Social workers—professionals trained to provide support and counseling to individuals and families who need help—deal with these issues on a practical, real-life level. Students can research the various types of services that social workers provide, and then consider how a social worker could be of assistance to the family Baldwin describes.

He looked at his mother. He repeated:
"He said he'd be back in five minutes."

"He said he'd be back in five minutes," said Sister McCandless with scorn, "don't look to me like that's no right answer. You's the man of the house, you supposed to look after your baby brothers and sisters—you ain't supposed to let them run off and get half-killed. But I expect," she added, rising from the chair, dropping the cardboard fan, "your Daddy'll make you tell the truth. Your Ma's way too soft with you."

He did not look at her, but at the fan where it lay in the dark red, depressed seat where she had been. The fan advertised a pomade[2] for the hair and showed a brown woman and her baby, both with glistening hair, smiling happily at each other.

"Honey," said Sister McCandless, "I got to be moving along. Maybe I drop in later tonight. I don't reckon you going to be at Tarry Service tonight?"

Tarry Service was the prayer meeting held every Saturday night at church to strengthen believers and prepare the church for the coming of the Holy Ghost on Sunday.

"I don't reckon," said Elizabeth. She stood up; she and Sister McCandless kissed each other on the cheek. "But you be sure to remember me in your prayers."

"I surely will do that." She paused, with her hand on the door knob, and looked down at Roy and laughed. "Poor little man," she said, "reckon he'll be content to sit on the fire escape *now*."

Elizabeth laughed with her. "It sure ought to be a lesson to him. You don't reckon," she asked nervously, still smiling, "he going to keep that scar, do you?"

"Lord, no," said Sister McCandless, "ain't nothing but a scratch. I declare, Sister Grimes, you worse than a child. Another couple of weeks and you won't be able to *see* no scar. No, you go on about your housework, honey, and thank the Lord it weren't no worse." She opened the door; they heard the sound of feet on the stairs. "I expect that's the Reverend," said Sister McCandless, placidly, "I *bet* he going to raise cain."[3]

"Maybe it's Florence," Elizabeth said. "Sometimes she get here about this time." They stood in the doorway, staring, while the steps reached the landing below and began again climbing to their floor. "No," said Elizabeth then, "that ain't her walk. That's Gabriel."

"Well, I'll just go on," said Sister McCandless, "and kind of prepare his mind." She pressed Elizabeth's hand as she spoke and started into the hall, leaving the door behind her slightly ajar. Elizabeth turned slowly back into the room. Roy did not open his eyes, or move; but she knew that he was not sleeping; he wished to delay until the last possible moment any contact with his father. John put

---

2. **pomade** (päm ād´) *n.* perfumed ointment.
3. **raise cain** slang for "cause trouble."

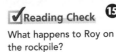

Reading Check ⓯

What happens to Roy on the rockpile?

The Rockpile ◆ 1153

⓭ **Critical Thinking**
Making a Judgment

- Ask students to consider the character of Sister McCandless. Be sure they understand that she is Elizabeth's friend and that she seems to take control of the situation when Roy is hurt.
- Have students read the bracketed passage. Then, ask them whether they think that Sister McCandless's scolding of John is justified or not. Possible response: Some students may feel that it is justified—John should have stopped Roy from going downstairs. Others may say it is not justified because John did try to stop Roy, and he is only a child himself, not a responsible adult.
- Encourage students to keep their judgment in mind as more is revealed about Sister McCandless's character.

⓮ **Critical Thinking**
Analyze

- Have students read the bracketed passage. Ask them to keep in mind their thoughts about Sister McCandless.
- Ask students: What do Sister McCandless's words reveal about her relationship with Elizabeth? Explain. Possible response: Students may say that Sister McCandless dominates Elizabeth, treating her as she would a child. They should note that she says Elizabeth is "worse than a child," and that she seems to usurp Elizabeth's responsibilities.

⓯ **Reading Check**

Answer: First, Roy's shirt is torn. Then, he is hit in the head and cut by a thrown tin can.

CUSTOMIZE INSTRUCTION FOR UNIVERSAL ACCESS

For Special Needs Students	For Less Proficient Readers	For English Learners
Students may need to pause and review the events of the story's plot. Be sure that students understand that Roy has gone to the rockpile against his parents' wishes; he has been hurt; and Elizabeth, John, and Sister McCandless are awaiting Roy's father.	Students may find the Reading Strategy exercise on p. 1152 challenging. Guide them to recognize that Elizabeth's glance at the clock is caused by her fear of Gabriel's imminent return. Use **Selection Support:** Reading Strategy, p. 292 to help students understand the family relationships.	Students might have difficulty with the dialogue between John, Elizabeth, and Sister McCandless. Encourage them to reread the dialogue, perhaps as they listen to the story read aloud on **Listening to Literature:** Audiocassette Side 38, Audio CD 22.

Baldwin and the Church

Evangelism refers to winning con-verts to Christianity. The evangelical church focuses on conversion, strict reliance on biblical scripture, and on preaching. Baldwin's childhood in the church is likely a major source of inspiration for "The Rockpile." The author's experiences as a preacher can be seen most clearly in *The Fire Next Time*, a long essay in which Baldwin directly addresses racism, its effects on society, and what must be done to combat it.

17 Reading Strategy

Identifying Cause and Effect

- Remind students that they have already learned a great deal about this family by examining cause and effect.

- Have students read the bracketed passage. Be sure they understand that Roy begins to cry when his father asks him what happened.

- Ask students the Reading Strategy question on p. 1154: How does Gabriel react to Roy's tears? **Answer:** He comforts Roy and reassures him, implying that he will not punish Roy no matter what happened.

- Encourage students to consider what the effect of Roy's tears on Gabriel suggests about the family dynamic.

---

his newspaper and his notebook on the table and stood, leaning on the table, staring at her.

"It wasn't my fault," he said. "I couldn't stop him from going downstairs."

"No," she said, "you ain't got nothing to worry about. You just tell your Daddy the truth."

He looked directly at her, and she turned to the window, star-ing into the street. What was Sister McCandless saying? Then from her bedroom she heard Delilah's thin wail and she turned, frowning, looking toward the bedroom and toward the still open door. She knew that John was watching her. Delilah continued to wail, she thought, angrily, *Now that girl's getting too big for that*, but she feared that Delilah would awaken Paul and she hurried into the bedroom. She tried to soothe Delilah back to sleep. Then she heard the front door open and close—too loud, Delilah raised her voice, with an exasperated sigh Elizabeth picked the child up. Her child and Gabriel's, her children and Gabriel's: Roy, Delilah, Paul. Only John was nameless and a stranger, living, unalterable testimony to his mother's days in sin.

"What happened?" Gabriel demanded. He stood, enormous, in the center of the room, his black lunchbox dangling from his hand, staring at the sofa where Roy lay. John stood just before him, it seemed to her astonished vision just below him, beneath his fist, his heavy shoe.

The child stared at the man in fascination and terror—when a girl down home she had seen rabbits stand so paralyzed before the barking dog. She hurried past Gabriel to the sofa, feeling the weight of Delilah in her arms like the weight of a shield, and stood over Roy, saying:

"Now, ain't a thing to get upset about, Gabriel. This boy sneaked downstairs while I had my back turned and got hisself hurt a little. He's alright now."

Roy, as though in confirmation, now opened his eyes and looked gravely at his father. Gabriel dropped his lunchbox with a clatter and knelt by the sofa.

"How you feel, son? Tell your Daddy what happened?"

Roy opened his mouth to speak and then, relapsing into panic, began to cry. His father held him by the shoulder.

"You don't want to cry. You's Daddy's little man. Tell your Daddy what happened."

"He went downstairs," said Elizabeth, "where he didn't have no business to be, and got to fighting with them bad boys playing on the rockpile. That's what happened and it's a mercy it weren't nothing worse."

He looked up at her. "Can't you let this boy answer me for hisself?"

Ignoring this, she went on, more gently: "He got cut on the fore-head, but it ain't nothing to worry about."

James Baldwin and the Church

Baldwin's choice of words, and often the subject matter of his stories, was influenced by the evangelical church, of which his father was a minister. In this story, many details reflect this influence:

- references to "the good Lord" and "saints"
- reference to the father as "the Reverend"
- mention of prayer services
- the fact that the mother and her friend call each other "Sister"
- conflicts between the family's strict religious values and the temptations of the neighborhood

As a teenager, Baldwin earned renown for his gifts as a preacher. He brought those same gifts, including the use of impassioned, rhythmic language, to his writing, creating prose of great beauty and power.

Reading Strategy
Identifying Cause and Effect How does Gabriel react to Roy's tears?

"You call a doctor? How you know it ain't nothing to worry about?"

"Is you got money to be throwing away on doctors? No, I ain't called no doctor. Ain't nothing wrong with my eyes that I can't tell whether he's hurt bad or not. He got a fright more'n anything else, and you ought to pray God it teaches him a lesson."

"You got a lot to say now," he said, "but I'll have *me* something to say in a minute. I'll be wanting to know when all this happened, what you was doing with your eyes *then*." He turned back to Roy, who had lain quietly sobbing eyes wide open and body held rigid: and who now, at his father's touch, remembered the height, the sharp, sliding rock beneath his feet, the sun, the explosion of the sun, his plunge into darkness and his salty blood; and recoiled, beginning to scream, as his father touched his forehead. "Hold still, hold still," crooned his father, shaking, "hold still. Don't cry. Daddy ain't going to hurt you, he just wants to see this bandage, see what they've done to his little man." But Roy continued to scream and would not be still and Gabriel dared not lift the bandage for fear of hurting him more. And he looked at Elizabeth in fury: "Can't you put that child down and help me with this boy? John, take your baby sister from your mother—don't look like neither of you got good sense."

John took Delilah and sat down with her in the easy chair. His mother bent over Roy, and held him still, while his father, carefully—but still Roy screamed—lifted the bandage and stared at the wound. Roy's sobs began to lessen. Gabriel readjusted the bandage. "You see," said Elizabeth, finally, "he ain't nowhere near dead."

"It sure ain't your fault that he ain't dead." He and Elizabeth considered each other for a moment in silence. "He came mightly close to losing an eye. Course, his eyes ain't as big as your'n, so I reckon you don't think it matters so much." At this her face hardened; he smiled. "Lord, have mercy," he said, "you think you ever going to learn to do right? Where was you when all this happened? Who let him go downstairs?"

"Ain't nobody let him go downstairs, he just went. He got a head just like his father, it got to be broken before it'll bow. I was in the kitchen."

"Where was Johnnie?"

"He was in here."

"Where?"

"He was on the fire escape."

"Didn't he know Roy was downstairs?"

"I reckon."

"What you mean, you reckon? He ain't got your big eyes for nothing, does he?" He looked over at John. "Boy, you see your brother go downstairs?"

"Gabriel, ain't no sense in trying to blame Johnnie. You know right well if you have trouble making Roy behave, he ain't going to listen to his brother. He don't hardly listen to me."

"How come you didn't tell your mother Roy was downstairs?"

John said nothing, staring at the blanket which covered Delilah.

Reading Strategy
Identifying Cause and Effect What is Gabriel's reaction to Elizabeth's efforts to downplay the incident?

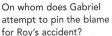

✓Reading Check ⑲
On whom does Gabriel attempt to pin the blame for Roy's accident?

The Rockpile ◆ 1155

---

⑱ **Reading Strategy**
Identifying Cause and Effect

- Briefly review student responses to the Reading Strategy question on p. 1154. Ask students to keep in mind what has been revealed about the family.

- Have students read the bracketed passage. Then, ask the Reading Strategy question on p. 1155: What is Gabriel's reaction to Elizabeth's efforts to downplay the incident? **Answer:** Gabriel responds angrily to his wife, threatening to punish her for Roy's accident, then shouting at her.

▶ **Monitor Progress** Ask students what Gabriel's words and actions following his return home reveal about the family dynamic. **Possible response:** Gabriel views himself as the head of his household; he is an authority figure and scolds his wife as if she were a naughty child. Roy appears to be his favorite child; Gabriel is overly protective of Roy and spoils him.

⑲ **✓Reading Check**

Answer: Gabriel attempts to blame John for Roy's accident.

CUSTOMIZE INSTRUCTION FOR UNIVERSAL ACCESS

For Less Proficient Readers	For Gifted/Talented Students	For Advanced Readers
The family discussion that begins with Gabriel's entrance would be a good point to play the **Listening to Literature** recording on Audiocassette Side 38 or Audio CD 22. Students can read along with the text and draw conclusions about the relationships within the family.	Call students' attention to the complicated relationships within this family. Some students may have direct personal experience with the complicated emotions that can develop between a step-child and step-parent. Instruct students to create collages that capture the emotions of this family, using whatever materials they prefer.	Ask students to consider this question: Is Gabriel a completely bad person? Students are likely to find both good—his tenderness for his family—and bad—his dominance and quick temper—in Gabriel. Instruct students to write brief but well-reasoned statements evaluating Gabriel's character.

⓴ Vocabulary Development

The Latin Prefix mal-

- Call students' attention to the word *malevolence* and its definition. Tell students that the Latin prefix *mal-* means "bad," "wrong," or "ill."

- Have students suggest words and phrases that contain this prefix, and list them on the chalkboard. Possibilities include: malfunction, maladjusted, malodorous, and malnutrition.

- Next, have students create their own definitions for these words, and check their answers in a dictionary.

Answers for p. 1156

Review and Assess

1. Possible response: Students may recall a time when they or a younger sibling disobeyed.

2. **(a)** They sit on the fire escape and watch the street. **(b)** Possible response: The street is forbidden because their parents see it as dangerous and filled with sinners.

3. **(a)** Gabriel is John's stepfather. **(b)** Possible response: Gabriel sees John as evidence of his wife's sinful past.

4. **(a)** Richard drowns in the river. **(b)** Possible response: Baldwin shows that the family is separate from and somewhat frightened by the community.

5. **(a)** He blames first Elizabeth and then John for Roy's injury. **(b)** Possible response: They have a strained relationship in which Gabriel is harsh and dominating. **(c)** Possible response: He remembers that she is his partner and the mother of his children.

6. Possible response: Students may wish to blame Roy himself for his injury. Students should support their opinions.

"Boy, you hear me? You want me to take a strap to you?"

"No, you ain't," she said. "You ain't going to taken no strap to this boy, not today you ain't. Ain't a soul to blame for Roy's lying up there now but you—you because you done spoiled him so that he thinks he can do just anything and get away with it. I'm here to tell you that ain't no way to raise no child. You don't pray to the Lord to help you do better than you been doing, you going to live to shed bitter tears that the Lord didn't take his soul today." And she was trembling. She moved, unseeing, toward John and took Delilah from his arms. She looked back at Gabriel, who had risen, who stood near the sofa, staring at her. And she found in his face not fury alone, which would not have surprised her; but hatred so deep as to become insupportable in its lack of personality. His eyes were struck alive, unmoving, blind

⓴ with <u>malevolence</u> —she felt, like the pull of the earth at her feet, his longing to witness her <u>perdition.</u> Again, as though it might be propitiation, she moved the child in her arms. And at this his eyes changed, he looked at Elizabeth, the mother of his children, the helpmeet given by the Lord. Then her eyes clouded; she moved to leave the room; her foot struck the lunchbox lying on the floor.

"John," she said, "pick up your father's lunchbox like a good boy."

She heard, behind her, his scrambling movement as he left the easy chair, the scrape and jangle of the lunchbox as he picked it up, bending his dark head near the toe of his father's heavy shoe.

malevolence (mə lev′ ə ləns) *n.* malice; spitefulness

perdition (pər dish′ ən) *n.* complete and irreparable loss; ruin

---

Review and Assess

Thinking About the Selection

1. **Respond:** Does this story call to mind any of your own childhood experiences? Explain.

2. **(a) Recall:** What do John and Roy do each Saturday morning? **(b) Deduce:** Why is the street "forbidden"?

3. **(a) Recall:** How is John related to Gabriel? **(b) Support:** What evidence is there that Gabriel's relationship with John is different from his relationship with the other children?

4. **(a) Recall:** What happens to the boy, Richard, at the river? **(b) Analyze:** Through this anecdote, what is Baldwin saying about this family's relationship to their community?

5. **(a) Recall:** Whom does Gabriel blame for Roy's injury? **(b) Draw Conclusions:** What conclusions can you draw about Gabriel's relationship with Elizabeth? Explain. **(c) Speculate:** Why do Gabriel's feelings toward Elizabeth soften at the end of the story?

6. **Make a Judgment:** Who do you think is responsible for Roy's injury?

1156 ◆ *Prosperity and Protest (1946-Present)*

✎ ASSESSMENT PRACTICE: Writing Skills

Punctuation   **(For more practice, see Test Preparation Workbook, p. 70.)**

Some tests require students to identify the best way to correct an error in punctuation. Use the following sample test item to demonstrate.

Because he had much of the responsibility of raising his eight siblings—James Baldwin claimed that he "never had a childhood."

Which is the best way to correct this passage?

A Because he had much of the responsibility of raising his eight siblings; James Baldwin claimed that he "never had a childhood."

B Because he had much of the responsibility of raising his eight siblings: James Baldwin claimed that he "never had a childhood."

C Because he had much of the responsibility of raising his eight siblings, James Baldwin claimed that he "never had a childhood."

D Correct as is

C correctly places a comma after an adverb clause preceding an independent clause.

Review and Assess

Literary Analysis

Setting

1. Find three details that describe the psychological environment of the story's **setting**—the mood and atmosphere of the neighborhood.
2. Find three details that describe the physical environment—the landmarks of the neighborhood.
3. What are some of the potential dangers the setting presents?
4. In what ways do you think the setting has influenced Gabriel's and Elizabeth's decisions about how to raise their children?

Connecting Literary Elements

5. (a) Use a chart like the one shown to analyze the rockpile, the main **symbol** in this story. (b) What does the rockpile represent?

The Rockpile				What it Means
What people say about it	Events linked with it	Details used to describe it	···▶ ···▶	

6. (a) What does "the toe of his father's heavy shoe," mentioned at the end of the story, symbolize? (b) In what way does this image capture John's relationship to Gabriel? (c) How would you define their relationship?

Reading Strategy

Identifying Cause and Effect

7. (a) What **causes** John to avoid telling his mother that Roy went to the rockpile? (b) What is the **effect** of his delay?
8. (a) What are the causes of Elizabeth's protectiveness toward John? (b) What is the effect on Gabriel of this protectiveness?

Extend Understanding

9. **Psychology Connection:** In this story, John is given a heavy responsibility: monitoring his brother's behavior. What problems might such responsibility create for a young boy like John?

Quick Review

The **setting** of a story is the time and place in which it occurs.

A **symbol** is a person, place, or object that has a meaning in itself but suggests other meanings as well.

To **identify cause-and-effect** relationships, note the circumstances that cause characters' actions and the effects their actions have on others.

 Take It to the Net
www.phschool.com
Take the interactive self-test online to check your understanding of the selection.

The Rockpile ◆ 1157

✳ ENRICHMENT: Further Reading

Other Works by James Baldwin

Go Tell It on the Mountain

Giovanni's Room

Another Country

Tell Me How Long the Train's Been Gone

Nobody Knows My Name

The Fire Next Time

Blues for Mr. Charlie

We strongly suggest that you preview these works before recommending them to students.

 Take It to the Net
Visit www.phschool.com for more information on James Baldwin.

Answers for p. 1157

Review and Assess

1. Details include the reckless games the children play on the rockpile, the "sinners" loitering in the street, the anxiety of John and Roy's parents.

2. Details include the rockpile, the crowds in the street, the river, the garbage strewn about the lot, and the fire escape from which John and Roy watch the neighborhood.

3. Possible response: There is the danger of succumbing to violence, of killing or being killed in the fight for survival.

4. Possible response: Because they feel the neighborhood is not safe, the parents impose strict rules on their children.

5. Possible responses: What people say about it: It cannot be removed; it is intriguing; it is a dangerous place; Events Linked With It: Children play recklessly; children fall and get hurt; Details: "mass of natural rock jutting out of the ground"; "slippery rock"; What it Means: It represents the dangers of the world outside from which Gabriel and Elizabeth want to shield their children.

6. Possible responses: (a) It symbolizes Gabriel's power over John. (b) It shows that Gabriel's authority in the family is crushing to John. (c) Their relationship is strained because John is not Gabriel's son.

7. Possible responses: (a) John does not tell his mother because he had "practically promised not to." (b) Roy gets hurt, and then everyone looks to John for an explanation.

8. Possible responses: (a) Elizabeth may be trying to compensate for the fact that Gabriel doesn't treat John with kindness. (b) It makes Gabriel angry.

9. Possible response: Students may say that John could become excessively anxious. John could feel he missed his childhood, as Baldwin did.

❶ Vocabulary Development

Word Analysis

1. to work improperly
2. producing an unpleasant scent
3. poorly adjusted to the conditions of life
4. a disease resulting from a poor diet

Spelling Strategy

1. recklessly
2. dressing
3. passed

Concept Development: Synonyms or Antonyms

1. antonyms
2. synonyms
3. synonyms
4. antonyms
5. antonyms
6. antonyms
7. synonyms
8. antonyms
9. antonyms

❷ Grammar and Style

1. "who seemed at a loss"; modifies *policemen*; nonrestrictive
2. "which spanned the river"; modifies *bridge*; restrictive
3. "who came home early on Saturdays"; modifies *father*; nonrestrictive
4. "which stood beside the rockpile"; modifies *house*; restrictive
5. "where it lay"; modifies *fan*; *restrictive*; "where she had been"; modifies *seat*; restrictive

Writing Application

The first sentence should contain a restrictive adjective clause, and the second a nonrestrictive adjective clause.

Integrate Language Skills

❶ Vocabulary Development Lesson

Word Analysis: Latin Prefix *mal-*

The Latin prefix *mal-* means "bad," "wrong," or "ill." Combined with the root *-vol-*, meaning "wish," *malevolence* means "ill will." Use this root to determine the meaning of each of these words.

1. malfunction   3. maladjusted
2. malodorous   4. malnutrition

Spelling Strategy

If a word ends in a double consonant, do not make a change when you add a suffix. For example, *engross* + *-ed* = *engrossed*. Correctly add the indicated suffix to the following words.

1. reckless + *-ly*   2. dress + *-ing*   3. pass + *-ed*

Concept Development: Synonyms or Antonyms

Identify each of the following pairs of words as either synonyms or antonyms.

1. intriguing, boring
2. benevolent, charitable
3. decorously, tastefully
4. latent, obvious
5. engrossed, detached
6. jubilant, despondent
7. arrested, halted
8. malevolence, kindness
9. perdition, salvation

❷ Grammar and Style Lesson

Restrictive and Nonrestrictive Adjective Clauses

Containing both a subject and a verb, **adjective clauses** add information about nouns in the main part of a sentence.

A **restrictive adjective clause** is necessary to complete the meaning of the noun or pronoun it modifies.

> **Restrictive:** He was afraid of the rockpile and the boys *who played there*. (essential; tells which *boys*)

A **nonrestrictive adjective clause** provides additional but inessential information and must be set off by commas.

> **Nonrestrictive:** Once a boy, whose name was Richard, drowned in the river. (nonessential; modifies *boy*)

WG Prentice Hall Writing and Grammar Connection: Chapter 19, Section 3

Practice Identify the adjective clause(s), and indicate the word it modifies. Then, state whether it is restrictive or nonrestrictive.

1. There were two white policemen, who seemed at a loss, walking in the street.
2. At the end of the street nearest the house was the bridge which spanned the river . . .
3. . . . made them think of their father, who came home early on Saturdays . . .
4. Then the small procession disappeared into the house which stood beside the rockpile.
5. He did not look at her, but at the fan where it lay in the seat where she had been.

Writing Application Write two sentences. In the first, use a restrictive adjective clause. In the second, use a nonrestrictive adjective clause.

TEACHING RESOURCES

The following resources can be used to enrich or extend the instruction for pp. 1158–1159.

Vocabulary

📓 **Selection Support:** Build Vocabulary, p. 290
📓 **Vocabulary and Spelling Practice Book** (Use this booklet for skills enrichment.)

Grammar

📓 **Selection Support:** Grammar and Style, p. 291
WG **Writing and Grammar**, Ruby Level, p. 455 ▣
▣ **Daily Language Practice Transparencies** ▣

Writing

WG **Writing and Grammar**, Ruby Level, p. 309 ▣
💿 **Writing and Grammar iText CD-ROM** ▣
▣ **Writing Models and Graphic Organizers on Transparencies**, p. 41

▣ **BLOCK SCHEDULING:** Resources marked with this symbol provide varied instruction during 90-minute blocks.

Writing Lesson

Roy's Journal

In "The Rockpile," Roy's actions spark a family crisis in which much is revealed about the family as a whole, but very little about Roy himself. Write a journal entry for Roy in which he discusses his inner thoughts and conflicts. Use appropriate language to express the genuine thoughts and feelings of a young boy.

Prewriting   Reread the story to create a timeline of events. Then, for each point on the line, jot down ideas about Roy's thoughts and feelings.

Drafting   As you draft Roy's journal, refer to your notes for detail. Keep the language personal and informal.

Revising   Look for opportunities to make the tone of the journal more personal. Replace words that may be too formal with more appropriate choices. Determine whether or not your writing provides new insight into Roy's behavior.

Model: Revising to Achieve a Personal Tone

When I heard my daddy coming up the stairs, I got real
                         snuck out

scared. I didn't want him to know I had ~~escaped my home~~.
    a good man

He's big, and he's ~~devout~~, and gets so mad.

> Replacing formal words with informal ones creates a personal tone.

 *Prentice Hall Writing and Grammar Connection: Chapter 14, Section 3*

Extension Activities

Listening and Speaking In a group, adapt "The Rockpile" as a **radio play.** Divide the story into scenes and develop a script. Keep the following tips in mind as you write and rehearse:

- Assign one person to be the narrator.

- Choose appropriate sound effects and music that evokes the time and place of the story.

Rehearse the play until you are satisfied that you are presenting it as effectively as possible. Then, perform it for the class. **[Group Activity]**

Research and Technology Using a wide range of sources, including the Internet, prepare an **illustrated report** comparing Harlem today with Harlem in the 1930s. Explain the reasons for any similarities and differences between Harlem past and Harlem present. Share your report with the class.

 Take It to the Net   www.phschool.com

Go online for an additional research activity using the Internet.

The Rockpile ◆ 1159

Lesson Support for p. 1159

❸ Writing Lesson

- Explain to students that their journal entries should express Roy's feelings about the story's conflicts.

- Instruct students to consider what they already know about Roy and his relationships with family members before they reread and create timelines.

- As they begin drafting, remind students that their primary goal is to convey Roy's feelings and conflicts in a believable way.

- Use the writing model on p. 1159 to guide students in achieving a personal tone. Make sure their work provides insight into Roy's behavior.

❹ Research and Technology

- Be sure that students understand that their reports should compare information about Harlem in the 1930s and today.

- Encourage students to work in small research groups, assigning research and presentation tasks.

- Remind students to look for images that they can use to illustrate their reports.

- Using the Research Report model in **Writing Models and Graphic Organizers on Transparencies,** p. 41, prepare students to draft and revise.

- Adapt the research paper rubric in **Performance Assessment and Portfolio Management,** p. 22, to assess students' reports.

CUSTOMIZE INSTRUCTION
For Universal Access

To address different learning styles, use the activities suggested in the **Extension Activities** booklet, p. 67.

For Visual/Spatial and Bodily/Kinesthetic Learners, use Activity 5.

For Interpersonal and Bodily/Kinesthetic Learners, use Activity 6.

For Logical/Mathematical Learners, use Activity 7.

from Hiroshima ✦ Losses ✦ Death of the Ball Turret Gunner

Lesson Objectives

1. **To analyze and respond to literary elements**
   - Literary Analysis: Implied Theme
   - Comparing Literary Works
2. **To read, comprehend, analyze, and critique nonfiction and poetry**
   - Reading Strategy: Drawing Inferences About Theme
   - Reading Check Questions
   - Review and Assess Questions
   - Assessment Practice (ATE)
3. **To develop word analysis skills, fluency, and systematic vocabulary**
   - Vocabulary Development Lesson: Latin Root: *-vol-*
4. **To understand and apply written and oral language conventions**
   - Spelling Strategy
   - Grammar and Style Lesson: Transitions and Transitional Phrases
5. **To understand and apply appropriate writing and research strategies**
   - Writing Lesson: Book Review
   - Extension Activity: Written Report
6. **To understand and apply listening and speaking strategies**
   - Extension Activity: Dramatic Reading

STEP-BY-STEP TEACHING GUIDE	PACING GUIDE
PRETEACH	
Motivate Students and Provide Background	
Use the Motivation activity (ATE p. 1160)	5 min.
Read and discuss author and background features (SE/ATE p. 1160)	10 min.
Introduce the Concepts	
Introduce the Literary Analysis and Reading Strategy (SE/ATE p. 1161) A	15 min.
Pronounce the vocabulary words and read their definitions (SE p. 1161)	5 min.
TEACH	
Monitor Comprehension	
Informally monitor comprehension by circulating while students read independently or in groups A	35 min.
Monitor students' comprehension with the Reading Check notes (SE/ATE pp. 1163, 1165, 1167, 1169, 1171, 1173)	as students read
Develop vocabulary with Vocabulary notes (SE pp. 1163, 1164, 1165, 1170, 1171; ATE p. 1163)	as students read
Develop Understanding	
Develop students' understanding of an implied theme with the Literary Analysis annotations (SE pp. 1165, 1167, 1168, 1171; ATE pp. 1165, 1167, 1168, 1171) A	5 min.
Develop students' ability to draw inferences about theme by using the Reading Strategy annotations (SE pp. 1167, 1173; ATE pp. 1164, 1166, 1170, 1173)	5 min.
ASSESS	
Assess Mastery	
Assess students' mastery of the Reading Strategy and Literary Analysis by having them answer the Review and Assess questions (SE/ATE p. 1175)	15 min.
Use one or more of the print and media Assessment Resources (ATE p. 1177) A	up to 45 min.
EXTEND	
Apply Understanding	
Have students complete the Vocabulary Development Lesson and the Grammar and Style Lesson (SE p. 1176) A	20 min.
Apply students' ability to write to the knowledge level of readers by using the Writing Lesson (SE/ATE p. 1177) A	45 min.
Apply students' understanding using one or more of the Extension Activities (SE p. 1177)	20–90 min.

A ACCELERATED INSTRUCTION:
Use the strategies and activities identified with an A.

UNIVERSAL ACCESS
● = Below Level Students
▲ = On-Level Students
■ = Above Level Students

Time and Resource Manager

PRINT 📖	TRANSPARENCIES	TECHNOLOGY
• **Beyond Literature,** Community Connection: Ethics of Warfare, p. 68 ▲ ■		• **Interest Grabber Video,** Tape 6 ● ▲ ■
• **Selection Support Workbook:** ● ▲ ■ Literary Analysis, p. 297 Reading Strategy, p. 296 Build Vocabulary, p. 294	• **Literary Analysis and Reading Transparencies,** pp. 135 and 136 ● ▲ ■	
		• **Listening to Literature** ● ▲ ■ Audiocassettes, Side 39 Audio CDs, CD 23
• **Literatura en español** ● ▲ • **Literary Analysis for Enrichment** ■		
• **Formal Assessment:** Selection Test, p. 294 ● ▲ ■ • **Open Book Test,** p. 202 ● ▲ ■ • **Performance Assessment and Portfolio Management,** p. 30 ● ▲ ■ • **PRENTICE HALL ASSESSMENT SYSTEM** ● ▲ ■	• **PRENTICE HALL ASSESSMENT SYSTEM** ● ▲ ■ Skills Practice Answers and Explanations on Transparencies	• **Test Bank Software** ● ▲ ■ • **Got It! Assessment Videotapes,** Tape 6 ● ▲
• **Selection Support Workbook:** ● ▲ ■ Grammar and Style, p. 295 • **Writing and Grammar,** Ruby Level ● ▲ ■ • **Extension Activities,** p. 68 ● ▲ ■	• **Daily Language Practice Transparencies** ● ▲ • **Writing Models and Graphic Organizers on Transparencies,** p. 95 ● ▲ ■	• **Writing and Grammar iText CD-ROM** ● ▲ ■ 🖥 *Take It to the Net* www.phschool.com

BLOCK SCHEDULING: Use one 90-minute class period to preteach the selection and have students read it. Use a second 90-minute class period to assess students' mastery of skills and have them complete one of the Extension Activities.

Prepare to Read

from Hiroshima ◆ Losses ◆
❶ The Death of the Ball Turret Gunner

Step-by-Step Teaching Guide for pp. 1160–1161

Motivation

What do today's young people fear most? Conduct a brief discussion in which students offer their responses to this question. Follow the discussion by explaining that about a half century ago, young people lived with the very real fear of atomic war and its massive destructive force. In elementary schools of the post-World War II age, students were taught to duck beneath their desks and cover their heads to protect themselves from bombs (a response that, from John Hersey's description, we know would have been futile in a real atomic bomb attack). Tell students that the selections they are about to read will give them a glimpse of the horrors of modern warfare and help them understand people's anxieties and fears in the aftermath of World War II.

▣ Interest Grabber Video

As an alternative, you may wish to play "Hiroshima Destruction" on Tape 6 to engage student interest.

❶ Background

More About the Authors

Hiroshima, the book excerpted here, grew from the idea that a first-person account of the bombing and its aftermath would be especially moving. The book begins a few hours before the explosion and follows the city until one year later. Hersey focuses on six survivors, including the four described here. These people—including two doctors and two members of the Christian clergy—are not representative of the population of Hiroshima; rather, they are meant to be recognizable for American readers, who may have known of the bombing only from such unpeopled photographs as those that illustrate this excerpt.

John Hersey (1914–1993)
Born in China to American parents and raised there until age ten, John Hersey returned repeatedly to East Asia during his long career as a war correspondent, novelist, and essayist.

In his twenty-five books and countless articles, Hersey combined a profound moral sensibility with the highest artistry. His novels and essays not only examine the moral implications of the major political and historical events of his day, they do so with high literary grace. In 1945, Hersey won a Pulitzer Prize for his novel *A Bell for Adano*, in which an American major discovers the human dignity of the Italian villagers who were his enemies in World War II.

The Atomic Bomb During the 1940s, Hersey traveled to China and Japan as a correspondent for *The New Yorker* and *Time* magazines. He also used these visits to gather material for his most famous and acclaimed book, *Hiroshima* (1946), a shocking, graphic depiction of the devastation caused by the atomic bomb that was dropped on the Japanese city of Hiroshima at the end of World War II. This remarkable report first appeared in *The New Yorker* on August 31, 1946. Wallace Shawn, then editor of *The New Yorker*, made the unprecedented decision to bump all of the magazine's other editorial content in order to publish Hersey's four-part article.

Stories of Inhumanity and Courage In 1950, Hersey published the novel *The Wall*, which tells of the extinction of the Warsaw ghetto by the Germans during World War II. Hersey's later works include *A Single Pebble* (1956), *The War Lover* (1959), *The Child Buyer* (1960), *The Algiers Motel Incident* (1968), *The Writer's Craft* (1974), *Blues* (1987), and *Fling and Other Stories* (1990).

Randall Jarrell (1914–1965)
Randall Jarrell was a talented poet, literary critic, and teacher whose work was praised by both writers and critics. His literary essays, many of which appear in his book *Poetry and the Age* (1953), have been credited with changing the critical tastes and trends of his time.

Literary Ambitions Born in Nashville, Tennessee, Jarrell graduated from Vanderbilt University, where he studied under writers Robert Penn Warren, Allen Tate, and John Crowe Ransom. All of these men would prove helpful in promoting Jarrell's career. Warren and Tate published Jarrell's early poetry and criticism, and Tate helped land Jarrell his first teaching job at Kenyon College.

During World War II, Jarrell enlisted in the U.S. Air Force. He served only briefly as a pilot, and spent the remaining war years as an aviation instructor, training pilots to fly the famed B-29 bombers that helped secure victory. Jarrell's war experiences provided him with the material for the poems in his books *Little Friend, Little Friend* (1945) and *Losses* (1948). These books rank among the finest literature to emerge from the war.

American Language Jarrell was a great admirer of the poetry of Robert Frost, and, like Frost, he wrote poems based on the sounds and rhythms of American speech. Jarrell's collections *The Seven-League Crutches* (1951) and *The Lost World* (1965) focus on childhood and innocence. *The Woman at the Washington Zoo* (1960) deals with the theme of aging and loneliness. "The Death of the Ball Turret Gunner"—a brief poem told in the first person of a soldier experiencing his last moments in a World War II bomber plane—is one of Jarrell's most famous works.

TEACHING RESOURCES

The following resources can be used to enrich or extend the instruction for pp. 1160–1161.

Motivation
▣ **Interest Grabber Video**, Tape 6

Background
📓 **Beyond Literature**, p. 68 ▪

Take It to the Net
Visit www.phschool.com for Background and hotlinks for the authors

Literary Analysis
🖼 **Literary Analysis and Reading Transparencies,** Implied Theme, p. 136

Reading
📓 **Selection Support:** Reading Strategy, p. 296; Build Vocabulary, p. 294 ▪

🖼 **Literary Analysis and Reading Transparencies,** Making Inferences About Theme, p. 135

 BLOCK SCHEDULING: Resources marked with this symbol provide varied instruction during 90-minute blocks.

Preview

Connecting to the Literature

You may have seen movies about World War II. You may even have a relative who experienced the war firsthand. Yet, it is probably still difficult for you to imagine what it was like to live through a conflict of such immensity. These selections will give you a better sense of the war and provide a picture of events that changed the world forever.

❶ Literary Analysis

Implied Theme

The **theme** is the central idea that a writer conveys in a work of literature. Most often a theme is **implied,** or revealed indirectly, through the writer's choice of details, portrayal of characters and events, and use of literary devices. These selections all present implied themes about war.

Comparing Literary Works

Usually, we expect works of journalism to be objective, while we expect poems to be subjective. These selections, however, challenge our expectations.

- An **objective account** of a story is one in which the narrator is an outside observer who reports events without emotion or bias.

  Hersey: A hundred thousand people were killed by the atomic bomb . . .

- A **subjective account** is one in which the narrator reveals his or her feelings about the events described.

  Jarrell: I woke to black flak and the nightmare fighters.

As you read these powerful pieces, compare how the authors mix objectivity and subjectivity in surprising and effective ways.

❷ Reading Strategy

Drawing Inferences About Theme

When the theme of a literary work is conveyed indirectly, it is up to the reader to **draw inferences,** or conclusions, by looking closely at the writer's choice of details, events, and characters. As you read, use a chart like the one shown to note important details that point to an implied theme.

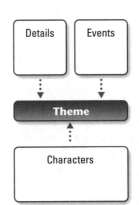

Vocabulary Development

evacuated (ē vak´ yoo āt´ id) *v.* to have made empty; withdrawn (p. 1163)

volition (vō lish´ ən) *n.* act of using the will (p. 1163)

rendezvous (rän´ dā voo´) *n.* meeting place (p. 1164)

philanthropies (fə lan´ thrə pēz) *n.* charitable acts or gifts (p. 1165)

incessant (in ses´ ənt) *adj.* constant; continuing or repeating in a way that seems endless (p. 1170)

convivial (kən viv´ ē əl) *adj.* fond of good company; sociable (p. 1171)

from Hiroshima / Losses / The Death of the Ball Turret Gunner ◆ 1161

---

❷ Literary Analysis

Implied Theme

- Remind students that the *theme* is the central idea conveyed in a literary work. Explain that an *implied theme* is revealed indirectly, rather than stated explicitly.

- Explain to students that they can identify the implied theme of a literary work by examining the characters, details, and literary devices the author employs.

- Use the Implied Theme transparency in **Literary Analysis and Reading Transparencies**, p. 136 to demonstrate how stories and poems can imply their themes.

- Encourage students to create similar charts in their notes as they read.

❸ Reading Strategy

Drawing Inferences About Theme

- Be sure students understand that if a work's theme is implied, a reader must draw inferences about it, based on the details the author includes.

- Present students with this line from Randall Jarrell's "Losses": . . . we burned, / The cities we had learned about in school—

- Guide students to recognize the contrast between education and destruction. What inference about the poem's theme can they draw? Possible response: The poem's theme is the apparent senselessness of war.

- Encourage students to use charts such as the one shown on p. 1161 to draw inferences as they read.

Vocabulary Development

- Pronounce each vocabulary word for students, and read the definitions as a class. Have students identify any words with which they are already familiar.

E-Teach

Visit E-Teach at www.phschool.com for teachers' essays on how to teach, with questions and answers.

CUSTOMIZE INSTRUCTION FOR UNIVERSAL ACCESS

For Less Proficient Readers	For English Learners	For Advanced Readers
Students may need additional help with the Reading Strategy, Drawing Inferences About Theme. Explain that when a work's *theme* is implied, as in the Literary Analysis focus, readers must draw inferences to understand the theme. Use the **Selection Support**: Reading Strategy, p. 296, to help students master the skill.	Students may need to take extra time decoding the details of the selections in order to draw inferences about their themes. Encourage them to pause periodically as they read to look up unfamiliar words and discuss the significance of the work's details.	Explain to students that in much of the literature of the twentieth century, the themes are implied, and readers must draw inferences. Encourage students to consider how the selections would be different if the themes were explicitly stated. Does drawing inferences about theme improve the experience of reading a literary work?

Step-by-Step Teaching Guide for pp. 1162–1174

CUSTOMIZE INSTRUCTION
For Intrapersonal Learners

Before they read, ask students to think about and record in writing their personal feelings about war. As they read, have them note particular phrases or descriptions that they find especially moving or disturbing. After they read, discuss how the three works affected their original feelings.

❶ About the Selection

World War II was a so-called "popular" war in which the issues that spurred the conflict were clearly defined. With the future of many of the nations of the world in grave danger, the majority of Americans believed that fighting the enemy was both just and necessary for survival. Nevertheless, technological advances in weaponry; the sheer magnitude of the global conflict; and the ability to report on the progress of the war from virtually any location around the world via print, radio, and film media, brought home the horrors of war in a new way. Although the antiwar movement did not become a political force until the 1960s, these works by Hersey and Jarrell take their place in the ranks of early antiwar literature.

❶ # FROM HIROSHIMA
John Hersey

1162 ◆ *Prosperity and Protest (1946–Present)*

TEACHING RESOURCES

The following resources can be used to enrich or extend the instruction for pp. 1162–1174.

Literary Analysis

📖 **Selection Support:** Literary Analysis, p. 297

Reading

🎧 **Listening to Literature Audiocassettes,**
Side 39 ▪

💿 **Listening to Literature Audio CDs,** CD 23 ▪

▪ **BLOCK SCHEDULING:** Resources marked with this symbol provide varied instruction during 90-minute blocks.

Background

In August 1945, American President Harry Truman was faced with a terrible decision. The world had been at war for six years. Germany had surrendered in May, but Japan refused to give up. The United States had just finished developing an atomic bomb. President Truman had to decide whether or not to use this new technology to bring an end to the war. On August 6, Truman ordered that the atomic bomb be dropped on the Japanese city of Hiroshima. Three days later, another bomb was dropped on Nagasaki. These two bombs killed more than 200,000 people and forced the Japanese surrender. Like so many events of World War II, the atomic bomb gave the world a new horror, as John Hersey so carefully documents in this selection.

At exactly fifteen minutes past eight in the morning, on August 6, 1945, Japanese time, at the moment when the atomic bomb flashed above Hiroshima, Miss Toshiko Sasaki, a clerk in the personnel department of the East Asia Tin Works, had just sat down at her place in the plant office and was turning her head to speak to the girl at the next desk. At that same moment, Dr. Masakazu Fujii was settling down cross-legged to read the Osaka *Asahi* on the porch of his private hospital, overhanging one of the seven deltaic rivers which divide Hiroshima; Mrs. Hatsuyo Nakamura, a tailor's widow, stood by the window of her kitchen, watching a neighbor tearing down his house because it lay in the path of an air-raid-defense fire lane . . . and the Reverend Mr. Kiyoshi Tanimoto, pastor of the Hiroshima Methodist Church, paused at the door of a rich man's house in Koi, the city's western suburb, and prepared to unload a handcart full of things he had evacuated from town in fear of the massive B-29 raid which everyone expected Hiroshima to suffer. A hundred thousand people were killed by the atomic bomb, and these [four] were among the survivors. They still wonder why they lived when so many others died. Each of them counts many small items of chance or volition—a step taken in time, a decision to go indoors, catching one streetcar instead of the next—that spared him. And now each knows that in the act of survival he lived a dozen lives and saw more death than he ever thought he would see. At the time, none of them knew anything.

The Reverend Mr. Tanimoto got up at five o'clock that morning. He was alone in the parsonage, because for some time his wife had been commuting with their year-old baby to spend nights with a friend in Ushida, a suburb to the north. Of all the important cities of Japan, only two, Kyoto and Hiroshima, had not been visited in strength by *B-san*, or Mr. B, as the Japanese, with a mixture of respect

◄ Critical Viewing How effectively do these remains of the sacred tree of a Hiroshima temple convey the physical and emotional devastation of the blast? Explain. **[Evaluate]**

evacuated (ē vak´ yōō āt´ əd) *v.* to have made empty; withdrawn

volition (vō lish´ ən) *n.* act of using the will

☑Reading Check ❹

What happened at exactly 8:15 in the morning on August 6, 1945?

from Hiroshima ◆ 1163

---

❷ **Vocabulary Development**

The Latin Root -vol-

- Call students' attention to the word *volition* and its definition. Tell students that the Latin word root *-vol-* means "to will" or "to wish."

- Have students suggest words and phrases that contain this root, and list them on the chalkboard. Possible answers: volunteer, malevolence, benevolence, and involuntary.

- Next, have students look up the meanings of these words in a dictionary.

- Have students write sentences in which they use these words correctly. Call on volunteers to read their sentences aloud—and to define the word "volunteer"!

❸ **▶Critical Viewing**

Possible response: The remains of the sacred tree convey the physical and emotional devastation of the blast quite effectively. First of all, the gnarled remnants of the tree and the bricks and debris scattered about illustrate the magnitude of physical damage. Perhaps more importantly, the fact that the decimated tree is a sacred one helps to underscore the emotional pain that the people of Hiroshima must have felt.

❹ **☑Reading Check**

Answer: At 8:15 that morning, the atomic bomb was dropped on the Japanese city of Hiroshima.

CUSTOMIZE INSTRUCTION FOR UNIVERSAL ACCESS

For Less Proficient Readers	For English Learners
Help students keep track of the characters in the excerpt from *Hiroshima* by making a chart with the following headings and filling it in as they read: 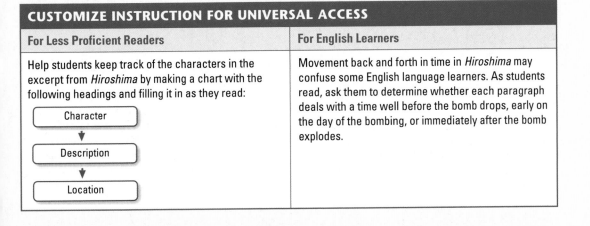 Character → Description → Location	Movement back and forth in time in *Hiroshima* may confuse some English language learners. As students read, ask them to determine whether each paragraph deals with a time well before the bomb drops, early on the day of the bombing, or immediately after the bomb explodes.

❺ Reading Strategy

Drawing Inferences About Theme

- Remind students that when the theme of a literary work is implied, rather than stated explicitly, readers must draw inferences about the theme based on details, events, and characters.

- Call students' attention to the chart modeled on p. 1161. Instruct them to prepare such a chart as they read.

- Have students read the bracketed passage. Ask them to use their charts to note the details, events, and characters it describes.

- Ask students what inferences they can draw about Hersey's theme based on these details, events, and characters.

  Possible response: Students may infer that Hersey implies that in a war, "the enemy" is actually made up of ordinary people no different from ourselves.

❻ Background

B-29 Bombers

The Allied bombing campaign against Japan carried out by the United States Army Air Force relied on the B-29. Coming at the very end of the war, the atomic bombing of Hiroshima and Nagasaki made it clear that long-range bombers which, like the B-29, could deliver nuclear weapons would be crucial in military strategy for the post-war world. After the war, the U.S. Air Force was established as a part of the Department of Defense, and the Strategic Air Command was put in charge of nuclear-armed bombers.

---

and unhappy familiarity, called the B-29*; and Mr. Tanimoto, like all his neighbors and friends, was almost sick with anxiety. He had heard uncomfortably detailed accounts of mass raids on Kure, Iwakuni, Tokuyama, and other nearby towns; he was sure Hiroshima's turn would come soon. He had slept badly the night before, because there had been several air-raid warnings. Hiroshima had been getting such warnings almost every night for weeks, for at that time the B-29s were using Lake Biwa, northeast of Hiroshima, as a <u>rendezvous</u> point, and no matter what city the Americans planned to hit, the Super-fortresses streamed in over the coast near Hiroshima. The frequency of the warning and the continued abstinence of Mr. B with respect to Hiroshima had made its citizens jittery; a rumor was going around that the Americans were saving something special for the city.

Mr. Tanimoto was a small man, quick to talk, laugh, and cry. He wore his black hair parted in the middle and rather long; the prominence of the frontal bones just above his eyebrows and the smallness of his mustache, mouth, and chin gave him a strange old-young look, boyish and yet wise, weak and yet fiery. He moved nervously and fast, but with a restraint which suggested that he is a cautious, thoughtful man. He showed, indeed, just those qualities in the uneasy days before the bomb fell. Mr. Tanimoto had been carrying all the portable things from his church, in the close-packed residential district called Nagaragawa, to a house that belonged to a rayon manufacturer in Koi, two miles from the center of town. The rayon man, a Mr. Matsui, had opened his then unoccupied estate to a large number of his friends and acquaintances, so that they might evacuate whatever they wished to a safe distance from the probable target area. Mr. Tanimoto had had no difficulty in moving chairs, hymnals, Bibles, altar gear, and church records by pushcart himself, but the organ console and an upright piano required some aid. A friend of his named Matsuo had, the day before, helped him get the piano out to Koi; in return, he had promised this day to assist Mr. Matsuo in hauling out a daughter's belongings. That is why he had risen so early.

Mr. Tanimoto cooked his own breakfast. He felt awfully tired. The effort of moving the piano the day before, a sleepless night, weeks of worry and unbalanced diet, the cares of his parish—all combined to make him feel hardly adequate to the new day's work. There was another thing, too: Mr. Tanimoto had studied theology at Emory College, in Atlanta, Georgia; he had graduated in 1940; he spoke excellent English; he dressed in American clothes; he had corresponded with many American friends right up to the time the war began; and among a people obsessed with a fear of being spied upon—perhaps almost obsessed himself—he found himself growing increasingly uneasy. The police had questioned

rendezvous (rän´dā vōō´) *n.* meeting place

𝓛iterature ❻
in context History Connection

◆ B-29 Bombers

The Second World War saw major advances in the technology of mechanized warfare—warfare that relied heavily on machines. The B-29 Superfortress bomber that Hersey mentions was an aircraft capable of long-range, heavy bombing runs. It was used frequently against Japan during 1944 and 1945. Firebomb B-29 raids against industrial cities in Japan totaled nearly 7,000 flights and dropped 41,600 tons of bombs.

✱ ENRICHMENT: Social Studies Connection

Hiroshima and Nagasaki

Share with the class the following information about Japan and the cities of Hiroshima and Nagasaki. Have one or more volunteers point out the places you cite on a wall map.

Japan is a chain of islands—which means that it can be attacked only by air or by sea. Its western neighbors are North and South Korea, Russia, and China. The four main islands of Japan are Hokkaido, Honshu, Shikoku, and Kyushu.

Hiroshima is a port city on the southwest coast of Honshu. Nagasaki is a port city on the west coast of Kyushu. Both had a certain amount of industry and military installations in 1945, but neither was as major a target as the capital, Tokyo, was. The cities were in large part destroyed by the bombs but were reconstructed throughout the 1950s. Today, both cities house important tourist sites and monuments that attract antiwar and antinuclear supporters from around the world.

him several times, and just a few days before, he had heard that an influential acquaintance, a Mr. Tanaka, a retired officer of the Toyo Kisen Kaisha steamship line, an anti-Christian, a man famous in Hiroshima for his showy philanthropies and notorious for his personal tyrannies, had been telling people that Tanimoto should not be trusted. In compensation, to show himself publicly a good Japanese, Mr. Tanimoto had taken on the chairmanship of his local *tonarigumi*, or Neighborhood Association, and to his other duties and concerns this position had added the business of organizing air-raid defense for about twenty families.

Before six o'clock that morning, Mr. Tanimoto started for Mr. Matsuo's house. There he found that their burden was to be a *tansu*, a large Japanese cabinet, full of clothing and household goods. The two men set out. The morning was perfectly clear and so warm that the day promised to be uncomfortable. A few minutes after they started, the air-raid siren went off—a minute-long blast that warned of approaching planes but indicated to the people of Hiroshima only a slight degree of danger, since it sounded every morning at this time, when an American weather plane came over. The two men pulled and pushed the handcart through the city streets. Hiroshima was a fan-shaped city, lying mostly on the six islands formed by the seven estuarial rivers that branch out from the Ota River; its main commercial and residential districts, covering about four square miles in the center of the city, contained three-quarters of its population, which had been reduced by several evacuation programs from a wartime peak of 380,000 to about 245,000. Factories and other residential districts, or suburbs, lay compactly around the edges of the city. To the south were the docks, an airport, and the island-studded Inland Sea. A rim of mountains runs around the other three sides of the delta. Mr. Tanimoto and Mr. Matsuo took their way through the shopping center, already full of people, and across two of the rivers to the sloping streets of Koi, and up them to the outskirts and foothills. As they started up a valley away from the tight-ranked houses, the all-clear sounded. (The Japanese radar operators, detecting only three planes, supposed that they comprised a reconnaissance.) Pushing the handcart up to the rayon man's house was tiring, and the men, after they had maneuvered their load into the driveway and to the front steps, paused to rest awhile. They stood with a wing of the house between them and the city. Like most homes in this part of Japan, the house consisted of a wooden frame and wooden walls supporting a heavy tile roof. Its front hall, packed with rolls of bedding and clothing, looked like a cool cave full of fat cushions. Opposite the house, to the right of the front door, there was a large, finicky rock garden. There was no sound of planes. The morning was still; the place was cool and pleasant.

Then a tremendous flash of light cut across the sky. Mr. Tanimoto has a distinct recollection that it travelled from east to west, from the city toward the hills. It seemed a sheet of sun. Both he and Mr. Matsuo reacted in terror—and both had time to react (for they were 3,500 yards, or two miles, from the center of the explosion). Mr. Matsuo dashed up

philanthropies (fə lan′ thrə pēz) *n.* charitable acts or gifts

Literary Analysis
Implied Theme In light of the bombing, what is ironic about an air-raid siren indicating only a "slight degree of danger"?

☑ **Reading Check** ❾
Why does Mr. Tanimoto move all the portable things in his church to a home farther from the town center?

from *Hiroshima* ◆ 1165

❼ **Literary Analysis**
Implied Theme

- Remind students that in many works of literature, the *theme* is not stated explicitly. Instead, it is *implied* through the characters, details, and literary devices.
- Have students read the bracketed passage. Be sure they are aware that the passage relates details of Mr. Tanimoto's actions just before the atomic bomb hit Hiroshima.
- Ask students the Literary Analysis question on p. 1165: In light of the bombing, what is ironic about an air-raid siren indicating only a "slight degree of danger"? **Answer:** This is an example of dramatic irony, because readers know what the characters do not: that the city is about to be destroyed by an atomic bomb.

▶ Monitor Progress Encourage students to discuss how this and other details might express the implied theme.

❽ **Critical Thinking**
Analyze

- Have students read the bracketed passage. Instruct them to visualize the scene Hersey describes here. How would they characterize it? **Possible response:** Students will likely respond that the scene is peaceful, even serene.
- Ask students: Considering what is about to happen—the atomic blast—why do you think Hersey includes this peaceful moment here? **Possible response:** This scene sharply contrasts with the chaos and devastation that is about to erupt, showing the suddenness and brutality of the atomic bomb attack.

❾ ☑ **Reading Check**

Answer: He moves the things in his church because the Japanese believed that Hiroshima would be bombed, perhaps very heavily.

Possible response: Students may say that they relate the devastation more to real people's lives now that they have read about some real people affected by the bombing.

11 **Reading Strategy**

Drawing Inferences About Theme

• Remind students that readers often must infer the theme of a literary work based on the details the author chooses to include.

• Have students read the bracketed passage. Then, ask them the Reading Skills question on p. 1167: What does the detail about the bleeding, dazed soldiers imply about the catastrophe that has just taken place?

Possible response: Whatever has happened was worse than anything the soldiers had anticipated; the attack was so unpredictable and immense a suitable defense was impossible.

▶ Monitor Progress Ask students, based on their responses, what this detail implies about Hersey's theme.

Possible response: Hersey conveys the idea that the atomic bomb is a weapon of tremendous, almost unthinkable power.

▲ **Critical Viewing** **10**
You may have seen photographs like this one of the aftermath of the Hiroshima bombing. Does Hersey's account change the way you view such pictures? Explain. **[Relate]**

the front steps into the house and dived among the bedrolls and buried himself there. Mr. Tanimoto took four or five steps and threw himself between two big rocks in the garden. He bellied up very hard against one of them. As his face was against the stone, he did not see what happened. He felt a sudden pressure, and then splinters and pieces of board and fragments of tile fell on him. He heard no roar. (Almost no one in Hiroshima recalls hearing any noise of the bomb. But a fisherman in his sampan on the Inland Sea near Tsuzu, the man with whom Mr. Tanimoto's mother-in-law and sister-in-law were living, saw the flash and heard a tremendous explosion; he was nearly twenty miles from Hiroshima, but the thunder was greater than when the B-29s hit Iwakuni, only five miles away.)

When he dared, Mr. Tanimoto raised his head and saw that the rayon man's house had collapsed. He thought a bomb had fallen directly on it. Such clouds of dust had risen that there was a sort of twilight around. In panic, not thinking for the moment of Mr. Matsuo under the ruins, he dashed out into the street. He noticed as he ran that the concrete wall of the estate had fallen over—toward the house rather than away from it. In the street, the first thing he saw was a squad of soldiers who had been burrowing into the hillside opposite, making one

---

☀ **ENRICHMENT: Social Studies Connection**

Radio Broadcasting

The Second World War occurred at a time when there was as yet only limited television broadcasting. Therefore, the most important source of up-to-the-minute news about the war was radio. This was true for Americans and their allies as well as for Japanese citizens such as Mrs. Nakamura. Radio broadcasting is still a vital link to the news of the day for thousands of people, many of whom keep the radio on as they go about their business at work.

The importance of radio news today may seem to be

eclipsed by that of television, but radio is still a vital news source. Just as in the golden age of radio (from 1925 until the early 1950s), today's on-air news reporters interview subjects and distill key ideas from masses of information. Encourage students to discuss how they get information about what is happening in your area, in the country, and in the world. Invite students to explore radio as a news source and consider what it was like to rely on radio as do Hersey's subjects.

of the thousands of dugouts in which the Japanese apparently intended to resist invasion, hill by hill, life for life; the soldiers were coming out of the hole, where they should have been safe, and blood was running from their heads, chests, and backs. They were silent and dazed.

Under what seemed to be a local dust cloud, the day grew darker and darker.

At nearly midnight, the night before the bomb was dropped, an announcer on the city's radio station said that about two hundred B-29s were approaching southern Honshu and advised the population of Hiroshima to evacuate to their designated "safe areas." Mrs. Hatsuyo Nakamura, the tailor's widow, who lived in the section called Nobori-cho and who had long had a habit of doing as she was told, got her three children—a ten-year-old boy, Toshio, an eight-year-old girl, Yaeko, and a five-year-old girl, Myeko—out of bed and dressed them and walked with them to the military area known as the East Parade Ground, on the northeast edge of the city. There she unrolled some mats and the children lay down on them. They slept until about two, when they were awakened by the roar of the planes going over Hiroshima.

As soon as the planes had passed, Mrs. Nakamura started back with her children. They reached home a little after two-thirty and she immediately turned on the radio, which, to her distress, was just then broadcasting a fresh warning. When she looked at the children and saw how tired they were, and when she thought of the number of trips they had made in past weeks, all to no purpose, to the East Parade Ground, she decided that in spite of the instructions on the radio, she simply could not face starting out all over again. She put the children in their bedrolls on the floor, lay down herself at three o'clock, and fell asleep at once, so soundly that when planes passed over later, she did not waken to their sound.

The siren jarred her awake at about seven. She arose, dressed quickly, and hurried to the house of Mr. Nakamoto, the head of her Neighborhood Association, and asked him what she should do. He said that she should remain at home unless an urgent warning—a series of intermittent blasts of the siren—was sounded. She returned home, lit the stove in the kitchen, set some rice to cook, and sat down to read that mornings Hiroshima *Chugoku*. To her relief, the all-clear sounded at eight o'clock. She heard the children stirring, so she went and gave each of them a handful of peanuts and told them to stay in their bedrolls, because they were tired from the night's walk. She had hoped that they would go back to sleep, but the man in the house directly to the south began to make a terrible hullabaloo of hammering, wedging, ripping, and splitting. The prefectural government,[1] convinced, as everyone in Hiroshima was, that the city would be attacked soon, had begun to press with threats and warnings for the completion of wide

---

1. **prefectural government** regional districts of Japan which are administered by a governor.

Reading Strategy
Drawing Inferences About Theme What does the detail about the bleeding, dazed soldiers imply about the catastrophe that has just taken place?

Literary Analysis
Implied Theme and Objective/Subjective Accounts What do the details about Mrs. Nakamura's tired children suggest about the author's objectivity?

Reading Check ⓭
Why are Mrs. Nakamura's children so tired?

from *Hiroshima* ◆ 1167

⓬ Literary Analysis

Implied Theme and Objective/Subjective Accounts

- Remind students that a literary work can present either an objective or a subjective account of the events it describes, depending upon the emotions the author reveals toward his subject.

- Have students read the bracketed passage. Be sure that they understand that Mrs. Nakamura's children are so tired she cannot bring herself to take them back to the "safe area" again.

- Ask students the Literary Analysis question on p. 1167: What do the details about Mrs. Nakamura's tired children suggest about the author's objectivity?
Possible response: These details suggest that Hersey sympathizes strongly with Mrs. Nakamura and other ordinary people; his is a subjective account.

- Encourage students to consider what Hersey's feelings—and the details through which he reveals them—imply about his theme.

⓭ ✔Reading Check

Answer: The children are so tired because Mrs. Nakamura brought them to the "safe area" at midnight, and they did not get home until two-thirty in the morning.

CUSTOMIZE INSTRUCTION FOR UNIVERSAL ACCESS

For Less Proficient Readers	For English Learners	For Gifted/Talented Students
Students might be confused by the transition from the moments following the explosion back to the moments preceding it. Guide them to understand that Hersey will show them the atomic blast from the perspectives of four different individuals.	Students may find Hersey's highly detailed descriptions of his subjects and their activities challenging. Allow them to first read the selection along with **Listening to Literature**, Audiocassette Side 39, Audio CD 23. Then, have them reread the descriptions carefully, pausing to look up any unfamiliar words.	Ask students to discuss Hersey's description of the atomic bomb's impact. Is this the first such description that they have read? If so, encourage them to look for photographs and videotaped images of nuclear explosions and their aftermath. Students can assemble a visual presentation for the class to complement Hersey's writing.

Implied Theme

- Be sure students recognize that the theme of Hersey's text is not stated explicitly—instead, Hersey implies his theme through the details he describes.

- Have students read the bracketed passage. Instruct them to pay close attention to the details about daily life in Hiroshima before the bomb.

- Ask students the Literary Analysis question on p. 1168: Why do you think the author included information about the citizens' attempts to defend their city and its population?
Possible response: The information is ironic because readers know that the defensive measures are futile; one cannot prepare for nuclear warfare.

▶ **Monitor Progress** Ask students to look at the picture on pp. 1168–1169 and explain how it illustrates the irony of the passage.
Possible response: The neighbor is knocking down his house to make way for a fire lane; however, the house will soon be hit by a bomb more devastating than any incendiary device ever seen.

🄯 **Literary Analysis**

Implied Theme

- Have students read the bracketed passage. Then, ask them to discuss Hersey's characterization of Mrs. Nakamura. How would they describe her experience of the war?
Possible response: Mrs. Nakamura has already suffered so much that it seems impossible she will have to endure more, but the reader knows that she will.

- Ask students what the description suggests about Hersey's implied themes.
Possible response: It implies a theme of the strength of the human spirit. Mrs. Nakamura embodies the resilience and strength of the human spirit.

fire lanes, which, it was hoped, might act in conjunction with the rivers to localize any fires started by an incendiary[2] raid; and the neighbor was reluctantly sacrificing his home to the city's safety. Just the day before, the prefecture had ordered all able-bodied girls from the secondary schools to spend a few days helping to clear these lanes, and they started work soon after the all-clear sounded.

🄮 Mrs. Nakamura went back to the kitchen, looked at the rice, and began watching the man next door. At first, she was annoyed with him for making so much noise, but then she was moved almost to tears by pity. Her emotion was specifically directed toward her neighbor, tearing down his home, board by board, at a time when there was so much unavoidable destruction, but undoubtedly she also felt a generalized, community pity, to say nothing of self-pity. She had not had an easy time. Her husband, Isawa, had gone into the Army just after Myeko was born, and she had heard nothing from or of him for a long time, until, 🄯 on March 5, 1942, she received a seven-word telegram: "Isawa died an honorable death at Singapore." She learned later that he had died on February 15th, the day Singapore fell, and that he had been a

---

2. **incendiary** (in sen′ dē er′ ē) *adj.* designed to cause fires.

1168 ◆ *Prosperity and Protest (1946–Present)*

Literary Analysis
Implied Theme Why do you think the author included information about the citizens' attempts to defend their city and its population?

◄ **Critical Viewing** 🔟

There are no people shown in this photograph—nor in many others—depicting the devastation wrought by the Hiroshima bomb. Does the lack of humanity lessen or intensify the power of the image? Explain. **[Assess]**

corporal. Isawa had been a not particularly prosperous tailor, and his only capital was a Sankoku sewing machine. After his death, when his allotments stopped coming, Mrs. Nakamura got out the machine and began to take in piecework herself, and since then had supported the children, but poorly, by sewing.

As Mrs. Nakamura stood watching her neighbor, everything flashed whiter than any white she had ever seen. She did not notice what happened to the man next door; the reflex of a mother set her in motion toward her children. She had taken a single step (the house was 1,350 yards, or three-quarters of a mile, from the center of the explosion) when something picked her up and she seemed to fly into the next room over the raised sleeping platform, pursued by parts of her house.

Timbers fell around her as she landed, and a shower of tiles pommelled her; everything became dark, for she was buried. The debris did not cover her deeply. She rose up and freed herself. She heard a child cry, "Mother, help me!" and saw her youngest—Myeko, the five-year-old—buried up to her breast and unable to move. As Mrs. Nakamura started frantically to claw her way toward the baby, she could see or hear nothing of her other children.

✔ Reading Check 🔟

What happens as Mrs. Nakamura stands watching her neighbor?

from *Hiroshima* ◆ 1169

🔟 ► **Critical Viewing**

Possible response: Students may say that the impact of the image is greater without people because the bomb appears to have erased all signs of life.

🔟 **Critical Thinking**

Analyze

- Have students read the bracketed passage. Then, ask them to describe their responses to this description of the blast.
  Possible response: Students may respond that this description is especially moving because of Mrs. Nakamura's impulse to protect her children.

- Ask students to explain why using a mother of three as one of his subjects would be an effective way for Hersey to make his points about war.
  Possible response: A mother's desire to protect her children is something every reader understands. The fate of a mother and her children will touch readers in a way that other subjects might not. The passage emphasizes the extreme vulnerability of the bomb's victims.

🔟 **✔ Reading Check**

Answer: The bomb exploded over Hiroshima, destroying her home as "everything flashed whiter than any white she had ever seen."

CUSTOMIZE INSTRUCTION FOR UNIVERSAL ACCESS

For Special Needs Students

Students might have difficulty following Hersey's shifts through time. Encourage them to create a chart using the following headings:

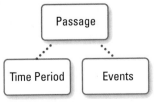

After completing their charts, suggest that students create brief summaries of each character's experience.

⑲ Background

World War II

Although World War II was a "popular" war with clearly defined issues involving crucial American and global interests, it was a conflict that included abhorrent actions on both sides. Hersey writes that the Japanese had "a fear of being spied upon," but they were not the only people who held such fears. After the attack on Pearl Harbor, the United States government rounded up Japanese American families living in the West and locked them up in detention camps for the duration of the war. While this action cannot be compared to the atrocities visited by Nazi Germany on the Jews of Europe, it nonetheless illustrates that thinking in terms of enemies versus allies can bring out irrational fears.

⑳ Reading Strategy

Drawing Inferences About Theme

• Remind students that when they read a literary work with an implied theme they must draw inferences about the theme from details in the text.

• Have students read the bracketed passage. Be sure they understand that a portion of Dr. Fujii's house hangs over the river and has stood fast against a number of floods.

• Ask students: Considering what is about to happen, what is Hersey saying about nuclear warfare with this description?
Possible response: Hersey compares the devastation of which nature is capable to the devastation caused by the bomb and finds the latter much more powerful.

In the days right before the bombing, Dr. Masakazu Fujii, being prosperous, hedonistic,[3] and at the time not too busy, had been allowing himself the luxury of sleeping until nine or nine-thirty, but fortunately he had to get up early the morning the bomb was dropped to see a house guest off on a train. He rose at six, and half an hour later walked with his friend to the station, not far away, across two of the rivers. He was back home by seven, just as the siren sounded its sustained warning. He ate breakfast and then, because the morning was already hot, undressed down to his underwear and went out on the porch to read the paper. This porch—in fact, the whole building—was curiously constructed. Dr. Fujii was the proprietor of a peculiarly Japanese institution: a private, single-doctor hospital. This building, perched beside and over the water of the Kyo River, and next to the bridge of the same name, contained thirty rooms for thirty patients and their kinfolk—for, according to Japanese custom, when a person falls sick and goes to a hospital, one or more members of his family go and live there with him, to cook for him, bathe, massage, and read to him, and to offer <u>incessant</u> familial sympathy, without which a Japanese patient would be miserable indeed. Dr. Fujii had no beds—only straw mats—for his patients. He did, however, have all sorts of modern equipment: an X-ray machine, diathermy[4] apparatus, and a fine tiled laboratory. The structure rested two-thirds on the land, one-third on piles over the tidal waters of the Kyo. This overhang, the part of the building where Dr. Fujii lived, was queer-looking, but it was cool in summer and from the porch, which faced away from the center of the city, the prospect of the river, with pleasure boats drifting up and down it, was always refreshing. Dr. Fujii had occasionally had anxious moments when the Ota and its mouth branches rose to flood, but the piling was apparently firm enough and the house had always held.

Dr. Fujii had been relatively idle for about a month because in July, as the number of untouched cities in Japan dwindled and as Hiroshima seemed more and more inevitably a target, he began turning patients away, on the ground that in case of a fire raid he would not be able to evacuate them. Now he had only two patients left—a woman from Yano, injured in the shoulder, and a young man of twenty-five recovering from burns he had suffered when the steel factory near Hiroshima in which he worked had been hit. Dr. Fujii had six nurses to tend his patients. His wife and children were safe; his wife and one son were living outside Osaka, and another son and two daughters were in the country on Kyushu. A niece was living with him,

---

3. **hedonistic** (he de nis´ tik) *adj.* indulgently seeking out pleasure.
4. **diathermy** (dī ə thur´ mē) *n.* medical treatment in which heat is produced beneath the skin to warm or destroy tissue.

⑲ World War II

World War II began in September 1939 when German forces, following the orders of the dictator Adolf Hitler, invaded Poland. In response to this unprovoked invasion, France and Great Britain declared war on Germany. Just over two years later, the United States entered the war when Japan, a German ally, launched a surprise attack on an American naval base at Pearl Harbor in Hawaii. The war continued to escalate during the early 1940s. More than two dozen nations were eventually drawn into the conflict, and tens of millions of soldiers were killed. By 1945, the tide had turned strongly in favor of the United States and its allies. In early May 1945, the German forces surrendered. Fighting continued in the Pacific however, as the Japanese refused to give up. The war finally ended in 1945 when the United States dropped two atomic bombs on the Japanese cities of Hiroshima and Nagasaki. The bombs killed more than 200,000 people and forced Japan's surrender.

incessant (in ses´ənt) *adj.* constant; continuing or repeating in a way that seems endless

---

✹ ENRICHMENT: Literature Connection

More About the Author

Commenting on John Hersey's *Hiroshima*, one reviewer wrote: "This is not a treatise. It is a factual account, in straightforward reportorial style, of what happened in Hiroshima on the morning of August 6, 1945, and in the sad days that followed. It is John Hersey at his best." Share this comment with students. Then, encourage them to discuss the reviewer's reactions.

Guide discussion by asking students if they agree that Hersey's book is "a factual account" written "in straightforward reportorial style." Students may feel that Hersey's attention to details of time and activity make the narrative factual and reportorial. Other students may feel that Hersey's focus on individuals makes his account less objective—and thus less reportorial—and more subjective.

and a maid and a manservant. He had little to do and did not mind, for he had saved some money. At fifty, he was healthy, <u>convivial</u>, and calm, and he was pleased to pass the evenings drinking whiskey with friends, always sensibly and for the sake of conversation. Before the war, he had affected brands imported from Scotland and America; now he was perfectly satisfied with the best Japanese brand, Suntory.

Dr. Fujii sat down cross-legged in his underwear on the spotless matting of the porch, put on his glasses, and started reading the Osaka *Asahi.* He liked to read the Osaka news because his wife was there. He saw the flash. To him—faced away from the center and looking at his paper—it seemed a brilliant yellow. Startled, he began to rise to his feet. In that moment (he was 1,550 yards from the center), the hospital leaned behind his rising and, with a terrible ripping noise, toppled into the river. The Doctor, still in the act of getting to his feet, was thrown forward and around and over; he was buffeted and gripped; he lost track of everything, because things were so speeded up; he felt the water.

Dr. Fujii hardly had time to think that he was dying before he realized that he was alive, squeezed tightly by two long timbers in a V across his chest, like a morsel suspended between two huge chopsticks—held upright, so that he could not move, with his head miraculously above water and his torso and legs in it. The remains of his hospital were all around him in a mad assortment of splintered lumber and materials for the relief of pain. His left shoulder hurt terribly. His glasses were gone. . . .

Miss Toshiko Sasaki, the East Asia Tin Works clerk, . . . got up at three o'clock in the morning on the day the bomb fell. There was extra housework to do. Her eleven-month-old brother, Akio, had come down the day before with a serious stomach upset; her mother had taken him to the Tamura Pediatric Hospital and was staying there with him. Miss Sasaki, who was about twenty, had to cook breakfast for her father, a brother, a sister, and herself, and—since the hospital, because of the war, was unable to provide food—to prepare a whole day's meals for her mother and the baby, in time for her father, who worked in a factory making rubber earplugs for artillery crews, to take the food by on his way to the plant. When she had finished and had cleaned and put away the cooking things, it was nearly seven. The family lived in Koi, and she had a forty-five-minute trip to the tin works, in the section of town called Kannonmachi. She was in charge of the personnel records in the factory. She left Koi at seven, and as soon as she reached the plant, she went with some of the other girls from the personnel department to the factory auditorium. A prominent local Navy man, a former employee, had committed suicide the day before by throwing himself under a train—a death considered honorable enough to warrant a memorial service, which was to be held at the tin works at ten o'clock that morning. In the large hall, Miss Sasaki and the others made suitable preparations for the meeting. This work took about twenty minutes.

21

22

convivial (kən viv´ ē əl) *adj.* fond of good company; sociable

Literary Analysis
Implied Theme and Objective/Subjective Accounts Is Hersey's description of Dr. Fujii objective or subjective? Explain.

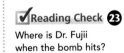
Reading Check **23**
Where is Dr. Fujii when the bomb hits?

from *Hiroshima* ◆ 1171

CUSTOMIZE INSTRUCTION FOR UNIVERSAL ACCESS

For English Learners	For Advanced Readers
Call students' attention to the use of the word *affected* at the top of p. 1171: "Before the war, he had affected brands imported from Scotland and America." Explain that *affected* here means "showed a liking for," with a connotation of trying to make an impression by putting on airs.	Students should recognize that Dr. Fujii is a less sympathetic character than Mr. Tanimoto, Mrs. Nakamura, or Miss Sasaki. He is "prosperous, hedonistic," and somewhat idle. Ask them to consider why Hersey might have included Dr. Fujii as a subject, despite his self-centered, pleasure-seeking lifestyle. Does this section of the text effectively advance Hersey's themes?

21 Literary Analysis
Implied Theme and Objective/Subjective Accounts

- Encourage students to recall Hersey's descriptions of Mr. Tanimoto and Mrs. Nakamura. Remind them that details in each description suggest that Hersey's has been a subjective account.
- Have students read the bracketed passage. Instruct them to consider carefully the details in Hersey's description of Dr. Fujii.
- Ask students the Literary Analysis question on p. 1171: Is Hersey's description of Dr. Fujii objective or subjective? Explain.
  Possible response: Hersey's description of Dr. Fujii appears to be objective, because there are no strongly emotional details. Some students may suggest that the magnitude of the destruction makes all of Hersey's descriptions subjective.

▶ Monitor Progress Encourage students to discuss how the description of Dr. Fujii develops Hersey's theme.

22 Critical Thinking
Analyze

- Have students read the bracketed passage. Point out that Hersey includes a number of mundane details about Miss Sasaki's morning. Ask students to list some of these details.
  Answer: Details include Akio's stomach upset, Miss Sasaki's making breakfast for her family and food for the hospital, and her long walk to work.
- Ask students: Knowing that the bomb is about to fall, how do these details affect your response to the text?
  Possible response: The details help you to relate to Miss Sasaki as a fellow human being, making the coming disaster seem more tragic and painful.

23 Reading Check
Answer: Dr. Fujii was on his porch overlooking the Kyo River.

Answers for p. 1172

Review and Assess

1. **Possible response:** Responses will probably focus upon the terrible destructive power of an atomic bomb.

2. **(a)** The bomb was dropped at eight-fifteen on the morning of August 6, 1945. **(b) Possible response:** Hersey's precision emphasizes the immensity of the attack; this one horrific event destroyed hundreds of thousands of lives in an instant.

3. **(a)** He repeatedly refers to the moment when the bomb exploded. **(b) Possible response:** By returning to the moment of the explosion, Hersey forces the reader to witness the bomb's destructive power again and again.

4. **Possible responses: (a)** Residents of the city expected to be bombed with conventional weapons; evacuation orders were given frequently; an air-raid siren sounded early every morning. **(b)** By describing the city before the blast, he shows readers Hiroshima as a living community before it is destroyed.

5. **(a)** She is crushed by books. **(b) Possible response:** The effect is sadly ironic. Miss Sasaki is crushed by the weight of "knowledge" and "learning"; the explosion that caused the books to fall, of course, was the fruit of many expert scientists' labors.

6. **(a)** They are merely ordinary citizens. **(b) Possible response:** By telling the story through the eyes of ordinary citizens, Hersey implies that the atomic bomb devastated everyone in the same way—regardless of background, class, or vocation.

7. **Possible response:** After reading this selection, students may feel that Truman's decision was wrong because the devastation visited upon ordinary citizens was so great. Other students may agree with Truman's decision because conventional warfare may have been equally deadly.

Miss Sasaki went back to her office and sat down at her desk. She was quite far from the windows, which were off to her left, and behind her were a couple of tall bookcases containing all the books of the factory library, which the personnel department had organized. She settled herself at her desk, put some things in a drawer, and shifted papers. She thought that before she began to make entries in her lists of new employees, discharges, and departures for the Army, she would chat for a moment with the girl at her right. Just as she turned her head away from the windows, the room was filled with a blinding light. She was paralyzed by fear, fixed still in her chair for a long moment (the plant was 1,600 yards from the center).

Everything fell, and Miss Sasaki lost consciousness. The ceiling dropped suddenly and the wooden floor above collapsed in splinters and the people up there came down and the roof above them gave way; but principally and first of all, the bookcases right behind her swooped forward and the contents threw her down, with her left leg horribly twisted and breaking underneath her. There, in the tin factory, in the first moment of the atomic age, a human being was crushed by books.

Review and Assess

Thinking About the Selection

1. **Respond:** What thoughts remain with you after reading this account of the bombing of Hiroshima?

2. **(a) Recall:** At what time and on what day was the bomb dropped on Hiroshima? **(b) Draw Conclusions:** Why do you think Hersey is so precise in noting the exact date and time?

3. **(a) Recall:** In describing each individual's experience, which moment does Hersey refer to again and again?
   (b) Interpret: What is the effect of Hersey's returning to this moment repeatedly?

4. **(a) Recall:** Note three details describing the city of Hiroshima in the hours preceding the bomb. **(b) Analyze:** Why does Hersey spend so much time describing the city before the blast?

5. **(a) Recall:** By what is Miss Sasaki crushed? **(b) Infer:** What effect do you think Hersey intended when he described Miss Sasaki's experience?

6. **(a) Classify:** Are the people Hersey portrays important decision makers or merely ordinary citizens?
   (b) Draw Conclusions: What is Hersey implying about the fates of individuals in the midst of war?

7. **Take a Position:** President Truman's hope that the atomic bomb would end the war proved true but at a huge cost. Do you think he made the right decision? Why or why not?

Losses

Randall Jarrell

It was not dying: everybody died.
It was not dying: we had died before
In the routine crashes—and our fields
Called up the papers, wrote home to our folks,
5   And the rates rose, all because of us.
We died on the wrong page of the almanac,
Scattered on mountains fifty miles away;
Diving on haystacks, fighting with a friend,
We blazed up on the lines we never saw.
10 We died like aunts or pets or foreigners.
(When we left high school nothing else had died
For us to figure we had died like.)

In our new planes, with our new crews, we bombed
The ranges by the desert or the shore,
15 Fired at towed targets, waited for our scores—
And turned into replacements and woke up
One morning, over England, operational.
It wasn't different: but if we died
It was not an accident but a mistake
20 (But an easy one for anyone to make).
We read our mail and counted up our missions—
In bombers named for girls, we burned
The cities we had learned about in school—
Till our lives wore out; our bodies lay among
25 The people we had killed and never seen.
When we lasted long enough they gave us medals;
When we died they said, "Our casualties were low."

Losses ◆ 1173

Reading Strategy
Drawing Inferences About Theme In lines 1–2, what surprising comments does the poet make about death?

✓**Reading Check** ㉖
Who is speaking?
Who are "we"?

CUSTOMIZE INSTRUCTION FOR UNIVERSAL ACCESS

For Less Proficient Readers	For Gifted/Talented Students	For Advanced Readers
Check students' comprehension by asking them what Jarrell means in lines 11–12 of "Losses." Be sure they understand he means that the fliers—"we"—were so young and untouched by death that they had no frame of reference other than the deaths of relatives, pets, and distant strangers to which to compare their own.	Encourage students to discuss their emotional responses to the images in Jarrell's very short poem, "The Death of the Ball Turret Gunner." Instruct students to capture those emotions in a visual representation of the poem's speaker before his death.	After they have completed the excerpt from *Hiroshima*, encourage students to consider whether or not Truman's decision to use the atomic bomb was justified. Students can conduct research on the topic, beginning with **Beyond Literature**, p. 68. Encourage them to form teams and stage a debate for the class.

Review and Assess

1. Possible response: While students may not have considered war from this perspective before reading the poem, they may agree with Jarrell's attitude. Student responses should be supported by citations from the poem.

2. **(a)** They die in "routine crashes," "Scattered on mountains," "Diving on haystacks," and "fighting with a friend." In all cases, they die like "aunts or pets or foreigners." **(b)** Possible response: They place little value on individual lives, even their own.

3. **(a)** They do not see the people they kill. **(b)** Possible responses: It demonstrates that part of the horror of modern warfare is its impersonal nature.

4. **(a)** He refers to it as a "dream of life." **(b)** Possible response: He might view life on earth as a dream because he is completely removed from it while experiencing the "nightmare" of the turret.

5. Possible responses: **(a)** "State" seems to refer to both the government and the fighter plane that is flown to support its war efforts. **(b)** He suggests that the state takes children from their mothers and drops them into war to fight and to die.

6. Possible response: Students may concede that some wars, such as World War II, are more justified than others, but may still feel that "good" is not an appropriate adjective for any war.

The Death of the Ball Turret Gunner

Randall Jarrell

A ball turret was a plexiglass sphere, or circular capsule, in the underside of certain World War II bombers; it held a small man and two machine guns. When the bomber was attacked by a plane below, the gunner, hunched in his little sphere, would revolve with the turret to fire his guns from an upside-down position.

From my mother's sleep I fell into the State,
And I hunched in its belly till my wet fur froze.
Six miles from earth, loosed from its dream of life,
I woke to black flak[1] and the nightmare fighters.
5 When I died they washed me out of the turret with a hose.

1. **flak** *n.* anti-aircraft fire.

Review and Assess

Thinking About the Selections

1. **Respond:** Do you share the poet's attitude toward war as he expresses it in "Losses"? Why or why not?

2. **(a) Recall:** In the first stanza of "Losses," in what variety of ways do the pilots die? **(b) Interpret:** What do these descriptions suggest about the pilots' attitude toward death?

3. **(a) Recall:** Do the pilots see the people they kill? **(b) Analyze:** What is the poet suggesting about the horror of modern warfare?

4. **(a) Recall:** In "The Death of the Ball Turret Gunner," which words does the gunner use to describe his view of life on Earth? **(b) Analyze:** In what way is this view of life related to the "nightmare" in the turret?

5. **(a) Interpret:** To what does the word "State" refer? **(b) Draw Conclusions:** What is the poet suggesting about the relationship between a soldier in a war and the government?

6. **Take a Position:** Jarrell based his poems on observations of World War II, a war that has been called "the good war." Is there such a thing as a "good war"? Explain.

ASSESSMENT PRACTICE: Writing Skills

Grammar and Usage	(For more practice, see Test Preparation Workbook, p. 71.)

The writing sections of many tests require students to choose the correct word to complete a sentence. Use the following sample item to show students how to recognize correct and incorrect grammar and choose the correct word to complete each sentence.

If you ever see photographs of the devastation of Hiroshima, _____ senses will be overwhelmed.

Choose the word or group of words that belongs in the blank.

A yourself   **C** you're
B your   **D** you

A, C, and *D* are not possessive forms. *B* is the correct possessive form.

Review and Assess

Literary Analysis

Implied Theme

1. (a) Which details in *Hiroshima* give clues to the **implied theme**? (b) What is that theme?
2. (a) In "Losses," what does line 26 imply about the value of the medals? (b) What is the poet saying about honor and valor in war?
3. In "The Death of the Ball Turret Gunner," what is the poet saying about the value of human life during war?
4. (a) Use a chart like the one shown to explore similarities and differences in Hersey's and Jarrell's portrayals of victims in war. (b) Do the three pieces share a common theme? Explain.

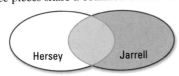

Comparing Literary Works

5. (a) In *Hiroshima*, which descriptions evoke the strongest emotions in you? (b) Is Hersey writing an **objective account** as a reporter or a **subjective account** as a commentator? Explain.
6. (a) Which lines in Jarrell's poems are stated as pure fact, seemingly without emotional bias? (b) What is the effect?

Reading Strategy

Drawing Inferences About Theme

7. (a) Explain the underlying meaning of this line from *Hiroshima*:

    . . . the night before the bomb was dropped, an announcer . . . advised the population . . . to evacuate to their designated 'safe areas.'

   (b) In what ways does that line help to communicate the theme?
8. In "Losses," the speaker notes, "We died like aunts or pets or foreigners." What does this line suggest about the poem's theme?

Extend Understanding

9. **Science Connection:** When the atom bomb was dropped on Hiroshima, no one knew about fallout, radiation sickness, or long-term contamination of the land. How might such knowledge have changed the decision to drop the bomb?

from Hiroshima / Losses / The Death of the Ball Turret Gunner ◆ 1175

Quick Review

An **implied theme** is the message the author suggests through details, characterization, and events but does not directly state.

In an **objective account,** the narrator is an outside observer who comments on the events without emotion. In a **subjective account,** the narrator reveals his or her feelings about the events described.

To **draw inferences about theme,** examine clues from the work for their underlying meanings.

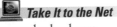 **Take It to the Net**
www.phschool.com

Take the interactive self-test online to check your understanding of these selections.

Answers for p. 1175
Review and Assess

1. Possible responses: **(a)** The details of the ordinary activities of Japanese citizens and the details of the physical impact of the bomb give clues about the theme. **(b)** The implied theme is the great destructive power of the bomb.

2. Possible responses: **(a)** The line suggests that the medals have little value, only signifying that someone has "lasted long enough." **(b)** Honor and valor have no real meaning in modern war.

3. Possible responses: The poet suggests that individual lives have no value in war.

4. Possible responses: **(a)** Hersey: Our "enemies" are ordinary people like ourselves; Jarrell: Our soldiers are not heroes but victims; Overlap: Victims of war are destroyed, regardless of the nature of their involvement with the conflict. **(b)** Students may respond that all three pieces imply that modern war is a purely destructive evil.

5. Possible responses: **(a)** Students may say that Mrs. Nakamura evoked the strongest emotions because of her young children. **(b)** Some students may feel Hersey's account is objective because of its reportorial style; others will say it is subjective because of the strong emotions involved.

6. **(a)** The first stanza of "Losses" and the last line of "The Death of the Ball Turret Gunner" seem to be pure fact. **(b)** The "facts" stated in these lines are of extreme horror, so the objective style heightens their effect.

7. Possible responses: **(a)** This line suggests that there are no "safe areas." **(b)** It communicates the theme by emphasizing the immensity of the bomb's destructive power.

8. Possible response: These words show that the deaths of the military pilots are not that important to anyone.

9. Possible response: Some students may feel that the United States would not have used the bomb had such effects been known. Others will feel that the desire to end the war would have outweighed even this knowledge.

ENRICHMENT: Further Reading

Other Works by the Authors

Works by John Hersey

A Bell for Adano

The Wall

Works by Randall Jarrell

Little Friend, Little Friend

The Woman at the Washington Zoo

We suggest that you preview these works before recommending them to students.

Take It to the Net
Visit www.phschool.com for more information on the authors.

Answers for p. 1176

❶ Vocabulary Development

Word Analysis

1. *volunteer*: a person who offers to do something

2. *malevolence*: the quality or state of wishing evil or harm to others

3. *benevolence*: an inclination or wish to do good; kindness

4. *involuntary*: a response or reaction over which one has no conscious control

Spelling Strategy

1. losses
2. parishes
3. crashes
4. reflexes
5. churches
6. glasses

Fluency: Sentence Completion

1. evacuated
2. volition
3. rendezvous
4. philanthropies
5. incessant
6. convivial

❷ Grammar and Style

Possible response: After Mr. Tanimoto cooked his own breakfast, he started for Mr. Matsuo's house. Later, as the two men set out, an air-raid siren went off. Then, the all-clear sounded. Suddenly, although there was no sound of planes, a tremendous flash of light cut across the sky. Both Mr. Tanimoto and Mr. Matsuo reacted in terror.

Writing Application

Students' paragraphs should present a chronological sequence of events. Details within paragraphs should be logically linked by transitions.

Integrate Language Skills

❶ Vocabulary Development Lesson

Word Analysis: Latin Root -vol-

The meaning of the word *volition*, "the act of using the will," is derived from the Latin root *-vol-*, meaning "to will" or "to wish." Using your knowledge of the roots, define each of the following words. Then, check your answers in a dictionary.

1. volunteer
2. malevolence
3. benevolence
4. involuntary

Spelling Strategy

The plural of words ending in *z, x, sh, ch,* or *s* is usually formed by adding *-es* to the base word. For example, *porch + -es = porches*. Write the plural of each of the following words.

1. loss
2. parish
3. crash
4. reflex
5. church
6. glass

❷ Grammar and Style

Transitions and Transitional Phrases

Transitions are words that show chronological, spatial, comparison and contrast, cause and effect, and order of importance relationships among ideas. Groups of words that function in the same way are called **transitional phrases.**

> **Transition:** *Then*, a tremendous flash of light cut across the sky.
>
> **Transitional phrase:** *At the time*, none of them knew anything.

Common transitions like *because, as a result, if, therefore, in addition, although, next, in contrast, similarly, despite,* and *recently* can clarify the connections between ideas.

Fluency: Sentence Completion

Select the word from the vocabulary list on p. 1161 that best completes each of these sentences.

1. The birds ___?___ their nest and never returned to it.

2. She did extra homework of her own ___?___.

3. Let's establish a ___?___ point, so we don't miss each other.

4. Among the financier's ___?___ was a fund to send young musicians to music camp.

5. The child's ___?___ whining bothered fellow train passengers.

6. The ___?___ friends attend parties together often.

Practice Add transitions or transitional phrases to the following paragraph.

> Mr. Tanimoto cooked his own breakfast. He started for Mr. Matsuo's house. The two men set out. An air-raid siren went off. The all-clear sounded. There was no sound of planes. A tremendous flash of light cut across the sky. Both Mr. Tanimoto and Mr. Matsuo reacted in terror.

Writing Application Write a series of sentences summarizing your activities during a typical day. Use transitions and transitional phrases to link ideas.

𝒲𝒢 *Prentice Hall Writing and Grammar Connection: Chapter 3, Section 2*

TEACHING RESOURCES

The following resources can be used to enrich or extend the instruction for pp. 1176–1177.

Vocabulary

📖 **Selection Support:** Build Vocabulary, p. 294

📖 **Vocabulary and Spelling Practice Book** (Use this booklet for skills enrichment.) ■

Grammar

📖 **Selection Support:** Grammar and Style, p. 295

𝒲𝒢 **Writing and Grammar,** Ruby Level, p. 37 ■

📖 **Daily Language Practice Transparencies**

Writing

𝒲𝒢 **Writing and Grammar,** Ruby Level, p. 272 ■

💿 **Writing and Grammar iText CD-ROM**

📖 **Writing Models and Graphic Organizers on Transparencies,** p. 95

■ **BLOCK SCHEDULING:** Resources marked with this symbol provide varied instruction during 90-minute blocks.

❸ Writing Lesson

Book Review

John Hersey's book *Hiroshima* was published in 1946. Imagine that, more than fifty years later, you have been asked to write a review of the book celebrating its anniversary. In your review, discuss the book as both a work of literature and an important historical document.

Prewriting	Reread the excerpt from *Hiroshima*. Speculate about the effect the book had on its first readers who were just learning about the power of nuclear weapons. Take notes about Hersey's use of description, and identify his attitude toward his subject.
Drafting	Begin with a vivid opening sentence. Then, describe the book and state why it is both a moving and an important piece of writing. Present point-by-point detail in your body paragraphs, and write a conclusion that reinforces Hersey's insights for modern readers.
Revising	Read your review to make sure you have conveyed a clear sense of the book. Determine whether you have appropriately targeted the knowledge level of your expected audience.

Model: Revising for Knowledge Level of Readers

the Japanese city of   on August 6, 1945
When the United States bombed Hiroshima, a catastrophic
power was unleashed. This event contributed to a fear of
nuclear war that would last for decades.

> An audience unfamiliar with an event requires the basic information added in revision.

W̶G Prentice Hall Writing and Grammar Connection: Chapter 13, Section 2

❹ Extension Activities

Listening and Speaking Present a **dramatic reading** of one of Randall Jarrell's poems. To prepare, try the following tips:

- Supplement the reading with evocative music and appropriate sound effects.
- Vary your tone of voice to draw out shades of meaning.
- Include visual aids, such as a photograph of a World War II bomber, to accompany your reading.

Research and Technology Using library and Internet sources, conduct research on the city of Hiroshima. Focus your investigation on the state of the city just before and after August 1945, when the bomb was dropped. Gather your findings in a **written report**.

 **Take It to the Net** www.phschool.com

Go online for an additional research activity using the Internet.

from Hiroshima / Losses / The Death of the Ball Turret Gunner ◆ 1177

---

❸ Writing Lesson

- Explain that students' book reviews should present assessments of *Hiroshima*, both as a literary work and as an historical document.
- After students reread and take notes on the selection, instruct them to write one-sentence assessments of the work.
- Students may construct outlines focusing on their assessments, using the model in **Writing Models and Graphic Organizers on Transparencies**, p. 95. Remind them to use material from their notes to support their assessments.
- As students revise, be sure that they include basic information appropriate for their audience.

❹ Listening and Speaking

- Explain that a dramatic reading is similar to a reading of a play. The reader uses vocal expression to show emotion and may incorporate visual elements, music, and sound effects.
- Have each participant choose one of the Jarrell poems. Provide time for students to locate and record music and other sounds. Students may also gather visual materials, such as photographs.
- Have students take turns performing for the class. Provide necessary audio/video equipment.
- Adapt the Speaking: Delivering a Speech rubric in **Performance Assessment and Portfolio Management,** p. 30, to assess students' dramatic readings.

CUSTOMIZE INSTRUCTION
For Universal Access

To address different learning styles, use the activities suggested in the **Extension Activities** booklet, p. 68.

- For Verbal/Linguistic and Logical/Mathematical Learners, use Activity 5.
- For Verbal/Linguistic Learners, use Activity 6.
- For Visual/Spatial Learners, use Activity 7.

Mirror ✦ In a Classroom ✦ The Explorer ✦ Frederick Douglass ✦ Runagate Runagate

Lesson Objectives

1. **To analyze and respond to literary elements**
   - Literary Analysis: Theme
   - Comparing Literary Works
2. **To read, comprehend, analyze, and critique poetry**
   - Reading Strategy: Interpreting
   - Reading Check Questions
   - Review and Assess Questions
3. **To develop word analysis skills, fluency, and systematic vocabulary**
   - Vocabulary Development Lesson: Latin Root: -cep-/-cept-
4. **To understand and apply written and oral language conventions**
   - Spelling Strategy
   - Grammar and Style Lesson: Parallel Structure
   - Assessment Practice (ATE)
5. **To understand and apply appropriate writing and research strategies**
   - Writing Lesson: Literary Analysis
   - Extension Activity: Multimedia Presentation
6. **To understand and apply listening and speaking strategies**
   - Extension Activity: Debate

STEP-BY-STEP TEACHING GUIDE	PACING GUIDE
PRETEACH	
Motivate Students and Provide Background	
Use the Motivation activity (ATE p. 1178)	5 min.
Read and discuss author and background features (SE/ATE pp. 1178, 1184) **A**	10 min.
Introduce the Concepts	
Introduce the Literary Analysis and Reading Strategy (SE/ATE p. 1179) **A**	15 min.
Pronounce the vocabulary words and read their definitions (SE p. 1179)	5 min.
TEACH	
Monitor Comprehension	
Informally monitor comprehension by circulating while students read independently or in groups **A**	35 min.
Monitor students' comprehension with the Reading Check notes (SE/ATE p. 1185)	as students read
Develop vocabulary with Vocabulary notes (SE pp. 1180, 1182; ATE p. 1181)	as students read
Develop Understanding	
Develop students' understanding of theme with the Literary Analysis annotations (SE/ATE p. 1185) **A**	5 min.
Develop students' ability to make interpretations by using the Reading Strategy annotations (SE p. 1184; ATE p. 1184)	5 min.
ASSESS	
Assess Mastery	
Assess students' mastery of the Reading Strategy and Literary Analysis by having them answer the Review and Assess questions (SE/ATE p. 1187) **A**	15 min.
Use one or more of the print and media Assessment Resources (ATE p. 1189) **A**	up to 45 min.
EXTEND	
Apply Understanding	
Have students complete the Vocabulary Development Lesson and the Grammar and Style Lesson (SE p. 1188) **A**	20 min.
Apply students' ability to use quotations by using the Writing Lesson (SE/ATE p. 1189) **A**	45 min.
Apply students' understanding using one or more of the Extension Activities (SE p. 1189)	20–90 min.

A **ACCELERATED INSTRUCTION:**
Use the strategies and activities identified with an **A**.

UNIVERSAL ACCESS
● = Below Level Students
▲ = On-Level Students
■ = Above Level Students

Time and Resource Manager

Reading Level: Average, Challenging, Challenging, Easy, Easy
Average Number of Instructional Days: 4

RESOURCES		
PRINT 📖	**TRANSPARENCIES** 📄	**TECHNOLOGY** 💿 🎧 📼
• **Beyond Literature,** Humanities Connection: Poetry of Protest, p. 69 ▲ ■		• **Interest Grabber Video,** Tape 6 ● ▲ ■
• **Selection Support Workbook:** ● ▲ ■ Literary Analysis, p. 301 Reading Strategy, p. 300 Build Vocabulary, p. 298	• **Literary Analysis and Reading Transparencies,** pp. 137 and 138 ● ▲ ■	
		• **Listening to Literature** ● ▲ ■ Audiocassettes, Side 39 Audio CDs, CD 23
• **Literatura en español** ● ▲ • **Literary Analysis for Enrichment** ■	• **Fine Art Transparencies, Volume 1,** Art Transparencies 20 ● ▲ ■	
• **Formal Assessment:** Selection Test, pp. 297–299 ● ▲ ■ • **Open Book Test,** pp. 205–207 ● ▲ ■ • **Performance Assessment and Portfolio Management,** p. 23 ● ▲ ■ • **PRENTICE HALL** ASSESSMENT SYSTEM ● ▲ ■	• **PRENTICE HALL** ASSESSMENT SYSTEM ● ▲ ■ Skills Practice Answers and Explanations on Transparencies	• **Test Bank Software** ● ▲ ■ • **Got It! Assessment Videotapes,** Tape 6 ● ▲
• **Selection Support Workbook:** ● ▲ ■ Grammar and Style, p. 299 • **Writing and Grammar,** Ruby Level ● ▲ ■ • **Extension Activities,** p. 69 ● ▲ ■	• **Daily Language Practice Transparencies** ● ▲ • **Writing Models and Graphic Organizers on Transparencies,** pp. 37–40 ● ▲ ■	• **Writing and Grammar iText CD-ROM** ● ▲ ■ 💻 *Take It to the Net* www.phschool.com

BLOCK SCHEDULING: Use one 90-minute class period to preteach the selection and have students read it. Use a second 90-minute class period to assess students' mastery of skills and have them complete one of the Extension Activities.

Step-by-Step Teaching Guide for pp. 1178–1179

Motivation

Ask students to suggest ways that they might cope with injustice and lack of opportunity. Would they give up? Protest actively? Express their anger in writing? Why or why not? Remind them that the writers of these poems protest through poetry.

Interest Grabber Video

As an alternative, play "Reading and Student Response" on Tape 6 to engage student interest.

❶ Background

More About the Authors

Sylvia Plath's father died during her childhood, leaving her mother to struggle financially. Plath's anger and sense of loss over this stayed with her, and is revealed in poems such as "Daddy" and "Medusa."

A staunch feminist, Adrienne Rich devoted much of her poetry to protesting male and female roles in American society. Rich carried her protests into real life as well. For example, she refused a National Medal of Honor in 1997 in protest of some of the policies of President Bill Clinton.

Gwendolyn Brooks's poetry became more political as her career progressed. She increasingly focused her work on building an African American protest community. In later years, Brooks was the poet laureate of Illinois.

In addition to his focus on social protest and interest in racial themes, Robert Hayden worked hard to perfect poetic techniques. From 1976–78, Hayden consulted about poetry at the Library of Congress.

Prepare to Read

❶ Mirror ◆ In a Classroom ◆ The Explorer ◆ Frederick Douglass ◆ Runagate Runagate

Sylvia Plath (1932–1963)

Despite her success as a writer, Sylvia Plath lived a short, unhappy life. In many of her poems, she expresses intense feelings of despair and deep inner pain. Born in Boston, Plath wrote poetry and received scholastic and literary awards as a youth. Although she suffered a nervous breakdown in her junior year, she graduated with highest honors from Smith College. She also studied at Cambridge University in England, where she met and married poet Ted Hughes in 1956. Her first book of verse, *The Colossus and Other Poems* (1960), was the only one published during her lifetime. Four more books of poetry and a novel, *The Bell Jar* (1963), were published posthumously.

Gwendolyn Brooks (1917–2000)

Gwendolyn Brooks was raised in a Chicago neighborhood known as "Bronzeville"—the setting for her first book, *A Street in Bronzeville* (1945). Although her early poems focus on suffering urban blacks who feel uprooted and are unable to make a living, Brooks's own youth was quite different. Her home was warm and her family loving, supportive, and confident that Brooks would find success as a writer. Brooks began writing poetry at the age of seven. In 1950, she became the first African American writer to win a Pulitzer Prize. After that, her reputation grew steadily, and she became one of the most highly regarded poets of our time.

Adrienne Rich (b. 1929)

Born in Baltimore, Maryland, Adrienne Rich is a poet and an essayist who is best known for her examination of women in society. Rich's career as a poet can be divided into two distinct stages. In the early part of her career, she wrote neatly crafted traditional verse. In contrast, her later poems are written in free verse and often explore deep personal feelings. Her first volume of poetry, *A Change of World* (1951), was published just after she graduated from Radcliffe College. Her most recent books are *Dark Fields of the Republic* (Poems 1991–1995) and *Midnight Salvage* (Poems 1995–1998). A new selection of her essays, *Arts of the Possible: Essays and Conversations*, and a new volume of poems, *Fox* (Poems 1998–2000), appeared in 2001.

Robert Hayden (1913–1980)

Born in Detroit, Robert Hayden was a young, politically active writer in the 1930s who protested not only the social and economic conditions of African Americans but also what he saw as the nation's inadequate care of the poor. Hayden was an extremely versatile writer who used a variety of poetic forms and techniques, focusing on a wide range of subjects. He published several collections of poetry, including *Heart-Shape in the Dust* (1940), *The Lion and the Archer* (1948), and *The Night-Blooming Cereus* (1972). His collection *A Ballad of Remembrance* received the Grand Prize for Poetry at the First World Festival for Negro Arts in 1966.

1178 ◆ *Prosperity and Protest (1946–Present)*

TEACHING RESOURCES

The following resources can be used to enrich or extend the instruction for pp. 1178–1179.

Motivation

Interest Grabber Video, Tape 6

Background

Beyond Literature, p. 69

 Take It to the Net

Visit www.phschool.com for Background and hotlinks for selections.

Literary Analysis

Literary Analysis and Reading Transparencies, Theme, p. 138

Selection Support: Literary Analysis, p. 301

Reading

Literary Analysis and Reading Transparencies, Interpreting, p. 137

BLOCK SCHEDULING: Resources marked with this symbol provide varied instruction during 90-minute blocks.

Preview

Connecting to the Literature

It is human nature to find fault with the situations, policies, and attitudes we experience in everyday life. While you may discuss your social concerns with your family and friends, some poets use their writing as a means of expressing their views.

❷ Literary Analysis

Theme

A poem's **theme** is the central idea it conveys. Poets suggest themes through the connotations of the words and images they choose. For example, in these lines about aging by Sylvia Plath, the words *drowned* and *terrible* have negative associations; thus, you can infer that the theme has something to do with the fear of growing old:

> In me she has drowned a young girl, and in me an old woman
> Rises toward her day after day, like a terrible fish.

As you read these poems, find clues to the themes in words and images that evoke either negative or positive responses.

Comparing Literary Works

Poetry has long been a vehicle for **social criticism.** In some poems, the social critique addresses topics we usually categorize as personal. In the poet's message, however, the personal takes on larger meaning. Other poems address large social themes and show the ways in which broad social problems affect the lives of individuals. All the poems you are about to read carry messages of social critique. As you read, examine the ways in which each one explores the intersection between the individual and the society of which he or she is part.

❸ Reading Strategy

Interpreting

In most poems, the central message is not directly stated. It is up to you to **interpret** it by looking for an underlying meaning in the words and images. Consider the connotations of the words and the associations they call to mind, and then try to determine what common thread ties them together. Use an organizer like the one shown to record words and images that will help you interpret the theme.

Words and Images	Potential Meaning

Vocabulary Development

preconceptions (prē´ kən sep´ shənz) *n.* ideas formed beforehand (p. 1180)

meditate (med´ ə tāt´) *v.* think deeply; ponder (p. 1180)

din (din) *n.* loud, continuous noise; uproar or clamor (p. 1182)

wily (wī´ lē) *adj.* sly; cunning (p. 1182)

Mirror / In a Classroom / The Explorer / Frederick Douglass / Runagate Runagate ◆ 1179

1179

CUSTOMIZE INSTRUCTION
For Interpersonal Learners

Through literature, the poets in this group protest attitudes and circumstances. Ask students to identify and describe values or attitudes that they might find difficult to accept. If they were poets living in each place, what might they feel compelled to challenge through their art?

❶ About the Selection

The speaker of this poem, a mirror, describes a woman's reaction to viewing her image day after day. The woman, aware that she is growing older, responds "with tears and agitation of hands."

❷ Background

Art

Mirror II **by George Tooker**

Born in 1920, George Tooker is an American painter whose style is known as "Magic Realism." Magic Realism is realistic art that uses everyday images symbolically, as Tooker uses the mirror in this painting. As in most of Tooker's paintings, the setting, lighting, and mood of *Mirror II* are clean, cold, and barren.

Use these questions for discussion:

1. In what way does the woman in the painting resemble the woman in the poem?
   Answer: Each woman searches "for what she really is"; each senses an older woman "rising toward her."

2. Do you think that the moods of the two works match? Explain.
   Answer: Yes; both works have serious and slightly fantastic moods.

❸ ▶ Critical Viewing

Answer: Both suggest that aging is an inevitable, though not necessarily welcome, part of the human condition.

---

❶ Mirror
Sylvia Plath

Mirror II, George Tooker, © Addison Gallery of American Art, Phillips Academy, Andover, Massachusetts

❷

❸ ◀ **Critical Viewing** The artist titled this painting *Mirror II*. What ideas are common to both the painting and poem? **[Connect]**

❹ **preconceptions** (prē′ kən sep′ shənz) *n.* ideas formed beforehand

meditate (med′ ə tāt′) *v.* think deeply; ponder

I am silver and exact. I have no <u>preconceptions</u>.
Whatever I see I swallow immediately
Just as it is, unmisted by love or dislike.
I am not cruel, only truthful—
5   The eye of a little god, four-cornered.
Most of the time I <u>meditate</u> on the opposite wall.
It is pink, with speckles. I have looked at it so long
I think it is a part of my heart. But it flickers.
Faces and darkness separate us over and over.
10 Now I am a lake. A woman bends over me,
Searching my reaches for what she really is.
Then she turns to those liars, the candles or the moon.
I see her back, and reflect it faithfully.
She rewards me with tears and an agitation of hands.
15 I am important to her. She comes and goes.
Each morning it is her face that replaces the darkness.
In me she has drowned a young girl, and in me an old woman
Rises toward her day after day, like a terrible fish.

1180 ◆ *Prosperity and Protest (1946–Present)*

TEACHING RESOURCES

The following resources can be used to enrich or extend the instruction for pp. 1180–1186.

Literary Analysis

📘 **Writing Models and Graphic Organizers on Transparencies,** pp. 37–40

Reading

📖 **Selection Support:** Reading Strategy, p. 300; Build Vocabulary, p. 298 ▪

🎧 **Listening to Literature Audiocassettes,** Side 39

💿 **Listening to Literature Audio CDs,** CD 23

Extension

📘 **Fine Art Transparencies, Volume 1,** Art Transparency 20
(After students have read "The Explorer," display Art Transparency 20. Call on volunteers to describe its overall impression and to speculate about the sights and sounds they would encounter if they were to experience the scene for themselves.)

▪ **BLOCK SCHEDULING:** Resources marked with this symbol provide varied instruction during 90-minute blocks.

IN A CLASSROOM

Adrienne Rich

Talking of poetry, hauling the books
arm-full to the table where the heads
bend or gaze upward, listening, reading aloud,
talking of consonants, elision,[1]
5   caught in the how, oblivious of why:
I look in your face, Jude,
neither frowning nor nodding,
opaque in the slant of dust-motes over the table:
a presence like a stone, if a stone were thinking
10   *What I cannot say, is me. For that I came.*

---

1. **elision** (ē lizh´ en) *n.* omission or slurring over of a vowel or syllable; often used in poetry to preserve meter.

Review and Assess

Thinking About the Selections

1. **Respond:** The speaker of "Mirror" maintains, "I am not cruel, only truthful—." If the truth hurts, do you think being truthful is cruel? Explain.

2. **(a) Recall:** What two reflecting surfaces does the speaker name? **(b) Infer:** Who is the speaker?

3. **(a) Recall:** In what way does the woman "reward" the speaker? **(b) Interpret:** Explain why she reacts this way.

4. **(a) Recall:** To whom does the woman turn? **(b) Interpret:** Why are they called liars?

5. **(a) Infer:** Who is the "old woman"? **(b) Draw Conclusions:** What are the woman's feelings about aging?

6. **Extend:** The woman searches the mirror for "what she really is." Can one's true self be seen in a mirror? Explain.

❹ Vocabulary Development

Latin Root -cep-/-cept-

- Point out the word *preconceptions* on p. 1180, and have a volunteer read the surrounding sentence aloud.

- Direct students' attention to the definition of *preconceptions,* and explain that the Latin word root *-cep-/-cept-* means "to take, hold, or seize."

- If time allows, refer students to the Vocabulary Development lesson on p. 1188. Have them look up the listed words in the dictionary.

Answers for p. 1181

Review and Assess

1. Accept reasonable responses.

2. **(a)** The speaker mentions a "four-cornered mirror" and a lake. **(b)** The mirror is the speaker in the poem.

3. **(a)** She rewards the speaker with tears and an agitation of hands. **(b)** She reacts that way because she is upset to see herself aging.

4. **(a)** She turns to "those liars, the candles or the moon." **(b)** They create deceptively complimentary images of the speaker.

5. **(a)** The old woman is the person the woman is becoming. **(b)** She is unhappy about aging and has difficulty accepting it.

6. Possible response: Students may say that a mirror can reveal physical traits but shows little of a person's feelings or thoughts.

❺ About the Selection

A person, identified only as "he," explores an apartment building, searching for "a still spot in the noise." His search for peace—for inner peace—is unsuccessful, however, as all he finds are noises connected with human activities and the frightening prospect of "choices, that cried to be taken."

Answers for p. 1182

Review and Assess

1. Students should support their responses.

2. **(a)** The "inner want" is peace of mind. **(b)** The title suggests that the speaker will explore in order to fulfill that inner want.

3. **(a)** He is searching in an apartment building. **(b)** No, he doesn't find it.

4. Possible responses: **(a)** The apartment building may represent the speaker's life, and the rooms represent his choices in life. **(b)** His actions and feelings might symbolize his inability to find solace and the limitations of the choices with which he is presented.

5. Possible response: People are afraid they will not be happy with the results of their decision.

❻ About the Selection

In this poem, the speaker describes the way Frederick Douglass will be remembered when freedom "is finally ours": not through statues, legends, poems, or wreaths, but through the lives that will realize the visionary's dream.

The Explorer

Gwendolyn Brooks

Somehow to find a still spot in the noise
Was the frayed inner want, the winding, the frayed hope
Whose tatters he kept hunting through the <u>din</u>.
A satin peace somewhere.
5 A room of <u>wily</u> hush somewhere within.

So tipping down the scrambled halls he set
Vague hands on throbbing knobs. There were behind
Only spiraling, high human voices,
The scream of nervous affairs,
10 Wee griefs,
Grand griefs. And choices.

He feared most of all the choices, that cried to be taken.

There were no bourns.[1]
There were no quiet rooms.

din (din) *n.* loud, continuous noise; uproar or clamor

wily (wī´ lē) *adj.* sly; cunning

1. **bourns** (bōrnz) *n.* limits; boundaries

Review and Assess

Thinking About the Selection

1. **Respond:** What did you see and hear as you read this poem?

2. **(a) Recall:** What is the "inner want" the poem's speaker expresses? **(b) Interpret:** In what way does the title of the poem relate to the "inner want"?

3. **(a) Recall:** Where is the explorer searching for the "inner want"? **(b) Assess:** Does he find it?

4. **(a) Interpret:** What might the explorer's apartment building symbolize? **(b) Interpret:** What might the explorer's actions and feelings symbolize?

5. **Apply:** Why do you think people often fear having to make choices?

Frederick Douglass¹

Robert Hayden

⑦

Part II, The Free Man, No. 30, The Frederick Douglass Series,
Jacob Lawrence, Hampton University Museum, Hampton, Virginia

When it is finally ours, this freedom, this liberty, this beautiful
and terrible thing, needful to man as air,
usable as earth; when it belongs at last to all,
when it is truly instinct, brain matter, diastole, systole,²
5   reflex action; when it is finally won; when it is more
than the gaudy mumbo jumbo of politicians:
this man, this Douglass, this former slave, this Negro
beaten to his knees, exiled, visioning a world
where none is lonely, none hunted, alien,
10 this man, superb in love and logic, this man
shall be remembered. Oh, not with statues' rhetoric,
not with legends and poems and wreaths of bronze alone,
but with the lives grown out of his life, the lives
fleshing his dream of the beautiful, needful thing.

---

1. **Frederick Douglass** American abolitionist (1817?–1895).
2. **diastole** (dī as′ tə lē′), **systole** (sis′ tə lē′) Diastole is the normal rhythmic dilation, or opening, of the heart. Systole is the normal rhythmic closing of the heart.

⑧ ▲ **Critical Viewing**
What impression of Douglass does this painting convey? **[Analyze]**

Review and Assess

Thinking About the Selection

1. **Respond:** What impression do you have of Frederick Douglass after reading this poem? What kind of person was he?

2. **(a) Recall:** What is the "beautiful and terrible" thing?
   (b) Infer: To whom does it not yet belong?

3. **(a) Recall:** In what ways does the speaker say that Douglass will not be remembered? **(b) Infer:** What does the speaker think are the limitations of statues and memorials?

4. **(a) Interpret:** In what way does the speaker say Douglass truly will be remembered? **(b) Analyze:** What does the speaker mean by "the lives fleshing his dream of the beautiful, needful thing"?

5. **Apply:** How do you think Frederick Douglass would respond to this poem? Explain.

Frederick Douglass ◆ 1183

---

⑦ Background: Art

Part II, The Free Man, No. 30, The Frederick Douglass Series by Jacob Lawrence

African American artist Jacob Lawrence utilizes bold geometric shapes and bright colors to depict the daily lives of ordinary black Americans as well as the lives of distinguished blacks. This painting is of the latter variety, part of a series of paintings completed during 1938 and 1939 on the life of Frederick Douglass. Use this question for discussion:

Does the painting correspond with the image of Frederick Douglass presented in the poem?
Possible response: Yes, because the poem alludes to a highly intelligent man "superb in love and logic," who would therefore probably be fond of reading.

⑧ ▶Critical Viewing

Answer: The impression is one of a thoughtful, scholarly Douglass.

Answers for p. 1183
Review and Assess

1. **Possible response:** Frederick Douglass had a difficult life, but he kept alive the dream of freedom for all.

2. **(a) Possible response:** Freedom is beautiful because it is dignifying and precious, especially after a long, hard struggle; it can also be terrible if it comes at a price. **(b)** Freedom does not yet belong to anyone because it is not yet instinctual.

3. **(a)** He won't be remembered by statue inscriptions, legends poems, or memorials.
   (b) Possible response: The speaker thinks statues and memorials are not vital or alive enough as tools for remembering.

4. **(a)** He will be remembered in the lives of those living out his dreams. **(b) Possible response:** He is referring to the lives who make Douglass's dream a reality by achieving the freedom for which he fought.

5. **Possible response:** Frederick Douglass would be proud to think that the work he began is still ongoing.

CUSTOMIZE INSTRUCTION FOR UNIVERSAL ACCESS

For English Learners	For Less Proficient Readers	For Gifted/Talented Students
Point out the words *diastole* and *systole* in line 4 of "Frederick Douglass." Have a volunteer read aloud the numbered footnote definitions. Explain to students that these words, which refer to the steady beating of the heart, suggest that for Douglass freedom is as necessary as breathing.	Direct students' attention to lines 2–3 of "Frederick Douglass." Help students understand the figurative ways in which Hayden describes freedom. Point out, for example, that the phrase *usable as earth* can be interpreted to mean "Freedom is as necessary to people as earth is."	Challenge students to interpret the meaning of "Frederick Douglass." Then, ask them to write an essay in which they compare and contrast Hayden's meanings with that of Paul Laurence Dunbar's poem about Frederick Douglass (p. 658).

❾ About the Selection

A chorus of voices conveys the risks, the rewards, and the emotions that accompany a journey on the Underground Railroad.

❿ Reading Strategy

Interpreting

• Have students read the bracketed text several times. Then, call on a volunteer to read it aloud.

• Discuss with students how the poetry invites a rapid and escalating pace and tone of voice.

▶ Monitor Progress Ask students the Reading Strategy question on p. 1184: Why do the words in lines 1–7 convey the feeling of running? Answer: The use of repetition, the lack of punctuation, and the non-stop litany of actions and imagery convey a sense of movement and of breathlessness.

❾ Runagate Runagate

Robert Hayden

Background

Although Robert Hayden's poetry spans the range of human experience, much of it reflects his passionate, lifelong interest in African American history. His first job after graduating from Detroit City College was to research local African American history with Detroit's Federal Writer's Project. Throughout his career as a professor of literature, Hayden continued to research and write about his heritage. In "Frederick Douglass," he pays tribute to the famous African American abolitionist. "Runagate Runagate" brings the experiences of the Underground Railroad vividly to life.

I

Runs falls rises stumbles on from darkness into darkness
and the darkness thicketed with shapes of terror
and the hunters pursuing and the hounds pursuing
and the night cold and the night long and the river

5   to cross and the jack-muh-lanterns beckoning beckoning
and blackness ahead and when shall I reach that somewhere
morning and keep on going and never turn back and keep on going

          Runagate[1]
                    Runagate
10   Runagate

Many thousands rise and go
many thousands crossing over

                              O mythic North
                    O star-shaped yonder Bible city[2]

15   Some go weeping and some rejoicing
some in coffins and some in carriages
some in silks and some in shackles

          Rise and go or fare you well

No more auction block for me
20   no more driver's lash for me

---

1. **Runagate** (run´ ə gāt) runaway; fugitive.
2. **star-shaped yonder Bible city** Bethlehem, a town in the free state of Pennsylvania.

Reading Strategy
Interpreting How do the words in lines 1–7 capture the feeling of running?

If you see my Pompey, 30 yrs of age,
new breeches, plain stockings, negro shoes;
if you see my Anna, likely young mulatto
branded E on the right cheek, R on the left,
25   catch them if you can and notify subscriber.[3]
Catch them if you can, but it won't be easy.
They'll dart underground when you try to catch them,
plunge into quicksand, whirlpools, mazes,
turn into scorpions when you try to catch them.

30   And before I'll be a slave
I'll be buried in my grave

North star and bonanza gold
I'm bound for the freedom, freedom-bound
and oh Susyanna don't you cry for me.

35   Runagate

              Runagate

II
Rises from their anguish and their power,

              Harriet Tubman,[4]

40   woman of earth, whipscarred,
              a summoning, a shining

              Mean to be free

And this was the way of it, brethren brethren,
way we journeyed from Can't to Can.
Moon so bright and no place to hide,
45   the cry up and the patterollers[5] riding,
hound dogs belling in bladed air.
And fear starts a-murbling, Never make it,
we'll never make it. *Hush that now,*
and she's turned upon us, leveled pistol
50   glinting in the moonlight:
Dead folks can't jaybird-talk, she says;
you keep on going now or die, she says.

Wanted   Harriet Tubman   alias The General
alias Moses   Stealer of Slaves
55   In league with Garrison   Alcott   Emerson
Garrett   Douglass   Thoreau   John Brown[6]

---

3. **subscriber** slave holder from whom the slaves are fleeing.
4. **Harriet Tubman** (c. 1820–1913) African American slave who escaped and led other slaves to safety in the North.
5. **patterollers** patrollers, hunting the escaped slaves.
6. **Garrison . . . John Brown** prominent abolitionists.

⑫ ▲ Critical Viewing
What inspiration might the moon have offered runaways? **[Hypothesize]**

⑬ ✓ Reading Check
To where is the speaker journeying? Why?

Runagate Runagate ◆ 1185

⑪ Literary Analysis
Theme
• Point out that Robert Hayden fills his poem with allusions to African American spirituals and folk songs.
• Ask students: How does this line from a spiritual illuminate the poem's theme?
Answer: The theme relates to the risks people take to be free, and this line expresses that even death is better than slavery.

⑫ ▶ Critical Viewing
Answer: By lighting their way during nighttime travel, the moon might have made the travelers' journey a bit easier.

⑬ ✓ Reading Check
Answer: The speaker is journeying north in the hope of finding freedom.

CUSTOMIZE INSTRUCTION FOR UNIVERSAL ACCESS

For Less Proficient Readers

Suggest that students visualize a thread of meaning linking the poem's words and images together, and point out that their interpretive challenge is to state what that thread of meaning may be. On the board, draw the following graphic organizer, depicting a thread linking images from "Runagate, Runagate." Have students reproduce the graphic, adding more images from the poem. Finally, ask them to write one sentence on a line labeled "Interpretation," stating the underlying idea that links the images together.

Stumbles on from darkness into darkness

North Star and bonanza gold

No more auction block for me

Answers for p. 1186

Review and Assess

1. Accept reasonable responses grounded in the poem.

2. **(a)** The poem describes a trip on the Underground Railroad. **(b)** They convey the feeling of hurrying in fear through sound and repetition.

3. **(a)** Harriet Tubman rises from their anguish and power. **(b)** She threatens to kill them if they try to give themselves up.

4. **(a)** Harriet Tubman is wanted dead or alive. **(b)** Slave owners will pay the reward.

5. **(a)** The poem's shifts in viewpoint from stanza to stanza reflect a chorus of voices. **(b)** The first seven lines voice the words of a slave on the run; the references to obstacles and the determination to "keep on going" are supporting examples. Lines 19–27 give the voice of a slave owner asking people to catch runaway slaves. Evidence of this are the descriptions of the slaves and the pleas to "catch them if you can." Lines 30–32 again represent the voice of a runaway slave. Lines 34–39 give the voice of a runaway slave describing Harriet Tubman. Lines 50–55 present the voice of a slave owner wanting Harriet Tubman captured or killed. The remaining lines of the poem present the voice of a runaway slave's impressions of the Underground Railroad.

6. **(a)** The risks involve being captured or killed. **(b)** Students should support their responses.

Armed and known to be Dangerous

Wanted   Reward   Dead or Alive

60 Tell me, Ezekiel, oh tell me do you see
mailed Jehovah[7] coming to deliver me?

Hoot-owl calling in the ghosted air,
five times calling to the hants[8] in the air.
Shadow of a face in the scary leaves,
shadow of a voice in the talking leaves:

65 Come ride-a my train

*Oh that train, ghost-story train
through swamp and savanna movering movering,
over trestles of dew, through caves of the wish,
Midnight Special on a sabre track movering movering,
first stop Mercy and the last Hallelujah.*

Come ride-a my train

Mean mean mean to be free.

---

7. **Ezekiel** (ē zē′ kē əl) . . . **Jehovah** (ji hō′ və) Ezekiel was a sixth-century B.C. Hebrew prophet; Jehovah is an Old Testament name for the Judeo-Christian God.
8. **hants** haunts; ghosts.

Review and Assess

Thinking About the Selection

1. **Respond:** How did your response change as the poem moved from stanza to stanza?

2. **(a) Recall:** What is being described in this poem? **(b) Interpret:** What feeling do the words "Runagate, Runagate, Runagate" convey? Explain.

3. **(a) Recall:** Who "rises from their anguish and their power"? **(b) Interpret:** In what ways does this person prevent the frightened fugitives from giving themselves up?

4. **(a) Draw Conclusions:** Whom do you think is wanted dead or alive? **(b) Draw Conclusions:** Who will pay the reward?

5. **(a) Interpret:** Do you think this poem reflects the experiences of a single speaker, or does it reflect a chorus of voices? Explain. **(b) Interpret:** If there is more than one voice, whose voices are they? Support your answers with examples from the poem.

6. **(a) Apply:** What do you think were some of the risks involved in the struggle for freedom? **(b) Take a Position:** If you had been in the situation of a "runagate," would you have put yourself at such risk? Explain.

✎ ASSESSMENT PRACTICE: Writing Skills

Sentence Structure   (For more practice, see Test Preparation Workbook, p. 72.)

Many tests require students to choose the best way to correct the structure of a sentence.

Robert Hayden wrote about folklore, mythology, spiritual matters, and he also wrote about historical events.

Choose the best way to write the passage.

A Robert Hayden wrote about folklore, mythology, and spiritual matters, he also wrote about historical events.

B Robert Hayden wrote about folklore, mythology, spiritual matters, historical events.

C Robert Hayden wrote about folklore, mythology, and spiritual matters, about historical events.

D Robert Hayden wrote about folkore, mythology, spiritual matters, and historical events.

D is correct. It is a complete sentence with parallel structure.

Review and Assess

Literary Analysis

Theme

1. (a) Using a chart like the one shown, list the sensory images used in "Runagate Runagate." (b) Explain how the words you have listed express the **theme** that a journey on the Underground Railroad was full of risk, danger, reward, and emotion.

Sight	Hearing	Smell	Touch	Taste

2. List three images in "The Explorer" that help to identify the theme.
3. (a) In "Frederick Douglass," what words does Hayden use to describe Douglass and his work? (b) Based on these words, what would you say is the theme of the poem?
4. In "Mirror," what does the line "I am important to her" suggest about the theme of the poem?

Comparing Literary Works

5. (a) In what ways do both "The Explorer" and "Frederick Douglass" express the longing for an end to struggle? (b) What are the struggles each poem addresses?
6. (a) In what way can "Mirror" be read as a poem of social critique? (b) What social change, if any, does the poem advocate?
7. (a) How does "Runagate Runagate" demonstrate the suffering of individuals caused by a social injustice? (b) Does the poem propose a specific social change, or not? Explain.

Reading Strategy

Interpreting

8. (a) In "Mirror," what is the significance of the word *swallow*? (b) How does this word contribute to the message of the poem?
9. What is the significance of the medical terms Hayden uses to describe a time when freedom is "diastole, systole, reflex action"?

Extend Understanding

10. **Cultural Connection:** Do you think most people share the attitude toward aging that the woman in "Mirror" has? Why or why not?

Mirror / In a Classroom / The Explorer / Frederick Douglass / Runagate Runagate ◆ 1187

Quick Review

The **theme** is the central message of a work of literature.

Literature of **social criticism** expresses the effects of social ills on individuals and often advocates change.

To **interpret** a work of literature is to determine its meaning by looking for messages in the words and images.

 Take It to the Net
www.phschool.com
Take the interactive self-test online to check your understanding of these selections.

Answers for p. 1187
Review and Assess

1. (a) **Sight:** Stumbles on from darkness into darkness; shapes of terror; blackness ahead; moon so bright; glinting in the moonlight; shadow of a face; **Hearing:** weeping; dogs belling; jaybird talk; hoot-owl calling; shadow of a voice; **Touch:** Night cold; silks and some in shackles; driver's lash; whip-scarred **(b)** These images all suggest the theme of people's willingness to make sacrifices and take risks for freedom.

2. Images might include "a still spot in the noise," "hunting through the din," and "no quiet rooms."

3. **(a)** He uses the words "visioning a world where none is lonely, none hunted." **(b)** The poem's theme is that Douglass's hard work has not yet been fully realized.

4. The poet thinks people care a lot about their looks.

5. **(a)** Both poems seek an end to a problem, though one is internal and the other is external. **(b)** "Explorer" describes an internal struggle for peace of mind; "Frederick Douglass" describes the struggle for freedom.

6. **(a)** "Mirror" can be said to critique society's obsession with youth and good looks. **(b)** It might advocate more respect for the elderly or an end to judging people based on their appearance.

7. **(a)** The poem describes how it feels to be pursued in the night by slave catchers. **(b)** The poem's power comes from its vivid description of a problem; it aims to inspire the reader to find a solution.

8. **(a)** The word *swallow* personifies the mirror and also indicates that the mirror takes in anything it sees without question. **(b)** The word contributes to the message that the mirror reflects the stark reality it takes in.

9. The medical terms describe involuntary phenomena that occur naturally without thinking, the way Hayden hopes freedom will occur for everyone.

10. Many older people do share the woman's attitude toward aging because of society's preoccupation with linking youth with good looks and usefulness.

ENRICHMENT: Further Reading

Other Works by the Authors

Works by Sylvia Plath
Ariel; The Bell Jar, "Daddy"

Works by Adrienne Rich
Dark Fields of the Republic: Poems 1991–1995; "Diving Into the Wreck"

Works by Gwendolyn Brooks
Bronzeville Boys and Girls; "The Bean Eaters"

Works by Robert Hayden
Angle of Ascent: New and Selected Poems; "Those Winter Sundays"

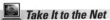 **Take It to the Net**
Visit www.phschool.com for more information on the authors.

❶ Vocabulary Development

Word Analysis

Students' poems should reflect knowledge of the precise meanings of the given words.

Spelling Strategy

Possible answers:

1. discover
2. preschool
3. redress
4. misconstrue

Fluency: Sentence Completion

1. meditate
2. preconceptions
3. din
4. wily

❷ Grammar and Style Lesson

1. The woman rewards the mirror's faithful accuracy with tears, tantrums, and depression.
2. High human voices are heard in one room, and the scream of nervous affairs is heard from another room.
3. There is no quiet or peace for the explorer.
4. The runagates escaped from slavery, some in coffins, some in carriages, some in silks, and some in shackles.
5. They saw the shadow of a face in the scary leaves and heard the shadow of a voice in the talking leaves.

Writing Application

Check to see that students have used parallel structure correctly.

Integrate Language Skills

❶ Vocabulary Development Lesson

Word Analysis: Latin Root -cep-/-cept-

The word *preconception*, like other English words such as *deception, inception, conception, concept, reception,* and *intercept,* derives from the Latin root *-cep-/-cept-,* meaning "to take, hold, or seize." Using these words, write a reflective poem about an experience you have had.

Spelling Strategy

A prefix added to a word does not affect the spelling of the original word. For example, when you add the prefix *pre-* to the word *conceptions,* you create *preconceptions.* Use the prefixes given with a word root you know to make new words.

1. *dis-*   3. *re-*
2. *pre-*   4. *mis-*

Fluency: Sentence Completion

Review the list of vocabulary words on page 1179. Then, select the word that best completes each sentence below.

1. The guru will ___?___ on the question I posed.

2. To keep the trial fair, the jurors had no ___?___ about the case.

3. The ___?___ of the machines was ear-splitting.

4. The raccoon is one of the most ___?___ of animals.

❷ Grammar and Style Lesson

Parallel Structure

Parallel structure is the expression of similar ideas in similar grammatical forms. Parallelism is especially helpful in poetry where it can add to the rhythm and sound of a poem. When writing, be careful to avoid faulty parallelism—the use of dissimilar grammatical structures to express similar ideas.

> **Example:** *when it is* truly instinct . . . / *when it is* finally won; *when it is* more / than the gaudy mumbo jumbo . . .

Practice Rewrite the following sentences using correct parallel structure.

1. The woman rewards the mirror's faithful accuracy with tears, tantrums, and getting depressed.

2. High human voices are heard in one room, and from another room comes the scream of nervous affairs.
3. There is no quiet place for the explorer and he's not finding any peace.
4. The runagates escaped from slavery, some in coffins, some in carriages, some in silks, and some were wearing shackles.
5. They saw the shadow of a face in the scary leaves and heard the shadow of a voice in the leaves that were talking.

Writing Application Write three sentences about a hero whose actions or attitudes you admire. In each sentence, use parallel structure to express your ideas eloquently.

WG *Prentice Hall Writing and Grammar Connection: Chapter 8, Section 4*

TEACHING RESOURCES

The following resources can be used to enrich or extend the instruction for pp. 1188–1189.

Vocabulary

📖 **Selection Support:** Build Vocabulary, p. 298

📖 **Vocabulary and Spelling Practice Book** (Use this booklet for skills enrichment.) ▪

Grammar

📖 **Selection Support:** Grammar and Style, p. 299

WG **Writing and Grammar,** Ruby Level, p. 154 ▪

📖 **Daily Language Practice Transparencies**

Writing

WG **Writing and Grammar,** Ruby Level, p. 311 ▪

💿 **Writing and Grammar iText CD-ROM**

Writing Models and Grapic Organizers on Transparencies, pp. 37–40

▪ **BLOCK SCHEDULING:** Resources marked with this symbol provide varied instruction during 90-minute blocks.

Writing Lesson

Literary Analysis

The purpose of a literary analysis is to show how various elements of a work of literature combine to convey an overall meaning or effect. Write a literary analysis of one of the poems you have just read.

Prewriting   Select a poem and read it several times, taking notes on how you will describe its overall effect or meaning. Gather examples of the poet's use of various elements such as imagery, personification, or metaphor to achieve this effect.

Drafting   Begin your analysis with a general statement about the poem and the points you will cover. Then, in a separate paragraph, support each point with examples and quotations from the poem. Conclude a well-phrased summary of your analysis.

Revising   Identify places in your draft at which you make important general statements about the poem. Strengthen your analysis by adding accurate quotations from the poem to support your interpretation.

Model: Using Quotations to Support Interpretation

Plath personifies the inanimate objects and contrasts them, giving them positive and negative human traits:
The mirror says, "I am not cruel, only truthful," but Plath adds, "Then she turns to those liars, the candles or the moon."

> Using direct quotations supports the interpretation of the poem.

 Prentice Hall Writing and Grammar Connection: Chapter 14, Section 4

Extension Activities

Listening and Speaking   With a group of classmates, stage a **debate** that answers these questions: What does freedom mean to you? Do you believe that everyone in present-day America is free? As you explore the issues raised by the questions, be sure to follow these rules:

- Allow each side to speak without interruption.
- Provide facts to support your ideas.

After both sides speak, give each one a chance for rebuttal. **[Group Activity]**

Research and Technology   In "Mirror," a woman is preoccupied with her appearance and upset at the signs of aging. With a partner, use magazine ads, song tracks, and oral commentary to create a **multimedia presentation** exploring our culture's emphasis on youth.

 Take It to the Net   www.phschool.com

Go online for an additional research activity using the Internet.

Mirror / In a Classroom / The Explorer / Frederick Douglass / Runagate Runagate ◆ 1189

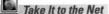

For My Children ✦ Bidwell Ghost

Lesson Objectives

1. **To analyze and respond to literary elements**
   - Literary Analysis: Lyric Poetry
   - Comparing Literary Works
2. **To read, comprehend, analyze, and critique poetry**
   - Reading Strategy: Reading in Sentences
   - Reading Check Questions
   - Review and Assess Questions
   - Assessment Practice (ATE)
3. **To develop word analysis skills, fluency, and systematic vocabulary**
   - Vocabulary Development Lesson: Related Words: *Heritage*
4. **To understand and apply written and oral language conventions**
   - Spelling Strategy
   - Grammar and Style Lesson: Sequence of Tenses
5. **To understand and apply appropriate writing and research strategies**
   - Writing Lesson: Ghost Story
   - Extension Activity: Multimedia-Cultural Presentation
6. **To understand and apply listening and speaking strategies**
   - Extension Activity: Dramatic Presentation

STEP-BY-STEP TEACHING GUIDE	PACING GUIDE
PRETEACH	
Motivate Students and Provide Background	
Use the Motivation activity (ATE p. 1190)	5 min.
Read and discuss author and background features (SE/ATE p. 1190) [A]	5 min.
Introduce the Concepts	
Introduce the Literary Analysis and Reading Strategy (SE/ATE p. 1191) [A]	15 min.
Pronounce the vocabulary words and read their definitions (SE p. 1191)	5 min.
TEACH	
Monitor Comprehension	
Informally monitor comprehension by circulating while students read independently or in groups [A]	15 min.
Monitor students' comprehension with the Reading Check notes (SE/ATE pp. 1193, 1195)	as students read
Develop vocabulary with Vocabulary notes (SE p. 1193; ATE p. 1193)	as students read
Develop Understanding	
Develop students' understanding of lyric poetry with the Literary Analysis annotations (ATE p. 1193) [A]	5 min.
Develop students' ability to read in sentences to understand the meaning of a poem by using the Reading Strategy annotations (ATE p. 1196)	5 min.
ASSESS	
Assess Mastery	
Assess students' mastery of the Reading Strategy and Literary Analysis by having them answer the Review and Assess questions (SE/ATE p. 1197)	15 min.
Use one or more of the print and media Assessment Resources (ATE p. 1199) [A]	up to 45 min.
EXTEND	
Apply Understanding	
Have students complete the Vocabulary Development Lesson and the Grammar and Style Lesson (SE p. 1198) [A]	20 min.
Apply students' ability to use sensory details in writing by using the Writing Lesson (SE/ATE p. 1199) [A]	45 min.
Apply students' understanding using one or more of the Extension Activities (SE p. 1199)	20–90 min.

[A] ACCELERATED INSTRUCTION:
Use the strategies and activities identified with an [A].

UNIVERSAL ACCESS
● = Below Level Students
▲ = On-Level Students
■ = Above Level Students

Time and Resource Manager

Reading Level: Average, Average
Average Number of Instructional Days: 2

PRINT	TRANSPARENCIES	TECHNOLOGY
• **Beyond Literature,** Cross-Curricular Connection: Geography, p. 70 ▲ ■		• **Interest Grabber Video,** Tape 6 ● ▲ ■
• **Selection Support Workbook:** ● ▲ ■ Literary Analysis, p. 305 Reading Strategy, p. 304 Build Vocabulary, p. 302	• **Literary Analysis and Reading Transparencies,** pp. 139 and 140 ● ▲ ■	
	Fine Art Transparencies, Volume 1, Art Transparency 11	• **Listening to Literature** ● ▲ ■ Audiocassettes, Side 40 Audio CDs, CD 23
• **Literatura en español** ● ▲ • **Literary Analysis for Enrichment** ■		
• **Formal Assessment:** Selection Test, p. 300 ● ▲ ■ • **Open Book Test,** p. 208 ● ▲ ■ • **Performance Assessment and Portfolio Management,** p. 15 ● ▲ ■ • **PRENTICE HALL ASSESSMENT SYSTEM** ● ▲ ■	• **PRENTICE HALL ASSESSMENT SYSTEM** ● ▲ ■ Skills Practice Answers and Explanations on Transparencies	• **Test Bank Software** ● ▲ ■ • **Got It! Assessment Videotapes,** Tape 6 ● ▲
• **Selection Support Workbook:** ● ▲ ■ Grammar and Style, p. 303 • **Writing and Grammar,** Ruby Level ● ▲ ■ • **Extension Activities,** p. 70 ● ▲ ■	• **Daily Language Practice Transparencies** ● ▲ • **Writing Models and Graphic Organizers on Transparencies,** p. 99 ● ▲ ■	• **Writing and Grammar iText CD-ROM** ● ▲ ■ **Take It to the Net** www.phschool.com

BLOCK SCHEDULING: Use one 90-minute class period to preteach the selection and have students read it. Use a second 90-minute class period to assess students' mastery of skills and have them complete one of the Extension Activities.

1190b

PRETEACH

Step-by-Step Teaching Guide for pp. 1190–1191

Motivation

How important is it that children learn about history and experiences of previous generations? In what ways can one generation help educate another when the world changes so drastically every year? Ask students to consider these questions and the ideas they would stress if they were to write a letter to the children of the future. What important lessons about life or what lessons from history would they want to convey? You might pair students to write the letters and then have the class compare their ideas with those expressed in McElroy's poem.

▣ Interest Grabber Video

As an alternative, play "Colleen McElroy" on Tape 6 to engage student interest.

❶ Background

More About the Authors

Colleen McElroy discovered her interest in the past and in stories as a young girl captivated by her grandmother's boudoir mirror and wind-up Victrola. Travel soon added a dimension to this "romance with language." It began during her childhood when she moved frequently with her mother and army sergeant stepfather, and continues to this day. Says McElroy about traveling and writing: "Each piece of writing is a new port of call, full of surprises and disappointments, pleasures and intrigue."

Louise Erdrich's experiences raising her five children have changed the way she writes. According to Erdrich, parenting has given her a perspective about the maturing process children begin and adults complete. She says that being a mother sometimes makes it hard to face the world's cruelties. A mother instinctively "protects the imagination against . . . [negative] intrusion."

Prepare to Read

❶ For My Children ◆ Bidwell Ghost

Colleen McElroy (b. 1935)

Like a modern-day explorer, Colleen McElroy enjoys experiencing new places and has traveled widely throughout the United States and abroad. This wandering spirit is reflected in many of her poems, which are inspired by people and scenes she has discovered during her travels. McElroy's love of travel has led her to embark on ancestral searches. Her many adventures on these searches have included island hopping in Fiji, exploring Malaysia, climbing Machu Picchu, and riding a motorcycle at age 58 across the Australian desert where she encountered aborigines. In her poetry, she often delves into her rich African American and Pacific Islander heritage to find connections between experiences of the past, realities of the present, and hopes for the future.

A Prolific Writer After growing up in St. Louis, Missouri, McElroy graduated from Kansas State University and earned a doctorate from the University of Washington, where she is now a professor of English. A prolific writer, she has published several collections of poetry, including *The Mules Done Long Since Gone* (1973), *Music from Home: Selected Poems* (1976), *Bone Flames* (1987), and *What Madness Brought Me Here* (1990). She has also published numerous short stories, as well as a travel memoir entitled *A Long Way from St. Louie* (1997).

She has received many awards and honors, including two fellowships from the National Endowment for the Arts, two Fulbright Creative Writing fellowships, a Jesse Ball DuPont Distinguished Black Scholar Fellowship, the Before Columbus American Book Award, and the Pushcart Prize.

In "For My Children," McElroy uses rich metaphors of her culture both past and present.

Louise Erdrich (b. 1954)

Louise Erdrich, whose Chippewa ancestry has shaped her identity, was born in Little Falls, Minnesota, the first of seven children. Her mother was of Chippewa and French descent, and her father was German American. Both of her parents were teachers at the Bureau of Indian Affairs school in Wahpeton, North Dakota, and they strongly encouraged Erdrich's storytelling skills.

A Writer's Education Erdrich entered Dartmouth College in 1972 as part of the school's first coeducational class. After receiving her undergraduate degree from Dartmouth, she taught poetry and writing to young people through a position at the State Arts Council of North Dakota. She then attended Johns Hopkins University, where she earned a master's degree in creative writing.

A Critically Acclaimed Writer Erdrich settled in central New Hampshire and published her first volume of poems, *Jacklight* (1984). Her debut novel, *Love Medicine* (1984), is the story of three Chippewa families living on a North Dakota reservation in the early part of the twentieth century. The novel, planned and written as part of a four-novel series set between 1912 and 1984, enjoyed great critical and commercial success. Erdrich's reputation grew with the publication of three sequels to the book, *The Beet Queen* (1986), *Tracks* (1988), and *The Bingo Palace* (1994). Her novel *The Antelope Wife* was published in 1998.

A Fruitful Career In 1989, Erdrich released a second volume of poetry, *Baptism of Fire*, and in 1991 she co-wrote *The Crown of Columbus*, which offers a Native American perspective of American historical events. Erdrich's most recent novel is *The Last Report on the Miracles at Little No Horse* (2001).

1190 ◆ *Prosperity and Protest (1946–Present)*

TEACHING RESOURCES

The following resources can be used to enrich or extend the instruction for pp. 1190–1191.

Motivation

▣ **Interest Grabber Video**, Tape 6

Background

📖 **Beyond Literature**, p. 70

💻 *Take It to the Net*
Visit www.phschool.com for Background and hotlinks for the selections.

Literary Analysis

📕 **Literary Analysis and Reading Transparencies**, Lyric Poetry, p. 140 ▣

Reading

📕 **Literary Analysis and Reading Transparencies**, Reading in Sentences, p. 139

📖 **Selection Support:** Reading Strategy, p. 304; Build Vocabulary, p. 302

 BLOCK SCHEDULING: Resources marked with this symbol provide varied instruction during 90-minute blocks.

Preview

Connecting to the Literature

The stories we hear from relatives, family friends, and neighbors help shape our awareness of our heritage. In different ways, both of these poems explore the mythic power of cultural heritage.

Literary Analysis

Lyric Poetry

Lyric poetry is melodic poetry that expresses the observations and feelings of a single speaker. Lyric poems were originally sung to the accompaniment of a stringed instrument called a lyre. Though rarely set to music today, lyric poems are still brief and melodic. Unlike narrative poems that tell stories, lyric poems focus on producing a single effect. In these lines from "Bidwell Ghost," for example, the speaker recalls vivid impressions of a fiery tragedy.

> It has been twenty years
>
> since her house surged and burst in the dark trees

As you read each poem, use a chart like the one shown to record the words and phrases that contribute to a single unifying effect.

Comparing Literary Works

Both of these poems speak about the past and its relation to the present. In "For My Children," the past is presented in a positive light, a pleasant place that holds a family's history. In "Bidwell Ghost," the past is seen in a terrifying light, as a dangerous place where the character experienced a great tragedy. Poets often use **flashbacks** to move back and forth in time. As you read, compare the use of this device to express the observations and feelings of a single speaker.

❸ Reading Strategy

Reading in Sentences

Like prose, many poems are written in sentences. They are also written in lines, but poets do not always complete sentences at the end of a line. Instead, a sentence may extend for several lines and then end in the middle of a line so that the poet can keep to a chosen rhythm and rhyme scheme. To understand the meaning of a poem, **read in sentences**. Notice the punctuation. Do not make a full stop at the end of a line unless there is a period, comma, colon, semicolon, or dash.

Vocabulary Development

shackles (shak´ əlz) *n.* restraints on freedom of expression or action (p. 1193)

heritage (her´ i tij´) *n.* something handed down from one's ancestors or from the past (p. 1193)

effigies (ef´ i jēz) *n.* likenesses; figures, such as dolls or statues (p. 1193)

For My Children / Bidwell Ghost ◆ 1191

---

❷ Literary Analysis

Lyric Poetry

- Tell students that as they read, they will focus on lyric poetry, in which words and phrases create a single unifying effect.

- After discussing the Literary Analysis instruction, have two volunteers read the poems aloud. Discuss each poet's use of vivid verbs such as *surged* and *burst* to create strong images.

- Model the use of the chart on the student page and direct students to complete a similar chart as they read the poems.

- Discuss the instruction under Comparing Literary Works. Guide students to understand how flashback provides information that contributes to the meaning of a lyric poem.

❸ Reading Strategy

Reading in Sentences

- Explain to students that reading in sentences helps readers better understand the meaning of a poem.

- Review with students the stops indicated by various types of punctuation. For example, a period indicates a longer pause than does a comma.

- Post the Reading in Sentences transparency, p. 143 in **Literary Analysis and Reading Transparencies**. Have volunteers read aloud the excerpts, first in lines and then in sentences. Discuss the differences in effect.

Vocabulary Development

- Pronounce each vocabulary word for students, and read the definitions as a class. Have students identify any words with which they are already familiar.

CUSTOMIZE INSTRUCTION FOR UNIVERSAL ACCESS

For Less Proficient Readers	For English Learners	For Advanced Readers
Students may find it difficult to capture a natural rhythm when reading poetry in sentences. To help them, read one or two stanzas of each poem aloud. Then, have students read aloud with you. If you wish, play **Listening to Literature**, Audiocassette 40 or Audio CD 23 to provide an additional reading model.	Before students can effectively read in sentences, they must clarify pronunciation and meaning of unfamiliar words. Preview the poems with students, modeling pronunciation of unfamiliar words. In particular, note the cultural references in "For My Children" and use the footnotes to inform your modeling.	Point out to students that poets sometimes use incomplete sentences. While this is technically incorrect, poets—and prose writers—may take liberties with grammar in order to create a particular effect. Challenge students to find examples of such poetic liberty and to analyze its effects.

 E-Teach

Visit E-Teach at www.phschool.com for teachers' essays on how to teach, with questions and answers.

Step-by-Step Teaching Guide
for pp. 1192–1196

CUSTOMIZE INSTRUCTION
For Intrapersonal Learners

Encourage students to respond to the poems by writing journal entries. Suggest that the entries take the form of poems based on their own cultural heritage or on stories that have been passed down to them.

❶ About the Selection

The speaker of "For My Children" searches for a heritage to share with her children, an African American heritage that extends "beyond St. Louis" all the way back "to Ashanti mysteries and rituals." As she delves into her store of tales, thoughts, and memories, she invokes many rich possibilities. She also discovers that the present and past are not as separate and discontinuous as they may seem—they mingle joyously in the children she observes.

❷ Background

Art

The Madonna and Child
by Momodou Ceesay

In this watercolor, contemporary artist Momodou Ceesay combines traditional elements of both African and European art. The effect is simultaneously tender and vibrant. The painting—filled with strong angles, vivid colors, and intense pattern repetition—pulses with life and contrast.

Use these questions for discussion:

1. How does the subject of the painting reflect the theme of the poem?
   Answer: The mother in the painting looks closely at the child, just as the speaker in the poem looks closely at her children to find links between the past and present.

2. How does the artist's use of color correspond to the images in the poem?
   Answer: The painting's vibrant colors appeal to the sense of sight; sensory images in the poem appeal to the sense of sight as well as hearing and touch.

❶

FOR MY CHILDREN
Colleen McElroy

❸ ▲ **Critical Viewing** In what ways does this painting reflect the heritage that the speaker seeks to hand on to her children? Explain. **[Analyze]**

1192 ◆ *Prosperity and Protest (1946–Present)*

TEACHING RESOURCES

The following resources can be used to enrich or extend the instruction for pp. 1192–1196.

Literary Analysis

📖 **Selection Support:** Literary Analysis, p. 305

Reading

🎧 **Listening to Literature Audiocassettes,** Side 40 ▪

💿 **Listening to Literature Audio CDs,** Side 23 ▪

Extension

📕 **Fine Art Transparencies, Volume 1,** Art Transparency 11 ▪

▪ **BLOCK SCHEDULING:** Resources marked with this symbol provide varied instruction during 90-minute blocks.

Background

In recent years, many Americans have become fascinated by oral history—the information gathered through interviews with individuals who can recall events and people of years past. Oral histories of families and communities are especially popular.

In societies without a written language, oral information that was passed down from one generation to the next took the place of written historical accounts. The speaker of "For My Children" is a collector of the oral history of her people. In telling this poem, she sifts through many facts and images of the past and passes on to the reader those she finds most striking.

I have stored up tales for you, my children
    My favorite children, my only children;
Of shackles and slaves and a bill of rights.
But skin of honey and beauty of ebony begins
5   In the land called Bilad as-Sudan,[1]
So I search for a heritage beyond St. Louis.

My memory floats down a long narrow hall,
    A calabash[2] of history.
Grandpa stood high in Watusi[3] shadows
10   In this land of yearly rituals for alabaster beauty;
Where effigies of my ancestors are captured
    In Beatle tunes,
And crowns never touch Bantu[4] heads.

My past is a slender dancer reflected briefly
15   Like a leopard in fingers of fire.
The future of Dahomey[5] is a house of 16 doors,
The totem of the Burundi[6] counts 17 warriors—
    In reverse generations.
While I cling to one stray Seminole.[7]

---

1. **Bilad as-Sudan** (bē läd´ äs sōō dan´) "land of the blacks," an Arabic expression by which Arab geographers referred to the settled African countries north of the southern edge of the Sahara.
2. **calabash** (kal´ ə bash´) *n.* dried, hollow shell of a gourd, used as a bowl or a cup.
3. **Watusi** (wä tōō´ sē) people of east-central Africa.
4. **Bantu** (ban´ tōō) Bantu-speaking peoples of southern Africa.
5. **Dahomey** (də hō´ mē) old name for Benin, in west-central Africa.
6. **Burundi** (boo rōon´ dē) country in east-central Africa.
7. **Seminole** (sem´ ə nōl´) Native American people from Florida.

The Madonna and Child 1990, Momodou Ceesay

shackles (shak´ əlz) *n.* restraints on freedom of expression or action

heritage (her´ i tij´) *n.* something handed down from one's ancestors or from the past

effigies (ef´ i jēz) *n.* likenesses; figures, such as dolls or statues

6 ✓**Reading Check**

What has the speaker stored up for her children?

For My Children ◆ 1193

---

3 ▶ **Critical Viewing**

Answer: The mother's traditional African clothing and the painting's stylized African landscape reflect the ancient African heritage McElroy describes.

4 **Vocabulary Development**

Related Words: *heritage*

- Call students' attention to the word *heritage* and its definition. Tell students that there are several words related to *heritage*.
- List the words presented in the Vocabulary Development Lesson on p. 1198: *heredity, inherit,* and *inheritance.* Have students suggest meanings for these words, using a dictionary if necessary.
- Invite students to write sentences using these words and the context of the two poems presented here.

5 **Literary Analysis**

Lyric Poetry

- Ask students to note details or allusions that they recognize in the bracketed stanza. List these on the chalk board.
  Possible responses: Students will likely recognize allusions to the Beatles and the Bantu and Watusi peoples.
- Lead students to see how the progression of images in the stanza contributes to a single effect, which illuminates the speaker's sense of her own history.
- Let students know that in Africa, the calabash gourd was dried and used as a container. The speaker compares her memory to such an ancestral gourd.
- Help students to interpret the remaining images and references, and summarize the stanza's effect. Students should note that the figure of the speaker's grandfather is pictured in a country celebrating "yearly rituals for alabaster beauty"—perhaps beauty pageants—and in which rock and roll tunes founded on black musical traditions make millions for white artists. The stanza closes with an image of purloined African royal crowns. The effect of the stanza is to evoke long years of exile and discrimination.

6 ✓**Reading Check**

Answer: She has stored up tales of their shared heritage.

Review and Assess

1. Urge students to generalize beyond the specific cultures mentioned in the poem.

2. (a) She addresses her children. **(b)** She wants to share stories of their heritage with them.

3. (a) She names the Watusi, Bantu, Seminole, Ashanti, and Ibo cultures. **(b)** The images suggest a grand and noble family, full of regal power. **(c)** Images include a house of 16 doors and a 17-warrior totem.

4. (a) She mentions the Mississippi and Congo rivers. **(b)** The Congo reflects the deep past and their African ancestry, while the Mississippi ties them to present-day America.

5. (a) The ancestral heritage of African Americans, with all its depth and grandeur, continues in current and future generations. **(b)** The speaker sees reflections of Africa—its physical landscape, art, and the beauty of its people—in the young children around her.

6. Possible responses: Children who are aware of their heritage can appreciate not only their own ancestral culture, but may also be more respectful of cultural diversity in general; they may be able to share their heritage with others; and they may develop more self-confidence.

---

20   My thoughts grow thin in the urge to travel
             Beyond Grandma's tale
      Of why cat fur is for kitten britches;
      Past the wrought-iron rail of first stairs
             In baby white shoes,
25   To Ashanti[8] mysteries and rituals.

      Back in the narrow hallway of my childhood.
             I cradled my knees
      In limbs as smooth and long as the neck of a bud vase,
      I began this ancestral search that you children yield now
30   In profile and bust
      By common invention, in being and belonging.

      The line of your cheeks recalls Ibo[9] melodies
             As surely as oboe and flute.
      The sun dances a honey and cocoa duet on your faces.
35   I see smiles that mirror schoolboy smiles
             In the land called Bilad as-Sudan;
      I see the link between the Mississippi and the Congo.

---

8. Ashanti (ə shän´ tə) people of western Africa.
9. Ibo (ē´ bō´) African people of southeastern Nigeria.

Review and Assess

Thinking About the Selection

1. **Respond:** Does this poem stir up thoughts about your own ancestors and cultural traditions? Why or why not?

2. **(a) Recall:** To whom does the speaker address this poem? **(b) Infer:** What is the speaker's reason for addressing the poem to them?

3. **(a) Recall:** Identify the cultures in which the speaker searches for evidence of her heritage. **(b) Analyze:** In the second and third stanzas, what impressions of her ancestors does the speaker convey? **(c) Analyze:** What images shape these impressions?

4. **(a) Recall:** Which two rivers does the speaker mention in the last stanza? **(b) Interpret:** Why might these two rivers be important to the speaker and to her children?

5. **(a) Interpret:** What is the poem's theme, or central message? **(b) Support:** What details or ideas in the poem support your interpretation?

6. **Apply:** In what specific ways might educating children about their heritage affect the choices they make in life?

1194 ◆ Prosperity and Protest (1946–Present)

✳ ENRICHMENT: Cultural Connection

Oral History

Oral history is as old as the study of history itself. As early as the fifth century B.C., the Greek historians Herodotus and Thucydides relied upon the oral accounts of survivors of wars to provide a basis for their written histories.

Among Native American cultures, such as the Chippewa from whom Louise Erdrich gains much of her identity, oral literature was the primary means of communicating the history and values of a people.

Oral literature includes oral histories, ritual drama, chanting, ceremonies, and songs, speeches, and narratives.

Today, interest in oral history has been advanced by the commitment of anthropologists, sociologists, historians, and artists who regard the oral tradition as a serious and vital part of all cultures.

BLOCK SCHEDULING: Resources marked with this symbol provide varied instruction during 90-minute blocks.

BIDWELL GHOST
Louise Erdrich

Winter, Ozz Franca

◀ Critical Viewing ❾
What features of this painting are reminiscent of phrases from the poem? Explain. **[Connect]**

Each night she waits by the road
in a thin white dress
embroidered with fire.

It has been twenty years
5   since her house surged and burst in the dark trees.
Still nobody goes there.

The heat charred the branches
of the apple trees,
but nothing can kill that wood.

✔Reading Check ❿
What is remarkable about the apple trees?

Bidwell Ghost ◆ 1195

---

❼ **About the Selection**

Like "For My Children," "Bidwell Ghost" is a multi-layered lyric poem that explores the effect of the past on the present. On one level, the poem presents a legend passed on to the poet and storyteller, who in turn passes it on to the reader. On another level, it probes the fate of a figure who is haunted and tormented by a tragic past.

❽ **Background**

Art

Winter by Ozz Franca

Like the Bidwell ghost, the figure in *Winter* emanates mystery and seems immersed in her own thoughts. The shadowy features give the figure an air of mystery. The red area adds warmth that could symbolize fire or blood.

Use these questions for discussion:

1. In what ways is the mood of this illustration similar to the mood of the poem?
   Answer: Both have dramatic, mysterious, and somber moods.

2. Does the illustration reflect the mental image you have of the Bidwell ghost? Explain.
   Possible response: The illustration mostly matches the image I formed while reading, however, the ghost in the poem wears a "thin white dress" while the figure in the illustration seems to be wrapped in a warm cloak.

❾ ▶ **Critical Viewing**

Answer: The woman in the painting appears to have a "blackened nest of hair," and the images of cold in the poem are reflected in her posture. Like the ghost, the woman in the painting stands alone, dressed in a white garment edged in flame-like color that suggests it has been "embroidered with fire."

❿ ✔**Reading Check**

Answer: They were charred by heat, but not killed.

⓫ Reading Strategy

Reading in Sentences

- Draw students' attention to the bracketed stanzas. Ask students how many sentences appear in these six lines.

  Answer: There are two sentences, each comprising one stanza.

- Ask students to read the stanzas as sentences, and note how Erdrich breaks the sentences into lines. What effect does this have on the reader?

  Answer: Students should note that Erdrich's line breaks work to divide the sentences into smaller units of meaning. This forces the reader to slow down and appreciate the solemnity of the account of the ghost.

Answers for p. 1196

Review and Assess

1. Students may have questions about the identity or history of the woman the poem describes.

2. **(a)** A house burned down. **(b)** A young woman was affected.

3. **(a)** She waits by the road for a ride to her old house. **(b)** Her behavior is strange, antisocial, and full of pain. **(c)** She might behave this way because she has been hurt by the loss of her home.

4. **(a)** They blossom. **(b)** It suggests that new life emerges despite crippling losses.

5. **(a)** The child is the ghost. **(b)** Erdrich uses this word to suggest that the ghost is vulnerable to pain and dependent on others.

6. Possible response: Ghosts are one way in which people deal with the mystery of death.

7. **(a)** She suggests that tragedy has an open-ended, permanent effect on people. **(b)** Students should be able to support their responses.

---

10 She will climb into your car
⓫   but not say where she is going
    and you shouldn't ask.

    Nor should you try to comb the blackened nest of hair
    or press the agates of tears
15 back into her eyes.

    First the orchard bowed low and complained
    of the unpicked fruit,
    then the branches cracked apart and fell.

    The windfalls sweetened to wine
20 beneath the ruined arms and snow.
    Each spring now, in the grass, buds form on the tattered wood.

    The child, the child, why is she so persistent
    in her need? Is it so terrible
    to be alone when the cold white blossoms
25 come to life and burn?

Review and Assess

Thinking About the Selection

1. **Respond:** What questions arose in your mind as you read this poem? Were they all answered? Explain.

2. **(a) Recall:** What occurred twenty years ago? **(b) Draw Conclusions:** Who or what was affected by that event?

3. **(a) Recall:** What does the Bidwell ghost do each night? **(b) Interpret:** How would you describe the Bidwell ghost's attitude or behavior? **(c) Speculate:** Why might the ghost feel or behave this way?

4. **(a) Recall:** What happens to the apple trees each spring? **(b) Analyze:** What does this image suggest about nature's resilience?

5. **(a) Analyze:** Who is "the child" in the final stanza? **(b) Speculate:** Why do you think the speaker uses this term?

6. **Speculate:** Why do you think people from so many cultures are fascinated with ghosts?

7. **(a) Interpret:** What does the poet suggest about the lasting impact of tragedy? **(b) Take a Position:** Do you agree with this idea? Explain.

✎ ASSESSMENT PRACTICE: Writing Skills

Identify Errors   **(For more practice, see Test Preparation Workbook, p. 73.)**

Many tests require students to identify the type of error in a written passage. Use the following sample test item to give students practice in this skill.

> Poets often use details of culture to add depth to their poems. The poem's details communicate its theme.

Read the passage and decide which type of error, if any, appears in the underlined section.

A Spelling error

B Capitalization error

C Punctuation error

D No error

Some students may choose *A*, thinking that *its* should have an apostrophe. Have a volunteer explain why this is not an error. Use this example to show students that some test items will contain no errors. D is the correct choice here.

█ BLOCK SCHEDULING: Resources marked with this symbol provide varied instruction during 90-minute blocks.

Review and Assess

Literary Analysis

Lyric Poetry

1. Describe, in your own words, the thoughts that the speaker expresses in the opening stanza of "For My Children."
2. In what way would you describe the "observations and feelings" the speaker expresses in "Bidwell Ghost"?
3. What is the single effect in (a) "For My Children" and (b) "Bidwell Ghost"?

Comparing Literary Works

4. In what ways are the Bidwell ghost and the apple trees alike?
5. Explain where the speaker's thoughts are "traveling" in the fourth stanza of "For My Children."
6. In "Bidwell Ghost," analyze the effect that the past has on the present. What connection can you find between the ghost and the people who see her? Use evidence from the poem for support.
7. Both "For My Children" and "Bidwell Ghost" consider the past as it affects the present. Does one of these poems seem more optimistic about the future? Explain.

Reading Strategy

Reading in Sentences

8. (a) By focusing on Louise Erdrich's use of punctuation, what do you notice about every stanza? (b) Why do you think Erdich chose to punctuate this poem as she did?
9. (a) Using a chart like the one shown, identify the figurative language in the last stanza of "For My Children." (b) Did reading the poem in sentences help you to understand the figurative language? Explain.

| Sentence 1 | ⋯▸ | Sentence 2 | ⋯▸ | Sentence 3 | ⋯▸ | **Interpretation** |

Extend Understanding

10. **Cultural Connection:** Could each poet's ancestral search be understood as a form of social protest? Explain.

For My Children / Bidwell Ghost ◆ 1197

Quick Review

Lyric poetry is melodic poetry that expresses the observations and feelings of a single speaker.

A **flashback** interrupts the chronological presentation of a narrative to relate an event of an earlier time.

To understand a poem's meaning, **read it in sentences,** pausing according to the punctuation rather than stopping automatically at the end of every line.

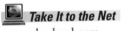 **Take It to the Net**
www.phschool.com
Take the interactive self-test online to check your understanding of these selections.

Answers for p. 1197
Review and Assess

1. The speaker would like to convey a heritage beyond that of slavery to her African American children.
2. The feelings reflect sadness, a sense of mystery, and helplessness.
3. **(a)** The single effect is inspirational. **(b)** The single effect is anguished.
4. They both return each spring.
5. They are traveling to her Ashanti heritage.
6. The past disturbs the present as the people who see the ghost recognize her pain but cannot help her.
7. Students will probably suggest that "For My Children" is more optimistic because it finds beauty and nobility in both the past and present.
8. **(a)** Most stanzas are complete sentences. **(b)** Possible response: The punctuation clarifies the separate images and gives the poem's mysterious events a sense of order.
9. **(a) Sentence 1:** The line of your cheek recalls Ibo melodies . . . ; **Sentence 2:** The sun dances . . . ; **Sentence 3:** Smiles mirror schoolboy smiles in the land of Bilad as-Sudan; **Interpretation:** A face is likened to music; the sun is personified; the children's smiles are likened to smiles of faraway children. **(b)** Reading in sentences makes it easier to isolate and understand the figurative language.
10. Possible response: "For My Children" could be read as a poem of social protest if the speaker feels that the country she lives in fails to acknowledge the power and dignity of her heritage.

✳ ENRICHMENT: Further Reading

Other Works by the Authors

Works by Colleen McElroy

Queen of the Ebony Isles

What Madness Brought Me Here: New and Selected Poems, 1968–1988

Driving Under the Cardboard Pines

Works by Louise Erdrich

Love Medicine

The Crown of Columbus

The Bingo Palace

 Take It to the Net
Visit www.phschool.com for more information on the authors.

Answers for p. 1198

❶ Vocabulary Development

Related Words

1. heredity
2. inheritance
3. heritage
4. inherit

Fluency: Synonyms

1. a
2. c
3. b

Spelling Strategy

1. memories
2. melodies
3. mysteries

❷ Grammar and Style

1. *waits*: present. The waiting takes place in the present.
2. *charred*: past. The charring was completed in the past.
3. *form*: present. The action of the buds' forming occurs in the present.
4. *come, burn*: present. All the action of the sentence is in the present tense.
5. *has wondered*: present-perfect. The action of this sentence started in the past and continues to the present.

Writing Application

Check to see that students have used the correct verb tense in the specified location.

Integrate Language Skills

❶ Vocabulary Development Lesson

Related Words: *heritage*

The word *heritage* means "something handed down from ancestors." It derives from the Latin word *heres*, meaning "heir," and usually refers more to cultural ideas, values, and tales than to objects or artifacts. Several English words, such as *heredity, inherit,* and *inheritance,* are related to this word. Use these four related words to complete the sentences below.

1. His slender physique is a result of ___?___.
2. The siblings' ___?___ included their uncle's prized collection of hand tools.
3. My twin cousins are very proud of their Scandinavian ___?___.
4. Children ___?___ physical characteristics from both parents.

❷ Grammar and Style Lesson

Sequence of Tenses

Using the correct **sequence of verb tenses** allows you to show the relationship of events in time. The *present tense* shows action that exists in the present. *The present-perfect tense* indicates something that began in the past and continues to the present. The *past tense* shows action that began and ended at a given time in the past.

Present: So I **search** for a heritage beyond St. Louis . . .

Present-Perfect: I **have stored** up tales for you . . .

Past: First the orchard **bowed** low and **complained** . . .

W̶G Prentice Hall Writing and Grammar Connection: Chapter 21, Section 2

1198 ◆ *Prosperity and Protest (1946–Present)*

Fluency: Synonyms

A synonym is a word that has a meaning similar to that of another word. Choose the best synonym for each of the first words.

1. effigies: (a) representations, (b) toys, (c) machines
2. shackles: (a) imprisoned, (b) worries, (c) chains
3. heritage: (a) folk art, (b) traditions, (c) society

Spelling Strategy

When forming the plural of a word that ends in a consonant plus *y*, change the *y* to *i* and add *es*. *Effigy* thus becomes *effigies*. Write the plural form of these words.

1. memory   2. melody   3. mystery

Practice Identify the tense of the italicized verbs in the following sentences, and then explain the relationship of events in time that the verbs express.

1. Each night she *waits* by the road.
2. The heat *charred* the branches of the trees.
3. Each spring now, in the grass, buds *form* on the tattered wood.
4. Is it so terrible to be alone when the cold white blossoms *come* to life and *burn*?
5. She *has wondered* about this all her life.

Writing Application Write three sentences about your own heritage. In the first sentence, use a verb in the present tense. In the second, use a verb in the present-perfect tense. In the third, use a verb in the past tense.

TEACHING RESOURCES

The following resources can be used to enrich or extend the instruction for pp. 1198–1199.

Vocabulary

📖 **Selection Support:** Build Vocabulary, p. 302

📖 **Vocabulary and Spelling Practice Book** (Use this booklet for skills enrichment.) 🖥

Grammar

📖 **Selection Support:** Grammar and Style, p. 303

W̶G **Writing and Grammar,** Ruby Level, p. 532 🖥

📱 **Daily Language Practice Transparencies**

Writing

W̶G **Writing and Grammar,** Ruby Level, p. 72

💿 **Writing and Grammar iText CD-ROM** 🖥

📱 **Writing Models and Graphic Organizers on Transparencies,** p. 99

📱 **BLOCK SCHEDULING:** Resources marked with this symbol provide varied instruction during 90-minute blocks.

Writing Lesson

Ghost Story

Ghost stories are common in Gothic fiction, folk literature, legends, and oral histories. Almost all ghost stories contain an element of mystery and eeriness; some also feature a noticeable air of humor or melancholy. Write a ghost story based on "The Bidwell Ghost."

Prewriting Reread the poem and take notes about the characteristics of the Bidwell ghost. Use a chart like the one shown to organize the poem's sensory details into categories. Then, decide which elements will best convey an aura of mystery.

Model: Categorizing Sensory Details

Sight	Hearing	Touch	Taste	Smell

Drafting Grab your audience's interest from the start with a vivid description of the setting or a description of an eerie event. As you develop your story, focus on building suspense by including descriptions, events, or hints that raise questions for readers. Be sure to answer most questions by the story's end.

Revising Read your story several times, both silently and aloud. Revise it to make it more suspenseful, adding or deleting as needed.

 Prentice Hall Writing and Grammar Connection: Chapter 5, Section 3

Extension Activities

Listening and Speaking Think of a tale or legend that you remember from childhood—or create one yourself—and share it in a **dramatic presentation.** Follow this procedure:

- Prepare by writing the story down and rehearsing your delivery without notes.
- When you practice the story, speak with emotion.
- Use pacing and gestures to heighten the story's suspense or interest level.

After you have practiced, give the presentation to the class.

Research and Technology In a small group, research and deliver a short **multimedia cultural presentation** about one of the African cultures mentioned in "For My Children"—Watusi, Bantu, Dahomey, Burundi, Ashanti, or Ibo. Describe the culture, and include posters, photographs, art, and music to present the culture in an interesting way. **[Group Activity]**

 Take It to the Net www.phschool.com

Go online for an additional research activity using the Internet.

---

❸ Writing Lesson

- Have students explore their associations with *ghosts* by creating a cluster diagram with the word *ghost* in the center.
- Refer students to the Story Map organizer, in **Writing Models and Graphic Organizers on Transparencies**, p. 99, to help them plan their stories.
- Review the Writing Lesson to guide students in developing their story.
- Use the Short Story rubric in **Performance Assessment and Portfolio Management**, p. 15 to evaluate students' stories.

❹ Research and Technology

- Make sure that all the listed cultures are assigned to at least one group of students. For groups focusing on the same culture, suggest divergent focal points for research.
- Discuss potential research sources, such as web sites for universities with African Studies programs.
- Invite students to present their reports as part of a cultural heritage festival.
- Use the Multimedia Presentation rubric in **Performance Assessment and Portfolio Management**, p. 13, to assess student presentations.

CUSTOMIZE INSTRUCTION
For Universal Access

To address different learning styles, use the following activities suggested in the Extension Activities booklet, p. 70.

For Verbal/Linguistic and Visual/Spatial Learners, use Activity 5.

For Verbal/Linguistic and Logical/Mathematical Learners, use Activity 6.

For Musical/Rhythmic and Bodily/Kinesthetic Learners, use Activity 7.

ASSESSMENT RESOURCES

The following resources can be used to assess students' knowledge and skills.

Selection Assessment

- 📖 **Formal Assessment,** p. 300
- 📖 **Open Book Test,** p. 208
- 📼 **Got It! Assessment Videotapes,** Tape 6
- 💿 **Test Bank Software**
- *Take It to the Net*
  Visit www.phschool.com for self-tests and additional questions on the selections.

Writing Rubric

- **Performance Assess. and Portfolio Mgmt.,** p. 15
- **Performance Assess. and Portfolio Mgmt.,** p. 13

PRENTICE HALL **ASSESSMENT** *SYSTEM*

- **Workbook**
- **Skill Book**
- **Transparencies**
- **CD-ROM**

The Writer in the Family

Lesson Objectives

1. **To analyze and respond to literary elements**
   - Literary Analysis: Static and Dynamic Characters
   - Connecting Literary Elements: Cultural Context

2. **To read, comprehend, analyze, and critique a short story**
   - Reading Strategy: Judging Characters' Actions
   - Reading Check questions
   - Review and Assess questions

3. **To develop word analysis skills, fluency, and systematic vocabulary**
   - Vocabulary Development Lesson: Greek Suffix: -itis

4. **To understand and apply written and oral language conventions**
   - Spelling Strategy
   - Grammar and Style Lesson: Commonly Confused Words: *affect* and *effect*
   - Assessment Practice (ATE)

5. **To understand and apply appropriate writing and research strategies**
   - Writing Lesson: Advice Column
   - Extension Activity: Costume Proposal

6. **To understand and apply listening and speaking strategies**
   - Extension Activity: Eulogy

STEP-BY-STEP TEACHING GUIDE	PACING GUIDE
PRETEACH	
Motivate Students and Provide Background	
Use the Motivation activity (ATE p. 1200)	5 min.
Read and discuss author and background features (SE/ATE pp. 1200, 1202) **A**	10 min.
Introduce the Concepts	
Introduce the Literary Analysis and Reading Strategy (SE/ATE p. 1201) **A**	15 min.
Pronounce the vocabulary words and read their definitions (SE p. 1201)	5 min.
TEACH	
Monitor Comprehension	
Informally monitor comprehension by circulating while students read independently or in groups **A**	35 min.
Monitor students' comprehension with the Reading Check notes (SE/ATE pp. 1205, 1207, 1209, 1211, 1213)	as students read
Develop vocabulary with Vocabulary notes (SE pp.1202, 1204, 1207; ATE p. 1202)	as students read
Develop Understanding	
Develop students' understanding of static and dynamic characters with the Literary Analysis annotations (SE pp. 1205, 1208, 1209, 1211, 1212; ATE pp. 1205, 1208, 1209,1211, 1213) **A**	5 min.
Develop students' ability to judge characters' actions by using the Reading Strategy annotations (SE pp. 1204, 1206, 1207; ATE pp. 1204, 1206, 1207)	5 min.
ASSESS	
Assess Mastery	
Assess students' mastery of the Reading Strategy and Literary Analysis by having them answer the Review and Assess questions (SE/ATE p. 1215)	15 min.
Use one or more of the print and media Assessment Resources (ATE p. 1217) **A**	up to 45 min.
EXTEND	
Apply Understanding	
Have students complete the Vocabulary Development Lesson and the Grammar and Style Lesson (SE p. 1216) **A**	20 min.
Apply students' ability to elaborate to support an argument by using the Writing Lesson (SE/ATE p. 1217) **A**	45 min.
Apply students' understanding using one or more of the Extension Activities (SE p. 1217)	20–90 min.

 ACCELERATED INSTRUCTION:
Use the strategies and activities identified with an **A**.

UNIVERSAL ACCESS
- ● = Below Level Students
- ▲ = On-Level Students
- ■ = Above Level Students

1200a

Time and Resource Manager

RESOURCES		
PRINT 📖	**TRANSPARENCIES** 🎴	**TECHNOLOGY** 💿 🎧
• **Beyond Literature,** Cultural Connection: Rituals of Mourning, p. 71 ▲ ■		• **Interest Grabber Video,** Tape 6 ● ▲ ■
• **Selection Support Workbook:** ● ▲ ■ Literary Analysis, p. 309 Reading Strategy, p. 308 Build Vocabulary, p. 306	• **Literary Analysis and Reading Transparencies,** pp. 141 and 142 ● ▲ ■	
		• **Listening to Literature** ● ▲ ■ Audiocassettes, Side 40 Audio CDs, CD 23
• **Literatura en español** ● ▲ • **Literary Analysis for Enrichment** ■		
• **Formal Assessment:** Selection Test, pp. 303–305 ● ▲ ■ • **Performance Assessment and Portfolio Management,** p. 10 ● ▲ ■ • **PRENTICE HALL** ASSESSMENT *SYSTEM* ● ▲ ■	• **PRENTICE HALL** ASSESSMENT *SYSTEM* ● ▲ ■ Skills Practice Answers and Explanations on Transparencies	• **Test Bank Software** ● ▲ ■ • **Got It! Assessment Videotapes,** Tape 6 ● ▲
• **Selection Support Workbook:** ● ▲ ■ Grammar and Style, p. 307 • **Writing and Grammar,** Ruby Level ● ▲ ■ • **Extension Activities,** p. 71 ● ▲ ■	• **Daily Language Practice Transparencies** ● ▲ • **Writing Models and Graphic Organizers on Transparencies,** p. 79 ● ▲ ■	• **Writing and Grammar iText CD-ROM** ● ▲ ■ 💻 *Take It to the Net* www.phschool.com

BLOCK SCHEDULING: Use one 90-minute class period to preteach the selection and have students read it. Use a second 90-minute class period to assess students' mastery of skills and have them complete one of the Extension Activities.

Motivation

Ask students to picture this situation: A young man whose father has recently died is asked by a family member to write a letter in his father's name, making it seem as though the father is still alive. Then, ask: What might be the purpose of such a letter? Will the young man refuse or comply? You might take an informal poll to ask students what they would do in a similar situation. After students have made their guesses and predictions, invite them to begin reading to learn the answers to these questions.

▭ Interest Grabber Video

As an alternative, play "Stages of Grief" on Tape 6 to engage student interest.

❶ Background

More About the Author

Running through much of Doctorow's work are themes about the individual struggling against corporate or government pressures. Doctorow saw the individual as outnumbered in twentieth–century society. While the young man in this story faces family rather than institutional pressures, he too struggles to follow his individual values.

Doctorow received many awards for his fiction, including the National Book Award (*Ragtime*), the American Book Award (*World's Fair*), and the PEN/Faulkner Award (*Billy Bathgate*).

Prepare to Read

❶ The Writer in the Family

E. L. Doctorow (b. 1931)

The literary work of Edgar Lawrence Doctorow defies strict categorization. It is distinguished by a unique and authoritative blend of fact and fiction—sometimes called "faction," a term first coined to describe Doctorow's work. Doctorow has always been fascinated by the political unrest, social rootlessness, and constant motion of his time; his literary experimentation, which pushes the limits of style, form, and content, both responds to and reflects an era brimming with contradiction and irony.

Early Years The son of a record store owner, Doctorow attended the respected Bronx High School of Science. He later studied philosophy and drama, which perhaps gave Doctorow a sense of staging and an understanding of character.

Rising to a Challenge As a reader for Columbia Pictures, Doctorow was dismayed at the inferior scripts he read. Certain he could create better stories, he began writing. In his first novel, *Welcome to Hard Times* (1960), Doctorow focused on stretching the boundaries of fiction set in the Old West by addressing serious themes of a kind not usually treated in such literature. During these early professional years, Doctorow combined writing with a successful career in book publishing. Editing the works of landmark authors such as Norman Mailer and James Baldwin added literary knowledge and versatility to Doctorow's own talents. He continued writing, producing novels, short stories, essays, plays, and screen adaptations that exhibit the same type of inventiveness demonstrated in his first novel.

Mixing Fact and Fiction Doctorow frequently incorporates fact and fiction into his writing to create powerful dramatic effects. *The Book of Daniel* (1971), for example, weaves factual details about Ethel and Julius Rosenberg—communists found guilty of treason and sentenced to die—into a story centering on the lives of fictional children parted from their parents amid political scandal.

Similarly Doctorow's 1975 novel, *Ragtime*, blends fictional characters with the invented and real experiences of historical figures such as Harry Houdini and J. P. Morgan. In his later books, including *In Loon Lake* (1980), *Waterworks* (1994), and *City of God* (2000), Doctrow continued his experimentations with narrative structure and content.

Acclaim and Success Unlike the work of many other experimental writers, Doctorow's books are crowd-pleasers. He does not sacrifice the elements of entertainment for the sake of aesthetic experiment. His books remain readable, rich, and enjoyable even as they challenge accepted ideas about the nature of literature. Perhaps this is the reason Doctorow has enjoyed both critical and popular success. He has won two National Book Critic Circle Awards, one for *Ragtime* and another for *Billy Bathgate* (1989). His memoir *World's Fair* (1986) won the American Book Award. Four of his novels have been made into major motion pictures, and a successful adaptation of *Ragtime* opened on Broadway in 1998.

The Creative Process As a best-selling novelist and professor of English at New York University, Doctorow has often spoken about fiction writing. In a 1990 lecture at the New York Public Library, he said of the creative process, "The writer sits alone in a room creating alternate worlds. . . . He does not just give the intellect, but the whole being of [a] character." Doctorow's short story "The Writer in the Family" gives additional insight into this remark: It is written from the point of view of a young writer who must invent his own father as a fictional character.

TEACHING RESOURCES

The following resources can be used to enrich or extend the instruction for pp. 1200–1201.

Motivation

▭ **Interest Grabber Video**, Tape 6 ▪

Background

▭ **Beyond Literature**, p. 71

▭ **Take It to the Net**
Visit www.phschool.com for background and hotlinks for "A Writer in the Family."

Literary Analysis

▭ **Literary Analysis and Reading Transparencies,** Static and Dynamic Characters, p.142

▭ **Selection Support:** Literary Analysis, p. 309

Reading

▭ **Literary Analysis and Reading Transparencies,** Judging Characters' Actions, p. 141 ▪

▭ **BLOCK SCHEDULING:** Resources marked with this symbol provide varied instruction during 90-minute blocks.

Preview

Connecting to the Literature

One of the most difficult aspects of life is coping with the loss of loved ones. In this story, the characters deal with such a loss in a complicated way that will probably surprise you.

Literary Analysis
Static and Dynamic Characters

Doctorow uses static and dynamic characters to create a heightened sense of contrast in his story.

- A **static character** is one whose attitudes and behavior remain essentially stable throughout a literary work.
- **Dynamic characters** experience a shift or change in attitude and behavior during the course of a work.

As you read "The Writer in the Family," organize a character list like the one shown, identifying each of the characters as either static or dynamic. Consider how the contrasts between these character types add to the story's impact.

Connecting Literary Elements

Characters arise in part from their **cultural context,** the economic and social environment that they inhabit. In this story, that context is the Bronx, a borough of New York City that includes a community of recent Jewish immigrants and their descendants. Set in the 1950s, the story focuses on a family for which "the journey . . . from the working class to the professional class" is the central goal. As you read, notice how the cultural context influences the characters' goals, aspirations, and values. Consider the impact that the aspirations of parents have on the lives of their children.

Reading Strategy
Judging Characters' Actions

The characters in this story bend the rules relating to a pivotal event in their lives—the death of a family member. Think about how you would behave if faced with similar circumstances. When you **judge the characters' actions,** you evaluate their behavior against moral or other criteria. While reading the story, consider the actions of each character. Then, decide whether or not you find them morally defensible.

Vocabulary Development

bronchitis (brän kīt′ is) *n.* inflammation of the lining of the major air passageways of the lungs (p. 1202)

cronies (krō′ nēz) *n.* close companions (p. 1202)

barometer (bə räm′ ət ər) *n.* instrument for measuring atmospheric pressure (p. 1204)

anthology (an thäl′ ə jē) *n.* collection of poems, stories, and so on (p. 1207)

Character

⋮

Condition at End of Story

⋮

Dynamic or Static?

The Writer in the Family ◆ 1201

---

❷ Literary Analysis
Static and Dynamic Characters

- Tell students that as they read "The Writer in the Family," they will focus on static (unchanging) and dynamic (evolving) characters. Read the instruction about static and dynamic characters aloud. Discuss examples of each character type from stories students have recently read.

- Use the Connecting Literary Elements instruction to point out that understanding cultural context will help students recognize the pressures for change experienced by Doctorow's characters.

- Note the chart on p.1201and model its use. Direct students to use it while reading in order to label characters as either static or dynamic.

❸ Reading Strategy
Judging Characters' Actions

- Remind students that judging characters' actions requires readers to enter the story situation, and thus engage in active reading.

- To judge characters' actions, readers must develop a set of standards. They should, however, judge in light of the circumstances of the story.

- Urge students to recall their knowledge of human behavior in judging characters' actions.

Vocabulary Development

- Pronounce each vocabulary word for students, and read the definitions as a class. Have students identify any words with which they are already familiar.

CUSTOMIZE INSTRUCTION FOR UNIVERSAL ACCESS

For Less Proficient Readers	For English Learners	For Advanced Readers
To help students better understand the story's characters, have them list the following family members: Jonathan, Ruth, Aunt Frances, Harold, and Jack. Tell students to take notes on what they learn about each character. These notes can help them decide whether each character is static or dynamic.	Give students clue words to help them remember the meanings of *static* and *dynamic.* For example, they might replace *static* with "no change" and *dynamic* with "change." As they evaluate characters for static or dynamic qualities, tell students to ask themselves "Has this character changed since the story began?"	Explain that there are a number of conflicts, both internal and external, in the story. Have students make a list of these conflicts and consider how each affects the development (or lack of development) of the characters.

 E-Teach

Visit E-Teach at www.phschool.com for teachers' essays on how to teach, with questions and answers.

Step-by-Step Teaching Guide for pp. 1202–1214

CUSTOMIZE INSTRUCTION
For Intrapersonal Learners

Have students reflect on the narrator's perceptions, motives, and actions. Encourage them to write a journal entry in which they both speculate about why Jonathan acts as he does and assess the ethics of his actions.

❶ About the Selection

This story raises a thorny question: Which is more important, loyalty or integrity? The relatives of a young man named Jonathan come up with an unusual scheme for maintaining the status quo within the family: They ask Jonathan to write a series of letters in the voice of his recently deceased father. The letters relieve the relatives of the difficult task of telling Jonathan's grandmother that her son has died. Jonathan goes along with the scheme until he realizes that the high value his family places on the status quo was a burden on his late father. By choosing integrity over loyalty, Jonathan makes a declaration of independence, both on his own and on his father's behalf.

❷ Vocabulary Development

The Greek Suffix -itis

- Draw students' attention to the word *bronchitis* and to its definition.

- Explain to students that the word includes the Greek suffix *-itis*, meaning "disease" or "inflammation." Tell them that *bronch* relates to *bronchus*, any of the major air passageways of the lungs.

- Invite students to brainstorm from a list of other diseases or conditions they know of that end with the suffix *-itis*.

---

❶ The Writer in the Family

E. L. Doctorow

Background

Most cultures have unique mourning rituals. For Jews, that ritual is called "shi'va." After a death, the family observes shi'va for seven days, during which time the mourners follow certain traditional rules. They remain at home and do not conduct business. Mirrors are covered, and comfortable furniture is exchanged for seating on low stools or the floor. Men and women neither shave nor cut their hair. Mourners do not wear new clothing or leather footwear. Traditionally, friends and fellow mourners join the family in their home to express sympathy and recite prayers. In "The Writer in the Family," the shi'va's ritual acknowledgment of death contrasts sharply with the pretense at the story's center.

---

❷ In 1955 my father died with his ancient mother still alive in a nursing home. The old lady was ninety and hadn't even known he was ill. Thinking the shock might kill her, my aunts told her that he had moved to Arizona for his bronchitis. To the immigrant generation of my grandmother, Arizona was the American equivalent of the Alps, it was where you went for your health. More accurately, it was where you went if you had the money. Since my father had failed in all the business enterprises of his life, this was the aspect of the news my grandmother dwelled on, that he had finally had some success. And so it came about that as we mourned him at home in our stocking feet,[1] my grandmother was bragging to her cronies about her son's new life in the dry air of the desert.

My aunts had decided on their course of action without consulting us. It meant neither my mother nor my brother nor I could visit Grandma because we were supposed to have moved west too, a family, after all. My brother Harold and I didn't mind—it was

bronchitis (brän΄ kit΄ is) *n.* inflammation of the lining of the major air passageways of the lungs

cronies (krō΄ nēz) *n.* close companions

---

1. **as we mourned . . . in our stocking feet** refers to the Jewish custom of not wearing leather footwear during the traditional mourning period known as shi'va.

1202 ◆ *Prosperity and Protest (1946–Present)*

TEACHING RESOURCES

The following resources can be used to enrich or extend the instruction for pp.1202–1214.

Literary Analysis

📄 **Writing Models and Graphic Organizers on Transparencies**, p. 79

Reading

📖 **Selection Support:** Reading Strategy, p. 308; Build Vocabulary, p. 306

🎧 **Listening to Literature Audiocassettes**, Side 40 ■

💿 **Listening to Literature Audio CDs**, CD 23 ■

■ **BLOCK SCHEDULING:** Resources marked with this symbol provide varied instruction during 90-minute blocks.

Laurence Typing, 1952, Fairfield Porter, Oil on canvas 40" x 30 1/8", The Parrish Art Museum, Southampton, New York, Gift of the Estate of Fairfield Porter

❹ ▲ **Critical Viewing** How might the boy in this picture use the familiar surroundings to help him concoct a believable letter? **[Connect]**

The Writer in the Family ◆ 1203

❸ ## Background

Art

Laurence Typing, by Fairfield Porter

This piece shows a young man typing in a homey setting. Both his surroundings and the typewriter suggest the 1950s—the time in which the story is set.

American artist Fairfield Porter (1907–1975) was born in Winnetka, Illinois. The subjects of his paintings are those he knows best—himself, his family, his friends, and the landscapes that surrounded him. The young man in the picture is the artist's son Laurence, who was born in 1936.

Use these questions for discussion:

1. What do the details in the picture tell you about the young man?
   Answer: He looks as if he is thinking hard about what he is typing. The books on the desk suggest that he is interested in intellectual pursuits.

2. What traits do you think the young man in the painting might share with the story's narrator?
   Answer: Traits might include seriousness, introspection, a good imagination, and a gift for writing.

❹ ▶ **Critical Viewing**

Answer: Students should note that in his letter, the narrator did an excellent job of imagining how his father would respond to and describe Arizona. They may therefore conclude that he would use the familiar surroundings in the room as the basis for comparisons in his letter.

CUSTOMIZE INSTRUCTION FOR UNIVERSAL ACCESS

For English Learners	For Special Needs Students	For Gifted/Talented Students
Help these students engage in the story by orienting them immediately to the central conflict. After students read the first paragraph, ask them these questions: Do you approve of the aunt's motives in not informing their mother about the death? Do you think this is the right thing to do? Why or why not?	Point out the word *cronies*, which the narrator uses to describe his grandmother's friends. Have students look up the word in a thesaurus to find synonyms for it. Guide them in grouping these synonyms into those with positive, negative, and neutral connotations.	Have students read the story's opening paragraph and identify its central conflict. Then, direct them to the Writing Lesson on p. 1217. After they read it, challenge students to take notes for such an advice column as they read. Urge them to think about the gray areas of the conflict. In other words, is there an absolute right or wrong?

- After students read the bracketed passage, guide them in identifying the aunts' actions.
  Answer: The aunts have decided to conceal Jack's death without consulting Jack's widow or children. Aunt Frances asks Jonathan to write letters to support the fiction of Jack's move.

- Ask students the Reading Strategy question on p. 1204: Which of the aunts' actions are controlling or manipulative? Explain.
  Answer: So far, all of the aunts' actions—concealing Jack's death, having Jonathan write letters as Jack, excluding Jack's widow from decisions—are manipulative and controlling.

always a nightmare at the old people's home, where they all sat around staring at us while we tried to make conversation with Grandma. She looked terrible, had numbers of ailments, and her mind wandered. Not seeing her was no disappointment either for my mother, who had never gotten along with the old woman and did not visit when she could have. But what was disturbing was that my aunts had acted in the manner of that side of the family of making government on everyone's behalf, the true citizens by blood and the lesser citizens by marriage. It was exactly this attitude that had tormented my mother all her married life. She claimed Jack's family had never accepted her. She had battled them for twenty-five years as an outsider.

⑤ A few weeks after the end of our ritual mourning my Aunt Frances phoned us from her home in Larchmont. Aunt Frances was the wealthier of my father's sisters. Her husband was a lawyer, and both her sons were at Amherst.[2] She had called to say that Grandma was asking why she didn't hear from Jack. I had answered the phone. "You're the writer in the family," my aunt said. "Your father had so much faith in you. Would you mind making up something? Send it to me and I'll read it to her. She won't know the difference."

That evening, at the kitchen table, I pushed my homework aside and composed a letter. I tried to imagine my father's response to his new life. He had never been west. He had never traveled anywhere. In his generation the great journey was from the working class to the professional class. He hadn't managed that either. But he loved New York, where he had been born and lived all his life, and he was always discovering new things about it. He especially loved the old parts of the city below Canal Street, where he would find ships' chandlers or firms that wholesaled in spices and teas. He was a salesman for an appliance jobber[3] with accounts all over the city. He liked to bring home rare cheeses or exotic foreign vegetables that were sold only in certain neighborhoods. Once he brought home a barometer, another time an antique ship's telescope in a wooden case with a brass snap.

"Dear Mama," I wrote. "Arizona is beautiful. The sun shines all day and the air is warm and I feel better then I have in years. The desert is not as barren as you would expect, but filled with wildflowers and cactus plants and peculiar crooked trees that look like men holding their arms out. You can see great distances in whatever direction you turn and to the west is a range of mountains maybe fifty miles from here, but in the morning with the sun on them you can see the snow on their crests."

My aunt called some days later and told me it was when she read this letter aloud to the old lady that the full effect of Jack's death came over her. She had to excuse herself and went out in the parking lot to cry. "I wept so," she said. "I felt such terrible longing for him. You're so right, he loved to go places, he loved life, he loved everything."

barometer (bə räm′ ət ər) n. instrument for measuring atmospheric pressure

2. **Amherst** Amherst College in Amherst, Massachusetts.
3. **jobber** industry jargon for a person who buys goods in quantity from manufacturers and sells them to dealers; a wholesaler or middleman.

⚜ ENRICHMENT: Math Connection

Trip Planner

In the story that Aunt Frances told her mother, Jack, Ruth, Harold, and Jonathan relocate to Arizona. Although today people can fly from New York to Arizona in several hours, in the 1950s, the trip would have been made by car, and it would have taken about a week. Have students compare the trip with one taken today. Would the same amount of time be needed? How much would such a trip cost? Have students map out a road trip for a family of four between New York and Phoenix. Ask them to work out an itinerary that takes into consideration where the family will eat, where they will stop for the night, and where they will get gasoline. Then, have students figure out the cost of such a trip. Students can also find out the mileage and cost of airplane tickets for four people from New York to Phoenix. Is it more economical for a family of four to drive or to fly to Phoenix today? Ask students to share their findings with the class.

We began trying to organize our lives. My father had borrowed money against his insurance and there was very little left. Some commissions were still due but it didn't look as if his firm would honor them. There was a couple of thousand dollars in a savings bank that had to be maintained there until the estate was settled. The lawyer involved was Aunt Frances' husband and he was very proper. "The estate!" my mother muttered, gesturing as if to pull out her hair. "The estate!" She applied for a job part-time in the admissions office of the hospital where my father's terminal illness had been diagnosed, and where he had spent some months until they had sent him home to die. She knew a lot of the doctors and staff and she had learned "from bitter experience," as she told them, about the hospital routine. She was hired.

I hated that hospital, it was dark and grim and full of tortured people. I thought it was masochistic[4] of my mother to seek out a job there, but did not tell her so.

We lived in an apartment on the corner of 175th Street and the Grand Concourse, one flight up. Three rooms. I shared the bedroom with my brother. It was jammed with furniture because when my father had required a hospital bed in the last weeks of his illness we had moved some of the living-room pieces into the bedroom and made over the living room for him. We had to navigate bookcases, beds, a gateleg table, bureaus, a record player and radio console, stacks of 78 albums, my brother's trombone and music stand, and so on. My mother continued to sleep on the convertible sofa in the living room that had been their bed before his illness. The two rooms were connected by a narrow hall made even narrower by bookcases along the wall. Off the hall were a small kitchen and dinette and a bathroom. There were lots of appliances in the kitchen—broiler, toaster, pressure cooker, counter-top dishwasher, blender—that my father had gotten through his job, at cost. A treasured phrase in our house: *at cost.* But most of these fixtures went unused because my mother did not care for them. Chromium devices with timers or gauges that required the reading of elaborate instructions were not for her. They

---

4. **masochistic** (mas´ ə kis´ tik) *adj.* deriving pleasure from physical or psychological pain.

Literary Analysis
Static and Dynamic Characters and Cultural Context What does this passage tell you about the cultural context of the speaker's family life?

❼ ✓Reading Check
How did the family manage financially after the father died?

The Writer in the Family ◆ 1205

❻ Literary Analysis
Static and Dynamic Characters and Cultural Context

- Invite a volunteer to read aloud the bracketed passage as students listen and visualize.
- Ask students the Literary Analysis question on p. 1205: What does this passage tell you about the cultural context of the speaker's family life?
  Possible response: It shows that both frugality and amassing symbols of success are valued. At the same time, Jonathan's mother clearly feels ambivalent about the focus on both economic success and frugality, rejecting items acquired for their status or appearance if they are not actually useful to her.

▶ Monitor Progress Have students name some key details in the setting that highlight the cultural context.

❼ ✓Reading Check
Answer: The narrator's mother takes a job in the hospital where her husband had died.

CUSTOMIZE INSTRUCTION FOR UNIVERSAL ACCESS

For Special Needs Students	For Less Proficient Readers	For English Learners
Give students an alternative method for understanding the cultural context around Jonathan's character. You might use photographs to show students apartments similar to Jack's or invite students to draw the setting as you read the bracketed passage from p. 1205 aloud.	To help students keep track of character development, have them summarize the narrator's role so far in the letter-writing scheme. Point out that the narrator went along with his aunt's unusual request. This suggests that while he is imaginative, he is also timid and obedient.	Review the bracketed passage on p. 1205 with students. Discuss unfamiliar words or phrases that could keep students from accurately visualizing the cultural context. For example, you might explain that an apartment *one flight up* is on the second floor.

Judging Characters' Actions

- Call on three volunteers to role-play the bracketed scene. Invite students to discuss and describe Mother's reaction.
  Answer: She is angry because Aunt Frances will not acknowledge Jack's death, thus controlling his life even after his death.

- Ask students the Reading Strategy question on p. 1206: Do you sympathize with Mother for her reaction? Why or why not?
  Answer: Most students will say that Mother's reaction is understandable. She is entitled to decide how her husband's death will be handled, and she is entitled to live truthfully, to grieve openly, and to try to move forward with her life. Aunt Frances's deception is preventing this.

▶Critical Viewing

The dress and hair styles as well as the somewhat formal postures and facial expressions place this photo in a time past.

were in part responsible for the awful clutter of our lives and now she wanted to get rid of them. "We're being buried," she said. "Who needs them!"

So we agreed to throw out or sell anything inessential. While I found boxes for the appliances and my brother tied the boxes with twine, my mother opened my father's closet and took out his clothes. He had several suits because as a salesman he needed to look his best. My mother wanted us to try on his suits to see which of them could be altered and used. My brother refused to try them on. I tried on one jacket which was too large for me. The lining inside the sleeves chilled my arms and the vaguest scent of my father's being came to me.

"This is way too big," I said.

"Don't worry," my mother said. "I had it cleaned. Would I let you wear it if I hadn't?"

It was the evening, the end of winter, and snow was coming down on the windowsill and melting as it settled. The ceiling bulb glared on a pile of my father's suits and trousers on hangers flung across the bed in the shape of a dead man. We refused to try on anything more, and my mother began to cry.

"What are you crying for?" my brother shouted. "You wanted to get rid of things, didn't you?"

A few weeks later my aunt phoned again and said she thought it would be necessary to have another letter from Jack. Grandma had fallen out of her chair and bruised herself and was very depressed.

"How long does this go on?" my mother said.

"It's not so terrible," my aunt said, "for the little time left to make things easier for her."

My mother slammed down the phone. "He can't even die when he wants to!" she cried. "Even death comes second to Mama! What are they afraid of, the shock will kill her? Nothing can kill her. She's indestructible! A stake through the heart couldn't kill her!"

When I sat down in the kitchen to write the letter I found it more difficult than the first one. "Don't watch me," I said to my brother. "It's hard enough."

▲ Critical Viewing
What details of clothing and mannerism place this photo in a time past?
[Analyze]

Reading Strategy
Judging the Characters' Actions Do you sympathize with Mother for her reaction? Why or why not?

"You don't have to do something just because someone wants you to," Harold said. He was two years older than me and had started at City College; but when my father became ill he had switched to night school and gotten a job in a record store.

"Dear Mama," I wrote. "I hope you're feeling well. We're all fit as a fiddle. The life here is good and the people are very friendly and informal. Nobody wears suits and ties here. Just a pair of slacks and a short-sleeved shirt. Perhaps a sweater in the evening. I have bought into a very successful radio and record business and I'm doing very well. You remember Jack's Electric, my old place on Forty-third Street? Well, now it's Jack's Arizona Electric and we have a line of television sets as well."

I sent that letter off to my Aunt Frances, and as we all knew she would, she phoned soon after. My brother held his hand over the mouthpiece. "It's Frances with her latest review," he said.

"Jonathan? You're a very talented young man. I just wanted to tell you what a blessing your letter was. Her whole face lit up when I read the part about Jack's store. That would be an excellent way to continue."

"Well, I hope I don't have to do this anymore, Aunt Frances. It's not very honest."

Her tone changed. "Is your mother there? Let me talk to her."

"She's not here," I said.

"Tell her not to worry," my aunt said. "A poor old lady who has never wished anything but the best for her will soon die."

I did not repeat this to my mother, for whom it would have been one more in the family <u>anthology</u> of unforgivable remarks. But then I had to suffer it myself for the possible truth it might embody. Each side defended its position with rhetoric, but I, who wanted peace, rationalized the snubs and rebuffs each inflicted on the other, taking no stands, like my father himself. Years ago his life had fallen into a pattern of business failures and missed opportunities. The great debate between his family on one side, and my mother Ruth on the other, was this: who was responsible for the fact that he had not lived up to anyone's expectations?

As to the prophecies, when spring came my mother's prevailed. Grandma was still alive.

One balmy Sunday my mother and brother and I took the bus to the Beth El cemetery in New Jersey to visit my father's grave. It was situated on a slight rise. We stood looking over rolling fields embedded with monuments. Here and there processions of black cars wound their way through the lanes, or clusters of people stood at open graves. My father's grave was planted with tiny shoots of evergreen but it lacked a headstone. We had chosen one and paid for it and then the stonecutters had gone on strike. Without a headstone my father did not seem to me to be honorably dead. He didn't seem to me properly buried.

My mother gazed at the plot beside his, reserved for her coffin. "They were always too fine for other people," she said. "Even in the old days on Stanton Street. They put on airs. Nobody was ever good enough for

Reading Strategy
Judging the Characters' Actions Do you agree with the narrator's statement that the letter-writing is dishonest? Why or why not?

anthology (an thäl´ ə jē) *n.* collection of poems, stories, and so on

**Reading Check** ⑩
In what way does the narrator deal with his aunt's inconsiderate remarks?

Judging Characters' Actions
- Read the bracketed passage aloud to students. Encourage them to monitor their emotional reactions as they listen.
- Ask students the Reading Strategy question on p. 1207: Do you agree with the narrator's statement that the letterwriting is dishonest? Why or why not?
Possible answers: Some students may say that the letter writing is both dishonest and wrong. Others may say that it is dishonest but not really wrong because it would be a painful blow for the old woman to find out that her son had died.

❿ ✔Reading Check
Answer: He refuses to repeat them to his mother.

CUSTOMIZE INSTRUCTION FOR UNIVERSAL ACCESS

For English Learners	For Less Proficient Readers	For Advanced Readers
Have students reread Jonathan's second letter on p. 1206. Point out the several sentence fragments in the letter. Explain that Jonathan has tried to give his father's letter an intimate, friendly tone, almost as if Jack were sitting there speaking to his mother. The sentence fragments add to this informal chatty feeling.	Draw students' attention to Jonathan's second letter on p. 1206. Explain that the phrase *fit as a fiddle* is a figure of speech that has been in use since the early 1600s. No one knows for sure its literal origins or meaning, but it has come to mean "feeling good."	Encourage students to point out how Jonathan uses his letter to "remake" his father. For example, Jack always wore suits and ties, and now Jonathan has him wearing slacks and short-sleeved shirts. Also, his businesses were unsuccessful, but Jack's Arizona Electric is very successful.

❶❶ Background

Art

Letters and Postcards
by Reid Christman

In this piece of art, letters and everyday objects add up to suggest a life story. Use this question for discussion:

How might Grandma add to the collection of objects in this piece of art? What would her additions suggest about her reaction to their contents?
Possible answers: She might post the letters from "Jack." Adding these letters to a collection of important mementos suggests Grandma's excitement over Jack's "success."

❶❷ ▶ Critical Viewing

Answer: A person who saves letters probably thinks of the contents as part of a personal history. Such a person might disapprove of the narrator because he is attempting to rewrite history.

❶❸ Literary Analysis

Static and Dynamic Characters

• Direct students to read the bracketed passage and then explain what Jonathan feels guilty about.
Answer: He feels guilty because he didn't want to be around his father when he was ill, and because he doesn't feel right about concealing his father's death.

• Ask students the Literary Analysis question on p. 1209: Judging by Jonathan's guilty reaction, would you say he is a static or a dynamic character?
Possible answer: Students may say that Jonathan is a dynamic character. Guilt over his past actions will probably cause him to change in the future.

them. Finally Jack himself was not good enough for them. Except to get them things wholesale. Then he was good enough for them."

"Mom, please," my brother said.

"If I had known. Before I ever met him he was tied to his mama's apron strings. And Essie's apron strings were like chains, let me tell you. We had to live where we could be near them for the Sunday visits. Every Sunday, that was my life, a visit to mamaleh. Whatever she knew I wanted, a better apartment, a stick of furniture, a summer camp for the boys, she spoke against it. You know your father, every decision had to be considered and reconsidered. And nothing changed. Nothing ever changed."

She began to cry. We sat her down on a nearby bench. My brother walked off and read the names on stones. I looked at my mother, who was crying, and I went off after my brother.

"Mom's still crying," I said. "Shouldn't we do something?"

"It's all right," he said. "It's what she came here for."

"Yes," I said, and then a sob escaped from my throat. "But I feel like crying too."

My brother Harold put his arm around me. "Look at this old black stone here," he said. "The way it's carved. You can see the changing fashion in monuments—just like everything else."

Somewhere in this time I began dreaming of my father. Not the robust father of my childhood, the handsome man with healthy pink skin and brown eyes and a mustache and the thinning hair parted in the middle. My dead father. We were taking him home from the hospital. It was understood that he had come back from death. This was amazing and joyous. On the other hand, he was terribly mysteriously damaged, or, more accurately, spoiled and unclean. He was very yellowed and debilitated by his death, and there were no guarantees that he wouldn't soon die again. He seemed aware of this and his entire personality was changed. He was angry and impatient with all of us. We were trying to help him in some way, struggling to get him home, but something prevented us, something we had to fix, a tattered suitcase that had sprung open, some mechanical thing: he had a car but it wouldn't start; or the car was made of wood; or his clothes, which had become too large for him, had caught in the door. In one version he was all bandaged and as we tried to lift him from his wheelchair into a taxi the bandage began to unroll and catch in the spokes of the wheelchair. This seemed to be some unreasonableness on his part. My mother looked on sadly and tried to get him to cooperate.

That was the dream. I shared it with no one. Once when I woke, crying out, my brother turned on the light. He wanted to know what I'd been dreaming but I pretended I didn't remember. The dream made me feel guilty. I felt guilty in the dream too because my enraged father knew we didn't want to live with him. The dream represented us taking him home, or trying to, but it was nevertheless understood by all of us that he was to live alone. He was this derelict back from death, but what we were doing was taking him to some place where he would live by himself without help from anyone until he died again.

At one point I became so fearful of this dream that I tried not to go to sleep. I tried to think of good things about my father and to remember him before his illness. He used to call me "matey." "Hello, matey," he would say when he came home from work. He always wanted us to go someplace—to the store, to the park, to a ball game. He loved to walk. When I went walking with him he would say: "Hold your shoulders back, don't slump. Hold your head up and look at the world. Walk as if you meant it!" As he strode down the street his shoulders moved from side to side, as if he was hearing some kind of cakewalk. He moved with a bounce. He was always eager to see what was around the corner.

The next request for a letter coincided with a special occasion in the house. My brother Harold had met a girl he liked and had gone out with her several times. Now she was coming to our house for dinner. We had prepared for this for days, cleaning everything in sight, giving the house a going-over, washing the dust of disuse from the glasses and good dishes. My mother came home early from work to get the dinner going. We opened the gateleg table in the living room and brought in the kitchen chairs. My mother spread the table with a laundered white cloth and put out her silver. It was the first family occasion since my father's illness.

I liked my brother's girlfriend a lot. She was a thin girl with very straight hair and she had a terrific smile. Her presence seemed to excite the air. It was amazing to have a living breathing girl in our house. She looked around and what she said was: "Oh, I've never seen so many books!" While she and my brother sat at the table my mother was in the kitchen putting the food into serving bowls and I was going from the kitchen to the living room, kidding around like a waiter, with a white cloth over my arm and a high style of service, placing the serving dish of green beans on the table with a flourish. In the kitchen my mother's eyes were sparkling. She looked at me and nodded and mimed the words: "She's adorable!"

My brother suffered himself to be waited on. He was wary of what we might say. He kept glancing at the girl—her name was Susan—to see if we met with her approval. She worked in an insurance office and was taking courses in accounting at City College. Harold was under a terrible strain but he was excited and happy too. He had bought a bottle of Concord-grape wine to go with the roast chicken. He held up his glass and proposed a toast. My mother said: "To good health and happiness,"

Literary Analysis
Static and Dynamic Characters Judging by Jonathan's guilty reaction would you say he is a static or a dynamic character?

Literary Analysis
Static and Dynamic Characters and Cultural Context What does this passage reveal about the family's cultural context?

15 ✓**Reading Check**
What recurring dream does the narrator experience?

⓮ Literary Analysis
Static and Dynamic Characters and Cultural Context

- Have a volunteer read the bracketed passage aloud. Then, ask students to describe how the narrator and his mother feel about meeting Harold's girlfriend.
  Answer: They are excited and want to make a good impression on the girlfriend.

- Ask students the second Literary Analysis question on p. 1209: What does this passage reveal about the family's cultural context?
  Answer: The family considers meeting Harold's girlfriend an important event, and possibly a precursor to marriage. Also, they have fine things that they care for well and wish to share with those they hold dear.

⓯ ✓Reading Check

Answer: He dreams that his father comes back from the dead but is "mysteriously damaged."

CUSTOMIZE INSTRUCTION FOR UNIVERSAL ACCESS

For Less Proficient Readers

Students who have trouble seeing the difference between static and dynamic characters may be helped by a visual demonstration. Draw the visual shown here on the board. Ask students which character each pair of figures represents. They should realize that Aunt Frances is static, while Jonathan is dynamic.

| deceitful | → | deceitful |

Static

| deceitful | → | honest |

Dynamic

CUNY (City University of New York) now comprises 20 campuses in New York's five boroughs. Ranging from Hunter College, which joined in 1870, to Medgar Evers College, which joined in 1968, the CUNY campuses offer more than 900 programs to its 200,000 students. In addition, some 150,000 New Yorkers participate in adult or continuing education programs. Prominent Americans such as Secretary of State Colin Powell graduated from the CUNY system.

and we all drank, even I. At that moment the phone rang and I went into the bedroom to get it.

"Jonathan? This is your Aunt Frances. How is everyone?"

"Fine, thank you."

"I want to ask one last favor of you. I need a letter from Jack. Your grandma's very ill. Do you think you can?"

"Who is it?" my mother called from the living room.

"OK, Aunt Frances," I said quickly. "I have to go now, we're eating dinner." And I hung up the phone.

"It was my friend Louie," I said, sitting back down. "He didn't know the math pages to review."

The dinner was very fine. Harold and Susan washed the dishes and by the time they were done my mother and I had folded up the gateleg table and put it back against the wall and I had swept the crumbs up with the carpet sweeper. We all sat and talked and listened to records for a while and then my brother took Susan home. The evening had gone very well.

Once when my mother wasn't home my brother had pointed out something: the letters from Jack weren't really necessary. "What is this ritual?" he said, holding his palms up. "Grandma is almost totally blind, she's half deaf and crippled. Does the situation really call for a literary composition? Does it need verisimilitude? Would the old lady know the difference if she was read the phone book?"

"Then why did Aunt Frances ask me?"

"That is the question, Jonathan. Why did she? After all, she could write the letter herself—what difference would it make? And if not Frances, why not Frances' sons, the Amherst students? They should have learned by now to write."

"But they're not Jack's sons," I said.

"That's exactly the point," my brother said. "The idea is *service.* Dad used to break his back getting them things wholesale, getting them deals on things. Frances of Westchester really needed things at cost. And Aunt Molly. And Aunt Molly's husband, and Aunt Molly's ex-husband. Grandma, if she needed an errand done. He was always on the hook for something. They never thought his time was important. They never thought every favor he got was one he had to pay back. Appliances, records, watches, china, opera tickets, . . . anything. Call Jack."

"It was a matter of pride to him to be able to do things for them," I said. "To have connections."

"Yeah, I wonder why," my brother said. He looked out the window.

Then suddenly it dawned on me that I was being implicated.

"You should use your head more," my brother said.

Higher Education

The City College that Harold and hi girlfriend attend revolutionized higher education for both immigrant and working-class New York families. An outgrowth of the Free Academy founded in 1847, City College proclaimed a mission to "let the children of the rich and poor take seats together. . . ." Low tuition costs made it possible for upwardly mobile students like Harold to gain the education they needed for access to the professional class. Today, a much larger CUNY (City University of New York) carries forth founder Townsend Harris's legacy to educate immigrant students from 145 countries, along with ethnically diverse native New Yorkers.

✹ ENRICHMENT: Cultural Connection

Passover

Aunt Frances tells Jonathan that she would invite him and his family for Passover if she thought his mother would accept the invitation. An eight-day festival, Passover is a Jewish celebration of freedom. It commemorates the angel of death "passing over" the homes of Israelites during a plague, and the subsequent flight of the Israelites from slavery in Egypt. The date of Passover varies, but it usually falls in March or April; it begins on the fifteenth day of the Hebrew month of Nisan.

Invite students with a Jewish background to explain more about Passover and the Seder—the ceremonial meal that families hold during the holiday period.

Yet I had agreed once again to write a letter from the desert and so I did. I mailed it off to Aunt Frances. A few days later, when I came home from school, I thought I saw her sitting in her car in front of our house. She drove a black Buick Roadmaster, a very large clean car with whitewall tires. It was Aunt Frances all right. She blew the horn when she saw me. I went over and leaned in at the window.

"Hello, Jonathan," she said. "I haven't long. Can you get in the car?"

"Mom's not home," I said. "She's working."

"I know that. I came to talk to you."

"Would you like to come upstairs?"

"I can't, I have to get back to Larchmont. Can you get in for a moment, please?"

I got in the car. My Aunt Frances was a very pretty white-haired woman, very elegant, and she wore tasteful clothes. I had always liked her and from the time I was a child she had enjoyed pointing out to everyone that I looked more like her son than Jack's. She wore white gloves and held the steering wheel and looked straight ahead as she talked, as if the car was in traffic and not sitting at the curb.

"Jonathan," she said, "there is your letter on the seat. Needless to say I didn't read it to Grandma. I'm giving it back to you and I won't ever say a word to anyone. This is just between us. I never expected cruelty from you. I never thought you were capable of doing something so deliberately cruel and perverse."

I said nothing.

"Your mother has very bitter feelings and now I see she has poisoned you with them. She has always resented the family. She is a very strong-willed, selfish person."

"No she isn't," I said.

"I wouldn't expect you to agree. She drove poor Jack crazy with her demands. She always had the highest aspirations and he could never fulfill them to her satisfaction. When he still had his store he kept your mother's brother . . . on salary. After the war when he began to make a little money he had to buy Ruth a mink jacket because she was so desperate to have one. He had debts to pay but she wanted a mink. He was a very special person, my brother, he should have accomplished something special, but he loved your mother and devoted his life to her. And all she ever thought about was keeping up with the Joneses."

I watched the traffic going up the Grand Concourse. A bunch of kids were waiting at the bus stop at the corner. They had put their books on the ground and were horsing around.

"I'm sorry I have to descend to this," Aunt Frances said. "I don't like talking about people this way. If I have nothing good to say about someone, I'd rather not say anything. How is Harold?"

"Fine."

"Did he help you write this marvelous letter?"

"No."

Literary Analysis
Static and Dynamic Characters In what ways do Aunt Frances's comments reveal that she is a static character?

Reading Check
Why does Aunt Frances return Jonathan's letter?

The Writer in the Family ◆ 1211

⓱ Literary Analysis

Static and Dynamic Characters

- Have students read the bracketed passage and rephrase Aunt Frances's comments in their own words.
- Then, ask students the Literary Analysis question on p. 1211: In what ways do Aunt Frances's comments reveal that she is a static character?
  Possible response: Aunt Frances's comments reveal that she has never questioned her decisions or actions—this shows that she is a static character. Her beliefs about how to handle Jack's death have not changed, nor have her views of Ruth.

▶ **Monitor Progress** Display the organizer from p. 1201, and have students complete it with information about Aunt Frances.

⓲ ✔Reading Check

Answer: She is unhappy because it reveals Jack's death.

CUSTOMIZE INSTRUCTION FOR UNIVERSAL ACCESS

For Advanced Readers

Point out to students that there is a great deal of irony in the conversation that Aunt Frances has with Jonathan. Discuss with students some examples of this irony: 1) Aunt Frances says that Jonathan's mother is strong-willed and selfish. However, Aunt Frances has also shown herself to be strong-willed and selfish; 2) Aunt Frances lists all the demands that Jonathan's mother made on Jack. It has been revealed, however, that Aunt Frances and her mother made many demands on Jack; 3) Aunt Frances refers to the "marvelous" letter, but the reader knows that she means the letter is anything but marvelous; 4) Aunt Frances says that she would invite the narrator's family for Passover if she thought that his mother would accept the invitation. However, it is likely that Aunt Frances does not extend the invitation because she does not accept them as part of the family and is making her point by not inviting them.

⑲ ▶ Critical Viewing

Answer: Students might say that in Aunt Frances's eyes, the car's sleek surface and modern style are signs of success.

After a moment she said more softly: "How are you all getting along?"

"Fine."

"I would invite you up for Passover if I thought your mother would accept."

I didn't answer.

She turned on the engine. "I'll say good-bye now, Jonathan. Take your letter. I hope you give some time to thinking about what you've done."

That evening when my mother came home from work I saw that she wasn't as pretty as my Aunt Frances. I usually thought my mother was a good-looking woman, but I saw now that she was too heavy and that her hair was undistinguished.

"Why are you looking at me?" she said.

"I'm not."

"I learned something interesting today," my mother said. "We may be eligible for a V.A. pension because of the time your father spent in the Navy."

That took me by surprise. Nobody had ever told me my father was in the Navy. "In World War I," she said, "he went to Webb's Naval Academy on the Harlem River. He was training to be an ensign. But the war ended and he never got his commission."

After dinner the three of us went through the closets looking for my father's papers, hoping to find some proof that could be filed with the Veterans Administration. We came up with two things, a Victory medal, which my brother said everyone got for being in the service during the Great War, and an astounding sepia photograph of my father and his shipmates on the deck of a ship. They were dressed in bell-bottoms and T-shirts and armed with mops and pails, brooms and brushes.

"I never knew this," I found myself saying.

"I never knew this."

"You just don't remember," my brother said.

I was able to pick out my father. He stood at the end of the row, a thin, handsome boy with a full head of hair, a mustache, and an intelligent smiling countenance. . . .

Neither the picture nor the medal was proof of anything, but my brother thought a duplicate of my father's service record had to be in Washington somewhere and that it was just a matter of learning how to go about finding it.

"The pension wouldn't amount to much," my mother said. "Twenty or thirty dollars. But it would certainly help."

I took the picture of my father and his shipmates and propped it against the lamp at my bedside. I looked into his youthful face and tried

▼ Critical Viewing
Affluent Aunt Frances drives a Buick Roadmaster like the one shown here. Judging from this image, why might she have chosen such a car? **[Connect]**

ENRICHMENT: Literature Connection

Great Sea Novels

Jonathan refers to his father's collection of Great Sea Novels. He states that the collection contains books by "Melville, Conrad, Victor Hugo, and Captain Marryat." Discuss what students know about each author. Share the following information:

• Herman Melville (1819–1891): an American author who worked on merchant ships and whalers; best known for novels of the sea such as *Moby-Dick* and *Billy Budd*.

• Joseph Conrad (1857–1924): a writer who was born in Poland but wrote in English and who spent much of his life on the sea. Two of his most famous novels are *Heart of Darkness* and *Lord Jim*.

• Frederick Marryat (1792–1848): an English novelist and naval officer who used his experiences at sea in his books; two of his novels are *Peter Simple* and *Mr. Midshipman Easy*.

to relate it to the Father I knew. I looked at the picture a long time. Only gradually did my eye connect it to the set of *Great Sea Novels* in the bottom shelf of the bookcase a few feet away. My father had given that set to me: it was uniformly bound in green with gilt lettering and it included works by Melville, Conrad, Victor Hugo and Captain Marryat. And lying across the top of the books, jammed in under the sagging shelf above, was his old ship's telescope in its wooden case with the brass snap.

I thought how stupid, and imperceptive, and self-centered I had been never to have understood while he was alive what my father's dream for his life had been.

Literary Analysis
Static and Dynamic Characters In what ways has Jonathan changed since the story's opening scene?

✔ **Reading Check** ㉑

What new information does Jonathan learn about his father's life?

⑳ Literary Analysis
Static and Dynamic Characters

- Direct students to read the bracketed passage at least twice. Have them consider it as they review the story in their minds.
- Ask a volunteer to read aloud the Literary Analysis question on p. 1212: In what ways has Jonathan changed since the story's opening scene?
  Possible response: At the beginning of the story, Jonathan has a tendency to try to please others, particularly his Aunt Frances. By the end of the story, he realizes that some things are more important, namely, being true to oneself and acting on one's beliefs. Also, Jonathan has learned a great deal about who his father really was.

㉑ ✔ Reading Check
Answer: He learns that his father was in the Navy during World War I, and that he received a medal for his service.

CUSTOMIZE INSTRUCTION FOR UNIVERSAL ACCESS

For Less Proficient Readers	For Advanced Readers
Help students see the significance of the final paragraph of the letter. Point out that in it, Jonathan pays tribute to his father's love of the sea. Emphasize that this tribute reflects the ways Jonathan's knowledge of his father has grown during the story.	Ask students what the *Great Sea Novels* collection suggests about Jack. Elicit from students that the book list suggests that Jonathan's late father liked adventure. Ironically, the story suggests that he didn't have a great deal of adventure in his life. Challenge students to locate other details in the story that suggest the character's love of adventure.

Answers for p. 1214

Review and Assess

1. Students should support their responses with details from the story.

2. **(a)** He has died. **(b)** She is told that he has moved to Arizona for health reasons. **(c)** Jonathan's aunts think that learning of her son's death will kill her.

3. **(a)** The aunts decide that Jonathan's grandmother should not be told of her son's death. Instead, Jonathan will write letters in his voice. **(b)** She is willing to be deceitful to protect her mother's feelings.

4. **(a)** He agrees to write the letters. **(b)** She feels the letters are an extension of the control under which she and her husband had lived. **(c)** They suggest that she values honesty and independence.

5. **(a)** His brother helps him to see that Frances is forcing him to do something he may not want to do; he sees that his father was frequently in the same situation. **(b)** His change suggests a message to Frances that she can no longer control Jack's family. **(c)** Possible answer: Jonathan will learn to make his own decisions rather than bow to pressure.

6. Students should support their responses with references to film, literature, or life experience.

7. Accept all well-supported answers.

On the other hand, I had written in my last letter from Arizona—the one that had so angered Aunt Frances—something that might allow me, the writer in the family, to soften my judgment of myself. I will conclude by giving the letter here in its entirety.

Dear Mama,
   This will be my final letter to you since I have been told by the doctors that I am dying.
   I have sold my store at a very fine profit and am sending Frances a check for five thousand dollars to be deposited in your account. My present to you, Mamaleh. Let Frances show you the passbook.
   As for the nature of my ailment, the doctors haven't told me what it is, but I know that I am simply dying of the wrong life. I should never have come to the desert. It wasn't the place for me. I have asked Ruth and the boys to have my body cremated and the ashes scattered in the ocean.
      Your loving son,
      Jack

Review and Assess

Thinking About the Selection

1. **Respond:** What did you find admirable or disappointing about the narrator?

2. **(a) Recall:** What has happened to Jonathan's father? **(b) Recall:** What is Jonathan's grandmother told about his father? **(c) Interpret:** What might happen to the grandmother if she were told the truth?

3. **(a) Recall:** What key decision is made about communicating with the narrator's grandmother? **(b) Analyze:** What does Aunt Frances's desire to conceal Jack's situation from their mother reveal about her character?

4. **(a) Recall:** What does Jonathan do to help his Aunt Frances with her plan? **(b) Infer:** How does Jonathan's mother feel about deceiving Grandma? **(c) Interpret:** What do these feelings suggest about her?

5. **(a) Interpret:** Why does Jonathan ultimately change his mind about what he is doing? **(b) Generalize:** What message does his change suggest? **(c) Hypothesize:** How do you think Jonathan will apply this insight to his life?

6. **Evaluate:** Do you think Doctorow's portrayal of a family in mourning is realistic? Explain.

7. **Take a Position:** How would you have responded had you been asked to write such letters? Explain.

✎ ASSESSMENT PRACTICE: Writing Skills

Grammar and Usage   **(For more practice, see Test Preparation Workbook, p. 74)**

Many tests require students to recognize and correct errors in grammar and usage. Use the following sample item to help students practice this skill.

   E.L. Doctorow has written numerous novels. Four of them <u>are made</u> into major motion pictures.

   Choose the best way to rewrite the underlined section of the passage. If the underlined section needs no change, choose "Correct as is."

A have been made   **C** could be made
B had been made   **D** Correct as is.

   The best way to rewrite the underlined section is to rewrite it for consistent verb tense. The correct answer is *A*.

Review and Assess

Literary Analysis

Static and Dynamic Characters

1. (a) Is Jonathan a **dynamic character**? (b) Cite three examples from the story to support your answer.
2. From the narrator's view, is the father a **static** or a **dynamic character**? Explain.
3. Identify Aunt Frances as either a static or a dynamic character. Support your answer.

Connecting Literary Elements

4. Use the **cultural context** of Jack's family to explain why Aunt Frances chooses Arizona as the fictional place for Jack's move.
5. (a) What cultural rituals and values bind the family together? (b) Which one divides them?
6. In what ways does the cultural context in which Jonathan lives contrast with that of Aunt Frances and her children?

Reading Strategy

Judging the Characters' Actions

7. (a) What do you think of Aunt Frances's behavior over the years? (b) In what way might her actions have contributed to her sister-in-law's bitterness toward the family?
8. (a) Contrast Aunt Frances's and Ruth's approach to death. (b) What values does each approach express? Record your answers and evidence in a chart like the one shown.

9. Who do you think was "right" at the end of the story? Why?

Extend Understanding

10. **Cultural Connection:** In today's society, doctors sometimes spare patients by not informing them of their terminal illnesses. Do you agree with this approach? Why or why not?

The Writer in the Family ◆ 1215

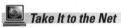

ENRICHMENT: Further Reading

Other Works by E.L. Doctorow

Welcome to Hard Times

The Book of Daniel

World's Fair

The Waterworks

Billy Bathgate

Ragtime

 Take It to the Net
Visit www.phschool.com for more information on E. L. Doctorow.

Answers for p. 1215

Review and Assess

1. **(a)** Jonathan is a dynamic character. **(b)** He decides to stand up to his aunt and not write the letters; he goes through the grieving process; and he sees his father in a new light.

2. Jack is a dynamic character from Jonathan's view. By the story's end, Jonathan remembers a very different man than he was at the story's beginning.

3. Aunt Frances is a static character. Throughout the story, she wants to keep things as they were.

4. Possible response: Aunt Frances's choice to set Jack in a successful Arizona retirement shows that for this family, which aspires to professional class status, retiring to Arizona symbolizes success.

5. Possible responses: **(a)** Jewish rituals such as shi'va unite the family, as does the desire to achieve middle class status. **(b)** Values about honesty and independence divide them.

6. Jonathan lives in a small Bronx apartment. His brother attends City University, a public school, and his father worked as a salesman. Aunt Frances lives in a wealthier community, is married to a lawyer, and sends her children to private colleges.

7. **(a)** Students may say that they disapprove of Frances's behavior. **(b)** Possible response: Aunt Frances's dislike and disregard for Ruth probably added to Ruth's bitterness. Ruth was resentful because she was never treated like an important member of the family.

8. **(a)** Ruth wants to grieve for a death and move on. Frances wants to deny a death ever occurred. **(b)** Students should support their own decisions about which approach is more productive.

9. Using their own moral codes, students should explain their responses.

10. Accept all reasonable responses.

❶ Vocabulary Development

Word Analysis

1. Inflammation of the sinuses
2. Inflammation of the appendix
3. Inflammation of a tendon
4. Inflammation of the tonsils

Spelling Strategy

1. beacon
2. bickered
3. waken
4. chorus

Concept Development: Sentence Completion

1. barometer
2. cronies
3. bronchitis
4. anthology

❷ Grammar and Style

1. *Affect*, a verb, is correct.
2. *Effect*, a noun, is correct.
3. *Effected* is wrong. The verb *affected* is correct.
4. *Affect* is wrong. The noun *effect* is correct.
5. *Affected*, a verb, is correct.

Writing Application

Paragraphs should be consistent with the characters and events of the story. Check to see that students have used both *affect* and *effect* correctly at least once.

Integrate Language Skills

❶ Vocabulary Development Lesson

Word Analysis: Greek Suffix *-itis*

The Greek suffix *-itis* means "disease" or "inflammation." *Bronchitis* means "inflammation of the bronchial tubes." With this knowledge, define each of the following words.

1. sinusitis
2. appendicitis
3. tendonitis
4. tonsillitis

Spelling Strategy

The "k" sound can be spelled with *ck, ch, cq,* or *q*. For example, in *bronchitis, ch* spells the "k" sound. When you are uncertain about the spelling of a word with the "k" sound, consult a dictionary. Complete the spelling of each word.

1. bea__on
2. bi__ered
3. wa__en
4. __orus

❷ Grammar and Style Lesson

Commonly Confused Words: *affect* and *effect*

Affect and *effect* are two examples of commonly confused words that look or sound alike but have different meanings. The word **effect** is most often used as a noun that describes the result of an action. **Affect** is most often used as a verb meaning "to act upon."

> **Correct use of *effect*:** . . . it was when she read this letter aloud to the old lady that the full **effect** of Jack's death came over her. (Here, *effect* is a noun meaning the full result.)

> **Correct use of *affect*:** Aunt Frances tried to **affect** every decision in the family. (Here, *affect* is a verb meaning "to influence.")

Concept Development: Sentence Completions

Review the vocabulary list on page 1201 and review the way each word is used in the context of the story. Then, select the vocabulary word that fits best in each of the following sentences.

1. According to the ___?___, it will probably rain in a day or two.
2. Grandpa and his ___?___ play golf every week.
3. My bout with ___?___ left me coughing for weeks.
4. We developed an ___?___ of short stories to share with the children.

Practice Name the part of speech for each italicized word, and explain whether or not the word is used correctly.

1. How did her husband's death *affect* Ruth?
2. Jack's illness had a serious *effect* on his business.
3. How was Jonathan *effected* by his family?
4. What *affect* might Arizona's climate have on bronchitis?
5. Aunt Frances was very *affected* by hearing Jonathan's first letter.

Writing Application Write a paragraph explaining the impact you think Jack's death had on Jonathan, using *affect* and *effect* at least once.

W̸G Prentice Hall Writing and Grammar Connection: Chapter 25, Section 2

TEACHING RESOURCES

The following resources can be used to enrich or extend the instruction for pp. 1216–1217.

Vocabulary

📖 **Selection Support:** Build Vocabulary, p. 306
📖 **Vocabulary and Spelling Practice Book** (Use this booklet for skills enrichment)

Grammar

📖 **Selection Support:** Grammar and Style, p. 307
W̸G **Writing and Grammar,** Ruby Level, p. 648
📖 **Daily Language Practice Transparencies** 📖

Writing

W̸G **Writing and Grammar,** Ruby Level, p. 226
💿 **Writing and Grammar iText CD-ROM**
📖 **Writing Models and Graphic Organizers on Transparencies,** p. 79

■ **BLOCK SCHEDULING:** Resources marked with this symbol provide varied instruction during 90-minute blocks.

❸ Writing Lesson

Advice Column

Doctorow's story explores Jonathan's difficult dilemma of how to handle the odd situation with his Aunt Frances. Write an advice column in response to a brief letter from Jonathan. As the columnist, propose specific actions and support your argument with solid reasoning and evidence.

Prewriting   First, list the elements of Jonathan's dilemma. Then, decide on the best advice. Identify several reasons to persuade Jonathan to follow your advice. Support your reasons with researched facts about the mechanisms people use to cope with grief.

Drafting   Begin your response by expressing sympathy for Jonathan's problem. Then, summarize your proposed action. Elaborate each point with logical arguments, reasons, or facts.

> ### Model: Elaborating to Support an Argument
>
> Tell your grandmother about your father's death because it is the honest thing to do. According to Dr. Sam Keigler, older people face death far more easily than do young people.

> Coherent reasons and expert evidence help support an argument.

Revising   Reread your column to be sure that Jonathan's problem and your response are clearly stated. Look for ways to strengthen your argument. Consider additional reasons and support you might add.

 Prentice Hall Writing and Grammar Connection: Chapter 11, Connected Assignment

❹ Extension Activities

Listening and Speaking As Jonathan, write and deliver a **eulogy** for his father's memorial service. Focus on the unique value of his father's life. Use the following tips as a guide:

- Identify two or three of Jack's special qualities.
- Give examples from his life.
- Explain how his father's presence enhanced Jonathan's life.

After you have rehearsed, present the eulogy to your class.

Research and Technology This story takes place in the 1950s. To prepare **a costume proposal** for a dramatic adaptation, conduct research to learn how the characters might have dressed and styled their hair. In a small group, look for photographs, illustrations, or actual clothing from older family members. Present your findings to the class. **[Group Activity]**

 **Take It to the Net**   www.phschool.com

Go online for an additional research activity using the Internet.

❸ Writing Lesson

- Review the story's central dilemma with students. Then, read through the Writing Lesson and help students address the prompt in the Prewriting section.
- Have students use the Problem/Solution Organizer, p. 79 in **Writing Models and Graphic Organizers on Transparencies,** to explore ideas for their advice columns.
- Urge students to focus first on identifying their central piece of advice. They can then develop supporting arguments.
- Use the Problem–Solution Essay rubric on p. 10 of **Performance Assessment and Portfolio Management** to assess student work.

❹ Listening and Speaking

- Review the definition of a eulogy with students, and invite any volunteers who have delivered or heard eulogies to share their knowledge.
- Encourage students to scan the selection for details that describe Jack.
- Remind students to use formal speaking guidelines in delivering their eulogies: Speak clearly and slowly, make eye contact, and confine movement to appropriate gestures.

CUSTOMIZE INSTRUCTION
For Universal Access

To address different learning styles use the activities suggested in the **Extension Activities booklet,**

For Interpersonal and Verbal/Linguistic Learners, Activity 5.

For Logical/Mathematic Verbal/Linguistic Learn Activity 6.

For Visual/Spatial L Activity 7.

ASSESSMENT RESOURCES

The following resources can be used to assess students' knowledge and skills.

Selection Assessment
- **Formal Assessment,** pp. 303–305
- **Got It! Assessment Videotapes,** Tape 6
- **Test Bank Software**

Take It to the Net
Visit www.phschool.com for self-tests and additional questions on "The Writer in the Family."

Writing Rubric
- **Performance Assessment and Portfolio Management,** p. 10

PRENTICE HALL
ASSESSMENT *SYSTEM*
- **Workbook**
- **Skill Book**
- **Transparencies**
- **CD-ROM**

Camouflaging the Chimera ✦ Ambush *from* The Things They Carried

Lesson Objectives

1. **To analyze and respond to literary elements**
   - Literary Analysis: First-Person Narrator
   - Comparing Literary Works
2. **To read, comprehend, analyze, and critique a [genre(s)]**
   - Reading Strategy: Picturing the Action
   - Reading Check questions
   - Review and Assess questions
3. **To develop word analysis skills, fluency, and systematic vocabulary**
   - Vocabulary Development Lesson: Concept Development: Words From War
4. **To understand and apply written and oral language conventions**
   - Spelling Strategy
   - Grammar and Style Lesson: Noun Clauses
   - Assessment Practice (ATE)
5. **To understand and apply appropriate writing and research strategies**
   - Writing Lesson: Newspaper [...]e
   - [...] Activity: Multimedia

[...]pply
[...]strategies

STEP-BY-STEP TEACHING GUIDE	PACING GUIDE
PRETEACH	
Motivate Students and Provide Background	
Use the Motivation activity (ATE p. 1218)	5 min.
Read and discuss author and background features (SE/ATE pp. 1218, 1220) [A]	10 min.
Introduce the Concepts	
Introduce the Literary Analysis and Reading Strategy (SE/ATE p. 1219) [A]	15 min.
Pronounce the vocabulary words and read their definitions (SE p. 1219)	5 min.
TEACH	
Monitor Comprehension	
Informally monitor comprehension by circulating while students read independently or in groups [A]	15 min.
Monitor students' comprehension with the Reading Check notes (SE/ATE p. 1223)	as students read
Develop vocabulary with Vocabulary notes (SE pp. 1221, 1222, 1223, 1224; ATE p. 1223)	as students read
Develop Understanding	
Develop students' understanding of first-person narration with the Literary Analysis annotations (SE pp. 1220, 1222; ATE pp. 1220, 1222) [A]	5 min.
Develop students' ability to envision the action in their reading by using the Reading Strategy annotations (SE p. 1224; ATE pp. 1221, 1223, 1224)	5 min.
ASSESS	
Assess Mastery	
Assess students' mastery of the Reading Strategy and Literary Analysis by having them answer the Review and Assess questions (SE/ATE p. 1227)	15 min.
Use one or more of the print and media Assessment Resources (ATE p. 1227) [A]	up to 45 min.
EXTEND	
Apply Understanding	
Have students complete the Vocabulary Development Lesson and the Grammar and Style Lesson (SE p. 1226) [A]	20 min.
[...] students' ability to use objectivity in their writing by using the Writing Lesson [...]p. 1227) [A]	45 min.
[...]dents' understanding using one or more of the Extension Activities (SE p. 1227)	20–90 min.

ACCELERATED INSTRUCTION:
[A] Use the strategies and activities identified with an [A].

UNIVERSAL ACCESS
● = Below Level Students
▲ = On-Level Students
■ = Above Level Students

Time and Resource Manager

Reading Level: Challenging, Average
Average Number of Instructional Days: 2

RESOURCES		
PRINT 📖	**TRANSPARENCIES**	**TECHNOLOGY** 💿 🎧
• **Beyond Literature,** Cross-Curricula Connection: Social Studies, p. 72 ▲ ■		• **Interest Grabber Video,** Tape 6 ● ▲ ■
• **Selection Support Workbook:** ● ▲ ■ Literary Analysis, p. 313 Reading Strategy, p. 312 Build Vocabulary, p. 310	• **Literary Analysis and Reading Transparencies,** pp. 143 and 144 ● ▲ ■	
		• **Listening to Literature** ● ▲ ■ Audiocassettes, Side 40 Audio CDs, CD 23
• **Literatura en español** ● ▲ • **Literary Analysis for Enrichment** ■		
• **Formal Assessment:** Selection Test, pp. 306–308 ● ▲ ■ • **Open Book Test,** pp. 214–216 ● ▲ ■ • **PRENTICE HALL ASSESSMENT SYSTEM** ● ▲ ■	• **PRENTICE HALL ASSESSMENT SYSTEM** ● ▲ ■ Skills Practice Answers and Explanations on Transparencies	• **Test Bank Software** ● ▲ ■ • **Got It! Assessment Videotapes,** Tape 6 ● ▲
• **Selection Support Workbook:** ● ▲ ■ Grammar and Style, p. 311 • **Writing and Grammar,** Ruby Level ● ▲ ■ • **Extension Activities,** p. 72 ● ▲ ■	• **Daily Language Practice Transparencies** ● ▲ • **Writing Models and Graphic Organizers on Transparencies,** p. 95 ● ▲ ■	• **Writing and Grammar iText CD-ROM** ● ▲ ■ 💻 *Take It to the Net* www.phschool.com

BLOCK SCHEDULING: Use one 90-minute class period to preteach the selection and have students read it. Use a second 90-minute class period to assess students' mastery of skills and have them complete one of the Extension Activities.

Motivation

Before reading the selections, share with students the Enrichment feature on p. 1222 of the Teacher's Edition about the Vietnam Veterans Memorial. Tell students that decades have passed since the war ended, yet crowds continue to visit this memorial, leaving mementos and notes. If possible, share photos and notes from Michael Katakis's book *The Vietnam Veterans Memorial*, or ask students who have seen the memorial to describe it and their response to it for the class. Lead students to reflect on how the war continues to haunt the many people who lived through that period, as these selections demonstrate.

▣ Interest Grabber Video

As an alternative, play "A Vietnam Veteran Remembers" on Tape 6 to engage student interest.

❶ Background

More About the Authors

Yusef Komunyakaa was born on April 29, 1947, in Bogalusa, Louisiana. He is the eldest of five children. Komunyakaa uses his childhood experiences to inform many of his works: His familial relationships, his maturation in a rural Southern community, and the musical environment afforded by the close proximity of the jazz and blues center of New Orleans provide fundamental themes for several of his volumes.

After serving in the Vietnam War, Tim O'Brien became a graduate student at Harvard. He was one of very few Vietnam veterans there at that time. Having the opportunity to do an internship at the *Washington Post*, he eventually left Harvard to become a newspaper reporter. O'Brien's career as a reporter gave way to his fiction writing after the publication of his memoir *If I Die in a Combat Zone, Box Me Up and Send Me Home*.

Prepare to Read

❶ Camouflaging the Chimera ◆ Ambush
from The Things They Carried

Yusef Komunyakaa (b. 1947)

"It took me fourteen years to write poems about Vietnam," said Yusef Komunyakaa (yōō´ sef kō mun yä´ kä) in 1994, shortly after winning the Pulitzer Prize for *Neon Vernacular*, the collection from which "Camouflaging the Chimera" is taken. "I had never thought about writing about it, and in a way I had been systematically writing around it." His book *Dien Cai Dau*, which is Vietnamese for "crazy," is also about Vietnam.

Opening the Creative Gates Komunyakaa was born in Bogalusa, Louisiana. He joined the army and went to Vietnam in 1965. Serving as an "information specialist," he reported from the front lines, edited a military newspaper called *The Southern Cross*, and earned a Bronze Star. After the war, he pursued his education, earning a B.A. at the University of Colorado, an M.A. at Colorado State University, and an M.F.A. at the University of California, Irvine. He then took a variety of teaching jobs and, in 1977, published his first collection of poetry. In 1983, he returned to his native Louisiana, working as a poet-in-the-schools in New Orleans. During this time, he let Vietnam resurface in his consciousness. "And it was as if I had uncapped some hidden place in me," Komunyakaa said. "Poem after poem came spilling out."

To date, Komunyakaa has published twelve poetry collections, as well as a collection of essays entitled *Blues Notes* (2000), and a libretto for an opera by composer T. J. Anderson. Komunyakaa teaches at Princeton University and is Chancellor of the Academy of American Poets.

Tim O'Brien (b. 1946)

No writer has more effectively captured the Vietnam War than Tim O'Brien. O'Brien has written five books that focus on the war, providing readers with vivid pictures of the fighting in the dense Vietnamese jungles and allowing them to share the fear and homesickness experienced by American soldiers during this bitter conflict.

The Essence of Things Born in Austin, Minnesota, O'Brien was drafted a month after graduating from college. Even though he was against the war, O'Brien reported for duty and was sent to Vietnam. He arrived in January 1969 and served near the village of My Lai, just months after an infamous massacre of its inhabitants by American soldiers. (The My Lai massacre plays an important part in his novel *In the Lake of the Woods*, published in 1994.)

After coming home in 1970, O'Brien attended graduate school at Harvard, and began writing essays about his experiences in Vietnam. His first published work, *If I Die in a Combat Zone, Box Me Up and Ship Me Home* (1973), is a memoir. Several subsequent novels include the National Book Award winner, *Going After Cacciato* (1978), and the widely praised *The Things They Carried* (1990), from which "Ambush" is taken. In this fictional memoir of Vietnam, the author artfully straddles the line between fact and fiction. The collection of interrelated stories centers around the men of Alpha Company, an infantry platoon. The book explores the very nature of storytelling and memory, and examines how the truths of fiction are sometimes more profound than those of life. O'Brien has said that he writes fiction ". . . to get at the essence of things, not merely the surface."

TEACHING RESOURCES

The following resources can be used to enrich or extend the instruction for pp. 1218–1219.

Motivation

▣ **Interest Grabber Video**, Tape 6 ▣

Background

▣ **Beyond Literature**, p. 72

 Take It to the Net
Visit www.phschool.com for background and hotlinks for the authors.

Literary Analysis

 **Literary Analysis and Reading Transparencies**, First-Person Narrator, p. 144 ▣

Reading

▣ **Selection Support:** Reading Strategy, p. 312; Build Vocabulary, p. 310

 **Literary Analysis and Reading Transparencies**, Picturing the Action, p. 143 ▣

▣ **BLOCK SCHEDULING:** Resources marked with this symbol provide varied instruction during 90-minute blocks.

Preview

Connecting to the Literature

Most soldiers who went to Vietnam were only a few years older than you are now. Imagine finding yourself in a jungle, far from home, where you might have to kill or be killed. This is the reality that faces the narrators of these works.

❷ Literary Analysis

First-Person Narrator

Sometimes, the most compelling stories are those told in the **first person,** by a narrator who uses the pronouns *I* and *we* and participates in the action. In these lines from "Ambush," the speaker describes hiding in wait for an enemy soldier:

> I did not hate the young man; I did not see him as the enemy; . . .
> I crouched and kept my head low.

As you read, notice how the use of the first-person point of view pulls you inside the narrator's mind, creating an intimate connection to the story.

Comparing Literary Works

These selections have many similarities. Both are narrated in the first person, describe soldiers waiting in ambush, and communicate the terror and moral ambiguity of war. However, one is a lyric poem, and the other is a story. An author's choice of form is one of the first and most important decisions he or she makes. **Form** creates the basic structure on which all matters of meaning and content are built. As you read these works, explore the ways in which the form of each one contributes to its power and meaning.

❸ Reading Strategy

Picturing the Action

Set during wartime in remote jungles, these selections are especially dramatic and vivid. Use the details the writers provide to **picture the action,** or form a mental image of what you are reading. When Komunyakaa writes, "We painted our faces & rifles/with mud from a riverbank," picture doing what he describes. These mental images will help the writing come alive. Record especially vivid details in a chart like the one shown.

Vocabulary Development

refuge (ref´ yōoj) *n.* shelter or protection from danger (p. 1221)

ambush (am´ boosh´) *n.* lying in wait to attack by surprise (p. 1222)

ammunition (am´ yōo nish´ ən) *n.* anything hurled by a weapon or exploded as a weapon (p. 1223)

muzzle (muz´ əl) *n.* front end of a barrel of a gun; the snout of an animal (p. 1223)

gape (gāp) *v.* stare, open-mouthed (p. 1124)

> **Sensory Details**
>
> ⬇
>
> **Action**
>
> ⬇
>
> **Vivid Verbs**

Camouflaging the Chimera / Ambush from The Things They Carried ◆ 1219

❷ Literary Analysis

First-Person Narrator

- Be sure students understand that a *first-person narrator* speaks directly to readers. First-person narrators take part in the action and reveal their thoughts or feelings, using the word *I.*

- Call students' attention to the example on p. 1219. Encourage them to consider what this narrator reveals about his state of mind.

- Use the First-Person Narrator transparency in **Literary Analysis and Reading Transparencies,** p. 144 to show what first-person narration reveals.

- Encourage students to maintain similar charts as they read the selections.

❸ Reading Strategy

Picturing the Action

- Explain to students that picturing the action a literary work describes can bring the work to life for a reader, enhancing its power.

- Point out to students that both selections contain vivid details that can help them to visualize what the authors describe.

- Use the example on p. 1219 to illustrate, instructing students to discuss what they picture. For further examples, use the Picturing the Action transparency in **Literary Analysis and Reading Transparencies,** p. 143.

- Encourage students to use a chart such as the one on p. 1219 to record details and envision the action as they read the selections.

Vocabulary Development

- Pronounce each vocabulary word for students, and read the definitions as a class. Have students identify any words with which they are already familiar.

 E-Teach

Visit E-Teach at www.phschool.com for teachers' essays on how to teach, with questions and answers.

CUSTOMIZE INSTRUCTION FOR UNIVERSAL ACCESS

For Less Proficient Readers	For English Learners	For Advanced Readers
To help these students picture the action of the selections, have them describe movies they have seen about the Vietnam War. Encourage them to focus their descriptions on the jungle terrain of the country, the protective camouflage worn by American soldiers, and the difficulties of fighting a guerilla war.	Picturing the action may be challenging for these students, especially if they are unfamiliar with the descriptive words the authors use. Encourage these students to read the selections, writing down any unfamiliar words. After looking up the words, have them reread, pausing this time to visualize.	To challenge these students, suggest that they move beyond picturing only the action. Encourage them to picture the emotional responses of the narrators and other characters in the selections. What might their facial expressions and body language reveal?

1219

Step-by-Step Teaching Guide for pp. 1220–1224

CUSTOMIZE INSTRUCTION
For Intrapersonal Learners

Before these students read the selections, ask them to consider their own ideas about military combat. Explain that wars frequently require soldiers to "kill or be killed." Ask students whether killing in the name of country is more acceptable than killing for other reasons.

❶ About the Selection

"Camouflaging the Chimera" is a suspenseful, first-person description of how it feels to lie in ambush for hours, waiting for the approach of enemy soldiers.

❷ Literary Analysis

First-Person Narrator

- Remind students that when a poem has a *first-person narrator*, the reader is drawn into the mind of the narrator, who participates in the action.

- Have students read the bracketed passage. Encourage them to try to enter the mind of the narrator.

- Ask students the Literary Analysis question on p. 1220: Who is the first-person narrator or speaker of this poem?
  Possible response: Students should recognize that the poem's first-person narrator is not a single soldier, but a group—thus, the use of "we."

- Use the First-Person Narrator transparency in **Literary Analysis and Reading Transparencies,** p. 144 to help students gain insight into the narrator's mind.

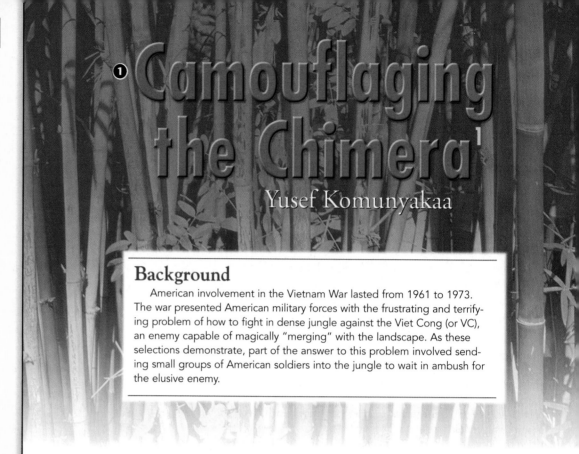

❶ # Camouflaging the Chimera[1]
Yusef Komunyakaa

Background

American involvement in the Vietnam War lasted from 1961 to 1973. The war presented American military forces with the frustrating and terrifying problem of how to fight in dense jungle against the Viet Cong (or VC), an enemy capable of magically "merging" with the landscape. As these selections demonstrate, part of the answer to this problem involved sending small groups of American soldiers into the jungle to wait in ambush for the elusive enemy.

❷

We tied branches to our helmets.
We painted our faces & rifles
with mud from a riverbank,

blades of grass hung from the pockets
5   of our tiger suits. We wove
ourselves into the terrain,
content to be a hummingbird's target.

We hugged bamboo & leaned
against a breeze off the river,
10   slow-dragging with ghosts

from Saigon to Bangkok,
with women left in doorways

Literary Analysis
First-Person Narrator
Who is the first-person narrator or speaker of this poem?

---

1. **Chimera** (ki´ mir´ ə) from Greek mythology, a firebreathing monster with a lion's head, a goat's body, and a serpent's tail.

1220 ◆ *Prosperity and Protest (1946–Present)*

TEACHING RESOURCES

The following resources can be used to enrich or extend the instruction for pp. 1220–1224.

Literary Analysis

📖 **Selection Support:** Literary Analysis, p. 313

🎧 **Listening to Literature Audiocassettes,** Side 40 ▪

💿 **Listening to Literature Audio CDs,** CD 23 ▪

reaching in from America.
We aimed at dark-hearted songbirds.

15 In our way station of shadows
rock apes tried to blow our cover,
throwing stones at the sunset. Chameleons

crawled our spines, changing from day
to night: green to gold,
20 gold to black. But we waited
till the moon touched metal,

till something almost broke
inside us. VC struggled
with the hillside, like black silk

25 wrestling iron through grass.
We weren't there. The river ran
through our bones. Small animals took refuge
against our bodies; we held our breath,

ready to spring the L-shaped
30 ambush, as a world revolved
under each man's eyelid.

refuge (ref´ yōōj) *n.*
shelter or protection
from danger

Review and Assess

Thinking About the Selection

1. **Respond:** What emotions did this poem evoke in you? Explain.
2. **(a) Recall:** Where does this poem take place?
   (b) Analyze: What obstacles and burdens does the speaker face?
3. **(a) Recall:** What runs through the soldiers' bones?
   (b) Support: What other images suggest that the speaker is merging with his surroundings? **(c) Interpret:** What does the speaker mean by his observation that "We weren't there"?
4. **(a) Interpret:** How would you describe the speaker's feelings toward the VC? Support your answer. **(b) Analyze:** Do the images in this poem suggest that the speaker is opposed to the war? Explain.
5. **(a) Define:** What is a chimera? **(b) Interpret:** What effect does the title have on your interpretation of the poem? Explain.
6. **Evaluate:** Komunyakaa has said, "I like connecting the abstract to the concrete." Has he succeeded in this poem? Explain.

Camouflaging the Chimera ◆ *1221*

❹ AMBUSH

from The Things They Carried

Tim O'Brien

When she was nine, my daughter Kathleen asked if I had ever killed anyone. She knew about the war; she knew I'd been a soldier. "You keep writing these war stories," she said, "so I guess you must've killed somebody." It was a difficult moment, but I did what seemed right, which was to say, "Of course not," and then to take her onto my lap and hold her for a while. Someday, I hope, she'll ask again. But here I want to pretend she's a grown-up. I want to tell her exactly what happened, or what I remember happening, and then I want to say to her that as a little girl she was absolutely right. This is why I keep writing war stories:

He was a short, slender young man of about twenty. I was afraid of him—afraid of something—and as he passed me on the trail I threw a grenade that exploded at his feet and killed him.

Or to go back:

Shortly after midnight we moved into the <u>ambush</u> site outside My Khe. The whole platoon was there, spread out in the dense brush along the trail, and for five hours nothing at all happened. We were working in two-man teams—one man on guard while the other slept, switching off every two hours—and I remember it was still dark when Kiowa shook me awake for the final watch. The night was foggy and hot. For the first few moments I felt lost, not sure about directions, groping for my helmet and weapon. I reached out and found three grenades and lined them up in front of me; the pins had already been straightened for quick throwing. And then for maybe half an hour I kneeled there and waited. Very gradually, in tiny slivers, dawn began to break through the fog, and from my position in the brush I could see ten or fifteen meters up the trail. The mosquitoes were fierce. I remember slapping at them, wondering if I should wake up Kiowa and ask for some repellent, then

1222 ◆ *Prosperity and Protest (1946–Present)*

Words From War

- Call students' attention to the words *ammunition* and *muzzle*, and their definitions. Explain to students that these are words that have entered the English language from the military and war.

- Have students suggest other words that come from war, and list them on the chalkboard. Possible responses: Students might mention *ambush*, *platoon*, and *grenade*.

- Have students look up the meaning of these words in a dictionary.

- Encourage students to discuss the impact of these words from war on the selections.

❽ Reading Strategy

Picturing the Action

- Remind students that by looking closely at the details in a literary work, they can picture the action, making the story come alive in their minds.

- Have students read the bracketed passage. Ask them to pay close attention to the details and visualize the scene the author describes.

- Ask students which images in the passage help them to visualize the scene. Possible response: Images may include the appearance and movement of the young Vietnamese man; the thickness of the brush; the grenade freezing as if a camera had clicked; and wisps of fog.

▶ Monitor Progress Ask students: How does picturing the action add to their understanding of these selections? Possible responses: Students should respond that for these selections—both of which are rich in sensory detail—picturing the action helps readers to understand the state of mind of the narrators and appreciate the impact of their experiences.

thinking it was a bad idea, then looking up and seeing the young man come out of the fog. He wore black clothing and rubber sandals and a gray <u>ammunition</u> belt. His shoulders were slightly stooped, his head cocked to the side as if listening for something. He seemed at ease. He carried his weapon in one hand, <u>muzzle</u> down, moving without any hurry up the center of the trail. There was no sound at all—none that I can remember. In a way, it seemed, he was part of the morning fog, or my own imagination, but there was also the reality of what was happening in my stomach. I had already pulled the pin on a grenade. I had come up to a crouch. It was entirely automatic. I did not hate the young man; I did not see him as the enemy; I did not ponder issues of morality or politics or military duty. I crouched and kept my head low. I tried to swallow whatever was rising from my stomach, which tasted like lemonade, something fruity and sour. I was terrified. There were no thoughts about killing. The grenade was to make him go away—just evaporate—and I leaned back and felt my mind go empty and then felt it fill up again. I had already thrown the grenade before telling myself to throw it. The brush was thick and I had to lob it high, not aiming, and I remember the grenade seeming to freeze above me for an instant, as if a camera had clicked, and I remember ducking down and holding my breath and seeing little wisps of fog rise from the earth. The grenade bounced once and rolled across the trail. I did not hear it, but there must've been a sound, because the young man dropped his weapon and began to run, just two or three quick steps, then he hesitated, swiveling to his right, and he glanced down at the grenade and tried to cover his head but never did. It occurred to me then that he was about

ammunition (am′ yōō nish′ ən) *n.* anything hurled by a weapon or exploded as a weapon

muzzle (muz′ əl) *n.* front end of a barrel of a gun; the snout of an animal

✓ **Reading Check** ❾

What does the speaker do when he sees the young man on the path?

Ambush from *The Things They Carried* ◆ 1223

❾ ✓ **Reading Check**

Answer: The speaker pulls the pin on a grenade and throws it at the young man to kill him.

CUSTOMIZE INSTRUCTION FOR UNIVERSAL ACCESS

For Special Needs Students	For Gifted/Talented Students	For Advanced Readers
These students may find these selections, both of which are rich in sensory detail, to be especially challenging. Instruct students to read descriptive sections slowly, marking any unfamiliar words and confusing passages for rereading.	Have these students study the photograph on p. 1223 and consider how it relates to the experiences O'Brien and Komunyakaa describe. Then, instruct them to create collages that illustrate the selections. Students should gather material for their collages from photographs and other artworks of the Vietnam War.	To help these students learn more about soldiers' experiences in Vietnam, direct them to the Vietnam Veterans' home page on the Internet: www.vietvet.org. Have students search the site for stories, poems, and pictures submitted by veterans in the Remembrances section. Students may present their findings to the class.

⑩ Reading Strategy

Picturing the Action

• Have students read the bracketed passage. Ask them to pay close attention to its details.

• Ask students the Reading Strategy question on p. 1224: Which images and words help you to imagine the action here?
Possible response: Possible images and words include the "popping noise" and "small white puff" of the grenade, the dead man's sandals being blown off, the man's face, and the "star-shaped hole."

Answers for p. 1224

Review and Assess

1. Possible response: Some students will argue that a father should be truthful; others will respect his decision to protect his daughter.

2. **(a)** He says, "There was no real peril." **(b)** Possible response: He means that he will never be able to accept that he killed without being in real danger.

3. **(a)** He is stunned and stares at the young Vietnamese man's body. **(b)** Kiowa tells him to accept the realities of war.

4. **(a)** He fantasizes that he watches the young man complete his walk along the path unharmed. **(b)** Possible response: It emphasizes the narrator's ambivalence about his wartime experiences.

5. Possible responses: **(a)** The first telling is objective, lacking details; the second is much more detailed and describes the narrator's emotions in depth. **(b)** Students may feel he chose this device to emphasize the complexity of war—there is no simple truth.

6. Possible response: Some students will argue that a killing in wartime is justified. Others will argue that no killing is ever "good."

---

to die. I wanted to warn him. The grenade made a popping noise—not soft but not loud either—not what I'd expected—and there was a puff of dust and smoke—a small white puff—and the young man seemed to jerk upward as if pulled by invisible wires. He fell on his back. His rubber sandals had been blown off. There was no wind. He lay at the center of the trail, his right leg bent beneath him, his one eye shut, his other eye a huge star-shaped hole.

⑩

It was not a matter of live or die. There was no real peril. Almost certainly the young man would have passed by. And it will always be that way.

Later, I remember, Kiowa tried to tell me that the man would've died anyway. He told me that it was a good kill, that I was a soldier and this was a war, that I should shape up and stop staring and ask myself what the dead man would've done if things were reversed.

None of it mattered. The words seemed far too complicated. All I could do was <u>gape</u> at the fact of the young man's body.

Even now I haven't finished sorting it out. Sometimes I forgive myself, other times I don't. In the ordinary hours of life I try not to dwell on it, but now and then, when I'm reading a newspaper or just sitting alone in a room, I'll look up and see the young man coming out of the morning fog. I'll watch him walk toward me, his shoulders slightly stooped, his head cocked to the side, and he'll pass within a few yards of me and suddenly smile at some secret thought and then continue up the trail to where it bends back into the fog.

Reading Strategy
Picturing the Action
Which images and words help you to imagine the action here?

gape (gāp) *v.* stare, open-mouthed

Review and Assess

Thinking About the Selection

1. **Respond:** If you had been the narrator, would you have told your nine-year-old this story? Why or why not?

2. **(a) Recall:** What does the narrator say to describe the degree of danger he faced? **(b) Interpret:** What does he mean when he says "And it will always be that way"?

3. **(a) Deduce:** How does the narrator react to the killing? **(b) Interpret:** In what way does Kiowa respond to the narrator's reaction?

4. **(a) Recall:** At the end of the story, what does the narrator fantasize? **(b) Interpret:** In what ways does this fantasy add to the story's meaning?

5. **(a) Compare and Contrast:** The narrator tells his story twice. Compare and contrast the short and long versions. **(b) Speculate:** Why do you think the author chose this narrative device?

6. **Make a Judgment:** Kiowa uses the expression "a good kill." Is there such a thing? Explain.

 ASSESSMENT PRACTICE: Writing Skills

Structure **(For more practice, see Test Preparation Workbook, p. 75)**

Many tests require students to combine sentences. Demonstrate with this example.

> Many people who have experienced war have horrifying memories. These memories will often stay with them for a lifetime.

Which of the following is the BEST way to combine the two sentences in the passage?

A Many people who have experienced war have horrifying memories, these memories stay with them for a lifetime.

B Many people who have experienced war have horrifying memories, stay with them for a lifetime.

C Many people who have experienced war have horrifying memories that stay with them for a lifetime.

D Staying with them for a lifetime, many people who have experienced war have horrifying memories.

A is a comma splice, *B* is a run-on, and *D* has a misplaced modifier. *C* is the correct answer.

Review and Assess

Literary Analysis

First-Person Narrator

1. In what specific ways does Komunyakaa's use of the **first-person narrator** help you enter the poem as a participant?

2. Do you think O'Brien's use of a first-person narrator makes you more sympathetic to the protagonist? Why or why not?

Comparing Literary Works

3. (a) Which of these works is informal and uses everyday speech? (b) Which is formal and uses complex imagery? (c) Can these differences be explained by the **form** of each work? Explain.

4. Despite the differences in form, what similarities do you find in the meaning of these two works? Record both similarities and differences in a diagram like the one shown.

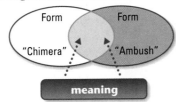

5. (a) How would you expect a poem to convey meaning in comparison with a story? (b) Are your expectations met by these works? Explain.

Reading Strategy

Picturing the Action

6. Explain how your ability to **picture the action** in this passage draws you into Tim O'Brien's world.

> . . . I remember the grenade seeming to freeze above me for an instant as if a camera had clicked, and I remember ducking down . . .

7. When you **picture** images such as "We hugged bamboo & leaned/against a breeze off the river" do you better understand and appreciate "Camouflaging the Chimera"? Explain.

Extend Understanding

8. **History Connection:** (a) What role does the jungle setting play in these works? (b) What role has the landscape played in other wars that Americans have fought?

 Quick Review

A **first-person narrator** uses the pronouns *I* and *we*, participates in the action of a literary work, and reveals his or her private thoughts, feelings, and perceptions.

The **form** of a work is its essential structure, for example, a lyric poem, short story, or one-act play. Form helps to shape the **meaning** and message of a work of literature.

To **picture the action,** use details from the work to see the events in your mind.

Take It to the Net
www.phschool.com

Take the interactive self-test online to check your understanding of these selections.

✳ ENRICHMENT: Further Reading

Other Works by the Authors

Works by Yusef Komunyakaa
Dien Cai Dau

Works by Tim O'Brien
Going After Cacciato
In the Lake of the Woods

 Take It to the Net
Visit www.phschool.com for more information on the authors.

1. **Possible response:** Komunyakaa uses sensory details that allow readers to imagine that they are part of the "we" who are in hiding.

2. **Possible response:** O'Brien's use of the first person allows readers to feel closer to, and therefore more sympathetic toward, the main character. It allows readers to enter more fully into the narrator's internal conflict.

3. **(a)** "Ambush" is informal, using everyday speech. **(b)** "Camouflaging the Chimera" is more formal, using complex imagery. **(c) Possible response:** The forms have much to do with the different levels of formality. Poetic imagery is more complex, while a fictional memoir uses everyday speech.

4. **Possible response:** "Chimera": Poem, with complex imagery and especially rich language; "Ambush": Fictional memoir, using everyday speech to describe what the narrator saw and felt; Overlap: Both works convey the confusion and horror of the Vietnam War.

5. **Possible responses: (a)** Students may expect a poem to convey meaning through briefly described yet complex images and a story to convey meaning through action and dialogue. **(b)** Students may find that these selections meet their expectations but also take on qualities of the other form.

6. **Possible response:** Readers are drawn into the story by imagining the grenade and seeing it freeze in the air, as the narrator sees it.

7. **Possible response:** Students may say that these images create a sensory experience that they might otherwise be unable to imagine.

8. **Possible responses: (a)** The setting has an enormous impact on the narrators—they blend into and become part of the landscape. **(b)** Landscape affects all wars by creating the conditions under which soldiers must fight. An example might be the desert landscape of the Persian Gulf War.

❶ Vocabulary Development

Concept Development

Possible response: To help them imagine an *ambush* attack, the recruits were sent to the underbrush to wait. Each soldier was given rounds of *ammunition* and a *grenade*, and assigned to a *platoon* of twenty others.

Spelling Strategy

1. dosage
2. enrage
3. village
4. foliage

Fluency: Context

1. I would seek *refuge*.
2. "Hold it by the *muzzle*."
3. I could only *gape* in amazement.
4. We might *ambush* her at lunch.
5. Guns and *ammunition* must be locked away separately.

❷ Grammar and Style

1. why I keep writing war stories
2. what was happening in my stomach
3. whatever was rising from my stomach
4. that the man would've died anyway
5. [that] you must've killed somebody

Writing Application

Paragraphs should clearly express an appropriate response to the selections and correctly use at least three noun clauses. The noun clauses should be underlined.

Integrate Language Skills

❶ Vocabulary Development Lesson

Concept Development: Words From War

Each war produces unique terms. World War I, for example, gave us *doughboy*, *over the top*, and *no man's land*. Many words of war, such as *ambush* and *ammunition*, have long since entered everyday language. Write a paragraph about a military practice maneuver using these words: *ammunition*, *ambush*, *platoon*, *grenade*.

Spelling Strategy

English words almost never end with the letter *j*, except for a few foreign derivatives. If a word ends with the *j* sound, always use *ge*, as in *refuge*. In your notebook, complete the spelling of these words.

1. dosa__   3. villa__
2. enra__   4. folia__

❷ Grammar and Style Lesson

Noun Clauses

A subordinate clause is a group of words with a subject and a verb that cannot stand by itself as a sentence. A **noun clause** is a subordinate clause that functions as a noun. Words that introduce noun clauses include *that*, *which*, *what*, *if*, *how*, *when*, *where*, *why*, *whatever*, *whoever*, and *whether*.

> **Subject:** *Whoever knows this* is wise.
>
> **Direct Object:** My daughter Kathleen asked *if I had ever killed anyone.*

In some cases, the word that introduces a noun clause is implied. For example, in the sentence "She knew I'd been a soldier," the introductory word *that* is implied.

W̶G̶ *Prentice Hall Writing and Grammar Connection: Chapter 19, Section 3*

1226 ◆ *Prosperity and Protest (1946–Present)*

Fluency: Context

Write a sentence responding to each of the following instructions. Include one vocabulary word from the list on page 1219 in each sentence.

1. Tell what you would do if you were caught outside in a thunderstorm.
2. Tell how a drill sergeant might instruct new recruits to hold a gun correctly when standing at ease.
3. Describe your reaction when your best friend reveals that she is from Mars.
4. Explain your strategy for capturing the leader of a rival team at camp.
5. Make a rule that would prevent children from injuring themselves with guns found in the home.

Practice Identify the noun clause in each sentence.

1. This is why I keep writing war stories.
2. . . . but there was also the reality of what was happening in my stomach.
3. I tried to swallow whatever was rising from my stomach. . . .
4. Later, I remember, Kiowa would try to tell me that the man would've died anyway.
5. . . . she said, "so I guess you must've killed somebody."

Writing Application Write a paragraph in response to these war writings by Komunyakaa and O'Brien. Use and identify at least three noun clauses.

TEACHING RESOURCES

The following resources can be used to enrich or extend the instruction for pp. 1226–1227.

Vocabulary

📖 **Selection Support:** Build Vocabulary, p. 310

📖 **Vocabulary and Spelling Practice Book** (Use this booklet for skills enrichment.) 📘

Grammar

📖 **Selection Support:** Grammar and Style, p. 311

W̶G̶ **Writing and Grammar,** Ruby Level, p. 460

📖 **Daily Language Practice Transparencies** 📘

Writing

W̶G̶ **Writing and Grammar,** Ruby Level, p. 80

💿 **Writing and Grammar iText CD-ROM**

📖 **Writing Models and Graphic Organizers on Transparencies,** p. 95

📖 **BLOCK SCHEDULING:** Resources marked with this symbol provide varied instruction during 90-minute blocks.

❸ Writing Lesson

Newspaper Article

The Vietnam War received intense journalistic coverage. Reporters from all media went to the jungle to gather stories for a public that was deeply divided about the war. As a newspaper reporter, write an article about the events Tim O'Brien relates in "Ambush."

Prewriting A newspaper article is supposed to be objective, even when relating the horrors of war. However, by stating clearly what they see and hear, reporters often communicate emotions as well. Reread "Ambush," and create an outline of the series of events that it describes.

Drafting Begin with a strong first paragraph, or lead, to hook your readers. Follow with a thorough description of the events.

> **Model: Drafting With Objectivity**
>
> The platoon waited in the dark all night. Mosquitoes swarmed, but otherwise, there was nothing but silence. Then, a young Viet Cong soldier appeared on the path. Tim lobbed a grenade. It was over quickly.

A newspaper article sticks to the facts.

Revising Review your account, and note language that too clearly reveals a bias. Replace any emotional language with simple and clear observations of events.

Prentice Hall Writing and Grammar Connection: Chapter 5, Section 3

❹ Extension Activities

Listening and Speaking Conduct an **interview** with a Vietnam War veteran about his or her experiences during the war. Use these tips to prepare:

- Choose a focus for your interview.
- Ask questions requiring in-depth, not "yes" or "no," responses.
- Ask questions about lessons that he or she feels can be learned from the war.

Record the interview on audio- or videotape, and share highlights with the class.

Research and Technology The Vietnam War was the first televised war. In a group, investigate the effect that media reports had on politics and protests in the 1960s. Then, create a **multimedia presentation** about the war. Use newspaper and magazine articles, photographs, political cartoons, television news reports, and protest songs. **[Group Activity]**

 **Take It to the Net** www.phschool.com

Go online for an additional research activity using the Internet.

ASSESSMENT RESOURCES

The following resources can be used to assess students' knowledge and skills.

Selection Assessment

- 📖 **Formal Assessment,** pp. 306–308
- 📖 **Open Book Test,** pp. 214–216
- 📼 **Got It! Assessment Videotapes,** Tape 6
- 💿 **Test Bank Software**

💻 **Take It to the Net**
Visit www.phschool.com for self-tests and additional questions on the selections.

PRENTICE HALL ASSESSMENT SYSTEM

- 📖 **Workbook**
- 📖 **Skill Book**
- 📄 **Transparencies**
- 💿 **CD-ROM**

---

❸ Writing Lesson

- Be sure students understand that their newspaper reports should use an objective tone to present the emotional details of the events O'Brien describes.
- Use the Outline transparency in **Writing Models and Graphic Organizers on Transparencies,** p. 95, to model outlining strategies for students. Instruct them to outline the events of "Ambush" as they reread the story.
- Remind students that the first paragraph of their reports should introduce the story in a way that will grab readers' attention.
- Before students revise, use the instruction on p. 1227 to guide them to remove biased and emotional language.

❹ Listening and Speaking

- Explain to students that in an interview, they can gather information by questioning a knowledgeable person.
- Instruct students to prepare by writing a list of questions in advance and anticipate follow-up questions. Possible questions include the following: Where did you serve? When did you arrive and leave? How did you cope with fear? What did you learn from your experience?
- Remind students to record their interviews. Students can work in small groups for technical support.
- Have students evaluate how well each interview achieved its purpose of getting the subject to describe memorable events and valuable lessons.

CUSTOMIZE INSTRUCTION
For Universal Access

To address different learning styles, use the activities suggested in the **Extension Activities** booklet, p. 72.

- For Verbal/Linguistic Learners, use Activity 5.
- For Verbal/Linguistic and Visual/Spatial Learners, use Activity 6.
- For Visual/Spatial Learners, use Activity 7.

The Crucible, Act I

Lesson Objectives

1. **To analyze and respond to literary elements**
   - Literary Analysis: Dialogue and Stage Directions
   - Connecting Literary Elements: Dramatic Exposition
2. **To read, comprehend, analyze, and critique a drama**
   - Reading Strategy: Questioning the Characters' Motives
   - Reading Check Questions
   - Review and Assess Questions
3. **To develop word analysis skills, fluency, and systematic vocabulary**
   - Vocabulary Development Lesson: Latin Root: *-grat-*
4. **To understand and apply written and oral language conventions**
   - Spelling Strategy
   - Grammar and Style Lesson: Pronoun Case in Incomplete Construction
   - Assessment Practice (ATE)
5. **To understand and apply appropriate writing and research strategies**
   - Writing Lesson: Defense of a Character's Actions (After Act IV)
   - Extension Activity: News Account
6. **To understand and apply listening and speaking strategies**
   - Extension Activity: Oral Report

STEP-BY-STEP TEACHING GUIDE	PACING GUIDE
PRETEACH	
Motivate Students and Provide Background	
Use the Motivation activity (ATE p. 1230)	5 min.
Read and discuss author and background features (SE/ATE p. 1230–1231)	15 min.
Introduce the Concepts	
Introduce the Literary Analysis and Reading Strategy (SE/ATE p. 1232)	15 min.
Pronounce the vocabulary words and read their definitions (SE p. 1232)	5 min.
TEACH	
Monitor Comprehension	
Informally monitor comprehension by circulating while students read independently or in groups	55 min.
Monitor students' comprehension with the Reading Check notes (SE/ATE pp. 1235, 1237, 1239, 1241, 1243, 1244, 1245, 1247, 1249, 1251, 1253, 1255, 1257, 1259, 1261)	as students read
Develop vocabulary with Vocabulary notes (SE pp. 1235, 1236, 1238, 1245, 1253, 1254, 1258)	as students read
Develop Understanding	
Develop students' understanding of dialogue and stage directions with the Literary Analysis annotations (SE pp. 1234, 1235, 1239, 1243, 1245, 1246, 1247, 1250, 1251, 1252, 1256, 1258, 1261; ATE pp. 1234, 1235, 1239, 1243, 1245, 1246, 1247, 1250, 1251, 1252, 1256, 1257, 1258, 1261)	10 min.
Develop students' ability to question the characters' motives by using the Reading Strategy annotations (SE pp. 1237, 1238, 1241, 1246, 1249, 1250, 1252, 1255, 1259, 1260, 1262; ATE pp. 1237, 1238, 1241, 1242, 1246, 1249, 1250, 1252, 1255, 1259, 1260, 1262)	5 min.
ASSESS	
Assess Mastery	
Assess students' mastery of the Reading Strategy and Literary Analysis by having them answer the Review and Assess questions (SE/ATE p. 1264)	15 min.
Use one or more of the print and media Assessment Resources (ATE p. 1264)	up to 45 min.
EXTEND	
Apply Understanding	
Have students complete the Vocabulary Development Lesson and the Grammar and Style Lesson (SE p. 1265)	20 min.
Apply students' understanding of the selection using one or more of the Extension Activities (SE p. 1265)	20–90 min.

A **ACCELERATED INSTRUCTION:**
Use the strategies and activities identified with an **A**.

UNIVERSAL ACCESS
● = Below Level Students
▲ = On-Level Students
■ = Above Level Students

Time and Resource Manager

RESOURCES		
PRINT	**TRANSPARENCIES**	**TECHNOLOGY**
• **Beyond Literature,** Cross-Curricular Connection: Social Studies, p. 73 ▲ ■		• **Interest Grabber Video,** Tape 6 ● ▲ ■
• **Selection Support Workbook:** ● ▲ ■ Literary Analysis, p. 317 Reading Strategy, p. 316 Build Vocabulary, p. 314	• **Literary Analysis and Reading Transparencies,** pp. 145 and 146 ● ▲ ■	
• **Literatura en español** ● ▲ • **Literary Analysis for Enrichment** ■		
• **Formal Assessment:** Selection Test, pp. 309–311 ● ▲ ■ • **Open Book Test,** pp. 217–219 ● ▲ ■ • **PRENTICE HALL ASSESSMENT SYSTEM** ● ▲ ■	• **PRENTICE HALL ASSESSMENT SYSTEM** ● ▲ ■ Skills Practice Answers and Explanations on Transparencies	• **Test Bank Software** ● ▲ ■ • **Got It! Assessment Videotapes,** Tape 6 ● ▲
• **Selection Support Workbook:** ● ▲ ■ Grammar and Style, p. 315 • **Writing and Grammar,** Ruby Level ● ▲ ■ • **Extension Activities,** p. 73 ● ▲ ■	• **Daily Language Practice Transparencies** ● ▲	• **Writing and Grammar iText CD-ROM** ● ▲ ■ **Take It to the Net** www.phschool.com

BLOCK SCHEDULING: Use one 90-minute class period to preteach the selection and have students read it. Use a second 90-minute class period to assess students' mastery of skills and have them complete one of the Extension Activities.

Background

A Streetcar Named Desire is the story of two sisters, Stella and Blanche, who are from a genteel Southern family. Stella has married Stanley Kowalski, a working-class man with no pretension to intellect or manners. When Blanche comes on a long visit, she reacts to Stanley with fear and loathing. In his turn, he realizes her contempt and resents it, believing she will try to turn Stella against him. In an act of brutal violence, Stanley eventually triumphs over the weaker Blanche. The film of Williams's play won an Academy Award for Vivian Leigh. While Marlon Brando did not win the Oscar that year, critics have said that his performance in the role of Stanley Kowalski had a more enduring influence on American film than any other.

▶ **Critical Viewing**

Answer: Students may mention the expressions on the actors' faces or the fact that they are standing so close together.

A Closer Look

Twentieth Century Drama: America on Stage

O'Neill, Hellman, Williams, and a host of American playwrights rewrote the rules of the theater.

It is opening night at a major American theater. You check your coat, find your seat, and flip through the *Playbill*. As the curtain rises, you are filled with anticipation of a bold, exciting, new play, like nothing you have ever seen.

No, it is not a big-budget musical with elaborate sets and fancy costumes. It is a night of talk—sometimes loud and angry, sometimes hushed and mournful, but always riveting.

For much of the twentieth century, the American theater was the center of the intellectual world. Great plays offered thrilling stories, crackling dialogue, and philosophical truth. The best American playwrights of the twentieth century chronicled different aspects of the American experience.

- **Thornton Wilder** (1897–1975), best known for the Pulitzer Prize-winning play *Our Town* (1938), revealed the secrets of small-town America.
- **Arthur Miller** (b. 1915) combined politics and realism to give America some of its most moving plays, including *Death of a Salesman* (1949) and *The Crucible* (1953) (see page 1232).
- **Lorraine Hansberry** (1930–1965) filled theaters with the stories of African Americans. Her play *A Raisin in the Sun* (1959) was the first drama by a black woman to be produced on Broadway.
- **Edward Albee** (b. 1928) shocked audiences with his psychological dramas, including the harsh and powerful *Who's Afraid of Virginia Woolf* (1962).

The American theater had not always been such a powerful forum. Before the 1920s, the American stage was known for light, escapist fare, and was a showcase for actors, not writers. It was Eugene O'Neill who introduced a new level of seriousness and ushered in a century of great drama.

America's First Great Playwright "I want to be an artist or nothing," Eugene O'Neill said at the age of twenty-five. He pursued that goal relentlessly. When he died forty years later, he had written more than fifty plays, and won the Nobel Prize and four Pulitzer Prizes.

▼ **Critical Viewing** This photograph shows Vivien Leigh as Blanche Dubois and Marlon Brando as Stanley Kowalski in Tennesse Williams's *A Streetcar named Desire*. In what ways does this scene depict the "raw power of human emotion"? **[Interpret]**

✳ ENRICHMENT: Theater Connection

Song and Dance

With the premiere of *Showboat,* the Broadway musical took its rightful place in American theater history. This show by Oscar Hammerstein II and Jerome Kern adapted a novel by Edna Ferber. In song, dance, and dialogue, it took on the difficult subject of miscegenation as well as the more popular, general theme of romance. This straightforward willingness to deal with serious issues in American society—in this case racial prejudice, in other shows gang warfare (*West Side Story*), urban loneliness (*Company*), and wife-beating (*Carousel*)—gives the Broadway musical a depth and passion that make it a serious genre of our theater.

Nearly all of O'Neill's work reflects his troubled childhood, and the rough-and-tumble experiences of his youth. When he was in his mid-twenties, hard living landed him in the hospital, where he pondered his life for the first time. "It was in this enforced period of reflection that the urge to write first came to me," he said.

O'Neill experimented with different styles—sometimes realistic, sometimes symbolic, and sometimes political. *Beyond the Horizon* (1920), his first play produced on Broadway, was a smash hit. *The Iceman Cometh* (1946) told the stories of dreamers and losers who frequent a waterfront saloon. *A Long Day's Journey Into Night* (1956), O'Neill's greatest play, recounted the playwright's traumatic childhood. It was not produced until after his death in 1953.

A Woman's Voice Lillian Hellman was born in 1905 in New Orleans, the daughter of a shoe salesman and a socialite. She became the most influential female playwright of the twentieth century.

In 1930, Hellman met detective novelist Dashiell Hammet, who was famous for stylish books like the *Thin Man* and *The Maltese Falcon*. Hammett became Hellman's mentor and encouraged her to shun cheap success for honest drama. Hellman's first play, *The Children's Hour*, appeared on Broadway in 1934. The tale of two female teachers whose lives are ruined by rumor and innuendo both captivated and shocked audiences.

From the late 1930s through the late 1940s, Hellman helped to shape a golden age of American theater. Her best-known work, *The Little Foxes* (1939), takes a harsh look at a rich and powerful Southern family. Her political drama *Watch on the Rhine* (1941) warned the world of the dangers of Nazism. By the time of her death in 1984, Hellman had paved the way for women writers to exert influence and express powerful views.

The Raw Power of Human Emotion Born in 1911, in rural Mississippi, Tennessee Williams was the son of a traveling salesman and a minister's daughter. While still a teenager, Williams became determined to be a writer.

Williams's first major play, *The Glass Menagerie*, appeared on Broadway in 1945, and was a huge hit. Based loosely on his own family, the play moved audiences with its compassion for a mother and sister who cling to their ever-fading dreams.

In 1947, the shy, sensitive Williams shocked audiences with the intensity of his play *A Streetcar Named Desire*. The play presented a hard-hitting story, filled with cruelty but also with beauty. Its effect on audiences was so great that it inspired dozens of writers to imitate it.

Williams wrote more than 60 plays. By the time he died in 1983, he had become one of the most influential—and imitated—writers of all time.

Background

Dashiell Hammet captured the era of Prohibition in his detective novel *The Thin Man* (1933). Nick and Nora Charles, a wealthy married couple spending the New Year's holiday in New York, move from speakeasy to cocktail party and back again as Nick sorts out a tangle of gangsters, liars, and cops to pin down a murderer. Nearly every conversation in the book takes place over cocktails, martinis, or whisky, and not a character in the book seems troubled by any concern for the 18th Amendment. Prohibition was repealed in 1933.

Hammet did not write plays, but his major novels were all filmed. *The Maltese Falcon*, starring Humphrey Bogart, is one of the great Hollywood classics. *The Thin Man*, which paired William Powell and Myrna Loy as Nick and Nora Charles, was so successful that it spawned a series of popular sequels, none as good as the original.

Critical Thinking

- Why do you think plays took so long to catch on in American society, when there was an important English theater all the way back in the 1500s?
  Answer: Puritans did not approve of theater and this disapproval permeated society.

**Step-by-Step Teaching Guide
for pp. 1230–1232**

Motivation

Have students think about situations in which they have been subjected to pressure from their peers or their families. Explain that they are about to read a play in which the population of an entire town splits into two factions—the accusers and the accused. Into this town come judges who try to force the accused to confess to the crimes of which they are accused. Those who refuse to confess will be sentenced to death.

▣ Interest Grabber Videotape

As an alternative, play "Arthur Miller" on Tape 6 to engage students' interest.

❶ Background

In an essay titled "*The Crucible* in History," Arthur Miller discussed his reasons for writing the play:

"In 1948, '49, '50, '51, I had the sensation of being trapped inside a perverse work of art, one of those Escher constructs in which it is impossible to know whether a stairway is going up or down. Practically everyone I knew, all survivors of the Great Depression of course as well as World War II, was somewhere within the conventions of the political left of center, one or two were Communist Party members, some were sort of fellow travelers, as I suppose I was. . . . I have never been able to believe in the reality of these people being actual or putative traitors any more than I could be, yet others like them were being fired from teaching or other jobs in government or large corporations. The unreality of it all never left me. . . . *The Crucible* was an attempt to make life real again, palpable and structured—a work of art created in order to interpret an anterior work of art that was called reality but was not."

Prepare to Read

❶ The Crucible

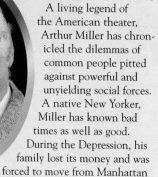

Arthur Miller (b. 1915)

A living legend of the American theater, Arthur Miller has chronicled the dilemmas of common people pitted against powerful and unyielding social forces. A native New Yorker, Miller has known bad times as well as good.

During the Depression, his family lost its money and was forced to move from Manhattan to more modest living quarters in Brooklyn. Although Miller graduated from Abraham Lincoln High School in 1932, he was forced to delay his enrollment at the University of Michigan for more than two years in order to raise money for tuition. He did so by working at a variety of jobs, including singing for a local radio station, driving a truck, and working as a stock clerk in an automobile parts warehouse.

Promising Playwright Miller first began writing drama while still in college. In 1947, his play *All My Sons* opened on Broadway to immediate acclaim, establishing Miller as a bright new talent. Two years later, he won international fame and a Pulitzer Prize for *Death of a Salesman* (1949), which critics hailed as a modern American tragedy.

His next play, *The Crucible* (1953), was less warmly received, because it uses the Salem witchcraft trials of 1692 as a means of attacking the anti-communist "witch hunts" in Congress in the 1950s. Miller believed that the hysteria surrounding the witchcraft trials in Puritan New England paralleled the contemporary climate of McCarthyism—Senator Joseph McCarthy's obsessive quest to uncover Communist party infiltration of American institutions.

In the introduction to his *Collected Plays* (1957), Miller described his perceptions of the atmosphere during the McCarthy era and the way in which those perceptions influenced the writing of *The Crucible*. He said, "It was as though the whole country had been born anew, without a memory even of certain elemental decencies which a year or two earlier no one would have imagined could be altered, let alone forgotten. Astounded, I watched men pass me by without a nod whom I had known rather well for years; and again, the astonishment was produced by my knowledge, which I could not give up, that the terror in these people was being knowingly planned and consciously engineered, and yet that all they knew was terror. That so interior and subjective an emotion could have been so manifestly created from without was a marvel to me. It underlies every word in *The Crucible*."

In the Shadows of McCarthyism During the two years following the publication and production of *The Crucible*, Miller was investigated for possible associations with the Communist party. In 1956, he was called to testify before the House Committee on Un-American Activities. Although he never became a member of the Communist party, Miller, like so many of his contemporaries, had advocated principles of social justice and equality among the classes. He had become disillusioned, however, by the reality of communism as practiced in the Soviet Union. At the hearings, he testified about his own experiences, but he refused to discuss his colleagues and associates. He was found guilty of contempt of Congress for his refusal, but the sentence was later overturned.

Hollywood Glamour In 1956, the spotlight was focused on Miller's personal life when he married glamorous film star Marilyn Monroe. Although he did little writing during their five-year marriage, he did pen the screenplay for a film, *The Misfits* (1961), in which Monroe starred. After their divorce, Miller wrote other noteworthy plays, including *The Price* (1968) and *The Last Yankee* (1993).

1230 ◆ *Prosperity and Protest (1946–Present)*

TEACHING RESOURCES

The following resources can be used to enrich or extend the instruction for pp. 1230–1232.

Motivation

▣ **Interest Grabber Video**, Tape 6: Arthur Miller

Background

📖 **Beyond Literature**, p. 73 ▣

 Take It to the Net
Visit www.phschool.com for Background and hotlinks for *The Crucible*.

Literary Analysis

📄 **Literary Analysis and Reading Transparencies**, Dialogue and Stage Directions, p. 146 ▣

Reading

📖 **Selection Support**: Reading Strategy, p. 316; Build Vocabulary, p. 314

📄 **Literary Analysis and Reading Transparencies**, Questioning the Characters' Motives, p. 145

 **BLOCK SCHEDULING:** Resources marked with this symbol provide varied instruction during 90-minute blocks.

❷ Background

In 1692, the British colony of Massachusetts was swept by a witchcraft hysteria that resulted in the execution of twenty people and the jailing of at least 150 others. The incident was not isolated. It is estimated that between 1 million and 9 million Europeans were accused of being witches and then executed in the sixteenth and seventeenth centuries. Many of these people were merely practicing folk customs that had survived in Europe since pre-Christian times. In addition, in an era when religion and politics were closely allied, witch hunts were often politically motivated. England's James I, for example, wrote a treatise on witchcraft and sometimes accused his enemies of practicing the black arts. It was a cry that resonated well among a superstitious populace.

For the New England colonies, however, the witchcraft episode was unusual, though perhaps inevitable. The colonists endured harsh conditions and punishing hardship in their lives. Finding themselves at the mercy of forces beyond their control—bitter weather, sickness and death, devastating fires, drought, and insect infestations that killed their crops—many colonists attributed their misfortunes to the Devil. They were fearful (some would say paranoid) people, and their Puritan faith stressed the biblical teaching that witches were real and dangerous.

In the small parish of Salem Village, many were quick to blame witchcraft when the minister's daughter and several other girls were afflicted by seizures and lapses into unconsciousness, especially after it was learned that the girls had been dabbling in fortunetelling with the minister's slave, Tituba. (They were not dancing in the woods, as portrayed in the play.) At first, only Tituba and two elderly women were called witches, but then the hunt spread until some of the colony's most prominent citizens stood accused. Many historians have seen a pattern of social and economic

animosity behind the accusations, but most feel that mass hysteria was also a strong contributing factor.

When *The Crucible* was first published, Arthur Miller added a note about the play's historical accuracy: "This play is not history in the sense in which the word is used by the academic historian. Dramatic purposes have sometimes required many characters to be fused into one; the number of girls involved in the 'crying-out' has been reduced; Abigail's age has been raised; while there were several judges of almost equal authority, I have symbolized them in Hathorne and Danforth. However, I believe that the reader will discover here the essential nature of one of the strangest and most awful chapters in human history. The fate of each character is exactly that of his historical model, and there is no one in the drama who did not play a similar—and in some cases exactly the same—role in history."

❷ Background

In 1643, the four colonies of New England—Plymouth, Massachusetts, Connecticut, and Rhode Island—formed a confederation called the United Colonies of New England. Each was the stronghold of a different religious body. The Plymouth Puritans were separatists who wanted a break from the Church of England. The Massachusetts Puritans were not separatist, but were still extremely conservative. Connecticut was governed by a Presbyterian system, while Rhode Island was home to Quakers, Anabaptists, and other free thinkers.

In 1660, Puritan Oliver Cromwell's reign over England came to an end with the restoration of the monarchy and the coronation of the Roman Catholic Charles II. Charles revoked the charters that guaranteed the American colonies self-government. This alarmed the Puritans on both economic and religious grounds; they wanted no interference with their profitable trade or with their systems of religion. This halt in colonial self-government would eventually lead to the American Revolution of the late 1700s. This resentment of authority was mirrored in the gradual changes to the Puritan system that finally erupted in the witchcraft trials.

Between 1662 and 1676, conflicts between the Indians and the Europeans escalated. In 1676, the all-out war known as King Philip's War ("King Philip" was a Wampanoag chief whose Indian name was Metacomet) broke out between them. Many on both sides were killed.

The Salem witchcraft trials grew out of this climate of unrest and fear of enemies attacking from all sides—the English king eroding colonial rights, Native Americans trying to repossess their land, and liberal factions within the church seeking to ease standards for membership (see Enrichment on p. 1248 of this teacher's edition).

❸ Literary Analysis

Dialogue and Stage Directions

- Let students know that stage directions have two purposes: to help those producing the play and to help readers. First, stage directions and dialogue provide guidelines about the playwright's intentions to the director and actors. Write the following quotation from the play on the chalkboard:

  PARRIS, *eagerly*: What does the doctor say, child?

- Point out that there are any number of ways the actor might read this line—listlessly, hopelessly, impatiently, rudely, and so on. The stage direction shows the actor what the writer intended.

- The second purpose of stage directions is to flesh out the script for readers. Descriptive details and indications of the characters' emotions help readers to picture a performance in their minds and to understand how the playwright conceived of the characters.

- Tell students that they can easily recognize the stage directions in *The Crucible* because they are printed in italic type.

❹ Reading Strategy

Questioning the Characters' Motives

- Motive is the answer to the question *Why?* Although a novelist can write passages that let a reader see into the thoughts and motives of the characters, most of the time a playwright allows the audience only to overhear conversations. When watching a play, the audience must interpret the characters' motives. Stage directions can help a reader of a play to some degree, but stage directions are usually quite brief.

Vocabulary Development

- Pronounce each vocabulary word for students, and read the definitions as a class. Have students identify any words with which they are already familiar.

 E-Teach

Visit E-Teach at www.phschool.com for teachers' essays on how to teach, with questions and answers.

1232

Preview

Connecting to the Literature

If you have ever observed the way a rumor spreads through your school or helped to spread one yourself, you know how easy it is to be swept along with a crowd, believing blindly rather than using your own judgment.

❸ Literary Analysis

Dialogue and Stage Directions

The written script of a drama consists of dialogue and stage directions.

- **Dialogue** refers to the words characters speak. Dialogue both advances the plot and reveals the characters' personalities and backgrounds.

- **Stage directions** usually indicate where a scene takes place, what it should look like, and how the characters should move and speak. Stage directions are usually set in italic type to distinguish them from dialogue.

As you read Act I of *The Crucible*, look for information about characters and events in the stage directions as well as in the dialogue.

Connecting Literary Elements

Dramatic exposition conveys critical information about a play's settings, props, characters, and even historical or social context. Most playwrights provide such information in the dialogue or stage directions. In *The Crucible*, Arthur Miller does something quite different, interjecting lengthy prose commentaries that contain a wealth of dramatic exposition. As you read Act I, gather details from these essay-like passages to help you enter the world of the play.

❹ Reading Strategy

Questioning the Characters' Motives

Like people in real life, characters in plays are not always what they seem. Often, we must **question the characters' motives**—their reasons for behaving as they do. Fear, greed, guilt, love, loyalty, and revenge are some of the driving forces behind human behavior. Use a chart like the one shown to examine the motives of each character in Act I.

Vocabulary Development

predilection (pred´ ə lek´ shən) *n.* pre-existing preference (p. 1235)

ingratiating (in grā´ shē āt´ iŋ) *adj.* charming or flattering (p. 1236)

dissembling (di sem´ bliŋ) *n.* disguising one's real nature or motives (p. 1238)

calumny (kal´ əm nē) *n.* false accusation; slander (p. 1245)

inculcation (in´ kul kā´ shən) *n.* teaching by repetition and urging (p. 1253)

propitiation (prə pish´ ē ā´ shən) *n.* action designed to soothe or satisfy a person, a cause, etc. (p. 1254)

licentious (lī sen´ shəs) *adj.* lacking moral restraint (p. 1258)

Character
Words and Actions
Motive

1232 ◆ *Prosperity and Protest (1946–Present)*

CUSTOMIZE INSTRUCTION FOR UNIVERSAL ACCESS

For Less Proficient Readers	For English Learners	For Advanced Readers
Remind students that stage directions are printed in italics. Have a small group of students read some of the play aloud. Ask them to pay close attention to the stage directions and try to follow them as they read the dialogue aloud.	Encourage students to get the most they can out of the stage directions, using context clues and sound-alike words, before they check dictionaries for definitions. Have them think about how a character would naturally speak a certain line.	Have students discuss how the stage directions affect their enjoyment and understanding of the play. Point out that the stage directions are not available to the audience watching the play in a theater. What does this suggest about Miller's intended audience?

The CRUCIBLE:[1]

Arthur Miller

---

1. **crucible** (krōō´ sə bel) *n.* heat-resistant container in which metals are melted or fused at very high temperatures; thus, a severe trial or test.

TEACHING RESOURCES

The following resources can be used to enrich or extend the instruction for pp. 1233–1263

Literary Analysis
📖 **Selection Support:** Literary Analysis, p. 317

TEACH

Step-by-Step Teaching Guide for pp. 1233–1263

CUSTOMIZE INSTRUCTION For Logical/Mathematical Learners

Ask students to trace the chain of causes and effects that lead toward the act's conclusion. Have students try to work out who is responsible for what happens at the end of the act. Is more than one person responsible? Which character do students think bears the greatest guilt for what happens?

❶ Background

Language

The word *crucible* comes from the Latin word for "cross." A crucible is any pot made of material strong enough to withstand the intense heat necessary to melt down metals. *Crucible* also means "a severe trial or test."

❷ About Act I

It is 1692 in Salem, Massachusetts. Betty Parris and Ruth Putnam have mysteriously fallen ill. Abigail, Betty's cousin, confesses to Reverend Parris that she and the other girls were dancing in the woods to chants sung by Tituba, Reverend Parris's West Indian slave. She denies his immediate suspicion that they were practicing witchcraft.

The Putnams are convinced that witchcraft is to blame for Ruth's illness. Parris has sent for Reverend Hale, an expert on the subject, in the hope that he can cure the girls.

John Proctor comes by looking for his servant Mary. Abigail reminds him of their love affair, and he sternly tells her that it is all over. Betty begins screaming, and soon the room is filled with people. Parris and the Putnams insist that it is witchcraft; Proctor, Rebecca Nurse, and Giles Corey are skeptical. Old conflicts between neighbors revive.

Hale enters and begins to ask questions. In mounting panic and hysteria, Betty and Abigail accuse Tituba of witchcraft. They begin to cry out other names as Parris and Hale agree to fetch the marshal.

❸ Literary Analysis
Dialogue and Stage Directions

- Point out the designation "An Overture" at the start of the stage directions. Tell students that in modern theater, an overture is a short piece of music that is played before the curtain goes up on Act I of an opera or a musical play. Overtures often consist of melodies and motifs that will be heard later in the show. Ask what Miller's calling this an overture suggests to them about this act.
  Answer: Act I may introduce themes and motifs that will be explored more fully in the later acts. It may be entirely expository in nature, like a musical overture. Its purpose may be simply to set a mood.

- Ask students the Literary Analysis question on p. 1234: What important information is revealed in the third paragraph of the stage direction?
  Answer: This paragraph identifies the two people on stage and their relationship to each other.

▶ Monitor Progress Have students find the place where they would first find out this information if they were attending a performance rather than reading the script.
  Answer: Some students may know that the cast is listed in order of appearance, so they might infer that the characters on stage are Reverend Parris and Betty Parris, and are related in some way. Other students will say they would not know until p. 1238 when Parris refers to Betty as his daughter.

CHARACTERS

REVEREND PARRIS	MARTHA COREY
BETTY PARRIS	REVEREND JOHN HALE
TITUBA	ELIZABETH PROCTOR
ABIGAIL WILLIAMS	FRANCIS NURSE
SUSANNA WALCOTT	EZEKIEL CHEEVER
MRS. ANN PUTNAM	MARSHAL HERRICK
THOMAS PUTNAM	JUDGE HATHORNE
MERCY LEWIS	DEPUTY GOVERNOR
MARY WARREN	DANFORTH
JOHN PROCTOR	SARAH GOOD
REBECCA NURSE	HOPKINS
GILES COREY	

ACT I

(An Overture)

A small upper bedroom in the home of REVEREND SAMUEL PARRIS, *Salem, Massachusetts, in the spring of the year 1692.*

There is a narrow window at the left. Through its leaded panes the morning sunlight streams. A candle still burns near the bed, which is at the right. A chest, a chair, and a small table are the other furnishings. At the back a door opens on the landing of the stairway to the ground floor. The room gives off an air of clean spareness. The roof rafters are exposed, and the wood colors are raw and unmellowed.

❸ *As the curtain rises,* REVEREND PARRIS *is discovered kneeling beside the bed, evidently in prayer. His daughter,* BETTY PARRIS, *aged ten, is lying on the bed, inert.*

At the time of these events Parris was in his middle forties. In history he cut a villainous path, and there is very little good to be said for him. He believed he was being persecuted wherever he went, despite his best efforts to win people and God to his side. In meeting, he felt insulted if someone rose to shut the door without first asking his permission. He was a widower with no interest in children, or talent with them. He regarded them as young adults, and until this strange crisis he, like the rest of Salem, never conceived that the children were anything but thankful for being permitted to walk straight, eyes slightly lowered, arms at the sides, and mouths shut until bidden to speak.

His house stood in the "town"—but we today would hardly call it a village. The meeting house was nearby, and from this point outward—toward the bay or inland—there were a few small-windowed, dark houses snuggling against the raw Massachusetts winter. Salem had been established hardly forty years before. To the European world the whole province was a barbaric frontier inhabited by a sect of fanatics who, nevertheless, were shipping out products of slowly increasing quantity and value.

1234 ◆ *Prosperity and Protest (1946–Present)*

Literary Analysis
Dialogue and Stage Directions What important information is revealed in the third paragraph of the stage direction?

CUSTOMIZE INSTRUCTION FOR UNIVERSAL ACCESS

For Gifted/Talented Students

Have students research childhood in early America. In the commentary above, Miller says that children were expected to "walk straight, eyes slightly lowered, arms at the sides, and mouths shut." Have students find out what Puritan children wore, how they were educated, what games they played, at what age they began working, and what the differences were between a boy's upbringing and a girl's. Ask students to research particularly Miller's observation that children were regarded simply as small adults. Can students find any evidence to the contrary? Have students share the results of their research with their classmates so that everyone has the background information to understand the context in which the girls of Salem began accusing adults of witchcraft.

No one can really know what their lives were like. They had no novel-ists—and would not have permitted anyone to read a novel if one were handy. Their creed forbade anything resembling a theater or "vain enjoyment." They did not celebrate Christmas, and a holiday from work meant only that they must concentrate even more upon prayer.

Which is not to say that nothing broke into this strict and somber way of life. When a new farmhouse was built, friends assembled to "raise the roof," and there would be special foods cooked and probably some potent cider passed around. There was a good supply of ne'er-do-wells in Salem, who dallied at the shovelboard[2] in Bridget Bishop's tavern. Probably more than the creed, hard work kept the morals of the place from spoiling, for the people were forced to fight the land like heroes for every grain of corn, and no man had very much time for fooling around.

That there were some jokers, however, is indicated by the practice of appointing a two-man patrol whose duty was to "walk forth in the time of God's worship to take notice of such as either lie about the meet-ing house, without attending to the word and ordinances, or that lie at home or in the fields without giving good account thereof, and to take the names of such persons, and to present them to the magistrates, whereby they may be accordingly proceeded against." This <u>predilection</u> for minding other people's business was time-honored among the people of Salem, and it undoubtedly created many of the suspicions which were to feed the coming madness. It was also, in my opinion, one of the things that a John Proctor would rebel against, for the time of the armed camp had almost passed, and since the country was reasonably—although not wholly—safe, the old disciplines were beginning to rankle. But, as in all such matters, the issue was not clear-cut, for danger was still a possibility, and in unity still lay the best promise of safety.

The edge of the wilderness was close by. The American continent stretched endlessly west, and it was full of mystery for them. It stood, dark and threatening, over their shoulders night and day, for out of it Indian tribes marauded from time to time, and Reverend Parris had parishioners who had lost relatives to these heathen.

The parochial snobbery of these people was partly responsible for their failure to convert the Indians. Probably they also preferred to take land from heathens rather than from fellow Christians. At any rate, very few Indians were converted, and the Salem folk believed that the virgin forest was the Devil's last preserve, his home base and the citadel of his final stand. To the best of their knowledge the American forest was the last place on earth that was not paying homage to God.

For these reasons, among others, they carried about an air of innate resistance, even of persecution. Their fathers had, of course, been per-secuted in England. So now they and their church found it necessary to deny any other sect its freedom, lest their New Jerusalem[3] be defiled and corrupted by wrong ways and deceitful ideas.

---

2. **shovelboard** game in which a coin or other disk is driven with the hand along a highly polished board, floor, or table marked with transverse lines.
3. **New Jerusalem** in the Bible, the holy city of heaven.

Literary Analysis
Dialogue, Stage Directions, and Dramatic Exposition In what way does the information Miller provides in these essay-like passages differ from the typical stage direction or dialogue?

predilection (pred′ əl ek′ shən) *n.* preexisting preference

Literary Analysis
Dialogue, Stage Directions, and Dramatic Exposition Why is this background information about Salem important to your understanding of the play?

5 ✔ **Reading Check**
What is a time-honored activity among the people of Salem?

The Crucible, Act I ◆ 1235

---

4 **Literary Analysis**
Dialogue, Stage Directions, and Dramatic Exposition

- What does the opening paragraph of the commentary (p. 1234) tell the reader about Parris? Why would Miller do this?
  Answer: The commentary prejudices readers against him by saying that he is a villain. Miller wants readers to know right away that Parris's motives are base.

- Ask students the first Literary Analysis question on p. 1235: In what way does the information Miller provides in these essay-like passages differ from the typical stage direction or dialogue?
  Answer: In this commentary, Miller speaks directly to the reader. He provides information about the historical figures and events on which his play is based.

- Ask students the second Literary Analysis question on p. 1235: Why is this background information about Salem important to your understanding of the play?
  Answer: Readers may not know much about the long-ago time and the place in which the play is set. This information fills in this background for readers.

▶ Monitor Progress What does the presence of this commentary suggest about Miller's intentions?
  Answer: Miller wanted his play to be read as well as performed. This commentary will not appear in a performance, so it is clearly written especially for the reader.

5 ✔ **Reading Check**
Answer: Minding one another's business is a time-honored activity among the people of Salem.

CUSTOMIZE INSTRUCTION FOR UNIVERSAL ACCESS

For Advanced Readers

Explain that the passage of lengthy prose commentary that appears here is one of several that appear throughout Act I. Tell students that these commentaries are included only for readers of the play—they are not part of its theatrical performance. Have students write brief critical essays discussing the reasons they think Miller included these commentaries and evaluating what they contribute to the play. Given that the theater audience does not read them or hear them, are they in any sense necessary? If not, why did Miller include them? What do they add to a reader's understanding and appreciation of the play? Might Miller have communicated the same information in dialogue, in a narration, or in other ways?

Questioning the Characters' Motives

- Have students paraphrase the motives Miller ascribes for the Puritan way of life in New England.
  Answer: The Puritans banded together to protect and perpetuate their religious beliefs.

- Ask students what they think might happen to any Puritans whose behavior did not conform to the community's beliefs.
  Answer: Such people would most likely be targeted by their watchful neighbors and turned over to authorities, since any sign of disunity would have been perceived as a threat to the ordered life of the community.

▶ Monitor Progress Have students keep this motivation for unity in mind as they continue reading Act I. Have them look for characters whose ideas seem to be different from those of their neighbors. What may happen to these characters later in the play?

❼ ▶ Critical Viewing

Answer: He is looking toward the sky, which suggests an attitude of prayer.

They believed, in short, that they held in their steady hands the candle that would light the world. We have inherited this belief, and it has helped and hurt us. It helped them with the discipline it gave them. They were a dedicated folk, by and large, and they had to be to survive the life they had chosen or been born into in this country.

The proof of their belief's value to them may be taken from the opposite character of the first Jamestown settlement, farther south, in Virginia. The Englishmen who landed there were motivated mainly by a hunt for profit. They had thought to pick off the wealth of the new country and then return rich to England. They were a band of individualists, and a much more <u>ingratiating</u> group than the Massachusetts men. But Virginia destroyed them. Massachusetts tried to kill off the Puritans, but they combined; they set up a communal society which, in the beginning, was little more than an armed camp with an autocratic and very devoted leadership. It was, however, an autocracy by consent, for they were united from top to bottom by a commonly held ideology whose perpetuation was the reason and justification for all their sufferings. So their self-denial, their purposefulness, their suspicion of all vain pursuits, their hard-handed justice, were altogether perfect instruments for the conquest of this space so antagonistic to man.

❻ But the people of Salem in 1692 were not quite the dedicated folk that arrived on the *Mayflower*. A vast differentiation had taken place, and in their own time a revolution had unseated the royal government and substituted a junta[4] which was at this moment in power. The times, to their eyes, must have been out of joint, and to the common folk must have seemed as insoluble and complicated as do ours today. It is not hard to see how easily many could have been led to believe that the time of confusion had been brought upon them by deep and darkling forces. No hint of such speculation appears on the court record, but social disorder in any age breeds such mystical suspicions, and when, as in Salem, wonders are brought forth from below the social surface, it is too much to expect people to hold back very long from laying on the victims with all the force of their frustrations.

The Salem tragedy, which is about to begin in these pages, developed from a paradox. It is a paradox in whose grip we still live, and there is no prospect yet that we will discover its resolution. Simply, it was this: for good purposes, even high purposes, the people of Salem developed a theocracy, a combine of state and religious power whose function was to keep the community together, and to prevent any kind of disunity that might open it to destruction by material or ideological enemies. It was forged for a necessary purpose and accomplished that purpose. But all organization is and must be grounded on the idea of exclusion and prohibition, just as two objects

---

ingratiating (in grā′ shē āt′ iŋ) *adj.* charming or flattering

The Execution of Stephen Burroughs for Witchcraft at Salem, Massachusetts in 1692, 19th-CenturyEngraving

❼ ▲ Critical Viewing
This nineteenth-century engraving shows the hanging of the Reverend Stephen Burroughs during the Salem witchcraft trials. What does this image suggest about the condemned man's state of mind? **[Infer]**

---

4. **junta** (hoon′ tə) *n.* assembly or council.

cannot occupy the same space. Evidently the time came in New England when the repressions of order were heavier than seemed warranted by the dangers against which the order was organized. The witch-hunt was a perverse manifestation of the panic which set in among all classes when the balance began to turn toward greater individual freedom.

When one rises above the individual villainy displayed, one can only pity them all, just as we shall be pitied someday. It is still impossible for man to organize his social life without repressions, and the balance has yet to be struck between order and freedom.

The witch-hunt was not, however, a mere repression. It was also, and as importantly, a long overdue opportunity for everyone so inclined to express publicly his guilt and sins, under the cover of accusations against the victims. It suddenly became possible—and patriotic and holy—for a man to say that Martha Corey had come into his bedroom at night, and that, while his wife was sleeping at his side, Martha laid herself down on his chest and "nearly suffocated him." Of course it was her spirit only, but his satisfaction at confessing himself was no lighter than if it had been Martha herself. One could not ordinarily speak such things in public.

8 Long-held hatreds of neighbors could now be openly expressed, and vengeance taken, despite the Bible's charitable injunctions. Land-lust which had been expressed before by constant bickering over boundaries and deeds, could now be elevated to the arena of morality; one could cry witch against one's neighbor and feel perfectly justified in the bargain. Old scores could be settled on a plane of heavenly combat between Lucifer[5] and the Lord; suspicions and the envy of the miserable toward the happy could and did burst out in the general revenge.

REVEREND PARRIS *is praying now, and, though we cannot hear his words, a sense of his confusion hangs about him. He mumbles, then seems about to weep; then he weeps, then prays again; but his daughter does not stir on the bed.*

The door opens, and his Negro slave enters. TITUBA *is in her forties.* PARRIS *brought her with him from Barbados, where he spent some years as a merchant before entering the ministry. She enters as one does who can no longer bear to be barred from the sight of her beloved, but she is also very frightened because her slave sense has warned her that, as always, trouble in this house eventually lands on her back.*

TITUBA, *already taking a step backward:* My Betty be hearty soon?

PARRIS: Out of here!

TITUBA, *backing to the door:* My Betty not goin' die . . .

PARRIS, *scrambling to his feet in a fury:* Out of my sight! *She is gone.* Out of my— *He is overcome with sobs. He clamps his teeth against them and closes the door and leans against it, exhausted.* Oh, my God! God help me! *Quaking with fear, mumbling to himself through his sobs, he goes to the bed and gently takes* BETTY'S *hand.* Betty. Child. Dear child. Will you wake, will you open up your eyes! Betty, little one . . .

---

5. **Lucifer** (lōō′ sə fər) the Devil.

Reading Strategy
Questioning the Characters' Motives
What do you learn here about Tituba's motives?

9 ✓ **Reading Check**
What accusation surfaces among the residents of Salem?

The Crucible, Act I ◆ *1237*

8 ❽ **Reading Strategy**
Questioning the Characters' Motives

• Miller's commentary suggests various motives for the accusations of witchcraft. Have students discuss these motives. Do they seem reasonable? Remind students that the penalty for witchcraft was death.
  Answer: Miller suggests that petty quarrels over property and other disagreements of long-standing caused people to accuse one another. Students may think that these are insufficient motives for what amounts to murder.

• Ask students the Reading Strategy question on p. 1237: What do you learn here about Tituba's motives?
  Answer: Tituba is afraid of Parris.

9 ❾ ✓ **Reading Check**
Answer: Some residents of Salem accuse others of witchcraft.

CUSTOMIZE INSTRUCTION FOR UNIVERSAL ACCESS

For Special Needs Students	For Gifted/Talented Students
Assign peer tutors for students. Have each pair work through the play a few pages at a time, reading the dialogue aloud. At natural breaks in the action, the tutor should make sure that his or her partner can identify the characters and summarize the action up to this point. Since most scenes in the play involve several characters, a few tutors and their partners may want to work together in a group.	Miller's richly metaphorical language was meant to be heard rather than read silently. Have students form a group in which to read the play aloud together. Readers can maintain the same roles or alternate so that everyone has a chance to read both major and minor characters. Have students discuss how hearing the language enriches their experience of the play.

- Draw students' attention to the vocabulary word, *dissembling*, on p. 1238. If necessary, discuss what kind of person has a capacity for dissembling.

- Ask students the first Reading Strategy question on p. 1238: Based on what stage directions have revealed about Abigail's personality, what can you conclude about her "worry" and "apprehension"?
  Answer: She isn't really worried or apprehensive.

⑪ Reading Strategy

**Questioning the Characters'
Motives**

- Ask students the second Reading Strategy question on p. 1238: Why is Parris so quick to dismiss the possibility that Betty's ailment is the result of "unnatural causes"?
  Answer: He knows that if people believe this rumor he will be in serious trouble.

- Why is Parris unwilling to tell the congregation that he discovered the girls dancing in the forest?
  Answer: They will blame him for being an irresponsible guardian.

He is bending to kneel again when his niece, ABIGAIL WILLIAMS, *seventeen, enters—a strikingly beautiful girl, an orphan, with an endless capacity for* <u>dissembling</u>. *Now she is all worry and apprehension and propriety.*

ABIGAIL: Uncle? *He looks to her.* Susanna Walcott's here from Doctor Griggs.

PARRIS: Oh? Let her come, let her come.

ABIGAIL, *leaning out the door to call to Susanna, who is down the hall a few steps:* Come in, Susanna.

SUSANNA WALCOTT, *a little younger than Abigail, a nervous, hurried girl, enters.*

PARRIS, *eagerly:* What does the doctor say, child?

SUSANNA, *craning around* PARRIS *to get a look at* BETTY: He bid me come and tell you, reverend sir, that he cannot discover no medicine for it in his books.

PARRIS: Then he must search on.

⑩ **SUSANNA:** Aye, sir, he have been searchin' his books since he left you, sir. But he bid me tell you, that you might look to unnatural things for the cause of it.

PARRIS, *his eyes going wide:* No—no. There be no unnatural cause here. Tell him I have sent for Reverend Hale of Beverly, and Mr. Hale will surely confirm that. Let him look to medicine and put out all thought of unnatural causes here. There be none.

SUSANNA: Aye, sir. He bid me tell you. *She turns to go.*

ABIGAIL: Speak nothin' of it in the village, Susanna.

PARRIS: Go directly home and speak nothing of unnatural causes.

SUSANNA: Aye, sir. I pray for her. *She goes out.*

ABIGAIL: Uncle, the rumor of witchcraft is all about; I think you'd best go down and deny it yourself. The parlor's packed with people, sir. I'll sit with her.

PARRIS, *pressed, turns on her:* And what shall I say to them? That my daughter and my niece I discovered dancing like heathen in the forest?

ABIGAIL: Uncle, we did dance; let you tell them I confessed it—and I'll be whipped if I must be. But they're speakin' of witchcraft. Betty's not witched.

PARRIS: Abigail, I cannot go before the congregation when I know you have not opened with me. What did you do with her in the forest?

ABIGAIL: We did dance, uncle, and when you leaped out of the bush so suddenly, Betty was frightened and then she fainted. And there's the whole of it.

PARRIS: Child. Sit you down.

ABIGAIL, *quavering, as she sits:* I would never hurt Betty. I love her dearly.

PARRIS: Now look you, child, your punishment will come in its time. But if you trafficked with spirits in the forest I must know it now, for surely my enemies will, and they will ruin me with it.

ABIGAIL: But we never conjured spirits.

1238 ◆ *Prosperity and Protest (1946–Present)*

dissembling (di sem′ blin) *n.* disguising one's real nature or motives

Reading Strategy
Questioning the Characters' Motives
Based on what stage directions have revealed about Abigail's personality, what can you conclude about her "worry" and "apprehension"?

Reading Strategy
Questioning the Characters' Motives Why is Parris so quick to dismiss the possibility that Betty's ailment is the result of "unnatural causes"?

PARRIS: Then why can she not move herself since midnight? This child is desperate! *Abigail lowers her eyes.* It must come out—my enemies will bring it out. Let me know what you done there. Abigail, do you understand that I have many enemies?

ABIGAIL: I have heard of it, uncle.

PARRIS: There is a faction that is sworn to drive me from my pulpit. Do you understand that?

ABIGAIL: I think so, sir.

PARRIS: Now then, in the midst of such disruption, my own household is discovered to be the very center of some obscene practice. Abominations are done in the forest—

ABIGAIL: It were sport, uncle!

PARRIS, *pointing at* BETTY: You call this sport? *She lowers her eyes. He pleads:* Abigail, if you know something that may help the doctor, for God's sake tell it to me. *She is silent.* I saw Tituba waving her arms over the fire when I came on you. Why was she doing that? And I heard a screeching and gibberish coming from her mouth. She were swaying like a dumb beast over that fire!

ABIGAIL: She always sings her Barbados songs, and we dance.

PARRIS: I cannot blink what I saw, Abigail, for my enemies will not blink it. I saw a dress lying on the grass.

ABIGAIL, *innocently:* A dress?

PARRIS—*it is very hard to say:* Aye, a dress. And I thought I saw—someone naked running through the trees!

ABIGAIL, *in terror:* No one was naked! You mistake yourself, uncle!

PARRIS, *with anger:* I saw it! *He moves from her. Then, resolved:* Now tell me true, Abigail. And I pray you feel the weight of truth upon you, for now my ministry's at stake, my ministry and perhaps your cousin's life. Whatever abomination you have done, give me all of it now, for I dare not be taken unaware when I go before them down there.

ABIGAIL: There is nothin' more. I swear it, uncle.

PARRIS, *studies her, then nods, half convinced:* Abigail, I have fought here three long years to bend these stiff-necked people to me, and now, just now when some good respect is rising for me in the parish, you compromise my very character. I have given you a home, child, I have put clothes upon your back—now give me upright answer. Your name in the town—it is entirely white, is it not?

ABIGAIL, *with an edge of resentment:* Why, I am sure it is, sir. There be no blush about my name.

PARRIS, *to the point:* Abigail, is there any other cause than you have told me, for your being discharged from Goody[6] Proctor's service? I have heard it said, and I tell you as I heard it, that she comes so rarely to the church this year for she will not sit so close to something soiled. What signified that remark?

---

6. **Goody** title used for a married woman; short for Goodwife.

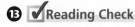

Literary Analysis
Dialogue What do his references to his "enemies" reveal about Parris's personality?

⑬ ✔**Reading Check**
What did Abigail and Betty do in the forest with Tituba?

The Crucible, Act I ◆ 1239

⑫ Literary Analysis
Dialogue and Stage Directions

- Ask students the Literary Analysis question on p. 1239: What do his references to his "ememies" reveal about Parris's personality? **Answer:** His statements suggest that he is a hostile, and even paranoid, man.

- Ask students why they think the girls danced naked in the woods when they knew they would be punished if they were caught. **Answer:** Abigail's statement, "It were sport," together with her feigned innocence and unwillingness to tell the truth suggest that Referend Parris' repressive ways prompted the girls to rebel.

⑬ ✔**Reading Check**
Answer: They danced.

CUSTOMIZE INSTRUCTION FOR UNIVERSAL ACCESS

For English Learners

Students may be puzzled by the unconventional English the play's characters speak. Write some examples from these two pages on the chalkboard:

- . . . he cannot discover no medicine for it . . .
- . . . he have been searchin' his books since he left you . . .
- It were sport, uncle!
- What signified that remark?

Explain that Miller wrote in a style that suggests the speech of early America. Grammar and spelling were not standardized at the time; rules of speech were much more lax than today. Help students "translate" the above examples into modern English. As students read the play, have them use context clues to figure out what the characters are saying.

⓮ Background

History

On February 9, 1950, Joseph R. McCarthy became a household name. On that day, he made a speech in which he claimed to have "here in my hand a list of 205 that were known to the Secretary of State as being members of the Communist Party and are still working and shaping the policy of the State Department." No such list was ever produced; when the Senate investigated McCarthy's charges, he was unable to come up with even one name. The Senate committee that followed up on McCarthy's accusations called them "the most nefarious campaign of half-truths and untruth in the history of the Republic." By 1954, McCarthy was discredited and his career was effectually over.

Although the era bears McCarthy's name, Congressman (later President) Richard M. Nixon was the first to use the tactics associated with his colleague from Wisconsin. In 1946, Nixon accused his opponent for a seat in the House of Representatives of being the puppet of a Communist-dominated committee. In a 1948 campaign, Nixon wrongfully accused another opponent of being a communist sympathizer. McCarthy's February 1950 speech was based in part on remarks Nixon had recently made in Congress.

ABIGAIL: She hates me, uncle, she must, for I would not be her slave. It's a bitter woman, a lying, cold, sniveling woman, and I will not work for such a woman!

PARRIS: She may be. And yet it has troubled me that you are now seven month out of their house, and in all this time no other family has ever called for your service.

ABIGAIL: They want slaves, not such as I. Let them send to Barbados for that. I will not black my face for any of them! *With ill-concealed resentment at him:* Do you begrudge my bed, uncle?

PARRIS: No—no.

ABIGAIL, *in a temper:* My name is good in the village! I will not have it said my name is soiled! Goody Proctor is a gossiping liar!

Enter MRS. ANN PUTNAM. *She is a twisted soul of forty-five, a death-ridden woman, haunted by dreams.*

PARRIS, *as soon as the door begins to open:* No—no, I cannot have anyone. *He sees her, and a certain deference springs into him, although his worry remains.* Why, Goody Putnam, come in.

MRS. PUTNAM, *full of breath, shiny-eyed:* It is a marvel. It is surely a stroke of hell upon you.

PARRIS: No, Goody Putnam, it is—

MRS. PUTNAM, *glancing at* BETTY: How high did she fly, how high?

PARRIS: No, no, she never flew—

MRS. PUTNAM, *very pleased with it:* Why, it's sure she did. Mr. Collins saw her goin' over Ingersoll's barn, and come down light as bird, he says!

PARRIS: Now, look you, Goody Putnam, she never—*Enter* THOMAS PUTNAM, *a well-to-do, hard-handed landowner, near fifty.* Oh, good morning, Mr. Putnam.

PUTNAM: It is a providence the thing is out now! It is a providence. *He goes directly to the bed.*

PARRIS: What's out, sir, what's—?

MRS. PUTNAM *goes to the bed.*

PUTNAM, *looking down at* BETTY: Why, her eyes is closed! Look you, Ann.

MRS. PUTNAM: Why, that's strange. *To* PARRIS: Ours is open.

PARRIS, *shocked:* Your Ruth is sick?

MRS. PUTNAM, *with vicious certainty:* I'd not call it sick; the Devil's touch is heavier than sick. It's death, y'know, it's death drivin' into them, forked and hoofed.

PARRIS: Oh, pray not! Why, how does Ruth ail?

MRS. PUTNAM: She ails as she must—she never waked this morning, but her eyes open and she walks, and hears naught, sees naught, and cannot eat. Her soul is taken, surely.

PARRIS *is struck.*

Literature in context — Social Studies Connec

⓮ History Repeats Itself

The Crucible was written in the early 1950s when fear of communism swept America. The fears were understandable—eastern Europe and China had recently fallen to communism—but they were also exploited for political ends. In Congress, a Republican senator named Joseph McCarthy leapt into the limelight when he charged that the State Department had been infiltrated by more than two hundred communists.

Leading a Senate investigation, McCarthy repeatedly charged that individuals who opposed his hearings were themselves communists; then he investigated them. The parallels between the events in Salem Village, as Miller depicts them, and ongoing events in Congress at the time Miller wrote the play are clear and deliberate.

✷ ENRICHMENT: History Connection

Ups and Downs of Communism

At no time was it illegal for a United States citizen to be a member of the Communist party. Before World War II, many American liberals espoused communist beliefs because they seemed an honorable alternative to the fascism that was sweeping Europe in the late 1930s. During this decade of the Great Depression, the United States was perhaps as close to a socialist state as it has ever been; the Roosevelt administration aided poor people to an unprecedented degree, sponsoring numerous public works projects and creating a welfare system. Communism, as the opposite of fascism, flourished in this atmosphere.

With the collapse of European fascism and the rise of Soviet Russia after World War II, Westerners began to turn against communism. Many believed it was simply fascism under another name—a system that began with high principles and ended in oppression and slavery.

PUTNAM, *as though for further details:* They say you've sent for Reverend Hale of Beverly?

PARRIS *with dwindling conviction now:* A precaution only. He has much experience in all demonic arts, and I—

MRS. PUTNAM: He has indeed; and found a witch in Beverly last year, and let you remember that.

PARRIS: Now, Goody Ann, they only thought that were a witch, and I am certain there be no element of witchcraft here.

PUTNAM: No witchcraft! Now look you, Mr. Parris—

PARRIS: Thomas, Thomas, I pray you, leap not to witchcraft. I know that you—you least of all, Thomas, would ever wish so disastrous a charge laid upon me. We cannot leap to witchcraft. They will howl me out of Salem for such corruption in my house.

A word about Thomas Putnam. He was a man with many grievances, at least one of which appears justified. Some time before, his wife's brother-in-law, James Bayley, had been turned down as minister at Salem. Bayley had all the qualifications, and a two-thirds vote into the bargain, but a faction stopped his acceptance, for reasons that are not clear.

Thomas Putnam was the eldest son of the richest man in the village. He had fought the Indians at Narragansett, and was deeply interested in parish affairs. He undoubtedly felt it poor payment that the village should so blatantly disregard his candidate for one of its more important offices, especially since he regarded himself as the intellectual superior of most of the people around him.

His vindictive nature was demonstrated long before the witchcraft began. Another former Salem minister, George Burroughs, had had to borrow money to pay for his wife's funeral, and, since the parish was remiss in his salary, he was soon bankrupt. Thomas and his brother John had Burroughs jailed for debts the man did not owe. The incident is important only in that Burroughs succeeded in becoming minister where Bayley, Thomas Putnam's brother-in-law, had been rejected; the motif of resentment is clear here. Thomas Putnam felt that his own name and the honor of his family had been smirched by the village, and he meant to right matters however he could.

Another reason to believe him a deeply embittered man was his attempt to break his father's will, which left a disproportionate amount to a stepbrother. As with every other public cause in which he tried to force his way, he failed in this.

So it is not surprising to find that so many accusations against people are in the handwriting of Thomas Putnam, or that his name is so often found as a witness corroborating the supernatural testimony, or that his daughter led the crying-out at the most opportune junctures of the trials, especially when—But we'll speak of that when we come to it.

PUTNAM—*at the moment he is intent upon getting* PARRIS, *for whom he has only contempt, to move toward the abyss:*[7] Mr. Parris, I have taken your

---

7. **abyss** (ə bis´) *n.* deep crack in the Earth.

Reading Strategy
Questioning the Characters' Motives
What does Miller tell you about Putnam's motives?

Reading Check
Why has Parris sent for Reverend Hale?

The Crucible, Act I ◆ 1241

⓯ Reading Strategy
Questioning the Characters' Motives

- Ask students the Reading Strategy question on p. 1241: What does Miller tell you about Putnam's motives?
  Answer: Putnam resents the fact that his brother-in-law was not accepted as minister of Salem. He avenged himself on the man who got the job by having him jailed.

- Why are the Putnams so eager to assume that the children are ill because they are bewitched?
  Answer: They apparently like making trouble for others. The stage directions "a twisted soul," "hard-handed," "vicious," and "for whom he has only contempt" all suggest that they are unhappy and bitter people who want to take out their unhappiness on others.

⓰ ✓Reading Check

Answer: Hale has experience in demonic possession.

Questioning the Characters' Motives

- Why does Abigail accuse Tituba and Ruth of "conjuring spirits"?
  Answer: Since Mrs. Putnam has already admitted that she asked Ruth to ask Tituba to communicate with the dead, Abigail makes a safe accusation. She won't be blamed for the accusation, nor will she be punished for her behavior in the woods.

- What does this passage reveal about the Putnams' motives for blaming Ruth's illness on witchcraft?
  Answer: They don't want to take any blame for having sent Ruth on a dangerous errand or making Ruth participate in the sin of "conjuring up the dead." Therefore, they look for a witch as a scapegoat.

18 ▶ **Critical Viewing**

Answer: Tituba is frightened of the consequences of this accusation. She doesn't expect her denials to be believed.

---

part in all contention here, and I would continue; but I cannot if you hold back in this. There are hurtful, vengeful spirits layin' hands on these children.

PARRIS: But, Thomas, you cannot—

PUTNAM: Ann! Tell Mr. Parris what you have done.

MRS. PUTNAM: Reverend Parris, I have laid seven babies unbaptized in the earth. Believe me, sir, you never saw more hearty babies born. And yet, each would wither in my arms the very night of their birth. I have spoke nothin', but my heart has clamored intimations. And now, this year, my Ruth, my only—I see her turning strange. A secret child she has become this year, and shrivels like a sucking mouth were pullin' on her life too. And so I thought to send her to your Tituba—

PARRIS: To Tituba! What may Tituba—?

MRS. PUTNAM: Tituba knows how to speak to the dead, Mr. Parris.

PARRIS: Goody Ann, it is a formidable sin to conjure up the dead!

MRS. PUTNAM: I take it on my soul, but who else may surely tell us what person murdered my babies?

PARRIS, *horrified:* Woman!

17 **MRS. PUTNAM:** They were murdered, Mr. Parris! And mark this proof! Mark it! Last night my Ruth were ever so close to their little spirits; I know it, sir. For how else is she struck dumb now except some power of darkness would stop her mouth? It is a marvelous sign, Mr. Parris!

PUTNAM: Don't you understand it, sir? There is a murdering witch among us, bound to keep herself in the dark. PARRIS *turns to* BETTY, *a frantic terror rising in him.* Let your names make of it what they will, you cannot blink it more.

PARRIS, *to* ABIGAIL: Then you were conjuring spirits last night.

ABIGAIL, *whispering:* Not I, sir—Tituba and Ruth.

PARRIS *turns now, with new fear, and goes to* BETTY, *looks down at her, and then, gazing off:* Oh, Abigail, what proper payment for my charity! Now I am undone.

PUTNAM: You are not undone! Let you take hold here. Wait for no one to charge you—declare it yourself. You have discovered witchcraft—

PARRIS: In my house? In my house, Thomas? They will topple me with this! They will make of it a—

Enter MERCY LEWIS, *the Putnams' servant, a fat, sly, merciless girl of eighteen.*

MERCY: Your pardons. I only thought to see how Betty is.

PUTNAM: Why aren't you home? Who's with Ruth?

MERCY: Her grandma come. She's improved a little, I think—she give a powerful sneeze before.

MRS. PUTNAM: Ah, there's a sign of life!

1242 ◆ Prosperity and Protest (1946–Present)

18 ▼ **Critical Viewing**
Abigail Williams has accused Tituba of conjuring up spirits. What can you infer about Tituba's reaction from her expression here? **[Infer]**

African Religion

The Puritans consider Tituba's ability to speak to the dead shocking and scandalous, but communication with the dead is a basic part of many African religions. In many religions derived from African cultures, the dead are honored and considered to be able to provide wisdom and advice to the living.

Vodoun, or voodoo, is a folk religion from the West Indies, which developed from Roman Catholic beliefs mixed with African religious practices.

In a voodoo ritual service, the priestess leads a gathering of people in song, drumming, dance, prayer, cooking, or animal sacrifice. As students read on, they will see that most of these details apply to the descriptions of what Tituba and the girls were doing in the woods. Ironically, a voodoo priestess is said to have the power to protect her followers from witchcraft.

MERCY: I'd fear no more, Goody Putnam. It were a grand sneeze; another like it will shake her wits together, I'm sure. *She goes to the bed to look.*

PARRIS: Will you leave me now, Thomas? I would pray a while alone.

ABIGAIL: Uncle, you've prayed since midnight. Why do you not go down and—

PARRIS: No—no. *To* PUTNAM: I have no answer for that crowd. I'll wait till Mr. Hale arrives. *To get* MRS. PUTNAM *to leave:* If you will, Goody Ann . . .

PUTNAM: Now look you, sir. Let you strike out against the Devil, and the village will bless you for it! Come down, speak to them—pray with them. They're thirsting for your word, Mister! Surely you'll pray with them.

PARRIS, *swayed:* I'll lead them in a psalm, but let you say nothing of witchcraft yet. I will not discuss it. The cause is yet unknown. I have had enough contention since I came; I want no more.

MRS. PUTNAM: Mercy, you go home to Ruth, d'y'hear?

MERCY: Aye, mum.

MRS. PUTNAM *goes out.*

PARRIS, *to* ABIGAIL: If she starts for the window, cry for me at once.

ABIGAIL: I will, uncle.

PARRIS, *to* PUTNAM: There is a terrible power in her arms today. *He goes out with* PUTNAM.

ABIGAIL, *with hushed trepidation:* How is Ruth sick?

MERCY: It's weirdish, I know not—she seems to walk like a dead one since last night.

ABIGAIL, *turns at once and goes to* BETTY, *and now, with fear in her voice:* Betty? BETTY *doesn't move. She shakes her.* Now stop this! Betty! Sit up now!

BETTY *doesn't stir.* MERCY *comes over.*

❿ MERCY: Have you tried beatin' her? I gave Ruth a good one and it waked her for a minute. Here, let me have her.

ABIGAIL, *holding* MERCY *back:* No, he'll be comin' up. Listen, now; if they be questioning us, tell them we danced—I told him as much already.

MERCY: Aye. And what more?

ABIGAIL: He knows Tituba conjured Ruth's sisters to come out of the grave.

MERCY: And what more?

ABIGAIL: He saw you naked.

MERCY: *clapping her hands together with a frightened laugh:* Oh, Jesus!

Enter MARY WARREN, *breathless. She is seventeen, a subservient, naive, lonely girl.*

MARY WARREN: What'll we do? The village is out! I just come from the farm; the whole country's talkin' witchcraft! They'll be callin' us witches, Abby!

MERCY, *pointing and looking at* MARY WARREN: She means to tell, I know it.

Literary Analysis
Dialogue and Stage Directions What does this conversation reveal about the two young women?

Literary Analysis
Dialogue and Stage Directions What are the contrasting character traits of Mary Warren and of Mercy Lewis?

❷❶ ✔Reading Check
Why do the Putnams believe there is witchcraft in Salem Village?

The Crucible, Act I ◆ *1243*

• Ask students to assess Abigail's character.
Answer: She is mean to the other girls. She is a leader who rules the group by inspiring fear. She is strong. She hates Goody Proctor.

• Ask students whether the other girls are likely to give Abigail away.
Answer: Betty and Mary seem too frightened of her to give her away, but Mary also seems frightened of the consequences of lying.

23 ▶ Critical Viewing
Answer: Betty exhibits pain and fear.

MARY WARREN: Abby, we've got to tell. Witchery's a hangin' error, a hangin' like they done in Boston two year ago! We must tell the truth, Abby! You'll only be whipped for dancin', and the other things!

ABIGAIL: Oh, *we'll* be whipped!

MARY WARREN: I never done none of it, Abby. I only looked!

MERCY, *moving menacingly toward* MARY: Oh, you're a great one for lookin', aren't you, Mary Warren? What a grand peeping courage you have!

BETTY, *on the bed, whimpers.* ABIGAIL *turns to her at once.*

ABIGAIL: Betty? *She goes to* BETTY. Now, Betty, dear, wake up now. It's Abigail. *She sits* BETTY *up and furiously shakes her.* I'll beat you, Betty! BETTY *whimpers.* My, you seem improving. I talked to your papa and I told him everything. So there's nothing to—

BETTY, *darts off the bed, frightened of* ABIGAIL, *and flattens herself against the wall:* I want my mama!

ABIGAIL, *with alarm, as she cautiously approaches* BETTY: What ails you, Betty? Your mama's dead and buried.

BETTY: I'll fly to Mama. Let me fly! *She raises her arms as though to fly, and streaks for the window, gets one leg out.*

ABIGAIL, *pulling her away from the window:* I told him everything; he knows now, he knows everything we—

BETTY: You drank blood, Abby! You didn't tell him that!

22 **ABIGAIL:** Betty, you never say that again! You will never—

BETTY: You did, you did! You drank a charm to kill John Proctor's wife! You drank a charm to kill Goody Proctor!

ABIGAIL, *smashes her across the face:* Shut it! Now shut it!

BETTY: *collapsing on the bed:* Mama, Mama! *She dissolves into sobs.*

ABIGAIL: Now look you. All of you. We danced. And Tituba conjured Ruth Putnam's dead sisters. And that is all. And mark this. Let either of you breathe a word, or the edge of a word, about the other things, and I will come to you in the black of some terrible night and I will bring a pointy reckoning that will shudder you. And you know I can do it; I saw Indians smash my dear parents' heads on the pillow next to mine, and I have seen some reddish work done at night, and I can make you wish you had never seen the sun go down! *She goes to* BETTY *and roughly sits her up.* Now, you—sit up and stop this!

But BETTY *collapses in her hands and lies inert on the bed.*

23 ▲ Critical Viewing
What emotion is conveyed in this image of Betty Parris's attempt to fly? Explain. **[Interpret]**

✳ **ENRICHMENT: History Connection**

Indians Versus Settlers

Abigail remembers seeing "Indians smash my dear parents' heads on the pillows next to mine." As the immigrant population rose, settlers took over more and more of what had been Native American territory. Native Americans retaliated by attacking the settlements.

At dawn on February 10, 1676, the Narragansett people attacked the tiny village of Lancaster, Massachusetts. They set fire to every building and

killed most of the settlers, except for a few whom they carried away and held for ransom. Ironically, the Narragansett were armed with guns for which they had once traded with the Europeans. Mary Rowlandson, freed after a £20 ransom was paid, published an account of the raid and her captivity. "Captivity narratives" such as hers were best-sellers in Puritan New England—they were among the very few books whose publication the Puritans allowed.

MARY WARREN, *with hysterical fright:* What's got her? ABIGAIL *stares in fright at* BETTY. Abby, she's going to die! It's a sin to conjure, and we—

ABIGAIL, *starting for* MARY: I say shut it, Mary Warren!

Enter JOHN PROCTOR. *On seeing him.* MARY WARREN *leaps in fright.*

Proctor was a farmer in his middle thirties. He need not have been a partisan of any faction in the town, but there is evidence to suggest that he had a sharp and biting way with hypocrites. He was the kind of man—powerful of body, even-tempered, and not easily led—who cannot refuse support to partisans without drawing their deepest resentment. In Proctor's presence a fool felt his foolishness instantly—and a Proctor is always marked for calumny therefore.

But as we shall see, the steady manner he displays does not spring from an untroubled soul. He is a sinner, a sinner not only against the moral fashion of the time, but against his own vision of decent conduct. These people had no ritual for the washing away of sins. It is another trait we inherited from them, and it has helped to discipline us as well as to breed hypocrisy among us. Proctor, respected and even feared in Salem, has come to regard himself as a kind of fraud. But no hint of this has yet appeared on the surface, and as he enters from the crowded parlor below it is a man in his prime we see, with a quiet confidence and an unexpressed, hidden force. Mary Warren, his servant, can barely speak for embarrassment and fear.

MARY WARREN: Oh! I'm just going home, Mr. Proctor.

PROCTOR: Be you foolish, Mary Warren? Be you deaf? I forbid you leave the house, did I not? Why shall I pay you? I am looking for you more often than my cows!

MARY WARREN: I only come to see the great doings in the world.

PROCTOR: I'll show you a great doin' on your arse one of these days. Now get you home; my wife is waitin' with your work! *Trying to retain a shred of dignity, she goes slowly out.*

MERCY LEWIS, *both afraid of him and strangely titillated:* I'd best be off. I have my Ruth to watch. Good morning, Mr. Proctor.

MERCY *sidles out. Since* PROCTOR'S *entrance,* ABIGAIL *has stood as though on tiptoe, absorbing his presence, wide-eyed. He glances at her then goes to* BETTY *on the bed.*

ABIGAIL: Gad. I'd almost forgot how strong you are, John Proctor!

PROCTOR, *looking at* ABIGAIL *now, the faintest suggestion of a knowing smile on his face:* What's this mischief here?

ABIGAIL, *with a nervous laugh:* Oh, she's only gone silly somehow.

PROCTOR: The road past my house is a pilgrimage to Salem all morning. The town's mumbling witchcraft.

ABIGAIL: Oh, posh! *Winningly she comes a little closer, with a confidential, wicked air.* We were dancin' in the woods last night, and my uncle leaped in on us. She took fright, is all.

PROCTOR, *his smile widening:* Ah, you're wicked yet, aren't y'! *A trill of expectant laughter escapes her, and she dares come closer, feverishly*

Literary Analysis
Dialogue, Stage Directions, and Dramatic Exposition What does Miller reveal about Proctor through this dramatic exposition?

calumny (kal´ əm nē) *n.* false accusation; slander

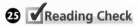
Reading Check
What does Mary Warren insist the girls do? How does Abigail react?

The Crucible, Act I ◆ 1245

---

24 Literary Analysis
Dialogue, Stage Directions, and Dramatic Exposition

• Ask students the Literary Analysis question on p. 1245: What does Miller reveal about Proctor through this dramatic exposition?
Answer: Proctor is a loner who relies on his own judgment. He is not necessarily popular. He doesn't like hypocrites.

• Have students speculate about the sins Proctor may have committed. Point out the stage direction describing Abigail "absorbing his presence, wide-eyed" and remind them of her desire to kill Proctor's wife.
Answer: Proctor and Abigail may have been lovers; Abigail is clearly attracted to him and hates his wife. Dialogue earlier in the play states that Goody Proctor avoids church because she doesn't want to "sit so close to something soiled," and that she threw Abigail out of her house.

25 ✓ Reading Check
Answer: Mary insists that they tell the truth. Abigail threatens violence if anyone talks.

Dialogue and Stage Directions

- Ask students the Literary Analysis question on p. 1246: What important information about Abigail's behavior and emotions is conveyed through these stage directions?
  Answer: The stage directions mention her "concentrated desire" and "grasping his hand." She wants Proctor.

- Ask students what Proctor's dialogue suggests about his intentions toward Abigail.
  Answer: He has made up his mind that the affair is over. He does not love her or want her to take his wife's place.

▶ Monitor Progress Given Abigail's character, how is she likely to react to this rejection?
  Answer: She may threaten Proctor. She has already "drunk a charm to kill Goody Proctor"; she may try something like that again.

27 Reading Strategy

Questioning the Characters' Motives

- Ask students the Reading Strategy question on p. 1246: What does this paragraph reveal about Abigail's motivation?
  Answer: She drank blood to kill Goody Proctor because she wants to take her place.

- Ask students to deduce Proctor's motivation for taking Abigail as a lover.
  Possible answers: He was captivated by her beauty. He responded to her feelings for him. He is not in love with his wife. His wife is, as Abigail says, a cold woman.

- Why is Proctor angry with himself? What does this suggest about him?
  Answer: His anger at himself after Abigail's remark about his wife suggests that he also has resented Elizabeth, and used this resentment as an excuse for his affair.

---

looking into his eyes. You'll be clapped in the stocks before you're twenty. *He takes a step to go, and she springs into his path.*

ABIGAIL: Give me a word, John. A soft word. *Her concentrated desire destroys his smile.*

PROCTOR: No, no, Abby. That's done with.

ABIGAIL, *tauntingly:* You come five mile to see a silly girl fly? I know you better.

26 PROCTOR, *setting her firmly out of his path:* I come to see what mischief your uncle's brewin' now. *With final emphasis:* Put it out of mind, Abby.

ABIGAIL, *grasping his hand before he can release her:* John—I am waitin' for you every night.

PROCTOR: Abby, I never give you hope to wait for me.

ABIGAIL, *now beginning to anger—she can't believe it:* I have something better than hope, I think!

PROCTOR: Abby, you'll put it out of mind. I'll not be comin' for you more.

ABIGAIL: You're surely sportin' with me.

PROCTOR: You know me better.

ABIGAIL: I know how you clutched my back behind your house and sweated like a stallion whenever I come near! Or did I dream that? It's she put me out, you cannot pretend it were you. I saw your face when she put me out, and you loved me then and you do now!

PROCTOR: Abby, that's a wild thing to say—

ABIGAIL: A wild thing may say wild things. But not so wild, I think. I have seen you since she put me out; I have seen you nights.

27 PROCTOR: I have hardly stepped off my farm this seven-month.

ABIGAIL: I have a sense for heat, John, and yours has drawn me to my window, and I have seen you looking up, burning in your loneliness. Do you tell me you've never looked up at my window?

PROCTOR: I may have looked up.

ABIGAIL, *now softening:* And you must. You are no wintry man. I know you, John. I *know* you. *She is weeping.* I cannot sleep for dreamin'; I cannot dream but I wake and walk about the house as though I'd find you comin' through some door. *She clutches him desperately.*

PROCTOR, *gently pressing her from him, with great sympathy but firmly:* Child—

ABIGAIL, *with a flash of anger:* How do you call me child!

PROCTOR: Abby, I may think of you softly from time to time. But I will cut off my hand before I'll ever reach for you again. Wipe it out of mind. We never touched, Abby.

ABIGAIL: Aye, but we did.

PROCTOR: Aye, but we did not.

ABIGAIL, *with a bitter anger:* Oh, I marvel how such a strong man may let such a sickly wife be—

PROCTOR, *angered—at himself as well:* You'll speak nothin' of Elizabeth!

**Literary Analysis
Dialogue and Stage Directions** What important information about Abigail's behavior and emotions is conveyed through these stage directions?

**Reading Strategy
Questioning the Characters' Motives** What does this paragraph reveal about Abigail's motivations?

ABIGAIL: She is blackening my name in the village! She is telling lies about me! She is a cold, sniveling woman, and you bend to her! Let her turn you like a—

PROCTOR, *shaking her:* Do you look for whippin'?

A psalm is heard being sung below.

ABIGAIL, *in tears:* I look for John Proctor that took me from my sleep and put knowledge in my heart! I never knew what pretense Salem was, I never knew the lying lessons I was taught by all these Christian women and their covenanted men! And now you bid me tear the light out of my eyes? I will not, I cannot! You loved me, John Proctor, and whatever sin it is, you love me yet! *He turns abruptly to go out. She rushes to him.* John, pity me, pity me!

The words "going up to Jesus" are heard in the psalm, and BETTY *claps her ears suddenly and whines loudly.*

ABIGAIL: Betty? *She hurries to* BETTY, *who is now sitting up and screaming.* PROCTOR *goes to* BETTY *as* ABIGAIL *is trying to pull her hands down, calling "Betty!"*

PROCTOR, *growing unnerved:* What's she doing? Girl, what ails you? Stop that wailing!

The singing has stopped in the midst of this, and now PARRIS *rushes in.*

PARRIS: What happened? What are you doing to her? Betty! *He rushes to the bed, crying, "Betty, Betty!"* MRS. PUTNAM *enters, feverish with curiosity, and with her* PUTNAM *and* MERCY LEWIS. PARRIS, *at the bed, keeps lightly slapping* BETTY'S *face, while she moans and tries to get up.*

ABIGAIL: She heard you singin' and suddenly she's up and screamin'.

MRS. PUTNAM: The psalm! The psalm! She cannot bear to hear the Lord's name!

PARRIS: No, God forbid. Mercy, run to the doctor! Tell him what's happened here! MERCY LEWIS *rushes out.*

MRS. PUTNAM: Mark it for a sign, mark it!

REBECCA NURSE, *seventy-two, enters. She is white-haired, leaning upon her walking-stick.*

PUTNAM, *pointing at the whimpering* BETTY: That is a notorious sign of witchcraft afoot, Goody Nurse, a prodigious sign!

MRS. PUTNAM: My mother told me that! When they cannot bear to hear the name of—

PARRIS, *trembling:* Rebecca, Rebecca, go to her, we're lost. She suddenly cannot bear to hear the Lord's—

GILES COREY, *eighty-three, enters. He is knotted with muscle, canny, inquisitive, and still powerful.*

REBECCA: There is hard sickness here, Giles Corey, so please to keep the quiet.

GILES: I've not said a word. No one here can testify I've said a word. Is she going to fly again? I hear she flies.

PUTNAM: Man, be quiet now!

Literary Analysis
Dialogue and Stage Directions What do these lines reveal about Mrs. Putnam's eagerness to see signs of witchcraft?

30  **Reading Check**
What effect does the psalm have on Betty? Why?

The Crucible, Act I ◆ 1247

28 **Literary Analysis**
Dialogue and Stage Directions

- Ask students what effect the sound of the psalm has in this scene.
  Answer: It frightens Betty. It is ironic because it accompanies Abigail's speech condemning virtue and praising sin.

- Ask students to analyze Abigail's speech beginning "I look for John Proctor." What does this speech tell them about Abigail? Does it alter their opinions of her? Does it make her more or less sympathetic?
  Answers: The speech suggests that the passion Abigail shared with John has made her question the values of Salem—purity, chastity, and virtue. She judges the people of Salem as hypocrites, because they share passion but preach against it. Students should sympathize with Abigail's suffering, and they may agree with her view of her neighbors.

29 **Literary Analysis**
Dialogue and Stage Directions

- Ask students the Literary Analysis question on p. 1247: What do these lines reveal about Mrs. Putnam's eagerness to see signs of witchcraft?
  Answer: She jumps to the conclusion that Betty's reaction to the psalm means that she is bewitched.

- How does Proctor react to Betty's screams?
  Answer: He asks why she screams instead of making an assumption.

▶ Monitor Progress Have students discuss what the characters' reactions suggest about them.

30 **Reading Check**
Answer: It seems to give her pain.

CUSTOMIZE INSTRUCTION FOR UNIVERSAL ACCESS

For English Learners	For Advanced Readers
Have a student read John's speech beginning "Abby, I may think of you" (p. 1246) aloud. Make sure students understand that when he says, "We never touched, Abby," he does not mean this literally—he is urging her to think and behave as if it had never happened and trying to tell her that on the deepest level, they never touched.	Ask students to analyze Abigail's motivation. They can begin with her actions in this conversation with Proctor and continue weighing her motives as they read further. Have students think about whether they sympathize at all with Abigail, or whether they condemn her entirely as they watch her begin to accuse people of witchcraft.

- Ask students what reputation Francis and Rebecca Nurse had had in the community until now.
  Answer: They had been greatly respected, and perhaps envied.

- Go over the information in the last two paragraphs of this passage with students. Clarify for them that bad feeling has arisen between the Putnam and Nurse clans over land.

- Draw students' attention to the last sentence in the passage, and define the word *iniquity*—"wickedness" or "unrighteousness."

- Ask students to summarize what Miller is suggesting when he says ironically that Mrs. Putnam's charge that Rebecca Nurse had "tempted her to iniquity" was more true than Mrs. Putnam realized.
  Answer: Students should recognize that the competitive envy between the two groups is prompting the Putnams' persecution of Rebecca Nurse. Miller is suggesting that although she may be unconscious of the fact, Mrs. Putnam's own resentment caused her to yield to the temptation of charging an innocent woman with a crime punishable by death—which is indeed iniquitous.

③② ▶**Critical Viewing**

Answer: Students may say that the rolled-up sleeves, open collar, and hoe suggest hard physical labor, and that the actor's expression is solemn and stern.

Everything is quiet. REBECCA *walks across the room to the bed. Gentleness exudes from her.* BETTY *is quietly whimpering, eyes shut.* REBECCA *simply stands over the child, who gradually quiets.*

And while they are so absorbed, we may put a word in for Rebecca. Rebecca was the wife of Francis Nurse, who, from all accounts, was one of those men for whom both sides of the argument had to have respect. He was called upon to arbitrate disputes as though he were an unofficial judge, and Rebecca also enjoyed the high opinion most people had for him. By the time of the delusion, they had three hundred acres, and their children were settled in separate homesteads within the same estate. However, Francis had originally rented the land, and one theory has it that, as he gradually paid for it and raised his social status, there were those who resented his rise.

Another suggestion to explain the systematic campaign against Rebecca, and inferentially against Francis, is the land war he fought with his neighbors, one of whom was a Putnam. This squabble grew to the proportions of a battle in the woods between partisans of both sides, and it is said to have lasted for two days. As for Rebecca herself, the general opinion of her character was so high that to explain how anyone dared cry her out for a witch—and more, how adults could bring themselves to lay hands on her—we must look to the fields and

③① boundaries of that time.

As we have seen, Thomas Putnam's man for the Salem ministry was Bayley. The Nurse clan had been in the faction that prevented Bayley's taking office. In addition, certain families allied to the Nurses by blood or friendship, and whose farms were contiguous with the Nurse farm or close to it, combined to break away from the Salem town authority and set up Topsfield, a new and independent entity whose existence was resented by old Salemites.

That the guiding hand behind the outcry was Putnam's is indicated by the fact that, as soon as it began, this Topsfield-Nurse faction absented themselves from church in protest and disbelief. It was Edward and Jonathan Putnam who signed the first complaint against Rebecca; and Thomas Putnam's little daughter was the one who fell into a fit at the hearing and pointed to Rebecca as her attacker. To top it all, Mrs. Putnam—who is now staring at the bewitched child on the bed—soon accused Rebecca's spirit of "tempting her to iniquity," a charge that had more truth in it than Mrs. Putnam could know.

MRS. PUTNAM, *astonished:* What have you done?

REBECCA, *in thought, now leaves the bedside and sits.*

PARRIS, *wondrous and relieved:* What do you make of it, Rebecca?

PUTNAM, *eagerly:* Goody Nurse, will you go to my Ruth and see if you can wake her?

REBECCA, *sitting:* I think she'll wake in time. Pray calm yourselves. I have eleven children, and I am twenty-six

③② ▼ **Critical Viewing**
Abigail calls John Proctor a "strong man." What details in this photograph support that idea? **[Interpret]**

Church Membership

Church membership among the Puritans was the result of religious conversion. Everyone in the community was expected to attend services, but only those who had been converted ("born again," in present-day terminology) were entitled to membership in the congregation and the power and privileges that went with membership (on p. 1249, Proctor refers to the ability to vote). Before 1662, only the children of church members were baptized and admitted to the church. However, as church membership fell, Boston

Puritans began to adopt the Halfway Covenant, which opened baptism and church membership to children of those who were virtuous Christians but not church members. Conservative congregations were violently opposed to this relaxation of standards, and some churches adopted the Halfway Covenant only after the Salem trials.

times a grandma, and I have seen them all through their silly seasons, and when it come on them they will run the Devil bowlegged keeping up with their mischief. I think she'll wake when she tires of it. A child's spirit is like a child, you can never catch it by running after it; you must stand still, and, for love, it will soon itself come back.

PROCTOR: Aye, that's the truth of it, Rebecca.

MRS. PUTNAM: This is no silly season, Rebecca. My Ruth is bewildered, Rebecca; she cannot eat.

REBECCA: Perhaps she is not hungered yet. *To* PARRIS: I hope you are not decided to go in search of loose spirits, Mr. Parris. I've heard promise of that outside.

PARRIS: A wide opinion's running in the parish that the Devil may be among us, and I would satisfy them that they are wrong.

PROCTOR: Then let you come out and call them wrong. Did you consult the wardens before you called this minister to look for devils?

PARRIS: He is not coming to look for devils!

PROCTOR: Then what's he coming for?

PUTNAM: There be children dyin' in the village, Mister!

PROCTOR: I seen none dyin'. This society will not be a bag to swing around your head, Mr. Putnam. *To Parris:* Did you call a meeting before you—?

PUTNAM: I am sick of meetings; cannot the man turn his head without he have a meeting?

PROCTOR: He may turn his head, but not to Hell!

REBECCA: Pray, John, be calm. *Pause. He defers to her.* Mr. Parris, I think you'd best send Reverend Hale back as soon as he come. This will set us all to arguin' again in the society, and we thought to have peace this year. I think we ought rely on the doctor now, and good prayer.

MRS. PUTNAM: Rebecca, the doctor's baffled!

REBECCA: If so he is, then let us go to God for the cause of it. There is prodigious danger in the seeking of loose spirits. I fear it, I fear it. Let us rather blame ourselves and—

PUTNAM: How may we blame ourselves? I am one of nine sons; the Putnam seed have peopled this province. And yet I have but one child left of eight—and now she shrivels!

REBECCA: I cannot fathom that.

MRS. PUTNAM, *with a growing edge of sarcasm:* But I must! You think it God's work you should never lose a child, nor grandchild either, and I bury all but one? There are wheels within wheels in this village, and fires within fires!

PUTNAM, *to* PARRIS: When Reverend Hale comes, you will proceed to look for signs of witchcraft here.

PROCTOR, *to* PUTNAM: You cannot command Mr. Parris. We vote by name in this society, not by acreage.

Reading Strategy
Questioning the Characters' Motives
What do the Putnams suggest by their remarks?

 34 ✔ **Reading Check**
What is Rebecca Nurse's effect on Betty? Why?

The Crucible, Act I ◆ 1249

33 **Reading Strategy**
Questioning the Characters' Motives

- Ask students the Reading Strategy question on p. 1249: What do the Putnams suggest by their remarks?
  Answer: They suggest that other people are to blame for their misfortunes.

- Ask students to summarize Rebecca's motives for her actions and comments in this sequence.
  Answer: Rebecca wants peace in the community. She doesn't want Hale coming among them because she doesn't welcome the strife that rumors of witchcraft will cause between neighbors. She is tolerant and calm and tries to make everyone else see reason and get along better.

- What was Parris's motive for calling Hale without consulting the congregation?
  Answer: He knows he is not popular in the parish. He doesn't want to call attention to his lack of control over his daughter and niece.

34 ✔ **Reading Check**
Answer: Rebecca Nurse's presence, which is filled with her calm strength, seems to quiet and soothe Betty.

CUSTOMIZE INSTRUCTION FOR UNIVERSAL ACCESS

For Gifted/Talented Students

Have students work as a group to make a large chart or diagram assessing the responsibility of each character for the trials that begin in Act II. Each student can choose one or two characters and carefully read through Act I, looking for speeches and actions in which this character sets something in motion that helps bring the town to the point of the trials. The diagram should clearly show what each character says and does that brings about this outcome. Students can create a bulletin-board display showing the results of their search for responsibility. The entire class can use the display as a springboard for a discussion of the issue of guilt in Salem. Remind students to consider the idea that apparently innocent characters like John Proctor may also bear some responsibility.

Questioning the Characters' Motives

- Ask students the Reading Strategy question on p. 1250: Of what charge does Parris accuse members of his congregation? What does this accusation reveal about him?
  Answer: Parris accuses the congregation of persecuting him, and suggests that this may be the work of the devil.

- Why does Parris preach "hellfire and damnation" when he knows this drives away the parishioners?
  Answer: He doesn't understand their needs. He is frightened and paranoid, and he reveals these emotions in his sermons.

36 Literary Analysis

Dialogue and Stage Directions

- Ask students the Literary Analysis question on p. 1250: How does the playwright indicate that Parris interrupts Proctor?
  Answer: The dash after the word *house* shows that Parris has cut Proctor off in midsentence.

- Have students identify the sources of the conflict between Parris and Proctor.
  Answer: Proctor thinks Parris is unfit to preach; he also thinks he is too much concerned with the material advantages of being a minister. Parris resents Proctor's contempt; he believes that the congregation should show their respect for the church by showing respect for his wishes.

- Why is everyone shocked when Proctor says he wants to join the faction against Parris?
  Answer: They live in a society where everyone agrees to accept the authority of the minister and the church.

▶ Monitor Progress Have students discuss who is right in this argument—Parris, Proctor, both to some degree, or neither? Have students give reasons for their opinions. Remind them to evaluate the men's opinions in the context of the time and place in which the play is set.

PUTNAM: I never heard you worried so on this society, Mr. Proctor. I do not think I saw you at Sabbath meeting since snow flew.

PROCTOR: I have trouble enough without I come five mile to hear him preach only hellfire and bloody damnation. Take it to heart, Mr. Parris. There are many others who stay away from church these days because you hardly ever mention God any more.

35 **PARRIS,** *now aroused:* Why, that's a drastic charge!

REBECCA: It's somewhat true; there are many that quail to bring their children—

PARRIS: I do not preach for children, Rebecca. It is not the children who are unmindful of their obligations toward this ministry.

REBECCA: Are there really those unmindful?

PARRIS: I should say the better half of Salem village—

PUTNAM: And more than that!

PARRIS: Where is my wood? My contract provides I be supplied with all my firewood. I am waiting since November for a stick, and even in November I had to show my frostbitten hands like some London beggar!

GILES: You are allowed six pound a year to buy your wood, Mr. Parris.

PARRIS: I regard that six pound as part of my salary. I am paid little enough without I spend six pound on firewood.

PROCTOR: Sixty, plus six for firewood—

PARRIS: The salary is sixty-six pound, Mr. Proctor! I am not some preaching farmer with a book under my arm; I am a graduate of Harvard College.

GILES: Aye, and well instructed in arithmetic!

PARRIS: Mr. Corey, you will look far for a man of my kind at sixty pound a year! I am not used to this poverty; I left a thrifty business in the Barbados to serve the Lord. I do not fathom it, why am I persecuted here? I cannot offer one proposition but there be a howling riot of argument. I have often wondered if the Devil be in it somewhere; I cannot understand you people otherwise.

PROCTOR: Mr. Parris, you are the first minister ever did demand the deed to this house—

36 **PARRIS:** Man! Don't a minister deserve a house to live in?

PROCTOR: To live in, yes. But to ask ownership is like you shall own the meeting house itself; the last meeting I were at you spoke so long on deeds and mortgages I thought it were an auction.

PARRIS: I want a mark of confidence, is all! I am your third preacher in seven years. I do not wish to be put out like the cat whenever some majority feels the whim. You people seem not to comprehend that a minister is the Lord's man in the parish; a minister is not to be so lightly crossed and contradicted—

PUTNAM: Aye!

PARRIS: There is either obedience or the church will burn like Hell is burning!

1250 ◆ *Prosperity and Protest (1946–Present)*

Reading Strategy
Questioning the Characters' Motives Of what charge does Parris accuse members of his congregation? What does this accusation reveal about him?

Literary Analysis
Dialogue and Stage Direction How does the playwright indicate that Parris interrupts Proctor?

PROCTOR: Can you speak one minute without we land in Hell again? I am sick of Hell!

PARRIS: It is not for you to say what is good for you to hear!

PROCTOR: I may speak my heart, I think!

PARRIS, *in a fury:* What, are we Quakers?[8] We are not Quakers here yet, Mr. Proctor. And you may tell that to your followers!

PROCTOR: My followers!

PARRIS—*now he's out with it:* There is a party in this church. I am not blind; there is a faction and a party.

PROCTOR: Against you?

PUTNAM: Against him and all authority!

PROCTOR: Why, then I must find it and join it.

There is shock among the others.

REBECCA: He does not mean that.

PUTNAM: He confessed it now!

PROCTOR: I mean it solemnly, Rebecca; I like not the smell of this "authority."

REBECCA: No, you cannot break charity with your minister. You are another kind, John. Clasp his hand, make your peace.

PROCTOR: I have a crop to sow and lumber to drag home. *He goes angrily to the door and turns to* COREY *with a smile.* What say you, Giles, let's find the party. He says there's a party.

GILES: I've changed my opinion of this man, John. Mr. Parris, I beg your pardon. I never thought you had so much iron in you.

PARRIS, *surprised:* Why, thank you, Giles!

GILES: It suggests to the mind what the trouble be among us all these years. *To all:* Think on it. Wherefore is everybody suing everybody else? Think on it now, it's a deep thing, and dark as a pit. I have been six time in court this year—

PROCTOR, *familiarly, with warmth, although he knows he is approaching the edge of Giles' tolerance with this:* Is it the Devil's fault that a man cannot say you good morning without you clap him for defamation? You're old, Giles, and you're not hearin' so well as you did.

GILES—*he cannot be crossed:* John Proctor, I have only last month collected four pound damages for you publicly sayin' I burned the roof off your house, and I—

PROCTOR, *laughing:* I never said no such thing, but I've paid you for it, so I hope I can call you deaf without charge. Now come along, Giles, and help me drag my lumber home.

PUTNAM: A moment, Mr. Proctor. What lumber is that you're draggin', if I may ask you?

---

8. **Quakers** members of the Society of Friends, a Christian religious sect that was founded in the mid-17th century and has no formal creed, rites, or priesthood. Unlike the Quakers, the Puritans had a rigid code of conduct and were expected to heed the words of their ministers.

Literary Analysis
Dialogue and Stage Directions What does this dialogue between Proctor and Giles reveal about the mood and atmosphere in Salem?

 Reading Check
How do Proctor's and Parris's beliefs about authority differ?

The Crucible, Act I ◆ *1251*

Questioning the Characters' Motives

- Ask students the Reading Strategy question on p. 1252: Why does Giles feel a "sudden will to work?"
  Answer: Giles has had enough of Putnam's company. He much prefers Proctor to Putnam and is glad to help Proctor do something that will annoy Putnam.

- Why does Putnam threaten Proctor and Corey?
  Answer: Putnam is greedy and belligerent. He will do whatever he must to hang on to property, even if it means making enemies of his neighbors.

40 Literary Analysis

Dialogue, Stage Directions, and Dramatic Exposition

- Ask students to characterize Mr. Hale. What is his area of expertise in the church?
  Answer: Mr. Hale is a learned man and an expert in demonology.

- Ask students the Literary Analysis question on page 1252: In this passage, what important information does Miller provide about his view of the world?
  Possible Answer: Miller introduces the idea that we, like the Puritans, are still gripped by the assumption that the world is neatly divided into clearly identifiable good and evil—the realms of God and the Devil.

PROCTOR: My lumber. From out my forest by the riverside.

PUTNAM: Why, we are surely gone wild this year. What anarchy is this? That tract is in my bounds, it's in my bounds, Mr. Proctor.

PROCTOR: In your bounds! *Indicating* REBECCA: I bought that tract from Goody Nurse's husband five months ago.

PUTNAM: He had no right to sell it. It stands clear in my grandfather's will that all the land between the river and—

PROCTOR: Your grandfather had a habit of willing land that never belonged to him, if I may say it plain.

GILES: That's God's truth; he nearly willed away my north pasture but he knew I'd break his fingers before he'd set his name to it. Let's get your lumber home, John. I feel a sudden will to work coming on.

PUTNAM: You load one oak of mine and you'll fight to drag it home!

GILES: Aye, and we'll win too, Putnam—this fool and I. Come on! *He turns to* PROCTOR *and starts out.*

PUTNAM: I'll have my men on you, Corey! I'll clap a writ on you!

Enter REVEREND JOHN HALE *of Beverly.*

Mr. Hale is nearing forty, a tight-skinned, eager-eyed intellectual. This is a beloved errand for him; on being called here to ascertain witchcraft he felt the pride of the specialist whose unique knowledge has at last been publicly called for. Like almost all men of learning, he spent a good deal of time pondering the invisible world, especially since he had himself encountered a witch in his parish not long before. That woman, however, turned into a mere pest under his searching scrutiny, and the child she had allegedly been afflicting recovered her normal behavior after Hale had given her his kindness and a few days of rest in his own house. However, that experience never raised a doubt in his mind as to the reality of the underworld or the existence of Lucifer's many-faced lieutenants. And his belief is not to his discredit. Better minds than Hale's were—and still are—convinced that there is a society of spirits beyond our ken. One cannot help noting that one of his lines has never yet raised a laugh in any audience that has seen this play; it is his assurance that "We cannot look to superstition in this. The Devil is precise." Evidently we are not quite certain even now whether diabolism is holy and not to be scoffed at. And it is no accident that we should be so bemused.

Like Reverend Hale and the others on this stage, we conceive the Devil as a necessary part of a respectable view of cosmology. Ours is a divided empire in which certain ideas and emotions and actions are of God, and their opposites are of Lucifer. It is as impossible for most men to conceive of a morality without sin as of an earth without "sky." Since 1692 a great but superficial change has wiped out God's beard and the Devil's horns, but the world is still gripped between two diametrically opposed absolutes. The concept of unity, in which positive and negative are attributes of the same force, in which good and evil are relative, ever-changing, and always joined to the same phenomenon—such a

Reading Strategy
Questioning the Characters' Motives Why does Giles feel a "sudden will to work"?

Literary Analysis
Dialogue, Stage Directions, and Dramatic Exposition What important information does Miller provide about his view of the world?

✳ ENRICHMENT: Literature Connection

Voltaire on the Inquisition

François-Marie Arouet, better known as Voltaire (1694–1778), is probably the best-known thinker of the French Enlightenment. The Spanish Inquisition (see p. 1253) was in power throughout Voltaire's lifetime, and it was the epitome of everything he despised about organized religion and Christianity in particular. Here is the opening of Voltaire's entry "On the Inquisition" from his *Philosophical Dictionary* (1764):

"The Inquisition is well known to be an admirable and truly Christian invention for increasing the power of the pope and monks, and rendering the population of a whole kingdom hypocrites."

concept is still reserved to the physical sciences and to the few who have grasped the history of ideas. When it is recalled that until the Christian era the underworld was never regarded as a hostile area, that all gods were useful and essentially friendly to man despite occasional lapses; when we see the steady and methodical inculcation into humanity of the idea of man's worthlessness—until redeemed—the necessity of the Devil may become evident as a weapon, a weapon designed and used time and time again in every age to whip men into a surrender to a particular church or church-state.

Our difficulty in believing the—for want of a better word—political inspiration of the Devil is due in great part to the fact that he is called up and damned not only by our social antagonists but by our own side, whatever it may be. The Catholic Church, through its Inquisition,♦ is famous for cultivating Lucifer as the arch-fiend, but the Church's enemies relied no less upon the Old Boy to keep the human mind enthralled. Luther[9] was himself accused of alliance with Hell, and he in turn accused his enemies. To complicate matters further, he believed that he had had contact with the Devil and had argued theology with him. I am not surprised at this, for at my own university a professor of history—a Lutheran,[10] by the way—used to assemble his graduate students, draw the shades, and commune in the classroom with Erasmus.[11] He was never, to my knowledge, officially scoffed at for this, the reason being that the university officials, like most of us, are the children of a history which still sucks at the Devil's teats. At this writing, only England has held back before the temptations of contemporary diabolism. In the countries of the Communist ideology, all resistance of any import is linked to the totally malign capitalist succubi,[12] and in America any man who is not reactionary in his views is open to the charge of alliance with the Red hell. Political opposition, thereby, is given an inhumane overlay which then justifies the abrogation[13] of all normally applied customs of civilized intercourse. A political policy is equated with moral right, and opposition to it with diabolical malevolence. Once such an equation is effectively made, society becomes a congerie[14] of plots and counterplots, and the main role of government changes from that of the arbiter to that of the scourge of God.

The results of this process are no different now from what they ever were, except sometimes in the degree of

---

9. **Luther** Martin Luther (1483–1546), German theologian who led the Protestant Reformation.
10. **Lutheran** member of the Protestant denomination founded by Martin Luther.
11. **Erasmus Desiderius** Erasmus (1466?–1536), Dutch humanist, scholar, and theologian.
12. **succubi** (suk′ yoo bī) female demons thought to lie on sleeping men.
13. **abrogation** (ab′ rō gā′ shən) abolishment.
14. **congerie** (kän′ jə rē′) heap; pile.

Literature in context   History Connection

 ♦ *The Inquisition*

Although Miller alludes to the Inquisition, a "court of justice" established by the Catholic Church during the 13th century, he does not describe it in the script of *The Crucible*. The Inquisition bears a close resemblance to the Salem witch hunts of the 1690s and to the Red Scare in the United States during the 1950s. In each case, a panel of judges decided allegations of heresy or treason. The Salem judges sentenced some individuals to death, as had the Catholic judges of the Middle Ages.

No one died in the 1950s as a result of Senator Joseph McCarthy's interrogations and accusations of communism. However, many suffered great damage to their personal and professional reputations and were unable to continue their careers and even their social lives for many years.

inculcation (in′ kul kā′ shən) *n.* teaching by repetition and urging

 ✔ **Reading Check**

What is Reverend Hale's experience with witchcraft?

The Crucible, Act I ◆ 1253

41 **Background**

History

The first Roman Catholic Inquisition was called in 1231. Anyone accused of heresy, witchcraft, or sorcery was brought before the inquisitor and offered the opportunity to confess. Anyone who did not confess was tried and interrogated. Beginning in 1252, torture was commonly used to extract confessions. A secular branch of the Inquisition sentenced condemned heretics to death. The Inquisition was at its most powerful in northern Italy and southern France until 1478, when Pope Sixtus IV created the Spanish Inquisition, headed by the infamous Torquemada, who probably condemned about 2,000 people to death at the stake. The Spanish Inquisition continued to wield power off and on until 1834, when it was permanently suppressed.

42 ✔ **Reading Check**

Answer: Hale has examined and acquitted one accused witch and her child. Most of his experience with witchcraft comes from books.

CUSTOMIZE INSTRUCTION FOR UNIVERSAL ACCESS

For Less Proficient Readers	For English Learners
The commentary that begins on p. 1252 is dense and complex, both in its language and its arguments. Have students break it down into paragraphs, find the main idea and key supporting details in each paragraph, and use these notes to summarize Miller's arguments. Students can then gather for a discussion of their reactions to what Miller says.	This commentary is filled with sophisticated and unfamiliar vocabulary. Assign peer tutors to help students read the commentary. Students learning English should try as much as possible to use context clues or cognates to define unfamiliar words before checking a dictionary.

- Ask students to summarize Miller's arguments about the devil in society and human beliefs about the devil.

  Answer: Miller asserts that in the same way that the Puritans ascribed negative events to the influence of the devil on witches, modern people attributed the ills of the world to communism and communists.

- Ask students whether they accept Miller's argument. Does he support his contention? What evidence does he use? Is his evidence convincing?

cruelty inflicted, and not always even in that department. Normally, the actions and deeds of a man were all that society felt comfortable in judging. The secret intent of an action was left to the ministers, priests, and rabbis to deal with. When diabolism rises, however, actions are the least important manifests of the true nature of a man. The Devil, as Reverend Hale said, is a wily one, and until an hour before he fell, even God thought him beautiful in Heaven.

The analogy, however, seems to falter when one considers that, while there were no witches then, there are Communists and capitalists now, and in each camp there is certain proof that spies of each side are at work undermining the other. But this is a snobbish objection and not at all warranted by the facts. I have no doubt that people *were* communing with, and even worshiping, the Devil in Salem, and if the whole truth could be known in this case, as it is in others, we should discover a regular and conventionalized <u>propitiation</u> of the dark spirit. One certain evidence of this is the confession of Tituba, the slave of Reverend Parris, and another is the behavior of the children who were known to have indulged in sorceries with her.

propitiation (prə pish´ ē ā´ shən) *n.* action designed to soothe or satisfy a person, a cause, etc.

 There are accounts of similar *klatches*[15] in Europe, where the daughters of the towns would assemble at night and, sometimes with fetishes,[16] sometimes with a selected young man, give themselves to love, with some bastardly results. The Church, sharp-eyed as it must be when gods long dead are brought to life, condemned these orgies as witchcraft and interpreted them, rightly, as a resurgence of the Dionysiac[17] forces it had crushed long before. Sex, sin, and the Devil were early linked, and so they continued to be in Salem, and are today. From all accounts there are no more puritanical mores in the world than those enforced by the Communists in Russia, where women's fashions, for instance, are as prudent and all-covering as any American Baptist would desire. The divorce laws lay a tremendous responsibility on the father for the care of his children. Even the laxity of divorce regulations in the early years of the revolution was undoubtedly a revulsion from the nineteenth-century Victorian[18] immobility of marriage and the consequent hypocrisy that developed from it. If for no other reasons, a state so powerful, so jealous of the uniformity of its citizens, cannot long tolerate the atomization of the family. And yet, in American eyes at least, there

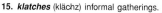

---

15. *klatches* (klächz) informal gatherings.
16. **fetishes** (fet´ ish iz) objects believed to have magical power.
17. **Dionysiac** (dī´ ə nis´ ē ak´) characteristic of Dionysus, Greek god of wine and revelry; thus, wild, frenzied, sensuous.
18. **Victorian** characteristic of the time when Victoria was queen of England (1837–1901), an era associated with respectability, prudery, and hypocrisy.

remains the conviction that the Russian attitude toward women is lascivious. It is the Devil working again, just as he is working within the Slav who is shocked at the very idea of a woman's disrobing herself in a burlesque show. Our opposites are always robed in sexual sin, and it is from this unconscious conviction that demonology gains both its attractive sensuality and its capacity to infuriate and frighten.

Coming into Salem now, Reverend Hale conceives of himself much as a young doctor on his first call. His painfully acquired armory of symptoms, catchwords, and diagnostic procedures are now to be put to use at last. The road from Beverly is unusually busy this morning, and he has passed a hundred rumors that make him smile at the ignorance of the yeomanry in this most precise science. He feels himself allied with the best minds of Europe—kings, philosophers, scientists, and ecclesiasts of all churches. His goal is light, goodness and its preservation, and he knows the exaltation of the blessed whose intelligence, sharpened by minute examinations of enormous tracts, is finally called upon to face what may be a bloody fight with the Fiend himself.

He appears loaded down with half a dozen heavy books.

HALE: Pray you, someone take these!

PARRIS, *delighted:* Mr. Hale! Oh! it's good to see you again! *Taking some books:* My, they're heavy!

HALE, *setting down his books:* They must be; they are weighted with authority.

PARRIS, *a little scared:* Well, you do come prepared!

HALE: We shall need hard study if it comes to tracking down the Old Boy. *Noticing* REBECCA: You cannot be Rebecca Nurse?

REBECCA: I am, sir. Do you know me?

HALE: It's strange how I knew you, but I suppose you look as such a good soul should. We have all heard of your great charities in Beverly.

PARRIS: Do you know this gentleman? Mr. Thomas Putnam. And his good wife Ann.

HALE: Putnam! I had not expected such distinguished company, sir.

PUTNAM, *pleased:* It does seem to help us today, Mr. Hale. We look to you to come to our house and save our child.

HALE: Your child ails too?

MRS. PUTNAM: Her soul, her soul seems flown away. She sleeps and yet she walks . . .

PUTNAM: She cannot eat.

HALE: Cannot eat! *Thinks on it. Then, to* PROCTOR *and* GILES COREY: Do you men have afflicted children?

PARRIS: No, no, these are farmers. John Proctor—

GILES COREY: He don't believe in witches.

Reading Strategy
Questioning the Characters' Motives
According to this passage, what motivates Reverend Hale to study and expose witchcraft?

Reading Check
What is the "armory" Hale brings with him to Salem?

The Crucible, Act I ◆ *1255*

Reading Strategy

Questioning the Characters' Motives

- Ask students the Reading Strategy question on p. 1255: According to this passage, what motivates Reverend Hale to study and expose witchcraft?
  Answer: Hale wants to cure people. He wants to best the devil in combat for human souls.

- How do students evaluate Hale's fitness for his task, based on the information in the commentary beginning on p. 1252?
  Answer: The case of the woman acquitted of witchcraft shows that Hale doesn't rush to judgment. However, he seems to rely too much on books and not on his own observations of people.

- What does Hale's recognition of Rebecca suggest about both characters?
  Answer: Rebecca's goodness is visible in her expression; Hale is observant enough to sense it.

Reading Check

Answer: It is an armory of "symptoms, catchwords, and diagnostic procedures."

- Ask students the first Literary Analysis question on p. 1256: What does this speech about the devil's precision reveal about Hale's understanding of human nature? **Answer:** Hale understands that people often want to find evidence of evil, and will sometimes fabricate it to meet that goal.

- Ask students the second Literary Analysis question on p. 1256: What does this dialogue reveal about Ann Putnam? **Answer:** She wants to blame someone—anyone—for the deaths of her children. She resents Rebecca Nurse's implied criticism of her for sending her daughter to Tituba.

PROCTOR, *to* HALE: I never spoke on witches one way or the other. Will you come, Giles?

GILES: No—no, John, I think not. I have some few queer questions of my own to ask this fellow.

PROCTOR: I've heard you to be a sensible man, Mr. Hale. I hope you'll leave some of it in Salem.

PROCTOR *goes.* HALE *stands embarrassed for an instant.*

PARRIS, *quickly:* Will you look at my daughter, sir? *Leads* HALE *to the bed.* She has tried to leap out the window; we discovered her this morning on the highroad, waving her arms as though she'd fly.

HALE, *narrowing his eyes:* Tries to fly.

PUTNAM: She cannot bear to hear the Lord's name, Mr. Hale; that's a sure sign of witchcraft afloat.

HALE, *holding up his hands:* No, no. Now let me instruct you. We cannot look to superstition in this. The Devil is precise; the marks of his presence are definite as stone, and I must tell you all that I shall not proceed unless you are prepared to believe me if I should find no bruise of hell upon her.

PARRIS: It is agreed, sir—it is agreed—we will abide by your judgment.

HALE: Good then. *He goes to the bed, looks down at* BETTY. *To* PARRIS: Now, sir, what were your first warning of this strangeness?

PARRIS: Why, sir—I discovered her—*indicating* ABIGAIL—and my niece and ten or twelve of the other girls, dancing in the forest last night.

HALE, *surprised:* You permit dancing?

PARRIS: No, no, it were secret—

46 **MRS. PUTNAM,** *unable to wait:* Mr. Parris's slave has knowledge of conjurin', sir.

PARRIS, *to* MRS. PUTNAM: We cannot be sure of that, Goody Ann—

MRS. PUTNAM, *frightened, very softly:* I know it, sir. I sent my child— she should learn from Tituba who murdered her sisters.

REBECCA, *horrified:* Goody Ann! You sent a child to conjure up the dead?

MRS. PUTNAM: Let God blame me, not you, not you, Rebecca! I'll not have you judging me any more! *To* HALE: Is it a natural work to lose seven children before they live a day?

PARRIS: Sssh!

REBECCA, *with great pain, turns her face away. There is a pause.*

HALE: Seven dead in childbirth.

MRS. PUTNAM, *softly:* Aye. *Her voice breaks; she looks up at him. Silence.* HALE *is impressed.* PARRIS *looks to him. He goes to his books, opens one, turns pages, then reads. All wait, avidly.*

PARRIS, *hushed:* What book is that?

MRS. PUTNAM: What's there, sir?

Literary Analysis
Dialogue and Stage Directions What does this speech about the devil's precision reveal about Hale's understanding of human nature?

Literary Analysis
Dialogue and Stage Directions What does this dialogue reveal about Ann Putnam's character and judgment?

ENRICHMENT: Science Connection

Infant Mortality

Although losing seven children at birth was unusual, infant mortality was high in Puritan New England. The simple explanation for Mrs. Putnam's losses is not witchcraft but the lack of medical science at the time.

New England had a bitterly cold climate. Houses were heated only by open fires and could not be cooled in hot weather except by leaving windows open. Flies and mosquitoes, which can spread disease, are prevalent throughout North America, and screens for doors and windows were far in the future. If crops did not do well, families went hungry; an undernourished mother might not have enough milk for her baby. Babies were as prone to illness then as they are now, but Puritans had no antibiotics with which to cure their children.

HALE, *with a tasty love of intellectual pursuit:* Here is all the invisible world, caught, defined, and calculated. In these books the Devil stands stripped of all his brute disguises. Here are all your familiar spirits—your incubi[19] and succubi, your witches that go by land, by air, and by sea; your wizards of the night and of the day. Have no fear now—we shall find him out if he has come among us, and I mean to crush him utterly if he has shown his face! *He starts for the bed.*

REBECCA: Will it hurt the child, sir?

HALE: I cannot tell. If she is truly in the Devil's grip we may have to rip and tear to get her free.

REBECCA: I think I'll go, then. I am too old for this. *She rises.*

PARRIS, *striving for conviction:* Why, Rebecca, we may open up the boil of all our troubles today!

REBECCA: Let us hope for that. I go to God for you, sir.

PARRIS, *with trepidation—and resentment:* I hope you do not mean to go to Satan here! *Slight pause.*

REBECCA: I wish I knew. *She goes out; they feel resentful of her note of moral superiority.*

PUTNAM, *abruptly:* Come, Mr. Hale, let's get on. Sit you here.

GILES: Mr. Hale, I have always wanted to ask a learned man—what signifies the readin' of strange books?

HALE: What books?

GILES: I cannot tell; she hides them.

HALE: Who does this?

GILES: Martha, my wife. I have waked at night many a time and found her in a corner, readin' of a book. Now what do you make of that?

HALE: Why, that's not necessarily—

GILES: It discomfits me! Last night—mark this—I tried and tried and could not say my prayers. And then she close her book and walks out of the house, and suddenly—mark this—I could pray again!

Old Giles must be spoken for, if only because his fate was to be so remarkable and so different from that of all the others. He was in his early eighties at this time, and was the most comical hero in the history. No man has ever been blamed for so much. If a cow was missed, the first thought was to look for her around Corey's house; a fire blazing up at night brought suspicion of arson to his door. He didn't give a hoot for public opinion, and only in his last years—after he had married Martha—did he bother much with the church. That she stopped his prayer is very probable, but he forgot to say that he'd only recently learned any prayers and it didn't take much to make him stumble over them. He was a crank and a nuisance, but withal a deeply innocent and brave man. In court, once, he was asked if it were true that he had been frightened by the strange behavior of a hog and had then said he knew it to be the Devil in an animal's shape. "What frighted you?" he

_____

19. **incubi** (in´ kyoo bī) spirits or demons thought to lie on sleeping women.

Literary Analysis
Dialogue, Stage Directions, and Dramatic Exposition Which details given in this background information explain Giles Corey's remarks about his wife, Martha?

Reading Check
How does Rebecca's concern for the children compare to Hale's and Parris's?

The Crucible, Act I ◆ *1257*

47 Literary Analysis
Dialogue and Stage Directions

• What makes the other characters feel that Rebecca is morally superior? Does Rebecca feel this way about herself?
Answer: The other characters see that Rebecca disagrees with their idea of the best solution to the problem. They know that Rebecca is good, and this puts pressure on them to agree with her. They dislike the pressure. Rebecca would never say that she was superior to them; she is thinking only of the children's well-being, not of herself.

48 Literary Analysis
Dialogue and Stage Directions, and Dramatic Exposition

• Ask students about their immediate responses to Giles Corey's anxiety about his wife's reading.
Possible answers: Students may think Giles lives in a period when women do not often read books, and is startled when they do. Other students may be horrified, and anticipate that Hale will suspect her of witchcraft simply because she reads.

• Ask students the Literary Analysis question on p. 1257: Which details given in this background information explain Giles Corey's remarks about his wife, Martha?
Answer: Giles may have forgotten his prayers because he was intimidated by Martha's presence and because he had only recently learned them.

49 Reading Check
Answer: Rebecca's main concern is for Betty's physical and spiritual comfort. Hale regards her almost as a scientific experiment. Parris is frightened for his child but also for his own position in the community.

- Ask students the Literary Analysis question on p. 1258: In what ways do Hale's questions to Betty suggest the answers he wants to hear?

Answer: He asks her instead of just waiting to see if she has anything to say.

- Ask students where they have seen this method of questioning before.

Answer: In the play's opening passages, Parris suggests to Abigail that she and the others were conjuring spirits, rather than just asking her what they were doing.

▶ Monitor Progress Point out that Hale repeats this method when he questions Abby about the soup. Ask students what they think of this method of questioning.

Answers: Students may object because it puts ideas into people's heads. When people are questioned about any serious crime, they can be so frightened that they may say anything; leading them is not the best way to find out the truth.

51 ▶ Critical Viewing

Answer: The photograph suggests that the girls are romping, dancing, literally "letting their hair down" and having fun.

was asked. He forgot everything but the word "frighted," and instantly replied, "I do not know that I ever spoke that word in my life."

HALE: Ah! The stoppage of prayer—that is strange. I'll speak further on that with you.

GILES: I'm not sayin' she's touched the Devil, now, but I'd admire to know what books she reads and why she hides them. She'll not answer me, y' see.

HALE: Aye, we'll discuss it. To all: Now mark me, if the Devil is in her you will witness some frightful wonders in this room, so please to keep your wits about you. Mr. Putnam, stand close in case she flies. Now, Betty, dear, will you sit up? PUTNAM *comes in closer, ready-handed.* HALE *sits* BETTY *up, but she hangs limp in his hands.* Hmmm. *He observes her carefully. The others watch breathlessly.* Can you hear me? I am John Hale, minister of Beverly. I have come to help you, dear. Do you remember my two little girls in Beverly? *She does not stir in his hands.*

PARRIS, *in fright:* How can it be the Devil? Why would he choose my house to strike? We have all manner of <u>licentious</u> people in the village!

HALE: What victory would the Devil have to win a soul already bad? It is the best the Devil wants, and who is better than the minister?

GILES: That's deep, Mr. Parris, deep, deep!

PARRIS, *with resolution now:* Betty! Answer Mr. Hale! Betty!

HALE: Does someone afflict you, child? It need not be a woman, mind you, or a man. Perhaps some bird invisible to others comes to you— perhaps a pig, a mouse, or any beast at all. Is there some figure bids you fly? *The child remains limp in his hands. In silence he lays her back on the pillow. Now, holding out his hands toward her, he intones:* In nomine Domini Sabaoth sui filiique ite ad infernos.[20] *She does not stir. He turns to* ABIGAIL, *his eyes narrowing.* Abigail, what sort of dancing were you doing with her in the forest?

ABIGAIL: Why—common dancing is all.

PARRIS: I think I ought to say that I—I saw a kettle in the grass where they were dancing.

ABIGAIL: That were only soup.

HALE: What sort of soup were in this kettle, Abigail?

ABIGAIL: Why, it were beans—and lentils, I think, and—

HALE: Mr. Parris, you did not notice, did you, any living thing in the kettle? A mouse, perhaps, a spider, a frog—?

PARRIS, *fearfully:* I—do believe there were some movement—in the soup.

ABIGAIL: That jumped in, we never put it in!

HALE, *quickly:* What jumped in?

ABIGAIL: Why, a very little frog jumped—

PARRIS: A frog, Abby!

---

20. **In nomine Domini Sabaoth sui filiique ite ad infernos** (in nō´mē nā dō´ mē nē sab´ ā äth sōō´ ē fē´ lēē kwā ē´ tā äd in fur´ nōs) "In the name of the lord of hosts and his son, get thee to the lower world" (Latin).

licentious (lī sen´ shəs) *adj.* lacking moral restraint

Literary Analysis
Dialogue and Stage Directions In what way do Hale's questions to Betty suggest the answers he wants to hear?

51 ▶ **Critical Viewing** Based on this photograph of Abigail and Tituba surrounded by other girls of Salem, how would you describe what actually happened in the woods? **[Interpret]**

HALE, *grasping* ABIGAIL: Abigail, it may be your cousin is dying. Did you call the Devil last night?

ABIGAIL: I never called him! Tituba, Tituba . . .

PARRIS, *blanched:* She called the Devil?

HALE: I should like to speak with Tituba.

PARRIS: Goody Ann, will you bring her up? MRS. PUTNAM *exits.*

HALE: How did she call him?

ABIGAIL: I know not—she spoke Barbados.

HALE: Did you feel any strangeness when she called him? A sudden cold wind, perhaps? A trembling below the ground?

ABIGAIL: I didn't see no Devil! *Shaking* BETTY: Betty, wake up. Betty! Betty!

HALE: You cannot evade me, Abigail. Did your cousin drink any of the brew in that kettle?

ABIGAIL: She never drank it!

HALE: Did you drink it?

ABIGAIL: No, sir!

HALE: Did Tituba ask you to drink it?

ABIGAIL: She tried, but I refused.

HALE: Why are you concealing? Have you sold yourself to Lucifer?

ABIGAIL: I never sold myself! I'm a good girl! I'm a proper girl!

MRS. PUTNAM *enters with* TITUBA, *and instantly* ABIGAIL *points at* TITUBA.

Reading Strategy
Questioning the Characters' Motives Why does Hale want to speak with Tituba?

 Reading Check

What important details does Parris add to Abigail's story? How does she explain them?

The Crucible, Act I ◆ 1259

Reading Strategy
Questioning the Characters' Motives

- Ask students the Reading Strategy question on p. 1259: Why does Hale want to speak with Tituba?
  Answer: Hale wishes to gain more information about Tituba's actions in the forest.

- Have students predict what is likely to happen when Tituba comes into the room. Have them base their predictions on what has happened since Hale's entrance.
  Answer: Hale is likely to question Tituba on the assumption that she is guilty of witchcraft.

- Point out that Hale also questions Abigail, assuming that she too is guilty of witchcraft. Have students note Abigail's response to these questions. What does her response suggest about her character?
  Answer: To divert attention from herself, she accuses Tituba. She points to Tituba as soon as Tituba enters the room. She is willing to sacrifice others to save herself.

Reading Check

Answer: Parris reveals that he saw a kettle being used to cook something, and that he saw something moving in it. Abigail claims it was only soup, and that a frog accidentally jumped in.

CUSTOMIZE INSTRUCTION FOR UNIVERSAL ACCESS

For Less Proficient Readers	For English Learners
Have students work together on cause-and-effect chains that trace the development of Act I from Parris's first questions to Abigail through the accusations of witchcraft that end the act. Students may want to consider causes that were in place before the play begins, such as Puritan disapproval of children having fun. They should also try predicting what will come of the accusations made at the end of the act.	To help students understand the complex set of motives and causes that drive the plot of the play, have them work together in groups with more proficient English speakers. Have students use a list of characters to brainstorm for dialogue and expository passages that reveal each character's motivations, and list these on the chalkboard. Then help students to create a timeline for the events in Act I, annotated with the characters' motivations for each action.

Reading Strategy

Questioning the Characters' Motives

- Ask students the first Reading Strategy question on p. 1260: What do you think Abigail is trying to do by accusing Tituba of making her "laugh at prayer"?
  Possible answers: Abigail is trying to divert attention from herself and her own guilt in trying to practice witchcraft against John Proctor's wife. On the previous page, Hale was beginning to accuse her of witchcraft.

- Why does Abigail attack Tituba rather than one of the other girls?
  Answer: Because Tituba is a slave and from a foreign culture, she is in a weak position. Abigail knows that her word will likely be taken against Tituba's.

55 Reading Strategy

Questioning the Characters' Motives

- Ask students the second Reading Strategy question on p. 1260: What does this dialogue reveal about Tituba's motives for her sudden confusion?
  Answer: Tituba confesses because Parris and Putnam tell her that the alternative is death.

- Why does Tituba not argue more strongly with Abigail?
  Possible answers: She is bewildered. She is shocked that Abigail has turned on her. She knows that no one will believe the word of a slave against that of the minister's niece. She doesn't want Abigail hanged.

ABIGAIL: She made me do it! She made Betty do it!

TITUBA, *shocked and angry:* Abby!

ABIGAIL: She makes me drink blood!

PARRIS: Blood!!

MRS. PUTNAM: My baby's blood?

TITUBA: No, no, chicken blood. I give she chicken blood!

HALE: Woman, have you enlisted these children for the Devil?

TITUBA: No, no, sir, I don't truck with no Devil!

HALE: Why can she not wake? Are you silencing this child?

TITUBA: I love me Betty!

HALE: You have sent your spirit out upon this child, have you not? Are you gathering souls for the Devil?

ABIGAIL: She sends her spirit on me in church; she makes me laugh at prayer!

PARRIS: She have often laughed at prayer!

ABIGAIL: She comes to me every night to go and drink blood!

TITUBA: You beg *me* to conjure! She beg *me* make charm—

ABIGAIL: Don't lie! *To* HALE: She comes to me while I sleep; she's always making me dream corruptions!

TITUBA: Why you say that, Abby?

ABIGAIL: Sometimes I wake and find myself standing in the open doorway and not a stitch on my body! I always hear her laughing in my sleep. I hear her singing her Barbados songs and tempting me with—

TITUBA: Mister Reverend, I never—

HALE, *resolved now:* Tituba, I want you to wake this child.

TITUBA: I have no power on this child, sir.

HALE: You most certainly do, and you will free her from it now! When did you compact with the Devil?

TITUBA: I don't compact with no Devil!

PARRIS: You will confess yourself or I will take you out and whip you to your death, Tituba!

PUTNAM: This woman must be hanged! She must be taken and hanged!

TITUBA, *terrified, falls to her knees:* No, no, don't hang Tituba! I tell him I don't desire to work for him, sir.

PARRIS: The Devil?

HALE: Then you saw him! TITUBA *weeps.* Now Tituba, I know that when we bind ourselves to Hell it is very hard to break with it. We are going to help you tear yourself free—

TITUBA, *frightened by the coming process:* Mister Reverend, I do believe somebody else be witchin' these children.

HALE: Who?

TITUBA: I don't know, sir, but the Devil got him numerous witches.

Reading Strategy
Questioning the Characters' Motives
What do you think Abigail is trying to do in accusing Tituba of making her "laugh at prayer"?

Reading Strategy
Questioning the Characters' Motives
What does this dialogue reveal about the motives for Tituba's sudden confession?

HALE: Does he! *It is a clue.* Tituba, look into my eyes. Come, look into me. *She raises her eyes to his fearfully.* You would be a good Christian woman, would you not, Tituba?

TITUBA: Aye, sir, a good Christian woman.

HALE: And you love these little children?

TITUBA: Oh, yes, sir, I don't desire to hurt little children.

HALE: And you love God, Tituba?

TITUBA: I love God with all my bein'.

HALE: Now, in God's holy name—

TITUBA: Bless Him. Bless Him. *She is rocking on her knees, sobbing in terror.*

HALE: And to His glory—

TITUBA: Eternal glory. Bless Him—bless God . . .

HALE: Open yourself, Tituba—open yourself and let God's holy light shine on you.

TITUBA: Oh, bless the Lord.

HALE: When the Devil come to you does he ever come—with another person? *She stares up into his face.* Perhaps another person in the village? Someone you know.

PARRIS: Who came with him?

PUTNAM: Sarah Good? Did you ever see Sarah Good with him? Or Osburn?

PARRIS: Was it man or woman came with him?

TITUBA: Man or woman. Was—was woman.

PARRIS: What woman? A woman, you said. What woman?

TITUBA: It was black dark, and I—

PARRIS: You could see him, why could you not see her?

TITUBA: Well, they was always talking; they was always runnin' round and carryin' on—

PARRIS: You mean out of Salem? Salem witches?

TITUBA: I believe so, yes, sir.

Now HALE *takes her hand. She is surprised.*

HALE: Tituba. You must have no fear to tell us who they are, do you understand? We will protect you. The Devil can never overcome a minister. You know that, do you not?

TITUBA, *kisses* HALE's *hand:* Aye, sir, oh, I do.

HALE: You have confessed yourself to witchcraft, and that speaks a wish to come to Heaven's side. And we will bless you, Tituba.

TITUBA, *deeply relieved:* Oh, God bless you, Mr. Hale!

HALE, *with rising exaltation:* You are God's instrument put in our hands to discover the Devil's agent among us. You are selected, Tituba, you are chosen to help us cleanse our village. So speak utterly, Tituba,

---

Literary Analysis
Dialogue and Stage Directions What techniques does Miller use to indicate that Tituba is making things up?

Literary Analysis
Dialogue and Stage Directions To what does Tituba confess in this dialogue?

 Reading Check
Who is the first person to name specific individuals?

The Crucible, Act I ◆ 1261

---

56 Literary Analysis

Dialogue and Stage Directions

- Ask students whether they think Tituba believes her own statements.
  Answer: Students should recognize that Tituba, in fear for her life, is saying anything she can think of that Parris wants to hear.

- Ask students the first Literary Analysis question on p. 1261: What techniques does Miller use to indicate that Tituba is making things up?
  Answer: Miller has Tituba repeat the questions she is asked, to gain time for thought, and then hesitate before she answers. Her hesitations are indicated with a dash.

57 Literary Analysis

Dialogue and Stage Directions

- Ask students the second Literary Analysis question on p. 1261: To what does Tituba confess in this dialogue?
  Answer: She confesses to witchcraft and to having seen an unidentified woman with the Devil.

- Point out that Tituba's "confession" is entirely the result of suggestions that Hale and Parris make to her. They prompt her, telling her what they want to hear, and she tries to satisfy them without actually accusing any innocent people.

58 Reading Check

Answer: Putnam, who asks about Sarah Good and Goody Osburn, is the first to name specific people.

CUSTOMIZE INSTRUCTION FOR UNIVERSAL ACCESS

For Special Needs Students	For Gifted/Talented Students
Have students work together to answer the Review and Assess questions on p. 1263. You might make this a homework assignment. The next day in class, students can gather in a group to discuss their answers. Have them go back to the text of the play to resolve any disagreements. Students can then answer the questions on p. 1264 in group discussion.	Through acting, students can better grasp the emotional upheaval of the events that end Act I. Encourage volunteers to play the roles of Hale, Parris, Abigail, Tituba, and Putnam through to the end of Act I, beginning from Parris's line, "How can it be the Devil?" on p. 1258. Have students run through, rehearse, and then perform their roles for the class. Ask students what emotions best describe the characters' motivations in this scene (fear, hysteria, hate, excitement, ambition, helplessness).

- Ask students the Reading Strategy question on p. 1262: What do you think motivates Hale to speak "kindly" to Tituba?
  Answer: He believes that she is trying her best to fight off the influence of the Devil. He is a compassionate man who truly wants to help.

- What motivates Tituba to name Goody Good and Goody Osburn?
  Answer: She responds to Hale's kindness. Putnam has just put these two names into her head, so she knows these are the names her questioners want to hear.

- What motivates Abigail to make this false confession?
  Answer: Abigail's motives are complex. She sees that a confession makes Tituba the center of attention and that Tituba's importance in the community has risen. Abigail wants to be important. Parris had already told her that her reputation was not good, and she wants to change that. She also wants to make sure that she is safe from any accusation about using witchcraft to kill Goody Proctor. She has also seen that a confession will guarantee safety from hanging.

turn your back on him and face God—face God, Tituba, and God will protect you.

TITUBA, *joining with him:* Oh, God, protect Tituba!

HALE, *kindly:* Who came to you with the Devil? Two? Three? Four? How many?

Tituba pants, and begins rocking back and forth again, staring ahead.

TITUBA: There was four. There was four.

PARRIS, *pressing in on her:* Who? Who? Their names, their names!

TITUBA, *suddenly bursting out:* Oh, how many times he bid me kill you, Mr. Parris!

PARRIS: Kill me!

TITUBA, *in a fury:* He say Mr. Parris must be kill! Mr. Parris no goodly man, Mr. Parris mean man and no gentle man, and he bid me rise out of my bed and cut your throat! *They gasp.* But I tell him "No! I don't hate that man. I don't want kill that man." But he say, "You work for me, Tituba, and I make you free! I give you pretty dress to wear, and put you way high up in the air, and you gone fly back to Barbados!" And I say, "You lie, Devil, you lie!" And then he come one stormy night to me, and he say, "Look! I have *white* people belong to me." And I look—and there was Goody Good.

PARRIS: Sarah Good!

TITUBA, *rocking and weeping:* Aye, sir, and Goody Osburn.

MRS. PUTNAM: I knew it! Goody Osburn were midwife to me three times. I begged you, Thomas, did I not? I begged him not to call Osburn because I feared her. My babies always shriveled in her hands!

HALE: Take courage, you must give us all their names. How can you bear to see this child suffering? Look at her, Tituba. *He is indicating* BETTY *on the bed.* Look at her God-given innocence; her soul is so tender; we must protect her, Tituba; the Devil is out and preying on her like a beast upon the flesh of the pure lamb. God will bless you for your help.

ABIGAIL *rises, staring as though inspired, and cries out.*

ABIGAIL: I want to open myself! *They turn to her, startled. She is enraptured, as though in a pearly light.* I want the light of God, I want the sweet love of Jesus! I danced for the Devil; I saw him; I wrote in his book; I go back to Jesus; I kiss His hand. I saw Sarah Good with the Devil! I saw Goody Osburn with the Devil! I saw Bridget Bishop with the Devil!

As she is speaking, BETTY *is rising from the bed, a fever in her eyes, and picks up the chant.*

BETTY, *staring too:* I saw George Jacobs with the Devil! I saw Goody Howe with the Devil!

PARRIS: She speaks! *He rushes to embrace* BETTY. She speaks!

HALE: Glory to God! It is broken, they are free!

1262 ◆ *Prosperity and Protest (1946–Present)*

Reading Strategy
**Questioning the
Characters' Motives**
What do you think
motivates Hale to speak
"kindly" to Tituba?

BETTY, *calling out hysterically and with great relief:* I saw Martha Bellows with the Devil!

ABIGAIL: I saw Goody Sibber with the Devil! *It is rising to a great glee.*

PUTNAM: The marshal, I'll call the marshal!

PARRIS *is shouting a prayer of thanksgiving.*

BETTY: I saw Alice Barrow with the Devil!

The curtain begins to fall.

HALE, *as* PUTNAM *goes out:* Let the marshal bring irons!

ABIGAIL: I saw Goody Hawkins with the Devil!

BETTY: I saw Goody Bibber with the Devil!

ABIGAIL: I saw Goody Booth with the Devil!

On their ecstatic cries—

THE CURTAIN FALLS

Review and Assess

Thinking About Act I

1. **Respond:** Were you surprised when the accusations against specific individuals multiplied? Explain.

2. **(a) Recall:** What is Betty's condition when the play opens? **(b) Recall:** What does Abigail say that she and Betty were doing in the forest? **(c) Infer:** What seems to be the main motivation for Reverend Parris's concern about the girls' behavior in the forest?

3. **(a) Recall:** What do Abigail, Betty, Mercy, and Mary discuss after Reverend Parris leaves his daughter's room? **(b) Interpret:** What events does this scene suggest may occur later in the play?

4. **(a) Recall:** Who is Reverend Hale? **(b) Recall:** Why is he contacted? **(c) Evaluate:** Do you think he is being fair and impartial so far? Why or why not?

5. **(a) Summarize:** Summarize Abigail's prior relationship with the Proctors. **(b) Interpret:** What does Betty's revelation about Abigail's actions in the forest suggest about Abigail's feelings for Goody Proctor?

6. **(a) Support:** What evidence suggests that sharp divisions exist among the people of Salem Village? **(b) Apply:** Name two others who may be accused. Explain your choices.

7. **Evaluate:** Which situations, if any, in contemporary life might cause an American town to be afflicted with a general hysteria? Explain.

The Crucible, Act I ◆ 1263

---

1. Students were probably surprised. One accusation would have been enough for the girls to escape punishment for their games in the woods.

2. **(a)** She is in a heavy sleep. **(b)** She says they were dancing. **(c)** He is afraid of how it may affect his position in the community if his enemies find out.

3. **(a)** They try to agree on what story they will tell; Abigail threatens the others with vengeance if they say that she tried to kill Goody Proctor. **(b)** It suggests that the girls will be asked what happened in the woods and that they will lie.

4. **(a)** He is a pastor from Beverly. **(b)** He is reputed to be an expert on demonic possession. **(c)** He does not rush to judgment, but he presumes guilt instead of innocence.

5. **(a)** Abigail was their servant and, briefly, John's lover. **(b)** Abigail is clearly filled with jealous hatred of her.

6. **(a)** Parris mentions having enemies who want to drive him from the pulpit. Rebecca mentions strife in the town. Proctor and Corey suggest that the Putnam family cheats and angers everyone. **(b)** Possible answer: Proctor and Rebecca may be accused because others resent them.

7. Students might refer to such actual events as unfounded accusations of child abuse at daycare centers, or some people's preparations for the end of the world at New Year, 2000.

✎ ASSESSMENT PRACTICE: Writing Skills

Grammar and Usage	(For more practice, use Test Preparation Workbook, p. 76)

Many tests require students to choose the best word to complete a sentence. Use this sample test item.

Among the plays written by Arthur Miller _____ *The Crucible, Death of a Salesman,* and *A View from the Bridge.*

Which word correctly completes this sentence:

A is   **C** was

B are   **D** remains

Since the subject ("the plays") is plural, the verb must be plural. Choice *B* is correct.

Review and Assess

1. Both stage directions and dialogue reveal that Abigail is a liar. Dialogue reveals that she hates Goody Proctor: "It's a bitter woman, a lying, cold, sniveling woman" and "You drank a charm to kill Goody Proctor!" Dialogue and stage directions show that she loves John: "I walk and walk about the house as though I'd find you comin' through some door." *She clutches him desperately.*

2. Stage directions mention her "concentrated desire" for him and indicate that she tries to touch him and make him touch her. They also mention her anger and resentment at his rejection.

3. **(a)** He wants the readers to understand the attitudes and beliefs in the time and place in which his play is set. **(b)** The comments are addressed to the reader; they will not be read or spoken in a staged performance.

4. The stage directions identify the time and place, describe the room, and identify the two characters currently on stage.

5. Their recent behavior is revealed in dialogue.

6. He compares the Inquisition and the Red Scare to the threat of witchcraft in Salem.

7. His main concern is to protect himself from those in the parish who would like to see him leave his position as minister.

8. Abigail wants John. Her threats make it clear that she doesn't want this becoming public knowledge.

9. He has a grudge against them and wants them accused without having to do so openly.

10. He criticizes greed and irresponsibility. Putnam is greedy for property; Parris is jealous of his salary and privileges. Both seek to blame others for their own misfortunes.

Review and Assess

Literary Analysis

Dialogue and Stage Directions

1. Use a chart like the one shown to analyze the character of Abigail Williams. To respond, combine details from her **dialogue** with Miller's descriptions of her in the **stage directions.**

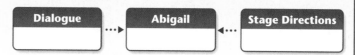

Dialogue		Abigail		Stage Directions

2. In the scene between Abigail and John Proctor, in what ways do the stage directions add to your understanding of their relationship?

Connecting Literary Elements

3. (a) Why does Miller include such extensive background information about seventeenth-century Salem and its inhabitants? (b) To whom is this information addressed? Explain.

4. What information is conveyed about the play's basic situation in the first three paragraphs of stage directions?

5. What technique does Miller use to provide important information about the recent activities of several village girls? Explain.

6. When Reverend Hale enters the scene, what two historic events does Miller compare in his **dramatic exposition**?

Reading Strategy

Questioning the Characters' Motives

7. What do Reverend Parris's comments and actions reveal about his **motivations**?

8. What do Abigail's actions in the forest and her threat to the girls reveal about her motives?

9. What is Putnam's motive for asking Tituba whether she saw Sarah Good or Goody Osburn in the woods?

Extend Understanding

10. **Cultural Connection:** Which elements of society does Miller seem to be criticizing through the characters of Reverend Parris and the Putnams? Explain.

1264 ◆ Prosperity and Protest (1946–Present)

TEACHING RESOURCES

The following resources can be used to enrich or extend the instructions for p. 1265

Vocabulary
- **Selection Support:** Build Vocabulary, p. 314
- **Vocabulary and Spelling Practice Book** (Use this booklet for skills enrichment.) ■

Grammar
- **Selection Support:** Grammar and Style, p. 315

- ✍ **Writing and Grammar,** Ruby Level, p. 572
- **Daily Language Practice Transparencies** ■

Writing
- ⊚ **Writing and Grammar iText CD-ROM**

Integrate Language Skills

❶ Vocabulary Development Lesson

Word Analysis: Latin Root -grat-

From *gratus*, Latin for "pleasing," comes the root *-grat-*, which means "pleasing" or "agreeable." An *ingratiating* attitude, for example, is one designed to please others. Explain how *-grat-* relates to the meaning of these words.

1. gratify   2. grateful   3. congratulate

Spelling Strategy

When adding a suffix that begins with a vowel to a word that ends in a silent *e*, drop the *e* and then add the suffix: *ingratiate* becomes *ingratiating*. For each word below, add the suffix given to form a new word.

1. ignite (*-ion*)   2. observe (*-ance*)

Concept Development: Context

Complete each of the following sentences with the appropriate vocabulary word from page 1232.

1. ____?____ can destroy a person's reputation.
2. Months of ____?____ helped me to learn.
3. He hid his true nature by ____?____.
4. His ____?____ behavior was scandalous.
5. To soothe their gods, they made sacrifices as an act of ____?____.
6. Her ____?____ manner pleased the customers.
7. With my ____?____ for history I knew I would enjoy *The Crucible*.

❷ Grammar and Style Lesson

Pronoun Case in Incomplete Constructions

In an **incomplete construction,** you may be uncertain about which form of pronoun to use. To decide, mentally complete the construction by inserting the missing words.

> **Example:** They want slaves, not such as *I*.
> (complete construction: *as I am*.)

Practice Choose the pronoun that best completes each sentence.

1. Proctor is not more sinful than (he, him).
2. Proctor has some affection for Abigail but cares more for his wife than (she, her).
3. Betty lies, but Abigail is craftier than (she, her).
4. "Blame her more than (I, me)," she says.
5. Abigail is manipulative, but Mercy Lewis is more cruel than (she, her).

Writing Application Write three sentences in which you compare two people. Use both proper nouns and correct pronouns in your sentences.

W̶G Prentice Hall *Writing and Grammar* Connection: Chapter 22, Section 2

Extension Activities

Writing Write a series of **news accounts** of the events in Salem as they might be described in a Boston newspaper of the day.

Listening and Speaking Working in a group, research and then report on the belief in witches in seventeenth-century Europe. Present your findings in an **oral report.** [Group Activity]

The Crucible, Act I ◆ 1265

ASSESSMENT RESOURCES

The following resources can be used to assess students' knowledge and skills.

Selection Assessment

- **Formal Assessment,** pp. 309–311
- **Open Book Test,** pp. 217–219
- **Got It! Assessment Videotapes,** Tape 6
- **Test Bank Software**
- **Take It to the Net**

  Visit www.phschool.com for self-tests and additional questions on *The Crucible*.

PRENTICE HALL ASSESSMENT SYSTEM

- **Workbook**
- **Skill Book**
- **Transparencies**
- **CD-ROM**

---

❶ Vocabulary Development

Word Analysis

1. To gratify means to please.
2. Someone who is grateful is pleased and thankful.
3. To congratulate means to express pleasure at someone's good fortune.

Spelling Strategy

1. ignition
2. observance

Concept Development: Context

1. Calumny
2. inculcation
3. dissembling
4. licentious
5. propitiation
6. ingratiating
7. predilection

❷ Grammar and Style Lesson

1. he
2. her
3. she
4. me
5. she

Writing Application

Have students check one another's sentences and use **Writing and Grammar,** Ruby Level, to resolve disagreements.

❸ Extension Activities

Writing Lesson

Students might write using seventeenth-century diction.

Listening and Speaking

Students' social studies teachers may be able to suggest sources of information for the report.

CUSTOMIZE INSTRUCTION
For Universal Access

To address different learning styles, use the following activities suggested in the **Extension Activities** booklet, p. 73.

For Visual/Spatial Learners, use Activities 5 and 7.

For Verbal/Linguistic Learners, use Activities 6 and 7.

For Interpersonal Learners, use Activity 7.

The Crucible, Act II

Lesson Objectives

1. **To analyze and respond to literary elements**
   - Literary Analysis: Allusion
   - Connecting Literary Elements: Historical Context

2. **To read, comprehend, analyze, and critique a drama**
   - Reading Strategy: Reading Drama
   - Reading Check Questions
   - Review and Assess Questions

3. **To develop word analysis skills, fluency, and systematic vocabulary**
   - Vocabulary Development Lesson: Greek Suffix: -logy

4. **To understand and apply written and oral language conventions**
   - Spelling Strategy
   - Grammar and Style Lesson: Commas After Introductory Words
   - Assessment Practice (ATE)

5. **To understand and apply appropriate writing and research strategies**
   - Writing Lesson: Additional Scene

6. **To understand and apply listening and speaking strategies**
   - Extension Activity: Wanted Poster

STEP-BY-STEP TEACHING GUIDE	PACING GUIDE
PRETEACH	
Motivate Students and Provide Background	
Use the Motivation activity (ATE p. 1230)	5 min.
Read and discuss author and background features (SE/ATE p. 1230–1231) [A]	5 min.
Introduce the Concepts	
Introduce the Literary Analysis and Reading Strategy (SE/ATE p. 1266) [A]	10 min.
Pronounce the vocabulary words and read their definitions (SE p. 1266)	5 min.
TEACH	
Monitor Comprehension	
Informally monitor comprehension by circulating while students read independently or in groups [A]	45 min.
Monitor students' comprehension with the Reading Check notes (SE/ATE pp. 1267, 1269, 1271, 1273, 1275, 1277, 1279, 1281, 1283, 1285)	as students read
Develop vocabulary with Vocabulary notes (SE pp. 1271, 1272, 1275, 1276, 1280, 1281, 1286; ATE p. 1276)	as students read
Develop Understanding	
Develop students' understanding of allusion with the Literary Analysis annotations (SE pp. 1269, 1276, 1280, 1285; ATE pp. 1269, 1270, 1276, 1277, 1280, 1285) [A]	5 min.
Develop students' ability to read drama by using the Reading Strategy annotations (SE pp. 1267, 1268, 1269, 1271, 1273, 1274, 1275, 1276, 1277, 1278, 1279, 1281, 1282, 1283; ATE pp. 1267, 1268, 1269, 1271, 1273, 1274, 1275, 1276, 1277, 1278, 1279, 1281, 1282, 1283)	5 min.
ASSESS	
Assess Mastery	
Assess students' mastery of the Reading Strategy and Literary Analysis by having them answer the Review and Assess questions (SE/ATE p. 1288)	15 min.
Use one or more of the print and media Assessment Resources (ATE p. 1288) [A]	up to 45 min.
EXTEND	
Apply Understanding	
Have students complete the Vocabulary Development Lesson and the Grammar and Style Lesson (SE p. 1289) [A]	20 min.
Apply students' understanding of the selection using one or more of the Extension Activities (SE p. 1289)	20–90 min.

 ACCELERATED INSTRUCTION:
Use the strategies and activities identified with an [A].

UNIVERSAL ACCESS
- ● = Below Level Students
- ▲ = On-Level Students
- ■ = Above Level Students

Time and Resource Manager

RESOURCES		
PRINT 📖	**TRANSPARENCIES**	**TECHNOLOGY** 🔊 🎧 📼
• **Beyond Literature,** Media Connection: Film Adaptations, p. 74 ▲ ■		• **Interest Grabber Video,** Tape 6 ● ▲ ■
• **Selection Support Workbook:** ● ▲ ■ Literary Analysis, p. 321 Reading Strategy, p. 320 Build Vocabulary, p. 318	• **Literary Analysis and Reading Transparencies,** pp. 147 and 148 ● ▲ ■	
• **Literatura en español** ● ▲ • **Literary Analysis for Enrichment** ■		
• **Formal Assessment:** Selection Test, pp. 312–314 ● ▲ ■ • **Open Book Test,** pp. 220–222 ● ▲ ■ • **ASSESSMENT SYSTEM** ● ▲ ■	• **ASSESSMENT SYSTEM** ● ▲ ■ Skills Practice Answers and Explanations on Transparencies	• **Test Bank Software** ● ▲ ■ • **Got It! Assessment Videotapes,** Tape 6 ● ▲
• **Selection Support Workbook:** ● ▲ ■ Grammar and Style, p. 319 • **Writing and Grammar,** Ruby Level ● ▲ ■ • **Extension Activities,** p. 74 ● ▲ ■	• **Daily Language Practice Transparencies** ● ▲	• **Writing and Grammar iText CD-ROM** ● ▲ ■ 💻 *Take It to the Net* www.phschool.com

BLOCK SCHEDULING: Use one 90-minute class period to preteach the selection and have students read it. Use a second 90-minute class period to assess students' mastery of skills and have them complete one of the Extension Activities.

❶ Literary Analysis

Allusion

- Review allusion by having students turn back to the stanza of Eliot's "The Love Song of J. Alfred Prufrock" (Unit 4) that begins, "No! I am not Prince Hamlet, nor was meant to be." Prufrock alludes to the tragic hero of Shakespeare's famous play. Point out that this allusion is also a metaphor. Prufrock goes on to compare himself to "an attendant lord" in the same play. Many allusions are metaphors or similes. For instance, if you accused a stingy friend of being "a real Scrooge," you would be alluding to the Dickens classic *A Christmas Carol* and also making a comparison that highlights your friend's miserly ways.

- Explain that the Bible was the only book most people in Salem had ever read. They heard passages from the Bible every Sunday, and people read their Bibles on their own. Members of a Puritan community knew the Bible so well that everyone could allude to it in conversation and the allusions would always be understood.

❷ Reading Strategy

Reading Drama

- Review the work students did with stage directions during their reading of Act I. Remind them that stage directions flesh out a script.

- Have students discuss the various ways the stage directions enriched their understanding of the events and characters in Act I.

Vocabulary Development

- Pronounce each vocabulary word for students, and read the definitions as a class. Have students identify any words with which they are already familiar.

E-Teach

Visit E-Teach at www.phschool.com for teachers' essays on how to teach, with questions and answers.

1266

Prepare to Read

The Crucible, Act II

❶ Literary Analysis

Allusion

An **allusion** is a brief reference within a work to something outside the work. Usually, an allusion relates to one of the following:

- Another literary work
- A well-known person
- A place
- A historical event

The Crucible makes many biblical allusions. For example, Act I contains a reference to the New Jerusalem, a term for the holy city of heaven. Use a chart like the one shown to record biblical allusions in Act II.

Connecting Literary Elements

To bring the Puritans to life on stage, Miller incorporates details of **historical context,** the key factors of life in the time period in which a literary work is set. Biblical allusions are one aspect of this re-creation of a historic time and place; the Puritans were a deeply religious people whose convictions help to set the play's action in motion. As you read, notice the ways in which Puritan ideas influence the action.

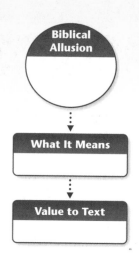

❷ Reading Strategy

Reading Drama

When you **read a drama** instead of watching the action and staging, you read the stage directions. Stage directions often interrupt the dialogue, but they provide critical information. As you read, pay close attention to the stage directions to understand the thoughts, attitudes, and behavior of the characters.

Vocabulary Development

pallor (pal′ ər) *n.* paleness (p. 1271)

ameliorate (ə mēl′ yə rāt) *v.* make better (p. 1271)

avidly (av′ id lē) *adv.* eagerly (p. 1272)

base (bās) *adj.* low; mean (p. 1275)

deference (def′ ər əns) *n.* courteous regard or respect (p. 1275)

theology (thē äl′ ə jē) *n.* the study of religion (p. 1276)

quail (kwāl) *v.* cringe from (p. 1280)

gingerly (jin′ jər lē) *adv.* cautiously (p. 1281)

abomination (ə bäm′ ə nā′ shən) *n.* something that causes great horror or disgust (p. 1286)

blasphemy (blas′ fə mē′) *n.* sinful act or remark (p. 1286)

TEACHING RESOURCES

The following resources can be used to enrich or extend the instruction for p. 1266.

Motivation

📼 **Interest Grabber Videotapes,** Tape 6

Background

📖 **Beyond Literature,** p. 74 ▪

💻 *Take It to the Net*

Visit www.phschool.com for Background and hotlinks for *The Crucible.*

Literary Analysis

📄 **Literary Analysis and Reading Transparencies,** Allusion, p. 148 ▪

Reading

📖 **Selection Support:** Reading Strategy, p. 320; Build Vocabulary, p. 318

📄 **Literary Analysis and Reading Transparencies,** Reading Drama, p. 147 ▪

 BLOCK SCHEDULING: Resources marked with this symbol provide varied instruction during 90-minute blocks.

Review and Anticipate

1 As Act I draws to a close, Salem is in the grip of mounting hysteria. What had begun as concern over the strange behavior of Betty—a reaction that may have stemmed from guilty feelings about her activities in the woods the night before—had swelled by the Act's end to a mass hysteria in which accusations of witchcraft were being made and accepted against a growing number of Salem's citizens. Which characters do you think will believe the accusations? Who do you think will be accused next?

ACT II

The common room of PROCTOR's *house, eight days later.*

At the right is a door opening on the fields outside. A fireplace is at the left, and behind it a stairway leading upstairs. It is the low, dark, and rather long living room of the time. As the curtain rises, the room is empty. From above, ELIZABETH *is heard softly singing to the children. Presently the door opens and* JOHN PROCTOR *enters, carrying his gun. He glances about the room as he comes toward the fireplace, then halts for an instant as he hears her singing. He continues on to the fireplace, leans the gun against the wall as he swings a pot out of the fire and smells it. Then he lifts out the ladle and tastes. He is not quite pleased. He reaches to a cupboard, takes a pinch of salt, and drops it into the pot. As he is tasting again, her footsteps are heard on the stair. He swings the pot into the fireplace and goes to a basin and washes his hands and face.* ELIZABETH *enters.*

2 ELIZABETH: What keeps you so late? It's almost dark.

PROCTOR: I were planting far out to the forest edge.

ELIZABETH: Oh, you're done then.

PROCTOR: Aye, the farm is seeded. The boys asleep?

ELIZABETH: They will be soon. *And she goes to the fireplace, proceeds to ladle up stew in a dish.*

PROCTOR: Pray now for a fair summer.

ELIZABETH: Aye.

PROCTOR: Are you well today?

ELIZABETH: I am. *She brings the plate to the table, and, indicating the food:* It is a rabbit.

PROCTOR, *going to the table:* Oh, is it! In Jonathan's trap?

ELIZABETH: No, she walked into the house this afternoon; I found her sittin' in the corner like she come to visit.

PROCTOR: Oh, that's a good sign walkin' in.

ELIZABETH: Pray God. It hurt my heart to strip her, poor rabbit. *She sits and watches him taste it.*

Reading Strategy

Reading Drama What important information do you learn about the amount of time passed between Act I and Act II?

3 ✓**Reading Check**

At what time of day does this scene take place?

The Crucible, Act II ◆ *1267*

TEACHING RESOURCES

The following resources can be used to enrich or extend the instruction for pp. 1267–1287.

Literary Analysis

📖 **Selection Support:** Literary Analysis, p. 321

TEACH

Step-by-Step Teaching Guide for pp. 1267–1287

CUSTOMIZE INSTRUCTION
For Musical/Rhythmic Learners

Have students listen to the musical and rhythmic qualities of Miller's language. Have them discuss the style in which he wrote the play and what listening to the language adds to their appreciation of it.

1 About Act II

The Proctors discuss the growing hysteria in Salem. Elizabeth urges John to tell the court that Abigail is a liar. They argue over his infidelity.

Hale arrives and questions the Proctors to discover whether they are good Christians. Some of their answers are unorthodox, but Hale is impressed with their honesty.

Cheever and Herrick enter with a warrant for Elizabeth's arrest. They find a doll with a needle in its belly and explain that Abigail was stabbed in the belly with a needle and blamed it on Elizabeth's spirit. Although Mary confesses to giving the doll to Elizabeth, the officials take Elizabeth away in handcuffs. Proctor threatens to expose Abigail unless Mary confesses that the accusations of witchcraft are lies.

2 Reading Strategy

Reading Drama

• Ask students the Reading Strategy question on p. 1267: What important information do you learn about the amount of time passed between Act I and Act II?
  Answer: Eight days have passed.

• Point out that John has tasted the stew, yet he acts surprised when Elizabeth tells him that it's rabbit. Why does he do this?
  Answer: He doesn't want her to know that he added salt.

• Have students read the first two lines on p. 1268. What do Proctor's actions suggest about his relationship with Elizabeth?
  Answer: He wants his stew to taste good, but he doesn't want to hurt Elizabeth's feelings by asking for more salt.

3 ✓Reading Check

Answer: at dusk

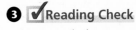

- Ask students the first Reading Strategy question on p. 1268: What do you learn about Elizabeth's feelings toward her husband from these stage directions?
  Answer: She finds it hard to show her feelings for him.

- Ask students to characterize the Proctors' relationship. Ask what their behavior suggests about their feelings for each other.
  Answer: There is tension between them. Each is careful to please the other. The effort they both make suggests that they care about their marriage and want to work through the tension.

- Ask students the second Reading Strategy question on p. 1268: How do these stage directions help prepare you for Proctor's remark that Elizabeth seems sad?
  Answer: She "would speak but cannot," and they are separated not only by the length of the room but also in their hearts.

- Why does Elizabeth try so hard to avoid friction? What does this suggest about her relationship with John?
  Answer: Elizabeth is afraid of John's anger. She is afraid of conflict. This suggests that the relationship is fragile; if they were sure of each other they wouldn't hesitate to quarrel.

PROCTOR: It's well seasoned.

ELIZABETH, *blushing with pleasure:* I took great care. She's tender?

PROCTOR: Aye. *He eats. She watches him.* I think we'll see green fields soon. It's warm as blood beneath the clods.

ELIZABETH: That's well.

PROCTOR *eats, then looks up.*

PROCTOR: If the crop is good I'll buy George Jacob's heifer. How would that please you?

❹ ELIZABETH: Aye, it would.

PROCTOR, *with a grin:* I mean to please you, Elizabeth.

ELIZABETH—*it is hard to say:* I know it, John.

He gets up, goes to her, kisses her. She receives it. With a certain disappointment, he returns to the table.

PROCTOR, *as gently as he can:* Cider?

ELIZABETH, *with a sense of reprimanding herself for having forgot:* Aye! *She gets up and goes and pours a glass for him. He now arches his back.*

PROCTOR: This farm's a continent when you go foot by foot droppin' seeds in it.

ELIZABETH, *coming with the cider:* It must be.

PROCTOR, *drinks a long draught, then, putting the glass down:* You ought to bring some flowers in the house.

ELIZABETH: Oh! I forgot! I will tomorrow.

PROCTOR: It's winter in here yet. On Sunday let you come with me, and we'll walk the farm together; I never see such a load of flowers on the earth. *With good feeling he goes and looks up at the sky through the open doorway.* Lilacs have a purple smell. Lilac is the smell of nightfall, I think. Massachusetts is a beauty in the spring!

ELIZABETH: Aye, it is.

There is a pause. She is watching him from the table as he stands there absorbing the night. It is as though she would speak but cannot. Instead, now, she takes up his plate and glass and fork and goes with them to the basin. Her back is turned to him. He turns to her and watches her. A sense of their separation rises.

PROCTOR: I think you're sad again. Are you?

ELIZABETH—*she doesn't want friction, and yet she must:* You come so late I thought you'd gone to Salem this afternoon.

❺ PROCTOR: Why? I have no business in Salem.

ELIZABETH: You did speak of going, earlier this week.

PROCTOR—*he knows what she means:* I thought better of it since.

ELIZABETH: Mary Warren's there today.

PROCTOR: Why'd you let her? You heard me forbid her go to Salem any more!

ELIZABETH: I couldn't stop her.

PROCTOR, *holding back a full condemnation of her:* It is a fault, it is a fault, Elizabeth—you're the mistress here, not Mary Warren.

ELIZABETH: She frightened all my strength away.

PROCTOR: How may that mouse frighten you, Elizabeth? You—

ELIZABETH: It is a mouse no more. I forbid her go, and she raises up her chin like the daughter of a prince and says to me, "I must go to Salem, Goody Proctor; I am an official of the court!"

PROCTOR: Court! What court?

ELIZABETH: Aye, it is a proper court they have now. They've sent four judges out of Boston, she says, weighty magistrates of the General Court, and at the head sits the Deputy Governor of the Province.

PROCTOR, *astonished:* Why, she's mad.

❻ ELIZABETH: I would to God she were. There be fourteen people in the jail now, she says. PROCTOR *simply looks at her, unable to grasp it.* And they'll be tried, and the court have power to hang them too, she says.

PROCTOR, *scoffing but without conviction:* Ah, they'd never hang—

ELIZABETH: The Deputy Governor promise hangin' if they'll not confess, John. The town's gone wild, I think. She speak of Abigail, and I thought she were a saint, to hear her. Abigail brings the other girls into the court, and where she walks the crowd will part like the sea for Israel.[1] And folks are brought before them, and if they scream and howl and fall to the floor—the person's clapped in the jail for bewitchin' them.

PROCTOR, *wide-eyed:* Oh, it is a black mischief.

ELIZABETH: I think you must go to Salem, John. *He turns to her.* I think so. You must tell them it is a fraud.

PROCTOR, *thinking beyond this:* Aye, it is, it is surely.

ELIZABETH: Let you go to Ezekiel Cheever—he knows you well. And tell him what she said to you last week in her uncle's house. She said it had naught to do with witchcraft, did she not?

PROCTOR, *in thought:* Aye, she did, she did. *Now, a pause.*

❼ ELIZABETH, *quietly, fearing to anger him by prodding:* God forbid you keep that from the court, John. I think they must be told.

PROCTOR, *quietly, struggling with his thought:* Aye, they must, they must. It is a wonder they do believe her.

ELIZABETH: I would go to Salem now, John—let you go tonight.

PROCTOR: I'll think on it.

ELIZABETH, *with her courage now:* You cannot keep it, John.

PROCTOR, *angering:* I know I cannot keep it. I say I will think on it!

ELIZABETH, *hurt, and very coldly:* Good, then, let you think on it. *She stands and starts to walk out of the room.*

PROCTOR: I am only wondering how I may prove what she told me, Elizabeth. If the girl's a saint now, I think it is not easy to prove she's

---

1. **part like . . . Israel** In the Bible, God commanded Moses, the leader of the Jews, to part the Red Sea to enable the Jews to escape from the Egyptians into Canaan.

Literary Analysis
Allusion What does Elizabeth's allusion to Moses' parting of the Red Sea reveal about Abigail's new standing in the community?

Reading Strategy
Reading Drama How would you describe Elizabeth's changing emotions as she challenges John?

❽ ✓Reading Check
What does Elizabeth want John to do?

The Crucible, Act II ◆ 1269

---

❻ Literary Analysis
Allusion

• Have students read the footnote at the bottom of the page. Ask the Literary Analysis question on p. 1269: What does Elizabeth's allusion to Moses' parting of the Red Sea reveal about Abigail's new standing in the community? **Answer:** The comparison between Abigail and Moses suggests that she has become a power in the community. The Israelites looked up to Moses because God spoke to him directly.

• Point out that the allusion to Moses is a simile—"the crowd will part *like* the sea for Israel." Have students find another simile in this passage and discuss its effect. **Answer:** Mary "raises up her chin like the daughter of a prince." This simile lets the audience picture Mary's newfound pride and self-importance.

❼ Reading Strategy
Reading Drama

• Ask students the Reading Strategy question on p. 1269: How would you describe Elizabeth's changing emotions as she challenges John? **Answer:** She feels frightened, then angry, then hurt.

• Ask students why they think Elizabeth feels the way she does. **Answer:** She is probably still upset about John's affair with Abigail. She wants him to prove that he no longer cares for Abigail. When he hesitates, she thinks it is out of love for Abigail.

❽ ✓Reading Check
Answer: She wants him to tell the court that Abigail's accusations of witchcraft are lies.

---

fraud, and the town gone so silly. She told it to me in a room alone—I have no proof for it.

ELIZABETH: You were alone with her?

PROCTOR, *stubbornly:* For a moment alone, aye.

ELIZABETH: Why, then, it is not as you told me.

PROCTOR, *his anger rising:* For a moment, I say. The others come in soon after.

ELIZABETH, *quietly—she has suddenly lost all faith in him:* Do as you wish, then. *She starts to turn.*

PROCTOR: Woman. *She turns to him.* I'll not have your suspicion any more.

ELIZABETH, *a little loftily:* I have no—

PROCTOR: I'll not have it!

ELIZABETH: Then let you not earn it.

PROCTOR, *with a violent undertone:* You doubt me yet?

ELIZABETH, *with a smile, to keep her dignity:* John, if it were not Abigail that you must go to hurt, would you falter now? I think not.

PROCTOR: Now look you—

ELIZABETH: I see what I see, John.

PROCTOR, *with solemn warning:* You will not judge me more, Elizabeth. I have good reason to think before I charge fraud on Abigail, and I will think on it. Let you look to your own improvement before you go to judge your husband any more. I have forgot Abigail, and—

ELIZABETH: And I.

PROCTOR: Spare me! You forget nothin' and forgive nothin'. Learn charity, woman. I have gone tiptoe in this house all seven month since she is gone. I have not moved from there to there without I think to please you, and still an everlasting funeral marches round your heart. I cannot speak but I am doubted, every moment judged for lies, as though I come into a court when I come into this house!

ELIZABETH: John, you are not open with me. You saw her with a crowd, you said. Now you—

PROCTOR: I'll plead my honesty no more, Elizabeth.

ELIZABETH—*now she would justify herself:* John, I am only—

PROCTOR: No more! I should have roared you down when first you told me your suspicion. But I wilted, and, like a Christian, I confessed. Confessed! Some dream I had must have mistaken you for God that day. But you're not, you're not, and let you remember it! Let you look sometimes for the goodness in me, and judge me not.

ELIZABETH: I do not judge you. The magistrate sits in your heart that judges you. I never thought you but a good man, John—*with a smile*—only somewhat bewildered.

PROCTOR, *laughing bitterly:* Oh, Elizabeth, your justice would freeze beer! *He turns suddenly toward a sound outside. He starts for the door as* MARY WARREN *enters. As soon as he sees her, he goes directly to her and grabs her by the cloak, furious.* How do you go to Salem when I forbid it? Do you mock me? *Shaking her.* I'll whip you if you dare leave this house again!

Strangely, she doesn't resist him, but hangs limply by his grip.

MARY WARREN: I am sick, I am sick, Mr. Proctor. Pray, pray, hurt me not. *Her strangeness throws him off, and her evident* <u>pallor</u> *and weakness. He frees her.* My insides are all shuddery; I am in the proceedings all day, sir.

PROCTOR, *with draining anger—his curiosity is draining it:* And what of these proceedings here? When will you proceed to keep this house, as you are paid nine pound a year to do—and my wife not wholly well?

As though to compensate, MARY WARREN *goes to* ELIZABETH *with a small rag doll.*

MARY WARREN: I made a gift for you today, Goody Proctor. I had to sit long hours in a chair, and passed the time with sewing.

ELIZABETH, *perplexed, looking at the doll:* Why, thank you, it's a fair poppet.[2]

MARY WARREN, *with a trembling, decayed voice:* We must all love each other now, Goody Proctor.

ELIZABETH, *amazed at her strangeness:* Aye, indeed we must.

MARY WARREN, *glancing at the room:* I'll get up early in the morning and clean the house. I must sleep now. *She turns and starts off.*

PROCTOR: Mary. *She halts.* Is it true? There be fourteen women arrested?

MARY WARREN: No, sir. There be thirty-nine now— *She suddenly breaks off and sobs and sits down, exhausted.*

ELIZABETH: Why, she's weepin'! What ails you, child?

MARY WARREN: Goody Osburn—will hang!

There is a shocked pause, while she sobs.

PROCTOR: Hang! *He calls into her face.* Hang, y'say?

MARY WARREN, *through her weeping:* Aye.

PROCTOR: The Deputy Governor will permit it?

MARY WARREN: He sentenced her. He must. *To* <u>ameliorate</u> *it:* But not Sarah Good. For Sarah Good confessed, y'see.

PROCTOR: Confessed! To what?

MARY WARREN: That she—*in horror at the memory*—she sometimes made a compact with Lucifer, and wrote her name in his black book—with

---

2. **poppet** doll.

pallor (pal′ ər) *n.* paleness

Reading Strategy
Reading Drama
What do these stage directions clarify?

ameliorate (ə mēl′ yə rāt′) *v.* make better

⓬ **Reading Check**
What are John and Elizabeth Proctor arguing about?

The Crucible, Act II ◆ 1271

- Ask students he Reading Strategy question on p. 1271: What do these stage directions clarify? **Answer:** They clarify Mary's physical weakness and John's change from fury to curiosity and pity.

- Ask students to infer why Mary is in such shaky physical condition. **Answer:** She has been in court all day; she has probably heard people condemned and arrested. She probably feels guilty and frightened because of her lies. She says she had to sit "long hours in a chair," which probably tired her out.

⓬ ✔**Reading Check**

Answer: They argue about Elizabeth's inability to forgive John and what she sees as his reluctance to cause trouble for Abigail.

CUSTOMIZE INSTRUCTION FOR UNIVERSAL ACCESS

For Advanced Readers

The Crucible is filled with figurative language and imaginative comparisons—similes, metaphors, and personification. Point out some examples on these two pages:

- . . . and still an everlasting funeral marches round your heart
- The magistrate sits in your heart that judges you.
- Oh, Elizabeth, your justice would freeze beer!

As students read the play, have them note especially striking metaphors and similes. When they are finished, ask them how Miller's figurative language contributes to the play.

The Hollywood Ten

In October 1947, the House Un-American Activities Committee turned its attention to Hollywood. J. Parnell Thomas, the chairman of the committee, announced that he had a list of 45 names of Hollywood writers and others who were implicated in subversive activities. Many actors, writers, and other artists were called before the committee and questioned.

The "Hollywood Ten" included writers Alvah Bessie, Herbert Biberman, Lester Cole, Edward Dmytryk, Ring Lardner Jr., John Howard Lawson, Albert Maltz, Samuel Ornitz, Adrian Scott, and Dalton Trumbo. All ten were considered "unfriendly" witnesses because they refused to answer the question, "Are you a member of the Communist party?"

In 1950, the Ten were fined $1,000 each and given prison sentences of up to one year. When they returned to Hollywood, they discovered that no major studio would hire them.

⓮ Critical Thinking

Evaluate

• Have students evaluate Mary's description of her reaction to Goody Osburn's denials. Do students think Mary really felt these things? Why or why not?
Answer: Students learned in Act I that Mary is a coward, easily led by the other girls, but that her inclinations are honest. They may say that Mary imagined her coldness and shortness of breath, or they may say that she really felt these things because of the pressure she was under.

• Have students evaluate Mary's evidence against Goody Osburn.
Answer: Students should agree with Proctor that there is no proof against Goody Osburn. She denied witchcraft, and her failure to repeat the commandments should not be enough to condemn her. The fact that Mary fell ill after Goody Osburn's visit is pure coincidence.

her blood—and bound herself to torment Christians till God's thrown down—and we all must worship Hell forevermore.

Pause.

PROCTOR: But—surely you know what a jabberer she is. Did you tell them that?

MARY WARREN: Mr. Proctor, in open court she near to choked us all to death.

PROCTOR: How, choked you?

MARY WARREN: She sent her spirit out.

ELIZABETH: Oh, Mary, Mary, surely you—

MARY WARREN, *with an indignant edge:* She tried to kill me many times, Goody Proctor!

ELIZABETH: Why, I never heard you mention that before.

MARY WARREN: I never knew it before. I never knew anything before. When she come into the court I say to myself, I must not accuse this woman, for she sleep in ditches, and so very old and poor. But then—then she sit there, denying and denying, and I feel a misty coldness climbin' up my back, and the skin on my skull begin to creep, and I feel a clamp around my neck and I cannot breathe air; and then—*entranced*—I hear a voice, a screamin' voice, and it were my voice—and all at once I remembered everything she done to me!

PROCTOR: Why? What did she do to you?

MARY WARREN, *like one awakened to a marvelous secret insight:* So many time, Mr. Proctor, she come to this very door, beggin' bread and a cup of cider—and mark this: whenever I turned her away empty, she *mumbled.*

ELIZABETH: Mumbled! She may mumble if she's hungry.

⓮ MARY WARREN: But *what* does she mumble? You must remember, Goody Proctor. Last month—a Monday, I think—she walked away, and I thought my guts would burst for two days after. Do you remember it?

ELIZABETH: Why—I do, I think, but—

MARY WARREN: And so I told that to Judge Hathorne, and he asks her so. "Goody Osburn," says he, "what curse do you mumble that this girl must fall sick after turning you away?" And then she replies—*mimicking an old crone*—"Why, your excellence, no curse at all. I only say my commandments; I hope I may say my commandments," says she!

ELIZABETH: And that's an upright answer.

MARY WARREN: Aye, but then Judge Hathorne say, "Recite for us your commandments!"—*leaning* avidly *toward them*—and of all the ten she could not say a single one. She never knew no commandments, and they had her in a flat lie!

PROCTOR: And so condemned her?

MARY WARREN, *now a little strained, seeing his stubborn doubt:* Why, they must when she condemned herself.

⓭ *Arthur Miller, Joseph McCarthy, and the Blacklist*
In the late 1940s, the House Un-American Activities Committee developed a "blacklist" of Hollywood screenwriters suspected of being Communists. For many years, film producers used this list to deny employment to these writers.

Arthur Miller himself was called before the House Un-American Activities Committee and asked to name people he had met at a meeting of alleged Communist writers. After refusing, Miller was convicted of contempt; later, he appealed and the contempt charge was overturned.

In 1999, Arthur Miller commented on the relationship between the "Red Scare" and the Salem witch trials. Miller said there were startling similarities in both the rituals of defense and the investigative routines. Three hundred years apart, both prosecutions were alleging membership in a secret, disloyal group.

avidly (av′ id lē) *adv.* eagerly

PROCTOR: But the proof, the proof!

MARY WARREN, *with greater impatience with him:* I told you the proof. It's hard proof, hard as rock, the judges said.

PROCTOR, *pauses an instant, then:* You will not go to court again, Mary Warren.

MARY WARREN: I must tell you, sir, I will be gone every day now. I am amazed you do not see what weighty work we do.

PROCTOR: What work you do! It's strange work for a Christian girl to hang old women!

MARY WARREN: But, Mr. Proctor, they will not hang them if they confess. Sarah Good will only sit in jail some time—*recalling*—and here's a wonder for you; think on this. Goody Good is pregnant!

ELIZABETH: Pregnant! Are they mad? The woman's near to sixty!

MARY WARREN: They had Doctor Griggs examine her, and she's full to the brim. And smokin' a pipe all these years, and no husband either! But she's safe, thank God, for they'll not hurt the innocent child. But be that not a marvel? You must see it, sir, it's God's work we do. So I'll be gone every day for some time. I'm—I am an official of the court, they say, and I—*She has been edging toward offstage.*

PROCTOR: I'll official you! *He strides to the mantel, takes down the whip hanging there.*

MARY WARREN, *terrified, but coming erect, striving for her authority:* I'll not stand whipping any more!

ELIZABETH, *hurriedly, as* PROCTOR *approaches:* Mary, promise you'll stay at home—

MARY WARREN, *backing from him, but keeping her erect posture, striving, striving for her way:* The Devil's loose in Salem, Mr. Proctor; we must discover where he's hiding!

PROCTOR: I'll whip the Devil out of you! *With whip raised he reaches out for her, and she streaks away and yells.*

MARY WARREN, *pointing at* ELIZABETH: I saved her life today!

Silence. His whip comes down.

ELIZABETH, *softly:* I am accused?

MARY WARREN, *quaking:* Somewhat mentioned. But I said I never see no sign you ever sent your spirit out to hurt no one, and seeing I do live so closely with you, they dismissed it.

ELIZABETH: Who accused me?

MARY WARREN: I am bound by law, I cannot tell it. *To* PROCTOR: I only hope you'll not be so sarcastical no more. Four judges and the King's deputy sat to dinner with us but an hour ago. I—I would have you speak civilly to me, from this out.

PROCTOR, *in horror, muttering in disgust at her:* Go to bed.

MARY WARREN, *with a stamp of her foot:* I'll not be ordered to bed no more, Mr. Proctor! I am eighteen and a woman, however single!

Reading Strategy
Reading Drama What change has Mary's participation in the court proceedings brought in her attitude toward the Proctors?

Reading Check
What evidence does Mary Warren use to prove that Goody Osborn is a witch?

The Crucible, Act II ◆ 1273

⓯ Reading Strategy
Reading Drama

- Ask students the Reading Strategy question on p. 1273: What change has Mary's participation in the court proceedings brought in her attitude toward the Proctors?
  Answer: Mary has acquired a sense of her own importance and will no longer accept being treated as a servant.

- Ask students whether this change in Mary is likely to be permanent or temporary, and why.
  Answer: Mary still seems very unsure of herself. She isn't used to standing up for herself. The change is probably temporary.

⓰ ✔Reading Check
Answer: Mary accuses her of mumbling; Goody can't name the commandments when challenged.

CUSTOMIZE INSTRUCTION FOR UNIVERSAL ACCESS

For Special Needs Students	For Gifted/Talented Students
Help students understand the Proctors' growing anxiety in the face of Mary's news. Proctor says of Abigail, "If the girl's a saint now, I think it is not easy to prove she's fraud, and the town gone so silly." Use this statement to help students think about the use and abuse of power. Discuss the frustration that John and Elizabeth must feel. What are students' experiences with lies? Of what past and present news stories of cover-ups in business or government are students aware?	Students probably have a fairly good working knowledge of courtroom procedure and rules from television dramas. Ask them to evaluate Mary's tale of what happens in the Salem courtroom by the modern standards they see depicted on television. How would a modern judge treat a display of screaming such as Mary describes? How would modern lawyers react to the "hard proof" Mary cites?

⓱ Reading Strategy

Reading Drama

- Ask students the Reading Strategy question on p. 1274: How do the stage directions "without conviction" affect your understanding of Proctor's line?
  Answer: He doesn't really believe what he says.

- Of whom is Elizabeth speaking when she says, "She wants me dead"? How do you know?
  Answer: She believes Abigail is the one who accused her. She knows that Abigail is jealous of her and wants to take her place.

- Why are the stage directions "reasonably" and "conceding" in Elizabeth's speeches enclosed in quotation marks?
  Answer: The quotation marks suggest that she is making an effort to appear reasonable and to appear to concede, when she's actually angry and upset.

PROCTOR: Do you wish to sit up? Then sit up.

MARY WARREN: I wish to go to bed!

PROCTOR, *in anger:* Good night, then!

MARY WARREN: Good night. *Dissatisfied, uncertain of herself, she goes out. Wide-eyed, both* PROCTOR *and* ELIZABETH *stand staring.*

ELIZABETH, *quietly:* Oh, the noose, the noose is up!

PROCTOR: There'll be no noose.

ELIZABETH: She wants me dead. I knew all week it would come to this!

PROCTOR, *without conviction:* They dismissed it. You heard her say—

ELIZABETH: And what of tomorrow? She will cry me out until they take me!

PROCTOR: Sit you down.

ELIZABETH: She wants me dead, John, you know it!

PROCTOR: I say sit down! *She sits, trembling. He speaks quickly, trying to keep his wits.* Now we must be wise, Elizabeth.

ELIZABETH, *with sarcasm, and a sense of being lost:* Oh, indeed, indeed!

PROCTOR: Fear nothing. I'll find Ezekiel Cheever. I'll tell him she said it were all sport.

ELIZABETH: John, with so many in the jail, more than Cheever's help is needed now, I think. Would you favor me with this? Go to Abigail.

PROCTOR, *his soul hardening as he senses . . . :* What have I to say to Abigail?

ELIZABETH, *delicately:* John—grant me this. You have a faulty understanding of young girls. There is a promise made in any bed—

PROCTOR, *striving against his anger:* What promise!

⓱

ELIZABETH: Spoke or silent, a promise is surely made. And she may dote on it now—I am sure she does—and thinks to kill me, then to take my place.

PROCTOR'S *anger is rising; he cannot speak.*

ELIZABETH: It is her dearest hope, John, I know it. There be a thousand names; why does she call mine? There be a certain danger in calling such a name—I am no Goody Good that sleeps in ditches, nor Osburn, drunk and half-witted. She'd dare not call out such a farmer's wife but there be monstrous profit in it. She thinks to take my place, John.

PROCTOR: She cannot think it! *He knows it is true.*

ELIZABETH, *"reasonably":* John, have you ever shown her somewhat of contempt? She cannot pass you in the church but you will blush—

PROCTOR: I may blush for my sin.

ELIZABETH: I think she sees another meaning in that blush.

PROCTOR: And what see you? What see you, Elizabeth?

ELIZABETH, *"conceding":* I think you be somewhat ashamed, for I am there, and she so close.

PROCTOR: When will you know me, woman? Were I stone I would have cracked for shame this seven month!

1274 ◆ *Prosperity and Protest (1946–Present)*

Reading Strategy
Reading Drama How do the stage directions indicating that Proctor speaks "without conviction" affect your understanding of his line?

✹ ENRICHMENT: Literature Connection

The Witch of Blackbird Pond

Elizabeth points out that her social position makes her less vulnerable to an accusation than "Goody Good that sleeps in ditches, nor Osburn, drunk and half-witted." In New England, those who were on the fringes of society were often the easiest targets for accusations of witchcraft.

In her award-winning novel *The Witch of Blackbird Pond,* Elizabeth George Speare tells the story of Hannah Tupper, a peaceful, gentle Quaker widow living just outside the Connecticut town of Wethersfield. Because Hannah is a Quaker, she does not attend religious services with the rest of the town and so no one will have anything to do with her socially. When a spiteful woman accuses Hannah of witchcraft, the community is only too eager to believe in her guilt. Although Hannah escapes with the help of two friends, many actual accused witches were not so fortunate.

ELIZABETH: Then go and tell her she's a whore. Whatever promise she may sense—break it, John, break it.

PROCTOR, *between his teeth:* Good, then. I'll go. *He starts for his rifle.*

ELIZABETH, *trembling, fearfully:* Oh, how unwillingly!

PROCTOR, *turning on her, rifle in hand:* I will curse her hotter than the oldest cinder in hell. But pray, begrudge me not my anger!

ELIZABETH: Your anger! I only ask you—

PROCTOR: Woman, am I so <u>base</u>? Do you truly think me base?

ELIZABETH: I never called you base.

PROCTOR: Then how do you charge me with such a promise? The promise that a stallion gives a mare I gave that girl!

ELIZABETH: Then why do you anger with me when I bid you break it?

PROCTOR: Because it speaks deceit, and I am honest! But I'll plead no more! I see now your spirit twists around the single error of my life, and I will never tear it free!

ELIZABETH, *crying out:* You'll tear it free—when you come to know that I will be your only wife, or no wife at all! She has an arrow in you yet, John Proctor, and you know it well!

Quite suddenly, as though from the air, a figure appears in the doorway. They start slightly. It is MR. HALE. *He is different now—drawn a little, and there is a quality of <u>deference</u>, even of guilt, about his manner now.*

HALE: Good evening.

PROCTOR, *still in his shock:* Why, Mr. Hale! Good evening to you, sir. Come in, come in.

HALE, *to Elizabeth:* I hope I do not startle you.

ELIZABETH: No, no, it's only that I heard no horse—

HALE: You are Goodwife Proctor.

PROCTOR: Aye; Elizabeth.

HALE, *nods, then:* I hope you're not off to bed yet.

PROCTOR, *setting down his gun:* No, no. HALE *comes further into the room. And* PROCTOR, *to explain his nervousness:* We are not used to visitors after dark, but you're welcome here. Will you sit you down, sir?

HALE: I will. *He sits.* Let you sit, Goodwife Proctor.

She does, never letting him out of her sight. There is a pause as HALE *looks about the room.*

PROCTOR, *to break the silence:* Will you drink cider, Mr. Hale?

HALE: No, it rebels my stomach; I have some further traveling yet tonight. Sit you down, sir. PROCTOR *sits.* I will not keep you long, but I have some business with you.

PROCTOR: Business of the court?

HALE: No—no, I come of my own, without the court's authority. Hear me. *He wets his lips.* I know not if you are aware, but your wife's name is—mentioned in the court.

base (bās) *adj.* low; mean

deference (def′ ər əns) *n.* courteous regard or respect

Reading Strategy
Reading Drama Why is the silent pause indicated by the stage directions important?

⑲ ☑**Reading Check**
What does Elizabeth fear that Abigail will do to her?

The Crucible, Act II ◆ *1275*

⑱ **Reading Strategy**

Reading Drama

- Ask students the Reading Strategy question on p. 1275: Why is the silent pause indicated by the stage directions important?
  Answer: The silence allows tension and suspense to build.

- Ask students how they reacted to the stage direction, "Quite suddenly, as though from the air, a figure appears in the doorway," before they read farther and learned that the figure was Hale.
  Answer: The figure's sudden appearance from nowhere suggests the supernatural. Given the atmosphere of witchcraft that Miller has created, students may have thought it was a witch, the Devil, or some other supernatural being.

- Once students learn that the figure is Hale, ask why they think Miller chooses to have him enter in this manner.
  Answer: Miller links Hale in the reader's mind with a spirit; the reader has to read on to find out whether he is a good or evil spirit.

- Ask students why Hale would come to the Proctors without the court's authority, and what the stage directions in the passage suggest about his intentions.
  Answer: He may not agree with the court's judgments so far. He may decide the time has come to rely on his own judgment. He may hope that he can help the Proctors.

⑲ ☑**Reading Check**

Answer: She fears that Abigail will denounce her as a witch.

CUSTOMIZE INSTRUCTION FOR UNIVERSAL ACCESS

For Gifted/Talented Students

Elizabeth urges John to speak privately to Abigail and convince her to confess her lies. Late in the original Broadway run of the play, Miller inserted a short scene to open Act III in which John fulfills this request. Partners can find Miller's scene and perform it for the class. (An excerpt is quoted on p. 1328 of this teacher's edition.) The whole class can debate on the value of such a scene. Does it add anything essential to the play or to the audience's understanding of Abigail and John? If not, what purpose does it serve?

Why do students think Miller decided to add this scene?

⑳ Reading Strategy

Reading Drama

- Ask students the Reading Strategy question on p. 1276: What do the stage directions reveal here about Elizabeth's true emotions?

  Answer: Elizabeth knows this is no laughing matter; she is horrified at the danger Rebecca may be in.

- Why is Elizabeth especially shocked on Rebecca's account?

  Answer: Everyone recognizes that Rebecca is a truly good person; Elizabeth probably realizes that if Rebecca isn't safe, then no one is safe, including herself.

㉑ Vocabulary Development

The greek Suffix -logy-

- Call students' attention to the word *theology* and its definition. Tell students that the word is derived from the Greek word *theo*, meaning "God," and the suffix *-logy*, meaning "the science or study of."

- Ask students to volunteer any other words they know that contain this suffix.

  Possibilities include: *biology, geology, anthropology, archaeology*

㉒ Literary Analysis

Allusion and Historical Context

- Ask students the Literary Analysis question on p. 1275: What do you know about the Puritans and their "plain style" that affects your interpretation of the golden candlesticks?

  Answer: The Puritans scorned material goods, especially in church; their churches were as plain as possible. They rejected the pageantry of Roman Catholicism. An insistence on gold candlesticks was not appropriate for a Puritan.

- Point out that Proctor has been to church roughly once every three weeks in the past year and a half. Ask students to evaluate this in terms of historical context.

  Answer: Today, this rate of attendance at church would be considered exemplary. However, according to the Puritans of Salem, who were expected to strictly keep the Sabbath, Proctor's attendance record is not good at all.

1276

PROCTOR: We know it, sir. Our Mary Warren told us. We are entirely amazed.

HALE: I am a stranger here, as you know. And in my ignorance I find it hard to draw a clear opinion of them that come accused before the court. And so this afternoon, and now tonight, I go from house to house—I come now from Rebecca Nurse's house and—

ELIZABETH, *shocked:* Rebecca's charged!

HALE: God forbid such a one be charged. She is, however—mentioned somewhat.

ELIZABETH, *with an attempt at a laugh:* You will never believe, I hope, that Rebecca trafficked with the Devil.

HALE: Woman, it is possible.

PROCTOR, *taken aback:* Surely you cannot think so.

HALE: This is a strange time, Mister. No man may longer doubt the powers of the dark are gathered in monstrous attack upon this village. There is too much evidence now to deny it. You will agree, sir?

PROCTOR, *evading:* I—have no knowledge in that line. But it's hard to think so pious a woman be secretly a Devil's bitch after seventy year of such good prayer.

HALE: Aye. But the Devil is a wily one, you cannot deny it. However, she is far from accused, and I know she will not be. *Pause.* I thought, sir, to put some questions as to the Christian character of this house, if you'll permit me.

PROCTOR, *coldly, resentful:* Why, we—have no fear of questions, sir.

HALE: Good, then. *He makes himself more comfortable.* In the book of record that Mr. Parris keeps, I note that you are rarely in the church on Sabbath Day.

PROCTOR: No, sir, you are mistaken.

HALE: Twenty-six time in seventeen month, sir. I must call that rare. Will you tell me why you are so absent?

PROCTOR: Mr. Hale, I never knew I must account to that man for I come to church or stay at home. My wife were sick this winter.

HALE: So I am told. But you, Mister, why could you not come alone?

PROCTOR: I surely did come when I could, and when I could not I prayed in this house.

HALE: Mr. Proctor, your house is not a church; your <u>theology</u> must tell you that.

PROCTOR: It does, sir, it does; and it tells me that a minister may pray to God without he have golden candlesticks upon the altar.

HALE: What golden candlesticks?

PROCTOR: Since we built the church there were pewter candlesticks upon the altar; Francis Nurse made them y'know, and a sweeter hand never touched the metal. But Parris came, and for twenty week he preach nothin' but golden candlesticks until he had them. I labor the earth from dawn of day to blink of night, and I tell you true when I look

1276 ◆ Prosperity and Protest (1946–Present)

Reading Strategy
Reading Drama What do the stage directions here reveal about Elizabeth's true emotions?

theology (thē ăl´ ə jē) *n.* the study of religion

Literary Analysis
Allusion and Historical Context What do you know about the Puritans and their "plain style" that affects your interpretation of the golden candlesticks?

✳ ENRICHMENT: History Connection

Puritan Ministers

Throughout Act I and on these two pages, John Proctor is severely critical of Reverend Parris. Parris resents this because "a minister is the Lord's man in the parish . . . not to be so lightly crossed and contradicted!"

The position of the minister in the parish was a radical innovation of Puritanism. The Roman Catholic view, which had dominated Europe for centuries, was that the Pope was the inheritor of the mantle of St. Peter. His priests were seen as assuming this divine authority. A Catholic priest, therefore, mediated between God and the congregation. A Puritan minister, however, was not believed to have any special authority given by the church, but was believed to have been directly chosen by God to preach his word. He was considered a teacher. Puritan ministers were well educated on doctrine and Scripture but were not considered to be better or holier than their parishioners.

to heaven and see my money glaring at his elbows—it hurt my prayer, sir, it hurt my prayer. I think, sometimes, the man dreams cathedrals, not clapboard meetin' houses.

HALE, *thinks, then:* And yet, Mister, a Christian on Sabbath Day must be in church. *Pause.* Tell me—you have three children?

PROCTOR: Aye. Boys.

HALE: How comes it that only two are baptized?

PROCTOR, *starts to speak, then stops, then, as though unable to restrain this:* I like it not that Mr. Parris should lay his hand upon my baby. I see no light of God in that man. I'll not conceal it.

HALE: I must say it, Mr. Proctor; that is not for you to decide. The man's ordained, therefore the light of God is in him.

PROCTOR, *flushed with resentment but trying to smile:* What's your suspicion, Mr. Hale?

HALE: No, no, I have no—

PROCTOR: I nailed the roof upon the church, I hung the door—

HALE: Oh, did you! That's a good sign, then.

PROCTOR: It may be I have been too quick to bring the man to book, but you cannot think we ever desired the destruction of religion. I think that's in your mind, is it not?

HALE, *not altogether giving way:* I—have—there is a softness in your record, sir, a softness.

ELIZABETH: I think, maybe, we have been too hard with Mr. Parris. I think so. But sure we never loved the Devil here.

HALE, *nods, deliberating this. Then, with the voice of one administering a secret test:* Do you know your Commandments, Elizabeth?

ELIZABETH, *without hesitation, even eagerly:* I surely do. There be no mark of blame upon my life, Mr. Hale. I am a covenanted Christian woman.

HALE: And you, Mister?

PROCTOR, *a trifle unsteadily:* I—am sure I do, sir.

HALE, *glances at her open face, then at* JOHN, *then:* Let you repeat them, if you will.

PROCTOR: The Commandments.

HALE: Aye.

PROCTOR, *looking off, beginning to sweat:* Thou shalt not kill.

HALE: Aye.

PROCTOR, *counting on his fingers:* Thou shalt not steal. Thou shalt not covet thy neighbor's goods, nor make unto thee any graven image. Thou shalt not take the name of the Lord in vain; thou shalt have no other gods before me. *With some hesitation:* Thou shalt remember the Sabbath Day and keep it holy. *Pause. Then:* Thou shalt honor thy father and mother. Thou shalt not bear false witness. *He is stuck. He counts back on his fingers, knowing one is missing.* Thou shalt not make unto thee any graven image.

Reading Strategy
Reading Drama What does this passage reveal about Proctor's attitude toward Parris as a minister.

✔ **Reading Check** ㉕

What aspects of the Proctor household does Hale question?

The Crucible, Act II ◆ *1277*

- Ask students the Reading Strategy question on p. 1277: What does this passage reveal about Proctor's attitude toward Parris as a minister?
  Answer: Proctor believes that Parris does not belong in the clergy. He distrusts Parris's fitness to give the sacraments.

- Have students go back to Act I and review the grounds for Proctor's criticism of Parris.
  Answer: Parris is greedy for the salary and benefits of his position. He summons Hale to the village without calling a meeting. His style of preaching has driven many people away from the church.

㉔ **Critical Thinking**
Interpret

- Ask students to name the commandment that John has left off the list. Ask why this omission is ironic.
  Answer: He has left out "thou shalt not commit adultery." This is ironic because this is the commandment he has broken.

- Point out the commandment "Thou shalt not bear false witness." Ask students to explain the irony of this commandment in view of the present events.
  Answer: The children and other accusers are bearing false witness against the accused, but they are praised for it rather than condemned.

- Tell students that for a Puritan, repeating the commandments in order was as usual as repeating the alphabet in order. Proctor, however, lists the commandments in random order (6, 8, 10, 2, and so on). What might this suggest to Hale?
  Answer: It reinforces Hale's realization that Proctor is not orthodox in his actions or beliefs. It probably prejudices Hale further against him.

㉕ ✔ **Reading Check**

Answer: He questions whether it is a Christian household.

Reading Drama

- Ask students the Reading Strategy question on p. 1278: How can you tell that Hale is beginning to grow suspicious of the Proctors?
  Answer: Hale is worried over John's failure to name all ten commandments. The stage directions "worried" and "disturbed and evasive" suggest that he doubts the Proctors.

- What does the stage direction "as though a secret arrow had pained his heart" suggest about Proctor? To what might the arrow allude?
  Possible answers: He repents having broken this commandment. He is ashamed.

- What is ironic about Proctor's statement, "I have no witness and cannot prove it, except my word be taken"?
  Answer: The same is true of all the accusations; they are made on people's unsupported word. Proctor is the only one who hesitates to accuse without witnesses, and yet he is the only one speaking the truth.

HALE: You have said that twice, sir.

PROCTOR, *lost:* Aye. *He is flailing for it.*

ELIZABETH, *delicately:* Adultery, John.

PROCTOR, *as though a secret arrow had pained his heart:* Aye. *Trying to grin it away—to* HALE: You see, sir, between the two of us we do know them all. HALE *only looks at* PROCTOR, *deep in his attempt to define this man.* PROCTOR *grows more uneasy.* I think it be a small fault.

HALE: Theology, sir, is a fortress; no crack in a fortress may be accounted small. *He rises; he seems worried now. He paces a little, in deep thought.*

PROCTOR: There be no love for Satan in this house, Mister.

HALE: I pray it, I pray it dearly. *He looks to both of them, an attempt at a smile on his face, but his misgivings are clear.* Well, then—I'll bid you good night.

ELIZABETH, *unable to restrain herself:* Mr. Hale. *He turns.* I do think you are suspecting me somewhat? Are you not?

HALE, *obviously disturbed—and evasive:* Goody Proctor, I do not judge you. My duty is to add what I may to the godly wisdom of the court. I pray you both good health and good fortune. *To* JOHN: Good night, sir. *He starts out.*

ELIZABETH, *with a note of desperation:* I think you must tell him, John.

HALE: What's that?

ELIZABETH, *restraining a call:* Will you tell him?

Slight pause. HALE *looks questioningly at* JOHN.

PROCTOR, *with difficulty:* I—I have no witness and cannot prove it, except my word be taken. But I know the children's sickness had naught to do with witchcraft.

HALE, *stopped, struck:* Naught to do—?

PROCTOR: Mr. Parris discovered them sportin' in the woods. They were startled and took sick.

Pause.

HALE: Who told you this?

PROCTOR, *hesitates, then:* Abigail Williams.

HALE: Abigail.

PROCTOR: Aye.

HALE, *his eyes wide:* Abigail Williams told you it had naught to do with witchcraft!

PROCTOR: She told me the day you came, sir.

HALE, *suspiciously:* Why—why did you keep this?

PROCTOR: I never knew until tonight that the world is gone daft with this nonsense.

HALE: Nonsense! Mister, I have myself examined Tituba, Sarah Good, and numerous others that have confessed to dealing with the Devil. They have *confessed* it.

Reading Strategy
Reading Drama How can you tell that Hale is beginning to grow suspicious of the Proctors?

CUSTOMIZE INSTRUCTION FOR UNIVERSAL ACCESS

For Less Proficient Readers

Help students take a stronger interest in the events of the play by imagining themselves as characters. Have students read the dialogue on page 1278 up to the point where Elizabeth insists that John tell Hale about Abigail. Ask students to imagine that they can advise the Proctors about what to say at this point. What advice would they give John and Elizabeth? Call on volunteers to act out the advice, and continue the scene with improvisation, each student taking a part.

For Advanced Readers

Ask students to write essays examining the levels of irony in *The Crucible*. You might start them off with the margin questions above. Have students look at the court proceeding in Act III and think about the irony in the judges' reactions to the testimony of both accusers and accused. Point out that Miller makes the audience or the reader "witnesses" to the proceedings. Ask students whether they think this irony is deliberate.

PROCTOR: And why not, if they must hang for denyin' it? There are them that will swear to anything before they'll hang; have you never thought of that?

HALE: I have. I—I have indeed. *It is his own suspicion, but he resists it. He glances at* ELIZABETH, *then at* JOHN. And you—would you testify to this in court?

PROCTOR: I—had not reckoned with goin' into court. But if I must I will.

HALE: Do you falter here?

PROCTOR: I falter nothing, but I may wonder if my story will be credited in such a court. I do wonder on it, when such a steady-minded minister as you will suspicion such a woman that never lied, and cannot, and the world knows she cannot! I may falter somewhat, Mister; I am no fool.

HALE, *quietly—it has impressed him:* Proctor, let you open with me now, for I have a rumor that troubles me. It's said you hold no belief that there may even be witches in the world. Is that true, sir?

PROCTOR—he knows this is critical, and is striving against his disgust with HALE and with himself for even answering: I know not what I have said, I may have said it. I have wondered if there be witches in the world—although I cannot believe they come among us now.

HALE: Then you do not believe—

PROCTOR: I have no knowledge of it; the Bible speaks of witches, and I will not deny them.

HALE: And you, woman?

ELIZABETH: I—I cannot believe it.

HALE, *shocked:* You cannot!

PROCTOR: Elizabeth, you bewilder him!

ELIZABETH, *to* HALE: I cannot think the Devil may own a woman's soul, Mr. Hale, when she keeps an upright way, as I have. I am a good woman, I know it; and if you believe I may do only good work in the world, and yet be secretly bound to Satan, then I must tell you, sir, I do not believe it.

HALE: But, woman, you do believe there are witches in—

ELIZABETH: If you think that I am one, then I say there are none.

HALE: You surely do not fly against the Gospel, the Gospel—

PROCTOR: She believe in the Gospel, every word!

ELIZABETH: Question Abigail Williams about the Gospel, not myself!

HALE *stares at her.*

PROCTOR: She do not mean to doubt the Gospel, sir, you cannot think it. This be a Christian house, sir, a Christian house.

HALE: God keep you both; let the third child be quickly baptized, and go you without fail each Sunday to Sabbath prayer; and keep a solemn, quiet way among you. I think—

GILES COREY *appears in doorway.*

GILES: John!

Reading Strategy
Reading Drama In what way do the stage directions help you to understand that Hale wants to believe that the Proctors are good people?

28 ✔ **Reading Check**
What does John Proctor tell Reverend Hale about Abigail Williams?

The Crucible, Act II ◆ 1279

27 **Reading Strategy**
Reading Drama

• Ask students the Reading Strategy question on p. 1279: In what way do the stage directions help you to understand that Hale wants to believe that the Proctors are good people?
Answer: "His own suspicion" agrees with what John says. He is "impressed" with John's reasoning.

• What do the stage directions and dialogue about witches suggest about Proctor's character?
Answer: He hates hypocrisy but realizes that a little hypocrisy is necessary to keep him out of danger. He doesn't really believe in witches, but he knows it is safer to say that he "will not deny them."

• What do Elizabeth's statements about witches suggest about her character?
Answer: Her honesty makes her brave enough to speak her mind.

28 ✔ **Reading Check**
Answer: He says that Abigail told him that the children's illness had nothing to do with witchcraft.

Allusion

- Ask students to explain the power of Francis's allusion to the "bricks and mortar of the church."
  Answer: The allusion is a metaphor that compares Rebecca to the church building. The church is the house of God, and the bricks and mortar are both the walls and the substance that holds the walls together. The allusion states directly that Rebecca is a good and holy woman, and states it powerfully by comparing her to the strong, lasting brick walls of the building.

- Have a volunteer read aloud Hale's speech beginning, "Nurse, though our hearts break . . ." Ask students to explain in what way the Devil is alive in Salem.
  Answer: The Devil is alive in the false accusations and the sin, envy, and spite that the Putnams, Abigail, and other characters vent on one another.

- Ask students the Literary Analysis question on p. 1280: What is the meaning of this allusion to the Devil?
  Answer: Hale compares Rebecca to Lucifer, the archangel who fell from heaven. (If necessary, refer students back to the commentary in Act I, p. 1253.)

PROCTOR: Giles! What's the matter?

GILES: They take my wife.

FRANCIS NURSE *enters.*

GILES: And his Rebecca!

PROCTOR, *to* FRANCIS: Rebecca's in the *jail!*

FRANCIS: Aye, Cheever come and take her in his wagon. We've only now come from the jail, and they'll not even let us in to see them.

ELIZABETH: They've surely gone wild now, Mr. Hale!

FRANCIS, *going to* HALE: Reverend Hale! Can you not speak to the Deputy Governor? I'm sure he mistakes these people—

HALE: Pray calm yourself, Mr. Nurse.

FRANCIS: My wife is the very brick and mortar of the church, Mr. Hale—*indicating* GILES—and Martha Corey, there cannot be a woman closer yet to God than Martha.

HALE: How is Rebecca charged, Mr. Nurse?

FRANCIS, *with a mocking, half-hearted laugh:* For murder, she's charged! *Mockingly quoting the warrant:* "For the marvelous and supernatural murder of Goody Putnam's babies." What am I to do, Mr. Hale?

HALE, *turns from* FRANCIS, *deeply troubled, then:* Believe me, Mr. Nurse, if Rebecca Nurse be tainted, then nothing's left to stop the whole green world from burning. Let you rest upon the justice of the court; the court will send her home. I know it.

FRANCIS: You cannot mean she will be tried in court!

HALE, *pleading:* Nurse, though our hearts break, we cannot flinch; these are new times, sir. There is a misty plot afoot so subtle we should be criminal to cling to old respects and ancient friendships. I have seen too many frightful proofs in court—the Devil is alive in Salem, and we dare not <u>quail</u> to follow wherever the accusing finger points!

PROCTOR, *angered:* How may such a woman murder children?

HALE, *in great pain:* Man, remember, until an hour before the Devil fell, God thought him beautiful in Heaven.

GILES: I never said my wife were a witch, Mr. Hale; I only said she were reading books!

HALE: Mr. Corey, exactly what complaint were made on your wife?

GILES: That bloody mongrel Walcott charge her. Y'see, he buy a pig of my wife four or five years ago, and the pig died soon after. So he come dancin' in for his money back. So my Martha, she says to him, "Walcott, if you haven't the wit to feed a pig properly, you'll not live to own many," she says. Now he goes to court and claims that from that day to this he cannot keep a pig alive for more than four weeks because my Martha bewitch them with her books!

Enter EZEKIEL CHEEVER. *A shocked silence.*

CHEEVER: Good evening to you, Proctor.

PROCTOR: Why, Mr. Cheever. Good evening.

quail (kwāl) *v.* cringe from

Literary Analysis
Allusion What is the meaning of this allusion to the Devil?

✳ ENRICHMENT: Literature Connection

Paradise Lost

Lucifer, an archangel who fell from heaven, is the central figure of *Paradise Lost,* the Renaissance epic by British poet John Milton (1608–1674). Milton was a Protestant, a supporter of Cromwell and the protectorate. His *Paradise Lost,* published in 1667, recounts the creation of hell and the subsequent battle for the soul of man between God and Satan. Some critics have protested that Milton's Satan, who declares that he prefers to reign in hell rather than serve in heaven, is much more appealing than his God.

Others have answered that this appeal mirrors the experience of humankind, which finds temptation more attractive than virtue. Still others point to Lucifer's powerful impact as a symbol of the erring human being, who tragically puts self before others or before God.

CHEEVER: Good evening, all. Good evening, Mr. Hale.

PROCTOR: I hope you come not on business of the court.

CHEEVER: I do, Proctor, aye. I am clerk of the court now, y'know.

Enter MARSHAL HERRICK, *a man in his early thirties, who is somewhat shamefaced at the moment.*

GILES: It's a pity, Ezekiel, that an honest tailor might have gone to Heaven must burn in Hell. You'll burn for this, do you know it?

CHEEVER: You know yourself I must do as I'm told. You surely know that, Giles. And I'd as lief³ you'd not be sending me to Hell. I like not the sound of it, I tell you; I like not the sound of it. *He fears* PROCTOR, *but starts to reach inside his coat.* Now believe me, Proctor, how heavy be the law, all its tonnage I do carry on my back tonight. *He takes out a warrant.* I have a warrant for your wife.

PROCTOR, *to* HALE: You said she were not charged!

HALE: I know nothin' of it. *To* CHEEVER: When were she charged?

CHEEVER: I am given sixteen warrant tonight, sir, and she is one.

PROCTOR: Who charged her?

CHEEVER: Why, Abigail Williams charge her.

PROCTOR: On what proof, what proof?

CHEEVER, *looking about the room:* Mr. Proctor, I have little time. The court bid me search your house, but I like not to search a house. So will you hand me any poppets that your wife may keep here?

PROCTOR: Poppets?

ELIZABETH: I never kept no poppets, not since I were a girl.

CHEEVER, *embarrassed, glancing toward the mantel where sits* MARY WARREN'S *poppet:* I spy a poppet, Goody Proctor.

ELIZABETH: Oh! *Going for it:* Why, this is Mary's.

CHEEVER, *shyly:* Would you please to give it to me?

ELIZABETH, *handing it to him, asks* HALE: Has the court discovered a text in poppets now?

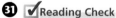 **CHEEVER,** *carefully holding the poppet:* Do you keep any others in this house?

PROCTOR: No, nor this one either till tonight. What signifies a poppet?

CHEEVER: Why, a poppet—*he gingerly turns the poppet over*—a poppet may signify—Now, woman, will you please to come with me?

PROCTOR: She will not! *To* ELIZABETH: Fetch Mary here.

CHEEVER, *ineptly reaching toward* ELIZABETH: No, no, I am forbid to leave her from my sight.

PROCTOR, *pushing his arm away:* You'll leave her out of sight and out of mind, Mister. Fetch Mary, Elizabeth. ELIZABETH *goes upstairs.*

HALE: What signifies a poppet, Mr. Cheever?

---

3. **as lief** (as lēf) *adv.* rather.

Reading Strategy
Reading Drama
How can you tell that Cheever does not at first believe the charges against Elizabeth?

gingerly (jin´ jər´ lē) *adv.* cautiously

31 ✔**Reading Check**
What turn of events causes Hale to feel he must defend the court?

The Crucible, Act II ◆ *1281*

- Ask students the Reading Strategy question on p. 1282: What do the stage directions reveal about Hale's true thoughts?
Answer: Hale is torn between his belief in Elizabeth's goodness and his belief in the evidence of the needle.

- Ask students to infer what really happened to Abigail at dinner.
Answer: Since Mary sewed the doll in court, Abigail probably saw her doing it. She probably saw Mary push the needle into the doll. She knew, therefore, that the doll would be in the Proctors' house with the needle in it. She stabbed herself with a needle to make her accusation match the "evidence."

▶ Monitor Progress Have students evaluate Abigail's character in light of her accusation of Elizabeth.
Answer: Abigail is desperate to have John even at the cost of having Elizabeth arrested and perhaps hanged.

CHEEVER, *turning the poppet over in his hands:* Why, they say it may signify that she—*he has lifted the poppet's skirt, and his eyes widen in astonished fear.* Why, this, this—

PROCTOR, *reaching for the poppet:* What's there?

CHEEVER: Why—*He draws out a long needle from the poppet*—it is a needle! Herrick, Herrick, it is a needle!

HERRICK *comes toward him.*

PROCTOR, *angrily, bewildered:* And what signifies a needle!

CHEEVER, *his hands shaking:* Why, this go hard with her, Proctor, this—I had my doubts, Proctor, I had my doubts, but here's calamity. *To* HALE, *showing the needle:* You see it, sir, it is a needle!

HALE: Why? What meanin' has it?

CHEEVER, *wide-eyed, trembling:* The girl, the Williams girl, Abigail Williams, sir. She sat to dinner in Reverend Parris's house tonight, and without word nor warnin' she falls to the floor. Like a struck beast, he says, and screamed a scream that a bull would weep to hear. And he goes to save her, and, stuck two inches in the flesh of her belly, he draw a needle out. And demandin' of her how she come to be so stabbed, she—*to* PROCTOR *now*—testify it were your wife's familiar spirit pushed it in.

PROCTOR: Why, she done it herself! *To* HALE: I hope you're not takin' this for proof, Mister!

HALE, *struck by the proof, is silent.*

CHEEVER: 'Tis hard proof! *To* HALE: I find here a poppet Goody Proctor keeps. I have found it, sir. And in the belly of the poppet a needle's stuck. I tell you true, Proctor, I never warranted to see such proof of Hell, and I bid you obstruct me not, for I—

Enter ELIZABETH *with* MARY WARREN. PROCTOR, *seeing* MARY WARREN, *draws her by the arm to* HALE.

PROCTOR: Here now! Mary, how did this poppet come into my house?

MARY WARREN, *frightened for herself, her voice very small:* What poppet's that, sir?

PROCTOR, *impatiently, points at the doll in* CHEEVER'S *hand:* This poppet, this poppet.

MARY WARREN, *evasively, looking at it:* Why, I—I think it is mine.

PROCTOR: It is your poppet, is it not?

MARY WARREN, *not understanding the direction of this:* It—is, sir.

PROCTOR: And how did it come into this house?

MARY WARREN, *glancing about at the avid faces:* Why—I made it in the court, sir, and—give it to Goody Proctor tonight.

PROCTOR, *to* HALE: Now, sir—do you have it?

HALE: Mary Warren, a needle have been found inside this poppet.

MARY WARREN, *bewildered:* Why, I meant no harm by it, sir.

PROCTOR, *quickly:* You stuck that needle in yourself?

Reading Strategy
Reading Drama What do these stage directions reveal about Hale's true thoughts?

MARY WARREN: I—I believe I did, sir, I—

PROCTOR, *to* HALE: What say you now?

HALE, *watching* MARY WARREN *closely:* Child, you are certain this be your natural memory? May it be, perhaps that someone conjures you even now to say this?

MARY WARREN: Conjures me? Why, no, sir, I am entirely myself, I think. Let you ask Susanna Walcott—she saw me sewin' it in court. *Or better still:* Ask Abby, Abby sat beside me when I made it.

PROCTOR, *to* HALE, *of* CHEEVER: Bid him begone. Your mind is surely settled now. Bid him out, Mr. Hale.

ELIZABETH: What signifies a needle?

HALE: Mary—you charge a cold and cruel murder on Abigail.

MARY WARREN: Murder! I charge no—

HALE: Abigail were stabbed tonight; a needle were found stuck into her belly—

ELIZABETH: And she charges me?

HALE: Aye.

ELIZABETH, *her breath knocked out:* Why—! The girl is murder! She must be ripped out of the world!

CHEEVER, *pointing at* ELIZABETH: You've heard that, sir! Ripped out of the world! Herrick, you heard it!

PROCTOR, *suddenly snatching the warrant out of* CHEEVER'S *hands:* Out with you.

CHEEVER: Proctor, you dare not touch the warrant.

PROCTOR, *ripping the warrant:* Out with you!

CHEEVER: You've ripped the Deputy Governor's warrant, man!

PROCTOR: Damn the Deputy Governor! Out of my house!

HALE: Now, Proctor, Proctor!

PROCTOR: Get y'gone with them! You are a broken minister.

HALE: Proctor, if she is innocent, the court—

PROCTOR: If *she* is innocent! Why do you never wonder if Parris be innocent, or Abigail? Is the accuser always holy now? Were they born this morning as clean as God's fingers? I'll tell you what's walking Salem—vengeance is walking Salem. We are what we always were in Salem, but now the little crazy children are jangling the keys of the kingdom, and common vengeance writes the law! This warrant's vengeance! I'll not give my wife to vengeance!

ELIZABETH: I'll go, John—

PROCTOR: You will not go!

HERRICK: I have nine men outside. You cannot keep her. The law binds me, John, I cannot budge.

PROCTOR, *to* HALE, *ready to break him:* Will you see her taken?

HALE: Proctor, the court is just—

Reading Strategy
Reading Drama What do the stage directions and Hale's comment reveal about his trust in Mary Warren?

35 ✔**Reading Check**
What does Cheever discover in the Proctor's home?

The Crucible, Act II ◆ 1283

---

33 Reading Strategy

Reading Drama

- Ask students the Reading Strategy question on p. 1283: What do the stage directions and Hale's comment reveal about Hale's trust in Mary Warren?
  Answer: He isn't ready to take her at her word.

- Why is Hale unwilling to trust Mary?
  Answer: Mary is easily persuaded to believe and do what she is told. Hale is a good judge of people and he can see that Mary is the type to lie under pressure.

34 Critical Thinking

Connect

- Have students connect Proctor's speech with the speech Hale makes on p. 1280 beginning, "Nurse, though our hearts break . . ." In what way is this speech a response to the previous one?
  Answer: Hale had said that the Devil was in Salem; Proctor identifies the Devil as "vengeance."

- Explain that "the keys of the kingdom" alludes to Jesus' statement to the apostle Peter: "I will give unto thee the keys of the kingdom of heaven" (Matthew 16:19). Ask students what connection Proctor makes.
  Answer: St. Peter uses his keys to let souls into heaven. Proctor is saying that by believing their accusations, the court has given the "little crazy children" the power to decide who will be saved and who will be damned.

35 ✔Reading Check

Answer: The evidence he finds supports Abigail's accusation of Elizabeth.

CUSTOMIZE INSTRUCTION FOR UNIVERSAL ACCESS

For Less Proficient Readers

Have students make a character web for Reverend Hale at the end of each of the four acts. Students should note changes in his behavior and attitude from each act to the next. Have them use their notes to trace Hale's character development throughout the play.

Background

Film

The photographs used to illustrate *The Crucible* are taken from the 1996 Hollywood film of the play, starring Daniel Day-Lewis, Winona Ryder, Joan Allen, and Paul Scofield. Arthur Miller wrote the screenplay for the film. Miller was pleased at the ability of film to "open wide enough to contain a whole society and move in close enough to see into a girl's heart." The film was shot near Salem, only a mile or so away from land once owned by John Proctor. About two hundred local people were used as extras in the film; most claimed descent from the victims of the witchcraft trials.

1284 ◆ Prosperity and Protest (1946–Present)

PROCTOR: Pontius Pilate![4] God will not let you wash your hands of this!

ELIZABETH: John—I think I must go with them. *He cannot bear to look at her.* Mary, there is bread enough for the morning; you will bake, in the afternoon. Help Mr. Proctor as you were his daughter—you owe me that, and much more. *She is fighting her weeping. To* PROCTOR: When the children wake, speak nothing of witchcraft— it will frighten them. *She cannot go on.*

PROCTOR: I will bring you home. I will bring you soon.

ELIZABETH: Oh, John, bring me soon!

PROCTOR: I will fall like an ocean on that court! Fear nothing, Elizabeth.

ELIZABETH, *with great fear:* I will fear nothing. *She looks about the room, as though to fix it in her mind.* Tell the children I have gone to visit someone sick.

She walks out the door, HERRICK *and* CHEEVER *behind her. For a moment,* PROCTOR *watches from the doorway. The clank of chain is heard.*

PROCTOR: Herrick! Herrick, don't chain her! *He rushes out the door. From outside:* Damn you, man, you will not chain her! Off with them! I'll not have it! I will not have her chained!

There are other men's voices against his. HALE, *in a fever of guilt and uncertainty, turns from the door to avoid the sight:* MARY WARREN *bursts into tears and sits weeping.* GILES COREY *calls to* HALE.

GILES: And yet silent, minister? It is fraud, you know it is fraud! What keeps you, man?

PROCTOR *is half braced, half pushed into the room by two deputies and* HERRICK.

PROCTOR: I'll pay you, Herrick, I will surely pay you!

HERRICK, *panting:* In God's name, John, I cannot help myself. I must chain them all. Now let you keep inside this house till I am gone! *He goes out with his deputies.*

PROCTOR *stands there, gulping air. Horses and a wagon creaking are heard.*

---

4. **Pontius** (pän´ shəs) **Pilate** (pī´ lət) Roman leader who condemned Jesus to be crucified.

Literary Analysis
Allusion To what biblical event, key to Puritan belief, does Proctor refer when he alludes to Pontius Pilate?

38 ◀ **Critical Viewing**
What thoughts or feelings do the facial expressions of Elizabeth Proctor, Reverend Parris, and the two deputies convey in this photo?

39 ✔ **Reading Check**
What happens to Elizabeth Proctor?

The Crucible, Act II ◆ *1285*

37 **Literary Analysis**
Allusion

• Provide some biblical background: Pontius Pilate knew that Jesus had been unjustly convicted, and he offered the people a choice: to crucify either Jesus or the robber Barabbas. The people chose Jesus, and Pilate literally washed his hands before the crowd as a symbol of his refusal to accept responsibility for Jesus' death. The figure of Pilate thus became notorious as an image of hypocritical innocence.

• Ask students the Literary Analysis question on p. 1285: What is the power of this biblical allusion?
Answer: Proctor insists that Hale, despite his protestations that he is acting in the interests of the law, does bear responsibility for what has happened.

• Ask students to evaluate the allusion. What does it suggest about Hale?
Answer: It suggests that even though Hale disclaims responsibility, he will knowingly allow the fraud to go forward.

38 ▶ **Critical Viewing**
Answer: They look deeply concerned.

39 ✔ **Reading Check**
Answer: She is arrested and charged with witchcraft.

Evaluate

- Why is Hale so unwilling to believe that Abigail is guilty of fraud and murder?

  Answer: To condemn so many innocent people to death, Abigail must be profoundly evil. Hale doesn't want to believe this of anyone. He prefers to blame it on the Devil rather than on a person.

- Ask students to explain in what way the Devil is involved in the court proceedings.

  Answer: The Devil exists in the evil that people do. Abigail has not literally seen the Devil—and neither has anyone else in Salem Village, for that matter—but she has done things that she knows to be wrong: drinking a charm to kill Elizabeth, having an affair with John, lying about Tituba and many others, and condemning people to death with false testimony.

HALE, *in great uncertainty:* Mr. Proctor—

PROCTOR: Out of my sight!

HALE: Charity, Proctor, charity. What I have heard in her favor, I will not fear to testify in court. God help me, I cannot judge her guilty or innocent—I know not. Only this consider: the world goes mad, and it profit nothing you should lay the cause to the vengeance of a little girl.

PROCTOR: You are a coward! Though you be ordained in God's own tears, you are a coward now!

HALE: Proctor, I cannot think God be provoked so grandly by such a petty cause. The jails are packed—our greatest judges sit in Salem now—and hangin's promised. Man, we must look to cause proportionate. Were there murder done, perhaps, and never brought to light? Abomination? Some secret blasphemy that stinks to Heaven? Think on cause, man, and let you help me to discover it. For there's your way, believe it, there is your only way, when such confusion strikes upon the world. *He goes to* GILES *and* FRANCIS. Let you counsel among yourselves; think on your village and what may have drawn from heaven such thundering wrath upon you all. I shall pray God open up our eyes.

HALE *goes out.*

FRANCIS, *struck by* HALE'S *mood:* I never heard no murder done in Salem.

PROCTOR—*he has been reached by* HALE'S *words:* Leave me, Francis, leave me.

GILES, *shaken:* John—tell me, are we lost?

PROCTOR: Go home now, Giles. We'll speak on it tomorrow.

GILES: Let you think on it. We'll come early, eh?

PROCTOR: Aye. Go now, Giles.

GILES: Good night, then.

GILES COREY *goes out. After a moment:*

MARY WARREN, *in a fearful squeak of a voice:* Mr. Proctor, very likely they'll let her come home once they're given proper evidence.

PROCTOR: You're coming to the court with me, Mary. You will tell it in the court.

MARY WARREN: I cannot charge murder on Abigail.

PROCTOR, *moving menacingly toward her:* You will tell the court how that poppet come here and who stuck the needle in.

MARY WARREN: She'll kill me for sayin' that! PROCTOR *continues toward her.* Abby'll charge lechery[5] on you, Mr. Proctor!

PROCTOR, *halting:* She's told you!

MARY WARREN: I have known it, sir. She'll ruin you with it, I know she will.

---

5. **lechery** (lech´ ər ē) *n.* lust; adultery—a charge almost as serious as witchcraft in this Puritan community.

abomination (ə bäm´ ə nā´ shən) *n.* something that causes great horror or disgust

blasphemy (blas´ fə mē´) *n.* sinful act or remark

PROCTOR, *hesitating, and with deep hatred of himself:* Good. Then her saintliness is done with. MARY *backs from him.* We will slide together into our pit; you will tell the court what you know.

MARY WARREN, *in terror:* I cannot, they'll turn on me—

PROCTOR *strides and catches her, and she is repeating, "I cannot, I cannot!"*

PROCTOR: My wife will never die for me! I will bring your guts into your mouth but that goodness will not die for me!

MARY WARREN, *struggling to escape him:* I cannot do it. I cannot!

PROCTOR, *grasping her by the throat as though he would strangle her:* Make your peace with it! Now Hell and Heaven grapple on our backs, and all our pretense is ripped away—make your peace! *He throws her to the floor, where she sobs, "I cannot, I cannot . . ." And now, half to himself, staring, and turning to the open door:* Peace. It is a providence, and no great change; we are only what we always were, but naked now. *He walks as though toward a great horror, facing the open sky.* Aye, naked! And the wind, God's icy wind, will blow!

And she is over and over again sobbing, "I cannot, I cannot, I cannot."

Review and Assess

Thinking About Act II

1. **Respond:** Which character do you find the most intriguing? Why?

2. **(a) Recall:** What does Mary Warren bring home to Elizabeth Proctor? **(b) Interpret:** What is the significance of this gift?

3. **(a) Recall:** What evidence is used to support Abigail Williams's assertion that Elizabeth Proctor is guilty of witchcraft? **(b) Assess:** Do you think the evidence is compelling? Why or why not?

4. **(a) Recall:** What does Sarah Good do to save herself from hanging? **(b) Draw Conclusions:** Why would such an action save her?

5. **(a) Recall:** According to John Proctor, what is "walking Salem" and writing the law in the community? **(b) Support:** What evidence would support Proctor's assertion?

6. **(a) Recall:** Who says the witchcraft trials are "a black mischief"? **(b) Analyze:** What is ironic about that remark?

7. **Analyze:** Why is it surprising that Rebecca Nurse is charged with witchcraft?

8. **Evaluate:** Do you find any irony in the fact that Ezekiel Cheever is the one who arrests Elizabeth Proctor? Why or why not?

The Crucible, Act II ◆ *1287*

ASSESSMENT PRACTICE: Writing Skills

Sentence Structure   (For more practice, see Test Preparation Workbook, p. 77.)

Many tests require students to identify correct sentence structure. Use this following sample test item.

Elizabeth is frightened, the court clerk and the magistrate enter.

Which is the best way to write this sentence?

A Although Elizabeth is frightened—the court clerk and the magistrate enter.

B Elizabeth being frightened, the court clerk and the magistrate enter.

C Elizabeth becomes frightened when the court clerk and the magistrate enter.

D correct as is

Only choice *C* is grammatically correct and shows the correct cause-and-effect relationship.

Review and Assess

1. God spoke directly to Moses and gave him the power to part the Red Sea; people believe that Abigail is possessed of special powers, as Moses was.

2. **(a)** Proctor implies that Hale refuses to take responsibility for his official actions. **(b)** It suggests that the innocent are being condemned.

3. Students should note that in the play, most often women accuse other women of witchcraft; the question is not simple. Students may feel that the low status of women, and especially of young girls, fuels the anger of accusers such as Abigail and Mary.

4. Proctor risks his social position by refusing to have his son baptized. He also risks his son's immortal soul. This suggests that Proctor's principles are of far greater importance to him than any interest he might have in what people think of him.

5. Since there were no laws against them, searches and arrests were not illegal. It suggests that the society had great faith in the correctness of its judges.

6. Make sure that students choose examples of lines that might be spoken with a variety of tones or emotions.

7. They describe how the actors are meant to move about the stage, how and whether they touch one another, and to whom their lines are addressed.

8. In a modern court, an accusation is not proof. A statement like Abigail's that a spirit is attacking her is not proof. A court official like Hale cannot visit suspects privately. Suspects are entitled to the protection of lawyers.

Review and Assess

Literary Analysis

Allusion

1. What does the biblical **allusion** to Moses and the parting of the Red Sea on page 1269 suggest about how the crowd views Abigail?

2. (a) What does John Proctor's allusion to Pontius Pilate on page 1285 imply about Proctor's opinion of Reverend Hale? (b) What does the allusion to Pontius Pilate imply about the witchcraft proceedings in Salem?

Connecting Literary Elements

3. In what way do details of **historical context,** including the status of women, explain why women were accused of witchcraft?

4. Knowing that keeping the Sabbath and attending church services were strictly enforced by the Puritans, how do you interpret John Proctor's exchange with Reverend Hale about the baptism of Proctor's sons? Explain.

5. The Puritans lacked laws to protect people from illegal searches and arrests. How does this fact add to your appreciation of the scene in which Elizabeth Proctor is apprehended?

Reading Strategy

Reading Drama

6. Using a chart like the one shown here, cite three examples of dialogue in which a character's attitudes would have been unclear to you if you had not read the stage directions.

Dialogue	Attitude Revealed in Stage Direction

7. In addition to characters' attitudes, what other significant information do the stage directions in Act II reveal to you?

Extend Understanding

8. **Social Studies Connection:** How are legal principles and evidence-gathering procedures different in America today than they were in the time in which the play is set? Explain.

Quick Review

An **allusion** is a brief reference within a literary work to another literary work, a well-known person, a place, or a historical event.

Considering the **historical context** of a literary work can help you better understand key factors about the work's setting, background, and culture.

When you **read drama,** pay close attention to dialogue and stage directions to enrich your understanding of the play's plot, characters, and themes.

 ***Take It to the Net***
www.phschool.com
Take the interactive self-test online to check your understanding of this selection.

TEACHING RESOURCES

The following resources can be used to enrich or extend the instruction for p. 1289.

Vocabulary
- **Selection Support:** Build Vocabulary, p. 318
- **Vocabulary and Spelling Practice Book** (Use this booklet for skills enrichment.)

Grammar
- **Selection Support:,** Grammar and Style, p. 319
- **Writing and Grammar,** Ruby Level
- **Daily Language Practice Transparencies**

Writing
- **Writing and Grammar iText CD-ROM**

BLOCK SCHEDULING: Resources marked with this symbol provide varied instruction during 90-minute blocks.

Integrate Language Skills

❶ Vocabulary Development Lesson

Word Analysis: Greek Suffix *-logy*

The Greek suffix *-logy* means "the science, theory, or study of." When combined with the Greek root *-theo-*, meaning "god," the word *theology* means "the study of religion." For each item below, identify a word that combines a root with the suffix *-logy*.

1. "star" __*logy*
2. "life" __*logy*
3. "earth" __ *logy*
4. "social" __*logy*

Spelling Strategy

For verbs that end in *-er*, add the suffix *-ence* to form nouns. For each of these words, use the suffix *-ence* to generate a noun.

1. differ
2. confer
3. prefer

Fluency: Words in Context

Explain why each statement is *true* or *false*.

1. Lying is *base* behavior.
2. To step *gingerly* is to stomp.
3. Someone who watches sports *avidly* probably knows very little about them.
4. Rude youngsters show *deference* to elders.
5. Puritans think witchcraft is an *abomination*.
6. A fearful animal may *quail* at the sight of a whip.
7. A minister is pleased to hear *blasphemy*.
8. A blushing person exhibits *pallor*.
9. The Puritans questioned their *theology*.
10. To *ameliorate* a situation is to make it better.

❷ Grammar and Style Lesson

Commas After Introductory Words

Use a **comma** to set off a mild interjection or another interrupter that introduces a sentence.

Examples: *Oh,* you're not done then.
Aye, the farm is seeded.

Practice Add commas to set off introductory words. If a sentence is correct as is, write *Correct.*

1. Hey did you ever see *The Crucible*?
2. Yes I saw a local theater group's production.
3. Well which characters are sympathetic?
4. I must admit that I found it unpleasant.
5. Perhaps but the problem could have been with the performance you saw.

Writing Application Write a brief scene using dialogue that involves two or more characters. Use commas to set off at least three introductory words.

Extension Activities

Writing Imagine that one of the citizens accused of witchcraft has disappeared. In a group, design a **wanted poster** that describes the individual and the reason he or she should be apprehended. [Group Activity]

Listening and Speaking Write and perform a **scene** that dramatizes the arrest of Rebecca Nurse. Make the style of your scene consistent with that of the rest of the play. Present the scene to your class.

 Prentice Hall Writing and Grammar Connection: Chapter 27, Section 2

The Crucible, Act II ◆ 1289

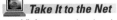

The Crucible, Act III

Lesson Objectives

1. **To analyze and respond to literary elements**
   - Literary Analysis: Dramatic and Verbal Irony
   - Connecting Literary Elements: Logical Fallacy

2. **To read, comprehend, analyze, and critique a drama**
   - Reading Strategy: Categorizing Characters by Role
   - Reading Check Questions
   - Review and Assess Questions

3. **To develop word analysis skills, fluency, and systematic vocabulary**
   - Vocabulary Development Lesson: Concept Development: Legal Terms

4. **To understand and apply written and oral language conventions**
   - Spelling Strategy
   - Grammar and Style Lesson: Subject and Verb Agreement in Inverted Sentences
   - Assessment Practice (ATE)

5. **To understand and apply appropriate writing and research strategies**
   - Writing Lesson: Character Sketch

6. **To understand and apply listening and speaking strategies**
   - Extension Activity: Monologue

STEP-BY-STEP TEACHING GUIDE	PACING GUIDE
PRETEACH	
Motivate Students and Provide Background	
Use the Motivation activity (ATE p. 1230)	5 min.
Read and discuss author and background features (SE/ATE p. 1230–1231) **A**	5 min.
Introduce the Concepts	
Introduce the Literary Analysis and Reading Strategy (SE/ATE p. 1290) **A**	15 min.
Pronounce the vocabulary words and read their definitions (SE p.1290)	5 min.
TEACH	
Monitor Comprehension	
Informally monitor comprehension by circulating while students read independently **A**	55 min.
Monitor students' comprehension with the Reading Check notes (SE/ATE pp. 1291, 1293, 1295, 1297, 1299, 1301, 1303, 1305, 1307, 1309, 1311, 1313)	as students read
Develop vocabulary with Vocabulary notes (SE pp. 1292, 1294, 1296, 1297, 1299, 1300, 1301, 1304, 1309; ATE p. 1294)	as students read
Develop Understanding	
Develop students' understanding of dramatic and verbal irony with the Literary Analysis annotations (SE /ATE pp. 1293, 1296, 1297, 1298, 1301, 1303, 1306, 1307, 1310, 1311, 1312, 1313, 1314) **A**	5 min.
Develop students' ability to categorize characters by role by using the Reading Strategy annotations (SE/ATE pp. 1291, 1292, 1293, 1294, 1295, 1299, 1301, 1304, 1305, 1309, 1311)	5 min.
ASSESS	
Assess Mastery	
Assess students' mastery of the Reading Strategy and Literary Analysis by having them answer the Review and Assess questions (SE/ATE p. 1316)	15 min.
Use one or more of the print and media Assessment Resources (ATE p. 1316) **A**	up to 45 min.
EXTEND	
Apply Understanding	
Have students complete the Vocabulary Development Lesson and the Grammar and Style Lesson (SE p. 1317) **A**	20 min.
Apply students' understanding of the selection using one or more of the Extension Activities (SE p. 1317)	45 min.
	20–90 min.

 ACCELERATED INSTRUCTION:
Use the strategies and activities identified with an **A**.

UNIVERSAL ACCESS
● = Below Level Students
▲ = On-Level Students
■ = Above Level Students

Time and Resource Manager

RESOURCES		
PRINT 📖	**TRANSPARENCIES**	**TECHNOLOGY** 💿 🎧 📼
• **Beyond Literature,** Career Connection: Law, p. 75 ▲ ■		• **Interest Grabber Video,** Tape 6 ● ▲ ■
• **Selection Support Workbook:** ● ▲ ■ Literary Analysis, p. 325 Reading Strategy, p. 324 Build Vocabulary, p. 322	• **Literary Analysis and Reading Transparencies,** pp. 149 and 150 ● ▲ ■	
• **Literatura en español** ● ▲ • **Literary Analysis for Enrichment** ■		
• **Formal Assessment:** Selection Test, pp. 315–317 ● ▲ ■ • **Open Book Test,** pp. 223–225 ● ▲ ■ • **PRENTICE HALL ASSESSMENT SYSTEM** ● ▲ ■	• **PRENTICE HALL ASSESSMENT SYSTEM** ● ▲ ■ Skills Practice Answers and Explanations on Transparencies	• **Test Bank Software** ● ▲ ■ • **Got It! Assessment Videotapes,** Tape 6 ● ▲
• **Selection Support Workbook:** ● ▲ ■ Grammar and Style, p. 323 • **Writing and Grammar,** Ruby Level ● ▲ ■ • **Extension Activities,** p. 75 ● ▲ ■	• **Daily Language Practice Transparencies** ● ▲	• **Writing and Grammar iText CD-ROM** ● ▲ ■ 💻 *Take It to the Net* www.phschool.com

BLOCK SCHEDULING: Use one 90-minute class period to preteach the selection and have students read it. Use a second 90-minute class period to assess students' mastery of skills and have them complete one of the Extension Activities.

❶ Literary Analysis

Dramatic and Verbal Irony

- Review the definition of irony from Kate Chopin's "The Story of an Hour" (p. 632). Remind students that irony is the difference between expectation and reality.

- List some examples of irony from Acts I and II of *The Crucible*. Have students decide whether these are examples of verbal or dramatic irony.

❷ Reading Strategy

Categorizing Characters by Role

- Work with students to fill in the chart on this page. Encourage them to reread parts of the play to refresh their memory about each character's role.

- Then, have students suggest other categories into which they can divide the characters. Have them discuss why categorizing characters is helpful.

Vocabulary Development

- Pronounce each vocabulary word for students, and read the definitions as a class. Have students identify any words with which they are already familiar.

E-Teach

Visit E-Teach at www.phschool.com for teachers' essays on how to teach, with questions and answers.

Prepare to Read

The Crucible, Act III

❶ Literary Analysis

Dramatic and Verbal Irony

Irony involves a contrast between what is stated and what is meant, or between what is expected to happen and what actually happens.

- In **dramatic irony,** there is a contradiction between what a character thinks and what the audience knows to be true.
- In **verbal irony,** a character says one thing but means something quite different.

Look for both forms of irony as you read Act III.

Connecting Literary Elements

In this act of the play, Miller challenges audiences to think critically. Beyond maintaining an awareness of irony, the audience must also weigh the logic presented in the court scene. There, Miller introduces a **logical fallacy,** an idea or argument that appears logical though it is based on a completely faulty premise. Judge Danforth explains his reasoning for believing the accusations of witchcraft. Though his thoughts seem logical, read them critically—all are based on a mistaken premise.

❷ Reading Strategy

Categorizing Characters by Role

The introduction of many characters in a drama can become confusing. It may be helpful to **categorize the characters**. One way you can classify characters in *The Crucible* is by the roles they play in the community. Using a chart like the one shown, identify the characters and their positions in Salem Village.

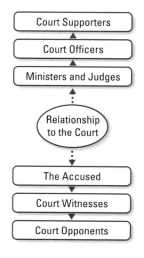

Court Supporters

Court Officers

Ministers and Judges

Relationship to the Court

The Accused

Court Witnesses

Court Opponents

Vocabulary Development

contentious (kən ten′ shəs) *adj.* argumentative (p. 1292)

deposition (dep′ ə zish′ ən) *n.* the testimony of a witness made under oath but not in open court (p. 1294)

imperceptible (im′ pər sep′ tə bəl) *adj.* barely noticeable (p. 1296)

deferentially (def′ ər en′ shəl lē) *adv.* in a manner that bows to another's wishes; very respectfully (p. 1297)

anonymity (an′ ə nim′ ə tē) *n.* the condition of being unknown (p. 1299)

prodigious (prə dij′ əs) *adj.* of great size, power, or extent (p. 1300)

effrontery (e frun′ tər ē) *n.* shameless boldness (p. 1300)

confounded (kən found′ id) *v.* confused; dismayed (p. 1301)

incredulously (in krej′ ōō ləs lē) *adv.* skeptically (p. 1304)

blanched (blancht) *adj.* paled; whitened (p. 1309)

TEACHING RESOURCES

The following resources can be used to enrich or extend the instruction for p. 1290.

Motivation

🎞 **Interest Grabber Video,** Tape 6

Background

📖 **Beyond Literature,** p. 75 ■

🖥 **Take It to the Net**

Visit www.phschool.com for background and hotlinks for *The Crucible*.

Literary Analysis

🖥 **Literary Analysis and Reading Transparencies,** Dramatic and Verbal Irony, p. 150 ■

Reading

📖 **Selection Support:** Reading Strategy, p. 324; Build Vocabulary, p. 322

🖥 **Literary Analysis and Reading Transparencies,** Categorizing Characters by Role, p. 149

▬ **BLOCK SCHEDULING:** Resources marked with this symbol provide varied instruction during 90-minute blocks.

❶ Review and Anticipate

Act II ends as Elizabeth Proctor is accused of witchcraft and carted off to jail as a result of the connivance of Abigail Williams. John Proctor demands that Mary Warren tell the court the truth; Mary, though aware of Abigail's ploys, is terrified of exposing her. Do you think John will convince Mary to overcome her fears and testify against Abigail? If he does convince her, how will the judges receive Mary Warren's testimony? Read Act III to see what happens in the Salem courtroom.

ACT III

The vestry room of the Salem meeting house, now serving as the anteroom of the General Court.

As the curtain rises, the room is empty, but for sunlight pouring through two high windows in the back wall. The room is solemn, even forbidding. Heavy beams jut out, boards of random widths make up the walls. At the right are two doors leading into the meeting house proper, where the court is being held. At the left another door leads outside.

There is a plain bench at the left, and another at the right. In the center a rather long meeting table, with stools and a considerable armchair snugged up to it.

Through the partitioning wall at the right we hear a prosecutor's voice, JUDGE HATHORNE's, *asking a question; then a woman's voice,* MARTHA COREY's, *replying.*

HATHORNE'S VOICE: Now, Martha Corey, there is abundant evidence in our hands to show that you have given yourself to the reading of fortunes. Do you deny it?

MARTHA COREY'S VOICE: I am innocent to a witch. I know not what a witch is.

HATHORNE'S VOICE: How do you know, then, that you are not a witch?

MARTHA COREY'S VOICE: If I were, I would know it.

HATHORNE'S VOICE: Why do you hurt these children?

❷ **MARTHA COREY'S VOICE:** I do not hurt them. I scorn it!

GILES'S VOICE, *roaring:* I have evidence for the court!

Voices of townspeople rise in excitement.

DANFORTH'S VOICE: You will keep your seat!

GILES' VOICE: Thomas Putnam is reaching out for land!

DANFORTH'S VOICE: Remove that man, Marshal!

GILES' VOICE: You're hearing lies, lies!

A roaring goes up from the people.

❸ 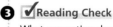 **Reading Check**

What accusation does Hathorne make of Martha Corey?

TEACHING RESOURCES

The following resources can be used to enrich or extend the instruction for pp. 1291–1315.

Literary Analysis

📖 **Selection Support:** Literary Analysis, p. 325

Reading

📖 **Selection Support:** Reading Strategy, p. 324

TEACH

Step-by-Step Teaching Guide for pp. 1291–1315

CUSTOMIZE INSTRUCTION
For Visual/Spatial Learners

Ask students to design a set for the play. Have them think about how the stage setting can affect the mood. Remind them that stage settings can be faithful to historical fact, but need not be; some of the most effective theatrical productions are set in different times and places from those called for in the script.

❶ About Act III

Proctor brings Mary to the court, and she confesses to Judge Hathorne and Governor Danforth. The officials and Parris are shocked and hesitate to believe her. Danforth brings in the girls and confronts them with Mary's testimony. Abigail says firmly that Mary is lying.

Proctor confesses to his affair with Abigail, explaining that jealousy of Elizabeth is the ground for all her lies and accusations. Abigail denies the affair. Elizabeth is brought into the room and asked about the affair. To protect John, she denies it.

As Hale and Danforth begin arguing about whom to believe, Abigail cries out that Mary's spirit, disguised as a yellow bird, is up in the rafters, threatening her. The other girls follow her lead and Mary breaks down and renounces her confession. Proctor and Corey are arrested as Hale denounces the court and the curtain falls.

❷ Reading Strategy

Categorizing Characters by Role

• Into which categories can you divide the voices heard in this opening to Act III?
  Answer: You can divide them into judges and witnesses.

• Ask students to give their opinions of the judges.
  Answer: They seem eager to convict Martha Corey. They insist on the proper court procedure when Giles tries to interrupt the examination of the witness.

❸  **Reading Check**

Answer: He accuses her of reading fortunes and harming the children.

1291

Categorizing Characters by Role

- Ask students the Reading Strategy question on p. 1292: Why do you think Giles makes this statement about Hathorne's status as a judge?

  Answer: Giles suggests that he and Hathorne are equals and that Hathorne has no right to call him names.

- Have students divide the characters who speak in this passage into two groups and explain their rationale.

  Possible answer: Hathorne, Herrick, Danforth, and Parris are in one group; Giles and Hale are in the other. The first group supports the proceedings of the court; the other tries to fight the court.

HATHORNE'S VOICE: Arrest him, excellency!

GILES' VOICE: I have evidence. Why will you not hear my evidence?

The door opens and GILES *is half carried into the vestry room by* HERRICK.

GILES: Hands off, damn you, let me go!

HERRICK: Giles, Giles!

GILES: Out of my way, Herrick! I bring evidence—

HERRICK: You cannot go in there, Giles; it's a court!

Enter HALE *from the court.*

HALE: Pray be calm a moment.

GILES: You, Mr. Hale, go in there and demand I speak.

HALE: A moment, sir, a moment.

GILES: They'll be hangin' my wife!

JUDGE HATHORNE *enters. He is in his sixties, a bitter, remorseless Salem judge.*

HATHORNE: How do you dare come roarin' into this court! Are you gone daft, Corey?

❹ **GILES:** You're not a Boston judge, Hathorne. You'll not call me daft!

Enter DEPUTY GOVERNOR DANFORTH *and, behind him,* EZEKIEL CHEEVER *and* PARRIS. *On his appearance, silence falls.* DANFORTH *is a grave man in his sixties, of some humor and sophistication that does not, however, interfere with an exact loyalty to his position and his cause. He comes down to* GILES, *who awaits his wrath.*

DANFORTH, *looking directly at* GILES: Who is this man?

PARRIS: Giles Corey, sir, and a more <u>contentious</u>—

GILES, *to* PARRIS: I am asked the question, and I am old enough to answer it! *To* DANFORTH, *who impresses him and to whom he smiles through his strain:* My name is Corey, sir, Giles Corey. I have six hundred acres, and timber in addition. It is my wife you be condemning now. *He indicates the courtroom.*

DANFORTH: And how do you imagine to help her cause with such contemptuous riot? Now be gone. Your old age alone keeps you out of jail for this.

GILES, *beginning to plead:* They be tellin' lies about my wife, sir, I—

DANFORTH: Do you take it upon yourself to determine what this court shall believe and what it shall set aside?

GILES: Your Excellency, we mean no disrespect for—

DANFORTH: Disrespect indeed! It is disruption, Mister. This is the highest court of the supreme government of this province, do you know it?

GILES, *beginning to weep:* Your Excellency, I only said she were readin' books, sir, and they come and take her out of my house for—

DANFORTH, *mystified:* Books! What books?

GILES, *through helpless sobs:* It is my third wife, sir; I never had no wife that be so taken with books, and I thought to find the cause of it, d'y'see, but it were no witch I blamed her for. *He is openly weeping.*

Reading Strategy
Categorizing Characters by Role Why do you think Giles makes this statement about Hathorne's status as a judge?

contentious (kən ten´ shəs) *adj.* argumentative

I have broke charity with the woman, I have broke charity with her. *He covers his face, ashamed.* DANFORTH *is respectfully silent.*

HALE: Excellency, he claims hard evidence for his wife's defense. I think that in all justice you must—

DANFORTH: Then let him submit his evidence in proper affidavit.[1] You are certainly aware of our procedure here, Mr. Hale. *To* HERRICK: Clear this room.

HERRICK: Come now, Giles. *He gently pushes* COREY *out.*

FRANCIS: We are desperate, sir; we come here three days now and cannot be heard.

DANFORTH: Who is this man?

❺ **FRANCIS:** Francis Nurse, Your Excellency.

HALE: His wife's Rebecca that were condemned this morning.

DANFORTH: Indeed! I am amazed to find you in such uproar. I have only good report of your character, Mr. Nurse.

HERRICK: I think they must both be arrested in contempt, sir.

DANFORTH, *to* FRANCIS: Let you write your plea, and in due time I will—

FRANCIS: Excellency, we have proof for your eyes; God forbid you shut them to it. The girls, sir, the girls are frauds.

DANFORTH: What's that?

FRANCIS: We have proof of it, sir. They are all deceiving you.

DANFORTH *is shocked, but studying* FRANCIS.

HATHORNE: This is contempt, sir, contempt!

❻ **DANFORTH:** Peace, Judge Hathorne. Do you know who I am, Mr. Nurse?

FRANCIS: I surely do, sir, and I think you must be a wise judge to be what you are.

DANFORTH: And do you know that near to four hundred are in the jails from Marblehead to Lynn, and upon my signature?

FRANCIS: I—

DANFORTH: And seventy-two condemned to hang by that signature?

FRANCIS: Excellency, I never thought to say it to such a weighty judge, but you are deceived.

Enter GILES COREY *from left. All turn to see as he beckons in* MARY WARREN *with* PROCTOR. MARY *is keeping her eyes to the ground;* PROCTOR *has her elbow as though she were near collapse.*

PARRIS, *on seeing her, in shock:* Mary Warren! *He goes directly to bend close to her face.* What are you about here?

PROCTOR, *pressing* PARRIS *away from her with a gentle but firm motion of protectiveness:* She would speak with the Deputy Governor.

DANFORTH, *shocked by this, turns to* HERRICK: Did you not tell me Mary Warren were sick in bed?

---

1. **affidavit** (af´ ə dā´ vit) *n.* written statement made under oath.

Literary Analysis
Dramatic and Verbal Irony and Logical Fallacy
What is illogical about Danforth's statement to Francis Nurse?

Reading Strategy
Categorizing Characters by Role In what sense could Danforth and Hathorne be classified together?

❼ ☑**Reading Check**
What has Martha Corey done that results in her arrest?

❺ # Literary Analysis
Dramatic and Verbal Irony and Logical Fallacy

- Ask students the Literary Analysis question on p. 1293: What is illogical about Danforth's statement to Francis Nurse?
  Answer: If Nurse is a good man as Danforth says, then Danforth shouldn't be surprised that he pleads for his wife's life; this is just what a good man would do.

- Why is Francis's statement, "We come here three days now and cannot be heard," ironic?
  Answer: The accusers have no trouble being heard; only the defenders of the accused are not listened to.

❻ # Reading Strategy
Categorizing Characters by Role

- Ask students the Reading Strategy question on p. 1293: In what sense could Danforth and Hathorne be classified together?
  Answer: Danforth and Hathorne are both authority figures.

- Ask students whether they perceive any difference between Hathorne and Danforth. If so, what?
  Answer: Hathorne is much quicker to condemn; Danforth listens to what people say, although he insists that proper procedure is followed.

❼ # ☑ Reading Check

Answer: Giles commented on her habit of reading; this led to her arrest.

CUSTOMIZING INSTRUCTION FOR UNIVERSAL ACCESS

For Less Proficient Readers

Use a chart to help students weigh the evidence in this trial. On the blackboard, draw a two-column chart, labeling the left side "For the Defense" and the right side "For the Prosecution." Explain to students the difference between *defense* and *prosecution*. Then, write several arguments or pieces of evidence in the chart, explaining how they help either side. Students can extend the chart as they read. Pause periodically to discuss students' charts and determine which side seems to be winning the trial.

❽ Vocabulary Development

Legal Terms: *deposition*

- Draw students' attention to the word *deposition* and its definition, "testimony of a witness made under oath but not in open court."

- Explain that the word comes from the French verb *deposer*, which means "to set down." A witness sets down his or her testimony in writing, to be used when the case comes to trial.

- Ask students to make note of other legal terms they encounter as they continue to read Act III.

❾ Reading Strategy

Categorizing Characters by Role

- Ask students the Reading Strategy question on p. 1294: Would Parris be so concerned about Mary Warren's testimony being heard in open court if he were not a community leader?

  Answer: He doesn't want her testimony heard at all, but especially not in open court, where members of his congregation might hear it.

- Why is Parris afraid of Mary's testimony?

  Answer: Parris knows that Mary's testimony will show that he has been a party to the fraud all along.

HERRICK: She were, Your Honor. When I go to fetch her to the court last week, she said she were sick.

GILES: She has been strivin' with her soul all week, Your Honor; she comes now to tell the truth of this to you.

DANFORTH: Who is this?

PROCTOR: John Proctor, sir. Elizabeth Proctor is my wife.

PARRIS: Beware this man, Your Excellency, this man is mischief.

HALE, *excitedly:* I think you must hear the girl, sir, she—

DANFORTH, *who has become very interested in* MARY WARREN *and only raises a hand toward* HALE: Peace. What would you tell us, Mary Warren?

PROCTOR *looks at her, but she cannot speak.*

PROCTOR: She never saw no spirits, sir.

DANFORTH, *with great alarm and surprise, to* MARY: Never saw no spirits!

GILES, *eagerly:* Never.

❽ **PROCTOR,** *reaching into his jacket:* She has signed a deposition, sir—

DANFORTH, *instantly:* No, no, I accept no depositions. *He is rapidly calculating this; he turns from her to* PROCTOR. Tell me, Mr. Proctor, have you given out this story in the village?

PROCTOR: We have not.

PARRIS: They've come to overthrow the court, sir! This man is—

DANFORTH: I pray you, Mr. Parris. Do you know, Mr. Proctor that the entire contention of the state in these trials is that the voice of Heaven is speaking through the children?

PROCTOR: I know that, sir.

DANFORTH, *thinks, staring at* PROCTOR, *then turns to* MARY WARREN: And you, Mary Warren, how come you to cry out people for sending their spirits, against you?

MARY WARREN: It were pretense, sir.

DANFORTH: I cannot hear you.

PROCTOR: It were pretense, she says.

DANFORTH: Ah? And the other girls? Susanna Walcott, and—the others? They are also pretending?

MARY WARREN: Aye, sir.

❾ **DANFORTH,** *wide-eyed:* Indeed. *Pause. He is baffled by this. He turns to study* PROCTOR'S *face.*

PARRIS, *in a sweat:* Excellency, you surely cannot think to let so vile a lie be spread in open court.

DANFORTH: Indeed not, but it strike hard upon me that she will dare come here with such a tale. Now, Mr. Proctor, before I decide whether I shall hear you or not, it is my duty to tell you this. We burn a hot fire here; it melts down all concealment.

PROCTOR: I know that, sir.

1294 ◆ *Prosperity and Protest (1946–Present)*

---

deposition (dep′ ə zish′ ən) *n.* the testimony of a witness made under oath but not in open court

Reading Strategy
Categorizing Characters by Role Would Parris be so concerned about Mary Warren's testimony being heard in open court if he were not a community leader?

✳ ENRICHMENT: History Connection

Cotton Mather

One important figure in Puritan Massachusetts who does not appear in the play is Cotton Mather (1663–1728), a Boston minister. In 1689, he became involved in a swirl of accusations of witchcraft in Boston. Mather published a book on the witchcraft case that many (including Reverend Hale) believed was partly responsible for the reactions of the Salem court. Mather was unable to attend the Salem trials, but he wrote letters urging caution in the acceptance of any testimony about spirits (such as Abigail averred about Elizabeth). However, Mather believed that unmistakably identified witches should be executed and urged "speedy and vigorous prosecution." The Salem judges, all of whom had close personal ties to Mather, took his advice. Popular legend has blamed Mather for much of the court's overzealousness ever since.

DANFORTH: Let me continue. I understand well, a husband's tenderness may drive him to extravagance in defense of a wife. Are you certain in your conscience, Mister, that your evidence is the truth?

PROCTOR: It is. And you will surely know it.

DANFORTH: And you thought to declare this revelation in the open court before the public?

PROCTOR: I thought I would, aye—with your permission.

DANFORTH, *his eyes narrowing:* Now, sir, what is your purpose in so doing?

PROCTOR: Why, I—I would free my wife, sir.

DANFORTH: There lurks nowhere in your heart, nor hidden in your spirit, any desire to undermine this court?

PROCTOR, *with the faintest faltering:* Why, no, sir.

CHEEVER, *clears his throat, awakening:* I—Your Excellency.

DANFORTH: Mr. Cheever.

CHEEVER: I think it be my duty, sir—*Kindly, to* PROCTOR: You'll not deny it, John. *To* DANFORTH: When we come to take his wife, he damned the court and ripped your warrant.

PARRIS: Now you have it!

DANFORTH: He did that, Mr. Hale?

HALE, *takes a breath:* Aye, he did.

PROCTOR: It were a temper, sir. I knew not what I did.

❿ DANFORTH, *studying him:* Mr. Proctor.

PROCTOR: Aye, sir.

DANFORTH, *straight into his eyes:* Have you ever seen the Devil?

PROCTOR: No, sir.

DANFORTH: You are in all respects a Gospel Christian?

PROCTOR: I am, sir.

PARRIS: Such a Christian that will not come to church but once in a month!

DANFORTH, *restrained—he is curious:* Not come to church?

PROCTOR: I—I have no love for Mr. Parris. It is no secret. But God I surely love.

CHEEVER: He plow on Sunday, sir.

DANFORTH: Plow on Sunday!

CHEEVER, *apologetically:* I think it be evidence, John. I am an official of the court, I cannot keep it.

PROCTOR: I—I have once or twice plowed on Sunday. I have three children, sir, and until last year my land give little.

GILES: You'll find other Christians that do plow on Sunday if the truth be known.

HALE: Your Honor, I cannot think you may judge the man on such evidence.

Reading Strategy
Categorizing Characters by Role Would you classify Parris or Danforth as a villain? Why or why not?

⓫ ✔Reading Check
What new testimony does Mary Warren give?

The Crucible, Act III ◆ 1295

Dramatic and Verbal Irony and Logical Fallacy

- **What is ironic about Danforth's statement, "I judge nothing"?**
  Answer: Danforth is a judge who makes life-and-death decisions.

- **Ask students the Literary Analysis question on p. 1296: In what way does Danforth's statement represent a logical fallacy?**
  Answer: He says he has no reason to suspect deception, but the events he is asked to believe are incredible by nature.

- **Share the Enrichment information below with students. Why is Parris's allusion to the story of Cain and Abel illogical?**
  Answer: Cain was not an upright man but a deliberate murderer; he killed his brother because he was jealous. Jealousy in this play motivates the accusers, not the victims.

DANFORTH: I judge nothing. *Pause. He keeps watching* PROCTOR, *who tries to meet his gaze.* I tell you straight, Mister—I have seen marvels in this court. I have seen people choked before my eyes by spirits; I have seen them stuck by pins and slashed by daggers. I have until this moment not the slightest reason to suspect that the children may be deceiving me. Do you understand my meaning?

PROCTOR: Excellency, does it not strike upon you that so many of these women have lived so long with such upright reputation, and—

PARRIS: Do you read the Gospel, Mr. Proctor?

PROCTOR: I read the Gospel.

PARRIS: I think not, or you should surely know that Cain were an upright man, and yet he did kill Abel.[2]

PROCTOR: Aye, God tells us that. *To* DANFORTH: But who tells us Rebecca Nurse murdered seven babies by sending out her spirit on them? It is the children only, and this one will swear she lied to you.

DANFORTH *considers, then beckons* HATHORNE *to him.* HATHORNE *leans in, and he speaks in his ear.* HATHORNE *nods.*

HERRICK: Aye, she's the one.

DANFORTH: Mr. Proctor, this morning, your wife send me a claim in which she states that she is pregnant now.

PROCTOR: My wife pregnant!

DANFORTH: There be no sign of it—we have examined her body.

PROCTOR: But if she say she is pregnant, then she must be! That woman will never lie, Mr. Danforth.

DANFORTH: She will not?

PROCTOR: Never, sir, never.

DANFORTH: We have thought it too convenient to be credited. However, if I should tell you now that I will let her be kept another month; and if she begin to show her natural signs, you shall have her living yet another year until she is delivered—what say you to that? JOHN PROCTOR *is struck silent.* Come now. You say your only purpose is to save your wife. Good, then, she is saved at least this year, and a year is long. What say you, sir? It is done now. *In conflict,* PROCTOR *glances at* FRANCIS *and* GILES. Will you drop this charge?

PROCTOR: I—I think I cannot.

DANFORTH, *now an almost <u>imperceptible</u> hardness in his voice:* Then your purpose is somewhat larger.

PARRIS: He's come to overthrow this court, Your Honor!

PROCTOR: These are my friends. Their wives are also accused—

DANFORTH, *with a sudden briskness of manner:* I judge you not, sir. I am ready to hear your evidence.

PROCTOR: I come not to hurt the court; I only—

---

2. **Cain . . . Abel** In the Bible, Cain, the oldest son of Adam and Eve, killed his brother, Abel.

1296 ◆ Prosperity and Protest (1946–Present)

Literary Analysis
Dramatic and Verbal Irony and Logical Fallacy
In what way does Danforth's statement represent a logical fallacy?

imperceptible (im´ pər sep´ tə bəl) *adj.* barely noticeable

✳ ENRICHMENT: Literature Connection

Cain and Abel

In the book of Genesis in the Bible, Cain offers God produce from his harvest, while Abel offers lambs from his flock. God accepts Abel's gift but rejects Cain's. Cain kills Abel out of jealousy.

John Steinbeck based his 1952 novel *East of Eden* on this biblical story. Cyrus Trask loves his son Adam, who fears and dislikes him, but is indifferent to Charles, who loves him devotedly. This causes terrible tension between the brothers. In the next generation, the pattern is repeated. Adam loves Aron, who is indifferent to him, but gives little thought to Caleb, who loves him. In their late teens, both boys offer birthday gifts to their father, who accepts Aron's but rejects Cal's. Passion and jealousy drive Cal to commit an act that leads to his brother's death.

DANFORTH, *cutting him off:* Marshal, go into the court and bid Judge Stoughton and Judge Sewall declare recess for one hour. And let them go to the tavern, if they will. All witnesses and prisoners are to be kept in the building.

HERRICK: Aye, sir. *Very deferentially:* If I may say it, sir. I know this man all my life. It is a good man, sir.

DANFORTH—*it is the reflection on himself he resents:* I am sure of it, Marshal. HERRICK *nods, then goes out.* Now, what deposition do you have for us, Mr. Proctor? And I beg you be clear, open as the sky, and honest.

PROCTOR, *as he takes out several papers:* I am no lawyer, so I'll—

DANFORTH: The pure in heart need no lawyers. Proceed as you will.

PROCTOR, *handing* DANFORTH *a paper:* Will you read this first, sir? It's a sort of testament. The people signing it declare their good opinion of Rebecca, and my wife, and Martha Corey.

DANFORTH *looks down at the paper.*

PARRIS, *to enlist* DANFORTH's *sarcasm:* Their good opinion! *But* DANFORTH *goes on reading, and* PROCTOR *is heartened.*

PROCTOR: These are all landholding farmers, members of the church. *Delicately, trying to point out a paragraph:* If you'll notice, sir—they've known the women many years and never saw no sign they had dealings with the Devil.

PARRIS *nervously moves over and reads over* DANFORTH's *shoulder.*

DANFORTH, *glancing down a long list:* How many names are here?

FRANCIS: Ninety-one, Your Excellency.

PARRIS, *sweating:* These people should be summoned. DANFORTH *looks up at him questioningly.* For questioning.

FRANCIS. *trembling with anger:* Mr. Danforth, I gave them all my word no harm would come to them for signing this.

PARRIS: This is a clear attack upon the court!

HALE, *to* PARRIS, *trying to contain himself:* Is every defense an attack upon the court? Can no one—?

PARRIS: All innocent and Christian people are happy for the courts in Salem! These people are gloomy for it. *To* DANFORTH *directly:* And I think you will want to know, from each and every one of them, what discontents them with you!

HERRICK: I think they ought to be examined, sir.

DANFORTH: It is not necessarily an attack, I think. Yet—

FRANCIS: These are all covenanted Christians, sir.

DANFORTH: Then I am sure they may have nothing to fear. *Hands* CHEEVER *the paper.* Mr. Cheever, have warrants drawn for all of these— arrest for examination. *To* PROCTOR: Now, Mister, what other information do you have for us? FRANCIS *is still standing, horrified.* You may sit, Mr. Nurse.

FRANCIS: I have brought trouble on these people: I have—

---

deferentially (def′ ər en′ shəl lē) *adv.* in a manner that bows to another's wishes; very respectfully

Literary Analysis
Dramatic and Verbal Irony
What makes Danforth's statement about the "pure in heart" an example of verbal irony?

 **Reading Check**
What document does Proctor present to the count?

The Crucible, Act III ◆ 1297

CUSTOMIZE INSTRUCTION FOR UNIVERSAL ACCESS

For Less Proficient Readers

One interesting aspect of Miller's play is that most of the characters are not entirely good or evil but a mix of faults and good qualities. Ask students to choose three or four characters and make a word web to describe each one. As students read Act III, they should note personality traits and brief quotations supporting their descriptions on the rays of the webs. Students can use these graphic organizers for a group discussion of the characters. As a follow-up, have them discuss what this mix of good and bad in each character suggests about the play's overall themes. How do the personalities relate to the play's events and outcome?

⓭ Literary Analysis
Dramatic and Verbal Irony

- Ask students the Literary Analysis question on p. 1297: What makes Danforth's statement about "the pure in heart" an example of verbal irony?
  Answer: It suggests that truth always prevails in court, when the audience has already seen innocent people condemned.

- What is ironic about Parris's insistence that the signers of the testament be summoned to court?
  Answer: By signing the testament, these people were trying to tell the truth and help others. Their punishment for this is that they are now all in danger from the court.

- Why is Parris's reaction to the testament ironic?
  Answer: Proctor says that all the signers are members of the church. Therefore, Parris's livelihood depends on these people. He should treat them well rather than suggesting that their actions are suspicious.

⓮ Critical Thinking
Making Judgments

- Which character is responsible for the arrest of the people on the list? How does he achieve this?
  Answer: Parris is responsible. He appeals to Danforth's pride by suggesting that the signers are not in favor of the court.

- What judgments can you make about both Danforth and Parris, given Danforth's decision to arrest the signers?
  Answer: Parris is manipulative; he will do anything to save himself from blame. Danforth can't stand to have the court criticized, and this affects his judgment.

⓯ ✔Reading Check

Answer: The document that Proctor presents says that Rebecca, Elizabeth, and Martha are all good Christian women. It is signed by 91 people.

Dramatic and Verbal Irony

- Why is Danforth's statement that "a person is either with this court or he must be counted against it" ironic?

  Answer: The court's job is to be impartial, not to assume the guilt of the accused as this court does. Proctor, Corey, and others who try to present actual evidence are ignored, but they are the ones trying to work by the rules of the court. Danforth is on the side of the accusers, ignoring the fact that their unsupported accusations flout the court's rules.

- Ask students the Literary Analysis question on p. 1298: In what sense is Proctor's quotation from the Bible ironic?

  Answer: It is ironic because so far in the play, harm has come to several characters who have done nothing but good.

DANFORTH: No, old man, you have not hurt these people if they are of good conscience. But you must understand, sir, that a person is either with this court or he must be counted against it, there be no road between. This is a sharp time, now, a precise time—we live no longer in the dusky afternoon when evil mixed itself with good and befuddled the world. Now, by God's grace, the shining sun is up, and them that fear not light will surely praise it. I hope you will be one of those. MARY WARREN *suddenly sobs.* She's not hearty, I see.

PROCTOR: No, she's not, sir. *To* MARY, *bending to her, holding her hand, quietly:* Now remember what the angel Raphael said to the boy Tobias.[3] Remember it.

MARY WARREN, *hardly audible:* Aye.

PROCTOR: "Do that which is good, and no harm shall come to thee."

MARY WARREN: Aye.

DANFORTH: Come, man, we wait you.

MARSHAL HERRICK *returns, and takes his post at the door.*

GILES: John, my deposition, give him mine.

PROCTOR: Aye. *He hands* DANFORTH *another paper.* This is Mr. Corey's deposition.

DANFORTH: Oh? *He looks down at it. Now* HATHORNE *comes behind him and reads with him.*

HATHORNE, *suspiciously:* What lawyer drew this, Corey?

GILES: You know I never hired a lawyer in my life, Hathorne.

DANFORTH, *finishing the reading:* It is very well phrased. My compliments. Mr. Parris, if Mr. Putnam is in the court, will you bring him in? HATHORNE *takes the deposition, and walks to the window with it.* PARRIS *goes into the court.* You have no legal training, Mr. Corey?

GILES, *very pleased:* I have the best, sir—I am thirty-three time in court in my life. And always plaintiff, too.

DANFORTH: Oh, then you're much put-upon.

GILES: I am never put-upon; I know my rights, sir, and I will have them. You know, your father tried a case of mine—might be thirty-five year ago, I think.

DANFORTH: Indeed.

GILES: He never spoke to you of it?

DANFORTH: No, I cannot recall it.

GILES: That's strange, he gave me nine pound damages. He were a fair judge, your father. Y'see, I had a white mare that time, and this fellow come to borrow the mare—*Enter* PARRIS *with* THOMAS PUTNAM. *When he*

---

3. **Raphael. . .Tobias** In the Bible, Tobias is guided by the archangel Raphael to save two people who have prayed for their deaths. One of the two is Tobias's father, Tobit, who has prayed for his death because he has lost his sight; the other is Sara, a woman who is afflicted by a demon and has killed her seven husbands on their wedding day. With Raphael's assistance, Tobias exorcises the devil from Sara and cures his father of blindness.

sees PUTNAM, GILES' *ease goes; he is hard.* Aye, there he is.

DANFORTH: Mr. Putnam, I have here an accusation by Mr. Corey against you. He states that you coldly prompted your daughter to cry witchery upon George Jacobs that is now in jail.

PUTNAM: It is a lie.

DANFORTH, *turning to* GILES: Mr. Putnam states your charge is a lie. What say you to that?

GILES, *furious, his fists clenched:* A fart on Thomas Putnam, that is what I say to that!

DANFORTH: What proof do you submit for your charge, sir?

GILES: My proof is there! *Pointing to the paper.* If Jacobs hangs for a witch he forfeit up his property—that's law! And there is none but Putnam with the coin to buy so great a piece. This man is killing his neighbors for their land!

DANFORTH: But proof, sir, proof.

GILES, *pointing at his deposition:* The proof is there! I have it from an honest man who heard Putnam say it! The day his daughter cried out on Jacobs, he said she'd given him a fair gift of land.

HATHORNE: And the name of this man?

GILES, *taken aback:* What name?

HATHORNE: The man that give you this information.

GILES, *hesitates, then:* Why, I—I cannot give you his name.

HATHORNE: And why not?

GILES, *hesitates, then bursts out:* You know well why not! He'll lay in jail if I give his name!

HATHORNE: This is contempt of the court, Mr. Danforth!

DANFORTH, *to avoid that:* You will surely tell us the name.

GILES: I will not give you no name. I mentioned my wife's name once and I'll burn in hell long enough for that. I stand mute.

DANFORTH: In that case, I have no choice but to arrest you for contempt of this court, do you know that?

GILES: This is a hearing; you cannot clap me for contempt of a hearing.

DANFORTH: Oh, it is a proper lawyer! Do you wish me to declare the court in full session here? Or will you give me good reply?

GILES, *faltering:* I cannot give you no name, sir, I cannot.

DANFORTH: You are a foolish old man. Mr. Cheever, begin the record. The court is now in session. I ask you, Mr. Corey—

PROCTOR, *breaking in:* Your Honor—he has the story in confidence, sir, and he—

PARRIS: The Devil lives on such confidences! *To* DANFORTH: Without confidences there could be no conspiracy, Your Honor!

HATHORNE: I think it must be broken, sir.

DANFORTH, *to* GILES: Old man, if your informant tells the truth let him come here openly like a decent man. But if he hide in <u>anonymity</u> I

Reading Strategies
Categorizing Characters by Role In which segment of the community would you classify Giles? Why?

anonymity (an´ ə nim´ ə tē) *n.* the condition of being unknown

⑱ ✔Reading Check
What is Giles Corey's defense? Explain.

The Crucible, Act III ◆ *1299*

---

⑰ Reading Strategy

Categorizing Characters by Role

- Ask students the Reading Strategy question on p. 1299: In which segment of the community would you classify Giles? Why?
  Answer: Giles is an opponent of the court. He fears it will condemn innocent people, such as his wife, George Jacobs, and the witness to Mr. Putnam's plan to accuse Jacobs.

- Do Danforth and Hathorne belong in the same category? What differences do you see between them?
  Answer: Hathorne is quicker to condemn. Danforth will do anything to protect the good name of the court, but he has a greater sense of justice than Hathorne. Students would probably still put both in the same category; neither is impartial as a judge should be.

⑱ ✔Reading Check

Answer: Corey claims that Putnam wanted Jacobs's property and therefore accused him. He mentions a witness to this whom he will not name.

CUSTOMIZE INSTRUCTION FOR UNIVERSAL ACCESS

For Gifted/Talented Students

In Act II, John Proctor accuses Elizabeth of judging him harshly: "I cannot speak but I am doubted, every moment judged for lies, as though I come into a court when I come into this house!" (p. 1270). Have students compare his conversation with Elizabeth in Act II to the court session that takes place in these pages of Act III. In what way is Elizabeth like the judges in the courtroom? In what way is she different? Remind students that Elizabeth judged John for something he did, while the court judges characters like Rebecca and Martha Corey for things they deny doing. Students can gather in a small group to compare and contrast Elizabeth and the judges.

Analyzing

- Ask students to analyze Danforth's character. What kind of person is he?

Answer: Danforth is a true Puritan. He believes in the idea of demonic possession and takes it for granted that no one would lie about such a thing. In a way, he is innocent and naive; he thinks it much more likely that a witch would deny being a witch than that a child would make a false accusation. He is impressed by some of what the other characters say, but only up to a point. Above all, he wants to protect the reputation of the court.

- Ask students to suggest the motivation for Danforth's feelings about the court.

Answer: Danforth's own good name is linked to the court's reputation.

---

must know why. Now sir, the government and central church demand of you the name of him who reported Mr. Thomas Putnam a common murderer.

HALE: Excellency—

DANFORTH: Mr. Hale.

HALE: We cannot blink it more. There is a <u>prodigious</u> fear of this court in the country—

DANFORTH: Then there is a prodigious guilt in the country. Are you afraid to be questioned here?

HALE: I may only fear the Lord, sir, but there is fear in the country nevertheless.

⑲ **DANFORTH,** *angered now:* Reproach me not with the fear in the country; there is fear in the country because there is a moving plot to topple Christ in the country!

HALE: But it does not follow that everyone accused is part of it.

DANFORTH: No uncorrupted man may fear this court, Mr. Hale! None! *To* GILES: You are under arrest in contempt of this court. Now sit you down and take counsel with yourself, or you will be set in the jail until you decide to answer all questions.

GILES COREY *makes a rush for* PUTNAM. PROCTOR *lunges and holds him.*

PROCTOR: No, Giles!

GILES, *over proctor's shoulder at* PUTNAM: I'll cut your throat, Putnam, I'll kill you yet!

PROCTOR, *forcing him into a chair:* Peace, Giles, peace. *Releasing him.* We'll prove ourselves. Now we will. *He starts to turn to* DANFORTH.

GILES: Say nothin' more, John. *Pointing at* DANFORTH: He's only playin' you! He means to hang us all!

MARY WARREN *bursts into sobs.*

DANFORTH: This is a court of law, Mister. I'll have no <u>effrontery</u> here!

PROCTOR: Forgive him, sir, for his old age. Peace, Giles, we'll prove it all now. *He lifts up* MARY'S *chin.* You cannot weep, Mary. Remember the angel, what he say to the boy. Hold to it, now; there is your rock. MARY *quiets. He takes out a paper, and turns to* DANFORTH. This is Mary Warren's deposition. I—I would ask you remember, sir, while you read it, that until two week ago she were no different than the other children are today. *He is speaking reasonably, restraining all his fears, his anger, his anxiety.* You saw her scream, she howled, she swore familiar spirits choked her; she even testified that Satan, in the form of women now in jail, tried to win her soul away, and then when she refused—

DANFORTH: We know all this.

PROCTOR: Aye, sir. She swears now that she never saw Satan; nor any spirit, vague or clear, that Satan may have sent to hurt her. And she declares her friends are lying now.

PROCTOR *starts to hand* DANFORTH *the deposition, and* HALE *comes up to* DANFORTH *in a trembling state.*

1300 ◆ *Prosperity and Protest (1946–Present)*

prodigious (prə dij′ əs) *adj.* of great size, power, or extent

effrontery (e frunt′ ər ē) *n.* shameless boldness

HALE: Excellency, a moment. I think this goes to the heart of the matter.

DANFORTH, *with deep misgivings:* It surely does.

HALE: I cannot say he is an honest man; I know him little. But in all justice, sir, a claim so weighty cannot be argued by a farmer. In God's name, sir, stop here; send him home and let him come again with a lawyer—

DANFORTH, *patiently:* Now look you, Mr. Hale—

HALE: Excellency, I have signed seventy-two death warrants; I am a minister of the Lord, and I dare not take a life without there be a proof so immaculate no slightest qualm of conscience may doubt it.

DANFORTH: Mr. Hale, you surely do not doubt my justice.

HALE: I have this morning signed away the soul of Rebecca Nurse, Your Honor. I'll not conceal it, my hand shakes yet as with a wound! I pray you, sir, *this* argument let lawyers present to you.

 DANFORTH: Mr. Hale, believe me; for a man of such terrible learning you are most bewildered—I hope you will forgive me. I have been thirty-two year at the bar, sir, and I should be <u>confounded</u> were I called upon to defend these people. Let you consider, now—*To* PROCTOR *and the others:* And I bid you all do likewise. In an ordinary crime, how does one defend the accused? One calls up witnesses to prove his innocence. But witchcraft is *ipso facto*,[4] on its face and by its nature, an invisible crime, is it not? Therefore, who may possibly be witness to it? The witch and the victim. None other. Now we cannot hope the witch will accuse herself; granted? Therefore, we must rely upon her victims—and they do testify, the children certainly do testify. As for the witches, none will deny that we are most eager for all their confessions. Therefore, what is left for a lawyer to bring out? I think I have made my point. Have I not?

HALE: But this child claims the girls are not truthful, and if they are not—

DANFORTH: That is precisely what I am about to consider, sir. What more may you ask of me? Unless you doubt my probity?[5]

HALE, *defeated:* I surely do not, sir. Let you consider it, then.

DANFORTH: And let you put your heart to rest. Her deposition, Mr. Proctor.

PROCTOR *hands it to him.* HATHORNE *rises, goes beside* DANFORTH, *and starts reading.* PARRIS *comes to his other side.* DANFORTH *looks at* JOHN PROCTOR, *then proceeds to read.* HALE *gets up, finds position near the judge, reads too.* PROCTOR *glances at* GILES. FRANCIS *prays silently, hands pressed together.* CHEEVER *waits placidly, the sublime official, dutiful.* MARY WARREN *sobs once.* JOHN PROCTOR *touches her hand reassuringly. Presently* DANFORTH *lifts his eyes, stands up, takes out a kerchief and blows his nose. The others stand aside as he moves in thought toward the window.*

PARRIS, *hardly able to contain his anger and fear:* I should like to question—

---

4. **ipso facto** (ip′ sō fak′ tō) "by that very fact"; "therefore" (Latin).
5. **probity** (prō′ bə tē) *n.* complete honesty: integrity.

---

confounded (kən found′ id) *v.* confused; dismayed

Literary Analysis
Dramatic and Verbal Irony and Logical Fallacy In what ways is Danforth's entire argument based on a faulty premise?

Reading Strategy
Categorizing Characters by Role Based on this scene, how would you classify Danforth?

✔**Reading Check**
What is Danforth's basic argument about witnesses and witchcraft?

The Crucible, Act III ◆ *1301*

🔵 Literary Analysis
Dramatic and Verbal Irony and Logical Fallacy

• Ask students the Literary Analysis question on p. 1301: In what ways is Danforth's entire argument based on a faulty premise?
Answer: Danforth does not allow for the possibility that an accused person may be innocent of witchcraft.

• Why is Danforth's insistence that lawyers are unnecessary ironic?
Answer: Since the court is so unwilling to listen to defenders of the accused or to accept their evidence, they need the legal protection that the court insists no innocent person needs.

🔵 Reading Strategy
Categorizing Characters by Role

• Ask students the Reading Strategy question on p. 1301: Based on this scene, how would you classify Danforth?
Answer: Students will probably classify Danforth as a villain.

• Does Danforth have any good or admirable qualities?
Answer: Students should see that Danforth is more inclined to listen to the defenders than any of the other officials, but he allows his judgment to be swayed by Parris, Hathorne, and others.

🔵 ✔ Reading Check
Answer: He argues that witchcraft is a crime with only two witnesses—the witch and the victim.

CUSTOMIZE INSTRUCTION FOR UNIVERSAL ACCESS

For Gifted/Talented Students

Ask students to imagine that they are lawyers appointed to represent Proctor, and have them rebut Danforth's argument (given in the speech beginning "Mr. Hale, believe me" on this page). Students should find the logical fallacies in Danforth's argument, point them out, and correct his faulty thinking. Students may want to work together or individually on their speeches. Volunteers can present their speeches to the class. If time allows, have students choose another argument in the play that is based on a logical fallacy. Have them repeat the exercise, sharpening both their written and oral skills of persuasion.

❷❸ ▶ Critical Viewing

Answer: Students will probably say that they don't find Danforth sympathetic or understanding.

DANFORTH—*his first real outburst, in which his contempt for* PARRIS *is clear:* Mr. Parris, I bid you be silent! *He stands in silence, looking out the window. Now, having established that he will set the gait:* Mr. Cheever, will you go into the court and bring the children here? CHEEVER *gets up and goes out upstage.* DANFORTH *now turns to* MARY. Mary Warren, how came you to this turnabout? Has Mr. Proctor threatened you for this deposition?

MARY WARREN: No, sir.

DANFORTH: Has he ever threatened you?

MARY WARREN, *weaker:* No, sir.

DANFORTH, *sensing a weakening:* Has he threatened you?

MARY WARREN: No, sir.

DANFORTH: Then you tell me that you sat in my court, callously lying, when you knew that people would hang by your evidence? *She does not answer.* Answer me!

MARY WARREN, *almost inaudibly:* I did, sir.

DANFORTH: How were you instructed in your life? Do you not know that God damns all liars? *She cannot speak.* Or is it now that you lie?

❷❸ ▼ Critical Viewing
In this movie still, Danforth conveys a feeling of sympathy or understanding for Mary Warren. Compare this portrayal with your own image of Danforth. **[Compare]**

1302 ◆ *Prosperity and Protest (1946–Present)*

CUSTOMIZING INSTRUCTION FOR UNIVERSAL ACCESS

For Less Proficient Readers

Students may have guessed that Mary would have to confront her friends in court. Invite students to consider the conflicts in that meeting. Use the following questions for discussion:

• Ask students whether they can think of a modern, real-life example of a person turning against his or her friends. Invite them to explain what happened.

• Have students predict what Mary's friends will do when they come into the courtroom. What do they predict Mary will do? Make sure they can support their predictions with details about Mary's behavior thus far.

MARY WARREN: No, sir—I am with God now.

DANFORTH: You are with God now.

MARY WARREN: Aye, sir.

DANFORTH, *containing himself:* I will tell you this—you are either lying now, or you were lying in the court, and in either case you have committed perjury and you will go to jail for it. You cannot lightly say you lied, Mary. Do you know that?

MARY WARREN: I cannot lie no more. I am with God, I am with God.

But she breaks into sobs at the thought of it, and the right door opens, and enter SUSANNA WALCOTT, MERCY LEWIS, BETTY PARRIS, *and finally* ABIGAIL. CHEEVER *comes to* DANFORTH.

CHEEVER: Ruth Putnam's not in the court, sir, nor the other children.

DANFORTH: These will be sufficient. Sit you down, children. *Silently they sit.* Your friend, Mary Warren, has given us a deposition. In which she swears that she never saw familiar spirits, apparitions, nor any manifest of the Devil. She claims as well that none of you have seen these things either. *Slight pause.* Now, children, this is a court of law. The law, based upon the Bible, and the Bible, writ by Almighty God, forbid the practice of witchcraft, and describe death as the penalty thereof. But likewise, children, the law and Bible damn all bearers of false witness. *Slight pause.* Now then. It does not escape me that this deposition may be devised to blind us; it may well be that Mary Warren has been conquered by Satan, who sends her here to distract our sacred purpose. If so, her neck will break for it. But if she speak true, I bid you now drop your guile and confess your pretense, for a quick confession will go easier with you. *Pause.* Abigail Williams, rise. ABIGAIL *slowly rises.* Is there any truth in this?

ABIGAIL: No, sir.

DANFORTH, *thinks, glances at* MARY *then back to* ABIGAIL: Children, a very augur bit[6] will now be turned into your souls until your honesty is proved. Will either of you change your positions now, or do you force me to hard questioning?

ABIGAIL: I have naught to change, sir. She lies.

DANFORTH, *to* MARY: You would still go on with this?

MARY WARREN, *faintly:* Aye, sir.

DANFORTH, *turning to* ABIGAIL: A poppet were discovered in Mr. Proctor's house, stabbed by a needle. Mary Warren claims that you sat beside her in the court when she made it, and that you saw her make it and witnessed how she herself stuck the needle into it for safe-keeping. What say you to that?

ABIGAIL, *with a slight note of indignation:* It is a lie, sir.

DANFORTH, *after a slight pause:* While you worked for Mr. Proctor, did you see poppets in that house?

ABIGAIL: Goody Proctor always kept poppets.

---

6. **augur bit** sharp point of an augur, a tool used for boring holes.

Literary Analysis
Dramatic and Verbal Irony In what ways are Danforth's statements examples of dramatic irony?

 Reading Check
According to Danforth, what is Mary Warren's fate—regardless of what she testifies? Why?

The Crucible, Act III ◆ *1303*

㉖ Reading Strategy

Categorizing Characters by Role

- Ask students the Reading Strategy question on p. 1304: How might Proctor classify Mary Warren? Why?
  Answer: Proctor feels sorry for her. He tries to help her.
- What do Parris's questions and comments suggest about his role in the play?
  Answer: He is one of the villains of the play. He continues to try to obscure the truth for his own ends. His questions are misleading and irrelevant.

㉗ Reading Strategy

Categorizing Characters by Role

- Ask students the Reading Strategy question on p. 1304: In what category would you place Hathorne? Explain.
  Answer: Students should classify Hathorne as a villain. He shows no real interest in hearing new evidence.
- Have students predict the effect of Mary's testimony on the judges. Have them give reasons for their predictions.
  Answer: Mary is so frightened that she speaks with little conviction. The judges probably won't believe her.

PROCTOR: Your Honor, my wife never kept no poppets. Mary Warren confesses it was her poppet.

CHEEVER: Your Excellency.

DANFORTH: Mr. Cheever.

CHEEVER: When I spoke with Goody Proctor in that house, she said she never kept no poppets. But she said she did keep poppets when she were a girl.

PROCTOR: She has not been a girl these fifteen years, Your Honor.

HATHORNE: But a poppet will keep fifteen years, will it not?

PROCTOR: It will keep if it is kept, but Mary Warren swears she never saw no poppets in my house, nor anyone else.

PARRIS: Why could there not have been poppets hid where no one ever saw them?

㉖ PROCTOR, *furious:* There might also be a dragon with five legs in my house, but no one has ever seen it.

PARRIS: We are here, Your Honor, precisely to discover what no one has ever seen.

PROCTOR: Mr. Danforth, what profit this girl to turn herself about? What may Mary Warren gain but hard questioning and worse?

DANFORTH: You are charging Abigail Williams with a marvelous cool plot to murder, do you understand that?

PROCTOR: I do, sir. I believe she means to murder.

DANFORTH, *pointing at* ABIGAIL, *incredulously:* This child would murder your wife?

PROCTOR: It is not a child. Now hear me, sir. In the sight of the congregation she were twice this year put out of this meetin' house for laughter during prayer.

DANFORTH, *shocked, turning to* ABIGAIL: What's this? Laughter during—!

PARRIS: Excellency, she were under Tituba's power at that time, . but she is solemn now.

GILES: Aye, now she is solemn and goes to hang people!

DANFORTH: Quiet, man.

㉗ HATHORNE: Surely it have no bearing on the question, sir. He charges contemplation of murder.

DANFORTH: Aye. *He studies* ABIGAIL *for a moment, then:* Continue, Mr. Proctor.

PROCTOR: Mary. Now tell the Governor how you danced in the woods.

PARRIS, *instantly:* Excellency, since I come to Salem this man is blackening my name. He—

DANFORTH: In a moment, sir. *To* MARY WARREN, *sternly, and surprised.* What is this dancing?

MARY WARREN: I—*She glances at* ABIGAIL, *who is staring down at her remorselessly. Then, appealing to* PROCTOR: Mr. Proctor—

Reading Strategy
Categorizing Characters by Role How might Proctor classify Mary Warren? Why?

incredulously (in krej´ ōō ləs lē) *adv.* skeptically

Reading Strategy
Categorizing Characters by Role In what category would you place Hathorne? Explain.

PROCTOR, *taking it right up:* Abigail leads the girls to the woods, Your Honor, and they have danced there naked—

PARRIS: Your Honor, this—

PROCTOR, *at once:* Mr. Parris discovered them himself in the dead of night! There's the "child" she is!

DANFORTH—*it is growing into a nightmare, and he turns, astonished, to* PARRIS: Mr. Parris—

PARRIS: I can only say, sir, that I never found any of them naked, and this man is—

DANFORTH: But you discovered them dancing in the woods? *Eyes on* PARRIS, *he points at* ABIGAIL. Abigail?

HALE: Excellency, when I first arrived from Beverly, Mr. Parris told me that.

DANFORTH: Do you deny it, Mr. Parris?

PARRIS: I do not, sir, but I never saw any of them naked.

DANFORTH: But she have *danced?*

PARRIS, *unwillingly:* Aye, sir.

DANFORTH, *as though with new eyes, looks at* ABIGAIL.

HATHORNE: Excellency, will you permit me? *He points at* MARY WARREN.

DANFORTH, *with great worry:* Pray, proceed.

HATHORNE: You say you never saw no spirits, Mary, were never threatened or afflicted by any manifest of the Devil or the Devil's agents.

MARY WARREN, *very faintly:* No, sir.

HATHORNE, *with a gleam of victory:* And yet, when people accused of witchery confronted you in court, you would faint, saying their spirits came out of their bodies and choked you—

MARY WARREN: That were pretense, sir.

DANFORTH: I cannot hear you.

MARY WARREN: Pretense, sir.

PARRIS: But you did turn cold, did you not? I myself picked you up many times, and your skin were icy. Mr. Danforth, you—

DANFORTH: I saw that many times.

PROCTOR: She only pretended to faint, Your Excellency. They're all marvelous pretenders.

HATHORNE: Then can she pretend to faint now?

PROCTOR: Now?

PARRIS: Why not? Now there are no spirits attacking her, for none in this room is accused of witchcraft. So let her turn herself cold now, let her pretend she is attacked now, let her faint. *He turns to* MARY WARREN. Faint!

MARY WARREN: Faint?

PARRIS: Aye, faint. Prove to us how you pretended in the court so many times.

Reading Strategy
Categorizing Characters by Role In what category is Parris? Explain your choice.

Reading Check
What information about Abigail does Danforth find shocking?

The Crucible, Act III ◆ 1305

Reading Strategy
Categorizing Characters by Role

- Ask students the Reading Strategy question on p. 1305: In what category is Parris? Explain your choice.
  Answer: Parris will do anything to divert attention from his own role in the fraud.

- Ask students: Into what category would you place John Proctor? Explain your answer.
  Answer: Students should classify Proctor as a hero or a good character. Even though Mary's ability to faint at will would help his case enormously, he doesn't berate or abuse her; he tries not to frighten her.

Reading Check
Answer: Danforth is shocked that Abigail laughed during church services.

Dramatic and Verbal Irony and Logical Fallacy

- Ask students the Literary Analysis question on p. 1306: In what sense does Danforth's question express a logical fallacy?

  Answer: Danforth's question assumes that Mary Warren's ability to faint depends on the presence of spirits.

- Then, ask students to speculate about why Mary was able to faint in the past, but cannot do so now.

  Answer: Mary had been stirred up by the frenzy around her—the other girls claimed they were affected by spirits, so Mary did, too.

31 ▶ Critical Viewing

Answer: The photograph shows a dramatic moment. Everyone is paying attention to what is happening. Everyone looks alert, intense, or frightened.

MARY WARREN, *looking to* PROCTOR: I—cannot faint now, sir.

PROCTOR, *alarmed, quietly:* Can you not pretend it?

MARY WARREN: I—*She looks about as though searching for the passion to faint.* I—have no *sense* of it now, I—

DANFORTH: Why? What is lacking now?

MARY WARREN: I—cannot tell, sir, I—

30 **DANFORTH:** Might it be that here we have no afflicting spirit loose, but in the court there were some?

MARY WARREN: I never saw no spirits.

PARRIS: Then see no spirits now, and prove to us that you can faint by your own will, as you claim.

MARY WARREN, *stares, searching for the emotion of it, and then shakes her head:* I— cannot do it.

PARRIS: Then you will confess, will you not? It were attacking spirits made you faint!

MARY WARREN: No, sir, I—

PARRIS: Your Excellency, this is a trick to blind the court!

MARY WARREN: It's not a trick! *She stands.* I—I used to faint because I—I thought I saw spirits.

DANFORTH: *Thought* you saw them!

MARY WARREN: But I did not, Your Honor.

HATHORNE: How could you think you saw them unless you saw them?

MARY WARREN: I—I cannot tell how, but I did. I—I heard the other girls screaming, and you, Your Honor, you seemed to believe them, and I—It

Literary Analysis
Dramatic and Visual Irony and Logical Fallacy
In what sense does Danforth's question express a logical fallacy?

31 ▼ **Critical Viewing**
In this scene, Parris and Danforth order Mary to pretend to faint. Analyze this movie still and describe the emotions conveyed by Parris, Danforth, Mary, and the girls. **[Analyze]**

were only sport in the beginning, sir, but then the whole world cried spirits, spirits, and I—I promise you, Mr. Danforth, I only thought I saw them but I did not.

DANFORTH *peers at her.*

PARRIS, *smiling, but nervous because* DANFORTH *seems to be struck by* MARY WARREN'S *story:* Surely Your Excellency is not taken by this simple lie.

DANFORTH, *turning worriedly to* ABIGAIL: Abigail. I bid you now search your heart and tell me this—and beware of it, child, to God every soul is precious and His vengeance is terrible on them that take life without cause. Is it possible, child, that the spirits you have seen are illusion only, some deception that may cross your mind when—

ABIGAIL: Why, this—this—is a base question, sir.

DANFORTH: Child, I would have you consider it—

ABIGAIL: I have been hurt, Mr. Danforth; I have seen my blood runnin' out! I have been near to murdered every day because I done my duty pointing out the Devil's people—and this is my reward? To be mistrusted, denied, questioned like a—

DANFORTH, *weakening:* Child, I do not mistrust you—

ABIGAIL, *in an open threat:* Let you beware, Mr. Danforth. Think you to be so mighty that the power of Hell may not turn *your* wits? Beware of it! There is—*Suddenly, from an accusatory attitude, her face turns, looking into the air above—it is truly frightened.*

DANFORTH, *apprehensively:* What is it, child?

ABIGAIL, *looking about in the air, clasping her arms about her as though cold:* I—I know not. A wind, a cold wind, has come. *Her eyes fall on* MARY WARREN.

MARY WARREN, *terrified, pleading:* Abby!

MERCY LEWIS, *shivering:* Your Honor, I freeze!

PROCTOR: They're pretending!

HATHORNE, *touching* ABIGAIL'S *hand:* She is cold, Your Honor, touch her!

MERCY LEWIS, *through chattering teeth:* Mary, do you send this shadow on me?

MARY WARREN: Lord, save me!

SUSANNA WALCOTT: I freeze, I freeze!

ABIGAIL, *shivering, visibly:* It is a wind, a wind!

MARY WARREN: Abby, don't do that!

DANFORTH, *himself engaged and entered by* ABIGAIL: Mary Warren, do you witch her? I say to you, do you send your spirit out?

With a hysterical cry MARY WARREN *starts to run.* PROCTOR *catches her.*

MARY WARREN, *almost collapsing:* Let me go, Mr. Proctor, I cannot, I cannot—

ABIGAIL, *crying to Heaven:* Oh, Heavenly Father, take away this shadow!

Without warning or hesitation, PROCTOR *leaps at* ABIGAIL *and, grabbing*

Literary Analysis
Dramatic and Verbal Irony Which kind of irony does Abigail's speech about her "blood runnin' out" demonstrate? Explain.

 Reading Check
What threat does Abigail level at Judge Danforth?

The Crucible, Act III ◆ 1307

 **Literary Analysis**
Dramatic and Verbal Irony

- Ask students the Literary Analysis question on p. 1307: Which kind of irony does Abigail's speech about her "blood runnin' out" demonstrate? Explain.
  Answer: Abigail describes herself as a victim when in fact she is the accuser. This is verbal irony.

- Why do Abigail and the others suddenly pretend to be cold and to see spirits?
  Answer: They want to reinforce Danforth's belief in their innocence, and they realize he is beginning to doubt them.

Reading Check

Answer: She implies that she may accuse him of witchcraft.

34 ▶Critical Viewing

Answer: Students may say that the high camera angle, showing the room from the point of view of the bird, is effective.

her by the hair, pulls her to her feet. She screams in pain. DANFORTH, astonished, cries, "What are you about?" and HATHORNE and PARRIS call, "Take your hands off her!" and out of it all comes PROCTOR'S roaring voice.

PROCTOR: How do you call Heaven! Whore! Whore!

HERRICK breaks PROCTOR from her.

HERRICK: John!

1308 ◆ Prosperity and Protest (1946–Present)

34 ▲Critical Viewing
Abigail pretends to be under the control of spirits. Does this scene from the movie effectively portray the scene in the play? **[Connect]**

DANFORTH: Man! Man, what do you—

PROCTOR, *breathless and in agony:* It is a whore!

DANFORTH, *dumfounded:* You charge—?

ABIGAIL: Mr. Danforth, he is lying!

PROCTOR: Mark her! Now she'll suck a scream to stab me with, but—

DANFORTH: You will prove this! This will not pass!

PROCTOR, *trembling, his life collapsing about him:* I have known her, sir. I have known her.

DANFORTH: You—you are a lecher?

FRANCIS, *horrified:* John, you cannot say such a—

PROCTOR: Oh, Francis, I wish you had some evil in you that you might know me! *To* DANFORTH: A man will not cast away his good name. You surely know that.

DANFORTH, *dumfounded:* In—in what time? In what place?

 PROCTOR, *his voice about to break, and his shame great:* In the proper place—where my beasts are bedded. On the last night of my joy, some eight months past. She used to serve me in my house, sir. *He has to clamp his jaw to keep from weeping.* A man may think God sleeps, but God sees everything. I know it now. I beg you, sir, I beg you—see her what she is. My wife, my dear good wife, took this girl soon after, sir, and put her out on the highroad. And being what she is, a lump of vanity, sir—*He is being overcome.* Excellency, forgive me, forgive me. *Angrily against himself, he turns away from the* GOVERNOR *for a moment. Then, as though to cry out is his only means of speech left:* She thinks to dance with me on my wife's grave! And well she might, for I thought of her softly. God help me, I lusted, and there *is* a promise in such sweat. But it is a whore's vengeance, and you must see it; I set myself entirely in your hands. I know you must see it now.

DANFORTH, *blanched, in horror, turning to* ABIGAIL: You deny every scrap and tittle of this?

ABIGAIL: If I must answer that, I will leave and I will not come back again!

DANFORTH *seems unsteady.*

PROCTOR: I have made a bell of my honor! I have rung the doom of my good name—you will believe me, Mr. Danforth! My wife is innocent, except she knew a whore when she saw one!

ABIGAIL, *stepping up to* DANFORTH: What look do you give me? DANFORTH *cannot speak.* I'll not have such looks! *She turns and starts for the door.*

DANFORTH: You will remain where you are! HERRICK *steps into her path. She comes up short, fire in her eyes.* Mr. Parris, go into the court and bring Goodwife Proctor out.

PARRIS, *objecting:* Your Honor, this is all a—

DANFORTH, *sharply to* PARRIS: Bring her out! And tell her not one word of what's been spoken here. And let you knock before you enter. PARRIS *goes out.* Now we shall touch the bottom of this swamp. *To* PROCTOR:

Reading Strategy
Categorizing Characters by Role Does Proctor's confession cause you to change the category to which you have assigned him? Why or why not?

blanched (blancht) *adj.* paled; whitened

Reading Check
What does John Proctor reveal about Abigail Williams?

The Crucible, Act III ◆ 1309

35 Reading Strategy
Categorizing Characters by Role

• Ask students the Reading Strategy question on p. 1309: Does Proctor's confession cause you to change the category to which you have assigned him? Why or why not?
Answer: Students are not likely to change their opinions of Proctor, since his confession is not new information to them and they knew that he planned to denounce Abigail.

• Ask students to predict what will happen when Elizabeth comes into the room. Have them give reasons for their predictions.

36 ✔ Reading Check
Answer: He reveals that he and Abigail were lovers.

- Ask students the Literary Analysis question on p. 1310: Which details in Elizabeth's exchange with Danforth reveal the dramatic irony at work in this scene?
  Answer: Elizabeth believes that defending her husband requires her to lie, but the audience knows that in this case, defending him requires her to tell the truth.

- Ask students why Elizabeth hesitates to answer Danforth's questions.
  Answer: She knows that lechery is a crime. She wants to protect John.

- Have students read ahead to Elizabeth's line, "Oh, God!" on p. 1311. Have them analyze the dramatic irony of the scene.
  Answer: Elizabeth is an honest woman who finds it very difficult to lie. The one time that the truth is most essential is the time she decides she must lie to protect someone. Once again in Salem, lies to the court have hurt the innocent and protected the guilty.

▶ Monitor Progress Ask students what might have happened if Elizabeth had told the truth.
Answer: The judges would have been much more inclined to doubt Abigail's accusations; she would have been arrested in any case as a harlot. John might also have been arrested, but lechery is not punishable by death.

Your wife, you say, is an honest woman.

PROCTOR: In her life, sir, she have never lied. There are them that cannot sing, and them that cannot weep—my wife cannot lie. I have paid much to learn it, sir.

DANFORTH: And when she put this girl out of your house, she put her out for a harlot?

PROCTOR: Aye, sir.

DANFORTH: And knew her for a harlot?

PROCTOR: Aye, sir, she knew her for a harlot.

DANFORTH: Good then. *To* ABIGAIL: And if she tell me, child, it were for harlotry, may God spread His mercy on you! *There is a knock. He calls to the door.* Hold! *To* ABIGAIL: Turn your back. Turn your back. *To* PROCTOR: Do likewise. *Both turn their backs*—ABIGAIL *with indignant slowness.* Now let neither of you turn to face Goody Proctor. No one in this room is to speak one word, or raise a gesture aye or nay. *He turns toward the door, calls:* Enter! *The door opens.* ELIZABETH *enters with* PARRIS. PARRIS *leaves her. She stands alone, her eyes looking for* PROCTOR. Mr. Cheever, report this testimony in all exactness. Are you ready?

CHEEVER: Ready, sir.

DANFORTH: Come here, woman. ELIZABETH *comes to him, glancing at* PROCTOR'S *back.* Look at me only, not at your husband. In my eyes only.

ELIZABETH, *faintly:* Good, sir.

DANFORTH: We are given to understand that at one time you dismissed your servant, Abigail Williams.

ELIZABETH: That is true, sir.

DANFORTH: For what cause did you dismiss her? *Slight pause. Then* ELIZABETH *tries to glance at* PROCTOR. You will look in my eyes only and not at your husband. The answer is in your memory and you need no help to give it to me. Why did you dismiss Abigail Williams?

ELIZABETH, *not knowing what to say, sensing a situation, wetting her lips to stall for time:* She—dissatisfied me. *Pause.* And my husband.

DANFORTH: In what way dissatisfied you?

ELIZABETH: She were—*She glances at* PROCTOR *for a cue.*

DANFORTH: Woman, look at me? ELIZABETH *does.* Were she slovenly? Lazy? What disturbance did she cause?

ELIZABETH: Your Honor, I—in that time I were sick. And I—My husband is a good and righteous man. He is never drunk as some are, nor wastin' his time at the shovelboard, but always at his work. But in my sickness—you see, sir, I were a long time sick after my last baby, and I thought I saw my husband somewhat turning from me. And this girl—*She turns to* ABIGAIL.

DANFORTH: Look at me.

ELIZABETH: Aye, sir. Abigail Williams—*She breaks off.*

**Literary Analysis
Dramatic and Verbal Irony** Which details in Elizabeth's exchange with Danforth reveal the dramatic irony at work in this scene?

DANFORTH: What of Abigail Williams?

ELIZABETH: I came to think he fancied her. And so one night I lost my wits, I think, and put her out on the highroad.

DANFORTH: Your husband—did he indeed turn from you?

ELIZABETH, *in agony:* My husband—is a goodly man, sir.

DANFORTH: Then he did not turn from you.

ELIZABETH, *starting to glance at* PROCTOR: He—

DANFORTH, *reaches out and holds her face, then:* Look at me! To your own knowledge, has John Proctor ever committed the crime of lechery? *In a crisis of indecision she cannot speak.* Answer my question! Is your husband a lecher!

ELIZABETH, *faintly:* No, sir.

DANFORTH: Remove her, Marshal.

PROCTOR: Elizabeth, tell the truth!

DANFORTH: She has spoken. Remove her!

PROCTOR, *crying out:* Elizabeth, I have confessed it!

ELIZABETH: Oh, God! *The door closes behind her.*

PROCTOR: She only thought to save my name!

HALE: Excellency, it is a natural lie to tell; I beg you, stop now before another is condemned! I may shut my conscience to it no more—private vengeance is working through this testimony! From the beginning this man has struck me true. By my oath to Heaven, I believe him now, and I pray you call back his wife before we—

DANFORTH: She spoke nothing of lechery, and this man has lied!

HALE: I believe him! *Pointing at* ABIGAIL: This girl has always struck me false! She has—

ABIGAIL, *with a weird, wild, chilling cry, screams up to the ceiling.*

ABIGAIL: You will not! Begone! Begone, I say!

DANFORTH: What is it, child? *But* ABIGAIL, *pointing with fear, is now raising up her frightened eyes, her awed face, toward the ceiling—the girls are doing the same—and now* HATHORNE, HALE, PUTNAM, CHEEVER, HERRICK, *and* DANFORTH *do the same. What's there? He lowers his eyes from the ceiling, and now he is frightened; there is real tension in his voice.* Child! *She is transfixed—with all the girls, she is whimpering, openmouthed, agape at the ceiling.* Girls! Why do you—?

MERCY LEWIS, *pointing:* It's on the beam! Behind the rafter!

DANFORTH, *looking up:* Where!

ABIGAIL: Why—? *She gulps.* Why do you come, yellow bird?

PROCTOR: Where's a bird? I see no bird!

ABIGAIL, *to the ceiling:* My face? My face?

PROCTOR: Mr. Hale—

DANFORTH: Be quiet!

PROCTOR, *to* HALE: Do you see a bird?

Reading Strategy

Categorizing Characters by Role What qualities or characteristics does Elizabeth now demonstrate?

38

39

Literary Analysis

Dramatic and Verbal Irony What does the audience know that Danforth does not know?

40 ✔ **Reading Check**

In what ways do John and Elizabeth's testimony differ? Why?

The Crucible, Act III. ◆ *1311*

---

38 **Reading Strategy**

Categorizing Characters by Role

- Ask students the Reading Strategy question on p. 1311: What qualities or characteristics does Elizabeth now demonstrate?
  Answer: She shows her love and protective feelings toward her husband.

- Ask students whether Elizabeth's action is heroic. If so, in what way?
  Possible answer: Elizabeth has done something that was very hard for her. She has committed the sin of lying in order to protect someone. This makes her action heroic, in spite of its unintended outcome.

39 **Literary Analysis**

Dramatic and Verbal Irony

- Ask students the Literary Analysis question on p. 1311: What does the audience know that Danforth does not know?
  Answer: The audience knows that the girls are pretending.

- Why does Abigail choose this moment to scream?
  Answer: She knows that Danforth may listen to Hale; she needs to distract attention from the conversation about adultery.

40 ✔ **Reading Check**

Answer: John says that Elizabeth knew that Abigail was a harlot; Elizabeth denies it.

CUSTOMIZING INSTRUCTION FOR UNIVERSAL ACCESS

For Special Needs Students

Check comprehension and help maintain student interest by having students ask questions of the characters. Have students generate a list of questions they would like to ask these characters at this point in the play:

Mary Warren

Danforth

John Proctor

Abigail

Elizabeth Proctor

Allow students to work in pairs and answer one another's questions, as in the following:

Question: Elizabeth, why did you lie in court?

Answer: I wanted to protect my husband.

Literature

The Scarlet Letter tells the story of Hester Prynne, a married woman living alone in Boston. When Hester's pregnancy becomes obvious, she is charged with adultery and condemned to wear the scarlet letter of the title, an *A* for adultery, on her clothing at all times. Hester accepts her punishment and continues to live in the community. She refuses to name the child's father. As her daughter Pearl grows older, readers realize that Pearl's father is the minister, Arthur Dimmesdale. In the end, Dimmesdale publicly confesses his love for Hester, acknowledges Pearl as his child, and dies. The novel is remarkable because the "fallen woman" is the heroine. Hester is the novel's only sympathetic character, just as Proctor, guilty of the same crime, is one of the few sympathetic characters in *The Crucible*.

42 Literary Analysis

Dramatic and Verbal Irony

- Ask students: Which type of irony do Abigail's words represent? Explain.
  Possible answers: Her words "She sees nothin'" represent verbal irony. They are true, but she intends everyone to think they are a lie.

- Ask students why the girls' repetition of Mary's words is ironic.
  Answer: All children play this mimicking game. It is ironic because it is a game played by innocent children, but the children here are not innocent and their actions have gone far beyond playing a game.

DANFORTH: Be quiet!!

ABIGAIL, *to the ceiling, in a genuine conversation with the "bird," as though trying to talk it out of attacking her:* But God made my face; you cannot want to tear my face. Envy is a deadly sin, Mary.

MARY WARREN, *on her feet with a spring, and horrified, pleading:* Abby!

ABIGAIL, *unperturbed, continuing to the "bird":* Oh, Mary, this is a black art to change your shape. No, I cannot, I cannot stop my mouth; it's God's work I do.

MARY WARREN: Abby, I'm *here!*

PROCTOR, *frantically:* They're pretending, Mr. Danforth!

ABIGAIL—*now she takes a backward step, as though in fear the bird will swoop down momentarily:* Oh, please, Mary! Don't come down.

SUSANNA WALCOTT: Her claws, she's stretching her claws!

PROCTOR: Lies, lies.

ABIGAIL, *backing further, eyes still fixed above:* Mary, please don't hurt me!

MARY WARREN, *to* DANFORTH: I'm not hurting her!

DANFORTH, *to* MARY WARREN: Why does she see this vision?

MARY WARREN: She sees nothin'!

42 **ABIGAIL,** *now staring full front as though hypnotized, and mimicking the exact tone of* MARY WARREN'S *cry:* She sees nothin'!

MARY WARREN, *pleading:* Abby, you mustn't!

ABIGAIL AND ALL THE GIRLS, *all transfixed:* Abby, you mustn't!

MARY WARREN, *to all the girls:* I'm here, I'm here!

GIRLS: I'm here, I'm here!

DANFORTH, *horrified:* Mary Warren! Draw back your spirit out of them!

MARY WARREN: Mr. Danforth!

GIRLS, *cutting her off:* Mr. Danforth!

DANFORTH: Have you compacted with the Devil? Have you?

MARY WARREN: Never, never!

GIRLS: Never, never!

DANFORTH, *growing hysterical:* Why can they only repeat you?

PROCTOR: Give me a whip—I'll stop it!

MARY WARREN: They're sporting. They—!

GIRLS: They're sporting!

MARY WARREN, *turning on them all hysterically and stamping her feet:* Abby, stop it!

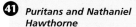
Literature in context History Connection

41 *Puritans and Nathaniel Hawthorne*

One of the many characters in *The Crucible* who have real historical counterparts is John Hathorne, a judge who took part in the Salem witchcraft trials. Hathorne's most famous descendant is the writer Nathaniel Hawthorne (see page 334), who lived in Salem during the nineteenth century. Hawthorne used the Puritan colonies of his ancestors as the settings for much of his work. In Puritan rigidity and repression he found an expression for his dark vision of the human soul.

Hawthorne's best-known novel, *The Scarlet Letter,* examines the repressive side of Puritanism and the hypocrisy and pain that such an atmosphere produced. His short stories "Young Goodman Brown" and "The Minister's Black Veil" also focus on New England's Puritan communities.

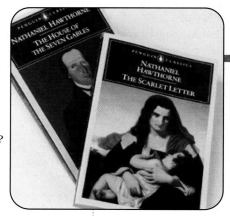

GIRLS, *stamping their feet:* Abby, stop it!

MARY WARREN: Stop it!

GIRLS: Stop it!

MARY WARREN, *screaming it out at the top of her lungs, and raising her fists:* Stop it!!

GIRLS, *raising their fists:* Stop it!!

MARY WARREN, *utterly confounded, and becoming overwhelmed by* ABIGAIL'S *—and the girls'—utter conviction, starts to whimper, hands half raised, powerless, and all the girls begin whimpering exactly as she does.*

DANFORTH: A little while ago you were afflicted. Now it seems you afflict others; where did you find this power?

MARY WARREN, *staring at* ABIGAIL: I—have no power.

GIRLS: I have no power.

PROCTOR: They're gulling[7] you, Mister!

DANFORTH: Why did you turn about this past two weeks? You have seen the Devil, have you not?

HALE, *indicating* ABIGAIL *and the* GIRLS: You cannot believe them!

MARY WARREN: I—

PROCTOR, *sensing her weakening:* Mary, God damns all liars!

DANFORTH, *pounding it into her:* You have seen the Devil, you have made compact with Lucifer, have you not?

PROCTOR: God damns liars, Mary!

MARY *utters something unintelligible, staring at* ABIGAIL, *who keeps watching the "bird" above.*

DANFORTH: I cannot hear you. What do you say? MARY *utters again unintelligibly.* You will confess yourself or you will hang! *He turns her roughly to face him.* Do you know who I am? I say you will hang if you do not open with me!

PROCTOR: Mary, remember the angel Raphael—do that which is good and—

ABIGAIL, *pointing upward:* The wings! Her wings are spreading! Mary, please, don't, don't—!

HALE: I see nothing, Your Honor!

DANFORTH: Do you confess this power! *He is an inch from her face.* Speak!

ABIGAIL: She's going to come down! She's walking the beam!

DANFORTH: Will you speak!

MARY WARREN, *staring in horror:* I cannot!

GIRLS: I cannot!

PARRIS: Cast the Devil out! Look him in the face! Trample him! We'll save you, Mary, only stand fast against him and—

ABIGAIL, *looking up:* Look out! She's coming down!

---

7. **gulling** fooling.

Literary Analysis
Dramatic and Verbal Irony In what ways does the idea of Abigail's "utter conviction" serve as an ironic statement?

 Reading Check
What do the girls do to undermine Mary Warren's testimony?

The Crucible, Act III ◆ *1313*

**Literary Analysis**
Dramatic and Verbal Irony

- Make sure students understand that Abigail has turned against Mary in order to fool Danforth and protect her own reputation.

- Ask students the Literary Analysis question on p. 1313: In what ways does the idea of Abigail's "utter conviction" serve as an ironic statement?

  Answer: It is impossible to feel utter conviction about something that one knows is untrue. However, it is Abigail's display of utter conviction that strengthens her case; Mary's hesitance and lack of conviction make her case look weak, though she is telling the truth.

44 ✔**Reading Check**

Answer: They pretend to see Mary's spirit walking in the rafters and trying to attack them.

CUSTOMIZE INSTRUCTION FOR UNIVERSAL ACCESS

For Less Proficient Readers

While they read Act I, students learned to question a character's motivation. Have students discuss Mary's motives for recanting her confession and supporting the other girls' lies. Remind them that Mary knows her actions will lead to the arrests and possibly the deaths of innocent people. Remind students of Abigail's forcefulness and her current popularity in the town, and have them think about situations in which they have been pressured to give in to the demands of classmates. Would students have reacted differently in Mary's situation?

45 Literary Analysis
Dramatic and Verbal Irony

- Ask students the Literary Analysis question on p. 1314: Which two words in these stage directions describing Abigail and Mary are an example of verbal irony?
  Answer: The words "infinite charity" are ironic because in feigning "charity," Abigail is once again acting out of self-interest.

- Why is Mary's accusation of Proctor ironic?
  Answer: Proctor is the only person who tried to help her crush the fraud.

▶ Monitor Progress Have students read Proctor's speech on p. 1315 and analyze its verbal irony.
  Answer: Proctor has tried to do the right thing—to show up the fraud—and for this he is condemned to hang for witchcraft. It is ironic that he is falsely condemned.

She and all the girls run to one wall, shielding their eyes. And now, as though cornered, they let out a gigantic scream, and MARY, *as though infected, opens her mouth and screams with them. Gradually* ABIGAIL *and the girls leave off, until only* MARY *is left there, staring up at the "bird," screaming madly. All watch her, horrified by this evident fit.* PROCTOR *strides to her.*

PROCTOR: Mary, tell the Governor what they—*He has hardly got a word out, when, seeing him coming for her, she rushes out of his reach, screaming in horror.*

MARY WARREN: Don't touch me—don't touch me! *At which the girls halt at the door.*

PROCTOR, *astonished:* Mary!

MARY WARREN, *pointing at* PROCTOR: You're the Devil's man!

He is stopped in his tracks.

PARRIS: Praise God!

GIRLS: Praise God!

PROCTOR, *numbed:* Mary, how— ?

MARY WARREN: I'll not hang with you! I love God, I love God.

DANFORTH, *to* MARY: He bid you do the Devil's work?

MARY WARREN, *hysterically, indicating* PROCTOR: He come at me by night and every day to sign, to sign, to—

DANFORTH: Sign what?

PARRIS: The Devil's book? He come with a book?

MARY WARREN, *hysterically, pointing at* PROCTOR, *fearful of him:* My name, he want my name. "I'll murder you," he says, "if my wife hangs! We must go and overthrow the court," he says!

DANFORTH'S *head jerks toward* PROCTOR, *shock and horror in his face.*

PROCTOR, *turning, appealing to* HALE: Mr. Hale!

MARY WARREN, *her sobs beginning:* He wake me every night, his eyes were like coals and his fingers claw my neck, and I sign, I sign . . .

HALE: Excellency, this child's gone wild!

PROCTOR, *as* DANFORTH'S *wide eyes pour on him:* Mary, Mary!

45 **MARY WARREN,** *screaming at him:* No, I love God; I go your way no more. I love God, I bless God. *Sobbing, she rushes to* ABIGAIL. Abby, Abby, I'll never hurt you more! *They all watch, as* ABIGAIL, *out of her infinite charity, reaches out and draws the sobbing* MARY *to her, and then looks up to* DANFORTH.

DANFORTH, *to* PROCTOR: What are you? PROCTOR *is beyond speech in his anger.* You are combined with anti-Christ,[8] are you not? I have seen your power; you will not deny it! What say you, Mister?

HALE: Excellency—

---

8. **anti-Christ** In the Bible, the great antagonist of Christ expected to spread universal evil.

Literary Analysis
Dramatic and Verbal Irony Which two words in these stage directions describing Abigail and Mary are an example of verbal irony?

DANFORTH: I will have nothing from you, Mr. Hale! *To* PROCTOR: Will you confess yourself befouled with Hell, or do you keep that black allegiance yet? What say you?

PROCTOR, *his mind wild, breathless:* I say—I say—God is dead!

PARRIS: Hear it, hear it!

PROCTOR, *laughs insanely, then:* A fire, a fire is burning! I hear the boot of Lucifer, I see his filthy face! And it is my face, and yours, Danforth! For them that quail to bring men out of ignorance, as I have quailed, and as you quail now when you know in all your black hearts that this be fraud—God damns our kind especially, and we will burn, we will burn together.

DANFORTH: Marshal! Take him and Corey with him to the jail!

HALE, *staring across to the door:* I denounce these proceedings!

PROCTOR: You are pulling Heaven down and raising up a whore!

HALE: I denounce these proceedings, I quit this court! *He slams the door to the outside behind him.*

DANFORTH, *calling to him in a fury:* Mr. Hale! Mr. Hale!

Review and Assess

Thinking About Act III

1. **Respond:** Which incident in Act III provoked the strongest emotional response in you? Why?

2. (a) **Recall:** Which three depositions are presented to the judges and on whose behalf? (b) **Analyze:** How do the judges discourage defenses of the accused?

3. (a) **Recall:** What does John Proctor confess to Danforth? (b) **Interpret:** Why does Proctor make this confession? (c) **Infer:** What does his confession reveal about his character?

4. (a) **Recall:** What is the lie Elizabeth Proctor tells Danforth? (b) **Analyze:** What are the consequences of her lie?

5. (a) **Recall:** What truth does Mary Warren reveal about her involvement with "spirits"? (b) **Analyze:** Why does she change her testimony and turn on John Proctor?

6. (a) **Recall:** What does Hale denounce at the end of Act III? (b) **Evaluate:** Do you find Hale sympathetic? Why or why not?

7. **Apply:** Imagine that Elizabeth Proctor had told Danforth the truth. In what way might the outcome of the trials have been different?

8. **Assess:** Who bears the most guilt for the fate of those hanged in the Salem witch trials—the girls who accused innocent people or the judges who sentenced them to death?

The Crucible, Act III ◆ 1315

✎ STANDARDIZED TEST APPLICATION: Writing Skills

Using Commas Correctly	**(For more practice, see Test Preparation Workbook, p. 77.)**

Many tests require students to identify errors in punctuation. Use this following sample test item.

DANFORTH I will have nothing from you Mr. Hale!

After which word should you insert a comma?

A I

B have

C you

D no comma needed

The name of the person being addressed must be set off with a comma. The correct answer is *C*.

Review and Assess

1. Sample answers: Abigail's cry, "She sees nothin'!", is an example of verbal irony; what she says is true, but she intends everyone to believe that it is false. Elizabeth's denial of knowledge of the affair between John and Abigail is a lie; ironically, but everyone believes it because of her reputation for honesty.

2. The audience knows that Proctor has confessed to the affair.

3. She achieves the opposite of what she wanted to achieve: Her husband is arrested, and the court's confidence in Abigail is restored.

4. Mary has the power to stop the proceedings by telling the truth.

5. Danforth does not allow for the possibility that an accused person may be innocent.

6. If an accusation is enough to condemn a person, there can be no justice.

7. **(a)** Parris cares only for the strong social position that the ministry gives him. Everything he does in the play is done only to protect himself. Hale is genuinely interested in theology and tries to do right. **(b)** Parris is a villain. Hale is a dynamic character who gives the audience hope that those on the side of the accusers may be brought to see reason.

8. **(a)** All three are easily led and frightened. None seems to have a conscience. **(b)** Students may sympathize with the girls' fears of punishment in Act I but are not likely to sympathize with their willingness to see innocent people hanged.

9. Elizabeth and Hale are dynamic characters. The others are static characters. Parris has been frightened throughout the play; Abigail has lied throughout; and Proctor has acted according to his conscience throughout.

10. Ask students to explain their answers.

11. Judges are supposed to be impartial. Both Danforth and Hale assume that those accused must be guilty before they hear any evidence.

Review and Assess

Literary Analysis

Dramatic and Verbal Irony

1. Using a chart like the one shown, list three examples of **dramatic and verbal irony** from Act III. Identify the type of irony and explain what each speaker really means.

Passage	Type of Irony	Analysis

2. What does the audience know that Elizabeth does not know when she testifies about her husband's behavior?

3. Why is the effect of Elizabeth's testimony ironic?

4. What is ironic about Mary Warren's statement, "I—have no power," when she is being interrogated in front of Abigail Williams?

Connecting Literary Elements

5. In Judge Danforth's dramatic exchange with Reverend Hale, what erroneous idea underlies all his reasoning about the legal proceedings? Explain.

6. In what sense does Danforth's **logical fallacy** have ramifications far beyond the conviction of John Proctor?

Reading Strategy

Categorizing Characters by Role

7. (a) Compare and contrast Reverend Parris with Reverend Hale. (b) How would you **categorize** the effectiveness of each in his role as minister?

8. (a) Which character traits would you ascribe to Betty Parris, Sarah Good, and Mercy Lewis? (b) Do you have sympathy for them? Why or why not?

9. Which characters would you classify as static (unchanging), and which would you classify as dynamic (changing or growing)? Why?

10. What other categories do you think would be useful for classifying the characters? Explain.

Extend Understanding

11. **Career Connection:** Which qualities of a good judge do you think are lacking in Hathorne and Danforth? Explain.

1316 ◆ *Prosperity and Protest (1946–Present)*

Quick Review

Dramatic irony occurs when there is a contradiction between what a character thinks and what the audience knows to be true.

Verbal irony occurs when a character says one thing but means something else.

A **logical fallacy** is an argument that appears logical but is based on a faulty premise.

To understand the characters' roles in a play, **categorize the characters** in meaningful ways.

 Take It to the Net
www.phschool.com
Take the interactive self-test online to check your understanding of this selection.

TEACHING RESOURCES

The following resources can be used to enrich or extend the instructions for p. 1317.

Vocabulary

📖 **Selection Support:** Build Vocabulary, p. 322

📖 **Vocabulary and Spelling Practice Book** (Use this booklet for skills enrichment.) 📄

Grammar

📖 **Selection Support:** Grammar and Style, p. 323

W&G **Writing and Grammar,** Ruby Level, p. 584

🖥 **Daily Language Practice Transparencies** 📄

Writing

W&G **Writing and Grammar,** Ruby Level, p. 97 📄

💿 **Writing and Grammar iText CD-ROM**

 **BLOCK SCHEDULING:** Resources marked with this symbol provide varied instruction during 90-minute blocks.

Integrate Language Skills

❶ Vocabulary Development Lesson

Concept Development: Legal Terms

The Crucible contains a number of legal terms. For example, a *deposition* is a legal document that contains the written testimony of a witness. Determine the meaning of each of these words from the context in which it appears in Act III. Then, use each word in a sentence.

1. prosecutor   2. contempt   3. perjury

Spelling Strategy

When adding an *-ly* suffix to a word that ends in a consonant, do not double or change the consonant. The words *deferentially* and *incredulously* follow this rule. Change each of the following adjectives into adverbs by adding the suffix *-ly:*

1. dubious   2. bountiful   3. obvious

Concept Development: Relationships

Review the vocabulary list on page 1290. Then, for each item below, indicate whether the paired words are synonyms or antonyms.

1. contentious, combative
2. deposition, testimony
3. imperceptible, obvious
4. deferentially, politely
5. anonymity, notoriety
6. prodigious, minuscule
7. effrontery, timidity
8. confounded, puzzled
9. incredulously, disbelievingly
10. blanched, darkened

❷ Grammar and Style Lesson

Subject and Verb Agreement in Inverted Sentences

In most sentences, the subject precedes the verb, but in an **inverted sentence** the verb comes first. Notice how the verb **agrees** in number with the subject of the following inverted sentences.

Plural: Now there $\underset{V}{\underline{are}}$ no $\underset{S}{\underline{spirits}}$ attacking her.

Practice Complete each sentence by choosing the correct form of the verb in parentheses.

1. There (is, are) a courtroom scene in Act III.
2. In the courtroom (sits, sit) many people.
3. Hearing the case (is, are) Danforth and Hathorne.
4. Here (is, are) Abigail and her cohorts.
5. Under suspicion (is, are) dozens of citizens.

Writing Application As Reverend Hale, write a letter to the editor of the Salem newspaper explaining why you now oppose the court's actions. Use three inverted sentences, and make your subjects and verbs agree in number.

W̶G *Prentice Hall Writing and Grammar Connection: Chapter 23, Section 1*

❸ Extension Activities

Writing Write a **character sketch** of Mary Warren in which you evaluate her strengths and weaknesses.

Listening and Speaking Draft and perform the monologue Elizabeth might give at the moment she learns the effect of her lie in court.

The Crucible, Act III ◆ 1317

EXTEND

Answers for p. 1317

❶ Vocabulary Development

Concept Development

Sample sentences are given.

1. attorney for the court: The prosecutor cross-examined the witness for the defense.
2. refusal to cooperate: The man who yelled at the judge was thrown out of court for contempt.
3. false testimony: Perjury is a crime because a witness swears an oath to tell the truth.

Spelling Strategy

1. dubiously
2. bountifully
3. obviously

Concept Development: Relationships

1. Synonyms	6. Antonyms
2. Synonyms	7. Antonyms
3. Antonyms	8. Synonyms
4. Synonyms	9. Synonyms
5. Antonyms	10. Antonyms

❷ Grammar Lesson

1. is	4. are
2. sit	5. are
3. are	

Writing Application

Check students' paragraphs.

❸ Extension Activities

Writing Lesson

Make sure that students' essays accurately reflect Mary's speeches and actions.

Listening and Speaking

If students prefer not to perform their monologues, allow them to work with partners. The writer can direct the other student's reading.

CUSTOMIZE INSTRUCTION
For Universal Access

To address different learning styles, use the following activities suggested in the **Extension Activities** booklet, p. 75.

For Verbal/Linguistic Learners, use Activities 5 and 6.

For Logical/Mathematical Learners, use Activity 7.

📺 **BLOCK SCHEDULING:** Resources marked with this symbol provide varied instruction during 90-minute blocks.

The Crucible, Act IV

Lesson Objectives

1. **To analyze and respond to literary elements**
   - Literary Analysis: Theme
   - Connecting Literary Elements: Extended Metaphor
2. **To read, comprehend, analyze, and critique a drama**
   - Reading Strategy: Applying Themes to Contemporary Events
   - Reading Check Questions
   - Review and Assess Questions
3. **To develop word analysis skills, fluency, and systematic vocabulary**
   - Vocabulary Development Lesson: Concept Development: Words From Myths
4. **To understand and apply written and oral language conventions**
   - Spelling Strategy
   - Grammar and Style Lesson: Commonly Confused Words
   - Assessment Practice (ATE)
5. **To understand and apply appropriate writing and research strategies**
   - Writing Lesson: Defense of a Character's Actions
   - Extension Activity: Compare and Contrast Chart
6. **To understand and apply listening and speaking strategies**
   - Extension Activity: Mock Trial

STEP-BY-STEP TEACHING GUIDE	PACING GUIDE
PRETEACH	
Motivate Students and Provide Background	
Use the Motivation activity (ATE p. 1230)	5 min.
Read and discuss author and background features (SE/ATE p. 1230–1231)	5 min.
Introduce the Concepts	
Introduce the Literary Analysis and Reading Strategy (SE/ATE p. 1318)	10 min.
Pronounce the vocabulary words and read their definitions (SE p. 1318)	5 min.
TEACH	
Monitor Comprehension	
Informally monitor comprehension by circulating while students read independently or in groups	45 min.
Monitor students' comprehension with the Reading Check notes (SE/ATE pp. 1319, 1321, 1323, 1325, 1327, 1329, 1331, 1333)	as students read
Develop vocabulary with Vocabulary notes (SE pp. 1322, 1324, 1326, 1329, 1331; ATE p. 1329)	as students read
Develop Understanding	
Develop students' understanding of theme with the Literary Analysis annotations (SE/ATE pp. 1319, 1320, 1321, 1324, 1325, 1326, 1327, 1329, 1330, 1331, 1333)	5 min.
Develop students' ability to apply a theme to contemporary events by using the Reading Strategy annotations (SE pp. 1321, 1323, 1332; ATE pp. 1321, 1323, 1332)	5 min.
ASSESS	
Assess Mastery	
Assess students' mastery of the Reading Strategy and Literary Analysis by having them answer the Review and Assess questions (SE/ATE p. 1335)	15 min.
Use one or more of the print and media Assessment Resources (ATE p. 1337)	up to 45 min.
EXTEND	
Apply Understanding	
Have students complete the Vocabulary Development Lesson and the Grammar and Style Lesson (SE p. 1336)	20 min.
Apply students' ability to analyze the evidence by using the Writing Lesson (SE/ATE p. 1337)	45 min.
Apply students' understanding using one or more of the Extension Activities (SE p. 1337)	20–90 min.

 ACCELERATED INSTRUCTION:
Use the strategies and activities identified with an .

UNIVERSAL ACCESS
● = Below Level Students
▲ = On-Level Students
■ = Above Level Students

Time and Resource Manager

Reading Level: Average
Average Number of Instructional Days: 4

PRINT 📖	TRANSPARENCIES	TECHNOLOGY 💿 🎧 📼
• **Beyond Literature,** Workplace Skills: Research, p. 76 ▲ ■		• **Interest Grabber Video,** Tape 6 ● ▲ ■
• **Selection Support Workbook:** ● ▲ ■ Literary Analysis, p. 329 Reading Strategy, p. 328 Build Vocabulary, p. 326	• **Literary Analysis and Reading Transparencies,** pp. 151 and 152 ● ▲ ■	
• **Literatura en español** ● ▲ • **Literary Analysis for Enrichment** ■		
• **Formal Assessment:** Selection Test, pp. 318–320 ● ▲ ■ • **Open Book Test,** pp. 226–228 ● ▲ ■ • **Performance Assessment and Portfolio Management,** p. 17 ● ▲ ■ • **PRENTICE HALL ASSESSMENT** *SYSTEM* ● ▲ ■	• **PRENTICE HALL ASSESSMENT** *SYSTEM* ● ▲ ■ Skills Practice Answers and Explanations on Transparencies	• **Test Bank Software** ● ▲ ■ • **Got It! Assessment Videotapes,** Tape 6 ● ▲
• **Selection Support Workbook:** ● ▲ ■ Grammar and Style, p. 327 • **Writing and Grammar,** Ruby Level ● ▲ ■ • **Extension Activities,** p. 76 ● ▲ ■	• **Daily Language Practice Transparencies** ● ▲ • **Writing Models and Graphic Organizers on Transparencies,** pp. 33–36 ● ▲ ■	• **Writing and Grammar iText CD-ROM** ● ▲ ■ 💻 *Take It to the Net* www.phschool.com

BLOCK SCHEDULING: Use one 90-minute class period to preteach the selection and have students read it. Use a second 90-minute class period to assess students' mastery of skills and have them complete one of the Extension Activities.

Theme

- Explain that a work's theme comprises both main idea and author's purpose. The theme is the concept that a writer most wants the reader to take away and think about. The plot, characters, and setting are all chosen to illustrate the theme. The theme is also the reason the author wrote the work. Miller wrote *The Crucible* because he wanted to express certain beliefs about human nature.

- Ask students to name some themes Miller introduced and developed during the first three acts.

  Possible answers: Unresolved conflicts between people can have tragic results; fear and hypocrisy are a deadly combination.

2 Reading Strategy

Applying Themes to Contemporary Events

- Share the Background information on the McCarthy era on p. 1240 of this teacher's edition.

- Remind students that in this case, "contemporary" does not refer to the present time; it refers to the time in which the play was written.

- Have students share what they know about the political climate in the United States during the years leading up to *The Crucible*. Remind them that during World War II, the enemies of the United States were fascist states. Ask students to notice any anti-fascist messages or themes in the play, such as Cheever's claim that he is only following the orders of the court when he arrests Elizabeth. What do students think this statement would have suggested to this play's contemporary audience?

  Answer: Students may recall that the same defense was offered at the Nuremberg trials by Nazi war criminals.

Vocabulary Development

- Pronounce each vocabulary word for students, and read the definitions as a class. Have students identify any words with which they are already familiar.

Prepare to Read

The Crucible, Act IV

1 Literary Analysis

Theme

A **theme** is the central idea or insight into life that a writer strives to convey in a work of literature. Like most longer works, *The Crucible* has several themes. One theme is that fear and suspicion are infectious and can turn into mass hysteria. Miller also touches upon the destructive power of guilt, revenge, and the failure of a judicial system fueled by ideology instead of justice. As you read Act IV, use a chart like the one shown to consider these and other themes that Miller conveys.

Connecting Literary Elements

An **extended metaphor** is a comparison that is developed throughout the course of a literary work. Miller's imagery of the seventeenth-century witch hunt in Salem builds a comparison to the events of the late 1940s and early 1950s in America, a time characterized by these intensified emotions:

- Fear of communism and a widespread hysteria that Communists had infiltrated the State Department.
- Panic based on witch hunt tactics—those who opposed McCarthy's hearings were charged with Communism themselves.

Notice Miller's ability to explore the events of his own era within the parallel context of the Salem witchcraft trials.

2 Reading Strategy

Applying Themes to Contemporary Events

The parallel between the events in Salem, as Miller depicts them, and ongoing events in Congress at the time Miller wrote the play are clear. As you read Act IV, think about what themes or messages Miller was conveying that specifically related to contemporary events.

Vocabulary Development

agape (ə gāp´) *adj.* wide open (p. 1322)

conciliatory (kən sil´ ē ə tôr´ ē) *adj.* tending to soothe anger (p. 1324)

beguile (bē gīl´) *v.* trick (p. 1324)

floundering (floun´ də riŋ) *n.* awkward struggling (p. 1324)

retaliation (ri ta´ lē ā´ shən) *n.* act of returning an injury or wrong (p. 1324)

adamant (ad´ ə mənt) *adj.* firm; unyielding (p. 1324)

cleave (klēv) *v.* adhere; cling (p. 1326)

sibilance (sib´ əl əns) *n.* hissing sound (p. 1326)

tantalized (tan´ tə līzd) *adj.* tormented; frustrated (p. 1329)

purged (pʉrjd) *v.* cleansed (p. 1331)

1318 ◆ *Prosperity and Protest (1946–Present)*

Topic

Events in Play

Theme

TEACHING RESOURCES

The following resources can be used to enrich or extend the instruction for p. 1318.

Motivation

▭ **Interest Grabber Video**, Tape 6

Background

▭ **Beyond Literature**, p. 76 ▪

▭ *Take It to the Net*

Visit www.phschool.com for Background and hotlinks for *The Crucible*.

Literary Analysis

▪ **Literary Analysis and Reading Transparencies**, Theme, p. 152 ▪

Reading

▭ **Selection Support:** Reading Strategy, p. 328; Build Vocabulary, p. 326

▪ **Literary Analysis and Reading Transparencies**, Applying Themes to Contemporary Events, p. 151

▪ **BLOCK SCHEDULING:** Resources marked with this symbol provide varied instruction during 90-minute blocks.

❶ Review and Anticipate

"Is every defense an attack upon the court?" Hale asks in Act III. Danforth observes, "A person is either with this court or he must be counted against it." Such remarks stress the powerlessness of people like John Proctor and Giles Corey against the mounting injustices in Salem. In pursuing justice, their efforts backfire, and their own names join the list of those accused. What do you think the final outcome will be? Who will survive, and who will perish? Read the final act to see if your predictions are correct.

ACT IV

A cell in Salem jail, that fall.

❷ *At the back is a high barred window; near it, a great, heavy door. Along the walls are two benches.*

The place is in darkness but for the moonlight seeping through the bars. It appears empty. Presently footsteps are heard coming down a corridor beyond the wall, keys rattle, and the door swings open. MARSHAL HERRICK *enters with a lantern.*

He is nearly drunk, and heavy-footed. He goes to a bench and nudges a bundle of rags lying on it.

HERRICK: Sarah, wake up! Sarah Good! *He then crosses to the other benches.*

SARAH GOOD, *rising in her rags:* Oh, Majesty! Comin',comin'! Tituba, he's here, His Majesty's come!

HERRICK: Go to the north cell; this place is wanted now. *He hangs his lantern on the wall.* TITUBA *sits up.*

TITUBA: That don't look to me like His Majesty; look to me like the marshal.

HERRICK, *taking out a flask:* Get along with you now, clear this place. *He drinks, and* SARAH GOOD *comes and peers up into his face.*

SARAH GOOD: Oh, is it you, Marshal! I thought sure you be the devil comin' for us. Could I have a sip of cider for me goin'-away?

HERRICK, *handing her the flask:* And where are you off to, Sarah?

TITUBA, *as* SARAH *drinks:* We goin' to Barbados, soon the Devil gits here with the feathers and the wings.

HERRICK: Oh? A happy voyage to you.

SARAH GOOD: A pair of bluebirds wingin' southerly, the two of us! Oh, it be a grand transformation, Marshal! *She raises the flask to drink again.*

HERRICK, *taking the flask from her lips:* You'd best give me that or you'll never rise off the ground. Come along now.

Literary Analysis

Theme In what ways do these stage directions describing an empty cell help to convey a theme?

❸

✔Reading Check

Who is Sarah Good talking about in this scene?

The Crucible, Act IV ◆ *1319*

TEACHING RESOURCES

The following resources can be used to enrich or extend the instruction for pp. 1319–1334.

Literary Analysis

📗 **Writing Models and Graphic Organizers on Transparencies,** pp. 33–36 ▪️

📖 **Selection Support:** Literary Analysis, p. 329

▪️ **BLOCK SCHEDULING:** Resources marked with this symbol provide varied instruction during 90-minute blocks.

TEACH

Step-by-Step Teaching Guide for pp. 1319–1334

CUSTOMIZE INSTRUCTION For Logical/Mathematical Learners

Have students discuss whether John Proctor qualifies as a tragic hero in the classical tradition. Review with them the definition of a tragic hero. Have them reread the play, looking for evidence to support their answers. Students may want to divide into two groups to debate the question.

❶ About Act IV

Parris pleads with the judges for a postponement of the hangings; he fears that the town will revolt if residents such as Rebecca Nurse are hanged without having confessed. Danforth agrees to a last attempt to persuade Proctor to confess and thus escape death. Elizabeth has the best chance to persuade him.

Left alone together, the Proctors ask each other's forgiveness. John asks whether he should falsely confess to witchcraft. Elizabeth tells him to do as he thinks best; she believes in his goodness either way.

Proctor confesses to having seen the Devil but refuses to name anyone else. He reluctantly signs his confession, but then tears it up, proclaiming that he prefers hanging to living a lie. The sentence is carried out as the curtain falls.

❷ Literary Analysis

Theme

- Ask students the Literary Analysis question on p. 1319: In what ways do these stage directions describing an empty cell help to convey a theme?
  Answer: This setting reminds the audience of the danger that the condemned prisoners are in.

- Ask what Sarah's comments about the devil suggest. Why are these comments ironic?
  Answer: Sarah's comments are ironic because she looks on the Devil as a blessed escape. Her comments make it clear that the real Devil is in the court and its false accusations and injustice.

❸ ✔Reading Check

Answer: the Devil

1319

❹ Literary Analysis

Theme

- Ask students the Literary Analysis question on p. 1320: What theme do you think Herrick's drunkenness on execution day implies? Answer: Herrick finds the proceedings too distasteful to face without the numbness of alcohol. This suggests that he, like others, knows injustice is taking place but feels powerless to stop it.

- What theme is implied in Danforth's statement, "There is a prodigious stench in this place"? Answer: The stench is of the crimes of the court rather than of the prisoners. The broad theme suggested here is that evil cannot take place without consequences.

TITUBA: I'll speak to him for you, if you desires to come along, Marshal.

HERRICK: I'd not refuse it, Tituba; it's the proper morning to fly into Hell.

TITUBA: Oh, it be no Hell in Barbados. Devil, him be pleasure man in Barbados, him be singin' and dancin' in Barbados. It's you folks—you riles him up 'round here; it be too cold 'round here for that Old Boy. He freeze his soul in Massachusetts, but in Barbados he just as sweet and—*A bellowing cow is heard, and* TITUBA *leaps up and calls to the window:* Aye, sir! That's him, Sarah!

SARAH GOOD: I'm here, Majesty! *They hurriedly pick up their rags as* HOPKINS, *a guard, enters.*

HOPKINS: The Deputy Governor's arrived.

HERRICK, *grabbing* TITUBA: Come along, come along.

TITUBA, *resisting him:* No, he comin' for me. I goin' home!

HERRICK, *pulling her to the door:* That's not Satan, just a poor old cow with a hatful of milk. Come along now, out with you!

TITUBA, *calling to the window:* Take me home, Devil! Take me home!

SARAH GOOD, *following the shouting* TITUBA *out:* Tell him I'm goin', Tituba! Now you tell him Sarah Good is goin' too!

In the corridor outside TITUBA *calls on—"Take me home, Devil: Devil take me home!" and* HOPKINS' *voice orders her to move on.* HERRICK *returns and begins to push old rags and straw into a corner. Hearing footsteps, he turns, and enter* DANFORTH *and* JUDGE HATHORNE. *They are in greatcoats and wear hats against the bitter cold. They are followed in by* CHEEVER, *who carries a dispatch case and a flat wooden box containing his writing materials.*

HERRICK: Good morning, Excellency.

DANFORTH: Where is Mr. Parris?

HERRICK: I'll fetch him. *He starts for the door.*

DANFORTH: Marshal. HERRICK *stops.* When did Reverend Hale arrive?

HERRICK: It were toward midnight, I think.

DANFORTH, *suspiciously:* What is he about here?

HERRICK: He goes among them that will hang, sir. And he prays with them. He sits with Goody Nurse now. And Mr. Parris with him.

DANFORTH: Indeed. That man have no authority to enter here, Marshal. Why have you let him in?

HERRICK: Why, Mr. Parris command me, sir. I cannot deny him.

❹ **DANFORTH:** Are you drunk, Marshal?

HERRICK: No, sir; it is a bitter night, and I have no fire here.

DANFORTH, *containing his anger:* Fetch Mr. Parris.

HERRICK: Aye, sir.

DANFORTH: There is a prodigious stench in this place.

HERRICK: I have only now cleared the people out for you.

DANFORTH: Beware hard drink, Marshal.

Literary Analysis
Theme What theme do you think Herrick's drunkenness on execution day implies?

CUSTOMIZE INSTRUCTION FOR UNIVERSAL ACCESS

For Gifted/Talented Students

Ask students to do some research on Barbados society and culture at the turn of the seventeenth century. How many ethnic groups and nationalities were represented in the population? What were race relations like? Which country ruled Barbados? What was the climate like? Which crops were grown? What were the communities like—villages like Salem, small farms, plantations, bigger cities? Which religions were dominant? What was the relationship between church and society? Have students use these and other questions to find out about Barbados and compare and contrast it with Salem. Ask students how they think the Puritans of Salem would have reacted to Barbados. Remind them that Parris, Betty, and Tituba all come from there. What effect does this contrast have on students' understanding of what happened in the woods?

HERRICK: Aye, sir. *He waits an instant for further orders. But* DANFORTH, *in dissatisfaction, turns his back on him, and* HERRICK *goes out. There is a pause.* DANFORTH *stands in thought.*

HATHORNE: Let you question Hale, Excellency; I should not be surprised he have been preaching in Andover[1] lately.

DANFORTH: We'll come to that; speak nothing of Andover. Parris prays with him. That's strange. *He blows on his hands, moves toward the window, and looks out.*

HATHORNE: Excellency, I wonder if it be wise to let Mr. Parris so continuously with the prisoners. DANFORTH *turns to him, interested.* I think, sometimes, the man has a mad look these days.

DANFORTH: Mad?

❺ HATHORNE: I met him yesterday coming out of his house, and I bid him good morning—and he wept and went his way. I think it is not well the village sees him so unsteady.

DANFORTH: Perhaps he have some sorrow.

CHEEVER, *stamping his feet against the cold:* I think it be the cows, sir.

DANFORTH: Cows?

❻ CHEEVER: There be so many cows wanderin' the highroads, now their masters are in the jails, and much disagreement who they will belong to now. I know Mr. Parris be arguin' with farmers all yesterday—there is great contention, sir, about the cows. Contention make him weep, sir; it were always a man that weep for contention. *He turns, as do* HATHORNE *and* DANFORTH *hearing someone coming up the corridor.* DANFORTH *raises his head as* PARRIS *enters. He is gaunt, frightened, and sweating in his greatcoat.*

PARRIS, *to* DANFORTH, *instantly:* Oh, good morning, sir, thank you for coming. I beg your pardon wakin' you so early. Good morning, Judge Hathorne.

DANFORTH: Reverend Hale have no right to enter this—

PARRIS: Excellency, a moment. *He hurries back and shuts the door.*

HATHORNE: Do you leave him alone with the prisoners?

DANFORTH: What's his business here?

PARRIS, *prayerfully holding up his hands:* Excellency, hear me. It is a providence. Reverend Hale has returned to bring Rebecca Nurse to God.

DANFORTH, *surprised:* He bids her confess?

PARRIS, *sitting:* Hear me. Rebecca have not given me a word this three month since she came. Now she sits with him, and her sister and Martha Corey and two or three others, and he pleads with them, confess their crimes and save their lives.

---

1. **Andover** During the height of the terror in Salem Village, a similar hysteria broke out in the nearby town of Andover. There, many respected people were accused of practicing witchcraft and confessed to escape death. However, in Andover people soon began questioning the reality of the situation and the hysteria quickly subsided.

Literary Analysis
Theme What theme does Miller convey through Hathorne's description of Parris?

Reading Strategy
Applying Themes to Contemporary Events What warning might the details about changes in Salem convey about the growing anti-Communist fear and suspicion in Miller's own time?

 ❼ ✔Reading Check

Why are so many cows wandering the roads?

The Crucible, Act IV ◆ 1321

---

❺ Literary Analysis
Theme

- Ask students the Literary Analysis question on p. 1321: What theme does Miller convey through Hathorne's description of Parris?
  Answer: Parris has lied from the beginning and bears a great deal of responsibility for the hysteria. Parris is now suffering from guilt and shame of having condemned innocent people to death. Miller suggests that evil will come back to haunt the person who commits it.

- Asks students to explain the irony in Danforth's line, "Perhaps he have some sorrow."
  Answer: Parris's sorrow lies in the horror he feels at his own complicity in the trials and executions, but Danforth assumes it is simply a private matter.

❻ Reading Strategy
Applying Themes to Contemporary Events

- Ask students the Reading Strategy question on p. 1321: What warning might the details about changes in Salem convey about the growing anti-Communist fear and suspicion in Miller's own time?
  Answer: The information about the conflict between Parris and the farmers suggests that Parris and perhaps the other accusers are beginning to lose the prominence they acquired when the trials began. In the same way, as fears about communism faded, McCarthy and his colleagues lost their reputations.

- What do Rebecca's different reported responses to Parris and Hale suggest about her and about the two ministers?
  Answer: Rebecca clearly despises Parris but likes Hale and is willing to listen to him. Her refusal to confess suggests that she is confident in her innocence.

- Ask students why Hale is trying to get the prisoners to confess.
  Answer: He wants to save their lives.

❼ ✔Reading Check

Answer: Their owners have been jailed or executed.

CUSTOMIZE INSTRUCTION FOR UNIVERSAL ACCESS

For Less Proficient Readers

Have students choose any two characters and make them the subject of a comparison-contrast essay. Possible pairings include Abigail and Elizabeth, Abigail and Mary, Cheever and Herrick, Hathorne and Danforth, Hale and Parris. Students can begin by making a word web for each character that lists his or her characteristics. They can then list the actions each character takes in the play. Finally, they can use these graphic organizers to pinpoint similarities and differences in the two characters. Students' essays should consider the effect of the two characters' differences, how each character serves as a foil for the other, and the thematic importance of the contrast between them.

Speculate

- Ask students why they think Abigail and Mercy have run away. Have them review the footnote about Andover at the bottom of p. 1321.

  Possible answers: Abigail is afraid that the tide of opinion in Salem will turn against the accusers, just as has happened in Andover. She doesn't want to stay in Salem when she knows her affair with John is over. She wants to start over somewhere else.

- Have students consider why Parris waited so long to tell Danforth of the girls' disappearance.

  Answer: He didn't want to admit that he was a poor guardian or that Abigail had made a fool of him.

❾ ▶Critical Viewing

Answer: He may be confessing that his niece has run away.

DANFORTH: Why—this is indeed a providence. And they soften, they soften?

PARRIS: Not yet, not yet. But I thought to summon you, sir, that we might think on whether it be not wise, to—*He dares not say it.* I had thought to put a question, sir, and I hope you will not—

DANFORTH: Mr. Parris, be plain, what troubles you?

PARRIS: There is news, sir, that the court—the court must reckon with. My niece, sir, my niece—I believe she has vanished.

DANFORTH: Vanished!

PARRIS: I had thought to advise you of it earlier in the week, but—

DANFORTH: Why? How long is she gone?

PARRIS: This be the third night. You see, sir, she told me she would stay a night with Mercy Lewis. And next day, when she does not return, I send to Mr. Lewis to inquire. Mercy told him she would sleep in *my* house for a night.

DANFORTH: They are both gone?!

PARRIS, *in fear of him:* They are, sir.

DANFORTH, *alarmed:* I will send a party for them. Where may they be?

PARRIS: Excellency, I think they be aboard a ship. DANFORTH *stands agape.* My daughter tells me how she heard them speaking of ships last week, and tonight I discover my—my strongbox is broke into. *He presses his fingers against his eyes to keep back tears.*

HATHORNE, *astonished:* She have robbed you?

PARRIS: Thirty-one pound is gone. I am penniless. *He covers his face and sobs.*

DANFORTH: Mr. Parris, you are a brainless man! *He walks in thought, deeply worried.*

PARRIS: Excellency, it profit nothing you should blame me. I cannot think they would run off except they fear to keep in Salem any more. *He is pleading.* Mark it, sir, Abigail had close knowledge of the town, and since the news of Andover has broken here—

DANFORTH: Andover is remedied. The court returns there on Friday, and will resume examinations.

PARRIS: I am sure of it, sir. But the rumor here speaks rebellion in Andover, and it—

DANFORTH: There is no rebellion in Andover!

PARRIS: I tell you what is said here, sir. Andover have thrown out the court, they say, and will have no part of witchcraft. There be a faction here, feeding on that news, and I tell you true, sir, I fear there will be riot here.

HATHORNE: Riot! Why at every execution I have seen naught but high satisfaction in the town.

PARRIS: Judge Hathorne—it were another sort that hanged till now. Rebecca Nurse is no Bridget that lived three year with Bishop before she married him. John Proctor is not Isaac Ward that drank his

1322 ◆ *Prosperity and Protest (1946–Present)*

agape (ə gāp´) *adj.* wide open

❾

▶Critical Viewing
In this court scene from execution day what might Parris be saying to Judge Danforth? **[Speculate]**

CUSTOMIZE INSTRUCTION FOR UNIVERSAL ACCESS

For Less Proficient Readers	For Gifted/Talented Students
Help students to make inferences about Hale, Parris, and Danforth by answering these questions: • What is each man's hope for the prisoners? (Parris wants the hangings postponed; Hale wants the prisoners to confess; Danforth wants the hangings over with.) • What is each man's greatest fear? (Parris fears a revolt in the town; Hale fears innocent people will die; Danforth fears others thinking he has put innocent people to death.) Have students create a three-column chart headed *Hale, Danforth,* and *Parris* to record their answers.	Ask students to write and perform a brief scene in which Mercy and Abigail decide to steal Parris's money and run away. Students should consider why the girls run, where they plan to go, and what they plan to do when they arrive. The scene should also discuss Abigail and Mercy's thoughts about the situation and the people they leave behind. How might Abigail feel knowing that her actions have probably condemned Proctor to death? How might both girls feel about leaving their homes?

family to ruin. *To* DANFORTH: I would to God it were not so, Excellency, but these people have great weight yet in the town. Let Rebecca stand upon the gibbet[2] and send up some righteous prayer, and I fear she'll wake a vengeance on you.

HATHORNE: Excellency, she is condemned a witch. The court have—

DANFORTH, *in deep concern, raising a hand to* HATHORNE: Pray you. *To* PARRIS: How do you propose, then?

 PARRIS: Excellency, I would postpone these hangin's for a time.

DANFORTH: There will be no postponement.

PARRIS: Now Mr. Hale's returned, there is hope, I think—for if he bring even one of these to God, that confession surely damns the others in the public eye, and none may doubt more that they are all linked to Hell. This way, unconfessed and claiming innocence, doubts are multiplied, many honest people will weep for them, and our good purpose is lost in their tears.

DANFORTH, *after thinking a moment, then going to* CHEEVER: Give me the list.

CHEEVER *opens the dispatch case, searches.*

PARRIS: It cannot be forgot, sir, that when I summoned the congregation for John Proctor's excommunication there were hardly thirty people come to hear it. That speak a discontent, I think, and—

DANFORTH, *studying the list:* There will be no postponement.

PARRIS: Excellency—

DANFORTH: Now, sir—which of these in your opinion may be brought to God? I will myself strive with him till dawn. *He hands the list to* PARRIS, *who merely glances at it.*

_____
2. **gibbet** (jib´ it) *n.* gallows.

Reading Strategy
Applying Themes to Contemporary Events
What might have happened if the McCarthy hearings had been postponed?

❶❶

✔ **Reading Check**
What has happened to Abigail?

The Crucible, Act IV ◆ *1323*

❿ **Reading Strategy**
Applying Themes to Contemporary Events

• Ask students the Reading Strategy question on p. 1323: What might have happened if the McCarthy hearings had been postponed?
Answer: The mood of the country might have changed and McCarthy might have lost his public support.

• Why does Danforth refuse to postpone the hangings?
Answer: He does not want to risk the court's reputation. He thinks that people will interpret a postponement as weakness or doubt, and he won't let that happen.

❶❶ ✔ **Reading Check**

Answer: Abigail, together with Mercy Lewis, has stolen money from her uncle and run away.

- Ask students to consider how Danforth's statement about being ready to hang any who might dare to "rise against the law" could be understood as a metaphor for what happened in the McCarthy hearings. How does the dialogue emphasize one of Miller's themes? Answer: Danforth's dialogue here is ironic, and reinforces Miller's theme of grotesque injustices inflicted on innocent citizens. The McCarthy hearings themselves were illegal, because membership in the Communist party was never illegal in the United States.

PARRIS: There is not sufficient time till dawn.

DANFORTH: I shall do my utmost. Which of them do you have hope for?

PARRIS, *not even glancing at the list now, and in a quavering voice, quietly:* Excellency—a dagger—*He chokes up.*

DANFORTH: What do you say?

PARRIS: Tonight, when I open my door to leave my house—a dagger clattered to the ground. *Silence.* DANFORTH *absorbs this. Now* PARRIS *cries out:* You cannot hang this sort. There is danger for me. I dare not step outside at night!

REVEREND HALE *enters. They look at him for an instant in silence. He is steeped in sorrow, exhausted, and more direct than he ever was.*

DANFORTH: Accept my congratulations, Reverend Hale; we are gladdened to see you returned to your good work.

HALE, *coming to* DANFORTH *now:* You must pardon them. They will not budge.

HERRICK *enters, waits.*

DANFORTH, *conciliatory:* You misunderstand, sir; I cannot pardon these when twelve are already hanged for the same crime. It is not just.

PARRIS, *with failing heart:* Rebecca will not confess?

HALE: The sun will rise in a few minutes. Excellency, I must have more time.

DANFORTH: Now hear me, and beguile yourselves no more. I will not receive a single plea for pardon or postponement. Them that will not confess will hang. Twelve are already executed; the names of these seven are given out, and the village expects to see them die this morning. Postponement now speaks a floundering on my part; reprieve or pardon must cast doubt upon the guilt of them that died till now. While I speak God's law, I will not crack its voice with whimpering. If retaliation is your fear, know this—I should hang ten thousand that dared to rise against the law, and an ocean of salt tears could not melt the resolution of the statutes. Now draw yourselves up like men and help me, as you are bound by Heaven to do. Have you spoken with them all, Mr. Hale?

HALE: All but Proctor. He is in the dungeon.

DANFORTH, *to* HERRICK: What's Proctor's way now?

HERRICK: He sits like some great bird; you'd not know he lived except he will take food from time to time.

DANFORTH, *after thinking a moment:* His wife—his wife must be well on with child now.

HERRICK: She is, sir.

DANFORTH: What think you, Mr. Parris? You have closer knowledge of this man; might her presence soften him?

PARRIS: It is possible, sir. He have not laid eyes on her these three months. I should summon her.

DANFORTH, *to* HERRICK: Is he yet adamant? Has he struck at you again?

conciliatory (kən sil′ ē ə tôr′ ē) *adj.* tending to soothe anger

beguile (bē gīl′) *v.* trick

floundering (floun′ dər iŋ) *n.* awkward struggling

retaliation (ri tal′ ē ā′ shən) *n.* act of returning an injury or wrong

adamant (ad′ ə mənt) *adj.* firm; unyielding

HERRICK: He cannot, sir, he is chained to the wall now.

DANFORTH, *after thinking on it:* Fetch Goody Proctor to me. Then let you bring him up.

HERRICK: Aye, sir. HERRICK *goes. There is silence.*

HALE: Excellency, if you postpone a week and publish to the town that you are striving for their confessions, that speak mercy on your part, not faltering.

DANFORTH: Mr. Hale, as God have not empowered me like Joshua to stop this sun from rising,[3] so I cannot withhold from them the perfection of their punishment.

HALE, *harder now:* If you think God wills you to raise rebellion, Mr. Danforth, you are mistaken!

DANFORTH, *instantly:* You have heard rebellion spoken in the town?

HALE: Excellency, there are orphans wandering from house to house; abandoned cattle bellow on the highroads, the stink of rotting crops hangs everywhere, and no man knows when the harlots' cry will end his life—and you wonder yet if rebellion's spoke? Better you should marvel how they do not burn your province!

DANFORTH: Mr. Hale, have you preached in Andover this month?

HALE: Thank God they have no need of me in Andover.

DANFORTH: You baffle me, sir. Why have you returned here?

HALE: Why, it is all simple. I come to do the Devil's work. I come to counsel Christians they should belie themselves. *His sarcasm collapses.* There is blood on my head! Can you not see the blood on my head!!

PARRIS: Hush! *For he has heard footsteps. They all face the door.* HERRICK *enters with* ELIZABETH. *Her wrists are linked by heavy chain, which* HERRICK *now removes. Her clothes are dirty; her face is pale and gaunt.* HERRICK *goes out.*

DANFORTH, *very politely:* Goody Proctor. *She is silent.* I hope you are hearty?

ELIZABETH, *as a warning reminder:* I am yet six months before my time.

DANFORTH: Pray be at your ease, we come not for your life. We— *uncertain how to plead, for he is not accustomed to it.* Mr. Hale, will you speak with the woman?

HALE: Goody Proctor, your husband is marked to hang this morning *Pause.*

ELIZABETH, *quietly:* I have heard it.

HALE: You know, do you not, that I have no connection with the court? *She seems to doubt it.* I come of my own, Goody Proctor. I would save your husband's life, for if he is taken I count myself his murderer. Do you understand me?

---

3. **Joshua . . . rising** In the Bible, Joshua, leader of the Jews after the death of Moses, asks God to make the sun and the moon stand still during a battle, and his request is granted.

Literary Analysis
Theme What themes do these descriptions of abandonment convey?

⓮

✔**Reading Check**
Why does Hale say he has returned to Salem?

The Crucible, Act IV ◆ 1325

⓭ Literary Analysis

Theme

- Ask students the Literary Analysis question on p. 1325: What themes do these descriptions of abandonment convey?
  Answer: Persecution of the innocent destroys the society it claims to be protecting.

- What theme does Danforth's refusal to postpone the hangings suggest?
  Answer: It suggests that unjust people, out of fear, shame, or pride, will perpetuate and defend their mistakes.

▶ **Monitor Progress** Hale's line, "Better you should marvel how they do not burn your province," is one of the play's many references to fire. Remind students that the play's title refers to a vessel that sits in the fire and holds molten metals or ores. Have the whole class discuss the themes suggested by the play's title.

⓮ ✔Reading Check

Answer: He says sarcastically that he comes to do the Devil's work. He has actually come to try to save lives.

CUSTOMIZE INSTRUCTION FOR UNIVERSAL ACCESS

For English Learners

Helps students to understand Hale's motives at this point in the play. Draw a detail web on the chalkboard. Explain that Hale now wants the accused and condemned prisoners to offer false confessions to save themselves. Write the following in the center of the web: *Hale wants the accused to lie to save themselves.* Ask students to find details from pp. 1325–1326 that suggest why Hale wants the prisoners to lie, and add these around the center of the web.

For Advanced Readers

As students approach the conclusion of *The Crucible*, have them decide which character in the play is the most compelling and write essays identifying and explaining their choices. Students need not choose a character they like or admire; they should choose the one who seems most fully realized, the character who is the most individual and memorable after they have closed the book. Students should explain what makes the character memorable—language? actions? motivations? other qualities?

⓯ Literary Analysis

Theme

- Ask students the Literary Analysis question on p. 1326: What theme or themes does Reverend Hale state in this speech?
  Answer: Hale suggests no principle is worth taking lives for.

- Ask students whether they agree with Hale. Why or why not?
  Answer: Students may say that each individual must make this decision for himself or herself. Proctor, for instance, must weigh his obligations to his family and his knowledge of his innocence against his unwillingness to lie. Remind students that to the Puritans, lying was a sin that could mean eternal damnation. The life after death that Puritans hoped for was considered much more important than life on earth; this was the reason Puritans lived so plainly and poorly.

⓰ ▶ Critical Viewing

Answer: They are concerned for each other; each can see that the other has suffered both mentally and physically. They both may feel some guilt over the situation they have helped to create.

ELIZABETH: What do you want of me?

HALE: Goody Proctor, I have gone this three month like our Lord into the wilderness. I have sought a Christian way, for damnation's doubled on a minister who counsels men to lie.

HATHORNE: It is no lie, you cannot speak of lies.

HALE: It is a lie! They are innocent!

DANFORTH: I'll hear no more of that!

⓯ HALE, *continuing to* ELIZABETH: Let you not mistake your duty as I mistook my own. I came into this village like a bridegroom to his beloved, bearing gifts of high religion; the very crowns of holy law I brought, and what I touched with my bright confidence, it died; and where I turned the eye of my great faith, blood flowed up. Beware, Goody Proctor— <u>cleave</u> to no faith when faith brings blood. It is mistaken law that leads you to sacrifice. Life, woman, life is God's most precious gift; no principle, however glorious, may justify the taking of it. I beg you, woman, prevail upon your husband to confess. Let him give his lie. Quail not before God's judgment in this, for it may well be God damns a liar less than he that throws his life away for pride. Will you plead with him? I cannot think he will listen to another.

ELIZABETH, *quietly:* I think that be the Devil's argument.

HALE, *with a climactic desperation:* Woman, before the laws of God we are as swine! We cannot read His will!

ELIZABETH: I cannot dispute with you, sir; I lack learning for it.

DANFORTH, *going to her:* Goody Proctor, you are not summoned here for disputation. Be there no wifely tenderness within you? He will die with the sunrise. Your husband. Do you understand it? *She only looks at him.* What say you? Will you contend with him? *She is silent.* Are you stone? I tell you true, woman, had I no other proof of your unnatural life, your dry eyes now would be sufficient evidence that you delivered up your soul to Hell! A very ape would weep at such calamity! Have the devil dried up any tear of pity in you? *She is silent.* Take her out. It profit nothing she should speak to him!

ELIZABETH, *quietly:* Let me speak with him, Excellency.

PARRIS, *with hope:* You'll strive with him? *She hesitates.*

DANFORTH: Will you plead for his confession or will you not?

ELIZABETH: I promise nothing. Let me speak with him.

A sound—the <u>sibilance</u> *of dragging feet on stone. They turn. A pause.* HERRICK *enters with* JOHN PROCTOR. *His wrists are chained. He is another man, bearded, filthy, his*

Literary Analysis
Theme What theme or themes does Reverend Hale state in this speech?

cleave (klēv) *v.* adhere; cling

sibilance (sib´ əl əns) *n.* hissing sound

⓰ ▼ Critical Viewing
From this movie still, what emotions do you imagine that John and Elizabeth Proctor are experiencing at this point?
[Infer]

eyes misty as though webs had overgrown them. He halts inside the doorway, his eyes caught by the sight of ELIZABETH. *The emotion flowing between them prevents anyone from speaking for an instant. Now* HALE, *visibly affected, goes to* DANFORTH *and speaks quietly.*

HALE: Pray, leave them Excellency.

DANFORTH, *pressing* HALE *impatiently aside:* Mr. Proctor, you have been notified, have you not? PROCTOR *is silent, staring at* ELIZABETH. I see light in the sky, Mister; let you counsel with your wife, and may God help you turn your back on Hell. PROCTOR *is silent, staring at* ELIZABETH.

HALE, *quietly:* Excellency, let—

DANFORTH *brushes past* HALE *and walks out.* HALE *follows.* CHEEVER *stands and follows,* HATHORNE *behind.* HERRICK *goes.* PARRIS, *from a safe distance, offers:*

PARRIS: If you desire a cup of cider, Mr. Proctor, I am sure I—PROCTOR *turns an icy stare at him, and he breaks off.* PARRIS *raises his palms toward* PROCTOR. God lead you now. PARRIS *goes out.*

Alone, PROCTOR *walks to her, halts. It is as though they stood in a spinning world. It is beyond sorrow, above it. He reaches out his hand as though toward an embodiment not quite real, and as he touches her, a strange soft sound, half laughter, half amazement, comes from his throat. He pats her hand. She covers his hand with hers. And then, weak, he sits. Then she sits, facing him.*

PROCTOR: The child?

ELIZABETH: It grows.

PROCTOR: There is no word of the boys?

ELIZABETH: They're well. Rebecca's Samuel keeps them.

PROCTOR: You have not seen them?

ELIZABETH: I have not. *She catches a weakening in herself and downs it.*

PROCTOR: You are a—marvel, Elizabeth.

ELIZABETH: You—have been tortured?

PROCTOR: Aye. *Pause. She will not let herself be drowned in the sea that threatens her.* They come for my life now.

ELIZABETH: I know it.

Pause.

PROCTOR: None—have yet confessed?

ELIZABETH: There be many confessed.

PROCTOR: Who are they?

ELIZABETH: There be a hundred or more, they say. Goody Ballard is one; Isaiah Goodkind is one. There be many.

PROCTOR: Rebecca?

ELIZABETH: Not Rebecca. She is one foot in Heaven now; naught may hurt her more.

PROCTOR: And Giles?

ELIZABETH: You have not heard of it?

Literary Analysis

Theme How does Miller's depiction of Elizabeth's attitude and behavior support his theme?

❿ ✔Reading Check

What does Hale urge Elizabeth Proctor to do?

The Crucible, Act IV ◆ *1327*

⓱ Literary Analysis

Theme

- Ask students the Literary Analysis question on p. 1327: How does Miller's depiction of Elizabeth's attitude and behavior support his theme?
  Answer: Miller's theme is that honesty and integrity are stronger than any attempt to break them down. Elizabeth shows that she can still triumph over her feelings because she knows herself to be honest.

- Why does John say that Elizabeth is a marvel?
  Answer: He admires her for her self-control given the terrible situation that she is in.

⓲ ✔Reading Check

Answer: He wants her to persuade John to confess and thus save his own life.

Film

The first film version of *The Crucible* was made in France in 1957 and released the following year in the United States. The film is called *Les sorcières de Salem* and stars the famous French actors Simone Signoret and Yves Montand as the Proctors. Both actors occasionally appeared in English-language films, notably *Room at the Top* (Signoret won an Academy Award for her performance in this film) and *Grand Prix* (Montand). The French screenplay was written by the philosopher Jean-Paul Sartre.

PROCTOR: I hear nothin', where I am kept.

ELIZABETH: Giles is dead.

He looks at her incredulously.

PROCTOR: When were he hanged?

ELIZABETH, *quietly, factually:* He were not hanged. He would not answer aye or nay to his indictment; for if he denied the charge they'd hang him surely, and auction out his property. So he stand mute, and died Christian under the law. And so his sons will have his farm. It is the law, for he could not be condemned a wizard without he answer the indictment, aye or nay.

PROCTOR: Then how does he die?

ELIZABETH, *gently:* They press him, John.

PROCTOR: Press?

ELIZABETH: Great stones they lay upon his chest until he plead aye or nay. *With a tender smile for the old man:* They say he give them but two words. "More weight," he says. And died.

PROCTOR, *numbed—a thread to weave into his agony:* "More weight."

ELIZABETH: Aye. It were a fearsome man, Giles Corey.

Pause.

PROCTOR, *with great force of will, but not quite looking at her:* I have been thinking I would confess to them, Elizabeth. *She shows nothing.* What say you? If I give them that?

ELIZABETH: I cannot judge you, John.

Pause.

PROCTOR, *simply—a pure question:* What would you have me do?

ELIZABETH: As you will, I would have it. *Slight pause:* I want you living, John. That's sure.

PROCTOR, *pauses, then with a flailing of hope:* Giles' wife? Have she confessed?

ELIZABETH: She will not.

Pause.

PROCTOR: It is a pretense, Elizabeth.

ELIZABETH: What is?

PROCTOR: I cannot mount the gibbet like a saint. It is a fraud. I am not that man. *She is silent.* My honesty is broke, Elizabeth; I am no good man. Nothing's spoiled by giving them this lie that were not rotten long before.

ELIZABETH: And yet you've not confessed till now. That speak goodness in you.

PROCTOR: Spite only keeps me silent. It is hard to give a lie to dogs. *Pause, for the first time he turns directly to her.* I would have your forgiveness, Elizabeth.

⑲ Literature in context — Media Connection

Being Abigail Williams

For more than four decades, no American film director chose to tackle Arthur Miller's challenging stage drama *The Crucible*. Finally, in 1996, Nicholas Hytner enlisted actors including Winona Ryder, Daniel Day-Lewis, and Joan Allen to star in a film based on a screenplay by Miller himself.

Ryder found playing Abigail Williams engrossing and disturbing. "I've heard Abigail called the villain of the piece, but I'm not so sure," she says. "She's never been given any power. . . . Abigail understands that she could get attention and power, so she goes with it. There's always a part of her that knows she is fooling, but I think she was convinced that spirits were attacking her. I see her as insane in a way, but so is the whole town. It's like a disease."

✳ ENRICHMENT: Literature Connection

In a scene inserted into *The Crucible* late in its original Broadway run, Abigail explains to Proctor why she will not renounce her testimony:

It were a fire you walked me through, and all my ignorance were burned away. It were a fire, John, we lay in fire. And from that night no woman dare call me wicked any more but I knew my answer. I used to weep for my sins when the wind lifted up my skirts; and blushed for shame because some old Rebecca called me loose. And then you burned my ignorance away. As bare as some December tree I saw them all—walking like saints to the church, running to feed the sick, and hypocrites in their hearts! And God gave me strength to call them liars, and God made men to listen to me, and by God I will scrub the world clean for the love of Him!

ELIZABETH: It is not for me to give, John, I am—

PROCTOR: I'd have you see some honesty in it. Let them that never lied die now to keep their souls. It is pretense for me, a vanity that will not blind God nor keep my children out of the wind. *Pause.* What say you?

ELIZABETH, *upon a heaving sob that always threatens:* John, it come to naught that I should forgive you, if you'll not forgive yourself. *Now he turns away a little, in great agony.* It is not my soul, John, it is yours. *He stands, as though in physical pain, slowly rising to his feet with a great immortal longing to find his answer. It is difficult to say, and she is on the verge of tears.* Only be sure of this, for I know it now: Whatever you will do, it is a good man does it. *He turns his doubting, searching gaze upon her.* I have read my heart this three month, John. *Pause.* I have sins of my own to count. It needs a cold wife to prompt lechery.

PROCTOR, *in great pain:* Enough, enough—

ELIZABETH, *now pouring out her heart:* Better you should know me!

PROCTOR: I will not hear it! I know you!

ELIZABETH: You take my sins upon you, John—

PROCTOR, *in agony:* No, I take my own, my own!

ELIZABETH: John, I counted myself so plain, so poorly made, no honest love could come to me! Suspicion kissed you when I did; I never knew how I should say my love. It were a cold house I kept! *In fright, she swerves, as* HATHORNE *enters.*

HATHORNE: What say you Proctor? The sun is soon up.

PROCTOR, *his chest heaving, stares, turns to* ELIZABETH. *She comes to him as though to plead, her voice quaking.*

ELIZABETH: Do what you will. But let none be your judge. There be no higher judge under Heaven than Proctor is! Forgive me, forgive me, John—I never knew such goodness in the world! *She covers her face, weeping.*

PROCTOR *turns from her to* HATHORNE; *he is off the earth, his voice hollow.*

PROCTOR: I want my life.

HATHORNE *electrified, surprised:* You'll confess yourself?

PROCTOR: I will have my life.

HATHORNE, *with a mystical tone:* God be praised! It is a providence! *He rushes out the door, and his voice is heard calling down the corridor:* He will confess! Proctor will confess!

PROCTOR, *with a cry, as he strides to the door:* Why do you cry it? *In great pain he turns back to her.* It is evil, is it not? It is evil.

ELIZABETH, *in terror, weeping:* I cannot judge you, John, I cannot!

PROCTOR: Then who will judge me? *Suddenly clasping his hands:* God in Heaven, what is John Proctor, what is John Proctor? *He moves as an animal, and a fury is riding in him, a* <u>tantalized</u> *search. I think it is honest, I think so; I am no saint. As though she had denied this he calls angrily at her:* Let Rebecca go like a saint; for me it is fraud!

Literary Analysis

Theme What theme does Miller convey through John Proctor's statement about honesty?

21 **tantalized** (tan′ tə līzd) *adj.* tormented; frustrated

22 ✔**Reading Check**

What sins does Elizabeth think she has committed?

The Crucible, Act IV ◆ 1329

CUSTOMIZE INSTRUCTION FOR UNIVERSAL ACCESS

For Special Needs Students	For English Learners
Help students prepare for the play's climax by reviewing the rise and fall of the play's action. Have students compile lists of the main events of the play, act by act, up to p. 1329. As a class, use the chalkboard to create a graph that shows the rise and fall of the plot. Tell students to write specific examples of events that have led to this crisis. As students read, have them add plot elements that contribute to the denouement, or resolution.	Help students understand that this intimate and powerful exchange between John and Elizabeth Proctor leads the audience swiftly toward the play's climax. Help students understand the conflicts faced by the characters. On the chalkboard, draw and label a T-chart headed "What is important to John" and "What is important to Elizabeth." In each column, list an example. Sample: "His wife's forgiveness" and "That John be true to himself." Ask students for additional examples from the play to complete the chart.

---

20 Literary Analysis
Theme

- Have students paraphrase Proctor's speech (beginning "I'd have you see some honesty . . ."). Answer: I might as well confess. Even though I would be lying, I have lied before. I need not pretend to be an honest man.

- Ask students the Literary Analysis question on p. 1329: What theme does Miller convey through John Proctor's statements about honesty? Answer: Miller shows that a man can be a hero in spite of having some flaws. Proctor's integrity is still strong.

- How has Elizabeth changed since her conversation with John in Act II? Answer: In Act II, she judged him because of his adultery; now she refuses to judge him. She has learned humility.

21 Vocabulary Development
Words From Myths

- Draw students' attention to the word *tantalized* on p. 1329, and tell students that words from myths most often are drawn from the names of mythic characters.

- Write the following words on the chalkboard and have students make inferences about their meaning by recalling the myths from which they are derived: *herculean, narcissism, protean.* Answers: *Herculean* is an adjective meaning "miraculously strong" and/or "able to accomplish many difficult tasks," as Hercules did in his legendary labors. *Narcissism* is the condition of being preoccupied with the self, like the mythic character Narcissus. *Protean* is an adjective describing things or people who are highly changeable or able to take on many forms or aspects. The word comes from the Greek sea god who could change his shape at will.

22 ✔Reading Check

Answer: She blames herself for coldness toward John.

1329

- Ask students the Literary Analysis question on p. 1330: Which details of Rebecca Nurse's character reinforce the theme of courage and personal integrity?
  Answer: her refusal to confess; her pleasure in seeing that Proctor is still alive; her compassion for him when she hears him give a false confession

- Suggest to students that Proctor's confession is doubly ironic; although he believes it to be false, it is actually true. Have them explore this irony and the theme it suggests.
  Answer: Miller suggests throughout the play that the Devil is not a supernatural being; the Devil exists in human beings and is manifested in their pride, avarice, envy, malice, and lies. John has indeed seen the Devil—in Abigail, in the Putnams, in Danforth, and even in himself.

Voices are heard in the hall, speaking together in suppressed excitement.

ELIZABETH: I am not your judge, I cannot be. *As though giving him release:* Do as you will, do as you will!

PROCTOR: Would you give them such a lie? Say it. Would you ever give them this? *She cannot answer.* You would not; if tongs of fire were singeing you you would not! It is evil. Good, then—it is evil, and I do it!

HATHORNE *enters with* DANFORTH, *and, with them,* CHEEVER, PARRIS, *and* HALE. *It is a businesslike, rapid entrance, as though the ice had been broken.*

DANFORTH, *with great relief and gratitude:* Praise to God, man, praise to God; you shall be blessed in Heaven for this. CHEEVER *has hurried to the bench with pen, ink, and paper.* PROCTOR *watches him.* Now then, let us have it. Are you ready, Mr. Cheever?

PROCTOR, *with a cold, cold horror at their efficiency:* Why must it be written?

DANFORTH: Why, for the good instruction of the village, Mister; this we shall post upon the church door! *To* PARRIS, *urgently:* Where is the marshal?

PARRIS, *runs to the door and calls down the corridor:* Marshal! Hurry!

DANFORTH: Now, then, Mister, will you speak slowly, and directly to the point, for Mr. Cheever's sake. *He is on record now, and is really dictating to* CHEEVER, *who writes.* Mr. Proctor, have you seen the Devil in your life? PROCTOR'S *jaws lock.* Come, man, there is light in the sky; the town waits at the scaffold; I would give out this news. Did you see the Devil?

PROCTOR: I did.

PARRIS: Praise God!

DANFORTH: And when he come to you, what were his demand?

PROCTOR *is silent.* DANFORTH *helps.* Did he bid you to do his work upon the earth?

PROCTOR: He did.

DANFORTH: And you bound yourself to his service? DANFORTH *turns, as* REBECCA *Nurse enters, with* HERRICK *helping to support her. She is barely able to walk.* Come in, come in, woman!

REBECCA, *brightening as she sees* PROCTOR: Ah, John! You are well, then, eh?

PROCTOR *turns his face to the wall.*

DANFORTH: Courage, man, courage—let her witness your good example that she may come to God herself. Now hear it, Goody Nurse! Say on, Mr. Proctor. Did you bind yourself to the Devil's service?

23

REBECCA, *astonished:* Why, John!

PROCTOR, *through his teeth, his face turned from* REBECCA: I did.

DANFORTH: Now, woman, you surely see it profit nothin' to keep this conspiracy any further. Will you confess yourself with him?

REBECCA: Oh, John—God send his mercy on you!

DANFORTH: I say, will you confess yourself, Goody Nurse?

Literary Analysis
Theme Which details of Rebecca Nurse's character reinforce the theme of courage and personal integrity?

REBECCA: Why, it is a lie, it is a lie; how may I damn myself? I cannot, I cannot.

DANFORTH: Mr. Proctor. When the Devil came to you did you see Rebecca Nurse in his company? PROCTOR *is silent.* Come, man, take courage—did you ever see her with the Devil?

PROCTOR, *almost inaudibly:* No.

DANFORTH, *now sensing trouble, glances at* JOHN *and goes to the table, and picks up a sheet—the list of condemned.*

DANFORTH: Did you ever see her sister, Mary Easty, with the Devil?

PROCTOR: No, I did not.

DANFORTH, *his eyes narrow on* PROCTOR: Did you ever see Martha Corey with the Devil?

PROCTOR: I did not.

DANFORTH, *realizing, slowly putting the sheet down:* Did you ever see anyone with the Devil?

PROCTOR: I did not.

DANFORTH: Proctor, you mistake me. I am not empowered to trade your life for a lie. You have most certainly seen some person with the Devil. PROCTOR *is silent.* Mr. Proctor, a score of people have already testified they saw this woman with the Devil.

PROCTOR: Then it is proved. Why must I say it?

DANFORTH: Why "must" you say it! Why, you should rejoice to say it if your soul is truly <u>purged</u> of any love for Hell!

PROCTOR: They think to go like saints. I like not to spoil their names.

DANFORTH, *inquiring, incredulous:* Mr. Proctor, do you think they go like saints?

PROCTOR, *evading:* This woman never thought she done the Devil's work.

DANFORTH: Look you, sir. I think you mistake your duty here. It matter nothing what she thought—she is convicted of the unnatural murder of children, and you for sending your spirit out upon Mary Warren. Your soul alone is the issue here, Mister, and you will prove its whiteness or you cannot live in a Christian country. Will you tell me now what persons conspired with you in the Devil's company? PROCTOR *is silent.* To your knowledge was Rebecca Nurse ever—

PROCTOR: I speak my own sins; I cannot judge another. *Crying out, with hatred:* I have no tongue for it.

HALE, *quickly to* DANFORTH: Excellency, it is enough he confess himself. Let him sign it, let him sign it.

PARRIS, *feverishly:* It is a great service, sir. It is a weighty name; it will strike the village that Proctor confess. I beg you, let him sign it. The sun is up, Excellency!

DANFORTH, *considers; then with dissatisfaction:* Come, then, sign your testimony. *To* CHEEVER: Give it to him. CHEEVER *goes to* PROCTOR, *the confession and a pen in hand.* PROCTOR *does not look at it.* Come, man, sign it.

purged (purjd) *v.* cleansed

Literary Analysis
Theme and Extended Metaphor How might Proctor's refusal to incriminate others relate to the McCarthy hearings of the 1950s?

 Reading Check
What does Danforth want Proctor to do?

The Crucible, Act IV ◆ *1331*

 Literary Analysis

Theme and Extended Metaphor

- Ask students the Literary Analysis question on p. 1331: How might Proctor's refusal to incriminate others relate to the McCarthy hearings of the 1950s?
  Answer: Many witnesses for the House Committee on Un-American Activities showed the same courage as Proctor and refused to name others.

- What theme does Proctor's cry, "I cannot judge another" suggest?
  Answer: Miller suggests that judging others is intrinsically wrong, that people should show compassion and understanding and not be quick to condemn. The actual judges in the play are criminals because they condemn the innocent to death.

25 ✔ **Reading Check**

Answer: He wants him to name the people he saw with the Devil and then to sign his confession.

Applying Themes to Contemporary Events

- Ask students the Reading Strategy question on p. 1332: Which notorious aspect of the McCarthy hearings might Miller be suggesting here?
  Answer: Miller alludes to those who betrayed their friends and acquaintances by naming names to the HUAC.

- Have students continue reading through Proctor's speech beginning "Because it is my name!" on p. 1333. Ask what theme is suggested by his insistence on keeping his name private.
  Answer: Proctor equates his name with himself—with his identity. His name symbolizes who he is. The honor of his name is a deeply personal thing and he is unwilling to betray it.

PROCTOR, *after glancing at the confession:* You have all witnessed it— it is enough.

DANFORTH: You will not sign it?

PROCTOR: You have all witnessed it; what more is needed?

DANFORTH: Do you sport with me? You will sign your name or it is no confession, Mister! *His breast heaving with agonized breathing,* PROCTOR *now lays the paper down and signs his name.*

PARRIS: Praise be to the Lord!

PROCTOR *has just finished signing when* DANFORTH *reaches for the paper. But* PROCTOR *snatches it up, and now a wild terror is rising in him, and a boundless anger.*

DANFORTH, *perplexed, but politely extending his hand:* If you please, sir.

PROCTOR: No.

DANFORTH, *as though* PROCTOR *did not understand:* Mr. Proctor, I must have—

PROCTOR: No, no. I have signed it. You have seen me. It is done! You have no need for this.

PARRIS: Proctor, the village must have proof that—

PROCTOR: Damn the village! I confess to God, and God has seen my name on this! It is enough!

DANFORTH: No, sir, it is—

PROCTOR: You came to save my soul, did you not? Here! I have confessed myself; it is enough!

DANFORTH: You have not con—

PROCTOR: I have confessed myself! Is there no good penitence but it be public? God does not need my name nailed upon the church! God sees my name; God knows how black my sins are! It is enough!

DANFORTH: Mr. Proctor—

PROCTOR: You will not use me! I am no Sarah Good or Tituba, I am John Proctor! You will not use me! It is no part of salvation that you should use me!

DANFORTH: I do not wish to—

PROCTOR: I have three children—how may I teach them to walk like men in the world, and I sold my friends?

26 DANFORTH: You have not sold your friends—

PROCTOR: Beguile me not! I blacken all of them when this is nailed to the church the very day they hang for silence!

DANFORTH: Mr. Proctor, I must have good and legal proof that you—

PROCTOR: You are the high court, your word is good enough! Tell them I confessed myself; say Proctor broke his knees and wept like a woman; say what you will, but my name cannot—

DANFORTH, *with suspicion:* It is the same, is it not? If I report it or you sign to it?

Reading Strategy Applying Themes to Contemporary Events
Which notorious aspect of the McCarthy hearings might Miller be suggesting here?

✷ ENRICHMENT: Literature Connection

What Happened Afterward

The following is the text of Miller's brief end note to *The Crucible*, titled "Echoes Down the Corridor."

Not long after the fever died, Parris was voted from office, walked out on the highroad, and was never seen again.

The legend has it that Abigail turned up later as a prostitute in Boston.

Twenty years after the last execution, the government awarded compensation to the victims still living, and to the families of the dead. However, it is evident that some people still were unwilling to admit their total guilt, and also that the factionalism was still alive, for some beneficiaries were actually not victims at all but informers.

(continued on p. 1333)

PROCTOR—*he knows it is insane:* No, it is not the same! What others say and what I sign to is not the same!

DANFORTH: Why? Do you mean to deny this confession when you are free?

PROCTOR: I mean to deny nothing!

DANFORTH: Then explain to me, Mr. Proctor, why you will not let—

PROCTOR, *with a cry of his whole soul:* Because it is my name! Because I cannot have another in my life! Because I lie and sign myself to lies! Because I am not worth the dust on the feet of them that hang! How may I live without my name? I have given you my soul; leave me my name!

DANFORTH, *pointing at the confession in* PROCTOR's *hand:* Is that document a lie? If it is a lie I will not accept it! What say you? I will not deal in lies, Mister! PROCTOR *is motionless.* You will give me your honest confession in my hand, or I cannot keep you from the rope. PROCTOR *does not reply.* What way do you go, Mister?

His breast heaving, his eyes staring, PROCTOR *tears the paper and crumples it, and he is weeping in fury, but erect.*

DANFORTH: Marshal!

PARRIS, *hysterically, as though the tearing paper were his life:* Proctor, Proctor!

HALE: Man, you will hang! You cannot!

PROCTOR, *his eyes full of tears:* I can. And there's your first marvel, that I can. You have made your magic now, for now I do think I see some shred of goodness in John Proctor. Not enough to weave a banner with, but white enough to keep it from such dogs. ELIZABETH, *in a burst of terror, rushes to him and weeps against his hand.* Give them no tear! Tears pleasure them! Show honor now, show a stony heart and sink them with it! *He has lifted her, and kisses her now with great passion.*

REBECCA: Let you fear nothing! Another judgment waits us all!

DANFORTH: Hang them high over the town! Who weeps for these, weeps for corruption! *He sweeps out past them.* HERRICK *starts to lead* REBECCA, *who almost collapses, but* PROCTOR *catches her, and she glances up at him apologetically.*

REBECCA: I've had no breakfast.

27 ▲ Critical Viewing
Judge Danforth says, "He who weeps for these weeps for corruption." What do you think the people surrounding the condemned are thinking? **[Analyze]**

Literary Analysis
Theme In what way does Proctor's change of heart reflect the themes of integrity and courage?

29 ☑ Reading Check
What decision does John Proctor finally make?

The Crucible, Act IV ◆ 1333

✸ ENRICHMENT: Literature Connection

What Happened Afterward

(continued from p. 1332)

Elizabeth Proctor married again, four years after Proctor's death.

In solemn meeting, the congregation rescinded the excommunications—this in March, 1712. But they did so upon orders of the government. The jury, however, wrote a statement praying forgiveness of all who had suffered.

Certain farms which had belonged to the victims were left to ruin, and for more than a century no one would buy them or live on them.

To all intents and purposes, the power of theocracy in Massachusetts was broken.

Answers for p. 1334

Review and Assess

1. **(a)** Students will probably be sad that Proctor dies. **(b)** Make sure students support their answers.

2. **(a)** Hale, Parris, and Danforth **(b)** Hale wants to save their lives; Parris wants them to confess because this will swing the town's sympathies back toward the court, Danforth wants their confessions to justify the entire proceedings.

3. **(a)** She steals Parris's savings and runs away. **(b)** She probably realized, like Parris, that the mood of the town no longer supported the court and that she was the most likely to suffer from this reaction since she was the greatest troublemaker.

4. **(a)** Proctor must choose between death and lying. **(b)** She wants him to live but knows in her heart that lying would be wrong.

5. **(a)** for falsely naming others as witches **(b)** He truly wants to live, but he renounces the confession when he realizes that he doesn't want to live as a dishonored man.

6. She believes that he did the right thing—he dies with honor.

7. Make sure students support their answers.

HERRICK: Come, man.

HERRICK escorts them out, HATHORNE *and* CHEEVER *behind them.* ELIZABETH *stands staring at the empty doorway.*

PARRIS, *in deadly fear, to* ELIZABETH: Go to him, Goody Proctor! There is yet time!

From outside a drumroll strikes the air. PARRIS *is startled.* ELIZABETH *jerks about toward the window.*

PARRIS: Go to him! *He rushes out the door, as though to hold back his fate.* Proctor! Proctor!

Again, a short burst of drums.

HALE: Woman, plead with him! *He starts to rush out the door, and then goes back to her.* Woman! It is pride, it is vanity. *She avoids his eyes, and moves to the window. He drops to his knees.* Be his helper!—What profit him to bleed? Shall the dust praise him? Shall the worms declare his truth? Go to him, take his shame away!

ELIZABETH, *supporting herself against collapse, grips the bars of the window, and with a cry:* He have his goodness now. God forbid I take it from him!

The final drumroll crashes, then heightens violently. HALE *weeps in frantic prayer, and the new sun is pouring in upon her face, and the drums rattle like bones in the morning air.*

Review and Assess

Thinking About Act IV

1. **(a) Respond:** How did you react to the ending of the play? **(b) Extend:** Would you recommend the play to a friend? Why or why not?

2. **(a) Recall:** Who seeks confessions from Rebecca Nurse and other condemned prisoners? **(b) Infer:** What motivates this person—or people—to seek these confessions?

3. **(a) Recall:** What unexpected action does Abigail take in this act? **(b) Draw Conclusions:** Why do you think she does this?

4. **(a) Recall:** What decision torments John Proctor? **(b) Interpret:** What conflict does Elizabeth experience as her husband seeks her guidance?

5. **(a) Recall:** What does John Proctor have "no tongue for"? **(b) Analyze:** Why does Proctor confess and then retract his confession?

6. **Interpret:** Why does Elizabeth say her husband has "his goodness" as he is about to be hanged?

7. **Evaluate:** Do you think John Proctor made the right decision? Why or why not?

⬥ ASSESSMENT PRACTICE: Writing Skills

Punctuation	(For more practice, see Test Preparation Workbook, p. 70.)

Many tests require students to identify errors in punctuation. Use this following sample test item.

PROCTOR   You have all witnessed it; what more is needed

With which punctuation mark should you end this sentence?

  A question mark   **C** exclamation mark
  B period   **D** comma

"What more is needed" is a question; the correct answer is *A*.

Review and Assess

Literary Analysis

Theme

1. Use evidence from the play to show how Arthur Miller conveys the **theme** that fear and suspicion are infectious and can produce a mass hysteria that destroys public order and rationality.
2. Cite evidence from the play that supports the theme that it is more noble to die with integrity than to live with compromised principles that harm others.
3. (a) In what ways do Hale's reactions to events compare to those of the other ministers and court officers? (b) What do these differences suggest about the ideas of integrity, pride, and vanity?
4. State and support another theme that you believe is central to the meaning of the play.

Connecting Literary Elements

5. Using a chart like the one shown, cite examples from the text that show how ideas such as witchcraft and "the work of the Devil" function in *The Crucible* as **extended metaphors** for Communism.

Passage From the Text	How It Relates to Communism

6. (a) What does the ending of the play suggest about the value of integrity and of holding fast to principles? (b) How might this idea relate to the McCarthy era?

Reading Strategy

Applying Themes to Contemporary Events

7. Based on the play's details, what criticisms might Miller be making about the way McCarthy's Senate committee dealt with those it questioned and those who criticized it?
8. What does the play suggest about the motives behind Senator Joseph McCarthy's political "witch hunts"? Explain.

Extend Understanding

9. **Social Studies Connection:** Given the nation's experience with McCarthyism, do you think a tragedy like the Salem witchcraft trials could occur today? Explain.

The Crucible, Act IV ◆ 1335

Quick Review

A **theme** is a central idea or insight about life revealed by a literary work.

An **extended metaphor** is a comparison that is developed through the course of a literary work.

To **apply a theme to a contemporary event**, draw a parallel between the central idea of a story and a current event.

 Take It to the Net
www.phschool.com
Take the interactive self-test online to check your understanding of this selection.

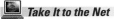

Answers continued

8. McCarthy probably acted out of base motives, just as HUAC did.
9. Students may say no because there are so many journalists and television and radio commentators that it is unlikely that something of the kind could continue. Other students may say that other "witch hunts" have taken place since the 1950s.

Answers for p. 1335

Review and Assess

1. The children feign illness in Act I because they fear punishment. Parris calls in Hale because he fears his enemies in the parish. John fails to denounce Abigail because he fears admitting to adultery. The fearful actions of the characters fuel the suspicions of witchcraft that drive events.
2. Those who die with integrity, such as Rebecca, Giles, and Proctor, are the good characters. They are honest, direct, and likable people.
3. (a) Hale's reactions, from Act I when he believes witchcraft to be present in Salem to Act IV when he knows that he has been wrong, are honest. He has no ulterior motives, as do the other men. (b) They suggest that although pride and vanity may prompt people to persecute others, even an honest man who makes a mistake can do great harm.
4. Answers will vary. Make sure students support their choice of theme with evidence from the text.
5. Possible answers: **Passage from the Text:** Danforth's questioning of Proctor ("When the Devil came to you did you see Rebecca Nurse in his company? . . . Did you ever see her sister Mary Easty . . . ? Did you ever see Martha Corey . . . ?") **How it Relates to Communism:** During the 1950s, many Americans feared Communism. They saw it as a secret force infiltrating American society. All of the details about witchcraft and the Devil in *The Crucible* suggest a similar idea of a secret evil engineered by individuals to penetrate the very fabric of society.
6. (a) The ending suggests that integrity is more important than any other virtue. (b) It suggests that those who withstood the pressures of the McCarthy era were heroes.
7. Like the committee members, the Salem judges presume guilt and accept accusation as proof.

continued

❶ Vocabulary Development

Word Analysis

Sample sentences are given.

1. Cereals are made from grains.
2. *Titanic* was the perfect name for the largest, strongest, fastest-moving ship ever built.
3. A narcissistic person's favorite possession is his or her mirror.

Spelling Strategy

1. basting
2. purify
3. serenity

Concept Development: Synonyms

1. b
2. a
3. b
4. a
5. c
6. c
7. c
8. a
9. b
10. b

❷ Grammar and Style Lesson

1. rose
2. raising
3. raised
4. risen
5. raised

Writing Application

Have students check one another's paragraphs.

Integrate Language Skills

❶ Vocabulary Development Lesson

Concept Development: Words From Myths

The word *tantalize* comes from the Greek myth about Tantalus a man tormented by the gods. Review the list of mythological figures below. Write a sentence for each, using the word in parentheses.

1. Ceres: The goddess of the harvest (*cereal*)
2. Titan: A race of giants with brute strength (*titanic*)
3. Narcissus: A boy punished by the gods for vanity (*narcissistic*)

Spelling Strategy

When you add a suffix beginning with a vowel to a word that ends in a silent *e*, drop the *e* before adding the suffix. For example, *tantalize* +*-ing* = *tantalizing*. For each word below, add the suffix indicated.

1. baste (*-ing*) 2. pure (*-ify*) 3. serene (*-ity*)

❷ Grammar and Style Lesson

Commonly Confused Words: *raise* and *rise*

Some words in English sound similar but function differently. For example, to **raise** means "to lift up"; it takes a direct object (a noun or pronoun that receives the action of the verb). To **rise** means "to go up or get up," and it does not take a direct object.

Verb	Present	Present Participle	Past	Past Participle
raise	raise, raises	raising	raised	(have) raised
rise	rise, rises	rising	rose	(have) risen

𝒲𝒢 *Prentice Hall Writing and Grammar Connection: Chapter 21, Section 1*

Concept Development: Synonyms

Select the letter of the word that is the closest in meaning to the first word.

1. agape: (a) dark, (b) open, (c) shocking
2. conciliatory: (a) soothing, (b) rude, (c) vengeful
3. beguile: (a) plead, (b) fool, (c) straighten
4. floundering: (a) groping, (b) jogging, (c) smelling
5. retaliation: (a) narration, (b) restatement, (c) revenge
6. adamant: (a) calm, (b) first, (c) stubborn
7. cleave: (a) depart, (b) grow, (c) adhere
8. sibilance: (a) hissing, (b) humming, (c) screaming
9. tantalized: (a) freed, (b) tempted, (c) danced
10. purged: (a) soothed, (b) washed, (c) filled

Practice Complete each sentence with the correct form of *rise* or *raise* in the tense indicated.

1. All (*past*) when the judge entered.
2. They were (*present participle*) the flag outside the courthouse.
3. Cries of witchcraft (*past*) a ruckus.
4. Spirits were reported to have (*past participle*) to the courtroom ceiling.
5. Citizens had (*past participle*) a rebellion.

Writing Application Write a paragraph in which you use the verbs *raise* and *rise* correctly.

TEACHING RESOURCES

The following resources can be used to enrich or extend the instruction for pp. 1336–1337.

Vocabulary

📖 **Selection Support**: Build Vocabulary, p. 326;

📖 **Vocabulary and Spelling Practice Book** (Use this booklet for skills enrichment.) 💻

Grammar

📖 **Selection Support**: Grammar and Style, p. 327

𝒲𝒢 **Writing and Grammar**, Ruby Level, p. 520

💻 **Daily Language Practice Transparencies**

Writing

𝒲𝒢 **Writing and Grammar**, p. 124 💻

💿 **Writing and Grammar iText CD-ROM**

BLOCK SCHEDULING: Resources marked with this symbol provide varied instruction during 90-minute blocks.

❸ Writing Lesson

Defense of a Character's Actions

Write an essay in which you defend the actions of an accused character in *The Crucible*. Like a good trial lawyer, you need not agree with your client's actions, but you must present the best defense possible to prove why he or she should not be found guilty.

Prewriting Skim the play to decide which character's actions you will defend. Record possible "pros" and "cons" in a two-column chart. You might discuss the character with others to come up with as complete a list of pros and cons as possible.

Model: Analyzing the Evidence

"Pros"	"Cons"
He is honest.	He angers quickly.
He is trustworthy.	He made a mistake.
He is loyal.	He is stubborn.

Drafting Begin by presenting the negative aspects of your character's actions. Then, move on to the positive aspects. In each case, cite specific evidence from the play. Use forceful, persuasive language to explain why the pros outweigh the cons.

Revising Make sure you have effectively refuted the negatives and included enough positive ideas to support the defense. Also, be sure that your word choice is clear, precise, and persuasive.

W̶G Prentice Hall Writing and Grammar Connection: Chapter 7, Section 2

❹ Extension Activities

Listening and Speaking Stage a **mock trial** to determine whether Danforth and Hathorne are guilty of murder for their roles in the Salem witch trials. Appoint a prosecutor, a defense attorney, defendants, witnesses, a jury, and a fair judge. Consider the following:

- Select prosecution and defense witnesses.
- Have both the defense attorney and the prosecutor give summations.

Present the trial to the class. [**Group Activity**]

Research and Technology Research the facts of the Salem witchcraft trials. Then, present a **comparison-and-contrast chart**, listing differences between the trials and the events in this play. For each difference, provide reasons Miller might have had for making those changes.

 Take It to the Net www.phschool.com

Go online for an additional research activity using the Internet.

---

❸ Writing Lesson

- Encourage students to try to defend Parris, Abigail, or one of the other less sympathetic or heroic characters.
- Model the drafting process for students by using Writing Process Model 6: Persuasive Essay, pp. 33–36 in **Writing Models and Graphic Organizers on Transparencies.**
- Use the Persuasive Speech rubric in **Performance Assessment and Portfolio Management**, p. 17, to evaluate students' essays.

❹ Extension Activity

Research and Technology

- Remind students that Miller had access to the Salem court records and that, in some places, he quotes verbatim from the transcripts.
- Have students consider why Miller made certain changes. You might tell them, for example, that Miller raised Abigail's age (the real Abigail was probably about 14) and invented the affair between her and John Proctor. How would the removal of this aspect of the play change it?

CUSTOMIZE INSTRUCTION
For Universal Access

To address different learning styles, use the following activities suggested in the **Extension Activities** booklet, p. 76.

For Musical/Rhythmic Learners, use Activity 5.

For Visual/Spatial Learners, use Activity 6.

For Intrapersonal Learners, use Activity 7.

ASSESSMENT RESOURCES

The following resources can be used to assess students' knowledge and skills.

Selection Assessment
- 📖 **Formal Assessment,** pp. 318–320
- 📖 **Open Book Test,** pp. 226–228
- 📼 **Got It! Assessment Videotapes,** Tape 6
- 💿 **Test Bank Software**

 Take It to the Net
Visit www.phschool.com for self-tests and additional questions on *The Crucible.*

Writing Rubric
- 📖 **Performance Assess. and Portfolio Mgmt.,** p. 17

 **PRENTICE HALL** *ASSESSMENT SYSTEM*

- 📖 **Workbook**
- 📖 **Skill Book**
- 📄 **Transparencies**
- 💿 **CD-ROM**

Lesson Objectives

1. To interpret an author's argument in a critical commentary
2. To understand the connection between a critical commentary and the literary work about which it is written
3. To apply the argument of a critical commentary to a literary work

About Critical Commentaries

- Have students read "About Critical Commentaries." Then, ask them to identify the two categories of such commentaries. Answer: The categories are those addressed to the work itself and those that make larger arguments.

- Encourage students to discuss the relative values of the two types of critical commentaries. Some students may say that a commentary on a literary work is more useful; others may be more interested in connecting literary works to larger themes.

- Ask students to explain which type of commentary they would prefer to write about the works in Unit 6. Possible response: Because some of the works in Unit 6 have contemporary themes, students may say they would prefer to write commentaries that address related social issues.

Reading Strategy

Interpreting an Author's Argument

- Have students read the information about the Reading Strategy.

- Be sure students understand that critical commentaries are arguments—the author makes an argument about a literary work, and possibly about related social issues.

- Review the How To chart on p. 1338 with students. Encourage them to use these strategies as they read.

- Explain that the language in critical commentaries is often dense with meaning. Encourage students to read slowly and look up unfamiliar words in a dictionary.

Critical Commentaries

About Critical Commentaries

A critical commentary is a piece of writing that analyzes and evaluates a work of art, an artistic performance, or a piece of literature.

- Some critical commentaries address the work itself—for example, discussing the strengths and weaknesses of a novel or a symphony.
- Other critical commentaries, like this piece by Arthur Miller, use the work as a springboard to a larger discussion. They might discuss particular works but then go on to offer the author's view of trends in society, of contemporary values, or of another issue of significance.

As the name suggests, critical commentaries express strong opinions. This does not mean, however, that they are not carefully planned and supported. Indeed, critical commentaries tend to be detailed and precise. Since their intent is largely persuasive, however, expect to find argumentative presentations and powerful use of language.

Reading Strategy

Interpreting an Author's Arguments

To gain the most from a critical commentary, interpret its arguments—the major points the author makes and the support he or she gives them. To interpret an argument, determine its meaning and importance, and then share it in terms that others can understand even if they have not read the work. While you may not choose to write about a commentary, deciding how to share its meaning is a good way to check your comprehension. These strategies can build your interpretive skills:

HOW TO	
Determine the Meaning	**Share the Meaning**
• After you read the commentary, write a sentence that asserts its main point. • Make sure your sentence is supported by the text. • List the evidence—examples, quotations, or other details—the author provides to support his or her view. • Notice how the author's word choice affects the message.	• Rewrite the main point as if you were sharing it with someone who had not read the commentary. • Summarize the author's argument. • Prepare a two-minute talk about the commentary. Explain its meaning and why it is important.

from *On Social Plays*

Arthur Miller

Time is moving; there is a world to make, a civilization to create that will move toward the only goal the humanistic, democratic mind can ever accept with honor. It is a world in which the human being can live as a naturally political, naturally private, naturally engaged person, a world in which once again a true tragic victory may be scored.

But that victory is not really possible unless the individual is more than theoretically capable of being recognized by the powers that lead society. Specifically, when men live, as they do under any industrialized system, as integers[1] who have no weight, no *person*, excepting as cus-

tomers, draftees, machine tenders, ideologists, or whatever, it is unlikely (and in my opinion impossible) that a dramatic picture of them can really overcome the public knowledge of their nature in real life. In such a society, be it communistic or capitalistic, man is not tragic, he is pathetic.[2] The tragic figure must have certain innate powers which he uses to pass over the boundaries of the known social law—the accepted mores[3] of his people—in order to test and discover necessity. Such a quest implies that the individual who has moved onto that course must be somehow recognized by the law,

> Here, Miller states his view. Notice how he uses such emotion-laden words as *impossible, overcome,* and *pathetic.*

---

1. **integers** (in´ tə jerz) *n.* numbers.

2. **pathetic** (pə the´ tik) *adj.* arousing pity.
3. **mores** (môr´ āz´) *n.* customs; unwritten laws.

---

from *On Social Plays*

- Explain to students that critical commentaries can be found in libraries and are a good way to learn more about the meaning of a literary work.

- Point out that in many of Arthur Miller's plays, such as *The Crucible*, characters are forced to battle with society over their rightful place in it. Given this concern, it should not surprise students that Miller's critical commentary moves beyond any specific work to speak to broader social issues.

- Have students read the selection and the notes that identify the elements of the commentary.

- Call students' attention to the first note. Ask them to explain Miller's view. Do the emotional words enhance Miller's argument? Explain.
  Possible response: Miller argues that because industrial societies rob people of their individuality, they cannot be tragic heroes in plays. Students may find the emotional words moving and effective, enhancing Miller's argument.

- Have students read the passage on p. 1340 identified by the second note as the point where Miller offers reasoning to support his view. Ask students: Is this effective support for Miller's argument?
  Possible response: Students who find Miller's reasoning compelling—who can relate emotionally to his concerns—will probably think it supports the argument effectively. Other students may want more concrete evidence.

CUSTOMIZE INSTRUCTION FOR UNIVERSAL ACCESS

For Less Proficient Readers	For English Learners	For Advanced Readers
These students may be challenged by the abstract nature of Miller's argument. Call attention to the first noted passage and explain that Miller believes that in industrial societies, people count only for the work they do and the money they spend. Ask students whether they have ever felt this way in their own society.	These students may find the dense language of Miller's essay difficult. Guide them through the first noted passage, asking them to pause and look up any unfamiliar words. Then, have them restate Miller's point in their own words. Encourage them to use this strategy to determine the meanings of other challenging passages.	After these students read the first noted passage, ask them to restate Miller's main argument. Then, ask them whether they agree with it. Some may agree that industrial society makes tragedy impossible; others may say that people still have personhood and can be tragic. Encourage students to debate the merit of Miller's argument.

from *On Social Plays*

- Remind students that in this critical commentary, Arthur Miller is using tragic drama as a springboard into a discussion of the impact of industrial society on individuals—he is connecting literature and social issues. One of students' goals as readers is to interpret Miller's argument.

- Call students' attention to the final note. Remind them that Miller has just stated that we can no longer tell the difference between a *tragic* character and a *pathetic* one. Then, ask students how Miller's use of words such as *industrial* and *integer* helps him make his point.
  Possible response: Students may say that these words remind readers of what Miller sees at the heart of the literary problem: In an industrial society, people are reduced to numbers—and thus cannot be truly tragic figures.

by the mores, by the powers that design—be they anthropomorphic[4] gods or economic and political laws—as having the worth, the innate value, of a whole people asking a basic question and demanding its answer. We are so atomized[5] socially that no character in a play can conceivably stand as our vanguard,[6] as our heroic questioner.

Miller offers this reasoning, whether based on his research or his personal observations, to support his view.

Our society—and I am speaking of every industrialized society in the world—is so complex, each person being so specialized an integer, that the moment any individual is dramatically characterized and set forth as a hero, our common sense reduces him to the size of a complainer, a misfit. For deep down we no longer believe in the rules of the tragic contest; we no longer believe that some ultimate sense can in fact be made of social causation,[7] or in the possibility that any individual can, by a heroic effort, make sense of it. Thus the man that is driven to question the moral chaos in which we live ends up in our estimate as a possibly commendable but definitely odd fellow, and probably as a compulsively driven neurotic.[8] In place of a social aim which called an all-around excellence—physical, intellectual, and moral—the ultimate good, we have set up a goal which can best be characterized as

The use of words like *industrial* and *integer* helps tie this point to the view that Miller stated earlier.

"happiness"—namely, staying out of trouble.[9] This concept is the end result of the truce which all of us have made with society. And a truce implies two enemies. When the truce is broken it means either that the individual has broken out of his ordained[10] place as an integer, or that the society has broken the law by harming him unjustly—that is, it has not left him alone to be a peaceful integer. In the heroic and tragic time the act of questioning the-way-things-are implied that a quest was being carried on to discover an ultimate law or way of life which would yield excellence; in the present time the quest is that of a man made unhappy by rootlessness and, in every important modern play, by a man who is essentially a victim. We have abstracted[11] from the Greek drama its air of doom, its physical destruction of the hero, but its victory escapes us. Thus it has even become difficult to separate in our minds the ideas of the pathetic and of the tragic. And behind this melting of the two lies the overwhelming power of the modern industrial state, the ignorance of each person in it of anything but his own technique as an economic integer, and the elevation of that state to a holy, quite religious sphere.

---

4. **anthropomorphic** (an´ thrə pō´ môr´ fik) *adj*: having human characteristics.
5. **atomized** (at´ ə mīzd´) *adj*. broken into small, disconnected pieces.
6. **vanguard** (van´ gärd´) *n*. leading part of an army or other group.
7. **social causation** social forces.
8. **neurotic** (nōō rät´ ik) *n*. person suffering from mental or emotional imbalance.

9. **a social aim . . . staying out of trouble** Miller is contrasting the ancient Greek ideal of *areté* (excellence; virtue) with the modern drives for conformity and comfort.
10. **ordained** (ôr dānd´) *adj*. assigned; appointed.
11. **abstracted** (ab strak´ tid) *v*. taken; separated.

CUSTOMIZE INSTRUCTION FOR UNIVERSAL ACCESS

For Special Needs Students	For Gifted/Talented Students
This selection may be very difficult for these students because of its long sentences and paragraphs and dense meaning. Have students work in pairs or small groups to rewrite the excerpt in their own words. Allow them time to go over the commentary, jotting down the main idea of each sentence. Then, have them write Miller's argument in language more accessible to students. Allow groups to present their new versions to the class.	After these students have read the selection, ask them whether they agree or disagree with Miller that tragedy in an industrial society is impossible. Place students in small groups based on their response. Challenge groups to write and perform a scene that either illustrates or criticizes Miller's argument. If students agree with Miller, they should create a character who is pathetic rather than tragic; if they disagree, their character should achieve true tragedy.

Check Your Comprehension

1. What does Miller mean when he calls people "integers"?
2. According to Miller, what must happen before a person can achieve "a true tragic victory" in the world?
3. Why does Miller disapprove of happiness as a goal?

Applying the Reading Strategy

Interpreting an Author's Arguments

4. When you interpret an argument, you must also determine its importance. Use a chart like the one shown to analyze your thoughts about Miller's commentary in "On Social Plays."

This critical commentary is important to . . .	
my understanding of *The Crucible* **because . . .**	**my understanding of Arthur Miller as a writer because . . .**
1. 2.	1. 2.

Activity

Writing a Critical Commentary

Select a story that you have recently read or a movie that you have recently seen. Identify which of the following statements most accurately represents your reaction to the story or film.

- "Life certainly is like that because . . . "
- "That was not true to life. In real life . . . "

In a brief critical commentary, use the story or movie as a springboard for sharing your views about some aspect of life.

Comparing Informational Materials

Critical Commentaries and Theater Reviews

Find a review of *The Crucible*. You might select a theater review from the play's debut in 1953 or a review of the 1996 film version. Analyze the ways in which the reviewer's comments about the society that Miller depicts differ from Miller's views as stated in "On Social Plays." Write a paragraph to compare and contrast the two commentaries.

Answers for p. 1341

Check Your Comprehension

1. He means that society defines people only by what they do for industry, either running machines or buying what they produce.

2. A person must be "recognized by the powers that lead society"—either the government or the gods—to achieve tragic victory.

3. He believes happiness means nothing more than "staying out of trouble."

Applying the Reading Strategy

4. Possible response: Left box: 1. it explains why the leaders of Salem tried to deny people their individuality; 2. it helps me to decide whether or not *The Crucible* is truly a tragedy; Right box: 1. it explains his concern for individuality in an industrial world; 2. it reveals that Miller tries to create *tragic* heroes, not *pathetic* ones.

Activity

Students' critical commentaries should identify both the work and the aspect of life it addresses, and should clearly state a main argument. Students should support their arguments with examples from the work and from life. Have students present their commentaries to the class and answer their classmates' questions.

Comparing Informational Materials

Possible response: Students may find reviews that point out the hostility of the society depicted by *The Crucible*, although the reviews will probably not use the work as a springboard the way that Miller does. Students will likely say that Miller's commentary is much more abstract and theoretical than the review.

Objectives

1. To write an essay analyzing literary trends
2. To analyze the ways in which different short stories address the same theme
3. To synthesize analyses of different stories into one argument about a literary trend
4. To use writing strategies to generate ideas, plan, organize, evaluate, and revise writing

Prewriting

- Explain to students that for this essay, they will need to choose stories that focus on the relationship between the individual and his or her family or community. Instruct students to use a chart like the one on p. 1342 to decide which stories in the unit have this focus.

- After they have identified stories they can analyze, have students ask the bulleted questions on p. 1342. If a student has difficulty answering questions about a story, it should not be included in the student's essay.

- Instruct students to take careful notes on the details in each story that reveal information about the characters' relationships. Notes should include quotations and page numbers.

- Explain to students that the thesis should sum up what the stories reveal about the individual within the family or community. Ask students to evaluate this sample thesis: "Individuals are in conflict with their families in two of these stories, but not in the third." Possible response: Students should recognize that this thesis does not synthesize the three stories. It is a poor thesis because it does not present one argument.

Writing About Literature

Analyze Literary Trends

During the period covered by this unit, issues of identity became a preoccupation in American life and literature. The changing role of women and the awareness that America is home to people of many cultural backgrounds added resonance to this preoccupation. Writers ask questions of identity in very personal ways: Who am I? Where do I come from? What is my role in my family and community?

To explore the variety of ways in which writers have answered these questions, complete the assignment outlined in the yellow box at right.

Prewriting

Find a focus. Use a chart like the one below to choose the characters and ideas that you want to analyze. Narrow your focus by answering these questions:

- Are the goals of the characters at odds with those of others?
- Are the beliefs of the characters in conflict with those of others?
- Do the actions of the characters reflect personal desires or the desires of others?

Use a self-sticking note to jot down ideas for the focus of your essay.

Model: Listing to Find a Focus

Possible focus: Explore conflict between materialism (status) and traditional values.

Story	Individual Characters	Family and Community	Notes
"The First Seven Years" p. 988	Miriam	Feld; Sobel; Max; aspiration for a better life; how is "better" measured?	Story shows conflict of values between materialism and depth of soul.
"Everyday Use" p. 1056	Dee	Dee is educated, sophisticated. Mother and Maggie are poor, uneducated.	Dee has "escaped," but she is the story's villain.

Gather details. Collect detailed information about the characters, including dialogue and descriptions. Note page numbers for future reference. These details will help you formulate your ideas.

Write a working thesis. A thesis is the focus, or main point, of your essay—the argument that you intend to prove. Your thesis may change as you write, but you need to have an idea of your intentions when you begin. Review your notes and write a thesis sentence.

1342 ◆ Prosperity and Protest (1946–Present)

Assignment:
A Question of Identity

Write an analytical essay that examines the fate of the individual within the family and community as it is depicted in at least three pieces of fiction from this unit.

Criteria:
- Analyze elements of plot and characterization from at least three stories.
- Identify larger trends or social forces to which characters are responding.
- Approximate length: 1,500 words.

Read to Write
Reread the texts to identify each character's goals and desires.

TEACHING RESOURCES

The following resources can be used to enrich or extend the instruction for pp. 1342–1343.

WG **Writing and Grammar**, Ruby Level, Chapter 14, pp. 298–317

Performance Assessment and Portfolio Management, p. 21

Writing Models and Graphic Organizers on Transparencies, p. 75

Writing and Grammar iText

Students can use the following tools as they complete their analyses of literary trends:

- Story Map Organizer
- Character Trait Word Bin
- Sentence Length Revising Tool

Drafting

Organize. Create an informal outline like the one shown below, and note where you will include quotations from the literature. Like your thesis, your outline may change as you clarify your ideas and determine the best way to present them.

Model: Creating an Informal Outline

I. **Introduction/thesis:** In these stories, those who seek new identities challenge traditional values.

II. **Example:** Feld wants Miriam to have a "better" life.

III. **Example:** Dee escapes the "backward" life of her family.

IV. **Conclusion:** To Dee, the quilt is an artifact, not something to use every day. In the same way, traditional values become quaint artifacts when abandoned by those seeking status.

Frame your ideas. Write an introduction that will grab the reader's attention. Consider beginning with a compelling quotation or detail. Then, write a strong conclusion that ends your essay with a memorable image or a statement that reinforces your main idea.

Revising and Editing

Review content: Revise to ensure a powerful argument. Make sure that your thesis is clearly stated and that you have proved it with evidence from the reading. Underline main ideas in your paper and confirm that each one is supported. Add more proof as needed.

Review style: Revise to cut wordy language. Check that you have found the clearest, simplest way to communicate your ideas. Omit unnecessary words.

Wordy: Miriam is not interested in or attracted to Max, but Feld pushes her to date him because he believes that Max, a college student, will be willing and able to give Miriam a life filled with luxury, wealth, and material comfort.

Revised: Miriam is not interested in the sullen Max, but Feld dreams that the college student will give her a comfortable life.

Publishing and Presenting

Give an oral presentation. Develop a brief talk for your class in which you detail your thesis. After your presentation, ask for questions and comments from your listeners.

WG *Prentice Hall Writing and Grammar Connection: Chapter 14*

Write to Learn

Writing is a tool for discovery, a way to figure out what you think and feel. This means that you may change your mind or get new ideas as you work. Allowing for this will improve your final draft.

Write to Explain

Do not simply summarize selections. Give examples from the reading to support your ideas.

Drafting

- Explain to students that an informal outline provides a way to organize the information they have gathered during the prewriting stage.

- Instruct students to include their theses in their outlines, as well as specific examples and quotes. Ask them to find the thesis in the model outline on p. 1343.
  Answer: The thesis is included under roman numeral I, "Introduction/thesis."

- Suggest that students begin by drafting their introduction and conclusion. Each of these paragraphs should communicate the essay's main point in an especially interesting way.

Revising and Editing

- On their drafts, have students underline or highlight their thesis and main points. Then, ask them to make sure that the thesis is clear and that all main points are supported with evidence from the stories. If they need more support, students should refer to their notes.

- Explain that sentences should make their points using only the words they really need. Ask students to explain why the Revised sentence on p. 1343 is more effective than the Wordy sentence.
  Possible response: Students should recognize that in the Wordy sentence, unneeded words block the idea.

Publishing and Presenting

- Encourage students to make notecards for their presentations. Students can prepare one card each for the introduction and conclusion, and one for each story.

- Encourage the class to ask questions after each presentation.

CUSTOMIZE INSTRUCTION FOR UNIVERSAL ACCESS

For Less Proficient Writers	For English Learners	For Advanced Writers
These students may have difficulty synthesizing analyses into one thesis. Encourage them to write their answers to the questions on p. 1342. Then, have students line up the answers for each story. Students should select three stories for which the answers are the same, so they can find one pattern for the thesis.	These students may find writing a clear thesis about characters' relationships difficult. If students have trouble finding appropriate words with which to state their arguments, have them use the Character Trait Word Bin on **Writing and Grammar iText CD-ROM.** They should look up any unfamiliar words.	Encourage these students to construct more challenging theses. Instead of selecting three stories that treat the theme in the same way, encourage these students to include at least one story that does not match. Their theses should account for the different ways the stories express the theme.

Lesson Objectives

1. To write a résumé for a job portfolio
2. To use writing strategies to generate ideas, plan, organize, evaluate, and revise writing

Model From Literature

Martín Espada writes of his work experiences in his poem "Who Burns for the Perfection of Paper" (p. 1100). Students' résumés will be far less personal than Espada's poem, but will present readers with a picture of the writer's experience.

Prewriting

- Encourage students to gather as many elements for their résumés as they can. Refer to the categories listed on p. 1344—work experience, education, honors, hobbies, interests, and extracurricular activities—and point out that résumés can include a wide range of experiences.

- Instruct students to use a checklist like the one on p. 1344 to choose which elements to include. Point out that on the model, only "Mow lawn" is not checked. Ask students to explain why it is left out. **Answer:** Mowing the lawn does not generally mean that one has the kinds of special skills indicated by "Videographer," "Mock Trial Team," and "Speak Hebrew."

- Have students use their charts to fit the selected experiences into one of three categories: work experience, activities, or skills. Be sure students recognize that all three are valuable.

- Remind students to sort their experiences chronologically. Point out that in many résumés, the most recent experiences are listed.

- Before students draft their essays, have them review the Rubric for Self-Assessment (p. 1347), so they know what is expected.

The **job portfolio** candidates submit to prospective employers usually consists of two main components—the **résumé**, which is a summary of one's qualifications and experience, and a cover letter that introduces the job seeker. Other elements of a job portfolio may include a list of references, a salary history, and writing or work samples. In this workshop, you will write a résumé designed to best show your strengths as a candidate for a job.

Assignment Criteria Your résumé should demonstrate the following characteristics:

- Name, address, and contact information provided in a highly visible format
- Clear summaries of the writer's work history, education, and related experience
- Information logically organized and provided in labeled sections and limited to one page
- Conventional formats, fonts, style, and spacing
- Formal and consistent use of language

To preview the criteria on which your résumé may be assessed, see the Rubric on page 1347.

Prewriting

Gather elements. Brainstorm for a **list** that thoroughly represents your work experience, education, honors, hobbies, interests, and extracurricular activities. The list may be messy and long; as you cut and focus your résumé you will not include every item, but it is helpful to begin by examining all the possibilities.

Select elements. Use a chart like the one shown to assess your list of items. Place a check beside those that best express your experience and skills. Then, select an appropriate category, such as work experience, activities, or skills, for each item. Note that many high school students do not have extensive work histories, but other activities, including experience on school clubs or responsibilities at home, can be mined for skills valuable to an employer.

Model: Selecting and Categorizing Experience

Include?	Item	Category
✓	Videographer	Work experience
✓	Mock Trial Team	Activities
✗	Mow Lawn	
✓	Speak Hebrew	Skills

Organize the timeline. Because you are a high school student, most employers will not look for a seamless work history, as they may with adult job seekers. However, it is useful to arrange items on your résumé to reflect an easily identifiable chronology.

TEACHING RESOURCES

The following resources can be used to enrich or extend the instruction for pp. 1344–1347.

Writing and Grammar, Ruby Level, Chapter 16, pp. 344–354

Writing Models and Graphic Organizers on Transparencies, p. 53–56

Writing and Grammar iText

Students can use the following tools as they complete their résumés:

- Self-Interview
- Timeline Organizer
- Descriptive Word Bank
- Sticky Notes Revising Tool

Student Model

Before you begin writing, read this student model and review the characteristics of an effective résumé.

Mark Israel Schilsky
123 Any Street
West Orange, New Jersey 00000
Telephone: (973) 555-5555 • E-Mail: mis@---.com

> Name and contact information are placed prominently at the top of the page and set in a larger font size.

OVERVIEW
Academically focused, hard-working, reliable high school student with strong interest in biology, seeking a laboratory internship for the summer; available from June 20 through August 25.

EDUCATION
West Orange High School, West Orange, NJ; will graduate in June 200-

> Clear labels like *Education* and *Honors* organize background and experience.

HONORS
NMSQT Commended Scholar, Biology II NJ Science League Sixth individually in all of NJ, Finalist NJ Governors School in the Sciences, Nominated to attend NJ Boys' State, Red Cross CPR/Lifeguard Certified, National Association of Biology Teachers Award for Excellence, National Youth Leadership Forum on Medicine Invitee, Recipient of Edward J. Bloustein Award for Academics, Eagle Scout Rank

WORK EXPERIENCE

Summer 2001 — **Laboratory Technician,** Duke University, Durham, NC
Performed PCR reactions, obtained DNA samples, and photographed electrophoresis gels.

9/99–present — **Videographer,** Temple Sharey-Tefilo, South Orange, NJ
Videotape celebrations, meetings, drama programs, and other special events; edit tapes, add special effects.

9/00–present — **Student Aide/Hebrew Teacher,** Temple Sharey-Tefilo, South Orange, NJ
Assist after-school teachers with children ages 5–7. Lead games and sports activities. Teach Hebrew to students, ages 9–11, 3–5 hours per week.

> Mark included dates, clearly set off to focus information.

SKILLS
• Computers: word processing, spreadsheets, graphics, HTML
• Microbiology laboratory procedures
• Knowledge Hebrew and Spanish

ACTIVITIES
• Mock Trial team
• Marching Band: Alto Sax Section Leader (1 yr)
• Varsity Spring Track
• School Musical: Program Editor, Stage Crew
• National Honor Society

> Mark provides a more complete picture of his personality by including information about his activities.

Student Model

- Explain that the Student Model is a sample, and that résumés may include more information.

- Point out to students that Mark's name is placed so that it is the very first thing a reader sees. Ask them why this might be important. **Possible response:** Students may say it is important because the name tells a potential employer who Mark is before the résumé tells what experience he has.

- Call students' attention to the headings Mark uses, and explain that they keep the résumé well organized. Ask students what distinguishes the headings from the other text.
  Answer: They are boldfaced, underlined, and written in capital letters.

- Ask students to review Mark's work experience. Point out that Mark has included clear, readable dates for each item.

- Finally, call students' attention to Mark's last heading, Activities. Explain that these items show employers that Mark is a well-rounded, motivated individual. Encourage students to take their own activities seriously and include them in their résumés.

Real-World Connection

Job portfolios in the workplace: Tell students that writing job portfolios and résumés may turn out to be the most important step of their careers—the *first* step. When they enter the job market, each of your students will need to write these documents in order to let prospective employers know who they are and what they can do. Encourage the class to see a résumé as a chance to show the world their very best.

CUSTOMIZE INSTRUCTION FOR UNIVERSAL ACCESS

For Less Proficient Writers	For English Learners	For Advanced Writers
These students may have difficulty selecting elements from their initial list to include in their résumés. Help students restate items from their list so that they fit an appropriate category. You can refer students to the Word Bins on **Writing and Grammar iText CD-ROM.**	Students who did not grow up in the United States may be unsure about what experiences they should include in their résumés. Point out that their fluency in their first languages and their familiarity with another culture are skills that many employers value very highly. These experiences should be emphasized in a résumé.	These students may be inclined to describe their experiences in too much detail. Discourage them from overwriting. Remind students that their résumés should be only one page long. Explain that their audience wants essential information communicated efficiently in a short space.

Drafting

- Make sure that students have already organized the items on their résumés into appropriate categories and chosen headings.

- Explain to students that before they begin to write, they must choose styles for their résumés. Have them read the examples of Whole Sentences and Phrases on p. 1346, and ask them to explain which is preferable.
  Possible response: Students should recognize that both are equally appropriate—as long as the résumé uses only one, consistently.

- Explain to students who are less familiar with résumés that there are standard elements employers expect to see. Review the checklist on p. 1346, and instruct students to use it to make sure their résumés include all of the standard elements.

- Remind students that they can change their résumés as they draft, if they need to.

Revising

- Have students read over the drafts of their résumés. Instruct them to ask themselves the following: Are my categories appropriate? Are they clearly labeled? Is the information in the right categories? Is the résumé organized consistently?

- Call students' attention to the example on p. 1346. Point out that Mark has found an item in the wrong category and moved it. He has also edited to limit the résumé to one page.

- Explain to students that the writing in their résumés should be not just consistent, but also active and specific—they should use active verbs and clear, concrete details. Refer students to the examples of Unspecific and Specific language on p. 1347.

Drafting

Select a style. Choose a style with which to convey information and apply it consistently as you draft. For example, use either whole sentences or phrases in your experience descriptions, but do not mix the two.

- **Whole sentences:** I edit videotapes and add special effects.
- **Phrases:** Edit videotapes; add special effects.

Adhere to standards. As you draft, use a checklist like the one shown to verify that you have included all standard and expected elements. Add any element that you may have overlooked.

Play to your strengths. If you, like many high school students, have had only limited work experience, use your résumé to emphasize academic and life experiences that show your capabilities. Stress skills related to the job for which you are applying.

Résumé Conventions

- ☐ **Heading** indicates name, address and contact information of the candidate.
- ☐ **Overview or Summary** provides a brief statement about the candidate.
- ☐ **Experience** lists details of work history.
- ☐ **Education** provides history of candidate's schooling and other training.
- ☐ **Skills** notes special abilities, such as computer training or fluency in a foreign language.
- ☐ **Honors/Awards/Activities/Memberships** is a flexible category used to show interests or hobbies.

Revising

Revise to make your format consistent. Make sure that you have followed a consistent organizational strategy throughout the résumé.

1. Check that your categories are clearly labeled, and the experience descriptions placed under the proper sections.
2. Check that all elements of the résumé are uniform. For example, the dates of your activities should be clearly indicated, and given in a consistent fashion—do not switch back and forth between styles.
3. Make sure that your résumé is only one page long. If it is too long, edit it so that it fits.

Model: Revising to Maintain Organizational Strategy

Summer 2001	**Laboratory Technician,** Duke University, Durham, NC
	Performed PCR reactions, obtained DNA samples, and photographed electrophoresis gels.
9/99–present	Mock Trial Team, West Orange High School, West Orange, NJ
	Served as defense attorney for mock trial cases.
	Honed research, public speaking, and team-building skills.
move to **Activities**	

Mark moved the description of his participation in the Mock Trial Team out of *Work Experience*, where it did not belong. He then edited it for length and placed it under *Activities*.

USING TECHNOLOGY IN WRITING

Explain that some word processing programs include résumé formatting tools. Encourage students to investigate these tools, using the Help tool and tutorials. Even if their programs do not offer a résumé format, students should be able to use such typesetting features as boldfacing, underlining, columns, and bulleted lists. Instruct students to use these features to help organize their résumés, but discourage them from using such features as nonstandard fonts. Students can also use the **Writing and Grammar iText CD-ROM.**

Revise to include active and specific language. The language you use in your résumé reveals your attitudes and seriousness of purpose. Avoid the use of unspecific or passive language. Use active verbs and specific descriptions.

Unspecific: Made brochures for public relations firm.

Specific: Researched, wrote, and edited four-color brochures for public relations firm.

Compare the model and the nonmodel. Why is the model more effective?

Nonmodel	Model
Watch children at after-school program.	Lead games and sports activities. Teach Hebrew to students ages 9–11.

Publishing and Presenting

Consider the following strategy to share your résumé with a wider audience.

Submit your résumé to an employer. Print your résumé on good-quality paper in a neutral color, such as white or ivory. When you read about a job you would like to pursue, send your résumé, along with a cover letter using standard business format. In your cover letter, you may wish to introduce yourself and elaborate on any talents or experiences that make you an excellent job candidate.

$\mathcal{W}_{G}$ *Prentice Hall Writing and Grammar Connection: Chapter 16*

Rubric for Self-Assessment

Evaluate your résumé using the following criteria and rating scale:

Criteria	Rating Scale				
	Not very				Very
How visibly does the résumé present the writer's name, address, and contact information?	1	2	3	4	5
How clear are the summaries of the writer's work history, education, and other experience?	1	2	3	4	5
How well organized is the résumé?	1	2	3	4	5
How well does the writer apply conventional formats, fonts, style, and spacing?	1	2	3	4	5
How formal and consistent is the writer's use of language?	1	2	3	4	5

Revising (continued)

- Have students read and compare the model and nonmodel on p. 1347. Then, ask the question above them: Why is the model more effective?
  Possible response: Students should recognize that the model uses concrete language and action-oriented verbs. These qualities make Mark's experiences sound more valuable.

- Remind students that it is important for résumés to be especially neat and free of errors. Instruct them to proofread for spelling and mechanical errors after revising and editing.

Publishing and Presenting

- Tell students to think about how they want their finished résumé to look to a potential employer— what font it should be in, what type of paper it should be printed on, and so on.

- Explain to students that the other major component of a job portfolio is a cover letter. A cover letter should draw attention to and elaborate on any skills or experiences that make the applicant especially well qualified for the position he or she is seeking.

Assessment

- Review the assessment criteria with the class.

- Encourage students to use the rubric on p. 1347 to score the Student Model résumé. Then, have them score their own résumés. Encourage them to revise any areas in which they received a low score.

TEST-TAKING TIP

Although it is not likely that students will be asked to write a résumé in a test situation, many tests do require students to work with such workplace documents as résumés and memoranda. Explain to students that familiarity with writing these documents will help them read and answer questions about them on a test. While workplace documents vary widely in format, nearly all share such characteristics as formal language, clear organization, headings and subheadings, concrete details, and a focus on conveying information efficiently in as little space as possible.

Analyze the Impact of the Media

Lesson Objectives

1. To analyze the impact of the media on the news and the democratic process
2. To analyze the explicit ways journalists can influence news coverage and public opinion
3. To analyze the implicit ways media makers can influence news coverage and public opinion

Analyze Explicit Influence

- Explain to students that an editorial is an explicit statement of a journalist's view on an issue. Editorials are one way that journalists and media makers can explicitly influence public opinion.

- Tell students that opinion forums are another explicit influence. By telling each other their opinions, participants in these discussions attempt to directly influence the forums' audience.

- If possible, show students videotape of a televised editorial and an opinion forum. Tell students to be on the lookout for opinion words such as "views," "thoughts," or "comments."

Analyze Implicit Influence

- Explain that media also influences public opinion implicitly. Have students read the comment on images of leaders on p. 1348. Then ask: How do the images of leaders chosen by news media influence public opinion? Possible response: When media makers broadcast flattering images of a leader, they communicate a positive message about him or her; an unflattering image communicates a negative message.

- Explain that the sequence of news stories on a television broadcast influences public opinion by directing the audience's attention and concerns toward the first stories covered.

- Tell students that journalists can also exercise influence by choosing what questions to ask leaders, because this determines what answers leaders can give and what information they can offer the public.

Both print and broadcast media can have a dramatic effect on the unfolding of the democratic process. As a potential voter, you must develop critical listening and viewing skills in order to analyze media activities and evaluate their effects. The strategies outlined below will help you understand some common points of media influence. The form on this page offers a starting point for actual analysis.

Analyze Explicit Influence

Journalists and media makers often hold strong views and sometimes seek to affect the political process by expressing their beliefs. Familiarize yourself with the usual forums for such statements of opinion.

Identify editorials. Talk-show hosts and journalists may deliver editorials that are intended to express opinions. Likewise, news shows may host discussions in which a variety of participants express opinions. Listen carefully as a participant is introduced. Words such as "views," "thoughts," or "comments" signal an opinion that listeners should evaluate.

Recognize opinion forums. Debate forums in which journalists express opposing views offer you the opportunity to hear many opinions. Note, however, that each speaker hopes to influence you to share a particular view.

Analyze Implicit Influence

Often, media makers exert indirect influence on elections or public opinion. Pay attention to these avenues of influence.

- **Images of leaders** When the media shows a candidate looking strong, it sends a positive message about that candidate. If the candidate looks tired or confused, the media has telegraphed a lack of support.

- **Reporting priorities** Media makers exert influence through the stories they report *and* the sequence in which they present them. The lead story of a television news show usually gets the largest audience, while stories reported later may reach a tiny audience. The placement of a story in the sequence may affect public perception.

- **Shaping attitudes** When journalists conduct interviews, the questions they ask influence the information you receive. To avoid accepting biased information, compare news sources.

(Activity: Listen and Analyze) For a week, analyze the coverage of an important story in at least one form of media. Use the feedback form shown here to analyze the impact of the coverage each day.

Feedback Form for Evaluating Media Influence

Rating System
+ = Present   − = Omitted

Explicit Influence of Reports
Editorial _____
Opinion Forum _____
How did these reports exert influence? What signals suggested opinion?

Implicit Influence of Reports
Persuasive images _____
Reporting priorities _____
Questioning priorities _____
Time issues _____

Answer the following question:
How might the media choices or elements that you noted affect the audience or even influence the outcome of a story?

CUSTOMIZE INSTRUCTION FOR UNIVERSAL ACCESS

For Special Needs Students	For English Learners	For Advanced Readers
These students may have trouble distinguishing between objective and subjective news. Tell them presenting opinions is a legitimate function of news media. Explain that explicit opinions are presented in editorials or opinion forums. If a segment on a news program is introduced as an editorial, students can assume it will present an opinion.	To help these students distinguish between objective and subjective news, show them the front page, editorials, and letters to the editor of a local newspaper. Explain that the front page is objective news, and editorials and letters are subjective. Letters to the editor in a newspaper are similar to opinion forums in television or radio news.	To help these students recognize editorials in audiovisual news media, encourage them to gather a word bank of opinion-oriented words such as "views," "thoughts," and "comments." Have them practice using these words before they try to recognize them in an actual news broadcast.

Assessment WORKSHOP

Punctuation, Usage, and Sentence Structure

Lesson Objective
To identify and correct errors in punctuation, usage, and sentence structure in a test situation

The writing sections of some tests examine your knowledge of the usage and mechanics of Standard Written English. Use the following strategies to help you answer test questions regarding punctuation, grammar and usage, and sentence structure:

- You can often identify errors by reading the sentence aloud, as if it were being spoken. Incorrect English usually sounds wrong, and you can learn to hear errors.
- Remember that punctuation marks act as symbols to readers, telling them where to stop, pause, read with a questioning tone, or read with excitement.
- Memorize the rules for specific grammatical structures, such as the use of *its* or *it's,* and the use of *who* and *whom,* that are a common source of errors.
- As you read, recognize correct and incorrect grammar— especially subject-verb agreement and pronoun usage.
- Learn to recognize structural errors, such as run-on sentences, sentence fragments, and misplaced modifiers.

Test-Taking Strategies

- Look carefully at all punctuation in each passage.
- Remember that there may be more than one error in each passage.
- Choose the answer that corrects *all* of the errors in the passage.

Applying Reading Strategies

Explain to students that envisioning the action in their minds, an important reading strategy for fiction, can help them to recognize errors in sentences. If a reader pays close enough attention, errors in punctuation, usage, or sentence structure interrupt envisioning and demand corrections.

Test-Taking Skills

- Have students read the sentence for the sample test item. Although there is little action to envision, encourage them to visualize as well as they can. Ask students whether they see an error in the sentence.
  Answer: Students should notice that the underlined section of the sentence contains a comma splice.
- Next, ask students to read through the answers for the sample item. Guide them to recognize that *A* is the correct answer because a semicolon should be used to separate two independent clauses.

Sample Test Question

Directions: Read the sentence, and then choose the letter of the best answer to the question.

Some automobiles require diesel fuel to run properly, some do not.

1. Which of the following choices is the best revision to the underlined passage?
   A properly; some do not
   B properly . . . some do not
   C properly: some do not
   D Correct as is.

Answer and Explanation

The correct answer is **A.** A semicolon should be used to separate two independent clauses.

Practice

Directions: Read the passage, and then choose the letter of the best answer to the question.

(1) It had been a long and hard-fought campaign, the voters were ready to make a choice. (2) With the qualifications of all the candidates in mind, the voters chose Dan O'Neill to be mayor. (3) Voters claimed that they were impressed with the full range of his positive attributes.

1. How would you correct sentence 1?
   A campaign: the voters
   B campaign; the voters
   C campaign The voters
   D Correct as is

Answer

The correct answer is *B*. The first sentence contains a comma splice—a comma is used to separate two independent clauses. Because there is an error, answer *D* is incorrect. Answer *A* is incorrect because the sentence after the colon does not summarize or explain the one before it. Answer *C* is incorrect because it needs a period after the word "campaign."

TEACHING RESOURCES

The following resources can be used to enrich or extend the instruction for pp. 1348–1349.

PRENTICE HALL
ASSESSMENT *SYSTEM*

- Workbook
- Skill Book
- Transparencies
- CD-ROM

RESOURCES

Suggestions for Sustained Reading R1

Glossary R7

Handbooks

Tips for Improving Reading Fluency R10

Literary Terms Handbook R12

Grammar and Mechanics Handbook R22

Summary of Grammar R22
Summary of Capitalization and Punctuation R24
Glossary of Common Usage R26

Internet Research Handbook R29

Citing Sources R31

Rubric Handbook R33

Preparing for College Entrance and AP™ Exams R37

Handbook of Academic Writing R40

College Application Essays R40
Writing About Literature R41

Formatting Business Letters R46

Commonly Misspelled Words R47

Indexes

Index of Authors and Titles R48

Index of Skills R50

Index of Features R57

Acknowledgments *(continued)* R58

Credits R61

SUGGESTIONS FOR SUSTAINED READING

Following are some suggestions for longer works that will give you the opportunity to experience the fun of sustained reading. Each of the suggestions explores one of the time periods, themes, or literary movements in this book. Many of the titles are included in the **Prentice Hall Literature Library**, featuring the **Penguin Literature Library.**

You may want to consult your teacher before choosing one of these longer works.

Unit 1: Beginnings–1750

The Interesting Narrative and Other Writings
Olaudah Equiano
Penguin Books, 1995

In the mid-eighteenth century, the young West African Olaudah Equiano was sold into slavery and shipped to the West Indies. There, his intelligence and curiosity enabled him to benefit from his travels with his master and from the education he received. After gaining his freedom, he traveled to England and joined the abolitionist cause, lecturing on the evils of slavery. It was British abolitionists who helped him publish his autobiography, *The Interesting Narrative of Olaudah Equiano.* This book and his other writings are not only a compelling argument against slavery, but also the "interesting" record of a compassionate and gifted man.

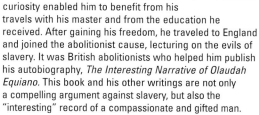

American Colonies: The Settling of North America
Alan Taylor
Penguin Books, 2001

The settling of the American colonies was not a simple, straightforward story but an interweaving of many narratives. Pulitzer Prize-winning author Alan Taylor does justice to this multifaceted history by explaining the roles that different peoples played in this process: enslaved Africans, Native American tribes, and European colonizers from England, the Netherlands, Spain, Russia, and France. In addition, Taylor expands his focus to include regions of the continent beyond the Eastern seaboard as well as ecological factors influencing colonial settlement.

The Four Voyages
Christopher Columbus, edited and translated by J. M. Cohen
Penguin Books, 1969

Imagine standing beside Christopher Columbus when, after a long and risky voyage across the Atlantic, he first arrived at the island of San Salvador. Readers can have this and other equally exciting experiences as they "travel" through *The Four Voyages.* This volume combines material from Columbus's own logbook and letters with contemporary biographies of him and letters from others who participated in his expeditions.

Chronicle of the Narváez Expedition
Alvar Núñez Cabeza de Vaca, translated by Fanny Bandelier
Penguin Books, 2002

In the early sixteenth century, Spain sent the Narváez expedition to the southern United States to claim vast territories for the Spanish empire. Cabeza de Vaca, who went on this journey, describes the fascinating but sad fate of this expedition. After being shipwrecked, members of the expedition traveled by foot all the way from Florida to California. Their numbers diminished until, by the end of the 9-year ordeal, only Cabeza de Vaca and three others remained.

Native American Literature
Prentice Hall
Pearson Prentice Hall, 2000

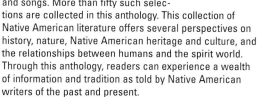

The literature of Native Americans from the Northeast through Central America is a rich and varied collection of myths and legends, poems, tribal histories, personal experiences, dreams, and songs. More than fifty such selections are collected in this anthology. This collection of Native American literature offers several perspectives on history, nature, Native American heritage and culture, and the relationships between humans and the spirit world. Through this anthology, readers can experience a wealth of information and tradition as told by Native American writers of the past and present.

To the Teacher:

Because great literature reflects all of life's realities, both positive and negative, classroom discussions of literature can raise sensitive and often controversial issues. Before you recommend novels, plays, and other literature to your students, you may want to consider the values and sensitivities of the community in which you teach, as well as the age and sophistication of your students. It is also a good policy to preview any literature that you are considering recommending to your students. The notes below offer some guidance on specific titles.

Unit 1

The Interesting Narrative and Other Writings
by Olaudah Equiano

This book deals with the kidnapping of children who are then sold into slavery, the horrors of the trip across the ocean on a slave ship, the mistreatment of slaves, and the suicides of several slaves. There is a good deal of Christian doctrine in this narrative.

American Colonies: The Settling of North America
by Alan Taylor

This book deals with many controversial topics, including Columbus's exploration, the conflicts between Europeans and Native Americans, and the enslavement of Native Americans and Africans.

The Four Voyages
by Christopher Columbus

In this book, the attitudes of the European explorers toward the natives of the islands may be offensive to some readers.

Chronicle of the Narváez Expedition
by Alvar Núñez Cabeza de Vaca

Both the Spanish explorers and the Native Americans treat each other very poorly in this book. Harsh conditions, cannibalism, and the killing of girl babies may disturb readers.

Native American Literature
Prentice Hall

Some of these selections depict violence, prejudice, and harsh living conditions and contain criticisms of white Americans, missionaries, and the U.S. government.

Unit 2

Rights of Man
by Thomas Paine

In referring to the rights of man, Paine is referring only to white men. Some of his opinions about the English monarchy and the Catholic Church may offend readers. There are also elements of anti-Semitism in the work.

The Federalist Papers
by Alexander Hamilton, James Madison, and John Jay

Some students may be disturbed by the fact that the framers of the Constitution did not include African Americans, Native Americans, or women in their concept of self-government.

The Anti-Federalist Papers and the Constitutional Convention Debates
Edited by Ralph Ketcham

Some students may be disturbed by the fact that neither the framers of the Constitution nor their opponents among the antifederalists included African Americans, Native Americans, or women in their concept of self-government.

Unit 2: A Nation Is Born (1750–1800)

The Autobiography and Other Writings
Benjamin Franklin
Penguin Books, 1986

Benjamin Franklin is one of America's best-loved Founding Fathers. He was a member of the Second Continental Congress and served on the committee that drafted the Declaration of Independence. Besides helping to establish the nation itself, he created many institutions—for example, a hospital, an academy, and a fire company—that were often the first ones of their type in the New World. In his *Autobiography,* Franklin reveals the qualities that enabled him to achieve success as a publisher, scientist, writer, politician, and diplomat.

Complete Writings
Phillis Wheatley
Penguin Books, 2001

Phillis Wheatley was an enslaved African who was brought to the United States as a child in 1761. She received her name from John Wheatley, the Boston tailor who purchased her. Wheatley and his wife realized Phillis's intelligence and provided her with an education that included such subjects as Latin, Greek, the Bible, and English and classical literature. Stimulated by her studies, Phillis won fame by publishing her first poem when she was just fourteen years old. She went on to write the many poems, translations, and letters in this volume, becoming America's first important black woman poet.

Rights of Man
Thomas Paine
Penguin Books, 1984

Thomas Paine was one of the most eloquent and widely read political authors of all time. His pamphlet "Common Sense" helped inspire the Declaration of Independence, and the first installment of his *Crisis* papers encouraged George Washington's army when it was enduring a difficult winter at Valley Forge. After the American Revolution,

Paine traveled to Europe and wrote *Rights of Man,* his defense of the French Revolution. In it, he argues against monarchy and for a republican form of government. He also sets forth ideas for curing society's ills, including a progressive income tax, popular education, and pensions. This book so infuriated the British government that it was banned. Today's readers, however, will marvel at Paine's prophetic insights.

The Federalist Papers
Alexander Hamilton, James Madison, and John Jay
Mentor, 1999

In 1787 and 1788, Alexander Hamilton, James Madison, and John Jay wrote eighty-five essays to persuade New Yorkers to adopt the new national Constitution. First published in newspapers, these articles were eventually collected in *The Federalist Papers.* Not only were they successful in their immediate purpose, but they have also survived more than 200 years as some of the wisest commentaries on government ever written. They explain, for example, how a political system of checks and balances, like the one embodied in the Constitution, can help protect against human vice and folly. In addition to the Papers themselves, this volume contains an introduction with detailed background information and an appendix with the text of the American Constitution.

The Anti-Federalist Papers and the Constitutional Convention Debates
Edited by Ralph Ketcham
Mentor, 1986

The perfect companion to *The Federalist Papers,* this volume provides a context for the debate surrounding the ratification of the Constitution. The introduction, for example, outlines both federalist principles and antifederalist political thought. It also provides a chronology of documents and important events. The many primary documents in the book itself are grouped into two sections: Part I, The Federal Convention of 1787, and Part II, Ratification of the Constitution. Readers can experience the birth of the nation as they follow debates on such essential issues as "State Equality in the Senate" and "Election and Term of Office of the National Executive."

Unit 3: A Growing Nation (1800–1870)

The Journals of Lewis and Clark
Edited by John Bakeless
Mentor, 1964

In 1803, Thomas Jefferson doubled the size of the United States by purchasing a tract of land west of the Mississippi River. Jefferson then sent Captains Meriwether Lewis and William Clark on an expedition to explore this vast, new territory. Readers will feel as if they are accompanying this historic expedition every step of the way as they read the journal entries of its two leaders. On this trek from the Missouri River to the Pacific coast, encounters with friendly and unfriendly Native Americans, awe-inspiring scenery, and grizzly bears are part of the daily routine.

The Scarlet Letter
Nathaniel Hawthorne
Pearson Prentice Hall, 2000

They were very few in number, but their courage, hard work, and intense perseverance enabled the Puritans who landed at Plymouth in 1620 to establish a colony. Though *The Scarlet Letter* was published in 1850, Nathaniel Hawthorne chose this setting—a world in which people lived simple lives and followed a strict moral code—for his masterpiece. The novel tells the story of Hester Prynne, who is branded as an outcast and struggles to create her own redemption.

Selected Writings of Ralph Waldo Emerson
Edited by William H. Gilman
Signet Classic, 1965

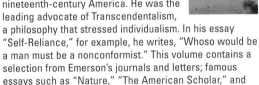

New England philosopher and poet Ralph Waldo Emerson was perhaps the most eloquent and influential author of nineteenth-century America. He was the leading advocate of Transcendentalism, a philosophy that stressed individualism. In his essay "Self-Reliance," for example, he writes, "Whoso would be a man must be a nonconformist." This volume contains a selection from Emerson's journals and letters; famous essays such as "Nature," "The American Scholar," and "Self-Reliance"; and Emerson's best poems, including "The Rhodora," "The Snow-Storm," and "Brahma." In addition, the editor, William H. Gilman, provides a foreword and a chronology of Emerson's life.

Walden and Civil Disobedience
Henry David Thoreau
Signet Classic, 1999

If Ralph Waldo Emerson was the leading advocate of Transcendentalism, his friend Henry David Thoreau was probably its leading practitioner. He lived the truths in which he believed. In 1845, for example, he built a wooden hut on the banks of Walden Pond near Concord, Massachusetts, and settled there for about two and a half years. *Walden* is the account of this attempt to live simply and independently. This grab bag of eloquence contains everything from vivid descriptions of nature to poems to a balance sheet of purchases. The essay "On the Duty of Civil Disobedience," prompted by Thoreau's opposition to slavery and to the war against Mexico, affirms that an individual's conscience has more authority than an unjust law. Its ideas still seem radical today.

Leaves of Grass
Walt Whitman
Signet Classic, 2000

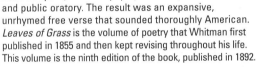

Walt Whitman invented American poetry by breaking free of British influence. While other American poets modeled their work on that of British writers, Whitman drew on unexpected sources such as opera, the newspaper, the Bible, and public oratory. The result was an expansive, unrhymed free verse that sounded thoroughly American. *Leaves of Grass* is the volume of poetry that Whitman first published in 1855 and then kept revising throughout his life. This volume is the ninth edition of the book, published in 1892.

Unit 3

The Scarlet Letter
by Nathaniel Hawthorne

This book's central subject is the accusation and punishment of a woman for engaging in adultery. Some students may feel that the public shaming that Hester endures at the hands of her fellow Puritans is disproportionate to her purported crime.

Selected Writings of Ralph Waldo Emerson
Edited by William H. Gilman

Emerson espouses religious beliefs that are contrary to most mainstream religious doctrines. Some students may be sensitive to these ideas.

Leaves of Grass
by Walt Whitman

Whitman's poems contain details about human sexuality, drinking, crime, slavery, the violence of war, suicide, prostitution, venereal disease, and various bodily functions. He occasionally uses dated ethnic, racial, and religious language and stereotypes that may be problematic.

Unit 4

Narrative of the Life of Frederick Douglass
by Frederick Douglass

Some students may feel angry and frustrated by the injustices of slavery and the countless cruel acts that went unpunished. The narrative contains many disturbing images of slaves being brutally beaten and whipped. References are made to adultery and to the rape of enslaved women by their masters. In one instance, a female slave is purchased for the purpose of "breeding." The word *nigger* is used occasionally.

The Adventures of Huckleberry Finn
by Mark Twain

In addition to depicting slavery and racism, the book contains negative racial stereotypes and offensive language, including frequent, casual use of the word *nigger*. Child abuse and alcoholism are also depicted.

Spoon River Anthology
by Edgar Lee Masters

Sensitive issues in these poems include adultery, sex without marriage, unwed motherhood, homosexuality, prostitution, venereal disease, abortion, rape, arson, murder, suicide, religious doubt, patriotic doubt, crooked business practices, dishonest politicians, and alcoholism.

My Ántonia
by Willa Cather

Racism, prejudice against immigrants, insensitivity toward the mentally retarded and developmentally disabled, and other biased attitudes are expressed in the novel.

The Sea-Wolf and Selected Stories
by Jack London

This volume includes scenes of violence and cruelty.

Unit 4: Division, Reconciliation, and Expansion (1850–1914)

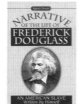

Narrative of the Life of Frederick Douglass
Frederick Douglass
Signet Classic, 1997

Frederick Douglass was born a slave in Maryland in the early 1800s. Intelligent, courageous, and persistent, he learned how to read and write even though the conditions of his servitude made it extremely difficult to gain such skills. After experiencing a number of masters and mistresses, both good and bad, Douglass escaped to New York and freedom. From there, he traveled to New Bedford, Massachusetts, where he found employment. He began to read the abolitionist publication the "Liberator," and soon launched a career as an antislavery speaker. In this narrative, Douglass not only conveys the facts of his early life, he also reveals the soul-destroying effects of slavery on master and slave alike.

The Adventures of Huckleberry Finn
Mark Twain
Pearson Prentice Hall, 2000

Ernest Hemingway once wrote that "all modern American literature comes from one book by Mark Twain called *Huckleberry Finn*." The most important part of this influential novel concerns the adventures of two "runaways" on the great Mississippi River. One is Huck Finn, the hero of the novel, who is escaping from his abusive father. The other is Jim, an enslaved African trying to gain his freedom. In the course of their travels, they meet a variety of memorable characters, and Huck experiences a conflict about the morality of slavery. Twain's novel has earned its place of honor in American literature through its skillful use of dialect, its vivid depiction of American life, and its compassionate analysis of race relations.

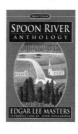

Spoon River Anthology
Edgar Lee Masters
Signet Classic, 1992

Edgar Lee Masters fled the small towns of his Illinois boyhood to become a big-city lawyer in Chicago. Yet in writing the poems of *Spoon River Anthology*, his most successful book, he drew heavily on his boyhood experiences. An interesting twist, however, is that the more than 200 townspeople in the book are all dead! They speak their free-verse poems from the graveyard, summing up their lives and expressing their angers, disappointments, ideas, dreams, and loves. Together, they provide a realistic picture of life in a small American town, a picture that is fascinating but not always pretty.

My Ántonia
Willa Cather
Pearson Prentice Hall, 2000

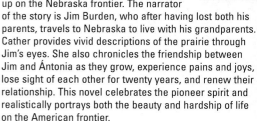

Willa Cather drew on her girlhood experiences to write *My Ántonia*. The book's heroine, Ántonia, is a self-reliant and spirited young Bohemian woman growing up on the Nebraska frontier. The narrator of the story is Jim Burden, who after having lost both his parents, travels to Nebraska to live with his grandparents. Cather provides vivid descriptions of the prairie through Jim's eyes. She also chronicles the friendship between Jim and Ántonia as they grow, experience pains and joys, lose sight of each other for twenty years, and renew their relationship. This novel celebrates the pioneer spirit and realistically portrays both the beauty and hardship of life on the American frontier.

The Sea-Wolf and Selected Stories
Jack London
Signet Classic, 1964

Fascinated by the conflict between wildness and civilization, Jack London wrote about this theme in many novels and tales. In his adventure story *The Sea-Wolf,* this conflict takes the form of a struggle between Wolf Larsen and Humphrey Van Weyden. Larsen is the captain of a seal-hunting ship, and as his first name suggests, he is fierce and cruel. Yet this complex man is also a student of philosophy. Van Weyden, who reluctantly becomes a crewman on the ship, is a believer in the value of civilization. The struggle between them takes place as the ship cruises the Pacific in search of seal herds. In addition to *The Sea-Wolf*, the book contains four stories by London, including "The Law of Life" and "All Gold Canyon."

Unit 5: Disillusion, Defiance, and Discontent (1914–1946)

The Great Gatsby
F. Scott Fitzgerald
Scribner, 1992

Fitzgerald's celebrated novel incorporates all of the glamour and decadence that characterized America in the 1920s. This tragic tale of broken dreams and ruined lives explores self-made millionaire Jay Gatsby's quest to win the love of the wealthy, beautiful—and married—Daisy Buchanan. The narrator of the story is Nick Carraway, a young Midwesterner who becomes Gatsby's neighbor on Long Island one summer. Nick is caught up in the dazzling lives of Gatsby, Daisy, and their wealthy friends until tragic circumstances reveal the emptiness of their values. The mysterious Gatsby, an impure man with a pure dream, is the perfect symbol of America in the Jazz Age.

The Grapes of Wrath
John Steinbeck
Penguin Books, 1967

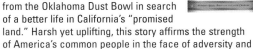

This powerful and moving novel is set during the period of severe economic hardship known as the Great Depression. It recounts the Joad family's journey from the Oklahoma Dust Bowl in search of a better life in California's "promised land." Harsh yet uplifting, this story affirms the strength of America's common people in the face of adversity and injustice.

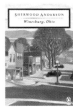

Winesburg, Ohio
Sherwood Anderson
Penguin Books, 1960

Inspired by Edgar Lee Master's *Spoon River Anthology*, Sherwood Anderson started to write a group of related stories about small-town life that became *Winesburg, Ohio*. He based his fictional town of Winesburg on his own hometown of Clyde, Ohio. Central to the book is young George Willard, the sympathetic character to whom others try to explain themselves. The characters who open up to George are isolated people who usually have trouble communicating. Among them are Dr. Parcival, a failed writer, and Enoch Robinson, who "was always a child." When George's mother dies and he begins to become a man, he is ready to leave Winesburg for "his future life in the city."

Poems by Robert Frost: A Boy's Will and North of Boston
Robert Frost
Signet Classic, 2001

This volume contains Frost's first two published books in their original form, *A Boy's Will* (1913) and *North of Boston* (1914). These books, which introduced Frost's distinctively New England voice and established him as a major poet, contain some of his best poems: "Mowing," "The Trial by Existence," "Mending Wall," and "After Apple-Picking," among others. *North of Boston* has many of the dramatic monologues that reveal Frost's skill in capturing memorable thoughts in down-to-earth speech.

Black Voices: An Anthology of African-American Literature
Edited by Abraham Chapman
Signet Classic, 2001

This volume collects the best African American literature of the twentieth century in a variety of genres: fiction, autobiography, poetry, and literary criticism. The fiction includes, among other works, Langston Hughes's humorous *Tales of Simple* and the dramatic prologue to Ralph Ellison's novel *Invisible Man*. Appearing in the autobiography section are such famous figures as Frederick Douglass, James Baldwin, and Malcolm X. The poetry section includes work by the Harlem Renaissance poets Langston Hughes, Claude McKay, and Countee Cullen, as well as the major post–World War II poets Robert Hayden and Gwendolyn Brooks. The last section features literary criticism by W.E.B. Du Bois, Alain Locke, Clarence Major, and others.

Unit 5

The Great Gatsby
by F. Scott Fitzgerald

In writing about race and ethnicity, Fitzgerald occasionally used terms that are considered offensive today. Most of the characters in the book are heavy drinkers, and there are numerous scenes that describe alcohol consumption. The novel relates the effects of an extramarital affair, although there are no explicit sexual references. The hit-and-run accident that results in Myrtle's death, Gatsby's murder, and Wilson's suicide may trouble students.

The Grapes of Wrath
by John Steinbeck

This novel depicts poverty, hardship, and social injustice in realistic detail. It contains references to drinking and smoking, sexual situations, coarse allusions, and derogatory language, as well as details of religious hypocrisy. It also criticizes greed and commercialism and is unsympathetic to banks and other large business interests.

Winesburg, Ohio
by Sherwood Anderson

These stories depict situations that involve homosexuality, pregnancy out of wedlock, sexual encounters, alcoholism, and physical violence.

Poems by Robert Frost: A Boy's Will and *North of Boston*
by Robert Frost

Several poems in *A Boy's Will* contain overtly religious references to God. Several poems in *North of Boston* deal with the subject of death.

Black Voices: An Anthology of African-American Literature
Edited by Abraham Chapman

Students may expect to encounter a number of sensitive issues, including profanity, suicide, violence, sexual innuendo, graphic language, and the use of the words *nigger* and *nigra*.

The Joy Luck Club
by Amy Tan

Hardships of a war-torn country, including death and the abandonment of children, may be distressing to some students. Divorce and the death of parents may also be uncomfortable subjects for some readers.

Daughters
by Paule Marshall

This novel contains scenes of adultery and rape and descriptions of female sexual pleasure. Abortions and miscarriages are described, though not in explicit detail. The book also contains profanity, slang references to homosexuals, and negative portrayals of many male characters.

On Nature: Great Writers on the Great Outdoors
Edited by Lee Gutkind

Sensitive issues in these essays include the trapping and killing of animals, drunkenness, foul language, sexual situations, religion, and descriptions of animal breeding.

Twentieth-Century American Drama
Prentice Hall

Our Town deals directly with death and includes references to one character's suicide.

In *The Glass Menagerie*, Tom abuses alcohol and Tom and Laura's father is also remembered as a problem drinker. The play focuses on Laura's physical disabilities and Amanda's belief that the only appropriate goals for Laura are marriage and a family. Also, Jim uses a derogatory term for German Americans.

Death of a Salesman includes scenes from Willy's adulterous affair with the Woman in Boston. There are references to the fact that both Biff and Happy steal things. Finally, the play concludes with Willy's suicide.

The Crucible deals with people who believed in the literal existence of Satan and witchcraft; their descriptions of evildoing may be disturbing. The play also includes references to adultery and John Proctor's use of the word *whore*. The play includes the wrongful execution of innocent people.

continued

Unit 6: Prosperity and Protest (1945–Present)

The Joy Luck Club
Amy Tan
Putnam, 1989

Organized as a group of sixteen related stories, *The Joy Luck Club* deals with mother-daughter relationships in the Chinese immigrant community of San Francisco. The title refers to the name of a club begun in 1949 by four immigrant Chinese women. Meeting regularly to play the Chinese game of mah jong, they snack, gossip, and tell one another their hopes and fears. The book is divided into four sections, two in which the mothers speak and two in which their American-raised daughters express themselves. Unexpectedly, one mother's sad family secret helps bridge the distance between the generations.

Daughters
Paule Marshall
Plume, 1992

The central character of this novel, Ursa Beatrice MacKenzie, is a Caribbean Islander working hard to achieve success in New York City. The story switches back and forth from the present to the past and alternates between New York and the Caribbean as Ursa confronts important issues in her life. These include starting a new job, ending a love relationship, and making peace with her father and mother. Readers will sympathize with her as she struggles to cope with the conflicting demands of different cultures.

On Nature: Great Writers on the Great Outdoors
Edited by Lee Gutkind
Most Tarcher/Putnam, 2002

This book of contemporary nature essays will appeal to those who love outdoor activities as well as to those who prefer mental exercise in an armchair. It features nonfiction by some of America's best contemporary authors: Joyce Carol Oates, Barry Lopez, Mark Doty, Diane Ackerman, John McPhee, and Bill Bryson, among others. Just a sample of the essay

R6 ◆ *Suggestions for Sustained Reading*

titles conveys the adventures that this book holds in store: "Killing Wolves," "Plain Scared," "The Spray and the Slamming Sea," "Love, War, and Deer Hunting," and "The Moon by the Whale Light."

Twentieth-Century American Drama
Prentice Hall
Pearson Prentice Hall, 2000

The plays in this volume represent some of the best work by America's greatest twentieth-century playwrights: *Our Town*, by Thornton Wilder; *The Glass Menagerie*, by Tennessee Williams; *Death of a Salesman* and *The Crucible*, by Arthur Miller; and *A Raisin in the Sun*, by Lorraine Hansberry. Wilder's innovative play, with its stage manager who addresses the audience, reveals the preciousness of everyday life in a typical American town. In Williams's poetic drama, harsh realities threaten the fantasies of a mother and daughter. Miller's *Death of a Salesman,* the tragedy of a common man, is as powerful as an ancient Greek tragedy about the downfall of a king. Hansberry documents several weeks in the life of an African American family, revealing the conflicting dreams of her characters.

Nonfiction Readings Across the Curriculum
Prentice Hall
Pearson Prentice Hall, 2000

These essays by well-known authors provide new and exciting ways of thinking about many subjects including literature, science, social studies, mathematics, sports, and the arts. This list, however, cannot do justice to the variety and liveliness of the essays. In a memoir, for example, author Beverly Cleary tells how she got started in her career and recalls some of the real-life people on whom she based her characters. Football great Joe Namath gives players a pep talk in his how-to essay from *Football for Young Players and Parents*. Readers will find that the enthusiasm of the writers in this volume is contagious.

continued from left column

Nonfiction Readings Across the Curriculum
Prentice Hall

Sensitive issues include racial prejudice against Asians and Asian Americans, Native Americans, and African Americans. Other issues include the horrors of war and the Holocaust.

abeyance (ə bā′ əns) *n.:* Temporary suspension

ablutions (ab lōō′ shənz) *n.:* Washing or cleansing the body as part of a religious rite

abundance (ə bun′ dəns) *n.:* A great supply; more than enough

acquiesce (ak′ wē es′) *v.:* Agree without protest

admonitory (ad män′ i tôr′ ē) *adj.:* Warning

adversary (ad′ vər ser′ ē) *n.:* Opponent; enemy

affliction (ə flik′ shən) *n.:* Something causing pain or suffering

aggregation (ag′ grə gā′ shən) *n.:* Group or mass of distinct objects or individuals

aggrieved (ə grēvd′) *adj.:* Offended; wronged

agues (ā′ gyōōz) *n.:* Fits of shivering

alacrity (ə lak′ rə tē) *n.:* Speed

alliance (ə lī′ əns) *n.:* Union of nations for a specific purpose

anarchy (an′ ər kē) *n.:* Absence of government

anathema (ə nath′ ə mə) *n.:* Curse

anomalous (ə näm′ ə ləs) *adj.:* Abnormal

antagonism (an tag′ ə niz′ əm) *n.:* Hostility

apparition (ap′ ə rish′ ən) *n.:* The act of appearing or becoming visible

appellation (ap′ ə lā′ shən) *n.:* Name or title

apprised (ə prīzd′) *v.:* Informed; notified

arduous (är′ jōō wəs) *adj.:* Difficult

arrested (ə rest′ id) *adj.:* Stopped

aspiration (as′pə rā′shən) *n.:* Strong ambition

asylum (ə sī′ ləm) *n.:* Place of refuge

audaciously (ô dā′ shəs lē) *adv.:* Boldly or daringly

autonomous (ô tän′ ə məs) *adj.:* Independent

avarice (av′ ər is) *n.:* Greed for riches

aversion (ə vur′ zhən) *n.:* Object arousing an intense or definite dislike

avuncular (ə vun′ kyōō lər) *adj.:* Having traits considered typical of uncles: jolly, indulgent, stodgy

bastions (bas′ chənz) *n.:* Fortifications

bayou (bī′ ōō) *n.:* Sluggish, marshy inlet

beguile (bē gīl′) *v.:* Charm or delight

bellicose (bel′ ə kōs) *adj.:* Quarrelsome

benevolent (bə nev′ ə lənt) *adj.:* Kindly; charitable

bivouac (biv′ wak) *n.:* Temporary encampment

blaspheming (blas fēm′ iŋ) *v.:* Cursing

blithe (blīth) *adj.:* Carefree

brazenness (brā′ zən nis) *n.:* Shamelessness; boldness; impudence

brutal (brōōt′ əl) *adj.:* Cruel and without feeling; savage; violent

buck (buk) *n.:* Male animal, especially a male deer

cacophony (kə käf′ ə nē) *n.:* Harsh, jarring sound

caper (kā′ pər) *n.:* Prank

capitulate (kə pich′ ə lāt′) *v.:* Surrender conditionally

celestial (sə les′ chəl) *adj.:* Of the heavens

chaos (kā′ äs) *n.:* Disorder of formless matter and infinite space, supposed to have existed before the ordered universe

claustrophobia (klôs′ trə fō′ bē ə) *n.:* Fear of being in a confined space

commiseration (kə miz′ ər ā′ shən) *n.:* Sympathy; condolence

conceits (kən sēts′) *n.:* Strange or fanciful ideas

confederate (kən fed′ ər it) *adj.:* United with others for a common purpose

conflagration (kän′ flə grā′ shən) *n.:* Big, destructive fire

congealed (kən jēld′) *v.:* Thickened or solidified

congenial (kən jēn′ yəl) *adj.:* Agreeable

conjectural (kən jek′ chər əl) *adj.:* Based on guesswork

conjectured (kən jek′ chərd) *v.:* Guessed

connate (kän āt′) *adj.:* Existing naturally; innate

consanguinity (kän′ saŋ gwin′ ə tē) *n.:* Kinship

consecrate (kän′ sə krāt′) *v.:* Cause to be revered or honored

conspicuous (kən spik′ yōō əs) *adj.:* Obvious; easy to see or perceive

consternation (kän′ stər nā′ shən) *n.:* Great fear or shock that makes one feel helpless or bewildered

contrition (kən trish′ ən) *n.:* Remorse for having done wrong

copious (kō′ pē əs) *adj.:* Plentiful; abundant

cornice (kôr′ nis) *n.:* Projecting decorative molding along the top of a building

cosmopolitan (käz′ mə päl′ ə tən) *adj.:* Common to or representative of all or many parts of the world

countenance (koun′ tə nəns) *v.:* Approve; tolerate

covertly (kō vərt′ lē) *adv.:* Secretly; surreptitiously

craven (krā′ vən) *adj.:* Very cowardly

crux (kruks) *n.:* Essential point

cunning (kun′ iŋ) *adj.:* Skillful in deception; crafty; sly

deference (def′ ər əns) *n.:* Respect; courtesy; regard

degenerate (dē jen′ ər it) *adj.:* Morally corrupt

deliberation (di lib′ ə rā′ shən) *n.:* Careful consideration

demarcation (dē′ mär kā′ shən) *n.:* Separation

depravity (di prav′ ə tē) *n.:* Corruption; wickedness

deprecated (dep′ rə kāt′ id) *v.:* Expressed disapproval of; pleaded against

depredations (dep′ rə dā′ shənz) *n.:* Acts of robbing or plundering

derivative (də riv′ ə tiv) *adj.:* Not original; based on something else

despotic (de spät′ ik) *adj.:* Harsh; cruel; unjust

despotism (des′ pət iz′ əm) *n.:* Government by absolute rule; tyranny

dictum (dik′ təm) *n.:* Formal statement of fact or opinion

digress (dī gres′) *v.:* Depart temporarily from the main subject

dilapidated (di lap′ ə dā′ tid) *adj.:* In disrepair

discern (di surn′) *v.:* Perceive or recognize; make out clearly

disdainfully (dis dān′ fəl ē) *adv.:* Showing scorn or contempt

dispatched (dis pacht′) *v.:* Sent off on a specific assignment

disposition (dis′ pə zish′ ən) *n.:* Inclination or tendency

distillery (dis til′ ə rē) *n.:* Place where alcoholic liquors are distilled

divines (də vīnz′) *n.:* Clergy

dogma (dôg′ mə) *n.:* Formalized and authoritative doctrines or beliefs

dolorous (dō′ lər əs) *adj.:* Sad; mournful

dominion (də min′ yən) *n.:* Power to rule

dusky (dus′ kē) *adj.:* Dim; shadowy

dyspepsia (dis pep′ shə) *n.:* Indigestion

efface (ə fās′) *v.:* Erase; wipe out

effaced (ə fāsd′) *adj.:* Erased; wiped out

effuse (e fyōōz′) *v.:* Spread out; diffuse

elusive (ē lōō′ siv) *adj.:* Hard to grasp

embankment (em baŋk′ mənt) *n.:* Mound of earth or stone built to hold back water or support a roadway

emigrants (em′ i grənts) *n.:* People who leave one area to move to another

eminence (em′ ə nəns) *n.:* Greatness; celebrity

engrossed (en grōst′) *adj.:* Occupied wholly; absorbed

entreated (en trēt′ id) *v.:* Begged; pleaded

epitaph (ep′ ə taf) *n.:* Inscription on a tombstone or grave marker

equanimity (ek′ wə nim′ ə tē) *n.:* Composure

equivocal (i kwiv′ ə kəl) *adj.:* Having more than one possible interpretation; uncertain

eradicate (e rad′ i kāt′) *v.:* Get rid of; wipe out; destroy

etiquette (et′ i kit) *n.:* Appropriate behavior and ceremonies

evitable (ev′ ə tə bəl) *adj.:* Avoidable

exalted (eg zôlt´ id) *adj.:* Filled with joy or pride; elated

excavated (eks´ kə vā tid) *v.:* Dug out; made a hole

expatriated (eks pā´ trē āt´ id) *adj.:* Deported; driven from one's native land

expedient (ik spē´ dē ənt) *n.:* Resource

exquisite (eks´ kwi zit) *adj.:* Very beautiful; delicate; carefully wrought

extort (eks tôrt´) *v.:* Obtain by threat or violence

extricate (eks´ tri kāt) *v.:* Set free

fallowness (fal´ ō nis) *n.:* Inactivity

fasting (fast´ iŋ) *v.:* Eating very little or nothing

feigned (fānd) *v.:* Pretended; faked

felicity (fə lis´ ə tē) *n.:* Happiness; bliss

finite (fī´ nīt) *adj.:* Having measurable or definable limits

flagrant (flā´ grənt) *adj.:* Glaring; outrageous

foppery (fäp´ ər ē) *n.:* Foolishness

foreboding (fôr bōd´ iŋ) *n.:* Presentiment

foreknowledge (fôr´ näl´ ij) *n.:* Awareness of something before it happens or exists

forestall (fôr stôl´) *v.:* Prevent by acting ahead of time

fortuitous (fôr tōō´ ə təs) *adj.:* Fortunate

frippery (frip´ ər ē) *n.:* Showy display of elegance

galvanic (gal van´ ik) *adj.:* Startling; stimulating as if by electric current

garrulous (gar´ ə ləs) *adj.:* Talking too much

genial (jēn´ yəl) *adj.:* Cheerful; friendly

geography (jē ôg´ rə fē) *n.:* The study of the surface of the Earth

glade (glād) *n.:* Open space in a wood or forest

glean (glēn) *v.:* Collect the remaining grain after reaping

gloaming (glō´ miŋ) *n.:* Evening dusk; twilight

grave (grāv) *adj.:* Serious; solemn

gregarious (grə ger´ ē əs) *adj.:* Sociable

guile (gīl) *n.:* Craftiness

hallow (hal´ ō) *v.:* Honor as sacred

heirs (erz) *n.:* People who carry on the tradition of predecessors

impelled (im peld´) *v.:* Moved; forced

imperially (im pir´ ē əl ē) *adv.:* Majestically

imperious (im pir´ ē əs) *adj.:* Urgent; imperative

impertinent (im pʉr´ tən ənt) *adj.:* Not showing proper respect

impious (im´ pē əs) *adj.:* Lacking reverence for God

importunate (im pôr´ chə nit) *adj.:* Insistent

importunities (im´ pôr tōōn´ ə tēz) *n.:* Persistent requests or demands

imprecations (im´ prə kā´ shənz) *n.:* Curses

improvident (im präv´ ə dənt) *adj.:* Shortsighted; failing to provide for the future

increment (in´ krə mənt) *n.:* Increase, as in a series

indecorous (in dek´ ər əs) *adj.:* Improper

indications (in´ di kā´ shənz) *n.:* Signs; things that point out or signify

ineffable (in ef´ ə bəl) *adj.:* Inexpressible; unable to be spoken

inert (in ʉrt´) *adj.:* Motionless

infallibility (in fal´ ə bil´ ə tē) *n.:* Inability to be wrong; reliability

infidel (in´ fə dəl) *n.:* Person who holds no religious belief

infinity (in fin´ i tē) *n.:* Endless or unlimited space, time, or distance

iniquity (in ik´ wə tē) *n.:* Sin

insatiable (in sā´ shə bəl) *adj.:* Constantly wanting more; unable to be satisfied

inscrutable (in skrōōt´ ə bəl) *adj.:* Not able to be easily understood

insidious (in sid´ ē əs) *adj.:* Secretly treacherous

insurgents (in sʉr´ jənts) *n.:* Rebels; those who revolt against established authority

interminable (in tʉr´ mi nə bəl) *adj.:* Seeming to last forever

intuitively (in tōō´ i tiv lē) *adv.:* Instinctively

invalided (in´ və lid´ id) *v.:* Released because of illness or disability

invective (in vek´ tiv) *n.:* Verbal attack; strong criticism

invoke (in vōk´) *v.:* Call on for help, inspiration, or support

jettisoned (jet´ ə sənd) *v.:* Thrown overboard to lighten the weight of a ship

jocularity (jäk´ yə lar´ ə tē) *n.:* Joking good humor

jubilant (jōō´ bəl ənt) *adj.:* Joyful and triumphant

labyrinth (lab´ ə rin*th*) *n.:* Intricate network of winding passages; maze

liberty (lib´ ər tē) *n.:* The condition of being free from control by others

limber (lim´ bər) *adj.:* Flexible

literalists (lit´ ər əl ists) *n.:* People who insist on taking words at their exact meaning

loath (lōth) *adj.:* Reluctant; unwilling

loathsome (lō*th*´ səm) *adj.:* Hateful; detestable

lulled (luld) *v.:* Calmed or soothed by a gentle sound or motion

luminary (lōō´ mə ner´ ē) *adj.:* Giving off light

magnanimity (mag´ nə nim´ ə tē) *n.:* Ability to rise above pettiness or meanness

maledictions (mal´ ə dik´ shənz) *n.:* Curses

malevolence (mə lev´ ə ləns) *n.:* Malice; spitefulness

malevolent (mə lev´ ə lənt) *adj.:* Mean-spirited; showing ill will

malice (mal´ is) *n.:* Ill will; spite

malign (mə līn´) *adj.:* Malicious; very harmful

malingered (mə liŋ´ gərd) *v.:* Escaped work or duty by pretending to be ill

manifest (man´ ə fest´) *adj.:* Evident; obvious; clear

manifold (man´ ə fōld´) *adj.:* In many ways

manuscript (man´ yōō skript´) *n.:* Written or typed document, especially one submitted to a publisher or printer

meticulous (mə tik´ yōō ləs) *adj.:* Extremely careful about details

moiling (mɔi´ liŋ) *v.:* Churning; swirling

mollified (mäl´ ə fīd´) *v.:* Soothed; calmed

monotonous (mə nät´ ən əs) *adj.:* Tiresome because unvarying

monotony (mə nät´ ən ē) *n.:* Tiresome, unchanging sameness; lack of variety

mortality (môr tal´ ə tē) *n.:* Death on a large scale, as from disease or war

motives (mōt´ ivz) *n.:* Reasons for action; inner drives

multifarious (mul´ tə far´ ē əs) *adj.:* Having many parts or elements; diverse

multitudinous (mul´ tə tōōd´ ən əs) *adj.:* Numerous

mundane (mun dān´) *adj.:* Commonplace; ordinary

munificent (myōō nif´ ə sənt) *adj.:* Generous

myriad (mir´ ē əd) *adj.:* Countless

negligence (neg´ li jəns) *n.:* Instance of failure, carelessness, or indifference

nonplused (nän´ plüsd´) *adj.:* Bewildered; perplexed

obeisance (ō bā´ səns) *n.:* Gesture of respect

obliterated (ə blit´ ər āt´ id) *v.:* Blotted out; destroyed

obstinacy (äb´ stə nə sē) *n.:* Stubbornness

obstinate (äb´ stə nit) *adj.:* Stubborn

obtuse (äb tōōs´) *adj.:* Slow to understand or perceive

ominous (äm´ ə nəs) *adj.:* Threatening

omnipotent (äm nip´ ə tənt) *adj.:* All-powerful

oppressed (ə prest´) *v.:* Kept down by cruel or unjust power or authority

oppresses (ə pres´ əz) *v.:* Weighs heavily on the mind

ornery (ôr´ nər ē) *adj.:* Having a mean disposition

oscillation (äs´ ə lā´ shən) *n.:* Act of swinging or moving regularly back and forth

ostentation (äs´ tən tā´ shən) *n.:* Boastful display

ostentatious (äs´ tən tā´ shəs) *adj.:* Intended to attract notice

pacify (pas´ ə fī´) *v.:* Calm; soothe

palisades (pal´ə sādz´) *n.:* Large, pointed stakes set in the ground to form a fence used for defense

palpable (pal´ pə bəl) *adj.:* Able to be touched, felt, or handled

parsimony (pär´ sə mō´ nē) *n.:* Stinginess

patriarch (pā´ trē ärk´) *n.:* Father and ruler of a family or tribe

pensive (pen´ siv) *adj.:* Thinking deeply or seriously

penury (pen´ yə rē) *n.:* Lack of money, property, or necessities

perdition (pər dish´ ən) *n.:* Complete and irreparable loss; ruin

peremptorily (pər emp´ tər ə lē) *adv.:* Decisively; commandingly

perfidy (pʉr´ fə dē) *n.:* Betrayal of trust

peril (per´ əl) *n.:* Danger

persevere (pʉr sə vir´) *v.:* Persist; be steadfast in purpose

pertinaciously (pʉr´ tə nā´ shəs lē) *adv.:* Holding firmly to some purpose

pervading (pər vād´ iŋ) *adj.:* Spreading throughout

pestilential (pes´ tə len´ shəl) *adj.:* Likely to cause disease

piety (pī´ ə tē) *n.:* Devotion to religious duties

pilfer (pil´ fər) *v.:* Steal

placid (plas´ id) *adj.:* Tranquil; calm; quiet

poignant (poin´ yənt) *adj.:* Sharply painful to the feelings

poise (poiz) *n.:* Balance; stability

posterity (päs ter´ ə tē) *n.:* All succeeding generations

precipitate (prē sip´ ə tāt´) *v.:* Cause to happen before expected or desired

prelude (prel´ yo͞od) *n.:* Introductory section or movement of a suite, fugue, or work of music

preposterous (pri päs´ tər əs) *adj.:* Ridiculous

prescient (presh´ ənt) *adj.:* Having foreknowledge

prodigious (prə dij´ əs) *adj.:* Of great power or size

profundity (prō fun´ də tē) *n.:* Intellectual depth

profusion (prō fyo͞o´ zhən) *n.:* Abundance; rich supply

propitious (prō pish´ əs) *adj.:* Favorably inclined or disposed

protruded (prō tro͞od´ id) *v.:* Jutted out

psychology (sī käl´ ə jē) *n.:* The science dealing with the mind and with mental and emotional processes

pugilistic (pyo͞o´ jə lis´ tik) *adj.:* Looking for a fight

querulous (kwer´ ə ləs) *adj.:* Inclined to find fault

radiant (rā´ dē ənt) *adj.:* Shining brightly

reaping (rēp´ iŋ) *v.:* Cutting or harvesting grain from a field

recompense (rek´ əm pens´) *n.:* Reward; repayment

recumbent (ri kum´ bənt) *adj.:* Resting

redolent (red´ əl ənt) *adj.:* Suggestive

redress (ri´ dres) *n.:* Atonement; rectification

refluent (ref´ lo͞o ənt) *adj.:* Flowing back

refulgent (ri ful´ jənt) *adj.:* Radiant; shining

repose (ri pōz´) *n.:* State of being at rest

repression (ri presh´ ən) *n.:* Restraint

retrospective (re trə spek´ tiv) *adj.:* Looking back on or directed to the past

reverential (rev´ ə ren´ shəl) *adj.:* Showing or caused by a feeling of deep respect, love, and awe

rueful (ro͞o´ fəl) *adj.:* Feeling or showing sorrow or pity

sagacious (sə gā´ shəs) *adj.:* Shrewd

salient (sāl´ yənt) *adj.:* Standing out from the rest

sallow (sal´ ō) *adj.:* Sickly; pale yellow

salutary (sal´ yo͞o ter´ ē) *adj.:* Beneficial; promoting a good purpose

scepter (sep´ tər) *n.:* Rod or staff held by rulers as a symbol of sovereignty

scintillating (sint´ əl āt´ iŋ) *adj.:* Sparkling

scourge (skʉrj) *n.:* Cause of serious trouble or affliction

scrabbling (skrab´ liŋ) *v.:* Scrambling

semi-somnambulant (sem´ i säm nam´ byo͞o lənt) *adj.:* Half-sleepwalking

sentience (sen´ shəns) *n.:* Capacity of feeling

sepulcher (sep´ əl kər) *n.:* Grave; tomb

serenity (sə ren´ ə tē) *n.:* Calmness

sinuous (sin´ yo͞o wəs) *adj.:* Moving in and out; wavy

slovenly (sluv´ ən lē) *adj.:* Untidy

smite (smīt) *v.:* Kill by a powerful blow

somnolent (säm´ nə lənt) *adj.:* Sleepy; drowsy

specious (spē´ shəs) *adj.:* Seeming to be good or sound without actually being so

squander (skwän´ dər) *v.:* Spend or use wastefully

stark (stärk) *adj.:* Stiff or rigid, as a corpse; severe

statistics (sta tis´ tiks) *n.:* The science of collecting and arranging facts about a particular subject in the form of numbers

stringency (strin´ jən sē) *n.:* Strictness; severity

subjugation (sub´ jə gā´ shən) *n.:* The act of conquering

sublime (sə blīm´) *adj.:* Inspiring awe or admiration through grandeur or beauty

subsistence (səb sis´ təns) *n.:* Means of support

subterranean (sub´ tə rā´nē ən) *adj.:* Underground

suffice (sə fīs´) *v.:* Be adequate; meet the needs of

suffrage (suf´ rij) *n.:* Vote or voting

sullen (sul´ ən) *adj.:* Sulky; glum

summarily (sə mer´ ə lē) *adv.:* Promptly and without formality

sundry (sun´ drē) *adj.:* Various; different

superfluous (so͞o pʉr´ flo͞o wəs) *adj.:* Excessive; not necessary

surmised (sər mīzd´) *v.:* Guessed

swag (swag) *n.:* Suspended cluster of branches

switch (swich) *n.:* Slender, flexible twig or whip

tempest (tem´ pist) *n.:* Violent storm

tempo (tem´ pō) *n.:* Rate of activity of a sound or motion; pace

terra firma (ter´ ə fʉr´ mə) *n.:* Firm earth; solid ground (Latin)

timorous (tim´ ər əs) *adj.:* Full of fear

trajectory (trə jek´ tə rē) *n.:* Curved path of an object hurtling through space

transient (tran´ zē ənt) *adj.:* Not permanent

tremulous (trem´ yo͞o ləs) *adj.:* Characterized by trembling

tremulously (trem´ yo͞o ləs lē) *adv.:* Fearfully; timidly

tumultuous (to͞o mult´ cho͞o wəs) *adj.:* Rough; stormy

tumultuously (to͞o mul´ cho͞o wəs lē) *adv.:* In an agitated way

tyranny (tir´ ə nē) *n.:* Oppressive and unjust government

unalienable (un āl´ yən ə bəl) *adj.:* Not to be taken away

unanimity (yo͞o´ nə nim´ ə tē) *n.:* Complete agreement

untoward (un tō´ ərd) *adj.:* Inappropriate or improper

unwonted (un wän´ tid) *adj.:* Unusual; unfamiliar

usurers (yo͞o´ zhərz) *n.:* Moneylenders who charge very high interest

usurpations (yo͞o´ sər pā´ shənz) *n.:* Unlawful seizures of rights or privileges

vagary (və ger´ ē) *n.:* Unpredictable occurrence

venerable (ven´ ər ə bəl) *adj.:* Worthy of respect

vigilance (vij´ ə ləns) *n.:* Watchfulness

vigilant (vij´ ə lənt) *adj.:* Alert to danger

visage (viz´ ij) *n.:* Appearance

vitality (vī tal´ ə tē) *n.:* Power to endure or survive; life force

vituperative (vī to͞o´ pər ə tiv) *adj.:* Spoken abusively

vociferation (vō sif´ ər ā´ shən) *n.:* Loud or vehement shouting

voluminous (və lo͞om´ ə nəs) *adj.:* Of enough material to fill volumes

waggery (wag´ ər ē) *n.:* Mischievous humor

wanton (wän´ tən) *adj.:* Senseless; unjustified

When you were younger, you learned to read. Then, you read to expand your experiences or for pure enjoyment. Now, you are expected to read to learn. As you progress in school, you are given more and more material to read. The tips on these pages will help you improve your reading fluency, or your ability to read easily, smoothly, and expressively.

Keeping Your Concentration

One common problem that readers face is the loss of concentration. When you are reading an assignment, you might find yourself rereading the same sentence several times without really understanding it. The first step in changing this behavior is to notice that you do it. Becoming an active, aware reader will help you get the most from your assignments. Practice using these strategies:

- Cover what you have already read with a note card as you go along. Then, you will not be able to reread without noticing that you are doing it.

- Set a purpose for reading beyond just completing the assignment. Then, read actively by pausing to ask yourself questions about the material as you read.

- Use the Reading Strategy instruction and notes that appear with each selection in this textbook.

- Stop reading after a specified period of time (for example, 5 minutes) and summarize what you have read. To help you with this strategy, use the Reading Check questions that appear with each selection in this textbook. Reread to find any answers you do not know.

Reading Phrases

Fluent readers read phrases rather than individual words. Reading this way will speed up your reading and improve your comprehension. Here are some useful ideas:

- Experts recommend rereading as a strategy to increase fluency. Choose a passage of text that is neither too hard nor too easy. Read the same passage aloud several times until you can read it smoothly. When you can read the passage fluently, pick another passage and keep practicing.

- Read aloud into a tape recorder. Then, listen to the recording, noting your accuracy, pacing, and expression. You can also read aloud and share feedback with a partner.

- Use the *Prentice Hall Listening to Literature* audiotapes or CDs to hear the selections read aloud. Read along silently in your textbook, noticing how the reader uses his or her voice and emphasizes certain words and phrases.

✔Reading Check

What common problem do many readers face?

✔Reading Check

In what ways will reading phrases rather than individual words affect your reading?

Understanding Key Vocabulary

If you do not understand some of the words in an assignment, you may miss out on important concepts. Therefore, it is helpful to keep a dictionary nearby when you are reading. Follow these steps:

- Before you begin reading, scan the text for unfamiliar words or terms. Find out what those words mean before you begin reading.
- Use context—the surrounding words, phrases, and sentences—to help you determine the meanings of unfamiliar words.
- If you are unable to understand the meaning through context, refer to the dictionary.

✔ **Reading Check**

Why should you look up words you do not know when reading an assignment?

Paying Attention to Punctuation

When you read, pay attention to punctuation. Commas, periods, exclamation points, semicolons, and colons tell you when to pause or stop. They also indicate relationships between groups of words. When you recognize these relationships you will read with greater understanding and expression. Look at the chart below.

Punctuation Mark	Meaning
comma	brief pause
period	pause at the end of a thought
exclamation point	pause that indicates emphasis
semicolon	pause between related but distinct thoughts
colon	pause before giving explanation or examples

Using the Reading Fluency Checklist

Use the checklist below each time you read a selection in this textbook. In your Language Arts journal or notebook, note which skills you need to work on and chart your progress each week.

Reading Fluency Checklist

❑ Preview the text to check for difficult or unfamiliar words.
❑ Practice reading aloud.
❑ Read according to punctuation.
❑ Break down long sentences into the subject and its meaning.
❑ Read groups of words for meaning rather than reading single words.
❑ Read with expression (change your tone of voice to add meaning to the word).

Reading is a skill that can be improved with practice. The key to improving your fluency is to read. The more you read, the better your reading will become.

LITERARY TERMS HANDBOOK

ALLEGORY An *allegory* is a story or tale with two or more levels of meaning—a literal level and one or more symbolic levels. The events, setting, and characters in an allegory are symbols for ideas or qualities. Many of Nathaniel Hawthorne's short stories, such as "The Minister's Black Veil" (p. 336), are allegories.

ALLITERATION *Alliteration* is the repetition of consonant sounds at the beginning of words or accented syllables. Sara Teasdale uses alliteration in these lines from her poem "Understanding":

> Your spirit's secret hides like gold
> Sunk in a Spanish galleon

ALLUSION An *allusion* is a reference to a well-known person, place, event, literary work, or work of art. Writers often make allusions to stories from the Bible, to Greek and Roman myths, to plays by Shakespeare, to political and historical events, and to other materials with which they can expect their readers to be familiar. In "The Love Song of J. Alfred Prufrock" (p. 718), T. S. Eliot alludes to, among other things, Dante's *Inferno,* Italian artist Michelangelo, Shakespeare's *Hamlet,* and the Bible. By using allusions, writers can suggest complex ideas simply and easily.

AMBIGUITY *Ambiguity* is the effect created when words suggest and support two or more divergent interpretations. Ambiguity may be used in literature to express experiences or truths that are complex or contradictory. Ambiguity often derives from the fact that words have multiple meanings.
See also Irony.

ANALOGY An *analogy* is an extended comparison of relationships. It is based on the idea that the relationship between one pair of things is like the relationship between another pair. Unlike a metaphor, an analogy involves an explicit comparison, often using the word *like* or *as*.
See also Metaphor, Simile.

ANECDOTE An *anecdote* is a brief story about an interesting, amusing, or strange event. An anecdote is told to entertain or to make a point. In the excerpt from *Life on the Mississippi* (p. 564), Mark Twain tells several anecdotes about his experiences on the Mississippi River.

ANTAGONIST An *antagonist* is a character or force in conflict with a main character, or protagonist. In Jack London's "To Build a Fire" (p. 608), the antagonist is neither a person nor an animal but rather the extreme cold. In many stories, the conflict between the antagonist and the protagonist is the basis for the plot.

See also Conflict, Plot, *and* Protagonist.

APHORISM An *aphorism* is a general truth or observation about life, usually stated concisely. Often witty and wise, aphorisms appear in many kinds of works. An essay writer may have an aphoristic style, making many such statements. Ralph Waldo Emerson was famous for his aphoristic style. His essay entitled "Fate" contains the following aphorisms:

> Nature is what you may do.
> So far as a man thinks, he is free.
> A man's fortunes are the fruit of his character.

Used in an essay, an aphorism can be a memorable way to sum up or to reinforce a point or an argument.

APOSTROPHE An *apostrophe* is a figure of speech in which a speaker directly addresses an absent person or a personified quality, object, or idea. Phillis Wheatley uses apostrophe in this line from "To the University of Cambridge, in New England":

> Students, to you 'tis given to scan the heights
See also Figurative Language.

ARCHETYPAL LITERARY ELEMENTS *Archetypal literary elements* are patterns in literature found around the world. For instance, the occurrence of events in threes is an archetypal element of fairy tales. Certain character types, such as mysterious guides, are also archetypal elements of such traditional stories. Archetypal elements make stories easier to remember and retell. In *Moby-Dick* (p. 354), Melville uses the archetype of a whale—like the biblical mammal in conflict with Jonah—to address man's conflict with nature.

ASSONANCE *Assonance* is the repetition of vowel sounds in conjunction with dissimilar consonant sounds. Emily Dickinson uses assonance in the line "The mountain at a given distance." The *i* sound is repeated in *given* and *distance*, in the context of the dissimilar consonant sounds *g–v* and *d–s*.

ATMOSPHERE *See* Mood.

AUTOBIOGRAPHY An *autobiography* is a form of nonfiction in which a person tells his or her own life story. Notable examples of autobiographies include those by Benjamin Franklin and Frederick Douglass. *Memoirs,* first-person accounts of personally or historically significant events in which the writer was a participant or an eyewitness, are a form of autobiographical writing.
See also Biography *and* Journal.

BALLAD A *ballad* is a songlike poem that tells a story, often one dealing with adventure and romance. Most ballads include simple language, four- or six-line stanzas, rhyme, and regular meter.

BIOGRAPHY A *biography* is a form of nonfiction in which a writer tells the life story of another person. Carl Sandburg's *Abe Lincoln Grows Up* is a biography of President Lincoln.
See also Autobiography.

BLANK VERSE *Blank verse* is poetry written in unrhymed iambic pentameter. An iamb is a poetic foot consisting of one weak stress followed by one strong stress. A pentameter line has five poetic feet. Robert Frost's "Birches" (p. 882) is written in blank verse.

CHARACTER A *character* is a person or an animal that takes part in the action of a literary work. The following are some terms used to describe various types of characters:

The *main character* in a literary work is the one on whom the work focuses. *Major characters* in a literary work include the main character and any other characters who play significant roles. A *minor character* is one who does not play a significant role. A *round character* is one who is complex and multifaceted, like a real person. A *flat character* is one who is one-dimensional. A *dynamic character* is one who changes in the course of a work. A *static character* is one who does not change in the course of a work.
See also Characterization *and* Motivation.

CHARACTERIZATION *Characterization* is the act of creating and developing a character. In *direct characterization*, a writer simply states a character's traits, as when F. Scott Fitzgerald writes of the main character in his story "Winter Dreams" (p. 744), "He wanted not association with glittering things and glittering people—he wanted the glittering things themselves." In *indirect characterization*, character is revealed through one of the following means:

1. words, thoughts, or actions of the character
2. descriptions of the character's appearance or background
3. what other characters say about the character
4. the ways in which other characters react to the character
See also Character.

CINQUAIN *See* Stanza.

CLASSICISM *Classicism* is an approach to literature and the other arts that stresses reason, balance, clarity, ideal beauty, and orderly form in imitation of the arts of ancient Greece and Rome. Classicism is often contrasted with *Romanticism*, which stresses imagination, emotion, and individualism.

Classicism also differs from *Realism,* which stresses the actual rather than the ideal.
See also Realism *and* Romanticism.

CLIMAX The *climax* is the high point of interest or suspense in a literary work. For example, Jack London's "To Build a Fire" (p. 608) reaches its climax when the man realizes that he is going to freeze to death. The climax generally appears near the end of a story, play, or narrative poem.
See also Plot.

CONFLICT A *conflict* is a struggle between opposing forces. Sometimes this struggle is internal, or within a character, as in Bernard Malamud's "The First Seven Years" (p. 988). At other times, this struggle is external, or between a character and an outside force, as in Jack London's "To Build a Fire" (p. 608). Conflict is one of the primary elements of narrative literature because most plots develop from conflicts.
See also Antagonist, Plot, *and* Protagonist.

CONNOTATION A *connotation* is an association that a word calls to mind in addition to the dictionary meaning of the word. Many words that are similar in their dictionary meanings, or denotations, are quite different in their connotations. Consider, for example, José García Villa's line, "Be beautiful, noble, like the antique ant." This line would have a very different effect if it were "Be pretty, classy, like the old ant." Poets and other writers choose their words carefully so that the connotations of those words will be appropriate.
See also Denotation.

CONSONANCE *Consonance* is the repetition of similar final consonant sounds at the ends of words or accented syllables. Emily Dickinson uses consonance in these lines:

But if he ask where you are hid
Until to-morrow,—happy letter!
Gesture, coquette, and shake your head!

COUPLET *See* Stanza.

CRISIS In the plot of a narrative, the *crisis* is the turning point for the protagonist—the point at which the protagonist's situation or understanding changes dramatically. In Bernard Malamud's "The First Seven Years" (p. 988), the crisis occurs when Feld recognizes that Sobel loves Miriam.

DENOTATION The *denotation* of a word is its objective meaning, independent of other associations that the word brings to mind.
See also Connotation.

DENOUEMENT *See* Plot.

DESCRIPTION A *description* is a portrayal, in words, of something that can be perceived by the senses. Writers create descriptions by using images, as John Wesley Powell does in this passage from "The Most Sublime Spectacle on Earth," his description of the Grand Canyon (p. 289):

> Clouds creep out of canyons and wind into other canyons. The heavens seem to be alive, not moving as move the heavens over a plain, in one direction with the wind, but following the multiplied courses of these gorges.

See also Image.

DEVELOPMENT *See* Plot.

DIALECT A *dialect* is the form of a language spoken by people in a particular region or group. Writers often use dialect to make their characters seem realistic and to create local color. See, for example, Mark Twain's "The Notorious Jumping Frog of Calaveras County" (p. 569).

See also Local Color.

DIALOGUE A *dialogue* is a conversation between characters. Writers use dialogue to reveal character, to present events, to add variety to narratives, and to arouse their readers' interest.

See also Drama.

DICTION *Diction* is a writer's or speaker's word choice. Diction is part of a writer's style and may be described as formal or informal, plain or ornate, common or technical, abstract or concrete.

See also Style.

DRAMA A *drama* is a story written to be performed by actors. The playwright supplies dialogue for the characters to speak, as well as stage directions that give information about costumes, lighting, scenery, properties, the setting, and the characters' movements and ways of speaking. Dramatic conventions include soliloquies, asides, or the passage of time between acts or scenes.

See also Genre.

DRAMATIC MONOLOGUE A *dramatic monologue* is a poem or speech in which an imaginary character speaks to a silent listener. T. S. Eliot's "The Love Song of J. Alfred Prufrock" (p. 718) is a dramatic monologue.

See also Dramatic Poem *and* Monologue.

DRAMATIC POEM A *dramatic poem* is one that makes use of the conventions of drama. Such poems may be monologues or dialogues or may present the speech of many characters. Robert Frost's "The Death of the Hired Man" is a famous example of a dramatic poem.

See also Dramatic Monologue.

DYNAMIC CHARACTER *See* Character.

EPIGRAM An *epigram* is a brief, pointed statement, in prose or in verse. Benjamin Franklin was famous for his epigrams, which include "Fools make feasts, and wise men eat them," and "A plowman on his legs is higher than a gentleman on his knees."

EPIPHANY An *epiphany* is a sudden revelation or flash of insight. The shoemaker in Bernard Malamud's "The First Seven Years" (p. 988) experiences an epiphany when he suddenly and thoroughly comprehends that the actions of his apprentice, Sobel, are motivated by his secret love for Miriam.

ESSAY An *essay* is a short nonfiction work about a particular subject. Essays can be classified as *formal* or *informal*, *personal* or *impersonal*. They can also be classified according to purpose, such as *analytical* (see the excerpt from *The Mortgaged Heart* on p. 1112), *satirical* (see "Coyote v. Acme" on p. 1118), or *reflective* (see Amy Tan's "Mother Tongue" on p. 1136). Modes of discourse, such as *expository*, *descriptive*, *persuasive*, or *narrative*, are other means of classifying essays.

See also Satire, Exposition, Description, Persuasion, *and* Narration.

EXPOSITION *Exposition* is writing or speech that explains, informs, or presents information. The main techniques of expository writing include analysis, classification, comparison and contrast, definition, and exemplification, or illustration. An essay may be primarily expository, as is William Safire's "Onomatopoeia" (p. 1115), or it may use exposition to support another purpose, such as persuasion or argumentation, as in Ian Frazier's satirical essay "Coyote v. Acme" (p. 1118).

In a story or play, the exposition is that part of the plot that introduces the characters, the setting, and the basic situation.

See also Plot.

FALLING ACTION *See* Plot.

FICTION *Fiction* is prose writing that tells about imaginary characters and events. Short stories and novels are works of fiction.

See also Genre, Narrative, Nonfiction, *and* Prose.

FIGURATIVE LANGUAGE *Figurative language* is writing or speech not meant to be taken literally. Writers use figurative language to express ideas in vivid and imaginative ways. For example, Emily Dickinson begins one poem with the following description of snow:

> It sifts from leaden sieves, / It powders all the wood

By describing the snow as if it were flour, Dickinson renders a precise and compelling picture of it.

See also Figure of Speech.

FIGURE OF SPEECH A *figure of speech* is an expression or a word used imaginatively rather than literally.

See also Figurative Language.

FLASHBACK A *flashback* is a section of a literary work that interrupts the chronological presentation of events to relate an event from an earlier time. A writer may present a flashback as a character's memory or recollection, as part of an account or story told by a character, as a dream or a day-dream, or simply by having the narrator switch to a time in the past.

FLAT CHARACTER *See* Character.

FOIL A *foil* is a character who provides a contrast to another character. In F. Scott Fitzgerald's "Winter Dreams" (p. 744), Irene Scheerer is a foil for the tantalizing Judy Jones.

FOLK LITERATURE *Folk literature* is the body of stories, legends, myths, ballads, songs, riddles, sayings, and other works arising out of the oral traditions of peoples around the globe. The folk literature traditions of the United States, including those of Native Americans and of the American pioneers, are especially rich.

FOOT *See* Meter.

FORESHADOWING *Foreshadowing* in a literary work is the use of clues to suggest events that have yet to occur.

FREE VERSE *Free verse* is poetry that lacks a regular rhythmical pattern, or meter. A writer of free verse is at liberty to use any rhythms that are appropriate to what he or she is saying. Free verse has been widely used by twentieth-century poets such as Leslie Marmon Silko, who begins "Where Mountain Lion Lay Down With Deer" with these lines:

I climb the black rock mountain
stepping from day to day
silently.

See also Meter.

GENRE A *genre* is a division, or type, of literature. Literature is commonly divided into three major genres: poetry, prose, and drama. Each major genre can in turn be divided into smaller genres. Poetry can be divided into lyric, concrete, dra-matic, narrative, and epic poetry. Prose can be divided into fiction and nonfiction. Drama can be divided into serious drama, tragedy, comic drama, melodrama, and farce.

See also Drama, Poetry, *and* Prose.

GOTHIC *Gothic* refers to the use of primitive, medieval, wild, or mysterious elements in literature. Gothic novels feature places like mysterious and gloomy castles, where horrifying,

supernatural events take place. Their influence on Edgar Allan Poe is evident in "The Fall of the House of Usher" (p. 308).

GROTESQUE *Grotesque* refers to the use of bizarre, absurd, or fantastic elements in literature. The grotesque is generally characterized by distortions or striking incongruities. *Grotesque characters*, like those in Flannery O'Connor's "The Life You Save May Be Your Own" (p. 972), are characters who have become bizarre through their obsession with an idea or a value or as a result of an emotional problem.

HARLEM RENAISSANCE The *Harlem Renaissance*, which occurred during the 1920s, was a time of African Ameri-can artistic creativity centered in Harlem, in New York City. Writers of the Harlem Renaissance include Countee Cullen, Claude McKay, Jean Toomer, and Langston Hughes.

HYPERBOLE *Hyperbole* is a deliberate exaggeration or overstatement, often used for comic effect. In Mark Twain's "The Notorious Jumping Frog of Calaveras County" (p. 569), the claim that Jim Smiley would follow a bug as far as Mexico to win a bet is hyperbole.

IAMBIC PENTAMETER *Iambic pentameter* is a line of poetry with five iambic feet, each containing one unstressed syllable followed by one stressed syllable (˘ ´). Iambic pen-tameter may be rhymed or unrhymed. Unrhymed iambic pen-tameter is called blank verse. These lines from Anne Brad-street's "The Author to Her Book" are in iambic pentameter:

And for thy, Mother, she alas is poor,
Which caused her thus to send thee out
of door.

See also Blank Verse *and* Meter.

IDYLL An *idyll* is a poem or part of a poem that describes and idealizes country life. John Greenleaf Whittier's "Snow-bound" (p. 274) is an idyll.

IMAGE An *image* is a word or phrase that appeals to one or more of the five senses—sight, hearing, touch, taste, or smell.

See also Imagery.

IMAGERY *Imagery* is the descriptive or figurative language used in literature to create word pictures for the reader. These pictures, or images, are created by details of sight, sound, taste, touch, smell, or movement.

IMAGISM *Imagism* was a literary movement that flourished between 1912 and 1927. Led by Ezra Pound and Amy Lowell, the Imagist poets rejected nineteenth-century poetic forms and language. Instead, they wrote short poems that used ordinary language and free verse to create sharp, exact, con-centrated pictures. Pound's poetry (p. 732) provides examples of Imagism.

IRONY *Irony* is a contrast between what is stated and what is meant, or between what is expected to happen and what actually happens. In *verbal irony*, a word or a phrase is used to suggest the opposite of its usual meaning. In *dramatic irony*, there is a contradiction between what a character thinks and what the reader or audience knows. In *irony of situation*, an event occurs that contradicts the expectations of the characters, of the reader, or of the audience.

JOURNAL A *journal* is a daily autobiographical account of events and personal reactions. For example, Mary Chesnut's journal (p. 536) records events during the Civil War.

LEGEND A *legend* is a traditional story. Usually a legend deals with a particular person—a hero, a saint, or a national leader. Often legends reflect a people's cultural values. American legends include those of the early Native Americans and those about folk heroes such as Davy Crockett.

See also Myth.

LETTER A *letter* is a written message or communication addressed to a reader or readers and is generally sent by mail. Letters may be *private or public*, depending on their intended audience. A *public letter*, also called a *literary letter* or *epistle*, is a work of literature written in the form of a personal letter but created for publication. Michel-Guillaume Jean de Crèvecoeur's "Letters From an American Farmer," excerpted on page 208, are public letters.

LOCAL COLOR *Local color* is the use in a literary work of characters and details unique to a particular geographic area. It can be created by the use of dialect and by descriptions of customs, clothing, manners, attitudes, and landscape. Local-color stories were especially popular after the Civil War, bringing readers the West of Bret Harte and the Mississippi River of Mark Twain.

See also Realism *and* Regionalism.

LYRIC POEM A lyric poem is a melodic poem that expresses the observations and feelings of a single speaker. Unlike a narrative poem, a lyric poem focuses on producing a single, unified effect. Types of lyric poems include the *elegy*, the *ode*, and the *sonnet*. Among contemporary American poets, the lyric is the most common poetic form.

MAIN CHARACTER *See* Character.

METAPHOR A *metaphor* is a figure of speech in which one thing is spoken of as though it were something else. The identification suggests a comparison between the two things that are identified, as in "death is a long sleep."

A *mixed metaphor* occurs when two metaphors are jumbled together. For example, thorns and rain are illogically mixed in "the thorns of life rained down on him." A *dead metaphor* is one that has been overused and has become a common expression, such as "the arm of the chair" or "nightfall."

METER The *meter* of a poem is its rhythmical pattern. This pattern is determined by the number and types of stresses, or beats, in each line. To describe the meter of a poem, you must scan its lines. *Scanning* involves marking the stressed and unstressed syllables, as follows:

Soon as | the sun | forsook | the eas|tern main
The peal | ing thun | der shook | the heav'n | ly plain;
— "An Hymn to the Evening," p. 172

As the example shows, each strong stress is marked with a slanted line (´) and each weak stress with a horseshoe symbol (˘). The weak and strong stresses are then divided by vertical lines (|) into groups called feet. The following types of feet are common in poetry written in English:

1. *Iamb:* a foot with one unstressed syllable followed by one stressed syllable, as in the word "around"
2. *Trochee:* a foot with one stressed syllable followed by one unstressed syllable, as in the word "broken"
3. *Anapest:* a foot with two unstressed syllables followed by one stressed syllable, as in the phrase "in a flash"
4. *Dactyl:* a foot with one stressed syllable followed by two unstressed syllables, as in the word "argument"
5. *Spondee:* a foot with two stressed syllables, as in the word "airship"
6. *Pyrrhic:* a foot with two unstressed syllables, as in the last foot of the word "imag|ining"

Lines of poetry are often described as *iambic, trochaic, anapestic,* or *dactylic.* Lines are also described in terms of the number of feet that occur in them, as follows:

1. *Monometer:* verse written in one-foot lines
   Évĭl
   Bĕgéts
   Évĭl

   —Anonymous
2. *Dimeter:* verse written in two-foot lines
   This ĭs | thĕ time
   ŏf thĕ trág|ĭc mán

   —"Visits to St. Elizabeth's," Elizabeth Bishop
3. *Trimeter:* verse written in three-foot lines:
   Óvĕr | thĕ win|tĕr glácĭĕrs
   Ĭ sée | thĕ súm|mĕr glów,
   Ănd through | thĕ wild-|piled snówdrĭft
   Thĕ wárm | rósebŭds | bĕlów.

   —"Beyond Winter," Ralph Waldo Emerson

4. *Tetrameter:* verse written in four-foot lines:

The sun | that brief | Decem|ber day
Rose cheer|less ov|er hills | of gray

—"Snowbound," p. 274

5. *Pentameter:* verse written in five-foot lines:

I doubt | not God | is good, | well-mean|ing, kind,
And did | He stoop | to quib|ble could | tell why
The lit|tle bur|ied mole | contin|ues blind

—"Yet Do I Marvel," Countee Cullen

A complete description of the meter of a line tells both how many feet there are in the line and what kind of foot is most common. Thus, the lines from Countee Cullen's poem would be described as *iambic pentameter. Blank verse* is poetry written in unrhymed iambic pentameter. Poetry that does not have a regular meter is called *free verse.*

MONOLOGUE A *monologue* is a speech delivered entirely by one person or character.

See also Dramatic Monologue.

MOOD *Mood,* or atmosphere, is the feeling created in the reader by a literary work or passage. Elements that can influence the mood of a work include its setting, tone, and events.

See also Setting *and* Tone.

MOTIVATION A *motivation* is a reason that explains a character's thoughts, feelings, actions, or speech. Characters are motivated by their values and by their wants, desires, dreams, wishes, and needs. Sometimes the reasons for a character's actions are stated directly, as in Willa Cather's "A Wagner Matinée" (p. 676), when Clark explains his reception of his aunt by saying, "I owed to this woman most of the good that ever came my way in my boyhood." At other times, the writer will just suggest a character's motivation.

MYTH A *myth* is a fictional tale that explains the actions of gods or heroes or the causes of natural phenomena. Myths that explain the origins of earthly life, as do the Onondaga, Najavo, and Modoc myths in this text, are known as origin myths. Other myths express the central values of the people who created them.

NARRATION *Narration* is writing that tells a story. The act of telling a story is also called *narration.* The *narrative,* or story, is told by a storyteller called the *narrator.* A story is usually told chronologically, in the order in which events take place in time, though it may include flashbacks and foreshadowing. Narratives may be true, like the events recorded in Mary Chesnut's journal (p. 536), or fictional, like the events in Flannery O'Connor's "The Life You Save May Be Your Own" (p. 972).

Narration is one of the forms of discourse and is used in novels, short stories, plays, narrative poems, anecdotes, autobiographies, biographies, and reports.

See also Narrative Poem *and* Narrator.

NARRATIVE A *narrative* is a story told in fiction, nonfiction, poetry, or drama. Narratives are often classified by their content or purpose. An *exploration narrative* is a firsthand account of an explorer's travels in a new land. Alvar Núñez Cabeza de Vaca's account of his exploration of the wilderness that is now Texas, "A Journey Through Texas," appears on page 32. "The Interesting Narrative of the Life of Olaudah Equiano" (p. 44) is a *slave narrative,* an account of the experiences of an enslaved person. A *historical narrative* is a narrative account of significant historical events, such as John Smith's *The General History of Virginia* (p. 72).

See also Narration.

NARRATIVE POEM A *narrative poem* tells a story in verse. Three traditional types of narrative verse are *ballads,* songlike poems that tell stories; *epics,* long poems about the deeds of gods or heroes; and *metrical romances,* poems that tell tales of love and chivalry.

See also Ballad.

NARRATOR A *narrator* is a speaker or character who tells a story. A story or novel may be narrated by a main character, by a minor character, or by someone uninvolved in the story. The narrator may speak in the first person or in the third person. An *omniscient narrator* is all-knowing, while a *limited narrator* knows only what one character does.

See also Point of View.

NATURALISM *Naturalism* was a literary movement among novelists at the end of the nineteenth century and during the early decades of the twentieth century. The Naturalists tended to view people as hapless victims of immutable natural laws. Early exponents of Naturalism included Stephen Crane, Jack London, and Theodore Dreiser.

See also Realism.

NONFICTION *Nonfiction* is prose writing that presents and explains ideas or that tells about real people, places, objects, or events. Essays, biographies, autobiographies, journals, and reports are all examples of nonfiction.

See also Fiction *and* Genre.

NOVEL A *novel* is a long work of fiction. A novel often has a complicated plot, many major and minor characters, a significant theme, and several varied settings. Novels can be classified in many ways, based on the historical periods in which they are written, the subjects and themes that they treat, the techniques that are used in them, and the literary movements that inspired them. Classic nineteenth-century novels include Herman Melville's *Moby-Dick* (p. 354) and Nathaniel Hawthorne's *The Scarlet Letter* (an extended reading suggestion). Well-known twentieth-century novels include F. Scott Fitzgerald's *The Great Gatsby* and Edith Wharton's *Ethan Frome* (recommended selections for extended reading). A *novella* is not as long as a novel but is longer than a short story. Ernest Hemingway's *The Old Man and the Sea* is a novella.

ODE An *ode* is a long, formal lyric poem with a serious theme that may have a traditional stanza structure. Odes often honor people, commemorate events, respond to natural scenes, or consider serious human problems.
See also Lyric Poem.

OMNISCIENT NARRATOR *See* Narrator *and* Point of View.

ONOMATOPOEIA *Onomatopoeia* is the use of words that imitate sounds. Examples of such words are *buzz*, *hiss*, *murmur*, and *rustle*.

ORAL TRADITION *Oral tradition* is the passing of songs, stories, and poems from generation to generation by word of mouth. The oral tradition in America has preserved Native American myths and legends, spirituals, folk ballads, and other works originally heard and memorized rather than written down.
See also Ballad, Folk Literature, Legend, Myth, *and* Spiritual.

ORATORY *Oratory* is public speaking that is formal, persuasive, and emotionally appealing. Patrick Henry's "Speech in the Virginia Convention" (p. 186) is an example of oratory.

OXYMORON An *oxymoron* is a figure of speech that combines two opposing or contradictory ideas. An oxymoron, such as "freezing fire," suggests a paradox in just a few words.
See also Figurative Language *and* Paradox.

PARADOX A *paradox* is a statement that seems to be contradictory but that actually presents a truth. Marianne Moore uses paradox in "Nevertheless" when she says, "Victory won't come / to me unless I go / to it." Because a paradox is surprising, it draws the reader's attention to what is being said.
See also Figurative Language *and* Oxymoron.

PARALLELISM *Parallelism* is the repetition of a grammatical structure. Robert Hayden concludes his poem "Astronauts" with these questions in parallel form:

What do we want of these men?
What do we want of ourselves?

Parallelism is used in poetry and in other writing to emphasize and to link related ideas.

PARODY A *parody* is a humorous imitation of a literary work, one that exaggerates or distorts the characteristic features of the original.

PASTORAL *Pastoral* poems deal with rural settings, including shepherds and rustic life. Traditionally, pastoral poems have presented idealized views of rural life. In twentieth-century pastorals, however, poets like Robert Frost introduced ethical complexity into an otherwise simple landsape.

PERSONIFICATION *Personification* is a figure of speech in which a nonhuman subject is given human characteristics. In "April Rain Song," Langston Hughes personifies the rain:

Let the rain sing you a lullaby.

Effective personification of things or ideas makes them seem vital and alive, as if they were human.
See also Figurative Language.

PERSUASION *Persuasion* is writing or speech that attempts to convince a reader to think or act in a particular way. During the Revolutionary War period, leaders such as Patrick Henry, Thomas Paine, and Thomas Jefferson used persuasion in their political arguments. Persuasion is also used in advertising, in editorials, in sermons, and in political speeches.

PLAIN STYLE *Plain style* is a type of writing in which uncomplicated sentences and ordinary words are used to make simple, direct statements. This style was favored by those Puritans who wanted to express themselves clearly, in accordance with their religious beliefs. In the twentieth century, Ernest Hemingway was a master of plain style.
See also Style.

PLOT *Plot* is the sequence of events in a literary work. In most fiction, the plot involves both characters and a central conflict. The plot usually begins with an *exposition* that introduces the setting, the characters, and the basic situation. This is followed by the *inciting incident*, which introduces the central conflict. The conflict then increases during the *development* until it reaches a high point of interest or suspense, the *climax*. The climax is followed by the end, or *resolution*, of the central conflict. Any events that occur after the resolution make up the *denouement*. The events that lead up to the climax make up the *rising action*. The events that follow the climax make up the *falling action*.
See also Conflict.

POETRY *Poetry* is one of the three major types of literature. In poetry, form and content are closely connected, like the two faces of a single coin. Poems are often divided into lines and stanzas and often employ regular rhythmical patterns, or meters. Most poems use highly concise, musical, and emotionally charged language. Many also make use of imagery, figurative language, and special devices such as rhyme.
See also Genre.

POINT OF VIEW *Point of view* is the perspective, or vantage point, from which a story is told. Three commonly used points of view are first person, omniscient third person, and limited third person.

In the *first-person point of view*, the narrator is a character in the story and refers to himself or herself with the first-person pronoun "I." "The Fall of the House of Usher" (p. 308) is told by a first-person narrator.

The two kinds of third-person point of view, limited and omniscient, are called "third person" because the narrator uses third-person pronouns such as "he" and "she" to refer to the characters. There is no "I" telling the story.

In stories told from the *omniscient third-person point of view*, the narrator knows and tells about what each character feels and thinks. "The Devil and Tom Walker" (p. 242) is written from the omniscient third-person point of view.

In stories told from the *limited third-person point of view*, the narrator relates the inner thoughts and feelings of only one character, and everything is viewed from this character's perspective. "An Occurrence at Owl Creek Bridge" (p. 508) is written from the limited third-person point of view.
See also Narrator.

PROSE *Prose* is the ordinary form of written language. Most writing that is not poetry, drama, or song is considered prose. Prose is one of the major genres of literature. It occurs in two forms: fiction and nonfiction.
See also Fiction, Genre, *and* Nonfiction.

PROTAGONIST The *protagonist* is the main character in a literary work. In "The Jilting of Granny Weatherall" (p. 846), the protagonist is the dying grandmother.
See also Antagonist.

QUATRAIN *See* Stanza.

REALISM *Realism* is the presentation in art of the details of actual life. Realism was also a literary movement that began during the nineteenth century and stressed the actual as opposed to the imagined or the fanciful. The Realists tried to write objectively about ordinary characters in ordinary situations. They reacted against Romanticism, rejecting heroic, adventurous, or unfamiliar subjects. Naturalists, who followed the Realists, traced the effects of heredity and environment on people helpless to change their situations.
See also Local Color, Naturalism, *and* Romanticism.

REFRAIN A refrain is a repeated line or group of lines in a poem or song. Most refrains end stanzas, as does "And the tide rises, the tide falls," the refrain in Henry Wadsworth Longfellow's poem (p. 260), or "Coming for to carry me home," the refrain in "Swing Low, Sweet Chariot" (p. 488). Although some refrains are nonsense lines, many increase suspense or emphasize character and theme.

REGIONALISM Regionalism in literature is the tendency among certain authors to write about specific geographical areas. Regional writers, like Willa Cather and William Faulkner, present the distinct culture of an area, including its speech, customs, beliefs, and history. Local-color writing may be considered a type of Regionalism, but Regionalists, like the Southern writers of the 1920s, usually go beyond mere presentation of cultural idiosyncrasies and attempt, instead, a sophisticated sociological or anthropological treatment of the culture of a region.
See also Local Color *and* Setting.

RESOLUTION *See* Plot.

RHYME *Rhyme* is the repetition of sounds at the ends of words. Rhyming words have identical vowel sounds in their final accented syllables. The consonants before the vowels may be different, but any consonants occurring after these vowels are the same, as in *frog* and *bog* or *willow* and *pillow*. End rhyme occurs when rhyming words are repeated at the ends of lines. Internal rhyme occurs when rhyming words fall within a line. *Approximate*, or *slant*, *rhyme* occurs when the rhyming sounds are similar, but not exact, as in *prove* and *glove*.
See also Rhyme Scheme.

RHYME SCHEME A *rhyme scheme* is a regular pattern of rhyming words in a poem. To describe a rhyme scheme, one uses a letter of the alphabet to represent each rhyming sound in a poem or stanza. Consider how letters are used to represent the *abab* ryhme scheme rhymes in the following example:

With innocent wide penguin eyes, three	a
large fledgling mocking-birds below	b
the pussywillow tree,	a
stand in a row.	b

—"Bird-Witted," Marianne Moore

See also Rhyme.

RHYTHM *Rhythm* is the pattern of beats, or stresses, in spoken or written language. Prose and free verse are written in the irregular rhythmical patterns of everyday speech. Consider, for example, the rhythmical pattern in the following free-verse lines by Gwendolyn Brooks:

Life for my child is simple, and is good.

He knows his wish. Yes, but that is not all.

Because I know mine too.

Traditional poetry often follows a regular rhythmical pattern, as in the following lines by America's first great female poet, Anne Bradstreet:

In critic's hands beware thou dost not come,

And take thy way where yet thou art not known
                                    —"The Author to Her Book"

See also Meter.

RISING ACTION *See* Plot.

ROMANTICISM *Romanticism* was a literary and artistic movement of the nineteenth century that arose in reaction against eighteenth-century Neoclassicism and placed a premium on imagination, emotion, nature, individuality, and exotica. Romantic elements can be found in the works of American writers as diverse as Cooper, Poe, Thoreau, Emerson, Dickinson, Hawthorne, and Melville. Romanticism is particularly evident in the works of the Transcendentalists.
See also Classicism *and* Transcendentalism.

ROUND CHARACTER *See* Character.

SATIRE *Satire* is writing that ridicules or criticizes individuals, ideas, institutions, social conventions, or other works of art or literature. The writer of a satire, the satirist, may use a tolerant, sympathetic tone or an angry, bitter tone. Some satire is written in prose and some, in poetry. Examples of satire in this text include W. H. Auden's "The Unknown Citizen" (p. 779) and Ian Frazier's "Coyote v. Acme" (p. 1118).

SCANSION *Scansion* is the process of analyzing a poem's metrical pattern. When a poem is scanned, its stressed and unstressed syllables are marked to show what poetic feet are used and how many feet appear in each line. The last two lines of Edna St. Vincent Millay's "I Shall Go Back Again to the Bleak Shore" may be scanned as follows:

But I | shall find | the sul|len rocks | and skies

Unchanged | from what | they were | when I | was young.
See also Meter.

SENSORY LANGUAGE *Sensory language* is writing or speech that appeals to one or more of the five senses.
See also Image.

SETTING The *setting* of a literary work is the time and place of the action. A setting may serve any of a number of functions. It may provide a background for the action. It may be a crucial element in the plot or central conflict. It may also create a certain emotional atmosphere, or mood.

SHORT STORY A *short story* is a brief work of fiction. The short story resembles the novel but generally has a simpler plot and setting. In addition, the short story tends to reveal character at a crucial moment rather than developing it through many incidents. For example, Thomas Wolfe's "The Far and the Near" (p. 786) concentrates on what happens to a train engineer when he visits people who had waved to him every day.
See also Fiction *and* Genre.

SIMILE A *simile* is a figure of speech that makes a direct comparison between two subjects, using either *like* or *as*. Here are two examples of similes:

The trees looked like pitch forks against the sullen sky.
Her hair was as red as a robin's breast.
See also Figurative Language.

SLANT RHYME *See* Rhyme.

SONNET A *sonnet* is a fourteen-line lyric poem focused on a single theme. Sonnets have many variations but are usually written in iambic pentameter, following one of two traditional patterns: the *Petrarchan*, or *Italian, sonnet*, which is divided into two parts, the eight-line octave and the six-line sestet; and the *Shakespearean*, or *English, sonnet*, which consists of three quatrains and a concluding couplet.
See also Lyric Poem.

SPEAKER The *speaker* is the voice of a poem. Although the speaker is often the poet, the speaker may also be a fictional character or even an inanimate object or another type of nonhuman entity. Interpreting a poem often depends upon recognizing who the speaker is, whom the speaker is addressing, and what the speaker's attitude, or tone, is.
See also Point of View.

SPIRITUAL A *spiritual* is a type of African American folk song dating from the period of slavery and Reconstruction. A typical spiritual deals both with religious freedom and, on an allegorical level, with political and economic freedom. In some spirituals the biblical river Jordan was used as a symbol for the Ohio River, which separated slave states from free states; and the biblical promised land, Canaan, was used as a symbol for the free northern United States. Most spirituals made use of repetition, parallelism, and rhyme. See "Swing Low, Sweet Chariot" (p. 488) and "Go Down, Moses" (p. 490).

STAGE DIRECTIONS *See* Drama.

STANZA A *stanza* is a group of lines in a poem that are considered to be a unit. Many poems are divided into stanzas that are separated by spaces. Stanzas often function just like paragraphs in prose. Each stanza states and develops a single main idea.

Stanzas are commonly named according to the number of lines found in them, as follows:

1. *Couplet:* a two-line stanza
2. *Tercet:* a three-line stanza
3. *Quatrain:* a four-line stanza
4. *Cinquain:* a five-line stanza
5. *Sestet:* a six-line stanza
6. *Heptastich:* a seven-line stanza
7. *Octave:* an eight-line stanza

STATIC CHARACTER *See* Character.

STREAM OF CONSCIOUSNESS *Stream of consciousness* is a narrative technique that presents thoughts as if they were coming directly from a character's mind. Instead of being arranged in chronological order, the events are presented from the character's point of view, mixed in with the character's thoughts just as they might spontaneously occur. Katherine Anne Porter uses this technique in "The Jilting of Granny Weatherall" (p. 846) to capture Granny's dying thoughts and feelings. Ambrose Bierce also uses the stream of consciousness technique in "An Occurrence at Owl Creek Bridge" (p. 508).

See also Point of View.

STYLE A writer's *style* includes word choice, tone, degree of formality, figurative language, rhythm, grammatical structure, sentence length, organization—in short, every feature of a writer's use of language. Ernest Hemingway, for example, is noted for a simple prose style that contrasts with Thomas Paine's aphoristic style and with N. Scott Momaday's reflective style.

See also Diction *and* Plain Style.

SUSPENSE *Suspense* is a feeling of growing uncertainty about the outcome of events. Writers create suspense by raising questions in the minds of their readers. Suspense builds until the climax of the plot, at which point the suspense reaches its peak.

See also Climax *and* Plot.

SYMBOL A *symbol* is anything that stands for or represents something else. A *conventional symbol* is one that is widely known and accepted, such as a voyage symbolizing life or a skull symbolizing death. A *personal symbol* is one developed for a particular work by a particular author. Examples in this textbook include Hawthorne's black veil and Melville's white whale.

SYMBOLISM *Symbolism* was a literary movement during the nineteenth century that influenced poets, including the Imagists and T. S. Eliot. Symbolists turned away from everyday, realistic details to express emotions by using a pattern of symbols.

See also Imagism *and* Realism.

THEME A *theme* is a central message or insight into life revealed by a literary work. An essay's theme is often directly stated in its thesis statement. In most works of fiction, the theme is only indirectly stated: A story, poem, or play most often has an *implied theme*. For example, in "A Worn Path" (p. 820), Eudora Welty does not directly say that Phoenix Jackson's difficult journey shows the power of love, but readers learn this indirectly by the end of the story.

TONE The tone of a literary work is the writer's attitude toward his or her subject, characters, or audience. A writer's tone may be formal or informal, friendly or distant, personal or pompous. For example, William Faulkner's tone in his "Nobel Prize Acceptance Speech" (p. 875) is earnest and serious, whereas James Thurber's tone in "The Night the Ghost Got In" (p. 898) is humorous and ironic.

See also Mood.

TRANSCENDENTALISM *Transcendentalism* was an American literary and philosophical movement of the nineteenth century. The Transcendentalists, who were based in New England, believed that intuition and the individual conscience "transcend" experience and thus are better guides to truth than are the senses and logical reason. Influenced by Romanticism, the Transcendentalists respected the individual spirit and the natural world, believing that divinity was present everywhere, in nature and in each person. The Transcendentalists included Ralph Waldo Emerson, Henry David Thoreau, Bronson Alcott, W. H. Channing, Margaret Fuller, and Elizabeth Peabody.

See also Romanticism.

GRAMMAR AND MECHANICS HANDBOOK

SUMMARY OF GRAMMAR

Nouns A **noun** names a person, place, or thing. A **common noun** names any one of a class of people, places, or things. A **proper noun** names a specific person, place, or thing.

Common Nouns	Proper Nouns
essayist	William Safire
city	New Orleans

Pronouns A **pronoun** is a word that stands for a noun or for words that take the place of a noun.

A **personal pronoun** refers to (1) the person speaking, (2) the person spoken to, or (3) the person, place, or thing spoken about.

	Singular	Plural
First Person	I, me, my, mine	we, us, our, ours
Second Person	you, your, yours	you, your, yours
Third Person	he, him, his, she, her, hers, it, its	they, them, their, theirs

A **reflexive pronoun** ends in -*self* or -*selves* and adds information to a sentence by pointing back to a noun or pronoun in the sentence.

> . . . They click upon *themselves*
> As the breeze rises, . . .
>
> — Frost, p. 882

An **intensive pronoun** ends in -*self* or -*selves* and simply adds emphasis to a noun or pronoun in the same sentence.

> The United States *themselves* are essentially the greatest poem.
>
> — Whitman, p. 434

Demonstrative pronouns (*this, these, that,* and *those*) direct attention to a specific person, place, or thing.

> *this* hat   *these* coats   *that* frame

A **relative pronoun** begins a subordinate (relative) clause and connects it to another idea in the sentence.

> The brave men, living and dead, *who* struggled here, have consecrated it . . .
>
> — Lincoln, p. 522

> I made a little book, in *which* I allotted a page for each of the virtues.
>
> — Franklin, p. 140

An **indefinite pronoun** refers to a noun or pronoun that is not specifically named.

> *Few* could refrain from twisting their heads toward the door; *many* stood upright and turned directly about; . . .
>
> — Hawthorne, p. 336

Verbs A **verb** is a word or group of words that expresses time while showing an action, a condition, or the fact that something exists.

An **action verb** is a verb that tells what action someone or something is performing.

> The sun that brief December day
> *Rose* cheerless over hills of gray, . . .
>
> — Whittier, p. 274

A **linking verb** is a verb that connects its subject with a word generally found near the end of the sentence. All linking verbs are intransitive.

> Her name *was* Phoenix Jackson.
>
> — Welty, p. 820

A **helping verb** is a verb that can be added to another verb to make a single verb phrase.

> Sir, we *have* done everything that could be done to avert the storm which is now coming on.
>
> —Henry, p. 186

Adjectives An **adjective** is a word used to describe a noun or pronoun or to give a noun or pronoun a more specific meaning. Adjectives answer these questions:

What kind?	*green* leaf, *tall* chimney
Which one?	*this* clock, *those* pictures
How many?	*six* days, *several* concerts
How much?	*more* effort, *enough* applause
Whose?	*Kennedy's* address, *my* name

The articles *the, a,* and *an* are adjectives. *An* is used before a word beginning with a vowel sound.

A noun or pronoun may sometimes be used as an adjective.

> *diamond* necklace   *summer* vacation

Adverbs An **adverb** is a word that modifies a verb, an adjective, or another adverb. Adverbs answer the questions *where*, *when*, *in what way*, or *to what extent*.

She came *yesterday*. (modifies verb *came*)

They were *completely* unaware. (modifies adjective *unaware*)

It rained *rather* often. (modifies adverb *often*)

Prepositions A **preposition** is a word that relates a noun or pronoun that appears with it to another word in the sentence. Prepositions are almost always followed by nouns or pronouns.

aboard the train   *among* us   *below* our plane

Conjunctions A **conjunction** is a word used to connect other words or groups of words.

A **coordinating conjunction** connects similar kinds or groups of words.

dogs *and* cats   friendly *but* dignified

Correlative conjunctions are used in pairs to connect similar words or groups of words.

both Prem *and* Sanjay   *neither* she *nor* I

A **subordinating conjunction** connects two complete ideas by placing one idea below the other in rank or importance.

Even before I asked, you knew . . .

A **conjunctive adverb** is an adverb used as a conjunction to connect complete ideas.

O'Connor portrayed social outcasts; *however*, she addresses society as a whole.

Interjections An **interjection** is a word that expresses feeling or emotion and functions independently of a sentence.

Oh, woe is me!

Subject and Verb Agreement To make a subject and verb agree, make sure that both are singular or both are plural.

He reads Hemingway.   *We read* Thoreau.

Phrases A **phrase** is a group of words, without a subject and verb, that functions in a sentence as one part of speech.

A **prepositional phrase** is a group of words that includes a preposition and a noun or pronoun.

beyond the horizon   inside the corral

An **adjective phrase** is a prepositional phrase that modifies a noun or pronoun by telling *what kind* or *which one*.

the book *on the table*   the size *of the classroom*

An **adverb phrase** is a prepositional phrase that modifies a verb, an adjective, or an adverb by pointing out *where*, *when, in what way,* or *to what extent*.

During the intermission before the second half of the concert, I questioned my aunt and found that the "Prize Song" was not new to her.

—Cather, p. 676

An **appositive phrase** is a noun or pronoun with modifiers, placed next to a noun or pronoun to add information and details.

I drop to Hawthorne, *the customs officer, measuring coal* . . .

—Lowell, p. 1014

A **participial phrase** is a participle that is modified by an adjective or adverb phrase or that has a complement. The entire phrase acts as an adjective.

Two or three men, *conversing earnestly together*, ceased as he approached, . . .

—Harte, p. 580

A **nominative absolute** is a noun or pronoun followed by a participle or participial phrase that functions independently of the rest of the sentence.

The preparations being complete, the two private soldiers stepped aside and each drew away the plank upon which he had been standing.

—Bierce, p. 508

An **infinitive phrase** is an infinitive with modifiers, complements, or a subject, all acting together as a single part of speech.

. . . some set *to mow*, others *to bind thatch*, some *to build houses*, others *to thatch them* . . .

—Smith, p. 72

Clauses A **clause** is a group of words with its own subject and verb.

An **independent clause** can stand by itself as a complete sentence. A **subordinate clause** cannot stand by itself as a complete sentence; it can only be part of a sentence.

An **adjective clause** is a subordinate clause that modifies a noun or pronoun by telling *what kind* or *which one*.

In compliance with the request of a friend of mine, *who wrote me from the East*, I called on good-natured, garrulous old Simon Wheeler . . .

—Twain, p. 569

A **subordinate adverb clause** modifies a verb, an adjective, an adverb, or a verbal by telling *where, when, in what way, to what extent, under what condition,* or *why*.

> *Whenever you like*, please visit.

A **noun clause** is a subordinate clause that acts as a noun.

> As I knew, or thought I knew, *what was right and wrong*, I did not see why I might not always do one and avoid the other.
>
> —Franklin, p. 140

SUMMARY OF CAPITALIZATION AND PUNCTUATION

Capitalization

Capitalize the first word in sentences, interjections, and incomplete questions. Also, capitalize the first word in a quotation if the quotation is a complete sentence.

> And then I said in perfect English, "Yes, I'm getting rather concerned."
>
> —Tan, p. 1136

Capitalize all proper nouns and adjectives.

> T. S. Eliot   Mississippi River   Harvard University
> Turkish   November   Puerto Rican

Capitalize a person's title when it is followed by the person's name or when it is used in direct address.

> Rev. Leonidas W. Smiley   General Robert E. Lee

Capitalize titles showing family relationships when they refer to a specific person, unless they are preceded by a possessive noun or pronoun.

> Granny Weatherall   my grandfather Mammedaty

Capitalize the first word and all other key words in the titles of books, periodicals, poems, stories, plays, paintings, and other works of art.

> *The Crucible*   "Anecdote of the Jar"

Capitalize the first word and all nouns in letter salutations and the first word in letter closings.

> Dear Henry,   Yours truly,

Punctuation

End Marks Use a **period** to end a declarative sentence, a mild imperative sentence, an indirect question, and most abbreviations.

> Pile the bodies high at Austerlitz and Waterloo.
>
> —Sandburg, p. 840

Use a **question mark** to end an interrogative sentence, an incomplete question, or a statement that is intended as a question.

> Was it even Kentucky or Tennessee?
>
> —Warren, p. 1017

Use an **exclamation mark** after an exclamatory sentence, a forceful imperative sentence, or an interjection expressing strong emotion.

> "Don't let him, sister!"
>
> —Frost, p. 888

Commas Use a comma before the conjunction to separate two independent clauses in a compound sentence.

> From my mother's sleep I fell into the State,
> And I hunched in its belly till my wet fur froze.
>
> —Jarrell, p. 1174

Use commas to separate three or more words, phrases, or clauses in a series.

> I spun, I wove, I kept the house, I nursed the sick, . . .
>
> —Masters, p. 669

Use commas to separate adjectives of equal rank. Do not use commas to separate adjectives that must stay in a specific order.

> She carried a thin, small cane made from an umbrella . . .
>
> —Welty, p. 820

Use a comma after an introductory word, phrase, or clause.

> Finding Tom so squeamish on this point, he did not insist upon it, . . .
>
> —Irving, p. 242

Use commas to set off parenthetical and nonessential expressions.

> My poor aunt's figure, however, would have presented astonishing difficulties to any dressmaker.
>
> —Cather, p. 676

Use commas with places, dates, and titles.

> Boston, Massachusetts   November 17, 1915
> Dr. Martin Luther King, Jr.

Use commas after items in addresses, after the salutation in a personal letter, after the closing in all letters, and in numbers of more than three digits.

Linden Lane, Princeton, N.J. Dear Marian,
Affectionately yours, 6,778

Use a comma to indicate words left out of an elliptical sentence and to set off a direct quotation.

In T. S. Eliot's poetry, allusions are perhaps the most prominent device; in Ezra Pound's, images.

"Well, Granny," he said, "you must be a hundred years old and scared of nothing."

—Welty, p. 820

Semicolons Use a semicolon to join independent clauses that are not already joined by a conjunction.

The old woman didn't change her position until he was almost into her yard; then she rose with one hand fisted on her hip.

—O'Connor, p. 972

Use semicolons to avoid confusion when independent clauses or items in a series already contain commas.

Before these events, the day was glorious with expectancy; after them, the day was a dead and empty thing.

—Twain, p. 564

Colons Use a colon before a list of items following an independent clause.

Great literature provides us with many things: entertainment, enrichment, and inspiration.

Use a colon to introduce a formal or a lengthy quotation.

In *The Member of the Wedding*, the lonely twelve-year-old girl, Frankie Addams, articulates this universal need: "The trouble with me is that for a long time I have just been an *I* person."

—McCullers, p. 1112

Quotation Marks A **direct quotation** represents a person's exact speech and is enclosed in quotation marks.

"Good," he said. "You will be able to play football again better than ever."

—Hemingway, p. 809

An **indirect quotation** reports only the general meaning of what a person said and does not require quotation marks.

One day I had said that Italian seemed such an easy language to me . . .

—Hemingway, p. 809

Always place a comma or a period inside the final quotation mark.

"Well, Missy, excuse me," Doctor Harry patted her cheek.

—Porter, p. 846

Place a question mark or an exclamation mark inside the final quotation mark if the end mark is part of the quotation; if it is not part of the quotation, place it outside the final quotation mark.

"Cornelia! Cornelia!" No footsteps, but a sudden hand on her cheek. "Bless you, where have you been?"

—Porter, p. 846

Use single quotation marks for a quotation within a quotation.

"'All right,' I say, 'I can't afford to pay
Any fixed wages, though I wish I could.'
'Someone else can.' 'Then someone else will
have to.'"

—"The Death of the Hired Man," Robert Frost

Underline or italicize the titles of long written works, movies, television and radio shows, lengthy works of music, paintings, and sculpture.

The Great Gatsby *Mary Poppins* Aida

Use quotation marks around the titles of short written works, episodes in a series, songs, and titles of works mentioned as parts of a collection.

"Winter Dreams" "Go Down, Moses"

Dashes Use dashes to indicate an abrupt change of thought, a dramatic interrupting idea, or a summary statement.

She'd had moments herself of picturing some kind of evil gene in her husband's ordinary, stocky body—a dark little egg like a black jelly bean, she imagined it.

—Tyler, p. 1028

Use dashes to set off a nonessential appositive or modifier when it is long, when it is already punctuated, or when you want to be dramatic.

. . . for some reason he was not completely sure of—it may have been the cold and his fatigue—he decided not to insist on seeing him.

—Malamud, p. 988

Hyphens Use a hyphen with certain numbers, after certain prefixes, with two or more words used as one word, with a compound modifier coming before a noun, and within a word when a combination of letters might otherwise be confusing.

fifty-four   daughter-in-law   up-to-date report

Apostrophes Add an apostrophe and *-s* to show the possessive case of most singular nouns.

Taylor's poetry   a poet's career

Add an apostrophe to show the possessive case of plural nouns ending in *-s* and *-es*.

the boys' ambition   the Cruzes' house

Add an apostrophe and *-s* to show the possessive case of plural nouns that do not end in *-s* or *-es*.

the men's suits   the deer's antlers

Use an apostrophe in a contraction to indicate the position of the missing letter or letters.

"You look like a saint, Doctor Harry, and I vow that's as near as you'll ever come to it."

—Porter, p. 846

GLOSSARY OF COMMON USAGE

adapt, adopt
Adapt is a verb meaning "to change." *Adopt* is a verb meaning "to take as one's own."

Washington Irving *adapted* many characters and situations from folk tales for his short stories.

Ezra Pound's followers *adopted* a spare style.

advice, advise
Advice is a noun meaning "an opinion." *Advise* is a verb meaning "to give an opinion."

The man ignores the *advice* of the old-timer.

How might you *advise* the younger generation?

affect, effect
Affect is almost always a verb meaning "to influence." *Effect* is usually a noun meaning "result." Effect can also be a verb meaning "to bring about" or "to cause."

An understanding of T. S. Eliot's multiple allusions can *affect* one's appreciation of his poetry.

In Cather's story, the concert has a profound *effect* on Aunt Georgiana.

The aim of persuasive writing is often to *effect* a change in the attitudes of the audience.

among, between
Among is usually used with three or more items. *Between* is generally used with only two items.

Among the writers of the Harlem Renaissance, Langston Hughes stands out.

In Frost's "Mending Wall," the speaker reports a conversation *between* himself and his neighbor.

as, because, like, as to
The word *as* has several meanings and can function as several parts of speech. To avoid confusion, use *because* rather than *as* when you want to indicate cause and effect.

Because Jonathan Edwards believed that his listeners' souls were in danger, he wanted them to repent.

Do not use the preposition *like* to introduce a clause that requires the conjunction *as*.

The Puritans reacted to music and dancing *as* one might expect: They considered that such entertainments were dangerous occasions for sin.

The use of *as to* for *about* is awkward and should be avoided.

Captain Ahab's bitter vehemence *about* the white whale must seem puzzling to the crew.

bad, badly
Use the predicate adjective *bad* after linking verbs such as *feel*, *look*, and *seem*. Use *badly* whenever an adverb is required.

Although Granny Weatherall looks *bad*, she is not at all happy to see Doctor Harry.

Elizabeth is *badly* shaken when Mr. Hooper refuses to remove the black veil.

because of, due to
Use *due to* if it can logically replace the phrase *caused by*. In introductory phrases, however, *because of* is better usage than *due to*.

Farquhar's failure to recognize the scout's trap may be *due to* his eagerness to aid a cause.

Because of Masters's ability to sketch characters accurately, his work became popular.

being as, being that
Avoid using the expressions *being as* and *being that*. Use *because* or *since* instead.

Because Whitman believed that new styles were needed in American poetry, he broke with traditional forms.

Since Shiftlet is more interested in the car than in Lucynell, it is hardly surprising that he abandons her.

beside, besides
Beside is a preposition meaning "at the side of" or "close to." Do not confuse *beside* with *besides*, which means "in addition to." *Besides* can be a preposition or an adverb.

When Clark sits *beside* Georgiana, he tries to imagine her emotions as she hears the music.

Besides Mr. Oakhurst, which other characters are run out of town?

Thomas Jefferson was the third president of the United States; he was a gifted architect, *besides*.

can, may
The verb *can* generally refers to the ability to do something. The verb *may* generally refers to being allowed or permitted to do something.

One of Ralph Waldo Emerson's major themes is that human beings *can* acquire from nature a sense of their own potential and autonomy.

May I borrow your copy of *The Grapes of Wrath*?

different from, different than
The preferred usage is *different from*.

In her powerful exploration of women's consciousness, Kate Chopin was *different from* the vast majority of her contemporaries.

due to the fact that
Replace this awkward expression with *because* or *since*.

Because Dexter Green cherishes his memories of the glamourous Judy Jones, it is not surprising that he is saddened by the knowledge that her youth and beauty have faded.

farther, further
Use *farther* when you refer to distance. Use *further* when you mean "to a greater degree."

The *farther* Phoenix Jackson travels in Eudora Welty's story "A Worn Path," the more her determination to reach her goal grows.

In his speech, Patrick Henry urges his countrymen to trust the British no *further*.

fewer, less
Use *fewer* for things that can be counted. Use *less* for amounts or quantities that cannot be counted.

The poem "The Red Wheelbarrow" uses *fewer* words than many other poems.

The train engineer felt *less* anticipation with each step.

good, well
Use the predicate adjective *good* after linking verbs such as *feel, look, smell, taste*, and *seem*. Use *well* whenever you need an adverb.

At the end of "Winter Dreams," Devon implies that Judy does not look as *good* as she used to.

Anne Tyler writes especially *well* about ordinary people and family relationships.

hopefully
You should not loosely attach this adverb to a sentence, as in "Hopefully, the rain will stop by noon." Rewrite the sentence so that *hopefully* modifies a specific verb. Other possible ways of revising such sentences include using the adjective *hopeful* or a phrase such as *everyone hopes that*.

William Faulkner wrote *hopefully* about mankind's ability to endure and prevail.

Mai was *hopeful* that she could locate some more biographical information about Jean Toomer.

Everyone hopes that Diane will win the essay contest.

its, it's
Do not confuse the possessive pronoun *its* with the contraction *it's*, standing for "it is" or "it has."

Perhaps the most memorable line in Emerson's poem "The Rhodora" is "Beauty is *its* own excuse for being."

Wallace Stevens's "Anecdote of the Jar" suggests that *it's* impossible to mediate completely between the wilderness and the world of civilization.

kind of, sort of

In formal writing, you should not use these colloquial expressions. Instead, use a word such as *rather* or *somewhat*.

> Robert Lowell's train of thought in "Hawthorne" is *rather* difficult to follow.

> Mary Chesnut is accurate but *somewhat* emotional.

lay, lie

Do not confuse these verbs. *Lay* is a transitive verb meaning "to set or put something down." Its principal parts are *lay, laying, laid, laid. Lie* is an intransitive verb meaning "to recline." Its principal parts are *lie, lying, lay, lain.*

> Stream-of-consciousness narration *lays* a special responsibility on the reader.

> The speaker of "I heard a Fly buzz—when I died—" *lies* in a silent room as her life slips away.

many, much

Use *many* to refer to a specific quantity. Use *much* for an indefinite amount or for an abstract concept.

> *Many* of William Faulkner's novels deal with the themes of pride, guilt, and the search for identity.

> *Much* of Mark Twain's fiction was influenced by his boyhood along the Mississippi.

may be, maybe

Be careful not to confuse the verb phrase *may be* with the adverb *maybe* (meaning "perhaps").

> The speaker *may be* the poet herself; in others, the speaker is clearly a different persona.

> The most memorable, and *maybe* the most ineffectual, character in T. S. Eliot's poetry is Prufrock.

plurals that do not end in -s

The plurals of certain nouns from Greek and Latin are formed as they were in their original language. Words such as *criteria, media,* and *phenomena* are plural and should not be treated as if they were singular (*criterion, medium, phenomenon*).

> In "Ars Poetica," Archibald MacLeish seems to deny that meaning is the most important *criterion* for the evaluation of poetry.

> The *phenomena* discussed by the "learn'd astronomer" in Whitman's poem may have included planetary orbits and the influence of the moon on the tides.

raise, rise

Raise is a transitive verb that usually takes a direct object. *Rise* is intransitive and never takes a direct object.

> Suspense *raises* readers' expectations.

> Flannery O'Connor published a collection entitled *Everything That Rises Must Converge.*

set, sit

Do not confuse these verbs. *Set* is a transitive verb meaning "to put (something) in a certain place." Its principal parts are *set, setting, set, set. Sit* is an intransitive verb meaning "to be seated." Its principal parts are *sit, sitting, sat, sat.*

> Phillis Wheatley's poem is so complimentary to Washington that it seems to *set* him on a pedestal.

> As Mrs. Mallard *sits* upstairs alone, she contemplates the death of her husband.

that, which, who

Use the relative pronoun *that* to refer to things or people. Use *which* only for things and *who* only for people.

> The poet *that* Lee liked best was Sylvia Plath.

> The Romantic movement, *which* emphasized emotions, took place during the early 1800s.

> The poet *who* was the first to read his work at a presidential inauguration was Robert Frost.

unique

Because *unique* means "one of a kind," you should not use it carelessly instead of the words "interesting" or "unusual." Avoid such illogical expressions as "most unique," "very unique," and "extremely unique."

> Some critics have argued that its themes make Herman Melville's *Moby-Dick* unique in literary history.

who, whom

In formal writing, use *who* only as a subject in clauses and sentences and *whom* only as an object.

> Walt Whitman, *who* grieved Lincoln's assassination, wrote a tribute to the slain president.

> F. Scott Fitzgerald, *whom* many have heralded as the voice of the Jazz Age, wrote *The Great Gatsby.*

Introduction to the Internet

The Internet is a series of networks that are interconnected all over the world. The Internet allows users to have almost unlimited access to information stored on the networks. Dr. Berners-Lee, a physicist, created the Internet in the 1980s by writing a small computer program that allowed pages to be linked together using key words. The Internet was mostly text-based until 1992, when a computer program called the NCSA Mosaic (National Center for Supercomputing Applications) was created at the University of Illinois. This program was the first Web browser. The development of Web browsers greatly eased the ability of the user to navigate through all the pages stored on the Web. Very soon, the appearance of the Web was altered as well. More appealing visuals were added, and sound, too, was implemented. This change made the Web more user-friendly and more appealing to the general public.

Using the Internet for Research

Key Word Search

Before you begin a search, you should identify your specific topic. To make searching easier, narrow your subject to a key word or a group of key words. These are your search terms, and they should be as specific as possible. For example, if you are looking for the latest concert dates for your favorite musical group, you might use the band's name as a key word. However, if you were to enter the name of the group in the query box of the search engine, you might be presented with thousands of links to information about the group that is unrelated to what you want to know. You might locate such information as band member biographies, the group's history, fan reviews of concerts, and hundreds of sites with related names containing information that is irrelevant to your search. Because you used such a broad key word, you might need to navigate through all that information before you could find a link or subheading for concert dates. In contrast, if you were to type in "Duplex Arena and [band name]," you would have a better chance of locating pages that contain this information.

How to Narrow Your Search

If you have a large group of key words and still do not know which ones to use, write out a list of all the words you are considering. Once you have completed the list, scrutinize it. Then, delete the words that are least important to your search, and highlight those that are most important.

These **key search connectors** can help you fine-tune your search:

AND: Narrows a search by retrieving documents that include both terms. For example: *baseball* AND *playoffs*

OR: Broadens a search by retrieving documents including any of the terms. For example: *playoffs* OR *championships*

NOT: Narrows a search by excluding documents containing certain words. For example: *baseball* NOT *history of*

Tips for an Effective Search

1. Remember that search engines can be case-sensitive. If your first attempt at searching fails, check your search terms for misspellings and try again.

2. If you are entering a group of key words, present them in order from the most important to the least important key word.

3. Avoid opening the link to every single page in your results list. Search engines present pages in descending order of relevancy. The most useful pages will be located at the top of the list. However, read the description of each link before you open the page.

4. Some search engines provide helpful tips for specializing your search. Take the opportunity to learn more about effective searching.

Other Ways to Search

Using Online Reference Sites How you search should be tailored to what you are hoping to find. If you are looking for data and facts, use reference sites before you jump onto a simple search engine. For example, you can find reference sites to provide definitions of words, statistics about almost any subject, biographies, maps, and concise information on many topics. Here are some useful online reference sites:

Online libraries

Online periodicals

Almanacs

Encyclopedias

You can find these sources using subject searches.

Conducting Subject Searches As you prepare to go online, consider your subject and the best way to find information to suit your needs. If you are looking for general information on a topic and you want your search results to be extensive, consider the subject search indexes on most search engines. These indexes, in the form of category and subject lists, often appear on the first page of a search engine. When you click on a specific highlighted word, you will be presented with a new screen containing subcategories of the topic you chose.

Evaluating the Reliability of Internet Resources

Just as you would evaluate the quality, bias, and validity of any other research material you locate, check the source of information you find online. Compare these two sites containing information about the poet and writer Langston Hughes:

Site A is a personal Web site constructed by a college student. It contains no bibliographic information or links to sites that he used. Included on the site are several poems by Langston Hughes and a student essay about the poet's use of symbolism. It has not been updated in more than six months.

Site B is a Web site constructed and maintained by the English Department of a major university. Information on Hughes is presented in a scholarly format, with a bibliography and credits for the writer. The site includes links to other sites and indicates new features that are added weekly.

For your own research, consider the information you find on Site B to be more reliable and accurate than that on Site A. Because it is maintained by experts in their field who are held accountable for their work, the university site will be a better research tool than the student-generated one.

Tips for Evaluating Internet Sources

1. Consider who constructed and who now maintains the Web page. Determine whether this author is a reputable source. Often, the URL endings indicate a source.
   - Sites ending in *.edu* are maintained by educational institutions.
   - Sites ending in *.gov* are maintained by government agencies (federal, state, or local).
   - Sites ending in *.org* are normally maintained by non-profit organizations and agencies.
   - Sites ending in *.com* are commercially or personally maintained.

2. Skim the official and trademarked Web pages first. It is safe to assume that the information you draw from Web pages of reputable institutions, online encyclopedias, online versions of major daily newspapers, or government-owned sites produce information as reliable as the material you would find in print. In contrast, unbranded sites or those generated by individuals tend to borrow information from other sources without providing documentation. As information travels from one source to another, it could have been muddled, misinterpreted, edited, or revised.

3. You can still find valuable information in the less "official" sites. Check for the writer's credentials, and then consider these factors:
   - Do not be misled by official-looking graphics or presentations.
   - Make sure that the information is updated enough to suit your needs. Many Web pages will indicate how recently they have been updated.
   - If the information is borrowed, notice whether you can trace it back to its original source.

Respecting Copyrighted Material

Because the Internet is a relatively new and quickly growing medium, issues of copyright and ownership arise almost daily. As laws begin to govern the use and reuse of material posted online, they may change the way that people can access or reprint material.

Text, photographs, music, and fine art printed online may not be reproduced without acknowledged permission of the copyright owner.

Citing Sources

In research writing, cite your sources. In the body of your paper, provide a footnote, an endnote, or a parenthetical citation, identifying the sources of facts, opinions, or quotations. At the end of your paper, provide a bibliography or a works-cited list, a list of all the sources you cite. Follow an established format, such as Modern Language Association (MLA) Style.

Works-Cited List (MLA Style)

A works-cited list must contain accurate information sufficient to enable a reader to locate each source you cite. The basic components of an entry are as follows:

- Name of the author, editor, translator, or group responsible for the work
- Title of the work
- Place and date of publication
- Publisher

For print materials, the information required for a citation generally appears on the copyright and title pages of a work. For the format of works-cited list entries, consult the examples at right and in the chart on page R32.

Parenthetical Citations (MLA Style)

A parenthetical citation briefly identifies the source from which you have taken a specific quotation, factual claim, or opinion. It refers the reader to one of the entries on your works-cited list. A parenthetical citation has the following features:

- It appears in parentheses.
- It identifies the source by the last name of the author, editor, or translator.
- It gives a page reference, identifying the page of the source on which the information cited can be found.

Punctuation A parenthetical citation generally falls outside a closing quotation mark but within the final punctuation of a clause or sentence. For a long quotation set off from the rest of your text, place the citation at the end of the excerpt without any punctuation following.

Special Cases

- If the author is an organization, use the organization's name, in a shortened version if necessary.
- If you cite more than one work by the same author, add the title or a shortened version of the title.

Sample Works-Cited Lists

Carwardine, Mark, Erich Hoyt, R. Ewan Fordyce, and Peter Gill. *The Nature Company Guides: Whales, Dolphins, and Porpoises.* New York: Time-Life Books, 1998.
Whales in Danger. "Discovering Whales." 18 Oct. 1999. <http://whales.magna.com.au/DISCOVER>

Neruda, Pablo. "Ode to Spring." *Odes to Opposites.* Trans. Ken Krabbenhoft. Ed. and illus. Ferris Cook. Boston: Little, Brown and Company, 1995.
The Saga of the Volsungs. Trans. Jesse L. Byock. London: Penguin Books, 1990.

An anonymous work is listed by title.

Both the title of the work and of the collection in which it is found are listed.

Sample Parenthetical Citations

It makes sense that baleen whales such as the blue whale, the bowhead whale, the humpback whale, and the sei whale (to name just a few) grow to immense sizes (Carwardine, Hoyt, and Fordyce 19–21). The blue whale has grooves running from under its chin to partway along the length of its underbelly. As in some other whales, these grooves expand and allow even more food and water to be taken in (Ellis 18–21).

Author's last name

Page numbers where information can be found

MLA Style for Listing Sources

Book with one author	Pyles, Thomas. *The Origins and Development of the English Language.* 2nd ed. New York: Harcourt Brace Jovanovich, Inc., 1971.
Book with two or three authors	McCrum, Robert, William Cran, and Robert MacNeil. *The Story of English.* New York: Penguin Books, 1987.
Book with an editor	Truth, Sojourner. *Narrative of Sojourner Truth.* Ed. Margaret Washington. New York: Vintage Books, 1993.
Book with more than three authors or editors	Donald, Robert B., et al. *Writing Clear Essays.* Upper Saddle River, NJ: Prentice-Hall, Inc., 1996.
Single work from an anthology	Hawthorne, Nathaniel. "Young Goodman Brown." *Literature: An Introduction to Reading and Writing.* Ed. Edgar V. Roberts and Henry E. Jacobs. Upper Saddle River, NJ: Prentice-Hall, Inc., 1998. 376–385. [Indicate pages for the entire selection.]
Introduction in a published edition	Washington, Margaret. Introduction. *Narrative of Sojourner Truth.* By Sojourner Truth. New York: Vintage Books, 1993. v–xi.
Signed article in a weekly magazine	Wallace, Charles. "A Vodacious Deal." *Time* 14 Feb. 2000: 63.
Signed article in a monthly magazine	Gustaitis, Joseph. "The Sticky History of Chewing Gum." *American History* Oct. 1998: 30–38.
Unsigned editorial or story	"Selective Silence." Editorial. *Wall Street Journal* 11 Feb. 2000: A14. [If the editorial or story is signed, begin with the author's name.]
Signed pamphlet	[Treat the pamphlet as though it were a book.]
Pamphlet with no author, publisher, or date	*Are You at Risk of Heart Attack?* n.p. n.d. [n.p. n.d. indicates that there is no known publisher or date]
Filmstrips, slide programs, and videotape	*The Diary of Anne Frank.* Dir. George Stevens. Perf. Millie Perkins, Shelley Winters, Joseph Schildkraut, Lou Jacobi, and Richard Beymer. Twentieth Century Fox, 1959.
Radio or television program transcript	"Nobel for Literature." Narr. Rick Karr. *All Things Considered.* National Public Radio. WNYC, New York. 10 Oct. 2002. Transcript.
Internet	*National Association of Chewing Gum Manufacturers.* 19 Dec. 1999 <http://www.nacgm.org/consumer/funfacts.html> [Indicate the date you accessed the information. Content and addresses at Web sites change frequently.]
Newspaper	Thurow, Roger. "South Africans Who Fought for Sanctions Now Scrap for Investors." *Wall Street Journal* 11 Feb. 2000: A1+ [For a multipage article, write only the first page number on which it appears, followed by a plus sign.]
Personal interview	Smith, Jane. Personal interview. 10 Feb. 2000.
CD (with multiple publishers)	Simms, James, ed. *Romeo and Juliet.* By William Shakespeare. CD-ROM. Oxford: Attica Cybernetics Ltd.; London: BBC Education; London: HarperCollins Publishers, 1995.
Signed article from an encyclopedia	Askeland, Donald R. "Welding." *World Book Encyclopedia.* 1991 ed.

RUBRICS

What is a rubric?

A rubric is a tool, often in the form of a chart or a grid, that helps you assess your work. Rubrics are particularly helpful for writing and speaking assignments.

To help you or others assess, or evaluate, your work, a rubric offers several specific criteria to be applied to your work. Then the rubric helps you or an evaluator indicate your range of success or failure according to those specific criteria. Rubrics are often used to evaluate writing for standardized tests.

Using a rubric will save you time, focus your learning, and improve the work you do. When you know what the rubric will be before you begin writing a persuasive essay, for example, you will be aware as you write of specific criteria that are important in that kind of an essay. As you evaluate the essay before giving it to your teacher, you will focus on the specific areas that your teacher wants you to master— or on areas that you know present challenges for you. Instead of searching through your work randomly for any way to improve it or correct its errors, you will have a clear and helpful focus on specific criteria.

How are rubrics constructed?

Rubrics can be constructed in several ways.
- Your teacher may assign a rubric for a specific assignment.
- Your teacher may direct you to a rubric in your textbook.
- Your teacher and your class may construct a rubric for a particular assignment together.
- You and your classmates may construct a rubric together.
- You may create your own rubric with criteria you want to evaluate in your work.

How will a rubric help me?

A rubric will help you assess your work on a scale. Scales vary from rubric to rubric but usually range from 6 to 1, 5 to 1, or 4 to 1, with 6, 5, or 4 being the highest score and 1 being the lowest. If someone else is using the rubric to assess your work, the rubric will give your evaluator a clear range within which to place your work. If you are using the rubric yourself, it will help you make improvements to your work.

What are the types of rubrics?

- A **holistic rubric** has general criteria that can apply to a variety of assignments. See p. R35 for an example of a holistic rubric.
- An **analytic rubric** is specific to a particular assignment. The criteria for evaluation address the specific issues important in that assignment. See p. R34 for examples of analytic rubrics.

SAMPLE ANALYTIC RUBRICS

Rubric With a 4-point Scale

*The following analytic rubric is an example of a rubric to assess a persuasive essay.
It will help you evaluate audience and purpose, organization, elaboration, and use of language.*

	Audience/Purpose	Organization	Elaboration	Use of Language
4	Demonstrates highly effective word choice; clearly focused on task.	Uses clear, consistent organizational strategy.	Provides convincing, well-elaborated reasons to support the position.	Incorporates transitions; includes very few mechanical errors.
3	Demonstrates good word choice; stays focused on persuasive task.	Uses clear organizational strategy with occasional inconsistencies.	Provides two or more moderately elaborated reasons to support the position.	Incorporates some transitions; includes few mechanical errors.
2	Shows some good word choices; minimally stays focused on persuasive task.	Uses inconsistent organizational strategy; presentation is not logical.	Provides several reasons, but few are elaborated.	Incorporates few transitions; includes many mechanical errors.
1	Shows lack of attention to persuasive task.	Demonstrates lack of organizational strategy.	Provides no specific reasons or does not elaborate.	Does not connect ideas; includes many mechanical errors.

Rubric With a 6-point Scale

*The following analytic rubric is an example of a rubric to assess a persuasive essay.
It will help you evaluate presentation, position, evidence, and arguments.*

	Presentation	Position	Evidence	Arguments
6	Essay clearly and effectively addresses an issue with more than one side.	Essay clearly states a supportable position on the issue.	All evidence is logically organized, well presented, and supports the position.	All reader concerns and counterarguments are effectively addressed.
5	Most of essay addresses an issue that has more than one side.	Essay clearly states a position on the issue.	Most evidence is logically organized, well presented, and supports the position.	Most reader concerns and counterarguments are effectively addressed.
4	Essay adequately addresses issue that has more than one side.	Essay adequately states a position on the issue.	Many parts of evidence support the position; some evidence is out of order.	Many reader concerns and counterarguments are adequately addressed.
3	Essay addresses issue with two sides but does not present second side clearly.	Essay states a position on the issue, but the position is difficult to support.	Some evidence supports the position, but some evidence is out of order.	Some reader concerns and counterarguments are addressed.
2	Essay addresses issue with two sides but does not present second side.	Essay states a position on the issue, but the position is not supportable.	Not much evidence supports the position, and what is included is out of order.	A few reader concerns and counterarguments are addressed.
1	Essay does not address issue with more than one side.	Essay does not state a position on the issue.	No evidence supports the position.	No reader concerns or counterarguments are addressed.

SAMPLE HOLISTIC RUBRIC

Holistic rubrics such as this one are sometimes used to assess writing assignments on standardized tests. Notice that the criteria for evaluation are focus, organization, support, and use of conventions.

Points	Criteria
6 Points	• The writing is strongly focused and shows fresh insight into the writing task. • The writing is marked by a sense of completeness and coherence and is organized with a logical progression of ideas. • A main idea is fully developed, and support is specific and substantial. • A mature command of the language is evident, and the writing may employ characteristic creative writing strategies. • Sentence structure is varied, and writing is free of all but purposefully used fragments. • Virtually no errors in writing conventions appear.
5 Points	• The writing is clearly focused on the task. • The writing is well organized and has a logical progression of ideas, though there may be occasional lapses. • A main idea is well developed and supported with relevant detail. • Command of the language is mature. • Sentence structure is varied, and the writing is free of fragments, except when used purposefully. • Writing conventions are followed correctly.
4 Points	• The writing is clearly focused on the task, but extraneous material may intrude at times. • A clear organizational pattern is present, though lapses may occur. • A main idea is adequately supported, but development may be uneven. • Sentence structure is generally fragment free but shows little variation. • Writing conventions are generally followed correctly.
3 Points	• Writing is generally focused on the task, but extraneous material may intrude at times. • An organizational pattern is evident, but writing may lack a logical progression of ideas. • Support for the main idea is generally present but is sometimes illogical. • Sentence structure is generally free of fragments, but there is almost no variation. • The work generally demonstrates a knowledge of writing conventions, with occasional misspellings.
2 Points	• The writing is related to the task but generally lacks focus. • There is little evidence of organizational pattern, and there is little sense of cohesion. • Support for the main idea is generally inadequate, illogical, or absent. • Sentence structure is unvaried, and serious errors may occur. • Errors in writing conventions and spelling are frequent.
1 Point	• The writing may have little connection to the task and is generally unfocused. • There has been little attempt at organization or development. • The paper seems fragmented, with no clear main idea. • Sentence structure is unvaried, and serious errors appear. • Poor word choice and poor command of the language obscure meaning. • Errors in writing conventions and spelling are frequent.
Unscorable	The paper is considered unscorable if: • The response is unrelated to the task or is simply a rewording of the prompt. • The response has been copied from a published work. • The student did not write a response. • The response is illegible. • The words in the response are arranged with no meaning. • There is an insufficient amount of writing to score.

STUDENT MODEL

Persuasive Writing

This persuasive letter, which would receive a top score according to a persuasive rubric, is a response to the following writing prompt, or assignment:

Write a letter to a government official strongly supporting an environmental issue that is important to you and urging the official to take a specific action that supports your cause.

Dear Secretary of the Interior:

It's a normal, carefree day in the forest. The birds are singing and all of the animals are relaxing under the refreshing glow of the sun. But suddenly the thunderous sound of a chain saw echoes throughout the woodlands, and trees fall violently. The creatures of the forest run in terror. Many of these beautiful creatures will starve to death slowly and painfully as their homes are destroyed, and this precious ecosystem will not be able to regrow to its previous greatness for many years to come.

> A descriptive and interesting introduction grabs the reader's attention and shows a persuasive focus.

This sad story is a true one in many places around the globe. We must slow deforestation and replant trees immediately to save our breathable air, fertile topsoil, and fragile ecosystems.

If entire forests continue to be obliterated, less oxygen will be produced and more CO_2 emitted. In fact, deforestation accounts for a quarter of the CO_2 released into the atmosphere each year: about 1–2 billion tons. Forests provide the majority of the oxygen on earth, and if these forests disappear our air will soon be unbreathable.

Second, deforestation results in a loss of topsoil. Many of the companies who are involved in deforestation claim that the land is needed for farms, but deforestation makes the land much less fertile because it accelerates the process of erosion. According to the UN Food and Agriculture Organization, deforestation has damaged almost 6 million square kilometers of soil.

> The writer supports the argument with facts and evidence, and also uses the persuasive technique of appealing to the reader's emotions.

Finally, if cutting doesn't slow, many species will die off and many ecosystems will be destroyed. The 2000 UN Global Environment Outlook says that forests and rain forests have the most diverse plant and animal life in the world. The GEO also notes that there are more than 1,000 threatened species living in the world's forests. Imagine someone destroying all of the houses in your neighborhood and leaving all of the residents homeless. This is how it is for the organisms that live in the forests.

In conclusion, deforestation must slow and trees must be replanted immediately, or we will lose clean air, topsoil, and many precious organisms. Furthermore, a loss in forests will result in a generation that knows very little about nature. So, to prevent the chaotic disturbance of peace in the forests, please do whatever you can to prevent deforestation. Vote YES on any UN bills that would help the condition of our world's forests.

> The conclusion restates the argument and presents a call to action.

Sincerely yours,

Jamil Khouri

Success on college aptitude and achievement tests depends in a large part on the work you have done throughout your school career. By investing a sensible amount of time in preparing for a college entrance or AP exam, however, you can ensure that you obtain the highest score of which you are capable. Follow the strategies in this workshop for college-entrance test preparation.

PREPARING FOR THE TEST

Choose and Register for Tests

To decide which tests you will take, find out from the colleges to which you are applying which tests they require and which tests they encourage. Then, consult with guidance counselors, search the Web, or use library resources to determine the registration deadline and fees, the exact location of the test site, and the time each test will be given. Register in advance to take the test at a convenient location and date.

Familiarize Yourself With the Test

To focus your studies for the test, use available resources, such as the College Board Web site or the most recent edition of a reputable prep book to determine the following:

- the topics and skills covered on the test
- the time each section of the test will take
- the number and type of questions in each section
- how the test is scored

Study for the Test

Begin preparing for the test well in advance of the date on which you will take it. Read through a guide or two on the test, determine what study suggestions will work for you, and take a practice exam or two.

Subject-Area Tests If you are taking an AP or SAT II exam, review class notes, textbooks, and papers that you have written.

Aptitude Tests for College Admission	
PSAT/ NMSQT	Preliminary Scholastic Aptitude Test / National Merit Scholarship Qualifying Test **General Description** A two-hour version of the SAT, covering verbal and math skills and including a writing section. **Why Take It** Most often taken by juniors to prepare for the SAT, to make contact with colleges, and to qualify for the National Merit Scholarship.
SAT	Scholastic Aptitude Test **General Description** An aptitude test of vocabulary, math, and reasoning skills. Mostly multiple-choice questions. **Why Take It** Most colleges require that applicants submit either SAT or ACT scores. **Sections** Three Verbal sections — 78 questions total; 1 hour 15 minutes. Three Math sections—60 questions total; 1 hour 15 minutes. One additional, 30-question "equating section" that is not counted toward score.
ACT	American College Test **General Description** An aptitude test of English, math, and science reasoning skills. More content-based than the SAT. Multiple-choice questions only. **Why Take It** Most colleges require that applicants submit either SAT or ACT scores. **Sections** One English section—75 questions; 45 minutes. One Math section—60 questions; 60 minutes. One Reading section—40 questions; 35 minutes. One Science Reasoning section—40 questions; 35 minutes.

The AP English Open Response Question
Use your knowledge of the structure of the test to aid you in preparing. For instance, the AP English Literature and Composition test traditionally offers an "open response" question. You must choose a work to comment on in response to the question asked.

For this case, you should prepare to address two to four classic novels or plays in advance. Select diverse works to make sure that if the question does not apply to one there is a good chance that it will apply to the other. (Consult with your teacher or other resources for a list of recommended works).

Review your notes on the works you select and reread significant passages. Reread any papers you have written on them. Then, write a paragraph or two introducing the core themes of each work and the means by which the writer conveys them. By writing on the works in advance, you store ideas and connections to explore on the test. You ensure that your ideas will flow well when you write the actual test essay.

Practice

A standardized test tests your ability to apply knowledge or insight—within definite time limits. You can practice this skill by timing yourself as you take practice tests.

Practice as if you are taking the actual test. You can find practice copies of tests online or in test prep books. Each time you take a practice test, set aside the amount of time you will be given to take the actual test. Set a timer or alarm clock to warn you ten minutes before time is up. As you take the test, practice the strategies recommended in the Use Basic Test-Taking Strategies section below.

Analyze your practice results. Taking a practice test will sharpen your test-taking skills only if you understand your results. After scoring your practice test, review your responses to the questions. If you chose the correct answer for a question, jot a note explaining why it is the right answer. If you chose the wrong answer, note why it is wrong and why the correct answer is the best choice. By analyzing your answers—correct or incorrect—you will begin to "think like the test" and will be able to answer questions more effectively.

USE BASIC TEST-TAKING STRATEGIES

The following strategies can help you get the best score of which you are capable on any standardized test.

Manage Time on the Test

Analyze the test. Find out in advance how much time is allowed for each section of the test. Then, calculate how much time it should take to complete one quarter or one third of each section.

Keep track of time. Bring a watch with you to the test. As you work, check the time at reasonable intervals. You might check the time after completing the first ten multiple-choice questions out of thirty or after completing the first essay.

Subject-Area Tests for College Placement	
SAT II	**General Description** Discipline-specific tests measuring command of a subject.
	Why Take It Some colleges may require SAT IIs for admission. Others use the scores to place students appropriately.
	Specifics All SAT II tests except the Writing test are multiple choice. Each takes an hour. The SAT II: Literature test divides 60 questions among 6 to 8 reading passages, covering poetry and prose from a broad range of periods.
AP exams	**General Description** Discipline-specific tests measuring command of a subject.
	Why Take It Participating colleges will award students college credit for achieving or bettering a given score.
	Specifics Formats vary with subject. The AP English Literature and Composition test traditionally features 50 to 55 multiple-choice questions divided among 4 to 5 reading passages (60 minutes) and 3 essay questions, including one "open response" (120 minutes total). Passages cover poetry and prose from a broad range of periods.

Adjust your pace. If you look at your watch after completing one third of a section and find out that you have used up half of your time, you should adjust your pace. Pick up speed—but do not rush. Remember, you do not need to answer every question to earn a respectable score.

Prioritize questions. Every question in a section counts for the same number of points, regardless of how difficult it may be. Prioritize questions. For a series of individual questions, as on the Analogies section of the SAT, you might simply skip the most difficult items and return to them later. On a test that features reading passages, quickly identify those passages that you are most confident you can analyze well, and work on the questions for these passages first. Return to the more difficult items when you have finished the easier ones.

Strategies for Answering Questions

The following strategies will aid you in answering the specific questions on the test.

Read passages effectively. First, skim a reading passage to get a general idea of its content. Then, read it carefully. When you encounter a word or idea that you do not understand, register it and move on. You may find a detail that clarifies it later.

The key to effective reading is to keep your focus. You need not understand everything in the passage. You do need to follow the main idea as it is developed from beginning to end. If you find your mind wandering—your eyes just running down the page without absorbing information—stop. Focus your attention, and keep reading.

After reading the passage, mentally sum up the main idea. When answering the questions on the passage, refer to the passage whenever necessary to confirm answers.

Read questions carefully. To test your reasoning skills, standardized tests ask questions that call on your ability to distinguish shades of meaning or make complex connections. For this reason, you must read every question with care, restating it in your own words to make sure you have understood it.

- Eliminate answer choices that are obviously wrong.
- Eliminate answer choices that contain a part that is obviously wrong.
- After eliminating one or more answer choices, choose the remaining answer that you think is likeliest to be correct.

Strategies for Essay Questions

To ensure that any essay you are called on to write for a test will command the attention of the person who will score it, use the following strategies.

Adapt your thesis from the question. The materials for the thesis of a test essay are right there in the test question. Read the question carefully. Then, jot down a thesis statement that mirrors the question, using key terms from the question, as in the example in the chart.

Motivate your thesis. To capture the attention of the person grading your essay, connect your thesis to a fundamental theme or issue. By doing so, you are showing your reader why he or she should care about your point.

For instance, you might face an essay question on Shakespeare's *The Tempest.* In your senior thesis, you may have written that the essential meaning of the play is to dramatize and reconcile opposing aspects of the human spirit. Imagination (Ariel), appetite (Caliban), revenge, and love all have their moment and are put in their proper place.

In the introduction to your test essay, you should restate that fundamental insight and say it in dramatic terms. Once you have stated the essential meaning or most important feature of the work, you can then motivate your thesis, as in the example below.

Sample question: In some works of literature, contrasts between characters are used to develop the central theme. Choose a work of literary merit and write a well-organized essay discussing how the writer uses character contrasts.

Sample preliminary thesis statement: In *The Tempest,* Shakespeare uses <u>contrasts between characters</u> such as Caliban and Ariel <u>to convey his theme</u> of the sorting out of oppositions in the human spirit.
[Thesis statement incorporates key terms from the question.]

Sample introduction (thesis plus motivation): In *The Tempest,* characters come in pairs. Each pair reflects a duality or conflict that defines the human spirit, from the quarrel between mind and body to the war of the sexes. Shakespeare uses contrasts between characters such as Caliban and Ariel to dramatize these dualities and, in the end, to reconcile them or at least to restore order to them.
[Motivates the thesis by connecting it to the meaning of the work as a whole]

Use precise and vivid language. As in any writing you do, choose words in your test essays that convey meaning precisely and create vivid images. If you are discussing Brutus's decision to join the conspirators in *Julius Caesar,* you might use the word *torn* instead of the word *undecided.*

If you are applying for admission to a college, you will probably need to submit an essay as part of your application. This essay is your introduction to a college applications committee. It will help committee members get a sense of you as a person and as a student. Review the chart at right for general strategies, and then follow the guidelines below to ensure that your college application essay does the best job presenting you.

Selecting a Topic

Read the essay question on the application form with care. Mark key criteria and direction words such as *describe* and *explain.* After you have written a first draft, check to make sure you have met all of the requirements of the question. Your essay has a better chance of succeeding if it meets the requirements exactly.

General Questions About You

The essay question on a college application may be as general as "Describe a significant experience or event in your life and explain its consequences for you." To choose the right topic for such a question, think of an event or experience that truly is meaningful to you—a camping trip, a volunteer event, a family reunion. Test the subject by drafting a letter about it to a good friend or relative. If you find that your enthusiasm for the subject grows as you write, and if your discussion reveals something about your growth or your outlook on life, the topic may be the right one for your essay.

Directed Questions

The essay question on an application may be more directed than a simple "tell us about yourself." For instance, you may be asked to select three figures from history you would like to meet and to explain your choices.

In such cases, do not give an answer just because you think it will please reviewers. Instead, consult your own interests and instincts. Your most convincing writing will come from genuine interest in the subject. You might discover the best topic by jotting down a diary entry or a letter to a friend in which you discuss possible subjects.

Style

Though an essay is a chance to tell something about yourself, it is also a formal document addressed to

Strategies for Writing an Effective College Application Essay

- **Choose the right topic.** If you have a choice of essay topics, choose the one that interests you.
- **Organize.** Use a strong organization that carries the reader from introduction to conclusion.
- **Begin with a bang.** Open with an introduction that has a good chance of sparking the reader's interest.
- **Elaborate.** Be sure to explain why the experiences you discuss are important to you or what you learned from them.
- **Show style.** Bring life to your essay through vivid descriptions, precise word choice, and sophisticated sentence structure, such as parallelism. Consider including dialogue where appropriate.
- **Close with a clincher.** Write a conclusion that effectively sums up your ideas.
- **Do a clean job.** Proofread your essay carefully to ensure that it is error-free.

strangers. Use a formal to semiformal style. Avoid incomplete sentences and slang unless you are using them for clear stylistic effect. Use words with precision, selecting one or two accurate words for what you mean, rather than piling up words in the hope that one of them will hit the mark.

Format

Most applications limit the length of essays. Do not exceed the allowed space or number of words. Your college application essay should be neatly typed or printed, using adequate margins. Proofread your final draft carefully. If you submit a separate copy of the essay (rather than writing on the application form), number the pages and include your name and contact information on each page.

Reusing Your Essay

Most students apply to a number of different colleges in order to ensure their admission to a school for the next semester. Once you have written a strong essay for one application, you should consider adapting it for others.

Do not submit a single essay to several schools blindly. Always read the application essay question carefully to ensure that the essay you submit fulfills all of its requirements.

By writing **criticism**—writing that analyzes literature—readers share their responses to a written work. Criticism is also a way for a reader to deepen his or her own understanding and appreciation of the work, and to help others to deepen theirs.

The information in this handbook will guide you through the process of writing criticism. In addition, it will help you to refine your critical perceptions to ensure that you are ready to produce work at the college level.

Understanding Criticism

There are a few different types of criticism. Each can enhance understanding and deepen appreciation of literature in a distinctive way. All types share similar functions.

The Types of Criticism

Analysis Students are frequently asked to analyze, or break into parts and examine, a passage or a work. When you write an analysis, you must support your ideas with references to the text, as in this example:

> **Conclusion:** In "Heat," the poet H.D. creates an enduring image of heat. There is no deeper meaning here; her task is to commemorate physical experience in words.
>
> **Support:** The poem's imagery gives heat solidity and depth. In the first stanza, the speaker asks the wind to "cut apart the heat" and, in the third stanza, to "plow through it," as if heat were a thick substance like earth.

Biographical Criticism Biographical criticism uses information about a writer's life to shed light on his or her work, as in this passage by Kenneth Silverman:

> Much of [Poe's] later writing, despite its variety of forms and styles, places and characters, is driven by the question of whether the dead remain dead. . . . [C]hildren who lose a parent at an early age, as Edgar lost Eliza Poe [his mother], invest more feeling in and magnify the parent's image. . . . The young child . . . cannot comprehend the finality of death. . . .

Historical Criticism Historical criticism traces connections between an author's work and the events, circumstances, or ideas that shaped the writer's historical era. For example, Jean H. Hagstrum analyzes William Blake's character of Urizen by showing how the character symbolizes the Enlightenment ideas of the scientist Isaac Newton and the philosopher John Locke.

> Urizen is also an active force. Dividing, partitioning, dropping the plummet line, applying Newton's compasses to the world, he creates abstract mathematical forms. Like Locke, he shrinks the senses, narrows the perceptions, binds man to the natural fact.

The Functions of Criticism

In each of the previous examples of criticism, you can find evidence of the following critical functions:

Making Connections All criticism makes connections between two or more things. For instance, the analysis of H.D.'s poetry connects different parts of a poem (the images of heat being cut or parted by a plow).

Making Distinctions Criticism must make distinctions as well as connections. In the analysis of "Heat," the critic distinguishes between two possible purposes for poetry: first, to create an enduring image and, second, to present a deeper meaning.

Achieving Insight By making connections and distinctions, criticism achieves insight. The analysis of H.D.'s poem reaches the insight that the poem stands on its own as a work of beauty apart from any deeper meaning.

Making a Judgment Assessing the value of a work is an important function of criticism. A critic may assess a work by comparing it with other works and by using a standard such as enjoyment, insight, or beauty.

"Placing" the Work Critics guide readers not by telling them *what* to think but by giving them *terms in which to think*. In the passage quoted above, Hagstrum helps us "place" Urizen. We cannot respond to Urizen, she reminds us, as if he were an individual like Macbeth or Holden Caulfield. Instead, we respond to him best by perceiving him as a historical force—the pursuit of reason—personified. The terms on which we appreciate and understand each of these characters are different.

Writing Criticism

Like all solid writing, a work of criticism presents a thesis (a central idea) and supports it with arguments and evidence. Follow the strategies below to develop a critical thesis and gather support for it.

Formulate a Working Thesis

Once you have chosen a work or works on which to write, formulate a working thesis. First, ask yourself questions like these:

- What strikes you most about the work or the writer that your paper will address? What puzzles you most?

- In what ways is the work unlike others you have read?

- What makes the techniques used by the writer so well-suited to (or so poorly chosen for) conveying the theme of the work?

Jot down notes answering your questions. Then, reread passages that illustrate your answers, jotting down notes about what each passage contributes to the work. Review your notes, and write a sentence that draws a conclusion about the work.

Gather Support

Taking Notes From the Work Once you have a working thesis, take notes on passages in the work that confirm it. To aid your search for support, consider the type of support suited to your thesis, as in the chart.

Conducting Additional Research If you are writing biographical or historical criticism, you will need to consult sources on the writer's life and era. Even if you are writing a close analysis of a poem, you should consider consulting the works of critics to benefit from their insights and understanding. For a more detailed explanation of the research process, see pages 694–699.

Take Notes

Consider recording notes from the works you are analyzing, as well as from any critical works you consult, on a set of note cards. A good set of note cards enables you to recall details accurately, to organize your ideas effectively, and to see connections between ideas.

If your thesis concerns . . .	look for support in the form of . . .
Character	• dialogue • character's actions • writer's descriptions of the character • other characters' reactions to the character
Theme	• fate of characters • patterns and contrasts of imagery, character, or events • mood • writer's attitude toward the action
Style	• memorable descriptions, observations • passages that "sound like" the writer • examples of rhetorical devices, such as exaggeration and irony
Historical Context	• references to historical events and personalities • evidence of social or political pressures on characters • socially significant contrasts between characters (for example, between the rich and the poor)
Literary Influences	• writer's chosen form or genre • passages that "sound like" another writer • events or situations that resemble those in other works • evidence of an outlook similar to that of another writer

One Card, One Idea If you use note cards while researching, record each key passage, theme, critical opinion, or fact on a separate note card. A good note card includes a brief quotation or summary of an idea and a record of the source, including the page number, in which you found the information. When copying a sentence from a work, use quotation marks and check to make sure you have copied it correctly.

Coding Sources Keep a working bibliography, a list of all works you consult, as you conduct research. Assign a code, such as a letter, to each work on the list. For each note you take, include the code for the source.

Coding Cards Organize your note cards by labeling each with the subtopic it concerns.

Present Support Appropriately

As you draft, consider how much support you need for each point and the form that support should take. You can provide support in the following forms:

- **Summaries** are short accounts in your own words of important elements of the work, such as events, a character's traits, or the writer's ideas. They are appropriate for background information.
- **Paraphrases** are restatements of passages from a work in your own words. They are appropriate for background and for information incidental to your main point.
- **Quotations of key passages** are direct transcriptions of the writer's words, enclosed in quotation marks or, if longer than three lines, set as indented text. If a passage is crucial to your thesis, you should quote it directly and at whatever length is necessary.

Quotations of multiple examples are required to support claims about general features of a work, such as a claim about the writer's ironic style or use of cartoonlike characters.

Revise Ideas as You Draft

When writing criticism, do not be afraid to revise your early ideas based on what you learn as you research or write further. As you draft, allow the insights—or the difficulties—that emerge to guide you back to the writer's works or other sources for clarification or support. What you discover may lead you to modify your thesis.

The chart above presents an example of the way this circular process can work.

DO's and DON'T's of Academic Writing

Avoid gender and cultural bias. Certain terms and usages reflect the bias of past generations. To eliminate bias in any academic work you do, edit with the following rules in mind:

- **Pronoun usage** When referring to an unspecified individual in a case in which his or her gender is irrelevant, use forms of the pronoun phrase *he or she.* Example: "A lawyer is trained to use <u>his or her</u> mind."

Stage of the Writing Process	The Developing Thesis Statement
Prewriting: A student rereads Sartre's story "The Wall" to find passages that support her thesis.	**First formulation:** "In his short story 'The Wall,' Sartre illustrates the belief that human life is ruled by inescapable fate."
Drafting: As the student summarizes the story's ending, she is struck by the fact that the narrator's final act has exactly the opposite effect from what he intended. She revises her thesis statement.	**Second formulation:** "In his short story 'The Wall,' Sartre demonstrates the power of fate by showing how the effects of a person's actions can completely contradict the person's intentions."
Revising: As the student rereads her first draft, she grows dissatisfied with her explanation of the story's ending. Why does the writer spend so much time showing the narrator's resignation to fate, only to have fate strike unexpectedly? She reworks her paper to support a new thesis statement.	**Final formulation:** "In his short story 'The Wall,' Sartre shows that 'fate' is a myth: However hard we try to resign ourselves to fate, we can never eliminate our responsibility for our own actions."

- **"Culture-centric" terms** Replace terms that reflect a bias toward one culture with more generally accepted synonyms. For instance, replace terms such as *primitive* (used of hunting-gathering peoples), *the Orient* (used to refer to Asia), and *Indians* (used of Native Americans), all of which suggest a view of the world centered in Western European culture.

Avoid plagiarism. Presenting someone else's ideas, research, or exact words as your own is plagiarism, the equivalent of stealing or fraud. Laws protect the rights of writers and researchers in cases of commercial plagiarism. Academic standards protect their rights in cases of academic plagiarism.

To avoid plagiarism, follow these practices:

- Read from several sources.
- Synthesize what you learn.
- Let the ideas of experts help you draw your own conclusions.
- Always credit your sources properly when using someone else's ideas to support your view.

By following these guidelines, you will also push yourself to think independently.

Forming Your Critical Vocabulary

To enhance your critical perceptions—the connections you find and the distinctions you make—improve your critical vocabulary. The following glossary shows contrasting pairs of critical terms. Some of these pairs define a spectrum along which you can place a work; others define simple opposites.

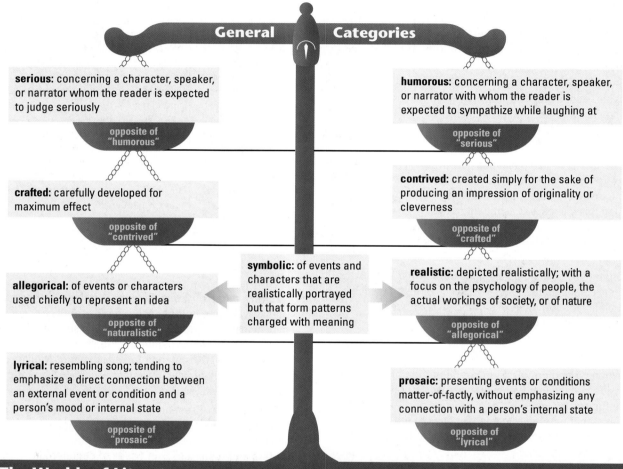

General Categories

serious: concerning a character, speaker, or narrator whom the reader is expected to judge seriously

opposite of "humorous"

humorous: concerning a character, speaker, or narrator with whom the reader is expected to sympathize while laughing at

opposite of "serious"

crafted: carefully developed for maximum effect

opposite of "contrived"

contrived: created simply for the sake of producing an impression of originality or cleverness

opposite of "crafted"

allegorical: of events or characters used chiefly to represent an idea

opposite of "naturalistic"

symbolic: of events and characters that are realistically portrayed but that form patterns charged with meaning

realistic: depicted realistically; with a focus on the psychology of people, the actual workings of society, or of nature

opposite of "allegorical"

lyrical: resembling song; tending to emphasize a direct connection between an external event or condition and a person's mood or internal state

opposite of "prosaic"

prosaic: presenting events or conditions matter-of-factly, without emphasizing any connection with a person's internal state

opposite of "lyrical"

The Worlds of Literature

In addition to categorizing elements and qualities of a work, critics categorize the imaginative world it assumes—the "rules" that govern actions and events in the work. Historically, the earliest literature projects a heroic world.

heroic, epic, or tragic world:	comic world:	naturalistic world:	farcical or absurd world:
a stern world governed by codes of conduct and divine judgments; characters are defined by moral qualities and are capable of significant, memorable actions (deeds)	a benevolent world temporarily disordered by confusions between appearance and reality, such as mistaken identity; characters are tested by the confusion, and order is restored	a world in which the actions of characters are of limited significance and the rules of reality are objective and unalterable, strictly limiting what is possible	a world in which characters are defined by ridiculous, exaggerated qualities and reality is replaced by mechanical, meaningless situations in which characters are trapped

Character

the people, animals, or other beings who perform or receive the action of a story

flat: marked by one dominant characteristic	**rounded:** having a complex set of characteristics
static: unchanging	**dynamic:** developing and growing
self-aware: acting with an understanding of his or her own motives and the consequences of his or her actions	**blind** or **fated:** acting with no understanding of his or her own motives or of the consequences of his or her actions

Plot

the narrated sequence of events in a work; the storyline, usually divided into an exposition (in which situation and characters are introduced), the rising action, the climax (or moment of greatest tension), the falling action, and the resolution

simple: telling of a single stream of events; each event affects the same set of characters	**complex:** telling of a number of streams of events, each involving a different set of characters (sets of characters may overlap)
dramatic: events unfold to build a maximum of tension or suspense, leading to a resolution	**episodic:** a series of loosely connected events occur, without building to a single, central climax or resolution
plot as driver: the question of "what happens next?" is intended to be the reader's primary interest in the work	**plot as vehicle:** the plot serves primarily to express a theme, display a character, or link together descriptions

Imagery

language used to suggest sensory experience, especially sensory experience linked by association to emotions and ideas

original: unique to the writer; distinctive	**conventional:** expected; patterned after previous work
sensual: devoted to recreating sensory experience	**metaphysical:** devoted to expressing abstract ideas or complicated analogies
effusive: pouring out; piled up	**patterned:** structured; controlled

Style

the distinctive features of a writer's choice of words and imagery, sentence length and structure, rhythm, and so on

elaborate: characterized by complex detail	**direct:** simple; to the point
sincere: attempting to convey ideas without drawing attention to the style of their presentation	**parodic:** drawing attention to style in order to mock a style that other writers' use seriously
straightforward: attempting to convey ideas directly	**ironic:** conveying ideas or attitudes by stating their opposites
conversational: resembling the style in which one friend might address another	**oracular:** suggesting that the writer is pronouncing deep truths without any particular concern that he or she be understood

Formatting Business Letters

Business letters follow one of several acceptable formats. In **block format** each part of the letter begins at the left margin. A double space is used between paragraphs. In **modified block format,** some parts of the letter are indented to the center of the page. No matter which format is used, all letters in business format have a heading, an inside address, a salutation, or greeting, a body, a closing, and a signature. These parts are shown and annotated on the model business letter below, formatted in modified block style.

Model Business Letter

In this letter, Yolanda Dodson uses modified block format to request information.

The **inside address** indicates where the letter will be sent.

A **salutation** is punctuated by a colon. When the specific addressee is not known, use a general greeting such as "To whom it may concern:"

The **body** of the letter states the writer's purpose. In this case, the writer requests information.

The **closing** "Sincerely" is common, but "Yours truly" or "Respectfully yours" are also acceptable. To end the letter, the writer types her name and provides a **signature.**

Students for a Cleaner Planet
c/o Memorial High School
333 Veterans' Drive
Denver, Colorado 80211

January 25, 20--

Steven Wilson, Director
Resource Recovery Really Works
300 Oak Street
Denver, Colorado 80216

Dear Mr. Wilson:

Memorial High School would like to start a branch of your successful recycling program. We share your commitment to reclaiming as much reusable material as we can. Because your program has been successful in other neighborhoods, we're sure that it can work in our community. Our school includes grades 9–12 and has about 800 students.

Would you send us some information about your community recycling program? For example, we need to know what materials can be recycled and how we can implement the program.

At least fifty students have already expressed an interest in getting involved, so I know we'll have the people power to make the program work. Please help us get started.

Thank you in advance for your time and consideration.

Sincerely,

Yolanda Dodson

Yolanda Dodson

Commonly Misspelled Words

The words on this page are ones that cause spelling problems for many people. As you review the list, check to see how many of the words give you trouble in your own writing.

abbreviate	bicycle	criticize	grammar	naturally	realize
absence	bookkeeper	cylinder	grievance	necessary	really
absolutely	boulevard	deceive	guarantee	negotiate	receipt
accelerate	brief	decision	guard	neighbor	recipe
accidentally	brilliant	defendant	guidance	neutral	recognize
accurate	bruise	definitely	handkerchief	nickel	recommend
ache	bulletin	delinquent	harass	niece	rehearse
achievement	buoy	dependent	height	ninety	relevant
acquaintance	bureau	descendant	humorous	noticeable	reminiscence
adequate	bury	description	hygiene	nuclear	renowned
advertisement	buses	desirable	immediately	nuisance	repetition
aerial	business	dessert	immigrant	obstacle	restaurant
aggravate	cafeteria	dining	independent	occasion	rhythm
agreeable	calendar	disappoint	individual	occurrence	ridiculous
aisle	campaign	disastrous	inflammable	omitted	sandwich
all right	canceled	discipline	interfere	opinion	satellite
aluminum	candidate	eighth	irritable	opportunity	schedule
amateur	captain	eligible	jewelry	optimistic	scissors
analysis	career	embarrass	judgment	outrageous	secretary
analyze	carriage	enthusiastic	knowledge	pamphlet	siege
ancient	cashier	entrepreneur	laboratory	parallel	sincerely
anecdote	category	envelope	lawyer	paralyze	solely
anniversary	ceiling	environment	legible	parentheses	sponsor
anonymous	cemetery	equipped	legislature	particularly	subtle
answer	census	equivalent	leisure	patience	superintendent
anxiety	certain	especially	liable	permanent	surveillance
apologize	characteristic	exaggerate	library	permissible	susceptible
appall	chauffeur	excel	license	perseverance	tariff
appearance	clothes	excellent	lieutenant	persistent	temperamental
appreciate	colonel	exercise	lightning	perspiration	theater
appropriate	column	existence	likable	persuade	threshold
architecture	commercial	extraordinary	liquefy	phenomenon	truly
argument	commitment	familiar	literature	physician	unmanageable
associate	committee	fascinating	maintenance	pneumonia	unwieldy
athletic	competitor	February	marriage	possession	usage
attendance	condemn	fiery	mathematics	prairie	usually
awkward	congratulate	financial	maximum	preferable	valuable
banquet	conscience	fluorescent	meanness	prejudice	various
bargain	conscious	foreign	mediocre	prerogative	vegetable
barrel	convenience	forfeit	mileage	privilege	voluntary
battery	cooperate	fourth	millionaire	probably	volunteer
beautiful	correspondence	fragile	minuscule	procedure	weight
beggar	counterfeit	gauge	miscellaneous	pronunciation	weird
beginning	courageous	genius	mischievous	psychology	whale
behavior	courteous	genuine	misspell	pursue	wield
benefit	criticism	government	mortgage	questionnaire	yield

Indexes

Index of Authors and Titles
Page numbers in *italics* refer to biographical information.

A
Account of an Experience with Discrimination, An, 547
Account of the Battle of Bull Run, An, 544
Acquainted With The Night, 892
Adamant, The, 1022
Adams, Abigail Smith, *202, 205*
Albee, Edward, *1228*
Alcott, Amos Bronson, *385*
Allisti Ti-Tanin-Miji (Rock Rainbow), 53
Alvarez, Julia, *1080, 1082*
Ambush, 1222
Ammons, A. R., *966, 966*
Anecdote of the Jar, 797
Anderson, Sherwood, *806, 815*
Antojos, 1082
Anxiety, 832
anyone lived in a pretty how town, 777
April Showers, 642
Ardella, 927
Ars Poetica, 798
Auden, W.H., *774, 779*
Autobiography of Benjamin Franklin, The, from, 140
Average Waves in Unprotected Waters, 1028

B
Baldwin, James, *1146, 1148*
Because I could not stop for Death, 420
Bidwell Ghost, 1195
Bierce, Ambrose, *506, 508*
Birches, 882
Black Man Talks of Reaping, A, 937
Bontemps, Arna, *934, 937*
Boulders Taller Than the Great Tower of Seville, 37
Bradford, William, *70, 78*
Bradstreet, Anne, *98, 102*
Brain — is wider than the Sky —, The, 426
Brooks, Gwendolyn, *1178, 1182*
Brown Chest, The, 1002
Bruchac, Joseph, 16
Bryant, William Cullen, *264, 267*
By the Bivouac's Fitful Flame, 441

C
Cabeza de Vaca, Alvar Núñez, *30, 32*
Caduto, Michael J., 16
Camouflaging the Chimera, 1220
Cather, Willa, *674, 676*
Cats, 688
Cervantes, Lorna Dee, *1096, 1098*
Chang, Diana, *1096, 1101*
Chesnut, Mary, *534, 536*
Chief Joseph, *594, 602*
Chicago, 838
Chopin, Kate, *632, 634*
Cisneros, Sandra, *1126, 1128*
Civil Disobedience, from, 412
Civil War, from, 536
Colt, Miriam Davis, *594, 596*
Columbus, Christopher, *60, 62*
Concord Hymn, 393
Confederate Account of the Battle of Gettysburg, A, 542

C (cont.)
Cooper, George, 481
Corn Planting, The, 815
Coyote v. Acme, 1118
Crane, Stephen, *474, 476*
Crèvecoeur, Michel-Guillaume Jean de, *202, 208*
Crisis, Number 1, The, from, 160
Crossing the Great Divide, 286
Crucible, The, 1233
Cullen, Countee, *934, 936*
Cummings, E. E., *774, 776, 777*

D
Death of the Ball Turret Gunner, The, 1174
Declaration of Independence, The, 156
de Hoyos, Angela, 451
Devil and Tom Walker, The, 242
Diamond Island: Alcatraz, 53
Dickinson, Emily, *418, 420, 422, 424, 425, 426, 427, 428*
Dillard, Annie, 301, *304*
Doctorow, E. L., *1200, 1202*
Doolittle, Hilda, *727, 737, 738*
Douglass, 658
Douglass, Frederick, *494, 497*
Dove, Rita, *1126, 1133*
Dream Variations, 928
Dunbar, Paul Laurence, *656, 658, 660*
Dust Tracks on a Road, from, 914

E
Earth on Turtle's Back, The, 16
Edwards, Jonathan, *106, 108*
Eliot, T.S., *716, 718*
Emerson, Ralph Waldo, *386, 388, 391, 393, 394*
Episode of War, An, 476
Equiano, Olaudah, *42, 44*
Erdrich, Louise, *1190, 1195*
Erdoes, Richard, 19
Espada, Martín, *1096, 1100*
Everyday Use, 1056
Explorer, The, 1182

F
Fall of the House of Usher, The, 308
Far and the Near, The, 786
Faulkner, William, *858, 860, 875*
Few Don'ts by an Imagiste, A, 729
First Seven Years, The, 988
First Snowfall, The, 272
Fitzgerald, F. Scott, *742, 744*
For My Children, 1192
For the Love of Books, 1133
Foster, Stephen, *474, 481*
Franklin, Benjamin, *138, 140, 146, 184, 191*
Frazier, Ian, *1110, 1118*
Frederick Douglass, 1183
Freeway 280, 1098
From the Dark Tower, 936
Frost, Robert, *880, 882, 885, 886, 888, 890, 892*
Fuller, Margaret, *385*

G
Garbage, from, 966

G (cont.)
General History of Virginia, The, from, 72
Gettysburg Address, The, 522
Gift Outright, The, 890
Go Down, Moses, 490
Gold Glade, 1017
Goss, Warren Lee, *534, 540*
Grass, 840
Great Figure, The, 735
Gulf War Journal, 553

H
H. D., *727, 737, 738*
Haley, Alex, 215, *217*
Hansberry, Lorraine, *1228*
Harjo, Joy, *1040, 1049*
Harte, Bret, *578, 580*
Hawthorne, 1014
Hawthorne, Nathaniel, *334, 336*
Hayden, Robert, *1178, 1183, 1184*
Heading West, 596
Heat, 738
Hellman, Lillian, *1229*
Hemingway, Ernest, *806, 809*
Henry, Patrick, *184, 186*
Here Is New York, from, 903
Hersey, John, *1160, 1162*
Hiroshima, from, 1162
Holmes, Oliver Wendell, *264, 270*
Hongo, Garrett, *1096, 1103*
Hughes, Langston, 449, *449, 924, 926, 927, 928, 929*
Hunger in New York City, 1102
Hurston, Zora Neale, *912, 914*
Huswifery, 100
Hymn to the Evening, An, 172

I
I Hear America Singing, 442
I heard a fly buzz — when I died —, 422
I, Too, 449
I Will Fight No More Forever, 602
i yearn, 946
In a Classroom, 1181
In a Station of the Metro, 734
In Another Country, 809
Inaugural Address, 197
Interesting Narrative of the Life of Olaudah Equiano, The, from, 44
Iroquois Constitution, The, from, 24
Irving, Washington, *240, 242*

J
Jackson, Stonewall, *534, 544*
Jarrell, Randall, *1160, 1173, 1174*
Jefferson, Thomas, *154, 156*
Jilting of Granny Weatherall, The, 846
Joseph, Chief, *594, 602*
Journal of the First Voyage to America, from, 62
Journey Through Texas, A, 32

K
Kennedy, John F., 196, *200*
King, Dr. Martin Luther, Jr., 180, *182*
Kingston, Maxine Hong, *1068, 1070*
Komunyakaa, Yusef, *1218, 1220*

L

Leaves of Grass, from, 434
Lee, Robert E., 520, 525
Letter from Birmingham City Jail, from, 180
Letter to Her Daughter from the New White House, 205
Letter to His Son, 525
Letters from an American Farmer, from, 208
Lewis, Meriwether, 284, 286
Life on the Mississippi, from, 564
Life You Save May Be Your Own, The, 972
Light Comes Brighter, The, 1021
Lincoln, Abraham, 520, 522, 523
London, Jack, 606, 608
Lonesome Dove, from, 626
Longfellow, Henry Wadsworth, 256, 258, 260
López de Cárdenas, García, 30, 37
Losses, 1173
Love Song of J. Alfred Prufrock, The, 718
Lowell, James Russell, 264, 272
Lowell, Robert, 1012, 1014
Lucinda Matlock, 669
Luke Havergal, 666

M

MacLeish, Archibald, 794, 798
Malamud, Bernard, 986, 988
Masters, Edgar Lee, 664, 669, 670
Matthews, Washington, 22
McCullers, Carson, 1110, 1112
McElroy, Colleen, 1190, 1192
McKay, Claude, 924, 930
McKim, Randolph, 534, 542
McMurtry, Larry, 626, 630
Melville, Herman, 352, 354
Mending Wall, 886
Miller, Arthur, 1228,1230, 1233, 1339
Minister's Black Veil, The, 336
Mint Snowball, 1047
Mirror, 1180
Moby-Dick, from, 354
Momaday, N. Scott, 1040, 1042
Moore, Marianne, 794, 800
Moore, Molly, 553, 558
Mortgaged Heart, The, from, 1112
Most Satisfied by Snow, 1101
Most Sublime Spectacle on Earth, The, 289
Mother Tongue, 1136
My Bondage and My Freedom, from, 497
My life closed twice before its close, 424

N

Names, The, from, 1042
Nature, from, 388
Navajo Origin Legend, The, from, 22
Negro Speaks of Rivers, The, 926
Night the Ghost Got In, The, 898
Nobel Prize Acceptance Speech, 875
Noiseless Patient Spider, A, 444
Notorious Jumping Frog of Calaveras County, The, 569
Nye, Naomi Shihab, 1040, 1047

O

Oates, Joyce Carol, 374, 382
O'Brien, Tim, 1218, 1222
Occurrence at Owl Creek Bridge, An, 508
O'Connor, Flannery, 970, 972

Of Modern Poetry, 796
Of Plymouth Plantation, from, 78
old age sticks, 776
Old Ironsides, 270
O'Neill, Eugene, 1228
On Social Plays, from, 1339
Onomatopoeia, 1115
Ortiz, Alfonso, 19
Ortiz, Simon, 1096, 1102
Outcasts of Poker Flat, The, 580
"Out, Out —", 888

P

Paine, Thomas, 154, 160
Paley, Grace, 832, 834
Parker, Arthur, C., 24
Pear Tree, 737
Pilgrim at Tinker Creek, from, 301
Plath, Sylvia, 1178, 1180
Poe, Edgar Allan, 306, 308, 326
Poetry, 800
Poor Richard's Almanack, from, 146
Porter, Katherine Ann, 844, 846
Pound, Ezra, 726, 729, 732, 734
Powell, John Wesley, 284, 289
Psalm of Life, A, 258

Q

Quindlen, Anna, 688, 691

R

Race at Morning, 860
Raven, The, 326
Reaction to the Emancipation Proclamation, 545
Recollections of a Private, 540
Red Wheelbarrow, The, 735
Refugee in America, 929
Rich, Adrienne, 1178, 1181
Richard Bone, 670
Richard Cory, 668
Right Stuff, The, from, 93
River-Merchant's Wife, The: A Letter, 732
Robinson, Edwin Arlington, 664, 666, 668
Rock Pile, The, 1148
Roethke, Theodore, 1012, 1021, 1022
Roots, from, 215
Runagate Runagate, 1184

S

Safire, William, 1110, 1115
Sánchez, Ricardo, 946, 947
Sandburg, Carl, 836, 838, 840
Second Inaugural Address, 523
Seeing, 301
Self-Reliance, from, 391
Sinners in the Hands of an Angry God, from, 108
Smith, John, 70, 72
Snowbound, from, 274
Snowstorm, The, 394
Song of Myself, from, 436
Soul Selects her own Society, The, 425
Speech in the Convention, 191
Speech in the Virginia Convention, 187
Stafford, William, 1012, 1019
Steinbeck, John, 766, 768
Stevens, Wallace, 794, 796, 797

Stopping by Woods on a Snowy Evening, 885
Storm Ending, 938
Story of an Hour, The, 634
Straw Into Gold: Metamorphosis of the Everyday, The, 1128
Suspended, 1049
Swing Low, Sweet Chariot, 488

T

Tan, Amy, 1126, 1136
Taylor, Edward, 98, 100
Thanatopsis, 267
There is a solitude of space, 427
There's a certain Slant of light, 424
This Is Just to Say, 736
Thoreau, Henry David, 385, 400, 402, 412
Thurber, James, 896, 898
Tide Rises, The Tide Falls, The 260
To Build A Fire, 608
To His Excellency, General Washington, 174
To My Dear and Loving Husband, 102
To Walt Whitman, 451
Toomer, Jean, 934, 938
Traveling Through the Dark, 1019
Tropics in New York, The, 930
Truth, Sojourner, 534, 547
Turner, Reverend Henry M., 534, 545
Turtle, The, 768
Twain, Mark, 472, 560, 562, 564, 569
Tyler, Anne, 1026, 1028

U

Unknown Citizen, The, 779
Updike, John, 1000, 1002

W

Wagner Matinee, A, 676
Walden, from, 402
Walker, Alice, 1054, 1056
Warren, Robert Penn, 1012, 1017
Water, is taught by thirst, 428
We Wear the Mask, 660
Welty, Eudora, 807, 821
Wharton, Edith, 642, 644
What For, 1103
Wheatley, Phillis, 170, 172, 174
When Grizzlies Walked Upright, 19
When I Heard the Learn'd Astronomer, 440
Where Is Here?, 374
White, E.B., 896, 903
Whitman, Walt, 432, 434, 436, 440, 441, 442, 444
Whittier, John Greenleaf, 265, 274
Who Burns for the Perfection of Paper, 1100
Wilder, Thornton, 1228
Williams, Tennessee, 1229
Williams, William Carlos, 726, 735, 736
Willie Has Gone to the War, 481
Wilson, Darryl Babe, 53, 58
Winter Dreams, 744
Wolfe, Thomas, 93, 96, 784, 786
Woman at War, A, from, 553
Woman Warrior, The, from, 1070
Worn Path, A, 821
Writer in the Family, The, 1202

Index of Skills

Literary Analysis

Alienation, 1097, 1105, 1106
Allegory, R12
Alliteration, R12
Allusion, 717, 719, 723, 1266, 1269, 1276, 1280, 1285, 1288, R12
Ambiguity, R12
Analogy, R12
Analytical essay, 1111, 1123, R14
Anapest, R16
Anecdote, 1041, 1044, 1051, R12
Antagonist, R12
Anticlimax, 785, 787, 788, 789, 791
Aphorism, 139, 149, 163, R12
Apostrophe, 99, 837, 841, R12
Approximate rhyme, R19
Archetypal literary elements, R12
Assonance, R12
Atmosphere, 1001, 1002, 1004, 1005, 1006, 1009. *See also* Mood
Audience, 155, 163
Author's point of view, 61, 65
Author's style, 31, 36, 39
Autobiography, 139, 141, 143, 145, 149, 495, 499, 501, 503, R12
    social context in, 913, 915, 916, 921
Ballad, R12, R17
Biography, R13
Blank verse, 881, 883, 885, 886, 888, 889, 892, 893, R13, R17
Character
    defined, R13
    dynamic, 1201, 1205, 1209, 1211, 1213, 1215, R13
    flat, R13
    grotesque, 971, 974, 976, 978, 979, 980, 983, R15
    main, R13
    major, R13
    minor, R13
    motivation of, 743, 747, 751, 753, 761, 763, 1055, 1057, 1058, 1059, 1060, 1065, R17
    static, 1201, 1205, 1209, 1211, 1213, 1215, R13
Characterization, 241, 675, 678, 679, 681, 685, 743, 746, 747, 750, 751, 752, 755, 759, 761, 763, 971, 974, 976, 979, 983, R13
    direct, 241, 253, 743, 763, 971, 983, R13
    indirect, 241, 253, 743, 763, 971, 983, R13
Cinquain, 257, R21
Classicism, R13
Climax, 633, 639, 653, 785, 787, 788, 789, 791, R13
    as plot element, 643, 653, 1081, R13, R18
Compare and contrast styles, 31
Compare and contrast themes, 692
Comparing literary works, 85, 483, 739
Conceit, 103
Concept and perception, 103
Conflict, 607, 610, 612, 613, 615, 616, 618, 619, 621, 623, 643, 653, 987, 989, 990, 991, 993, 994, 996, 997, R13
    external, 607, 623, 987, 997
    internal, 607, 623, 987, 997
    as plot element, 643, 653, 1081
Connotation, R13
Consonance, R13
Conventional symbol, R21
Couplet, 177, 257, R21

Crisis, R13
Cultural context, 1201, 1205, 1209, 1215
Cultural details, 27
Dactyl, R16
Dead metaphor, R16
Denotation, R13
Denouement, 1081, R18. *See also* Plot
Description, 285, 293, R14
Descriptive essay, R14
Development, 1081, R18. *See also* Plot
Dialect, 575, 859, 861, 863, 865, 866, 867, 877, R14
Dialogue, 913, 921, 1232, 1234, 1235, 1239, 1243, 1245, 1246, 1247, 1250, 1251, 1252, 1256, 1257, 1258, 1261, 1264, R14
Diaries, journals, and letters, 534, 535, 536, 538, 540, 545, 549
Diction, 185, 187, 193, 433, 434, 438, 445, 521, 522, 524, 527, 1013, 1014, 1017, 1018, 1021, 1023, R14
Dimeter, R16
Direct address, 99
Direct characterization, 241, 253, 743, 763, 971, 983, R13
Drama, R14
Dramatic exposition, 1232, 1235, 1245, 1252, 1257, 1264
Dramatic irony, 607, 623, 633, 639, 1290, 1293, 1296, 1297, 1298, 1301, 1303, 1306, 1307, 1310, 1311, 1313, 1314, 1316, R16
Dramatic monologue, 717, 719, 720, 723, R14
Dramatic poem, R14
Dynamic character, R13
Elegy, R16
Elements of plot, 643, 646, 647, 651, 653
    climax, 643, 653. *See also* Climax
    conflict, 643, 653. *See also* Conflict
    exposition, 643, 653, 1081, R14
    falling action, 643, 653, R18
    resolution, 643, 653, 1081, R18
    rising action, 643, 653, 785, 787, 791, R18
Emotional appeals, 43, 49
End rhyme, 657, R19
English sonnet, R20
Epic, R17
Epigram, R14
Epiphany, 987, 989, 990, 991, 993, 994, 995, 996, 997, R14
Epistle, 203, 206, 209, 211, R16
Essay, 1111, 1112, 1116, 1120, 1122, 1123, R14
    analytical, 1111, 1123, R14
    descriptive, R14
    expository, 1111, 1123, R14
    formal or informal, R14
    narrative, R14
    personal or impersonal, R14
    persuasive, R14
    reflective, 1127, 1128, 1130, 1131, 1134, 1136, 1137, 1138, 1140, 1142, R14
    satirical, 1111, 1123, R14
Exact rhyme, 419
Exploration narrative, 31, 33, 35, 36, 37, 39, R17
Exposition, 643, 653, 1081, R14
Expository essay, 1111, 1123, R14
Expressing emotions, 103
Extended metaphor, 935, 939, 1318, 1324, 1331, 1335
External conflict, 607, 623, 987, 997
Eyewitness perspective, 65

Falling action, 643, 653, R18
Fiction, R14
Figurative language, R14
Figures of speech, 99, R15
Firsthand accounts, 71
First-person narrator, 679, 1219, 1220, 1222, 1225
First-person point of view, 675, 685, 808, 829, 1055, 1058, 1065, R19
Flashback, 845, 850, 852, 855, 1081, 1084, 1093, 1191, 1197, R15
Flat character, R13
Foil, R15
Folk literature, R15
Foreshadowing, 1027, 1029, 1030, 1032, 1033, 1034, 1037, R15
Form, 1219, 1225
Formal essay, R14
Free verse, 433, 434, 436, 438, 445, R15, R17
Genre, R15
Gothic style, 307, 314, 320, 324, 329, 331, R15
Grotesque characters, 971, 974, 976, 978, 979, 980, 983, R15
Harlem Renaissance, R15
Heptastich, R21
Historical context, 1266, 1276, 1288
Historical influences, 76
Historical narrative, 535, 549, R17
Humor, 563, 570, 572, 573, 575, 897, 899, 907
Hyperbole, R15
Iamb, R16
Iambic pentameter, R15, R17
Identity, 1127, 1131, 1134, 1137, 1140, 1142
Idyll, R15
Image, R15
Imagery, 795, 802, 935, 939, R15. *See also* Imagism; Imagist poetry
Imagism, 727, R15. *See also* Imagery; Imagist poetry
Imagist poetry, 728, 730, 732, 733, 739, R15. *See also* Imagism; Imagery
Impersonal essay, R14
Implied theme, 1161, 1165, 1167, 1168, 1171, 1175, R21
Inciting incident, 1081, R18
Indirect characterization, 241, 253, 743, 763, 971, 983, R13
Informal essay, 897, 898, 899, 901, 905, 907, R14
Internal conflict, 607, 623, 987, 997
Internal rhyme, 657
Irony, 607, 610, 613, 615, 621, 623, 633, 639, R16
    dramatic, 633, 639, 1290, 1293, 1296, 1297, 1298, 1301, 1303, 1306, 1307, 1310, 1311, 1313, 1314, 1316, R16
    situational, 633, 639, R16
    verbal, 633, 639, 1290, 1293, 1296, 1297, 1298, 1301, 1303, 1306, 1307, 1310, 1311, 1313, 1314, 1316, R16
Italian sonnet, R20
Journal, 61, 63, 65, R16. *See also* Diaries, journals, and letters
Legend, R16
Letter, R16
    business, R46
    personal, 549
    public and private, 203, 206, 209, 211, R16
    See also Diaries, journals, and letters
Limited narrator, R17

Limited third-person point of view, 808, 829, 1069, 1077, R19
Literary periods, 116
Literary letter, R16
Literary themes, 218, 692
Literary trends, 452, 948, 1342
Local color, 579, 584, 587, 591, R16
Logical fallacy, 1290, 1293, 1296, 1306, 1316
Lyric poetry, 1191, 1197, R16
Main character, R13
Major character, R13
Meaning, 163, 1225
Memoirs, 1069, 1071, 1077
Metaphor, 401, 408, 414, 935, 939, R16
   dead, R16
   extended, 1318, 1331, 1335
   mixed, R16
Meter, 266, 268, 271, 272, 273, 276, 277, 279, 281, R16
Metrical romance, R17
Minor character, R13
Mixed metaphor, R16
Monologue, 373, R17
Monometer, R16
Mood, 257, 261, 266, 268, 273, 277, 279, 281, 595, 600, 603, R17
Motivation, R17. See also Character, motivation of
Myth, R17
Narrative, R17
Narrative accounts, 71, 74, 75, 76, 81, 82, 84, 85
Narrative essay, R14
Narrative poem, R17
Narrator, 808, 817, 822, 827, 829, R17
   first-person, 678, 829, 1219, 1220, 1222, 1225
   limited, R17
   omniscient, R17
   See also Point of view
Naturalism, 475, 480, 483, R17
Nonfiction, R17
Novel, R17
Novella, R18
Objective account, 1161, 1167, 1171, 1175
Objective point of view, 507, 517
Octave, R21
Ode, R16, R18
Omniscient narrator, R17
Omniscient third-person point of view, R19
Onomatopoeia, R18
Oral tradition, 15, 18, 24, 27, R18
Oratory, 107, 111, 113, R18
Origin myths, 15, 17, 18, 19, 23, 24, 27
Oxymoron, R18
Parable, 335, 338, 342, 344, 345, 346, 347, 349
Paradox, R18
Parallelism, 185, 193, R18
Parody, R18
Pastoral, 881, 883, 886, 889, 893, R18
Pentameter, R17. See also Iambic pentameter
Personal essay, R14
Personal letter, 549
Personal symbol, R21
Personification, 171, 177, 837, 841, R18
Persuasion, 155, 156, 157, 158, 163, R18
Persuasive essay, R14
Petrarchan sonnet, R20
Plain style, R18
Plot, 1081, 1083, 1084, 1088, 1089, 1091, 1093, R18
   climax, 1081, 1093, R18
   denouement, 1081, 1093, R18
   development, 1081, 1093, R18
   elements of. See Elements of plot

exposition, 1081, 1093, R18
   falling action, 643, 653, R18
   inciting incident, 1081, 1093, R18
   resolution, 1081, 1093, R18
   rising action, 643, 653, 785, 787, 791, R18
Poetry, R19
   lyric, 1191, 1197
   of praise, 171, 177
   theme of, 1179, 1187
Point of view, 507, 510, 514, 517, 808, 810, 815, 817, 822, 823, 825, 826, 827, 829, R19
   author's, 61, 65
   first-person, 675, 685, 808, 829, 1055, 1058, 1065, R19
   limited third-person, 808, 829, 1069, 1077, R19
   objective, 507, 517
   omniscient third-person, R19
   See also Narrator
Primary source documents, 203, 206, 211
Private and public letters, 203, 206, 211, R16
Prose, R19
Protagonist, R19
Public speaking, 107
Puritan plain style, 99, 101, 103
Purpose, 163
Pyrrhic, R16
Quatrain, 257, R21
Realism, 475, 480, 483, R13, R19
Real-life events, 71
Reflective essay, 1127, 1128, 1130, 1131, 1134, 1136, 1137, 1138, 1140, 1142, R14
Refrain, 487, 489, 491, R19
Regionalism, 579, 581, 584, 587, 590, 591, R19
Repetition, 185, 193
Resolution, 643, 653, 1081
Restatement, 185, 193
Rhetorical questions, 185
Rhyme, 657, 660, 661, R19
Rhythm, R20
Rising action, 643, 653, 785, 787, 788, 791, R18
Rites of passage, 1041, 1051
Romanticism, R13, R20
Round character, R13
Satire, 775, 781, R20
Satirical essay, 1111, 1123, R14
Scanning, R16. See also Scansion
Scansion, R20. See also Scanning
Secondhand account, 71
Sensory language, R20
Sermon, 107, 109, 111, 113
Sestet, R21
Setting, 320, 1147, 1149, 1150, 1152, 1157, R20
Shakespearean sonnet, R20
Short story, R20
Simile, 795, 798, 800, 802, R20
Single effect, 307, 308, 314, 315, 317, 318, 320, 321, 322, 324, 326, 329, 331, 643, 647, 653
Situational irony, 633, 639, R16
Slant rhyme, 419, 423, 429, 657, 661, R19
Slave narrative, 43, 46, 49, R17
Social context in autobiography, 913, 915, 916, 921
Social Criticism, 1179, 1187
Sonnet, R16, R20
Speaker, 661, 665, 667, 671, 925, 931, R20
Speech, 185, 187, 188, 193
Spiritual, 486, 487, 491, R20
Spondee, R16
Stage directions, 1232, 1234, 1235, 1239, 1243, 1245, 1246, 1247, 1250, 1251, 1252, 1256, 1257, 1258, 1261, 1264
Stanza, 257, 258, 261, R21

Static character, R13
Stream-of-consciousness, 507, 514, 517, 845, 846, 849, 850, 851, 852, 853, 855, R21
Style, 401, 404, 408, 414, 1013, 1014, 1017, 1018, 1021, 1023, R21
   author's, 31, 36, 39
   compare and contrast, 31
Subjective account, 71, 1161, 1167, 1171, 1175
Suspense, 1027, 1032, 1033, 1034, 1037, R21
Symbol, 335, 338, 347, 349, 353, 355, 357, 358, 360, 363. 365, 366, 367, 368, 371, 767, 770, 771, 1147, 1149, 1150, 1157, R21
Symbolism, R21
Tercet, R21
Tetrameter, R17
Theme, 353, 358, 366, 368, 371, 767, 770, 771, R21
   compare and contrast, 692
   evaluate, 218
   implied, 1161, 1165, 1167, 1168, 1171, 1175, R21
   of play, 1318, 1319, 1320, 1321, 1325, 1326, 1327, 1329, 1330, 1331, 1333, 1335
   of poem, 1179, 1187
Third-person limited point of view, 507, 517
Third-person omniscient point of view, 241, 243, 244, 247, 250, 253
Tone, 495, 501, 503, 595, 596, 598, 600, 603, 661, 775, 781, 1111, 1120, 1123, R21
Transcendentalism, 387, 388, 391, 397, R21
Trends
   analyze, 1342
   compare and contrast, 452
   evaluate, 948
Trigger feelings, 43
Trimeter, R16
Trochee, R16
True rhyme, 657, 661
Venn diagram, 31
Verbal irony, 633, 639, 1290, 1293, 1296, 1297, 1298, 1301, 1303, 1306, 1307, 1310, 1311, 1313, 1314, 1316, R16
Voice, 1097, 1104, 1105, 1106
Word choice, 1001, 1002, 1004, 1009
Writer's styles, 285, 293

Reading Strategies

Advertisements, comparing editorials and, 169
Attitudes, recognizing, 665, 671
Author's arguments, interpreting, 1338, 1341
Author's purpose, 61, 65. See also Purpose
Background information, 1069, 1070, 1071, 1072, 1074, 1077
Background knowledge, 521, 526, 527
Blank verse, 881, 884, 887, 891, 893
Cause and effect
   identifying, 1147, 1151, 1152, 1154, 1155, 1157
   relationships, 225
Challenging a text, 387, 397
Characters
   categorizing by role, 1290, 1292, 1293, 1294, 1295, 1299, 1301, 1304, 1305, 1309, 1311, 1316
   conclusions about, 743, 745, 749, 757, 758, 763
   contrasting, 1055, 1057, 1063, 1065
   identifying with, 808, 812, 818, 822, 829, 987, 990, 995, 997, 1081, 1086, 1088, 1093
   judging actions of, 1201, 1204, 1206, 1207, 1215

questioning motives of, 1232, 1237, 1238, 1241, 1246, 1249, 1250, 1252, 1255, 1259, 1260, 1262, 1264
Charged words, 155, 161, 163
Chronological order, identifying, 507, 512, 514, 517
Clarifying, 675, 685
    meaning, 171, 177
    sequence of events, 845, 848, 855
Clues to the theme, 767, 769, 771
Complex sentences, 71
Conclusions, 139, 142, 149
    about characters, 743, 745, 749, 757, 758, 763
Context clues, 107, 112, 113, 701
Contrast, 31
Cultural details, 15, 17, 21, 22, 26, 27
Diagrams, 71
Distinguishing fact from opinion, 203, 209, 211, 535, 541, 543, 544, 549
Drama, 1266, 1267, 1268, 1269, 1271, 1273, 1274, 1275, 1276, 1277, 1278, 1279, 1281, 1282, 1283, 1288
Editorials, 166
Events
    anticipating, 643, 649, 651, 652, 653
    applying themes to contemporary, 1318, 1321, 1323, 1332, 1335
    clarifying sequence of, 845, 855
    putting them in order, 1027, 1031, 1037
Experience, relating to your own, 1041, 1042, 1051
Facts, 203, 209, 211, 535, 541, 543, 544, 549
Faulty modes of persuasion, 166, 169
Flashback, 1027, 1037
Generalizations, 459
Historical context, connecting to, 935, 938, 939
Historical details, 475, 477, 478, 483
Hyperbole, 897, 904, 907
Identify with characters, 808, 812, 818, 822, 829, 1081, 1086, 1088, 1093
Images, 419, 421, 429
    associating with life, 257, 259, 261
Inferences, 459
Inferences
    about cultural attitudes, 241, 243, 244, 250, 253
    about meaning, 335, 339, 341, 343, 345, 349
    about poet's attitude, 433, 435, 437, 445
    about speaker, 925, 928, 931
    about theme, 1161, 1167, 1173, 1175
Interpreting
    author's arguments, 1338, 1341
    poetry, 657, 661, 1179, 1184, 1187
Ironic details, 633, 636, 637, 639
Line of reasoning, 1111, 1113, 1123
Listening, 487, 491, 717, 718, 721, 723
Locating information on Web sites, 88, 91
Logical modes of persuasion, 166, 169
Meaning, 775
    clarifying, 171, 177
    relating structure to, 775, 778, 780, 781
Newspaper editorial, 166
Opinions, 203, 209, 211, 535, 541, 543, 544, 549
Paraphrasing, 99, 102, 103, 795, 796, 802, 1013, 1022, 1023
Persuasion, logical and faulty modes of, 166–169
Persuasive appeals, 185, 193
Picturing the action, 1219, 1224, 1225
Predicting, 607, 609, 612, 614, 617, 620, 623, 785, 791, 971, 975, 976, 979, 980, 983

Punctuation, 1349
Purpose, 913, 917, 918, 921
    establishing, 495, 503
    See also Author's purpose
Questioning the text, 579, 585, 589, 591
Regional dialect, 563, 567, 570, 571, 575
Responding, 595, 597, 601, 603, 837, 841
Senses, engaging, 728, 731, 739
Sentence-completion questions, 955
Sentences
    breaking down, 71, 73, 75, 77, 78, 85, 307, 310, 313, 319, 324, 327, 331
    breaking down long, 859, 862, 868, 870, 877, 1001, 1009
    complex, 71
    inverted, 171, 177
    reading in, 1191, 1197
Sentence structure, 1349
Signal words, 31, 34, 38, 39
Spatial relationships, 285, 288, 293
Structure, 775
    relating to meaning, 775, 778, 780, 781
Summarizing, 43, 49, 266, 268, 269, 271, 277, 278, 279, 281, 1097, 1102, 1104, 1106
Symbols, 353, 356, 361, 365, 367, 371
Time words, 31
Theme
    applying to contemporary events, 1318, 1321, 1323, 1332, 1335
    connections to unit, R1, R2, R3, R4, R5, R6
    finding clues to, 767, 769, 771
Usage, 1349
Web sites, 88–91
Writer's message, 1127, 1131, 1134, 1138, 1140, 1142
Writer's philosophy, 401, 404, 405, 407, 409, 412, 414

Grammar and Style

Absolute phrase, 1094
Abstract noun, 740
Action verb, 66, R22
Active voice, 50
Adjectival modifiers, 724
Adjective, 114, R22
    correct use of, 1038
    participles as, 282
    placement of, 940
Adjective clause, 254, 1158, R23
Adjective phrase, R23
Adverb, 114, 1038, R22
Adverb clause, 624, 1010
Adverb phrase, R23
Agreement, subject and verb, 178, 1317
Analogies, 484
Antecedent and pronoun agreement, 446
Apostrophe, R26
Appositive, 640, 1124
Appositive phrase, 640, R23
Capitalization, R24
    of proper nouns, 550
Clause, R23. See also Adjective clause; Adverb clause; Noun clause
Collective noun, 372
Colon, R25
Commas, R24
    after introductory words, 1289
    in series, 908
Common noun, R22
Common usage glossary, R26

Commonly confused words
    like and as, 484
    raise and rise, 1336
    See also Usage
Comparative adjectives and adverbs, 114
Compound sentence, 28, 518
    coordinating conjunctions in, 592
Concrete noun, 740
Conjunction, R23
Conjunctive adverb, 212, R23
Coordinate adjective, 332
Coordinating conjunction, R23
    in compound sentences, 592
Correlative conjunction, 504, R23
Dash, 764, R25
Declarative sentence, 842
Demonstrative pronoun, R22
Dialogue, punctuating, 830
Direct address, 104, 492
Direct quotation, R25
Double negative, 194, 576
Elliptical clause, 1052
Exclamation mark, R24
Exclamatory sentence, 842
Gerund, 430
Gerund phrase, 654
Helping verb, R22
Hyphen, R26
Imperative sentence, 842, 856
Incomplete constructions, pronoun case in, 1265
Indefinite pronoun, R22
Independent clause, R23
Indirect quotation, R25
Infinitive, 415, 894
Infinitive phrase, 415, 894, R23
Intensive pronoun, 686, R22
Interjection, R23
    punctuation of, 662
Interrogative sentence, 842
Introductory words, comma after, 1289
Inverted word order, 262
Inverted sentence, subject and verb agreement in, 1317
Irregular verbs, 878
Linking verb, 66, R22
Negatives, double, 194, 576
Nominative absolute, R23
Nonrestrictive adjective clause, 1158
Nonrestrictive participial phrase, 792
Noun, 740, R22
Noun clause, 672, 1226, R24
Objective case, 150
Parallel coordinate elements, 922
Parallelism, 164
Parallel structure, 528, 772, 1188
Parentheses, 782
Participial phrase, 294, 792, 1107, R23
Participle as adjective, 282
Passive voice, 50
Past participle, 282, 294, 1107
Past tense, 40, 932, 1198
Perfect tense, 40
Period, R24
Phrase, R23
Plural possessive noun, 86
Preposition, R23
Prepositional phrase, R23
Present participle, 282, 1107
Present perfect tense, 932, 1198
Present tense, 1198
Pronoun, R22
    antecedent agreement and, 446
    appositive, with, 1124

demonstrative, R22
indefinite, R22
intensive, 686, R22
personal, R22
reflexive, 686, R22
relative, R22
Pronoun case, 150
in incomplete constructions, 1265
Proper noun, 550, R22
Punctuation, R24
for dialogue, 830
for interjections, 662
for quotation within quotation, 1078
See also entries for specific punctuation marks
Question mark, R24
Quotation marks, 830, 1078, R25
Reflexive pronoun, 686, R22
Relative pronoun, R22
Restrictive adjective clause, 1158
Restrictive participial phrase, 792
Semicolon, 212, 518, R25
Sentence
complex, 1143
compound, 1143
inverted, 1317
simple, 1143
varying length, 398
varying openers, 350
Sentence fragment, 604, 1066
Sentence structure, 1143
Sentence types, 842
Sequence of tenses, 1198
Series, commas in, 908
Singular and plural possessive nouns, 86
Style, 114
Subject complements, 803
Subjective case, 150
Subject and verb agreement, 178, 1024, 1317, R23
Subjunctive mood, 984
Subordinate adverb clause, R24
Subordinate clause, R23
Subordinating conjunction, R23
Superlative adjective and adverb, 114
Transitional phrase, 1176
Transitions, 1176
Usage
adapt, adopt, R26
advice, advise, R26
affect, effect, 1216, R26
among, between, R26
as, because, like, as to, R26
bad, badly, R26
because of, due to, R26
being as, being that, R27
beside, besides, R27
can, may, R27
different from, different than, R27
due to the fact that, R27
farther, further, R27
fewer, less, R27
good, well, R27
hopefully, R27
its, it's, R27
kind of, sort of, R28
lay, lie, R28
like, as, 484
many, much, R28
may be, maybe, R28
plurals that do not end in *-s,* R28
raise, rise, 1336, R28
set, sit, R28

that, which, who, R28
unique, R28
who, whom, 998, R28
Verb, R22
action, R22
helping, R22
irregular, 878
linking, 66, R22
and subject agreement, 178, 1024, 1317, R23
Verb tenses, 40, 932
sequence of, 1198

Vocabulary

Analogies, 150, 262, 484, 894, 922, 1052, 1066
Antonyms, 50, 86, 178, 282, 332, 398, 492, 576, 662, 764, 1094, 1158, 1317
Context, 40, 114, 254, 518, 782, 792, 803, 908, 984, 998, 1226, 1265, 1289. *See also* Words in context
Definitions, 194, 878, 1107, 1124
Denotations, 446
Etymologies, 212
Forms of *appear,* 740
Forms of *guile,* 662
Forms of *peril,* 86
Glossary, R7
Latin terms, 604
Legal terms, 1317
Music, words from, 686
Myths, words from, 1336
Prefixes
ac-, 164
ad-, 740
auto-, 1107
con-, 1052
di-, 724
dis-, 40
dys-, 856
ex-, 254
fore-, 640
im-, 40, 50, 350
in-, 40, 50, 350
mal-, 372, 1158
mono-, 576
multi-, 294
ob-, 550
omni-, 114
pre-, 1188
pro-, 772
re-, 178
sub-, 908
trans-, 1038
Related words
brutal, 842
exhaust, 1024
heritage, 1198
Relationships, 1317
Schwa, 114
Sentence completion, 504, 550, 624, 856, 932, 1038, 1078, 1143, 1176, 1188, 1216
Suffixes
-able, 282, 803
-ance, 212
-ary, 878
beginning with vowels, 150, 842, 1094, 1143, 1265, 1336
-ence, 212, 1289
-ery, 878
-ety, 856
-fold, 104
-ful, 894
-ial, 686
-ible, 282, 803

-ic, 764, 1124
-ious, 724
-itis, 1216
-ity, 194, 856
-less, 1078
-logy, 1289
-ly, 1078, 1317
-ness, 1078
-or, 430
-ory, 654
-sion, 294, 1107
-th, 104
-tion, 28, 294, 1107
Synonyms, 28, 50, 66, 86, 282, 332, 350, 372, 398, 415, 430, 528, 592, 654, 672, 724, 740, 842, 940, 1024, 1094, 1158, 1198, 1317, 1336
True or false, 164, 772
Word choice, 604, 640, 1010
Word endings
-ance, 1052
-ant, 1052
-ate, 550
double consonant, 1038, 1066, 1158
-ed, 86, 492, 604
-ence, 415, 1052
-ency, 415
-ent, 415, 504, 1052
-er, 1289
-ess, 430
-ing, 1038
-ion, 550
-re, 178
-ss, 528
-w, 984
-y, 624, 640, 1198
Word matching, 212
Word meanings, 104, 294, 686, 830
Word roots
-archy-, 528
-aud-, 1078
-bel-, 592
-bene-, 504
-cep-, 1188
-cept-, 1188
-cre-, 940
-doc-, 1066
-doct-, 1066
-equi-, 350
-face-, 262
-fid-, 164
-finis-, 430
-flict-, 66
-flu-, 415
-fus-, 446
-graph-, 922
-grat-, 1265
-greg-, 484
-ject-, 624
-lib-, 932
-litera-, 998
-lum-, 894
-man-, 654
-manu-, 654
-mort-, 40
-patr-, 282
-pose-, 672
-press-, 492
-psych-, 782
-radi-, 398
-satis-, 803
-scrib-, 1143
-script-, 1143
-sim-, 1010

-sol-, 984
-somn-, 764
-summa-, 518
-temp-, 792
-ten-, 1124
-terr-, 908
-val-, 830
-vid-, 50
-vigil-, 150
-voc-, 332
-vol-, 1176
Word suffixes
   -es, 1176
Words in context, 40, 254, 518, 792, 908, 1289
   See also Context
Words from music, 686
Words from myths, 1336
Words from Spanish, 1094
Words from war, 1226
Word sounds,
   a-consonant-e, 484
   ai, 484
   ch, 1216
   ci, 332
   ck, 1216
   cq, 1216
   dg, 922
   e, 842
   ge, 792, 1226
   gn, 830
   ign, 518
   j, 792
   kn, 830
   l, 932
   ll, 932
   ph, 672, 908
   ps, 782
   q, 1216
   qu, 66, 592
   th, 398
   ti, 332
y as vowel, 662

Critical Thinking and Viewing

Analyze, 18, 23, 25, 26, 48, 69, 77, 101, 102,
   109, 112, 129, 134, 148, 153, 159, 162, 173,
   176, 186, 189, 190, 192, 207, 232, 245, 252,
   271, 273, 280, 288, 292, 309, 396, 408, 411,
   413, 420, 421, 423, 425, 435, 439, 441, 442,
   467, 482, 502, 516, 523, 537, 541, 544, 564,
   590, 596, 601, 608, 652, 669, 684, 722, 779,
   780, 787, 790, 799, 801, 814, 819, 828, 910,
   914, 929, 930, 936, 938, 964, 965, 982, 1007,
   1008, 1016, 1018, 1020, 1022, 1036, 1046,
   1048, 1050, 1086, 1092, 1099, 1103, 1105,
   1114, 1115, 1117, 1132, 1135, 1141, 1156,
   1172, 1174, 1183, 1192, 1194, 1196, 1206,
   1214, 1221, 1263, 1287, 1306, 1315, 1333,
   1334
Analyze art, 712
Anticipate, 1270
Apply, 84, 102, 207, 210, 269, 330, 392, 393,
   411, 482, 489, 502, 526, 541, 568, 574, 590,
   668, 669, 670, 780, 790, 814, 819, 840, 927,
   929, 938, 1046, 1050, 1076, 1132, 1182, 1183,
   1186, 1194, 1315
Assess, 20, 210, 280, 292, 325, 328, 330, 390,
   425, 477, 614, 622, 652, 828, 900, 930, 1169,
   1182, 1287, 1315
Cause and effect, 23, 94, 112, 330, 390, 622,
   960, 1114
Classify, 112, 162, 207, 736, 902, 1099, 1101,
   1105, 1117, 1172

Compare, 291, 450, 548, 580, 860, 1070, 1082,
   1302
Compare and contrast, 6, 23, 44, 148, 173, 210,
   292, 348, 356, 370, 421, 427, 435, 441, 444,
   465, 547, 548, 586, 601, 614, 622, 684, 722,
   734, 770, 778, 797, 813, 885, 906, 917, 937,
   996, 1015, 1016, 1062, 1064, 1074, 1092,
   1101, 1105, 1117, 1141, 1224
Connect, 17, 52, 72, 160, 162, 208, 216, 234,
   269, 273, 280, 325, 337, 344, 377, 390, 393,
   425, 440, 441, 444, 479, 490, 502, 516, 526,
   546, 548, 561, 568, 571, 634, 638, 645, 668,
   669, 676, 684, 690, 722, 735, 736, 762, 768,
   790, 800, 816, 821, 839, 847, 854, 864, 882,
   889, 891, 903, 906, 928, 977, 994, 1003,
   1008, 1020, 1029, 1036, 1048, 1056, 1076,
   1090, 1092, 1098, 1099, 1101, 1116, 1119,
   1129, 1132, 1135, 1149, 1180, 1195, 1203,
   1212, 1308
Contrast, 23, 260, 274, 427, 481, 498, 548, 668,
   790, 1015
Criticize, 292, 413
Deduce, 101, 176, 190, 411, 780, 854, 876,
   1018, 1020, 1050, 1105, 1156, 1222, 1224
Defend, 252, 525
Define, 210, 390, 731, 799, 876, 1018, 1114, 1221
Describe, 56
Distinguish, 102, 516, 628, 731, 770, 840, 902,
   1022, 1114, 1132, 1139
Draw conclusions, 9, 38, 46, 48, 77, 84, 102,
   131, 133, 140, 162, 173, 190, 192, 252, 259,
   260, 269, 271, 273, 280, 292, 348, 392, 413,
   421, 423, 441, 442, 502, 574, 590, 600, 622,
   638, 710, 762, 840, 906, 938, 963, 972, 1008,
   1036, 1046, 1050, 1076, 1132, 1156, 1172,
   1174, 1181, 1186, 1196, 1287, 1334
Evaluate, 23, 63, 77, 84, 112, 148, 159, 162,
   173, 192, 207, 210, 252, 259, 260, 271, 273,
   288, 292, 370, 390, 413, 439, 442, 444, 490,
   516, 568, 574, 601, 602, 622, 638, 652, 731,
   736, 737, 738, 762, 770, 778, 780, 797, 819,
   824, 869, 874, 891, 892, 901, 920, 927, 929,
   936, 1008, 1018, 1048, 1049, 1076, 1092,
   1105, 1114, 1117, 1122, 1163, 1214, 1221,
   1263, 1287, 1315, 1334
Evaluate an advertisement, 706
Explain, 210
Extend, 38, 112, 190, 273, 280, 428, 435, 516,
   799, 801, 876, 906, 1016, 1334
Form a hypothesis, 237
Generalize, 18, 48, 64, 148, 207, 288, 370, 392,
   439, 722, 738, 801, 874, 891, 892, 982, 1008,
   1020, 1214
Hypothesize, 38, 64, 84, 93, 181, 364, 380, 554,
   568, 574, 876, 906, 1043, 1185, 1214
Infer, 11, 18, 26, 38, 48, 64, 74, 77, 83, 144, 148,
   153, 176, 190, 199, 248, 267, 271, 273, 280,
   286, 287, 288, 325, 348, 361, 370, 390, 393,
   436, 439, 441, 482, 488, 489, 526, 541, 548,
   566, 568, 574, 590, 602, 617, 622, 638, 668,
   669, 670, 722, 738, 790, 814, 819, 828, 854,
   874, 887, 891, 892, 902, 920, 927, 930, 936,
   938, 982, 1008, 1016, 1020, 1036, 1046,
   1048, 1064, 1076, 1092, 1105, 1117, 1136,
   1141, 1172, 1181, 1183, 1194, 1208, 1214,
   1236, 1242, 1263, 1315, 1326, 1334
Interpret, 4, 5, 18, 64, 68, 77, 84, 101, 112, 128,
   148, 152, 159, 162, 173, 174, 176, 192, 252,
   259, 260, 269, 287, 292, 316, 325, 330, 348,
   370, 385, 390, 392, 393, 410, 421, 423, 425,
   427, 428, 435, 444, 480, 482, 489, 490, 496,
   509, 513, 516, 541, 568, 590, 638, 652, 668,
   669, 670, 676, 684, 722, 731, 734, 736, 738,

762, 778, 780, 790, 797, 798, 799, 801, 809,
   814, 819, 828, 840, 854, 874, 876, 884, 887,
   889, 891, 892, 911, 927, 929, 930, 936, 982,
   996, 1008, 1016, 1018, 1020, 1022, 1035,
   1036, 1048, 1064, 1076, 1092, 1099, 1101,
   1102, 1105, 1114, 1132, 1135, 1141, 1172,
   1174, 1181, 1182, 1183, 1186, 1194, 1196,
   1214, 1221, 1224, 1228, 1244, 1248, 1258,
   1263, 1287, 1315, 1334
Interpret a pattern, 711
Judge, 79, 112
Make a decision, 448
Make an inference, 708. See also Infer
Make a judgment, 100, 162, 392, 411, 441, 569,
   622, 722, 762, 770, 780, 887, 967, 982, 996,
   1020, 1022, 1117, 1122, 1156, 1181, 1224
Modify, 427, 754
Predict, 988
Read a graph, 236, 468
Read a map, 230, 470
Recall, 18, 23, 26, 38, 48, 64, 77, 84, 101, 102,
   112, 148, 159, 162, 173, 176, 190, 192, 207,
   210, 252, 259, 260, 269, 271, 273, 280, 288,
   292, 325, 330, 348, 370, 390, 392, 393, 396,
   411, 413, 421, 423, 425, 427, 428, 435, 439,
   441, 442, 444, 482, 489, 490, 502, 516, 526,
   541, 548, 568, 574, 590, 601, 602, 622, 638,
   652, 668, 669, 670, 684, 722, 731, 734, 736,
   738, 762, 770, 778, 780, 790, 797, 799, 801,
   814, 819, 828, 840, 854, 874, 876, 884, 887,
   889, 891, 892, 902, 906, 920, 927, 929, 930,
   936, 938, 982, 996, 1008, 1016, 1018, 1020,
   1022, 1036, 1046, 1048, 1050, 1064, 1076,
   1092, 1099, 1101, 1105, 1114, 1117, 1122,
   1132, 1135, 1141, 1156, 1172, 1174, 1181,
   1182, 1183, 1186, 1194, 1196, 1214, 1221,
   1224, 1263, 1287, 1315, 1334
Relate, 157, 176, 425, 428, 464, 617, 652, 668,
   722, 814, 1166
Respond, 18, 23, 26, 38, 48, 64, 77, 84, 101,
   102, 112, 148, 159, 162, 173, 176, 190, 192,
   207, 210, 252, 259, 260, 269, 271, 273, 280,
   288, 292, 325, 330, 348, 370, 390, 392, 393,
   396, 411, 413, 421, 423, 425, 426, 427, 428,
   435, 439, 441, 442, 444, 482, 489, 490, 502,
   516, 526, 541, 548, 568, 574, 590, 601, 602,
   622, 638, 652, 668, 669, 670, 684, 722, 731,
   734, 736, 738, 762, 770, 778, 780, 790, 797,
   799, 801, 814, 819, 828, 840, 854, 874, 876,
   884, 887, 889, 891, 892, 902, 906, 920, 927,
   929, 930, 936, 938, 982, 996, 1008, 1016,
   1018, 1020, 1022, 1036, 1046, 1048, 1050,
   1064, 1076, 1092, 1099, 1101, 1105, 1114,
   1117, 1122, 1132, 1135, 1141, 1156, 1172,
   1174, 1181, 1182, 1183, 1186, 1194, 1196,
   1214, 1221, 1224, 1263, 1287, 1315, 1334
Speculate, 32, 146, 148, 190, 204, 207, 273,
   288, 325, 392, 396, 402, 421, 423, 443, 516,
   548, 553, 556, 560, 602, 622, 638, 658, 668,
   670, 731, 776, 778, 799, 854, 874, 884, 887,
   889, 902, 927, 996, 1016, 1018, 1020, 1022,
   1082, 1114, 1135, 1141, 1156, 1196, 1224,
   1322
Summarize, 26, 413, 526, 541, 906, 1036, 1141,
   1263
Support, 62, 63, 64, 79, 162, 247, 260, 286, 325,
   389, 392, 413, 422, 436, 502, 874, 889, 902,
   920, 938, 1046, 1050, 1122, 1156, 1194,
   1221, 1263, 1287
Synthesize, 26, 101, 159, 176, 207, 348, 396,
   444, 602, 730, 801, 891

Take a position, 26, 77, 148, 192, 210, 252, 280, 348, 370, 390, 411, 421, 428, 482, 548, 601, 602, 622, 652, 684, 686, 734, 828, 874, 902, 930, 1036, 1064, 1099, 1114, 1135, 1172, 1174, 1186, 1196, 1214

Writing
Writing Applications

Advertisement, 213
Advice column, 1217
Analytical essay, 218, 263, 1125
Analytic essay, 577
Assessment, R37, R38, R39
Autobiographical writing, 118, 151
Biographical criticism, R41
Book review, 1177
Character analysis, 725, 765, 1079
Character defense, 1337
Character sketch, 1317
Character study, 373
College admission essay, 505
Commentary on speeches, 195
Comparing narratives, 87
Comparison-and-contrast essay, 793, 941, 1108
Criticism,
    biographical criticism, R41
    critical commentary, 1338, 1341
    critical essay, 519
    critical evaluation of philosophical essay, 399
    critical response, 909, 1025
    critical review, 593, 879
    historical criticism, R41
Defense of character's actions, 1337
Definition, 804
Deposition, 985
Descriptive writing,
    natural wonder, 295
    in paragraph, 66, 484
Diary entry, 529
Direct address, 104, 492
Editorial, 416, 687
Editor's review of manuscript, 741
Essay, 941
    analytical, 218, 263, 1125
    analytic, 577
    college admission, 505
    comparison and contrast, 793, 941, 1108
    critical, 519
    on historical context, 773
    philosophical essay, 399
    problem-and-solution, 220, 551
    reflective, 105, 493, 641, 1053
    on use of repetition, 843
Evaluation of persuasion, 115
Explorer's journal, 41
Firsthand biography, 673
Ghost story, 1199
Historical criticism, R41
Imitating an author's style, 447
Introduction to an anthology, 895
Introduction to poetry reading, 783
Job portfolio, 1344
Journal, 1159
Letter
    to an author, 431, 1144
    personal, 213
Literary analysis, 625, 1189
Literary criticism, 333
Manuscript, editor's review of, 741
Memorial speech, 831
MLA citations, R31, R32
Moment of inspiration, 923

Monument inscription, 179
Multimedia presentation, 950
Museum placard, 51
Narration, 118, 454
News account, 1265
Newspaper article, 1227
New version of story, 1095
Oral report on the voyage, 67
Parallel coordinate elements, 922
Parallelism, 164
Parenthetical citations, R31
Personality profile, 999
Personal letters, 213
Personal narrative, 655
Persuasion, 166
Persuasive essay, 165
Poem to honor hero, 663
Poetry comparison, 933
Position paper on development, 605
Poster, 693
Précis, 283
Problem-and-solution essay, 220
Proposal to the principal, 165
Reference list, 699
Reflective composition, 454
Reflective essay, 105, 493, 551, 641, 1053
Research paper, 694
Research writing, 694
Response-to-literature essay, 351
Response to short story, 351
Résumé, 1344–1347
Retelling a story, 29, 255
Review of short story, 1067
Social worker's report, 1039
Stream of consciousness monologue, 857
Symbol analysis, 1011
Thesis, 1342
Transitions, 1176
Varying sentence length, 398
Wanted poster, 1289
Workplace writing, 1344, R46
Works-cited list, 699, R31
Writing for assessment, R37, R38, R39

Writing Strategies

Argument
    anticipating opponents', 416
    elaborating to support, 625
    refuting, 333
    revising for powerful, 1343
Background, providing necessary, 804
Beginning, middle, and end, 283
Cause and effect, 151, 923, 1039
Character study summary, 373
Charting
    to analyze audience, 694
    to analyze similarities and differences, 692
Chronological order, 1011
Citing sources
    MLA-style, R31, R32
    relevant citations, 399
Cluster diagram, 447, 999
Conclusion
    based on evidence, 116, 693
Context, providing, 213
Details
    clustering to generate, 999
    descriptive, 105
    gathering, 29, 87, 241, 551, 641, 783
    organizing by main idea and, 698
    sensory, categorizing, 1199
    of support, 783
    for vivid character, 857, 1095

Direct quotation, R43
Drafting,
    editing, 117
    to elaborate on an idea, 879
    grouping ideas, 693
    grouping selections, 693
    for objectivity, 1227
    updating a story, 255
    writing a summary, 373
Elaborating, 67
    to add emotional depth, 655, 1053
    for information, 765
    for stronger statement, 1108
    to support an argument, 625, 1217
    for vividness, 67
Episode, isolating an, 118
Evidence, analyzing, 1337
Exact quotations, 351
Experience
    freewriting to tap personal, 493
    relating to, 1041, 1042, 1051
    selecting and categorizing, for
        résumé, 1344
Field report, 485
Forceful language, 165
Idea notebook, 118
Identifying
    criteria, 1025
    points of comparison, 941
Internal documentation, 773
Introduction, R39
Isolating an episode, 118
Language, using specific, 687
Listing
    to find focus, 1342
    and itemizing, 454
Main idea, organizing by, 117
Main impression, creating, 663
Manuscript preparation, R31, R32
Objectivity, drafting for, 1227
Opponents' arguments, anticipating, 416
Order of importance, 698
Organizing
    clearly and logically, 431, 505
    common methods of, 698
    composition, 456
    events in chronological order, 51
    into paragraphs, 117
    presentations, 952
    selecting approach for, 698
    to show comparison, 577
    significant events, 120
Outline
    creating informal, 1343
    devising working, 453
Paragraph development, 117
Peer Review, 17
Persuasive writing, 179
Plagiarism, R43
Precise details, 41, 485
Prewriting, R42
Publishing, 121, 223, 699
Quotations
    adding, 195
    to connect themes, 933
    direct, R43
    exact, 351
    from the story, 519
    to support interpretation, 1189
    from the text, 909
Refuting an argument, 333

Revising, 29, 41, 51, 67, 87, 105, 115, 117, 120–121, 151, 165, 179, 195, 213, 255, 263, 283, 333, 351, 447, 485, 493, 551, 577, 625, 641, 783, 804, 857, 923, 933, 941, 999, 1025, 1039, 1053, 1095, 1199, 1337
  for accuracy, 698, 725
  to add dialogue, 120
  to add emotional appeal, 831
  to add evaluation, 219
  to add persuasive language, 529
  to add precise details, 1067
  for balance, 456
  for brevity and clarity, 741
  to build contrast, 793
  to clarify sequence, 952
  for clear organization, 1011
  for coherence, 605
  to connect contradictory information, 843
  to cut wordy language, 1343
  to focus on criteria, 949
  to include evaluative modifiers, 593
  to include precise language, 1144
  to maintain organizational strategy, 1346
  for personal tone, 1159
  for powerful argument, 1343
  to provide support, 1079
  for readers' knowledge level, 1177
  sentences, 453
  to show cause and effect, 985
  to smooth transitions, 895, 952
  by taking opposing view, 222
  for thoroughness, 693
  for variety, 699
  to vary media, 953
  to vary sentences, 457
  for word choice, 121, 223
Sentences
  revising, 457
  varying length and structure of, 453
Source citations (MLA-style), R31, R32
  See also Citing sources
Specific language, 687
Summarizing written texts, 123
Thesis, formulating, 218
Transitional words, 673, 1125
Transitions
  for clarity, 1125
  to show place, 295
Unity, building, 115

Listening and Speaking

Attack ad hominem, 700
Autobiographical narrative, 122
Campaign speech, 923
Cause-and-effect flowchart, 1095
Choral reading, 493
Class discussion, 673, 999
Class improvement plan, 151
Collage, 447
Communication techniques, evaluating, 954
Contrasting interpretations, 687
Conversation, 857, 1011
Critique persuasive arguments, 700
Cultural heritage, 1108
Debate, 51, 195, 416, 1189
  forums, 1348
  informal, 105, 741
Dr. Martin Luther King, Jr., 115
Dramatic presentation, 1199
Dramatic reading, 179, 283, 333, 551, 941, 1177
Dramatic reenactment, 29

Editorials, 1348
Enactment, 255, 625
Eulogy, 593, 895, 1217
Evaluation, 1025
Explicit influence, 1348
False causality, 700
Group discussion, 783
Implicit influence, 1348
Informal debate, 105, 741
Interview, 213, 458, 577, 773, 793, 1108, 1227
Media analysis, 458, 1348
Mock Supreme Court hearing, 529
Mock trial, 1337
Monologue, 351, 373, 687, 1317
Musical analysis, 1053
Musical presentation, 485
Music in media, 458
News reports, 165
Opening statement, 1125
Opinion forums, 1348
Oral interpretation, 605, 663
Oral presentation, 505, 699
Oral reports, 115, 1265
Panel discussion, 1079
Persuasive arguments, critique of, 700
Persuasive speech, 87
Persuasive techniques, 224
Poetry reading, 431
Political speech, 1039
Presentation, 67, 765, 933, 999
  dramatic, 1199
  evaluating, 954
  musical, 485
  oral, 505, 699
  tourism, 295
Public service announcement, 399
Radio broadcast, 458, 879
Radio play, 1159
Readers Theatre, 985
Recording of ocean sounds, 263
Red herring, 700
Role-play, 725, 909, 1011
Round-table discussion, 804
Scene, 1289
Sequel, 831
Sight gags, 458
Soliloquy, 641
Sound effects, 458
Speech, 41, 122, 655, 1144
Stand-up comedy routine, 843
Summary, 519
Television talk show, 1067
Tourism presentation, 295

Research and Technology

Advertisement, 213
African languages presentation, 1067
Anthology, 493
  class, 1053
  poetry, 1108
Body language presentation, 985
Booklet, 625
Cartoon strip, 773
Charts, 67
Class anthology, 1053
Collection of poems, 804
Comparison-and-contrast chart, 1337
Costume Proposal, 1217
Cultural research, 999
Debate, 879
Definition essay, 485
Discussion, 333

Display, 195
Essay, 255, 263, 485, 1125
Expedition map, 295
Exploration booklet, 41
Feature article, 1011
Flowchart, 655
Folk tale collection, 923
Graphic display, 105, 179
Handbook, 115
Illustrated booklet, 673
Illustrated report, 1159
Illustration for poem, 741
Immigration report, 1079
Internet
  copyrighted material on, R30
  evaluating reliability of sources on, R30
  introduction to, R29
  key word search, R29
  narrowing search, R29
  online reference sites, R29
  subject searches, R30
  tips for effective search, R29
  See also Web sites
Interpretive presentation, 895
Logo design, 29
Marketing brochure, 605
Menu, historically accurate, 87
Model or map of battlefield, 551
Multimedia cultural presentation, 1199
Multimedia presentation, 505, 1189, 1227
Multimedia report, 577, 1095
Musical presentation, 687
Oral presentation, 283, 351, 416, 1025
Oral report, 641, 857
Poster, 933
Précis, 165
Profile, 399
Prospecting and mining report, 593
Report, 373, 431, 447, 663, 725, 765, 843, 909
  illustrated, 1159
  immigration, 1079
  multimedia, 577, 1095
  oral, 641, 857
  research, 831, 941, 1039
  team, 1144
  written, 783, 793, 909, 1177
Research presentation, 51
Research report, 831, 941, 1039
Team report, 1144
Travel brochure, 151
Visual model, 519
Web sites, 529
  home page of, 89
  interior page of, 90
  locating information on, 88
  See also Internet
Written report, 783, 793, 909, 1177

Index of Features

Assessment Workshop

Cause-and-effect relationships, recognizing, 225
Context clues, 701
Inferences and generalizations, 459
Punctuation, usage, and sentence structure, 1349
Sentence-completion questions, 955
Test-taking strategy, 123, 225, 459, 955
Written texts, summarizing, 123

Closer Look, A

All the News That's Fit to Print: Colonial Newspapers, 152
Captivity Narratives: Colonial Pulp Fiction, 68
Harlem Renaissance: A Cultural Revolution, The, 910
Mark Twain: The American Bard, 560
Transcendentalism: The Seekers, 384
Twentieth Century Drama: America on Stage, 1228

Connections

American Speechmaking, 196
Defining an American, 214
Emergence of an American Voice, The, 448
Facing Troubled Times, 832
Fireside and Campfire: Views of Nature, 300
Forging New Frontiers, 626
From Every Corner of the Land, 946
Living in a Changing World, 688
Meeting of Cultures, 52
Pioneer Spirit, 92
Shadows of the Imagination, 374
Voices for Freedom, 180
War Diaries, Journals, and Letters, 552

Listening and Speaking Workshops

Ad hominem, attack, 700
Attitudes, shaping, 1348
Bandwagon effect, 700
Circular reasoning, identify, 700
Communication methods and techniques, evaluating, 954
Editorials, identify, 1348
Evidence, identify, 224
Explicit influence, analyze, 1348
False causality, 700
Generalizations, challenging, 700
Images of leaders, 1348
Implicit influence, analyze, 1348
Information, critique, 700
Media, analyzing, 458, 1348
Objectivity and subjectivity, weigh, 954
Opinion forums, recognize, 1348

Persuasive purposes and techniques, 224
Presentations, evaluate, 954
Priorities, reporting, 1348
Purpose, recognizing, 954
Reasoning, critique, 700
Red herring, 700
Speech, 122
Structure, analyze, 954
Support, evaluate, 224

Literature in Context

American Experience
  American Railroad, 789
  Angel of the Battlefield, 539
  America's Love for the Western, 584
  Arthur Miller, Joseph McCarthy, and the Blacklist, 1272
  European Influence on American Literature, 251
  Jazz Age, 760
  Jonathan Edwards, Puritans, and Sermons of Fear, 340
  Moving West, 599
  New American Voices, 1073
  New Yorker Magazine, 1004
  Poe and the Gothic Tradition, 312
  Rooming House, The, 992
  Slave Narratives, 500
  Southern regionalism, 981
  Two Influential Writers, 872
  World War II, 1170
  Zora Neale Hurston Rediscovered, 919
Cultural Connection
  Fitzgerald's Elusive Women, 756
  James Baldwin and the Church, 1154
  Proverbs, 147
Economics
  Slave Trade, 47
Geography Connection
  Sierra Nevada, 582
History Connection
  B-29 Bombers, 1164
  Battle of Shiloh, 511
  Biblical Imagery, 110
  Dogs and the Yukon, 611
  Dominican Republic, 1085
  House Calls, 848
  Inquisition, 1253
  Legend of the White Whale, 359
  Mayflower, 80
  Puritans and Nathaniel Hawthorne, 1312
  Olympus, 406
  Socrates, 142
  "The War to End All Wars", 811
  Women and Publishing, 650
Humanities Connection
  Hudson River School, 290
  Jefferson, Locke, and the Social Contract, 158

  Whale as Archetype, 362
Literature Connection
  A Guide to Yoknapatawpha County, 866
Media Connection
  Being Abigail Williams, 1328
Music Connection
  Wagner Operas, 680
Mythology Connection
  Centaur, 1045
Social Studies Connection
  Higher Education, 1210
  History Repeats Itself, 1240
  Pocahontas, 76

Reading Informational Materials

Author's arguments, interpreting, 1338, 1341
Comparing informational materials
  critical commentaries and theatre reviews, 1341
  editorials and advertisements, 169
Contrasting informational materials
  modern proclamations, 532
  patterns of organization, 299
  web sites and other reference sources, 91
Critical commentaries, 1338
Editorials, evaluating, 169
Information, locating appropriate, 88, 91
Logical and faulty modes of persuasion, 166, 169
Memorandums, 296
Newspaper editorials, 166
Online information, 88
Public documents, 530
Public relations documents, 942

Writing Workshops

Analyze literary trends, 1342
Autobiographical narrative, 118
Drafting, 117, 120, 219, 220, 222, 453, 456, 693, 698, 952, 1343, 1346
Editing, 117, 219, 453, 693, 1343
Job portfolio, 1344
Literary periods, analyze, 116
Literary themes, evaluate, 218
Literary trends, compare and contrast, 452
Multimedia presentation, 950
Prewriting, 116, 118, 218, 452, 454, 692, 694, 950, 1342, 1344
Problem-and-solution essay, 220
Publishing and presenting, 117, 121, 219, 223, 453, 457, 693, 699,
Reflective composition, 454
Research paper, 694
Revising, 117, 120, 219, 222, 453, 456, 693, 698, 952, 1343, 1346

Estate of Gwendolyn Brooks "The Explorer" from *Blacks by Gwendolyn Brooks,* published by The David Company, Chicago, IL. Copyright © 1987, renewed by Third World Press, Chicago, IL, 1991. Used by permission of The Estate of Gwendolyn Brooks.

Diana Chang "Most Satisfied by Snow" from *Most Satisfied by Snow* by Diana Chang. Copyright by Diana Chang. Used by permission of the author.

Sandra Dijkstra Literary Agency for Amy Tan "Mother Tongue" by Amy Tan. Copyright © 1990 by Amy Tan. First appeared in *Threepenny Review.* Reprinted by permission of the author and Sandra Dijkstra Literary Agency.

Doubleday, A division of Random House, Inc. "The Adamant" and "The Light Comes Brighter," copyright 1938 by Theodore Roethke, from *The Collected Poems of Theodore Roethke* by Theodore Roethke. From *Roots* by Alex Haley, copyright © 1976 by Alex Haley. Used by permission of Doubleday, a division of Random House, Inc.

Rita Dove Rita Dove, "For the Love of Books," first published as part of the *Introduction to Selected Poems,* Pantheon Books/Vintage Books, © 1993 by Rita Dove.

Farrar, Straus & Giroux, Inc. "Coyote v. Acme" from *Coyote V. Acme* by Ian Frazier. Copyright © 1996 by Ian Frazier. "The Death of the Ball Turret Gunner" and "Losses" from *The Complete Poems* by Randall Jarrell. Copyright © 1969 by Mrs. Randall Jarrell. "Hawthorne" from *The Union Dead* by Robert Lowell. Copyright © 1959 by Robert Lowell. Copyright renewed © 1987 by Harriot Lowell, Caroline Lowell, and Sheridan Lowell. "The First Seven Years" from *The Magic Barrel* by Bernard Malamud. Copyright © 1950, 1958 and copyright renewed © 1977, 1986 by Bernard Malamud. Excerpt from *The Right Stuff* by Tom Wolfe. Copyright © 1979 by Tom Wolfe. From "Homage to Mistress Bradstreet" by John Berryman from *Homage to Mistress Bradstreet and Other Poems.* Copyright © 1948, 1956, 1958, 1959, 1967, 1968 by John Berryman.

Fulcrum Publishing "The Earth on Turtle's Back" from *Keepers of the Earth: Native American Stories and Environmental Activities for Children,* by Michael J. Caduto and Joseph Bruchac (© 1988) Fulcrum Publishing, 350 Indiana St., #350, Golden, CO 80401, 800-992-2908. Used by permission.

Graywolf Press "Traveling through the Dark" copyright 1962, 1998 by the Estate of William Stafford. Reprinted from *The Way It Is: New and Selected Poems* with the permission of Graywolf Press, Saint Paul, Minnesota.

Harcourt Brace & Company "A Worn Path" from *A Curtain of Green and Other Stories,* copyright 1941 and renewed 1969 by Eudora Welty. "The Jilting of Granny Weatherall" from *Flowering Judas And Other Stories,* copyright 1930 and renewed 1958 by Katherine Anne Porter. "Chicago" and "Grass" from *Chicago Poems* by Carl Sandburg, copyright 1916 by Holt, Rinehart and Winston, Inc.; renewed 1944 by Carl Sandburg. "The Life You Save May Be Your Own" from *A Good Man Is Hard To Find And Other Stories,* copyright © 1953 by Flannery O'Connor and renewed 1981 by Regina O'Connor. This material may not be reproduced in any form or by any means without the prior written permission of the publisher. "Everyday Use" from *In Love & Trouble: Stories of Black Women,* copyright © 1973 by Alice Walker. Reprinted by permission of Harcourt Brace & Company.

Joy Harjo "Suspended" by Joy Harjo from *In Short: A Collection of Brief Creative Nonfiction,* edited by Judith Kitchen and Mary Paumier Jones. Copyright © 1996. Reprinted by permission of the author.

HarperCollins Publishers, Inc. "Bidwell Ghost" from *Baptism of Desire* by Louise Erdrich. Copyright © 1990 by Louise Erdrich. "Seeing" from *Pilgrim at Tinker Creek* by Annie Dillard. Copyright © 1974 by Annie Dillard. Used by permission of HarperCollins Publishers, Inc. "Where Is Here" taken from *Where Is Here?* by Joyce Carol Oates. Copyright © 1992 by The Ontario Review, Inc. First published by The Ecco Press in 1992. From *Dust Tracks On a Road* by Zora Neale Hurston. Copyright 1942 by Zora Neale Hurston. Copyright renewed 1970 by John C. Hurston. Used by permission.

HarperCollins Publishers, Inc. and Faber & Faber Ltd. "Mirror" from *Crossing the Water* by Sylvia Plath. Copyright © 1963 by Ted Hughes. Originally appeared in *The New Yorker.* Used by permission of HarperCollins Publishers, Inc.

HarperTorch, An imprint of HarperCollins Publishers, Inc. "Old-Time Cowboys in the Modern World" by John Graves from *A JOHN GRAVES READER.*

John Bret-Harte "The Outcasts of Poker Flat" by Bret Harte from *SELECTED STORIES OF BRET HARTE.*

Harvard University Press "There's a certain Slant of light" (#258), "Because I could not stop for Death" (#712), "There is a solitude of space" (#1695), "My life closed twice before its close—" (#1732), "I heard a Fly buzz—when I died" (#465), and "The Soul selects her own Society" (#303) by Emily Dickinson from *The Poems of Emily Dickinson,* Thomas H. Johnson, ed., Cambridge, Mass.: The Belknap Press of Harvard University Press, Copyright (c) 1951, 1955, 1979 by the Presidents and Fellows of Harvard College. Reprinted by permission of the publishers and the Trustees of Amherst College.

Henry Holt and Company, Inc. "Acquainted with the Night" and "The Gift Outright" from *The Poetry of Robert Frost* edited by Edward Connery Latham, Copyright 1928, © 1969 by Henry Holt and Co., © 1970 by Lesley Frost Ballantine, © 1942, 1956 by Robert Frost. Reprinted by permission of Henry Holt and Company, LLC. "Out, Out—" and "Mending Wall" from *The Poetry of Robert Frost* edited by Edward Connery Lathem. Copyright 1944, © 1958 by Robert Frost, © 1967 by Lesley Frost Ballantine, Copyright 1916, 1930, 1939, © 1969 by Henry Holt and Company, Inc.

Houghton Mifflin Company "Ars Poetica" by Archibald MacLeish from *NEW AND COLLECTED POEMS,* 1917–1982. Copyright © 1985 by the Estate of Archibald MacLeish. Reprinted by permission of Houghton Mifflin Company. All rights reserved.

Houghton Mifflin Company and The Estate of Carson McCullers From *The Mortgaged Heart* by Carson McCullers. Copyright 1940, 1941, 1942, 1945, 1948, 1949, 1953, © 1956, 1959, 1963, 1971 by Floria V. Lasky, Executrix of The Estate of Carson McCullers. Used by permission of Houghton Mifflin Company and The Estate of Carson McCullers.

International Creative Management, Inc. "Ambush" by Tim O'Brien from *THE THINGS THEY CARRIED*.

The Estate of Martin Luther King, Jr., c/o Writer's House Inc. "Letter from Birmingham City Jail " ("Why We Can't Wait") by Martin Luther King, Jr. Reprinted by arrangement with The Heirs to the Estate of Martin Luther King, Jr. c/o Writers House as agent for the proprietor. Copyright 1963 Martin Luther King, Jr., renewed 1991 by Coretta Scott King.

Alfred A. Knopf, Inc., a division of Random House, Inc. "The Brown Chest" from *The Afterlife: and Other Stories* by John Updike, copyright © 1994 by John Updike. "I, Too," "Refugee in America," "Dream Variations," "The Negro Speaks of Rivers," and "Ardella" from *The Collected Poems of Langston Hughes* by Langston Hughes, copyright © 1994 by The Estate of Langston Hughes. "A Noiseless Flash" from *Hiroshima* by John Hersey, copyright 1946 and renewed 1974 by John Hersey. "Ancedote of the Jar" from *The Collected Poems of Wallace Stevens* by Wallace Stevens, copyright 1954 by Wallace Stevens. From *The Woman Warrior* by Maxine Hong Kingston, copyright © 1975, 1976 by Maxine Hong Kingston. From *Of Plymouth Plantation 1620–1647* by William Bradford, edited by Samuel Eliot Morison. Copyright 1952 by Samuel Eliot Morison and renewed 1980 by Emily M. Beck. Used by permission of Alfred A. Knopf, a division of Random House, Inc.

Latin American Literary Review Press, "Freeway 280" by Lorna Dee Cervantes from *Freeway 280*. Copyright by Latin American Literary Review, Volume V, Number 10. Used by permission.

Liveright Publishing Corporation, a subsidiary of W. W. Norton & Company, Inc. "Frederick Douglass." Copyright © 1966 by Robert Hayden, from *Collected Poems of Robert Hayden* by Robert Hayden, edited by Frederick Glaysher. "Storm Ending," from *Cane* by Jean Toomer. Copyright 1923 by Boni & Liveright, renewed 1951 by Jean Toomer. "Runagate Runagate." Copyright © 1966 by Robert Hayden, from *Collected Poems of Robert Hayden* by Robert Hayden, edited by Frederick Glaysher. "anyone lived in a pretty how town." Copyright 1940, © 1968, 1991 by the Trustees for the E.E. Cummings Trust, "old age sticks." Copyright © 1958, 1986, 1991 by the Trustees for the E.E. Cummings Trust, from *COMPLETE POEMS: 1904–1962* by E.E. Cummings, edited by Fumage. Used by permission of Liveright Publishing Corporation.

Louisiana State University Press, "Dunbar" by Anne Spencer from *Time's Unfading Garden: Anne Spencer's Life and Poetry,* edited by J. Lee Greene. Copyright © 1977 by Lousiana State University Press. Reprinted by permission of Louisiana State University Press.

Archives of Claude McKay "The Tropics in New York" from *The Poems of Claude McKay* by Claude McKay, Harcourt Brace, publisher, copyright © 1981.

Elaine Markson Literary Agency, Inc. "Anxiety" from *Later the Same Day* by Grace Paley (Farrar, Straus and Giroux, 1985). Copyright © 1985 by Grace Paley. All rights reserved.

Ellen C. Masters, c/o Hillary Masters, POA "Richard Bone" and "Lucinda Matlock" from *Spoon River Anthology* by Edgar Lee Masters, published by Macmillan Co. Used by permission.

N. Scott Momaday From *The Names: A Memoir* by N. Scott Momaday published by Harper & Row Publishers, Inc. Copyright © 1976 by N. Scott Momaday. Reprinted by permission of the author.

William Morris Agency, Inc. "Gold Glade" by Robert Penn Warren from *New and Selected Poems*. Copyright © 1985 by Robert Penn Warren. Reprinted by permission of William Morris Agency, Inc., on behalf of the author.

New Directions Publishing Corporation "Heat" and "Pear Tree" by H. Doolittle, *Collected Poems, 1912–1944*. Copyright © 1982 by the Estate of Hilda Doolittle. "In a Station of the Metro" and "The River-Merchant's Wife: A Letter" by Ezra Pound, from *Personae*. Copyright © 1926 by Ezra Pound. "The Great Figure," "The Red Wheelbarrow," and "This is Just to Say" by William Carlos Williams, from *Collected Poems Volume 1: 1909-1939*. Copyright 1938 by New Directions Publishing Corporation. Used by permission of New Directions Publishing Corporation. Excerpts form "The Imagist Manifesto" from *Literary Essays of Ezra Pound,* edited with an introduction by T.S. Eliot. Copyright 1918, 1920, 1935 by Ezra Pound.

The New York Times "Onomatopoeia" by William Safire from *You Could Look It Up*. Copyright © 1988 by The Cobbett Corporation. Originally appeared in *The New York Times*. Reprinted by permission.

W. W. Norton & Company, Inc. "Garbage" by Ammons A.R. from *Garbage*. Copyright © 1993 by A.R. Ammons. From "Civil Disobedience" reprinted from *Walden and Civil Disobedience, A Norton Critical Edition,* by Henry David Thoreau, edited by Owen Thomas. Copyright ©1966 by W. W. Norton & Company, Inc. "Who Burns for the Perfection of Paper" from *City of Coughing and Dead Radiators* by Martin Espada. Copyright © 1993 by Martin Espada. Used by permission of W. W. Norton & Company, Inc.

W. W. Norton & Company, Inc. and Adrienne Rich "In a Classroom" from *Time's Power: Poems 1985–1988* by Adrienne Rich. Copyright © 1989 by Adrienne Rich. All rights reserved. Used by permission.

Harold Ober Associates, Inc. "The Corn Planting" from *Sherwood Anderson Short Stories,* edited by Maxwell Geismar. © 1962 by Eleanor Anderson. "A Black Man Talks of Reaping" by Arna Bontemps. Copyright © 1963 by Arna Bontemps. Reprinted by permission of Harold Ober Associates Incorporated.

Simon J. Ortiz "Hunger in New York City" from *Woven Stone* by Simon J. Ortiz. Published by University of Arizona Press, 1992 © 1976 by Simon J. Ortiz. Used by permission of Simon J. Ortiz.

Penguin Books Ltd. "Melting Snow" by Kobayashi Issa (18 lines) from THE PENGUIN BOOK OF JAPANESE VERSE translated by Geoffrey Bownas and Anthony Thwaite (Penguin Books, 1964) Translation copyright © Geoffrey Bownas and Anthony Thwaite, 1964.

Plimoth Plantation Excerpt from Plimoth Plantation Web site (www.plimoth.org).

Princeton University Press From *Walden* by Henry David Thoreau. Copyright © 1971 by Princeton University Press. Used by permission of Princeton University Press.

Random House, Inc. "The Unknown Citizen," copyright 1940 & renewed 1968 by W.H. Auden, from *W.H. Auden: Collected Poems.*

"The Writer in the Family" from *Lives of the Poets* by E. L. Doctorow, copyright © 1984 by E. L. Doctorow. "Cats" from *Living Out Loud* by Anna Quindlen, copyright © 1987 by Anna Quindlen. "Race at Morning" from *Big Woods* by William Faulkner, copyright © 1955 by The Curtis Publishing Company. Used by permission of Random House, Inc.

Russell & Volkening, Inc. "Average Waves in Unprotected Waters" by Anne Tyler. Copyright © 1977 by Anne Tyler. This story originally appeared in *The New Yorker,* February 28th, 1977. Reproduced by permission of Russell & Volkening as agents for the author.

Estate of Ricardo Sanchez "i yearn" by Ricardo Sanchez. Copyright © 1975 by Ricardo Sanchez. Reprinted by permission of the Estate of Ricardo Sanchez.

Scribner, a division of Simon & Schuster, Inc. "The Far and the Near" from *Death to Morning* by Thomas Wolfe. Copyright © 1935 by Charles Scribner's Sons; copyright renewed © 1963 by Paul Gitlin. "In Another Country" from *Men Without Women* by Ernest Hemingway. Copyright 1927 by Charles Scribner's Sons. Copyright renewed 1955 by Ernest Hemingway. Reprinted with the permission of Scribner, a division of Simon & Schuster.

Scribner, a division of Simon & Schuster and The Literary Estate of Marianne Moore "Poetry" from *The Collected Poems of Marianne Moore* by Marianne Moore. Copyright © 1935 by Marianne Moore, copyright renewed © 1963 by Marianne Moore and T.S. Eliot. Used by permission of Scribner, a division of Simon & Schuster, Inc., and The Literary Estate of Marianne Moore.

Scribner, a division of Simon & Schuster and Melanie Jackson Agency, LLC "Gulf War Journal from a Woman at War" from *A Woman at War* by Molly Moore. Copyright © 1993 by Molly Moore. Used by permission of Scribner, a division of Simon & Schuster and Melanie Jackson Agency, LLC.

Simon & Schuster, Inc. from *Lonesome Dove* by Larry McMurtry. Copyright © 1985 by Larry McMurtry. Used by permission of Simon & Schuster.

Sterling Lord Literistic, Inc. "The Crisis, Number 1" by Thomas Paine from CITIZEN TOM PAINE. Copyright by Howard Fast. Used by permission of Sterling Lord Literistic, Inc.

Estate of William Stafford "Traveling Through the Dark" from *Stories That Could Be True: New and Collected Poems* by William Stafford. Copyright © 1960 by William Stafford. Used by permission.

Charles Scribner's Sons, a division of Simon & Schuster, Inc. "Winter Dreams" by F. Scott Fitzgerald, from *All The Sad Young Men*. Copyright 1922 by Frances Scott Fitzgerald Lanahan; copyright renewed 1950. "Richard Cory" from *The Children of the Night* by Edwin Arlington Robinson, published by Charles Scribner's Sons.

Syracuse University Press "The Iroquois Constitution" from *Parker on the Iroquois: Iroquois Uses of Maize and Other Food Plants; The Code of Handsome Lake; The Seneca Prophet; The Constitution of the Five Nations* by Arthur C. Parker, edited by William N. Fenton (Syracuse University Press, Syracuse, NY, 1981). Used by permission.

Rosemary Thurber and the Barbara Hogenson Agency, Inc. "The Night the Ghost Got In" copyright 1933, © 1961 by James Thurber. From *My Life and Hard Times*, published by Harper & Row. Reprinted by arrangement with Rosemary Thurber and the Barbara Hogenson Agency. All rights reserved.

University of Nebraska Press, Reprinted from the *Journals of the Lewis and Clark Expedition, volume 5,* edited by Gary E. Moulton by permission of the University of Nebraska Press. Copyright © 1988 by the University of Nebraska Press. Used by permission.

The University of North Carolina Press "To His Excellency, General Washington" and lines from "An Hymn to the Evening" from *The Poems of Phillis Wheatley* edited and with an introduction by Julian D. Mason, Jr. Copyright © 1966 by The University of North Carolina Press, renewed 1989. Used by permission of the publisher.

University of Texas Press and the author "El Corrido de Gregorio Cortez" from *With His Pistol In His Hand: A Border Ballad And Its Hero* by Americo Paredes, Copyright © 1958, renewed 1986. By permission of the author and the University of Texas Press.

USA Today and Robert N. Wiener Pro bono work headlined "Lawyers leave poor behind" by Robert N. Wiener, from *USA Today* (September 25, 2000). Copyright © 2000 by *USA Today.* Used by permission.

Viking Penguin, Inc., a division of Penguin Putnam, Inc. From "On Social Plays," copyright © 1955, 1978 by Arthur Miller, from *The Theater Essays of Arthur Miller* by Arthur Miller, edited by Robert A. Martin. From *The Crucible* by Arthur Miller, copyright 1952, 1953, 1954, renewed © 1980, 1981, 1982 by Arthur Miller. "The Turtle (Chapter 3)" from *The Grapes of Wrath* by John Steinbeck, copyright 1939, renewed © 1967 by John Steinbeck. Used by permission of Viking Penguin, a division of Penguin Putnam Inc.

Wesleyan University Press "For My Children" by Colleen McElroy from *What Madness Brought Me Here*. "Camouflaging the Chimera" by Yusef Komunyakaa from *Neon Vernacular*. "What For" by Garrett Kaoru Hongo from *Yellow Light*. Used by permission of Wesleyan University Press.

Joel White, for the Estate of E.B. White From "Here Is New York" by E.B. White from *Essays of E.B. White*.

Darryl Babe Wilson "Diamond Island: Alcatraz" by Darryl Babe Wilson. Copyright © 1991 by Darryl Babe Wilson. Reprinted by permission of the author.

Yale University Press From *Mary Chesnut's Civil War,* edited by C. Vann Woodward. Copyright © 1981 by C. Vann Woodward, Sally Bland Metts, Barbara G. Carpenter, Sally Bland Johnson, and Katherine W. Herbert. All rights reserved. Reproduced by permission of the publisher, Yale University Press.

Note: Every effort has been made to locate the copyright owner of material reprinted in this book. Omissions brought to our attention will be corrected in subsequent editions.

CREDITS

Cover and Title Page: *Travel by Ox-Drawn Covered Wagons,* Artist unknown, Courtesy of the Bancroft Library, University of California, Berkeley; **xxiii** Mark Lewis/Tony Stone Images; **vi** Nicole Galeazzi/Omni-Photo Communications, Inc.; **vii** *Red Jacket,* George Catlin, From the Collection of Gilcrease Museum, Tulsa, Oklahoma; **ix** *The Declaration of Independence,* John Trumbull, Yale University Art Gallery; **x** Stock Newport, Inc.; **xii** *Young Soldier: Separate Study of a Soldier Giving Water to a Wounded Companion* (detail), 1861, Winslow Homer, Oil, gouache, black crayon on canvas, 36 x 17.5 cm., United States, 1836–1910, Cooper-Hewitt, National Museum of Design, Smithsonian Institution, Gift of Charles Savage Homer, Jr., 1912-12-110, Photo by Ken Pelka, Courtesy of Art Resource, New York; **xiv** Digital Imagery ©Copyright 2001 PhotoDisc, Inc.; **xv** *School Bell Time,* 1978. From the Profile/Part I: The Twenties series (Mecklenburg County), Romare Bearden, 29 1/4 x 41" Collection: Kingsborough Community College, The City University of New York; ©Romare Bearden Foundation/ Licensed by VAGA, New York, NY; **xvi** Corel Professional Photos CD-ROM™; **xviii** Pocumtuck Valley Memorial Association, Memorial Hall Museum, Deerfield, Massachusetts; **1** *World Map,* 1630, Jan Jansson, The Huntington Library, Art Collections and Botanical Gardens, San Marino, CA; **2** (1492) CORBIS-Bettmann, (1558) Victoria & Albert Museum, London/Art Resource, NY, (1608) *John Smith* (detail), The National Portrait Gallery, Smithsonian Institution, Washington, D.C./Art Resource, NY, (1620) The Granger Collection, New York, **3** (1675) North Wind Picture Archives, (1727) Corel Professional Photos CD-ROM™, (1741) The Granger Collection, New York; **5** North Wind Picture Archives; **6** (t.) North Wind Picture Archives, (b.) Colonial Williamsburg Foundation; **9** The Bettmann Archive; **11** North Wind Picture Archives; **13** *Oneida Chieftain Shikellamy,* Unknown American, c.1820, 45 1/2" x 32", oil on canvas, Philadelphia Museum of Art. The Collection of Edgar William and Bernice Chrysler Garbisch; **14** Silver Burdett Ginn; **16** Nicole Galeazzi/Omni-Photo Communications, Inc.; **20** *Dreamwalker,* Nancy Wood Taber, colored pencil, courtesy of the artist; **25** *Red Jacket,* George Catlin, From the Collection of Gilcrease Museum, Tulsa; **32–33** Corel Professional Photos CD-ROM™; **34** *Painting of Cabeza de Vaca, Esteban, and their companions among various Texas Indian tribes,* Tom Mirrat, The Institute of Texan Cultures, San Antonio, Texas; **37** Jeff Greenberg/Photo Researchers, Inc.; **42** *Olaudah Equiano* (detail), National Portrait Gallery, Smithsonian Institution, Washington, D.C./Art Resource, NY; **44** National Maritime Museum, London; **46** Courtesy of the Library of Congress; **52** *Native American male* (Wailaki tribe), Edward S. Curtis, Courtesy of the Southwest Museum, Los Angeles, Photo #N.40042; **56–57** *San Francisco,* 1849, Attributed to Joshua Pierce, Oil on canvas, Photo by John Lei/Omni-Photo Communications, Inc.; **58** Courtesy of the author; **59** *Building the Fort,* ca. 1960, Julien Binford, oil on canvas, 86" x 101", The Jamestown Yorktown Educational Trust; **60** Erich Lessing/Art Resource, NY; **62** Astrolabe, Museum fur Kunst und Gewerbe, Hamburg; **63** CORBIS-Bettmann; **68** Peabody Museum of Archaeology and Ethnology, Harvard University; **69** The Rosenbach Museum & Library; **70** (l.) *John Smith* (detail), National Portrait Gallery, Smithsonian Institution, Washington, D.C./Art Resource, NY, (r.) CORBIS-Bettmann; **72** *The First Day at Jamestown, 14th May 1607,* from "The Romance and Tragedy of Pioneer Life" by Augustus L. Mason, 1883, William Ludlow Sheppard/Bridgeman Art Library, London/New York; **74** Print Collection, Miriam and Ira D. Wallach Division of Art, Prints and Photographs, The New York Public Library, Astor, Lenox and Tilden Foundations; **76** Architect of the Capitol; **79** *The Coming of the Mayflower,* N.C. Wyeth, from the Collection of Metropolitan Life Insurance Company, New York City, photograph by Malcolm Varon; **80** *The Mayflower in Plymouth Harbor,* William Halsall, Burstein Collection/ CORBIS; **83** Cary Wolinsky/Stock, Boston; **92** NASA; **95** Audio Visual Archives at the John F. Kennedy Library; **96** AP/Wide World Photos; **97** *Pilgrims Going to Church,* George Henry Boughton, Collection of The New York Historical Society; **98** *The Puritan,* Augustus Saint-Gaudens, The Metropolitan Museum of Art, Bequest of Jacob Ruppart, 1939 (39.65.53) All Rights Reserved; **100** Crewel Work Chair Seat Cover, Gift of Samuel Bradstreet, Courtesy, Museum of Fine Arts, Boston; **106** CORBIS-Bettmann; **109** *The Puritan,* c. 1898, Frank E. Schoonover, Oil on canvas, Collection of The Brandywine River Museum, Gift of Mr. and Mrs. Jacob J. Foster; **118** David Young-Wolff/PhotoEdit; **124–125** *Washington Crossing the Delaware,* Emanuel Gottlieb Leutze, oil on canvas, H.149 in., W.255 in. (378.5 x 647.7cm.) The Metropolitan Museum of Art, Gift of John S. Kennedy, 1897. (97.34), Copyright © 1992 By the Metropolitan Museum of Art; **126** (1748) The Granger Collection, New York, (1776) Courtesy, Independence National Historical Park Collection; **127** (all) The Granger Collection, New York; **129** Courtesy, American Antiquarian Society; **131** ©Archive Photos; **135** *George Washington* (Vaughan portrait), Gilbert Stuart, Photograph ©Board of Trustees, National Gallery of Art, Washington, Andrew Mellon Collection; **136** ©Archive Photos; **137** *Miss Liberty,* Abby Aldrich Rockefeller Folk Art Center, Williamsburg, VA; **138** *Benjamin Franklin* (detail), c.1790, Pierre Michel Alix, National Portrait Gallery, Smithsonian Institution, Washington, D.C./Art Resource, New York; **140** *Quaker Meeting,* Courtesy, Museum of Fine Arts, Boston. Reproduced with permission. ©2000 Museum of Fine Arts, Boston. All Rights Reserved; **142** ©British Museum; **144, 146** The Granger Collection, New York; **152** ©Bettmann/CORBIS; **153** (t.) CORBIS, (b.) Smithsonian Institution, Photo no. 86-4091; **154** (r.), (l.) The Granger Collection, New York; **156** Corel Professional Photos CD-ROM™; **157** Yale University Art Gallery; **158** Ron Watts/ CORBIS; **160** Munson-Williams-Proctor Institute Museum of Art, Utica, New York; **170** *Phillis Wheatley* (detail), Unidentified artist after Scipio Moorhead, National Portrait Gallery, Smithsonian Institution, Washington, D.C./Art Resource, New York; **172–173** Corel Professional Photos CD-ROM™; **174** New York State Historical Association, Cooperstown; **181, 182** UPI/ CORBIS-Bettmann; **183** *George Washington standing on the platform,* Penn State Capitol, Harrisburg, Photo: Brian K. Foster. Courtesy Senate Communications; **184** (l.) *Patrick Henry* (detail), c.1835, James Barton Longacre after Lawrence Sully, The National Portrait Gallery, Smithsonian Institution, Washington, D.C./Art Resource, New York, (r.) The Granger Collection, New York; **186** *Patrick Henry Before the Virginia House of Burgesses 1851,* Peter F. Rothermel, Red Hill, The Patrick Henry National Memorial, Brookneal, Virginia; **189** Courtesy of the Library of Congress; **191** The American Philosophical Society; **196** Bettmann/CORBIS; **199** *Retroactive I,* Robert Rauschenberg, 1964, Wadsworth Atheneum, Hartford, Connecticut, Gift of Susan Morse Hilles, ©Robert Rauschenberg/Licensed by VAGA, New York, NY; **200** AP/ Wide World Photos; **201** 18th c. New England needlework, Colonial Williamsburg Foundation; **202** (l.) The Granger Collection, New York, (r.) CORBIS-Bettmann; **204** *Building the First White House,* 1930, N.C. Wyeth, Copyrighted © by the White House Historical Association, photo by the National Geographic Society; **208** *Independence (Squire Jack Porter),* 1858, Frank Blackwell Mayer, National Museum of American Art, Smithsonian Institution, Bequest of Harriet Lane Johnson, Art Resource, New York; **214** Owen Franken/Stock, Boston; **216** *Dance Africa,* 1996, Synthia Saint James, Courtesy of the artist; **217** AP/Wide World Photos; **220** ©The Stock Market/Michal Heron; **226–227** *Niagara Falls, about 1832–1840,* Thomas Chamber, © Wadsworth Atheneum, Hartford, Ella Gallup Sumner and Mary Catlin Sumner Collection; **228** (1804) Seltzer, *Lewis' First Glimpse of the Rockies,* The Thomas Gilcrease Institute of Art Tulsa, Oklahoma, (1804 France) Giraudon/Art Resource, NY, (1814) The Granger Collection, New York, (1825) Samuel S. Spaulding Collection, Buffalo and Erie County Historical Society, (1829) Adam Woolfit/CORBIS; **229** (1831 France) Christie's Images/SuperStock, (1831) Image Select/Art Resource, NY, (1838) The Granger Collection, New York; **232** The Granger Collection, New York; **234** The National Portrait Gallery, Smithsonian Institution/Art Resource, NY; **237** American Steel Foundries; **238** Copyrighted by the White House Historical Association, Photograph by the National Geographic Society; **239** *Fredericksburg Refugee Family at Campfire,* D.E. Henderson, Gettysburg National Military Park Museum; **240** *Washington Irving* (detail), Daniel Huntington, National Portrait Gallery, Smithsonian Institution, Washington, D.C./Art Resource, New York; **245** *The Devil and Tom Walker,* 1856, John Quidor, oil on canvas, 68.8 x 86.6 cm. © The Cleveland Museum of Art, Mr. and Mrs. William H. Marlatt Fund, 1967.18; **246** Walking stick, King Georges County, Virginia, 1846, carved wood with ink decoration, 37 x 2 inches in diameter, Abby Aldrich Rockefeller Folk Art Center, Williamsburg, VA; **247** Yale University Art Gallery, New Haven. The Mabel Brady Garvan Collection; **248** Leonard Lee Rue III/Stock, Boston; **250** Index Stock Photography, Inc.; **251** Ron Watts/CORBIS; **256** *Henry Wadsworth Longfellow* (detail), Thomas B. Read, The National Portrait Gallery, Smithsonian Institution, Washington, D.C./Art Resource, New York; **258** Stephanie Maze/Woodfin Camp & Associates; **264** (b.) The Granger Collection, New York, (t.) *William Cullen Bryant* (detail), Unidentified photographer, The National Portrait Gallery, Smithsonian Institution, Washington, D.C./Art Resource, New York, (m.) CORBIS-Bettmann; **265** (t.) *John Greenleaf Whittier* (detail), 1881, William Notman, The National Portrait Gallery, Smithsonian Institution, Washington, D.C./Art Resource, New York, (b.) The Granger Collection, New York; **267** *Kindred Spirits,* Asher B. Durand, New York Public Library, Astor, Lenox and Tilden Foundations; **270** Charles Krups/AP/Wide World Photos; **272** ©Ulrike Welsch; **274** *Old Holley House, Cos Cob,* John Henry Twachtman, Cincinnati Art Museum, John J. Emery Endowment; **276–277** Digital Imagery ©Copyright 2001 PhotoDisc, Inc.; **284** (r.) *John Wesley Powell* (detail), Edmund Clarence Messer, The National Portrait Gallery, Smithsonian Institution, Washington, D.C./Art Resource, NY, (l.) The Granger Collection, New York; **286** (r.) *Draught of the Falls and Portage of the Missouri River* (Clark's map of the Missouri River), Missouri Historical Society, Clark Papers, Voorhis #1, 2 July 1805, ink on paper, L/A 464b., (l.) *Lewis and Clark with Sacajawea at the Great Falls of the Missouri,* Olaf Seltzer, #0137.871. The Thomas Gilcrease Institute of Art, Tulsa, Oklahoma; **287** *White Salmon Trout,* ink on paper (Clark's drawing of salmon from his journal), Missouri Historical Society MHS Archives, entry before 17 March 1806. L/A #407b; **289** Corel Professional Photos CD-ROM™; **291** *Grand Canyon with Rainbow,* 1912, Thomas Moran, oil on canvas, 25" x 30" (63.5 x 76.3cm) Collection of the Fine Arts Museums of San Francisco, Gift of

Mr. and Mrs. Robert Gill through the Patrons of Art and Music (1981.89); **300** Tammy Rice/The Learning Source; **302** ©Visuals Unlimited; **304** Thomas Victor; **305** *Mysterious Night*, ca. 1895, watercolor on board, 30-1/2 x 21-1/2 inches, Morris Museum of Art, Augusta, GA; **306** CORBIS-Bettmann; **309** "I at length . . ., " Edgar Allen Poe's Tales of Mystery and Imagination (London: George G. Harrap, 1935), Arthur Rackham, Print Collection, Miriam and Ira D. Wallach Division of Art, Prints and Photographs, The New York Public Library; Robert Astor, Lenox and Tilden Foundations; **312** Ron Watts/CORBIS; **316** Steve Mohlenkamp/Index Stock Photography, Inc.; **323** ©2000 The Munch Museum/The Munch-Ellingsen Group/ Artists Rights Society (ARS), New York; **328** *The Raven*, 1845, Edmund Dulac, The Granger Collection, New York; **334** *Nathaniel Hawthorne* (detail), 1862, Emanuel Gottlieb Leutze, The National Portrait Gallery, Smithsonian Institution, Washington, D.C./Art Resource, New York; **337** New York State Historical Association, Cooperstown, New York; **340** Ron Watts/CORBIS; **344** *Cemetery*, Peter McIntyre, Courtesy of the artist; **352** The Granger Collection, New York; **356** *Captain Ahab on the deck of the Pequod*, 1930, pen and ink drawing, The Granger Collection, New York; **357** Stock Newport, Inc.; **359** CORBIS; **361** *Moby-Dick*, 1930, pen and ink drawing, The Granger Collection, New York; **362** The Whaling Museum; **364** *Moby-Dick*, 1930, pen and ink drawing, The Granger Collection, New York; **369** Culver Pictures, Inc.; **375** Phil Schermeister/CORBIS; **377, 380** Digital Imagery ©Copyright 2001 PhotoDisc, Inc.; **382** Alex Oliveira/Globe Photos; **383** *Early Morning at Cold Spring*, 1850, oil on canvas, 60 x 48" Asher B. Durand, Collection of the Montclair Art Museum, Montclair, New Jersey; **384** ©Lee Snider; Lee Snider/CORBIS; **385** (b.) Courtesy of the Library of Congress, (t.) Hulton-Deutsch Collection/CORBIS; **386** *Ralph Waldo Emerson* (detail), Frederick Gutekunst/The National Portrait Gallery, Smithsonian Institution, Washington, D.C./Art Resource, NY; **389** *Sunset*, Frederick Edwin Church, Munson-Williams-Proctor Institute Museum of Art, Utica, New York; **393** Leonard Harris/Stock, Boston; **394** Frank Whitney/The Image Bank; **400** The Granger Collection, New York; **402** Owen Franken/PNI; **406** Burstein Collection/ CORBIS; **408** ©The Stock Market/Dan McCoy; **410** ©Lee Snider; Lee Snider/CORBIS; **417** *Walden Pond Revisited*, 1942, N.C. Wyeth, tempera, possibly mixed with other media on panel, 42 x 48" Collection of the Brandywine River Museum, Bequest of Miss Carolyn Wyeth; **418** The Granger Collection, New York; **420** *Waiting Outside No. 12*, Anonymous, Crane Kalman Gallery; **422** *Room With a Balcony*, Adolph von Menzel, Staatliche Museen Preubischer Kulturbesitz, Nationgalerie, Berlin; **426** Frederic Edwin Church, American, 1826–1900. *Twilight in the Wilderness*, 1860s. Oil on canvas, 101.6 x 162.6 cm. © The Cleveland Museum of Art, 1997, Mr. and Mrs. William H. Marlett Fund, 1965.233; **432** The Granger Collection, New York; **440** *The Lawrence Tree*, 1929, Georgia O'Keeffe, Wadsworth Atheneum, Hartford, The Ella Gallup Sumner and Mary Catlin Sumner Collection, ©1998 The Georgia O'Keeffe Foundation/Artists Rights Society (ARS), New York; **443** *The Reaper*, c.1881, Louis C. Tiffany, oil on canvas, National Academy of Design, New York City; **448–449** *Nobody Around Here Calls Me Citizen*, 1943, Robert Gwathmey, oil on canvas, H. 14-1/4" x W. 17" Collection Frederick R. Weisman Art Museum at the University of Minnesota, Minneapolis, Bequest of Hudson Walker from the Ione and Hudson Walker Collection. ©Estate of Robert Gwathmey/Licensed by VAGA, New York, NY; **449** *Langston Hughes* (detail), c.1925, Winold Reiss, The National Portrait Gallery, Smithsonian Institution, Washington, D.C./Art Resource, New York; **450** *Mandolin*, Rosa Ibarra, Courtesy of the artist; **451** Photo by M&A Productions; **454** Digital Imagery ©Copyright 2001 PhotoDisc, Inc.; **460–461** *The Fall of Richmond*, Currier & Ives, SuperStock; **461** (t.) *Portrait of Abraham Lincoln* (detail), William Willard, The National Portrait Gallery, Smithsonian Institution, Washington, D.C./Art Resource, New York, (b.) The Granger Collection, New York; **462** (all) The Granger Collection, New York; **463** (1886), (1903), (1908) The Granger Collection, New York, (1881) CORBIS-Bettmann; **464** CORBIS-Bettmann; **465** (both) Courtesy of the Library of Congress; **467** Nebraska State Historical Society; **471** *Six O'Clock, Winter*, 1912, John Sloan, The Phillips Collection; **472** *Samuel Longhorne Clemens (Mark Twain)* (detail), 1935, Frank Edwin Larson, The National Portrait Gallery, Smithsonian Institution, Washington, D.C./Art Resource, New York; **473** *Fight for the Standard*, oil on canvas, H 26 3/4 inches, W 21 1/2 inches, Wadsworth Atheneum, Hartford. The Ella Gallup Sumner and Mary Catlin Sumner Collection Fund; **474** (l.) CORBIS-Bettmann, (r.) The Granger Collection, New York; **476** Courtesy of the Library of Congress; **479** Courtesy National Archives; **480** Museum of the Confederacy, Richmond, Virginia; **481** *Young Soldier: Separate Study of a Soldier Giving Water to a Wounded Companion* (detail), 1861, Winslow Homer, Oil, gouache, black crayon on canvas, 36 x 17.5 cm., United States, 1836–1910, Cooper-Hewitt, National Museum of Design, Smithsonian Institution, Gift of Charles Savage Homer, Jr., 1912-12-110, Photo by Ken Pelka, Courtesy of Art Resource, New York; **488** Courtesy of the Library of Congress; **494** *Frederick Douglass* (detail), c. 1844, Attributed to Elisha Hammond, The National Portrait Gallery, Smithsonian Institution, Washington, D.C./Art Resource, New York; **496** *The Chimney*

Corner, 1863, Eastman Johnson, oil on cardboard, 15 1/2 x 13 in., Munson-Williams-Proctor Institute Museum of Art, Utica, New York; Gift of Edmund G. Munson, Jr.; **498** *A Home on the Mississippi*, 1871, Currier & Ives, The Museum of the City of New York, Harry T. Peters Collection; **500** Ron Watts/CORBIS; **506** CORBIS-Bettmann; **508** Superstock; **509** The Kobal Collection; **520** (l.) *Portrait of Abraham Lincoln* (detail), William Willard, The National Portrait Gallery, Smithsonian Institution, Washington, D.C./Art Resource, New York, (r.) *Robert E. Lee* (detail), 1864–1865, Edward Caledon Bruce, The National Portrait Gallery, Smithsonian Institution, Washington, D.C./Art Resource, New York; **523** CORBIS; **525** Buddy Mays/ CORBIS; **532** Courtesy of the Library of Congress; **533** *Newspapers in the Trenches '64*, William Ludwell Sheppard, Museum of the Confederacy, Richmond, Virginia, Photography by Katherine Wetzel; **534** Courtesy of the Library of Congress; **537** Courtesy of the Library of Congress; **539** Ron Watts/CORBIS; **542** Andre Jenny/Focus Group/PictureQuest; **544, 546** The Granger Collection, New York; **547** Bettmann/CORBIS; **552** Sygma; **555** Chip Hires/Liaison International; **556** D. Hudson/ Sygma; **558** The Washington Post; **559** *The Old Stage Coach of the Plains*, 1901, Frederic Remington, oil on canvas, Amon Carter Museum, Forth Worth; **560** (b.) Corel Professional Photos CD-ROM™, (t.) Courtesy National Archives; **561** ©Bettmann/ CORBIS; **562** *Samuel Longhorne Clemens (Mark Twain)* (detail), 1935, Frank Edwin Larson, The National Portrait Gallery, Smithsonian Institution, Washington, D.C./Art Resource, New York; **564** *Paddle Steamboat* Mississippi, Shelburne Museum, Shelburne, Vermont, Photo by Ken Burris; **566** The Historic New Orleans Collection, Museum/Research Center; **569** *Mark Twain (Samuel L. Clemens) Riding the Celebrated Jumping Frog*—an English caricature, 1872, Frederic Waddy, The Granger Collection, New York; **571** The Granger Collection, New York; **572** ©Craig K. Lorenz/Photo Researchers, Inc.; **578** The Granger Collection, New York; **580** *Edge of Town*, Charles Ephraim Burchfield, The Nelson-Atkins Museum of Art, Kansas City, Missouri; **582** Corel Professional Photos CD-ROM™; **584** Ron Watts/CORBIS; **586** Esbin/Anderson/Omni-Photo Communications, Inc.; **594** *Chief Joseph* (detail), 1878, Cyrenius Hall, National Portrait Gallery, Smithsonian Institution, Washington, D.C./Art Resource, New York; **596** Kansas State Historical Society; **599** Ron Watts/ CORBIS; **600** Kansas State Historical Society; **602** National Museum of American History, Smithsonian Institution; **606** CORBIS-Bettmann; **608** Wayne Lynch/DRK Photo; **611, 614** Corel Professional Photos CD-ROM™; **617** Annie Griffiths/DRK Photo; **618–619** CORBIS; **626** Corel Professional Photos CD-ROM™; **628** *Open Range*, 1942, Maynard Dixon, oil on canvas, 34 1/2 x 39" Museum of Western Art, Denver. #36.79. Bernard O. Milmoe, Photographer.; **630** AP/Wide World Photos; **631** *Channel to the Mills*, 1913, Edwin M. Dawes, oil on canvas, 51 x 39 1/2 in. Minneapolis Institute of Arts, anonymous gift; **632** The Granger Collection, New York; **635** *Afternoon in Piedmont (Elsie at the Window)*, c. 1911, Xavier Martínez, Collection of The Oakland Museum of California, Gift of Dr. William S. Porter; **636** Corel Professional Photos CD-ROM™; **642** ©Archive Photos; **644** *Memories*, 1885–86, William Merritt Chase, oil on canvas, Munson-Williams-Proctor Institute Museum of Art, Utica, New York; **648** Digital Imagery ©Copyright 2001 PhotoDisc, Inc.; **650** Bettmann/CORBIS; **656** The Granger Collection, New York; **658** Stock Montage, Inc.; **664** (l.) *Edwin Arlington Robinson* (detail), 1933, Thomas Richard Hood, The National Portrait Gallery, Smithsonian Institution, Washington, D.C./Art Resource, New York, (r.) *Edgar Lee Masters* (detail), 1946, Francis J. Quirk, The National Portrait Gallery, Smithsonian Institution, Washington, D.C./Art Resource, New York; **666** Horst Oesterwinter/International Stock Photography, Ltd.; **668** *The Thinker (Portrait of Louis N. Kenton, 1900)*, Thomas Eakins, The Metropolitan Museum of Art, Kennedy Fund, 1917, Copyright © 1967, 1984 by The Metropolitan Museum of Art; **670** Joel Greenstein/Omni-Photo Communications, Inc.; **674** CORBIS-Bettmann; **676** George Schreiber (1904–1977), *From Arkansas*, 1939, oil on canvas, Sheldon Swope Art Museum, Terre Haute, Indiana; **680** Robbie Jack/CORBIS; **682** The Granger Collection, New York; **688** Tim Davis/Photo Researchers, Inc.; **690** ©Julie Habel/CORBIS; **691** John Barrett/Globe Photos; **694** ©The Stock Market/José L. Peláez; **702–703** Edward Hopper, American, 1882–1967, *Nighthawks*, oil on canvas, 1942, 84.1 x 152.4 cm, Friends of American Art Collection, 1942.51, ©2000 The Art Institute of Chicago. All Rights Reserved; **704** (1915) CORBIS-Bettmann, (1919) National Archives, (1920) Bettmann/CORBIS, (1929) The Granger Collection, New York; **705** (1931) *The Persistence of Memory*, 1931, Salvador Dali, The Museum of Modern Art, New York. Given anonymously. Photograph © 2000 The Museum of Modern Art, New York, (1939) SuperStock, (1941) The Granger Collection, New York, (1945) Alfred Eisenstaedt, Life Magazine © Time Warner; **706** Culver Pictures, Inc.; **707** Museum of Connecticut History; **708** Culver Pictures, Inc.; **710** Courtesy of the Library of Congress; **712** Photographs and Prints Division, Schomburg Center for Research in Black Culture, The New York Public Library, Astor, Lenox and Tilden Foundations; **714** Historical Pictures Collection/Stock Montage, Inc.; **715** *No Place to Go*, 1935, Maynard Dixon, Oil on canvas, 25 x 30 inches. The Herald Clark Memorial Collection, Courtesy of Brigham Young University Museum of Fine Arts. All

Rights Reserved. Photo by David W. Hawkinson; **716** *T. S. Eliot* (detail), 1888–1965, Sir Gerald Kelly, The National Portrait Gallery, Smithsonian Institution, Art Resource, New York; **720** Corel Professional Photos CD-ROM™; **726** (l.) The Granger Collection, New York, (r.) *William Carlos Williams* (detail), The National Portrait Gallery, Smithsonian Institution, Washington, D.C./Art Resource, NY; **727** CORBIS-Bettmann; **730** The Granger Collection, New York; **733** Zha Shibiao, Chinese, 1615–1698, Qing dynasty. Shibiao, *Waiting for the Moon* from *Landscape Album in Various Styles*, 1684. Album of twelve leaves, ink or ink and color on paper; each 29.9 x 39.4 cm. © The Cleveland Museum of Art, 1998, Gift of Mr. and Mrs. Severance A. Millikin, 1955.37; **735** *The Figure 5 in Gold*, 1928, Charles Demuth, oil on composition board. H. 36 in. W. 29-3/4 in. (91.4 x 75.6 cm) Signed (lower left): C.D. Inscribed (bottom center): W.C.W. (William Carlos Williams), The Metropolitan Museum of Art, Alfred Stieglitz Collection, 1949. (49.59.1). Photograph Copyright © 1996 By the Metropolitan Museum of Art; **737** Adam Jones/Photo Researchers, Inc.; **738** *Overhanging Cloud in July*, Charles Burchfield, Collection of Whitney Museum of American Art. Purchase, with funds from the Friends of the Whitney Museum of American Art (60.23). Photography Copyright © 2000: Whitney Museum of American Art; **742** *F. Scott Fitzgerald* (detail), David Silvette, The National Portrait Gallery, Smithsonian Institution, Washington, D.C./Art Resource, New York; **744** Corel Professional Photos CD-ROM™; **748–749** *Golf Course—California*, 1917, George Wesley Bellows, Oil on canvas, 30 x 38 inches, Collection Cincinnati Art Museum, The Edwin and Virginia Irwin Memorial, 1966.6; **750** Digital Imagery ©Copyright 2001 PhotoDisc, Inc.; **754** *The Morning Sun*, c. 1920, o/c, 50 x 40 ins., Pauline Palmer, Collection Rockford Art Museum, Gift of the Friends of American Art, 1922; **756** Bettmann/ CORBIS; **758** Digital Imagery ©Copyright 2001 PhotoDisc, Inc.; **760** Ron Watts/CORBIS; **766** UPI/CORBIS-Bettmann; **768** ©The Stock Market/Milt/Patti Putnam; **774** (l.) *E. E. Cummings* (detail), 1958, Self-Portrait, The National Portrait Gallery, Smithsonian Institution, Washington, D.C./Art Resource, New York, (r.) CORBIS-Bettmann; **776** *Remember Now the Days of Thy Youth*, 1950, Paul Starrett Sample, Oil on canvas, 34 x 48 inches, Hood Museum of Art, Dartmouth College, Hanover, NH; Gift of Frank L. Harrington, class of 1954; **779** *The Turret Lathe Operator*, 1925, Grant Wood, oil on canvas, 18" x 24", Cedar Rapids Museum of Art, Cedar Rapids, Iowa, Cherry Burrell Charitable Foundation Collection. Courtesy Associated American Artists, ©Estate of Grant Wood/Licensed by VAGA, New York, NY; **784** *Thomas Wolfe*, 1938, Soss Melik, The National Portrait Gallery, Smithsonian Institution, Washington, D.C./Art Resource, New York; **786** *Stone City, Iowa*, 1930, Grant Wood, Joslyn Art Museum, Omaha, Nebraska, ©Estate of Grant Wood/Licensed by VAGA, New York, NY; **789** Ron Watts/CORBIS **794** (t.l.) The Granger Collection, New York, (t.r.) CORBIS-Bettman, (b.) AP/ Wide World Photos; **797** Silver Burdett Ginn; **798, 799** Index Stock Photography, Inc.; **800** *Untitled*, 1964, Alexander Calder (one of seven lithographs in series), 19 1/2 x 25 1/2", Solomon R. Guggenheim Museum, New York, Gift of the artist, 1965, Photo by David Heald, © The Solomon R. Guggenheim Foundation, New York, ©1998 Estate of Alexander Calder/Artists Rights Society (ARS), New York; **805** *Do It Yourself Landscape*, 1962, Andy Warhol, Museum Ludwig, Cologne, photo courtesy of Rheinisches Bildarchiv Köln. ©1998 Andy Warhol Foundation for the Visual Arts/ARS, New York; **806** (l.) Larry Burrows/Life Magazine © Time Warner Inc., (r.) CORBIS-Bettmann; **807** Thomas Victor; **809** American Red Cross; **811** Verlag Suddeutscher-Bilderdienst; **812** ©FPG International LLC; **813** Digital Imagery ©Copyright 2001 PhotoDisc, Inc.; **816** © Ryan Beyer/Stone; **820** *Miz Emily*, Joseph Holston, 24" x 16", Holston Reproductions; **824** *Georgia Red Clay*, 1946, Nell Choate Jones, oil on canvas, 25 x 30 inches, 1989.01.094, Morris Museum of Art, Augusta, Georgia; **833** Jay Dorin/Omni-Photo Communications, Inc.; **834** Thomas Victor; **835** *The Tower*, 1920, Charles Demuth, Tempera on pasteboard, 23 1/4 x 19 1/2 in. (58.4 x 49.4 cm) Initialed and inscribed in pencil on reverse: After Christopher Wren (?) Provincetown, Mass./1BO (?)—CD, Columbus Museum of Art, Ohio; Gift of Ferdinand Howald, 31.146; **836** *Carl Sandburg*, Miriam Svet, The National Portrait Gallery, Smithsonian Institution, Washington, D.C./Art Resource, New York; **838** Stock Montage, Inc.; **840** Corel Professional Photos CD-ROM™; **844** *Garden of Memories*, 1917, Charles Burchfield, The Museum of Modern Art, New York. Gift of Abby Aldrich Rockefeller (by exchange). Photograph ©2000 The Museum of Modern Art, New York; **848** ©Bettmann/CORBIS; **852** ©1993 J. Fishkin. All Rights Reserved; **858** *William Faulkner* (detail), Soss Melik, The National Portrait Gallery, Smithsonian Institution, Washington, D.C./Art Resource, New York; **860** Superstock; **863** Digital Imagery ©Copyright 2001 PhotoDisc, Inc.; **864** *Winter in Southern Louisiana*, 1911, Ellsworth Woodward, oil on canvas, Collection of Mississippi Museum of Art, Jackson, Purchase by Mississippi Art Association and Art Study Club, 1912.005; **869** *Old Man and The Boy*, John Head, Russell A. Fink Gallery; **871** Digital Imagery ©Copyright 2001 PhotoDisc, Inc.; **872** Ron Watts/CORBIS; **873** Corel Professional Photos CD-ROM™; **880** Dimitri Kessel/Life Magazine; **882–883, 885** Corel Professional Photos CD-ROM™; **886** Dewitt Jones/Woodfin Camp & Associates; **888** Corel Professional Photos CD-ROM™; **890** UPI/CORBIS-Bettmann; **892** Ellis Herwig/ PNI; **896** (l.) CORBIS-Bettmann, (r.) AP/Wide World Photos; **898, 900, 901** *My Life and Hard Times*, Copyright ©1933 by James Thurber. Copyright © renewed 1961 by James Thurber. Reprinted by arrangement with Rosemary A. Thurber and The Barbara Hogenson Agency; **903** Culver Pictures, Inc.; **910** Bettmann/ CORBIS; **911** *Zora and Langston*, Phoebe Beasley, Bettmann/CORBIS; **912** Courtesy of the Estate of Carl Van Vechten, Joseph Solomon, EXECUTOR, The National Portrait Gallery, Smithsonian Institution, Washington, D.C./Art Resource, New York; **914** ©Hulton Getty/Archive Photos; **917** *School Bell Time*, 1978 From the Profile/Part I: The Twenties series (Mecklenburg County), Romare Bearden, 29 1/4 x 41" Collection: Kingsborough Community College, The City University of New York; ©Romare Bearden Foundation/ Licensed by VAGA, New York, NY; **919** Ron Watts/CORBIS; **924** (l.) *Langston Hughes* (detail), c. 1925, Winold Reiss, The National Portrait Gallery, Smithsonian Institution, Washington, D.C./Art Resource, New York, (r.) The Granger Collection, New York; **926** Corel Professional Photos CD-ROM™; **928** *Girls Skipping*, 1949, Hale Woodruff, oil on canvas, 24" x 32", Private Collection. Courtesy of Michael Rosenfeld Gallery, New York; **930** Michael Skott/The Image Bank; **934** (b.) UPI/CORBIS-Bettmann, (t.) *Countee Cullen* (detail), c. 1925, Winold Reiss, The National Portrait Gallery, Smithsonian Institution, Washington, D.C./Art Resource, New York, (m.) *Jean Toomer* (detail), c. 1925, Winold Reiss, Gift of Laurence A. Fleischman and Howard Garfinkle with a matching grant from the National Endowment of the Arts, The National Portrait Gallery, Smithsonian Institution, Washington, D.C./Art Resource, New York; **937** *Hoeing*, Robert Gwathmey, Oil on canvas, 40" by 60 1/4" (101.6 cm by 153 cm) Carnegie Institute Museum of Art, Pittsburgh, Pennsylvania, Patrons Art Fund, 44.3. Photograph by Richard Stoner, ©Estate of Robert Gwathmey /Licensed by VAGA, New York, NY; **938** Corel Professional Photos CD-ROM™; **946** Huipil (blouse) from the Tarascans of Michoacan. Embroidered cotton. Museo de Indumentaria Mexicana, Mexico City, D.F. Mexico. Schalkwijk/Art Resource, NY; **947** Rikard Sergei Sanchez/Arte Público Press; **950** © Ian Shaw/Stone; **956–957** *Telephones* (detail), 1954, Colleen Browning, oil on plywood, 14 x 32.5" (33.56 x 82.55 cm) Signed, lower right. Butler Institute of American Art. Museum purchase, 1955; **958** (1952) Nancy Crampton, (1955) Leviton/Black Star, (1969) The Granger Collection, New York, (1972) Peter Garfield/Folio, Inc., (1972 China) UPI/CORBIS-Bettmann; **959** (1982) ©1985 Peter Marlow/Magnum Photos, Inc., (1987) ©Larry Downing/ Woodfin Camp & Associates, (1990) ©The Stock Market/Wes Thompson, (1997) ©Dan Groshong/CORBIS Sygma; **960** The Granger Collection, New York; **965** *Down 18th Street*, 1980, Wayne Thiebaud, Hirshorn Museum and Sculpture Garden, Smithsonian Institution, Museum Purchase with Funds Donated by Edward R. Downe, Jr., 1980. Photography by Ricardo Blanc; **967** ©Mark Bolster/International Stock Photography, Ltd.; **968** Digital Imagery ©Copyright 2001 PhotoDisc, Inc.; **969** *Television Moon*, 1978–79, Alfred Leslie, oil on canvas, Wichita Art Museum, gift of Virginia and George Ablah; **970** Flannery O'Connor Collection, Ina Dillard Russel Library, Georgia College; **972** *Deep Fork Overlook*, Joan Marron-LaRue, Courtesy of the artist; **977** *Black Walnuts*, Joseph Pollet, Collection of Whitney Museum of American Art. Purchase and gift of Gertrude Vanderbilt Whitney, by exchange (52.30). Photograph Copyright © 2000: Whitney Museum of American Art; **981** Ron Watts/CORBIS; **986** Nancy Crampton; **988** Culver Pictures, Inc.; **992** Ron Watts/CORBIS; **994** ©The Stock Market/ Shiki; **1000** Thomas Victor; **1003** Corel Professional Photos CD-ROM™; **1004** Ron Watts/CORBIS; **1007** ©The Stock Market/Dick Frank Studios 1996; **1012** (b.r.) Kit Stafford, (t.l.) Rollie McKenna, (b.l.) *Robert Penn Warren* (detail), 1935, Conrad A. Albrizio, The National Portrait Gallery, Smithsonian Institution, Washington, D.C./Art Resource, New York, (t.r.) AP/Wide World Photos; **1014–1015** *Crowninshield's Wharf, Around the Wharf are the Vessels America, Fame, Prudent, and Belisaurius*, George Ropes, Peabody Museum of Salem, Photo by Mark Sexton; **1017** Corel Professional Photos CD-ROM™; **1019** Tim Lynch/Stock, Boston; **1021** Corel Professional Photos CD-ROM™; **1026** Diana Walker; **1028** © Fred Charles/Stone; **1035** *Girl Looking at Landscape*, 1957, Richard Diebenkorn, oil on canvas, 59 x 60 3/8 inches (149.9 x 153.4 cm), Gift of Mr. and Mrs. Alan H. Temple, 61.49, Collection of Whitney Museum of American Art, photograph by Geoffrey Clements, N.Y., Photograph copyright (c) 1997: Whitney Museum of American Art; **1040** (b.) Photo by Michael Nye, (m.) Photo by Paul Abdoo, (t.) Thomas Victor; **1043** *Passion of Paints*, ©1997 Bob Peters, Exclusively represented by Applejack Licensing International; **1045** Museo de Santa Cruz/Bridgeman Art Library, London/ New York; **1047** Culver Pictures, Inc.; **1049** *Getting Down*, Joseph Holston, 14" x 14", Holston Originals; **1054** Thomas Victor; **1056** Jeff Greenberg/Omni-Photo Communications, Inc.; **1061** Museum of English Rural Life/© Dorling Kindersley; **1062** Lee Russell/CORBIS; **1063** Jeff Greenberg/Omni-Photo Communications, Inc.; **1068** ©Anthony Barboza/Life Magazine; **1070** AP/Wide World Photos; **1073** Ron Watts/CORBIS; **1074–1075** © Matt Lambert/Stone; **1080** Prentice Hall; **1082** *Fruit Vendor*, 1951, Olga Costa, Museo de Arte Moderno,

Art Credits ◆ R63

Mexico. © Olga Costa—SOMAAP, Mexico, 1999; **1087** Richard Bickel/ CORBIS; **1090** Andre Jenny/Focus Group/PictureQuest; **1096** (m.l.) Shelley Rotner/Omni-Photo Communications, Inc., (t.) Georgia McInnis/Courtesy of Arte Público Press, (m.r.) Marlene Fostor, (b.) Rollie McKenna; **1098** *Untitled*, Peter Malone, Chen/Art Resource, NY; **1100** Collins/ Monkmeyer; **1101** Corel Professional Photos CD-ROM™; **1102** Mitchell Funk/The Image Bank; **1103** ©John Lemker/Animals Animals; **1109** *My Mother's Book of Life*, 1987, Lee Lawson, acrylic on panel, 34 x 30 in., Photo courtesy of Pomegranate Artbooks; **1110** (t.) The Granger Collection, New York, (m.) © 1996 Sigrid Estrada, (b.) AP/Wide World Photos; **1112** © Paul Edmondson/Stone; **1115** *Blam*, 1962, ©Roy Lichtenstein, oil on canvas, 68 x 80 in.; **1116** © Annabelle Breakey/Stone; **1119, 1120, 1121** Warner Bros./ Photofest; **1126** (m.) Robert Foothorap, (t.) AP/Wide World Photos, (b.) Robert Severi/Liaison International; **1129** *Biography*, 1988, Marina Gutierrez, Courtesy of the artist; **1133** Digital Imagery ©Copyright 2001 PhotoDisc, Inc.; **1136** Jim McHugh; **1139** Gary Gay/The Image Bank; **1145** *Choke*, 1964, Robert Rauschenberg, Oil and screenprint on canvas, 60" x 48", Washington University Gallery of Art, St. Louis, Gift of Mr. and Mrs. Richard K. Weil, 1972, ©Robert Rauschenberg/Licensed by VAGA, New York, NY; **1146** Thomas Victor; **1148** *Push to Walk*, collage 48" x 48" Phoebe Beasley; **1153** ©Telegraph Colour Library 1998/FPG International LLC; **1160** (t.) AP/Wide World Photos, (b.) Rollie McKenna; **1162** FPG International Corp.; **1164** ©CORBIS; **1166** FPG International Corp.; **1168–1169** Courtesy National Archives; **1170** Ron Watts/CORBIS; **1173, 1174** Stock Montage, Inc.; **1178** (b.r.) Pach/CORBIS-Bettmann, (t.l.) AP/Wide World Photos, (b.l.) Thomas Victor, (t.r.) CORBIS-Bettmann; **1180** *Mirror II*, George Tooker (1920–1938), Egg tempera on gesso panel, 20 x 20 in., 1968.4, Gift of R. H. Donnelley Erdman (PA 1956), Addison Gallery of American Art, Phillips Academy, Andover, Massachusetts. All Rights Reserved; **1183** *Part II, The Free Man, No. 30*, The Frederick Douglass Series, Jacob Lawrence, Hampton University Museum, Hampton,

Virginia; **1185** © Pekka Parviainen/Science Photo Library/Photo Researchers, Inc.; **1190** (r.) Thomas Victor, (l.) Nihad Becirovic; **1192** *The Madonna and Child*, 1990, Momodou Ceesay, Dialogue Systems, Inc.; **1195** *Winter*, Ozz Franca, Oil, 24 x 18", Edition of 1999 s/n, Courtesy of The Hadley Companies; **1200** Andrea Renault/Globe Photos; **1203** *Laurence Typing*, 1952, Fairfield Porter, oil on canvas, 40 x 30 1/8 inches, The Parrish Art Museum, Southampton, New York, Gift of the Estate of Fairfield Porter; **1205** Digital Imagery ©Copyright 2001 PhotoDisc, Inc.; **1206** Courtesy of Rebecca Graziano; **1208** Letters and Postcards, Reid Christman, 24" x 18" (61cm x 45.7cm) Fredrix linen canvas; **1212–1213** Courtesy of General Motors; **1218** (r.) AP/ Wide World Photos, (l.) Photo by Mandy Sayer; **1220** Brian Parker/Tom Stack & Associates; **1222–1223** P.J. Griffiths/Magnum Photos, Inc.; **1228** ©Bettmann/CORBIS; **1229** (t.) Courtesy of the Library of Congress, (b.) Oscar White/CORBIS; **1230** AP/ Wide World Photos; **1231** *The Trial of Two "Witches" at Salem, Massachusetts, in 1662*, Howard Pyle, The Granger Collection, New York; **1234** © James Cotier/Stone; **1236** *The Execution of the Reverend Stephen Burroughs for Witchcraft at Salem Massachusetts*, in 1692, 19th century engraving, The Granger Collection, New York; **1240** AP/Wide World Photos; **1242, 1244, 1248** Photofest; **1253** Musée Condé, Chantilly, France/Bridgeman Art Library, London/New York; **1254** Digital Imagery ©Copyright 2001 Photo-Disc, Inc.; **1259** Photofest; **1267** © James Cotier/Stone; **1270** Photofest; **1272** Ron Watts/CORBIS; **1280** Pocumtuck Valley Memorial Association, Memorial Hall Museum, Deerfield, Massachusetts; **1284** Photofest; **1291** © James Cotier/Stone; **1295** © Joe Sohm/ Stone; **1302, 1306, 1308** Photofest; **1310** Richard Stoddard; **1312** Penguin USA; **1319** © James Cotier/Stone; **1323, 1326** Photofest; **1328** ©Reuters/Brad Rickerby/Archive Photos; **1333** Photofest; **1339** Digital Imagery ©Copyright 2001 PhotoDisc, Inc.; **1344** Brent Jones/Stock, Boston

Staff Credits

The people who made up the *Prentice Hall Literature: Timeless Voices, Timeless Themes* team—representing design services, editorial, editorial services, market research, marketing services, media resources, online services & multimedia development, production services, project office, and publishing processes—are listed below. Bold type denotes the core team members.

Susan Andariese, Rosalyn Arcilla, Laura Jane Bird, Betsy Bostwick, **Anne M. Bray,** Evonne Burgess, **Louise B. Capuano, Pam Cardiff,** Megan Chill, Ed Cordero. Laura Dershewitz, Phillip Fried, **Elaine Goldman,** Barbara Goodchild, Barbara Grant, **Rebecca Z. Graziano, Doreen Graizzaro,** Dennis Higbee, **Leanne Korszoloski,** Ellen Lees, David Liston, **Mary Luthi, George Lychock,** Gregory Lynch, Sue Lyons, **William McAllister,** Frances Medico, Gail Meyer, Jessica S. Paladini, Wendy Perri, Carolyn Carty Sapontzis, **Melissa Shustyk, Annette Simmons, Alicia Solis,** Robin Sullivan, Cynthia Sosland Summers, Lois Teesdale, **Elizabeth Torjussen, Doug Utigard,** Bernadette Walsh, Helen Young

Additional Credits

Gregory Abrom, Robert Aleman, Diane Alimena, Michele Angelucci, Gabriella Apolito, Penny Baker, Sharyn Banks, Anthony Barone, Barbara Blecher, Helen Byers, Rui Camarinha, Lorelee J. Campbell, John Carle, Cynthia Clampitt, Jaime L. Cohen, Martha Conway, Dina Curro, Nancy Dredge, Johanna Ehrmann, Josie K. Fixler, Steve Frankel, Kathy Gavilanes, Allen Gold, Michael E. Goodman, Diana Hahn, Kerry L. Harrigan, Jacki Hasko, Evan Holstrom, Beth Hyslip, Helen Issackedes, Cathy Johnson, Susan Karpin, Raegan Keida, Stephanie Kota, Mary Sue Langan, Elizabeth Letizia, Christine Mann, Vickie Menanteaux, Kathleen Mercandetti, Art Mkrtchyan, Karyl Murray, Kenneth Myett, Stefano Nese, Kim Ortell, Lissette Quinones, Erin Rehill-Seker, Patricia Rodriguez, Mildred Schulte, Adam Sherman, Mary Siener, Jan K. Singh, Diane Smith, Barbara Stufflebeem, Louis Suffredini, Lois Tatarian, Tom Thompkins, Lisa Valente, Ryan Vaarsi, Linda Westerhoff, Jeff Zoda

Prentice Hall gratefully acknowledges the following teachers who provided student models for consideration in the program.

Kate Anders, Suzanne Arkfeld, Elizabeth Bailey, Bill Brown, Diane Cappillo, Mary Chapman, Deedee Chumley, Terry Day, Cheryl Devoe, Dan Diercks, Ellen Eberly, Nancy Fahner, Terri Fields, Patty Foster, Joanne Giardino, Julie Gold, Christopher Guarraia, Dianne Hammond, Jo Higgins, Pauline Hodges, Gaye Ingram, Charlotte Jefferies, Bill Jones, Ken Kaiser, Linda Kramer, Karen Lopez, Catherine Lynn, Ashley MacDonald, Kathleen Marshall, LouAnn McCarty, Peggy Moore, Ann Okamura, Will Parker, Maureen Rippee, Tucky Roger, Terrie Saunders, Marilyn Shaw, Ken Spurlock, Mary Stevens, Sandra Sullivan, Wanda Thomas, Jennifer Watson, Amanda Wolf